THE CORRESPONDENCE OF ROBERT TOOMBS, ALEXANDER HAMILTON STEPHENS, AND HOWELL COBB • ROBERT AUGUSTUS TOOMBS AND ALEXANDER HAMILTON STEPHENS AND HOWELL COBB

Publisher's Note

The book descriptions we ask booksellers to display prominently warn that this is an historic book with numerous typos or missing text; it is not indexed or illustrated.

The book was created using optical character recognition software. The software is 99 percent accurate if the book is in good condition. However, we do understand that even one percent can be an annoying number of typos! And sometimes all or part of a page may be missing from our copy of the book. Or the paper may be so discolored from age that it is difficult to read. We apologize and gratefully acknowledge Google's assistance.

After we re-typeset and design a book, the page numbers change so the old index and table of contents no longer work. Therefore, we often remove them; otherwise, please ignore them.

We carefully proof read any book that will sell enough copies to pay the proof reader; unfortunately, most don't. So instead we try to let customers download a free copy of the original typo-free book. Simply enter the barcode number from the back cover of the paperback in the Free Book form at www.RareBooksClub.com. You may also qualify for a free trial membership in our book club to download up to four books for free. Simply enter the barcode number from the back cover onto the membership form on our home page. The book club entitles you to select from more than a million books at no additional charge. Simply enter the title or subject onto the search form to find the books.

If you have any questions, could you please be so kind as to consult our Frequently Asked Questions page at www.RareBooksClub.com/faqs.cfm? You are also welcome to contact us there.

General Books LLC™, Memphis, USA, 2012.

❦ ❦ ❦ ❦ ❦ ❦ ❦ ❦

OP THE
American Historical Association
FOR
THE YEAR 1911
IN TWO VOLUMES
VOL. II
THE CORRESPONDENCE OF ROBERT TOOMBS, ALEXANDER
H. STEPHENS, AND HOWELL COBB
EDITED BY ULRICH B. PHILLIPS
THE CORRESPONDENCE OF ROBERT TOOMBS,
DER H. STEPHEN
HOWELL COBB.
ALEXANDER H. STEPHENS, AND EDITED BY ULRICH BONNELL PHILLIPS, Ph. D., *Professor of American History in the University of Michigan,*
Honorary Member of the Georgia Historical Society.
CONTENTS.
Page.
Preface 7
Chronology of Robert Toombs, Alexander H. Stephens, and Howell Cobb-13
Calendar of the letters of Toombs, Stephens, and Cobb heretofore printed-17
Calendar of the letters of Toombs, Stephens, and Cobb here printed 31
Correspondence of Robert Toombs, Alexander H. Stephens, and Howell Cobb 53
5
PEEFAOE.

In the period of agitation over Southern grievances, South Carolina was the convinced and headlong member of the group of Southern States while Georgia maintained a distinctly deliberative attitude. It was chiefly the action of Georgia which determined on the one hand that there should be no resort to secession in 18491850 under the provocation of the Wilmot Proviso, and on the other hand that the South as a unit should strike for independence in 1860-61 in an endeavor to escape the menace of control by the Republican party. The dearth of contemporary documents exhibiting the problems, views, and purposes of the leaders of southern public opinion in the time of the secession movement has long been regretted by students. The publication by the American Historical Association of Dr. J. F. Jameson's Calhoun correspondence twelve years ago illuminated southern politics, particularly in South Carolina. The present volume, while chiefly relating to Georgia, supplements and continues the general theme of the Calhoun papers.

The collection now printed embraces the correspondence of Robert Toombs, Alexander H. Stephens, and Howell Cobb, partly because they were the most prominent public men of Georgia in the fifties, and partly because their correspondence has reached the editor's hands more abundantly than that of any of their contemporaries. The careers of Toombs and Stephens were so intertwined that they are inseparable by the historian. Bosom friends from early manhood to ripe old age, their policies were almost identical upon virtually every question except that of the expediency of secession after the election of Lincoln. The only general divergence in their points of view was that while Stephens was always dominated by a scrupulous regard for constitutionality, Toombs had little concern in technicalities of any sort, but devoted his scrutiny to the general soundness of public law and finance and to the integrity of representatives. In spite of their agreement in policies, therefore, the speeches and writings of the one reiterate less often than they supplement those of the other. Howell Cobb was usually not an intimate colleague of these two. He entered public life as a Democrat while Toombs and Stephens were Whigs. The three joined forces to procure the enactment and popular endorsement of the Compromise of 1850; but after Cobb's election as governor of Georgia in 1851 the coalition fell apart. In the middle and later fifties after Toombs and 7

Stephens had abandoned the Whig party the prevalence of faction among the Democrats prevented them from any cordial reunion with Cobb. For a brief period at the end of the decade Toombs and Cobb jointly worked for secession in opposition to the unconvinced unionism of Stephens; but before the first year of the war was past the original grouping was resumed; for Cobb became a champion of President Davis while Toombs and Stephens agreed in denouncing the cardinal policies of Davis in internal affairs as both tyrannical and ruinous. Finally the three were again harmonious in their views of the reconstruction programme until Cobb's untimely death. But whether in mutual accord or opposition, the letters of the three men and their respective friends combine to give a rounded view of each successive problem which confronted them. A principal purpose of the editor has been to enable the student to put himself in the places of these men and see current affairs of their time through their eyes. To this end a large number of letters written by other contemporaries to one or another of the trio has been included in this volume. Many of these are from writers of little fame, but are perhaps not less significant on that account. The letters of John H. Lumpkin and Thomas D. Harris, for example, give glimpses of the political machinery of the time; those of Henry L. Benning and George D. Phillips embody some remarkably sound and searching analyses of the sectional situation; those of George S. Houston and George W. Jones narrate contemporary developments in Alabama and Tennessee respectively; while those of Thomas W. Thomas give beautiful illustration of the sentiments and psychology of a typical though obscure " fire-eater ". Very few of the letters here assembled are in reply to one another; but in many instances letters written by various men at about the same time when read in a group give a fairly full view of the situation with which each of them deals. This consideration has led the editor to present the whole collection in a single chronological series.

Material for the life of Stephens is already fairly plentiful in convenient form. The collection of his writings and speeches by Cleveland (1866), Stephens's own "War between the States" (1868-70) and "Reviewers Reviewed" (1872), the intimate biography by Johnston and Browne (1878), the recent life by Pendleton (1907), and the so-called "Recollections" edited by Mrs. Avary (1910) leave little to add beyond the gleaning of his private correspondence. For Cobb's career, on the contrary, nothing has been accessible but the Congressional Globe and the almost negligible "Memorial Volume of Howell Cobb" edited by Samuel Boykin (1870). Of Toombs there has been the somewhat slender biography by Stovall (1892) and an excellent appreciation by Reed in his "Brothers' War ". To these is about to be added a biography of Toombs by the present editor,[1] now in press, which is in considerable part a commentary upon the documents printed in this volume. In view of the disproportionate attention previously given to the lives of the three men it is perhaps fortunate that the present collection bears more fully upon the careers of Toombs and Cobb than upon that of Stephens.

The letters here printed have been drawn mainly from a few manuscript collections. Of these by far the greatest in bulk is the mass of Howell Cobb papers in the possession of his daughter, Mrs. A. S. Erwin of Athens, Georgia. These papers, comprising numerous letters from Cobb to his wife and to his brother-in-law, Colonel John B. Lamar, and multitudinous ones addressed to Cobb by many correspondents, were stored confusedly with miscellaneous other things in trunks and boxes, and apparently had not been explored for decades past except by seekers for Confederate postage stamps. Mrs. Erwin kindly permitted the editor to take home to New Orleans some thousands of these letters and keep them until such copies as he desired had been made and verified. She required, however, that the copies be sent to her for inspection and " elimination" by herself and her brother, Judge Andrew J. Cobb of the supreme court of Georgia. The omissions in the letters printed are properly indicated. The letters from the Erwin collection are indicated by the letter " E ", printed beside the heading of each.

The second collection in point of size was made by the late John C. Reed of Atlanta, in 1906, from among the papers belonging to the estate of Alexander H. Stephens. Colonel Reed's intention was to use these letters, most of which were written by Toombs to Stephens, in the preparation of a biography of Toombs. For a time Colonel Reed, at the instance of the present editor, also contemplated preparing these letters for documentary publication; but he found himself unable to decipher them satisfactorily. Colonel Reed's failing health, followed by his death in January, 1910, put an end to his project for a life of Toombs. The Reed collection consists almost wholly of letters written to Alexander H. Stephens. More than half were written by Robert Toombs, and most of the remainder were from Thomas W. Thomas, Howell Cobb, and Joseph E. Brown. All of the important letters in the Reed collection (more than three-fourths of the whole number of them) are here printed. They are designated by the letter " R " at the heading of each.

A third but much smaller collection in private possession came to the editor's hands also through the good offices of his invaluable friend Colonel Reed. These are the papers of the late

J. Henly Smith, now owned by Mr. Burgess Smith of Atlanta. Their chief content is of letters from Alexander H. Stephens to J. Henly Smith, 1 The Macmlllan Company, New York, 1913. virtually all of which are here printed. They are designated by the letter " S " in the headings. The remaining chief private contributors of documents in their possession are Mr. W. J. DeRenne of Wormsloe, Savannah, Georgia, and Mr. J. K. Smith of Grand Rapids, Michigan. Extensive inquiries by the editor in person and through very numerous friends in his native State of Georgia have satisfied him that the existence of other important collections of Toombs, Stephens, or Cobb letters in private hands is quite improbable. It is well known that Toombs in particular did not preserve his correspondence.

A general search in public repositories has revealed collections valuable for this purpose only in the library of the Historical Society of Pennsylvania and in the manuscripts division of the Library of Congress at Washington. Most of the items drawn from the former, all of which are indicated by the abbreviation "Pa.", are letters of Howell Cobb to James Buchanan. The documents printed from the manuscripts in the Library of Congress, designated by the letters "L. C. ", comprise letters from Toombs and Stephens to John J. Crittenden, George W. Crawford, and James Thomas, and from Stephens to J. Barrett Cohen.

A considerable number of letters drawn from old newspaper files and rare pamphlets are also included in this volume. But so far as the editor is aware nothing is here printed which is not conveniently accessible, with the exception of a single letter, from Toombs to Crittenden, whose substance is necessary for the understanding of other letters which closely precede and follow it. A calendar of letters of Toombs, Stephens, and Cobb, as well as a calendar of the letters now printed, and a chronology, all prepared by the editor, are prefixed to this volume.

The letters now printed have been carefully selected from the much greater bulk of those at command with a view to the fullest possible illustration by such means of the careers of Toombs, Stephens, and Cobb, and of the history of the South and the Union during their time. The necessity of economizing space has led to the general exclusion of addresses, subscriptions and signatures, and to the occasional omission of passages from the texts. Except as regards the letters from the Erwin collection the editor alone is responsible for these omissions. He has omitted nothing from a regard to conventional decorum, nothing from a desire to shield the reputation of any person concerned, and nothing to support any policies or causes. In particular, the matter omitted from the letters of Toombs to Stephens relates mainly to law cases in which they were of counsel. Many of the names in these passages are undecipherable, and the material appears to be of no historical importance.

The editor has not always reproduced peculiarities of spelling, capitalization and punctuation in the originals. Letters which show a marked illiteracy on the part of their writers, however, are printed *literatim;* and it has been thought advisable to show Toombs's habit of doubling some of his final consonants.

In addition to Mrs. Erwin, Judge Cobb, Colonel Reed, Mr. Burgess Smith, Mr. J. K. Smith, and Mr. DeRenne mentioned above, and to the editor's wife whose aid in the preparation of the documents has been very great, acknowledgment of cordial assistance rendered is due to Miss Julia A. Flisch of Augusta, Georgia, Professor R. P. Brooks of the University of Georgia, Mr. H. C. Erwin of Athens, Georgia, Colonel A. R. Lawton and Mr. William Harden of Savannah, Georgia, Dr. Thomas M. Owen of Montgomery, Alabama, Miss Gertrude E. Byrne of New Orleans, Mr. W. R. Benjamin of New York, and Mr. Gaillard Hunt and Mr. J. C. Fitzpatrick of Washington. If a dedication were appropriate to such a book as this it would be devoted to the memory of the editor's lamented friend who did so much to make the work possible, the scholarly, gallant and devoted John C. Reed, Captain in the Confederate States Army, and ever afterward "Colonel" by loving courtesy.

Ulrich B. Phillips.

The University Of Michigan, *March 15,1913*. CHRONOLOGY OF ROBERT TOOMBS, ALEXANDER H. STEPHENS AND HOWELL COBB.

1810, July 2. Robert Toombs born in Wilkes County, Ga. 1812, February 11. Alexander H. Stephens born in Wilkes County, Ga. 1815, September 7. Howell Cobb born in Jefferson County, Ga. (Cobb's parents removed to Athens, Clarke County, Ga., in his early youth.) 1824-1827. Toombs a matriculate in the University of Georgia (Franklin College) at Athens, Ga. 1828. Toombs graduated at Union College, Schenectady, N. Y. 1829-30. Toombs a student of law in the University of Virginia. 1830. March. Toombs admitted to the bar; began the practice of law at Washington, Ga. 1830. Toombs married Miss Julia A. DuBose. 1828-1832. Stephens a student in the University of Georgia, graduating in 1832. 1832. Stephens taught school at Madison, Ga. 1833. Stephens taught school in Liberty County, Ga. 1834. July 22. Stephens admitted to the bar; began the practice of law at

Crawfordville, Ga.

1830-1834. Cobb a student in the University of Georgia, graduating in 1834. 1835. May 26. Cobb married Miss Mary Ann Lamar, daughter of a wealthy planter in central Georgia. 1836. Cobb admitted to the bar; began the practice of law at Athens, Ga. 1836. Cobb a candidate for presidential elector on the Van Buren ticket. 1836. Stephens elected to the Georgia House of Representatives; reelected in 1837, 1838, and 1839. 1837. Cobb appointed solicitor-general of the western circuit of Georgia, serv ing until 1840. 1837. Toombs elected to the Ge-

orgia House of Representatives; re-elected in 1838, 1839, 1840, 1842, and 1843. 1842. Cobb elected to United States House of Representatives as a Democrat. 1843, October. Stephens elected to United States House of Representatives as a
Whig.
1843, December 4-1844, June 17. Twenty-eighth Congress, first session. Cobb and Stephens in the House. 1844, January 13 and 18. Speeches by Cobb on the reception of anti-slavery petitions. 1844, February 9. Speech by Stephens on the law for election of Congressmen by districts. 1844, October. Toombs elected to the United States House of Representatives as a Whig. 1844, December 2-1845, March 3. Twenty-eighth Congress, second session. Cobb and Stephens in the House. 1845, January 22. Speech by Cobb advocating the annexation of Texas. 1845, January 25. Speech by Stephens advocating the annexation of Texas. 1845, December 1-1846, August 10. Twenty-ninth Congress. first session. Cobb.
Stephens and Toombs in the House. 1846, January 8 and April 14. Speeches by Cobb on the Oregon question. 1846, January 12. Speech by Toombs on the Oregon question. 1846, June 16. Speech by Stephens on the Mexican War. 1846, July 1. Speech by Toombs on the tariff. 1846, July 7. Speech by Stephens on the public lands. 1846, December 7-1847, March 3. Twenty-ninth Congress, second session. Cobb,
Stephens and Toombs in the House. 1847, January 8. Speech by Toombs opposing the acquisition of territory from
Mexico.
1847, February 9. Speech by Cobb on the Mexican War.
1847, February 12. Speech by Stephens on the Mexican War.
1847, December 6-1848, August 14. Thirtieth Congress, first session. Cobb, Stephens and Toombs in the House. 1848, February 2. Speech by Cobb on the Mexican War. 1848, July 1. Speeches by Toombs and Cobb on the state of party politics. 1848. Toombs and Stephens promoted the nomination and election of Zachary Taylor as President. 1848, December 4-1849, March 3. Thirtieth Congress, second session. Cobb,
Stephens and Toombs in the House. 1849, February 17. Speech by Stephens on the treaty with Mexico. 1849, December 3-1850, September 30. Thirty-first Congress, first session. Cobb, Speaker, Stephens and Toombs Members of the House. 1849, December 13 and 22. Speeches by Toombs obstructing the organization of the House. 1850, February 27. Speech by Toombs on the admission of California. 1850, June 15. "Hamilcar speech" by Toombs on the right of slaveholders to emigrate into the Territories. 1850, August 9. Speech by Stephens on the Texan boundary. 1850, September 7. Speech by Toombs advocating the enactment of the compromise bills. 1850, September and October. Joint canvass of Georgia by Toombs, Stephens and Cobb to procure a popular indorsement of the compromise legislation. 1850, December 10-14. Georgia State convention, controlled by Toombs, Stephens and Cobb, adopted the "Georgia Platform" December 14, indorsing the compromise. During this convention Toombs, Stephens and Cobb launched Constitutional Union Party in Georgia. 1850, December 2-1851, March 3. Thirty-first Congress, second session. Cobb,
Speaker, Stephens and Toombs Members of the House.
1851, October. Cobb elected governor of Georgia as the candidate of the Consti tutional Union Party. 1851, December. Toombs elected to the United States Senate as a Constitutional Unionist. 1851, December 1-1852, August 1. Thirty-second Congress, first session.
Stephens and Toombs in the House. 1852, April 27. Speech by Stephens on the political situation. 1852, July 3. Speech by Toombs on the presidential campaign. 1852, December 3-1853, March 3. Thirty-second Congress, second session.
Stephens and Toombs in the House. 1853, January 13. Speech by Stephens on the Galphin claim. 1853. Attempt by Toombs and Stephens to revive the Whig Party. Defeated in this by the rise of the Republican Party in 1854, Toombs and Stephens became Democrats. 1853, December 3-1854, August 7. Thirty-third Congress, first session. Toombs in the Senate, Stephens In the House. 1854, February 17. Speech by Stephens on the Kansas-Nebraska bill. 1854. February 23. Speech by Toombs on the Kansas-Nebraska bill. 1854, July 20. Speech by Toombs on the homestead bill. 1854, July 31. Speech by Toombs on the rivers and harbors bill. 1854, December 4-1855, March 3. Thirty-third Congress, second session. Toombs in the Senate, Stephens in the House. 1855. October. Cobb elected to United States House of Representatives. 1855, December 3-1856, August 18. Thirty-fourth Congress, first session. Toombs in Senate, Stephens and Cobb in the House. 1856, January 24. Lecture by Toombs on slavery, in Tremont Temple, Boston,
Mass.
1856, February 28. Speech by Toombs on affairs in Kansas. 1856, May 1. Speech by Toombs on the action of the Naval Retiring Board. 1856, June 23, 24 and 29. Introduction and discussion by Toombs of the Toombs bill for the admission of Kansas. 1856, July 10. Speech by Cobb on Brooks's assault upon Sumner. 1856, June 28. Speech by Stephens on the admission of Kansas. 1856, August 21-August 30. Thirty-fourth Congress, second session. Toombs in the Senate, Stephens and Cobb in the House. 1856, December 1-1857, March 3. Thirty-fourth Congress, third session. Toombs in Senate, Stephens and Cobb in the House. 1857, January 6. Speech by Stephens on the Kansas question. 1857, January 6. Speech by Toombs on the Iowa contested senatorial election. 1857, March 4-1860, December 8. Cobb, Secretary of the Treasury in Buchanan's Cabinet. 1857, December 7-1858, June 14. Thirty-fifth Congress, first session. Toombs in
Senate, Stephens in the House.

1858, January 28. Speech by Toombs on the increase of the Army. 1858, March 18 and 22. Speeches by Toombs on the Kansas question. 3858, May 13. Speech by Toombs on the Galphin claim. 1858, May 24, 25 and 26. Speeches by Toombs on the log-rolling practices in the voting of river and harbor appropriations. 1858, December 6-1859, March 3. Thirty-fifth Congress, second session. Toombs in Senate, Stephens in the House. 1859, February 9. Speech by Toombs on the revenue and expenditures. 1859, February 12. Speech by Stephens on the admission of Oregon. 1859, December 5-1860, June 25. Thirty-sixth Congress, first session. Toombs in Senate. 1860, January 24. "Door-sill speech" by Toombs on the invasion of States. 1860, May 21. Speech by Toombs on the Davis resolutions regarding slavery in the Territories. 1860. November 13. Speech by Toombs before the Georgia Legislature, advocating secession. 1860. November 14. Speech by Stephens before the Georgia Legislature, opposing secession. 1860, December 3-1861, March 3. Thirty-sixth Congress, second session. Toombs in Senate until January 12. 1861, January 7. Speech by Toombs on the grievances and Intentions of the

South (his farewell speech to the Senate). 1861, January 19. Secession of Georgia.

1861, February 4-March 16. Provisional Congress of the Confederate States, first session, at Montgomery, Ala. Cobb president of the Congress, Toombs and Stephens Members from Georgia. 1861, February 9. Stephens elected Vice-President of the Confederate States under the provisional constitution. 1861, February 27-July 24. Toombs Secretary of State in the Confederate Cabinet.

1861, April 29-May 21; July 20-August 81; September 23 and November 18; 1862, February 17. Provisional Congress of the Confederate States, second, third, fourth, and fifth sessions, at Richmond, Va. Cobb president, Toombs a Member from Georgia. 1861, July 15. Cobb commissioned colonel in the Confederate Army, assigned to the command of the Sixteenth Georgia Regiment of Infantry, operating in Virginia. 1861, July 19. Toombs commissioned brigadier general in the Confederate Army, assigned to the command of a brigade of Georgia troops operating in Virginia. 1861, November 6. Stephens elected Vice-President of the Confederate States under the permanent constitution. 1861, November 19. Toombs elected to the Confederate Senate from Georgia, but declined the election. 1862, February 3. Cobb promoted to be brigadier general. 1863, March 4. Toombs resigned his commission in the Confederate Army. 3863, September 9. Cobb promoted to be major general, assigned successively to the command of military districts in Florida and Georgia. 1863, October-1864, December. Toombs in command of a regiment of the

Georgia State Guard, aiding in obstructing Sherman's invasion of Georgia.

1864, March 16. Speech by Stephens before the Georgia Legislature censuring the administration of President Davis.

1865, February 5. Stephens participated in the Hampton Roads conference with

President Lincoln.

1865, May 11. Arrest of Stephens by the United States military authorities. He was imprisoned at Fort Warren, in Boston Harbor. Toombs escaped arrest by flight to Cuba and Europe. 1865, May 24. Arrest of Cobb by the United States military authorities; released May 28. 1865, October 12. Release of Stephens from imprisonment. 1866, January. Stephens elected United States Senator from Georgia, but was not allowed by the Senate to take his seat. 1868, July 23. Speeches by Toombs and Cobb at the "bush arbor" meeting,

Atlanta, Ga., censuring the Republican program of reconstruction. 1868, October 9. Death of Cobb in New York City.

1868. Publication of the first volume of Stephens's "Constitutional View of the

War between the States ". 1870. Publication of the second volume of Stephens's " Constitutional View of the.

War between the States". 1873. Stephens elected to the United States House of Representatives, serving from 1873 to 1882.

1877, July 11-August 25. Georgia constitutional convention at Atlanta. Toombs a delegate and leader in the work of providing a new constitution for the State. 1882, October. Stephens elected governor of Georgia. 1883, March 4. Death of Stephens at Atlanta, Ga. 1885, December 15. Death of Toombs at Washington, Ga. CALENDAR OF THE LETTERS OF TOOMBS, STEPHENS AND COBB HERETOFORE PRINTED.

In making this calendar two classes of items have been excluded: (1) Letters printed in fragments. These appear by hundreds in Johnston and Browne's Life of Alexander H. Stephens. Nearly all of them are letters from A. H. Stephens to Linton Stephens and to Richard Malcolm Johnston. (2) Purely routine official communications of trivial moment. These comprise (a) reports and letters of transmittal addressed by various officials to Howell Cobb as Speaker of the United States House of Representatives (printed in the House Executive Documents, Thirty-first Congress), (6) letters of transmittal by Howell Cobb when Secretary of the Treasury, conveying documents on various topics to Congress (printed in the Executive documents of the Senate and House, Thirty-fifth and Thirty-sixth Congresses), and (o) some of the military reports and letters from or to Howell Cobb and Robert Toombs during their service in the field in the war for southern independence (printed in the War of the Rebellion Official Records). Such official communications as have been deemed of any historical significance, however, have been included in the calendar.

Alexander H. Stephens, Athens, Ga., August 6, 1828, to Aaron Grier Stephens. University of Georgia commencement; anti-tariff public opinion. M. L. Avary, Recollections of A. H. Stephens, N. Y., 1910, pp. 8, 9.

Alexander H. Stephens, Washington, D. C, February 11, 1845, to his constituents. The votes of the southern Whigs upon Texan annexation. H. Cleveland, Alexander H. Stephens in Public and Private, Philadelphia 1866, p. 71.

Alexander H. Stephens, Washington, D. C, December 5, 1848, to John J. Crittenden. Urges Crittenden to come to Washington to aid in shaping the affairs of the incoming Taylor administration. Mrs. C. Coleman, Life of J. J. Crittenden, Philadelphia, 1873, I, 328, 329.

Robert Toombs, Washington, D. C, January 22, 1849, to J. J. Crittenden. The Preston bill; the project of a southern phalanx in Congress. Coleman, Crittenden, I, 335, 336 (reprinted herein).

Robert Toombs, Washington, D. C, April 23, 1850, to J. J. Crittenden. The policy of the southern Whigs in regard to the compromise bills. Coleman, Crittenden, I, 364-366. (Letter published under erroneous date of Apr. 25, 1850.)

Alexander H. Stephens, Washington, D. C, February 17, 1852, to J. J. Crittenden. Invites Crittenden to respond to a toast at a Washington's Birthday celebration. Coleman, Crittenden, II, 27.

Linton Stephens, Milledgeville, Ga., 1852, to Alexander H. Stephens. Concerning the writer's approaching marriage. Avary, Stephens, pp. 89, 90.

Alexander H. Stephens, Crawfordville, Ga., November 17, 1856, to Benjamin H. Hill. Demands an explanation. B. H. Hill, jr., Life of B. H. Hill, Atlanta, 1893, p. 20.

Benjamin H. Hill, Lagrange, Ga., November 18, 1856, to Alexander H. Stephens. Disclaims unkind animus. Hill, Life of Hill, pp. 20-22. 73566—13 2 17

Alexander H. Stephens, Crawfordville, Ga., November 22, 1856, to Benjamin H. Hill. Demands categorical reply to previous inquiry. Hill, Life of Hill, p. 22.

Benjamin H. Hill, Lagrange, Ga., November 24, 1850, to Alexander H. Stephens. Justification of utterances. Hill, Life of Hill, pp. 22-24.

Alexander H. Stephens, Crawfordville, Ga., November 29, 1856, to Benjamin H. Hill. Challenge to duel. Hill, Life of Hill, p. 24.

Benjamin H. Hill, Lagrange, Ga., December 6, 1856, to Alexander H. Stephens. Declines challenge. Hill, Life of Hill, p. 25.

Alexander H. Stephens, Washington, D. C, December 12, 1856, to the editor of the Augusta, Ga., Chronicle and Sentinel. Posts Hill for falsehood and cowardice. Hill, Life of Hill, pp. 25, 26.

Alexander H. Stephens, Crawfordville, Ga., March 13, 1857, to Williams Rutherford. Legislative history of the Western & Atlantic Railroad. Cleveland, Stephens, pp. 605-611.

Alexander H. Stephens, Crawfordville, Ga., March 17, 1857, to Williams Rutherford. Continuation of the legislative history of the Western & Atlantic Railroad. Cleveland, Stephens, pp. 611-621.

Howell Cobb, Treasury Department, Washington, D. C, December 8, 1857, to John C. Breckenridge, Vice-President. Report of the Secretary of the Treasury on the state of the finances for the year ending June 30, 1857. (S. Ex. Docs., 35th Cong., 1st sess., vol. 1, No. 1; H. Ex. Docs., 35th Cong., 1st sess., vol. 1, No. 3.)

Howell Cobb, Treasury Department, Washington, D. C, January 29, 1858, to James L. Orr, Speaker of the House. Revision and codification of the revenue laws. (H. Ex. Docs., 35th Cong., 1st sess., vol. 9, No. 50.)

Howell Cobb, Treasury Department, Washington, D. C, May 19, 1858, to John C. Breckenridge. The present condition of the finances. (S. Ex. Docs., 35th Cong., 1st sess., vol. 13, No. 60.)

Howell Cobb, Treasury Department, Washington, D. C, May. 19, 1858, to James L. Orr. Asks provision for an additional loan of $15,000,000. (H. Ex. Docs., 35th Cong., 1st sess., vol. 13, No. 127.)

Howell Cobb, Treasury Department, Washington, D. C, December 6, 1858, to John C. Breckenridge. Report of the Secretary of the Treasury on the state of the finances for the year ending June 30, 1858. (S. Ex. Doca, 35th Cong., 2d sess., vol. 1, No. 3.)

Alexander H. Stephens, Washington, D. C, March 2, 1859, to John C. Breckenridge and others. Declines proffer of public dinner. Cleveland, Stephens, pp. 124, 125, footnote.

Howell Cobb, Treasury Department, Washington, D. C, December 22, 1859, to John C. Breckenridge. Report of the Secretary of the Treasury on the state of the finances for the year ending June 30, 1859. (S. Ex. Docs., 36th Cong., 1st sess., vol. 5, No. 3.)

Alexander H. Stephens, Crawfordville, Ga., January 21, 1860, to John J. Crittenden. Criticizes plans of amending the Constitution and of launching a new political party. Cleveland, Stephens, pp. 656-660.

Alexander H. Stephens, Crawfordville, Ga., January 26, 1860, to S. J. Anderson. Disavows desire for the Democratic presidential nomination. War of the Rebellion Official Records, series 2, vol. 2, p. 605.

Henry Cleveland, Augusta, Ga., March 25, 1860, to Alexander H. Stephens. Inquires whether Stephens will permit the use of his name for the Presidency. Cleveland, Stephens, pp. 141, 142.

Alexander H. Stephens, Crawfordville, Ga., April 8, 1860, to Henry Cleveland. Forbids the use of his name at the Charleston convention. Cleveland, Stephens, pp. 142-144.

Robert Collins and others, Macon, Ga., May 5, 1860, to Alexander H. Stephens. Request for the opinion of Stephens concerning the rupture of the Charleston convention. Cleveland, Stephens, p. 661.

Alexander H. Stephens, Crawfordville, Ga., May 9, 1860, to Robert

Collins and others. Reviews the political situation and recommends the sending of delegates from Georgia to the adjourned Democratic National Convention at Baltimore. Cleveland, Stephens, pp. 661-668; Johnston and Browne, Stephens, pp. 357-364.

Alexander H. Stephens, Crawfordville, Ga., June 29, 1860, to S. J. Anderson. Laments the rupture at Charleston. War of the Rebellion Official Records, series 2, vol. 2, pp. 605, 606.

Alexander H. Stephens, Crawfordville, Ga., July 1, 1860, to Dr. Z. P. Landrum. The political situation. Cleveland, Stephens, pp. 678-684; A. H. Stephens, War between the States, II, 685-691.

Alexander H. Stephens, Crawfordville, Ga., August 2, 1860, to S. J. Anderson. States his intention of canvassing Georgia in behalf of Douglas. War of the Rebellion Official Records, series 2, vol. 2, p. 607.

Alexander H. Stephens (Crawfordville, Ga., Aug. 30?), 1860, to Linton Stephens. Apprehensions of secession. Avary, Stephens, p. 55.

J. A. Hambleton, Atlanta, Ga., October 25, 1860, to Alexander H. Stephens. Requests Stephens to introduce Douglas at Atlanta. Avary, Stephens, p. 55.

Alexander H Stephens, Crawfordville, Ga., November 25, 1860, to a citizen of Georgia residing in New York. The problem of maintaining southern rights; the prospect of secession. Cleveland, Stephens, pp. 162, 163.

Abraham Lincoln, Springfield, Ill., November 30, 1860, to Alexander H. Stephens. Requests a copy of Stephens's speech to the Georgia Legislature. Cleveland, Stephens, facsimile, facing p. 150; Stephens, War between the States, facsimile, facing II, 266.

Alexander H. Stephens, Crawfordville, Ga., November 30, 1860, to George T. Curtis. Apprehensions of secession and war. Cleveland, Stephens, pp. 159, 160.

Howell Cobb, Treasury Department, Washington, D. C, December 4, 1860, to William Pennington (Speaker). Report of the Secretary of the Treasury on the State of the Finances for the Year Ending June 30, 1860. (H. Ex. Docs., 36th Cong., 2d sess., vol. 2, No. 2.)

Alexander H. Stephens, Crawfordville, Ga., December 14, 1860, to Abraham Lincoln. Vouches for the substantial correctness of the newspaper report of his speech; deplores the perilous condition of the country. Cleveland, Stephens, facsimile of draft, facing p. 150; Stephens, War between the States, facsimile of draft, facing II, 266.

Abraham Lincoln, Springfield, Ill., December 22, 1860, to Alexander H. Stephens. The people of the South have no cause to fear that a Republican administration would interfere directly or indirectly with slaveholding in the South. Cleveland, Stephens, facsimile, facing p. 150; Stephens, War between the States, facsimile, facing II, 266; Johnston and Browne, Stephens, p. 371.

Alexander H. Stephens, Crawfordville, Ga., December 30, 1860, to Abraham Lincoln. Republican fanaticism the cause of southern apprehensions. Cleveland, Stephens, pp. 151-154; Stephens, War between the States, II, 267-270; Johnston and Browne, Stephens, pp. 371-373.

Alexander H. Stephens, Crawfordville, Ga., January 8, 1861, to S. J. Anderson.

The secession prospect in Georgia. War of the Rebellion Official Records, series 2, vol. 2, pp. 609, 610. Martin J. Crawford and James Jackson, Washington, D. C, January 15, 1861, to Robert Toombs or Thomas R. R. Cobb. The House of Representatives has refused to consider the Crittenden resolutions. W. R. O. R., ser. 1, vol. 53, p. 119.

Alfred Iverson and others, Washington, D. C, January 16, 1861, to Robert Toombs and Cobb. Senate has substituted Clark's resolutions for Crittenden's and laid the whole subject on the table. W. R. O. R., ser. 1, vol. 53, p. 119.

Robert Toombs, Milledgeville, Ga., January 24, 1861, to Fernando Wood. Inquires whether any arms consigned to the State of Georgia have been seized by public authorities at New York. Frank Moore, Rebellion Record, Vol. I, documents, p. 26.

Fernando Wood, New York January 25, 1861, to Robert Toombs. States with regret that arms consigned to the State of Georgia have been seized by New York State police, but the city of New York is not responsible for the "outrage." Frank Moore, Rebellion Record, Vol. I, documents, p. 26.

Samuel R. Glenn, Washington, D. C, January 31, 1861, to Alexander H. Stephens. Requests statement of views. Cleveland, Stephens, p. 160.

Alexander H. Stephens, Montgomery, Ala., February 8, 1861, to Samuel R. Glenn. Declines to add to his public utterances in private correspondence. Cleveland, Stephens, pp. 160, 161.

John Perkins, jr., and others, Montgomery, Ala., February 9, 1861, to Alexander H. Stephens. Notification of election as Vice-President. W. R. O. R., ser. 4, vol. 1, pp. 101, 102.

Francis W. Pickens, Charleston, S. C, February 13, 1861, to Howell Cobb. Status of Fort Sumter. W. R. O. R., ser. 1, vol. 1, pp. 254-257.

Robert Toombs, Department of State, Montgomery, Ala., March 16, 1861, to William L. Yancey, Pierre A. Rost, and A. Dudley Mann. Instructions as special commissioners to Europe. J. D. Richardson, Messages and Documents of the Confederacy, Nashville, 1905, II, 3-8.

Robert Toombs, Department of State, Montgomery, Ala., March 16, 1861, to W. L. Yancey, P. A. Rost, and A. D. Mann. The duties of commissioners. Richardson, II, 9-11.

Andrew B. Roman, Martin J. Crawford, and John Forsyth, Washington, D. C, March 20, 1861, to Robert Toombs. "You have not heard from us because there is no change. If there Is faith in man we may rely upon the assurances we have as to the status. Time is essential to a peaceful issue of this mission. In the present posture of affairs precipitation is war. We are all agreed." W. R. O. R., ser. 1, vol. 1, p. 277.

"Commissioners" (i. e. Crawford, Roman, and Forsyth), Washington, D. C, March 28, 1861, to Robert Toombs. "The Senate has adjourned *sine die.* There is a dead calm here." W. R. O. R., ser. 1, vol. 53, p. 137.

Robert Toombs, Savannah, Ga., March 21, 1861, to D. P. Walker. Georgia troops for use against Fort Pickena W. R. O. R., ser. 4, vol. 1, p. 181; Confederate Records of Georgia, III, 31, 32.

L. P. Walker, Montgomery, Ala., March 22, 1861, to Robert Toombs. Georgia troops. W. R. O. R., ser. 4, vol. 1, p. 184; Confederate Records of Georgia, III, 32.

Robert Toombs, Savannah, Ga., March 23, 1861, to L. P. Walker. Impasse regarding Georgia troops. W. R. O. R., ser. 4, vol. 1, p. 184; Confederate Records of Georgia, III, 34.

Martin J. Crawford and Andrew B. Roman, Washington, D. C, April 2, 1861, to Robert Toombs. "The war wing presses on the President; he vibrates to that side.... Their form of notice to us may be that of the coward, who gives it when he strikes. Watch at all points."... W. R. O. R., ser. 1, vol. 1, p. 284.

Robert Toombs, Department of State, Montgomery, Ala., April 2, 1861, to W. L. Yancey, P. A. Rost, and A. D. Mann. Ratification by five States has put the Confederate constitution into effect. Richardson, II, 12, 13.

Martin J. Crawford, A. B. Roman, and J. Forsyth, Washington, D. C, April 5, 1861, to Robert Toombs. Armament in preparation by the United States Government. "Be ever on your guard. Glad to hear that you are ready." W. R. O. R., ser. 1, vol. 1, p. 289.

Martin J. Crawford, J. Forsyth, and A. B. Roman Washington, D. C, Apr. 6, 1861, to Robert Toombs. Rumor stronger that the armaments are intended for Sumter and Pickens. W. R. O. R. ser. 1, vol. 1, p. 287.

Alexander H. Stephens, Montgomery, Ala., April 18,1861, to L. P. Walker. The acceptance of State troops by the Confederate government. W. R. O. R., ser. 4, vol. 1, p. 224.

Robert Toombs, Department of State, Montgomery, Ala., April 24, 1861, to W. L. Yancey, P. A. Rost, and A. D. Mann. Reduction of Fort Sumter; secession of Virginia; proclamation offering to grant letters of marque and reprisal. Richardson, II, 13-18.

Alexander H. Stephens, Richmond, Va., April 25, 1861, to Robert Toombs. Report as commissioner from the Confederate States to Virginia. W. R. O. R., ser. 4, vol. 1, p. 242.

William L. Yancey and Pierre A. Rost, Paris, France, May 10, 1861, to Robert Toombs. Consideration in Great Britain and France of the question of recognizing Confederate independence. Richardson, II, 19, 20.

Robert Toombs, Department of State, Montgomery, Ala., May 17, 1861, to John T. Pickett. Instructions as Confederate agent to Mexico. Richardson, II, 20-24.

Robert Toombs, Department of State, Montgomery, Ala., May 18, 1861, to W. L. Yancey, P. A. Rost, and A. D. Mann. The policies of the Confederate government; the prospect of secession by North Carolina; the enthusiasm of the southern people. Richardson, II, 26-34.

Albert Pike, Little Rock, Ark., May 20, 1861, to Robert Toombs. The Confederate enlistment of Indian troops; treaties contemplated with the Indian tribes. W. R. O. R., ser. 1, vol. 3, pp. 580, 581.

William L. Yancey and A. D. Mann, London, May 21, 1861, to Robert Toombs. Report of interview with Lord John Russell. Richardson, II, 34-38.

Robert Toombs, Department of State, Montgomery, Ala., May 24, 1861, to W. L. Yancey, P. A. Rost, and A. D. Mann. Removal of Confederate capital to Richmond. Richardson, II, 38, 39.

William L. Yancey, P. A. Rost, and A. D. Mann, London, June 1, 1861, to Robert Toombs. Further interviews with Lord John Russell; British public opinion. Richardson, II, 39-41.

Robert Toombs, June 21, 1861, to Alexander H. Stephens. Urges the promotion of the Confederate cotton-loan project. Avary, 67, 68.

John B. Floyd, near Wytheville, Va. , July 1, 1861, to Howell Cobb. Requests aid in procuring arms. W. R. O. R., ser. 1, v. 51, pt. 2. p. 153.

William L. Yancey and A. D. Mann, London, July 15, 1861. to Robert Toombs. Attitude of the French and British Governments. Richardson, II, 42-46. Robert Toombs, Department of State, Richmond, Va., July 22, 1861, to Charles 1. Helm. Instructions as Confederate special agent to the Spanish, British, and Danish West Indies. Richardson, II, 46-48.

John T. Pickett, Mexico, July 28, 1861, to Robert Toombs. Affairs in Mexico. Richardson, II, 49.

William L. Yancey and A. D. Mann, London, August 1, 1861, to Robert Toombs. Public opinion in Great Britain and France; difficulty of communication with the Confederate Government. Richardson, II, 53, 54.

William L. Yancey, P. A. Rost, and A. D. Mann, London, August 7, 1861, to Robert Toombs. The Queen's speech to Parliament. Richardson, II, 50-59.

Walker Fearn, London, August 14, 1861, to Robert Toombs. Transmits copy of note addressed by the Confederate commissioners to the British Secretary of State for Foreign Affairs. Richardson, II. 60.

Jefferson Davis, Richmond, Va., September 21,1861, to Howell Cobb. Presentation of colors and sword on behalf of members of Congress. W. R. O. R., ser. 4, vol. 1, p. 615.

Howell Cobb, Yorktown, Va., October 21,1861, to R. M. T. Hunter. Indorsement of Magruder. W. R. O. R., ser. 1, vol. 4, p. 6S5.

Judah P. Benjamin, Richmond, Va. , February 18, 1862, to Howell Cobb. Instructions to arrange with Gen. Wool for exchange of prisoners. W. R. O. R.

, ser. 2, vol. 3, pp. 800, 801.

Howell Cobb, Norfolk, Va., February 23, 1862, to J. P. Benjamin. Progress in negotiation with Wool. W. R. O. R., ser. 2, vol. 3, p. 803.

Howell Cobb, Norfolk, Va., February 26, 1862, to J. P. Benjamin. Wool's delay in negotiations. W. R, O. R., ser 2, vol. 3, pp. 807, 808.

Howell Cobb, Norfolk, Va., February 28, 1862, to John B. Wool. Position of the Confederate Government regarding exchange of prisoners. W. R. O. R., ser. 2, vol. 3, pp. 338-340.

Howell Cobb, Norfolk, Va., March 1, 1861, to J. P. Benjamin. United States Government has withdrawn its proposals. W. R. O. R., ser. 2, vol. 3, p. 809.

Howell Cobb, Richmond, Va., March 4, 1862, to J. P. Benjamin. Final report of failure of negotiations with Wool. W. R, O. R., ser. 2, vol. 3, p. 812.

Benjamin Huger, Norfolk, Va., March 11, 1862, to Howell Cobb. Incloses letter of Wool to Cobb. W. B.. O. R., ser. 2, vol 3, p. 817.

Howell Cobb, Suffolk, Va., March 12, 1861, to J. P. Benjamin. Incloses letter from Wool. W. R. O. R., ser. 2, v. 3, p. 817.

Howell Cobb, Headquarters Second Brigade, Second Division, Army of the Peninsula, April 22, 1861, to L. McLaws. Report of engagement at Lee's Mill, April 16,1862. W. R. O. R., ser. 1, vol. 11, pt. 1, pp. 416-418.

Robert Toombs, "In the field," July 7, 1862, to A. Coward. Report of operations on June 27, 1862. W. R. O. R., ser. 1, vol. 11, pt. 2, pp. 695, 696.

Robert Toombs, near Westover, Va., July 7, 1862, to A. Coward. Report of operations on July 1,1862. W. R. O. R., ser. 1, vol. 11, pt. 2, pp. 696-698.

Alexander H. Stephens, Sparta, Ga., July 17, 1862, to G. W. Randolph. Recommends that persons who have procured substitutes be exempted from conscription. W. R. O. R., ser. 4, vol. 2, pp. 6, 7.

Howell Cobb, Headquarters Second Brigade, August 12, 1862. Report of battles of Savage Station and Malvern Hill. W. R. O. R., ser. 1, vol. 11, pt. 2, pp. 748-750.

Alexander H. Stephens, Richmond, Va., September 8, 1862, to James M. Calhoun. Conflict of civil and military authority in the government of Atlanta. Cleveland, Stephens, pp. 747-749; Stephens, War between the States, II, 786-788; Johnston and Browne, Stephens, pp. 421-423.

Howell Cobb, Opequon Crossing, September 22, 1862. Report of the battle of Crampton's Pass, September 14, 1862. W. B. O. R., ser. 1, v. 19, pt. 1, pp. 870, 871.

Samuel Cooper, Richmond, Va., November 11,1862, to Howell Cobb. Assignment of Cobb to command of the district of middle Florida. W. R. O. 'R., ser. 1, voL 14, p. 677.

G. T. Beauregard, Charleston, S. C, November 21, 1862, to Howell Cobb. Inquires concerning resources for defense of the district of middle Florida. W. B. O. R., ser. 1, vol. 14, p. 684.

Howell Cobb, Columbus, Ga., December 3, 1862, to G. T. Beauregard. Resources for the defense of the district of middle Florida. W. R. O. R., ser. 1, vol 14, pp. 697, 698.

Howell Cobb, Columbus, Ga., December 3, 1862 to adjutant and inspector general, C. S. Army, unofficial request for permission to increase forces by recruiting. W. R. O. R., ser. 1, vol. 14, pp. 696, 697.

Howell Cobb, Tallahassee, Fla., December 8, 1862, to Thomas Jordan. Troops in middle and east Florida. W. R. O. R., ser. 1, vol. 14, p. 702.

Howell Cobb, Tallahassee, Fla., December 9, 1862, to G. T. Beauregard. Asks authority to raise additional troops in Florida, and that all troops thereafter raised be left in the State for its defense. W. B. O. B., ser. 1, vol. 4, pp. 703-705.

Thomas Jordan, Charleston, S. C, December 10, 1862, to Howell Cobb. Regrets that no additional troops can be supplied Cobb. W. B. O. B., ser. 1, vol. 14, pp. 707-709.

Howell Cobb, Quincy, Fla., December 11, 1862, to Thomas Jordan. The defenses of St. Marks. W. B. O. B., ser. 1, vol. 14, p. 710.

James M. Chambers and James F. Bozeman, "on boat *Indian,"* December 20, 1862, to Howell Cobb. Defenses of the Apalachicola Biver. W. B. O. E., ser. 1, vol. 14, pp. 731, 732.

Howell Cobb, Quincy, Fla., December 22, 1862, to G. T. Beauregard. Defenses of the Apalachicola Biver. W. E. O. B., ser. 1, vol. 14, pp. 728-731.

Thomas Jordan, Charleston, S. C, December 29,1862, to Howell Cobb. Defenses of the Appalachicola Elver. W. E. O. E., ser. 1, vol. 14, p. 737.

James A. Seddon, Bichmond, Va., December 30, 1862, to Howell Cobb. The red-tape of recruiting. W. B. O. E, ser. 1, vol. 14, pp. 737, 738.

J. J. Williams, Tallahassee, Fla., January 11, 1863, to HoweU Cobb. Topographical report. W. E. O. E., ser. 1, vol. 14, pp. 751-753.

Howell Cobb, Quincy, Fla., January 12, 1863, to J. A. Seddon. Plans for recruiting troops in Florida. W. E. O. E., ser 1, vol. 53, pp. 271-273.

Howell Cobb, Headquarters district of middle Florida, January 17, 1863 to Thomas Jordan. Transmits Capt. Williams's topographical report. W. B. O. B., ser. 1, vol. 14, p. 751.

J. A Seddon, Bichmond, Va., January 20, 1863, to Howell Cobb. The raising of troops. W. B. O. B., ser. 1, vol. 53, pp. 276, 277.

Howell Cobb, January 28, 1863. Circular concerning recruitment of troops in Florida. W. B. O. B., ser % vol. 53, p. 278.

Howell Cobb, Quincy, Fla., January 29, 1863, to J. A. Seddon. The raising of troops. W. B. O. E., ser. 1, vol. 53, pp. 277, 278.

J. A Seddon, Bichmond, Va., March 23, 1863, to Howell Cobb. Orders aid given to Gen. Finegan. W. B. O. E., ser. 1, vol. 14, p. 842.

Howell Cobb, Quincy, Fla., April 28, 1863, to J. A. Seddon. Progress and problems in recruiting. W. B. O. B., ser. 1, vol. 14, p. 920.

Alexander H. Stephens, Crawfordville, Ga,, June 12, 1863, to Jefferson Davis. Proffers services for a mission to Washington concerning exchange of prisoners. Stephens, War between the States, II, 558-561.

Jefferson Davis, Richmond, Va., July 2, 1863, to Alexander H. Stephens. Commission to establish cartel for exchange of prisoners. Stephens, War between the States, II, 779, 780. W. B. O. R., ser. 2, vol. 6, p. 54.

Alexander H. Stephens. Richmond, Va., July 8, 1863, to Jefferson Davis. Reports refusal of United States Government to participate in proposed conference. W. R. O. R., ser. 2, vol. 6, pp. 94, 95.

Howell Cobb, Quincy, Fla., July 10, 1863, to Thomas Jordan. Conditions on the Appalachicola River. W. R. O. R., ser. 1, vol. 28, pt. 2, pp. 189, 190.

John F. O'Brien, Charleston, S. C, July 21, 1863, to Howell Cobb. Defenses of the Appalachicola Biver. W. B. O. B., ser. 1, vol. 28, pt. 2, p. 214.

J. G. Shorter, Montgomery, Ala., August 4, 1863, to Howell Cobb. Asks assistance' in arresting deserters. W. B. O. B., ser. 1, vol. 28, pt. 2, pp. 273, 274.

Howell Cobbf Quincy, Fla., August 11,1863, to Thomas Jordan. Transmits communication of governor of Alabama (Shorter). W. B. O. B., ser. 1, vol. 28, pt. 2, pp. 272, 273.

Clifton H. Smith, Charleston, S. C, August 13, 1863, to Howell Cobb. Fortifications at Columbus, Ga. W. E. O. B., ser. 1, vol. 28, pt. 2, p. 279.

Howell Cobb, Headquarters district of middle Florida, August 17, 1863, to John Milton. Defenses of Apalachicola. W. B. O. B., ser. 1, vol. 28, pt. 2, p. 453.

Howell Cobb, of Houston County, Ga., Perry, Ga., August 24, 1863, to Alexander H. Stephens. Recommends a presidential dictatorship for the Confederacy. Cleveland, Stephens, pp. 172, 173. The name of the writer, suppressed by Cleveland, is here supplied from the original MS. Howell Cobb, of Houston County, was a cousin of Howell Cobb, of Clarke County, whose correspondence is published in this volume.

Alexander H. Stephens, Crawfordville, Ga., August 29, 1863 to Howell Cobb, of Houston County. Disapproves plan of dictatorship. Cleveland, Stephens, pp. 173, 174.

Howell Cobb., Quincy, Fla., September 4, 1863. to Thomas Jordan. Defenses of Columbus, Ga. W. B. O. E., ser. 1, vol. 28, p. 338.

Samuel Cooper, Eichmond, Va., September 10, 1863, to Howell Cobb. Organization of Georgia State troops for local defense. W. B. O. B., ser. 4, vol. 2, p. 798.

Howell Cobb, Atlanta, Ga., September 14, 1863, to Samuel Cooper. Progress in organizing Georgia State troops. W. B. O. E., ser. 4, vol. 2, p. 807.

Howell Cobb, Atlanta, Ga., September 28, 1863, to Samuel Cooper. Organization and officering of Georgia State troops. W. B. O. B., ser. 4, vol. 2, pp. 831-833.

Howell Cobb, Atlanta, Ga., September 29, 1863, to Samuel Cooper. The officering of Georgia State troops according to Georgia laws. W. B. O. B., ser. 4, vol. 2, pp. 834, 835. Confederate Becords of Georgia, vol. 3, p. 420.

Howell Cobb, Atlanta, Ga., October 3, 1863, to W. W. Mackall. Strength and distribution of Georgia State troops. W. B. O. B., ser. 1, vol. 52, pt. 2, pp 536, 537.

J. A. Seddon, Eichmond, Va., October 5, 1863, to Howell Cobb. The officering of Georgia State troops. W. E. O. B., ser. 4, vol. 2, p. 854; Confederate Becords of Georgia, III, 421, 422.

Joseph E. Brown, Marietta, Ga., October 15, 1863, to Howell Cobb. The officering of Georgia State troops. W. B. O. R., ser. 4, vol. 2, p. 878; Confederate Becords of Georgia, III, 423, 424.

Howell Cobb, Atlanta, Ga., October 18, 1803, to Joseph E. Brown. The officering of Georgia State troops. W. R. O. R., ser. 4, vol. 2, p. 878; Confederate Records of Georgia, III, 424, 425.

Howell Cobb, Atlanta, Ga., October 18, 1863, to J. A. Seddon. The officering of Georgia State troops. W. R. O. R., ser. 4, vol. 2, p. 877; Confederate Records of Georgia, III, 422, 423.

J. A. Seddon, Richmond, Va., October 27, 1863, to Howell Cobb. The officering of Georgia State troops. Confederate Records of Georgia, III, 425, 426.

G. T. Beauregard, Charleston, S. C, October 31, 1863, to Howell Cobb. The availability of Georgia State troops for the defense of Charleston. W. R. O. R., ser. 1, vol. 28, p. 465.

Howell Cobb, Atlanta, Ga., November 7, 1863, to Samuel Cooper. The organization of the Georgia State Guard. W. R. O. R., ser. 1, vol. 31, pt. 3, p. 649.

Alexander H. Stephens, November 14, 1863, to Richard Malcolm Johnston. Constitutional doctrines; prospects of the war. Cleveland, Stephens, pp. 175-181.

Howell Cobb, Atlanta, Ga., January 1, 1864, to Col. Gorgas. Request for 5,000 stand of small arms. W. R. O. R., ser. 1, vol. 32, pt. 2, pp. 506, 507.

Howell Cobb, Atlanta, Ga., January 9, 1864, to J. A. Seddon. Request authority to organize new companies and regiments from the Georgia State Guard whose term is about to expire. W. R. O. R., ser. 4, vol. 3, p. 13.

J. A. Seddon, Richmond, Va., January 25, 1864, to Howell Cobb. "It Is not thought expedient to organize new companies, but to retain all of conscript age to fill up the old." W. R. O. R., ser. 4, vol. 3, p. 43.

Howell Cobb, Atlanta, Ga., January 26, 1864, to J. A. Seddon. Reiterates request for organization of new companies. W. R. O. R., ser. 4, vol. 3, pp. 38, 39.

Howell Cobb, Atlanta, Ga., February 4, 1864, to J. A. Seddon. Supply of recruits and provisions in Georgia surprisingly large. W. R. O. R., ser. 4, vol. 3, pp. 74, 75.

Samuel Cooper, Richmond, Va., February 7, 1864, to Howell Cobb. Asks recommendation of some Georgia colonel or brigadier for appointment as commander of the cantonment for prisoners about to be established at Andersonvllle, Ga. W. R. O. R., ser. 2, vol. 6, p. 925.

J. A. Seddon, Richmond, Va., February 12, 1864, to Howell Cobb. Thanks Cobb for his zeal. W. R. O. R., ser. 4, vol. 3, p. 113.

Alexander H. Stephens, Crnwfordville, Ga., April 8, 1864, to Herschel V. Johnson. The *habeas corpus* controversy between Stephens and Davis. W. R. O. R., ser. 4, vol. 3, pp. 278-280.

Howell Cobb, Macon, Ga., April 19, 1864, to Samuel Cooper. Report of the mustering out of the Georgia State Guard. W. R. O. R., ser. 4, vol. 3, p. 310.

Howell Cobb, Macon, Ga., April 21, 1864, to Joseph E. Brown. Exemptions from conscription. W. R. O. R., ser. 4, vol. 3, pp. 347-349; Confederate Records of Georgia, III, 504-509.

Howell Cobb, Macon, Ga., April 28, 1864, to Samuel Cooper. Reserve corps smaller than expected. W. O. R., ser. 4, vol. 3, p. 344; Confederate Records of Georgia, III, 503.

Alexander H. Stephens, Crawfordvllle, Ga., April 29, 1864, to J. A. Seddon. The tax in kind; the prospective dearth of provisions. Cleveland, Stephens, pp. 786-790.

J. A Seddon, Richmond, May 2, 1864, to Howell Cobb. The organization of the Georgia reserves. W. R. O. R., ser. 4, vol. 3, pp. 371, 372.

Joseph E. Brown, Milledgeville, Ga. , May 5, 1864, to Howell Cobb. Conscription exemptions. W. R. O. R., ser. 4, vol. 3, pp. 381-386; Confederate Records of Georgia, III, 515-527.

Howell Cobb, Macon, Ga., May 5, 1864, to Samuel Cooper. Report of inspection of prison stockade at Andersonvilla W. R. O. R., ser. 2, vol. 7, pp. 119, 120.

Howell Cobb, Macon, Ga., May 10, 1864, to J. A. Seddon. Recommends disbandment of certain local organizations. W. R. O. R., ser. 4, vol. 3, p. 462.

Howell Cobb, Macon, Ga., May 12, 1864, to Joseph E. Brown. Conscription and exemptions. W. R. O. R., ser. 4, vol. 3, pp. 417-422; Confederate Records of Georgia, III, 529-540.

Samuel Cooper, Richmond, Va., May 15, 1864, to Howell Cobb. Orders two regiments to Richmond. W. R. O. R., ser. 1, vol. 36, pt. 2, p. 1011.

J. A. Seddon, Richmond, Va., May 18, 1864, to Howell Cobb. Policies concerning the Georgia reserve. W. R. O. R., ser. 4, vol. 3, p. 463.

Joseph E. Brown, Milledgeville, Ga. , May 20, 1864, to Howell Cobb. Conscription and exemptions. W. R. O. R., ser. 4, vol. 3, pp. 431-439; Confederate Records of Georgia, III, 541-558.

Howell Cobb, Macon, Ga., May 21, 1864, to J. A Seddon. Organization of reserves. W. R. O. R., ser. 4, vol. 3, pp. 439, 440.

Howell Cobb, Macon, Ga., May 23,1864, to Joseph E. Brown. The conscription controversy. W. R. O. R., ser. 4, vol. 3, pp. 442-444; Confederate Records of Georgia, III, 562-566.

Joseph E. Brown, Atlanta, Ga., May 30, 1864, to Howell Cobb. The conscription controversy. Indorsed by Howell Cobb, June 6,1864: "This communication and the author are alike unworthy of further notice." W. R. O. R., ser. 4, vol. 3, pp. 455-457; Confederate Records of Georgia, III, 569-573.

Howell Cobb, Macon, Ga., May 31, 1864, to J. A. Seddon. Recommends disbandment of Howard's battalion. W. R. O. R., ser. 4, vol. 3, pp. 457, 458.

Howell Cobb, Macon, Ga., June 5, 1864, to Samuel Cooper. Report upon the organization of the Georgia reserves. W. R. O. R., ser. 4, vol. 3, pp. 473-475.

Howell Cobb, Macon, Ga., June 6, 1864, to J. A. Seddon. Burden of prisoners of war. W. R. O. R., ser. 2, vol. 7, p. 203.

Howell Cobb, Macon, Ga., June 7,1864, to Samuel Cooper. Conflict of Confederate and Georgia governments over conscription. W. R. O. R., ser. 4, vol. 3, p. 476; Confederate Records of Georgia, III, 578.

J. A. Seddon, Richmond, Va., June 9, 1864, to Howell Cobb. Indorses the disbandment of Howard's battalion. W. R. O. R., ser. 4, vol. 3, p. 478.

Howell Cobb, Macon, Ga., July 15,1864, to J. A. Seddon. Asks ruling as regards conscription exemptions. W. R. O. R., ser. 1, vol. 52, pt. 2, p. 707; Confederate Records of Georgia, III, 591.

J. A. Seddon, Richmond, Va., June 18, 1864, to Howell Cobb. Conscription exemptions. W. R. O. R., ser. 4, vol. 3, p. 502; Confederate Records of Georgia, III, 581, 582.

Alexander H. Stephens, Crawfordvllle, Ga., June 22, 1864, to Herschel V. Johnson. The *habeas corpus* controversy. Cleveland, Stephens, pp. 790-795.

J. A. Seddon, Richmond, Va., June 27, 1864, to Howell Cobb. Asks recommendation of men for appointment as district commissioners of claims. W. R. O. R., ser. 4, vol. 3, p. 516.

Howell Cobb, Athens, Ga., July 1, 1864, to J. A. Seddon. Plans for checking Sherman's invasion. W. R. O. R., ser. 1, vol. 38, pt. 5, p. 858.

Jefferson Davis, Richmond, Va., July 6, 1864, to Howell Cobb. Conscription. W. R. O. R., ser. 4, vol. 3, p. 532; Confederate Records of Georgia, III, 588.

J. A. Seddon, Richmond, Va., July 16, 1864, to Howell Cobb. The controversy with Gov. Brown. W. R. O. R., ser. 4, vol. 3, p. 538; Confederate Records of Georgia, III, 592. Howell Cobb, Macon, Ga., July 18, 1864, to J. A. Seddon. Inquiry concerning conscription. W. R. O. R., ser. 4, vol. 3, p. 542. J A Seddon, Richmond, Va., July 19, 1864, to Howell Cobb. Conscription exemptions. W. R. O. R., ser. 4, vol. 3, p. 543. Howell Cobb, Macon, Ga., July 21, 1864, to J. A. Seddon. Conscription exemptions. W. R. O. R., ser. 1, vol. 52, pt. 2, p. 710. J. A. Seddon, Richmond, Va., July 21, 1864, to Howell Cobb. Conscription exemptions. Confederate Records of Georgia, III, 596. J. B. Hood, Atlanta, Ga., July 31, 1864, to Howell Cobb. Stoneman's raid.

W. R. O. R., ser. 1, vol. 38, pt. 5, p. 935. Howell Cobb, Macon, Ga., August 1, 1864, to Samuel Cooper. The defeat of

Stoneman's raid. W. R. O. R., ser. 1, vol. 38, pt. 3, p. 972. F. A. Shoup, Atlanta, Ga., August 10, 1864, to Howell Cobb. Inquires the strength of the Andersonville garrison. W. R. O. R, ser. 1, vol. 38, pt. 5, p. 954.

Jefferson Davis, Richmond, Va., August 11, 1864, to Howell Cobb. Controversy with Gov. Brown. W. R. O. R., ser. 4, vol. 3, p. 580. Howell Cobb, Macon, Ga., August 12, 1864, to J. A. Seddon. Urges that no more prison camps be established in Georgia. W. R. O. R., ser. 2, vol. 7, p. 585.

Howell Cobb, Macon, Ga., August 31,1864, to William M. Browne. The supporting force for the bureau of conscription. W. R. O. R., ser. 4, vol. 3, p. 613.

Jefferson Davis, Richmond, Va., September 1, 1864, to Howell Cobb. Asks reinforcement of Hardee. W. R. O. R., ser. 1, vol. 39, pt. 2, p. 811.

Jefferson Davis, Richmond, Va., September 3, 1864, to Howell Cobb. Reinforcement of Hardee. W. R. O. R. , ser. 1, vol. 39, pt. 2, p. 813.

J. B. Hood, Lovejoy's Station, Ga. , September 6, 1864, to Howell Cobb. Orders reinforcement of Andersonville garrison. W. R. O. R., ser. 1, vol. 38, pt. 5, p. 1025.

J. A. Seddon, Richmond, Va., September 15, 1864, to Howell Cobb. Instructions concerning impressment of supplies. W. R. O. R., ser. 4, vol. 3, pp. 644, 645.

Alexander H. Stephens, Crawfordville, Ga., September 22, 1864, to Isaac Scott and others. The cause of liberty; the peace movement in the North.

Cleveland, Stephens, pp. 191-196. Alexander H. Stephens, Crawfordville, Ga., September 22, 1864, to a committee.

Approves resolutions of the Georgia legislature endorsing state sovereignty and advocating a peace movement, but deprecates the employment of any other machinery than that of the Confederate government. Frank Moore,

Rebellion Record, Vol. II, documents, pp. 182-184. J. B. Hood, Palmetto, Ga., September 3, 1864, to Howell Cobb. Assignment of

Cobb to the command of the district of Georgia. W. R. O. R., ser. 1, vol. 39, pt. 2, p. 882. J. B. Hood, Carley's House, Ga., October 1, 1864, to Howell Cobb. Orders obstruction of the Georgia Railroad. W. R. O. R., ser. 1, vol. 39, pt. 3, p. 788.

Alexander H. Stephens, Crawfordville, Ga., October 1, 1864, to William King.

Declines Sherman's overture for negotiations. Cleveland, Stephens, pp. 196, 197; Johnston and Browne, Stephens, p. 472. Howell Cobb, Macon, Ga., October 7, 1864, to Samuel Cooper. The detailing of troops. W. R. O. R., ser. 1, vol. 39, pt 3, p. 801.

J. A. Seddon, Richmond, Va., October 11, 1864, to Howell Cobb. Conscription exemptions. W. R. O. R., ser. 1, vol. 52, pt. 2, p. 760; Confederate Records of Georgia, III, 638, 639. Howell Cobb, Macon, Ga., October 22, 1864, to J. A. Seddon. Conscription exemptions and Georgia Militia. W. R. O. R., ser. 1, vol. 52, pt. 2, pp. 764-766; Confederate Records of Georgia, III, 639-642. Howell Cobb, Lovejoy's Station, Ga., November 2, 1864, to George W. Brent.

Plans for operating against Atlanta. W. R. O. R., ser. 1, vol. 39, pt. 3, p. 878.

Alexander H. Stephens, Crawfordvllle, Ga., November 4, 1864, to Alexander J. Marshall. Constitutional doctrines. Cleveland, Stephens, pp. 796-804.

J. B. Hood, near Florence, Ala., November 11, 1864, to Howell Cobb. The obstruction of Sherman's advance. W. R. O. R., ser. 1, vol. 39, pt. 3, p. 911.

Howell Cobb, Macon, Ga., November 14, 1864, to J. A. Seddon. Control of Georgia Militia. W. R. O. R., ser. 4, vol. 3, p. 822.

Robert Toombs, Macon, Ga., November 17, 1864 to Joseph E. Brown. Retreat of Georgia Militia before Sherman's advance. W. R. O. R. , ser. 1, vol. 44, p. 862; Confederate Records of Georgia, III, 673.

John C. Whitner, Augusta, Ga., November 18, 1864, to Howell Cobb. The records of the Confederate Provisional Congress. W. R. O. R., ser. 4, vol. 3, pp. 1016-1018.

Jefferson Davis, Richmond, Va., November 21, 1864, to Alexander H. Stephens. Demands a personal explanation. W. R. O. R., ser. 4, vol. 3, p. 840.

Alexander H. Stephens, Richmond, Va., December 13, 1860, to Jefferson Davis. Strictures upon the conduct of Davis in rejecting plans for a peace movement. W. R. O. R., ser. 4, vol. 3, pp. 934-040.

Howell Cobb, Macon, Ga., December 17, 1864, to Jefferson Davis. The records of the Confederate Provisional Congress. W. R. O. R., ser. 4, vol. 3, pp. 1015, 1016.

Howell Cobb, Macon, Ga., December 25, 1864, to G. T. Beauregard. The military prostration of Georgia. W. R. O. R., ser. 1, vol. 44, p. 989.

Howell Cobb, Macon, Ga., December 25, 1864, to J. A. Seddon. Recommends resort to voluntary enlistments in place of conscription. W. R. O. R., ser. 4, vol. 3, pp. 964, 965.

G. T. Beauregard, Charleston, S. C, December 28, 1864, to Howell Cobb. Operations near Savannah. W. R. O. R. , ser. 1, vol. 53, pp. 385, 386.

J. A. Seddon, Richmond, Va., December 30, 1864, to Howell Cobb. Urges enforcement of conscription. W. R. O. R., ser. 4, vol. 3, p. 981.

Howell Cobb, Macon, Ga., January 2, 1865, to J. A. Seddon. Organization of a cavalry brigade for the Georgia Reserve. W. R. O. R., ser. 4, vol. 3, p. 991.

Jefferson Davis, Richmond, Va., January 6, 1865, to Alexander H. Stephens. Reply to strictures of Stephens. W. R. O. R., ser. 4, vol. 3, pp. 1000-1004.

Howell Cobb, Macon, Ga., January 8, 1865, to J. A. Seddon. Deprecates enlistment of negroes in Confederate Army. W. R. O. R., ser. 4, vol. 3, pp. 1009, 1010.

J. A. Seddon, Richmond, Va., January 19, 1865, to Howell Cobb. Disapproves project of enlistment in new organizations, and urges vigor in conscription. W. R. O. R., ser. 4, vol. 3, pp. 1030, 1031.

Howell Cobb, Augusta, Ga., January 20, 1865, to Jefferson Davis. Desperation and disaffection in Georgia; recommends restoration of Joseph E. Johnston and abandonment of conscription. W. R. O. R., ser. 1, vol. 53, pp. 393, 394.

William M. Browne, Augusta, Ga., January 28, 1865, to Howell Cobb. Hindrances to conscription. W. R. O. R., ser. 4, vol. 3, pp. 1048, 1049.

Howell Cobb, Augusta, Ga., January 11, 1865, to J. A. Seddon. Local organizations refuse to obey Cobb's orders to mobilize. W. K. O. R., ser. 1, vol. 47, pt. 2, p. 1055.

Alexander H. Stephens, J. A. Campbell, and R. M. T. Hunter, Petersburg, Va.,
January 30, 1865, to TT. S. Grant. Peace conference. Stephens, War between the States, II, 797. Thomas T. Eckert, City Point, Va., February 1, 1865, to Alexander H. Stephens,
J. A. Campbell, and R. M. T. Hunter. Peace conference. Stephens, War between the States, II, 796. Alexander H. Stephens, J. A, Campbell, and R. M. T. Hunter, City Point, Va.,
February 1, 1865, to Thomas T. Eckert. Peace conference. Stephens, War between the States, II, 801. Alexander H. Stephens, J. A Campbell, and R. M. T. Hunter, City Point, Va.,
February 1, 1865, to U. S. Grant. Peace conference. Stephens, War between the States, II, 799. Howell Cobb, Macon, Ga., February 1, 1865, to J. A. Seddon. The complaint of the commandant of conscripts. W. R. O. R., ser. 4, vol. 3, p. 1048. Alexander H. Stephens, J. A. Campbell, and R. M. T. Hunter, City Point, Va.,
February 2, 1865, to Thomas T. Eckert. Peace conference. Stephens, War between the States, II, 802. Abraham Lincoln, Washington, D. C, February 10, 1865, to Alexander H. Stephens. Exchange of two prisoners. Cleveland, Stephens, facsimile, facing p. 199.

Howell Cobb, Macon, Ga., March 16,1865, to Cuvier Grover. Delivery of prisoners of war. W. R. O. R., ser. 2, vol. 8, p. 403.

Alexander H. Stephens, Milledgeville, Ga., January 22, 1866, to J. F. Johnson and others. Declines to permit the use of his name as candidate for the United States Senate. Cleveland, Stephens, p. 204; Johnston and Browne, Stephens, pp. 489, 490.

H. R. Casey and others, Milledgeville, Ga., January 29, 1866, to Alexander H. Stephens. Asks whether Stephens will serve if elected United States Senator. Cleveland, Stephens, p. 205; Johnston and Browne, Stephens, p. 490.

Alexander H. Stephens, Milledgeville, Ga., January 29, to H. R. Casey and others. Would not decline if elected. Cleveland, Stephens, p. 205; Johnston and Browne, Stephens, p. 490.

C. G. Memminger, September 17, 1867, to Alexander H. Stephens. The Confederate cotton-loan project. Avary, Stephens, p. 66.

Alexander H. Stephens, Crawfordville, Ga., October 22, 1868, to the editors of the Baltimore Statesman. Review of A. T. Bledsoe's review of Stephens' War between the States. A. H. Stephens, Reviewers Reviewed, N. Y., 1872, pp. 9-28.

Alexander H. Stephens, Crawfordville, Ga., June 4, 1869, to the editors of the National Intelligencer. Reply to communication of S. S. Nicholas. Stephens, Reviewers Reviewed, pp. 39-50.

Alexander H. Stephens, Crawfordville, Ga., June 23, 1869, to the editors of the National Intelligencer. Reply to the reply of S. S. Nicholas. Stephens, Reviewers Reviewed, pp. 53-60.

Alexander H. Stephens, Crawfordville, Ga., August 17, 1869, to the editors of the Augusta (Ga.) Constitutionalist. Reply to Horace Greeley's criticism of Stephens' War between the States. Stephens, Reviewers Reviewed, pp. 137-146.

Alexander H. Stephens, Crawfordville, Ga., August 31, 1869, to the editors of the New York World. Reply to review of Stephens' War between the States, by George T. Curtis.

Stephens, Reviewers Reviewed, pp. 91-114.

Alexander H. Stephens, Crawfordville, Ga., September 25, 1869, to the editors of the New York World. Reply to reply by Curtis. Stephens, Reviewers Reviewed, pp. 123-136.

Alexander H. Stephens, Crawfordville, Ga., June 25, 1870, to the editors of the Memphis Appeal. Reply to communication of Alexander M. Clayton. Stephens, Reviewers Reviewed, p. 149.

Alexander H. Stephens, Crawfordville, Ga., July 6, 1870, to B. Barksdale. Reply to an editorial in the Jackson (Miss.) Clarion. Stephens, Reviewers Reviewed, pp. 157-159.

Alexander H. Stephens, Crawfordville, Ga., July 13, 1870, to Charles Ellis. Reply to editorial in the Savannah Republican. Stephens, Reviewers Reviewed, pp. 177-179.

E. Barksdale, Jackson, Miss., July 16,1870, to Alexander H. Stephens. Reply to Stephens' reply. Stephens, Reviewers Reviewed, pp. 159-162.

Alexander H. Stephens, Crawfordville, Ga., August 6, 1860, to E. Barksdale. Reply to Barksdale's reply. Stephens, Reviewers Reviewed, pp. 169-171.

E. Barksdale, Jackson, Miss., August, 1870, to Alexander H. Stephens. Sur rejoinder. Stephens, Reviewers Reviewed, pp. 171, 172. Alexander H. Stephens, Crawfordville, Ga., August 28, 1870, to E. Barksdale.

Rebuttal. Stephens, Reviewers Reviewed, pp. 173-176. Alexander H. Stephens, Crawfordville, Ga., September 21, 1870, to the editor of the Augusta, Ga., Constitutionalist. Reply to speeches of Amos T. Aker man. Stephens, Reviewers Reviewed, pp. 188-195. Alexander H. Stephens, Crawfordville, Ga., October 28,1870, to John W. Forney.

Reply to editorial in the Washington Sunday Morning Chronicle. Stephens, Reviewers Reviewed, pp. 180-187. Alexander H. Stephens, Crawfordville, Ga., November 19, 1870, to the editor of the Atlanta New Era. Reply to an editorial. Stephens, Reviewers Reviewed, pp. 196-207.

Alexander H. Stephens, Crawfordville, Ga., December 2, 1870, to the editor of the Atlanta New Era. Reply to the New Era's reply. Stephens, Reviewers Reviewed, pp. 214-225.

Alexander H. Stephens, 1871, to a friend. Reminiscences of antebellum politics. Avary, Stephens, pp. 15-29.

F. A. P. Barnard, New York, February 16, 1878, to Alexander H. Stephens.

Thanks for Stephens's speech at presentation of Lincoln's portrait Johnston and Browne, Stephens, p. 538.

CALENDAR OF THE LETTERS OF TOOMBS, STEPHENS AND COBB HERE PRINTED.

Page.

Robert Toombs to Alexander H. Stephens, January 1, 1844. Georgia politics;

Whig affairs 53

John W. H. Underwood to Howell Cobb, February 2, 1844. Resents the abolition agitation 54

Thomas Ritchie to Howell Cobb, February 8, 1844. The Democratic campaign. 55 Thomas Ritchie to Howell Cobb, May 6, 1844. Dissension among Virginia

Democrats upon Texan annexation and Van Buren's candidacy 56

Alexander H. Stephens to James Thomas, May 17, 1844. Censure upon the

Texan policy of Tyler and Calhoun 57

Thomas Ritchie to Howell Cobb, May 23, 1844. The problem of the Baltimore convention 59

Alexander H. Stephens to James Thomas, July 16, 1844. The Whig campaign in Georgia 59

Wood Hinton to Howell Cobb, January 7, 1845. Inquiry for a haven for emancipated slaves 60

Robert Toombs to Alexander H. Stephens, January 24, 1845. Tariff, Texas, and slavery 60

J. W. Burney to Howell Cobb, January 31, 1845. Texan annexation 62

Alexander H. Stephens to James Thomas, February 11, 1845. Texan annexation 62

Junius Hillyer to Howell Cobb, February 15, 1845. Texan annexation 63

Robert Toombs to Alexander H. Stephens, February 16, 1845. Texan annexation 63

George D. Phillips to Howell Cobb, February 21, 1845. Texan annexation 65

George D. Phillips to Howell Cobb, February 25, 1845. Texan annexation; the superintendentship of the United States branch mint at Dahlonega, Ga 66

Alexander H. Stephens to Howell Cobb, February 27, 1845. Facilities for travel between Georgia and Washington 68

William B. Wofford to Howell Cobb, December 14, 1845. Georgia politics... 69 George D. Phillips to Howell Cobb, December 30, 1845. The Oregon question. 69 Alexander H. Stephens to George W. Crawford, February 3, 1846. The Galphin claim; the Oregon question 71

Robert Toombs to George W. Crawford, February 6, 1846. The Galphin claim; the Oregon question 72

Howell Cobb to his wife, April 3, 1846. Oregon 75

John P. King to Howell Cobb, May 7, 1846. The Mexican War 75

Howell Cobb to his wife, May 10, 1846. The Mexican War 76

Thomas R. R. Cobb to Howell Cobb, May 12, 1846. Enthusiasm in Georgia for a war with Mexico 76

Albon Chase to Howell Cobb, May 20, 1846. Oregon, Mexico, and local politics. 77

William Hope Hull to Howell Cobb, May 22, 1846. Mexico and Oregoxi 78

Howell Cobb to his wife, June 4, 1846. Mexico and Oregon 79

John B. Lamar to Howell Cobb, June 8, 1846. Plantation investments; Calhoun; Woodbury 80

Howell Cobb to his wife, June 14, 1846. Office seeking, tariff, Oregon 81 31

Page.

John B. Lamar to Howell Cobb, June 24, 1846. Georgia Whig opposition to the

Mexican War 82

Charles J. McDonald to Howell Cobb, July 7, 1846. In championship of State rights 84

James F. Cooper to Howell Cobb, July 8, 1846. Local politics 85

John H. Lumpkin to Howell Cobb, November 13, 1846. Democratic party problems 86

Edward J. Harden to Howell Cobb, May 3, 1847. Prospects of the presidential campaign 87

Thomas R. R. Cobb to Howell Cobb, June 23, 1847. The Mexican War 88

Isaac E. Holmes to Howell Cobb, August 21, 1847. The Wilmot Proviso 88

Robert Toombs to James Thomas, November 19, 1847. Shortcomings of the

Georgia supreme court 88

Luther J. Glenn to Howell Cobb, December 1, 1847. The Wilmot Proviso 89

Hopkins Holsey to Howell Cobb, December 3, 1847. Georgia politics; corporation charters; the popular election of judges 89

Hopkins Holsey to Howell Cobb, December 31, 1847. Congressional politics; the Wilmot Proviso 91

Joseph Henry Lumpkin to Howell Cobb, January 21, 1848. Current politics; the pro-slavery position 94

Luther J. Glenn to Howell Cobb, February 12, 1848. Current politics 95

Lucius Q. C. Lamar to Howell Cobb, February 15, 1848. Inquiry for congressional reports 96

Henry L. Benning to Howell Cobb, February 23, 1848. Analysis of the sectional position and prospects of the Whig and Democratic Parties; proposal of a Democratic programme 97

Robert Toombs to James Thomas, April 16, 1848. Disapproval of Clay's candidacy 103

Robert Toombs to James Thomas, May 1, 1848. Further discussion of Clay... 104 Thomas W. Thomas to Howell Cobb, May 27, 1848. Local petition; current politics 105

Thomas R. R. Cobb to Howell Cobb, May 31, 1848. The nomination of Cass.. 106

Thomas W. Thomas to Howell Cobb, June 5, 1848. In praise of Cass 107

James C. Dobbin to Howell Cobb, June 15, 1848. Current politics; slavery in the Territories 107

W. C. Daniell to Howell Cobb, June 20,1848. The presidential campaign 109

Henry R. Jackson to Howell Cobb, June 21,1848. Current politics 110

Thomas Smith to Howell Cobb, June 27, 1848. The slavery issue in the presidential campaign I11

W. C. Daniell to Howell Cobb, July 1,1848. Democratic prospects in Georgia; secession contemplated by the writer 113

Thomas W. Thomas to Howell Cobb, July 7, 1848. The presidential campaign in Georgia 114

James Jackson to Howell Cobb, July 9,1848. Democratic prospects in Georgia. 115 John B. Lamar to Howell Cobb, July 12, 1848. The necessity of a prompt settlement of the question of slavery in the Territories 116

John H. Lumpkin to Howell Cobb, August 22, 1848. Democratic affairs in

Georgia and east Tennessee 116

Alexander H. Stephens to the editor of the Federal Union, August 30, 1848. Views upon the constitutionality of slavery in the Territories 117

George Fries to Howell Cobb, September 4, 1848. Democratic prospects in
Ohio 124

Page.

Ausburn Birdsall to Howell Cobb, September 8, 1848. Whig policies in New
York 125

Richard French to Howell Cobb, September 10, 1848. Current politics 126

George S. Houston to Howell Cobb, September 23, 1848. Democratic prospects in Alabama 126

Alexander H. Stephens to John J. Crittenden, September 26, 1848. Whig prospects in Georgia 127

Robert Toombs to John J. Crittenden, September 27, 1848. The presidential campaign 127

Alfred Iverson to Howell Cobb, October 17,1848. The Democratic campaign in Georgia 129

James F. Cooper to Howell Cobb, October 20, 1848. Whig and Democratic activities in northeastern Georgia 130

George S. Houston to Howell Cobb, October 23, 1848. Campaign prospects... 131

Thomas D. Harris to Howell Cobb, October 29, 1848. Democratic prospects in Pennsylvania, etc 132

Howell Cobb to a committee of citizens in Charleston, S. C, November 47, 1848. Comparison of northern Whig and Democratic attitudes upon the slavery issue 133

Robert Toombs to John J. Crittenden, November 9,1848. The Whig victory in Georgia 135

John Forsyth to Howell Cobb, November 10, 1848. The Democratic defeat; personal inquiry 136

James F. Cooper to Howell Cobb, November 11, 1848. Democratic losses in northeastern Georgia 137

Mark A. Cooper to Howell Cobb, November 20, 1848. Suggestion of a United
States ordnance foundry in the South 137

Howell Cobb to his wife, December 21, 1848. Debate upon the slave-trade in the District of Columbia 138

John H. Lumpkin to Howell Cobb, December 25, 1848. Calhoun's movement for consolidating the South 138

Alexander H. Stephens probably to George W. Crawford, December 27,1848.
The Galphin claim 138

Robert Toombs to John J. Crittenden, January 3, 1849. Censures Calhoun's efforts to organize a southern phalanx in Congress; hopes Clay will be kept out of the Senate; 139

Robert Toombs to John J. Crittenden, January 22, 1849. A plan for adjusting the question of slavery in the new Territories; the Calhoun movement 14p

William Hope Hull to Howell Cobb, January 26,1849. Popular quietude despite the excitement of the politicians 142

Hopkins Holsey to Howell Cobb, January 29, 1849. The sectional issue as affecting the Whig and Democratic parties 142

Howell Cobb to his wife, February 1, 1849. Current politics 145

Alexander H. Stephens to John J. Crittenden, February 6, 1849. Urges Crittenden to accept office in Taylor's Cabinet 146

Robert Toombs to John J. Crittenden, February 9, 1849. Current affairs; the Preston bill 146

Hopkins Holsey to Howell Cobb, February 13, 1849. The peril of southern rights and the problems of southern Democrats 148

Thomas W. Thomas to Howell Cobb, February 16, 1849. Indorses Cobb's opposition to Calhoun's southern-rights movement 152

Hopkins Holsey to Howell Cobb, February 24,1849. The prospective necessity of disunion as a refuge from northern aggressions 152 73566—13 3 Page.

Alexander H. Stephens to George W. Crawford, March 2, 1849. The Galphin claim; local politics 155

John H. Lumpkin to Howell Cobb, March 12,1849. Southern rights and Democratic regularity 15(3

George S. Houston to Howell Cobb, March 14, 1849. The popularity of the southern-rights movement in Alabama 157

John W. Burke to Howell Cobb, March 22, 1849. The predicament of a Unionist editor in a southern-rights community 157

George S. Houston to Howell Cobb, March 22, 1849. Alabama politics 158

Thomas D. Harris to Howell Cobb, May 8, 1849. Cobb's prospects for the Speakership 158

Howell Cobb to James Buchanan, June 2, 1849. Asks Buchanan's indorsement of his policy 159

James B. Bowlin to Howell Cobb, June 6, 1849. The campaign against Benton in Missouri 159

John H. Lumpkin to Howell Cobb, June 6, 1849. The contest between

Union and southern-rights policies within the Democratic party of Georgia 160

James Buchanan to Howell Cobb, June 12,1849. A testimonial indorsing Cobb's policy and praising his abilities 161

John H. Lumpkin to Howell Cobb, June 13, 1849. Local Democratic affairs.. 163

Howell Cobb to James Buchanan, June 17, 1849. Personal explanation 163

Lewis Cass to Howell Cobb, June 19, 1849. Indorses Cobb's policy 164

Robert Toombs to Mrs. Chapman Coleman, June 22, 1849. Censures John M. Clayton as an intriguer exerting an evil influence upon President Taylor 165

George S. Houston to Howell Cobb, June 26,1849. The adversity of the Unionist Democrats in Alabama 166

Thomas D. Harris to Howell Cobb, June 28, 1849. Democratic party affairs in Georgia and Alabama 167

Henry L. Benning to Howell Cobb, July 1, 1849. The northern Democrats are falling irretrievably under anti-slavery control. Dissolution of the Union is the only preventive of universal abolition. The South in establishing her independence should establish a consolidated republic rather than a confederacy 168

George S. Houston to Howell Cobb, July 28, 1849. Democratic faction strife in Alabama 172

George S. Houston to Howell Cobb, August 10, 1849. Victory of the Unionist Democrats in Alabama 173

Thomas W. Thomas to Howell Cobb, August 19 1849. Local politics in
Georgia 173

John L. Robinson to Howell Cobb, August 24, 1849. Democratic victory in
Ohio; prospects as to the Speakership in Congress 174

Alfred Iverson to Howell Cobb, October 6, 1849. Local Democratic affairs 175

John H. Lumpkin to Howell Cobb, October 19, 1849. Local Democratic affairs. 176

Howell Cobb to his wife, November 27, 1849. Speakership prospects 176

Howell Cobb to his wife, December 2, 1849. Democratic caucus on the Speakership 177

Howell Cobb to his wife, December 4, 1849. The Speakership contest in the
House 177

Henry R. Jackson to Howell Cobb, December 8, 1849. The Speakership 178

Howell Cobb to his wife, December 20, 1849. Sectional strife in the Speakership contest 179

Howell Cobb to his wife, December 22,1849. Cobb's election as Speaker under a plurality rule 179
Page.

James Buchanan to Howell Cobb, December 29, 1849. Congratulations; recommends Stanton of Tennessee for appointment on the Committee on Ways and Means 180

Howell Cobb to his wife, January 11, 1850. Affairs at Washington 181

W. C. Daniell to Howell Cobb, January 23, 1850. Asks aid in distributing copies of Stringfellow's '' Scriptural Defense of Slavery" 182

Howell Cobb to his wife, February 4, 1850. The tabling of a Wilmot Proviso resolution in the House 182

John B. Lamar to Howell Cobb, February 7, 1850. Apprehensions that the safeguarding of southern rights will necessitate disunion; personal affairs... 182

Howell Cobb to his wife, February 9, 1850. Disapproves Clay's speech on his proposed compromise 183

Alexander H. Stephens to James Thomas, February 13, 1850. The doubtful prospect of permanently allaying the sectional discontent 184

George D. Phillips to Howell Cobb, March 10, 1850. The sectional issue in Georgia Democratic affairs 184

Hiram Warner to Howell Cobb, March 17, 1850. Urges the adjustment of the sectional issue prior to the meeting of the projected Nashville convention... 186

Robert Toombs to Linton Stephens, March 22, 1850. Dispraises the personnel of the Georgia Legislature and of Congress; is hopeful that the sectional issue will soon be adjusted 188

Williams Rutherford, jr., to Howell Cobb, April 16,1850. Current politics.. .-. 189

Lewis Cass to Howell Cobb, May 5, 1850. Congressional negotiations 190

Thomas R. R. Cobb to Howell Cobb, May 7,1850. Union sentiment in Georgia. 191

John B. Lamar to Howell Cobb, July 3, 1850. The compromise 191

Alexander H. Stephens to the editors of the National Intelligencer, July 3, 1850. The Texan boundary and southern rights 192

Absalom H. Chappell to Howell Cobb, July 10, 1850. Disunion sentiment among the Georgia Democrats; urges Cobb to issue a Unionist address to his constituents 193

William H. Morton to Howell Cobb, July 10, 1850. Local disunion sentiment; urgent need of compromise legislation 194

Alexander H. Stephens to the editors of the Baltimore Clipper, July 13, 1850.
Contradicts a newspaper canard 195

Howell Cobb to William Hope Hull, July 17, 1850. Advocates the Clay compromise 196

John H. Lumpkin to Howell Cobb, July 21, 1850. The action of the Nashville convention has fostered disunion sentiment among the Georgia Democrats; the Whigs are Unionist 206

John H. Lumpkin to Howell Cobb, July 29, 1850. Local agitation of the sectional issue; urgency of compromise legislation 208

D. M. Haley to Howell Cobb, August 2, 1850. Questions the constitutional authority of Congress to take territory from Texas 209

Howell Cobb to his wife, August 10, 1850. The prospects of the compromise.. 210

James A. Meriwether to Howell Cobb, August 24, 1850. Local disunion agitation; the need of compromise legislation 210

Robert Toombs to Millard Fillmore, September 9, 1850. Charles J. Jenkins declines the Secretaryship of the Interior 212

William Woods to Howell Cobb, September 15, 1850. Local sentiment on the compromise 212

Luther J. Glenn to Howell Cobb, September 21, 1850. The question in Georgia of accepting or rejecting the compromise..... 213 Page.

John H. Lumpkin to Howell Cobb, October 5, 1850. The Unionist campaign for delegates to the Georgia convention 214

Howell Cobb to John B. Lamar, October 10, 1850. Progress of the Unionist campaign 215

Alexander W. Buel to Howell Cobb, October 12, 1850. The sectional issue in Michigan politics 215

M. C. Fulton to Howell Cobb, November 6, 1850. Unionist sentiment in North Carolina and Virginia; popularity of Cobb 217

Robert Toombs to Howell Cobb, January 2, 1851. The action of the Whig and Democratic caucuses upon the question of indorsing the compromise 218

Benjamin Balche to Howell Cobb, January 10, 1851. Plans for promoting a "National Union" party 220

Howell Cobb to Absalom H. Chappell and others, February 7, 1851. Indorsing the plans of the Constitutional Union Party in Georgia 221

Joseph H. Lumpkin to Howell Cobb, February 10, 1851. Constitutional Union
Party affairs 227

Robert Toombs to Absalom H. Chappell and others, February 15,1851. Indorsing the Constitutional Union movement 227

John H. Lumpkin to Howell Cobb, February 16, 1851. Problems of the Constitutional Unionists 229

Thomas W. Thomas to Howell Cobb, April 14,1851. Advises Cobb not to accept a gubernatorial nomination 230

S. T. Chapman to Howell Cobb, April 24, 1851. Current politics 232

Robert Toombs to John J. Crittenden, April 25, 1851. Current politics 232

James F. Cooper to Howell Cobb, May 5, 1851. The quandary of the Union Democrats 233

John Calvin Johnson to Howell Cobb, May 22, 1851. Local politics 234

S. T. Chapman to Howell Cobb, June 11,1851. The gubernatorial campaign in
Georgia 236

James A. Meriwether and others to Howell Cobb, June 18, 1851. Notification of
Cobb's nomination for the governorship of Georgia by the Constitutional Union party 236

Alexander H. Stephens to Howell Cobb, June 23, 1851. Campaign issues in
Georgia 237

Howell Cobb to James A. Meriwether and others, June 24, 1851. Acceptance of the gubernatorial nomination 238

A. H. Kenan to Alexander H. Stephens, July 3, 1851. Warns Stephens that
Toombs is aspiring to the United States Senate 241

John B. Lamar to Howell Cobb, July 3, 1851. The secessionist campaign in South Carolina 242

Henry S. Foote to Howell Cobb, July 9,1851. Unionist prospects in Mississippi. 242

Robert E. Martin to Howell Cobb, July 13, 1851. The Georgia campaign 242

Andrew J. Donelson to Howell Cobb, July 15, 1851. National Democratic affairs 244

Samuel W. Flournoy to Howell Cobb, July 18, 1851. The Georgia campaign.. 245

E. G. Cabaniss to Howell Cobb, August 1,1851. The Georgia campaign 246

John H. Lumpkin to Howell Cobb, August 1, 1851. The Georgia campaign... 247

Howell Cobb to John Rutherford and others, August 12, 1851. The right of secession in theory and practice 249

Alexander H. Stephens to Howell Cobb, September 1, 1851. The Georgia campaign 260

W. P. Jones and others to Howell Cobb, September 11,1851. The Georgia campaign 260 Page.

Robert Toombs to Howell Cobb, October 11, 1851. Congratulates Cobb on his election as governor; announces his own candidacy for the Senate 261

George Ashmun to Howell Cobb, October 11, 1851. Congratulations to Cobb; politics in Massachusetts 261

Andrew J. Donelson to Howell Cobb, October 22,1851. The problem of Democratic regularity as regards the Georgia Constitutional Unionists 262

Andrew J. Donelson to Howell Cobb, October 26, 1851. Current affairs 264

Thomas D. Harris to Howell Cobb, November 23, 1851. Current affairs 264

Alexander H. Stephens to Howell Cobb, November 24,1851. Affairs at Washington 264

Alexander H. Stephens to Howell Cobb, November 26, 1851. The contest between the Constitutional Union and Southern Rights parties for the regular Democratic standing 265

Thomas D. Harris to Howell Cobb, November 29,1851. The House Democratic caucus at Washington 267

Alexander H. Stephens to Howell Cobb, December 5, 1851. The Democratic caucus 268

George W. Jones to Howell Cobb, December 7,1851. The Democratic caucus. 269

Alexander H. Stephens to Linton Stephens, December 10,1851. Party adjustments and problems in Congress 271

George W. Jones to Howell Cobb, January 25,1852. Democratic conditions and prospects 275

John Slidell to Howell Cobb, January 28, 1852. Views on the Democratic situation 275

Thomas D. Harris to Howell Cobb, February 2, 1852. The embarrassments of
Union Democrats 277

Howell Cobb to C. W. Denison, February 3, 1852. Declines support for the Vice-Presidency on a ticket with Webster 278

Hopkins Holsey to Howell Cobb, February 6,1852. The situation of the Union Democrats 279

John B. Lamar to Howell Cobb, February 12,1852. The quandary of the Union Democrats 280

William Hope Hull to Howell Cobb, February 14,1852. Advice that the Union Democrats make overtures for rejoining the Southern Rights Democrats 280

Alexander H. Stephens to Messrs. Fisher and De Leon, February 25, 1852. The expediency and finality of the compromise 282

John E. Ward and Henry R. Jackson to Howell Cobb, February 28,1852. The position of the Union Democrats 284

John H. Lumpkin to Howell Cobb, March 2, 1852. Local Democratic proceedings 287

John B. Lamar to Howell Cobb, March 8, 1852. Local proceedings; the Democratic prospect 287

Thomas D. Harris to Howell Cobb, April 7, 1852. Party affairs at Washington.. 289

John B. Lamar to Howell Cobb, April 12,1852. Local political developments.. 289

George W. Jones to Howell Cobb, April 14,1852. Advice to the Union Democrats of Georgia 290

Lewis Cass to Howell Cobb, April 15, 1852. Presidential prospects 291

John Milledge to Howell Cobb, April 17,1852. Plans for the Georgia Constitutional Union party convention 291

Andrew J. Donelson to Howell Cobb, April 25, 1852 293

Andrew J. Donelson to Howell Cobb, May 10, 1852. Presidential prospects; personal affairs 294

William B. Wofford to Howell Cobb, May 21,1852. Current politics 295

Henry Hull, jr., to Howell Cobb, May 25, 1852. The Baltimore Democratic convention 295 Page.

Robert Toombs to Howell Cobb, May 27, 1852. Presidential prospects 297

Thomas D. Harris to Howell Cobb, May 28, 1852. The Baltimore convention. 298 John H. Lumpkin to Howell Cobb, June 6, 1852. The nomination of Pierce.. 299

James Jackson to Howell Cobb, June 8, 1852. The Baltimore convention 300

George W. Jones to Howell Cobb, June 13, 1852. Campaign prospects 301

John B. Lamar to Howell Cobb, June 22,1852. Party problems in Georgia... 302

Philip Clayton to Howell Cobb, June 28, 1852. Politics at Washington 303

Alexander H. Stephens to the editor of the Augusta, Ga., Chronicle and Sentinel, June 28, 1852. Repudiates the nomination of Scott and advocates the running of an independent ticket 304

John B. Lamar to Howell Cobb, July 1,1852. The embarrassments of the Union Democrats in Georgia 307

John H. Lumpkin to Howell Cobb, July 11, 1852. Union Democratic plans.. 308

Orion Stroud to Howell Cobb, August 2,1852. Invites an expression of views. . 311

Howell Cobb to Orion Stroud, August 4,1852. The course of the Union Democrats 311

Henry R. Jackson to Howell Cobb, August 7, 1852. The disintegration of the Constitutional Union party in Georgia 316

John B. Lamar to Howell Cobb, August 10,1852. The official dissolution of the Constitutional Union party 316

Philip Clayton to Howell Cobb, August 25,1852. The attitude of newspapers at Washington 317

Howell Cobb to his wife, August 27, 1852. The prospect of Democratic harmony in Georgia 318

Henry L. Benning to Howell Cobb, September 2, 1852. Hopes of Democratic reunion; apprehensions of eventual necessity of disrupting the Union to prevent northern tyranny 318

George D. Phillips to Howell Cobb, September 15,1852. Hopes for Democratic reunion 319

Howell Cobb to John B. Lamar, September 18, 1852. The failure of the plan for Democratic fusion 320

Francis J. Grund to Howell Cobb, October 29,1852. The campaign in Pennsylvania 321

Robert Toombs to John J. Crittenden, December 15, 1852. Satisfaction at the election of Pierce 322

Lewis Cass to Howell Cobb, December 18,1852. Cabinet prospects 322

John B. Lamar to Howell Cobb, January 12,1853. Political prospects 323

George W. Jones to Howell Cobb, February 11,1853. Conjectures as to Pierce's Cabinet 323

JohnB. Lamar to Howell Cobb, February 14,1853. Current affairs 324

Thomas D. Harris to Howell Cobb, February 15,1853. Cabinet conjectures 325

Alexander H. Stephens to James Thomas, February 22,1853. Current affairs... 325 George W. Jones to Howell Cobb, March 10,1853. Pierce's inaugural address... 326 L. B. Mercer to Howell Cobb, April 10, 1853. Pierce's appointments; politics in Tennessee 326

George W. Jones to Howell Cobb, May 19, 1853 327

John H. Lumpkin to Howell Cobb, July 2,1853. The gubernatorial nomination in Georgia 329

Alexander C. Morton to Howell Cobb, July 2, 1853. Local politics 330

John W. Forney to Howell Cobb, July 29,1853. Presidential appointments 330

John L. Ketcham to Howell Cobb, August 9, 1853. The problem of proving a negro's claim to freedom 331

William Hope Hull to Howell Cobb,

August 16, 1853. The gubernatorial campaign in Georgia 334 Page.

Lucius Q. 0. Lamar to Howell Cobb, September 21, 1853. Georgia senatorial candidacies 335

Thomas D. Harris to Howell Cobb, October 13, 1853. Current politics 336

John T. Grant to Howell Cobb, October 18, 1853. Georgia politics 337

Thomas C. Howard and H. K. Green to Howell Cobb, December 3, 1853. Georgia politics 337

John H. Lumpkin to Howell Cobb, December 28, 1853. The senatorial campaign in Georgia 338

Colin M. Ingersoll to Howell Cobb, January 20, 1854. National Democratic embarrassments over the Kansas-Nebraska bill 339

Robert Toombs to W. W. Burwell, February 3, 1854. The Kansas-Nebraska bill 342

Stephen A. Douglas to Howell Cobb, April 2, 1854. The Kansas-Nebraska bill. 343 Thomas H. Bayley to Howell Cobb, May 6, 1854. The Kansas-Nebraska bill... 343 Alexander H. Stephens to W. W. Burwell, May 7, 1854. The Kansas-Nebraska bill 343

Alexander H. Stephens to W. W. Burwell, May 8, 1854. Opposes any agreement by the United States to abandon privateering 344

Alexander H. Stephens to J. W. Duncan, May 26, 1854. The passage of the

Kansas-Nebraska bill; affairs in Cuba 345

Alexander H. Stephens to W. W. Burwell, June 26, 1854. The position of the southern Whiga 346

Alexander H. Stephens to W.W. Burwell, June 27, 1854. The southern Whigs. 347

Howell Cobb to his wife, October 1, 1854. Cobb's political prospects 347

Howell Cobb to James Buchanan, December 5, 1854. The political outlook;

Buchanan the most eligible presidential candidate for the Democratic party 348

Alexander H. Stephens to W. W. Burwell, December 30, 1854. The affairs of the Southern Quarterly Review 349

Thomas W. Thomas to Alexander H. Stephens, May 5, 1855. Requests a statement of Stephens's views 350

Robert Toombs to T. Lomax, June 6, 1855. Denounces the Know-nothing party. 350

Alexander H. Stephens to Thomas W. Thomas, June 7, 1855. Georgia politics.. 353 Robert Toombs to Alexander H. Stephens, June 21, 1855. Account of a trip to

England 353

Thomas D. Harris to Howell Cobb, October 15, 1855. The Speakership prospect. 355

Howell Cobb to his wife, December 23, 1855. The Speakership contest 356

Robert C. Winthrop to Howell Cobb, January 5, 1856. The Speakership contest. 357

Howell Cobb to his wife, February 2, 1856. Banks's election as Speaker 358

Robert Toombs to Thomas W. Thomas, February 9, 1856. Party and sectional affairs; estimate of Howell Cobb 359

Thomas W. Thomas to Alexander H. Stephens, February 25, 1856. The Kansas issue 361

Thomas R. R. Cobb to Howell Cobb, March 4, 1856. Presidential prospects 362

Howell Cobb to, April 21, 1856. Indorsement of Buchanan 363

Robert Toombs to George W. Crawford, May 17, 1856. Current affairs 364

Junius Hillyer to Howell Cobb, May 28, 1856. Current affairs 365

Robert Toombs to George W. Crawford, May 30, 1856. Current affairs 365

Gazaway B. Lamar to Howell Cobb, May 31, 1856. Brooks's assault upon Sumner 365

John E. Ward to Howell Cobb, June 3, 1856. The Cincinnati convention 367

Alexander H. Stephens to Thomas W. Thomas, June 16, 1856. Comparison of Buchanan's position in 1856 with that of Scott in 1852 367 Page.

John E. Ward to Howell Cobb, July 5, 1856. Political prospects 372

James Buchanan to Howell Cobb, July 10, 1856. Current politics 373

Howell Cobb to James Buchanan, July 14, 1856. Relations between Buchanan and Pierce 374

William Hope Hull to Howell Cobb, July 14, 1856. Relations with Pierce; campaign prospects 375

James Buchanan to Howell Cobb, July 22, 1856 376

Howell Cobb to James Buchanan, July 27, 1856. Campaign prospecta 377

Howell Cobb to James Buchanan, August 3, 1856. Relations with Pierce 378

Howell Cobb to James Buchanan, August 4, 1856. Prospects in Maryland 379

Howell Cobb to James Buchanan, August 14, 1856. The Maryland situation.. 379 Robert Toombs to Alexander H. Stephens, September 3, 1856. The campaign in

Georgia 380

Thomas W. Thomas to Alexander H. Stephens, September 5, 1856. The Georgia campaign 380

J. Branham to Howell Cobb, September 15, 1856. The campaign 381

Jeremiah S. Black to Howell Cobb, September 22, 1856. Advice for the South in the event of Fremont's election 382

Robert Toombs to Alexander H. Stephens, December 1, 1856. Buchanan's policies 383

Alexander H. Stephens to Thomas W. Thomas, December 12, 1856. Stephens's challenge to B. H. Hill for a duel 384

Lucius Q. C. Lamar to Howell Cobb, December 17, 1856. Current personal and political affairs 385

Alexander H. Stephens to Thomas W. Thomas, December 29, 1856. Review of Stephens's controversy with B. H. Hill 386

Howell Cobb to his wife, January 6, 1857. Cabinet prospects 389

Thomas W. Thomas to Alexander H. Stephens, January 12, 1857. Stephens's controversy with Hill; current local and national politics 389

Robert Toombs to Thomas W.

Thomas, February 5, 1857 394

Robert M. McLane to Howell Cobb, February 14, 1857. Cabinet negotiations and prospects 395

John W. Forney to Howell Cobb, February 18, 1857. Current politics 396

James Buchanan to Howell Cobb, February 21, 1857. Appointment of Cobb as
Secretary of the Treasury 397

Robert Toombs to Alexander H. Stephens, February 24, 1857. Cabinet negotiations; the tariff bill 397

Robert Toombs to Alexander H. Stephens, March 10, 1857. Current affairs... 398 Howell Cobb to —, March 30, 1857. Refuses leave of absence to a Federal official for the purpose of political campaigning 398

Robert Toombs to W. W. Burwell, March 30, 1857. The Cuban question; personal affairs 399

Howell Cobb to Alexander H. Stephens, June 10, 1857. Urges Stephens not to retire from Congress 400

Thomas W. Thomas to Alexander H. Stephens, June 15, 1857. The Kansas question 400

Howell Cobb to Alexander H. Stephens, June 17, 1857. The Kansas question.. 401 Howell Cobb to Alexander H. Stephens, June 18, 1857. The Kansas question.. 402

Robert Toombs to W. W. Burwell, July 11, 1857. The Kansas question 403

Thomas R. R. Cobb to Howell Cobb, July 15 1857. The Kansas question 404

Lucius Q. C. Lamar to Howell Cobb, July 17, 1857. The Kansas question 405

Howell Cobb to Alexander H. Stephens, July 21, 1857. The Kansas question.. 406 Howell Cobb to Alexander H. Stephens, July 23, 1857. Current local and national politics 407 Page.

Robert Toombs to Alexander H. Stephens, August 3, 1857. Toombs's candidacy for reelection to the Senate 408

Robert Toombs to Alexander H. Stephens, August 4, 1857. The Georgia campaign 409

Alexander H. Stephens to the voters of the eighth congressional district of Georgia, August 14, 1857. Announcement of candidacy for reelection to Congress; the Kansas question 409

Robert Toombs to Alexander H. Stephens, August 15, 1857. The Georgia campaign 420

Howell Cobb to Alexander H. Stephens, September 3, 1857. Current politics.. 421 Howell Cobb to Alexander H. Stephens, September 12, 1857. Kansas affairs.. 422 Howell Cobb to Alexander H. Stephens, September 19, 1857. Kansas affairs.. 423 Howell Cobb to Alexander H. Stephens, October 9, 1857. The panic of 1857; current politics:424

Howell Cobb to Alexander H. Stephens, October 19, 1857. Current politics.-425 Robert Toombs to W. W. Burwell, November 20, 1857. Personal and political affairs 425

Thomas W. Thomas to Alexander H. Stephens, January 12, 1858. Censures the course of Buchanan and Cobb on the Kansas question 427

Thomas W. Thomas to Alexander H. Stephens, January 21, 1858. Censures
Wise and Buchanan 428

Thomas W. Thomas to Alexander H. Stephens, February 7, 1858. The arrest of William Walker; the Kansas question 429

Joseph E. Brown to Alexander H. Stephens, February 9, 1858. Contemplates secession in the event of the denial of statehood to Kansas with the Lecompton constitution 431

Robert Toombs to James Buchanan, March 2, 1858. The Kansas question 432

Joseph E. Brown to Alexander H. Stephens, March 26, 1858. The Kansas issue and prospective secession 432

Robert Toombs to Alexander H. Stephens, March 28, 1858. The course of the southern Know-nothings on the Kansas question 433

Robert Toombs to James Buchanan, April 18, 1858. The English bill 433

Joseph E. Brown to Alexander H. Stephens, May 7, 1858. Satisfaction at the
Kansas adjustment; local affairs 434

Howell Cobb to William F. Colcock, May 22, 1858. Instructs Colcock, collector of customs at Charleston, S. C, to refuse clearance papers to a vessel intended for bringing Africans to the United States 434

Stephen D. Dillaye to Howell Cobb, June 8, 1858. Censure of Cobb's use of the patronage in the New York customhouse 439

Howell Cobb to John Robbins, jr., and others, July 3, 1858. Fourth of July sentiments 439

Howell Cobb to James Buchanan, August 2, 1858. Treasury affairs 440

Howell Cobb to James Buchanan, August 4, 1858. Disputes over the Treasury patronage 440

Howell Cobb to James Buchanan, August 6, 1858. The patronage dispute 441

Howell Cobb to James Buchanan, August 7, 1858. Current affairs 442

Howell Cobb to Alexander H. Stephens, September 8, 1858. Declines to support Douglas for the Presidency 442

Joseph E. Brown to Alexander H. Stephens, May 5, 1859. Current affairs 444

Joseph E. Brown to Alexander H. Stephens, June 4, 1859. The Democratic situation 444

Joseph E. Brown to Alexander H. Stephens, June 21, 1859. Current politics.. 445 Howell Cobb to James Buchanan, July 25, 1859. Treasury affairs 446 Page.

Alexander H. Stephens to J. Henly Smith, July 29, 1859. The African slavetrade 446

Robert Toombs to Alexander H. Stephens, August 27, 1859. Georgia politics.. 447

Howell Cobb to James Buchanan, October 7, 1859. The thwarting of filibusters. 447

Alexander H. Stephens to J. Henly Smith, November 10, 1859. Current affairs. 447

Howell Cobb to Alexander H. Stephens, November 14, 1859. Apprehensions of. Republican ascendency 448

Robert Toombs to Thomas W. Thomas, December 4, 1859. Contemplates secession if a Republican is elected President 449

Alexander H. Stephens to J. Henly Smith, December 17, 1859. Political prospects 450

Robert Toombs to Alexander H. Stephens, December 26, 1859 451

Robert Toombs to Alexander H. Stephens, December 28, 1859. The deadlock over the Speakership 452

Joseph E. Brown to Alexander H. Stephens, December 29, 1859. Democratic proceedings in Georgia 453

Robert Toombs to James Buchanan, December 29, 1859. Advice of Pericles to the Athenians pertinent to current American politics 453

Joseph E. Brown to Alexander H. Stephens, January 5, 1860. The Democratic situation in Georgia 453

Alexander H. Stephens to J. Henly Smith, January 6, 1860. Popular apathy.. 454

Robert Toombs to Alexander H. Stephens, January 5, 1860. The Speakership contest J 454

Robert Toombs to Alexander H. Stephens, January 11, 1860. The prospect regarding the Democratic presidential nomination 455

Howell Cobb to John B. Lamar, January 15, 1860. Personal attitude toward the Democratic nomination 456

Alexander H. Stephens to J. Henly Smith, January 22, 1860. Attitude upon the question of disunion 457

Robert Toombs to Alexander H. Stephens, January 31, 1860. The Speakership struggle 458

Alexander H. Stephens to J. Henly Smith, February 4, 1860. The Speakership election; the national prospect 459

Robert Toombs to Alexander H. Stephens, February 10, 1860. Sectional issues. 460

Alexander H. Stephens to J. Henly Smith, February 24, 1860. Current affairs.. 462

Alexander H. Stephens to Dr. Henry R. Casey, March 9, 1860. Forbids the use of his name in connection with the presidential nomination 463

Robert Toombs to Alexander H. Stephens, March 16, 1860. Presidential prospects 464

Alexander H. Stephens to J. Henly Smith, March 18, 1860. Howell Cobb's presidential candidacy 465

Alexander H. Stephens to J. Henly Smith, April 14, 1860. Advice as to correspondence for the Southern Confederacy of Atlanta 467

Robert Toombs to Alexander H. Stephens, April 20, 1860. Speculation upon the Charleston nomination 467

Robert Toombs to Alexander H. Stephens, May 5, 1860. The proceedings of the Charleston convention 468

Robert Toombs to Alexander H. Stephens, May 7, 1860. The split in the Democratic Party 469

Alexander H. Stephens to J. Henly Smith, May 8, 1860. Laments the Democratic split 470

Howell Cobb to Robert Collins and others, May 9, 1860. Advice to Georgia Democrats 471

Robert Toombs to Robert Collins and others, May 10, 1860. Advice to Georgia Democrats 475

Robert Toombs to Alexander H. Stephens, May 12, 1860. Declines to join movement in favor of Douglas 477

Robert Toombs to Alexander H. Stephens, May 16, 1860. Comparison of views. 478

Howell Cobb to John B. Lamar, May 22, 1860. Plans for the Baltimore Democratic convention 479

Robert Toombs to Alexander H. Stephens, May 26, 1860. Argument against Douglas 480

Robert Toombs to Alexander H. Stephens, June 9, 1860. The impossibility of Democratic union 481

Alexander H. Stephens to J. Henly Smith, June 17, 1860. The Democratic situation 481

John A. Cobb to John B. Lamar, June 20, 1860. The Baltimore convention... 482

Alexander H. Stephens to J. Henly Smith, July 2, 1860. The hopelessness of Douglas's candidacy 483

Alexander H. Stephens to J. Henly Smith, July 4, 1860. Current affairs 486

Alexander H. Stephens to J. Henly Smith, July 10, 1860. Territorial doctrines; Lincoln's personal merit; the inadvisability of disunion 486

Alexander H. Stephens to J. Henly Smith, July 15, 1860. Denies the rumor that he will support the Breckinridge ticket 488

Alexander H. Stephens to J. Henly Smith, July 24, 1860. Current affairs 488

Thomas W. Thomas to Alexander H. Stephens, July 30, 1860. Complains of a personal injury 489

Thomas W. Thomas to Alexander H. Stephens, August 8, 1860. Accepts an explanation 490

Alexander H. Stephens to J. Henly Smith, August 8, 1860. Current affairs; gloomy apprehensions 490

Alexander H. Stephens to J. Henly Smith, August 25, 1860. Campaign excitement in Georgia 491

Alexander H. Stephens to J. Henly Smith, August 30, 1860. The prospect for Douglas 493

Alexander H. Stephens to J. Henly Smith, September 6, 1860. Campaign conjectures 493

Alexander H. Stephens to J. Henly Smith, September 10, 1860. The campaign. 494

Alexander H. Stephens to J. Henly Smith, September 12, 1860. The legitimacy of the Douglas and Breckinridge nominations; campaign prospects 494

Alexander H. Stephens to J. Henly Smith, September 15, 1860. The gloomy prospect 496

Alexander H. Stephens to J. Henly Smith, September 16, 1860. Defends his own consistency 497

Alexander H. Stephens to J. Henly Smith, September 30, 1860. The campaign for Douglas in Georgia 500

Alexander H. Stephens to J. Henly Smith, October 13, 1860 500

Alexander H. Stephens to J. Henly Smith, November 8, 1860. The news of Lincoln's election 502

Alexander H. Stephens to J. Henly Smith, November 21, 1860. The distressing prospect 503

Alexander H. Stephens to J. Henly Smith, November 23, 1860. Advocates retaliatory legislation 503

Alexander H. Stephens to, November 25, 1860. The problem of securing southern rights 504

Howell Cobb to the people of Georgia, December G, 1860. Reviews the political situation ana recommends the secession of Georgia 505 Page.

Howell Cobb to his wife, December 7, 1860. Prospective resignation from the Cabinet 516

Howell Cobb to James Buchanan, December 8, 1860. Resignation of the secretaryship of the Treasury 517

James Buchanan to Howell Cobb, December 10, 1860. Accepts Cobb's resignation: 518

Howell Cobb to his wife, December 10, 1860. Resignation from the Cabinet; plans for canvassing for secession in Georgia 518

Robert Toombs to E. B. Pullin and others, December 13, 1860. Advises testing the Republicans in Congress in regard to southern rights before resorting to secession 519

William Henry Trescot to Howell Cobb, December 14, 1860. The programme in South Carolina 522

Thomas R. R. Cobb to Howell Cobb, December 15, 1860. The campaign in Georgia 522

Mrs. Jacob Thompson to Mrs. Howell Cobb, December 15, 1860. Affairs at Washington 522

Thomas R. R. Cobb to Howell Cobb, December 19, 1860. The campaign for secession 524

A. Hood to Howell Cobb, December 19, 1860. The campaign in Georgia 524

Robert Toombs to the people of Georgia (telegram), December 23, 1860. Proceedings in the Senate committee of 13; Georgia should promptly secede... 525

Charles F. M. Garnett to Howell Cobb, December 28, 1860. Indorses a manufacturer of cannon shells 525

Alexander H. Stephens to J. Henly Smith, December 31, 1860. The secession prospect 526

Robert Toombs to the Augusta, Ga., True Democrat, January 1, 1861. (Telegram.) Cabinet changes 528

Mrs. Robert Toombs to Alexander H. Stephens, January 1, 1861. Departure from Washington 528

William Porcher Miles to Howell Cobb, January 14, 1861. The prospect of southern independence 528

William Henry Trescot to Howell Cobb, January 14, 1861. The progress of secession 529

Jacob Thompson to Howell Cobb, January 16, 1861. Cabinet affairs 531

George I. Durham to Howell Cobb, January 17, 1861. The secession movement in Texas 533

Raphael Semmes to Howell Cobb, January 26, 1861. Advice concerning a navy for the Southern Confederacy 533

Junius Hillyer to Howell Cobb, January 30, 1861. Prospects concerning the border States; the tariff question for the Confederacy 535

Augustus R. Wright to Howell Cobb, February 1, 1861. The mission from Georgia to Maryland 536

Howell Cobb to his wife, February 3, 1861. The assembling of the Montgomery convention 536

Howell Cobb to his wife, February 6, 1861. Prospects concerning the Confederate Presidency 537

Junius Hillyer to Howell Cobb, February 9, 1861. The prospect of northern acquiescence in southern independence 538

Gazaway B. Lamar to Howell Cobb, February 9, 1861. Urges the Confederate Government to avoid the provocation of the North to hostilities 538

T. Allan to Howell Cobb, February 11, 1861. The predicament of southern government clerks at Washington 540 Page.

Junius Hillyer to Howell Cobb, February 11, 1861. The problem of the border States 541

R. K. Hudgins to Howell Cobb, February 11, 1861. The course of a southern sympathizer in the United States Navy 642

Joseph E. Brown to Alexander H. Stephens, February 12, 1861. Military affairs 543

Richard H. Clark to Howell Cobb, February 16, 1861. The prospect of hostilities 543

Howell Cobb to his wife, February 20, 1861. Conjectures regarding the Confederate Cabinet 544

C. W. Cottom to Howell Cobb, February 22, 1861. Seeks to change his field of journalistic activity from Minneapolis to Georgia or Alabama 544

Gazaway B. Lamar to Howell Cobb, February 22, 1861. Financial advice to the Confederate Government 545

L. K. Bowen to Howell Cobb, February 25, 1861. Excitement at Baltimore.. 546 Raphael Semmes to Howell Cobb, February 28, 1861. Flans for a lighthouse bureau in the Confederate Government 546

John A. Cobb to Howell Cobb, March 4, 1861. Presentation of pistols by Col. Colt 547

William Badham, jr., to Howell Cobb, March 6, 1861. Affairs in North Carolina 547

E.B. Hartto Howell Cobb, March 7, 1861. Affairs in New York City 648

Gazaway B. Lamar to Howell Cobb, March 9, 1861. Financial advice to the Confederate Government 549

Thomas R. R. Cobb to Howell Cobb, March 19, 1861. Confederate revision of laws 551

A. M. Evans to Howell Cobb, March 20, 1861. Patronage and sentiment in northeastern Georgia 551

Gazaway B. Lamar to Howell Cobb, March 25, 1861. Confederate finance 652

Howell Cobb to James Buchanan, March 26, 1861. The rosy prospects of the Confederacy 554

Gazaway B. Lamar to Howell Cobb, March 28, 1861. Confederate finance 555

Howell Cobb to his wife, March 31, 1861. Conditions in Mobile 557

Robert Toombs to Alexander H. Stephens, April 6, 1861. Current affairs at Montgomery 558

Howell Cobb to his wife, April 7,

1861. Conditions in New Orleans 569

John W. H. Underwood to Howell Cobb, April 11, 1861. Factional politics in Georgia 560

Gazaway B. Lamar to Howell Cobb, April 13, 1861. The military situation... 561

Robert Toombs to Howell Cobb, April 23, 1861. Military events in Virginia and Maryland 562

Alexander H. Stephens to R. Schleiden, April 26, 1861. The question of peace or war 563

Augustus B. Longstreet to Howell Cobb, May 1, 1861. Advocates free trade for the Confederacy 564

Joseph E. Brown to Alexander H. Stephens, May 4, 1861. Urges the garrisoning of the Georgia coast 565

Howell Cobb to his wife, May 10, 1861. Current affairs 565

Williams Rutherford, jr., to Howell Cobb, May 14, 1861. Current affairs 566

Howell Cobb to his wife, May 18, 1861. Current affairs 568

Robert Toombs to Alexander H. Stephens, June 8, 1861. The military situation. 568

Thomas W. Thomas to Alexander H. Stephens, June 17, 1861. The organization and equipment of troops in Georgia 570

Joseph E. Brown to Alexander H. Stephens, June 25, 1861. The aiming of Georgia regiments

Joseph E. Brown to Alexander H. Stephens, July 8, 1861. Progress in organizing Georgia troops

Gabriel Toombs to Alexander H. Stephens, July 31, 1861. Appeal for Stephens's influence to dissuade Robert Toombs from entering the Confederate military service

Howell Cobb to bis wife, August 6, 1861. The prospect of peace

Thomas W. Thomas to Alexander H. Stephens, August 21, 1861. Stephens's visit to camp.'

Joseph E. Brown to Alexander H. Stephens, August 22, 1861. Current affairs..

Thomas W. Thomas to Alexander H. Stephens, September 12, 1861. Sickness among the troops

Thomas W. Thomas to Linton Stephens, September 20, 1861. Sickness of the regimental officers

Pvobert Toombs to Alexander H. Stephens, September 22, 1861. Current affairs

Joseph E. Brown to Alexander H. Stephens, September 28, 1861. Georgia politics

Robert Toombs to Alexander H. Stephens, September 30?, 1861. Criticism of the military passiveness of the Confederate Government

Robert Toombs to Alexander H. Stephens, October 3, 1861. The military situation

Thomas W. Thomas to Alexander H. Stephens, October 5, 1861. Sentiment in the Army

Thomas W. Thomas to Alexander H. Stephens, October 10, 1861. Georgia politics; the incompetence of President Davis

Thomas W. Thomas to Alexander H. Stephens, October 17, 1861. A colonel's tribulations on the march

Howell Cobb to his wife, November 13, 1861. A reconnoissance in the Peninsula

Howell Cobb to his wife, December 9, 1861. Manoeuvers against McClellan's army

Thomas R. R. Cobb to Alexander H. Stephens, December 18, 1861. A question of discipline

Thomas V. Thomas to Alexander H. Stephens, December 31, 1861. Public opinion in Georgia

C. G. Memminger to Howell Cobb, January 1, 1862. Current affairs

Howell Cobb to his wife, February 18, 1862. Current affairs

Howell Cobb to his wife, February 22, 1862. The situation at Norfolk

Howell Cobb to his wife, February 25, 1862. Arrangements for the exchange of prisoners

Robert Toombs to Alexander H. Stephens, March 4, 1862. Current affaire

Howell Cobb to John B. Lamar, March 7, 1862. The military situation

Robert Toombs to Alexander H. Stephens, March 24, 1862. Current affairs...

Robert Toombs to Alexander H. Stephens, March 28, 1862. Brigade experiences

Howell Cobb to his wife, April 15, 1862. The situation in the Peninsula

Robert Toombs to Alexander H. Stephens, May 17, 1862. Operations in the Peninsula

Robert Toombs to George Hill and others (telegram), June 11, 1862. Defies the authority of local committees to regulate plantation industry Page.

Thomas W. Thomaa to Alexander H. Stephens, June 19, 1862. Personal affairs 595

John C. Whitner to Howell Cobb, June 28, 1862. The records of the Confederate Congress 5%

Joseph E. Brown to Alexander H. Stephens, July 2, 1862. The Confederate conscription act 597

John C. Whitner to Howell Cobb, July 2, 1862. The records of the Confederate constitutional convention 599

Robert Toombs to Alexander H. Stephens, July 14, 1862. The battles before Richmond 599

John B. Lamar to Mrs. Howell Cobb, August 9, 1862. Plantation affairs 602

John C. Whitner to Howell Cobb, August 12, 1862. The records of the Confederate constitutional convention 602

Robert Toombs to Alexander H. Stephens, August 22, 1862. Arrest of Toombs by Longstreet's order 603

Joseph E. Brown to Alexander H. Stephens, September 1, 1862. Conflict of civil and military jurisdiction in Atlanta 605

Howell Cobb to his wife, September 6, 1862. The Antietam campaign 606

Howell Cobb to his wife, September 17, 1862. The Antietam campaign 606

Robert Toombs to Linton Stephens, December 1, 1862. Georgia politics 607

James M. Smythe to Howell Cobb, December 17, 1862. Death of Thomas R. R. Cobb 609

Joseph E. Brown to Alexander H.

Stephens, January 30, 1863. Suggests Linton
Stephens for the governorship of Georgia 610
Joseph E. Brown to Alexander H. Stephens, February 16, 1863. Suggests Toombs for the governorship of Georgia 610
Robert Toombs to Alexander H. Stephens, March 2, 1863. Toombs announces his resignation from the Army 611
Robert Toombs to his brigade in the Army of Northern Virginia, March 5, 1863.
Farewell address 612
Howell Cobb to his wife, March 13, 1863. Affairs in Florida 613
Joseph E. Brown to Alexander H. Stephens, March 16, 1863. The availability of Toombs as a gubernatorial candidate 614
Howell Cobb to his wife, April 1, 1863. Operations in Florida 614
Robert Toombs to Alexander H. Stephens, April 21, 1863. Economic studies.. 615 Howell Cobb to James A. Seddon, May 14, 1863. Declines appointment as head of the Quartermaster General's Department 616
Joseph E. Brown to Alexander H. Stephens, May 21, 1863. Brown announces his candidacy for reelection as governor 617
Joseph E. Brown to Alexander H. Stephens, May 29, 1863. The gubernatorial prospect 618
Robert Toombs to W. W. Burwell, June 10, 1863. Current affairs 619
Thomas W. Thomas to Alexander H. Stephens, July 2, 1863. A question of conscription 620
Robert Toombs to Alexander H. Stephens, July 14, 1863. The problem of defending Georgia against invasion 621
Joseph E. Brown to Alexander H. Stephens, August 12, 1863. Despondency in
Georgia.' 621
Robert Toombs to the editor of the Augusta, Ga., Constitutionalist, August 12, 1863. Criticism of the financial policies of the Confederate Government.. 622 Joseph E. Brown to

Alexander H. Stephens, August 22, 1863. Affairs in
Georgia 627 Page.
Robert Toombs to W. W. Burwell, August 29, 1863. The gloomy prospect for the Confederacy 628
Robert Toombs to Alexander H. Stephens, November 2, 1863. Toombs announces his candidacy for the Confederate Senate 630
Joseph E. Brown to Alexander H. Stephens, November 27, 1863. The senatorial election 630
Howell Cobb to Alexander H. Stephens, January 2, 1864. Current affairs 631
Joseph E. Brown to Alexander H. Stephens, January 4, 1864. Current affairs.. 631 Joseph E. Brown to Alexander H. Stephens, January 28, 1864. The military situation in Georgia 632
Joseph E. Brown to Alexander H. Stephens, February 13, 1864. Requests a conference 633
Joseph E. Brown to Alexander H. Stephens, February 20, 1864. The suspension of *habeas corpus* 633
Joseph E. Brown to Alexander H. Stephens, March 4, 1864. The planning of a governor's message 634
Benjamin H. Hill to Alexander H. Stephens, March 14, 1864. Comparison of views on the situation 634
Robert Toombs to Alexander H. Stephens, April 1, 1864. Criticism of Confederate policy 637
Joseph E. Brown to Alexander H. Stephens, April 5, 1864. *Habeas corpus;* current politics 639
Joseph E. Brown to Alexander H. Stephens, April 12, 1864. The *habeas corpus* controversy 640
Joseph E. Brown to Alexander H. Stephens, April 19, 1864. The *habeas corpus* controversy 641
Joseph E. Brown to Alexander H. Stephens, May 5, 1864. The *habeas corpus* controversy 642
Joseph E. Brown to Alexander H. Stephens, May 11, 1864. A judicial appointment 643
Joseph E. Brown to Alexander H. Stephens, June 6, 1864. The defense of Atlanta 644
Joseph E. Brown to Alexander H.

Stephens, June 17, 1864. The control of a newspaper 644
John H. Winder to Howell Cobb, July 9, 1864. An emergency at Andersonville. 644
Howell Cobb to his wife, July 14, 1864. The siege of Atlanta 645
Howell Cobb to his wife, July 18, 1864. Stoneman's raid 646 iawell Cobb to his wife, July 20, 1864. The military situation in Georgia... 647 II Cobb to his wife, July 22, 1864. The siege of Atlanta: 648
'» Cobb to his wife, July 23, 1864. The Battle of Atlanta 648
E. Brown to Alexander H. Stephens, August 17, 1864. The services of -=p Militia 649 m to Howell Cobb, August 29, 1864. Affairs in Florida 650
Mexander H. Stephens, August 30, 1864. The siege of 651
'der H. Stephens, September 23, 1864. Advises -man.! 652
T. Stephens, September 30, 1864. Current 653 iphens, Octob'., 1864. A proposed con *t* 653
'mb-864. The consistency of 654 Page.
Howell Cobb to his wife, November 16, 1864. Sherman's preparations for his march through Georgia 655
An anonymous writer to Howell Cobb, January 3, 1865. Urges the enlistment of negro troops 656
Howell Cobb to his wife, January 16, 1865. Current affairs 658
Howell Cobb to his wife, January 31, 1865. Current affairs 659
Robert Toombs to Alexander H. Stephens, March 16, 1865. Current affairs... 660
Robert Toombs to Alexander H. Stephens, March 23, 1865. Local conditions.. 661 Jefferson Davis to Mrs. Howell Cobb, March 30, 1865. Controversy between
Davis and the Confederate Senate 661
Joseph E. Brown to Alexander H. Stephens, April 25, 1865. Policy under the
Sherman-Johnston armistice 662
Howell Cobb to his wife, April 27, 1865 662
Howell Cobb to William H. Seward,

July 18,1865. Bespeaks consideration for
Jefferson Davis 663

J. D. Collins to John A. Cobb, July 31, 1865. Industrial conditions 665

J. D. Hoover to Howell Cobb, August 31, 1865. Current affairs 666

Mrs. Jefferson Davis to Mrs. Howell Cobb, September 9,1865. Pereonal affairs. 667

Howell Cobb to Andrew Johnson, October 17, 1835. Application for amnesty. 668 George Hillyer to Howell Cobb, November 7, 1865. Cobb's application for amnesty 669

Joseph E. Brown to Alexander H. Stephens, November 9, 1865. Georgia politics 670

Howell Cobb to his wife, November 18,1865. The prospect of amnesty 671

Howell Cobb to his wife, December 7,1865. Current affaire 672

Robert Toombs to Alexander H. Stephens, December 15, 1865. Toombs writing from exile, expresses his irreconcilable opposition to reconstruction 673

J. B. Eustis to Howell Cobb, January 6, 1866. Conditions in Louisiana 676

Joseph E. Brown to Alexander H. Stephens, March 2, 1866. Current politics.. 677

Joseph E. Brown to Alexander H. Stephens, March 3, 1866. Reconstruction.. 677

William M. Browne to Howell Cobb, March 28, 1866. Reconstruction 677

A. C. Niven to Howell Cobb, April 9, 1866. Reconstruction 679

Alexander H. Stephens to J. Barrett Cohen, June 6, 1866. *Habeas corpus* 680

Alexander H. Stephens to J. Barrett Cohen, July 4, 1866. Reconstruction 681

Josephus Anderson to Howell Cobb, September 8, 1866. The effect of freedom upon the negroes 682

Howell Cobb to Daniel E. Sickles, September 12, 1866. Asks intercession in favor of Jefferson Davis f

Howell Cobb to his wife, December, 1866. The paralysis of plantation industry

Joseph E. Brown to Alexander H. Stephens, December 8, 1866. The relief the poor in Atlanta

John C. Rutherford to Howell Cobb, March 20, 1867. Reconstruction

Alexander H. Stephens to J. Barrett Cohen, May 25, 1867. Ref

Alexander H. Stephens to J. Barrett Cohen, July 15,1867. *v*

Howell Cobb to his wife, September 1, 1867. Reconstruct

Jeremiah S. Black to Howell Cobb, September 23, 1867.

Alexander H. Stephens to J. Bwrett Cohen, October 20

Robert Toombs to Alexander H. S tephens, Novembpthe cotton tax

Robert Toombs to Alexander H. ''ephpnegro judge

Howell Cobb to J. D. Hoover, r the South 73566—13 1...
Page.

Jeremiah S. Black to Howell Cobb April, 1868?. The corruption of the Federal Government 694

William M. Browne to Howell Cobb, May 12, 1868. The presidential campaign 695

Gazaway B. Lamar to Howell Cobb, May 15, 1868. Politics at Washington. ... 696

L. Q. Washington to Howell Cobb, May 31, 1868. National politics 697

Jefferson Davis to Howell Cobb, July 6, 1868. Plan of Davis to become a cotton factor at Liverpool 698

Mrs. Jefferson Davis to Mrs. Howell Cobb, July 6, 1868. Personal affairs 699

Alexander H. Stephens to J. Barrett Cohen, July 17,1868. Current affairs 700

Bird B. Chapman to Alexander H. Stephens, July 21, 1868. Current politics.. 701 An anonymous writer to Howell Cobb, August 3, 1868. Urges the champions of southern rights to keep silent during the presidential campaign 702

Robert Toombs to Alexander H. Stephens, August 9, 1868. Georgia politics.. 702 John M. Johnson to Howell Cobb, September 22,1868. Conditions in Georgia.. 704 Mrs. Jefferson Davis to Mrs. Howell Cobb,

October 22, 1868. Condolence; affairs of the Davis family 704

Robert Toombs to Alexander H. Stephens, December 11, 1868. Affaire of the
University of Georgia 706

Robert Toombs to Alexander H. Stephens, January 24, 1870. Georgia politics. 707 Robert Toombs to Alexander H. Stephens, February 8, 1870. Georgia politics. 708 Alexander H. Stephens to J. Barrett Cohen, April 16, 1870. Personal affairs.. 708

Alexander H. Stephens to J. Barrett Cohen, August 8, 1870. South Carolina politics 708

Alexander H. Stephens to J. Barrett Cohen, October 25, 1870. South Carolina politics 709

Robert Toombs to Alexander H. Stephens, November 19, 1870. Personal affairs 710

Dudley M. Du Bose to Alexander H. Stephens, December 21, 1870. Georgia politics 711

Robert Toombs to Alexander H. Stephens, December 30,1870. Georgia politics. 711 Robert Toombs to Alexander H. Stephens, December 30, 1870. The lease of the Western & Atlantic Railroad 711

Alexander H. Stephens to Francis P. Blair, May 8, 1871. Carl Schurz and the
Liberal Republican movement 713

Robert Toombs to Alexander H. Stephens, January 21,1872. Georgia politics. 716 lexander H. Stephens to J. Barrett Cohen, July 2, 1872. The Greeley move -vnent 717 ander H. Stephens to J. Barrett Cohen, March 2, 1873. Georgia politics.. 717 ' Toombs to Alexander H. Stephens, March 14, 1874. The lease of the
"3'rn & Atlantic Railroad 718 . oombs to Alexander H. Stephens, November 6, 1874. Current poli . 721

Alexander H. Stephens, March 10, 1875. Current politics.. 721-ander H. Stephens, October 30, 1876. The presidential 722 r H. Stephens, December 17, 1876. The Hayes 723

T. Stephens, December 28, 1876. The Hayes 725 .. Apr 24, 1877. The Hayes-Tilden .«m. 727 Pi LETTERS

HEBE PRINTED Hi _

Robert Toombs to L. M. Trammell, April 26,1877. Advocates the call of a convention to revise the constitution of Georgia 727

Robert Toombs to Alexander H. Stephens, November 2, 1877. The campaign for the ratification of the new constitution of Georgia 731

Robert Toombs to Alexander H. Stephens, January 25, 1878. The free-ailver question 732

Robert Toombs to Alexander H. Stephens, January 30, 1879. Current affairs. 734

Robert Toombs to Alexander H. Stephens, March 10, 1879. Current politics.. 736

Robert Toombs to Alexander H. Stephens, April 2, 1879. The monetary question in Congress 737

Robert Toombs to Alexander H. Stephens, March 25, 1880. Current politics.. 739

Robert Toombs to Alexander H. Stephens, April 25, 1880. Current politics.. 740

Alexander H. Stephens to J. Barrett Cohen, June 26, 1881. Notice of Jefferson Davis's "The Rise and Fall of the Confederate Government" 742

Alexander H. Stephens to J. Barrett Cohen, September 18, 1881. Invitation for a visit 742

Robert Toombs to Alexander H. Stephens, February 19,1882. Personal affairs. 742 THE CORRESPONDENCE OF ROBERT TOOMBS, ALEXANDEB H. STEPHENS AND HOWELL OOBB.

Edited By Ulbich B. Phillips.

Robert Toombs To Alexander H. Stephens. R.

Washington ga., *Jan. 1st, 18*

Dear Stephens,... The session2 passed off well. We succeeded in carrying everything but the Court8—lost that in the Senate by three votes. When I was at Milledgeville I thought its passage would have injured the *party* but benefitted the country; but from the general regret expressed at its loss among the people since we adjourned, I am inclined to think it would have been popular with the people. The session is decidedly popular with all classes. The people are better pleased than they have been for many years with their legislature, and I begin to think our power in Georgia is tolerably firmly fixed. Our election for Congress took place to-day. I have not heard from all the precincts, but from what we have heard Wilkes will give a considerably increased majority to Clinch,5 say over 100 votes. I have no doubt of his election by at least four thousand. The Democrats made a false move on the Rail Road question,8 which I think will very seriously affect them in the Cherokee counties.7 They made a party question of its abandonment. The Whigs stood up well in the House and tolerably in the Senate. We had to gild the pill a little for them. But I have no doubt but that a large majority of the people are opposed to its abandonment, and since our adjournment I see some of the Democratic papers are inclined to claw off. Even the Columbus Times talks *softly* on the subject.

The congressional district bill is a fair one. We had to gerrymander a little in order to give the Democrats their third district— 1 Erroneously dated Jan. 1, 1843, in the original. 'Of the State legislature.

"A bill to establish a supreme court for the State of Georgia. 4 Whig.

« Duncan L. Clinch, Whig candidate for Congress. He was elected in place of John Mlllen, deceased.

The question of completing or ahandoning the Western & Atlantic Railroad, then under construction by the State of Georgia.

'The northwestern portion of Georgia, recently vacated by the-Cherokee Indians.

the first instance I expect of a party's ever doing that thing for the benefit their opponents. The Senatorial district bill *looks* strong but is in fact weak— we could have done much better with greater appearance of fairness but every Senator *almost* was fixing for himself. Crawford 1 is much pleased and says we have left him the State government in such condition that if it is not satisfactorily administered it will be *his* fault. Write me as often as you can. It will give me pleasure to attend to any business for you.

John W. H. Underwood 2 To Howell Cobb. E.

Clarksville, Geo., *February 2nd, J844.*

My Dear Sir: I hope you are not too deeply engaged with the affairs of this great republic to pass idly by a letter from one of your constituents in the true sense of the word. I am a native Georgian and true American citizen, and feel a deep and abiding interest in the perpetuity of our institutions, and I feel that I hazard nothing when I say that the continual agitation of the abolition question will blow into fragments, aye into dust that cannot be seen, our glorious Union which cost the blood of the best set of men that ever lived or died. It is not the South that alone is interested in this momentous question. The same torch (lit by the abolitionists of the North) that will consume our humble cottages at the South will also cause the northeastern horizon to coruscate with the flames of northern palaces.

Sir, it is no spirit of flattery that I say I felt proud as a Georgian when I read your manly effort in favour of the extension of the 21st rule. For myself, if I was in Congress I would forestall the agitation of the question, if the Members of Congress from the non-slaveholding States will force discussion upon that question. The true course, in my humble opinion, for the Southern Members to pursue would be to shake the dust of the Capitol from their feet and return to the bosom of their families. Come back to us, and we will take such measures as will best defend us from their incendiary proceedings and will convince the sticklers for the right of petition that there is another appeal when life, liberty and property are at stake.

I am as ardently attached to our Union and institutions as any man, but when our Northern brethren, forgetful of the spirit of compromise which resulted in the formation of our Constitution, and regardless of our rights as

members of this Union, force issues upon us which were intended by the framers of our government to be buried and closed forever, it is time that we should hold them as we hold the rest of mankind, "enemies in war, in peace friends." I am opposed to any temporizing on this question; it should be met at the 1 George W. Crawford, then governor of Georgia.
2 Member of Congress from Georgia, 1859-1861. threshold, at the door; the assailants should be met and never suffered to enter the citadel till they walk over our prostrate bodies. What will it avail us at the South for the incendiaries to cease their work after our throats are cut and our houses burned? Sir, the negroes in Georgia are already saying to each other that great men are trying to set them free and will succeed, and many other expressions of similar import. And if the agitation of the subject is continued for three months longer we will be compelled to arm our Militia and shoot down our property in the field. If the thing is not already incurable, tell the agitators we had rather fight them than our own negroes, and that we will do it too. They shall not skulk behind our negro population and thus save themselves; if fighting must be done, we will fight white folks at the North—those who are moving heaven and earth to provoke insurrection at the South. I have expressed myself as I feel, and it is the feeling of the whole South. Please let me hear from you.

Thomas Ritchie 1 To Howell Cobb. E.

Richmond va., *February 8th, 1844.*

Dear Shi: Your polite but laconic note prompts me to address you. You cheer me with the history you give me, and as your information preceded our late glorious convention I am in hopes the skies are brighter than when you wrote me. I will thank you for any information you may be able to impart to me on this subject. I take a very deep interest in the success of the Republican candidate and in the defeat of Mr. Clay. I consider his election is calculated to ring the knell of most of our great Republican principles.

A reunion has taken place between the friends of Calhoun and Van Buren in Virginia. Our late State convention has happily brought it about. Am I too sanguine in hoping that the moral effects of our example will extend to Georgia? I received a letter from Governor McDonald the other day in which he says that the Republicans are about to make a great rally in that State at the convention they are about to hold in June or July. Is it not possible to rouse up the Republicans of Georgia immediately and to unite them together more firmly and energetically in the way we have done? Could not you and your colleagues address your friends there and call upon them to put forth their strength directly? I hope to see the press ot Georgia and of N. Carolina and of Tennessee come out without delay trumpet-tongued.

I beg you to communicate as soon as is convenient what is going on among our friends.

The veteran editor of the Richmond Enquirer, and afterwards of the Washington Union.

Mr. Cobb,1 first in the H. of R. and then in the U. S. Senate, and the particular friend of Mr. Crawford,2 was my correspondent from Washington to the day of his death. Are you related to that estimable man and esteemed statesman?

The enclosed memorandum has been put into my hands and I must ask you to assist me in answering it. My impression is that I have seen a letter from Mr. Crawford, changing his views of the Bank of the U. States. Be so good as to drop me a line upon it and enclose me a copy of Mr. Crawford's letter if you have such a one at your disposition, or write me where I am to obtain the information.

Thomas Ritchie To Howell Cobb. E. Private.

Richmond va.—*Monday evening— May 6, 18.*

My Dear Sir: I am deeply sensible of the kindness you have shown me and the confidence you have reposed in me by your candid and manly letter. It is worthy of the character which I have heard ascribed to you by those who personally know you.

For 40 years (on Thursday next) have I been the Editor of a paper—and never have I seen the Republican party in so much danger. We are breaking up into factions. The great Dictator marching on to power with a strong and invincible party at his heels whilst we are divided by miserable contests and contemptible jealousies.

You ask me to interpose my good offices between the contending presses at Washington. I might as well attempt to stop the Ocean with a bullrush. The Globe *now* will hearken to no good counsels. An arrogant spirit presides over it at the very moment that it should most conciliate and bind us together. And again my able and noble friend, Dromgoole,8 whose only fault in the world is on some occasions a dogged *tenax propositi,* is rushing before the public, instead of treating me like his real friend, and I trust in God, if not as able at least as pure and disinterested a politician as himself, by remonstrating with me privately, if he thought I had done wrong, and seeking by arguments to which I am never deaf, to bring me right. But, sir, Dromgoole is groping in the dark. He does not know the sentiment of Virginia. She will demand the annexation of Texas if it can be obtained. But he does not know the condition of things in relation to the presidential slate. Dromgoole and a hundred Globes cannot stop the current of public sentiment in the South. I send you confidentially a letter I received to-day from a Republican.

i Howell Cobb, Congressman from Georgia, 1807-1812, uncle of the Howell Cobb to whom this letter is addressed. William H. Crawford, Senator from Georgia, 1807-1813; United States minister to France, 1813-1815; Secretary of the Treasury, 1816-1825; presidential candidate, 18241825. 'George C. Dromgoole, congressman from Virginia, 1835-1837, 1845-1847.

He is a lawyer in Petersburg. Don't

show it but return it to me. I reed. 5 others of a similar character yesterday from different parts of the State.

I have this moment received the proceedings of the Democrats of this county (Henrico) assembled today at their Court House. The oldest, staunchest Republicans unanimously voted for relieving W. H. Roane and his colleagues of the Baltimore convention, from their instructions to vote for V. B.1 and leaving them to their *sound discretion*. You know the character of W. H. Roane (former U. S. Senator and the devoted friend of Mr. V. B.). It was *he* not /, who passed the *last Resolution* which the Globe and Dromgoole attack. The meeting of Henrico to-day was about at one time, I understand, to instruct the Baltimore delegates to vote for no man who was not for Texas. As it was, they expressed their earnest desire for their Baltimore delegates to procure the nomination of a Democrat friendly to the immediate annexation of Texas.

I spoke very freely to Mr. Stiles, about what I thought was the duty of our friends in Congress, for no member, unless he be a delegate to the B. convention, to have anything to say to the presidential election and for them only to collect information about the candidates and await the public sentiment.

Do write me now and then. Inform me what is going forward.

P. S. Do cultivate the acquaintance of my friend, Gen. Bayley, the new member.

Alexander H. Stephens To James Thomas.2 L. C.

Washington, D. C., *May 17,18U*Dear Thomas, Your favour from Savannah was duly received yesterday and I feel greatly obliged to you for it. I was not unapprised of the movements of the Locos at home upon the *new issue* got up by Captain Tyler, nor was I at all surprised at it, as I remarked in the House. So soon as the late tariff bill " humbug " was disposed of I had no doubt as a party, like most men when publicly condemned in the last court, they would in mass cut out for Texas! And so it seems what I predicted as a result has come to pass. But it will avail them nothing. Mr. Tyler may consider that the people of this country are as much lost to all sense of national honor as he is of personal, and that they place no higher estimation upon good faith than he does, but he will find himself mistaken and will be brought to see that they do not look upon breach of faith, meanness and perfidy in the same light that he does. I wish I had time to write you a full letter upon this subject but I have not. Suffice it to 1 Van Buren.

« A prominent attorney of Sparta, Ga., whose daughter married Stephens's half-brother Linton Stephens in 1852.

say that the whole annexation project is a miserable political humbug got up as a ruse to divide and distract the Whig party at the South, or peradventure with even an ulterior view—that is the dissolution of the present Confederacy. That is not yet quite free from disguise but I only believe it lies near Mr. Calhoun's heart. And as for Tyler, he would willingly destroy a country which he has word illegible deceived and betrayed when he is satisfied that he can no longer be its chief ruler. He and Calhoun both know that the Senate would never prove themselves so lost to all sense of national honor and good faith as to ratify their treaty. This they know well. As for Tyler I do not know but he fool-like did think that perhaps others had as little regard for these qualities as himself and had as little abhorrence for meanness and perfidy as himself. But Calhoun knew better. It is all a trick—one of his desperate moves or strokes to produce dissention in the country for his own personal aggrandizement. But as I said, he will not succeed. Van Buren will be nominated at Baltimore, a kind of schism? will ensue and the dissenters will run a *Texas* man for the South and Van Buren will run at the *North,* and the whole for the purpose if possible of driving the election to the House where they know Van Buren will be elected. For it is now the general belief that without some such trick Clay's election is inevitable. So far as Tyler is concerned in the project it has been for his own aggrandizement. So far as Calhoun is concerned it has been done to set? up a *Southern party*. So far as the *Locos* are concerned—I mean by them the old Simon pures, it has been to distract the Whigs, upon the old principle "divide and conquer". But again I say it will not succeed. When the people of Georgia see all these facts and know everything relating to the treaty it will be by all sensible men of all parties I think universally condemned. But I have not time to give you details. You may have seen it said in the papers that he (Tyler) has actually called out our military forces and stationed two regiments on the confines of *Texas* and several sail in the Gulph—a virtual declaration of war—without consulting Congress. This is true, and a greater outrage upon the constitution has never been committed by any President. I should not be surprised if he is impeached.

P. S. I have not got time to look over the above? to see if spelling is correct.

Marginal P. S. Chappell1 is completely off, and every Whig should know it.

» Absalom H. Chappell, Democratic congressman from Georgia, 1843-1845, standing for reelection in 1844.

Thomas Ritchie To Howell Cobb. E. Richmond va., *May 23,18U*

My Dear Sir: If you had asked me to square the circle or solve the longitude I should as soon have undertaken it as to have advised you upon the problem which you have proposed to me. If you will give us a strong available candidate on whom our party will rally, *tu eris mAhi magnus Apollo.*

As one step towards seeing your way out of the fog, I advise you to make the acquaintance of my friend W. H. Roane who is a delegate from this district. You will find him a man after your own heart. Tell him, if you please, that we are only strengthened in the opinion which he entertained when he left us, that it is in vain to expect to carry Virginia with our friend

Van Buren.

If we have no Texas candidate but Capt. John Tyler he will carry off a few thousands from Mr. V. B. which *per se* would be sufficient to defeat Mr. V. B. in Virginia.

My eldest son, W. F. Ritchie, carries this hasty letter with him. Pie is an alternate delegate to the Baltimore convention. He has seen all my correspondence and knows the public sentiment of Virginia as well as I do. He will go into the convention and carry out the wishes of his constituents of the Abingdon district and he goes in also as *no man's man*—not even his father's—as I have written Mr. Colquitt. I pray you to make him welcome in Washington.

Alexander H. Stephens To James Thomas. L. C.

Macon, Ga., *July 16,1844* Dear Thomas, Your favour of the 8th inst. came to hand a few days ago just as I was getting in the cars on my departure from home, and I have not had time since then or rather an opportunity of sufficient word illegible to send you an earlier answer. I will if it is in my power be with you on the 27th inst. but I am not certain that I can. The day before I shall be at Crawfordville where I hope also to meet you, and on the 24th I shall be at Washington I expect. The travel and fatigue I fear will be almost too much for me. I am here to day, and to morrow shall if nothing prevents go over to Clinton where there is to be a meeting the next day. Meriwether 1 and E. A. Nisbet are to be there. Jenkins and myself were at Eatonton last Saturday; and in all parts I have been in, as well as those from which I have heard, the prospect is good. In some counties it is reported that we will sustain loss etc., but upon a close examination I find that in nearly all instances the rumor is false. The Locos seem determined to do what they can by gasconnading, 1 James A. Meriwether, Eugeniua A. Nisbet, and Charles J. Jenkins were Georgia Whig leaders. and the only effect of it is I think to arouse the Whigs and make them energetic, and that is all we want. Chappell from what I learn here will be badly beaten in this district. I am informed by the most intelligent and observing men in such matters that he will do us no injury in this and Monroe county and no other county except Upson and Meriwether, and very little in those. My news from Cherokee is good. Miller and Lumpkin 2 have had a meeting and discussion at Decatur, in which they say Miller got decidedly the advantage. Lumpkin complained of ill health and got out in that way. The Whigs are up and doing. I saw here last night men from Cobb, Pike, Monroe, Twiggs and Pulaski and all are zealous. Colquitt and Haralson3 and young Alford and Samford and Chappell were all here last week and literally stormed the castle, but to no effect. And I assure you the prospect as far as I have seen is quite as good for our carrying the State as it was at the same time in 1840, if not better—and there is no comparison hardly between the indications now and this time last year, for our people are now fully up and aroused, and this is all we have ever wanted in order to succeed at an election.

Wood Hinton To Howell Cobb. E.

Georgia, Jackson County, *Jan. 7,1845.* Sir: I have one request to make of you that is this there are some negroes property to be Transported into some free State in the United State thare are maney opinions about it some say that it cannot be dun on a count that thare is no state that will receive them this question you can decide. I dont want you to make this a publick question in the House but to talk with the Members of Illinois or Indiana as they are the two nearest free States to me I am told that their States will not receive Negroes from a slave holding state and that they have past a law to that effect and a penalty if any is carried there this point you can decide.. . That question is one of importance to me and this business if actd on will stop the mouths of many I sincerely request of you for me Will confer special favour.

Robert Toombs To Alexander H. Stephens. R.

Washington ga., *J any. 24th, 1845.* Dear Stephens,... I can hear nothing of local politics. There is a dead calm. The report of the Finance Committee is doing us much good. It has struck the Locos dumb. Crawford's adminis

J In the congressional election of 1844, Absalom H. Chappell was narrowly defeated in the third district by his Whig opponent, Washington Poe.
2 John H. Lumpkin, Democrat, defeated H. V. M. Miller in the fifth district by a heavy majority.
» Hugh A. Haralson was elected in the fourth district. Colquitt, Alford and Samford were Democratic speakers in the campaign, but were not candidates. tration has certainly been eminently successfull and has made him very popular. If we can get him to run again we can carry the State and retrieve our fortunes in Georgia. The course of the Democracy in Congress on Texas and the tariff is doing them mischief in this State, and if our local press would handle those questions now in the present calm of the public mind much could be made out of them; but very few of our papers are worth a straw. As soon as I get able I shall open upon them in several of the papers. Now is the proper time to affect the public mind. I did not see how you voted on that Rail Road iron question. That duty ought to be repealed or greatly reduced. It should be a *low* revenue duty *only.* 1st. Because it is greatly to the interest of the country to encourage internal improvements and thereby cheapen internal transportation which benefits all classes and especially the agricultural classes. 2ondly. R. R. iron not being an article of general consumption, competition is not likely to become sufficient within a reasonable time to cheapen the article and compensate for the duty. Hence the duty will continue to be a bounty to the manufacturer, and under that state of facts *no article* ought to be protected. I am able only to suggest my objections and not enforce them. The most foolish thing Mr. Clay did during the campaign was to write that foolish letter to Pennsylva-

nia pledging his opposition to any modification of the tariff of 1842. It is a good law but it is not perfect; nor did human ingenuity ever make a perfect revenue law. It never will. His letter to Bronson and his N. Carolina speech contained the true doctrine on the tariff. I am unwilling to go an inch further. I care not a fig for the clamors of that American Beotia (Pennsylvania). If the whole duty on R. R. iron was repealed her agonies would give me no pain. Annexation by Congress gives me considerable trouble. I am in great doubt about it. The words of the Constitution *ex vi termini* are sufficient to embrace the case, and I am clear from the action of the Convention that the Convention did not intend to limit the power to the admission of States from the then territory of the United States. I think the Convention were then looking to the acquisition of Louisiana. It was absolutely necessary to our western States. I am therefore clear in the opinion, nothwithstanding Mr. Jefferson's opinion to the contrary, that the acquisition of Louisiana by treaty and then its admission was perfectly constitutional; but I am not clear that it would have been constitutional without such previous acquisition by treaty. But from the best reflection I can give it, it being a question of doubt, I would decide it in favour of the popular will and, I therefore honestly believe, the public safety and the safety of the Union, and go for Foster's plan. Benton's division of the territory will not answer. I would yield nothing upon the slavery question below 36 degrees latitude—and I don't like that. Congress has no right to interfere with the social relations of the inhabitants of *any* State. And the Missouri Compromise was all wrong and could only be defended because it *practically* yielded nothing.

J. W. Burney To Howell Cobb. E.

Monticello ga., *31st Jany., 1845.*
Dear Sir: Many of our citizens had assembled at the Post office this morning to hear the Texas news. When we saw the measure had passed the H. of R., and that Messrs. Stephens and Clinch had voted with the rest of our delegation there was a general exclamation of " well done good and faithful servant ". Our Whig friends joined in the expression of their joy. I beg you to tender to Mr. Stephens (to whom I am not known) my sincere thanks for this vote. The question is *vital* to us. His superior love of country to party entitles him to great credit. Can it be that Judge Berrien1 will not pursue a like course? Now is the time for him to show himself to be above party influence. Do all, all work to carry this great question through the Senate. We are satisfied here with the Resolutions as they passed the House, tho we would have preferred the Missouri Compromise being stricken out. But concessions must be made, and the people of Georgia will agree to any thing reasonable on the subject to get the country.

I have troubled you too much already, but felt as if it was my duty to say this much.

We shall now look with great anxiety to the other end of the Capitol for favorable action.

Alexander H. Stephens To James Thomas. L. C.

Washington, D. C., *Feb. 11, 1845.*
Dear Thomas, Let me know what you think of my speech upon Texas and what the Whigs of Hancock think of my vote upon the same. From the Chronicle and Sentinel2 I infer that they do not sustain it; but certainly they forget the true position of the Whigs of Georgia last year upon that subject. I haven't time to say more. No news here. Benton it is thought will defeat the measure in the Senate. He wishes it kept open. Polk has not got here yet, and nobody knows who will be in his cabinet.

1 John McPherson Berrien, Senator from Georgia, 1825-1829, Attorney General in Jackson's Cabinet, 1820-1831; Senator again (as a Whig), 1841-1852. The Chronicle and Sentinel of Augusta was a leading Whig organ in Georgia.

Junius Hillyer1 To Howell Cobb. E.

Athens, ga., *Feb. 15th, 1846.*

Dear Howell, I have just returned from Clark court and in the morning I must start to Walton, but I cannot longer defer writing to you. You must accept as my excuse for not having written often that I have constantly visited Chase's2 office and had the pleasure of seeing your letters to him, so that through that channel I have been in constant communication with you and from Chase, Mitchell and others you have I thought been so far in communication with me as to make it not very important for me to address you directly.

It is true our editors do not speak with as much zeal on Texas as I think they ought but I do believe that our people are looking with a deep interest on the issue of the question in the Senate; what will be the fate of the bill I do not know but I do believe that if annexation is defeated the wrath of the people of Georgia will be visited on the Whigs after such a sort that they will feel the effects of it during the lives of the present generation. We take for granted since the report of the committee that our Senator Mr. Berrien will oppose it. That his doing so will be against the wishes of a very large majority it seems to me he must know. It is for him however to reconcile it to his conscience to vote directly contrary to the known will of his constituents. Do your best. Let not the measure be lost....

Robert Toombs To Alexander H. Stephens. R.

Washington ga., *Feb. 16th, 1845.*
dear S[t]ephens,8 I received your letter of 9th and hardly know what to write you about my prospects of getting to Taliaferro. I tell myself every five or six days that I am getting well but the slightest exercise or labour brings back the pains in my shoulders, arms and legs. I *hope* to get there but I fear I shall not be able, tho' I should dislike to be able and not have you there. Therefore unless very inconvenient I wish you would come. My physician thinks that I am clear of rheumatism and that my present pains are the result of spinal irritation which he says fre-

quently succeeds as severe attacks as mine. I doubt he is right about it. I am generally free from pain when at rest but the slightest motion even writing a letter is accompanied with pain. I am thus particular that you may judge somewhat for yourself.

1A Democratic leader resident at Athens, Ga., Cobb's home. He was judge of the superior court of Georgia (western circuit), 1841-1845; Congressman from Georgia, 18511855; Solicitor of the United States Treasury, 1857-1861.- Albon Chase, editor of the " Southern Banner," at Athens, Ga.

'Corner of the original letter mouse-eaten.

I have not answered the Times because I am wholly unequal to the labour. Except my letters to you I have not written as much as a sheet of paper since I was taken sick, until day before yesterday I wrote about half that amount to Berrien. As soon as I am able I shall give him a touch. The Whigs generally, indeed universally except Jenkins, as far as I have seen or heard from them, are satisfied with the course of yourself and Clinch on the Texas question. My means of knowing their opinions are of course limited. I have heard of no single man who objects to the *terms* of annexation embraced in the resolutions. A good many differ with you as to the *mode,* but you are a sufficient judge of the popular mind that the *mode* exerts no influence upon the people generally. Many who differ with you as to the *mode* think that your own course will have a good effect upon the state of opinion here by killing it off as a party question. It may have that effect, but I am not without my misgivings. If Berrien could have voted with you I think such would likely have been the case, but his voting the other way, connected with the fact that the measure will be lost by the votes of *slaveholding* Senators will I think prevent that result. From that state of facts I fear it will still be a party question in the South. In that event the divisions of the Whig party even on the *mode* of annexation must needs be an element of weakness and not of strength. The *terms* of annexation are certainly very favourable to the South, better than I ever supposed could pass either branch of Congress; and I deeply regret that the form in which they come up prevents their passage through the Senate. I see nothing but evil to our party and the country that can come out of this question in future. You ought to send copies of your speech to all of our editors for immediate publication. It will put you right before the country. Your speech is a good one, tho' I have rarely found myself differing with you on so many points. I concur with you in but one of your reasons for desiring annexation and that is that it will give power to the slave states. I firmly believe that in every other respect it will be an unmixed evil to us and not without natural *disadvantages* as well as advantages. Tho' I can not bring myself to concur with you on the constitutional question, I shall not commit myself publicly on that point without further time and a more full investigation. It strikes me that a satisfactory answer to your argument drawn from the admission of N. Carolina and K. Island is to be found in the Constitution itself. Altho' the government was to go into operation on the ratification of nine states the other states could by the very terms of the Constitution come in at any time afterwards. I hope and trust the question will take such a direction in the Senate as not to bring our friends even in apparent collision. Archer's report1 gave me the backache to read it. Its style is really ridiculous. It is either a long ways behind or *before* the age. He " writes bombast and calls it a style." Write me as soon as you get this whether you will come to T. Court. Come if you can and let us talk over these matters. For I can not write. We must commence the spring campaign early and vigorously.

George D. Phillips2 To Howell Cobb. E.

Clarksville ga., *21si Feb. 1846.*

Dear Sm: I have just returned from a trip to Texas and if my voice could reach Washington and my opinions have any, the slightest influence on grave Senators, that beautiful country would soon be a portion of our Confederacy. I have seen and conversed with and freely mixed with all classes and do assure you if Texas is not now annexed it never can be with their consent. The property holders and higher classes of the people are anxious for the Union but the middle and lower classe decidedly opposed to it, whilst but few people of property are now immigrating to the country, and vast numbers from Ark., Misso., Illinois, Indiana, Ohio, etc., to say nothing of the swarms from foreign countries are nearly to a man against annexation. Should the measure not succeed now many of its warm advocates will drop off and the issue between competitors for Congress in Texas at their next election will be, annexation or no annexation, and when that issue comes the anti-annexationists will be in the majority. I was not fully satisfied of the importance of Texas to our sountry in a military point of view until I travelled into the cor iry. Nor would Oregon be worth a baubee to us without Texas; we'sJ'iver could protect it, and if we do not get the last I hope we will be ise enough to surrender the latter; and if I had a seat in Congress I n4ver would favour any project for the occupation of Oregon until wle had got Texas, but on the contrary throw every impediment in the wjay, even give it up to England or the devil.

I What is Tom Benton about; is he yet sowing the wind? He will sHirely reap the whirlwind for his past acts. It is thought by many he will break up the harmony of the Democratic party. I think not; he may fume, fret and denounce, but he has lost caste, he is no longer the big gun he was with the people, he is denounced from Geo. to the Colorado.

1 William S. Archer, of Virginia, chairman of the Senate Committee on Foreign Affairs, had presented a report, Feb. 4, 1845, contending that Texas could be annexed only by treaty, and not by act of Congress. 'A leading Democrat of northeastern Georgia, a

keen critic of public affairs. 73566—
13 5

What a misfortune Yancey did not bore his man through just for the honor of Old Rip;1 but whatever is, is right!

I did intend being in Washington on the 4th and see *little Jemmy* invested with the proud mantle of Washington and Jackson, but my long trip and the delicate state of my wife's health will prevent; so I shall remain quiet until you get home and visit us at our Court.

George D. Phillips To Howell Cobb. E.

Habersham County, Ga., *Feb. £5,1845.* Dear Sir: I wrote you a few days ago that the Texas question, as decided now, would stand decided forever. I would stake my ears against a Romish crucifix, that time proves the correctness of this opinion; but I would qualify in this particular: if President Polk convenes an extra Congress and Texas be thereby annexed, even under less favourable circumstances than those secured by the House Resolutions, Texas will assent, provided there be no restrictions on the subject of slavery embraced. The wit of man could not devise a plan of annexation to which they would assent if at any future time any portion of Texas, or rather any State formed out of Texas territory, should give rise even to a discussion in Congress on the question of negro slavery. Her public lands are more than enough to pay her public debt, and she feels indifferent on that subject. You need not indulge the least fear that Texas will fall a prey to English diplomacy, intrigue, or money. I had my doubts and fears until I visited the country and mixed with her people freely, the elite and the clod-pole. Save the immigrants from the West, and probably those from abroad, all, all are Americans, and better, Southern, and dyed in the wool. And I hazard nothing in saying Texas will-sustain and defend Southern rights and Southern institutions or (,,;ase to exist as a free people. Nor will Texas permit England to guarantee her independence. She is conscious of having a better guarantee in the strong arms and brave hearts of her sons; and if she is not received by the U. S., or her independence acknowledged by the powers that be, as soon as a new state of things becomes settled in Mexico she will wring from Mexico that acknowledgement. There is now a strong feeling in all the states from the Rio del Nort to the Table Lands to amalgamate with Texas; an invading army of 2000 men would certainly take possession of 4 states. As those who are resolved not to fight are easily whipd, all that Texas will desire of Uncle Sam will be to keep her Indians at home. As to Mexico and her own savages, she can take care of them.

1 This alludes to the bloodless duel between William L. Yancey, of Alabama, and Thomas L. Cllngman, of North Carolina. "Old Rip" (Rip Van Winkle) was a nickname of the State of North Carolina.

The last mail brought us intelligence that Congress had decided to establish a territorial government in Oregon. The slavery question did not apply there; but to us it involved the question of power, and if I had been clear that the whole country to the 54th deg. N. L. belonged to us, I never could have supported the measure in advance of a settlement of the Texas question. With me it would have been: no Texas, no Oregon, or both simultaneously. I have never seen any conclusive evidence of our titles to Oregon north of 49, and doubt if such proof is extant. If so, where will I find it? If I am not deceived, Oregon will prove a Pandora's Box. For a foot of Maine I was willing to fight; for Texas I would fight the world, because the world would be impertinently interfering with our concerns; but for Oregon north of 49,I would not quarrel....

There is I find an extraordinary effort making to remove Mr. Cooper, superintendent of the mint,1 from office; and that Dr. Singleton should have the motley crowd almost passeth belief and that too to wear the slippers. Does it not require some credulity to believe this, yet it is so. You know the Dr. is a dull plodding man, and if he were again in office and remained there for half a century he could not be as well qualified for the office as Mr. Cooper was the first week he entered it. Under the Dr.'s administration depositors had to wait from two to four weeks for coin. Some improvement took place when Rosignol was in office, but since Mr. Cooper has been in depositors often get their gold coin as soon as the assay can be made. Mr. Rosignol was an efficient man but his manners rendered him unpopular and it was said, perhaps with some truth, he killed two birds with one stone, served a bank and Uncle Sam too; and for this I presume was removed. Mr. Cooper is easy and polite in his intercourse with all who have business at the mint. If any charges of improper conduct have been brought against him I have not heard them; and it would be difficult to imagine one so correct and unexceptionable in his conduct that such a being as Harrison Riley could not bring a charge against. I presume they dare not attack Mr. Cooper on the ground of want of qualification. No change could be made for the better on that score. Do depositors of gold bullion want him removed? No, and he may challenge to the proof. I speak of honorable, intelligent gentlemen. Many two-and-sixpence depositors may have signed a petition. To what kind of a petition would you fail to get signers? You might get forty in Washington to emancipate my negroes and compel them to cut my throat. But if they really have, as I hear, 6000 petitioners for the removal, I have no doubt but 9/10 of them never were in the mint, made a deposit of gold or know Mr. Cooper, and further that 9/10 of them are Whigs. If Mr.

11. e., the United States branch mint at Dahlonega, Ga.

Cooper or his friends were to get up counter petitions they could beat the celebrated Abolition petition a stone's throw. That I think had 7 thousand names. We could get 20 thousand in Geo. The truth is this: Dr. Singleton wants the office for the money. Harrison Riley, than whom the devil is not more artful, hates Mr. Cooper because he is a gentleman and a Democrat, and wishes to get him out of the county, and others whom I could name cooperate from interested motives. In justice to Maj. C. and in justice to your constituents I hope you and every Democratic Member of Congress of both houses will call on President Tyler and put this low and dirty effort down, by the correct representations. It is said Mr. C. is some way related to the President; if so, there may be more danger than if no such connection existed. If any importance is attached to six thousand then ask a suspension of any action until a counter petition of 10,000 can be sent on; and if the matter is reserved for the Presidentelect, do not in the fulness of heartfelt rejoicing and the pageantry of oiling the head of our triumphant Chief make you forget to call on him, the whole of you, Judge Colquitt at your head, and prevent an honest man and faithful officer from being thrown overboard to gratify a land pirate and his porpoise coadjutor. I write in haste and amidst confusion, but have no doubt wearied you. Adieu.

Alexander H. Stephens To Howell Cobb. E.

Steamboat Wilmington (near Charleston Harbour, Thursday Morning), *27 Feb. 1845.* Dear Cobb, According to promise I drop you a line, though I write on the boat where I am rocked and shaken so I fear you can not read it. I have had a fine and comfortable travel so far, and expect soon to take leave of the sea and its dangers. I never had a smoother passage from Wilmington to Charleston. The wind was perfectly calm and the sea at rest. Touching the stages, I ascertained that there is a daily line from Raleigh to Columbia—two horse, I was told. It leaves Raleigh at 2 p. m., and after being out *two nights* arrives at Columbia at 8 p. m. the *third night.* Another line leaves the Wilmington railroad at the breakfast house Warsaw, for Fayetteville and Columbia. That is the best route, and it gives you an opportunity of judging of the probable state of the weather— as you can pay to that place, and then if the weather threatens to be bad you can take that line. It leaves the railroad 45 miles from Wilmington; is a four horse coach, but did not look to me as if it could carry more than six. It is a small and slender looking *North Carolina* affair. But I can say no more.

William B. Wofford1 To Howell Cobb. E.

MillEDGEvillE ga., *Hth Decbr., 1845.* Dear Sir, I reed. yours of the 5th inst. by due course of mail. The President's views as expressed in his Message on all subjects is well received by his friends, and in fact it has sealed the lips of his political inimies.

The bill organising a Supream Court has passed and Judge Warner has bin nominated by our friends as the democratic candidate and the Whigs are pledged to elect him.

Much good feeling exists at this place with our friends and marke what I now tel you two years hence the Democratic Party in Georgia will stand erect. I am busy ingaged in preparing materiels for the campain of 1847. I compel the Feds to vote on all important questions and there dishonest political course is pointed out to them all most every day in the Senate and I am certain it would gratify you to witness how they hang there heads and bear it without oping there mouths.

Fountain G. Moss is the gentleman that I wish appointed post master at Hollingsworth P. Off. in my neighbourhood the petition sent last year states the reson which makes it desirable to have Mr. Moss appointed in place of Mr. Wynn please have the business attended without fail.

I enclose you two dollars Send me the Washington Union and the balance I will pay you on site. I mean the weekley paper.

N. B.—Give my compliments to Colquitt and the balance of the delegation from Georgia excep Berrien and his people.

George D. Phillips To Howell Cobb. E.

Clarksville ga., *Deer. 30th, 185.* Dear Sir: Enclosed you will receive a letter from our friend Col. Lumpkin to me apprising me he had collected a certain amot. of money which was held subject to my order.... Will you do me the kindness to speak to the Col. on the subject, or if you choose shew him his letter, which will refresh his recollection, and receive the amot., and likewise do me the farther favor to hand it to Thomas Ritchie with whom I am in arrears. No doubt you sometimes call on the venerable old gentleman whose grey head and tremulous hand is more formidable to the Whigs than an army with banners. This will give you some trouble perhaps, but we cannot live without troubling one another, and you *do not know how much trouble I may have on your account yet.* Be it however much or little I shall 1 A prominent Democratic politician of northeastern Georgia, at this time a member of the Georgia legislature. 'l. e., the Whigs. not make out my bill. I could send the statement of Maj. Walker if I thought it were necessary, but the Col. might think I questioned his honor, or some such thing; and I have a great disinclination to be called out in Cold Weather. I will however drop him a line. The President's Message has set all our mountain folks to thinking and talking. Every one understands, or thinks he understands, all about the Oregon question; and I heard a crowd on Christmas, not one of whom knew on which side of the Rocky Mountains Oregon was, swear they would support and fight for Polk *all over the world,* that he was right, and we would have Oregon and thrash the British into the bargain. As to the tariff, they despised it—they never liked it—and Polk had shewn it was not the poor man's friend. But about locking up the public money, they were not so sure he was right,—it had better circulate from hand to hand, as people could then get money for their work. After the Message had been elaborately execrated? by the meeting, my summing up was that our mountain population (save a few rabid Whigs) were sound to the core, and let peace or war betide they would do their duty. Bagatelle aside, this Oregon affair must prove a rough customer to us and England. I am no advocate of quarrels, much less protracted ones, and decidedly prefer a fight, though it results in a bloody nose, to the latter, and therefore feel anxious that the question should be settled; but I must be permitted to doubt if either England or the U. S. has pursued the most politic course, and think if negotiations *could* be resumed the controversy would be settled with scarcely a shade's variation from the terms previously offered and rejected. But how can the confab be reopened? Neither power will make the first advance; each to a great extent have taken their position, and pride prompts to its maintenance. That our old ally and best transatlantic friend in bye-gone days begins to look on us with green eyes there can be no doubt. Her conduct in relation to Texas, her notions of a balance of power, etc., prove it, and war with England will demonstrate it fully. We should therefore not precipitate a conflict, but with energy prepare for it by increasing our navy and fortifying the most assailable points. The opinion expressed by many distinguished men that England cannot war with us, is a strange delusion. With her stock of cotton on hand and the supplies she can get from Brazil, Egypt and the E. Indies, not one of her spindles would stop for two or three years; and as to her want of breadstuffs, she can feed her suffering thousands on the water and in Canada as cheaply as at home. Her press gangs are now superseded by the necessities of the people, and the difficulty would be to restrain enlistments. And has she ever had such a time to carry out those objects which she so anxiously desires, as the present? She is at peace with all Christendom, her population redundant, the Catholic fanatics of Ireland would forget repeal to join the crusade against slavery; and France, colonizing France, not at all relishing our declarations as to European powers interfering with the affairs of N. America, would stand aloof and feel no desire that the strife should cease until both were whipped.

But if Oregon is ours, although I regret it is not under instead of on the Pacific, we must have it unless we voluntarily yield a part; and I think the President has immortalised himself in taking the stand he has. I hope Congress will act on the subject with caution, prudence, and firmness. Let us ever be in the right and trust to our valor and the God of battles for the issue.

The winter has been excessively cold and has kept me at home, but shall leave in a few days for Ala. The vote on the adm. of Texas was nobly done. Write to Tom Rush to go to Congress. He has talents of a high order, and the people wish him to go, but he is disinclined. Do write to him at Nacogdoches.

Alexander H. Stephens To George W. Crawford.1 L. C.

Washington, D. C, *Feb. 3,1846.*
Dear Crawford, Yours in relation to the Galphin claim came to hand last night and I will examine the case you cite. I turned over the papers relating to the claim to Judge Berrien some weeks ago whp I think likewise turned them over to Mr. McDuffie who is to bring the subject before the Senate. This I think the better course. They have more time in the Senate, and being a smaller body are more disposed to attend to the real merits of the case. If a favourable report can be got through that body it will stand a much better chance in our House. And should it come there I would do all that labour, research and investigation can do to effect its passage. I have bestowed a good deal of attention to the subject and am clearly of opinion that it is founded in right and justice and ought to be passed. Our time however for some weeks, as you see from the papers, has been taken up almost exclusively with the Oregon debate, and when we will bring that to a close I am wholly unable to conjecture. Every one in the House I believe (myself alone excepted) i is desirous of making a speech upon the subject. Even those who have spoken are anxious many of them to make another. But I suppose the debate will be ended in the House when it is taken up in the Senate, which will take place next week. It is a subject I feel no disposition to speak upon in its present shape and condition, and I partake very little of that excitement in relation to it which seems to prevail amongst others. I am for our rights as far as they are clear, and in maintaining them thus far I should not suffer myself to be in 1 Governor of Georgia, 1843-1847, Secretary of War in Taylor's Cabinet, 1849-1850. lie was for many years attorney for the Galphin claimants.
fluenced by any considerations growing out of a fear or apprehension of war. Nor do I conceive that the questions of peace or war are at all involved in terminating the joint occupancy under the convention of 1818. It seems to me that such a measure would only bring about a settlement of our boundary, which ought to be done, as our people are new going there in large companies for the purpose of colonizing. Whether this will lead to a rupture with England or not I cannot pretend to say. It ought not, and will not if properly managed. But one thing is certain, our government will have to recede from the position of Mr. Polk that our "title to the whole of the territory is clear and unquestionable ", or war will be inevitable unless I greatly mistake the temper of the British Government. The war however will not be the result of the giving the notice but subsequent legislation taking possession of the whole of the country. And this I am not prepared to do, and will not do, for I do not think our rights clear to that extent. And I moreover think that the whole subject is proper for negotiation and settlement upon terms of mutual compromise. And if I may go a step further I think this will be the result of the whole matter. If the notice is given, negotiations (if the President does his duty) will be opened, he will recede from his position, and the controversy will ultimately be ended in some sort of amicable adjustment. I can not bring myself to the belief that war will result. But enough of this. I am doing what I can to facilitate the settlement

of the amount of our state at the Treasury Department, but my progress is slow. I sent you some papers upon this subject a few days ago.

P. S.—My health is good, much better than it has been for several years.

Robert Toombs To George W. Crawford. L. C.

Washington, D. C, Ho. or Reps., *Feb. 6,181$.* Dear Crawford, I received your letter of the 31st ult. last night. Lest you may not receive the speech I first sent, I send you another by this mail. The authorities on the Galphin claim to which you refer I will consult in a few days. I think from your statement of the case it is "in pint. " This is a very bad body before which to argue such a question, but if it can be got through the Senate and is backed by a strong report in this House I think it could be got through without much difficulty. A majority report *favourable* would certainly settle it, but the committees of this House are very badly constituted for any just purpose. They are nearly as rabid against all sorts of claims as the Locos in the Georgia legislature. They have promised a good deal in the way of reform, and instead of honestly retrenching actual abuses, which they have neither the honesty or the firmness to do, they desire to retrench by defeating all sort of claims, honest as well as dishonest, against the government.

I suppose you have the defective receipts sent you by Mr. Stephens. You will perceive from the nature of the objections that it is impossible ever to settle with the government without legislation, and I am decidedly of opinion that a gross appropriation for a full settlement will be the very best we can do, if we can carry it. If you can get the Secretary of War to recommend or acquiesce in it, it can I think be carried, and I very much wish you could bring him to that point. Without it I see little or no chance of ever getting any considerable portion of the remaining claim, if indeed we can get anything more.

I am glad to hear from you that you will not be obliged "to stop" during your administration. I had supposed your only resource against such a calamity would be in the act of 1843 authorizing you to raise money to pay off that debt by new 6 per cents. You will probably recollect at that time I favoured that policy in any event. I don't care to pay that debt. I would much prefer letting it remain the 25 or 30 years, when I doubt not its interest and much of the principal can be paid from the road,1 and the experience of the last five years is very conclusive that all railroads judiciously located will pay, and I think ours will be one of the very best in the South. I perceive from the newspapers that you are adopting the policy of raising the wind by means of the 6 per cents. If they are pressed gradually on the market they will rise, unless we have war.

I do not think a war in the least probable. Mr. Polk never dreamed of any other war than a war upon the Whigs. He is playing a low grog-shop politician's trick, nothing more. He would be as much surprised and astonished and frightened at getting into war with England as if the Devil were to rise up before him at his bidding. The Democratic Party had declared our title to "all Oregon" "clear and unquestionable." Mr. Polk adopted and asserted the same thing in his inaugural speech. Both moves were political blunders. It became necessary to retrieve them. He was bound to offer 49. He supposed as the British Government had refused that proposition when made with more advantageous additions than were embraced in his proposition that that Government would do so again. It was an affectation of moderation when he knew that it was the best we could ever get. He withdraws the proposition and begins his game of "bluster," with the full conviction that the Whig Party, true to their fatality to blunders, would raise the shout of peace, peace, and which would make him, the vilest poltroon that ever disgraced our Government, the head of the war party. His party were already committed to him to 54 40', they would stand by him, and he expected finally to be forced by the British Whigs and Southern Calhoun men to compromise; but he greatly

'The Western & Atlantic Railroad.

hoped that he would not be forced even to this alternative until he had "all Oregon" on every Democratic banner in the Union for his "second heat. " I have not the least doubt but that he fully calculated that the "notice" would be rejected by a combination between the Whigs and Calhoun men of this Congress, and then he could have kept it open for a new presidential campaign. That these were the objects of the Administration I have not the least doubt. Hence I urged the Whigs to stand up and give him the *power* to give the notice whenever he thought proper, which would have "blocked" him. But they would save themselves and their party for the same reason that the lad did in scripture, "because" their friends "had much goods. " Wall street howled, old Gales was frightened into fits at the possibility of war, and the Whig press throughout the country screamed in piteous accents peace, peace, with the vain foolish hope of gaining popular confidence by their very fears, and like the magnetic needle, they expected to tremble into peace. Nothing could be more absurd. If we have peace they are disarmed, and whatever may be the terms of accommodation they will be estopped from uttering a word of complaint. If war comes, no people were ever foolish enough to trust its conduct to a "peace party," for very good sufficient reasons. If the country should be beaten and dishonored they will be called upon to patch up a dishonorable peace, but in no other event.

There is another view of this question, purely sectional, which our people don't seem to understand. Some of our Southern papers seem to think we are very foolish to risk a war to secure anti-slave power. They look only at the surface of things. If we had control of the government and could control this question, I have not the least doubt that Calhoun is right in saying that his "masterly inactivity" policy is the only one which ever could acquire " all Oregon ". It can never be done in any other way except to give the notice and stand still, which would effect the same object-rightfully; but notice and action *never will secure all Oregon.* Mark the prediction. Notice will force an early settlement. That settlement will be upon or near the basis of 49, and therefore a loss of half the country. Now one of the strongest private reasons which governs me is that I don't care a fig about *any* of Oregon, and would gladly get ridd of the controversy by giving it all to anybody else but the British if I could with honor. The country is too large now, and I don't want a foot of Oregon or an acre of any other country, especially without "niggers." These are some of my reasons for my course which don't appear in print.

I deeply regret that the Whigs, especially of the Senate, have given and will give a different direction to the question. If Polk wants war he can make it in spite of any let or hindrance from them. If he does not want it, he will not need their aid to keep out of it; but they "gabble" and "chatter" about the peace of the country and the horrors of war as if they had any real power over either question....

P. S.—We are still on Oregon. The question will be taken on Monday. "Notice" will pass this time, in what form is doubtful, but I think unqualified. Negotiations are undoubtedly renewed and are now pending on the subject.

Howell, Cobb To His Wife. E.
Washington City, *3rd April, 1846.*
My Dear Wife,... On the day that you left, Genl. Cass made a *great* speech on Oregon. Up to 54.40 was his position, and the general opinion is expressed that it is the ablest and most effective effort that has been made on the subject. It will add greatly to the number of 54.40 men with the masses, whose honest impulses will teach them to sympathise with the views he has put forth. On the next day Col. Benton made a regular attack upon Cass, which has led to the most exciting and animating debate that I have ever witnessed in Congress. You will see it reported in the papers and it will afford you a faithful picture of the grappling of great intellects. Upon the whole, Cass seems to be victor in the fight, and the effort of Benton to paralyze the effort of Cass's speech will be foiled...

John P. King1 To Howell Cobb. E.
Augusta, Ga., *May 7, 181fi.* ... P. S.—Exciting news from Mexico this morning; this only could be reasonably expected. I have *(entre nous)* never seen any reasons of expediency for sending Taylor to the Bio Grande. Why insultingly *heard* this poor feeble distracted people? They have been hardly dealt with, and why not give them some decent chance to cover up their humiliation, which they certainly would have done by negociation ere long if our cannon had been kept out of their sight. I should not be much surprised if we were on the eve of a long and distracting war with all the attendant evils of debts, taxes, tariff, and the *finale* of all ambitious Republics—a military despotism. I hope to God that we may not yet have cause to wish that both Texas and Oregon had been ingulphed before they were heard of by the people of the United States.

1 United States Senator from Georgia, 1833-1837, president of the Georgia Railroad & Banking Co., 1841-1878.

Howell Cobb To His Wife. E.
Washington City, *10th May, 181fi.*
My Dear Wife,... The city has been in great excitement since yesterday evening in consequence of the news we received from our Army in Texas. It is now settled that we are at war with Mexico, and on tomorrow the President is to send in to Congress a war message, and immediately legislation will be had for the prompt and energetic enforcement of our rights against Mexico. When the Union1 of Monday night reaches you, you may expect to find an account of some pretty exciting scenes in Congress. At least that is the impression of those with whom I have talked (principally our own mess). I confess I do not feel so warlike myself. I prefer a foeman worthy of my steel. The reflection that we are so eager to avenge ourselves upon this poor, imbecile, self-distracted province, and at the same time sacrifice rights more "clear and unquestionable" to appease the threatened anger of her Brittanic Majesty, is to me humiliating in the extreme. However I will do my duty in both cases honestly and fearlessly, and trust the result to God and my country. The impression is beginning to be made upon the public mind here that this war with Mexico will render our negotiation with England more difficult and more doubtful of a pacific termination, as it is thought that English policy will be found to unite its interest with Mexican arms,—and thus we may after all the miserable pandering of American legislation to British arrogance, find ourselves engaged in war with England before the twelve months of notice shall have expired. All is speculation at present, and must continue so until the effect of what we have done shall be seen.

Thomas R. R. Cobb 2 To Howell Cobb. E.
Athens, Ga., *May 12, 181fi.*
My Dear Brother,... Toombs misrepresented me on the Oregon question. The Senate's Resolutions as amended by Owen met my hearty approbation. I preferred that there should be embodied in the resolutions a willingness to negotiate during the 12 mos.

Nobody talks of Oregon now. It is Mexico and War. I never saw the people more excited. A volunteer company could be raised in every county in Georgia. Our government has permitted itself to be insulted long enough. The blood of her citizens has been spilt on her own soil. It appeals to us for vengeance. Can we hesitate 1 Thomas Ritchie's newspnper, the Washington Union.

'Brother of Howell Cobb, a lawyer and anthor of a digest of the laws of Georgia, 1851, and of a legal treatlso on slavery, 1858. Be was not active In politics until the secession crisis In 1860-61. He became a brigadier-general in the Confederate army, and was killed in the battle of Fredericksburg.

to deal out a just retribution? It is the general opinion here that England is pulling the wires. The quicker we know it the better. Let Congress act and that quickly....

Albon Chase 1 To Howell Cobb. E.

Athens ga., *May 20, 181fi.*

Dear Sir: I have at length mustered sufficient resolution to commence a letter to you; but as through approaching age these tasks are becoming arduous, I know not how I shall get through it. Though for some time silent, I have not been unmindful of your favors, and most sincerely do I thank you for the letters you have written me; and I would be especially obliged, whenever any thing of interest occurs in Congress on a Thursday that you would let me know by that night's mail. It will enable me sometimes to gain a week in publishing news.

I perceive by your late letters to myself and others that you are in no very amiable humor with some of us for our want of zeal and interest in some things which you have much at heart. But you must recollect that while you are in a whirl of excitement, we are but lookers-on and keep quite cool. I am not disposed to argue any point connected with the Oregon or Texas controversy. I am ranked here as a 54 40' man, though I do not hesitate to avow that I would yield much for the sake of peace. I would take 49 if England offered it, to avoid a greater evil than the failure to obtain possession of our territory north of that line. And in this I, at least, am not inconsistent with myself; for if while at peace, Mexico had entered into a negotiation relative to boundary, I would not insist upon the whole country east of the Rio Grande for the whole length of that river. I would have been gratified at a compromise with her even, for the sake of peace. But it is too late now, and it may ere long be too late in regard to Oregon.

You seem to think I have not defended you as I ought. I certainly have not condemned your course, and I have defended all the positions you have taken in Congress. This no other editor in Georgia has done. I really have no fault to find with any of your votes, though I think I should have given mine for the notice as it finally passed, when I found nothing better could be gotten. That I have not defended you, is simply because you have not been attacked so far as I have seen. I have no fancy for making a fuss when there is no occasion for it.

And now in reference to another subject. Hope Hull showed me your letter in reply to one from him, and he requests me to give some reasons for the course which I suppose he suggested. Your 1 Editor of the Southern Banner, Athens, Ga.

friends here have not thought it best to make any movement towards a nomination at present, for various reasons. The Whigs are making no public effort to get up opposition to you, but are evidently waiting to see if some disaffection may not be excited, with a view to take up any of our men who can get a little Democratic support and who will consent to be run by them. If we hold a convention they will secretly operate upon the selection of delegates; they will find agents to present other names besides yours before the convention; they will endeavor to get up some feeling, especially on the Oregon question (and a great many Democrats disagree with you there), and they will strain every nerve to induce one of the defeated candidates to run against you. By a convention we shall show where our disaffection is, if there is any. It will concentrate and give vitality to that disaffection and I fear produce unpleasant results hereafter. We have no doubt that you are the choice of the district and that you could be triumphantly nominated; but we think our permanent harmony would be best maintained by considering you the candidate of course, unless some movement adverse to this view should be made. If any county holds a meeting and suggests any other name, or calls for a convention, of course we must hold it; but I think if we can, we had better let every thing remain quiet. You need feel no delicacy on the subject, or any doubt as to your position. Any very small opposition to you, having the faintest hope of success, would make itself known. If such should appear, we will promptly call a convention to say who is our choice; but if none manifests itself, you should be flattered at the fact that while you are in the field your constituents are satisfied and no one disputes your claim.

Mr. Calhoun, I see, is getting farther and farther off. Who will go with him? Can you tell? I think I shall have to read him out before long. Please let me hear from you, and I will endeavor to be more punctual hereafter.

William Hope Hull 1 To Howell Cobb. E.

Atheks ga., *May 22,18S.* Dear Howell, We are pretty quiet here in the midst of the general war fever. I believe there will be an effort made to raise a company for Texas, but I doubt its success. Clarke county is too much under the influence of Whiggery to have much enthusiasm in the matter. By the way, speaking of the Texas question, I am afraid the Democratic party is about to take untenable ground about the boundary there. The Rio de Norte is the western boundary, but not for its whole course. No possible logic can prove that Santa 1A neighbor and warm personal and political friend of Cobb.

Fe and the other towns on the east side of the river on its upper streams, were ever a portion of Texas. The true line would leave the river somewhere above Mier, and follow the mountains north, leaving a large section between the line and the upper parts of the river. You may think all this very superfluous on my part, but I have not yet seen the distinction drawn by any one in Congress, nor by Ritchie, and you may depend upon it is a serious consideration and worthy of attention. I think you seem a little "riled" that your friends here have not taken up the cudgels on your behalf on the 54.40 question. We acted, as we thought, for the best, not only for you but for the party. If an attempt had been made to rally the party upon the " whole of Oregon "

I do verily believe it would have split us in fragments, and for aught I can see would have given the Whigs and "moderate men" a majority. But by letting the thing be quiet and not fanning the embers of opposition, I think that all disaffection will die away and produce no unpleasant consequences. The same way we reason about a convention. I have no question that there is opposition to you in the breasts of some professed Democrats, but it has taken no open and distinct form, and if no fuss is made it will die of itself; but if we called a convention, though (I beg you to observe) I have no doubt as to the issue and am not at all afraid but that you would break down your opponents and be nominated and elected in spite of them,—still feelings might be engendered and factions started which might do us very serious injury hereafter. For this reason we thought it best to say nothing until towards August or thereabouts, when our papers will put up your name as a matter of course; and I presume there will be no opposition. In the meantime, however, if a call is made for a convention by your enemies, we shall not object, but shall go into it confident of a decided majority for you. I have given you with perfect candor my views on the subject, in which I concur with the most of your friends in Athens. Mr. Calhoun has killed himself about here as far as *Democratic* support goes. I have not heard the first Democrat sustain his course on the War bill. If he intended to quit us he could not have chosen a time nor a topic on which he could do us less harm in Georgia.... You speak in yours of the prospect of a settlement of the Oregon dispute. I am unable to see the signs of it in anything that has come to my knowledge. I wish you would let me into the secret in your next....

Howell Cobb To His Wife. E.

Washington Cmr, *4th June, 1846.*

My Dear Wife,... The prospect of winning much glory in the battle field is growing extremely unpromising. The news from Mexico indicates that the war there is fast drawing to a close, and it is now anticipated with much certainty that in a very short time our peaceful relations will be restored with that ill fated people. With England too the bow of peace spans our horizon. The last accounts from Great Britain have quieted all fears of a rupture with her about Oregon. So much so that in both countries the opinion is generally indulged and freely expressed that the Oregon dispute may be considered as approaching its final and peaceful adjustment. It is reported here that Mr. Pakenham has received instructions from his government to offer a settlement on the basis of 49 and the mutual? free navigation of the Columbia river. If this be true, we shall soon see a treaty to that effect made and ratified by the Senate, much to the disappointment of *us* 54.40 men, though in the end *we* shall be benefited by the result so far as popularity and public confidence is concerned...

John B. Lamar 1 To Howell Cobb. E.

Macon ga., *June 8th, 1846.*

Dear Howell, Yours of the 31st ult. came duly to hand. I had considered all things maturely and determined not to sell my property as I intimated there was a probability of my doing in a previous letter. I have weighed matters and concluded to toil on in my old vocation the balance of my life, for fear I might by chance do worse by attempting a change. In changing my investment from its present shape to funds I might make some mis-step and ruin myself. It is dangerous for a man unused to controlling large sums of money to have the disposition of them. Such matters require experience. I find by your letter on the subject that your *first thoughts* were exactly the same as my *second* ones. You are right. I have a great many fancy ideas, but I seldom act hastily on any of them. I usually wait for "the sober second thought" in matters of moment. And the second thought is to hold on and " let well enough alone ". Planting is a troublesome business that does not pay well. It has its risks like every other business. But sum up everything and it is about as safe as most other modes of investing money. My taste leads me to a roving life, and on that account I have desired my means in such shape as to afford me a good income with little trouble. But it cannot fall to the lot of all who desire it to live like " Childe Harold " or Jabez Jackson, and so I will content myself with my fate, and steal off to Europe only now and then...

You say in the last sentence of your letter—" Have I erred in my course about Mr. Calhoun? I will not claim any great foresight. but 1 A prosperous planter with estates in central and southwestern Georgia. He managed the plantations of his sister. Mrs. Howell Cobb, as well as bis own, and was one of Howell Cobb's chief political advisers.

have I not blundered along amazing well?" I see it " sticking out" that Lumpkin1 has shown you my letter to him. I gave my confessions to John because I knew he would sympathise with me in the premises, which I had nothing to expect from such an old Hunker as you. Yes you have been about half right in your opinions, and I have been a little over half wrong I confess, and you take the opportunity to hint it, very modestly however. Well, when a man finds that he has been following a "will o' the wisp" all his life you are glad to see him rub his eyes and look about for a genuine light to guide his way, I suppose. Woodbury, "ciphering Levi", is the next man I look to as embodying my principles. But if he can't get the Granite State right side up again I am afraid I can't make him available. If he can manage that, you may feel yourself duly authorized to announce him as my candidate for the Presidency. I believe him to be the purest patriot in the United States.

Howell Cobb To His Wife. E.

Washington City, *1bth June, 1846.*

My Dear Wife,... Most unexpectedly to me I received a note on Sunday morning from Genl. Harden2 announcing his arrival in the city. The General is in good health and fine spirits. He is determined to have an office if one is to be had, and I am determined to render him all the aid in my power to carry out his wishes. Mr. Polk's feelings are of the kindest character towards him, and he has expressed to me his determination to provide for him at the very earliest time when an appointment shall offer itself. I do hope that our efforts may be successful. Certainly no applicant for office stands in greater need than our old friend in whose cause my feelings are so deeply enlisted.

Today in the House we succeeded in taking up the tariff bill by a majority of about thirty, and shall be engaged in its discussion for the next two weeks or more. As I have been honored with the chair during this debate I shall not have the same time to devote to my letters and business as heretofore. As you know, much of my writing was done at my desk in the House. So you must not complain if my letters should not reach you as punctually as heretofore.

What will be done with this vexed question of the tariff I am not able to say. Many indulge a strong hope and belief that we shall be able to pass such a bill as will give satisfaction to the country. I am not so sanguine myself- The course pursued by the Southern democracy about Oregon has had the effect of alienating the good feelings of many of our northern and western democrats and thereby rendering the harmonious and united action of the party more difficult than it would have been had all the South stood square up upon that great question as *some of us* did. I fear the effect that is likely to be produced in the success of the democratic party by the unfortunate collisions which have arisen during the present session. Conscious of having fully and faithfully performed my own duty, I have no personal responsibility resting upon my shoulders which I am not willing and prepared fully to shoulder.
..

I have been engaged pretty much during today in getting letters for Mr. Gardner of the Constitutionalist, who has involved himself in a quarrel with his neighbours of the Chronicle and Sentinel about the charge of Mr. Wise pulling Mr. Polk's nose. All an infamous lie; but at the same time, as Gardner seemed to attach some importance to the proof, I have promised it for him; and if the editors of the Chronicle and Sentinel have any sense of shame left they will blush upon its perusal.

Dear Howell, In a previous letter I mentioned that there was, with few exceptions, a patriotic spirit among the Whigs to sustain the country in the war against Mexico. So there was as long as the first generous impulse lasted. But a change has come over the spirit of their dream. And I do verily believe if the raising of volunteers had been postponed to this time the Whig leaders and presses would take such an attitude as to prevent any member of their party from volunteering, thereby making, literally, a Democratic war. They are perfectly rabid. The tone of their editorials and conversations on the subject of the administration and the war generally is of such a virulent character as to be actually loathsome. I had no idea that the rancor of party spirit, as potent as it is, could carry men so far from all just ideas of patriotism, when the country is engaged in a war.

They are now looking on the action of Congress with regard to the tariff with the eagerness of hyenas and jackals, waiting only for the onslaught to be over to rush on to the work of mutilation. The duty on tea and coffee is the object on which they gloat. It is there they expect—if the duty is laid—to find a vulnerable point to go before the prejudices of the people with during the next Congressional campaign. They already smile a malignant smile in anticipation of the havoc they expect to deal with this pitiful weapon. And in order to render it effective they are preparing the way ingeniously by industriously endeavouring to dampen or extinguish 1 The Constitutionalist and the Chronicle and Sentinel were the two leading newspapers of Augusta, Ga.
altogether every ardent feeling in their party for the success of our arms in the contest with the Mexicans. If they can succeed in making the rank and file of their party feel as little interest as themselves in the matter, and the apathy spreads into our ranks, they will then have a fair field for clap-trap. But if, as I think must be the case in spite of their treasonable purposes, the people of both parties continue to look with interest to our army and its operations, they will signally fail. They underrate the patriotism and intelligence of the people. During times of peace and quiet the people collectively, like individual men, are easily appealed to through the pocket nerve. A penurious man, if every generous sentiment is not extinguished by avarice, will make sacrifices for a brother who requires his aid; and a mass of men, penny saving tho' they be, when the honor of their country is at stake will feel a generous emotion of patriotism arise in their breasts and stifle every petty feeling of avarice.

When the cry of tea and coffee is proclaimed from the stump, as it will be, it can be easily met by telling how Ward and Fannin were butchered; the mangled corpses of Cross and the soldiers who fell into the hands of the Mexicans will raise a feeling stronger than the strongest decoction of which coffee is capable. And then Palo Alto and Resaca de la Palma will rouse feelings of pride, and every man, woman and child is vulnerable there. The victories achieved by our army all feel a *personal* interest in. A man may be very peacefully inclined, but still he loves military glory in a secret corner of his heart and is proud to be one of a nation who can exhibit its strength on the battle field. Men have a very ingenious way of appropriating a share in such things to themselves, altho' they have had no hand in the matter. If you ever noticed it, a man from Massachusetts is prouder than one from Connecticut. And a South Carolinian is haughtier than a Georgian, because there have been more battles fought in the former than the latter. A Massachusetts man, see him where you will, looks and feels like he was a cap stone of the Bunker Hill monument. And a S. Carolinian supposes that when you see him it naturally reminds you of Eutaw, and the Cowpens. I have observed this propensity to identify one's self with the glories of his locality carry itself from deeds to the capabilities of the soil. Thus, notice most men from Mississippi, and they seem to feel like the personification of an acre of land which could produce a 500 weight bag of cotton without the aid of manure, while a gentleman from North Carolina where the soil has not so much a reputation abroad, is usually not so assuming in his bearing. This is an odd fancy of my own, but nevertheless men are very proud of noble deeds done by others if there is the least excuse for appropriating any tithe of it however indirectly, and appeal to a man's pride of country and he is vulnerable. No talk about coffee can compete with a fanfaronade about roaring cannon and charging squadrons. Every man is at heart a soldier, altho' he may never have borne a musket or seen a bomb shell-fired from a mortar. His ignorance of such things only increases his respect and admiration. I think you may feel safe about the coffee if I am any judge of human nature, especially as you can spare a few voters who may be devotees to that beverage. But if you charge yourself with a full load of Mexican cruelty and perfidy and of American chivalry, you will find few people proof against it. There are few men in your district who will admit that they would not if called on "fight, bleed and die" in defense of their country; to pay a few cents more on the pound for coffee to raise money to support our volunteers who have gone to Mexico, is much cheaper when they consider it maturely than "bleeding and dying," however patriotic the latter evolutions may be. Tell a man that a regiment composed of 930 enthusiastic Georgians have gone to defend the honour of the country and expose themselves to the rigours of an almost tropical climate, while he is left at home to make and gather his crop and enjoy the society of his family and the comforts of home, and all that is required of him is to pay a few cents on a pound of coffee to sustain the brave fellows, and he will see at once that he has decidedly the best of the bargain, even putting it on the score of dollars and cents. If in addition to this the duty on iron and sugar is reduced the proposition will be a plainer one and leave but little fulcrum space for the lever which the Whigs are calculating on wielding with such effect.

P.S.—I shall not go north before you return, if at all. I shall go to your house and spend most of my summer, I think.

Charles J. Mcdonald 1 To Howell Cobb. E.

Macon ga., *7th July, 1846.* Dear Cobb, I am here, and a moment's leisure gives me the opportunity to inquire of you what the Democratic party intend to do? Can it be possible that the unanimity of the committee which reported on the proceedings of the Memphis Convention is an indication of Ahe mind of Congress on the subject? It is reported that a majority of the democratic members of Congress from Virginia will follow that committee in trampling down the cherished doctrines of her Jeffersons and Madisons on the construction of the Constitution of the United States. It is by the strict construction alone, which they practiced and enjoined, that Congress can be kept within the bounds prescribed for it by the people who formed the i Governor of Georgia, 1839-1843; candidate for the governorship in 1851 on the Southern Rights ticket, defeated by Howell Cobb. Judge of the supreme court of Georgia, 1856-1861.

instrument which gave it being. The people never intended to give their representatives the right to assume power by implication. The power to regulate commerce gives no authority to create roads or canals. It is the authority to prescribe the rules or laws which shall govern the commercial intercourse between the States. It is to be hoped that the perilous doctrine will be at once rebuked. Mr. Madison about twenty years ago vetoed a bill with such objects. Can you get the Maysville veto for me? I suppose all the high protectionists will, to a man, support a doctrine which will draw from the Treasury annually twenty millions of dollars. That sum can be lost in the unfathomable bed of the Mississippi every year without any improvement in its ever varying channel. Will the whole Democracy of the West be drawn from their positions by the apparent interest of their constituents in the stupendous expenditures to which this policy will give rise? These men are too apt to be swerved from duty by an interested ambition. No political death is so sweet as that in which a man falls a sacrifice to noble principles. I have not heard from you on this subject, but I take it for granted that you are not a convert to this new faith. Let me hear from you.

I am sorry to hear of the dissensions in the Democratic ranks at Washington. Can they not be healed? The party have treated Mr. Polk unkindly in not sustaining his patriotic measures in regard to our foreign relations. They have given the Whigs a decided advantage, and the whole course of Congress in regard to the Oregon question has shown the ignoble spirit that would concede to power what it would maintain against a nation less able to defend its usurpations.

Why has Mr. Polk passed by the army, which distinguished itself in the late battles, in making his appointments?

James F. Cooper1 To Howell Cobb. E.

Dahlonega, Ga., *July 8,1846.* My Dear Sir: Since I wrote you last I have not heard a syllable further relative to Wofford's pretensions... Since we published the call for our meeting on the 4th, I have conversed freely with the rank and file of the Democracy on the subject, and find that they are entirely undivided in your favor, showing that there has been no tampering with them as yet. They have heard of no other claims, and of course I did not mention them. It were a pity to destroy such a blessed unanimity. On the 4th we clinched the thing in Lumpkin.[2] A great many people were here to attend a muster

[1] Superintendent of the United States branch mint at Dahlonega, Ga.
[2] Lumpkin County, whose county seat was Dahlonega.

and there was no dissenting voice. You will glide in again without, I think, the slightest opposition. The Whigs are doing nothing that I hear of.

If those disaffected Buckeyes and Hooziers sacrifice McKay's Bill on the altar of Oregon, it will be ruinous to us at the next general election—say the governor's. We cannot elect a governor unless you reduce the tariff. We shall moreover lose all the closely contested congressional districts—Jones's, Towns's, etc. Stephens and Toombs will be immovable in their places.

I am now keeping house at the mint, and when you visit Lumpkin this fall we will be glad to see you and your family with us. You might make this a depot of your family from which you could branch off to Union, Habersham, etc.

John H. Lumpkin [1] To Howell Cobb. E.

Rome ga., *13th Nov., 1846.* Dear Cobb, Your letter of the 10th inst. was received by last night's mail. I agree with you that the Southern democracy have not redeemed their pledges to their Northern allies; that while we have contended for and obtained the whole of Texas, we have sacrificed and given up one half of our claim to Oregon—and this of itself is enough to account for the defeats that our friends have met with in Pa., N. Y., and other Northern and Northwestern States. But is this the cause of our disasters? I think not entirely. Indeed I incline to the opinion that our Northern allies are not prepared to support some of the cardinal measures of the Democratic party. With the Southern' portion of our party a tariff for revenue only is a cardinal principle, and we cannot consent to compromise this principle, even for success itself. But in Pennsylvania and in New York and some other states North and East this doctrine is repudiated by those who claim to be associated with us in principles. I need not inform you that such Democrats received no encouragement or countenance in the legislation of the last session of Congress. I am not surprised therefore that these men have been repudiated at home. In fact I rejoice that Whigs have superseded such Democrats as Dr. Leib, Yost, Black etc. etc. , and for my part I had rather be in the minority than to be in the majority controlled by such men. The bill making appropriations for rivers and harbours caused a similar division among our own friends in different sections of the Union, and has likely contributed in some degree to these disastrous results. But shall we give up our opposition to protective tariff and to these extravagant appropriations on this account? By no means. Let us

A leading Democrat of northwestern Georgia, Member of Congress, 1843-1849 and 1855-1857; judge of the superior court of Georgia (Cherokee circuit), 1849-1850; a close friend and voluminous correspondent of Howell Cobb.

commence the contest anew and have nothing to do with any man or set of men who combine for our destruction; and if we have not the power to accomplish positive good, we may have power to prevent harm and prevent our destruction. Some of our warm and influential Democrats in this section of the State are disposed to censure the President and his Cabinet and attribute these results to the want of management in our Executive. I disagree with all such. I do not believe that Genl. Washington, or Genl. Jackson in his prime, could have directed the ship of state with more ability. Indeed, no man living or dead could have produced harmony and ensured success with such conflicting and discordant materials. I am amazed when I see what was accomplished at the last session, and can never censure the President for any of these disastrous results. I differ with the President in one point only, and that is purely a question of policies, and that is in regard to appointing men to office who do not agree with him in principle. I do not mean such as are politically opposed to him alone, but such as do not sustain the great, leading measures of his administration that are nominally identified with the Democratic party. More of this when we meet. I shall be with you in Augusta on the first. Mrs. L. unites with me in regards to Mrs. Cobb.

Edward J. Harden[1] To Howell Cobb. E.

City or Washington, *3d May, 1847.* My Dear Friend, The newspapers are so far ahead of me that I can inform you of nothing that is new. At the President's some evenings since I told him that I saw that it was suggested by a writer published in the Constitutionalist of Augusta, that he ought to run again for the Presidency. He said no, that he had honor enough and was content to retire; but I think in the course of the conversation he said it depended on the people. I think he would be glad to serve for another term. He told me that we ought not to let Berrien come back in the Senate—that he was troublesome. Virginia you see has come out badly—the Whigs have not given larger votes than usual, but the democrats held back. It is attributed here to the influence of Mr. Calhoun entirely, and Bagby[2] thinks that influence will be felt severely in Alabama. In fact he thinks Calhoun and Webster will coalesce, and it may be that Webster's Southern journey is in connection with such a plan. Great preparations are made for his reception in Charleston. But nothing but death can prevent Taylor from being the next President. Men, women and children are rising up in his favor; and Blair (Blair and Rives) says that the democrats

[1] Judge of the city court of Savannah, Ga., 1845-1847; United States Indian commissioner, 1847; author of "The Life of George M. Troup", Savannah, 1859.
[2] Arthur P. Bagby, Senator from Alabama.

ought to be the first to nominate him,

so as not to let the Whigs have the forestalling of his opinions and action. Bagby thinks the Calhoun influence will operate strongly in Georgia also. I hope not. I see you will have a covention in June to choose a candidate for governor. I am told Herschel Johnson is spoken of. If a strong man is not started we shall be beaten.

I am afraid this commission will not last long enough for my comfort. I am tired asking favors of my friends, but don't you think a resolution, a recommendation of the convention in my favor, would be beneficial to me? If so set the ball to rolling. Abb will probably be a member, and I can influence all of the low country to join in it. I would be glad to hear from you on this subject.

P. S.—I have been so rudely used by the Indian claimants that I was advised and did arm myself....

Thomas R. R. Cobb To Howell Cobb. E.

Athens ga., *June 23rd, 1847* Dear Bro., I have today got the copy deed and send you a copy immediately. All are pretty well. No news from Taylor. News by the Caledonia just got here. For myself I want no mediation from England. She meddles too much in our affairs anyhow. I am opposed to this Government dismembering Mexico. Let us whip her decently and give her a good government, such as the *people* wish. If they *afterwards* wish to be annexed we can do it. I am for *extending the area of freedom,* but not by *war.* The odious doctrine upon which Britain acts of taking territory for *the expenses* of the war is anti-Democratic. Let the glory of our government be that *not one* citizen lives under its laws that is not there by *choice....*

Isaac E. Holmes1 To Howell Cobb. E.

Charleston S. C., *Aug. 21st, %7.* Dear Sir, I wish the Southern Representatives would consent to act together without regard to Whig or Democrat. The Wilmot Proviso is paramount to all Party. We are in great danger. The North is resolved to crush Slavery—are we equally in the South resolved at all hazards to defend it? What say you for Benton's proposal to have a Northern President, without regard to the Wilmot Proviso?

Robert Toombs To James Thomas. L. S.

Washington, Ga., *Nov. 19, 18fl.* Dear Thomas, I did not receive your favour of the 20th Oct. touching the Gilbert case until I returned home yesterday, and was not

'Congressman from South Carolina, 1839-1851.

aware that the case had been taken up at all until I heard it had been decided by the Supreme Court.1 The Supreme Court is becoming a perfect nuisance. Unless we can get a lawyer on the bench, it will go down. I have disliked to say so heretofore, but from a careful inspection of its decisions I am well satisfied that the Court has committed more errors than it ever corrected; and I think such is becoming the general opinion of the profession.

Luther J. Glenn 2 To Howell Cobb. E.

Milledgeville ga., *December 1, 1847.* Dear Sir: After a four days' discussion in the Senate on the Wilmot proviso and the war and the acquisition of Territory, the vote was taken last night. The Whigs took high ground against the war and denounced it as infamous and iniquitous. They also went against any further acquisition of territory, occupying pretty much the position of Mr. Clay in his Lexington speech. You will see that a resolution was introduced declaring that the people of Georgia will adhere to the Missouri Compromise line in the division of territory that may hereafter be acquired by the General Government. It was lost by a vote of 20 to 26. Of the twenty who voted for it, 18 are D. and 2 Whigs; of those who voted against it 21 are Whigs and 5 Democrats. I think the Democrats who voted against it, were the vote to be taken over, would record their votes in favor of it. As for the Whigs, they are right in a political point of view, in opposing it, if they desire to preserve the unity of the party North and South.

The Whigs I think will endeavour to nominate Genl. Taylor for the Presidency. One of them, to wit Clayton, asked me this morning if I would not vote for resolutions of that character.

The Legislature will hardly adjourn till after Christmas. I know it will not, if the business even now before it be acted upon....

Hopkins Holsey 3 To Howell Cobb. E.

Athens ga., *Dec. 3rd, 1847.* Dr. Sir: I drop you a few hastily penn'd lines this morning in acknowledgement of your various favors since you left us. You are too well aware of the distraction of an editor's attention, and even sometimes of his brain, to hold me to strict accountability as a correspondent. I beg you to be assured once for all that your communications are not only at all times welcomed, but the contents duly garnered in my recollection, to be rendered available at the proper time 1 The supremo court of Georgia, then but recently established.
'A Democrat o£ Athens, Ga., at this time a member of the Georgia legislature. Editor of the Southern Banner, Athens, Ga. and opportunity. From the many valuable extracts and suggestions so kindly furnished me, selections were made for publication, but the thronging intelligence of the war, elections, and legislative proceedings, to say nothing of the new and mighty questions which are springing upon us, unavoidably postponed them. But the day is not far distant when we shall have need of them in full sway. You will have perceived from the papers the exciting questions of domestic policy which have just arisen among us. Among them none are more prominent than granting "liberal charters" to manufacturing companies, and the election of judges by the people. I think you will regret with me to see our friends, particularly of the press, divided upon this question or remaining silent upon it. The Banner, you will perceive, is yet fighting the battles of *radical* Democracy against the *conservative* tendencies of Whiggery, and I regret to say a portion of the so-styled Democ-

racy, with what effect remains to be seen. You will have seen that the *Augusta Constitutionalist* has unfortunately taken ground in favor of the "liberal charters" recommended by Mr. Crawford in his last Message, and also against the Democratic measure of electing the judges by the people. On the side of the Banner this controversy shall be conducted with unalterable firmness, whilst at the same time it will endeavor to avoid any asperities which may close the door to conciliation. A course of this kind, backed by the general voice of the Democracy, may eventually succeed in winning erring friends back to the fold. When they find they can not lead the party they must necessarily fall back upon the party grounds, unless prevented by the harshness which is too apt to spring up in a controversy among friends. I am persuaded that the suggestions of Mr. Crawford are parcel of a design to quench the growing spirit of Democracy everywhere manifested throughout the Union, and particularly in Georgia. The object is to *ride us down by the Massachusetts policy of incorporated wealth,* under the false plea of "developing our resources." What may be the result of this question at Milledgeville I am not prepared to give you a satisfactory solution. Your brother (Thomas), who spent some time there in the early part of the session, is quite confident that the legislature will not grant the charters without the principle upon which we insist, of *'individual responsibility.* I hope it may be so. You will have seen that a call has been made by the Banner upon the party to stand firm, and also upon the Governor to protect us by his veto. A letter has also been addressed to our friend Jackson (of Walton) requesting him to see the Governor upon the subject and state the necessity, in case the legislature should give countenance to the scheme, of his preserving the party by his firmness. We have a great many Democrats interested in giving way to it, and it is possible, at least, that our hopes may have, at last, to rest upon our Governor. This scheme once riveted upon us we are down, done, and I fear forever. We have no hopes of carrying the popular election of judges at this session of the legislature—not more than half of our own party in the Senate being in favor of it. But the subject will be pressed until the public mind is properly enlightened, when there can be but little doubt of its success. There is but little local news among us. The picture of things in general being pretty much as you left it with the exception of change in the seasons. The winter has been mild until within a few days—some snow and sleet. The papers notify us of your arrival in Washington, where you will soon be a participant in the opening drama. The whole country looks upon the ensuing session as one of the most stormy in our annals, but the developments of popular sentiment in the late elections are too plain to permit us to despair of the country. The House is one way and the people the other. Excuse these generalities. As I am desirous of knowing *everything* which transpires in Congress, will you do me the favor to call at once upon the editor of the *Union* and request him to send me his *daily* paper, we paying the difference if necessary. P. S.—Please write frequently, unreservedly.

Hopkins Holsey To Howell Cobb. E.

Athens, Ga., *Dec.* 31st, 1847. Dr. Sir: I avail myself of a leisure moment to reply to your communication of the1. Your favor in sending to this office the National Intelligencer is duly appreciated, in as much as the editor of the Union admits that his reports of the proceedings of Congress, thus far, have not been accurate. I find this to be the case particularly in regard to Mr. Giddings's instructions to the Judiciary Committee relative to the slave trade in the District of Columbia. These instructions as reported in the Intelligencer open up the whole question of property in slaves; and the double vote of Mr. Winthrop, in first deciding the tie vote against the South, and afterwards upon the correction of the Journal repeating his position, is peculiarly unfortunate for the Southern Whigs. It is also an unlucky omen for them that *Northern Democrats* were the only members from the non-slaveholding states, voting against the agitation of the question. In the other wing of the Capitol a similar mishap seems to have befallen them almost at the same time upon the movement of John P. Hale on the same subject, in the disposition of which I observe *all* the Northern democratic Senators voting with the entire South to lay the question of reception on the table, and *all* the Northern Whigs voting against it.

1 Blank in the original.

Previous to this conclusive demonstration by the Northern Democrats in both Houses came the resolutions by Mr. Dickinson of New York, which assume the same ground taken by Mr. Dallas in Pennsylvania last summer. Satisfactory as this position must be to us in all respects (leaving out the absolute monomania of the Calhoun faction) it becomes us to ascertain, before we adopt it as the basis of our action in the next campaign, whether the Northern Democracy will rally to its support? This is the all important preliminary question to be decided before we can properly solve that other question, whether we should take the basis of Mr. Buchanan or Mr. Dallas. I perceive in your letter the expression of a belief that our Northern friends will come to the support of Dallas and Dickinson and Cass ground. By the bye, this is the first and most gratifying intimation that we have here of Gen. Cass's position. Resuming the question which of these two propositions, leaving the matter to be settled by the Territories or adopting the Missouri basis, will best unite the Northern Democracy, I can only say at this distance you have a better opportunity of judging than I can possibly have as to the actual state of things North. If our friends there are of the opinion that they can stand better upon one of these propositions than the other, of course we should let them have their own way. They are certainly better judges than we can be of what they may be able to effect. It is needless to say to you that the Southern Democrats will be satisfied with either position.

You will however agree with me that great caution should be observed by us in weighing the evidences of the state of Northern feeling. Buchanan, Dallas, Cass are all for the Presidency; and may not the fact that Mr. Buchanan having broken ground on the Missouri basis have operated upon the other two to vary their positions from his, and thus mislead us? Both of the latter have numerous friends who will adhere to their positions, and could we be assured they were sufficiently numerous to give tone to the Northern Democracy, the question would be settled. But I apprehend that the surer data of conjecture on our part should be laid deeper in the nature of things than the mere personal or immediate political attachments to individuals, however prominent they may be.

Upon a survey of the whole ground, I must express to you my strong apprehension that our Northern friends can not be brought to any other position with half the strength that they would rally to the Missouri basis. You will perceive that I treat it alone as a practical question. Let me now assign you a few reasons. First, the Herkimer men in New York will not yield to Mr. Dickinson's or Dallas's ground. Their pride, their passions, are all enlisted against it. Secondly, the Democrats of New Hampshire occupy the same ground as the Radicals of New York. If we adopt the Missouri basis may we not yet hope that both of these States will yet be saved? The ground of my hopes may be found in Clingman's speech. It is difficult to convince our Northern friends that Congress has not the complete control of this question. You know how they stood in relation to the constitutional power over the District. The Missouri basis will enable them to retain their constitutional prepossessions and yet to seek refuge from an unjust, unequal or destructive exercise of the power.

The South on the other hand may retain its constitutional opinions and yet yield to the Missouri basis for the sake of peace and harmony. This idea that constitutional questions may not be compromised is all fallacious. In Mr. Jefferson's letter to Mr. Cartwright on the powers of the state and federal governments, speaking of questions of this nature he says, " if they can neither be avoided or compromised," etc.

There is however another and more conclusive view in favor of occupying the compromise ground to which I ask your attention. *Henry Clay* holds the card in his hand which he is yet to play upon this subject. He will wait for us to shew our hands. If he finds we have adopted Mr. Dickinson's ground—*he will himself trump us with the Missouri Compromise, and win the game* m *spite of us!* Clingman's speech shews how easily it could be done. Mr. Clay is the father (if I mistake not) of that Compromise. He will rally his party to it and kill us with the word *Union.* We might struggle in vain. The Democratic party of Georgia is already committed, in the convention of last spring. Our press, with but one exception, are committed also. Virginia is committed, South Carolina even is now committed by a unanimous vote to abide the Missouri line. Leading politicians all through the South are committed. We can not war against a position which we have already sanctioned." If the issue should be formed by the two parties in this manner, Mr. Clay would sweep through the non-slaveholding States with irresistible power, and find none but a partial check, at least in the South. I am therefore of the opinion that, strengthened as the Compromise has been by the recent developments in the South, and strong as it must be in the nature of things North, that we should never relinquish it. *We must occupy it in the Baltimore Convention or the Whigs will, and kill us off at the South with our men weapons.* You will have observed also in the recent democratic meeting at the Museum in Philadelphia that the Missouri line was adopted. This is at least evidence of the state of feeling and opinion among our Northern friends. It was *unanimously* adopted.

The Herkimer men will send delegates to the convention. So will the Conservatives. Both delegations should be admitted. The Ultras will eventually find so strong a current against them, that *they* would fain *compromise.* But if that word is not to be known in the Convention, they will return home enemies to the party. This will probably be the case with the N. Hampshire delegation also. It may also be the case with Maine and Rhode Island. Besides, the Compromise is so intimately blended with the idea of *preserving the Union* that hosts of men of *all parties,* North and South, will follow the banner upon which it may be inscribed. If we do not write it upon ours, the Whigs will upon theirs, and we must fall under its influence.

P. S.—The Ultras, North, says that Dallas's proposition virtually excludes Union. That's their feeling—we must respect it, though erroneous. Exclusion either way would weaken the bonds of *Union,* and thus our own shaft would recoil upon us.

Joseph Henry Lumpkin1 To Howell Cobb. E.

Athens, ga., *J any. 21st, 1848.*

My Dear Sir: On my return from Savannah this morning I found your letter of the eighth of this month waiting my arrival. I sincerely regret that any reference to the extract of my letter to you in Bennett's Paper should have given you any concern, for I repeat what I said to you before, that I neither desired nor intended any concealment of my change of opinion towards Mr. Clay. Whether General Taylor will or will not submit himself to be used by the very men who would have defeated his election could they have done so, I cannot say. He has been faithfully warned, / *know,* not to do so, but to compel these leaders to surrender *to him* at discretion and to make no terms with them; he has been further admonished to beware of the rock on which Mr. Clay's barque has been so signally wrecked, as every Statesman should be who when his government is engaged in a foreign war will with unfilial hand? expose the nakedness of his parent country.

For the bold and decided stand taken by Mr. Buchanan and other distinguished Democrats at the North, the South owes them a deep debt of gratitude; for myself however, I never for a moment believed that the North would take the responsibility of dissolving the American Union upon a *false issue,* even when slavery was the subject. And I believe at this very moment that the institution stands upon a firmer basis than it ever has done since the formation of the Republic. Had the Abolitionists let us alone we should have been guilty, I verily believe, of political and social suicide by emancipating the African race, a measure fatal to them, to ourselves, and to the best interest of this Confederacy and of the whole world. The violent assaults of these fiends have compelled us in self defence to 1 Chief-justice of the supreme court of Georgia, 1845-1867. investigate this momentous subject in all of its bearings, and the result has been a firm and settled conviction that duty to the slave as well as the master forbids that the relation should be disturbed; and notwithstanding Mr. Webster's false declaration as the result of his personal observations among us, there is but one mind among the whole of our people upon this subject. And we never will submit for one moment to the smallest aggression upon our constitutional rights. Respecting this property even Judge Warner,1 Massachusetts man as he is, declared to me a few days since that dearly as he was attached to the Union, he would not hesitate a moment to advocate its immediate dissolution should the principle of the Wilmot Proviso be engrafted upon our system. I repeat that my mind was never more at ease than at present upon this subject.

Having been at home so short a time, I know nothing of the local news. Your friends are all well. Tom and myself leave again tomorrow for Talbotton where the Supreme Court sits on Monday next; he was appointed at Savannah Assistant Reporter, and I thing it altogether likely that after this year Kelly will retire from the business. There is nothing unpleasant between Col. Franklin and himself.

Lother J. Glenn To Howell Cobb. E. Mcdonough ga., *Feby. 12, '48.*

Dear Sir:.... I may be mistaken, but such is the fierceness of the opposition of the Whigs to the Mexican war that I apprehend an increase of taxes for the purpose suggested by you, by the last Legislature, would not have gone down well with the people.

They (the Whigs in this county) are even making a " great to do" over the appropriations for bringing home the remains of Cols. McIntosh and Echols. I believe however with Mr. Brown, in the war meeting at New York, that there is a "just God" and that retributive justice will yet overtake them, though just here they seem confounded hard to " run down."

You ask me to explain the vote in the Senate on the preamble to the Taylor resolutions. I will do it to the best of my recollection, remarking at the outset that I was not one of the "six" who voted against it. If I recollect aright, the Preamble set forth nothing but the military qualifications of Taylor, concluding with the declaration that he had "mind or intellect" enough to make a president. When the vote was about to be taken on the "preamble and resolutions" Mr. Forman (a Democratic Senator) called for a division of the preamble from the resolutions. I begged him to withdraw his call, in order that we might vote upon the whole. Refusing to do so, I 1 Hiram Warner, a native of Massachusetts, was at this time an assooiate-justlce of the supreme court of Georgia. « thought at the time that I was compelled to vote for the Preamble, though the next morning he and myself, I recollect, expressed our regret that we had done so, and I moved a reconsideration of the whole action of the Senate upon the subject, which was lost by one vote, "Waters voting against it though he had promised me to vote for it. I regret that the resolutions did not pass the House, for then the Whigs of Georgia would have another obstacle in their way of going into a convention. It seems from the " signs of the times" that the contest in the Democratic Convention will lie between Cass and Woodbury. Between them it would be with me a difficult matter to decide. I have always admired the sternness of Mr. Woodbury in advocating the rights of the South, and believe there is no firmer or purer man. Since Genl. Cass's letter to Nicholson made its appearance, I confess much if not all of the doubt and suspicion that before rested upon my mind relative to his soundness on the ""Wilmot Proviso" has been removed, and perhaps he would be stronger in the South than Mr. W. or any other Northern man. I am with you, however, in the support of the "nominee" of the convention, provided he be sound on the slavery question. I was much pleased with the "skeleton " of your speech, in the Intelligencer. You brought to light one vote in the house, which I have long wanted to see, and that was the amendment of the New York Member to confine Genl. Taylor in his operations to the east bank of the Rio Grande, or rather to bring him back to the " undisputed territory of the U. States "....

P. S.—I have a serious notion of moving to Atlanta in the course of the present year. What think you of the step, so far as professional prospects are concerned?

Lucres Q. C. Lamar 1 To Howell Cobb. E.

Covington, Ga., *Feb. 15th, 18$.*

Dear Sir: As I have no personal acquaintance with our immediate representative, Hon. Mr. Haralson, I hope you will excuse the liberty I have taken in addressing you this letter. I wish you to have sent to me some paper devoted *exclusively* to the reporting of the proceedings of Congress. I do not know whether the amount enclosed is sufficient or not. If it be too small, please have the paper sent on at once anyhow, and I will immediately make up the deficit—if too large I would be glad if you would purchase for me last year's Congressional Globe and Appendix. I would be gratified also to have the speeches of *McLane* of Maryland, Foote, Rhett and *Bedinger,* that is if they can be *conveniently* obtained. The truth is that 1 JuRtlet Lamar was at this time a young lawyer at Covington, Ga. His carper In public life was as Congressman and Senator from Mississippi, colonel In the Confederate army. Secretary of the. Interior under President Cleveland, and Associate Justice of the United States Supreme Court, the reports of the speeches in the Union are so provokingly meagre and defective that I never look at them. Your speech for instance (which I think sincerely is the best *on your side* of the session), as found in the Intelligencer, is most unmercifully mutilated in the Union. I should not trouble you with this very small matter had I any other means of ascertaining the name of the paper I wish—one that gives us your speeches accurately and in extenso.

Henry L. Benning1 To Howell Cobb. E.

Columbus ga., *83d Feby., 1848.*

Dear Howell, You ask me to write you soon and fully my views of Cass's letter and Dickinson's resolution. I have had so much to do lately that I could not attempt an answer until now, although your letter of the 3d inst., has been on hand for a fortnight. What you require of me involves, I think, my opinion as to the course which ought to be pursued by the democatic party to secure the next Presidency. On a question of such magnitude I am not prepared to speak with confidence; and yet upon your invitation... I will venture a suggestion or two.

First then, I do not object to Mr. Dickinson's resolutions. Still I must say that they are not precisely *the thing* according to my notion of what the exigency demands. The sins are chiefly sins of omission. The resolutions do not declare what principle ought to govern in *the interval* between the time of acquiring territory and the time at which the people thereof may choose to settle those " questions of domestic policy ", which it is left to them to settle.

Again, they very indistinctly, if at all, condemn the *principle* of the Wilmot proviso. If I am not mistaken in that principle, it is that *Congress* may prohibit slavery in acquired territory *as long as it remains territory.* Now, Mr. D's resolutions say no more than that Congress cannot do anything inconsistent with the right of the people of the territories to form themselves into States equally sovereign with the old states. The W. Proviso principle is not inconsistent with this right. That which it is inconsistent with is the right of the people of the territories to hold slaves therein if Congress forbids.

Once more, no general principle is announced by the resolutions upon the question of the quantity of territory we ought to require from Mexico in a treaty of peace. Perhaps these omissions are merits, but I venture to think not, and more audacious still, to send you what I deem the remedy in three resolutions, or rather two, ac 1 A lawyer of Columbus, Ga., previously a college chum of Howell Cobb's, and always a keen student of public affairs; associate-justice of the supreme court of Georgia, 18531861; brigadier-general in the Confederate army.
73566—13 7 companying this. The first is new, the second, one of Mr. D's unchanged, and the third is the other of his with some additions important but not in my opinion affecting the abstract principle on which the resolution rests.

Why these alterations? Let us consider for a moment the strength of the two parties in a sectional point of view. We see the Whig majorities, both certain and expected, chiefly in the free states, the Democratic in the slave. We see also already organized in some of the important free states a third party having naturally more sympathy with the Whigs than with the Democrats, and in the other free states no inconsiderable amount of the same third party in the state of raw material. If we add together the votes of the certain free Whig states, 51, and of those in which the abolitionists are supposed by the Whigs to have a casting vote, viz, N. Y. 36, Pa. 26, Ind. 12, Me. 9, N. H. 6, we shall have 51 plus 84 equals 135. Now even allowing for Wisconsin, 143 elects, so that those free states with either Ky. 12, N. C. 11, or Mo. 8, may dictate their man. We see too in New York strong symptoms of this abolition element becoming truly formidable, and in Pa. we distrust somewhat—a very little—the ability of the new soldiers under the banner of free trade to resist the temptation which the enemy will assuredly offer them in the resurrection of the Act of 1842. Further, we behold the Whigs in their conventions, legislatures and public meetings North already adopting the Wilmot Proviso, and on the other hand the Democrats generally ejecting the "perilous stuff" from their stomachs, as witness the letters and speeches of Buchanan, Dallas, Cass, etc., Dickinson's resolutions, and the general tone of the press. Seeing all this and much more of the same sort, are we not obliged to infer as a thing accomplished, 1st: That the Whigs *intend* to bid for Abolition bodaciously? And 2d: That they can *afford* to bid higher for it than can the Democrats, supposing the latter base enough to enter the lists? And are we not bound also to admit that true policy demands of the Democrats to endeavor to counteract the effect of the fusion of the two factions into one? Can this be done at all except by looking to the slave states?

If, however, we carry the slave states, we have but 117 votes. It *won't do,* then, to hazard the loss of much of our strength in the free states. The problem is to gain South and not lose North. It is the aim of the resolutions which I send you to solve it.

First then, I say that the Whigs reckon without their host when they count upon absorbing abolition, because they will nominate either Clay or Taylor; and the abolitionists, the honestly mad ones, will die at the stake before they will vote for the reprobate who dares say in word or deed that man may hold property in man— may traffic and trade in human flesh—particularly when his opponent will be a non-slaveholder and a patriot competent to utter any amount of innocent but "moral and religious sentiment" against the "peculiar institution." What says 1844? Has Mr. Clay set his negroes free since? And Genl. Taylor, a sugar planter, on the poisonous banks of the Mississippi; he is in a much worse predicament, beyond the reach of any fable in iEsop, because by his avowed innocence of all knowledge of political questions and by his self-imposed inexorable taciturnity he will not be able even to tell the abolitionists so much as that he believes slavery to be a great moral and political evil.

But suppose this eccentric faction shedding from its humid hair pestilence upon the nations shall, contrary to the best founded expectations, flying from its orb, sink into the sun of Whiggery. Console yourself because you could not by *any* possibility prevent it, and because all will not be lost. Democracy will have over-balancing accessions from other sources. The last four years have been fruitful in the product of every good thing, including voters, both indigenous and naturalized. It is not extravagant, I think, for our party to reckon upon two thirds of the former and nine tenths of the latter. Why there are but three modes, or rather two and a half, suggested for conducting the war—to fight, to tax, and to take—which is one; to back clean out of a conquered country, telling the cutthroats that we were unrighteously, unconstitutionally, and damnably there from the first, which is two—to back partly out to an unnamed line, going we only know from ocean to ocean, across the continent where it is all desert and mountain, and there to fight to the very death, provided always that any enemy should dare come up and knock a chip off of Jonathan's head—which is half a one. Now, will any but the old fools (of all fools the worst you know) take up with the second or third of these plans? The young have no more sense than to believe that war is war—blood, chains, gold, territory, and no more "sentiment" than to smite, to rivet, to sieze, and to annex. They feel that woe to the vanquished is weal to the victor. We may call these young fellows ours. How many are there? The New York Herald says 800,000— two thirds of that number are 530,000, half of which 260.000 would be the excess in our favor. Of them 160 or 170 thousand are in the free states. Then the naturalized vote must be quite large. Again, how Democratic the Army is becoming, even the regulars. Every letter from it will be a personal appeal to father, brother, friends, to put down those who give aid and comfort to the enemy. Above all, our annexation policy must bring recruits from all classes and quarters. All this being so, are we not able to despise the nauseous compound?

How, then, are we to " gain South"? I say by the principle contained in the last clause of the third of the resolutions, declaring that citizens of the slave states may settle with their slaves in the acquired teritory *until* such time as the people thereof see fit to forbid it by legislation. The adoption of this will not carry a single slave into such territory, not one, but it will carry many a vote into the ballot box. Mere barren option, never to be availed of tho' it is, still the candidate who refused it could not at the South in a contest with one who *conceded* it stand a fire of blank cartridges. What Hotspur felt is nature:

I'd give thrice as much lnnd to any well deserving friend.

But in the way of *Bargain* I'd cavil on the ninth part of a hair.

But won't its adoption do us more harm at the North than even so much good as this at the South can outweigh? It is not possible. Remember how far Dickinson's untouched resolutions go. These say "it is best" (mind you only expediency) to leave questions of domestic policy, that is whether there shall or shall not be slavery. to the people of the territory. So then it is best to let the people there make it a *slave* territory if they will. Going *thus* far will not damage us, it is agreed. Why? Because the good sense of the people North *sees* that such a permission is a mere vanity. Like laying duties upon cotton—or coal at Newcastle. Now how much further does my amendment go? It only affirms that it is best (expediency too) on many momentous accounts *to permit* the citizens of all the states to have an equal right of removal into the acquired territory and of holding there as property whatever they held as such where they came from. It does not affirm that such " citizens " have a *right* to do this or that Congress has not the *right* to forbid it. The constitutional question, so difficult, such a tool of death in the hands of madmen whether at the North or the South, is honorably and fairly got rid of, as indeed it is in Dickinson's original resolution to the extent to which it goes. For the most that can be made out of the expression "by leaving ", "by permitting" is that it is *doubtful* whether Congress has power on this subject "to bind and to loose" and therefore that it ought not to interfere to do either. Now, if the reasons assigned by Buchanan, Cass, etc., are sufficient to prove the harmlessness of leaving the question of slavery to the people of the territory, they are equally sufficient to prove the harmlessness of permitting all citizens to remove into the territory with their slaves and there to hold them in bondage. Those reasons amount to this, that the *interest* of slaveholders will prevent them from wishing to cross the Rio Bravo with their slaves, and so of course the people to pass the laws on the subject to slavery, being all non-slaveholders, will prohibit it. Why is it the interest of the slaveholder to keep away? On account of incompatibility of soil, climate, productions, danger of loss by facilities for escape, and on account of the region being now by the laws of Mexico free. Every one of these reasons will still affect the interest of the slaveholder to the same extent if my amendment should be adopted. It may be said that onejpf those reasons, viz: that drawn from the fact that the territory is now by law free and a slave going there would become free on touching the soil, would not apply if slave owners were "*permitted*" to take their slaves and hold them as such in the territory. Practically it is all the same. I submit that a prudent slaveholder will be as shy of putting himself and his slaves in the power of Mexican laws *to be made,* as of those already made. Very well. The good sense of Northern Democracy can as easily see this as the other. and the prospect of carrying Ky. , N. C., and Md., *with* the principle, and of losing S. C. and all that she can influence, without it, will make the scales fall from their eyes in a trice. One thing is never to be forgotten, that committed as the party is, it cannot in its wildest dreams hope for the vote of an abolitionist, and further, that the action of the abolitionists a9 a party as to keeping embodied or subsiding into Whiggery will depend upon what the Whigs do and *not upon anything* that we can do, unless we undo all that we have done. In such a case ought we not to follow the dictates of ordinary prudence?

If the war continues we ought to proclaim some such principle as that embodied in the first resolution. If we elect our man with that as one of bur battle cries, be sure Mexico won't waste minutes before she will come with a decent proposition for peace. And I think the sooner the thing is done the better. Let it have time to feel its way into grace and favor and for the Whigs to commit themselves against it. However, as to "grace and favor", there is no fear that it will need friends. True, we shall continue to hear the dog-in-the-manger growl of the Charleston Mercury. He has been so long only showing his teeth that we have come to believe that is all they were made for. All North it will out run the Cholera, as Prince John said to Jesse.1 Bye the bye, I have just seen the N. Y. Herald's account of the Utica convention. The address is able, not so well written as that of the Albany convention. There is one good thing in it, the declaration that they don't make W. Provisoism a *test,* a *sine qua non.* This being so, it has occurred to me that our Baltimore convention could not by any possibility have evidence enough presented to it to decide which to admit, Hunkers or Barnburners, nor the heart to risk making *martyrs* of *the innocent,* to the triumph of the guilty, and that therefore it would be obliged as a matter of sheer conscience not to be at home to New York but still to do a good part by her all the same as if she were admitted inside. That is, nominate some man staunch, staunch as Chimborazo, on 1" Prince John" Van Buren, to Jesse Hoyt. all the *test* questions, the *sine qua nons,* so that both divisions of the democracy may be gratified. Howell, I am death for Equity. Now, equality is equity. By presenting such a candidate the two wings will " spread " themselves in rivalry to speed the common body. What do you think of this. Bright, ain't it.

Well, this is the hand which I want to deal you at Baltimore. I am bound to say that there are some good cards in it. And anybody can play it. Genl. Cass is a good old man, Dallas is a gentleman, Buchanan is touched with the tariff, a man of vigor, tho', very great, sufficient doubtless to bear letting that drop out of his veins. I care not so much for the player as the cards.

Yes, the grand thing for success is harmony, unanimity in the principles and measures to be sent before the country in the address and resolutions respecting the war question and the territory question, chiefly the last. You Democrats in the House have nothing to do, being a minority, except to ascertain this common ground, compare notes, yield a little, and it will be yielded unto you. Keep the slavery question out of the way of any public discussion in the convention. What the convention does ought to be done without delay, without fuss, with perfect unity and perfect unanimity. Let its work instantly spring forth complete in every part, like Minerva from the head of Jupiter. If there is a will there is a way. There are Democrats in Congress from nearly every State, and what they can all agree upon be sure they can get their several state delegations to Baltimore to agree upon. And then, out of abundance of caution, let one member of Congress, if possible, from each state go down to Baltimore as a lobby member, an organ of assimilation. You know we shall all be strangers to one another. Why can't we organize victory. I see I have written reams. It shows at least that I take interest in the cause and that I am disposed to accomplish the object of your letter, that is (ain't it?) to enable you fellows at Washington to find out which way the wind blows. Write to me again. Speak out. Condemn what I have proposed if it ought to be done, tell me what's better—above all tell me the probable " platform " as well as the man. Dix and Shunk I forgot about. Either will do well, so far as I am at present advised.

P. S.—Tell Iverson I will answer his in a day or two, and show him this. I don't care who sees it.

Send me the address and resolutions of our last convention at Baltimore, if you can do it easily.

Resolutions enclosed with the foregoing. Resolved: That the United States have the intelligence and the virtue and the power to administer with safety, with justice and with equity any quantity of territory which they may honorably acquire from any foreign nation. *Resolved:* That true policy requires the government of the United States to strengthen its political and commercial relations upon this continent by the annexation of such continuous territory as may conduce to that end and can be justly obtained, and that neither in such acquisition nor in the territorial organization thereof can any conditions be constitutionally Imposed or institutions be provided for or established inconsistent with the right of the people thereof to form a free sovereign state with the powers and privileges of the original members of the confederacy. *Resolved:* That in organizing a territorial government for territory acquired by common blood and common treasure, and conferring in its achievement common glory, the principles of self government will be best promoted, the spirit and meaning of the Constitution best observed, the sentiments of justice of equality and of magnanimity best consulted, the self sacrificing love for the Union best maintained and strengthened, and the shining examples of mutual forbearance and compromise set us by our fathers in every dark day of our past career best emulated, by leaving all questions which concern the Domestic policy of such territory to the unrestrained Legislation of the people thereof, and until such legislation forbid, by permitting the citizens of every state to settle therein and to hold as property there whatever they may have held as property in the states from which they came.

Robert Toombs To James Thomas. L. C.

Washington, D. C. *Apr. 16, 1843.*

Dear Thomas, I received your letter of the 9th inst. today and I am very glad to hear you are improving. You did not state to what point in Kentucky you expected to direct your steps. I have an extensive acquaintance with the public men of Kentucky and could give or furnish you letters to almost any point, and if you know where you will probably remain longest and will write me I will procure such letters as would no doubt greatly increase the comfort and pleasure of your trip. I could send them to any point you might designate, if you are about leaving. Mr. Crittenden, my particular friend and messmate, will leave here for Kentucky about the first of June on a gubernatorial canvass in Kentucky. I will commend you to him especially, and I hope you may fall in with him somewhere in the state, if not at Frankfort, his residence. I will send by this mail or the next some letters for Louisville where I suppose you will most likely land in Kentucky. I hope you will find it convenient to call by Washington. There is much to see here to interest an intelligent stranger; men, if not things.

Clay has behaved very badly this winter. His ambition is as fierce as at any time of his life, and he is determined to rule or ruin the party. He has only power enough to ruin it. Rule it he never can again. In February while at Washington he ascertained that the Kentucky convention would nominate Taylor. He procured letters to McMillen? that he would decline when he went home, and the Taylor men from Kentucky under this assurance wrote home to their friends not to push him off the track by nominating Taylor. Mr. Clay never intended to comply, but without now having the boldness to deny it he meanly hints at having changed his determination. Bah! He now can deceive nobody here. The truth is he has sold himself body and soul to the Northern Anti-slavery Whigs, and as little as they now think it, his friends in Georgia will find themselves embarrassed before the campaign is half over. I find myself a good deal denounced in my district for avowing my determination not to vote for him. It gives me not the least concern. I shall never be traitor enough to the true interests of my constituents to gratify them in this respect. I would rather offend than betray them. Mr. Botts of the House and Mr. Berrien of the Senate and Mr. Buckner of Kentucky are the only three men from the slave states who prefer Mr. Clay for our candidate, and there are not ten Southern representatives who would not support Genl. Taylor against him if he were nominated. The real truth is Clay was put up and pushed by Corwin and McLean, Greeley & Co. to break down Taylor in the South. Having made that use of him they will toss him overboard at the convention without decent burial. It is more than probable that a third candidate may be brought forward, and Scott stands a good chance to be the man. For my part I am a Taylor man without a second choice.

Robert Toombs To James Thomas. L. C.

Washington, D. C, *May 1, 1848.*

Dear Thomas, I received your letter of the 26th inst. by the last mail. I will send you today by this mail, or tomorrow at farthest, several letters for Louisville etc., and will direct to you at Louisville others for Lexington and the neighborhood in Kentucky. I send you one today for Mr. Crittenden who will be at home (Frankfort) about the 12th or 14th of June. Besides, I have commended you to him and Mrs. Crittenden, who are now here and living with me. You will find Mrs. C. a most amiable and agreeable lady, and Crittenden the very prince of good fellows. I know not his superior in all the earth, in all those qualities of head and heart which we most love and respect. I think Frankfort, his residence, is on the way to Lexington from Louisville. You must by no means omit to stop there if Mr. C. is at home when you pass.

The political chauldron is yet boiling and bubbling with increased energy. Mr. Clay's prospects now seem to be very gloomy even for the nomination of the convention. I do not think it at all probable, if indeed it is possible, for him to get it. Those demonstrations at the North were only intended to destroy Taylor, and the very men who were nominated and instructed expressly to vote for him will set about to manage him out of it. He has nobody to blame but himself, for I candidly and honestly warned him of the treachery, and designated the traitors. But his insane ambition blinded him, and he must drink the bitter draft of disappointment which I would have gladly (from the recollections of the past) dashed from his lips.

The machinations of the petty demagogues in my district give me no concern. I am sorry that so large a number of the honest and patriotic Whigs of the district have allowed themselves to be misled by the contrivances of artful knaves and by their own devotion to Mr. Clay. This latter class will all come right when they know the whole truth of the matter, and will in good time thank me for pursuing their interests rather than following them in error. But however this may be, I prefer to displease rather than betray them. Mr. Clay occupies a position towards the strong anti-slavery men of the

North that would make his election the greatest possible danger to the South, and I shall never do any act to aid it, whatever may be the consequences personally to me. If my party choose to run him I only ask to be released of public duty, and I shall quietly drop into my former pursuits so congenial to my tastes, my interests and mental preparation. Whatever they may think of it, I have truly served the people from a sense of duty. There is no office within the reasonable probabilities of my attainment which I could afford to take under the government. My avarice would turn me to my profession rather than to public employment. Therefore I should at any time surrender my trust with greater pleasure than I ever accepted it. But while I have it, I will maintain the public interest and my own honor at any and every hazard of the popular displeasure. Our public men are becoming the veriest cowards that ever disgraced the earth. Mr. Clay has not five friends of his nomination in both branches of Congress; but eight tenths of them are afraid to open their lips upon the subject to the public. I would not hold office upon such terms. Give my best respects to your wife and daughter and Mrs. Bell. We should be very happy to see you here in Washington on your return South.

Thomas W. Thomas1 To Howell Cobb. E.

Elberton ga., *May 27th, 1848.* Dear Sir: Inclosed herewith I send a petition praying Congress to establish a line of stages from the village of Anderson to connect with the Georgia Rail Road, via Elberton. We will be much obliged if you will give yourself the trouble to present it and see that it is acted on and either granted or refused. The impression prevails very generally that such things are always treated with contempt and suffered 1A lawyer and editor of Elberton, Ga.; judge of the superior court of Georgia (northern circuit), 1855-1859; colonel of the Fifteenth Regiment of Georgia infantry in the Confederate army, 1861-1862.
to die in silence, and I would beg leave to suggest that you take such action in the matter as will be seen in the usual newspaper reports of the proceedings in Congress. Such a course will at least be good policy in this—the people here will see you have done your duty. Petitions for the same purpose as the one inclosed will probably be forwarded by the people of Oglethorpe and Anderson district, but whether these go or not we wish you to act on ours. We stand greatly in need of mail facilities, and if our rights are withheld much longer, I believe the people will secede and form an independent republic bounded by Broad River and Savannah. Such a movement is not only justified by the declaration of independence, but will be in accordance with the spirit of the age. Of the 330 signers a larger proportion than one-tenth sign by "his mark ",—a lamentable but overwhelming proof of the necessity of the light of letters....

Among the names I sent you in the neighborhood of Broad River P. O. was one Henry Stephens. He lately got a speech from you on the Mexican War. He says the Whigs have been lying on Polk about originating the war. He says this speech has Gen. Taylor's letter in it, and it was Taylor " that sent them troops from one river to tother. " We are all curious to know who has been nominated, though we have no anxiety about the result. We have a perfect confidence the Baltimore Convention will give us a man sound on Southern rights. I have not heard a single man express himself for any favorite, though all expect if Polk is not renominated the candidate will be a northern man. Every day serves to strengthen the conviction that we can beat Gen. Taylor as easily as Clay. I can count at least a half dozen Whigs who have pledged themselves not to vote for Taylor on any conditions. I send below a short list of democrats whom I expect you have not got.

Thomas R. R. Cobb To Howell, Cobb. E.

Athens ga., *May Slat, 1848.* Dear Brother, I return you the order which I negligently omitted to endorse.

We have the nominations. I am " reconciled," not very much " delighted." I am not a great admirer of Cass, although I think it a generous act on the part of Northern Democrats to nominate both anti-Wilmot Proviso men. I think a more *judicious* ticket could have been selected. Michigan and Kentucky are too close together to have *both* candidates. I don't see what strength Butler carried to Cass that any Southern man would not have carried, and more especially Quitman. And on the score of military glory, Scott or Taylor if nominated will overshadow that of either. King of Alabama would have been a much more *judicious* nomination, although I would vote for no man sooner than GenL Butler. These are my first impressions. Every county in the district will be represented in the approaching Convention. You will be unanimously nominated, from all I can learn. There will be some difference of opinion as to the Elector. Most of the delegates are for Genl. Wofford if he wants it. McMillan, I think, is rather working to get it, and has friends in Elbert, Madison and Jackson. Hillyer is talked of also, and I would not be surprised if Griffin is looking at it...

Thomas W. Thomas To Howell Cobb. E.

Elberton, Ga., *June 5th, 1848.* Dear Sir: The last mail brought us the news of Gen. Cass's nomination, and with it came a whig paper charging him with having voted for the Wilmot Proviso. My recollection of the facts is this, the Proviso was attached to the three million bill in the House and sent to the Senate where on motion to amend it was struck out, Gen. Cass voting for the striking out. In this shape it was sent back to the House and passed without the Proviso. If my memory serves me, this was the only time the question ever came up in the Senate and Gen. Cass recorded his vote in favor of the South. Please send me the Senate journal showing all his votes on the question. I am under so many obligations to you for favors of this kind that I dislike to trouble you, and wish you to attend to my request only in case it be convenient. The Democrats here are highly gratified with the nominations and are prepared to give them a united support. Cass in my humble judgment is a perfect embodiment of progressive democracy as opposed to what the Whigs call conservatism, which in plain English means putting the people in ward, to save them from their pretended ignorance and folly; and the question is not only between free-trade and protection, but also whether we shall govern ourselves or have guardians. Cass went for 54.40, is now for the acquisition of Mexican territory, free trade, the independent treasury, and hates the British; and therefore must be worthy of democratic suffrage.

James C. Dobbin 1 To Howell Cobb. E.

Fayettevtllk N. C, *June 15th, 1848.*

My Dear Sir: Your esteemed favour in reply to my first communication was duly received, and its perusal gave me no little pleasure, awakening, as it did, pleasing recollections of incidents during my brief political career in Washington.

I think, my dear sir, I am not deceived in inferring from the spirit and tenor of your letter that an occasional correspondence will not be unacceptable, and will serve but to keep alive that kindly 1 Member of Congress from North Carolina, 1845-1847.
attachment which I trust neither time nor separation will extinguish. Still, plunged as I have been for many months in the laborious practice of the law, I cannot but occasionally abandon the courthouse and stroll into the avenue of politics. They have rather forced me to consent to become a candidate for our Legislature. I have no opposition, and of course will have a quiet time, and a little dish of Legislative politics may not be disagreeable. Well, the agony is over and Cass and Butler are nominated, and Taylor and Fillmore; and although it has produced some sensation, the tickets seem to have been anticipated by the popular mind. We have had a large Democratic meeting here and responded very zealously to the nomination of Cass and Butler. Judge Strange and myself addressed them. The meeting was large, enthusiastic, and everything passed off well.

I struggled hard to prove Cass orthodox on the slavery question, and I would not have done so had I suspected him. And his letter to Nicholson is certainly liberal and magnanimous for a Northern man. I was provoked at Yancey's conduct in the convention. The introduction of his resolution1 was unnecessary. The resolution reported by the committee was comprehensive. There was no evidence that Cass had wrong views, and the adoption of Yancey's resolution squinted very much towards a suspicion of Cass and looked too much like pressing nice, hair-spliting distinctions on the subject upon our Northern democratic friends, whose liberality should be appreciated but not abused. My *own notion is that the Territorial Legislature* while legislating *as such* and for the Territory and for territorial purposes *has no right* to pass a law to prohibit slavery. Because if we adopt that doctrine we at once practically exclude the slaveholder forever. The Territory acquired is filled at the time of acquisition with *non-slaveholders.* The Legislature meets and a law excluding slavery is enacted. This will exclude the slaveholder, for he can't get there to repeal the law. I regard the Territory as the *common* property of the *States.* And the *people* of each *State* have a right to enjoy it *with* or *without* their peculiar property. But when the people are meeting to pass a fundamental law, to adopt a Constitution and to ask admission into the Union as a State, *then* the *prohibition or establishment* of slavery becomes a subject for legitimate action. It will not do for us to admit that the first Legislature in New Mexico can pass a law immediately and exclude every slaveholder from the territory—if we do, are we not admitting that it is not the property of each and all the States? But I do not think Cass has *publicly*—certainly not in his Nicholson letter—expressed any opinion contravening my position. He says " leave to the people affected by the question " its regu 1 Proclaiming the doctrine of congressional non-intervention with slavery in the Territories. See footnote 1, p. Ill, *infra.* lation. He does not say that he thinks the Territorial Legislature can prohibit it. I hope he will not say so. Because it may never in all probability become a practical question on which he as President could act. Yet the expression of such an opinion would prejudice him in the South with many, very many.

But enough of this. When you write me give me your views. I can not express to you my feelings about the Whigs' nomination. If they succeed, my confidence in popular virtue and intelligence will be a little shaken. I know much virtue and much intelligence will vote the ticket. I regard it as evidence that the Whigs are afraid of their principles. They know the people are against them. They put up "Old Zac " and surround him with a blaze of military glory, and just behind him is Fillmore lurking, holding ready to fasten upon the country all the odious and rejected measures of the Whig Party. Can they succeed? What do our friends think of it? I was pleased to see that yourself and *distingue* were on the tour, lionizing. That is right. I have given up South Carolina and am afraid of Georgia and Louisiana. Massachusetts will bolt. Ohio will vote for Cass, so likewise Pennsylvania. But for those miserable Barnburners, New York would be all right. The South will have a hard fight. The slavery question and " Old Zac" being a slaveholder may for a moment shake some of the faithful—but I have faith in our *Principles* and in *Providence.*

I can't say much to please you about North Carolina. Reid is doing his best. I don't think he will succeed, although he has sprung up a suffrage question which is taking well. I do think we will carry the legislature. There is a strong probability of it.

But enough of politics. Tell Stephens I heartily appreciate his remembering me so kindly and assure him that the feeling is cordially reciprocated. I like Stephens. With all his bad politics he is a generous hearted fellow and of brilliant genius.

By the by, lest I forget it, *in confidence,* a friend of mine wishes to go abroad. Do you know of a vacancy—Naples, Rome, Belgium, etc., etc. Remember this when you write...

W. C. Daniell 1 To Howell Cobb. E.

Near Gainesville ga., *20th June, 1848.* My Dear Sir: If the Report of Fremont's last exploration has been printed and you have a spare copy you will oblige me by sending it to me. I would not ask this of you if I knew where to purchase a copy.

I fear that the Whigs have by the nomination of Taylor imposed the duties of a laborious and arduous campaign upon the Democratic 1 A substantial planter whose summer home lay in Cobb's congressional district. leaders in this state. I was taken sick the day I reached Savannah from my plantation. I have only recently recovered my strength since my arrival here. I can therefore say but little of the manner in which Cass's nomination has been received, but as far as I have heard there is every disposition among our friends to yield him their support. It would not by any means be safe to count on his getting the vote of this State, though I hope he may. Woodbury would have been a stronger man with us here, but I suppose that Cass has been chosen because he was deemed the strongest in the country.

I see Old Bullion1 is out in a new part, and seems to be quite pleased to play the second fiddle. How are the mighty fallen. No one has asked him to be and no paper has (I believe) spoken of him as a candidate for the Presidency this time, and it is quite manifest I think that he does not mean to be forgotten and consequently overlooked. He is in a worse box than my friend (Calhoun) whom he denominated to Crittenden (so said Toombs who was present) as the "Nigger King."

Henry R. Jackson " To Howell Cobb. E.

Savannah ga., *21st June, 1848.* My Dear Cousin, Since the reception of your last letter I have been so constantly occupied with some vexatious law business which has kept me on the run in Savannah and taken me up into the country, that I have actually been unable to find the letter to reply to it. I have not said so much in opposition to the Calhoun clique as was my disposition, because I did not think it altogether a prudent course. With reference to those papers of the Dem. party in Georgia that had advocated the Florida and Alabama resolution, I have not sought a collision, either with the Constitutionalist or the Telegraph, because I thought the probabilities strong that both of these papers, if let alone, would eventually come out warmly for Cass, should he be the nominee of the Convention. I did not think that angry collision would operate beneficially for the party. Therefore I contented myself with simply expressing my own views fully and firmly. As events have proved, both the Constitutionalist and Telegraph are out for Cass, and are consequently thrown into opposition themselves to the Calhoun, Yancey and Charleston Mercury clique. I think it better that this should be so than that they should have been excited into animosity by a general onslaught upon them on the part of the other presses of the State.

But in the name of all that is rational, what induced the Georgia delegates in the national convention to vote for that resolution of 1 Thomas H. Benton.

a A lawyer, editor, and Democratic politician of Savannah, Ga., judge of the superior court of Georgia (eastern circuit), 1849-1853, brigadier-general in the Confederate army. Yancey's1 After having voted for the nomination of Cass, how *could* they vote for the resolution (a pack of nonsense in itself) with the interpretation put upon it by Yancey himself? Did they not perceive that it would operate prejudicially to us in Georgia? And how could they at any rate vote for such outrageous nonsense?

My views always have coincided with yours upon this subject. I am as clear as daylight in my ideas upon it. Gen. Cass is right throughout. He has suggested the only ground upon which a Southern man can stand, and I am convinced that reflection will bring all Southern Democrats (not disposed to quit the party *at any rate)* to his zealous support...

Thomas Smith 2 To Howell Cobb. E.

Versailles indiana, *June £7,,48.* Dr. Sir: Knowing the tax imposed by business, ceremony, and a little real friendship, on Members of Congress, I have refrained writing to many friends that I really wished to. Under this state of feeling I would not write you or trouble you now if I did not think and fear that a momentous political crisis was about developing that is destined shortly to shake our political fabrick. In this Confederacy the Democratic party, long in the ascendant, has had to conciliate and compromise sectional interests and feelings. In this spirit the Slavery question has been put on the ground of non-interference on the part of the Genl. Govmnt. On that basis the democratic party has planted itself. If it can maintain that position, it is the only position that it can maintain in the free states, and is there a Southern man so blind as not see it and so uninformed as not to know it?

To drive us from this ground, the Whigs and abolitionists have agitated for the last 10 or 15 years. Their denunciation of the South, Southern dictation and Southern influence, has been fierce, and their appeals have been powerful and pathetic in favour of the poor *negro.* To meet these arguments and such invective has required all the talent and forbearance of the Democratic party. The Democratic free-state creed commends itself strongly to the sober sense of community, and those that attempt to overturn it can't but show the incendiary's *torch* and the assassin's *knife—*" in their fury the hope of the Union is lost". The Democratic South in our conventions, in Congress, and at the ballot box has shown the same conciliatory spirit,—

in making our last and former nominations 1 Yancey had offered the following as an amendment to the report of the committee on resolutions at the Baltimore convention: "Resolved, That the doctrine of non-interference with the rights of property of any portion of this confederation, be it In the States or in the Territories, by any other than the parties interested In them. is the true republican doctrine recognized by thl» body." This resolution was defeated, 246 to 38.

Congressman from Indiana, 1839-1841 and 1843-1847.

they have been foremost in favor of *free-state men*. But in the nomination of the present *Whig* candidate it is manifest to all the people, and they can't but see the finger of the South in it, and the dictatorial and domineering spirit they have shown in forcing their man upon the Convention.

It has forced some fears upon the Democrats, as well as confusion and dismay into the Whig ranks, and utter disgust into the abolition breasts. The consequence of all will be to very much widen the breach between the free and slave states of the Union. In the late Whig convention the South showed neither quarter nor respect to the North. She gave not a vote for a Northern man....

But the point to which I wish to call your attention is this: the fear amongst the democratic party is that the South may so far unite on the nominal Whig candidate as to give him all the South, in disregard of the friendly spirit the free states have always shown you. If this shall be the case I cannot doubt that much democratic sympathy will be lost you, and a falling off amongst your friends in these states, that time can never *cure*. Because it is so plain the nomination of *Taylor* is a Southern Whig trick, against the feelings of the Whig party, to catch up other thtvn Whig votes in the South, and against the sense and sentiment of the nation, that union of effort of all parties will be made against the South before his term of office, if elected, shall expire. You know that North nothing but a free-state union of effort is wanting to disfranchise the South, so far as the Presidential office is concerned; and what so well calculated to produce that result as such palpable tricks as the South has just perpetrated in the nomination of a man without talent and the independence to speak out boldly his opinions and his party fealty.

In taking such a man at such a time it must be there is something impure in it. Something behind the curtain. But it will out. If the old General shall ever be called by the people *unanimously* or *spontaneously* to the Presidency, he will find the need of opinions and fixed principles. His administration, or that of any man, must proceed upon fixed principles, and the better they are matured the better he will bear up under the responsibilities of the office.

You are aware that every Whig in Congress and out of it in all the free States in the Union by their votes, speeches and action in the primary assemblies, amongst the people, and many of the democrats, are committed to the principles of the Wilmot Proviso, and if *Taylor* is elected, unless they back out from their present position, which they dare not do, it will be engrafted upon the legislation of the next four years. In this great contest the South brings their General into the field unarmed. His anxiety to lead the motley forces of federalism compels him to put on the no-party badge, and to command without a sword or the armor the Constitution has put upon him for his own protection and that of the States. Mr. Jefferson says: the President's negative was given him for his own protection, the protection of the States and the judiciary, against the aggressions of Congress. But I presume as he has voluntarily divested himself of the protection the Constitution in vested him with, to get office, he expects to put it on in the heat and smoke of the battle. Let him not think so. If he does it, he will be shot down by his own forces and confederates; and if Tyler was denounced a traitor, he will be justly denounced an arch traitor. It is distinctly understood he will veto none of the people's measures.

Of the success of the Democratic Ticket, Cass and Butler, in this region there is no room to doubt. I have never seen in favor of any democratic ticket so ardent a spirit manifested by the party. I think in this county there is not a dissenting voice. *Indiana* may be set down for Cass and Butler by a large majority over all opposition. Even should Hale run, and Mr. Van Buren lead the Barnburners, we can beat them all.

I wish to know from you, my dear sir, what Georgia will do in the premises.

I have bored you with a very prosing long letter.

Our very best respects to your Lady and friends.

W. C. Daniell To Howell Cobb. E. Hall County ga., *1st July, 1848.*

My Dear Sir: I received yours addressed to me at Savannah last night. I have been so much at home since my arrival here—more than a month—that I could give you but little information of the way in which the nominations have been received, but for the arrival last night of my friend Dr. Bailey from Savannah. He has been traveling leisurely up, and taking a deep interest in the cause of Democracy, has made inquiry everywhere on his way. Moving in a private conveyance out of the great thoroughfares, he tells us of what may be deemed, to a considerable extent at least, the spontaneous movement of the people.

He authorizes me to say to you that having travelled over the same country just four years ago, he can say with much confidence that up to this time there is more unanimity and enthusiasm among the Democracy now than there was then, whilst the Whigs are lukewarm. Where there are malcontent Democrats they vote for Taylor. The malcontent Whigs are near two to one of the Democrats, and they will not vote at all. The only malcontent Democrats he heard of were in Hancock. 73566—13 8

He thinks that King's1 Whig opponent will take off some 300 to 400 votes, which with the Democratic vote, should the Democrats run no candidate, which he deems the best policy, may elect Seward.2

But at present no one can see the issue that may be made in the coming presidential campaign. What is Van Buren doing? Do give me what light you can on his and Dodge's recent nominations at Utica. Is he no longer a "Northern man with Southern principles?"

If Taylor should, as I have supposed, repudiate the pledges of the Louisiana delegation in the Whig convention, what will the Whigs do? If the movement of the Barnburners should come to the head indicated by Van Buren's letter—of which I have only heard, but which assures me that he will accept a nomination of promise and that he deemed such a nomination (of promise) very probable when he wrote—where can we find the men to elect Cass or any other Democrat? If the hostility to Slavery has become so extended as to tempt Martin Van Buren to bow low and worship at its shrine for the highest office in the gift of the people, how long will it be before our own security will require that we withdraw from those who deem themselves contaminated by our touch? And how long before we shall deem those our best friends who would tell us that our only dependence is upon ourselves?

Thomas W. Thomas To Howell Cobb. E.

Elberton, Ga., *July 7th, 1848.* Dear Sir: I wrote you by the last mail in relation to the inquiries contained in yours of the 20th June and promised to write again when I could procure better information. I saw here last Tuesday, Col. John D. Watkins from the neighborhood of Petersburg and had a conversation with him about the prospects of democracy in that quarter. He informs me it is true Speed has declared for Taylor and has been that way inclined for a year past. I learn also it is extremely doubtful that Speed voted for Polk, and the general impression is he voted with the Whigs in that contest. Watkins says he (Speed) can't influence a single other vote, and all the democrats there besides, are unanimous and enthusiastic for Cass. A little to my surprise I learned that Dr. Danelly and he both are, and have been all the time, out and out Cass men. At our celebration here on the 4th a Mr. Vinson Hubbard, heretofore considered a Democrat, offered a toast the substance of which was that Gen. Taylor might be elected and fill the office as Washington did.

1 Thomas B. King, Whig Congressman from Georgia, 1839-1843 and 1845-1849, defeated Joseph W. Jackson In the congressional election of 1848 by a heavy majority. He resigned from Congress In 1849, when President Taylor sent him to California to promote a state-forming movement there. James L. Seward, Member of Congress from Georgia, 1853-1859, did not enter the campaign of 1848.

This looks a little dangerous and I think it probable he will support Taylor, though we shall not cease until after the election in our efforts to reclaim him. He is a poor man and is living on land free of rent, belonging to a strong Whig, and this possibly explains the heresy. The toast he gave however hints at the only quarter whence we may expect danger in the present campaign. The fool-idea constantly harped upon by the Whig press, of having a second Washington in the chair of state, has turned some weak heads. It had begun to tell upon the public mind before the democratic press noticed the operation, and now we should work vigourously and direct our attack to this point. Our Editors are much to blame in this matter. They seemed to have a sort of reverence for Taylor, which was very ill-timed, and refused to lay hands upon him, even after he was nominated by the Whig convention of Georgia. What is once acquiesced in by a party, though but for a short time, is hard afterwards to be contested, and we are now reaping the fruits of having indulged in the weakness of admiring military prowess. As far as my humble efforts could go, I at an early day charged Taylor with being a Wilmot Proviso man. Notwithstanding he was already the candidate of the Whig party in Georgia, the Democratic press differed with me and took the trouble to write and publish articles to show that I was wrong, thereby defending a Whig candidate. In the Constitutionalist of July 21st, 1847 you will find the charge made by me, fully sustained by documents, and in the same paper a reply by the editor defending Taylor. I am glad to see they are getting back in the right track, and the only difficulty is they may not have time to undo all the mischief they have wrought. I throw out these views to you because you may do something to help these Democratic Taylor champions out of the fog. From a close observation of the prejudices and opinions of the people around me I am satisfied they are well grounded. Could not you send Vinson Hubbard (at Elberton) some document showing Taylor had at last succumbed and taken purely a party position, also one of the same sort to Jesse Dobbs?

James Jackson 1 To Howell Cobb. E.

Monroe ga., *July 9th, 1848.* My Dear Cousin,... In reference to Politicks, the state of feeling could not be better in Georgia than it now is. I do not know and have not heard of one Democrat who will not give the ticket his cordial support. The movement of the Barn Burners in New York must strengthen Cass in all the South. If the Southern Democracy do not now go heart and soul for the regular Democratic ticket, they

'Judge of the superior court of Georgia (western circuit), 1849-1857.

will deserve all the evils which you predict will result from the ascendency of their natural foes. Georgia, you know, is always doubtful. I consider her as safe as can be predicted of any state so shifting in Politicks. We have the majority and must succeed, for the Democrats are united and, about here, enthusiastic....

I attended the late convention at Milledgeville, and have the vanity to believe that I convinced Gardner in five minutes that Holsey 1 and himself had been quarreling over an abstraction—a judicial, not a political question, and one with which the President will have no more to do than the man in the moon. If he will check Congress it is all we can ask of him, and all *Calhoun could* do were he President himself. How do you like our resolutions—I think they are " tip-top "....

John B. Lamar To Howell Cobb. E. American Hotel, New York, *July 12th/Ifi.*

Dear Howell, Don't forget my passports, as I sail on Monday in the ship Fidelia for Liverpool.

P. S.—I hope to God Congress will not adjourn before the nigger question is settled about the newly acquired territory. If it does adjourn and leave that question open until after the Presidential election the "cake is all dough " with this Union, you may depend upon it. Now is the time to settle it while both parties are disposed to conciliate to effect their ends, but if you wait until after election the successful party will have no inducement, and the defeated party too much exasperated, to yield anything. I hope Congress will not adjourn until the question is settled; and if you love your country better than president making, you will use all your influence to have it settled before you adjourn. It is more important than people are aware of generally to settle the question before Congress adjourns.

John H. Lumpkin To Howell Cobb. E.

Athens, East Tennessee, *22 August, 1848.* Dear Cobb, I reached the Stone Mountain on the morning of the 16th inst., the day after the democratic mass meeting, and I found our friends firm, united, enthusiastic and confident of success. As the meeting was over, I passed on the line of the road,2 and I saw democrats from all the counties in my district and they assured me that the democracy would do their whole duty for Hackett,8 and for Cass and Butler. I did not see Hackett, nor did I go to Rome, but I came to this place to see my family as fast as the publick conveyances 1 James R. Gardner, of the Augusta Constitutionalist, and Hopkins Holsey, of the Southern Banner, at Athens, were leading Democratic editors in Georgia. 3 The Georgia and the Western & Atlantic Railroads. » Thomas C. Hackett, of Marietta, Ga. , Member of Congress, 1849-1851. would take me. I found my wife and children in good health, and my blue eyed boy that I had never seen, the largest and finest child I have. I shall leave here tomorrow for Georgia, and will go by appointment to Cumming. During next week I shall go through Walker county and see Aycock and such as are disaffected there, and I will go from there to Summerville and from thence to Rome. Our democratic friends in this part of Tennessee are doing their duty, and the result of the late elections has given them confidence and hope, and discouraged our political opponents. A. V. Brown has passed on through this section of East Tennessee and he is now above here making speeches. Govr. Jones1 is in company with him. Gentry2 has a list of appointments on his return home from Congress. He will be accompanied wherever he goes. I have no fears for the result in this State. I have seen many Clay Whigs since I came here who do not think that any booby can make a President. I am satisfied that there are many here who feel and act just as John M. Botts did while we were at Washington. Colquitt and McAllister visited Marietta from the Stone Mountain, and from there this week they will be at Canton, and next week at Cumming. You must be sure and attend the district mass meeting to be held in Cass county. I am in good health.

Alexander H. Stephens To The Editor Of The Federal Union.3

Clinton, Ga. *30th, Aug., 1848.* Mr. Editor: In passing through this place, I have just seen your paper of yesterday's date which contains some enquiries addressed to me, to which I cannot hesitate to give a prompt reply "in such reasonable length and respectful terms" as to secure, I trust, a place in your columns.

And that I may be distinctly understood, I will give the entire communication and my answer to each enquiry in order:

To The Hon. A. H. Stephens:

It is known to you, that your motion to lay upon the table the "Compromise bill" of the Senate, during the late session of Congress, has produced considerable excitement in this district. You have been nominated as the Whig candidate for re-election. If you should have opposition, it is scarcely to be doubted that this bill will be the main issue involved in the canvass. It is therefore eminently desirable that your sentiments should be clearly understood as to what are the rights of the South and how far they are affected by the bill. A careful perusal of your speech has left our mind in doubt as to yonr opinion upon several essential points. We therefore venture respectfully to propound to you a few interrogatories, to which we ask a reply.

L Do you believe that Congress has the right under the Constitution, to prohibit slavery in the territories belonging to the United States?

1 Aaron V. Brown and George W. Jones were leading Democrats in Tennessee. Meredith P. Gentry, a Whig Congressman from Tennessee, 1839-1843 and 1845-1853.
'From the Federal Union, Milledgerllle, Ga., Sept. 12, 1848.
'The Clayton compromise hill.

To your first enquiry I answer, that I do not believe that Congress has the right, either in honor, justice or good faith, to prohibit slavery in the territories belonging to the United States and thus to appropriate the public Domain entirely to the benefit of the people of the non-slaveholding states—and hence I have uniformly voted against the Oregon bill which contained a section excluding slavery, notwithstanding most if not all my Democratic colleagues have repeatedly voted for a bill organizing a Government there with such exclusion—and notwithstanding Mr. Polk has lately signed a bill which contained such an exclusion.

So far as New Mexico and California are concerned, and towards which your enquiries are doubtless mainly directed, there is no express provision in the Constitution which applies either directly or indirectly to them. They are to be considered as acquired by conquest, and there is no article or clause in the Constitution that relates in the remotest degree to the government of conquests. I do not believe that the framers of the Constitution contemplated that such a contingency would ever happen—and hence the silence of the Constitution upon that subject. But as the Supreme Court of the United States have repeatedly held the doctrine that the power to make conquest does belong to the General Government, though not expressly granted, it is not my purpose to say anything upon that point now. The only point in your enquiry relates to the government of the conquest, and to that point I answer explicitly that I consider the conquest, according to the best authorities upon the laws of nations, as belonging to the *people* of the United States—to all the citizens of the United States, the South as well as the North. When the treaty is fully complied with these provinces will constitute a public domain acquired by the common valor, blood and treasure of all. And in the government of them the rights and interests of the South should be looked to, guarded and protected as well as the North by all proper and necessary laws. Until they are admitted into the United States the government of them must devolve upon Congress or such territorial legislatures as may be created and authorized by Congress. And any legislation by Congress or by the territorial legislatures which would exclude slavery would be in direct violation of the rights of the Southern people to an equal participation in them and in open derogation of that equality between the states of the South and North which should never be surrendered by the South. And I hold also that any legislation by Congress or by the territorial legislatures which does not secure and protect the rights of the South as fully and as completely in the enjoyment of their property in slaves as it does the rights of the people of the North in the enjoyment of their property in these territories is manifestly unjust, in violation of the rights of the South, and a surrender of that equality between the different members of this confederacy which shall never be made by my sanction.

Your second enquiry is in the following words: II. From your replies to Mr. Stanton of Tennessee, on pages 10 and 11 of your speech, we clearly infer that it is your opinion that the Constitution of the United States does not guarantee to the slaveholder the right to remove with his property into any territory of the United States and to be protected in the undisturbed use and enjoyment of his slaves as property. Do we properly construe your meaning?

And in reply you will allow me to say that you seem greatly to misapprehend my answer to Mr. Stanton. The purport of my answer to him was (I have not the speech before me) that the Constitution did secure and guarantee the rights of the master to his slave in *every state and territory of the Union* where slavery was not prohibited by law. But that it did not establish it in any territory or State where it was so prohibited. And the same I reaffirm. It is too plain a question to admit of argument. It is one of those truths which under our system of government may be considered as a political axiom. Everybody knows that the Constitution secures and guarantees property in slaves in Georgia and in all the slave States, but that it does not secure the use and enjoyment of such property in New York or any of the States where slavery is prohibited.

Your third question is in the following words: III. If the right spoken of in the 2d question does exist under the Constitution in reference to territory generally, does it exist in relation to New Mexico and California?

And in answer to it I say that I hold that the Constitution does secure and guarantee the rights of the master to property in his slave in all the territories belong to the United States where slavery is not prohibited. With regard to the territories, the same principle holds which is applicable to the states. I do not maintain the position that slavery cannot be maintained without positive law. But I say that according to all the decisions of all the courts I have ever seen in all civilized nations, it cannot be maintained and protected where it is prohibited by express law. In all the states of this Union where it is not prohibited, the Constitution secures and protects it; but in those states where it is prohibited it does not protect it further than to provide for the recapture of runaway slaves—and the same principle I have no doubt from the decisions of the Supreme Court would by that tribunal be held to be applicable to the territories. By the Missouri Compromise slavery was prohibited from all.that portion of the Louisiana cession out of Missouri, North of 36:30 degrees of North latitude. Slavery by that Compromise was in effect *abolished* in all that territory. For by the laws in force in the territory at the time of the acquisition slavery was recognised and had existence. There is a large territory now unoccupied which is embraced in the provisions of that Compromise and from which by that Compromise slavery is prohibited. And can any man believe that if a slaveholder should carry his slave into that territory where slavery is prohibited, that the Supreme Court of the United States would recognise his right and protect him in holding his slave there?

It is not my purpose now to speak of the constitutionality of the Missouri Compromise—I am speaking of it as a practical question under the decisions of the Supreme Court; and according to principles settled by that Court, does any man believe that the rights of the master would be protected by that Court in that territory, or any other territory of the United States, where slavery is prohibited, until the prohibition is removed by competent authority, any more than in a State where slavery is prohibited? In New Mexico and California slavery was abolished and prohibited by express law at the time of the conquest. And according to the decisions of the Supreme Court of the United States, which no man can gainsay or deny; (I mean the *fact* of the decisions; I do not now speak of their correctness), all the laws which were of force at the time of the conquest will continue in force until altered by competent authority, *except such as were inconsistent with the Constitution of the United States* or the stipulations of the treaty. Is the prohibition of slavery by the local law of any state or place inconsistent with the Constitution of the United States? If it is, those laws of New Mexico and California will become abrogated and necessarily cease to operate upon the final fulfilment of the treaty stipulations. But if the prohibition of slavery by the local law of any state or place is not inconsistent with the Constitution according to the decisions of the Supreme Court, they will of course remain of force until altered by competent authority. My own opinion is, that neither the existence of slavery or non-existence of it by the local law of any place is inconsistent with any provision of the Constitution. The Constitution extends over states where slavery exists as well as where it is prohibited. Slavery depends upon the law of the place, which may be *either written or unwritten.* And where it exists the Constitution protects it, but it does not establish it where it is prohibited.

I have heard some argue that the laws in New Mexico and California prohibiting slavery there were similar to the laws concerning the establishment of religion. I consider the cases totally different. for this plain reason: An established religion is inconsistent with an *express provision of the Constitution.*

But the non-existence or prohibition of slavery by the local law of any State or place is not inconsistent with any provision of the Constitution. It is in vain for any man to attempt to deceive himself or others upon this point. And it is worse than in vain to attempt to make the Southern people believe that any right was secured to them by the late proposed Compromise bill which without any legal protection referred the matter to the Supreme Court. The only right it *pretended* to secure was the right of a law suit—and that existed without the Compromise just as amply and as fully as it did under it. And under the circumstances if any man can suppose that the Court, at the end of the suit, would decide in favor of the rights of the Southern people, he cannot doubt but that the same decision would be made even if the Wilmot Proviso were passed.

But to proceed to your fourth question, which is as follows: IV. We infer from the tenor of your speech that you do not believe the right exists in relation to New Mexico and California, because of the decrees of 1829 and 1837 abolishing slavery throughout the Republic of Mexico. If so, what right of the South is surrendered by the Compromise bill, and how is it surrendered?

To this I answer that your inference is entirely wrong. I do believe that we of the South have a right to an equal participation in this acquisition, notwithstanding the decrees and acts of Mexico abolishing and prohibiting slavery in New Mexico and California—and a right that I never intend to abandon or surrender by my vote. It is the right which belongs to us as a portion of the conquerors of the country. It is public property, belonging as I have said before to all the citizens of the country—to the people of the South as well as the North. It is common property, and the principles applicable to it are well expressed by Vattel, as follows: *All the members* of a corporation have an *equal right* to the *use* of the *common 'property.* But respecting the *manner of enjoying it, the body of the corporation may make such regulations as they think proper,* provided that those regulations be *not inconsistent with that equality of right which ought to be preserved in a communion of property.* Thus a corporation may determine the use of a common forest or a common pasture, either allotting it to all the members, according to their wants, or allotting each an equal share, but *they have no right to exclude any one of the members,* or to *make a distinction to his disadvantage,* by assigning him a less share than that of the others. (Vattel's Law of Nfations, 113.)

These are the principles I hold: Congress has no right to exclude the South from an equal share, and it is the duty of Congress to see that the rights of the South are as amply protected as the rights of the North. And it was this right of legal protection for the property of the South that was surrendered in that bill. If Congress has the power to declare exactly how far the interests of the North shall be protected, if they have the power to extend the Missouri Compromise line, they certainly have the power to say in clear and distinct words that up to that line on the South the rights of the South shall be protected—and not after prohibiting us from going North of that line leave us to contest with the Courts our rights on the South of it. This is what the Compromise bill did. It excluded us from the whole of Oregon, and left us to the Courts to decide whether we should be allowed to carry and hold our property in New Mexico and California. For such a Compromise I shall never vote. Your fifth question is as follows:

V. If by virtue of the Constitution of the United States, we have not the right to carry our slaves into these territories, we ask, upon what principle do you claim It, in behalf of your constituents? Do you claim it, upon the broad principle of justice arising from the fact that It is the fruit of common blood and common treasure? If so, do you expect Congress, constituted as it now is, or is hereafter likely to be, will ever recognise this principle of justice, and by positive legislation authorise the extension of slavery into those territories?

And in answer I say, that I do claim it "*upon the broad principle of justice arising from the fact that it is the fruit of common blood and common treasure."* And I do expect that Congress constituted as it is will recognise this principle of justice when the South presents an unbroken front, as it ought to do, against paying one dollar for the territories unless this justice is awarded to them; and you will here permit me to bring to your mind a reminiscence not inapplicable on the present occasion. When the annexation of Texas was at first started by Mr. Tyler, by a treaty which left this question of vital importance to the South unsettled, I opposed it. I was then bitterly assailed by the paper which you now conduct for opposition to this great Southern measure upon all occasions when I addressed the people of Georgia. In 1844, I declared that I was in favor of the annexation of Texas upon proper principles—but I was utterly opposed to the Tyler treaty for several reasons, the *main one of which was that the slave question was left open in it, the rights of the South were not secured by it,* and that I should never vote for any plan of annexation that did not settle this question in the compact of union and secure these rights in terms clearly and distinctly defined. This position I maintained in your own city, and if you will turn to the files of the Federal Union and examine an editorial of the first week in July, 1844, I think you will see that this position of mine was alluded to and it was denounced as amounting to a total opposition to the whole measure and it was said (I quote from memory) that I *was insisting upon what never could be obtained.* But I had taken my position firmly, not to be deterred by any *fears* or *alarms* or *denunciations.* And from that position and its success a profitable lesson may now be learnt. I made a speech in Congress when a plan for annexation similar to the Tyler treaty was offered, in which I maintained the same position and stated the only grounds upon which I should vote for annexation. They were the same grounds which I had advocated throughout 1844. Seven Southern Whigs stood by me—we held the balance of power in the House. And when all other plans offered (and there were a number) failed (neither of which secured the rights of the South), then Mr. Brown (after conference with me and others) offered his with the Missouri Compromise in it; and that passed by my vote and the other seven Whigs, and it could not have passed in the Committee of the Whole House without our votes, as the proceedings of the House will show. The firm and inflexible course I and seven other Southern Whigs took upon that question *secured the rights of the South and obtained the establishment of the Missouri Compromise,* which it was said by the Federal Union could never be obtained. And if a similar course shall be taken and maintained by all parties at the South, the same Compromise or one as good can be obtained again. I have taken the same stand now and I intend to maintain it in defiance of all assaults and denunciations that may be made against me from any and every quarter.

The sixth and last of your enquiries, is as follows: VI. If you should be of opinion that we have the constitutional right to carry our slaves into these territories, would you sooner risk the recognition and vindication of that right before Congress where there is a decided majority in both branches against us, or before the Supreme Court where it is well known that a majority of the Bench are from slaveholding States?

We are aware, that you deprecate in very strong terms any reference to the complexion of the Supreme Court upon this subject. Tour deprecation may be the result of a sentiment which we by no means condemn. Yet we do not agree with you in its application in this instance. The South are in a minority, we fear a doomed minority, on this subject, and we are therefore disposed to vindicate our rights by all honorable means. We certainly should not refuse to accept justice because the tribunal to whom we apply are supposed to be favorable to our cause. With all deference to your views on this point, we must be indulged in the belief that your indignation savors more of transcendentalism than of sound, practical statesmanship.

To this I answer that I consider the reference of this subject to the Supreme Court as a total abandonment of the question by the South. According to repeated decisions of that court upon the principles involved in it, I cannot see how any man can look upon it in any other light. But I will here say, that I am opposed to referring any political question to that court. And as a Representative in Congress, as long as I shall have the honor of remaining there, I shall never avoid responsibility by turning any question over to the Supreme Court or any other body. I shall, as I have heretofore done, maintain the equal and just rights of my constituents upon all questions; and I shall demand that they be clearly and distinctly recognised by Congress, that they may be amply *protected* by all others before whom they may come for action; and when these rights are left to the courts to determine, by my sanction they shall be so clearly set forth and defined that the courts *shall be bound to protect them, in their decisions.* And I say to you and the people of the 7th. Congressional District, that I shall never return as your and their Representative and tell them I have *secured their* rights by getting an act passed which will enable them to carry their slaves to California and New Mexico to encounter a law suit whenever they get there, which will cost more than their slaves are worth. If I can never get a better compromise for them than such an one as that, I shall never agree to any at all. They have that right independently of any thing I can do for them, and that is a right which no act of Congress can deprive them of.

George Fries 1 To Howell Cobb. E. Hanoverton, Ohio, *Sept. 4th '45.*

My Dear Sir: When we parted at Washington I promised to write as soon as I had looked over the whole field in Ohio and scanned well our political prospects. I have been home two weeks and have spent near all that time in traveling over my district, and, in company with Col. Weller, over part of the Western Reserve. On my way home I passed through the Reserve from Cleveland, and then saw clearly that the Taylor party *there* was " among the things that were." Since then, Root, Giddings and Crowell have been renominated (I may be mistaken as to the latter)—all anti-Taylor men. Indeed all the strong Whigs on the Reserve are out against Taylor. Among democrats, in that section of the state, there is very little defection. I attended with Weller immense massmeetings last week at New Lisbon, Youngstown, Carrollton and Steubenville.

Youngstown is on the Reserve. I have never seen but one as large a meeting in my life. The best men of our party were there, and assured us that, whilst Van Burenism was eating out the vitals of Whiggery, it would take it as long to fatten on what it gets off democracy as it would have required those asses to have fattened that are said in the good old Book to have " snuffed up the East wind." The truth is, the democracy in that quarter have been whipped long enough to stand up to anything.

In my district—where Tappan resides—we have some trouble, but much less than the Whigs. From present appearance I think Van Buren will take off five to ten Whigs to one democrat. So will it be in the whole southern, southwestern, N. W., and southeastern part of the state. Take it all in all then, I am happy to say that i Member of Congress from Ohio, 1845-1849.

we are all as sanguine of success for Cass in this state as we are that the sun will rise and set. If you or your Southern friends have a doubt of Ohio, lay it aside. All's well, rest assured of that.

Of Weller's prospects let me say a word. If *all* the factions that have heretofore opposed us should unite on Ford, he will be elected. This I think they cannot do. So Weller thinks; and all appearances now indicate that Ford's prospects are daily declining. He has thus far not *dared* to define his position. Let him do that, either for Taylor or Van Buren, and his game is up. As he now stands both factions doubt him, and from both will there be a loss. The few Van Buren democrats will go Weller. So much for Ohio. How stands Georgia? Will you be sure to carry her for Cass? And what is the state of feeling and prospects of success in the whole South? I trust you will write as soon as possible and state *to me* what we may look for with certainty. There are some here who fear the South.

I had a glorious trip home. Mr. Turner and family were in company to Cleveland, both in good health and both speaking very frequently of you, your wife and sister in terms that showed clearly that they remembered you all with friendly and grateful hearts.

I hope you'll remember me to your sister, and say that I regretted very much not having had time to call before my departure, to bid her good-bye. I hope we shall see you all next winter.

Ausburn Birds All 1 To Howell Cobb. E.

Binghamton, N. Y., *Sept. 8th, 184S.* Dear Sir: I sent you by yesterday's mail, a copy of the Albany Evening Journal, the leading whig paper in this State, in which you will find a full endorsement of the platform laid down at Buffalo *as the old Whig platform.* I send you herewith to-day a printed circular recently issued by the Whig State Central Committee, which is now being circulated throughout the State. I can vouch for its genuineness. The Whigs and Barnburners seem to vie with each other in the present crusade against the South. The Democratic party which supports Cass and Butler are the only advocates of a strict adherence to the Constitution and its compromises to be found in the North. Can it be possible that in such a contest the South will fail to stand by the Constitution, its own interests, and by its Northern friends? I will not permit myself to doubt that it will be found equal to the emergency. The idea is strange to us indeed, that Southern votes are to be given to aid sectional disorganizers and disunionists. It cannot—it ought not to be so. He that does not *protect* as well as provide for his own household is truly worse than an infidel.

1 Member of Congress from New York, 1847-1849.

Richard French 1 To Howell Cobb. E.

Mount Sterling, Ky., *Septr. 10th 1848.*

Dear Sir: As Kentucky is to go for General Taylor in November next, I feel anxious to know what Georgia and the other Southern States, particularly South Carolina and Florida, will do. I think you can decide for Georgia, and give the reason for the hope that is in you for the others. In my quarter of the Union, Kentucky excepted, prospects for Cass and Butler are good.

The slave question in Ky. has taken deeper hold and awakens more concern than usual. Many I think regard the crisis as at the door—but I fear, notwithstanding, the Whigs have their hearts so zealously set upon *availability,* that even *that* question will not controul them. How does Mr. Stephens prosper under his motion and vote to lay the compromise Bill on the Table? Knowing Members of Congress abhor long letters, I withhold much that I might say. Congratulating you upon your safe return home and tendering to you my ardent desire for your return to Congress, I remain as ever.

George S. Houston 2 To Howell Cobb. E.

Athens ala., *23d Septr., 1848.* My Dear Sir: I have not recd. a copy or no. of the Union since I left Washington altho I ordered it and have since written for it. I am therefore behind the news. In truth, we have so little political excitement here that we speakers are passing round to the Courts and have even quit speaking. They have so entirely given up Ala., that they make no fight, and of course we can't keep it up. I have not found one solitary de-

mocrat who is going to vote for Taylor. My information from Ohio, Michigan, Ill., Inda., Iowa, Wiscn., is that the "*free soil*" movement will injure the whigs more than it will us, and that we are certain of all of those States. N. York is gone—without hope. Maine and N. Hampshire are all of the New England states we need expect, tho R. M. McLane writes me that he thinks our chance decidedly the best for Maryland, N. Jersey and Delaware. How is Georgia about *these times?* ... I notice that Cone used up Stephens. I fear that may injure us in yr. State. What say you? Will it do so? They are trying to make a martyr of Stephens. They tried to get up some feeling here, but we soon killed it off. I have only made a speech or two since I came home. Mrs. Houston's health is so bad I can't leave home, and I fear I will not be able to do so any at all before the election. What is your news from Florida and Louisiana? Have you any? Have you any fear of Pennsylvania? Tennessee is very doubtful—no doubt of it. But I think it will vote for Taylor.
1 Member of Congr5mom Kentucky, 1835-1837, 1843-1845, and 1847-1840. Member of Congress iron Alahama, 1841-1849, and 1851-1861.

Alexander H. Stephens To John J. Crittenden.1 L. C.

Crawfordville, Ga.,, *26, Sep. 1848.*
Dear Snt: I reached home a few days ago and found your kind letter, for which I felt truly obliged to you. You have doubtless heard of the occurrence2 which put me out of the canvass in this state for three weeks past and upwards. I am now recovering slowly. My right hand is still in bad condition and I fear I shall never be able to use it as formerly. I now can only scribble with my left hand—but enough of this. Our election for Congress comes off next Monday and trust we shall send you a good report. The Democrats however are making a most desperate fight. But I think you may rely on Georgia for Taylor. It is true I can't form so satisfactory an opinion as if I had been in the field for the last few weeks. But I know we were gaining fast when I was amongst them. The whole campaign since then has rested entirely upon the shoulders of Mr. Toombs, and I assure you he has done gallant service. The *real Clay* men here as elsewhere I believe are doing nothing for Taylor, while many of them are openly in opposition; but I think we shall triumph notwithstanding.

We were greatly rejoiced to hear of your great triumph in Kentucky. The Locos in Congress were making extravagant brags just before the election but I would not permit myself even to feel apprehension. Remember me kindly to Mrs. Crittenden. I cannot say more now and I fear that you cannot read what I have said.

Robert Toombs To John J. Crittenden. L. C.

Washington, Ga., *Sept. 27th, 1848.*
Dear Snt: Upon reaching home two nights since after an absence of three weeks, I found your letter of the 2nd inst. It gave me real pleasure to find that you corroborated some of the good accounts I had received from the West, especially from Ohio. We are in the midst of a bitter fight among editors and candidates; but there is so little excitement among the people that one can hardly tell which way the current is moving. You have doubtless seen that Stephens was cut down by a cowardly assassin on the 3rd inst. He is yet unable to get out. His invaluable services have been thus far wholly lost in the campaign, which has thrown double duty on me. I have not been at home but four days since I arrived in Georgia. Stephens is getting well slowly—the muscles connecting the thumb and forefinger of his right hand were cut asunder and the wound extended down to the junction of the two. This is now his most serious wound, those on the body being nearly well and doing well. His physi 1 United States Senator from Kentucky, Attorney-General, etc.
Assault upon Stephens by F. H. Cone at Atlanta, Ga., Sept. 3, in which Stephens's right band was severely injured, cians are still under some apprehension that he will have to lose the hand to escape lockjaw, tho' the chances of such a calamity are daily lessening, and I hope all may yet be well with him.

The Democrats here are fighting for existence, and fight with a determination I never before witnessed. They refrain from opposing Taylor in any way, but furiously denounce Fillmore all the time. We were turning the tide very well on to him until that infernal letter of 1838 to the abolitionists was dug up. That has fallen upon us like a wet blankett and has very much injured us in the State. It gave an excuse to all Democrats who wanted to go back to their party to abandon Taylor. Our election takes place next Monday for Members of Congress—I feel confident of our carrying five—I think the chances with us for six Members out of the eight. We shall carry the state I think *certainly* for Taylor, but by a *hard, close* vote. But it will be done. The Congressional election I think will show between 500 and 1000 votes in our favour which will settle the matter for Old Zach by between 2,000 and 4,000 votes. We can lose the popular vote on Members of Congress by 1,000 and carry the State, tho' that would make it a desperate conflict. The Clay men in the State will do nothing; some of them would be glad to lose it with the hope of breaking down Stephens and myself in the State. They will lessen my vote in my district some two or three hundred unless I can get them from the Democrats. I think I shall do so. Had not Mr. Clay put himself up there would not have been even a contest in Georgia, the friends of Clay being the only men here who ever dared to attack Taylor. But I will no longer fatigue you with speculations or facts on our State politics. You may set this state down *safe* and *certain* for Taylor, in my judgment.

Florida I still hear is safe, not much dispute about it I think. Alabama is in a perfect turmoil—we have gained more leading respectable Democrats in that State than in any other in the Union. They count pretty confidently on carrying their State and the Democrats greatly fear it. But after witnessing the power of party drill in Georgia, I must confess I have but small hope of overcoming their large majority in that State. I think Carolina will go for Cass. Calhoun, Burt and Woodard and Simpson profess neutrality!! What miserable creatures! I think the solution of all this is that Calhoun found all the upper part of the State strongly against him and was afraid to risk an avowal for Old Zach; but, thank God, the contest will make a party in the State. Charleston is with us by a large majority, and will return Holmes,1 who stands firm for Taylor. In many other districts there are warm contests going on, but the Mercury having been forced to come out for "the equivocating betrayer of Southern rights" I take to be pretty conclusive evidence 1 As Member of Congress.

of how the State will go. Calhoun stands off too, in order to make a Southern party "all his own" on slavery in the new Territories. Poor old dotard, to suppose he could get a party now on any terms!! Hereafter treachery itself will not trust him. I hear nothing from Mississippi—definite. Louisiana I think altogether safe. My accounts from Tennessee agree with yours, tho' our friends there will have a harder fight than they expected. Your election greatly disheartened me,—I knew if the Democracy could so thoroughly rally against you in Kentucky we should have rough work everywhere; and all the subsequent elections have strengthened that conviction. If we are safe in Ohio we shall elect Taylor, but if we lose Ohio I much fear the result.

I suppose after the New York flare up we shall have no more of the "Sage of Ashland." I think no man in the nation is now so heartily and justly despised by the Whig party in the Union as Mr. Clay, and I doubt not but that the feeling is heartily reciprocated by him. Upon the whole, tho' our prospects are not so good as I had hoped and expected, still I firmly believe we shall succeed in electing Genl. Taylor. Every day of my own time shall be given to that object until the sun goes down on the 7th Nov. If we succeed handsomely in Georgia next week it will greatly improve Taylor stock in the South, and I now believe we shall. I will write you next week. I shall be able to tell before you could learn thro' the newspapers and will write or telegraff you as soon as I have sufficient information to know all about it.

Mrs. Toombs and the girls are at home and very well. She complains a good deal at my absence but she is becoming herself warmly enlisted for " Old Zach." She sends her best love to Mrs. Crittenden and yourself, and says her greatest interest in the success of Genl. Taylor arises from the hope that she may then again have the pleasure of meeting you all in Washington. Lou and Sally send love to both of you. My kindest regards to Mrs. C. Hoping I shall be able to send you cheering news next week.

P. S.—I find talking politics to two or three gentlemen and writing you a letter at the same time "a mixed up" business, as I fear you will find on reading it. Write me the first pieces of good news you hear.

Al/FRED IVERSON 1 TO HOWELL COBB. E.

Columbus ga., *Oct. 17, '48.* Dr. Sir: We are much mortified at the result of the late election in the 2d Dist. I will not stop to explain the causes; but say what is more important, that we shall make the most powerful effort that the 'Democratic Congressman from Georgia. 1817-1849, judge of the superior court of Georgia (Chattahoochee circuit), 1849-1853, United States Senator, 1855-1861, brigadier-general in the Confederate army. 73566—13 9 party has ever made to increase it in November. I think the whole district is roused up and are at work and will continue to the end. In this county we shall send our strongest men into every district and ride from house to house the week before the election and see every Democrat and arrange to bring out every one to the polls. We are also writing to our leading men in the other counties and sending out missionaries. Maj. Howard starts next week to Irwin and will remain until after the election, and will visit Lowndes, Ware, Appling and Telfair also. A company are also to go out from Albany to the same region. I think we shall swell our majority in the dist. from 100 to 200 over Wellborn's1 vote.

There is more defection in our ranks than I or anyone supposed a month ago, but nevertheless things are getting better, and most of the recusants will come back or not vote at all.

We cannot but consider the State as doubtful, however, and unless the most powerful exertions are made, we shall lose it. Had you not better go up to Lumpkin and Union a week before the election and traverse the country and aid in bringing out the full vote? These counties did not do well in Oct. They ought to do better by at least 100 votes in Nov. The 5th Dist. did not do as well as I expected. Cass and Murray ought to have given 300 larger majority, and Paulding should have done better. We hope for 3,500 in Novr., in that District, and if our leading men *work* they will give it. We shall do a little better in the 3d and 7th, and probably fall off some in the 4th and also in the 1st. The result in Pennsylvania makes things look a little squally, and the vote of Georgia may decide the election. We shall carry Ohio, but Georgia will be needed to make an election. Let us make a desperate effort to carry it. I should like to hear from you.

James F. Cooper To Howell Cobb. E.

Dahlonega ga., *Octo./20/48.* My Dear Sir: The great Whig barbecue has come and gone, and some Democrats are left yet to tell the tale. I will not venture to estimate the numbers. Without much trouble however I could give the *names* of all the visitors. The Whigs are no doubt much mortified. After circulating Hand Bills far and wide, riding, drumming, coaxing, etc. , they succeeded in getting together a crowd altogether smaller than wd. assemble at 24 hours notice that Colquitt wd. speak. The orators were Berrien, Hull, and our old semper parati Peeples, and Underwood. Gen. Clinch was the chairman and, it is said, *really made a speech!* Our County of Lumpkin, I believe, is entitled to the honor of drawing out the maiden speech from this veteran of Whiggery.

i Marshall J. Wellborn, Democratic Member of Congress from Georgia, 1849-1851.

The Whigs accuse us of keeping back the "cracked-heel" Democracy from their meeting. The "sore-eyed" fellows were not there, it is true, but some staunch Democrats from each of our sixteen election districts were present and we improved the opportunity of supplying each district with tickets. We have succeeded in furnishing every point in Lumpkin and Union with a full supply of Cass and Butler tickets, and we have the assurance that every Democratic voter will be seen by our committee men between now and the 7th November, and that all will be at the polls. This Whig powwow has not only facilitated our organization and *equipment,* but it will also operate to awaken the suspicions of our forces. and they will be out to a man.

The 5th and 6th Districts will give a majority of 6,000 votes— can the Whigs ever ride with that" load of poles "?

Never have I seen our Democracy more united and determined. Every hour since the October election has added new vigor and energy to our ranks. I could not have believed that one month could work such a change. The days of '44 are upon us here again, without perhaps as much excitement but with more organization and sterner determination to do our whole duty.

The vote of Georgia for Cass and Butler is as sure as any future event unless some untoward events happen to the Democracy of Middle and Lower Georgia, for I assure you that the estimate of 6.000 majority is based upon probable and reliable data....

Gilmer will be the banner county. In October she voted only 700 votes and gave 420 majority. She can easily vote 12 or 1,-300 and her majority will be proportional.

George S. Houston To Howell, Cobb. E.

Athens, ala., *23d Octr., 1848.* My Dear Sir: What the *diel* have you been about? Why have you let the Whigs gain so in Geo.? We have many accounts here as to the vote of Geo. The one now most relied upon is that we have a majority of 264 in the popular vote, and that " *aint much no how?* But to be serious, I am uneasy now for the first time. The news here is that we have Geo. by 264 votes, the Whigs have Penna., by near 5,000, and Florida by something, leaving Ohio doubtful in this election. Well, I think we will get Ohio and probably your State. What do you think of it yourself? I suppose the difficulty between Judge Cone and Stephens injured us some votes, probably a good many. Not that I think Cone was in fault, for I don't know who is in fault; but for the reason that Cone is a large man and Stephens a weakly man, and Cone used a knife. I may be wrong, but these are my own suppositions, so I count upon the votes of Geo. Florida I never claimed. I am greatly at a loss to account for the vote of Penna. Our friends there assured me in the strongest terms that we were certain of Penna., and continued to do so up to within a few days of the election. I hope we have yet carried our *Governor,* but I judge not. I yet claim the state for Cass and B., and without it we will find it very difficult indeed to elect our men. I have always set Geo. down as doubtful; and with Penna., I gave C. and Butler 153 votes, seven over an election. Take off Penna. 26 and we have 127, lacking 19 of a majority. Geo. 10, (do you say so?) and then we must get 9 more, and one chance to do it is in Maryland, Del., N. J., Connt., Tennessee, La., and probably Florida. Give me your views fully. The Whigs here are in some spirits lately, and offering to bet. I could get bets here that Taylor will be elected. The Whigs will bet on Taylor. There is no excitement at all in Ala. Our majority in this state will be from 7,000 to 10,000, we Demos. think.

Thomas D. Harris1 To Howell Cobb. E.

Washington D. C., *Oct. 29th, 1848.*

Dear Col., I thank you for the several letters which you have been kind enough to write me in reference to the prospect in Georgia. I hope the 7th of November may find her on the side of democracy and the country. I should have no doubt of it were it not for the military glory of old Taylor which I somewhat fear may dazzle a sufficient number of soft customers to carry the day.

If we are to lose the State of Pennsylvania it will simply be because we have not democrats enough in the State to prevent it. I think I may safely say that I now *know* our friends are at work in good earnest in the good old commonwealth. The defaulting Democrats at the last election, with all others who are lukewarm, are being visited by Committees appointed for that purpose to the end that all may be brought to the polls. The idea is an admirable one and if properly executed must tell powerfully in our favor.

In reference to Wilmot's dist. and other infected portions of the state, I had hoped to be specially advised before this time. Perhaps I may receive a letter tomorrow or next day. If so I will send it to you. In the meantime you would doubtless like to have such information as we have from that dist. Birdsall and Dickinson are both at this time in that part of the state, the first of whom as I understand has written to Washington that Wilmot makes no active opposition to Cass, and that if he does anything against him it is done very quietly. He thinks he will permit his people to vote as they please, and expresses the opinion that the dist. will give an increased majority in November on Longstreth. I do not know Mr. B., but learn that he is quite a politician and a shrewd calculator.

1 A member of the clerical staff of the United States House of Representatives, a devoted friend of Howell Cobb.

It is said moreover that Judge Thompson writes from the Erie district that Cass will carry the State by 10,000. Job Mann writes that we shall carry the state if we are active, and adds that *we are active.*

In short, sir, every democrat hereabouts feels and believes that the State will be ours as sure as the 7th of November rolls around and if it goes against us all be wretchedly disappointed a second time.

I wrote to Holden the other day, of N. C. Standard, to know the prospects in the old North State, and reed. in reply a most unexpectedly encouraging letter. He says the free-soil movement there will greatly distract the Whig party, which taken in connexion with the great activity of the democratic party affords a well grounded hope for carrying the State for Cass and Butler.

In reference to Ohio, it is generally conceded that Cass must carry it against any and all combinations.

N. Jersey we hope and believe will go with us. At all events the Whigs there are dreadfully scared and the democrats are in fine spirits.

Tennessee it is said is sure for Cass and Butler. I *know* this is the opinion of old Cave Johnson and I hear also that the President thinks with him.

Louisiana,—La Sere writes Wm. I. Brown very recently that Cass and Butler will carry that state without any sort of difficulty. He speaks of it as not at all doubtful. So you see we hear comfortable news on all sides. I pray the result may not show that our friends were to sanguine. In reference to myself, I think I should be entirely confident if I could be quite sure the people wouldn't turn fools on account of old Leatherhead's military fame.

Howell Cobb To A Committee Of Citizens In Charleston, S. C.1

Athens ga., *November ?,* Gentlemen: I have the honor to acknowledge the receipt of your circular, accompanied by the proceedings of the "Democratic Taylor Party" of Charleston on the first instant.

Flattered with this evidence of your confidence I cannot hesitate to express to you the feelings which the reception of your communication under the circumstances by which we are now surrounded has excited.

My attention having been called in your circular to the proceedings of your meeting, I have been induced to give it a somewhat critical examination. Whilst I find in that paper much to admire and approve, I must express my unfeigned regret that the able pen which 1 From an incomplete draft in the handwriting of Howell Cobb among the Erwin papers. claims its authorship has failed to trace the history of the interesting question which it discusses in many aspects in which it is our interest as well as our duty to consider it.

No truth is more plainly written in the political history of our country than the one which teaches us of the continued inroads which northern fanaticism has unceasingly attempted upon our peculiar institutions. Forgetful of the active and profitable part which their fathers took in the measures which led to the permanent establishment of domestic slavery in the South, a portion of the northern people have waged a relentless warfare upon our rights, interests and feelings. It has been conducted with an energy that never tires and marked with an enthusiasm that fanaticism alone can enkindle. However insignificant its first beginnings may have been, I agree with you in the opinion you have expressed that it has now reached a point which challenges our attention and demands our most serious consideration. That we may read in the history of the last few months the fact that there exists on the part of a large portion of the northern people a settled purpose to deny to us our constitutional right to an equal participation in the Mexican territory so recently purchased with our joint blood and treasure, no one will pretend to call in question. This determination so recently sealed with the most solemn testimonial known to our constitution and laws puts at rest all doubt and cavilling upon this point. The extent to which it may cause itself to be felt in the legislative department of the government only remains to be seen.

In now setting upon the proper policy to be pursued by the South for the further maintenance of her just and constitutional rights we must institute a more scrutinizing inquiry into the political associations by which we are surrounded than seems to have occupied the attention of those who prepared the preamble and resolutions adopted at your meeting. I do not flatter myself that I shall be enabled to furnish you with any new facts upon a subject which has so properly claimed your serious attention, but I cannot refrain from a brief reference to some which you have omitted in this connection and which according to my apprehensions deserve to be most deliberately considered.

The course which the two political parties of the North have pursued towards the South is widely different, and it becomes us as well in reference to the duty we owe to ourselves as to others to mark that difference. It may save us from a false step in an important and delicate duty, and in any contingency can be productive of no harm. I will not stop now to trace the history of the abolition question in the halls of Congress as connected with the reception of abolition petitions, nor can it be necessary to remind you, Gentlemen, that during that eventful struggle the records of Congress will be searched in vain for the vote of a single Northern Whig given in favor of the exclusion of these petitions; and yet they were excluded for years by the almost united votes of Southern representatives with the aid of Northern democratic votes. Would it not therefore be unjust to adopt the language so often used by Southern men that all the north of both parties are equally untrue and unsound upon the slavery question?

But we approach a practical test and one which bears upon the point of our investigation. The North threatens to exclude us from the newly acquired territories of New Mexico and California by the enforcement of the Wilmot proviso. How stand the parties at the

North upon this issue? Whilst a sufficient number of the Northern democrats both in the Senate and the House of Representatives have been found who in addition to the united Southern vote would defeat this measure so justly odious to us and thereby save the South from this gross aggression upon her rights, not a single Northern Whig in either branch of Congress has yet been produced who was willing to cast his vote in opposition to this measure of wrong and injustice. Does this fact speak no language of interest to the South? Was there nothing in it to command your consideration or awaken your sense of gratitude towards one portion of our Northern brethren whilst you complain with so much justice and propriety of the daring outrage sought to be done us by the other? Are friends and foes to be treated alike with indifference and scorn? Do we regard with the same feelings and emotions the men who have invoked all the powers of the General Government for our oppression and those who have with us declared that our peculiar institutions, whether in the states or territories, cannot be reached by any legislative act of the United States government?

For myself I have been disposed to regard with feelings of a vastly different character these two classes of Northern men. Taught by my experience and observation to look to the northern democracy whenever I sought for the friends of the South upon this important question beyond our own limits, I have watched their movements with an anxious interest and have as yet seen no cause to regret the confidence which I have been disposed to place in their professions of regard for our constitutional rights. When they consented and indeed urged the nomination of a distinguished citizen for the Presidency who had openly avowed his opposition to the Wilmot proviso I had indulged the hope that...

Robert Toombs To John J. Crittenden. L. C.

Atlanta, Ga., *Nov. 9th, 1848.* Dear Crittenden, The telegraff being out of order, you may get our glorious news by this before you receive it otherwise.

I am on my way to my plantation, having passed thro' the lower portion of the State last night.

The thing is settled, *Io triumphe,* Georgia will give Old Zach 2,000 majority. I have worked hard and feel amply rewarded—now "whatever sky is above me, I have a heart for every fate. "

I leave in five minutes for the West. John Forsyth 1 To Howell Cobb. E. Columbus, Geo., *Nov. 10th, 1848.*

Dear Sir: The disastrous defeat which the Democracy has just suffered makes it necessary for me to attempt to carry out a wish I have long cherished. It is to pursue my editorial profession in a field of wider influence and greater profit than can be attained in this nook of country. My preference is for Washington, the focus of political intelligence and influence, and my desire is to be connected with the organ of the Democracy in that city.

It has occurred to me that the egress of Mr. Hein from the Union office, or perhaps the declining years of the father of the press, Mr. Ritchie himself, might afford the opening I desire. Personally unacquainted with Mr. Ritchie and knowing that your relations with him are near if not intimate and confidential, I have taken the liberty of addressing you this letter to enquire, first if you can now give me the information I desire; or second if you cannot, to request you if you think proper, to make the necessary enquiries for me and pave the way for a correspondence with Washington on the subject.

Two years ago in Mexico my friend Col. H. R. Jackson and myself indulged ourselves in some dreamy plans and speculations of some joint and future arrangement of this sort. If your reply should lead me to hope that my hopes can be compassed I propose to invite him to embark with me in the undertaking.

A flood of terrible political news has been pouring in upon us with lightning speed since the great battle day. We are beaten at all points and have truly " lost all but our honor." My presages for the future looking to the country (not to party) are gloomy enough. I foresee that the South has to submit to the degradation by exclusion from a joint domain, or push resistance to the verge if not over the verge of revolution of the Government.

The Whigs in our streets are even now preparing excuses for Gen. Taylor, in the event that he "holds his hand " when "the Proviso" is presented to him. The *party* will uphold him in it. But enough of politics. We have both "supped full" of it, this week and you are ready to exclaim, *Parce, puer, jam satis!* 1A Democratic newspaper editor at Columbus, Ga.

James F. Cooper To Howell Cobb. E.

Dahlonega, Ga., *Nov. 11, 1848.* My Dear Sir: We have a few more returns,—

Gilmer 855 402 453 majority
Haberhsam 353 majority
Forsyth __. 119 majority
Union 235

The result is certainly as extraordinary as disastrous. Our calculations were based upon the well known fact that the people did not vote in October and that they certainly would vote in November. As to the turn out our expectations are fully realized, but hundreds of democrats have come to the polls only to vote against us. We were assured that there were no changes against us and we do not now know who have been the traitors. We know no democrat of standing who has voted for Taylor. Is it not extraordinary that so large a wing of the democratic party has deserted without a solitary leader at their head? The rank and file have rebelled by regiments, and yet we do not and never will know the individual traitors. We have been stabbed in the dark. Dr. Phillips was confident of a gain of 200 in Habersham. Chastain claimed more in Gilmer. Foster was equally confident of Forsyth. So were we all in Lumpkin. This wholesale defection is entirely unexpected and inexplicable. I can not even console you with an explanation other than the indisputable truth that very many Democrats have voted for Taylor.

Give my compliments to Bill Dearing and tell him that if I ever come to Athens, which I much doubt, we will discuss those oysters.

Mark A. Cooper1 To Howell Cobb. E.

Iron Works Geo., *20 Novr., 1848.* Dear Sir: It has been suggested to me recently by a gentleman of character coming from another State that the attention of Congress would again be invited to the subject of a national foundry South by the Chief of the Ordnance Department; and that by an earnest and early effort a bill may pass for such an establishment to be located by a Board of Ordnance Officers, leaving them the whole South to select in and every part of each State. Your active efforts will be all important at the start. We are willing to give every State and every place a chance, and at that think you may secure it for Georgia. She will be one of the first in the Union. Why not make her so in your time? What say you? Will you lay hold of it? Write me at your earliest convenience and oblige.

1 Congressman from Georgia, 1839-1843, proprietor of iron works near Rome, Georgia.

Howell Cobb To His Wife. E.

Washington City, *21st Dec, 1848.*

My Dear Wife, I was all packed and ready to start home tonight; but am prevented from carrying my intention into effect by the fact that today there was sprung upon the House the most important question which will be before us during the session. I allude to a motion to abolish the slave trade in the District of Columbia. Under the circumstances my friends say I must not leave, and I do not feel myself that I would be doing right to leave my seat at a moment when so important a question is pending. There is great excitement and it may continue for several days. As soon as this question is disposed of I shall start but it is impossible now to name a day.

I write in haste and in the midst of the excitement of the House.

John H. Lumpkin To Howell, Cobb. E.

Washington City, *25th Dec, 1848.* My Dear Friend, I have just returned from my dinner at the Irving Hotel. We had an excellent Christmas dinner, and my friend the Hon. A. H. Stephens fulfilled his engagement and dined with myself and Judge Iverson. He had called this day to see Mr. Calhoun with a view to determine on the time for the meeting of the committee on behalf of the Southern members. No time has up to this been agreed on. Stephens is chairman, but he says he intends to yield to the committee the right to elect their chairman. Clayton of Del., Chapman, Md., Bayley, Va., Venable of N. C, Calhoun of S. C, Cabell of Fla., King of Ala., Foote of Miss., Downs of La., Rusk of Texas, Sebastian of Arkansas, Achison, Mo. and Morehead of Kentucky and Gentry of Tennessee compose that committee. They are all men of calmness and deliberation, with the exception of Venable, Calhoun and Foote. I cannot tell you anything as to the probable course they may think proper to pursue.

Alexander H. Stephens, Probably To George W. Crawford.

L.C.

Ho. Of Reps., Washington, D. C, *Dec 27, 1848.* Dear Sir: Your letter of the 19th inst. (I believe) was duly received, and from the enclosed letters you will see that I have not forgotten the " Golphin claim " even in the midst of all the excitement the "Free-Soilers" and the factionists of the South have been able to get up about "Niggers"— and you will see that the same "official insolence" you met with still reigns in the Comptroller's office. I called on him as soon as I got over the fatigue of travel in getting here—and the rascal told me his report would be made the next week. After that week was out I addressed a note to Mr. Walker. His reply I send you. Yesterday I sent him another. Today I got the answer I send you. I shall today write to him and request him if he has any difficulty in deciding upon the report when made, to suspend his opinion until "old George" can have a hearing. I think the subject better be postponed for the incoming administration. And now for other matters. "Old Zac" will not be here until late in February, and he will not make any arrangements for a cabinet until he gets here. On this you may rely. Who will constitute his cabinet no one can even conjecture. But I think Georgia will be represented in it.

There has been a great effort here to break up his forces before he gets on the field. The scheme however will fail. The "freesoilers" and the Locos will do their best to effect it; but it will be as fruitless an attempt as their combined efforts to defeat his election....

Excuse my left hand writing.

Robert Toombs To John J. Crittenden. L. C.

Washington, D. C., *Jan. 3, 1849.*1 My Dear Sir: Since I wrote you last the surface of the political sea has looked calm and unruffled except the new Carolina movement;2 but in truth under the surface all is commotion and intrigue. This Southern movement is a bold strike to disorganize the Southern Whigs and either to destroy Genl. Taylor in advance or compel him to throw himself in the hands of a large section of the democracy at the South. The Southern Democracy are perfectly desperate. Their Northern allies, they clearly see, will unite with the Freesoilers; and even now the peace is broken between them forever. Almost every man of the Southern Democrats have joined Calhoun's movement. After mature consideration, we concluded to go into the meeting in order to control and crush it; it has been a delicate business but so far we have succeeded well and I think will be able to overthrow it completely on the 15th Inst.

The action of these Southern Democrats is based not on the conviction that Genl. T. can *not* settle our sectional difficulties, but that he *can* do it. They do not wish it settled,—" Hinc lachrymae ". The Northern Whigs have receded on the District of Columbia question, and will come square up to sound, safe ground on slavery in the

District. As to the cursed " Slave pens ",8 we will try to trade them off 1 Erroneously dated Dec. 3, 1848, in the original. The meeting alluded to at the end of the Brst paragraph occurred on Jan. 15, 1849. Cf. U. B. Phillips, "Life of Robert Toombs," pp. 60-63; J. F. Jameson, ed., " Correspondence of J. C. Calhoun," pp. 761, 762.

A movement, led by Calhoun, looking to the union of the South for the defense of Southern interests, regardless of Whig and Democratic affiliations. a This alludes to the proposed abolition of the slave-trade In the District of Columbia. to advantage. No honest man would regret their annihilation, if done rightly. The territorial question I think, this gold fever by drawing a large American population into California, will make more easy to adjust. Upon the whole I see nothing desperate in settling these legacies of Polk's administration unless we have treason in our own ranks. The temper of the North is good, and with kindness, and patronage skilfully adjusted, I think we can work out of present troubles, preserve the Union, and disappoint bad men and traitors.

We have the greatest solicitude about the course of Mr. Clay. He must be kept out of the Senate if Genl. Taylor's friends in your legislature are strong enough to do it. That he is deeply hostile to Genl. T. we have abundant evidence under his own hand. That he is determined to come here and to make a party of his own, and perhaps join the Free-soilers, I have very strongest reasons to believe. Indeed as far as Stephenson of Cinci. can be relied on as his exponent, / know. The details I am not at liberty to give—I may have it in a few days and will then again write you. Therefore Taylor's friends in Kentucky must prevent his election if possible. Clayton is thoroughly friendly to Genl. T's success, and I think Tom Corwin is too. He has been battered so in Ohio by the Free-soilers, he begins to hate them; besides, he must fight them for existence.

Webster is I fear deeply hostile, but all the rest of Massachusetts may be relied on, and I think the true policy is to set up a great man in Mass. over him by bringing Lawrence or some other fit person into the cabinett from that State. He will then be much more easily managed. He has acted very badly in Massachusetts. You see I am just thinking aloud in writing you, so as to give you the result of my observation and reflections on current events here. Nothing is developed, but everything in embryo.

Your son Col. Thomas is here. He has not yet finished his business but it promises well and I think will be adjusted to your satisfaction. Mrs. T. is well and sends her best love to Mrs. C. She says she will write to her soon. She desires to be kindly remembered to you. My best respects to Mrs. C. Write me when at leisure.

P. S.—We hear nothing from the Genl. except that he has called you to his service. You must not think of declining. The sentiment is universal here that it is of the first importance to the success of Genl. T's administration and to the country that you should come.

Robert Toombs To John J. Crittenden.1 L. C.

Washington, D. C, *Jany. 22, 1849.*
Dear Crittenden, We have been in a good deal of trouble here for the last month about this slavery question but I now believe we begin 1 Published once before In Mrs. Chapman Coleman, " Life of John J. Crittenden," I, 335, 336.
to see the light. I came here very anxious to settle the slavery question before the 4th. of March. The longer it remains on hand the worse it gets; and I am confident it will be harder to settle after than before the 4th. of March. We have therefore concluded to make a decided effort at it now. Preston1 will this morning move to make the territorial bills the special order for an early day, which will bring the subject before us. We shall then attempt to erect all of California and that portion of N. Mexico lying west of the Sierra Membres into a state as soon as she forms a constitution and asks it, which we think the present state of anarchy there will soon drive her to do. This will leave out a very narrow strip, not averaging more than 15 or 20 miles, between this California line and the Rio Grande line of Texas. This Texas line the Democrats are committed to, and some of our worst Northern Whigs (Corwin, etc.) say, if that line is established they will vote this slip with it to Texas. I think we can carry this, or something very like it. The principle I act upon is this: It cannot be a slave country; we have only the point of honor to save; this will save it, and rescue the country from all danger from agitation. The Southern Whigs are now nearly unanimous in favour of it, and will be wholly so before the vote is taken. We know nothing of Genl. Taylor's policy but we take it for granted he would be willing to any honorable settlement which would disembarrass his administration from the only question which threatens to weaken and distract it. If you see any objections to it, write me immediately; for we will keep ourselves in a situation to ease off if it is desirable to do so. I have a strong opinion in favour of its propriety and practicability, and with a perfect knowledge of the hopes, fears, cliques, and combinations of both parties, I do not hesitate to say now is the very best time to force it to a settlement.

We have completely foiled Calhoun in his miserable attempt to form a Southern party. We found a large number of our friends would go into the miserable contrivance and we all then determined it was best to go in and control if possible the movement. We had a regular flareup in the last meeting, and at the call of Calhoun I told them briefly what we were at. I told him that the Union of the South was neither possible nor desirable until we were ready to dissolve the Union; that we certainly did not intend to advise the people now to look anywhere else than to their own government for the *prevention* of apprehended evils; that we did not expect an administration which we had brought into power would do any act or permit any act to be done which it would become necessary for our safety to rebel at; and that we thought that the Southern opposition 1 William B. Preston, Member of Congress from Virginia, 1847-1849; Secretary of the Navy, 1849-1850. could not be sustained by their own friends in acting on such an hypothesis; and that we intended to stand by the government until it committed an overt act of aggression upon our rights, which neither we nor the country ever expected. We then by a vote of 42 to 44 voted to recommit his report (we had before this tried to kill it directly but failed). We hear the committee have whittled it down to a weak milk and water address to the whole Union. We are opposed to any address whatever, but the Democrats will probably outvote us tonight and put forth the one reported; but it will not get more than two or three Whig names. Col. Thomas is here and I am sorry to say has not succeeded as well as we expected; but I suppose he keeps you advised. Mrs. T. joins me in kindest regards to Mrs. C. and yourself. Don't think of not coming into the administration. There is but one opinion here as to its necessity.

William Hope Hull1 To Howell Cobb. E.

Athens ga., *J any. 26,1849*. Dear Howell, We are all knocking along here in the same old way. The Col.2 is still going it on the *resistance* string— but I don't think the party about here are at all disposed to dance to that tune. I never in my life saw as great a fuss got up by Congressmen and Editors with so little corresponding excitement among the people. I am perfectly annoyed by the course of our party press in Georgia. Holsey is the most moderate among them. Even the *Cassville Pioneer*, where I had hoped for better things, has run mad as well as the rest of them. I see in the Federal Union a long letter from somebody in Washington advising public meetings to be gotten up in all the counties in the State by way of showing a popular feeling. It will not be done in Clark, at least I think not. Is it not perfectly farcical that the people who own slaves should be perfectly quiet, and we who own none should be lashing ourselves into a rage about their wrongs and injuries?...

Hopkins Holsey To Howell Cobb. E.

Athens ga., *J any. 29th, 1849*. Dear Sir: I acknowledge the receipt of three letters from you detailing the proceedings of the several meetings of Southern members of Congress, the last of which was on the 22nd Inst. I sit down to write you in haste, barely throwing off a few suggestions. It is with regret that I observe the democratic party of the South divided as to the proper course of action. The object of those 1 A cousin of Howell Cobb, active In his political support.
Col. Hopkins Holsey, editor of the Southern Banner.
who are in favor of Mr. Calhoun's address1 is clearly to prepare the South for counteraction to the Wilmot Proviso in case Gen. Taylor should sign it. There cannot in the present state of things be any popular action upon it, for the very reason that the Whig masses believe Gen. Taylor will not sanction it. Any attempt to get up such action would defeat the object of those who sign the address. It will therefore be simply laid before the people as a note of preparation should the emergency arise. You are aware that my inclination is to meet that emergency with a determination that shall vindicate Southern rights. Such you have no doubt perceived is the course of the democratic party very generally, as indicated not only by the tone of all the Southern democratic journals as well as by the action of Virginia, S. Carolina, Florida, and perhaps N. Carolina. The tide has evidently taken that direction *from the force of the question,* and cannot be arrested. You will discover that, so far as *disorganization* of either party at the South is concerned, the "Whigs thus far are more disorganized at home than we are. It is evidently so in Virginia and North Carolina. The spring elections will shew it and be in our favor. In Florida, the vote being unanimous, the parties stand upon the same ground. If one is disorganized, the other is also. Let us look at it now in a general sense applied to the whole Union. If the Southern Whigs and Democrats take the same ground, both parties are disorganized or neither. If the democrats take resistance ground as a party and a portion of the whigs cooperate with them as is likely, they will be strong enough to hold out inducements to the Northern democracy to hold on, and advocate a compromise in the next Presidential contest. The disorganization of the democratic party can only take place in case the Southern Whigs in mass should take ground with Gen. Taylor should he sign the Proviso. The leaders may and probably will— even a large portion of the rank and file—but not enough to carry a single Southern state, provided the Southern democrats are united. If new parties are to be formed upon the strength of the question, then both parties will be disorganized and a reorganization of federal parties take place. I hope however that this may not occur. The Union of the democratic party South upon the Virginia resolutions2 1 This address to the Southern people, adopted at a meeting of Southern Senators and Representatives at Washington, Jan. 22, 1849, in spite of opposition by Toombs, Cobb, and others, urged the union of Southerners in resistance to Northern aggression, regardless of previous party ties. The address as published bore the names of 48 signers, all of whom were Democrats. The address is reprinted in Calhoun's " Works," VI, 290-313.

The resolutions here referred to were unanimously adopted by the Virginia legislature March 8, 1847, and reenacted with additions January 20, 1849. They read In part: "Resolved, That if... the fearful issue shall be forced upon the country, which must result from the adoption and attempted enforcement of the proviso aforesaid the Wilmot Proviso as an act of the general government, the people of Virginia can have no difficulty in choosing between the only alternatives that will then remain, of abject submission to aggression and outrage on the one hand, or determined resistance on the other, at all hazards and to the last extremity." Niles' Register, LXXV, 73; H. V. Ames, "State Documents on Federal Relations," pp. 244-246.

will sweep every thing before it in the South and induce our friends North to hold on. This is all they want—to see the South acting as one man. They will be with us in that event.

I however agree with you that an address should be put forth doing ample justice to the noble band at the North who have fought our battles.1 Perhaps such an address is fully as, if not more important than the other. Why not put forth two addresses at different periods, or modify the present address so as to do justice to our Northern friends, and impress upon the South the necessity of dissolving connection with Northern Whiggery. Perhaps the last course would be best, and *if so modified* I can not see the least objection to signing it, unless we are to succumb to Taylor and the Northern fanatics. If you cannot agree upon a modified address, could there not be an understanding that another shall soon be put forth by the *democrats alone,* shewing the position of parties North towards us, and the hopes we entertain if the South proves true to herself that they will settle the question at the proper time. If this agreement can be made we shall then be united, and every Southern Democratic member might then sign both addresses. I trust that our friends will either modify the address so that all can sign it, or enter into some arrangement that will secure unanimity. For my own part I cannot act with the Taylor and Fillmore "National party" on the Wilmot Proviso question unless it is in a way I do not expect will take place, viz., a compromise of the question and the preservation of our rights.

If Taylor should sign the Wilmot Proviso, this " National party" would be out beating up recruits. I cannot join them. I love the Union for its justice,—it is a beautiful idea in that dress; but I can not and will not bow down to a fanatical majority in Congress clothed with the garment of " the Union." I do not know your determination in the event Taylor and Fillmore should raise their "national party" banner to enforce the Proviso. I have given you mine very candidly. You see very clearly that the current is setting in the direction of my position. In conversation with Col. John Lamar a week or two since he agreed entirely with me. But we must not make a contingency the ground of separation even should it ever take place upon the happening of such contingency. I will frankly state what you already know, that our friends here are divided to some extent upon the course of action in the event to which I have alluded. The Union may prove too strong for the continuance of slavery. But I do not as yet see the sign. On the 1 To oppose the argument of the Calhoun address of Jan. 22, Howell Cobb and John H. Lumpkin, of Georgia, and Linn Boyd and Beverly L. Clarke, of Kentucky, all Democrats, issued an address to their constituents, Feb. 26, 1849, praising the loyalty of Northern Democrats toward Southern rights and contending that the maintenance of the nationwide Democratic party afforded the surest moans of securing Southern interests. contrary I see the reverse in the action of three southern states already if not four. I believe if their legislatures were all in session at this time their action would be the same as that of Virginia, etc., with but few exceptions. The question is disorganizing the whigs a great deal more than it is us. I dismiss all fears upon the subject of disorganization of the one party more than the other. If there should be any difference it would be in our favor provided the democrats will act harmoniously together. This we should do. Which wing of the two divisions at Washington springing out of the recent meeting should yield, if either must; the larger or the smaller? But I hope neither, for I think you might all act together by one of the plans above suggested unless you disagree as to final action in the contingency alluded to.

As to Gayle, much as I would prize a single Whig recruit in the cause of Southern rights, he should not be a stumbling block, a weight to sink the democratic ship. He should not be regarded in the necessity of a modified address that would unite the democratic party.

It will be a party address at any rate; and if it drives him off, *de minimis non curat.* There is not enough of the Whig element to prize it so highly on such an occasion. Finally, we must not be like the girl looking in the well, and go to crying if the baby should fall into the well.

Howell Cobb To His Wife. E.

Washington City, *1st Feb., 1849.* My Dear Wife.... I see from the Savannah Republican that the whig papers have commenced their war upon me and I suppose that the democratic press will soon follow suit. Well, I am prepared for it, and I do assure you that I never felt less solicitude about a personal result in my life. My own feelings are unaccountable to myself. I am unable to account for my indifference on any other principle than the unlimited approval which my conscience gives to everything I have done. Don't understand me as referring to the great question itself about which so much excitement exists; for on that point I do feel deeply anxious for the result and can see in the present state of things nothing to cheer the friends either of the South or the Union. In the whigs I have no confidence, from Genl. Taylor down to the lowest lackey of the crew, and as the democrats are now blindly following the erratic call of the madcap South Carolinian, God only knows what is to be the end of what we hardly yet see the beginning. But I will not annoy you with politics, though your familiarity with the debates may have whetted your appetite for this kind of food.... 73566— 13 10

Alexander H. Stephens To John J.

Crittenden. L. C.

Washington, D. C., *6 February, 1849.* Dear Sir: You must have patience and bear with me. Nothing but a full consciousness of the importance of the subject compels me to send you these lines. You must forego all objection, and take the head of General Taylor's cabinet. It is a matter about which you cannot hesitate—you owe it to him, to yourself, to your friends, and to the country. I tell you the " crisis" requires it. Those who took the responsibility of advocating the nomination and election of General Taylor must not *flinch* from the equal and perhaps greater responsibility of standing by and defending his administration. I am convinced that he will be most *desperately* assailed. The fact that he has been elected by the people without the aid of schemers and intriguers and without any pledge save to serve the country faithfully, having no friends to reward and no enemies to punish!! will of itself arouse a bitter hostility by a set of *leeches* who look upon the public offices as nothing but spoils for political hacks to revel on. But he will be much more bitterly, while perhaps more insidiously, assailed by one whom I need not name to you—I can not be mistaken—I never was deceived a second time by any man. And all that disappointment and envy and ambition and hate and *revenge* can actuate a malignant heart to do will be done by him in a reckless spirit of " Ruling or Ruining ". You must bear with me. I speak plainly—I know what is ahead—I shall not and do not here say anything to provoke hostilities from that quarter; but my instinct tells me to be ready for the fight. General Taylor has the confidence of the country—he deserves it—and I have no fears but he will maintain it. He got it, however, by *fighting* in the first instance, and he will maintain it the same way, though on a different field. And to meet the emergency his friends must stand firmly by him. Let what will come. Let the forces be 5 to 1—headed by the " great chief " of the tribe, every one of the Young Indians must do his duty. We must have no *Indiana militia* in the coming contest. You must therefore come—I do not solicit, or suggest or ask; I speak in language positive and absolute. For upon your decision in this matter depends more than you are aware of. *You must not refuse.* I write in haste, but not from my impulses.

Robert Toombs To John J. Crittenden. L. C.

Washington, D. C., *Feb. 9, 1849.*1 Dear Sir: Yesterday I reed your favour of the 1st inst. and hasten to say a word in reply to that part of it which was personal to myself.

1 Wrongly dated Jan. 9, 1849, in the original. Preston's bill, alluded to in this letter. was introduced on Feb. 7, 1849. Cf. "Congressional Globe," 30th Cong., 2d sess., p. 477; U. B. Phillips, "Life of Robert Toombs," p. 63.

Nothing could give me more pleasure than the appointment of Gov. Crawford to Genl. Taylor's cabinett; and it would give me increased pleasure if it were done in lieu of myself. I have known Crawford long and well; and there are but few abler and no purer men in America, and he has administrative qualities of an unusually high order. I have an unaffected repugnance to official station, and my interests harmonize with my inclinations in this respect. Politics with me is but an episode in life, not its business; and I assure you with perfect candour I have not an unaccomplished personal wish in that connexion. My apology for saying this in relation to myself is the tenor of your letter and desire to disembarass you wholly from any allusion to the subject to Genl. Taylor in connexion with my name. I have no feeling but gratification at his inclinations toward Gov. C, which is increased from a slight apprehension that he might be misled in another quarter in Georgia, which would have given me real pain and his friends in Georgia great, and I must add, just dissatisfaction.

Mr. Preston made his speech and proposed his bill on Tuesday. His speech was a very good one and its effect very happy. We shall carry the measure easily in the House. It meets with its bitterest opposition from Calhoun's tail and Giddings's. New England and New York want to hold off until next session. Their object is unmistabably to make themselves necessary to the adm. in carrying it, and demanding terms for their service. We shall bring them in I think, but if not we can carry it without them. The only difficulty is in the Senate. Webster, Benton and Calhoun and his tail are its great opponents there. The two first have no tail, and we are daily shortening that of the latter. Both parties are unanimous for the bill from Georgia (except Berrien); and we shall carry the majority of the Democratic party North and South, which will prevent any party injury. I consider the question for all practical purposes as now settled whatever may be its fate at this session.1

Col. T. is still here; his business is now prospering well. The Senate's Military Committee will report unanimously against the legality of the proceedings of the Court Martial, which I hear will be satisfactory to the President.

I have written you very hastily that it might go by the first mail after receiving yours. Julia is very well and sends her best regards to Mrs. C. and yourself. We both hope very much to see you and her before the 4th of March and leave you quietly installed.

1 Toombs's hopes for the success of the Preston plan of adjustment were soon dashed. By a vote of 91 to 87 in committee of the whole, Feb. 27, a proviso was attached to the bill, prohibiting slavery in the area of the proposed State; and when just afterwards the bill as amended was put upon its adoption, not a single vote was cast in its favor.

Hopkins Holsey To Howell Cobb. E.

Athens, Ga., *Feby. 13th, 1849.*

My Dear Friend, I received your letter in reply to mine by due course of mail and another favor from you by the mail of this morning. I shall communicate freely with you as you request, in regard to the present position of the democratic party. I find in your letter of reply that you supposed an allusion had been made by me to the possibility of your supporting the Taylor and Fillmore "National party" in the event of Taylor's signing the Wilmot restriction or any other obnoxious measure to our section of the country deeply involving our interests. Nothing was farther than this from my intention. The allusion was only to my own position, that I could never consent to join that party on such a question. I am gratified to find that you think and will act with me should Taylor dare to make himself the instrument of coercing us into these odious measures. I perceive the force of your position whilst looking alone to an adjustment by Congress. Your ground of observation is better than mine—but I cannot perceive the probability of an adjustment" that will or ought to be satisfactory to us either at this or the ensuing session of Congress. The last election has placed this question beyond any concession from the North. The democrats in that region have fought their last fight for us I fear, my friend. I do not blame them. They can not stand any longer on Southern ground. They have been betrayed by some and wantonly repudiated by others. As men they are obliged to yield to a storm, which the damning ingratitude of Southern Whigs have aided, to prostrate them into the very dust. The Northern Whigs have heaped insult and injury upon us, have never quailed in their crusade against our rights, and have compelled the majority of the Southern people to kiss the rod which smites them. When this lesson is taught by the past *where is the hope of the future?*

The difficulty now lies in the fact that neither party hereafter will court the South. The Northern democracy will not because both Van Buren and Cass have fallen victims to their Southern alliance. The Northern Whigs will not court where they have found they could subdue by an unyielding firmness. Could they now find the least inducement to yield and thus take the place of the Democrats there would be some hope of preserving our rights and the Union. A few aspirants to office may do it but the mass of the party never will. Again they have the fate of the Democrats before them and see that they may share the same fate. Under these circumstances I see not a single ray of hope. Gen. Taylor and his Southern friends will never join the Northern democracy as advised by Burke. He was right. It is the only way to save the Union.

A new state of things you will perceive has arisen out of the last election. The Northern Democrats, judging from passing events, are now becoming through the *necessity of the case* as strong in their anti-slavery position as the Whigs, if not more so. It is the natural result of the election, and nothing can change it but what I do not expect,—the total dissolution between the Northern and Southern Whigs. They must have that assurance and believe that the South will forever prove true to her Northern friends. But they can never get it; nay, it is almost if not entirely *too late* to give it. *The die is cast.* The result is melancholy, deplorable, damning to the Southern Whigs. But it is done; and all that we have to do now is to adapt ourselves to this new state of things. We are taught by it to prepare for the worst. The Southern address can not possibly get up any popular excitement. The Democrats of the South only can move. The Whigs you know will not budge whilst Taylor is in the clouds. The few attempts which have been made are failures. But it has had and will have the effect to make men take their positions in the event of Taylor being against the South. Look at Virginia and Florida, to say nothing of North and South Carolina. The Democratic party of the South is taking position in favor of bold measures. The tone of its press is conclusive and *without exception,* even in the mountains. You think Douglas's bill will pass. I do not think as it stands it will be acceptable to the Southern Democracy. It does not settle the territorial question. It may come up at the very next session. New Mexico is too large as made by the bill. It admits the Mexican population to vote. It is in fact a substantial yielding of the question by us and a practical triumph of the fanatics. The Southern people, you are aware, are now more sensitive than ever. They are not willing to give up the substance for the shadow.

They are wrought up, by the late movement in Congress, into a greater jealousy than ever of their rights. I speak of the slaveholding interest and those who are connected with it. There is an ultra feeling roused up in their bosoms which they did not feel before. They will not tolerate what they would and did before. If you tell them that Douglas's bill organizes the new territory into *States* and the principle of excluding them contended for by the restrictionists is not carried out, they will tell you that the whole population that is to decide the question is north of 36£ degrees, and that the North gets the whole territory as a matter of course. They would be willing for the population north of the line to decide the question for the territory north of the line but not for that south of it. Besides they will raise objections to naturalising and entitling to the rights of citizenship the Mexican mixed population; and all of this they will tell you consistently with their professions (before the election) that the people of the territories should decide the question for themselves. They will object to the *kind of people* made citizens by the bill in New Mexico. The feature of the bill which authorizes them to form a state constitution makes them so *per se.* Another objection they will raise consistently with the principle of self government avowed before the election, and that is that the territories if organized as such, or the States, particularly New Mexico, are too large; that they meant territories of the usual size and with a fair chance for introduction and settlement by them under the usual preliminary organization. They will say that so far as the principle of the bill is concerned the whole territory might as well have been organized into a state government with the population north of the Missouri line to exclude slavery south of it. They will look upon the restriction as *practically* carried by the bill and feel that the North has got all the territory by a mere manoeuvre. They will consider that a willingness on their part to yield to this practical usurpation of the whole would be construed into a craven desire to sneak behind a mere form in order to preserve their domestic institution in the states and that the North, encouraged by so plain an indication of surrender, will move on step by step to the emancipation of their slaves directly or indirectly in the States. The bill assumes that it is a mere point of honor for which the South is contending, and not for an actual bonafide participation in the territory. Be this as it may, the question is will even the point of honor or equality be saved by a practical surrender of the whole territory to the North. There would be no difficulty in adhering to Gen. Cass's principle of local self government if States or territories were formed south of the Missouri line as well as North of it.

I know that Douglas's bill is an administration measure and it is natural for the administration to desire its passage. But for the above reasons I do not think it will give satisfaction to the Southern democracy. I have heard an occasional expression to this effect from plain men among us.

Nothing short of a real, bona-fide, practical division of the territory in just proportions will stand the public judgment. I see not the least possibility of such a partition being made by the North in the state of mind into which it has been thrown by the results of the last election. The Northern Whigs see that they have friends in the South who will aid them in carrying out the restriction if it assumes the shape of law; they saw by the election that they had friends who would adhere to them in any extremity—in short that the South had quailed. The Northern democrats are obliged from that result to follow in the wake of their firmer opponents, if not to outstrip them in zeal. Man is but mortal and when conquered by the defection of allies to whom he turned in the last resort for aid, will yield to the storm, both from a desire of self preservation and from disgust at perfidy and ingratitude. These great principles in human action warn us to expect nothing from the North. I give up the Northern democracy as a sacrifice to their own noble bearing, a sacrifice by the blindness of some and the design of others among the Southern Whigs. My heart bleeds at the unavoidable separation, but my judgment pronounces the doom as unavoidable. We shall part as brethren sundered by a fiat which we could not avert. From the day of the election of Taylor and Fillmore this Union became divided into mere sectional parties and its existence endangered. We saw it before the election, we proclaimed it in solemn admonitions to the people in the canvass. You will recollect the eloquent appeals made by our friend Hope Hull upon this subject. I fear his prophecies are about to be realized. I have but little confidence now in the stability of the Union unless the South succumbs entirely to aggression. This she may do, but I do not think she will. The struggle will be great, but she will recover, although it may be by a small majority of the people at first.

And now, my dear friend, let me say to you that it is the force of the question that is sweeping the Democratic ranks at the South. Neither personal hatreds or attachments will have any effect. Men will ally on this question with their most bitter personal enemies and part with their best friends. Great questions always make new parties among men. If this does not, none other can. I feel gratified that there is not any radical difference between us. I am for no popular excitement at this time, because it would be not only unwise but impracticable. The address has and will produce none in the way of popular meetings or resolves, for the reasons before mentioned. But it has prepared the minds of men for the emergency which may arise. I rejoice to find you resolved should that emergency arise to act in concert with those who may defend the rights of the South. I infer this much from the first part of your letter in reply to mine, and only doubt it from the subsequent part in which you say you will not join either the Taylor and Fillmore "national party" or the Southern sectional party. I think you will find upon reflection that an intermediate course will be impracticable. There can be neither neutrality or a third party in such a contest. You will see that when the question of Union or disunion is made it will directly involve the question of slavery in the States and that the question of slavery made by the emergency will involve that of Union or disunion. As surely as the Wilmot restriction, in terms, is passed by Congress and signed by Taylor, the question of Union or disunion will come up. Those who side for the Union will admit that the institution of slavery is seriously endangered but that the Union ought to be stronger than the rights of the slaveholders. This view of the question is already taken by some of our friends as well as political opponents. When this ground is taken, emancipation will follow as a matter of course the triumph of the Union party. The question will be one of an appalling nature and will array men of both sides, who now act together, in the bitterest opposition. There can be no neutrality, no middle ground in such a contest.

You are aware that the natural tendency of party action is for the democrats to side against Gen. Taylor if he should sign the restriction. It is easy and natural. Although the same tendency exists with the Whigs to side with him, yet there is a countervailing principle of interest in the property involved which will drive all but the aspirants to office and weak minded men connected with the slave interest into opposition against him. Those considerations will give a large majority sooner or later to the party in opposition, as evidenced in all the Southern states which have yet taken action upon the subject.

Pray excuse this long and tedious letter. It has been dictated by the magnitude of the subject and the recollection of the cordial good feeling and pleasant intercourse between us. Nothing but the emergency spoken of can separate us; and I hope even that will be incompetent to the task.

Thomas W. Thomas To Howell Cobb. E.

Elberton ga., *Feb. 16th, 1849.* Dear Sir:... As one of your constituents I take great pleasure in saying I heartily approve of your course in relation to the Southern address, and you may always count on my approbation in any step against disunion. I am informed some of the democracy here would have preferred your signing the address; and I would not be surprised if some dissatisfaction did not exist here and in other parts of the district along the river where they are a little tainted with Calhounism. I have expressed my opinion of the address in a communication to the Constitutionalist which I send off with this. The article is signed Jackson, and you will find me in the breach along with you if you should get into trouble about withholding your signature....

Hopkins Holsey To Howell Cobb. E.

Athens, Ga., *Feby. 24th, 1849.*

My Dear Friend, I have sat down to answer your letter of the 18th inst. sooner, than I expected...

You express a doubt whether the exciting question which is now unfortunately dividing the democratic party will be adjusted at the present session of Congress. You will observe my friend how they correspond precisely with my anticipations expressed in previous letters.

I fear that you will find this adjustment ever at hand and still fleeing before you. My apprehensions are built upon the nature of man and the passions and interests which are the great springs of his action. Appearances may for a while indicate that they will not perform their usual functions, but their final operation is as certain as that of any of the known and fixed laws in physics. My views of the springs of human action tell me that the Northern democracy have fought their last battle for our constitutional rights. They are but *men,* noble specimens I grant you, and must yield to the storm. I have no recrimination for them—on the contrary, nothing but love and admiration. My heart bleeds at the unavoidable separation. If ever this Union should be destined to be rent asunder the guilt will not be upon their heads. If civil blood should flow, not one drop of theirs should ever be shed by a southern man. *Democracy* alone should be the shibboleth that should pass them unharmed through the strife. But we do not differ about their former position. The only question is as to the future. Although I behold rare examples of magnanimity in a portion of them who still adhere to their ancient ground, I must believe that the Democratic masses cannot and will not follow them. They are noble instances of self sacrifice upon the altar of country. They immortalize those who make the sacrifice. *Charles Brown!1* What a noble, what a wonderful man! I thank you for his speech. It is enough of itself to sever the unhallowed union between the Southern and Northern Whigs. But blindness, fatal blindness is both the error and the crime of the larger portion of the Southern people. Many cannot, and many will not see! It is to be hoped that Gen. *Cass* will exhibit a similar example of self immolation. It will not only gain him the brightest laurel that ever adorned his brow but may do much towards arresting the menacing tendency of things in the North and staying the march to a dissolution of the Union. But on this point my hopes are not bright I must confess. Nothing but an assurance that the South will hereafter be true to herself, and of course to the Northern democracy, can ever repair the blow inflicted by the last election. I do not believe that as rational men they will ever feel conscious of this assurance. As long as Southern whiggery adheres to her fatal Northern connections a doubt will hang over the Northern democracy as to the firmness of the South; and doubt on this question is fatal. If I could suppose for a moment that it was possible for the Southern Whigs to "march 1 Charles Brown, a Democratic Congressman from Pennsylvania, had delivered a speech In the House, Feb. 3, 1849, on abolition and slavery, In reply to Richard W. Thompson of Indiana. Appendix to "Congressional Globe," 30th Cong., 2d seas., pp. 114-120.

straight over to the democratic party," as Burke so forcibly put it, I should have hope both for the security of our rights and the integrity of the Union. This is a *sina qua non* which looks morally impossible, and with its failure a cloud hangs like a pall upon the Union. It is needless to tell *you* my devotion to this Union. It has been if possible a passion, something beyond the mere calculations of judgment. I am devoted to it still as a bond of justice and fraternal love. Its wreck would be the greatest calamity which ever befel our race. But believe me when I say to you that I have lost faith in its continuance much longer. The question which threatens it is the *only* one which can endanger it. *That may,* and I fear will dissolve it at no distant day. I do not fear it alone from the present aspect of the question, although much may depend upon its adjustment. I believe if the South now falters the least, if she takes any thing short of *real, practical reciprocity,* she will indicate a feeling that will bring upon her in no very short time increased aggression and final ruin. The fanatics are watching us closely. If we quail, we are inevitably doomed. It is this particular juncture which imparts a peculiar delicacy to the least surrender.

Douglas's bill will not suit the present state of the public mind in the South; Preston's is worse. The principle of self government recognized by us in the canvass will not be acknowledged to extend to any other than territories or states of the usual size and in the ordinary mode of organization. Both bills are founded upon a mere quibble.

If we are so weak that we must be satisfied with it, then be it so. But it will be a fatal indication. You misapprehend me when you suppose I am for " sectional party " as a remedy. I think we are forced by circumstances which are beyond our control to assume bold ground, say of defence, or separation in the last resort. I look only to the consummation of the aggressive measures pending, alone to the emergency. All my views upon this subject depend upon that contingency. They rest as you know upon a condition. You will not look at the possibility of the happening of the contingency. I look at it as not only possible but probable. And now my dear friend let me say to you that men and leaders are nothing in this matter. It is the strength of the question alone which is bearing down every thing before it in the Southern states. You know that Calhoun is no favorite with me. He is not even guiltless in producing this crisis. But extremes are destined to act together on this question. We will not *follow* Calhoun, but must cooperate with him in resisting the encroachment. In short you will find that a large portion of the Southern Whigs themselves will finally come into the resistance movement. *Toombs* is pledged to it in the emergency and *Stephens* even has recently warned the House that the South will not submit. What now says the address which you could not find it consistent with your judgment to subscribe? I fear that between Toombs and Stephens on the one hand and your South Carolina friends on the other you will occupy a position which however it may coincide with your judgment will be regretted by many of your most devoted friends... The first thing you will see is that if they cannot take Taylor away from their Northern allies on the question of slavery, they will be acting in concert with Calhoun. Finally you cannot be insensible of the fact that the Virginia and Florida ground is sweeping the South by an overwhelming majority. The tide is irresistible.

Alexander H. Stephens To George W. Crawford. L. C.

Crawfordville, Ga., *Mch. 2, 1849.*

Dear Crawford, When I saw you in Augusta I expected and intended to write to you long before this time. But I had hardly got home before I was hurried off to Gwinnett Court to attend a case for our Sheriff of great importance to him, and I was detained there all the week. Yesterday was the first day I have had to myself since my return from Washington. And the first thing now that presses itself upon my mind is a letter I found in the office here from a man who says he is entitled to a portion of the Galphin claim. I enclose it to you that you may inform me whether his claim is well founded. You know all the facts. With your answer return the letter. If he is entitled, I will go down and see Dr. Galphin about it, and if not I shall have nothing to do with it.

I hope Dr. Robertson will be appointed inspector of drugs in Charleston, and that Moiise may get a place in the custom house there. I hope also that James Herring whom I know well may be appointed Postmaster at LaGrange, Ga. Tell Collamer to be cautious in making removals in our State.

I find there is a great effort in the interior of the State to create excitement and agitation on the slave question. How it will succeed I cannot now conjecture. Jones's paper would have more influence if Dr. Lee was not considered as the author and director of its tone. Can you not get him appointed Comr. of Patents? I left the petition for him with J. M. Clayton. It was strong and respectable. His appointment would do us great good negatively and positively. One more subject. Grieve,1 of Milledgeville, wants a *chargeship* somewhere in Europe. Can't you get him sent to Sardinia or some such place? I wish you could. Kenan desires it, and it would gratify me to see him gratified in particular.-.

I saw several of the bar of the Western Circuit at Gwinnett— Whigs and Democrats, and saw a great many people from all parts 1 Miller Grieve was an editor of the Southern Recorder; Augustus H. Kenan was a prominent Whig, of Milledgeville, Ga. of the State on the railroad, and I need not say that your appointment has given general and universal satisfaction. Judge Hill1 is going to make a strong pull for the nomination for Governor. My own opinion is that Trippe2 is the proper man. Towns it is thought will not run in consequence of his health. If not, Johnson8 or Lumpkin4 will most probably be selected. Write to me and let me know how you get on and how you like "old Zack" and your associates. Remember me to Sam Anderson. I wrote to him yesterday. The weather here now is fine and spring rapidly approaching.

John H. Lumpkin To Howell Cobb. E.

Hermon ga., *12th March, 181$.* Mi Dear Cobb, I have been here long enough to have had a full and free conversation with my father5 on the subject of Mr. Calhoun's Address and the reasons we have assigned for withholding our signatures to it. And it gives me pleasure to assure you that he approves of our course and will stand by us to the last, if no other man in Georgia does. And he says that he thinks that when the democratic party of Georgia shall be in full possession of all the movements of the wire workers that they will meet with merited rebuke and condemnation at their hands. Be this as it may, I am much encouraged since I have seen him and talked with him; and you may rely upon his doing all that he can to sustain us. You recollect that I gave one of our addresses to Col. Nathan Bass of Eatonton before I left Augusta. When I arrived at my father's I found the proceedings of the Eatonton meeting published in the Federal Union. The resolution was presented to that meeting by Col. Bass; and I am not surprised, now that I know this fact, that he was so much excited. He has too many negroes to be entrusted with the management of such a question. But these resolutions are responsive to Mr. Calhoun's address; and in fact determine to organize a Southern sectional party and to disregard either democratic or whig, and to make the love of negroes and the defence of their rights connected with them as paramount to every other consideration. This is all well enough, if by this course they could do more to arrest the threatened aggressions upon their rights than any other; but it is idle and worse than idle to suppose that they can do as much by pursuing such a course as they could by adhering to the Democratic party of the Union. But they have at least verified our conjecture in regard to the effect 1 Edward Y. Hill, of LaGrange, Ga., secured the Whig nomination for governor, hut was defeated by George W, Towns who was reelected. Robert P. Trippe, Congressman from Georgia, 1855-1859. Herschel V. Johnson, judge of the buperior court of Georgia (Ocomulgee circuit), 1849-1853; governor ,f Georgia, 1853-1857; vvlce-presldentlal candidate on the Douglas ticket, 1860. 'John H. Lumpkin, e Wilson Lumpkin, governor of Georgia, 1831-48,35; U. S. Senator, 1837-1841. or result of this Southern address, to wit, that it would result in the organization of a southern sectional party. But these resolutions show another thing that I was in some doubt concerning until I read them. They disclose the fact that this Southern party is ready to go over to the support of Genl. Taylor and his administration upon a *certain contingency,*—and that contingency, I now know, is if Genl. Taylor shall sustain the rights of the South or the views of the Southern Sectional party on this question. I now look forward to the time when the democratic party of the south will become purged of Calhoun, Calhoun men, and Calhounism and those left to sustain the principles and measures of the democratic party may be a corporal's guard; but I had rather be of that number and know that I am maintaining Southern rights and democratic principles, than to be wafted on a popular breeze to fame and distinction on incorrect principles. I want you to write to me and keep me advised of all the movements about Athens. I am in good health. Give my respects to Mrs. Cobb and all my relations.

George S. Houston To Howell Cobb. E.

Athens ala., *14 March, 1849.* My Dear Sir: I arrived at home Sunday night, and Monday was circuit court. A meeting was called to approve the Southern Address, and after its organization a debate arose between the leader and "getter up" of it and myself, which consumed the balance of the day and of course killed off the meeting for the present; and I believe *for ever.* I was badly fatigued from my travel, but I assure you I made a good speech. I at least defeated all action by the meeting. I find *very general discontent* amongst my friends for my not signing the address, tho' I am satisfying them pretty well—at least they can't beat me. I can beat any man who will *run at me,* at least I think so. I dislike to run, but will probably have to do it. Write me and tell me how you find things. Send me anything good for us that you may see. My Senatorial prospects are blasted.

John W. Burke To Howell Cobb. E.

Cassville, Geo., *March 22, 1849.* My Dear Sir: The article in my last paper in speaking of your address has brought down a shower of curses upon my head from the old Calhoun democrats about here, and there is many an one. What must I do? I have spoken my sentiments; and I will sink my paper and go back to Athens before I will say a word in favor of Mr. Calhoun, or the Southern movement. I have no good will for the former; and I abhor the latter. The old gentleman with whom I board, Dr. Potter, says it won't do and I must go with the tide. But I wont—I can't. An old fellow came into my office this evening and remarked that he liked my paper very well but he hoped I would not say anything more in favor of Cobb and Lumpkin. I told him I would stand up for you as long as I lived. He said he was a democrat, and would support me, but he knew Mr. Calhoun was a friend to the South and he thought I ought to be silent unless I could speak a word in his favor. I told him I could not speak a word for him, and furthermore I would not, and that altho I was alone of all the Georgia Dem. press, I would say all I could to still the troubled waters and conciliate the Northern Democracy. He found he could make nothing, and he left. I shall lose many friends but I have the satisfaction in knowing that *I am honest* and *right.*

Can't you make some of the Democrats of Athens take the *Standard?.* ..

Do write to *Lumpkin* for me. He may do me some good in Cherokee if he will. A line from you to him would be of service to me and received kindly.

George S. Houston To Howell Cobb. E.

Athens ala., *22d March, 1849.* My Dear Sir: I have just returned from court in another of my counties, and have to say that the people are with me very warmly. Some of my friends all through my district think I should have signed the address; but I find none—not one have I found—who says he will for that act vote against me, and indeed the politicians are all coming to my side. I am in a bother and would like your opinion, but I fear I can't hear from you in time. Many—*very many*— of my friends desire me to be a candidate for the Senate. I am well satisfied that it will injure me to be elected to the House and then run for the Senate. I think the first would defeat the last. My district is open for me, the aspirants have all taken ground publickly that they will not run for Congress if I do. So I can now be elected without opposition, no doubt of that. I am stronger than I ever was. My election to the Senate is doubtful for the reason that South Ala. is offended at me for not signing the address. If I had signed I could have been elected. I think my chance right good anyway. Mrs. Houston's health is delicate, quite so. Now tell me what you think about these things. To give up the House may be to be thrown entirely out, but even if that be the result I shall not regret it. You know I wish to

Thomas D. Harris To Howell Cobb. E.

Washington D. C, *May 8, 1849.* Mr Dear Cobb,... How agreeable it would be to see you elected Speaker of the next House; and yet, with a bare democratic majority, how difficult it would prove to concentrate every Democratic vote upon you. Those Connecticut democrats, for instance, whose election was brought about by declaring in favor of the proviso, might feel themselves constrained to support one for that office whose views on that question are more in unison with their own. But I must hope for the best. Should we run well upon the Whigs in Ky., Tenn., and N. Carolina, and hold our own in the remaining States, we may have a *sound* working majority, in which event your election certainly would be unquestionable. In the present state of the canvass I hesitate not to say that in no event can the next House present an Administration majority. It will certainly be antiTaylor. If we lose none in Ky. or Tennessee and gain one each in Md., N. C., Ala. and Mississippi and two in Indiana, we shall have a majority of two, exclusive of three free-soil democrats....

Howell Cobb To James Buchanan. Pa.

Athens, Ga., *2nd June, 1849.*

Dear Sir: It may become necessary for me to show the people of Georgia the feelings and views of the leading men of our party as to the course pursued by the Southern members of the last Congress. I enclose to you a copy of an address which I sent to my constituents with three others; and the object of this letter is to request your views on the subject. The truth is that there is an effort made by some of the *peculiar* friends of Calhoun to put down those of us who refused to follow his lead, and I desire to arm myself with the necessary weapons of defence if the war should continue to be waged. Though I would prefer such a letter from you as I could publish if it should become necessary, yet I will receive one under such restrictions as you may think proper to impose.

Allow me to request an early reply.

James B. Bowlin To Howell Cobb. E.

St. Louis mo., *June 6, 1849.* Dear Cobb, I send you by this mail a speech of Col. Benton on slavery in general and Calhoun in particular. We are in a terrible political snarl, and God only knows how it is to terminate. The issue has sprung up, as you will perceive, by Calhoun's taking our State into his bailiwick alongside of S. Carolina and Va. A few of his agents smuggled through the Legislature a set of extreme resolutions, not from any practical effect they were likely to have, but to head Benton. On his part he goes almost to the length of the other extreme, as you will see, and boldly makes fight at the hustings. In this dilemma it is hard for an honest man with Southern feelings and principles and yet a devoted lover of the Union to know where he is. The active leaders against Benton are his old foes. They never were honest in anything politically, and no doubt arranged the succession before rendering the throne vacant. But as the question is one of property, always a delicate subject, they lead off large numbers of good old-fashioned Union democrats, and they are replaced by the whigs who are almost uniformly for Benton's positions. This is the way the fight stands. They do not meet him, but bay him with meetings at a distance and scatter as old Bullion comes lumbering after them.

The speech I send you is his first. We have heard from one or two others made, but not received them here yet; and if they come I'll send them. You will see he gives Calhoun no quarters, and brings to light some singular facts. Calhoun's name is odious here, and Benton will keep it as prominent in the fight as possible, and will give it particular Hell in the progress of events. His opponents dread the title, and to show it not merited try to beat Benton in denouncing him, so that he has a fair show for unenviable notoriety in this fight. If Benton can force on them the livery of Calhoun and disunion he'll make them odious enough to scare children with. They had as well undertake to lead the church in the livery of the devil.

Benton fights boldly from a proud consciousness of victory, though it should be a victory at the expense of his party. For he has already drawn them fully into the ridiculous position of resting this question with the people, the whole people, and not with his party, which at once gives him some 40.000 Whig votes the start, to begin on, which virtually yields him the victory. But if he should be successful, and yet a majority of the Democrats should decide against him, the effect would be a Whig victory, and one from which we could not soon recover.

I have taken no part. I tell them my cause is before them and when my constituents fault it I'll defend it, but I'll certainly not kick until I feel the spur.

You have no doubt seen what a terrible fire we had here on the night of the 17th of last month. It was certainly one of the most terrific and at the same time grand sights I ever saw. About 400 houses in the very heart of the city were all in flames at once, looking like an ocean of fire.

John H. Lumpkin To Howell Cobb. E.

Rome ga., *6th June, 1849.* Dear Cobb,... I was not able to attend the democratic meeting here yesterday. They have appointed Hackett. Printup and myself delegates to the convention and adopted some preliminary arrangements for the nomination of a senator in the 47th senatorial district in July next.

Since Hackett's return he has manifested a disposition to go as a delegate to the convention, and James M. Spurlock, who is thoroughly with you and myself and also in Hackett's confidence, advised me to consent that Hackett should go and assured me that he would act with us. And Hackett in my presence yesterday morning said that no resolution should be passed approving the Southern address. You have seen him and have talked with him and can say whether it was good policy to send him as a delegate or not. Printup is as true as steel and may be relied on. L. W. Crook has been appointed from Chattooga, and will go. I don't know how he is affected towards us.... I have written letters to prominent men in every county in my district on this subject and they all assure me that all is right. I wrote to James Morris but received no answer. I wrote to James Edmondson, and he wrote me that delegates would be sent down that would not permit the passage of any resolutions that would remotely reflect upon you and myself.

Col. Jos. E. Brown1 of Canton wrote me that he was a delegate and expected to go and he should resist any attempt to pass any resolution approving the Calhoun address. Tumlin is with us and will see that delegates go down who will sustain us. Col. Murphy is with us and promised me he would go down to Milledgeville as a delegate. Jos. Henry Lumpkin of Oglethorpe writes me that he will go down from Oglethorpe county for our benefit. I shall continue to use my efforts until the convention meets. And I am determined to be there myself and see if I cannot aid you in rolling back the assaults that have been made upon us. Fouche2 is against any issue on this subject and approves of the article in last week's Southern Banner and says that they contain his views and are so well expressed that he will republish it in this week's issue. I cannot think that we shall have any difficulty with him hereafter.

James Buchanan To Howell Cobb. E.

Wheatland, Near Lancaster pa., *12 June, 1843.* My Dear Sir: I regret exceedingly to learn from yours of the 2nd instant that an attempt has been made from any quarter to impair your standing with the Democratic party of the South for the reason that you did not deem it proper to become a party to the late address of a portion of the Southern Representatives in Congress to the 1 Then a member of the Georgia senate, later governor and chief-justice of Georgia, United States Senator, etc. 3 Simpson Fouche, a Democratic editor at Rome, Ga.

73566—13 11 people of the South on the subject of slavery. Whilst it would ill become me to decide between those gentlemen who signed and those who refused to sign this address, I yet do not hesitate to declare that in my opinion there is not a member of the House of Representatives who has been more able and efficient than yourself in advocating and defending on all suitable occasions the rights and institutions of the South against the assaults of abolitionists and quasi-abolitionists of every shade and description. Indeed I should consider it a serious misfortune to the country, and especially to the South at the present critical moment, to lose the services in Congress of a gentleman of your abilities, experience and well known influence in the House. Without flattery I can sincerely declare that I know no Southern Democratic member who possesses in a more eminent degree than yourself the confidence of all those Democrats in the North who like myself have identified our political fate with the maintenance of the constitutional rights of the South on the question of slavery.

When the subject of an address from the Southern members of Congress without distinction of party on the subject of slavery was first agitated, I augured from it the happiest results. Had all united, this would have elevated the question above the range of mere party politics, and would have strongly appealed to the love of union with which every good man throughout the country is inspired. After it was known however that the address would be signed by Democrats alone, with only one or two exceptions, it was easy to foresee that in the public estimation of the north it would sink however undeservedly to the level of a mere party question. Such has proved to be the fact: and it has done no good in this portion of the Union. What has been its effect in the South I have not the means of judging. Should it prove to be instrumental in dividing and consequently weakening the Democracy in the slaveholding states, all of whom have the same object in view, this consequence would be truly deplorable.

I have not a copy of the address in my possession nor can I find one in Lancaster. I would thank you to send me a copy.

Should the convention about to assemble at Pittsburg to nominate a candidate for canal commissioner make a judicious selection, and this I have no reason to doubt, the state will again wheel handsomely into the Democratic line on the second Tuesday of October. The Democrats of Pennsylvania who voted for General Taylor are generally disgusted with his administration, and there is considerable dissatisfaction among the Whigs.

John H. Lumpkin To Howell Cobb. E.

Rome ga., *13th June, 1849.* My Dear Cobb, This is my birth-day and I am now thirty-seven years old, and I commemorate it simply by writing you this line to assure you that I am in good health and my family all as well as usual. I had occasion to write a letter to Govr. Towns a few days ago in behalf of my friend John Jolly of Cumming who through me applied for an office on the railroad. He has been recently removed by Mr. Colamer from the post office at Cumming because he is not ashamed or afraid to call himself a democrat. My application to the Govr. however was unsuccessful. In concluding my letter I took the liberty to enquire of him what the editor of the Federal Union meant by the course he was lately pursuing and to suggest that he was regardless of the harmony of the democratic party and had but little care whether the fall elections were successful or not. In reply to this portion of my letter the Governor replied, "As regards the feelings of the editor of the Federal Union toward yourself and Mr. Cobb I am satisfied he is not unfriendly to either of you and I have satisfied myself that he did not write the offensive articles referred to by you. In his paper of last week in reply to the Southern Banner he takes the same ground of that paper and I think is decidedly opposed to any agitation of the subject. The two articles in the Federal Union I think myself were unfortunate. I may be deceived. I can hardly believe that it was the intention of the articles to reflect upon you and Mr. Cobb, altho' they will admit of that construction. In a word, I believe it is the settled purpose of the party in the center of the State to have no further agitation of the southern address, to avoid censure of any of the delegation as regards this matter. I do trust that this will be the course pursued in the convention, and that we will adopt the Virginia resolutions or some other of like character upon which we can unite harmoniously. If the convention should not act in harmony the party in this State will be defeated both in the Legislature and for Governor." I give you all that portion of his letter that refers to this subject that you may know how he stands. He has written to Fouche, the Editor of the Southerner. in the very same vein, as I learn from Fouche. The convention will be held on the 11th July, and that is the second week of our court. If I can possibly leave court I will be there.

Howell Cobb To James Buchanan. Pa.

Athens ga., *June 17th, 1849.* Dear Sir: I am truly obliged to you for the flattering manner in which you are pleased to speak of my position with the northern democracy. My letter however led you into an error, as I was not as explicit as I should have been.

I have no difficulties to encounter in my own district. My own election took place last fall; and even if it was yet to come off, I have the gratification of knowing that my course on the slavery and all other questions meet with the entire approval of my democratic constituents. It is in other portions of the State that the effort is made to make the Calhoun address the test of democratic fellowship. I will send you a copy of this address and by comparing it with the one I enclosed you in my last letter, you will find that the issue I have made upon Calhoun, is the purpose of organizing a *Southern sectional party* to supplant in the south the *democratic party.* Such I have no doubt is his purpose, and for that object he prepared it and *designedly* failed to make any discrimination between Northern Democrats, Whigs and abolitionists. You will observe that the whole point of my address is directed to that fact; and unless I am sustained, the result must be the disruption of the democratic party as a *national* party, which would be the accomplishment of Calhoun's schemes ever since I have been in public life.

I am happy to learn that the prospect with the democracy in Pennsylvania is so promising. The same feeling exists in Georgia towards Taylor and his administration; indeed his name has almost become a bye-word and reproach. Our dangers arise in another quarter. Calhoun is our evil genius; and unless he is stopt in his career we shall be overwhelmed in our fall elections. If his friends continue to force upon the people the issue of a southern party which he has made by his address we must work for certain defeat.

My object in desiring to have the liberty of publishing your letter was only to use it in case it became necessary. It shall not be made public.

Lewis Cass To Howell Cobb. E.

Detroit, Mich., *June 19, 1849.* Dear Sir: I have just received your letter and hasten to reply to it. As you are anxious I should transmit my answer without delay I have time only to write very briefly and to give you my general impressions. I read with much care the circular signed by yourself and Messrs. Boyd, Clark and Lumpkin immediately after it was published; and it seemed to me the views you presented to your constituents were such as well became Southern statesmen. You did justice to the Democracy of the North and exposed with equal truth and severity the course of the Whig party upon the great questions affecting the South. You are perfectly right in your views. The Northern Democracy are opposed to those extreme issues which would array one great portion of the Union against another and might eventually lead to a dissolution of the Union.

P. S.—My Dear Sir: It was impossible for me to write a letter fit for publication within the period you mentioned. I have therefore sent you the accompanying hasty views which I hope will answer your purpose. You can refer to them if you please as my opinions on the subject but keep the letter out of the papers.

Robert Toombs To Mrs. Chapman Coleman.1 L. C.

Washington, Ga., *June 22nd, 1849.*

My Dear Madam: I was surprised and greatly pained at the receipt of your letter of the 5th inst. I had the most explicit assurances from Washington that your wishes would be gratified without the most remote reference to any contingency whatever. That was the reason I sent you what turns out to be my premature congratulations. The complaints against Mr. Clayton2 are exceedingly numerous and I fear but too well founded; and what is still more to be deplored, they are from Genl. Taylor's firmest and staunchest friends.

I have not been disappointed in him—your father well knows my opinion of him—his appointment was a fatal step in Genl. T's administration. Genl. Taylor is in a new position, his duties and responsibilities are vast and complicated, and besides, he is among strangers whose aims and objects are not known to him. Therefore that he should commit mistakes, even grave errors, must be expected; but I have an abiding confidence that he is honest and sincere and will repair them when seen. If I am mistaken in this, no man in the nation will more bitterly repent the events of the last eighteen months than I will, and I think in that event I shall have made my last Presidential campaign.

I know your father's disposition to put the kindest and most charitable construction upon everybody's acts, and therefore he will hunt out some plausible excuse for Clayton's letter. I think it was mean and contemptible to the last degree. You can not appreciate its unutterable meanness unless you had seen as I did, the positions of the two men in the political events of the session of '47-8. The one with the Presidency in his own grasp, thrusting it aside and standing generously and firmly by Genl. Taylor and cheering up his handfull of friends in the darkest hour of his fortunes; the other weak, timid and vacillating, watching the fortunes of each of the prominent candidates and enlisting under each with sole reference to his prospects for the day, and finally when the crisis came, in the very despair of irresolution, he covered himself with little Delaware merely to escape being found on the losing side. Give our best respects to Mr. Coleman and remember us most kindly to your father and mother. We are all in fine health.

1 Daughter of John J. Crittenden. John M. Clayton, of Delaware, Secretary of State In Taylor's Cabinet.

George S. Houston To Howell, Cobb. E.

(Strictly Private.)

Athens ala., *26 June, 1849*. My Dear Sir: I have this moment recd. yours of the 17th instant and give you a word in reply. *Alabama is gone, " hook and line "*, and no mistake. The Calhoun men will have the state unless the Whigs get it, which is at least possible if not probable. As to the resolution of the convention endorsing and censuring, it is susceptible of no satisfactory explanation. It was first and mainly intended to kill off Hilliard 1 but with about as much desire to kill me off. Again there was not one single delegate in the jconvention from *North Ala.* They stood aloof being determined to bind themselves in no way to vote for Chapman. 2. There was no thought in this end of the state that any such movement would be made in that body,— no one thinking the people had delegated them to do any such act. 3. The Calhoun men have controuled the last two or three State conventions in Ala., and I have no doubt they will continue to do so again (and I feel ashamed to say it). Col. King,2 as you know, having a *childish overweening desire to be elected to the Senate,* signed the address; and his friends, taking *their cue* from it, are pressing the address with more *violence* and *zeal* than even the Calhoun men, if possible. They are, or seem to be, determined to get ahead of the *Chivalry*3 and all, for the purpose of getting him back into the Senate. So our State is gone, and you may so set it down. My district is the only part of it that is sound; but a rabid Calhoun man will be elected, and then it will go too. The man I beat two years ago will be elected. He is an old nullifier and enemy of mine... Chapman has very fully allied himself with the Calhoun men,... and he has strength in some two or three of our best and largest and purest Democratic counties in North Ala., *in his old district.* He has taken sides against Cobb,5 and they may defeat him and I fear they will. The great presumption is that he will transfer to those counties the Calhoun feeling. If so the thing is ended forever, for they have always been a part of our main strength. The two papers (democratic) and the whig press in my district have opened the most bitter war upon the Chivalry, as the Whig papers are doing all over the state, and we may yet be able to do something; but if so it has yet to be done and by the hardest fighting. Our friends are generally afraid of the slavery question. They don't like to encounter it. You may consider me " *on the shelf*" for years if not forever. My deepest regret now is that I did not run 1 Henry W. Hilliard, Whig Congressman from Alabama, 1845-1851.
2 William R. King, then Senator from Alabama. 3 The extreme Southern-rights element, led by William L. Yancey. 4 David Hubbard, a Democrat, defeated by Houston in 1847. W. R. W. Cobb, Democratic Congressman from Alabama, 1847-1861. for Congress, and I would do so even now if I could with propriety and honor. I could start now and beat them all badly. Write me often. I will send you a Hilliard paper with some good articles in it.

Thomas D. Harris To Howell Cobb. E.

Dalton ga., *June £8, 1849.*

My Dear Friend, Seeing your name in the published list of delegates to the Democratic State Convention I have determined to say to you very hurriedly a few words in reference to the prime business of the convention to wit—the nomination of a candidate for Governor. I shall speak bluntly and truthfully—after this fashion: Should Towns be the nominee, Hill's majority in Oct. will equal if not exceed that of old Taylor's. There can be no mistake about it. I had misgivings before I came to Cherokee; but now after passing through Paulding, Chattooga, Floyd, Walker, to this place, and hearing as much through others from counties where I have *not* been as I have heard with my own ears in counties where I *have been* I should despise myself were I not to give the alarm. Don't let gentlemen deceive themselves. Gentlemen of the convention will think and speak as some think and speak in Cherokee, thus: the democratic opponents of Towns are a few disappointed office seekers only, all of whom with those few if any who sympathize with them will come up to the scratch on the day of trial. *But it will not be so.* Mark it and believe it! Towns as our standard bearer will tear the democracy of Cherokee into tatters and prostrate the party in the State for years to come. Now, sir, what is to be done?... The *individual* enters not into my thought. It is the party I would save, and could I feel that he, Towns, could lead us to victory I should go for him zealously in convention. The party—the good old party—the only honest party in this country—is all I think of in penning these disjointed lines. *And I want that party saved.*

Praying that the present incumbent may have the cleverness to disembarrass his friends by either voluntarily and in good temper withdrawing his name or by previous understanding gracefully declining to accept the nomination, thereby saving the feelings of his own especial supporters in the convention, I would respectfully suggest two names either of which in my opinion would rally enthusiastically the whole democratic party and ride triumphantly over the Federal opponent,—first W. T. Colquitt, 2d. Jim Cooper. The latter would call to the polls the last fraction of a democrat in the mountains. Whilst the former might do quite as well, and in other portions of the State perhaps better. Lumpkin must not run. His policy at this time should be to lie quiet. His failing to sign the Southern address might and would be used somewhat to his prejudice. One year from today that difficulty will have ceased to exist.

Do you apprehend any action of the convention in reference to the Southern address? Certainly that body will scarcely be so rash as to attempt to denounce these Southern Members of Congress who failed to sign it—if so, I shall blush for the party. I have no idea however that any considerable number of delegates were selected with any such view; and if not there can be no danger of the introduction of this firebrand. Plant yourselves upon the Virginia resolutions, and then go home.

I was at the convention in Montgomery. The party is full of fire and will elect the Governor by 10,000 majority. Hilliard will be defeated by a man named Pugh.1 A resolution denouncing these whigs and democrats of the South who refused to sign the Calhoun address was introduced at the conclusion of its proceedings by a delegate from Montgomery, the object of which was to aid in Milliard's defeat. There was no particular disposition to censure Houston or Cobb; and had H. been a candidate the resolution would not have been introduced. Cobb they cared nothing for. This feature of the convention's proceedings was designed to kill Hilliard.

Henry L. Benning To Howell Cobb.
E.

Columbus ga., *1 July, 1849.* Dear Howell, Until a day or two ago I thought I should be in the convention for the nomination of Governor on the 11th of this month. My calculation was founded on a mistake of the day on which Randolph inferior court is to be held. Business of importance requires me to attend that court; and I now find that its session conflicts with that of the convention. I had wished to be one of the convention, not on account of the nature or importance of the object for which it has been called—the nomination of a candidate for Governor—but on account of the bearing which its action may have on the future policy of the party, and more especially on account of the manner in which it ought to consider your own position. Everybody is agreed that Towns should be renominated but everybody is not agreed as to propriety of your course on the "Southern Address" or upon the question whether any and if so what notice ought to be taken of it by the convention. Indeed it will manifestly require all the skill and forbearance and concession of which the convention shall be master, to dispose of this subject so as to secure the concurrence of all concerned. It having been one of the most earnest wishes of my heart to serve you in relation to it to the very utmost verge of what respect for some very deep seated convictions of my own would permit, I had rejoiced in my appointment as a delegate from this county. Being however, owing to the cause above mentioned, de 1 James L. Pugb, Congressman from Alabama, 1859-1861.

prived of the pleasure of attending the convention, and of thus getting an opportunity of a personal interview with you, I take the liberty of friendship to express to you in writing some views which I think are worthy of your consideration.

First then it is apparent, horribly apparent, that the slavery question rides insolently over every other everywhere—in fact that is the only question which in the least affects the result of elections. It is not less manifest that the whole North is becoming ultra anti-slavery and the whole South ultra pro-slavery. Hence very small acts of deviation from the prevailing course of conduct of either section, being so conspicuous from their rarity, will attract immense animadversion. Is not this true? Can the Hunker democracy of the North be now depended on by the democracy of the South? To say nothing of their course in the last Congress, which you understand so well, witness the action of Connecticut in the recent elections, the sentiments contained in the Hunker address in New York, the open and formal going over of the Hunkers to the Barnburners in Vermont, and the recent resolutions of the Maine Legislature, the coalition with or rather the merger into the Barnburners by the Hunkers of Wisconsin, the tone of the Indiana Democracy, the election of Chase as senator in Ohio by Democrats, and over and above all, the bold unmasking of Benton in his avowal at Jefferson City of his adhesion to ' free-soilism.' Hunkerism is manifestly giving away— it has already yielded— throughout the North. Old associations, old pledges, old hopes, perhaps convictions, may for awhile keep a few old leaders of the Northern democracy in their old position on the slavery questions; but the body and the present leaders of the party are gone, gone forever. What inference do I ask you to draw from all this? The inference that your long cherished wish to keep up the unity of the Democratic party is now vain, and that you ought not to sacrifice yourself and your usefulness to your state in holding on to a chimera.

No doubt this wish so natural and so attractive had much to do with your refusal to sign the Southern Address.

At that time there might be a hope of the democratic party being able to protect the institution of slavery from abolitionism; now it is painfully obvious that it cannot protect itself from annihilation, except by falling in with the anti-slavery current. Indeed the frank democrats of the North admit this and justify their bowing of the knee to Baal by the example of the South in refusing to support Cass after he had taken a satisfactory pro-slavery position. Add to this the desire to corner Taylor and the Whigs on the slavery question, and you will see motive enough to place the democrats of the North in a position next Congress where it will be utterly impossible for any Southern man to stand and live. Surely however it can be but a little time, whether so soon as next Congress or not, before, owing to the causes now at work, the North and the South must stand face to face in hostile attitude. What I would have you consider is this: is it not better voluntarily to take at once a position, however extreme, which you know you must and will some time take, than to take it by degrees and as it were on compulsion? Why sacrifice your usefulness by pursuing a course which however magnanimous it may be must end in failure, when by so doing you lay yourself liable to ineradicable imputations which you know but which none but you will be able to know are groundless and false? Why put yourself in a situation where though innocent everybody will believe you guilty? Already your not co-operating in the Southern convention subjects you to mis-construction. Of all the democrats I have heard express an opinion on that subject there has been but *one* who justified your course whilst a few bitterly denounced it and the rest the great body in consideration of your undoubted fidelity, of your long and valuable services to the party, and to some extent of the reasons which you *assigned* in your address for your justification, barely excused it. This feeling towards you is not calculated to be changed for the better by the course which the Northern democracy, for the sake of which you did what you did, will hereafter pursue on the slavery question. A long period of past fidelity on the part of the Northern democracy to the South as it is in the constitution will be forgotten by us in a moment of treachery. That moment is coming. And when it comes, the reasons for your justification assigned in your address will too have lost their effect. What then, secondly, should you do in order to put yourself right before the country? Nothing certainly but what is consistent with the sense of propriety and duty which we all know you entertain to yourself and state. You ought to indicate your *future* course with unmistakeable distinctness. This convention furnishes you with a fine opportunity to accomplish the object. What would meet the case would be I think about this. Let the Virginia Resolutions be reported by a committee and then let an additional resolution be offered by *you,* founded upon the indication of the position which the Northern democracy are assuming, developed since those resolutions were passed by the Virginia Legislature, acknowledging our obligations to our Northern brethren for their conduct in the past but expressing our apprehensions for their course in the future, and recommending in the event of the passage by Congress of the Wilmot proviso or of any law affecting slavery in the District of Columbia or any other law founded on similar principles, the Legislature to be convened forthwith and when convened recommending it to call a convention of the Southern States. This coming from you, and enforced by some remarks in which you can explain your position and set yourself fully right according to the very truth of the matter with the party, will be hailed with acclamation. I do but indicate the principle on which I think the thing ought to be done. Doubtless the details may be varied and improved, and I am inclined to believe too that this course will not only be best for you, your own personal honor and duty being considered, but will also have a good effect, if anything can have it, upon the North. When *you* take such a stand they will feel that the South is not gasconading but has in reality mischief in her; and if that does not stay their hand nothing will.

Now having said so much to you on your own account it is proper that I tell you in a few words my position on the slavery question and the duty of the South, in order that you may make due allowance for anything in what I have said which appears exaggerated or extreme. I think then *1st,* that the only safety of the South from abolition universal is to be found in an *early* dissolution of the Union. I think that the Union by its *natural and ordinary* working is giving anti-slavery-ism such a preponderance in the Genl. Government, both by adding to the number of free states and diminishing the number of slave, that it (anti-slavery-ism) will be able soon to abolish slavery by act of Congress and then to execute the law. I no more doubt that the North will abolish slavery the very first moment it feels itself able to do it without too much cost, than I doubt my existence.

I think that as a remedy for the South, dissolution is not enough, and a Southern Confederacy not enough. The latter would not stop the process by which some states, Virginia for example, are becoming free, viz. by ridding themselves of their slaves; and therefore we should in time with a Confederacy again have a North and a South. The only thing that will do when tried every way is a *consolidated* Republic formed of the Southern States. That will put slavery *under the control of those most interested* in it, and nothing else will; and until that is done nothing is done. You see therefore that I am very extreme in my opinions and that you must weigh them as you weigh what I recommend to you. During the last six months I have given much attention to this problem of problems to the South, and have made up my own mind in my own way. I am no Calhoun man. He in fact is off the stage; the coming battle is for other leadership than his, a leadership that is of this generation, not of the past.

To return a second to the old subject. For myself I should not object to the introduction and adoption of the Va. Resolutions as the full expression of our present party position; and I think that by a little adding that may be effected. But there is no telling what some Hotspur may do. He might introduce a resolution that would compel a vote directly upon your course, and if such a vote were taken it would betray a great want of unanimity in the party upon the most important and exciting of all possible subjects, whereas by taking time by the forelock in some such manner as that which I have ventured to suggest you would forestall all such fellows— indeed kill them with joy. In conclusion I must beg you to realize the present emergency. Let your eye take in the whole case at one view—see nothing but the facts as they are, and then decide in the light of the evidence and that only. If you do, I am sure for the reason that I confide in my own judgment, that you must come to the conclusion to which I have come. The fundamental thing is the conviction that the Northern Democracy is no longer trustworthy. That being so, it dictates our course just the same, let the defection proceed from one cause or another. We must act upon what is, not upon what produced it.

George S. Houston To Howell Cobb. E.

Athens ala., *28th July, 1849*. Dear Cobb, I recd. yours giving me an account of your state convention. I am glad it passed off well. If I had suspected that ours would have acted the fool... I would have gone down; but none of us ever suspected such a thing till it was done; and I hardly think I could have prevented it, for the contest seems to be between the King men and the Chivalry who will go the greatest length. The whole thing is moved on by Senatorial aspirants and their friends. At least such is my opinion; and old Govr. Clay1 it seems has entered the lists and with zeal has gone into the contest. His doing so is intended to hurt me—for even yet, with the Southern address and all, I am the strongest man in North Ala. and it does injure me because he is *11 of kin*" to the Huntsville Democrat, the leading democratic paper in North Ala., and of course it has drawn the sword upon me and assails the non-signers with violence. I am safe in my district with the people, and I think every democrat who goes from it to the Legislature except one will be for me, and that one is an aspirant. My district furnishes two or three competitors for the Senate but they can't touch me. I think, tho', the Calhoun men are determined on my defeat. They will probably form almost any sort of combination to do it. This is my opinion, and I think I will be defeated; indeed I must say that there seems to be no escape for me....

Old Benton has injured us by his course. He is making issue with Calhoun; and the people hate him so much that they all feel willing to join any one to defeat him....

1 Clement C. Clay, sr., ex-governor of Alabama.

George S. Houston To Howell Cobb. E.

Athens ala., *10th August, 1849*.

My Dear Sir: Our elections are over; the results not yet known. David Hubbard is my successor, an old nullifier, tho' he had nothing to say about the "*CaZhoun address.*'" I once during the canvass heard he did, but when I asked him about it he denied it; he however is of *that stripe*. The address men ran at Cobb1 very hard, with a talented man, and all the democratic papers in the State except those in my district against Cobb, and yet he has triumphed by about *1,000* majority. Geo. W. Jones re-elected without opposition. J. H. Thomas re-elected. And W. Johnson also; and I have but little doubt of Hilliard's success. So you see all of the "*anti-Calhoun Address*" men have triumphed in these parts or hereabouts. I missed it by not coming back, which I could easily have done; but I did not see it soon enough. Even yet my chance for the Senate is right good if we have the Legislature, which is exceedingly doubtful. I think the Whigs have it. My district has elected five Whigs, one from my own county. I have had nothing to do with the State election. The democratic State convention treated me so badly I determined for the present to hold still. They are now most gloriously rebuked— I mean the Chivalry—in the State. All the non-signers elected who ran, and if they continue to control one party in the state they will break it down if they have not now done so. You may well guess I feel a little better than some time ago.

P. S.—If in looking over the list of members elected in this State you see any of your friends elected, or see where you can strike a good lick, you must write a line.

Thomas W. Thomas To Howell Cobb. E.

Elberton ga., *Aug. 19th, 1849*. Dear Sir: I find the opinion prevailing quite extensively among the democrats here that Holsey of the Banner is sympathizing with Benton against Calhoun, and that you are backing him in it. It has been suggested to me by several prominent democrats within the last ten days that such seemed to be the fact. Everything I have seen from Holsey on the subject expresses my sentiments exactly; but still there is no denying his course is not agreeable to some of your constituents—some too who are worthy and reliable democrats—and since I can see no need for your shouldering the responsibility of his editorials I have taken the liberty of telling them you have nothing to do with his paper and can rightfully be held accountable therefor no more than myself. They have got hold of the idea that he writes entirely under your dictation—by what process of reasoning I am unable to say—and this I am sure cannot be true. After endeavoring to trace this impression to its source I am compelled to believe it is a spontaneous and not a pumped-up combustion as far as it goes. There is but one copy of the Banner taken in the county that I know of; but the obnoxious editorials have been circulated by extracts in the Chronicle and Constitutionalist. I don't attach much importance myself to what I have herein stated; but still I thought it would not be amiss to put you in possession of the facts.

We have a glorious prospect of sending a democratic senator from this district. The Whigs are hopelessly split up. They were compelled to call a convention to settle their differences (the first time such a thing was ever done here) and the result has given general dissatisfaction. I can count up a dozen delegates to their convention who are openly out for the democratic candidate. Wm. B. White who was before their convention for the nomination electioneers strongly for Lindsey H. Smith, our candidate. And better than all, the quarrel can not be reconciled. Smith told me enough Whigs pledged themselves voluntarily to vote for him the first day he declared himself to elect him.

John L. Robinson To Howell Cobb. E.

Rushville, Indiana, *Aug. 24th, 18Jf9.*

Dear Cobb, The result of the recent election in the South and West gives us ground to hope that we may be able to control the next House, at least to organize it by the election of Democratic officers. In this State we have emphatically and finally routed and prostrated Taylor and Taylorism, electing eight reliable Democrats, 1 Taylor man and 1 Free-soiler with Democratic sympathies and who will, I think go with us for Speaker and the other officers of the House.

But my object in writing you is to learn something of the condition of things among the Southern Democracy. You know you can communicate with me frankly on this subject, as I doubt not it will be the sincere desire of both of us to shape our action in the organization so as to insure the success of sound Democratic officers. French I think can without doubt unite every section of our friends for Clerk but the more important question is who can we unite upon for Speaker? Will Mr. Calhoun's friends support you? If not of course you cannot be elected, nor would allow your name used. The Northern or free State Democracy will I think prefer you to any other man. *Sub rosa* I have been informed that as between Winthrop and a Democrat the free-soilers would vote with us if we would take up Gov. McDowell. He is poor timber however, I fear. for Speaker. And could he get the Calhoun interest? Then again I have heard the name of Jno. A. McClernand of Ill. mentioned as one who could command all the Calhoun vote. I don't know but there is some truth in this; but I fear no one of the free-soilers would vote for him and fear we must get one or two of them or a like number from the Whigs proper to succeed. Let me hear from you freely on this subject. For myself I will cheerfully vote for *any man* (if he is not a Taylor man) whom a majority of the Democrats may designate, and I shall try and be on the ground early and use all my influence (feeble though it be) to promote harmonious action and keep down and strangle the baleful spirit of sectional feeling or faction, let it show from what quarter it may; and I know I can say as much for my Democratic colleagues, all of whom are new members except Brown and myself, and who got into Congress *as Democrats* and nothing else.

Joe Wright's majority in this state for Governor will reach nearly 10,000, and we would have beat McGaughey for Congress if he had had any regular opposition. My own majority is 772 and would have been at least 1,200 but for the cholera which happened to be in every German township in the district. Taylor's majority was 415 last fall....

Alfred Iverson To Howell Cobb. E.

Columbus ga., *Oct. 6th, 1849.* Dear Cobb, It seems to be pretty clear that we shall have a majority in the Legislature. You know my wishes as to the judgship. Bethune is a candidate, and *perhaps* Ingram of Harris may be also. I do not fear either of *them.* But there is another Richmond in the field! Yesterday the report was rife in the street that Sturgis would be a candidate to be supported by Alexander and Hines Holt, McDougall and Col. Jones. I asked him this morning about it. He said he was not a candidate at present but would be if he saw a chance to be elected. I have no doubt that he will be a candidate, and a strong effort will be made to cast the Whig vote upon him with the hope of detaching Dems. enough to elect him.... Now what can you do for me? What members can you influence? Under the circumstances I must call upon all my friends for their " aid and comfort." Can you do anything with Wofford? I am a little afraid of the old Clark party associations and sympathy operating upon him. I do not know the members from Franklin. Perhaps you can control them and those from Jackson and Madison and Walton. You will be at Milledgeville, of course, and I hope to meet you there on Saturday before the Legislature meets. We must all unite in an effective effort. to renovate the senatorial and congressional districts and to impress other matters of policy upon the Legislature. Let me hear from you soon.

Dear Cobb, I returned from Chattooga court last night and found your letter addressed to me from Clarkesville, Ga. Before this you have learned that I am in the field as a candidate for Judge of this circuit, and I am not only a candidate but I am anxious to be elected; and I rely very much upon your aid and influence in the contest. I am assured that I shall obtain all of my circuit except Jack Jones, Talley of Lumpkin, and it is probable that Shackleford may vote for Horner; the rest I think are for me against either of my opponents. I am therefore the decided choice of my circuit; and with your influence I do not doubt but that a majority of the democratic party will be for me. But the danger is that a few of the Calhoun Democrats have crept into the Legislature, and their hostility to me will prevent me from obtaining a majority of all the votes polled. It is the policy of all minorities to take up the weaker candidate and defeat if possible the one who is the favorite of the party in power. If this game is played I am defeated without the hope of success. And all the gratification I can have under these circumstances will be that I shall have it in my power to defeat them also. Judge Wright, Judge Underwood and Judge Trippe are for me, and I have no hesitation in saying that a majority of the whig party in this circuit prefer me to any other democrat. And will not Toombs and Stephens prefer me to any man whom this Calhoun faction may strive to elect over me? Will they and the whig party be willing to see Jack Howard and a few such mad-caps put me down because I do not subscribe in blank to every thing that Mr. Calhoun may say? Colquitt writes me that his son Alfred is a candidate for secretary of the senate. He is anxious for his election. James Cooper is a candidate, and so is my townsman Tel. Cuyler. James Jackson writes me that he is a candidate for Judge and will not be a candidate for the secretary of the senate. Armstrong of Macon is also a candidate for the same office. I shall be at Milledgeville on Saturday before the legislature meets, and you must be there also, and I must be elected the judge of this circuit. It is an important movement and will do much to save Cobb and Lumpkin and the integrity of the democratic party.

Washington City, *27th Nov., 1849.*

My Dear Wife, I reached Washington today, though I see my arrival here announced in the papers for several days ago....

About the Speakership I have learned but little and that not very favorable to. my own success. There are as yet but few members here and nothing certain can therefore be known; but I now believe that I shall be beaten. The very game that I anticipated is being played off upon me. The report is busily circulated that I cannot get the Calhoun men and therefore cannot be elected, which is inducing the party to look to others who can command their support. Boyd at present seems to be the man, and I should not be surprized if it should result in his election. I am, you see, prepared for the worst, and really feel less anxious than I supposed I should.

Howell Cobb To His Wife. E.

Washington City, *2d Dec., 18$.* My Dear Wife, Before this letter reaches you you will have heard the result of the election of Speaker, though it has not yet taken place. The telegraph will communicate it to the papers sooner than a letter can possibly reach you. Last night our party met in caucus and I was nominated without much trouble on the first ballot. Today great doubts are entertained of the result. The Carolina delegation are understood to be against me irrecoverably, and unless they come into my support together with some southern whigs I must be defeated. But it is useless to speculate, as you will know all about it before you read these calculations. I shall be content with any result that may come. In getting the nomination over the strong opposition made against me I have gained a sufficient triumph *for the present.* I can give you no news because we have had no talk about any thing but the election of speaker, etc. This has afforded food for all the gossip, and until the election is over we shall hear nothing of any thing else....

Perhaps I ought to add in the way of political news that the whigs are in as bad a stew as ourselves. Five Whigs, including three from Ga., retired from the whig caucus last night and have sworn vengeance against Winthrop, though they do not say what they will do when we come to vote in the House. ...

Howell Cobb To His Wife. E.

Washington City, *4th Dec., 1849.*

My Dear Wife, I have just received your fourth letter and must acknowledge its receipt, though I can do nothing more as I am literally overwhelmed with company and have not a *single moment* to write. I write this letter in a crowded room with the most exciting conversation going on around me.

I thought that I would be able tonight to notify you of the result of the election of Speaker, but I cannot. We have had two days of voting without making a selection and no one can possibly see the end. I have come to the conclusion that my election is *impossible.* 73566—13 12

I have been sustained in the most flattering manner by my party, and feel as triumphant as if I was elected. / *am satisfied* Mr. Calhoun and his friends have treated me well. They gave me their support with as much cordiality as I had any right to expect. It is true they were warmly opposed to my nomination and used every effort as I believe to defeat it; but being nominated, they voted for me, except Holmes and Woodward.

I have been defeated by the Northern free-soil Democrats who would vote for no southern man. If the disaffected southern whigs support me I can yet be elected, but I have no hope of it and feel now that I am *triumphant* but not *elected.* ...

Henry R. Jackson To Howell Cobb. E.

Savannah, Ga., *Dec. 8, 1849.*

My Dear Cousin, We are all anxiously looking for the final result of the Speaker's election. I am glad to see that Colcock of Carolina (a gentleman every inch of him) has stood up to you with other Carolinians. Do not think me intrusive in suggesting to you to cultivate Colcock (as the saying is). He is a man of considerable strength in Carolina. Cultivate all of the Carolinians who are at all disposed to be friendly. Come into as little collision with Calhoun as possible. Not that he can crush you! far from it! but you are in a position to drag? anything at the South you may desire, with a little forbearance. Excuse this from one who you know would only suggest such things with a view to your best interests. Calhoun can never be a leading politician. It is wise therefore to cultivate his friends as far as can be consistently done.

By this time you are either elected Speaker or defeated. If elected accept my hearty congratulations. If defeated you know as well as anyone that it is a small matter when considered in comparison with the long public career which awaits you if you wish it.

I write now to say to you that the proprietors of the Georgian have written to Francis J. Grand to act as a correspondent for our paper. Do you know him? If not will you make his acquaintance and suggest to him your willingness to confer with him and aid him in his correspondence with the Georgian? I write this at the suggestion and with the approval of my partner.

You will at once see the importance of advising with him at times. Let me hear from you in reference to this.

I have just returned from the circuit. A man should not blow his own trumpet—but I may say to you that I have succeeded far better than I *dreamed* I could succeed when elected. I keep as cool as a cucumber. Do you doubt it? I simply say that a prominent Whig mentioned to me that I undoubtedly possessed an advantage over Fleming which was that of keeping *calm.* I do not doubt that you think it *strange;* but one act of rascality like that played upon me in Milledgeville can excite me more than a thousand trials.

Howell Cobb To His Wife. E.

Washington City, *20th Dec., 1849.* My Dear Wife, I received a letter from you by last night's mail, and should have replied to k but for the fact that I was compelled to go to a caucus and did not get back to my room until after midnight.

We have had a democratic caucus every night for the last three days and shall have another tomorrow night. So far they have resulted in no good but have produced the most embittered feelings between the different portions of the party. The introduction of the slavery question in their debates has so completely alienated the north from the south that I believe it to be utterly impossible ever again to unite the party on any man. Many of my warmest friends from the north have said to me that they could never vote for me again, though personally they would be as much gratified at my success as at the. start, but the threats and menaces of southern men (which will go home to their constituents) would destroy their position at home if they should now return to me, as it would seem to be done under the influence of these belligerent taunts. Others are insisting that I should be renominated. Others want to vote for me anyhow. Some few will do it but I am determined not to be a candidate again if my wishes and feelings control the matter. Many of the whigs are willing that I should be elected provided the democrats would give them certain committees. I have repudiated the proposition and peremptorily refused to take the office upon those terms so you see that we are " far from land," and there is no earthly prospect that I shall be Speaker. The two parties (whig and democrat) appointed a committee of conference who are to report to the meeting tomorrow night. But as we will not consent to the proposition just referred to, I see no chance of any agreement, and I believe that nothing will come of it.

I think it more than probable that the matter will finally be brought to a close by the adoption of the plurality rule, which will elect the candidate having the highest number of votes; and my opinion is that in the present state of things and feeling that it will elect Mr. Winthrop; but as I have frequently said to you it is useless to conjecture, as all is in doubt and uncertainty.

Howell Cobb To His Wife. E.

Washington City, *22d Dec., 1849.* My Dear Wot;, The long agony is over and as you have doubtless seen by the telegraphic accounts I have been elected Speaker. And now the question is whether it is most to be rejoiced over or regretted. I confess that for many days my feelings have all been averse to my own success. Apart from the consideration that it lengthens our absence from each other, which disturbs me much, it involves me in responsibilities and labors far greater than any I have ever yet had to encounter. These reflections have depressed my spirits and also made me regret that my aspirations have been gratified. I have before me a delicate and arduous duty, and shall endeavour to act upon the rule which has so far borne me through all my trials and troubles, to wit—*to do what I believe to be right,* and trust the consequences to that Arbiter of human events whose unerring judgment will give to every one as he deserves of his strengthening grace and support.

I must throw myself for some time upon your indulgence as my labors will be very great for a few weeks. I shall not only have all the committees to arrange—a herculean task from which I almost shrink—but the members have all run out of money and my duty requires me to make arrangements for receiving and disbursing thousands of dollars, as you know they are all paid by the Speaker. My room is crowded with company and I am now trespassing on hours past midnight to drop you this line.

Your many inquiries about the scenes which have been transpiring here for the. last few days must be postponed to some later day when I will give you a full account of all that has taken place.

You will see by the papers that I was finally elected by the plurality rule. / *voted against the rule throughout,* so that I am not liable to the charge of conducing to my own elevation by resorting to an unknown expedient. The rule was adopted principally by whig votes, but they avowed at the time that they believed it would result in my election. "'

I was elected without the aid of either whig or free-soil votes and my election was despaired of even at the last vote, because I refused *to the last moment to make any pledge whatever* though pressed by my friends to do so. I said to them that I was the only calm and collected man in the House and therefore could not waive my own judgement for them.

I have done nothing to procure my election. Indeed all my personal efforts have been directed to my defeat for the last two weeks.

James Buchanan To Howell Cobb. E.

Wheatland, Neab Lancaster pa., *29 December, 1849.* My Dear Sir: I most cordially congratulate you upon your election as Speaker. I felt anxious for your success, both for public and private reasons. A Southern Speaker at the present moment, elected by Northern Democratic votes, is an event of the most propitious character. In this part of the world many of us believed and for one I desired that the South should shew themselves to be in earnest and convince their Northern brethren that the Slave question was above party. This once done and the question is settled consistently with Southern rights. I was sorry therefore to find the Southern Whigs with three or four exceptions voting in mass for a Wilmot Proviso man for Speaker. Clingman presented a strange contrast. One day he was ready to dissolve the Union rather than submit to the Wilmot Proviso; and the next he voted for Winthrop, its most respectable and powerful advocate. But I hope to be in Washington in a fortnight or three weeks and shall not trouble you further at present with my reflections. My chief object in writing at present has been to bring Stanton of Tennessee to your notice; *and this emphatically without any suggestion direct or indirect on his part.* He is now with me and will leave here to-day. It is difficult at any time to select a suitable Chairman of the Ways and Means; and it is all important at the present moment that an able and industrious man should be placed in that position. I wish Father McKay were now in Congress. I do not suggest that Stanton should have that place, but as second on the committee his services would be invaluable. I know him well. He is able, faithful, industrious and persevering. Among the younger members of the last Congress I considered him the most promising. For practical sense and sound judgment he has but few superiors. This is purely my own suggestion and you will value it at what it may be worth.

Howell Cobb To His Wife. E. Washington City, *11th Jany., 1850.*

My Dear Wife,... Since I last wrote to you we have been engaged in the House pretty constantly in the election of a Clerk, and only succeeded on yesterday in electing one. Mr. Campbell the old clerk (a Whig) was the successful candidate by the aid of a few southern democratic votes, which has produced quite an excitement and added no little to the bad sectional feeling which already existed among the members.

I was required yesterday *in the line of my duty* to dine with the Attorney-General. Our company consisted of the Judges of the Supreme Court, the British Minister (Sir Henry Bulwer), Mr. Webster, the Vice-President, Mr. McAllister of Ga., Mr. Gales and myself. You see it was quite an affair among the dignitaries of Washington. Like all such entertainments it was not a very agreeable entertainment to me, though quite as much so as one of the kind could be. Necessarily a great deal of formality and all that kind of thing. This part of my business is the most unpleasant to me. I never had much taste for such things at any time and it is becoming more and more insipid in proportion as the necessity for it increases. I could pass my time far more agreeably with my little boys at a circus or monkey show by way of variety than to be seated up wine bibbing with swell heads of the metropolis. Whatever judgment others may pass upon this exhibition of my taste, I may safely appeal to three little gentlemen of my acquaintance with a certainty of a favorable decision....

W. C. Daniell To Howell Cobb. E. Savannah ga., *23rd January, 1850.* Dear Sir: Last summer I became acquainted with the Revd. Mr. Stringfellow of Va., in consequence of seeing his scriptural vindication of slavery which is the most complete which I have seen. The edition was out and I could not obtain a single copy which I wanted for the purpose of republication at home. Recently he has notified me of his intention to publish another edition at Washington. I have ordered 1,000 copies and ask as a favour of you to apply to Mr. Seddon who will supply you with one hundred copies which I ask the favour of you to frank throughout your district. I know you must be fully engaged and would not thus tax you under ordinary circumstances; but the object I have in view will I think excuse me in your eyes....

Howell Cobb To His Wife. E. Washington City *4th Feby., 1850.* My Dear Wife,... Today we had a vote in the House on the Wilmot proviso resolution introduced by Root; and for the first time since that question has been up we succeeded by a very decided vote in laying it on the table. It augurs well for the country and I trust may be considered as foreshadowing a favorable and honorable adjustment of this truly vexed and harassing question. God grant that it may be so and that the storm will blow over, leaving us a happy prosperous and united people....

John B. Lamar To Howell Cobb. E. Macon, Ga., *Feb. 7th, 1850.* Dear Howell, On my return from Sumter on Sunday evening, yours of 29th ult. came to hand.... Whenever Sister is ready I shall take pleasure in escorting her, the young ladies and the "young fry" on to Washington. I have written to her not to fail to arrange with your sisters to accompany her. It will doubtless be pleasant to themselves and highly useful to her. As I suppose from the Speaker being the only high functionary the Democracy have his house will be somewhat a headquarters of the patriotism and fashion of the party... I am rather disposed to believe you will be the last of the Speakers, from the present clouds on the political horizon. I see no chance to adjust the difficulty with honour to our section and satisfactorily to the North.

Since I came home I have spent several days in bringing up my Congressional reading in the Union and Globe; and the speeches there which together with the Legislative proceedings North and my knowledge of the people there make me conclude the chance to be bad for a settlement to be made honourable to us. If it is not settled during this session all hope is gone of the Union.

I am making my mind up for the worst. If the matter can not be settled without the degradation of exclusion of us by Congress from all the new territory and without abolition in the Dist., then the sooner the Union is dissolved the better. You may not admire my taste, but Clingman's speech corresponds with my ideas and feelings.

I think while we do everything we can to preserve the Union without suffering ourselves to be degraded into inequality, at the same time we ought to be admonished by every indication at the North to begin to cast about for the consequences of the dissolution of the Union when it comes—as come it must I fear. I know your loyalty to the Union, and without flattery I think I may say but for your influence Georgia would have been more rampant for its dissolution now than South Carolina ever was. You have moderated the feelings of the people here; but as great as your influence has proven on two occasions, pardon me when I beg you to keep yourself in a position where you will not have to breast the storm raised by the passage of the Wilmot Proviso as applied to the territory south of the Compromise line and abolition of slavery in the Dist.

The price of cotton has raised the price of land, so there is no chance of buying you a cleared plantation now. And during such prices it would be folly to take hands from making cotton in Baldwin to clear the place in Dooly, so we shall have to let planting affairs remain in "statu quo." Your places in Baldwin have averaged over 300 bags each year for 1848 and 1849; and as I think they will not fall under that for some years to come, we can afford to wait a more propitious season to buy a new place.

Howell Cobb To His Wife. E.

Washington City, *9th Feby., 1850.* My Dear Wife,... Mr. Clay has made his great speech on the slavery question and I fear that no good is to result from it. It will in my judgment have a bad effect on the public mind of the north, as it will induce with them the opinion that he expresses southern sentiment, which is very far from being the fact. The excitement is unabated here on that subject and will doubtless continue until there is a final adjustment of the whole matter. That such will be the ultimate result I will not permit my mind seriously to doubt. I have great confidence in the virtue and intelligence of the American people and so believing I must look sanguinely to the period when all patriotic hearts will and can unite in saying " all is well."

My labors are extremely onerous and keep me constantly employed. Having undertaken, I will go through with the task, but no consideration would induce me again to be speaker of the House. *It don't pay.*

Alexander H. Stephens To James Thomas. L. C.

Ho. Of Reps., Washington, D. C., *Feb. 13,1850.* Dear Thomas,... We have no news here at this time of interest or importance. What is to be the result of the slavery question I can not tell. I suppose however that some adjustment of it will be made—some adjustment of it for the present. But when I look to the future and consider the causes of the existing sectional discontent, their extent and nature I must confess that I see very little prospect of future peace and quiet in the public mind upon this subject. Whether a separation of the union and the organization and establishment of a Southern Confederacy would give final and ultimate security to the form of soceity as it exists with us, I am not prepared to say. I have no doubt if we had unity, virtue, intelligence and patriotism in all our councils, such an experiment might succeed. But unfortunately for our country at this time, we have if I am not mistaken too much demagogism and too little statesmanship. Most of the *fighting resolves* of our Legislatures I fear are nothing but gasconade put forth by partisan leaders for partisan effect. If our people really mean to fight, if their minds are made up upon this alternative, they should say so, and they should make the declaration in Congress too plain to admit of equivocal readings. But if they do not intend to resort to the *ultima ratio* of all nations they should cease in that sort of braggadocio which will in end result in their own degradation. But enough. I did not commence this with any intention of giving you a dissertation on the present *crisis* of public affairs.

George D. Phillips To Howell Cobb. E.

Farm Hill, Habersham County ga., *March 10th, 1850.* Dear Sir: You have seen the action of the Geo. legislature on the all absorbing question of Southern Rights,1 and you can readily 1 The Georgia legislature had adopted on February 8 a Relies of resolutions denouncing the anti-slavery proposals then pending in Congress. The eighth resolution in the conceive that many of your friends and constituents are anxious to have your views and opinions in relation thereto. Both parties in Geo. are divided to some extent. This is unfortunate but was to be expected, at least in the 5 & 6 Congressional dists.1 where the question in controversy between the N orth and South has been perhaps less anxiously watched than in other parts of the State and from erroneous views entertained by some in relation to your position and Judge Lumpkin's on the Oregon bill.

You will recollect the conversation we had in Milledgeville on Gartrell's Resolutions, the 8th of which might have been construed into a direct censure against the late President, yourself, and others. Well that resolution was the most troublesome bone of contention in committee, and I never ceased my attacks on it until its phraseology was changed as it now is. To have gone farther would have been to abandon our constitutional rights in all the territories, past and present, which I never will do; and yet I am accused of making war against you, from having perhaps been too active in pressing the resolution through the committee and House. Now this is an issue that I do not want forced on me. I seek nothing and desire nothing. It can do me no good and may do you and others harm. In a short discussion between Genl. Wofford and myself a few days ago he charged the committee with making an attack on you. I repelled it mildly and let it pass. If it is renewed as it may be and as I know some desire it should be it will have a tendency to produce still further division in our party. The Genl. took the position in the senate, and is making an effort, at home to sustain it, that the South in this controversy should take the Missouri Compromise line and ask no more. He seems to forget that that line is not. offered and has been repudiated by the North in Congress. We claim the whole of our constitutional rights as equal co-owners of every foot of California; but for the sake of Union would do as heretofore, compromise on the Missouri line, having all other questions, and particularly that in relation to fugitive slaves, settled. Now sir this is the hour when every man and especially those in high places should speak out and speak plainly. Such has ever been your habit and I hope to hear from you as soon as practicable. For myself I am for equality or disunion, and I am sure this is the predominant feeling of Georgia.

series reads: "*Resolved,* That In the event of the passage of the Wllmot Proviso by Congress, the abolition of slavery in the District of Columbia, the admission of California as a State In its present pretended organization, or the continued refusal of the non-slaveholding States to deliver up fugitive slaves as provided in the Constitution, it will become the immediate and imperative duty of the people of this State to meet in convention to take into consideration the mode and measure of redress ". Text printed in H. V. Ames, " State Documents on Federal Relations ", pp. 259-201. 1 The fifth and sixth congressional districts comprised the northwestern and northeastern portions of the State, respectively.

Hiram Warner1 To Howell Cobb. E.

Greenville ga., *17th March, 1850.*

Dear Sir: Although I am no politician I very reluctantly obtrude myself upon your attention for the purpose of making a single suggestion in relation to the slavery question, in which we all feel a deep and abiding interest. The Nashville convention it is supposed will meet in June. I see that it has been stated that all action by Congress in relation to the settlement of that question will probably be deferred until after the meeting of that convention. My own opinion is that the question had better be settled before that convention meets, if it can be, for several reasons. That convention may not be *unanimous* as to the proper course to be pursued; and then the South will present a *divided* front and weaken its moral force. If they should be unanimous, composed as I fear it may be of *ultra* politicians who have nothing to lose but everything to gain by secession, or more properly speaking revolution, they may resolve to take such ultra grounds for a settlement of the difficulty as the people of the non-slaveholding States cannot sanction; and besides it will look like dictation on the part of the Southern States, and the North may refuse on that account; whereas nothing of that kind can operate upon them if the question is settled before the convention meets— to say nothing of the *everlasting claim* which certain individuals might suppose they would have upon the slaveholders of the South by having the question settled by what they would consider the action of the convention, when according to my judgment if the question can be settled at all it can be as well settled without the convention as with it.

Now if the North intends to settle this question and to give to the South equal rights in the common territory of the Union, she will settle on the basis of the Missouri Compromise line; and with that I shall be content, and the people of the Southern states will be content in my judgment. What the Southern people want (I mean the real stakeholders) is the right to take their slave property into the common territory south of that line and to enjoy it without *disturbance.* In that proposition there is something just and tangible; and if that right should be refused by the North our people can be rallied to fight up to that line.

It is a position which our people can take and maintain without any apprehension of disgrace by being compelled by the force of circumstances to back out from it, which can not be said of all the propositions which have been assumed and insisted upon, as *indis* 1 Born In Massachusetts, 1802; judge of the superior and supreme courts of Georgia. 1833-1840 and 1845-1853; Congressman from Georgia, 1855-1857; member of the Georgia convention of 1861, voting against secession. *pensdbly* necessary to protect the rights of the South. The great object of the Nashville convention it is said is to effect a settlement of the existing difficulty; but suppose that convention should commit the Southern people to such measures as the North could not sanction; what then is to be done? Why fight for an abstraction or for an issue from which no *practical* good can result, or abandon the *ultimatum* in disgrace? I for one do not desire to be placed in that predicament.

When I fight, if fight I must, let me fight for some *practical* object, something that will benefit me and my countrymen—something for which I will be justified in the sight of God and all mankind. Such an issue would be presented by the Missouri Compromise line. If the North refuse us our rights south of that line then it will afford *plenary* evidence that they intend to exclude us for all time from an equal enjoyment of the common territory of the Union and we can act upon that evidence—but surely there is yet enough of justice and patriotism among our Northern brethren to settle this vexed question now and forever upon the basis of the Missouri Compromise line. But what I most desired to say to you is that according to my view of things this question had better be settled if possible before the meeting of the Nashville convention, and thereby obviate the necessity of that convention, which I fear may not do as much good as might be desirable and may do much harm.

If California is admitted with her boundary limited to 36-30 or some other equivalent, then Genl. Taylor's project of admitting the whole territory as a state will be defeated, the question will be settled, and no thanks to him; and he will have to bear the odium of his admitted interference through his agent Mr. King, in attempting to bring it all in as *free* territory. The people here I do not think are as yet properly aroused as to this question, but it is my impression a settlement upon the basis of the Missouri Compromise will be satisfactory.

Judge Hill and my brother were nominated by the convention at Fayetteville last week as delegates from this congressional district to the Nashville convention, and I hope Genl. Wofford will go from your dist. I have thus hastily and confidentially given you some of my views, knowing at the same time you are in a situation to form a much more correct opinion upon the subject than I possibly can pretend to be; yet I know you will consider them in that friendly spirit in which they have been dictated. With my best wishes for your success in the discharge of the arduous duties which necessarily devolve upon you in your present position, I beg you to accept the assurance of my very high regard and friendship.

"robert Toombs To Linton Stephens.1 R.

Washington, D. C., *March 22nd, 1850.*

Dear Linton, I received your letters and have been constantly promising myself to acknowledge and thank you for them, but we have been in a whirlwind of excitement a good deal of the time here. and I have been sorely pressed with public questions, a heavy committee business and a good deal of private and professional business, which has worked me almost to the total exclusion of my correspondence. I am now getting some relief, and promise amendment for the future. I think your advent into public life was not well timed to improve your estimate of political morals; but lest the last Georgia legislature may work unfavourably on your mind, I think it but giving humanity fair play to say they were the greatest set of scoundrels that even the Democrats ever cursed the country with. I have never known such an utterly base and unprincipled majority as you had to deal with. I thought Alec and I caught the worst lot in 1839 when the whiskey insurrection overthrew the Whigs, but they were good natured drunkards and clever fellows in comparison with the lot you met with last winter, and what was worse, you had some bad fellows from our own line to deal with.

The present Congress furnishes the worst specimens of legislators I have ever seen here, especially from the North on both sides. There is a large infusion of successful jobbers, lucky serving-men, parishless parsons and itinerant lecturers among them who are not only without wisdom or knowledge but have bad manners, and therefore we can have but little hope of good legislation. With a large number of them their position is chiefly valued for the facilities it gives them for a successful foray upon the national treasury.

We have a tolerable prospect for a proper settlement of the slavery question. I should think it a strong prospect if it were not that the Calhoun wing of the South seem to desire no settlement and may perhaps go against any adjustment which would likely pass. The settlement will probably be in the main on the basis of Bell's proposition as backed by Webster. We will take that with a clause putting the rights of property of American citizens under American laws, and I think we have some chance to get it. But as I send you my speech I will not inflict a "nigger" letter upon you. Abe told me yesterday that you spoke of coming on this summer, or rather first of May. We shall be keeping house in a very pleasant part of the city and you must spend your time with us when you come. Mrs. T. sends a special message hereby to the same effect and we shall expect you as 1 Half-brother of Alexander H. Stephens; member of the Georgia House of Representatives, 1840-1853, and of the Georgia Senate, 1853-1854, judge of the supreme court of Georgia, 1859-1860, lieutenant-colonel of the BUfteenth Regiment of Georgia Volunteers in the Confederate Army.

our guest. Your brother has not been well for the last fortnight; but is about, or was out yesterday. Today I have not yet seen him. How is John Bird? Give him my best respects and tell him to write me the news.

Williams Rutherford, Jr.,1 To Howell Cobb. E.

Crawford Co. ga., *April 16th, 1850.*

Dear Howell, I suppose you have leisure enough by this time to read a letter from me. Entering as you did upon new and untried duties amidst difficulties unparalleled in the history of the government, I was conscious that your time would be fully occupied as well as your mind, and did not follow my inclination to write you a letter of congratulation upon your election. During the time the election was in suspense I felt as much anxiety on your account as any one of your numerous friends. And no event gratified me more sincerely than your success. In reading the ballotings I felt provoked at Stephens and Toombs that they did not vote for you. It seemed to my mind so clear that it was their duty to have voted for you that I did not doubt but that they would have *greedily* seized the opportunity to have shown their friendship when they could have done it without the least sacrifice of party obligation. There must have been some good reason operating upon their minds, which no doubt they have explained to you. Let me know what it was. I am not satisfied with the explanation given by the Recorder. That is, that you had not pledged yourself to so construct the committees as to prevent the "Wilmot proviso" from being forced upon the house. A reason of this sort had no weight with them in the case of Gen. Taylor; and he did not pledge himself. Yet these gentlemen plead and voted for him and justified their course (in my eyes if not in yours) on the ground that he was a Southern man and strongly identified with us, making such a pledge an idle waste of breath. Their confidence in you could not have been increased by a pledge.

Several speeches and the Patent Office report for 1848 under your frank have reached me for which I return my sincere thanks. The speeches are *great* speeches, from great men on the *great topic of the day*; and I think it fortunate that they are all printed on the same sized paper, as I intend to have them bound. I have read Mr. Wellborn's today, or rather finished it, and was highly gratified to find so good a spirit pervade the whole. The time for *vaporing* has past, and men should speak out the words of " truth in soberness." I am much pleased with both of his resolutions. Although agreeing with Berrien and Calhoun that the north has no *right* to claim our exclusion 1 Afterwards professor of mathematics In the University of Georgia.

from one foot of the territory, yet as they do claim it most earnestly and there is no *practical* benefit in our setting up a counter claim to any above 36 30' I am for settling the controversy by adopting that line. I have now most of the speeches of distinguished men on the slavery question with the exception of Mr. Calhoun's and Mr. Cass's—both of these I should be pleased to get in *pamphlet* form. And as I intend to make a book of such speeches I should like to get one or two of those on the other side provided they are from distinguished men and in statesmanlike form. Pick a good opportunity and make one yourself and let me have a copy. Mr. Calhoun, my beau ideal of a great man, is dead!! I think he has clearly vindicated himself from the charge that he *desired* disunion: in his dying effort. He has taken the true? ground in my opinion, that the true Union can alone be maintained by a rigid adherence to the Constitution. Like him I believe it ceases to be desirable when it ceases to be for the "*common welfare*" Ever since I have been able to form any definite opinion with regard to our form of government I have held to the *right of secession*. But have never desired the *occasion*. That a state has the *right* I have never doubted, any more than I have doubted that one partner has the right to withdraw from a firm when it ceases to be for his " welfare." And I never could see why this *could not* be done peaceably. It may bring about war but not necessarily.

I am about done planting, and with better prospects than I ever had. The new land which made me such fine corn last year, I have now in cotton. This together with the best of my old land will I think with the same disasters make me double the cotton made last year. But you know I am sanguine, and will make proper allowances...

Lewis Cass To Howell Cobb. E.
Washin., D. C., *May 6, 1850.*

My Dear Sir: I intended to call upon you today; but the weather is so bad and I am so much afraid of interrupting you in your devotional duties that I have concluded to drop you this note.

Mr. Clay made his report yesterday, and as I am anxious that that part of it which refers to Douglas's bills should meet your approval, I would suggest to you whether you had not better call upon him and converse with him upon the subject. From the way in which he spoke to me of you yesterday I am sure he esteems you and that you may safely talk with him upon this subject.

Thomas K. R. Cobb To Howell Cobb. E.
Milledgeville ga., *May 7th, 1850.*
Dear Brother,... There is nothing passing within my knowledge in the political world in your district worth your attention. The *people* are for the Union, and will sustain you in any honest effort to compromise honorably the question. *My own* feeling is that the abolition of the slave trade in the District is not only *allowable* but *desirable*. The only fear is to make the people understand the question when these demagogues cry out "Abolition." The good hearted and honest will be with you. Unfortunately their voice is seldom *raised* and never *heard*. I speak of this question, as I see it rumored that it is included in the proposition of the Compromise Committee....

John B. Lamar To Howell Cobb. E.
Macon, Ga., *July 3rd, 1850.*

Dear Howell, Yours of the 26th came to hand. I shall be in Washington before long. I have been detained longer than I expected in arranging to have my house tin-roofed and newly plaistered. I am nearly through, and shall leave as soon as I can get off, taking the Cowpens in my route.

The friends of the Compromise of the Committee of 13 have handed round a call for a public meeting to be held on Saturday evening at the Council Chamber. It is headed with the name of A. H. Chappell and had 104 signatures when I saw it last. You may judge from this fact how true the assertions of some of the Democratic papers are that the Compromise has no friends here. The Democratic press in middle Georgia is in the hands of those who are leading the party to the devil. Their audacious assertions have heretofore been treated as idle and harmless bravadoes; but as they are now doing mischief there seems to be a spirit rising among the people to speak out and let their representatives in Congress know what public sentiment really is.

Col. Chappell has been addressed by some of his friends to learn his views on the Compromise. He has replied in a letter which will be printed by Saturday. It is the ablest production of his pen that I ever saw and will carry force with it from the candor and truth of all its statements. I will send you a copy of it. He is out and out for the Senate Compromise.

The game playing by some of the Democratic presses is to browbeat our representatives in Congress into the belief that the people are opposed desperately to the Senate Compromise and if they vote for it their doom is sealed. It is queer how impudently they utter what everybody knows to be untrue. As an example, a press in this place in a paper of yesterday italicized these words—" the Compromise has no friends in the South and never had "; and a few hours after its appearance the above alluded to call of a meeting of the friends of the Compromise numbered over a hundred highly respectable names. I can say to you do what is right and pay no attention to what the papers say. The people will be with you in supporting the Compromise.

The noise and bluster of a few presses in Georgia is no more the voice of the people than the delegates to the Nashville Convention were their representatives.

Alexander H. Stephens To The Editors or The National Intelligencer.1

House Of Representatives, *July 3, 1850.* Gentlemen: In your paper of this morning I notice the following editorial:

We take it for granted that there is foundation, of some kind or other, for the statement in the following extract from the Washington correspondence of the New York Journal of Commerce. If it be all really true, the gallant State of Texas is about to march an Army into the Territories of the United States, and against an armed station of the United States within them; and we are to have news of it in less than six weeks from this time! Let us hope, however, that the worthy correspondent of the Journal is prematurely alarmed for the safety of Santa Fe and the detachment of the army whose duty it will be to defend it:

"Correspondence Of The Journal Of Commerce,

"*Washington, Saturday, June 29, 1850. "*There will be some startling intelligence from Texas in less than six weeks from this time. Texas will send an adequate force at once, as is supposed, to effect her objects—probably 2,500 men. There are at Santa F6 about two hundred Texan camp followers, who take an interest in favor of the Texans. The troops of the United States, under Col. Munroe, number about five or six hundred, to which six hundred are about to be added. The Texans in this city are of the opinion that Texas, supported as she is by the sympathies of the whole South, will arrest the United States military officers, and bring them to trial for obstructing the operation of her laws. Should the adjustment bill be defeated, there is no doubt that Texas will absorb New Mexico, and if the United States interfere the Southern States will give her all the aid she needs."

From this it seems that you hold it to be the "duty" of the "army" of the United States now stationed at Santa Fe to defend, without authority of law, the military occupation of that portion of New Mexico lying this side of the Rio Grande against any attempt of Texas to maintain her claim by extending her jurisdiction over it.

Your right to entertain such an opinion it is not my object to question. But I wish to say to you, lest you may be mistaken in the opinions of others, thatthe first Federal gun that shall be fired 1 From the National Intelligence". Washington, D. C, July 4, 1850.

against the people of Texas, without the authority of law, will be the signal for the freemen from the Delaware to the Rio Grande to rally to the rescue. Whatever differences of opinion may exist in the public mind touching the proper boundary of Texas, nothing can be clearer than that it is not a question to be decided by the *army.* Be not deceived, and deceive not others. *"Inter armes leges silent."* When the "Rubicon" is passed, the days of this Republic will be numbered. You may consider the "gallant State of Texas" too weak for a contest with the army of the United States. But you should recollect that the cause of Texas, in such a conflict, will be the cause of the entire South. And whether you consider Santa F6 in danger or not, you may yet live to see that fifteen states of this Union, with seven millions of people, "who, knowing their rights, dare maintain them," cannot be *easily* conquered!" *Sapientibws verbum sat."*

Absalom H. Chappell 1 To Howell Cobb. E.

Macon ga., *July 10th, 1850.* My Dear Sir: The state of things is such as is filling thousands of the best men in Georgia with deep alarm. The Democratic party of this section of the State is becoming rapidly demoralized in reference to the great question of the preservation of the Union. The game of the destructives is to use the Missouri Compromise principle as a medium of defeating all adjustment and then to make the most of succeeding events, no matter what they may be, to infuriate the South and drive her into measures that must end in disunion. We, or rather a few of us here, have done and are doing our utmost to check the torrent. The mass of the Whig party is taking the right course, but the number lost and likely to be lost from their ranks is not small.

The only effectual check however to which we can look must come from that party, and from the Democrats of your district and Hackett's.

It is of the very last importance that you should without delay throw yourself fully into the breach by an address to your constituents. Prepare I beseech you and send out at once such an address. It would have immense weight throughout the State and especially in the up-country. It will do incalculable good, and what is more, prevent incalculable and irremediable evil. There must be some counterpoise to the influence of McDonald's name with the "old panel," or all will be lost. Nothing can arrest the heady current that is now sweeping every thing to ruin, but to make the leaders and as 1 A prominent politician of central Georgia. 73568— 13 13 pirants in the movement feel that they are dimming and damning their prospects of office.

If any other Representative or Senator from Georgia, Whig or Democrat, can be prevailed on to come out with an address to the people in behalf of any course of compromise, pacification and adjustment that is not hopeless of being passed, he will be rendering the country greater service than he has ever before had the opportunity of rendering.

I send you a copy of a letter I have recently written in reply to the request of some friends.

P. S. Since writing the above, I have seen Geo. R. Hunter of Crawford, the leading and most influential Democrat in Crawford County. He is pursuing a conservative and patriotic course, but tells me there is a very strong disposition among the Democrats of that county to rush to the most deplorable lengths. I think Hunter's influence will hold the majority of them within patriotic bounds. The Whigs there are behaving right almost to a man thus far. It will be found that the Whigs are more united for what you and I deem a proper course than the Democrats are against it.

Again I entreat you to throw yourself fully and strongly into the breach by an address to your constituents.

William H. Mohton To Howell Cobb. E.

Athens ga., *10th July, 1850.* My Dear Sir: Your old friend Wm. L. Mitchell, Chief Engineer on the State Road was here last Monday and took it on himself to go round the town and see as many of the country people as he could to get them to sign a call for the 20th inst. to take into consideration the ratification of the proceedings of the Nashville convention. He has left town, but committed the business to Mr. Wm. Clayton, as I understand, to increase the signatures and agitate the people to resistance. I look on this movement of Mitchell's as a direct attack on you and your influence in this district. I think he will be put down, and his movement also. He is a professed Disunionist, and it seems to me all who go with the Nashville convention are ultimately to fall into that position. There are many people who may be misled. I would be glad if you could come and be here on the 20th inst., which is the day they have proposed meeting. Your presence would put a quietus to him and his following. Congress has had the agitation of the slavery question too long before them, and they ought to settle it on the compromise of the Senate. If things are managed right Genl. Cass could be elected next president. The Whig party had it in their power to settle all difficulty, and Mr. Webster made a start that way; but they as a party at the north are behind the times. The Democrats may yet settle everything right if they will, and yet be sustained at home, as Gen. Cass will be. The doctrine of non-intervention must succeed, and the country will be safe. S. Carolina will secede, but we can and must put a stop to it in Georgia. She will have to be taught a lesson that it would have been better to give her in 1832.

Poor Gen. Taylor has got no friends in Georgia nor in the south that I know of. I don't think there are 10 men in this state who would now vote for him for anything. His fall is as low as his military fame was high. The Northern Whigs won't do, and I hope Webster will abandon them. The Democrats are better and if they will, can save the country from further agitation, and again reinstate themselves in power. You know I am a warm Whig; but I will drop them and any one else who does not go for peace and the union.

Alexander H. Stephens To The Editors Of The Baltimore Cupper.1

Washington D. C., *13th July, 1850.* Messrs. Editors: My attention has just been called to a communication in your paper of this morning, over the signature of *Henrico,* (copied from the Philadelphia Bulletin,)2 purporting to give the incidents attending the illness of Gen. Taylor, preceding his death, which contains statements in reference to myself and colleague, Mr. Toombs, under a protestation of "repeating merely what" the correspondent "knew to be true," that I cannot permit to go to the country uncontradicted. I did not see General Taylor during his last illness, nor did my colleague, Mr. Toombs. The last interview I had with him was several days before his attack, and never, in any interview I had with him, was there the slightest allusion made in the remotest degree whatever, to the subject stated by Henrico. And I feel warranted in saying the same in relation to my colleague, Mr. Toombs. I deem it, therefore, a duty as well to myself as to the memory of the honored and illustrious dead, to say that the statement of the Bulletin's correspondent in this particular is without the shadow of foundation.

1 From the Chronicle and Sentinel (Augusta, Ga.), July 20, 1850. The "Henrico" communication was a newspaper canard reporting that Toombs and Stephens had visited President Taylor while he was suffering In his last iliness and had threatened that unless he should aid the pro-slavery cause In the legislation then pending In Congress they would cause the House of Representatives to censure him for his participation In the settlement of the Galphin claim. Stephens account of what actually occurred to give occasion for this report Is printed In A. H. Stephens, Recollections, M. L Avary ed., N. T., 1910, p. 26.

Howell Cobb To William Hope Hull.1

Washington City, *July 17th, 1850.*

Dear Sir: Having received a number of letters asking my opinion on the various propositions which have been suggested for the settlement of the slavery question, I have determined... to make this communication as an answer to them all.

In order that we may form a reliable judgment upon the proper basis of a settlement of our existing difficulties, it is necessary that we should consider their origin and progress. A brief analysis of these points will aid us materially in arriving at a proper conclusion, if our object is, as it should be, the elucidation of truth. I do not propose to go farther back in our history than the acquisition of our Mexican territories—although a review of the annexation of Texas, and the causes which led to the war which resulted in these acquisitions, would not be wholly uninstructive in the investigation. In my anxiety to economize time, I shall forego any disposition I might feel, under more favorable circumstances, to indulge in the trains of reflection which this branch of the subject would naturally suggest. It is a duty which others have performed in a very satisfactory manner, and I leave it where they have placed it.

When the war with Mexico was brought to a close we found ourselves as the result of that memorable conflict the owners of a vast territory, almost wholly unpeopled and represented to abound in mineral and other resources which were likely, with its other natural advantages, to render its settlement and future policy an object of anxious solicitude to the people of the different sections of the Union. As diversified as are the character, interests and prejudices of our people, scattered over a widely extended country, following pursuits imbibing prejudices and educated with thoughts, feelings and passions as variant as the soil, climate and habits of our extended domain would naturally produce, it was yet found that there existed but one element of discord which was likely to have a material effect in the adoption of the proper policy to be pursued in reference to this new and vast addition to our territorial limits.

It is hardly necessary to say that the institution of African slavery in the Southern States constituted this only element. The people of the South with unparalleled unanimity asserted *their right* under the guarantees and provisions of the Constitution to remove into these common territories, the purchase of their blood and treasure, in common with their brethren of the North, and to carry with them their slave property, just as the people of the other sections of the Union could remove with their property of any other char 1 From the Chronicle and Sentinel, Augusta, Ga., Aug. 20 and 21, 1850.
acter. The North on the other hand asserted that it was their right and duty to prevent the settlement of those territories with slave property, by the exercise of a power claimed by them to reside in the Congress of the United States. They declared that Congress had the power and should exercise it to pass laws prohibiting the people of the South from emigrating to that country with their slaves. Such a law was proposed and has been urged from that day to the present time with all the influence which fanatical zeal and sectional prejudice could bring to bear in its favor. This law is known to the country under the familiar title of the " Wilmot Proviso," its object and purposes being such as I have attributed to it. These were the antagonistical principles which the two sections of the country had arrayed against each other, the South declaring *her constitutional right* to go with her slave property into the territories, the North declaring at the same time her constitutional right and duty to prevent it by congressional legislation.

This controversy thus begun raised the question of the constitutional rights of the South in relation to this matter. The South with a conscious confidence in the constitutional right which she asserted repudiated the idea that Congress was the proper forum before whom this issue was to be tried. She would not recognize in Congress a constitutional arbiter of her rights under that solemn compact which holds us together and prescribes our various duties and relationships under the federal government, and therefore firmly resolved not to submit tamely to such judgment as Congress might see fit to pass upon her rights if such judgment should be in violation of those rights which she declared to be solemnly guaranteed to her by the Constitution of the country.

It is not necessary for the purposes of this investigation here to inquire either after the time, place or manner for the constitutional ascertainment of these rights. It is sufficient to know that the South *denied to Congress* the exercise of any such power. It was thus, then, that we of the South presented the issue to our brethren of the North, utterly denying that the Constitution conferred any power upon Congress either to exclude us from the common territories of the Union or to decide upon our constitutional right in regard to them. We asked no recognition of the first principle laid down at the hands of Congress, for that would have involved us in the absurdity of seeking Congressional action at the very time that we were denying the power to act; but *we did demand* a conformity to the second position which we assumed, and that was that Congress could not and should not by its legislation, or in other words by the adoption of the Wilmot Proviso, exclude us from participating in the settlement of those territories with our property of every description.

To this demand a portion of our northern brethren gave a prompt and satisfactory response. With us they denied the power which had been claimed for Congress to legislate on the subject; with us they regarded the people upon whose happiness and prosperity such legislation was to operate as a more fit and appropriate tribunal for the decision of so momentous a question as the nature and character of the laws and institutions under which they were to live. At what time this power could be properly exercised by the people of the territories was a point upon which diversity of opinion existed, but all agreed in denying its existence in Congress. The South and a portion of the North being thus agreed upon the great point at issue, to wit: *that Congress could not constitutionally legislate upon the subject,* we very naturally set to work to agree upon *a basis of action.* We erected a platform conformable to our agreed opinions— that platform was Non-intervention, truly and powerfully expressive of the principle it was intended to represent. Those northern statesmen who thus nobly and generously responded to our constitutional demands took upon themselves the discharge of a labor and duty of no ordinary magnitude. A strong current of passion and prejudice had been set in motion by the inflammatory appeals of sectional partisans. It was sweeping every thing before it in its ruthless course and threatened to bury beneath its turbid waters any and every patriotic spirit who might have the temerity to throw himself into the breach and attempt to arrest its onward progress; but there were men of iron nerves and patriotic hearts who dared to do their duty in this trying crisis. They met this maddened spirit of aggression with a stern and unbending defiance. They had counselled with us around the altars of our common country, and having agreed with us that the doctrine of Non-intervention was the doctrine of the Constitution they went forth, panoplied in that sacred armor, to do battle in the cause of truth and justice and right. They now return to us, after a hard and desperate but triumphant struggle, with the fruits of victory—and we are told, "Touch them not, for they will turn to ashes on your lips."

In the progress of this vexed question we have given a still more substantial evidence of our confidence in the constitutional principle we have asserted and our willingness to abide by its operation. It was upon this doctrine that the South gave its support to the plan of settlement known as the "Clayton Compromise bill." It is unnecessary for me to examine the details of that bill, for none will deny that its only merit which commended it to southern support was drawn from the consideration that it repudiated congressional legislation on the subject of slavery and left the adjudication of the constitutional question of our rights in the territories to the only tribunal having jurisdiction over the subject. *Non-intervention* was the basis upon which the bill rested, and as such it received the warm and cordial support of a large portion of the southern people, and when it was defeated by those who demanded congressional interference the dissatisfaction and regret of the southern mind was expressed in loud and deep denunciations of those who were charged with the high offence of having sacrificed by the defeat of this measure the best interests of the South at the shrine of mere party devotion. I do not propose to break the train of my present reflections by stopping to inquire into the correctness of that charge—I simply refer to it to illustrate the deep and settled conviction which had fastened itself upon the public mind of the South that in the doctrine of non-intervention we should find an ample guaranty for the protection of our constitutional rights on this subject. I have spoken of it as the doctrine *of the South.* I am aware that there were some who from the beginning have held a different opinion, as the facts to which reference has just been made very clearly show; but I cannot be at fault in saying that the number of those who dissented from the doctrine, was comparatively small, and I know that with my own political party it was universally approved and sanctioned.

I have taken this review of the past history of this question for the purpose of bringing clearly and distinctly before our minds *the true issue* which has divided the two sections of the country, distracting our national councils and alienating the hearts and affections of our people one from another. Let us bear constantly in mind the origin of the controversy, the points of difference which have separated us, and more particularly the principles upon which we have heretofore stood, in order that we may decide correctly and honestly how far these principles will be violated or sustained in any mode of adjustment that we may be required to examine. With me these principles, which in common with the people of the South I am so deeply committed to, shall constitute the touch-stone by which I will test the soundness of the proposed modes of settlement which I am now called upon to consider.

There are three plans before the country for the settlement of this question, which it seems principally engage the public mind. The one or the other of these will doubtless be ultimately adopted, but which of them is destined to be successful it is impossible now to say, and indeed much depends upon the course which the South may adopt in reference to them.

The plan of the late administration (Gen. Taylor's) which proposes to admit California as a State, to be followed in rapid succession by the admission of New Mexico and other States without much reference either to the character or number of the people who may inhabit the territory, is obnoxious to so many and such grave objections and has met with so little favor with the people of the South that I deem it unnecessary to bestow upon its consideration even a passing notice. It has received the universal condemnation of our people, and is discarded as utterly worthless and odious. A large portion of the South is now urging the adoption of the Missouri Compromise line, as not only a satisfactory but *the only* satisfactory mode of settlement. It possesses many advantages which have commended it to the favor of southern men, and has been regarded during the whole progress of the controversy by some as eminently 'suited to the purpose of quieting this harrassing sectional agitation and giving repose to the public mind. I may be permitted to express my regret that it did not sooner find favor with many of its present warmest advocates in our State. There was a time when the prospect of adopting it was far more promising than at present. In the early history of our present difficulties I was among the number of those who believed that the South could with justice and propriety acquiesce in that mode of settlement, notwithstanding her constitutional objections to Congressional legislation on the subject. My reasons for so believing have been so frequently presented to the people of my district that it would be worse than superfluous to repeat them. It will be recollected by those who are at all familiar with our Congressional history that I have given votes in accordance with this view of the subject, nor will it fail to attract their attention that those votes thus given have been made the subject of the severest censure by some of those who are now most solicitous for the adoption of a similar policy. I may be permitted to express in a passing word the gratification it has afforded me to witness "this change which has come over the spirit of their dreams."

In order however to understand the comparative merits of this and another mode of settlement, which I shall present to your consideration, it will be necessary to look at the practical details of the plan as proposed to be carried out by those who give it their preference.

The friends of the Missouri Compromise line are willing to admit California as a State with her southern limits restricted to the parallel of latitude 36 deg. 30 m. This, with the organization of territorial governments north of that line in the balance of the territory prohibiting slavery and south of the line permitting it, constitutes the main features of their plan of settlement. There is some diversity of sentiment among them upon the question of recognizing the existence of slavery in such territorial governments as may be formed south of the line 36 deg. 30 m.; but whether recognized by Congress or not, no one proposes to force the institution of slavery into any portion of the territory against the wishes of the people who may emigrate there and inhabit it; so that at last its existence there must depend, as it should, upon the decision of the people of the territories. This fact should be borne in memory to prevent the public mind from falling into the fatal error of supposing that the adoption of Missouri Compromise line was the absolute establishment of slavery in any portion of that country. Such a result does not necessarily follow upon this mode of adjustment. Soil, climate and the general adaptation of the country to slave labor are the great elements that must mould and regulate the institutions of those territories if left free from the operation of Congressional restrictions, and hence it is that we have heretofore been so willing to repose in confidence upon the constitutional doctrine of non-intervention. Such is the plan of settlement which the friends of the Missouri Compromise line propose. I have already referred to the fact that this mode of adjustment had heretofore received my approval. It still commends itself to my favor, and hence I am prepared again to give it my vote and support. I have observed that with some this measure has been regarded as antagonistical to all of the other modes of adjustment which have been proposed. I cannot give my assent to this view of the matter. It does not follow as a necessary consequence that our approval of this proposition precludes us from the favorable consideration of other terms of settlement which may be offered. Whilst we give to this the fullest appreciation of its merits we shall not fail fairly to scan the terms of other propositions with a sincere desire to arrive at a proper conclusion in reference to them all. It is in this spirit that I have considered them; and to this spirit among our people do I commend the conclusions to which my reflections have brought my mind.

The remaining plan of settlement which I desire to consider is the bill of the Senate committee of thirteen, of which Mr. Clay was chairman. It proposes the admission of California as a State with her present boundary, the organization of territorial governments for the balance of the country upon the principle of "non-intervention" in reference to the subject of slavery, and the settlement of the boundary between Texas and New Mexico. These are the only objects of the bill about which any sectional diversity of opinion exists. Serious objections have been urged to the admission of California as a State in consequence of the great irregularities which attended the organization of her State government, as well as the improper influences which, it is alleged, were brought to bear upon her people in the formation of her State constitution. In these objections there is much force, and I shall not pretend to justify or approve of the course of proceedings which have brought about the present state of things. It is only necessary for me to know that these objections are not so grave and formidable in their character as to require at my hands the entire rejection of California as a state when the question is prescribed to me as part of a general system of settlement by which peace and quiet is to be restored to my country, torn and distracted by the most angry and alarming dissensions. We have the satisfaction of knowing that the constitution which California presents to us has received the sanction and approval of her people, and that in the progress of time, should the inhabitants of that country be satisfied that their interest and prosperity require a change of their fundamental law, the power exists with them to alter, change and modify it at pleasure. The mere fact that her constitution excludes the institution of slavery constitutes no valid or constitutional objection to her admission as a State. The right of the people to pass upon this and all kindred questions in the organization of their State governments is a principle which needs only to be stated to be admitted and sanctioned. There is no principle, I am sure, which has received a more universal approval among southern statesmen than the one I have just asserted, and I entertain no apprehension that it will be seriously questioned at the present time. I find myself however relieved from the necessity of examining critically this branch of the subject from the fact that the friends of each plan of settlement are agreed upon the one point of the admission of California as a State. It is true that there are some who are opposed to her admission on constitutional grounds, and who could not therefore give their support to any measure of adjustment of which this feature was a constituent part; but I feel quite certain that the number who entertain this extreme position is comparatively small. With the great majority of those who have seriously considered of the settlement in question there has been a general concurrence of assent to the admission of California as a State. The point of difference between the friends of the Missouri Compromise basis and the bill I am now considering, so far as the admission of California is concerned, is limited to the question of boundary. The former insist upon restricting her southern boundary to the latitude of 36 deg. 30 min.; and with such restriction they would support her admission, notwithstanding the objections to which I have alluded; and you will bear in mind that those objections apply in the one case as well as in the other. This being true, it narrows this branch of the subject to the isolated point whether or not this difference of boundary is of sufficient magnitude and importance as to justify the warm supporters of the one plan in their irreconcilable opposition to the other. If the admission of California with restricted boundaries be a measure just and acceptable to the South, I am at a loss to understand how her admission with more extended boundaries can be regarded as a measure justifying the extreme and violent opposition which has been threatened to it. I am fully aware of the feeling of opposition entertained by our people to the admission of California as a State as a separate and distinct measure; but I am considering it as a part of a general system of adjustment, and in that light I feel confident that you will agree with me in the conclusion that there does not exist between the two propositions such a broad difference as many are disposed to think.

The next feature in the Senate bill worthy of our notice is the organization of territorial governments for the remaining portions of the territories, upon the principles of "non-intervention." I have been gratified to observe in the public discussions on this branch of the subject that this part of the adjustment has received the sanction of many of those who have opposed it as a whole. Others, I regret / to say, have been uncandid enough not to notice it at all, thereby leaving the impression that it contained no such provision, whilst a few have repudiated the doctrine, to which they were heretofore so fully committed, as unworthy of their further support. I can entertain no doubt that with the great mass of our people there will be found a general approval of this feature of the bill. Indeed, how can it be otherwise? It is a practical assertion of the constitutional principle for which we have so long and anxiously contended. It virtually repudiates the odious doctrine of aggression threatened in the enforcement of the "Wilmot Proviso," leaving the decision of the subject where we have always desired that it should be left, where the Constitution has put it, in the hands of the people, to be decided by their free and unrestricted will under the operation of those great natural causes and influences to which I have already referred. Whatever may be said by others, the democratic supporters of " nonintervention" can find, no cause of complaint in this feature of the settlement.

If we should institute a comparison between this feature of the present bill and the corresponding feature of the Missouri line basis we should find that the former possesses decided advantages over the latter, unless we are prepared to admit that we have been wholly at fault in our assertion of the constitutional right of the people to remove into any portion of the common territory with their slave property. Taking it for granted that the South is not willing to make this humiliating confession, let us look at the comparative advantages of the two plans. Whilst the present bill opens the whole country not included within the limits of California to the operation of our doctrine of " non-intervention," and thereby secures to our people the constitutional right to go into any portion of it with their slave property, the other plan positively excludes them from all that portion of it lying north of 36 30', leaving only the territory south of that line accessible to them. Even granting that the right which the Constitution gives us is recognized by Congress—*a tribunal whose jurisdiction we deny*—still, as I have before remarked, that does not necessarily ensure the existence of slavery there unless those natural causes which must control the ultimate decision of the question should favor that result, causes which will operate, in my humble judgment, as effectually in the one case as in the other. If so, the advantages of the present plan are just to the extent of the country lying north of 36 30', from which under the other settlement we should be excluded by positve prohibition. In any view of the subject I must regard this provision of the bill as wholly free from objection.

This brings me to the last provision of the Senate bill, which provides for the settlement of the boundary between Texas and New Mexico. The opponents of this measure assert that this portion of the bill proposes to take from Texas a large portion of her territory and transfer it to New Mexico. I will not stop to discuss the title of Texas to the boundary which she claims. I hold that her claim to that boundary is good, but it is unnecessary at this time to give my reasons for that opinion. Others however entertain a different opinion, and we find the ablest statesmen of the country entertaining widely different sentiments in regard to it. The question must be settled in some way and by some tribunal, and I can see no constitutional objection to a settlement of a question of boundary between one of the States of the Union and the territory of the United States by Congress, with the assent and approval of that State. It is not sought in this instance to coerce Texas into the terms of settlement which are proposed; her free assent is asked, and if denied, the parties are respectively remanded to their former rights, and the offer of settlement becomes a nullity. It would seem to be a sufficient reply to all the objections which have been made to this provision of the bill that it is a matter peculiarly belonging to Texas to determine upon; and being identified with the South in the preservation of the institution of slavery, we should be the last to object to her as the final arbiter to decide upon the subject. If the terms offered are derogatory to her character, destructive of her interest and violative of her rights as a sovereign State, she will doubtless reject them and rely upon other means to preserve her domain from the ruthless invasion of the United States. It is alleged however that this measure proposes to rob Texas of a large portion of her territory where slavery now exists by law, for the purpose of dedicating it to free-soil. This is indeed a strange argument in the mouth of those who have held with me the doctrine of our constitutional rights in all the territories, which I have already discussed. How is this cession of country to be given up to free-soil? Does not the same bill propose to organize over it a territorial government on the principles of "non-intervention," *our own favorite doctrine* which we have unceasingly declared by word and votes gave to us our full constitutional rights in the territories? Standing then where we have always stood, firmly poised upon this great constitutional principle,

I deny that there is in this proposition any surrender of slave territory offered up, as is charged, to propitiate free-soil fanaticism. Indeed, so far from this being true, the very fact that slavery now exists by law in that portion of the territory which Texas cedes to the United States will greatly strengthen the Southern position of its constitutional existence throughout the territory to which it may be annexed.

No one who has observed the events of recent occurrence in connection with this subject can fail to appreciate the pressing importance of its early and satisfactory adjustment. The contest which is likely to take place between the State of Texas and the people of New Mexico residing within the disputed territory presents a more urgent argument for its speedy adjudication than any political considerations which I can offer. It appeals to the justice and patriotism of the country in terms which demand an early and prompt response. The advantages which Texas would derive from this settlement of her disputed boundary are of no inconsiderable importance. The pecuniary equivalent which she would receive from the Government for the cession she is asked to make would enable her to throw off a heavy debt which now hangs like an incubus over her, bearing down the energies of her people, and driving from her borders the tide of population which is ever rolling towards our newly settled countries. I entertain no doubt that from the new impetus which would be given to her settlement and consequent increased prosperity, she would soon furnish her sister States of the South a far more acceptable equivalent for the surrendered territory—if indeed it should turn out to be surrendered—in the new sisterhood of Southern States which she would be enabled to lead to our national altar for admission as States into the Union.

I have thus far discussed this bill without reference to any amendments that might be made to it, avowing my willingness to support it as it now stands. I entertain no doubt that the bill could and would be amended in one important provision if the support of the entire South could thereby be obtained in its favor. I allude to the southern boundary of California. The southern boundary could be restricted to the latitude of 35 deg. 30 min., a natural boundary, by the co-operation of the present friends of the measure and the southern members. Such a change would probably lose the bill a portion of its northern support, but the united vote of the South would more than compensate for such loss, and would in my opinion secure its success in this amended form. But I regret to say that such proposed amendment fails to conciliate the southern opposition to the bill.

I have now given you with candor and frankness the views which I entertain of the two propositions for the settlement of this vexed question. I have endeavored to run a parallel between them, comparing their respective advantages and disadvantages. I cannot regard either of them as free from objection, yet I have been unable to discover in either objections of a character grave and imposing enough to preclude me from giving it my support. The one comes to me under the sanction of a precedent which in a past crisis of the country gave quiet and repose to an agitated and distracted people. whilst the other commends itself to my favor by the sound and salutary principles of constitutional right in which it is conceived.

I shall not add to the length of this letter by a discussion of the other bills reported by the Senate committee on the subjects of the slave trade in the District of Columbia and fugitive slaves. They are not necessarily connected with the subject I have been considering, and my views can be presented to my constituents at some other time. They are separate and distinct bills, and not provisions of the Compromise bill as is erroneously supposed by many.

There are other grave and important considerations which I should be pleased to bring to the notice of our people in connection with this settlement and the probable effect of its rejection. but for the present I forbear.

John H. Lumpkin To Howell Cobb.
E.

Rome, ga., *21 July, 1850.*

My Dear Cobb, I was much gratified to receive a letter from you after your long silence, and more delighted to understand from your letter that with the aid of the new administration the measure of adjustment proposed by Mr. Clay as the chairman of the committee of thirteen would be passed substantially as it is.

Since I last wrote you the Nashville convention has been held, and with a view of defeating any measure of settlement they have proposed a settlement on the basis of the old Missouri Compromise line, with slavery prohibited north of 36.30 and recognized by express enactment south of that line. I say to defeat any settlement, because they say that they will accept nothing less, which to my mind under the circumstances is equivalent to saying that it is their ultimatum, their sine qua non; and they do not even wish that to be tendered them. And I say this because they have always repudiated this compromise heretofore as unconstitutional, and they have only proposed it now when it is known to be impracticable, and as a measure always popular with the democracy at the South, and as a measure better calculated than any other to rally on as the antagonist plan of settlement to the one proposed by Mr. Clay, and the one most likely to pass both houses of Congress. And they are holding meetings in my portion of the state to ratify the proceedings of the Nashville convention, and they will obtain I fear a large majority of the democratic party, who will go along with them upon the ground that they prefer the Missouri Compromise line to any other measure of compromise or settlement, and not because they will not accept or abide the measure of the committee of 13, should it pass both houses of Congress. The democrats in the last Legislature have done us great mischief, and I fear that they have yielded themselves up into the hands of wild and visionary spirits, and once committed they will follow them to destruction. The Whig party in this section are united to a man for a settlement of the question and the preservation of the Union. The democrats, I am sorry to inform you, are divided; and I fear a majority of the democrats now prefer the Nashville platform or the Missouri Compromise line to any mode of settlement. A majority of the democrats are however for a settlement in good faith; but the danger is that they will be committed by the ultras for an impractical mode of settlement, and when that mode fails and some other succeeds they may be induced to form a portion of a party now organizing for resistance and a dissolution of the Union.

Wm. L. Mitchell and various other prominent individuals I have met with are in favor of a dissolution of the Union *per se* (as I understand uncle Jos. H. Lumpkin has written to you he is), and newspaper editors have become bold enough to insert communications in their columns without any remark of disapprobation, openly advocating an immediate dissolution of the Union. And this is what Fouche, Colquitt, and all that class of men in the South desire.... A meeting was held on the fourth day of July in Cobb. Fouche, Stiles, McDonald and Joe Brown were the only persons invited or who attended; and they had everything in their own way. They studiously concealed from the people their ulterior purposes, and carefully arranged it so that no one opposed to them should be heard on that occasion. A meeting has been called by Fouche, our delegate to the Nashville Convention, for the friends of Southern Rights to meet in this county on the 23rd inst. to ratify the proceedings of the Nashville Convention. Court was here last week and will continue here this week. I was in attendance on the court last week and I am compelled to be absent at Hamilton County circuit court this week, and this was known to them, and they have made this appointment, in my opinion, to avoid my presence. I shall endeavor through my friends who remain here to get them to postpone the meeting until I can return home, and give notice for the whole people of the county to come together; and if they will do this we shall put them down. If this is not done, we shall call a larger meeting in favor of a just and amicable settlement of the slavery question and the preservation of the Union; and in this way we shall control publick sentiment on this question. Scott, Printup and myself are for the settlement, Fouche, Cuyler and Barclay Terhune against it, and Judge Hooper is on the Bench and a neutral. Mitchell, a Whig, is against the Clay compromise; Judge Underwood, Alexander, Coulter, Trammel, and in fact all the other Whig lawyers and Whigs, are for the Clay compromise. Let the bill or bills proposed by the committee of 13 pass, and I will insure it that two-thirds of the people of Georgia will be for the Union as it is, and against all resistance and all dissolution. But for God's sake let it pass at once, and so not keep us longer in suspense. I saw Billy Woods yesterday; he is sound and he assured me that the people of the mountains are with you and for a settlement of the question.

Col. Hackett is now at Rowland's Springs. I understand he is improving and has gained some strength since he arrived there. Hopes are now entertained that he will recover. The appointment of my old friend T. Butler King, Secretary of the Navy, will not give much strength to the Administration at this time in this state. His mission to California has not given him any strength with Southern men of either party. John W. H. Underwood is now here and has purchased property and intends to move here this fall. He is not for either plan of settlement. In other words he does not like either of them, but if passed will acquiesce. He will not be a member of a resistance party. Doct. H. V. M. Miller occupies the same position. All who are for resistance and for disunion will be found in the ranks of the democratic party; and if their history should be known, they will be found out to be old Nullifiers in 1832.

John H. Lumpkin To Howell Cobb.
E.

Rome ga., *29 July, 1850.* Dear Cobb, I have been absent from home for a few days and I have been very sick also during the time. I am however now on foot and able to give you a short letter. Fouche and some others designed to hold a meeting in this county in my absence and without my knowing it. But I accidentally ascertained the fact, and conferred with some of my friends and told them how to manage in my absence. I told them to propose a postponement of the meeting to some future day, upon the ground that they desired all the people of the county invited, and a full expression of publick sentiment in regard to the measures proposed for a settlement of the slavery issues. If this was not agreed to, then marshall all the strength that they could and defeat the passage of Resolutions ratifying the proceedings of the Nashville Convention, or to vote down any Resolutions that proposed the Missouri Compromise line as an ultimatum or sine qua non. And to be sure not to permit resolutions to pass denouncing the measures now pending before the Senate for settlement of all the questions in dispute. I am told that the majority of the meeting were opposed to the " factionists ", " agitators ", and " disunionists ", and they had the sagacity to see it, and moved themselves to postpone the meeting until the 15th of August, and proposed to have free discussion before the people upon all the proposed plans for a settlement of the controversy. This was agreed to, and thus the meeting adjourned over until that time. The Democrats here are divided now, and the Whigs are to a man for a settlement of the question upon the basis of the Clay Compromise substantially. There may be here and there an exception. But I hazard nothing when I say the Whigs here are unanimous for the settlement of the question upon the basis of Mr. Clay's Bill. And you may say this to Stephens and Toombs. ... Why does not the Senate pass the pending bills at once? If this was done the question would be settled, and my word for it, the disunionists would be scattering in all this region of country. This is the fight I want to see made. I will be then where I was in 1832, on the old Jackson and Union platform, and I shall never despair of the result. But if new parties are formed or reorganized at the South, one thing must be incorporated into *our platform* as a fundamental principle,—we take no new country after a given day. It is to such that we owe all of our present divisions in the democratic party at the South. I will endeavor to avoid such breakers in future.

D. M. Haley To Howell Cobb. E.

Canton, Mississippi, *Augt. 2d, 1850.* Dear Sir: I have just read your letter to Mr. H. Hull of the 17th July last in which you admit the title of the State of Texas to be good to the territory she claims. As a Southern man and one in favour of a Constitutional Union of these Confederate States, I will take the liberty to ask of you to point out to me or any of the Members in Congress from this State (as I have the honor of an acquaintance with them) the clause of the Constitution of the United States that gives Congress the power to purchase territory from a State and then put the same under Territorial Government by an act of Congress? I have examined that instrument in vain to find such a clause. I consider such a power assumed by Congress to be of more danger to the South than almost any act that Congress could do for the safety of the free institutions of our beloved country.

Believe me to be a friend of the Union on constitutional principles, upon the broad principles of equality to all the citizens of 73566—13 14

Union, North and South, East and West, as laid down by our fathers that created it and brought it into existence.

You will please excuse the liberty of a stranger and a whig, but I claim this liberty as we are all American citizens and have the same object in view, the peace and happiness of all.

I have written several letters to the Honl. A. G. Brown of the House over which you preside, who can give you the assurance of my fidelity to my country and liberty to man, here and elsewhere.

Howell Cobb To His Wife. E.

Washington, D. C, *Aug. 10, 1850.* My Dear Wife,... You will see that the Senate has passed the Texas boundary bill. If we can carry it through the House as I hope and believe we shall, it will save us from the most imminent cause of danger to the Union, and will in my opinion greatly expedite the ultimate and rapid settlement of the whole slavery question. It is hard to say whether the temper of the House is getting worse or better. Sometimes my opinion inclines one way, and then the other. Upon the whole I feel encouraged to look for a settlement at an early day pretty much upon the basis of the Clay compromise bill, though I almost fear to express an opinion upon the action of this Congress, as I have in some respects missed the mark heretofore. From the beginning I have thought that the question would be settled and upon this basis, and trust that the result will show that in this main particular I have been right...

James A. Meriwether 1 To Howell Cobb. E.

Eatonton ga., *84th August, 1850.*

My Dear Sir: I read your letter a few days since and was very much pleased with its tone. Your views are sound and wholesome. Another duty will shortly devolve on you; of writing another in favor of preserving and maintaining the Union.

The treasonable assemblage which was advertised as a part of the performances of the week came off at Macon a day or two since. The crowd was not exactly as great as that which Lafayette met at New York, yet it was large enough to find accommodation at the hotels, without the necessity of camping, or lying out. In truth it was a stupendous failure, so felt and acknowledged. A gentleman present informs me that there were not eight hundred of the fireeaters on the ground, and he says they recommended disunion as the true policy. The godlike Rhett and his adjutant Yancey preached most eloquently in behalf of treason....

1 Judge of the superior court of Georgia (Ocomulgee circuit), 1845-1849.

I have recently read the resolutions of a so-called Southern meeting at Washington, and without knowing who I shall hit, I will say, that the representative who votes for them will find himself without a constituency. You cannot imagine how perfectly quiet the whole people are on the subject of all the stir and fuss at Washington, and they are heartily sick and disgusted at the pretended excitement there. Nobody at home, Whig or Democrat, believes that any man there feels what he expresses of ultraism. Party harness sets very loosely on the people of Georgia at this time, and we are prepared to adjust it according to the principles of the man, either as he is for or against the Union. As for my own part, I will never vote for any man whose devotion to the Union is not beyond suspicion, and by his conduct evinces his opposition to the factious feelings of the day.

I have no question that Gov. Towns will call a convention if California is admitted into the Union, and then comes the issue at once, Union or disunion. I have not the first fear of the result. The traitors who seek its dissolution will not muster a corporal's guard.

California ought to be admitted; she is entitled to admission, and I hope all the representatives from Georgia will rise superior to mere sectional prejudices, which their constituents do not approve, and vote for it. With the exception of a few who fear Calhoun's ghost will haunt them if they *do right,* this district is unanimous so far as I can learn. If the disunionists force the alternative upon us of disunion or fight, I shall take the latter. In truth, before I will submit to disunion for anything that is likely to occur, I will spend the balance of my days in the tented field, and I am persuaded this is the sentiment of nine tenths of the Whigs and three fourths of the democrats. I do most sincerely trust that our representatives at Washington will rebuke by their patriotic course this factious, sectional and treasonable course....

I have had a great horror of civil war, believing it was likely to follow the treasonable course of certain men in Georgia; but I have made up my mind to submit to its curses, and am now ready for the contest.

The impression I see prevails at Washington among our Senators that if California is admitted into the Union the Gov. will convene a convention! There is no law authorizing any such act on his part. The Legislature authorized him to call a convention provided *California and New Mexico* were admitted as a state, but not for the admission of California alone....

Your position is one which will enable you to do a great deal of good to the country. Take, then, all the measures which have passed the Senate and pass them through the House. They are based on the principles of eternal right, and ought to prevail.

If I should have happened to have run across your path, you must excuse it to that devotion and anxiety I feel to save the Union from destruction and our common country from unnecessary excitement....

Robert Toombs To Millard Fillmore.1

Washington, D. C, *Sept. 9, 1850*. Mr. Toombs had the honor of receiving the President's note this evening and regrets with him the declension of Mr. Jenkins.2 Mr. T. thinks that if it be agreeable to the President, it will be best to publish Mr. Jenkins's letter. In view of recent events Mr. T. thinks its publication would be advantageous to the friends of the administration in the South.

William Woods To Howell Cobb. E. Dahlonega ga., *Sept. 15th, 1850*. Dear Sir: The news of the final passage of the California Bill reacht here today. Some ar pleasd and some displeasd. The Governor will call a Convention there is no doubt, and the action of Congress will come directly before the people. The contest is going to be one of excitement and troubel such as I have before said to you I did not desire to witness, but I am no disunionist, nor neither do I think a majority of my section of the State will be; not satisfied entirely with the passage of the Bill, yet we ar willing to abide the action of Congress. I have bin mixen amonst the people for the last three weeks at the Courts and I find nearly all the leading Democrats opposed to the Bill, and some of them ready to do enything for redress. Some for non intercourse, and some for cesesion and some openly declare there preference to disolve the union than submit.

r
I have circulated a number of your copys of your letter in this County and Union. Some of the Ultrys hardly would recieave them; they curse you loud and often; they to mostly Democrats. Some of them ar purposing to swap you and Lumpkin for Stephens and Tooms, *to wit* such men as our very worthy friend G. N. Lester and meny other good and trew Democrats. This is rather prevoken, but I think we will be able to stand up to them and in the mean time advance the true intrest of our country.

I hope you may land safely home and reddy to enter into the political struggle that now awaits us. I have evry confidence your l MS. (autograph note) in the possession of the Buffalo, N. Y., Historical Society, Fillmore papers, vol. 9, no. 6. It is indorsed: "Hon. R. Toombs, Washington, Sept. 9, 1850. Relative to publishing letter of Mr. Jenkins declining appointment of Secretary of Department of the Interior.

1 Charles J. Jenkins, then a prominent Georgia Whig; author of the " Georgia Platform," 1850; governor of Georgia, 1865-1868. presents and influence will serve much to the furtherance of the course advocated by your friends in your own native State.

Luther J. Glenn To Howell Cobb. E. Mcdonouoh ga., *Sept. 21st, 1850.*

My Dear Sir: I would have been glad to have heard from you more frequently during the present session of Congress, and I should be more gratified to see you when you return from Washington. I fear however that I shall not have that pleasure.

No one is more truly rejoiced than myself that the exciting question of the day has been settled by Congress, and peace and quiet once more restored to the country—at least would be but for the convention that will be called in Georgia. You have doubtless seen that it is the intention of the Governor to call the convention. In some portions of the State the election of delegates will produce an angry and excited contest. With us I don't think there will be much excitement. We have but few "Fire Eaters," and none that are very rampant. The Whigs in this county are united to a man, while but *very few* of the Democrats will favor any measure looking to secession or a dissolution. Gov. McDonald's name has done more for the cause of the "Ultras" in this quarter than everything else beside. Being an old Union man, their Governor, and once having been judge of this circuit, there are many who think that whatever he says and does is " law and gospel."

I am astonished that the Governor should have been caught in the trap: but so it is, and it is now necessary, he doubtless thinks, to get every other Democrat "to cut off his tail." In this however he will be mistaken. The people are not ready to sacrifice the best government ever established, to redress "imaginary evils" existing in a distempered fancy at a distance of three thousand miles or more.

The fire-eaters have made high calculations upon the accession of Messrs. Toombs and Stephens to their cause. Since the "latter day " revelations of those gentlemen, however, the stock has fallen.

I confess I have not been able to comprehend the course of those gentlemen, unless it be that they intended to place themselves in such a position that they might, without incurring the charge of inconsistency, join either the "house of York or Lancaster," as circumstances might make it prudent. Many of their own party, in this county *at* least, have not approved of the "mysterious course" they have seen proper to pursue.

On the issue of union or disunion, the latter will not be able to muster a corporal's guard in this county..

The great object of the fire-eating papers has been to excite prejudice in their favor by abusing you. I think their abuse will recoil upon their own heads.

John H. Lumpkin To Howell Cobb. E.

Rome ga., *5 Octr., 1850.* Dear Cobb, I congratulate you on your return home from Washington, after the longest and most important session of Congress that I have ever known. You have had a most laborious session, and ought to have some liesure and repose during this and the next month. But it is most important that you should mingle with the people and make speeches. We have made our arrangements for a tremendous massmeeting of the Union party at Kingston. It will come off on the 8th of Novr. next, and you must not make any engagement that will interfere with it. It has been made principally to enable you to meet the people of Cherokee. We intend to make arrangements for 20,000 persons and we shall use every effort to induce them to turn out. The Cherokee country is sound to the core. They are for the Union and against any measure that will place the State in a hostile attitude to the Federal Government. As soon as the California Bill passed and Towns issued his weak and ill advised proclamation calling a convention of the people the fire-eating press took ground for secession, and Colquitt, Benning, and others of that ilk, came out openly for secession. But the people refused to throw up their caps and shout for the dissolution of the Union. In fact they met with no encouragement from the masses in all this region of country. They had the sagacity to see it, and immediately tacked, and said that they were not for secession, but some measure of resistance,—not to the measures that had been enacted exactly; but in as much as this spirit of abolition was increasing and must necessarily progress, that they thought that the convention should declare, when it met, at what point and for what actual aggression the future resistance should be taken. Some are for making Georgia a military camp and await an aggression that would come shortly, and thus they are attempting under the lead of Colquitt to change the issue. Their meeting at Kingston was a complete failure, not exceeding 1,000 men present, and one half of them at least for the Union and against these fire-eaters. In Floyd, Paulding and Chattooga, all is right. Tumlin is here and says that Cass county will be overwhelmingly for the Union. In Murray the contest may be close, under the new issue, but my impression is that James Morris can carry that county if he will run, and he is a Union man. In Walker county the Democrats are afraid to coalesce with the Whigs, for fear it will inure to the benefit of the Whig party and its principles. They are however Union men and are reliable men. I have an appointment to speak in Chattooga this day week. I shall go from there to Walker court the next week, and I will try and put our friends right. I shall go from there to Dade, and I rely upon their standing up firmly for the Union. They are my old friends. In Gilmer, Chastain is leading the Union party, and he says that there is not a disunionist in that county. In Union and Lumpkin Wm. Woods writes me that all is right. In Cherokee and Forsyth all would be right if we had any prominent man who would take the field. I have written to some of my old friends there, but I cannot hear from them. In Cobb I fear we shall lose that county through the influence of John Anderson and McDonald. In Gwinnett, Simmons says that we have no cause to be alarmed; and Murphy writes me that De Kalb is for the Union. We have got these ultras at last. Write me and let me known the prospect in your district.

Howell Cobb To John B. Lamar. E.

Athens ga., *10th Oct., 1850.* Dear John, I have written to the committee at Macon that I cannot be there on the 17th—the day now appointed for their meeting—but I have said to them that I would attend a meeting on the 4th or 5th of Nov. if it was desirable to them. It will therefore depend upon themselves whether or not I shall make a speech there at all.

Since my return to Athens I have not been able to ascertain with certainty the state of the public mind throughout my district. I have only spoken so far in this and Jackson counties. In these two counties there are not exceeding fifty democrats against me whilst the majority of the whigs are with me. In the other counties of the district I hear that there is equal unanimity among the democrats in my support. Dougherty has taken the other side and is seeking to rally the whigs with him. His calculation seemed to be that he could hold the Whigs together and carry off a sufficient portion of the democrats, to give him the control of the district, but he will be wofully disappointed. I have no doubt that I could be reelected tomorrow by double the majority I ever received in the dis.

We shall have a most exciting and angry contest in the state, and in some sections a very doubtful one—though I entertain no doubt that we shall have a large majority of the convention....1

Alexander W. Buel 2 To Howell Cobb. E.

Detroit mich., *Oct. 12th, 1850.* Dear Sir: After our long and eventful session at Washington I am happy in reporting myself amongst my constituents, and in avail 1 A great majority of unionist delegates was elected to the Georgia convention. It met at Mllledgeville in December and by a vote of 237 to 19 adopted resolutions, known as the "Georgia Platform," accepting the compromise as a hasis of the continuance of the Union, though asserting that any further northern aggressions ought to be resisted by the State of Georgia, by secession if necessary, in last resort. The text is printed in M. W. Cluskey, "Political Text Book," pp. 599, 600; H. V. Ames, "State Documents on Federal Relations," pp. 272, 273.

'Congressman from Michigan, 1849-1851; defeated for reelection, 1850.

ing myself of the first convenient opportunity for carrying out your suggestion at our last interview.

I took the liberty a few days since of sending you notice of my *xinanimous* renomination upon the *first* vote, believing that by so doing I could not better serve your wish to be informed of the views of my constituency in relation to the great measures of compromise and conciliation which distinguish the acts of our late session. For myself I could desire no stronger endorsement of my course, and as such it is of course gratifying to me; but it is the more gratifying as it not only sustains me, but that system of policy and measures so patriotically advocated by yourself and others from every section of the Union. In fact, my constituency almost without regard to party have rejoiced over the late adjustment in nearly every feature. There is a strong disinclination in the minds of our people to encourage any further attempts at mere empty agitation over the schemes of fanatical demagogues.

Still it is evident that certain agitators who are following in the lead of Seward and certain others of his fanatical sect are desperately engaged to continue if possible the agitation upon the strength of the fugitive slave bill. All sorts of persuasions and misrepresentations are resorted to and just now fiercely pushed, to affect the Congressional elections of this fall. This matter is working chiefly in the Whig party, which however is becoming permanently distracted. Sewardism is likely to divide the Whigs of the North badly. A large portion of them is becoming sound and conservative in relation to a continuance of agitation. We have just had a case under the law, which has produced here a little excitement. The abolitionists seized hold of it, excited our colored population; and to insure an execution of the law without riot or disturbance, some military was called out; but depend upon it the excitement is grossly exaggerated. The show of excitement was in fact mainly expressive of a determination upon the part of nine tenths of our people to see that the law and constitution were faithfully observed.. It is possible however that the law in some of its details may be a little defective and require amendment, but that can be better ascertained when the law shall have been fairly and practically tested. My vote for this bill is constantly arrayed in the papers in large letters, and I am denounced by the fanatics in no measured terms. I may lose a few votes, but if this issue is to be pressed upon me, I am advised that I shall receive a considerable vote from those who usually differing from me in politics, are yet determined to support me in my course upon the adjustment. At all events, I stand upon my votes fearlessly, and I boldly proclaim that upon this subject I will stand by the Constitution or fall in its defence.

To you personally let me say in frankness and sincerity, our people at the North feel that much is due for the independent and patriotic course which you yourself pursued under circumstances so calculated to try one's firmness and wisdom. Allow me to add that no one participates in that feeling more cordially and sincerely than I do. We shall in the course of events soon meet again at the Capital, but in the mean time I shall be pleased to hear from you.

M. C. Fulton To Howell Cobb. E. Strawberry Plains, East Tennessee, *Nov. 6th, 1850.*

Dear Sir: I have passed through a portion of 3 States since I saw you, and I find the sentiment of the whole section through which I have travelled all in favor of Union, with the exception of South Carolina; and even there I found several *Union Men,* but many of them, it is said, being dependent upon their own exertions for a support, do not express their views and feelings because they are so greatly in the minority. In S. C. the great difficulty is that the people never have but one side of the question. If it could be in that State as in Ga. and other States where the people are all informed by means of public discussions, the public mind would be very different, even in S. C., from what it now is. I suppose no man in the State has yet dared to make a speech in favor of Union. I met one fellow along the road between Pendleton and Greenville who asked me what Ga. was going to do. I told him; whereupon he expressed great astonishment that Ga. should be willing to disgrace herself so much. I replied she would only add to her honor and credit by going, as I hoped she would ever do, for the Constitution and the Union and against *treachery* and South Carolina. I found however after talking with him that he really knew nothing of the true character of the late *settlement,* except California was admitted as a free State and Texas had been bribed, and all that kind of stuff. I told him what the adjustment was. He seemed to be surprised at it very much, and could see nothing wrong in all that, and said if that was so, he would prefer to stay in the Union; and so would many others, perhaps thousands even in that State, I have no doubt, if they were correctly informed. Men who understand this matter are for disunion *per se* with few exceptions, and they labor to lead the people after them and resort to misrepresentation and other discreditable means to effect their purposes. The people in Clingman's district say he is in advance of them and that he is only trying to regain the popularity he lost some years ago by voting against the 21st Rule and for which he was once defeated I believe before the people for Cong. All are for Union in the old North State. I was told that more than f of the people would sustain the Union. In Tennessee the same thing is true. The people all approve of your course and speak of your chance for Vice Pres. or Pres. being as good or better than any man in the South; they like Foote's late course, but do not respect him. It is different with you. All speak favorably of you and they all entertain a deep feeling of respect for you which they do not for Foote. They already, Sir, here speak of the old distinctions of Whig and Democrat as done away with pretty much, and now look to the formation of a party of national character upon Union and compromise ground. They say here however that the repeal of the Fugitive Law or the abolition of slavery in the District will dissolve the Union; and I am convinced that such will be the result in the event that either of these should transpire. Sam Knox thinks that Franklin County will go for Union by at least 400-500. I trust Ga. will do right. She is looked to with great interest now, and great hopes are entertained that she will give a quietus to all this agitation and the whole race of agitators.

P. S.—I have since writing the above had opportunity to form some opinion of the feeling of the people in this state, Virginia. They are all in favor of the compromise to a man, I believe. I could write you much of what I have heard and seen that might interest you, but will only say that I have spoken with no man, of public men, that does not approve of your course, and they all seem to know you.

Robert Toombs To Howell Cobb. E. Washington, D. C, *Jan. 2. 1851.*
Dear Cobb, I duly recd. your letter. We have had the strangest state of things here for four days that has ever been witnessed in this country, and really I am more at a loss for the interpretation thereof than I have ever been before. The Democratic party met on Saturday night and voted down a resolution endorsing the Compromise. They laid it on the table under various pretexts, and then nominated their officers. The Southern Whigs called upon me pretty generally when I came here and wanted to know where they were to go. I advised them to tender a strong Compromise resolution to their caucus, and secede upon its rejection. My object was to cutt them all off from their national organization and therefore shut them out of the Whig national convention if one should be held. This I deemed more important as Graham and old Gales, etc., were now trying to bring M embers of Congress into the National Whig caucus. Contrary to all expectation, the National Whigs of the North in the very desperation of their defeat, backed by some members of the Cabinett, came right out and passed the resolution, "jam up." This took everybody by surprise and created great fluttering in the Democratic ranks. The measure is not yet understood here generally. It is supposed here to be a Whig effort at nationalization. Such a result was neither intended nor expected by those Northern Whigs who voted for it; but they desired to cutt loose from their Free-soil allies at any and every hazard, and Brooks and others avowed themselves ready to vote for a Democrat on the Compromise. Therefore this movement will greatly strengthen and not weaken our line. The Democratic movement was more complicated. The "fire-eaters" (many of them) would not go into the caucus, because they wanted the resolution beaten and were afraid to vote against it, and they alleged that Geo. W. Jones got the resolution from you, and Venable and the fire-eaters generally of the South openly boasted that it was a lick at you. But the controlling element in defeating the resolution was the clerkship. Forney played this game desperately. He got all the Free-soilers to go for himself on the undertaking to apply no tests which would exclude them from the party; and he found it necessary, to carry out his policy, to take a Compromise Democrat. He therefore got them all to go on Boyd. He already had the Southern fire-eaters, who have finished their treaty with Buchanan, and it was absolutely necessary to carry out his purposes to get some one in Boyd's line. Boyd I don't think has anything at all to do with ulterior objects. In fact he is openly for Butler of Ky. His only connection was he wanted the Speakership, and they offered it to him, and he openly advocated the adoption of the resolution. Therefore from this brief view of the leading points you will perceive the real state of the case is much less formidable than it looks to be. A large number of Compromise Democrats tell me they are determined to bring the defeated resolutions in the house and compel them to stand up. They will pass by a large majority, which tends much to unhorse the coalition. Our party took no part, but only looked on. I was doubtful at the time which was best; I am now sure our course was the best. I have had two long interviews with Donelson. He is thoroughly with us, but he does not understand the ropes about Washington. I fear his hostility to Buck1 will lead him into premature trouble. I have advised him strongly against making any issue on anybody of his party until the time comes. Buck is undoubtedly against the Compromise and has complained to D. of misrepresenting his position. He says he was for 36 30', not the Compromise. This position you will understand without another word. *It is the key to his whole position,* and unless he fears their weakness he will unite with the fire-eaters. We have been here but forty eight hours, and these are 1 Buchanan.

my best readings of the times. They may be wrong; I give them to you confidentially for your own reflection and advice....

Benjamin Balche To Howell Cobb. E. Newburyport, Mass., *J any 10, 1851.*
Dear Sir: Herewith is inclosed the most important bill of the session, for presentation at the earliest day and moment by some good man of influence who can appreciate the importance of this work and of this bill, involving as it does hundreds of millions of wealth and the best interests of every section of the Union.

It is the most important measure ever presented in Congress by which to perpetuate our glorious Union under one National Government and by which to establish a national prosperity upon an enduring foundation, and by which regardless of cost to concentrate the trade and commerce of the world in our own country.

This is but one of the 12 important measures upon which the American people will establish their National Union party upon an *enduring foundation,* and by which they will sweep the Union in its support whether Mr. Clay, Mr. Webster or Mr. Cass, have "privately " expressed their " disapprobation " of such a " Union party" or not.

The Platform is as broad as our Union and wide and high enough for all parties to unite in peace and union.

Its principles are democratic, out and out, its issues are comprehensive, and its measures are dictated by the concentrated national wisdom and exalted patriotism worthy of our country, of the people, and of the age.

The American People will have this National Union party, established upon constitutional and patriotic grounds, and upon a foundation lasting as the Earth and Heavens, whether the political office seekers of Washington like it or not.

The National Union party will have their National Union convention at Washington on the 22nd Feby. next, at the time and place appointed, when their 12 Issues and Measures which will sweep the Union in their support will be adopted by acclamation, whether the Whig party or Democratic party like them or not, and before which measures and issues all other measures of either party will be sunk deep in oblivion.

P. S.—The independent ticket and nomination of the National Union party is, for President, Millard Fillmore, for Vice Prest., Howell Cobb.

P. S. 2. I want this bill presented on Monday, by yourself or some other friend of the Union, away from all New England interests or influences. Let it be referred to the Committee of the whole on the State of the Union and not be placed in jeopardy by a reference to any subordinate committee whatever. Let it be presented by Judge Bowlin or some man opposed to Whitney's and Benton's Plan.

Howell Cobb To Absalom H. Chappell And Others.1

Washington D. C, *Feb. 7,1851.*

Gentlemen: My public duties will detain me in Washington until the close of the session. It will therefore be out of my power to be personally present at your proposed celebration of the 22d of February, though in spirit and heart I shall be with you, prepared to give to the noble cause in which you are engaged, the pledge of an honest heart and an untiring spirit.

You are happy in the selection of a day particularly appropriate to the object of your assemblage. How could the descendants of our revolutionary fathers more aptly exhibit their reverence for the memory of the father of his country, than by dedicating its return to solemn counsellings, for the preservation and perpetuity of that inestimable Union, purchased by their blood and transmitted to us as our proudest and richest heritage? If the immortal spirit of that venerated sage could again put on its mortality and move in our midst, what could be more grateful to his feelings than to witness the consecration of his own birth-day to the cause of that noble Union which he hoped might be perpetual.

A few months since and the stoutest hearts were appalled with the dangers which threatened the integrity of the Republic. A question involving the most dangerous issue which can ever arise in our country was rapidly dividing the people of. the Union into sectional organizations—thus driving the old ship of state with frightful velocity upon almost certain destruction. The contest in our own State arising out of this question is yet fresh in the recollection of our people. It was warm and spirited, exhibiting the fact that there existed in the public mind a due appreciation of the momentous consequences involved in its decision. I trust that the lessons of wisdom which it inculcated will not soon be forgotten, and that the beneficial results which the triumph of just and constitutional principles then promised to the country will be fully realized in the future history of the Republic. Whether or not this just and well-founded hope is destined to a realization or a disappointment, is entirely dependent 1 From a pamphlet report of proceedings bearing the caption: "*Union Celebration in Macon, Ga., on the Anniversary of Washington's Birthday, Feb. t2, 1851,"* pp. 4-7. The Constitutional Union party had been launched at a meeting in Milledgeville, Ga., Dec. 12, 1850. Toombs, Stephens, and Cobb were Its chief sponsors. The persons to whom this letter was addressed were a committee of arrangement for the "Union Celebration" which was intended to promote the fortunes of the new party. upon the wisdom and firmness of those who have participated in bringing about the present prosperous and happy state of public affairs.

The dangers which so universally threatened a few months ago the peace and quiet of the country, involving the very existence of the Union, have been avoided and turned aside; but it would be a criminal blunder to suppose that they had been entirely overcome and destroyed. So long as the causes which brought about these dangers shall continue to exist, so long will the duty of the watchful sentinel remain to be performed. So long as the fiendish spirit of fanaticism is found warring upon the Constitution, and the disunionist is attempting to poison the hearts of the people with a spirit of hatred to the Union of our fathers, so long will the obligation rest upon all true friends of the Union to unite their hands and hearts in defending a common country from the treasonable assaults of a common enemy.

It requires only a brief reference to the past, and a glance at the future, to satisfy any candid and intelligent mind that these elements of danger are yet in existence to be met and overcome, as they may from time to time develop themselves to the country. A sectional majority had threatened by the exercise of a disputed power to trample upon the constitutional rights of the minority. The people of the South declared that there existed no constitutional power in this government to exclude them from the free and equal participation of the territory acquired by the joint blood and treasure of the whole country. Whilst a Northern majority threatened a disregard of this constitutional right, a threat which they proposed to execute by the passage of that odious measure, familiarly known to the country as the Wilmot Proviso—the South also demanded the execution of a voluntary obligation assumed by their Northern brethren, to deliver to us our fugitive slaves, who might escape or be enticed into the non-slaveholding States. This demand had long been neglected, until the obligation itself was felt, in many portions of the country, to be an unmeaning clause of the Constitution. These were the elements of distraction which were so rapidly loosening the bonds that held together our Union, and every patriotic heart in the land watched with the intensest anxiety the progress of that long and arduous struggle, which was to decide these momentous issues. That decision was made—the wisdom; intelligence and patriotism of the country were found adequate to the task which the emergency created. In the series of adjustment measures passed at the last session of Congress on the various branches of the slavery question, is found the record of a fair, just and honorable settlement of this alarming question.

It only now needs to be considerd *final,* and then will I grant that the danger is entirely over and the Republic is safe. But unfortunately for the future peace and quiet of the country, this settlement is not regarded in that light by a large portion of the people. At the North, a clamor has been raised for the repeal of the fugitive slave law, by that restless and fanatical crew, whose hostility to the South and her institutions has rendered them proverbially infamous in the estimation of all good citizens. But the abolitionists do not content themselves with a demand for the repeal of this part of the compromise. They denounce the whole settlement as a base surrender to the demands of the South, and in the continued agitation of the question of slavery, seek the destruction of the Union, because that Union guards and protects the South by its constitutional provisions, in the undisturbed enjoyment of its peculiar institutions. I speak of the opponents of this settlement at the North as abolitionists, as I do not feel disposed to discriminate between the open and avowed abolitionists, and that class of mongrel politicians who sympathize with their treasonable sentiments, but decline from motives of policy to wear their outward livery.

In the South the spirit of opposition to these adjustment measures is equally violent and determined. It is unnecessary for the purpose of this investigation to look beyond the limits of our own State. In the canvass of last year is found abundant evidence of the truth of the proposition. The tone of the public press and the impassioned addresses of public speakers exhibited the fierce and violent opposition of a portion of our citizens to the compromise measures. If all other means were denied to us of measuring the extent of their opposition, we might form some estimate of its controlling influence in view of the fact that it sundered their party relationships and drove the advocates of resistance to an open repudiation both of their party and their principles. It requires deep-rooted feeling and unswerving fixedness of purpose to produce such results.

In the organization of " The Southern Rights party " of Georgia, we see the truth of the statement here made— a sectional organization based upon sectional feelings and views, and having its origin in a spirit of hostility to the late action of the Government on the subject of slavery. Those citizens who have united in this movement repudiate all national alliances as dangerous in their tendency and incompatible with the successful defence of Southern rights and honor. They profess to regard the compromise measures as violative of the spirit, if not the letter of the Constitution, nor do they hesitate to avow that in the adoption of those measures, the rights and honor of the South have been disregarded and trampled upon. It would be an unjust imputation upon their spirit and patriotism to suppose that they intend to yield a faithful acquiescence in measures which they regard as so unjust and dishonorable to them. In truth their very organization into a sectional party, thereby withdrawing themselves from their former party association, accompanied with the charge of bad faith upon their Northern associates who have stood true and firm to the National pledge ought to be considered as ample notice to all intelligent men of their determination not to acquiesce in the action of Congress. With some the avowal is openly made with a boldness worthy of a better cause, whilst others would fain conceal their ultimate purposes in the hope of enticing into their ranks a portion of the honest and sincere friends of the Union upon the basis of the late compromise. With what effect, it remains yet to be seen.

The professions of this "Southern Rights party" are strangely inconsistent with their position and known sentiments. They proclaim to the country their attachment and devotion to the Union, and in some instances claim to be its only true friends. Is it not too strong a demand upon our credulity to ask of us to put confidence in these professions? Whence originates their love of the Union? Is it in the wrongs and injuries it inflicts upon them—in the humiliation and disgrace they feel in submitting to its laws and government? They either deceive themselves or seek to impose upon others. I hold it to be impossible for any true-hearted man to feel love and devotion for a government, which in his judgment oppresses and dishonors him. Let every man in the South imbibe the passions and prejudices of these peculiar friends of the Union, and it may be pertinently asked. How long will the Union withstand the assaults of its enemies? With whom do the Southern Rights men of Georgia sympathize in their political associations? Beyond the limits of their own section they know no friends worthy of their confidence and alliance. It is their pride and boast that they form no political association with any of our northern brethren—the North presents no material for party organization sound and honest enough to command their respect and induce their alliance. In connexion with this view of the subject it is appropriate to the day and occasion of your assemblage, gentlemen, to ask of our countrymen to hearken to the voice of the father of his country as it rises from the tomb, warning them against the dangerous and destructive tendencies of sectional organizations, and the men who would seek through them to instil into the hearts of the people enmity against the Union of their revolutionary fathers.

All the sympathies of the Southern Rights party of Georgia are with sectional men, sectional issues and sectional associations. It aspires not to the more enlarged basis of a national organization. In a sister State the same issue is presented, in a bolder and more startling proposition. There, the object of immediate secession is proclaimed in plain and explicit terms. A dissolution of the Union is regarded as the only remedy that can be resorted to for existing grievances. It is urged upon the people with all the power and eloquence of her ablest men. No one will deny that the tide of disunion sentiment is rolling with increasing volume through the entire limits of South Carolina, needing only the alliance of a single neighboring State to determine their policy for an immediate dissolution of the Union.

In view of this important condition of things in a sister State on our immediate borders, and knowing as we do that all the sympathies of this Southern Rights organization in our own State are enlisted in the same cause, it becomes the duty of wise and prudent men to regard with anxious and jealous care its various movements. The open disunionists of South Carolina and the Southern Rights party of Georgia entertain a common opinion on the compromise measures of the last session. They both consider the action of the government, in this respect, as violative of their rights and honor, and consequently regard an acquiescence in them as humiliating and dishonoring. The one demands an immediate dissolution of the Union, as the only adequate remedy for the wrong inflicted; the other pursues a milder and more politic course, with a consciousness that, in the end, a similar result will be reached. Thus it is that a feeling of hostility to the government is being diffused through our State, preparatory to the occasion which will justify an open avowal in favor of disunion.

I have made this brief reference to the state of public opinion in the different sections of the country on the slavery question for the purpose of showing that the danger which so lately threatened the Union is not entirely overcome. It brings to our consideration the important inquiry—What is the true policy to be adopted by the friends of the Union to avert these dangers in the future? My own opinion is that the Union organization of Georgia has adopted the true, safe and judicious policy. You regard the late compromise measures as the recognition of those great constitutional principles for which the South has always contended. In the repudiation of the Wilmot Proviso, and the enforcement of the Constitutional obligation to deliver up fugitive slaves, the North have given practical evidence of their intention to stand, in good faith, by the Constitutional Union of their fathers—recognizing and enforcing all the rights guaranteed by that solemn compact to their brethren of the South. Looking upon the basis of that settlement as the recognition of sound constitutional principles, you propose to regard it as a final disposition of past issues, and to require the application of the same principle to any future controversy that may arise out of the question 73566—13 15 of slavery. In this view of the subject you have my full and hearty concurrence. I believe it is the only policy that will give lasting peace and quiet to the country, maintain the rights of the South, and preserve the Union inviolate. In order that this object may be effected you tender your aid and co-operation to your fellow-citizens of all sections who agree with you in these views—thus endeavoring to unite the friends of these measures in a common effort to sustain them against the combined opposition of their enemies.

The success of this movement decides, in my honest judgment, the fate of the Union. It may be that there are friends of this settlement whose opinions on other subjects are so antagonistic to those of the great body of the supporters of the compromise as to preclude the hope of their cooperation; but it is true of a few only, and the difficulties arising from this source will not be of sufficient magnitude to encompass the path of the mass of those who are prepared to stand firmly upon the platform of the settlement. Your success, gentlemen, is not dependant, as some have idly supposed, upon the organization of a National Union Party. It is a narrow view of the subject so to regard it. On the contrary, among the number of those who have discountenanced the formation of such a National party are to be found the names of many able and distinguished men, who look to the success of the Union organization in Georgia as decisive of the ultimate triumph of the great principle upon which it is based. Your organization has laid down a sound and patriotic principle—*a faithful adherence to the compromise measures of the last session of Congress.* It is your platform—upon it you stand, and extend the right hand of fellowship to your fellow-citizens, wherever found, who are willing and prepared to stand by your side and unite with you in its maintenance and support. It matters not to you whether the organization under which this principle triumphs be known as the Union, or the Republican, or the Democratic party, or by any other name. It is the *success of the principle,* not *the name of the party,* which engages your thoughts and enlists your energies. That you will be gratified in the triumphant success of the principle I entertain no shadow of doubt. Be firm and steadfast in your organization—true to the pledge you have given—and a brilliant triumph awaits your patriotic efforts in the cause of the South and the Union.

The Union organization of our State has been violently assailed, and the motives of its friends and supporters traduced and misrepresented. This was to be expected, and furnishes satisfactory evidence that its power and influence has already been felt by those whose insidious assaults upon the Union have been arrested by it. The Union men of Georgia have done much in the last six months for their country, but their labors are not yet over, and I trust they will not rest from them until they have made permanent the peace and quiet they have so nobly contributed to bring about. / *renew to them the offer of my hand and my heart in the good cause.*

Joseph H. Lumpkin To Howell Cobb. E.

Macon ga., *Feb. 10th, 1851.* My Dear Sir: I have delayed writing to you hitherto because I had nothing definite to say—I address you for the reason that I have....

Gov. Towns intends, from what I have heard, to reassemble the Legislature in *May* to reorganize the Congressional districts. Now it is needless to remind you that *June* has been designated as the' time for holding a convention of the Constitutional Union party to nominate a candidate for Governor, and that the month of May is prior in point of time to that of June. Put these simple facts together and you have all I wish to say. No stone will be left unturned to reorganize the old state parties. That done, and I leave you to judge as to what will follow. Something must be done and done quickly and done effectually. Had not the new *state* party better be cemented and consolidated regardless of any other organizations elsewhere? It is not advisable in my judgement to form in advance of the state a great national central party. Let the state take the lead and the other will follow of course. A firm and decided movement of this sort on the part of Georgia will exert a controlling influence in the other states. Thousands are in suspense, not knowing what to do. *They are waiting to hear from you.* Let national parties and national candidates alone then for the present and strike boldly for Georgia, leaving the party to form such national alliances hereafter as circumstances may dictate and justify.

I write in haste and in confidence. I send you six dollars to pay for the Tri-weekly *Intelligencer,* from the 20th Jany. 1851 to 20th Jany. 1852. Take a receipt.

P. S.—You can be Governor, if you desire it. Either your district or John's should furnish the candidate. Warner would be a highly acceptable candidate. The Court cannot spare him.

Robert Toombs To Absalom H. Chappell And Others.1

Washington D. C, *Feb. 15th, 1851.*

Gentlemen: I have received' your polite invitation to unite with you in the celebration of the birthday of Washington. I regret that my public duty here will deprive me of that pleasure.

I most heartily approve your purpose to make the birthday of the father of his country the occasion of paying honor to his memory 1 *Union Celebration in Macon, Ga., on the Anniversary of Washington's Birthday, Feb. 22, 1851,* pp. 7, 8. Letter addressed to the committee of arrangement.
and of taking counsel together for the preservation of that Union which he esteemed so important to the protection of the liberties of his country.

The anniversary of the day which gave him to liberty, is appropriately dedicated to the perpetuation of its best safe-guard, constitutional union.

I agree with you, gentlemen, in the opinion that the crisis demands the union of the friends of the peace measures, of the last session of Congress, for the sake of the Union. It is known to you that those measures separately and in all their details did not meet with my approval. I did not and do not now believe that the bills for the establishment of Territorial governments for New Mexico and Utah were such as the South had a right to demand, but they contained all she did demand; and I supported them in conformity with the deliberate and frequently expressed opinions of an overwhelming majority of the people of the South. I shall now maintain them, at least until the question between us is settled. The principle engrafted upon the territorial bills is non-intervention with slavery— whether it be right or wrong, its truth has heretofore been maintained with singular unanimity and fervidness by the South, and by none more strenuously than by those who now affirm that we have lost the whole territory by the bills referred to.

As the opinion of this class of persons do not govern themselves, it ought not to surprise them that they control nobody else. My own contempt for their opinions or denunciations has been too often expressed before assembled thousands of the people of Georgia to need repetition here. They were either ignorant of the rights of their country, or basely betrayed them; in either event they are no longer worthy of public confidence, and such has been the verdict of the people. Our opponents at the South can give us but little trouble; we can easily settle with them at the ballot box. The only exception to this in the South may be South Carolina, and I think we may safely calculate upon her *prudence,* no matter how many secession delegates she may send to her convention. Such seems to be the repugnance of her resistance men to separate State action. that I think we may solely rely upon her having enough of that "rascally virtue" to save us and herself from extreme measures. This is not the case with the North—we may need the cartridge box to settle with her. British emissaries are stirring up fools, fanatics and free-negroes there to resist the will of the American people as constitutionally expressed in their public laws. I believe Mr. Thompson is the first British emissary who has dared to disturb the peace of this country since the summary execution of his countrymen Ambrister and Arbuthnot. Gen. Jackson had many admirers, he may have imitators in New England. Mr. T. had better not rely too much upon the extinction of the feeling of the Revolution, even in Boston.

The present Government of the United States is true to its duties and to the laws and constitution of the land; it will maintain them with a firmness equal to any emergency, with a constancy and courage as prolonged as the conflict.

The existing political organizations of the North, both Whig and Democrat, are wholly unequal to the present crisis. Their antecedents are continual stumbling blocks in the path of safety and duty. If either were sound I should not hesitate to advise you to promote its success. But both have degenerated into mere factions, adhering together by the common hope of public plunder. Their success would benefit nobody but themselves, and would be infinitely mischievous to the public weal. The Whigs and Democrats of Massachusetts are struggling between Sumner and Winthrop; it is a contest in which the friends of the country have not the slightest interest. The success of the principles of either would be equally fatal to the safety and existence of the Republic. The Whigs and Democrats of New York and Ohio are thoroughly denationalized. Indeed, there is no non-slaveholding State in which the free-soil Whigs do not control the Whig organization, and none in which the Democratic free-soilers do not control it, except in N. Jersey, Pennsylvania, Indiana, Illinois and Iowa. Our safety, and the safety of the country therefore, lies in refusing all cooperation with either the Whig or Democratic parties of the North, and a thorough union with the sound men of both these parties, in a United National party. If this is impracticable, we ought to stand aloof from both and support none but a sound National candidate.

Apart from the question of slavery, another great question is rising up before us to become a " fixed fact" in American politics. It is, and has the will of a majority, sometimes called the higher law, in antagonism to our constitutional compact. If the first succeeds, we have no other safety except in secession; if the latter, "liberty and Union, may be forever one and inseparable ". In all these questions it is our true policy to stand by those who agree with us— repudiate those who differ from us. We are beleaguered by enemies at the North and the South. Let us not falter in our duty.—The Constitution and Union is worth a struggle. Who will falter in this glorious conflict?

John H. Lumpkin To Howell Cobb. E.

Rome ga., *16th Feby., 1851.* Dear Cobb, I have been very anxious to hear from you ever since the commencement of this session. I want to know what is the prospect of organizing a constitutional union party, national in its character. I see that Mr. Ritchie, Genl. Cass and sundry other prominent Democrats who were and are for the compromise measures of the last session of Congress oppose this new party organization. What is to be the result? We cannot act in concert with the Southern Rights Democrats of Georgia, even were they willing to unite and act in concert with the national Democratic party. But they are not willing to go into a national Democratic convention and abide in good faith its result, and it is therefore idle and worse than idle to think of acting and cooperating with that class of men. I gave up the national Democratic party with reluctance, and never did do so until the issue was forced upon me against my consent, but I am now satisfied that a national party organization upon the basis of the compromise measures of the last session is the only barrier against factions and fanatics at the two extremes of the Union. But I fear that interest and ambitious schemes of aspiring politicians of the two old parties will prevent this organization, and if so what is to become of the Union and those Democrats in Georgia who have perilled all for the Union—I am anxious to hear from you on this subject and shall anxiously await your reply.

I have held Floyd and Cass courts, and shall leave home tomorrow for Cherokee court, and will not return home until after Murray county superior court. A letter written immediately would reach me at Cumming, Forsyth county, or at Dahlonega, Lumpkin County. I am much pleased with my new position, and I flatter myself after I become a little more familiar with my duties I shall get along very well.

Tell Mr. Ritchie that the Democratic party in Georgia are divided, and that the Union Democrats can never expect to act with the disunionists again. They are not national or conservative, but are factious, sectional and nondescript, and they have indulged in a strain of abuse against the Union Democrats that can never be forgotten or forgiven. The Union organization in Georgia is firmly established, and would gladly see it national in its character, but if in this they are disappointed they will either act alone or as a separate independent party, or with that political party that is more hostile to abolitionists at the north or disunionists at the south. This leaves my family in good health. Mrs. Lumpkin sends her respects to you.

Thomas W. Thomas To Howell Cobb E.

Warrenton ga., *April 14th, 1851.* Dear Sir: I am detained here a short time on my way home from Milledgeville and will avail myself of the opportunity to write you a short letter on matters of public concern. I see it stated in the Banner that you expect to retire from Congress, and the intimation is thrown out that you may possibly be induced to yield to what seems to be the general wish of the Union party by accepting the nomination for Governor. Now I do not wish you to become the candidate for Governor;

and I am sure you will excuse one of the old panel for speaking thus plainly and giving a brief statement of his reasons. The Whig wing of the Union party—so far as I have had an opportunity to become informed—are nearly unanimous for your nomination, but I am induced to believe your Democratic friends would prefer your remaining in Congress. It is mainly under your lead they have been induced to get on the Union platform; and they will continue to have more confidence in the movement if you remain in the field where you can aid in directing and controlling in person the future movements of the grand union army. These views I have heard many of them express, and I think them well founded for many reasons. In your absence questions involving former party principles might arise, and the fire-eaters could appeal to the Union Democrats to desert the cause and insist most positively by way of reason that you would not have voted with the Whig Union men if you had been there. This is one of the many ways your absence would lay us open to attack. The office of Governor has got to be a very small affair anyhow, requiring only the sharpness and closeness of an executor or administrator in making good bargains and saving small matters, to administer with credit and popularity. Unfortunately this is the very sort of talent you lack, for I once saw you give a negro at the Governor's house half a dollar for holding your hat, and if you manage in that way with the Western and Atlantic road the state of Georgia will have a good large bill to foot at the end of your administration. If you accept the nomination you will be elected of course by 40 or 50 thousand majority, and then in all probability you will be laid on the shelf for life. Look back through the last fifteen years, and there is not a man who survived politically the office of governor, and but one man (Senator Dawson) whose reputation could stand even a nomination for that post. It is very complimentary to you for the Whig Union men to be so unanimous in your favor, and your friends of the old panel acknowledge and appreciate their liberality; but we have the best right to be consulted. We don't want your reputation risked (for it is a pure risk with everything to lose and nothing to gain) and damaged and you kept out of sight for the next four years by this little matter of being governor. I agree to the policy of running some Democrat and some old-panel Democrat at that, but we can find a man whose ambition will be crowned by the office and his deserts too, and who can't be so useful elsewhere. I have written hastily and without reserve and in accordance with what I expressed to Tom Cobb at Madison court. I presume it needs no apology for so doing. I have stood up to you and the cause in my small sphere long enough and strong enough not to be suspected of any hidden design against either.

S. T. Chapman To Howell Cobb. E. Journal And Messenger Office, Macon, Ga., *April 24th, 1851.*

Dear Sir: I received a few days since a long and very interesting letter from Mr. Buchanan in regard to the present aspect of political affairs. It was in response to one from me which accompanied some copies of our paper. Mr. B. seems to think that unless we of the South can present an undivided front in favour of some conservative man who can command the support of a portion of the North, that Gen. Scott will be the next President. He however advises *against* any movement in his behalf in our approaching convention. I wd. be happy to show you his letter, though it is marked *Confidential,* and will do so when we meet.

Be good enough to let me hear from you at length on these points? Mr. Buchanan by the way begged me to present you with his kindest regards; and upon the question of the Compromise referred us to his letter to the Phila. Committee of November last— by the way an admirable document.

I am sorry that I have not time and strength to write you at length in regard to the aspect of political affairs in this section. The Union organization stands firm. Campbell and his coadjutors, you see, are preparing to bring off their convention the week before ours. Their object is well understood here. They intend to nominate some Union Democrat, for the purpose of producing confusion if possible in our deliberations. I can learn of no one thus far who will consent to serve them, though they have offered the nomination to three or four. As to the Union candidate, the public mind seems settled. *You* are the universal favorite; and however averse you may be to wear the harness we must venture to place it upon you. Milledgeville, I know, is not a desirable place of residence; still I think you can afford to endure it at least for a single term, especially as the election would be regarded as a triumphant vindication of your course in the last Congress as well as a signal rebuke to those who have attempted to put you down in the state. It is useless to blink the question. The spirit of disunion and revolution has only been temporarily subdued. It is not yet prostrate in the State...

Robert Toombs To John J. Crittenden. L. C.

Washington, Geo., *April 25th, 1851.* Dear Crittenden, There is a little fire-eating paper published at Athens, Georgia, for which Judge Berrien last winter tried to get the printing of the P. Office advertisements; but upon the representations of Stephens and others of our delegation Mr. Hall refused the request and gave Judge Berrien his reasons, placing the refusal expressly upon its disloyal course towards the Union, and gave the advertisements to the Southern Banner printed at the same place. Since that time the paper has been steadily denouncing Fillmore and his cabinett as unsound on the slavery question, using what little power it had in trying to weaken his friends and administration. Within the last ten days it has been selected by the State Department as the "By Authority" publisher of the laws of Congress! What does this mean? It is much commented on in Georgia, and just now is doing us harm under the idea that it is "a straw" indicating some change in Washington. I have supposed that there must be some mistake about it; but it is feared in very influential quarters that it is intended to put Berrien and his few friends in position and endeavor to reorganize the Whig party upon some other basis in the state. Now I have no desire to indicate to the administration its policy, much less to control it, more especially as its recent course towards the N. York and Ohio Whigs does not meet the approbation of myself or those who act with me; but if it is not an improper thing I should like to know how this thing was done.

I have abandoned my European trip this year. Events in Georgia will make it necessary for me to remain at home and again enter into the political arena. Mrs. T. and the girls are in good health and we are all enjoying the leisure and comfort of home. Give our best regards to Mrs. Crittenden.

James F. Cooper To Howell Cobb. E.

Columbus ga., *May 5, 1851.*

My Dear Sir:... I am one of the convention to assemble at Milledgeville in June, a delegate from Cobb County, one of four, all *democrats.* We have something more to do than to nominate a governor. I think it is our duty to assume some attitude which will enable Georgia to appear in the Democratic national convention of 1852. We are entitled to a voice in the selection of a presidential candidate and we ought to have it. I am in the Union organization, but I reserve the privilege of supporting the democratic nominee for President. I can go for Fillmore or Webster only in preference to Yulee, Rhett, Jeff. Davis or Democrats of that stamp, but as the Democratic party will surely nominate a conservative I expect to support the nomination.

It is prejudicial to the democracy to hold off from the convention; by so doing we sacrifice all claims for consideration by that body. The nomination will be made without reference to us and our support. We will be treating it with contempt and showing great ingratitude to those true and loyal Democrats who have stood so firmly by the Constitution. Will you venture to advise a course? How would it answer to lay down a declaration of faith conforming to the old Baltimore platform, incorporating with it the Compromise measures of the last Congress? Wd. not such a declaration of principles entitle us to a voice at Baltimore no matter by what party name we are called? The Whigs of Georgia must be conscious that there is nothing left of their party; and they will not be tenacious of their federal doctrines. Toombs, Stephens and Dawson have voted to sustain the Tariff of 1846, and against the Improvement Bill. I can't see what they lack now of being Democrats—if so, there should be no objection to such a declaration as would give us practical political weight.

I wd. be glad to hear from you a suggestion upon this topic.

You have seen that I am *talked* of for Congress in the 5th. It is only talk—others are *figuring* for the distinction, and I am ashamed to mingle with the scramble. As usual my *modesty* is my destruction.

John Calvin Johnson To Howell Cobb. E.

(Confidential.)

Watkinsville, Ga., *May 22nd, 1851.*

Dear Cobb, Pardon me if in "these troublous times" I offer a suggestion or two for the good (as I believe) of our party.

You will be nominated for Governor, and Wofford perhaps for Congress—both originally Democrats. W. J. Hill of Walton for Senator, making three Union Democrats on one ticket to be voted for by the Union Whigs of Clarke county. Now what is to be done in relation to the nomination for Representatives? I unhesitatingly answer, nominate Y. L. G. Harris and Richd. Richardson, the old Members. Many of our people do not yet appreciate the truth that Whiggery and Democracy are defunct in Georgia. Some Whigs in the Union ranks here have not yet buried their political animosity against you; they never liked Wofford, and think him a very unfit successor to the late "Speaker of the House". They have not been accustomed to voting for Democrats; and believing that a majority of the Union Party are Whigs, they cannot see the honesty, they say, of all the offices being appropriated by the Old Democrats. We shall have more prejudices to combat and overcome in Clarke, than in any county in Georgia, and I believe that you as well as I have some county pride and want the thing "done up brown" here. I believe it is generally believed that two originally Whigs will be nominated for House of Representatives, but some say that an untried man will be run in Athens. This will not do. Young Harris is a strong man on this side of the river. It is however said by some that Harris does not wish to run. Those who say this are some Fire Eaters who wish it so because they dread his popularity, and some Union men who have other reasons. I know that he will cheerfully run if nominated, and I know that he would rather gracefully retire than be driven from the track. Caution must be observed in our first nominations, or we may be wofully deceived in the vote of Clarke county. I try to make our friends regard your nomination as a State affair; but you live in Clarke. Wofford sticks in their gizzard. Hill is a Democrat—and I again repeat, nominate the old representatives, and it will not so much appear like a prostration of Whiggery in Clarke. I have no feeling on the subject myself, but I watch things closely. The Fire Eaters are moving heaven and earth to carry this county. They have efficient wire workers—on this side of the river they have the advantage in drill sergeants—and we must proceed cautiously and with policy. I know in your position you must be prudent; but you can drop a word or two confidentially to some one or two of your active friends in Athens, and have public sentiment settled as to Harris and Richardson before the nomination, which should take place before the nomination for Congress, rather to sweeten that pill which will be a bitter one to many on our side of the river. Think of these things, and I believe you will come to the conclusion that I am right. Bye the bye, is not the Banner ranting rather too much about the right of secession? Would it not be better to charge home upon them a sympathy with South Carolina and a desire to secede, than discuss the abstract right? When a house is on fire it is needless to inquire how the fire originated, but how it can be extinguished—so with this question. Ought Georgia to secede? The fire-eaters over here are very anxious to discuss the question and are glad to see the Banner going it, but I do not wish to gratify them and always stop them by asking them "if they are in favor of secession for causes now existing?" They are not quite ready yet, but I understand one or two have said that they wish South Carolina would secede. Let not old party prejudices be revived in this county. Let us proceed cautiously in our first nominations and in future there will be no difficulty, but a false step now might cripple us in old Clarke.

P. S.—Under existing circumstances, I am sorry to say that our Union Democrats over this way are firmer to their integrity than the Whigs. I know yet of no positive defections in our ranks, but I occasionally hear " an ominous growl" that I do not like.

S. T. Chapman To Howell Cobb. E.
Journal And Messenger Office,

Macon, Ga., *June 11th, 1851.* My Dear Sir: Yours of the 7th reached me last night on my return from Savannah. The point on which I desired to hear from you was one to which you refer in the conclusion. I know your views and temperament too well to suppose that you would consent to any thing in the shape of concealment. In fact I urged upon the members the importance of assuming a distinct position upon that question, upon the very ground that unity of opinion was necessary to success. The right of secession, as claimed by our opponents, must be either a useless abstraction, or a revolutionary sentiment leading directly to the destruction of the government. In its practical operation it is intended to cover the retreat of South Carolina from the Union. One of the delegates to the disunion convention openly avowed this—nay, he contended that a state had not only the right to secede but that the moment one seceded the others were absolved from the contract and the Union no longer would exist. Their object in assuming these positions was two-fold: 1. They desired to impress the people that by seceding Carolina would do no wrong, and, 2. That the moment she secedes the citizens of other states are absolved from their allegiance to the general government. Your letter I think met all these issues fairly, ably, and unanswerably. For this reason I desired and recommended that it be read before the committee. Unfortunately that committee was composed of short-sighted, timid men, men who looked to expediency rather than principle as their guide, men who preferred to establish their own consistency at the sacrifice of everything. They took a different course. I have yielded a reluctant assent under the full belief that you would come out promptly in your avowal of sentiment. You ask my opinion as to the time and manner. I answer, the sooner the better. I would do it either in my letter of acceptance or in an address to the people of the state. If the latter, I would simply accept and then intimate an intention to publish the address in a few weeks. The latter should be printed in pamphlet form and sent into every captain's district in the state. I merely throw this out as a suggestion....

James A. Meriwether And Others To Howell Cobb.1

Eatonton ga., *18 June, 1851.* Sir: At a convention recently held of the Constitutional Union party, you were unanimously nominated as their candidate for the 1 From the Union, Washington, D. C, July 2, 1851. The committee comprised James A. Meriwether, William Hope Hull, John Milledge, W. B. Wofford, and Thomas W. Thomas. Chief Magistracy of Georgia. The undersigned were appointed a committee to notify you of your nomination and to solicit your acceptance.

In the performance of this duty we may add that many of that convention were those with whom you have hitherto agreed upon the political issues which have divided the country: many were there who have hitherto differed from you on those issues. Yet *all,* animated by an ardent love for the preservation of that government, which has been transmitted to us by Washington, now, when an imperilled Union demands the loyalty of every patriotic heart, forgetting all past differences of mere loyalty, and striving after a higher and nobler object, have united to save that Union itself.

Not only has the spirit of fanaticism elsewhere, but that of ultraism among us, sought to destroy the principles of our government as expounded by Washington, Jefferson and Madison; but it has ever sought to lay its sacrilegious hands upon the government itself and to throw into revolution and anarchy that which is the *fmest, happiest and best* on earth.

To avoid this calamity and to preserve this Union upon the principles of the Constitution have united the hearts and purposes of that portion of the people of Georgia who were represented in the late convention of the Constitutional Union party. By that party, with such principles, you have been nominated as a candidate for the Chief Magistracy of Georgia.

Permit us to add the expression of our individual preferences as to its acceptance.

Alexander H. Stephens To Howell Cobb. E.

Crawfordville, Ga., *23 June, 1851.* Dear Cobb, I have been extremely ill—but am now better—am able to sit up, that is all. I cannot walk out yet. I see you are going to have a bitter and heated contest. You must be wide awake with all your wits at command from the word go. No time is to be lost. You have an adroit and wily competitor. Take the stump and keep it on all suitable occasions. I see the Macon meeting has been propounding questions. These I should like to answer for you. They would ask me no more questions this campaign, I venture. I would give them short, explicit and unequivocal answers with just argument enough to clinch what I had to say. Let what you say be pointed not prolix. Show to the first that the settlement is better than 14 slave states asked. Show what Calhoun contended. Show what he said about the Mexican laws the last day he was in the Senate. Show what the Georgia Whigs and Democrats asked and show what they got

In reference to the calling out of the militia, etc., maintain the right of the President and duty of the President to execute the law against all factious opposition whether in Mass. or S. C. Maintain the power to execute the fugitive slave law at the North and the power to execute the Revenue or any other law against any *lawless* opposition in S. C. Turn the whole force of this upon the *revolutionary* movement in S. G, and urge all good citizens who value law and order and the rights of liberty and property to stand by the supremacy of the law. This is the life and soul of a republic. Warn the good people of Georgia to beware of revolution—refer to France— and plant yourself against the factionists of S. C., upon the constitution of the country. The right of secession treat as an abstract question. It is but a right to change the Govt., a right of revolution, and maintain that no just cause for the exercise of such right exists. And keep the main point prominent, that the only question now is whether we should go into revolution or not. S. C. is for it. This is the point to keep prominent. I wish I had strength to write more or to give you my views more at large. Our central committee must be at work soon. There never was a more bitter contest I expect in our state than will be this fall. Our opponents will leave no stone unturned no lie untold and no dollar they can raise unspent. You must be up and awake.

Howell Cobb To James A. Meriwether And Others.1
Athens ga., *June 24,1851.*

Gentlemen: I have this day received your letter of the 18th instant, informing me of my nomination, by the convention of the Constitutional Union party of Georgia, for the office of governor. With a full appreciation of the honor which the convention has conferred upon me I accept the nomination, and if elected will endeavor faithfully to discharge the duties of the office.

The resolutions adopted by your convention present in distinct terms to the people of the State an issue involving the peace and re pose of the country, if not the very existence of the Union. No one can overestimate the importance of the decision which is to be pronounced by the people upon it, and it is only in a due estimate of the consequences dependent upon the result that we can look for a judgment worthy of the intelligence and patriotism of our fellowcitizens.

During the exciting scenes that characterized the deliberations of the last Congress on the slavery question the public mind was di 1 From the Union, Washington, D. C, July 2, 1851. The committee consisted of James A. Meriwether, William Hope Hull, John Milledge, W. B. Wofford, and Thomas W. Thomas.

rected with intense anxiety to the action of our national legislature. Every patriotic heart in the land felt that the issues of life and death were involved in the final adjustment of that angry and exciting contest which was threatening the overthrow of the noblest structure ever erected by human wisdom—the *American Union.* That result, so long and anxiously looked for by the people of the states, was at length consummated by their representatives, in the adoption of those bills familiarly known to the country as the "adjustment" or "compromise measures." I do not propose at this time to discuss those measures: it would not be altogether appropriate to the occasion even if I felt impelled to such a course by the apprehension of any doubt existing in the public mind in reference to my views on this subject. I have alluded to the subject as introductory to another, growing out of those measures, which challenges in an emphatic manner the public attention from recent political movements in our own and neighboring states.

When, in consequence of the passage of the compromise bills by Congress, the people of Georgia were summoned to a convention to consider of the course and policy which the adoption of those measures required them to pursue, we all felt that circumstances had devolved upon our State a responsibility of no ordinary character, but one which the intelligence and patriotism of her people peculiarly adapted her to assume. The anxiety manifested in reference to the action of that convention was not confined to the limits of our own State. It was felt throughout the length and breadth of the Union, and was second in intensity only to the solictude which had previously been exhibited about the adoption of the measures which had caused its assemblage. The questions which that convention was called upon to consider were discussed by the public press, by our public speakers, in private conversation—indeed in every mode known to the political canvass—with unusual warmth and marked ability. It is certainly no reflection upon any previous political struggle in our State to say that on no former occasion was there more talent, learning, research, and patriotism brought into requisition than by the respective friends and advocates of the various policies indicated in the course of the canvass. The representatives selected under these circumstances assembled in convention—a body of as wise and patriotic men as ever before convened in any State in the Union. They came fresh from the people, fully intrusted with their wishes and empowered to speak authoritatively for them; and in the name of their constituencies they placed upon the records of our State the enlightened judgment of an honest and patriotic people. It is unnecessary for me here to speak of the action of the convention in detail. It is of too recent occurrence and therefore too familiar to the people to require a recital of it. Not only will it be remembered what was the action of the convention but it should likewise be borne in mind that it met the approving voice of the people throughout the State.

The universal sentiment of approval which greeted the representatives upon their return to their respective constituencies was rendered the more striking and remarkable by the feeble and occasional mutterings of the few restless and discontented spirits who withheld their sanction. Who supposed at that time that there would have been arrayed in a few months a political organization in the State, based upon a repudiation of this wise, just, and enlightened judgment of the people?

If the people of Georgia are prepared to reverse a decision so recently and solemnly made and madly to rush the ship of state into the gulf of disunion in obedience to the summons of a neighboring State, then it is manifest that I am not the man to select for their chief magistrate; for while I concede that the South has cause of complaint against the North for their conduct in the past in connexion with the question of slavery, yet I must in candor declare that there is nothing which in my judgment will justify us in dissolving a government formed by Washington and his immortal compeers, and which the committee are right in pronouncing " the freest, happiest, and best in the world." It will be a dark day for liberty throughout the world when this step is taken.

The effect produced throughout the Union by the action of that convention is not only grateful to our feeling of State pride, but should not be without its influence upon our minds when we are invited to a reconsideration of the decision which was then pronounced. With our sister States of the South, and with the patriotic friends of the Union everywhere, the action of that convention was hailed with exhibitions of unbounded applause. The highest encomiums were passed upon the wisdom, intelligence, and patriotism of its members as exhibited in their firm and unyielding devotion to the rights of the South, the constitution of the country, and the Union of the States. Georgia, already proudly pre-eminent among her sister States, was thus elevated to a yet higher and nobler position. As one of her citizens, I give to the action of her convention my warm, cordial, and unreserved approval, and am prepared to give to the maintenance of her decision my best efforts. She has declared in the most solemn manner that " she can, *consistently with her honor,* abide by the general scheme of pacification." In that declaration I fully concur. When I give to this action of her convention my unqualified approval, I do not feel that my native State has required me. as one of her citizens, to submit to an act *of degradation.* I will not cast upon her the ungrateful reflection that she has taxed the allegiance of her citizens to the extent of requiring at her hands a humiliating submission to a condition of *degradation* and *inequality* among her sister States. It is with far different feelings that I regard her action. I look upon her in the proud position which she occupies in this confederacy of States, and feel no blush of shame mantling my cheeks as I read her history in the past, realize her present preeminence, and look forward to the bright prospect which the future opens up before her. Should however the time ever arrive when the conditions of her remaining in the confederacy are *degradation* and *inequality,* I shall be prepared with her " to resist, with all the means which a favoring Providence may place at her disposal," even *(as a last resort)* "to a disruption of every tie which binds her to the Union," any and every power that seeks to put her upon such debasing terms. Nor am I particular by what name this resistance may be characterized—whether secession, revolution, or anything else; for no one can for a moment doubt that should this fearful collision ever come, the issue will be decided only by the arbitrament of the sword. Where constitutions end revolutions begin.

But to my mind the future presents no such gloomy forebodings. So far we have maintained the honor of our state and at the same time preserved the Union. A firm and unyielding adherence to the principles laid down by our convention will insure the future peace and repose of the country and will enable us, in common with our brethren of the American Union, to realize all those blessings which the future has in store for our country if we will prove true to the high destiny to which we have been called. Let Georgia then remain firm in the decision she has made, and not invite by a vacillating course a renewal of sectional strife and jealousies.

A. H. Kenan 1 To Alexander H. Stephens. R.

Milledgevtlle ga., *July 3rd, '51.* Dear Stephens, I drop you a line upon a matter of some interest to us both—are you aware that Toombs is looking to the Senate? Would it not be best for you to occupy the field first? I have seen many mutual friends of ours from the adjoining counties who will give you a warm support for the Senate, but who at the same time say that if you run for the district you must then serve, etc. I should have written you before upon this subject but from motives of delicacy. I am now satisfied that if it is your wish to go to the Senate, the policy of the move? requires that you should at once make your election—this will give you the advantage of position. Let me hear from you.

1A prominent politician of central Georgia. 73566—13 16

John B. Lamar To Howell Cobb. E. Macon ga., *July 3rd, 1851.*

Dear Howell, I send herewith the proceedings of a meeting held on Sullivan's Island in S. C. Also the comments of the Sav. Georgian on them. I call your attention especially to Rhett's toast of " co-operation," which means for S. C. to secede and force Ga. and the South to follow her. Also to his hailing McDonald and recognizing

Mc's "bugle" as identical with his own.

You will also perceive that the Sav. Georgian in trying to evade Mr. Rhett's association commits himself unqualifiedly to the very issue until now they have dodged, viz.: that their object is to cause the people of Georgia to stultify themselves by repudiating the Georgia Platform and recanting their opinions of last year.

Henry S. Foote 1 To Howell Cobb. E.

Jackson miss., *July 9th, 1851.* My Dear Sir, It gives me great pleasure to comply with your very reasonable request touching the article to which you did me the honor of calling my attention. This man seems to lie with as much facility as some of his stripe in our own state. I am gratified to learn from your letter the favorable condition of things in Georgia; though never since your nomination have I at all doubted the result of the contest there.

I always told you that Mississippi was one of the most reliable Union States in the Confederacy. We will prove this to be literally true in September. Quitman and Quitmanism are *dead* in Mississippi forever.

Heaven grant you length of days and much multiplied honor as I have ever deemed you worthy to enjoy!

Robert E. Martin To Howell Cobb. E.

Greensboro ga., *13th July, 1851.* My Dear Sir: Yesterday I met with Col. John Lamar in his way to Athens. I requested him to write you as soon as he reached Athens and say to you that I thought it advisable that your first appointment after you get back from southwestern Ga. should be made for Greensboro. I saw Stephens yesterday. He says he will be with you at any time you will appoint. A few persons in this county appear a little refractory. They were greatly encouraged and strengthened on the 4th inst. by a *stump talk* from Judge Dougherty; McDonald, W. Lumpkin and Smyth were present also. No one of them had any influence save Dougherty. It is intended to give you 1 United States Senator from Mississippi, etc.

a dinner at this place. I am of opinion that the place is a bad one. For myself, I should greatly prefer that you should send an appointment here on your own hook, without the form of an invitation or promise of a dinner. A public dinner can't be given these days without the question being raised why brandy was or was not used.

As I expect you will meet the people of Greene, I will state to you their objection to you. In the first place the old Whigs say you are a Democrat. This you can easily answer by telling them that God in his great mercy and wisdom made you so.

They say that you voted for the Wilmot proviso, and that it was a bargain entered into between Toombs, Stephens and yourself that you should be a candidate for Governor of Ga. before you left Washington City. And Judge Dougherty adds that you, with all others who stand upon the resolutions of the Ga. Convention, are too great disunionists for him; that you are ready to dissolve the government for a cause far too frivolous for him. You see I have answered the first objection myself, the remaining ones I leave for you.

From what I have said, I do not wish you to understand that McDonald can under any circumstances receive over 250 votes. Even that is or will be considered a great triumph for Greene county. You can greatly reduce this amt. A few days past I requested Mr. Brown to see Nickelson and a few others, and for them to write you to know when you could be here. By some means, Oscar Dawson got wind of it and offered to first write you himself to learn when you could attend, and then that the Comt. could be appointed and write you. Now, my own opinion is that he has not nor will not write. For that reason I do so myself, and again give it as my opinion that you had best write to James B. Nickelson or James L. Brown of this place that you will be in Greensboro by such time, and for them to make it known to the people, and if you wish you can inform Stephens of it in time for him to attend also.

Don't feel under the least restraint in writing to Nickelson or Brown for want of personal acquaintance. They are both good and true, and have the cause of Cobb and the Union greatly at heart, and will do all in their power to promote the good cause. If your appointment for Dooly was a day later, I would be there.

On the railroad yesterday I met with McCay of Americus. He told me that whilst in Cobb county he witnessed bets that your majority in the Cherokee country would be 15.000 votes. This was also stated by another gentleman who stated that within the last 2 weeks he had visited the greater part of that section of the state, and that it was generally a conceded point that your majority in Cherokee alone would not be less than from 12 to 15,000. If this be so, may the Lord have mercy upon them.

Andrew J. Donelson 1 To Howell Cobb. E.

New York, *July 15, 1851.*

Dear Sir: I am rejoiced to learn that there is now little fear of your election to the Chief Magistracy of the Empire State of the South, and that you have not dissolved your connection with the Democratic party.

I have been appointed a member of the Democratic national committee, vice Hon. David S. Kaufman (one of your associates in Congress) deceased, and am extremely desirous of procuring reliable intelligence as to the present condition of the Democratic organization throughout the country. Baltimore without doubt will be the place for holding the next convention, from time-honored associations and former triumphs, and the only open question now is what month the convention will be held. May or June are named, and several members of the committee go for the postponement till June, as the Whigs profit considerably by holding their convention after ours. A thorough reorganization is forming among the National Democracy of the North; and you may depend upon it that all the conventions to be held hereafter will specially endorse the compromise measure, especially the fugitive slave law. A majority of the people of the North are law abiding, but are sometimes misled by designing demagogues to overstep their bounds.

In 1852 this city can be relied upon by the National Democracy as true to the Union and the Constitution. The tone of the public sentiment is perfectly conservative on the slavery question, and the agitation of Southern institutions is condemned on every occasion.

If you would furnish me with a list of the more prominent "Union " Democrats of your State, I could make a good use of them in the coming contest. Politics are so mixed up in your State that I would be at a loss to know who are now known as National Union Democrats.

New Hampshire, you will see, presents Judge Woodbury as her first choice for the Presidency; in Pennsylvania Mr. Buchanan had a majority in both of the Democratic State conventions, but will not be nominated until March 1852 when the State convention meets at Harrisburgh to choose Delegates to the Dem. national convention. Gen. Houston is the choice of the people of Texas and has many friends at the North, prominent National Democratic journals having him indiscriminately for the Presidency and VicePresidency. No man in the nation will be found supporting the national nominees of the party, whatever the result more than Gen. Houston; and as it seems to be now conceded by a great portion of the 1 Editor of the Washington Union, 1351-1852, defeated candidate of the Know-nothing party for the Vice-Presidency, 1856.
press that the North is entitled to the Presidential nomination, Gen H. when the time arrives will waive his claims most gracefully, and place himself in the hands of his friends, and campaign it for the nominees of the party.

Samuel W. Flournoy To Howell Cobb. E.

Columbus ga., *July 18th, 1851.* Dear Sir: Since your speech in this place on the 9th inst., your opponents are industriously circulating the report that you maintained on that occasion the right of the Federal Government to use force to control one of the States of the Union in case such State should in its sovereign capacity secede from the Union. My own understanding of your doctrine was different. You contended, if I understood you correctly, that all governments were governments of force, but that under the existing laws of the United States the government of the common country was only authorized to use the military power to control individuals and suppress mobs and other combinations of men too strong to be controlled by the civil authority.

Having so understood your opinions, in an article of the 15th inst., published in the Columbus Enquirer, among other things the following extract will be found:

But according to the views; or pretended views rather, of our opponents there is but one thing now that is worth talking about, and that is the abstract, naked right of secession. This right Mr. Cobb admitted, and in express terms avowed that when a State in its sovereign capacity and by its regularly constituted and constitutional agents took its course, that the Federal Government had no legal or constitutional authority to control such State by force. Is this Federal doctrine? He was opposed however to disunion, secession and agitation and contended that the Union could only be maintained by compromise, conciliation, and mutual affection. The government rested and must rest on the hearts of the people, and the attempt now making to render It odious and bring it into disrepute was but little better than treason against the liberties of man.

Now, sir, it is denied that this extract embodies the views presented by you as to the abstract right of secession, or the want of legal and constitutional power on the part of the Federal Government to resort to force to control the action of a Sovereign State. If you have a spare moment at Americus, will you be good enough to drop me a short line as to the correctness of my understanding as embodied in this extract. Our opponents are in a condition just now to take advantage of everything and poison the public mind by every misrepresentation. It is a part of my business to correct such misrepresentations and stand by the friends of the Union in the great struggle now waging throughout the South. Hence this trespass on your time.

I desire you to understand this as coming individually from the writer without consultation with anybody, and without any purpose of using your reply in any other way than you may expressly permit. All I desire is that your opinions may be fairly before your constituents, and that under the banner you are bearing aloft we may all gain a triumph that may effectually silence the disunionists, secessionists, and that whole breed of croaking agitators with whom we have to contend.

I send you a number or two of the *Times,* and some other papers that may be useful to you.

Be kind enough to let me know what seems to be the state of public feeling wherever you have been since you left our city.

Give me any suggestions that you may deem of importance at the present time. All you may say will be in the strictest confidence, unless you may otherwise direct or permit.

In your movements through the interior, and particularly in the upper part of the State, I should like above all things once in a while to have your opinion of the prospects before us. I know that this is asking rather too much; but still the people's servant must indeed be a servant. Beat the race by all means, and if I see you no more until then, I trust to be present when you deliver your inaugural address as the Chief Magistrate of Good Old Georgia, our native State.

E. G. Cabaniss To Howell Cobb. E. Forsyth ga., *August 1,1851.* Db. Sib: The Rev. J. C. Simmons, the minister in charge of this circuit, has just now called on me and informed me that their camp meeting in this county about eight miles from this place will embrace the 28th inst., the day you have appointed to address the citizens of Monroe. It becomes necesary that you should appoint another day. Our superior court commences on the Monday following the 28th, and if you wait until your return from Twiggs to speak here, it would be during court when I fear from the crowded state of our criminal docket sufficient time might not be allowed you. The camp meeting commences on the 25th and continues until the 30th inst. We would prefer that you should come previous to that time if it should suit your convenience. Suppose you make your appointment to speak here on the 21st and in Twiggs on the 23d inst. I will thank you to notify me of the time you will be here as soon as you can, in order that we may have bills printed and posted up.

The fire-eaters show considerable mortification and chagrin at your Culloden speech. They were disappointed in not hearing something with which to find fault. They dread the impression made by it, and hence the mortification so visible in their countenances. Some of them are even mad because you gave no cause of offence and said nothing that they can answer. The main objection which has been urged is that the law prohibiting the slave trade in the D. C. is not the same as the law of Maryland on that subject. Some are so rude as to charge you with making a wilful misstatement. Foremost in making this charge is their candidate for senator in this district. Your statement is the same which I saw frequently in the published debates while the Compromise bills were under discussion, made by Mr. Clay and others, and I have no doubt of its truth; but in order to silence their clamors and to defend you from the charge of wilfully stating an untruth, if you have any paper containing the law of Maryland— it was copied into some of them during the debate in Congress—I will thank you to send it to me, or put me in possession of authority with which to defend you. The charge itself is too captious to do you any injury, but I wish to confound the man who made it.

John H. Lumpkin To Howell Cobb. E.

Rome ga., *Aug. 1, 1851.* Dear Cobb, I have had nothing from you since your nomination except the newspaper accounts of your progress in the southwestern counties of the State. As a matter of course you will be at Athens at the Commencement, and I would be glad to meet you there and confer with you; but my court will be in session in Cass county at that time. I saw Toombs a few weeks since, and he informed me that it was your intention to visit the Cherokee counties about the middle of August and to address the people of each county. I have informed our friends that such was your design and I can assure you that we shall give you everywhere a favorable reception. Every effort has been made to carry the Cherokee democrats from us, and to some extent our opponents have succeeded in imposing on the uninformed the grossest deceptions. They claim to be Union men, and allege that McDonald is the democratic candidate, and that you have joined the Whigs; and many honest democrats have been induced to go for McDonald because of their old hostility to the Whigs as political opponents. But we have been active and industrious in our efforts to counteract these movements and sustain our former ascendancy on the issue of Union or disunion. McDonald was the strongest man that the fire-eaters could run in this section of the State. He lives in this section of the State, and he is known personally to most if not all of the voters, and he was twice voted for by the Democrats in this section of the State for Governor, and it requires industry to keep the old line democrats off of him. This will satisfy you of the necessity of coming up here as soon as your arrangements will permit. And you must if you can canvass all the counties in this circuit. McDonald was at court here last week, and he was bowing and shaking the people by the hand very familiarly. He made a good impression, and we had all of our forces here in the field against him. Chastain and Stiles opened the Congressional campaign at this place on Thursday last. They were limited to 45 minutes each and both of them spoke twice. I was not present but I saw the effect that was produced on the Union men and on the disunionists and I am satisfied that the victory of Chastain was complete. There was some fear among some of the Union men who did not know Chastain that he would be a drawback upon you in this district, but the speech he made here has satisfied all that he is the superior of Stiles on the stump. McDonald did not go to the meeting at Rome, but he is now on a tour through the counties above this with Mr. Stiles. They were both in Chattooga county at Summerville last Saturday, and McDonald did not make a speech but made some explanations to the people from the rostrum vindicating himself against false accusations. On Monday he was in company with Mr. Stiles at LaFayette and he has since gone to Ringgold and will be at Trenton in Dade county. Col. Chastain, to their astonishment, dropped in upon them on Monday at LaFayette, and he brings a good report from that county, and especially from the gathering to hear Stiles.

On yesterday our senatorial convention met at the Floyd Springs, 15 miles above this, and Col. Joseph Walters of Floyd was unanimously nominated the candidate of the Union party for the senate. He is an old Union Jackson democrat, and was a delegate to the convention last fall that formed, or aided in forming, the Union party. Wm. T. Price, formerly a Whig, was nominated as the candidate of the Union party for Representative. The Union candidates must succeed by at least 500 majority in Floyd, and I should not be supprised if our majority went to 800 votes. I have done all that I shall be able to do in this county until the election. In Chattooga and in Gordon the contest will be close, but I think we shall carry both of these counties. A few aspiring men for the sake of the county offices in Chattooga have done a great deal against the Union party, but I think we shall still carry that county. In Walker our friends expect a large majority. Col. Saml. Farris is our candidate for senate in Walker and Dade. And all that is necessary for you to do to secure the entire vote in Dade county is to go there in person and become acquainted with these people. Fulton and his family connections and their influence will probably be against you in the county of Dade. The remainder of the people will go for you. If I could go there with you and introduce you in person, I could carry them all for you.

We had a free barbecue and a free discussion at the Floyd Springs yesterday. Chastain, Chisholm and Wofford spoke for the Union party, and James M. Spurlock represented the fire-eaters. Our friends assure me that it all went off well. Chisolm assures me that the Union men are gaining ground in Paulding county, and I am assured that the same is true of Cass. In Murray the Bishop influence in that county will go for you and against McDonald and this without doubt will give us this county. And Chastain informs me that Gilmer and Union will be almost united. The contest in Cobb and Forsyth will be close and the latter will be warm, but in Cherokee and Lumpkin all will be well notwithstanding the course pursued by a few of Cooper's friends at the start when Chastain was nominated. It is a small affair, and most of them are already reconciled now....

Howell Cobb To John Rutherford And Others.1

Athens ga., *August 12th, 1851.*

Gentlemen: I did not receive your letter until my return from the lower part of the State, about the first of the present month, and have not therefore replied to it at an earlier day.

As I have received communications from other parts of the State on the same and kindred subjects, I have determined in this reply to consider the questions involved at some length, as I desire that it may be considered as responsive to the various communications to which I have referred.

Your letter propounds the two following interrogatories: 1st. "Do you believe that a State by virtue of her sovereignty, has the right peaceably to secede from the Union, or is it your opinion that the General Government has the constitutional authority to coerce her to remain in the Union? And should a call be made upon the militia to aid in attempting to coerce a seceding State, would you if in the Executive office obey such requisition? 2d. "Do you believe that the late acts of Congress termed the 'Compromise' were constitutional, just and equitable?"

I shall consider these questions in the inverse order in which you have proposed them.

In order that I may be distinctly understood in reference to the late acts of Congress, termed the " Compromise," I consider it proper to make a brief reference to each of the six bills which composed that 1 From the Southern Recorder, Milledgevllle, Ga., Aug. 19, 1851. The letter was addressed to a committee of the citizens of Macon, Ga.

compromise, and shall in that way be enabled to give the most satisfactory answer to your second interrogatory...-1

The bill for the suppression of the slave trade in the District of Columbia was objected to by Southern men principally on the ground of the penalty which it provides. That feature is taken from the laws of Maryland, and it will be remembered that all that now remains of the district was originally a part of the State of Maryland. In 1816 the State of Georgia prohibited the introduction of slaves into this State for sale, under a penalty of a fine of five hundred dollars and imprisonment in the penitentiary for four years for each slave brought into the State for sale. This law was repealed in 1842 and re-enacted in 1843 and again repealed at the session of 1849. The penalty for the violation of the District law is the liberation of the slave, which is, as I have said, the same penalty provided by the Maryland law for a violation of their Act upon the same subject. There was as far as I could learn but one voice among the people of the district on this subject. They all desired it.

The Fugitive Slave bill is the only remaining measure of the compromise to be considered—I wish it was practicable without extending this communication to too great a length to incorporate into it the leading provisions of the bill. It must suffice however to state that it was prepared by one of the most extreme advocates of Southern rights in Congress. It contains every provision that was demanded by the South, and I have yet to meet with the first man who claims more at the hands of Congress on this subject than this bill grants. Congress in the adoption of this bill has in my judgment exhibited a willingness and determination fully to discharge the obligation which the constitution imposes for the delivery of our fugitive slaves.

I have now rapidly referred to each of the compromise measures, and you will see that whilst, in the language of the Georgia Convention, I do not wholly approve of all these measures, yet I see in them no violation of our constitutional rights, nor is there in my opinion anything which forbids on the part of our people an *honorable acquiescence* in these measures. Such was the decision of the people of this State last fall, as recorded by their delegates in the convention of last November. If I did not regard the settlement as fair and honorable I would not be found among the advocates of the Georgia Platform. It is not simply because Georgia has decided the question that I maintain her decision, but because she has made a wise, just and patriotic decision. If I thought that Georgia had made a decision that subjected her citizens to terms of inequality 1The material here omitted virtually repeats the substance of Cobb's letter to W. H. Hull, July 17, 1850, above printed, in regard to the organization of Utah and New Mexico, the adjustment of the Texan boundary, and the admission of

California.

and degradation, I would as a loyal citizen submit to her will until I could induce her, if in my power, to abandon so humiliating a position; and such I presume is the position of every honorable man within her limits. It is, therefore, right and proper that the people should know not only who will submit to the decision of the State, but also who approves and will sustain that decision.

Your first interrogatory directs my attention to the question of secession, and you have put the issue upon the right of a State to secede from the Union without just cause. As this right is claimed by many as a constitutional right, and by all of those who advocate it in its modern acceptation as consistent with constitutional obligations, I shall consider it at some length with reference to its constitutional bearings.

When asked to concede the right of a State to secede at pleasure from the Union, with or without just cause, we are called upon to admit that the framers of the constitution did that which was never done by any other people possessed of their good sense and intelligence—*that is to provide in the very organization of the government for its own dissolution.* It seems to me that such a course would not only have been an anomalous proceeding, but wholy inconsistent with the wisdom and sound judgment which marked the deliberations of those wise and good men who framed our Federal Government. Whilst I freely admit that such an opinion is maintained by many for whose judgment I entertain the highest respect, I have no hesitation in saying that the convictions of my own judgment are well settled that no such principle-was contemplated in the adoption of our constitution. If it was the purpose of the framers of the constitution to subject the perpetuity of the Union to the will and indeed, I may add, the caprice of each State, it is a most remarkable fact that a principle of such vast importance, involving the very existence of the republic, should have been left an open question to be decided by inferences and metaphysical deductions of the most complicated character. When one rises from a careful study of the constitution of the United States he feels impressed with its wonderful adaptation to the wants and interests of this growing people. Not only does he find wise and judicious provisions and guarantees for the state of the country as it then existed, but with prophetic wisdom its framers seem to have penetrated the future, accommodating the government to the necessities and requirements of its present increased population and extended resources. I am not prepared to admit that the men who exhibited so much care and foresight in reference to all the various parts of this complicated machine would have left to vague conjecture the existence of the important and vital power now claimed for each State of dissolving at pleasure the Union which had cost them and their compatriots so much toil and labor and anxiety. If they had intended to provide for the destruction of that noble structure which they were then erecting with all the care and wisdom of able statesmen and devoted patriots by such simple and obvious means as the withdrawal of any State from the confederacy, they would have manifested their intention by some plain and palpable provision of the constitution. Such a course would have been characteristic of the honest, practical and enlightened statesmen of the convention. Their failure to do so carries the strongest conviction to my mind that no such principle was recognized by them. In connection with this view of the subject the inquiry forces itself upon our minds if each State reserved the right to withdraw at pleasure from the Union, why was there so much difficulty encountered by the friends of the constitution in obtaining its ratification by the different States? There were few if any who were opposed to the formation of the Union after the constitution had been submitted to the States for ratification, provided they could engraft certain amendments upon it. The policy of adopting the constitution on condition that these amendments should be acceded to was urged with great earnestness in the conventions and among the people of several of the States, but was finally abandoned on the ground that it would be a conditional ratification and therefore inadmissible. On this point I must refer to the opinion expressed by Mr. Madison, who has been called " *the father of the constitution"* and to whose exposition of that sacred instrument the republican party have been accustomed to look with such implicit confidence. Mr. Madison says: "My opinion is that a reservation of a right to withdraw if amendments be not decided on under the form of the constitution within a certain time is a conditional ratification, that it does not make New York a member of the new Union, and consequently that she would not be received on that plan. Compacts must be reciprocal; this principle would not in such a case be preserved. *The constitution requires an adoption in toto and forever"*

If the right was reserved to each State to withdraw, it would have been an act of supererogation on the part of New York or any other State to declare in advance that she would withdraw or secede if the amendments she proposed to the constitution were not adopted. If the right existed it could be exercised as well without as with the condition annexed to her ratification of the constitution, and the assertion of it would have been a useless interpolation and a nullity. It was not so regarded however at the time by those who had been active participants in the framing of the constitution. Mr. Madison considered the reservation of a right to withdraw from the Union as "a condition that would vitiate the ratification." He says further in writing to Mr. Hamilton on this subject: " *The idea of reserving a right to withdraw* was started at Richmond and considered a conditional ratification which was itself *abandoned* as worse than a rejection."

If the opinion of Mr. Madison which I have here referred to be well founded, it puts an end to this controversy. There can be no doubt about the fact that he did not recognize the right of each State to secede from the Union at her own pleasure. In addition to the facts which I have just considered, there is a strong illustration of the opinion that prevailed among the framers of the constitution on this subject in the action of the States of North Carolina and Rhode Island. These States refused to come into the Union until some time after the ratification of the constitution. They were not opposed to the formation of the Federal Union, but like some of the other States they were unwilling to adopt the constitution as it then stood. If it had been a recognized and undoubted principle that each State was bound to remain in the Union only so long as it suited its own convenience, no one doubts that these States instead of withholding their assent to the constitution after it had been adopted by the requisite number, would have come at once into the Union with the intention of immediately withdrawing from it upon the refusal of the other States to adopt such amendments as they desired; but regarding the effect of their ratification of the constitution in an entirely different light from the secessionists of the present day, they adopted quite a different policy. So far as we can gather light and information from the opinions and actions of the men who framed and adopted the constitution, it all goes to strengthen and confirm the conviction I have already expressed against the existence of any such right.

The political history of the country from the time of the declaration of independence to the adoption of the constitution is confirmatory of the correctness of the opinion I have expressed. In the original articles of confederation it is more than once declared that the object was to form *a perpetual Union.* Those articles of confederation were found too weak and inefficient to carry out the great purposes of the people in the establishment of a general government, and hence it was that in its own language was the present constitution adopted for the purpose of forming *"A more perfect union."* It would be a reflection both upon the integrity and the wisdom of the framers of the constitution to say that they abandoned "*a perpetual Union*" to form *a more perfect one* and in doing so adopt *a temporary, conditional Union.* Such, however, is the construction placed by the seccessionists upon the action of those great and good men to whose energy and wisdom and patriotism we are indebted for our present noble and glorious Union.

The policy of our government during its whole existence looks to the continuance and perpetuity of the Union. Its temporary and conditional existence is nowhere impressed either upon its domestic or foreign policy. It has for more than half a century pursued the even tenor of its way, growing in strength and increasing in usefulness, taking deeper and deeper hold upon the hearts and affections of the people, illustrating the great American principle of free government and reflecting upon its inspired founders the highest and brightest honors. Whilst I do not propose to illustrate these views by a detailed review of the action of the government, I cannot forbear to refer to one portion of our history which is strongly corroborative of the correctness of the position I have assumed. When the people of the United States determined upon the purchase of the Louisiana territory and effected that desirable object at the cost of a considerable amount of money and by the exercise of a questionable constitutional power, it will not be said that they did so for the benefit of those who then inhabited the country nor indeed for those who might subsequently remove there. They were prompted to the acquisition of that vast and valuable territory by considerations of public policy affecting their interests and welfare as citizens of the various States of the Union. The commercial and military advantages to the United States from the possession of that country were so great and important that its acquisition was considered almost an act of self-protection. Will it now be said that the people of Louisiana possess the right to deprive the remaining States of the Union of all the interests and advantages which they have bought and *paid for* out of their own treasury by withdrawing or seceding from the Union at will?

Louisiana is as free, sovereign and independent as any other State in the Union, and if this right exist in any one State, it exists in all without reference to the mode by which the territory was acquired out of which the State is formed. I apprehend that the people of the United States did not for a moment entertain the idea that in admitting Louisiana into the Union they had thus periled all the advantages of that important acquisition by placing it in the power of a single State to deprive the Union of commercial and military advantages and resource's of inestimable value purchased by the joint treasure of all the States and now held by them as beyond the reach of any price or consideration that could be offered in exchange for them. These remarks apply with equal force to all the territorial acquisitions made by the United States where States have been or may hereafter be formed and admitted into the Union, and the same principle might be forcibly illustrated by reference to the action of the government on subjects of a kindred character; but it cannot be necessary and I will not extend this view to any greater length.

When the right of a State to secede from the Union at will is conceded, we have put the existence of the government at the disposal of each State in the Union. The withdrawal of one is a dissolution of the compact which holds the States together; it is no longer the Union that the constitution formed, and the remaining States are absolved from all moral obligation to abide longer by their compact. I say moral obligation, because the argument of the secessionists denies the existence of any binding legal obligation. By admitting the doctrine of the secessionists we are brought to the conclusion that our Federal Government, the pride and boast of every American patriot, the wonder and admiration of the civilized world, is nothing more than a voluntary association, temporary in its character, weak and imbecile in the exercise of its powers, incapable of self-preservation, claiming from its citizens allegiance and demanding annual tribute from their treasure, and yet destitute of the power of protecting their rights or preserving their liberties. If this be the true theory of our government, what is the constitution of the United States that we should estimate it so highly? Where is its binding force, that we should hold to its provisions with such unyielding tenacity? Individuals cannot violate their compacts or set aside at pleasure their mutual obligation without the assent of the other parties. Nations cannot recklessly disregard their treaty stipulations without incurring the consequences of violated faith. But our constitution, the revered monument of revolutionary patriotism and wisdom which we have been taught to regard with reverential feeling, is doomed to fall below the standard of national treaties and individual contracts. It has formed a Union founded upon mutual sacrifices and concessions, made by the several component parts for the greater benefits to be derived by each from the combined cooperation of all, and now we are told that there is no obligation to observe that Union beyond the pleasure of the parties to it, and that the constitution can be annulled by the act of any State in the confederacy.

I do not so understand our government; I feel that I owe my allegiance to a government possessed of more vitality and strength than that which is drawn from a voluntary obedience to its laws. I hold that no government is entitled to any allegiance that does not pass wise and just laws and does not possess the power to enforce and execute them.

I am fully aware of the fact that the effort is now being made to render the denial of a State to dissolve the Union odious in the public estimation, by presenting to the public mind in connection with it a frightful picture of an armed soldiery and a military despotism. I have no fears of the judgment that our enlightened countrymen will pass on this controversy—and surely I could not complain of any consequence that should result from my avowal of doctrines which I have imbibed from the teachings of Mr. Madison, Gen. Jackson, Judge Crawford, and their republican associates. It does not follow however as a necessary consequence of the principles which I have laid down, that military coercion is to be used against a State that may attempt the exercise of this revolutionary right.

Whilst I deny the right of a State to secede and thus dissolve the Union, I would not attempt by the strong arm of military power to bring her citizens back to their allegiance unless compelled to do so in defence of the rights and interests of the remaining States of the Union. We should not recognize her separate independence, nor could we allow our own interests to be periled by sanctioning any alliance she might be disposed to make with any foreign government. In our desire to inflict no injury upon a wandering sister we should not forget the duty which the government owes to those who remain firm and true to their allegiance and whose claim upon its protection and support should not be lightly regarded. The laws of self protection would require at the hands of the government that due regard should be had for the protection of the rights and interests of the other States, and to that demand it would be bound to respond. If one of these States should in a mad hour attempt to secede from the Union, and the kind and indulgent policy which I have indicated should be resorted to, I have no doubt that in a very short time such State would feel it to be both her duty and interest to retrace her wandering steps and return to the embrace of the sisterhood. This opinion is founded upon the high estimate I place upon the value of the Union to each and all of the States that compose it. It would require the experience of only a short absence to teach the wanderer the benefits and advantages from which she had voluntarily exiled herself.

Such are the general views which I entertain on this subject, and I have freely expressed them. I have discussed it as a mere abstract question, and in that light I regard it. Whatever differences of opinion may exist among the true friends of the Union on the abstract question of the right of secession, I apprehend that when it assumes a practical shape there would be but slight shades of difference as to the policy and effect of our action. There are many who hold to the doctrine of the right of a State to secede from the Union, with whom I do not differ practically. They grant the abstract right of secession but claim for the remaining States the right to protect themselves from any injurious consequences that might flow from the exercise of that abstract right by the seceding State. It is only necessary to state the two propositions to show that in the end the practical operation of their principles would lead to the same results that I would reach by the enforcement of the doctrines which I have avowed. Our difference is theoretical, not practical, and therefore constitutes no impediment in the way of our cordial co-operation.

We all hold that just and wise laws should be enforced and executed, whilst we are prepared to oppose acts of injustice and oppression by all the means in our power, to the rupture of every tie that binds us to any government. No government, however wisely and honestly administered, can be maintained in the absence of binding obligations on its citizens to obey its laws and power to enforce their execution on recusant parties. Hence I cannot consent to the doctrine that our government is destitute of these powers essential to its vitality and existence. The claim which I have urged in behalf of the Federal Government cannot be abandoned without endangering the frame-work of our admirable system, nor is there any serious danger to be apprehended from its improper exercise. Its true strength, based upon the existence of these powers, is to be found in the justice and wisdom of its legislation; these are the true and only safe avenues to the hearts and affections of the people, wherein are found the strong pillars of support to a free government. I do not entertain the idea for a moment that our government can be maintained by the strong arm of military power when it ceases to bestow the blessings upon the people for which it was formed. Whenever it becomes the instrument of wrong and oppression to any portion of the people by unjust laws and degrading legislation, it will cease to be the Union formed by our revolutionary fathers, and possessing no further claims upon our allegiance and support, should that period ever unfortunately arrive, we will not fail to prove ourselves as true to the principles of liberty and equal rights as our honored and venerated fathers; nor will we stop to look at the provisions of a violated constitution for the mode or measure for the redress of our grievances.

I have so far considered the question in reference to the doctrine of the constitutional right of a State to secede without just cause, at her own will and pleasure, and I think I have shown that it is unsupported either by principle or authority. On the other hand, I admit the right of a State to secede for just causes, to be determined by her self. Being a party to the compact, which the constitution forms, she has the right which all other parties to a compact possess to determine for herself when, where and how the provisions of that compact have been violated. It is equally clear that the other parties to the compact possess a corresponding right to judge for themselves, and there being no common arbiter to decide between them, each must depend for the justification of their course upon the justice of their cause, the correctness of their judgment and their power and ability to maintain their decision.

The right of a State to secede in case of oppression or " a gross and palpable violation" of her constitutional rights, as derived from the reserved sovereignty of the States, I am prepared to recognize. In 73566—13 17 such case each State, in the language of the Kentucky and Virginia resolutions of 1798-'99, is to be the judge, not only of the "infractions," but of the "mode and measure of redress." It is the just right of the people to change their form of government when in their opinion it has become tyrannical in a mode not provided for in the constitution, and is therefore revolutionary in its character and depends for its maintenance upon the stout hearts and strong arms of a free people.

In connection with this branch of the subject, a question arises which in the opinion of some is of considerable importance. It is, whether or not the citizens of a State thus resuming her sovereign powers would be liable to the charge of treason in conforming to the requirements of their State government. I refer to this particularly only in consideration of the importance attached to it by others. From what I have said it will clearly appear that I hold that they would not be. In my opinion, no man commits treason who acts in obedience to the laws and authorities of a regular organized government, such as we recognize our State governments to be.

But there is a question, gentlemen, involved in your interrogatories, which rises in magnitude far above any which I have yet considered. It involves the important inquiry, whether in the event of a State seceding from the Union, and the Executive of the United States making a requisition for troops to coerce her back, I, if elected Governor of Georgia, would obey that requisition. This question may become a practical one. I sincerely trust and hope it never will. Under the existing laws of the United States the President has no power to order out the militia to coerce a seceding State. Neither the Act of 1795 nor the Act of 1807 would apply in such an emergency. Those Acts apply to cases where individuals, acting without the authority of any State government, resist by force the laws of the United States—to riots and insurrections—to such cases as we were apprehensive a few months since might be manifested in opposition to the Fugitive Slave Law in portions of the Northern States. That this is the true construction to be placed upon the Acts will be apparent from the conduct of Gen. Jackson in a former period of our history, when the State of South Carolina threatened to secede from the Union. He then found it necessary to invoke the aid of additional legislation by Congress. His appeal to the then Congress resulted in the passage of the law familiarly known as "the Force Bill;" but that act being temporary in its object and character has lost all of its vitality and long since ceased to be of force, having expired by its own limitation. In the contingency involved in your question it would be necessary that the President, if his views of right and policy led him to coercion, should ask of Congress additional legislation, and it would be for them to determine whether or not they would grant it. If a State should secede and the President should recommend to Congress such legislation and Congress should grant it, then your question would become practical, and I am prepared to answer it fully, freely, and frankly. It would be the most fearful issue that ever the people of this country have been called on to decide since the days of the revolution—so momentous, so vital to the interests of the people of Georgia, that I should feel bound to ascertain the will of that people before I acted. I should endeavor to be the *Executive of the will of the people of Georgia.* To ascertain that will, I should convene the Legislature of the State, and recommend to them to call a convention of the people, and it would be for that convention, representing the people upon that naked issue, to determine whether Georgia would go out of the Union and ally herself and peril her destinies with the seceding State, or whether she would remain in the Union and abide the fortunes of her other sisters. And as Georgia spoke, so would I endeavor, if her Executive, to give power and effect to her voice.

But if a collision of arms between the States comprising our glorious confederacy should ever come, it requires no prophet to predict the result. The Union would fall beneath the weight of revolution and blood, and fall, I fear, to rise no more. It was formed in the hearts of the American people—it can only be preserved in their hearts. When any very large portion of its inhabitants look upon it as *oppressing and degrading* them, when they cease to revere it as the legacy of Washington and the inheritance of the blood of the revolution, its vitality will be gone, and empty parchments, though aided by military force, can never hold it together. Hence we see the abolitionists of the North denouncing it as "a covenant with hell," and hence we hear the disunionists of the South inflaming the hearts of the people against it, announcing that they have been degraded and oppressed by it, and preparing eventually to overthrow it. They are wise men, they understand the workings of the human heart, and they well know that when the heart feels that wrong, indignity and insult have been heaped upon a man, unless he be indeed a craven spirit, a blow will follow. Prepare the hearts of the people to hate the Union of their fathers, and the battle is won—they are ready to fight against it. Hence, bebeving as I do that the late Compromise is such, in the language of the Georgia Platfrom, " as she can in honor abide by," I have used every effort in my power to stay this ceaseless and ruinous agitation North and South, and to keep the constitution and the Union where our fathers erected them—firmly on the foundation of the people's hearts.

Alexander H. Stephens To Howell Cobb. E.

Crawfordvtlle, Ga., *1st September, 1851*. Dear Cobb, Your letter was received this morning. I cannot meet you according to request. I have an appointment for the 6th inst. at Sparta. All next week I shall be in my district. I am still feeble, but able to talk. I hope I shall continue to hold my feet. I was in Morgan, Baldwin and Burke last week. The news is good everywhere. We shall carry Burke. The contest is hot. The friends everywhere are up and active. My engagements extend to the election.

W. P. Jones 1 And Others To Howell Cobb. E.

Palmetto, Geo., *Sept. 11th, 1851.*

Dear Sir: In consequence of some arrangements which have been entered into between the Union party and Southern Rights party, we feel it our duty to inform you of the arrangements.

When Mr. Menefee and Jones returned from Atlanta, every Union man they spoke to in relation to giving a barbecue on the 24th were anxious to have discussion by both parties, and they made the offer to the S. Rights party, which after a good deal of quibbling they accepted.

One of our party made the following offer to them, which they accepted and would accept of no other, and we thought it better to accede to it, than that they should go off and boast that we offered to let them come into the discussion and then backed out. They would have spread it all over the country that we were afraid of discussion and it would have had a bad effect upon those Union men that wanted discussion on both sides, and besides we will get a greater number of the S. Rights party out; and still another reason, there will be so many people here we were afraid that we could not feed them all ourselves. You may look for the largest crowd here that you have addressed this year. The terms of debating are as follows: A Union man is to speak an hour, a S. R. the 2nd hour, a Union man the 3rd hour a S. R. the 4th and the same order to be observed throughout.

So you see the conclusion depends upon which party is the longest winded.

Please drop us a line to let us know what you think of the arrangement.

We would also state that a Southern Rights man remarked that when you heard of the arrangement you would not come, that you would be sick. But we would say to you that there is more need of your coming now than ever.

1 Jones was chairman of a committee of the Constitutional Union party, at Palmetto, Ga.

P. S.—We have not heard from Stephens. Will you use your influence to get him here and any other speaker that you can get to come? The oposite party will have all their strength out; we only know of two they will have, Colquitt and Smythe.

Robert Toombs To Howell Cobb. E.

Washington, Ga., *Oct. 11, 1851.*

Dear Cobb, Don't you hear these howlings rolling over toward the rocky mountains? We have glory enough for one day. Heard from all my district but Elbert. If she does her duty we shall have two thousand majority in the 8th. Stephens reaches near 3,000 majority. I think you will whale him out about 16,000.1

John B. Weems of my town wants to be one of your secretaries. He is very competent, steady and fine talents. You cannot do better, and besides if you can do it conveniently it will make a place for our friend Thomas W. Thomas of Elbert as solicitor, which he very much desires. Write to me immediately to Washington.

I have announced myself in the field against Berrien.2

George Ashmun s To Howell Cobb. E.

Springfield, Mass., *Oct. 11,1851.* My Dear Sir: I cannot help giving you my congratulations upon the very handsome result of your State election. I hear it with as much satisfaction as I ever heard of a Whig triumph—for, whatever may have been the form of the contest, *true Whig* 4 principles were at stake.

In this State we have a singular struggle going on. Democracy and Free-soilism have openly married as in Ohio—and we Whigs, having shaken our skirts clear of the abolitionism which has fouled them too much and too long, are making fight single-handed against the coalition. The result is very doubtful; but one satisfactory result will follow at any rate. The Whig party in this State is purified and brought out of the mire of sectionalism on to the high ground of nationalism. The old leaders of the Democracy are equally sound; but they are overborne and have no power.

I suppose that there are those who charge you with being no longer a Democrat, for I see that Jeff. Davis claims his to be the only true Democracy; but probably you and I should not agree any better about tariffs and annexations than ever.

1 The vote for Cobb in tbe gubernatorial election was 57,397, against 38,824 for Charles J. McDonald. *1.* e., as a candidate for tbe United States Senate. Whig congressman from Massachusetts, 1845-1851. You may call them Democratic; names are nothing. Footnote in the original J

At any rate I rejoice over the splendid triumph which you have achieved, for every reason except one—namely that it will keep you for a while out of Congress.

You will be back again tho' after a while—or your people are not the sensible men I take them for.

Andrew J. Donelson To Howell Cobb. E.

Washington City, *Oct. 22d, 1851.*

Dr. Sir: I owe you many apologies for delay in answering your favors of the 7th and 10th inst. The first was not reed. until I had written my article headed Georgia Elections; but they were both before me when I penned the next one headed with your name. You will find in today's paper under the head of " the Union of the Democratic party," a more pointed and perhaps more difficult attempt to reconcile matters in the South. It is written under the smart of some feeling that the papers apparently in the interest of Messrs. Buchanan and King are eternally firing at the Washington Union as not sound on the question of Southern or States' rights. I have made my mark, and must leave to time and such friends as yourself to suggest what more is proper to extricate us from division in the democratic ranks.. ..

You will have great difficulty in keeping the road open to a national convention of the Democratic party. Although it is certain that none but compromise men can be nominated as the candidates of the party, yet to make this point the test in the selection of delegates to the convention is not so easily maintained. Your opponents for instance in Georgia may in many cases bring their organization to bear in the appointment of delegates who will profess a determination to submit to the verdict of the people on the compromise, but who will be not the less bent on using their political power as a punishment to those who have defeated their designs as *secessionists;* and your friends distrusting such a party may be unwilling to act with it at all. Messrs. Stephens and Toombs too may wish to save for the benefit of the Whigs this party test, and thus increase the tendency to leave you a prey to the conflict of ancient prejudices.

I think it beyond all question that the Whigs have lost the Presidency. This is because as a party in the North they are less sound than the democrats on the compromise. The anti-slavery sentiment is the root of the evil which that measure will extirpate; and this sentiment was the one which the Whigs employed in the last Presidential election and which they cannot disown without the loss of power. Seeing this fact, Messrs. Stephens and Toombs ought not to separate from you, because you look to a national democratic platform upon which may come some men that may be unsound. If they will help you cordially, he consequence may be that none of the constituencies may commit the error of appointing delegates who are not known to be cordially on the Georgia Platform. In a short time it may be expected that the excitement created by the Nashville convention will pass away, and the old parties will naturally assume their relations on the other great issues which have divided them.

You have achieved a great victory and have laid the foundation of public character which men of all parties must recognize as placing you in all time to come in the list of our great men. I hope that your course will still be progressive and increase the means of benefitting the people who have entrusted to you their highest interests.

It is difficult for me to steer my course so as to please all our aspirants to the Presidency. I can only say that as to persons I feel neutral and shall hope to remain so. It is my aim to be firm and uncompromising in the support of principles and doctrines, leaving to the Democractic party the selection of the man the most proper to give practical effect to these principles and doctrines.

Douglas is here and talks modestly. I think he is stronger at this moment that either Cass or Buchanan. Marcy is coming forward in New York; but it is not believed that the Barnburners and Hunkers are yet cordially united except on State questions. My belief is that no New Yorker will get the vote of New York; and that we shall lose the State unless the Barnburners come into the support of a Compromise man.

You speak of commending me to Messrs. Stephens and Toombs. You must prepare them to find me an old fashioned democrat of the Jackson school, and standing firmly on the democratic platform as a compromise man. I do not the less appreciate however their noble and patriotic co-operation with you against the disorganization of the South, and shall hope that when they know us better they will find us not unworthy of their friendship in other respects.

My belief is that the scheme of many here to run Mr. Fillmore as the Union Whig will not be carried out. The Virginia elections will prove that no impression has been made in that State which can change the current of former party associations. It will still be democracy and whiggery there. Scott's gunpowder will be at last the only card of the latter party, and it will be used rather to protect the retreat of such leaders as Seward and Johnston than to gain a victory.

I shall be always glad to hear from you. See my article of this morning and let me know if I do not cover strongly enough the compromise as a democratic national test.

P. S.—The contest for Speaker, I think, will be between Boyd of Kentucky, Jones of Tennessee, Disney of Ohio, and Bayley of Va. Andrew J. Donelson To Howell Cobb. E.

Private. Washington D. C., *Oct. 26th, 1851.*

Dr. Sir: You cannot but have observed that the secession party in the South has looked to Buchanan for ultimate support. The consequence is a scheme to organize the House on that basis. It is in the face of such a fact that I suggest to you the propriety of guarding your Union friends in Georgia against committing themselves for Forney, whose whole influence is against the position you occupy. His *hurrah* for *Cobb and Foote* at the Tammany Hall must not mislead you. There has never been a line in his paper that was not written in the opposite interest.

P. S. The recent movement at Tammany I will write you specially about tomorrow.

Thomas D. Harris To Howell Cobb. E.

Washington, D. C., *Novr. 23, 1851.*

Dear Governor, From information received but a moment since, I can but regard the election of Forney to the Clerkship as a fixed fact. Virginia, which I had been led to believe would go for Judge Young, is almost unanimous for the former gentleman (Street of that state being my informant). This being the fact, all the other Southern states will be certain to follow in her track. Now sir I feel myself tottering. and it may be, yea will be, to my fall if no helping hand shall come to the rescue. Will you address Forney a letter, as well as Boyd and such other gentlemen as you may think it proper to approach?

I will write you daily after Wednesday next, and perhaps tomorrow, Monday.

This will reach you on Thursday, and you will have no time to lose if you determine to write as above desired. Boyd, I feel almost sure, will be Speaker.

Alexander H. Stephens To Howell Cobb. E.

Washington, D. C., *Nov. ®4, 1851.*

Dear Cobb, I intended to write you a long letter today but I have not had the time. I have been *bored* to death all day, and now just at 12 p. m. I have only one moment before going to sleep, which hangs heavily upon me, to say that I got here safely last night. Have got a little of the run of things here which I wish to give you, but it would be useless to do so, or rather to attempt it, without going into details which I cannot do tonight, and will therefore defer it until tomorrow or some other day. I am the only member from Georgia in the city. Disney, Bayley, Boyd and G. W. Jones are the candidates for the Speakership. Forney and Young are candidates for the Clerkship. There are very few members here yet. Forney? has been making a very bad speech in New York, it is said. I have not seen it. There is a great deal to be done here before a great many men who think themselves wise get their eyes open. The *mission* of the Constitutional Union party is not fulfilled yet. The Union newspaper man has not exactly got " the hang of" the " schoolhouse " yet. Keep all things straight in Georgia, and we shall "try" to keep up this end of the log, though it is a great deal the biggest. Good-night.

Alexander H. Stephens To Howell Cobb. E.

Washington, D. C., *Nov. ₤6,1851.*

Dear Cobb, Your letter of the 23rd inst. came to hand this evening. The report of the committee on election in the Jasper county case was received a day or two ago. I shall write to Chappell tonight. I think he ought to contest the seat, provided that by a rejection of the Slaughter precinct in Jasper he would be elected in the District. I do not know how that would of itself affect the result.

The Columbus Times you sent also came to hand this evening. There is evidently a great or strong inclination on the part of the leading S. R.1 men throughout the South to fall into line. But their object I fear is not only to fall into line, but to *leap* far beyond the proper and safe line for Southern men to occupy. They are in other words inclined, as is usually the case with men of their temperament, to go from one extreme to another. Two months ago *no party* at the North with them was sound enough to be *trusted*. Now they are ready to go into a party caucus with the *National Democracy* without any inquiry into the past or any assurance for the future. We shall have more trouble from them in getting a purgation of the North than from any other quarter. Without them you are right in saying we have the game in our own hands, but with them it will be difficult to effect any good. They are as vindictive as conquered subjects—and they are willing now, I believe, to combine with Preston King, Rantoul and Wilmot under the name of Democracy to wreak their vengeance upon all who have stood in their way in their mad ambition to overthrow the Government. As for the protection of Southern Rights, I must be excused for saying I do not believe it ever entered into their designs or formed any part of their objects. I have had full and free conversations with men of all parties since I have been here, and while it is true I can not pretend to be able to give you any very accurate conjecture as to the turn events will ultimately take, yet I will venture to state what the probabilities are at this present writing. A caucus of the *Democratic party* (eo 1 Southern Rights.

nomine) will be held Saturday night. At this all will attend who have been published in the Union newspaper as Democrats (including Preston King "et omne id genus ") except the Georgia Union Democrats. They will not attend. At this caucus resolutions will be offered affirming the Compromise and taking position against any future agitation of the slave question. If this is resisted and voted down, there will be a "flare up" and withdrawal. This I think would be the best possible result. For I am certain, or at least feel assured from what I see and hear at this place, that if the resolutions should pass *"nem. con."* it will only be done with a mental reservation on the part of some and with the absence of others who will still profess to belong to the fraternity. For there is no mistaking the evidence of our senses, especially where it is so abundant, that there is a great unsoundness with a large portion of the Northern Democrats upon the subject of slavery. I had a long free and frank interview yesterday with Mr. Donelson, the editor of the Union. He is simply a man of expedients. He is for bolstering up and using palliatives. He is neither for North or South, but out and out for *Democracy* and nothing else. I endeavored to open his eyes, and hope I did to some extent. Today I had a long interview with George W. Jones and found him thoroughly right. He told me that he should offer resolutions such as I have indicated. I suggested to him to offer one in addition to such as he named, declaring a warm attachment to the Union upon the principles of those he stated, or in other words upon the condition of the Compromise measures (as they are called) being sustained in good faith by the Northern members of the confederacy. This I wanted as a test for the S. It. men from the South. If they come amongst us I wanted them, as you say, to follow not to lead. They are conquered, and I am willing to grant them *quarters* with all my soul, but they must march in with their flag down. He did not say whether he would comply with the suggestion or not. I wish I had then known what had passed between you and him on that subject. I will endeavor, or at least open the way, to get to see his resolutions before the meeting. The Pennsylvania Democrats have not been acting fairly with us, as I fear, in the late canvass. Their sympathies were with McDonald. After the victory was won and their friends *defeated,* then they shouted *huzza* for Cobb and Democracy because it was to their *interest* to do so. I am not disposed to *trust* such men far. I have heard a good deal on this point, from unquestionable authority, which grieved me. King of Ala. was also in that line. Dickinson of New York is true as steel I think. I have a good deal to say to you about candidates for the Presidency which I cannot do now for want of time. As for the Speakership all is yet in a fog. Not members enough here to form any opinion. My *opinion* now is that the contest will narrow down to Boyd and Disney, though there is no telling what a day may bring forth. For clerk the contest will lie between Young and Forney. I am for Young, and think he will be elected unless he submits to a caucus, in which event Forney may beat him. I told Harris today to tell Young not to go into caucus. Foote is here, and what he is doing I do not know, but I *expect* is trying to rally the Democracy on Cass. He is a f—l, and I almost wish he had been beaten. Hillyer is here—got in last night. I saw him today, and find him "right side up. " I am well pleased with "*bearings.*" I shall not look for Toombs before day after tomorrow, Friday. Dawson writes to me that he shall be here by Saturday or Sunday. My health is quite as good as it was when I left home. The weather here is cold for the season. I got here Sunday evening in a snow storm, and it snowed all day yesterday again. Today it is all melted, but we have a clear cool atmosphere. Remember me to Mrs. Cobb and the little boys, and accept for yourself my best wishes privately and publickly—that is as an individual citizen and a public officer. I shall write to you again before long.

Thomas D. Harris To Howell Cobb. E. Washington D. C., *Now. 29, 1851.* Dear Governor, The democratic party meet in half an hour from this time in caucus; and I propose giving you such items of its action as may be gleaned from members passing in and out during its sitting, so that the letter may start off in the morning's mail. Charly Stewart1 stands at the door and has promised to report the number in attendance.

A resolution will be introduced by a member from Tennessee (Polk)2 declaring in favor of the Compromise as a finality, and of its rigid enforcement in all its parts. As at present advised, there may some trouble grow out of this move, but it will pass. I await the working cauldron.

Charly reports about eighty in caucus, and Richardson of Ill. in the chair....

11 o'clock. Bad feeling in caucus. Polk's resolution, which was brief, reasonable and fair, was proposed to be amended by Bob Johnson,8 in the form of a long senseless preamble and resolutions with a dozen or two of Whereases. Stanton of Tenn. then moves a resolution to the effect that it is inexpedient *at this time* to say anything about the Compromise, and postponing the whole subject to the meeting of the democratic National Convention. Whereupon Carter of Ohio 1 Probably Charles E. Stuart, Congressman from Michigan, 1847-1S49 and 1851-1853, Senator, 1853-1859. William H. Polk, Congressman from Tennessee, 1851-1853, brother of James K. Polk. 'Robert W. Johnson, Congressman from Kentucky, 1847-1853, Senator, 1853-1861. moves to lay the whole thing upon the table, and calls the previous question; this latter proposition carried by twenty-odd majority. A number of Southern men leave the caucus, among them Bayley, Polk, Jones and Gorman of Indiana. Boyd nominated by 20 over Disney; Forney by 40 over Young; Glossbrenner and Johnson largely, and McNew for door-keeper.

Too late for the mail, and my letter will be kept open during tomorrow.

Sunday Morning. Called to see Stephens this morning; found him in a very bad humor. He wants to beat Boyd and Forney, and asked me to see Gorman and send him to his room, which I did; and Gorman is now with him. He hopes to prevail upon G. to run for Speaker....

Alexander H. Stephens To Howell Cobb. E.

Washington, D. C., *Dec. 5, 1851*. Dear Cobb, The newspapers will inform you of what we are doing here. Boyd is speaker, and you see how it was brought about. I regretted very much that I could not vote for him in consequence of his connection with Free Soilers in his nomination. Had Boyd declined the nomination he would have got the entire Southern vote and a large portion of the Northern Whig vote and all the *sound* Northern Democratic vote. When the caucus voted down Polk's proposition Gorman and a number of other Northern Democrats seceded from the meeting. Gorman is as true a man as lives. He told me himself that he would not belong to a party that allowed Preston King1 and Rantoul to be members of it. But the difficulty was with men in high quarters. The attempt is now making and has been making to reorganize the Democratic party, *eo nomine* without any regard to principles or the past. "Bygones" are to be "bygones." Read the leader in the Union this morning. A man may be a disunionist and a good Democrat, and an abolitionist and still a good Democrat. The foulest of all coalitions is now at work— Southern Rights men and Abolitionists. What is to be the result I can not tell. But I do not permit myself to believe that it can succeed. Joseph W. Jackson2 sitting in caucus with Chauncey L. Cleveland!—and not only that, but voting to refer questions of great political importance to a national convention of which Robert Rantoul is a member! We are however in the beginning of new questions the end whereof is not yet seen. The Whig party is dead. It made a galvanic struggle in caucus, but it may be considered as disabandonned sic. I mean the national organization. There are 1 Preston King, of New York, Robert Rantoul, of Massachusetts, and Chauncey L. Cleveland, of Connecticut, mentioned below, were conspicuous Anti-slavery Democrats. Democratic Congressman from Georgia, 1850-1853.

a great many *sound men* of that party now at the North who are ready for a new movement, and in a few months many of the Democratic organizations will be ready for the same. The fire-eaters South hate nobody as much as they do you. They have it now reported that the movement in caucus came from you, and they claim the result as a triumph over you and the Georgia combination. They will hear something of coalition hereafter. I write this in great haste and would have written before but for my engagements in hunting winter quarters, moving, etc. In my next I will give you some suggestions. Buchanan I fear has had something of an intrigue with certain men down South—*Verbum sap.* But all will come out in due time.

George W. Jones 1 To Howell Cobb. E.

Washington, D. C., *Deer. 7, 1851*. Dear Cobb, I have just received and read your favor of the 3rd inst. Your surprise at the telegraphic account of the fate of the compromise resolution offered by my colleague, Major Polk, in the Democratic caucus was not greater than my disappointment and regret at the result. The resolution was short, simple, concise and direct, written by myself, and offered with my approbation. It merely declared that the series of acts passed during the first session of the thirty-first Congress, known as the Compromise, are regarded as a final adjustment and permanent settlement of the question therein embraced, and should be maintained and executed in good faith. R. W. Johnson of Ark. offered a substitute, embracing first about the same thing and then embracing the abolition of slavery in the District of Columbia, in the forts, arsenals, dock yards, Territories, and the slave trade between the States. Whereupon my colleague F. P. Stanton moved to refer the whole subject to the National Convention; and thereupon D. K. Cartter of Ohio moved to lay the whole subject upon the table, which was carried in the affirmative, our old friend Jos. W. Jackson, R. W. Johnson, A. G. Penn, F. P. Stanton and other Southern members voting in the affirmative—many taking the ground that it was neither the time nor place for such proceedings but that it was the appropriate and legitimate duty and function of the National Convention soon to assemble to declare principles and erect a platform for the party, all or nearly all admitting that the Democratic party would regard and sustain the Compromise as a final settlement of the sectional questions, but that some of them preferred going along smoothly and gently leading their constituencies in to acquiescence and support of the Compromise, rather than by a frank and manly declaration of that intention run the risk of 1 Congressman from Tennessee, 1843-1853, and 1855-1850.

throwing off a few freesoilers. When the resolutions were laid upon the table, I announced to the Caucus that I could not longer act with it and declined to take any part in the nominations or proceedings of that body. The nominations were made, Preston King, Robert Rantoul, Jr., and C. F. Cleveland voting in caucus for the nomination of Linn Boyd, which was and should be regard ed by all honorable men as as full an endorsement of the Compromise as the voting for a resolution could be, but not exactly in the same form and words.

When the members assembled in the Hall on Monday morning, before proceeding to vote for Speaker, I announced to the assembled members that I should vote for Linn Boyd of Kentucky, he sitting within five feet of me, not because he was the nominee of the caucus, but because I knew him to be a sound Democrat and a true and tried Compromise Union man, which he did not deny,—when quite a debate sprang up between Stanley, Meade, Savage, Brooks, Richardson and others, during which the proceeding of the Whig caucus was brought to light and exposed. It was all a trick—a finesse—and intended more to pave the way of the few Conservative Whigs of the North out of their own party into the Democratic party than to unite and rally the Whig party upon the Compromise. In that debate our friends regained to some extent the lost ground by the worse than blunder of the Saturday night Caucus.

I think there will be a resolution introduced into the House very soon declaring the Compromise as a finality of the questions embraced, when all will have to come to the scratch and make a record of their intention upon this subject, which will, I trust, put us, as the lawyers say, *rectus in, curia,* or rather, as I would say, right before the people and the country.

Even Preston King as I understand (for I have not discoursed him on the subject) expresses himself as exceedingly anxious that all agitation shall cease and the past be forgotten, and that harmony, union and cooperation shall be the characteristics of the Democratic party for the future. Really his *ilk* are very much like whipped spaniels, and from present appearances he will not be disposed to give us any trouble this session. If the Democratic Caucus had adopted the resolution our nominees would have received perhaps one hundred and fifty votes. I have seen some letters and articles from high sources in the North deprecating and regretting the fate of Polk's resolution. Nevertheless the Democratic party is *the* party of the Compromise, the country, the nation—the country, and under the banner of the Compromise and the Union, they must and will rally; and in that sign they will conquer. Who will be the nominees no one can tell or give even a reliable guess. But whoever they may be, all except a few fire-eaters, concur in opinion that they will be Compromise-Union men. Fear not; our friends in the North do not intend to take any "*step backward*" on the slavery question—the mass of the Democrats of the North are sound and more determined than ever; but there are those among them who feel somewhat committed and embarrassed and do not feel inclined to take too bold a stand at the start, but rather to leave the good work of coming fully to the support of the Compromise to the silent but equally certain operation of time. This course I do not approve personally, but prefer, as the thing is right, to say so even at the hazard and certainty of sloughing off all the rotten and unsound limbs and branches at both extremities. Do not despair. but hope that all will yet be right.

Boyd has great difficulty and perplexity in forming his committees. Bayley voted against him. There have been many protestations by the Democratic members against the appointment of Bayley to the Chairmanship of the Ways and Means, and a decided expression of preference in favor of my appointment to that position.... I think Geo. S. Houston of Alabama will be appointed. Genl. Bayley will probably be at the head of Foreign Affairs, with his assent. I must refer you to the debate which sprang up in the House preceding the election of Speaker, as reported in the Congressional Globe, for the exposure of the Whig caucus resolutions. Orin Fowler said there was but about forty present, and they were not counted, the vote was not called—no ayes and noes taken nor record made. Some voted against and some did not vote at all—they made no nominations, but came into the House voting about loose....

I shall be exceedingly gratified to hear from you at all times, and particularly after the receipt of this to know if this explanation makes things look any better. All the Democrats or nearly so here admit that it will be right for the Democratic national convention to adopt resolutions in regard to the Compromise. What the character of the resolution will be when adopted, there seems to be but one opinion: that is, its endorsement and adoption as a finality.

Alexander H. Stephens To Linton Stephens. R.

Washington, D. C., *10th December, 1851.* Dear Brother, Your two letters, one of the 5th and the other of the 6th inst. were received this morning. In reply to your inquiries about the state of things here I can only say that very much to my surprise and regret I am bound to believe that a coalition has been entered into between the Southern Rights men and the Free-Soilers under the name and style of a reorganization of the Democratic party. The failure to pass the Compromise resolutions in the so-called Democratic caucus was owing to this union of opposing elements. Boyd was nominated and elected Speaker by that combination. His constitution of the committees can leave no doubt as to the leading principle with him. You see the most violent Anti-Compromise men from both sections of the Union are given the most prominent positions, while the *friends* of those measures are kept in the background. This was a very mean act in Boyd. You will see the committees in the papers. I call your attention to a few names. On the first committee—Elections, for instance, Disney from Ohio, who voted for the Wilmot Proviso, is made chairman, and Ashe of N. C, a fire-eater, stands next to him. For Claims, Daniel of N. O, an opponent of the Compromise out and out, is Chairman, with Edgerton of Ohio, an anti-slavery Democrat next to him. The Chairman of my committee on Commerce is a New York Anti-Compromise Democrat, while Fuller of Me., a truer and better man, stands below him. Fuller was with us on the settlement in feeling thoroughly, as Cobb knows, and voted with us on several occasions. But I need not go through with the list. Burt you see is chairman of one of the most important committees. Millson of Va. is also chairman of a committee, an out and out opponent of the settlement. So even Cutter of Ohio, Thurston of R. I. and Stuart of Mich., and Bartlett of Vt. on the other side, all against the Compromise and all chairmen of committees, to say nothing of the prominent position of others less conspicuous than chairmen. Gorman of Indiana, one of the truest men that ever came to Congress from the North, and one who seceded from the caucus because of the failure to pass Polk's Resolution, has a subordinate place on a committee. He stands below Burt, an open enemy to the Union. This shows the ruling spirit in the organization of the House. Houston of Ala. is put at the head of the Ways and Means, from no reason I believe but his known opposition to Cobb. My opinion is that Cobb has some bitter enemies where he little expected it; and I am disposed to think, not without some authority, that his confidence has been abused. This you may say to him. Indeed you may show him this letter. But tell him it is only for the purpose of putting him on his guard. I could give him several reasons for what I say which I do not feel at liberty to mention in this way. At this time I have no doubt that it is the determination of the small fry now at Washington, who have the control of the Democratic party North and South, to form a perfect *coalition* between the two extreme wings of their respective divisions, whose ruling spirit will be, as Calhoun said, "the cohesive principle of public plunder. " The spoils is all they go for. But I cannot believe that the country is prepared for such corruption. I have no doubt that Southern Rights men are— such as figured in the late meeting in Milledgeville—and even the S. C. chivalry; but I do not believe that the body of our people are prepared to sanction such a foul conspiracy against their rights, interests, purposes and honor. We are now in a great *crisis* in our history. If the South, if *Georgia,* succumbs to this movement and gives in her adhesion, we are gone people. Now is the time for firmness. We must teach the tricksters that the destinies of this great country are not to be bartered away in this manner. The Whig party, so-called, put itself right in *caucus.* That was a great point. But there will be no national Whig convention. And I trust there will be no Whig organization kept up. The true men must get together, and act together without any regard to past party names. The contest will be between the *coalitionists* and the Spoilsmen on the one hand, and the Conservatives or Constitutional Union men on the other. It is the object here to drive Georgia into a division on the old lines. It is thought that she cannot maintain her present position. As a part of this scheme it is the earnest desire of the *tricksters* to keep up the Whig party. This is the reason for taking Toombs from the Ways and Means and putting Stanley in his place. It is thought that *he* will keep up the fight on the old line. A part of all this policy is to *cut Cobb down*—to get him out of position with the Democracy. He is getting too high in the estimation of some of the *little jealous souls* that he helped to raise to that humble position they now occupy. To *sack him* they will now unite with men who would have hung him and them with "a grape vine" (in their own language) twelve months ago, if they had got the power. I refer now to such men as Stanton of Tenn. and Houston of Ala. These mean rascals little know what is in store for them, unless I misjudge the people. I have said you may show this letter to Mr. Cobb but I do not wish you to show it to anybody else, which will be a sufficient restraint upon him when he reads this part of it; for it is hastily written and not intended in any way for public use. It is simply a detail of some facts, given just as I should speak them out were I with you. The position of our friends in the Legislature at this time is important, responsible and delicate. The issue before them pregnant with great results. If they can maintain their front with calmness, boldness and firmness, and stand upon their own ground, all will be saved. If they falter which I can not permit myself to believe all will be gained.1 Let the world know that we stand upon our own platform and adhere to our own principles, through weal through woe, now and forever. Georgia saved the Union last fall, and she may be the instrument in saving it again by compelling a purgation of National parties. The Whig party has already undergone the process. It remains only now to compel the Democratic organization to pass through the same or a similar lustration. Without this her work will be but half done, and the mission of the Constitutional Union party be only half 1 Error In original. Should be " all will be lost. " 73566—13 18 accomplished. Developments have not yet sufficiently displayed the probable future of events for me to give you at this time any suggestions as to the *course* they should adopt for their coming Presidential contest. I will write to you again on that point. At present I should only inculcate the idea that we must not join the *coalitionists,* that we must preserve our organization, and that we must have a man, like Caesar's wife, above suspicion. In a few weeks we shall see many shiftings and turnings on the board. And when the observant eyes of all the aspirants to the high office of President see that Georgia stands firm to her principles, we shall not be without a man who will put himself right on the questions. This is my opinion. The elements here are too discordant to harmonize long when the outward pressure is removed. The present condition of affairs, it is said, has been brought about at Buchanan's suggestion. That he has been acting badly I think *more than probable*. Time alone can bring the matter properly to light. If it should thereafter be made to appear that he has been intriguing in this way we must take up Dickinson, or some other such man, and beat him into lint.

I said in the outset that I was surprised at Boyd's conduct. I thought he had more good sense, to say nothing of patriotism. It seemed to me that he had but one road to pursue to make a man of himself and to build up a great national party composed of the ablest and truest men of the Republic—a party that might have lived and survived the contests of a quarter of a century—but instead of pursuing that course he has lost all by yielding to the fragments of contemptible factions who have been whipped at home and now try to reestablish themselves in public confidence by forming a piratical compact for public plunder and robbery. But enough. You said you were anxious to see what course Toombs and I took in the proceedings at the organization. We did not attend either caucus—none of the Union men from Georgia did. We did not vote for Boyd because we then feared the coalition which since has disclosed itself. Toombs and I voted for Hillyer. The others voted for Bay ley. What will the Southern Rights men of Georgia who abused Cobb so about his committees say of Boyd's committees? I mean those men who lately shouted so loudly in Milledgeville at their return to the *National Democracy,* who were so sound upon slavery— what will they say to his making Seymour, Free-Soiler from N. Y., Chairman of the Com. on Commerce, Olds of Ohio, Chr. Com. on Post Offices and Post Roads, Timothy Jenkins of N. Y. *pledged to vote to abolish slavery in this District,* Chairman of the Com. on Private Land Claims, besides the others mentioned before. Cobb was in their opinion a traitor for putting Giddings and P. King and Allen where they could do no harm; but I suppose Boyd will be lauded for putting men holding the same principles in the highest places of honor.

George W. Jones To Howell Cobb. E.

Washington D. C., *January 25, 1852.* Dear Cobb, I have seen and read the article in the Macon Journal and also your letter to Judge Murphy upon the propriety of the Union party of Georgia sending delegates to the Democratic national convention. Both are right in spirit,. principle and temper. All the Compromise men will be required in that convention to save the party and the country—with me the party and the country are synonymous terms. I send you the resolutions of the Tennessee Democratic State convention of the 8th inst. They will do, if adhered to in good faith. But to be candid with you. I have little or no hope that the Compromise will be adopted by the Baltimore convention as a finality, though many of our friends think otherwise. I see that the Union convention of Alabama recommend the holding of a Union national convention in this city in June next. The fire-eaters' convention of Mississippi have appointed delegates to the Baltimore convention. The fire-eaters of the South and the Democratic free-soilers of the North will all have delegates there, who will be of course opposed to any expression favorable to the Compromise,—a failure to do which in my opinion will be suicidal, fatally so. I have just had a conversation casually with one of our extremist friends of the South. He said that no Southern Compromise man can be elected—that is, said he, such a one as Foote or Cobb. I am confident that no disunionist or free-soiler can be elected as a Democrat. The Democrats are so sanguine here of success next fall that it is regarded almost as high treason against the party to express a doubt of its success. The wish and desire of some of the Northern men is to get up the excitement on Kossuth and his doctrines so high that it will over ride all other questions, and the canvass go off under it. Of course we cannot very well premise what will be the state of things, until after the Baltimore convention shall have met and adjourned. Upon its action depends the success or defeat of the Democratic party and the weal or woe of the country; therefore send delegates.

John Slidell1 To Howell Cobb. E.

New Orleans la., *28 J any., 1852.* Mt Dear Sir: I have your letter of 12 inst. You ask me to let you know *how far we are apart.* I cannot discover that we are at all so. I am as anxious to purge the party of abolitionists and unqualified disunionists as you or any one else can be; but in doing this we must take care that they do not carry with them the very large body of democrats both North and South who did not approve of the 1 Congressman from Louisiana, 1843-1845, United States Senator, 1853-1861, etc.

compromise and who are unwilling that its endorsement *now* shall be made a test of party faith. In the slaveholding states generally the whig party was nearly unanimous in favor of the compromise, while in most of them a large minority and in some a majority of the democratic party were opposed to it. In this state (and I believe, Texas) a very great majority of our party approved of the compromise; yet those who were opposed are sufficiently numerous to make our defeat certain in any contest when their support shall be withheld. If this be the case in Louisiana what can be hoped for in any other Southern state should a course be pursued that would have the appearance even of proscribing those who were opposed to the compromise. All that we can ask from them is acquiesence, not opposition. This has been very adroitly and happily done in the late Alabama convention. I presume that you will have seen the resolution. If not, you can readily find it. It seems to me to come up to your idea of finality, and I think will command the concurrence of every Southern Democrat whom we would desire to retain. As to the Rhetts, Yanceys, &c, the sooner and the more effectually we get rid of them the better; and if in the Baltimore convention we adopt a resolution deprecating all modification of the fugitive slave law, it will relieve us at the same time of the Van Burens, Blairs, etc. With such a declaration, I have no doubt of the election of our candidate; but I would infinitely prefer defeat to a victory purchased by truckling to the abolitionists or disunionists. As to the idea of peaceable secession, I consider it one of those harmless follies which can only derive importance from being seriously discussed, and would leave those who entertain it to the quiet enjoyment of the abstraction. The remedy can easily be applied if an attempt be made to carry it out in practice. I infer from your letter that you do not approve of the course suggested by a majority of the Union members of the legislature in Georgia to abandon old party organizations and to hold aloof from the national conventions of the two great parties. I hope that I am right in this inference and that your union democrats will either separately or in concert with their brethren with whom they disagree only on the subject of the compromise be represented at the Baltimore convention. If the Union whigs with you are as honest in their declarations of willingness to fraternise with us, you can aid in giving them a candidate whom they can support. If you do not, you leave the game in the hands of the secessionists, so far at least as Georgia is concerned. Excuse me for what may seem intrusive counsel on a matter which you must necessarily understand much better than I, but it is sometimes well even on subjects with which we are most familiar to know how they appear to those who see them from a different point of view and without the excitement that always follows such a struggle as that through which you have lately passed. While I have strong preferences for Mr. Buchanan, as well on account of personal intimacy as of my conviction of his superior fitness and availability, I need scarcely say that I have still more at heart the reorganization of our party on sound principles, and that if such a consummation can be more surely attained by another nomination I am prepared to sustain it, and that whoever may be the candidate, he will have my cordial support. I say whoever may be the candidate, because I feel sure that only a sound Union Democrat can by any possibility be nominated at Baltimore.

Pray let me know what you and your friends purpose doing in regard to the convention.

Thomas D. Harris To Howell, Cobb. E.

Washington D. C, *Feb. 2, 1852.*

Dear Governor, I am just this moment in receipt of yours of the 28th ultimo, and make haste to acknowledge it for the purpose of saying that I will seek an early opportunity to make known to "X" your wish to have a line from him, and will also endeavor to have such other knowing friends as I may safely approach to write you from time to time as occasion may suggest.

For my poor short-sighted self, I can offer no other apology for my silence than my incapacity to see and understand things as they are. The times are troubled, and ominous givings out fill the ear at every corner of the streets. In the darkness which broods over Washington City I can see the shadowy outlines of ugly monsters moving stealthily to and fro, bent upon the destruction of all good.

It is plain to the humblest discernment, though, that there exist in the Democratic party the elements of destruction, which if not skilfully managed will splinter it into a thousand atoms. How fatal the error at the commencement of the present session in failing to affirm the Compromise in caucus by the adoption of Polk's resolution! And yet I do not know, with the counsels then prevailing, that it could have been otherwise...

If Polk's resolution had been adopted in caucus, this day there would scarcely have been two parties in Ga., Fla., Ala. and Mississippi. The fire-eaters would have been bound hand and foot, and could have done nothing but follow quietly the patriotic lead of the Union party.

An idea prevails here that neither of the prominent aspirants for the Presidency will be nominated. Douglas's stock particularly is very low just now. Buchanan in the dark, Cass and Butler in front, but yet a long ways off. Some of the Western men begin to suggest the name of Genl. Lane as a fitting man to rally upon as a compromise in the event of failing to unite upon another. Lane himself is a true Union man, and he and his friends are in *good faith* the friends of Cass. This idea, or something like it, may grow more important as things are developed. Stone, a member from Kentucky, thinks Butler may not unite his own delegation in convention. He himself, who is a delegate, prefers Lane or Bright.

A portion of the fire-eaters in the present Congress are presumptuous and dictatorial, and are growing less and less in favor every day. Both here and at home it seems that nothing can appease them but the overthrow of yourself and such as you. This is the sacrifice they ask at the hands of the National Democracy, who sympathized with you in your late fight for the Union. It is the price of their support and cooperation with the democratic party in the great fight of the present year. They will fail in its accomplishment.

Grund has just stepped in, and I read him your letter. He was evidently flattered by your good opinion of him, and authorizes me to say that he will write you fully and without reserve at an early day.

After things shall begin to assume an understandable shape, I will write you often.

Howell Cobb To C. W. Denison.1

Milledgeville ga., *Feby. 3, 1852.*

Dear Sir: Since I wrote to you I have read the two first numbers of your paper, Our Country, and I feel that it is due alike to you and myself that I should address you this letter. I must say to you in that perfect candor, which I trust has ever characterized my political conduct, that you have wholly misapprehended my position on some of the important issues which have divided the people into political parties.

Without pretending to discuss these issues I will state in a few words some of the points of difference. First on the tariff question. I was a member of Congress when the tariff of '46 was passed, and gave that measure my warm and cordial support, and since that time have opposed any modification of it and shall continue to do so unless the circumstances of the country would justify such modifications as would relieve it of some of its objectionable protective features; in a word, I am what is known in the political world as a free-trade man. Secondly on the subject of internal improvements, and more particularly the improvement of rivers and harbors, I have been uniformly opposed to the whole system, and regard it as the most fruitful source of profligacy and corruption that our federal system is liable to.

1From a draft In Howell Cobb's handwriting among the Erwln papers. Denison had announced In Our Country, of which he was the editor, a ticket for the campaign of 1852 with Webster for Tresident and Cobb for Vice-President.

These are the two leading questions of political difference between the parties of our country, and you perceive that my position is entirely different from what you had supposed it to be. It may strike you as singular that there should exist irreconcilable difficulties on these questions between you and myself, when Whigs and Democrats of Georgia are prepared to unite in the same national organization. The reason is that upon these issues there exists a wide difference between the Whigs of Massachusetts and Georgia; but I do not propose now to consider that matter.

Upon that more vital and important question involving the constitutional obligations of the Federal Government in connection with the institution of slavery, I am happy to find we are more nearly agreed. *The finality of the compromise and its faithful enforcement* are essential elements to any political organization who may desire the confidence and cooperation of the South. I gave you in my last letter my opinion of the best mode of effecting that desirable result. That opinion remains unchanged and I shall act upon it; and I deeply regret that all who agree upon this paramount question cannot be brought into united and harmonious cooperation, but it is too painfully apparent that such a result is not likely to be effected.

As I have gone thus far in explaining to you my position on these questions, I ought and will add one word in reference to Mr. Webster. I gratefully appreciate the distinguished services which he rendered the country in the adoption of the compromise measures, and have regarded with similar feelings his patriotic efforts for the faithful enforcement of that adjustment. He deserves, and the country accords to him, this merited applause, but it is due to that perfect candor which I intend shall mark this communication, to say to you that *no man*—Whig or Democrat, great or small—can or ever will receive the support of the South for the presidency who advocates the doctrines avowed by Mr. Webster in his Buffalo speech. I will not say more—I could not say less.

Hopkins Holsey To Howell, Cobb. E.
(Private.)

Athens, Ga., *Feby. 6th, 1852.* Dr. Sir: I write to you in advance to apprise you of an article which will appear in the next Banner, upon the necessity of some demonstration at Washington in relation to the Compromise which shall inspire confidence in the National Democracy and bring our Whig Union friends to consent to the appointment of delegates to Baltimore. In the article alluded to you will find one extracted from the last issue of the *Republican* (R. I.) *Herald* that is sound to the core. I will remark to you that in the same issue in which these views appear the Herald mounts the *Cass and Butler* flag *for the first time.* I take this to be a favorable indication from Gen. Cass and his Northern friends, and my impression is that the article in the Republican Herald was called forth by a notice in a previous issue number of the Banner.

I have written a letter to Hillyer to be shewn to our Union delegates in Congress, beseeching them to take up Foote's Resolution or its equivalent, and *pass it at once*—at any rate to make some Democratic demonstration at Washington in relation to acquiescence in and finality of the Compromise, which shall inspire confidence and encourage our movement towards the Baltimore convention among our Whig Union friends. Our central committee will probably wait for some demonstration of this kind before calling the convention to appoint delegates to Baltimore. I suggest to you the propriety of writing to our friends at Washington, impressing upon them the *absolute necessity of some demonstration upon the Compromise question which shall inspire confidence and bring the Union party of the South cheerfully and harmoniously into the Baltimore convention.* I shall also press this view in my paper in the proper form and manner. My course is sustained by our Union friends in this part of the country.

P. S.—There is some reluctance among the Union Whigs here about going into the Baltimore convention under the unfavorable impression made by the democratic caucus at the beginning of the session. This error must be repaired *as soon as possible.*

John B. Lamar To Howell Cobb. E.
Macon ga., *Feb. 12, 1852.* Dear Howell, I saw Chappell today after you left. He says that he has come to the deliberate conclusion that we will not be received into the Baltimore convention with a recognition of the Ga. Platform, and feels no disposition that we should present a delegation there to be rejected. He seems afraid you are moving too fast for your friends. He is open to conviction on the subject. I wish you could have seen him....

William Hope Hull To Howell Cobb. E.
Athens ga., *Febry. U, 1852.* Dear Howell, I received your letter and have carefully cogitated on its contents. We have done nothing here yet for two reasons. first our court sat but two and a half days and it rained all the time as bad as it commonly does and there was nobody at court, so that holding a political meeting was out of the question, and secondly I think we had better postpone the matter in this county until we can be strengthened by examples elsewhere. The old Whig feeling is stronger here than anywhere I know. We have had to keep every democrat in the background to keep the thing together heretofore and I have no hope of bringing them into the Baltimore movement unless there is a general acquiescence elsewhere. There is at present very strong feeling here against it, and I believe there will be a break up whenever it is broached. Foster had a letter from Stephens which he read us. Stephens is *dead out* against the whole movement. I do not know anything about Toombs; but if he is going with us he ought to come out and say so very soon. If he is with Stephens it is useless to talk about keeping any considerable portion of

our whig strength. The question will then arise, " where are we to go?" I am now satisfied from the course things are taking that a Union party (which I have fondly hoped would be organized) is out of the question. We cannot become Whigs—that is absurd—then we must be Democrats. If the Whigs would go with us and be Democrats it would be all well. We would keep up our Union organization and could govern the policy of Georgia and act in full fellowship with the National Democracy. But I suppose the Whigs will break off. Then I say we must fall back on the Democratic line, and of course act with those who are with us. If this be sound, then why have two delegations to Baltimore? Why weaken the Democratic party by divisions and strife and give over the State to the Whigs? In plain terms—if we are to be Democrats why not be Democrats, and let past quarrels be forgotten? Of course no abandonment of principles must be required from anybody, but the party must affirm principles on which all can agree, and pass by in silence those on which they differ. You will perceive from these remarks that my conclusion is that if we have to break with the Whigs we must act with the Southern Rights Democrats.

I see no pith in the idea of keeping up two organizations, both claiming to be Democrats, and refusing to act together. In fact I believe it to be impracticable. The Baltimore convention, if two delegations are sent there, will follow the New York precedent, and admit them both. Both will support the nominee, and how can they help coalescing? We must get on the best way we can, and squabble it out with the Calhoun clique, as we used to do, in the party bounds. In all these remarks I go on the supposition that there is no certain assurance that the Baltimore convention will take a position and nominate a man more satisfactory to the South than the Whig convention will. My belief is, and on this I reason, that both conventions will do about the same thing, pass indefinite resolutions, dodge all the issues made on the Compromise, and that both will nominate men that Southern men can support if they want to. If there is any reason to believe that the Baltimore convention will be clearly and undeniably more satisfactory than the other, then I would first try to get the Whigs to join us in sending delegates to Baltimore, and if I failed there I would agree to wait until after the nominations, in the hope of getting all true Union men to vote the Democratic ticket. I believe we could do it without difficulty if we could show them that the Democratic candidate was nearer to us than the Whig.

To sum up the whole matter, I hold that we must have some party of a size to be respectable. If there is any reasonable certainty of keeping the Union party together, let us do so. If not, let us reunite with the Democrats from whom we have divided, and let us act as soon as we make up our minds. Our convention should meet first. If we break up in a row, the Democrats should enter into immediate treaty with the other convention, to harmonise the party on the old issues. To this end our convention should meet two days before the other. These are simply the views of your humble servant. I have not expressed them in public nor have I consulted with anyone here on the propriety of them. I offer them to you and I hope you will reflect on them before you determine on a different course. Remember me to Mrs. Cobb.

Alexander H. Stephens To Messrs. Fisher And De Leon.1

Washington, D. C., *Feb. 25,1852.* Messrs. Fisher And De Leon, I notice in your editorial of this morning, the following comments on a letter of mine, lately published in the Chronicle and Sentinel, of Augusta, Ga.:

This brings to us a state of things on which we beg the Southern public men and people to pause and ponder. Towards the close of the struggle on the Compromise in Congress, it was well ascertained that there were enough of Northern men who would have voted for 36.30 rather than pass no bill. But what was the insuperable difficulty? Why, that a number of Southern men had already yielded to the Compromise, and it was seen that if it was rejected and better terms obtained, and as a matter of course by some Northern votes, the effect would be fatal to the Southern men who had yielded. Northern men could not vote for 36.30 without prostrating the very Southern men with whom they were on the very best terms. And now since, as Mr. Stephens admits, the question is not yet settled, and will have yet to be settled, we beseech all Southern men to beware of again committing the mistake of standing in the. way of the acknowledgment of the rights of their own section.

To this I ask the privilege of presenting a word in reply. You say that it was well ascertained before the passage of those measures in the last Congress, which have been denominated the Compromise, that there were enough Northern men who would have voted for 1 From the Federal Union, Milledgevllle, Ga., March 16, 1852. 36.30, rather than pass no bill. Now will you inform the country who those Northern men were? A fact *then* so well ascertained, can certainly be stated *now.*

Again, will you inform the country what you mean by *"voting for 36.JO?"* Do you mean the extension of the provisions of the Missouri Compromise, by which slavery was forever prohibited *north* of that line, leaving the people *south* of it to do as they pleased upon the subject of slavery? If so, was it not much better for the South, and much more consistent with the great republican principle upon which our government rests, to let the people do as they pleased over the whole territory up to 42 deg. north latitude, just as the Utah and New Mexican bills, which passed, provide, than to have the people *restricted* in any portion of the territory?

As the "Compromise" as you call it now stands, the people so far as the action of the government is concerned have the privilege of doing as they please upon the subject of African slavery—as well north of 36.30 as south of it. Do you mean to say that it would have been juster to the South or more republican in principle for Congress to have restricted this privilege to the line of 36.30?

One question more. Do you mean to say that it was well ascertained that there were enough Northern men who were ready to vote for the *recognition and protection* of slavery south of 36.30, provided it were *forever excluded* north of that line? If so, will you be kind enough to give the names of those Northern men?

For myself I can say that if any such well ascertained fact existed I knew nothing of it. If there was a single Southern man in the House of which I was a member who was in favor of *recognising and 'prohibiting by law* the right to hold slaves in any of these territories, it was unknown to me then and now, and I should like you to name any such one, and give the country the evidence of your assertion by any vote or public act that will sustain it. The events of that period are too fresh in the recollection of all to be forgotten. And I ask you if it was not a well *ascertained* fact then and long before that an overwhelming majority of the South denied the power of Congress to *legislate* upon the subject of slavery in the territories, either for or against it? Was not this the doctrine of Mr. Calhoun, the great leader of the South, in this controversy? Was it not a "well ascertained " fact that upon this ground he was opposed to the Missouri Compromise upon principle?

To what then did I "retreat," as you say in another part of your editorial? Is it not a very notorious fact that I was most bitterly assailed throughout the South for maintaining that we had the right to claim *protection* in the territories? Am I now to be charged with "*retreating*" because I did not join those who were for breaking up the Union, because they did not get what they charged me with being " *a, traitor*" to the interests of those I represented, for *asking?* Was it, or is it a "*retreat*" to say to the South that they were and are bound in *honor,* to say nothing of *patriotism,* to *abide* by that action of their government which was in conformity with the demands of a large majority of her own people?

You will allow me to say very respectfully that I did not " admit" in the letter to which you allude that "the question was not settled." I said and repeat that the *crisis* that called into existence the new organization in Georgia, based upon the principle of maintaining the settlement which has been made, has not passed by—that the same elements which then produced such agitation in the country still exist, and which can only be arrested by a national organization upon the principles of that formed in Georgia. And do not the indications of the times warrant this assertion? Do we not see men of the South who twelve months ago were doing all in their power to render the government *odious* and *hateful* in the estimation of the people now uniting with those of the North whose allies had denounced the Union as "*a league with death*" and "*covenant with hell!*"

The preservation of the Union upon the principles of the Constitution should be the choicest object of a patriot. But if that combination which is now forming shall be successful, and the government shall fall into the hands of those who were so recently bent upon its destruction, what hope will the future present? Should not " good men and true" in all sections of the country and without regard to past party distinctions who are in favor of the "settlement " which has been made unite and keep the Union with its destinies in the hands of its *friends,* instead of permitting it by the foulest of all conditions to be seized by its *enemies?* It was for this object the new organization in Georgia was formed. And to the principles of that organization the people of this country must come sooner or later, if that bright future of peace, quiet, prosperity and progress is in store for us which every true friend of his country should devoutly desire.

John E. Ward And Henry R. Jackson To Howell Cobb. E.

Savannah ga., *FeVy 28th, 1852.* Dear Sir: Having heard that you will be in Washington in the course of a few days, we would respectfully suggest that you avail yourself of the opportunity thus afforded you to impress upon the minds of our political friends whom you will meet at the Capitol the importance of taking a correct position upon the slavery question in the Baltimore convention. It is to be feared that errors may be prevalent as to the state of public opinion upon this subject in Georgia, and more especially among the elements of the old Democratic party. A stranger to the *"personnel"* of our recent State organizations would be naturally led into serious mistakes by the simple fact that nearly the entire press which was democratic at the period of the adoption of the Compromise bills, has advocated the aims and principles of the Southern Rights party. Violent during the contests which immediately followed the Compromise, upon what was termed the Southern question, they have recently become marvellously silent in reference to it; and after having openly, repeatedly and emphatically abjured all connexion with the National Democracy as being unsound upon that question they, or at least many of them, now intimate a willingness to support the nominee of the Baltimore convention, it matters not what position that body may assume in reference to the Compromise. To conclude from the past tone of these papers that the large body of the old Democratic party in Georgia were embraced in the Southern Rights organization would be a capital error; to infer from their present tone that the people of Georgia, or the Democracy of Georgia, *will be content with anything short of a fledge from the Baltimore convention of the finality of the Compromise measures would be a still more fatal mistake.*

The Union Democrats in this State have never for a moment wavered in their confidence in the power and will of the National Democracy to sustain the Constitution and to save the Union. Fortified by this idea they have resolutely contended against the *secession views* which have long been entertained by a school of Southern politicians which have always injured and weakened, never benefitted or strengthened the Democratic party, which did more to defeat Gen. Cass in 1848, we firmly believe, than all of Gen. Taylor's military fame. For months before his nomination he was assailed by this sect of politicians; they endeavoured to scatter far and wide into the Southern mind the seed of suspicion against him and the men of the North who sustained him; they disturbed the unanimity and dignity of the convention that nominated him; and finally did more to injure him by a tame and heartless support than they could have done by open hostility.

The secession views to which we refer were rampant in the late violent conflicts in this State; and you are perfectly familiar with the arguments in which they clothed themselves, as also with the arguments by which they were successfully met. While the idea of *compromise being binding upon any party of northern politicians* was sneered at and hooted at on the one hand—while corruption was imputed to all Northern statesmen and integrity allowed to none, on the other hand the Union men of the State continually pointed to the Northern Democracy and to Northern Democratic statesmen by *name,* as having shown themselves true to the constitutional rights of the South. We believe that the people of Georgia signified their acquiescence in the late compromise measures *mainly became they relied upon the National Democracy to carry them honestly and faithfully out.* Certain it is that but for this confident hope secession would have carried the day. Is it now to be disappointed? Such of course will be the desire of all extreme men who wish continued agitation and a disruption of the Union; it will confirm their prophecies and advance their darling project. But what effect will it have upon Union men, and more especially upon Union Democrats? If, after the death-struggle through which we have passed, waged upon the grounds to which we have referred, it should become apparent that the National Democratic party by their silence in the Baltimore convention have intimated their willingness to open again the fiery issues of 1850, that too with a view to conciliate the very men who have come to them lashed from their own sectional position of war upon all national organizations, they can expect, they will have a right to expect, nothing further from the Union Democrats of the South. Disappointed, disheartened, indignant, those Democrats cannot be rallied to the support of the nominee of the Baltimore convention. His defeat in Georgia will be as certain as was the defeat of Gov. McDonald.

On the other hand if the convention should affirm the finality of the Compromise measures, it requires but a glance at the present posture of parties in Georgia to show that the State will cast her suffrages for the Democratic candidate by a large majority. The Union Democrats will of course go heartily into his support. The Southern Rights Democrats will from the necessity of the case be compelled to do the same thing. It is possible that a few of the most violent of the violent may follow the example of Yancey and others in Alabama, but the masses of the party will gladly return to their old standard. *They will have no rational pretext for refusing to do so.* Their leaders cannot sustain themselves before the people in a sectional attitude. The accessions from the body of the Whig party, it matters not what the Whig convention may do, will be unquestionably large. The triumph of the Democratic party proper in Georgia will be complete. We should suppose that the same would be the case in other Southern States similarly situated.

Pardon us for thus trespassing upon your time. Our excuse is to be found in a deep anxiety for the success of the Democratic party as the embodiment of the great constitutional principles for which, in common with yourself, we have always contended.

P. S.—I send you by this mail a number of the Sav. Georgian. Notice the extract from the *Pennsylvanian* in one column and in the next the editorial remarks upon Mr. Webster's Union speech. Are not the *secession* views of this paper as plainly intimated as language can convey them? Are Northern Democrats to be cajoled by the idea that they are lulled to sleep forever? and are we to be thus chided, even with "*treachery*", by our old political allies, because we have been compelled to act with Union Whigs in order to save the country? We venture to say that no Union Democrat in this part of the nation who has any respect for himself will act with men who countenance these things.

John H. Lumpkin To Howell Cobb.
E.

Rome ga., *2nd March, 1852.* Dear Cobb, I have only time to say to you that we have appointed our delegates from this county to the Milledgeville convention. Col. Waters, Wm. T. Price, Mr. Knowles, and myself were appointed. Three of us are *decidedly* in favor of sending delegates to the Baltimore convention—Price, Waters and myself, and the other is opposed to the policy. We had to consent to this arrangement, to prevent a division before the meeting of the convention. From what I can learn the other adjacent counties in this region of country will all send delegates in favor of being represented in the Baltimore convention. Dr. H. V. M. Miller who arrived here to day from Augusta, I find, is uncompromisingly the advocate of sending delegates to the Baltimore convention. And he says that two months hence and all the Union men will favor this line of policy. Col. J. W. H. Underwood returned yesterday from Jackson county superior court and he says that every thing is right in that quarter and that Judge Jackson, Hope Hull, Holsey and Peeples assured him that your old district was sound on this question. And if the Democratic members of Congress would pass Foote's resolution that now lies on the table of the Senate, it would settle the controversy in our favor at once at the South. The Union party would at once rally to the Democratic convention. I shall go from this to Athens, Tennessee, tomorrow and return back on Monday to Cass superior court, and delegates will be appointed from there during the first week of the court, and I will see to it that everything is done up correctly in that county. Col. Ward, Col. Milner, Col. Johnson, Col. Tumlin and Capt. Wofford are arranging everything in that county. This leaves all well.

John B. Lamar To Howell Cobb. E. Macon, Georgia, *March 8th, 1852.*

Dear Howell, We have seen your arrival in Washington announced in the Union some days since.... I wrote you at Washington some days since, which I presume you have read before this.

We had a meeting here on Tuesday last and appointed Chappell, Armstrong, Gresham and Holt delegates to the Milledgeville Convention. There was some contrariety of opinion as to the propriety of sending delegates to Baltimore, growing out of the rejection of Polk's resolution and the apparent disposition of our friends at Washington to evade an open expression of opinion on the finality of the Compromise, and their pandering to the insolent pretensions of the fire-eaters. The meeting passed off quite harmoniously, by the passage of a "finality" resolution, and referring the matter to the Convention to assemble at Milledgeville on the 22nd of April.

If our friends at Washington will be true to us, all will go well here for the national Democratic candidate. I mean by that, if they will come out unequivocally and plant themselves on the finality of the Compromise. I have read a recent letter from Mr. Buchanan and the editorials of the Washington Union, in which they say that the finality of the Compromise is now universally conceded and seem to imply that any expression of opinion to that effect is supererogation. I cannot appreciate such reasoning. It looks too much like dodging. If our people are really in earnest in the belief that the Compromise is final, why be ashamed to say so in Baltimore or anywhere else?

The conduct of the Democratic party at Washington this session toward us has shaken my faith in the honesty of public men. We have stood by the national Democracy under the abuse of a portion of our party in Georgia for five years; the very head and front of our offending in their eyes has been that we were too national and were too much affiliated with the Northern Democracy. For the last two years we have stood in the breach and stood the fire from that faction at the South who now arrogate to be " *the Democracy.* " And after all this we have seen that miserable faction taken by the hand at Washington and their insolent pretensions recognized, and the cold shoulder turned on us. Such ingratitude is enough to make one feel like he could " turn Turk and stone the church." To think that our loyalty to the Democracy has ever been for a moment looked upon as doubtful by any honest man in Washington is incredible. I do not believe it. But I do believe that such political dwarfs as Douglas,... seeing us about to carry the people of Georgia as one man into the support of a *worthy candidate* of the Democratic party for the Presidency,... manage to slam the door in the faces of those who were eager to go with us, and thus please the fire eating faction and get them to *talk* of supporting him. It is all talk... . General Cass is the man our people can centre on, if he and his friends will take the stand on the finality of the Compromise.

Thomas D. Harris To Howell Cobb. E. Washington D. C., *April 7, 1852.*

Dear Governor, I believe I have nothing to say to you which can prove interesting. Monday's proceedings in the House were characterized with very great anxiety and solicitude, which reached every member present. I was glad to see at the same time but little or no evidence of violent and angry feeling. Those proceedings will have reached you before this does, and if I am not greatly mistaken you and every Georgian will clearly see that we have no party to look to in the North for support in the maintenance of our rights but the *democratic party.* If this were a doubtful proposition before, it is now clearly and unmistakeably settled. The Southern man who now doubts would not believe were an Angel from heaven to declare the truth. I actually feel sorry for those southern Whigs who still hug to their deluded bosoms the hope of building up the Whig party South....

Clearly the best course to be pursued by them is to shake off whatever of Whiggery hangs about them, and go over at once and entirely to the democratic party. True we have some bad men in our midst, both North and South. This can't be helped; nothing is pure on earth. Let them, the Whigs, join us and maybe we'll be the better able to whip out the wolves from among us.

We begin to feel here that the young Giant's prospects are on the wane, and that old Cass's are looming up. Uncertainty however still envelops the whole thing. If I can go as a delegate to the Baltimore convention, without embarrassment in *any quarter,* I should very much like to do so.

John B. Lamar To Howell Cobb. E. Macon ga., *April 12th, 1852.*

Dear Howell, As far as I have conversed with Whigs I think there is a decided reaction taking place in reference to Baltimore about here. They are satisfied that Scott will be the nominee of the Philadelphia convention. And the vote on Jackson and Hillyer's resolutions has convinced them that the N. and S. Whigs are split beyond remedy. Seeing that they must finally support the Baltimore nominee, they are losing their decided tone of opposition to sending delegates; and in some instances I have found Whigs who have concluded under all the circumstances that course is best.

The worst feature is that for the last six weeks the counties round here have been acting on the advices from Dawson, and many of 73566—13 19 them have instructed their delegates against Baltimore. This will produce some trouble I fear. All will depend on the course Jenkins pursues whether we have a tornado on the 22nd.

George W. Jones To Howell Cobb. E.

Washington, D. C, *April H, 185£.*
Dear Cobb, It is a misfortune that the Virginia convention failed to adopt the finality of the Compromise. It was the lead followed by the Southern rights convention of Georgia, which together have in the estimation of some weakened the chances of the adoption by the Baltimore convention of the Compromise finality. I am inclined to think that the Baltimore convention will do right on that subject. If it shall, and give us Cass as the nominee, I think we shall have a certain victory. You know the condition of things here and the almost impossibility of forming a reliable opinion on subjects connected with the Presidency. But some things cannot be mistaken. Jackson's resolution, and also that of Hillyer, were adopted under circumstances and by a vote which compares most favorably for the Democracy. As shown by those votes and the known position of the Democratic absentees there is a decided Democratic Compromise majority in the House from each of the sections and consequently in the aggregate. Not so with the Whigs. By the same means the fact is established that while the Southern Whigs in the House are almost unanimous for the Compromise, being one third of the Southern vote and one third of the Whig party in the House, the Northern wing of the Whig party is from four to five to one against the Compromise; and consequently a majority of the Whigs of the House are against the Compromise, as are a majority of the Whigs of the whole Union. The prospects of Douglas have been on the wane since you left here; those of Cass brightening. It is now pretty generally conceded that Cass will be the strong man in the Baltimore convention, starting with a majority of the delegates. Many of his friends confidently anticipate his nomination. The Union party convention of Georgia should by all means adopt the Compromise, the resolutions of Jackson and Hillyer, and send delegates to Baltimore and ask to be admitted, in my opinion. But if it shall be thought best by your convention not to ask to be admitted, still they should be then ready to endorse the proceedings and approve the nomination, if what they think is right shall be done by the Baltimore convention. It will place you all right before the country and in the party and give an impetus and moral force to the nomination which will materially contribute to that success which all confidently anticipate will crown the labors of the Baltimore convention, if its counsels shall be wise and its action prudent.

Lewis Cass To Howell Cobb. E.
Washington, D. C., *April 15,1852.*

My Dear Sir: I have requested my colleague Gov. Felch to post you a few copies of the Union. It contains an article which puts me right upon some points which have been much misunderstood. I venture to take the liberty to ask you to cause it to be republished in such of the Democratic Union papers as may be willing to insert it and as you may be willing to ask to do such a thing.

We are talking as usual. But since you left here, if a modest man may speak of himself, I suppose I may say, that my prospects have grown much brighter. At least my friends say so; and I have to believe it. *The Democratic Mirror f* has come out. It is dead. Never was there a clearer act of political suicide. I think there is a good deal of *softening* here and a greater desire to bring our whole party together. I wish you were here that I might talk with you fully and freely.

John Milledge To Howell Cobb. E.
(Private.)

Savannah ga., *April 17th, 1852.* My Dear Gov., I am here after a day's hard travel and as I had no one to engage in conversation with I concluded I would "look on," and if any *winning horses* were seen would write you. The more I think of our approaching convention the more I am persuaded that on its good management will depend the harmony and the happiness of all concerned in it, for the future. Allow me therefore, with due deference and confidence in your own experience and knowledge of men, to offer a few suggestions which if they coincide with your views should be acted on promptly. In the first place I think either *Andrews,1 Booster,2* or *Thomas*3 of Hancock should be called to the chair to organize. Either of these gentlemen will do. After the names of the delegates are recorded etc. and the body ready to elect their president, no one could be selected more fit *in every* respect than R. R. Cuyler, Esq.4 He is an old Whig, accustomed to public speaking, and can with quiet taste, "dignity and propriety," point out in the most winning and inviting style the most expeditious and comfortable route to Baltimore to those who feel somewhat disposed to stay at home *for the present.* Cuyler is a railroad man, has been exceedingly successful in managing one company as its president, 1 Garnett Andrews, of Washington, Ga., judge of the superior court of Georgia (northern circuit), 1834-1845 and 1853-1855.

Ell H. Baxter, judge of the superior court of Georgia (northern circuit), 1849-1853. James Thomas, of Sparta, Ga. President of the Central of Georgia Railroad Co. for many years. and I see no good reason why the stock in this new enterprize should not under him command a *premium.* He is therefore of all others the man for president. I shall take the responsibility of directing his mind thitherwards. What say you to this? But let us continue. I am inclined to the opinion that after his address a motion should be made to adjourn; to meet at 3 or 4. After meeting, the usual motion for the appointment of a committee would be in order. The reason why I prefer to adjourn after his speech is this: that both he and the members during the interval can find out each other and their views, and thus be better prepared to appoint the committee. After which the convention will of course again adjourn until morning. Now the size and character of that committee. There is somewhat in both these points. If there is a large and able com., the wrangling, if there should be any (which I sincerely hope will not be the case) will take place in the committee room and thus expend itself. If the report should be harmonious or carried by anything like a respectable majority the convtn. will adopt it. Besides a better chance to argue and consult, the leading men having " *acquiesced"* the others will see no great objections in the way. What will be the matter of that report? I will not attempt to say. I know one thing, that if I were on that committee I should, even if alone and unaided, attempt to remove the old Whig trash that is now lying *on the track*. It is nothing but a dead log anyhow which was thrown across the road in 1848, cut asunder from the root which gave it life, beauty and strength. It has died and is rotten and can never be used again. It would crumble to pieces by the touch of a child. I sympathize with my old associates, personally I mean— for having been in the race with them once I have continued until last year to run with them after a shadow, the substance having departed. You remember Sancho Panza hanging on all night to the limb of a tree, in great distress of mind on account of his imminent peril— what was his relief and joy when he found in the morning that he was only an inch and a quarter from the ground!" How much suffering," said he, "could I have spared myself had I have *let go,* and fallen at once." Apply the comparison—they have got to fall certain; yet they hang on in dread and pain. What a pity some one who had dropt off would not act! Now the convention, coming from the Whig portion of it, should assume the responsibility and take courage enough for this deed. Suppose a resolution be incorporated in the report declaring that all the old issues contended for by the Whig party had been finally disposed of, and that whereas it was not the interest of the South again to enter into a contest with the other party for a tariff for protection, or a U. S. Bank, etc. , but that as there was union of sentiment and harmony of feeling among us all on these points under the present policy and measures of the govt., be it resolved that no sacrifice of principle or honor would attach to those who heretofore acted with that party, by joining the Democratic party, which from the evidences before us were our most reliable friends for the protection of our rights and the salvation of our Union. This is the idea. It would have a benign effect. You see at once-the force and controlling influence such a declaration proceeding from such a body would have on the outsider. Having confidence in the integrity and patriotism of such men as composed it, they would be satisfied and sustained in their new positions, and feel comfortable. If this, or something like it is not done, you observe, in case of a split or the disbanding of the CConstitutional TJnion party what an unpleasant position these men will be left in. In my opinion this point should be the first to be taken, and when this is recognized as a fixed fact all things will go right...

Andrew J. Donexson To Howell Cobb. E.

(Private.) washington, D. C., *26th April, '62.*

My Dear Sir: Your note without date is received. My course is taken with a view to the circumstances which surround me. Self defence will make it more belligerent, but it can never be as strong as it ought to be until our party leaders cease to undermine each other. The Forsyth and Fisher charge of coalition has been noticed, but not in the manner it will be in a few days if Borland makes the movement he threatens.

The Cass stock is rising, but the array against him is not the less active and bitter.

We have not the particulars of your convention. It is said that the Democratic portion of it will send delegates to Baltimore, not to take seats but to be ready to concur in the nomination if made on proper principles. Mississippi, I understand, will have delegates from both parties, each claiming to be sound and orthodox. The practical effect will be a compromise in which each will vote for the same men if the Compromise is accepted as a finality.

Powerful combinations are at work to frighten us from our position and to let each party nominate without reference to the *finality* question. Carter of Ohio, King of New York and such men are the most prominent in this move. They cannot succeed, or if they do Scott is elected President without trouble.

1 In the sessions of the Constitutional Union party convention, at Milledgeville, Apr. 22 and 23, 1852, a stormy debate occurred over the proposal to send delegates to the Baltimore Democratic convention. James Jackson and A. H. Kenan were the leading speakers in favor of the proposal, and Thomas W. Thomas and Charles J. Jenkins, its leading opponents. The convention adjourned without taking definite action. Thereupon the Union Democrats among the delegates held a convention of their own and appointed a delegation to Baltimore.

Cass counts upon 15 votes in New York on the first ballot and thinks that no bait can take off Dickinson. If so he must get the nomination, as I cannot think Virginia will hold out against the sense of a large majority in order to enable 1/3 to dictate the President. Douglas cannot be brought forward whilst Cass is in the field. Buchanan and Marcy have active friends here, but I do not see how they can combine their force so as to produce the nomination of either if Dickinson remains true to Cass. A new man is talked of as the necessary result of all this management, and Boyd is more often mentioned than anyone else. But I see no evidence to justify the belief that the suggestion will have influence to disturb the other combinations. In my judgment Cass will have a large majority of the convention and that if he is not the nominee there will be a dissolution of the party. It is generally admitted that he will reach one hundred and fifty on the 3d ballot. If so it is not probable that there can be union on any one else.

The Whigs are worse off than we are, and will be forced to run Scott.

Andrew J. Donelson To Howell Cobb. E.

Washington D. C, *May 10th, 1852.*

Dr. Sir: You will see from my card in this morning's Union that I retire from the editor's chair. This step was necessary in as much as my private means did not allow me to incur any greater expenditure; and no certain prospect existed of aid from the Democratic party. Genl. Armstrong will conduct the paper until he sees what is the feeling of the Baltimore convention. All this is the result of the baneful influence of the presidential schemers. Freesoil and secession are allowed to play what pranks? they please, because leading men standing on our platform are unwilling to provoke their wrath.

There is so much smoke now in the political atmosphere that it is difficult to see precisely the places of the objects the most prominent. Cass is still ahead, but his friends are not energetic. He is too quiescent. One count is all that he will be able to obtain is a majority on the second or third ballot; but then comes the tug of war. Buchanan expects to hold off three fourths of the South, and with the aid of Douglas and Marcy to hold in check much more than one third of the whole convention. This combined influence embracing in its circle all the *isms* may defeat a nomination.

My idea is that Cass is our strongest man, and that if he is thrown overboard we are defeated as a party unless we pass strong resolutions on the compromise and place a new man upon that platform who may command strength enough for a nomination. Scott will be our opponent, and will beat us if we make a mistake in our tactics.

A great effort will be made to prevent any Compromise expression at Baltimore. If so we may as well disband, for Scott will then have himself proved a better compromise man than Fillmore, and in my judgment he will be so strong that a separate ticket in the South will be unavailing.

But why should I trouble you? My own sacrifice here is a better comment on the true feeling of our party in Congress than any resolutions yet passed.

P. S.—You ought to come here. All may be lost if judicious men are not on the spot to prevent the intrigues of the active participants in this struggle. We have at least ten candidates for what is called the chance *of a new man.*

William B. Wofford To Howell Cobb. E.

Hollingsworth ga., *May 21st, 1852.*
Dear Sir: I was very desirous to have been down at the convention; but the indisposition of my family at the time prevented me from doing so. I was pleased with the course taken by our Democratic friends in sending delegates to the Baltimore convention. If that convention adopts the compromise measures, the Union party "will still be united in Georgia. I was much disappointed at the course taken by Mr. Stephens, and I fear that all is not right with Mr. Toombs; but so far the Union party in this part of the State are still together in feeling, and I trust things will be so conducted at Baltimore as to keep us so. I take the liberty to say to you that our friends in Cass county feel a deep interest in the expected change of the State Road 1 by the way of Cassville. My boy, Capt. Wofford, is very desirous for the change to be made; and if you have any legal patronage to bestow in that section of the state I should be pleased for you to give him some aid in that way. Please write me on the receipt of this letter and give me your views fully relative to our political prospects.

Henry Hull, Jr. To Howell Cobb. E.

Athens, Georgia, *May 25, 1852.*
Dear Sir: The mail of last night brought a letter to Hope from you, and as I knew the address to be your writing, I opened it to see if I could do anything for you in Hope's absence. He left us yesterday morning for Baltimore. It is true he had been in some doubt as to going, and I think was mainly induced to go because he thought you desired that he should. I advised him to go and 1The Western & Atlantic Railroad.
am glad that he has gone. I see that there will be a Fillmore delegation from Georgia to the Whig convention and I am glad of it, for while I do not think Mr. Fillmore stands any chance of nomination or election yet I think it due to the firm stand which he has constantly maintained towards the Compromise to express at least the decided preference of the Whigs of Georgia for him over old Scott. I think as Whigs they owe Mr. Fillmore the fullest expressions of confidence and approbation, and as Union men they can do no less than say we are willing to support him if the party nominating him will stand up to the Compromise in full.

I am glad that the Union convention acted just as they did. It is all right as it now stands. The large majority of the party were not *willing* to go into the Democratic convention, and had a decided aversion to the Whig convention. It was well I think not to force them to either. And now let the delegates from the state to *both* do their best to obtain such a nomination and such a platform as will suit the Union men of the South, and I have no fears of the ultimate result. If the Whigs put up Scott, whatever a few men may say, I think the whole strength of the party in Georgia will sustain the democratic candidate. If Mr. Fillmore should receive the nomination of the Whigs with an endorsement of the Compromise, and Gen. Cass is the Democratic candidate, I think certainly the large proportion of the old Whigs will support Fillmore, and it would be hard to give them a reason why they should not. For myself I am determined to support that party which in its principles and candidates comes *square-est* up to the Compromise and the Georgia Union Platform.

I wish they would nominate you, when Cass and Buchanan and Marcy and Douglas, etc., etc., quarrel among themselves. But we shall see before long what we shall see! Permit me to take this occasion to tender my thanks for the honour of being one of your "aide-de-camps." I shall be ready on all occassions to perform the duties of my station, to support and sustain you, and consider my especial duty to attend upon Mrs. Cobb at *all times* when I can contribute to her enjoyments. Say so to her for me. If you go to the North again can't you manage to call on me to attend you? When will you come to Athens? I hope to see you and your family at your own house some time in the summer. My wife regrets every day almost the absence of Mrs. Cobb and hopes to see her soon.

If you have some hour of leisure and nothing else to do write me your own views and wishes as to the state of parties and politics in the country and the state.

Robert Toombs To Howell Cobb. E. Washington, D. C., *May 27,1852.*

Dear Cobb, I recd. your letter of the 30th Apl. the day I left home, and would have answered it before; but on the 2d day after my arrival here I was taken down again with rheumatism, and only got up four or five days ago. My health is rapidly improving, and I now think I shall be " myself again" in a few days. I concur with you in opinion that the supplemental movementl may be made available for much good, and I apprehend no danger from it. The Fillmore movement in Georgia is a bad one, but will have a good effect now with the Democratic convention. I have written a letter to Georgia very decidedly against, which I suppose you will see before you get this. You will perceive it looks to the future and is intended to prepare the public mind for decisive action. The Democratic convention will unquestionably adopt the Compromise by a great majority. It will be full, fair and explicit. Of this I do not entertain a doubt. Even the fire-eaters are whipped on this point, and will " go it blind." Buchanan is now anxious for it and has brought in his men, and I am certain that question is settled. It is becoming so strong here that it is confidently expected that even the Whig convention will come up to it to save Scott's friends in the South; but this is doubtfull. There is great doubt who will be the nominee of the Democratic convention. Douglas has greatly weakened within ten days, and Cass and Buchanan are now clearly in the ascendant, though neither of them can make a show for two-thirds of the party. If they combine, one or the other can be nominated. This you will readily see is difficult, if not impossible. I think you will see great obstinacy among the friends of the leading candidates, who begin to think that taking a third man will not pay and I think they will fight hard against all outsiders.

The Scott men are very confident; but I do not think much of their skill and tactics. It is certain that quite a number of the pretended friends of Fillmore in Tennessee, Kentucky and Virginia are really for Scott and will back him if they dare to do it. I have kept quiet in order not to alarm the scoundrels, that they may carry out their treachery. I would prefer their success in their convention, because Scott's nomination cannot embarrass us under any circumstances. That of Fillmore, with a reputation in favour of the Compromise, would much embarrass us in the South. I prefer to wing? the Scott men, and with that view I wrote the letter to Georgia. If the Democratic convention do as I expect, pass sound resolutions and give us a sound man we shall have no trouble; and Stephens will i The movement of the Union Democrats toward supporting the national Democratic party. cooperate freely whenever they get in his and our line. He agrees with me as to the prospects of their doing so. The delegates are coming in rapidly. I saw your letter to Donelson yesterday, and have been expecting Jackson today. Buck's friends will try to rule out the Union Democrats from Georgia. I think they will fail. The Southern Rights delegates who have arrived, to wit Wiggins and Warner, have both given in to Buck—so Venable tells me this morning. They found " Little Dug " below par when they got here and immediately, as you would know, tacked about and deserted him.

There is now great apparent feeling on both sides; but the Compromise has carried the count ry. Fire-eaters and free-soilers are rapidly knocking under, and will mostly fall into line. I will let you hear from me as soon as the convention acts. For the present, as Old Ritchie says, " the skies are bright and brightening."

Thomas D. Harris To Howell Cobb. E.

Washington D. C., *May 28, 1852.*

Dear Governor, This is Friday evening and the city is thronged almost to suffocation by delegates to the convention, and innumerable outsiders who came along to help make the nominations. Jim Jackson, Hull, Lumpkin, Rice, Kenan, Armstrong, Jones, Hood and one or two other Union delegates are on hand, whilst Milledge, Tumlin, Ward and somebody else are looked for tomorrow.

We apprehend we shall scarcely be able to come to terms with the fire-eaters. They are willing I think to affirm the Compromise, but insist upon casting the vote in convention as a unit to be determined by a majority vote of the delegates. Our ultimatum, which you are already aware of, is to be allowed to go in with equal privileges and cast 5 of the ten votes. As at present advised, the matter will go before the convention, and our friends will stand firmly by us.

The feeling, if I am not more mistaken than I ever was, is strongly in favor of Cass. So much so indeed that I hope strongly for his nomination.... Douglas is not much spoken of; but I shall be afraid to the last lest he be nominated. The Fire-eaters speak of Buchanan, but are they not in heart for Douglas?...

Toombs talks boldly of late and declares himself out and out for the Democratic nominee, provided the Compromise is affirmed. I am glad of it, and the more so because the fire-eaters seek to discourage the nomination of Cass by declaring the fixed purpose of a large part of their party not to support his election—he, Cass, being understood to be the choice of Toombs. I meet this sort of talk by assuring our friends that for every fire-eater's vote lost, we shall gain 3 Union Whig votes. I go to Baltimore tomorrow to engage rooms for our delegation. This is written you not for its importance or interest. The Telegraph will soon after its receipt begin to give you more important information.

John H. Lumpkin To Howell Cobb. E.

Baltimore md., *6 June, 1852.* Dear Cobb, The convention has adjourned, and before this reaches you the news will have reached you what has been done. The strong men have been thrown over board and Genl. Pierce of New Hampshire and Col. Wm. R. King of Ala. are the nominees of the convention. This was the best that could be done, and under all the circumstances we have much reason to congratulate ourselves on the result. It was in my opinion morally impossible to nominate Genl. Cass, and there was at all times great danger of the nomination of S. A. Douglas, and therefore I consider the nomination of Genl. Pierce an open and consistent friend of Genl. Cass and the compromise measures as a safe deliverance for the Union party of Georgia and the South.

The Union democrats were not received either by the convention or the Georgia democratic delegation in the spirit I had anticipated. We were however, admitted, without any power to do much good or much harm. They have done us the justice to admit that we were democrats in principle and that we represented a portion of the democratic party of the State of Georgia, but we were admitted jointly with the Southern Rights delegation, they having 21 and we 17 delegates present. This prevented us from doing any thing but to destroy their power to do harm. They desired to run and insist on the nomination of Mr. Douglas; and we as you know desired the nomination of Genl. Cass. A few of their men preferred Mr. Buchanan to Mr. Douglas, and by combining with them we were enabled to cast the vote of Georgia for Buchanan; and we continued to adhere to him until the time had passed when the nomination of Douglas was much feared. And then they were enabled to secure a majority of the joint delegation to vote for Douglas, which they did twice, while we on behalf of the Union delegates protested against it as reflecting the views of the Union democrats of Georgia; and thus we effectually destroyed all the moral effect of this vote. It was at our instance that Georgia was the fourth State to cast the vote of Georgia for Genl. Pierce, and when we agreed to this course in support of Virginia, North Carolina, Alabama, Mississippi and other southern states followed, and they gave Genl. Pierce the nomination at once. We had it announced when we cast the vote of the State for him that both delegations were united upon him and the moral effect upon the convention was irresistible. I shall leave here this afternoon for New York and after spending a few days there I shall return back to Washington City.

Judge Jackson leaves here this afternoon for Washington to confer with Mr. Toombs and our other friends there. He will no doubt write you fully from that place.

James Jackson To Howell. Cobb. E. Washington City, *8th June, 1852.*

My Dear Cousin, I have declined writing to you up to this time because things have been in such confusion that I could not (and I believe no one else could) see the end or give you any reliable information as to what that end might be. The Southern R ights") delegation made a dead fight to exclude us from the convention, after all their protestations for harmony at home. We had 17 delegates, they 21, and the committee before whom Cohen and myself argued the right of the respective delegates admitted both to act, jointly however, and as a unit cast the vote of the state. We hesitated at first as to what course we should pursue, but finally concluded to retain our seats for two reasons—1st to keep Georgia from voting for Douglas, 2d to avoid a separation from the national Democracy. We acted in this matter by the advice of our Cass friends, who thought it better to hold the State on Buchanan than by our retiring to allow it to go for Douglas. With the exception of Bass, Stiles and Bailey, the whole S. R. Delegation was for Douglas 1st choice, and but for our remaining would have gone for him when he was rising and might possibly have nominated him. This is well understood and our position and services known to the Cass and Buchanan men.

...

Several delegates were anxious to press you for Vice-President but I told them you did not want it and if they voted for you I should withdraw your name.

The result of the whole matter is this, we have a platform entirely satisfactory and a *Cass man* for the nominee. The platform and the man are both entirely satisfactory to both Toombs and Stephens. I came back here on purpose to see them, and have conversed with them freely and fully. And now one word as to our policy. These S. R. Delegates who wanted us kicked out of the convention are now as sweet and kind as cooing doves and anxious for a *joint* address to the Democratic party for a great ratification meeting in Georgia. This I shall decline, because we must carry Whigs with us in the new organization, and we shall carry thousands. To do this we should wait until the Whigs hold their convention. It seems to be settled that they will run Scott with no platform. After this a mass meeting of all friends of the nomination whether heretofore Union or fire-eater, Whig or Democrat, should be called to nominate an electoral ticket and run it through Georgia. This is the view Mr. Toombs takes of the policy, and I think he is right. By a premature arrangement with the fire-eaters we might drive off the Whig masses. By prudent conduct we may make Georgia a unit....

Pierce was Cass's first choice after himself, and all his friends, McLane particularly, are well pleased with the general results. I shall leave in a day or two for Philadelphia where Hope Hull is waiting for me.

George W. Jones To Howell Cobb. E.

Washington, D. C., *June 13, 1852.* Dear Cobb, Yours of the 7th has been received. Notwithstanding the defeat of Cass in the convention, the nomination of Pierce by that body and the adoption of the platform is a more complete triumph of the Compromise Democrats of the South than the nomination of Cass would have been. Pierce is not only willing to acquiesce in and abide by, but he has "set the seal of his *emphatic approbation* to the Compromise measures of 1850." In fact he believes them "*wise, liberal and just*" and is for maintaining and executing them in good faith. In many respects I believe he is the very best man the convention could have selected. The more I learn of him and his course the more I am pleased with his nomination. He is open, frank and explicit, bold and decided, with intellect sufficient to conceive, comprehend and determine the right, and moral courage and firmness to avow and carry out that right. In short he is a Democrat of the old line— the original panel—one after my own heart, no taint of protective tariff, internal improvements, banks, exclusive privileges, class legislation, extravagant expenditures of the public moneys, abolition, free-soilism or sectional prejudices to mar or tarnish the brightness of his escutcheon. Whigs and abolitionists admit that he is gentleman above reproach, a democrat of the strictest sect, devoid of guile, equivocation or evasion, and that he is richly endowed in a preeminent degree with that priceless jewel without which no man is fit for President or any other public station—*common sense,* by means of which he has acquired a thorough knowledge of men and the true principles of our systems of government and the wants and interests of the people for whom and whose protection and benefit alone those systems were adopted. When the man and his character private and public shall be known he will be appreciated by the democracy everywhere. Indeed already we have here the most cheering evidences of the complete, harmonious, cordial and enthusiastic union of the democracy, in every locality heard from, in support of the Democratic ticket, Pierce and King. The reunion in New York is a guaranty of our success in that great State. A similar result is confidently anticipated in the Keystone. With Fillmore as the Whigs' candidate Ohio is certain for our ticket. But as Scott will in all probability be their nominee, the vote of the Buckeye is doubtfull.

Quite a number of the Southern Whig delegates are now in this city on their way to Baltimore, many of them are uncompromising for Fillmore— others are avowedly for him but at heart desire the nomination of Scott, as the most of the Whigs think that Scott is the only man with whom they have any hope of carrying New York, Pennsylvania or Ohio. I look upon his nomination as a fixed fact without any platform other than he may erect in his letter of acceptance, which will in no event go beyond a declaration to execute *all the laws* and not to use the *vetos* to defeat the will of Congress. With such a candidate and platform we shall have an easy victory in the South, tho' our friends in some of the Northern States will have war to the knife, as in such a contest all the free-soil votes and influences will be concentrated on the Whig candidate. But elect our ticket we must and will. The peace and quiet of the country and the perpetuity of the Constitution demand it most imperiously.

Preston King, C. F. Cleveland & Co. are for Pierce and King—so is Venable, Bocock, Averett and all of that school. I have heard of barely one calling himself a democrat who refuses to support the nominees, and that individual is Norton S. Townsend, the English abolition successor of Joseph M. Koot, from the Yankee reserve in Ohio. Write.

P. S.—The Southern rights men and free-soilers lost all in the convention except the defeat of Cass, the best friend the South had in the Senate in 1850 from a free State. Orr of S. C. made a speech for Pierce and King. He told me that the Mercury and other secession papers in his state are against the nominations, and that he was glad of it.

John B. Lamar To Howell Cobb. E.

Macon ga., *June 22/52* Dear Hdwell, The despatch from Baltimore has come at last and Scott is the nominee, with Graham of N. C. for Vice President.

P. S.—Will the Union party convene and resolve themselves into the Democratic party and put out a ticket? Or will the two wings— disjecta membra—of the old Democratic party unite and have a "new deal" in the way of putting out an electoral ticket? Write and give me your views in confidence about the matter. My impulses are all for the former, if the Whigs are willing to form a permanent Democratic party with us. The nomination of Scott disbands the two sections of Whigs forever and I should think they would have no other course. But if they are to act with us it must be a permanent organization....

Philip Clayton To Howell Cobb. , (Confidential.) Treasury Department, Second Auditor's Office washington, D. C,

June 28th, 1852.

Dear Howell, I send you a report of Ogle's speech at the Lancaster Convention, taken from the N. Y. Herald. The political world is upon the eve of a Revolution. The Administration now stands upon a pivot, with great power to do good and make themselves, or evil and ruin the country. Since the nomination of Johnston in Pennsylvania and the endorsement of Scott, with the proceedings thereon, the Administration if it holds to the declaration that they consider the Compromise a final settlement of the slavery question must repudiate the proceedings. If they do so boldly they will take the country by storm, if they approve or dally they are damned. I believe the Administration will repudiate, the proprietors of the Republic are for cutting loose from free-soil Whiggery at the North and planting themselves upon the Union organization. We are waiting anxiously the return of the President to see which way the cat will jump. If he only had such a man as Toombs in his Cabinet all would be well, but everyone of them need nerve. I have strong hopes they will do right. They have their destiny in their own hands. The Union newspaper is equally at fault in his sympathies with the Anti-Compromise men South. He should repudiate McDonald, Trousdale, Quitman, Davis *et id omne genus,* for it is utterly impossible to reconcile those men and their followers to the Conservative Democrats of the North. I have pleaded with Donelson to take a different course but he persists that he will have a Democrat for the next President or none. He is at heart with the Union organization, but is doing everything upon earth to defeat them in the South. His support of you and Foote, as he avowed in his paper, is hypothetical. Another evil resulting from his course is this, by sympathizing with the Southern Anti-Compromise men he gives an excuse to the Whig papers to sympathize with the Northern Anti-Compromise men, for as objectionable as the Pennsylvania Whig platform is, it is more national than the Southern Ultraists. The Union organization must sympathize with all true friends of the Compromise wherever found, and if the Administration acquiesces in the Scott platform and the Union newspaper continues its half horse and half alligator course we ought, that is the Union party, to have an organ in this city that would reflect our sentiments.

I hope, however, the Administration will take the proper course and that Donelson will come to his senses. Let me hear from you about things in general and the state of feeling in particular. What effect is the secession question going to have in the contest.

Alexander H. Stephens To The Editor Of The Augusta, Ga., Chronicle And Sentinel.1

Washington, D. C, *June 28th, 1852.*
Dear Sir: I am pleased to see the stand you have taken upon the nomination of General Scott. His letter of acceptance is out in the papers of this morning, and comes far short of satisfying the just expectations of the South. He seems studiously to have avoided giving the Whig Platform (which embraces the Compromise measures) his endorsement. He accepts the nomination "with the resolutions annexed," but does not express his concurrence in them. He takes the nomination *with the encumbrance*—this is the plain English of his letter. And for his " adherence to the principles set forth in the resolutions ", he offers " no other pledge or guarantee than the known incidents of a long life now undergoing the severest examination." Amongst these *"known incidents"* there is *not one* in favor of the Compromise, but on the contrary, some of the most noted of these "*incidents*" within the last eighteen months, to go no farther back, are facts of most significant import in their bearing upon a proper construction of this declaration. He has not only refused ever since the passage of the acts known as the Compromise to give them his public approval, but has suffered his name to be held up as a candidate for the Presidency in Pennsylvania and Ohio by their open and avowed enemies. And in the convention that conferred this nomination on him he permitted himself to be used by the *Freesoilers* in that body to *defeat* Mr. Fillmore and Mr. Webster under whose auspices they were passed, and who were renounced by the North because of their adherence of the policy by which they have been sustained. If he be in *good faith* in favor of these measures, as some *pretend to believe,* why did he suffer their *enemies* to use him to *defeat* their *tried friends?* This question may be evaded but it cannot be satisfactorily answered. He is the *favorite* candidate of the *Free-soil* wing of the Whig party, and as such in my judgment he is not entitled to the support of any Southern man who looks to the protection of the rights of the South and the Union of the States.

1 From the Augusta Chronicle and Sentinel, July 7, 1852.

I said on a late occasion in the House that I did not think that the people of Georgia "*ought to vote for any man for President who was not known to the country to be openly and unequivocally in favor of the Compromise measures, with the faithful execution of the Fugitive Slave Law included?* And I need hardly add, I suppose, that I am of the same opinion still. It is not enough that the resolutions of the convention are good and sound. The men who are to be brought into power and who are to execute them should be equally sound and explicit. "Principles not men" may be a very appropriate " motto" for a partizan politician who never " bolts" a nomination, but I prefer another which is just about as long, though considered more comprehensive,—it is "Principles *and men."* I want correct principles and also reliable men to carry them out. The principles of the convention that nominated General Scott as set forth in their resolutions are good—I approve them fully and cordially—but they have been committed to the hands of a candidate who gives no certain or unequivocal guarantee, if elected, for their support and maintenance. What then is to be done? perhaps you may be ready to ask. In reply to such a question at this time I have only to say that my present object is not so much to give an opinion touching what *should* be done as it is to point out what *should not* be done. Our Convention is soon to assemble; the whole subject will be before them. And I can but believe that their wisdom and patriotism will dictate such course as will be consistent with the rights, interests, honor and dignity of the State. Georgia by her firmness and integrity of purpose has already gained a distinction never before attained by any State of the Union. She has compelled both the two "great parties ", as they are called, to incorporate in their creeds the principles upon which she planted herself in the memorable contest of 1850. Whether this has been done from *policy* or *from choice* it is immaterial now to enquire. But the duty which that State owes to herself and to the country in my judgment does not end here. It is important that what has been acknowledged in *theory* (whether from policy or choice) shall be performed in *practice.* Our mission will be but half fulfilled until that is done. This is the great end and object to which the Convention should look. And its action should be governed by no motive but a desire to pursue the surest way and to adopt the best means of accomplishing that purpose. How can the successful maintenance of our principles be best secured? Ought we with this object in view to support either of the present nominees, or should we run an independent ticket? These are the practical questions.

Besides what I have said already, there are other considerations which present themselves before deciding the first of these questions.

73566—13 20

Both the parties at Baltimore, it is conceded, have by majorities in each endorsed our principles; but both of them permitted the association, affiliation and fellowship of *Freesoilers* in their counsels— the *FreesoUer8,* it is true, were in a minority in both, but they were a minority of considerable strength; and whether either of these parties, so organized and so constituted, can efficiently maintain and carry out in Congress the principles set forth in their respective platforms, if brought into power with their present discordant materials, is a question yet to be solved, and one which we should gravely consider before we think of committing our destiny to the guardianship and protection of either of them. Notwithstanding the endorsement by the Democratic party of the Compromise, yet Preston King, Mr. Van Buren, and others of like principles are recognized in the party as good Democrats, though they have changed none of their opinions upon that subject. The same is true of Seward and his allies in reference to the Whig party. Why then should we be hasty to fall into the ranks of either of these parties? For myself I assure you I have no such inclination. What can any man hope from any such alliance? Would it not be better and safer to maintain our ground and to stand aloof from both, at least until we have some practical evidence that some good object is to be gained by our co-operation with one or the other? Some perhaps may say that if Georgia should stand out and cast her vote for some other man then the election may be thrown into the House! Suppose it should be? There is just where the constitution has provided that it shall be determined, in case the electoral college shall fail to make a choice. And would it not be one of the best things for the country at this time if the election could be brought into the House? It would be a decisive step towards putting an end to these party conventions and irresponsible bodies of men who now virtually make choice of our Chief Magistrates, to the entire subversion of the theory of the Constitution. And it would greatly aid in the formation of parties in the Government upon legitimate and correct principles, by bringing those to act together in the administration who agree upon the leading questions of the day irrespective of those outside organizations which now so much obstruct such co-operation.

But I have said more on this point than I intended. From these views, though general, you will perceive that I am opposed to our taking up either of the present nominees, but in favor of putting up and running an independent ticket. By pursuing this course we shall maintain our integrity, stand by our principles, and sustain no possible loss so far it respects either our rights, interests or honor. If anybody can say as much of either of the other alternatives. I am quite at a loss to conjecture the grounds upon which he rests his assumptions.

John B. Lamar To Howell Cobb. E. Macon, Ga., *July 1st, 1852.*

Dear Howell, I received Henry Jackson's letter containing the determination of yourself. Ward, Arnold, Andrews, etc., and have sent a copy of it to John Henry Lumpkin, Steve Thomas, E. R. Browne of Americus and others.

You must be back by the 15th. It is highly necessary. Everything is in a very unorganized state. Holsey's editorial in his last paper, announcing the dissolution of the Const itutional Union party and giving the members of each party leave to go where they please, will promote confusion and cause many delegates to stay away. I wrote to Steve Thomas and urged him to write to Wofford, Morris and other leading men and post them up.

I received a letter from Lumpkin yesterday in which he says he will not put himself out of the pale of Democracy by going to the Const. Union convention. I wrote to him and urged him to go.

A few days ago E. R. Browne of Americus wrote to know if we could not get some of our men on the electoral ticket, professing a willingness however, rather than cause disturbance, to vote for the ticket as it is. I gave him the points and no doubt he will go right. I mention these things to shew you what a state men's opinions are in. We have not a single paper to look to as an index of the opinions of the leading men of our party. Holsey has done a great deal of damage. In his first piece where he badgered the Southern Rights men and demanded they should take down their ticket, he only produced exasperation. In his next issue he says he demanded 54 40' when he meant to take 49, and gave our enemies the idea that we were disposed to supplicate. And after the breach had been widened through his imprudent editorials beyond mending, then he comes out and proclaims the Constitutional Union organization disbanded, which has thrown everything into confusion (and led the Whigs moreover to believe that his proclamation was made under the mistaken impression we had, that we were to unite with the S. R. and reorganize the Democratic party and cast off our Whig friends cooly, when they no longer could serve our purpose. This is the idea that is disseminated among the Whigs to exasperate them against you).

The fire-eaters... boast about the streets that we can not put out a ticket that will carry 5,000 votes. Every thing is as bad as it can be. And it will require your presence on the 15th to put things in a train to prevent our defeat. Hadn't you better write to Lumpkin, Jim Jackson, Tumlin and others immediately to fail not in being in Milledgeville on the 15th.

The fire-eaters are playing for the Whig vote. 1st. By exasperating them against you. 2. they have an idea of buying over somebody with Dawson's seat in the Senate. They had their plans laid for Dawson before he committed himself to Scott.

I tell you the fire-eaters have their organization compact, and their plans all laid and their people excited, and it will require your utmost skill to *ward off ruin*. Their whole aim is at you, and it will require Generalship on your part to prevent defeat. I give you this candid state of facts, knowing that *what depresses other men only stimulates you to action.*

John H. Lumpkin To Howell Cobb. E.

Rome ga., *July 11th, 1852.* Dear Cobb, I reed. a line from you written at New York on the 5th inst. informing me that you would be at home by the 15th and urging me without failure on my part to be at the Union Convention.

I have been absent from home and neglected my business and family so much of late that I cannot, I regret to inform you, be at the convention without serious inconvenience to myself and much personal sacrifice. *But my heart is with you, and m/y destiny is Unked with that of yourself and the Union Democracy of Georgia that have so kindly and generously sustained you and myself in the struggles that have convulsed the country for two years or more.*

I indulged the hope when I reached home that it was even probable that the Southern Rights party, who claimed to be democrats and the friends of Pierce and King, would be willing to withdraw the electoral ticket which they had nominated and unite with the Union Democracy in the call of a convention of the friends of Pierce and King, and agree that a ticket should be nominated that would fairly and equally represent all sections and divisions of the friends of Pierce and King. It seemed to me that this was right and proper in itself and if they were truly the friends of the Democratic nominees and desired their success in the State more than they did to crush you and the Union democracy that this line of policy would have been voluntarily pursued. But in these just and reasonable expectations I confess I have been disappointed and I am now satisfied that it is as easy for oil and water to mix and mingle as it is for the two divisions of the Democracy to unite. I am satisfied that they care nothing for the National Democratic party, its principles or its candidates, but they have been forced by us to give an unwilling and reluctant support to that party to save themselves from utter annihilation. In fact if we can succeed in obtaining over them one more triumph we shall take from them the rank and file, or a large majority of them, and the leaders, whether Pierce or Scott should be elected, will propose to organize another sectional party, with the hope of succeeding in carrying out their designs. Finding that all efforts to harmonize upon terms of equality were fruitless and unavailing, I was and still am in favor of another electoral ticket for Pierce and King. My opinion was that the best mode of bringing out the ticket was through the agency of the executive committee of the Union Democratic organization to call together a convention of the Union Democratic party and let them put out a ticket and invite all who agreed with them and who were opposed to the Southern Rights organization to unite and act with us in the support of the ticket. This plan commended itself to my favor upon two grounds, first because those of us who had participated in the action of the National Democratic convention could not in my opinion consistently with strict party obligations go into any convention outside of the National Democratic party. I went to the Baltimore convention as a Democrat, was received as such and participated in all their proceedings, and I do most cordially approve of all they have done, platform, candidates and all, and in fact I have more attachment today for the National Democracy than I have ever had—because they have shown themselves sound upon all the questions that have lately divided us at the South. How could I under these circumstances go into the Union convention before it is pledged to the support of the Democratic nominees? I know that the argument of our friends is that we are not to conceal the fact that we are for Pierce and King and that we cannot go with them unless they should nominate a ticket for them, and that the intention of the Union Democracy who go there is to change the Union organization into a Democratic organization and then nominate a Pierce and King electoral ticket. If you make these facts known to the publick in advance of the meeting of the convention, no whigs will go with you there but such as are willing to be represented in the Union Democratic organization; and if you conceal it from the publick, as has been done at least in this section of the state, when you attempt to change the Union into a democratic organization you make an issue with Union whigs which I fear will prove troublesome to you and all other Union democrats at the convention. In fact I am inclined to think that the only issue that you will have at the convention will be upon this question, the union whigs insisting that while they support the democratic nominees, as they will for the most part be willing to do from this section of the state, that you must not insist on their doing so as democrats; while your interest and principles and those of the Union democracy that you represent requires that we should not be outside of the National Democratic organization. And this is the second ground of objection that presents itself to my mind against participating in the deliberations of the Union organization. But when I learned through Judge Henry R. Jackson that a majority of our leading and influential friends differed with me in the line of policy I had marked out for myself and were urging it upon the Union democracy to send delegates to this convention and were relying upon my cooperation in this movement, I at once wrote to influential friends in all the Cherokee counties that the line of policy that our friends had marked out for us was to send Pierce and King delegates to the convention that was called to meet on the 15th instant and be prepared then and there to put up an electoral ticket for Pierce and King; and I have received letters from most of these counties assuring me that delegates would be there from almost all the counties, pledged for Pierce and King. And where they have not yet sent delegates they will be prepared to cooperate with us in the support of a Union Pierce and King ticket. We have sent delegates of the right sort from this county, Polk, Paulding, Chattooga, Cass, Gordon, Cherokee, Cobb and Forsyth, and I hope from other counties. From Walker we shall have no delegation, but Thos. G. McFarland assures me that the Union Whigs will cooperate with us in this movement. The whigs in this city are more decidedly against us than anywhere else I have heard from, and it is in a great measure owing to the position of John R. Alexander. I am glad to inform you that the Union democracy are unanimous here, and throughout this country so far as I can learn, in favor of another electoral ticket; and I indulge the hope that many of the Southern Rights men who formerly opposed us will now be willing to unite with us on the ground that the Southern Rights party have manifested a spirit of proscription towards us. The people who are not controlled by the hopes of office will not countenance in their leaders this bitter and vindictive spirit of proscription. I hope that Mr. Toombs will now feel he is at liberty to take position in favor of a separate Union democratic ticket. He owes this to himself; but more especially does he owe this to you and myself, who were mainly instrumental in giving him his present position on the ground that he would act with us in favor of the National democratic nominees.

The Southern Rights men are very vindictive towards you and would immolate you had they the power and have been making great efforts of late to separate from you some of your friends, but there is no traitor in the ranks of the Union democracy, and you have no friend that would not throw himself between you and the most deadly blow aimed at your vitals. The men who are associated with you are willing to fight until they conquer. A purer and a more gallant set of men never have been associated in any political organization...

Orion Stroud To Howell Cobb.2
Monroe ga., *2d. August, 1852.*

Dear Sir: I am one of those who desire to see harmony prevail among the friends of Pierce and King in our State. It does seem to me to be miserable policy to run two tickets for the same men. It may endanger the loss of the State to those candidates whom you and I prefer to all others.

From my knowledge of your principles and character, I am satisfied that your views and feelings on this subject have been misunderstood and are grossly misrepresented. Will you be kind enough to give to an old friend— one who has always supported you— those views that harmony may if possible prevail, and all the friends of Pierce and King be united honorably upon one ticket.

Howell Cobb To Orion Stroud.2
Athens ga., *August 4th, 1852.*

Dear Sir: Your letter asking my views in regard to the present condition of political affairs in our State has been received, and I take great pleasure in replying to it at once—more especially as my opinions have been both misunderstood and misrepresented.

In no presidential election which has occurred of late years has there existed a greater unanimity of sentiment with the people of Georgia than the one now about to take place. This is not surprising when we reflect upon the issues which are involved in it. The only matter of surprise is that there should be any dissentient voice in our state to the election of Gen. Pierce and Col. King. I do not propose to review the political excitements of the last two years— but a recollection of the issues which have been passed upon in that time by the people of Georgia, and the unanimity with which the 1 At this time the regular Whigs In Georgia, led by Senator William C. Dawson, had nominated an electoral ticket in Scott's behalf, while Toombs and Stephens had announced that they would support neither Scott nor Pierce, but favored the launching of an Independent movement In behalf of Daniel Webster for the Presidency. The Union Democrats, locally called the "Tugalo" party, then summoned a fresh convention of the moribund Constitutional Union party. When this met, at Milledgeville, July 15, the Tugaloes had a majority, but when they forced through a resolution for the nomination of a Pierce ticket, the Whigs bolted. The Tugaloes then nominated an independent ticket of Pierce electors.

'From the Federal Union, Milledfievllle, Ga., Aug. 17, 1852, reprinted from the Southern Banner. Athens, Ga. public mind has affirmed the policy adopted by the convention of 1850, present ample ground for both regret and surprise that there should now exist any serious difference of opinion among us as to the course which our past pledges and future interests require us to pursue. The people of Georgia had determined "to stand to and abide by the Compromise." This was the principle upon which the Union party of Georgia was organized. It was its peculiar province to maintain it. It looked to a national party organization as the instrumentality through which that object was to be effected, regarding sectional parties, founded necessarily upon sectional issues, as the most dangerous elements of disunion to which our federal system was subject. Our policy and pledge was to affiliate with that national party which would present to the country a platform of principle in accordance with the decision which the people of Georgia had pronounced in favor of the finality of the Compromise and candidates pledged to the faithful maintenance of those principles.

In common with a large portion of the Union party, I confidently looked to the action of the national Democratic Party with the certain conviction that it would present such a platform and such candidates. This opinion has been too frequently expressed, and is too familiar to all who have attached sufficient importance to my opinions to inform themselves upon the subject, to require a repetition.

I simply take occasion to remind you, as one who I well remember concurred with me then, that my opposition to the Southern Address was based upon the conviction that justice was not done in that paper to the Northern Democracy who in all the past, as in their more recent votes upon Jackson's and Hillyer's resolutions, and in their course in the National Democratic convention, have proved themselves *in the main* to be the true supporters of the constitutional rights of the South.

On the other hand I had no expectation that the national Whig party would pursue a similar policy. In the language of a distinguished Georgian, I knew that "it was denationalized." It had become the mere instrument of wrong and injustice to the South, under the direction and control of W. H. Seward and his abolition associates. Whilst I appreciated the patriotic services of both Mr. Clay and Mr. Fillmore and the few Northern Whigs who stood by them in this bitter contest, I have always believed that they would be abandoned by the great body of the Northern Whigs, and that the latter would be victimized by the Seward influence for his course upon the Compromise measures. All these anticipations have been fully realized by the action of the late Whig Convention at Baltimore. Mr. Fillmore was cast aside by that Convention for no other reason *but because he had approved the Compromise and opposed its repeal or modification.* When the Convention sought to cover up this procedure by the flimsy pretext of adopting Compromise resolutions, which were voted against by a majority of the friends of the successful candidate and which were nominally supported by men known to be opposed to them from their past and present course on this great question, they offered an insult to the intelligence of the country which deserves to be rebuked by every honest and patriotic man in the land. The nomination of Gen. Scott was scarcely wanting to stamp the Northern Whig party as a sectional, higherlaw organization. Nor will all the military glory which has been-won by the successful chieftain of many hard-fought battles blot out from our recollection *the stern and indisputable facts* which have marked his nomination as the triumph of Seward and abolitionism over the nationality and patriotism of the Whig party. Gen. Scott ought and will not receive the votes of any considerable portion of the people of Georgia.

In thus refusing their support to him, the people of Georgia do not merely express their opposition *to the man*—that is comparatively a matter of secondary consideration—they also pass judgment *upon the Northern Whig party* which has become so demoralized by its sectional principles and policy, as to be thus solemnly pronounced unworthy of Southern confidence and association. Without some sudden and miraculous change we may safely regard the people of Georgia as *firmly* and *forever* separated from the Northern Whig party.

Nor have I been disappointed in my anticipations of the action of the national Democratic party. It has not only adopted a platform upon the compromise in accordance with the declared sentiments of a large majority of the people of Georgia, but it has done so with a clearness of expression and unanimity of sentiment which should satisfy the most skeptical and prejudiced mind of the good faith with which it has been done and with which it will be observed. If additional evidence is wanting to convince the incredulous and confirm the doubting, it would be found in the character and position of the man selected as the organ and instrument to carry out those principles. Gen. Pierce, in common with the democracy of New Hampshire, has given to the compromise measures *his "emphatic approbation",* and in accepting the nomination of the convention for the presidency has expressed his warm and cordial approval of the platform of principles which they had adopted. Besides all of this we find in a long and patriotic public service, which has not unfrequently thrown him into contact with this foul spirit of abolitionism, repeated proof of his fidelity to the constitution in the maintenance of the just rights of the South. Of Col. King I need only say that his votes on the Compromise bills are recorded in every instance with those representatives from Georgia who have been the friends and defenders of that settlement. For these reasons, thus hastily thrown together, I feel it my duty as a Union man, even if unaffected by other considerations connected with my democratic principles, to give to the election of Pierce and King my most cordial support. It presents to Union men the only measure in my judgment of nationalizing their principles and of giving them permanence and efficiency in the administration of our Federal Government.

It is admitted by the great body of our people that the Whig party and Gen. Scott offer no such considerations to induce our support and confidence. If their success was dependent upon the people of Georgia it would indeed be a foregone conclusion against them. I do not consider it necessary to discuss that subject farther.

Another proposition is submitted for our consideration. It is found in the appeal made to the Union Whigs of Georgia, to bring into the field a third candidate for the Presidency in the person of Mr. Webster. They are asked to *throw away* their votes upon this ticket rather than to vote for Gen. Pierce, against whom no other objection can be successfully urged with Union Whigs except that *he is a democrat and the nominee of the democratic party.* I would put it to the candor and frankness of our Union Whig friends, if they can expect or hope to carry out the principles of the Union organization by casting their votes for a man who can in no probable contingency obtain *the electoral vote of a single state in the union?* I say nothing for the present of *the past* and *present* opinions of Mr. Webster on the great constitutional principles involved in the issues which have just convulsed the country almost to dissolution. Before they determine upon the course which this policy indicates, I would ask them to consider the question I have just propounded; and also to refresh their memories with another perusal of his Buffalo speech.

The considerations I have presented will no doubt produce upon other minds the same effect which my own has experienced. Indeed there is such clear and unmistakable evidence of this fact throughout our State that no one doubts that *a large majority* of the people of Georgia are in favor of the election of Gen. Pierce. He will probably receive the largest vote ever given in Georgia to any presidential candidate since the unanimous vote given to Gen. Jackson in 1831—and this brings me to the consideration of the question to which you have called my attention in reference to the electoral tickets now before the people in favor of the same candidates, Pierce and King. To give a full expression to my opinions on this point would require a review of the causes which led to a dismemberment of the old parties in Georgia and the organization in their stead of the Union and Southern Rights parties. I forbear for the present at least from going into that discussion, and shall content myself with a simple statement of the present state of things in reference to the electoral tickets growing out of those divisions, accompanied with a frank avowal of what I have believed and do still believe ought to be done in the matter.

The Southern Rights party, assuming the name of the Democratic party, met *previous to the meeting of the Baltimore convention* and placed their electoral ticket before the people of Georgia. Up to the time that the National Democratic convention adopted their platform upon the Compromise and presented their candidates in accordance with it, there was no assurance of the unanimity with which that platform and candidates would be sutained by the people of the State. From the time however that it was seen and known that this concurrence of sentiment existed in favor of the Democratic nominees, I have favored the proposition to run but one electoral ticket. I could not myself support a ticket nor ask my friends to support it in the selection of which we had not participated and which its leading friends and supporters pertinaciously insisted should not be disturbed. for the purpose of conciliation and compromise. As some of their more liberal and just minded advocates have admitted, it was asking Union men to do what under similar circumstances they would not have been willing to have done themselves. Under these circumstances the Union Convention had no other course left them but to nominate an electoral ticket of their own and stand by it to the end, unless a fair and honorable compromise could be made in the selection of one electoral ticket which could unite all the friends of Pierce and King in its support. Both before and since the action of the Union Convention I have at all times not only expressed a willingness but urged the propriety and policy of making such a compromise of the electoral ticket, and thereby producing union of action and harmony of feeling among all the friends and supporters of Pierce and King. Such has been and still is my policy. If divisions exist and continue and there should result from them any unhappy consequences, the fault will not be with me or my frineds. In my opinion however the vote of the state for Pierce and King under any contingencies that may arise is certain, a result which relieves the matter of much of its embarrassment with those who look alone to the vote of the State in the present presidential election. Still I concur with you that all should unite upon a ticket honorable to all, and I repeat if this object be not attained the fault shall not be mine.

Henry R. Jackson To Howell Cobb. E.

Savannah, *Aug. 7th, 1852.*

My Dear Sir: I drop you a line to say that my friend, Mr. Jno. Owens, will go from this city to meet the executive committee of the Union party on Tuesday next. He will accept of your previous kind invitation and will be your guest during his sojourn in your city.

From present indications I fear that the Union Whigs are generally abandoning our standard. They are certainly doing so here. An article in the Savannah Republican of this morning I have no doubt expresses their views and wishes. In fact it has been clear for some time past that the masses would not cordially unite with us. I am afraid that such is the case generally through the state. What is to be done under these circumstances becomes a matter of serious reflection. Much responsibility will devolve upon the executive committee; and I trust that you will have reliable intelligence from all parts of the State.

John B. Lamar To Ho Well Cobb. E.

Macon ga., *Aug. 10th, 1852.* Dear Howell,... The executive committee met to day, Owens, Hill of Troup, Hood and self present. We came to the conclusion as soon (after the 17th and 18th) as the electors are heard from to publish an address disbanding the Constitutional Union party and giving the reasons therefor—the principal of which is the rally of the Whigs on a 3rd candidate endangering the success of Pierce and K., calling for sacrifices at the hands of those who have the interest of the country at heart more than selfish views; the expense of convening the Legislature and uncertainty of action of that body; with a delicate allusion to the awful responsibility assumed by the Southern Rights Democrats in persisting in excluding a host of the friends of P. and K. from any participation in the ticket.1

This course places them in this situation. If their ticket succeeds it is owing to our self sacrifice; if it fails it is owing to their obstinacy and presumption. I think the most dignified course is to withdraw our ticket, give up our organization and let the country judge us by our acts. It would not be long before they would seek our alliance if many such pieces as "Peace maker" from Walton Co., in Augusta Constitutionalist of 8th (Sunday) opened their eyes to a sense of their situation, provided we Dems. became disgusted at their course and staid at home at the election...

1 Shortly after this time the executive committee of the Constitutional Union party of Georgia issued a formal address dissolving the party.

Philip Clayton To Howell Cobb. E.
Treasury Dept.—2nd Aud. Oft., *Washington, D. C, August 25th, 1852.*

Dear Howell, If you have had time to read the Union and Republic newspapers you will have perceived that they were both fighting shy as to the Constitutional Union party. I thought at one time I had the Republic safe but the coalition in New York knocked every thing into pye, and I now fear that they are, with the Administration, within the embraces of that boa-constrictor Seward, and will be crushed to death. They begin to feel the difficulty of their position, and I have no doubts secretly wish that at the meeting of the designated convention in New York on the 11th of next month the Woolly Heads and Silver Greys will part company never to meet again. The blunder however has been committed and they can never recover from it. The position of Donelson was similar, only his dangers lay in another section of the Republic. At one time he evidently sympathized with McDonald and Quitman, but a trip to Tennessee and the result of the election in that state and Alabama opened his eyes, and he will in future do better. I got him to publish your letter to the Macon Committee with some comments; and I think hereafter he will defend you warmly. He said to me the other day that if he had known as much before the late Southern elections as he does now relative to the position of the fire-eaters of the South he should have given his influence in favor. of Shields against Collier. You may rest assured that the stock of the Constitutional Union party is rising, and men who thought that its existence was of the mushroom order begin to believe that it will control the destiny of the Republic. I learn that Trousdale will buckle on his sword in favour of the General Government against a refractory State.

I think the effort of the Northern Democratic press, with Donelson at their head, to rally the fire-eaters of the South upon the old Democratic platform was an egregious error and they will see it. In the first place it was treating the Union Democrats of the South with base ingratitude. They occupied precisely the same position as to questions growing out of the compromise that the Administration did in seeking an alliance with Seward and Co. The great error in both has been that instead of controling events they endeavoured to resist them.

If we are successful in Georgia by a very decided majority I think the "trio as they term it, will be able to dictate terms in the next Presidential race.

Let me hear from you when you can. I still hold to it that your majority cannot be under 10,000, and honestly believe it until the contrary is shewn. In the language of the old song, " I was not born in the woods to be scared by an owl." 1 Toombs, Stephens, and Cobb.

Howell, Cobb To His Wife. E.

Milledgeville, Ga., *Aug. 27, 1852.*
My Dear Wife, Politically things look well. The addresses of the executive committee are well received here with all Pierce and King men, and there is an enthusiastic spirit in favor of a compromise. Judge Johnson1 (I understand) is warmly in favor of it. Col. Wingfield of Putnam expressed the most anxious solicitude for the success of the movement and told me that he would call a meeting in Putnam to respond. If the same feeling should be exhibited in other portions of the State, there will be a regular love feast at Atlanta on the 18th Sept.2 Nothing can now prevent our complete triumph but the rash counsel of imprudent men. If we avoid *any discussion of details* until the 18th all will pass off well. Otherwise we might get up a useless quarrel upon immaterial points and ruin everything. From this section of the State, Southern Rights and Union men *all* speak of going to the meeting at Atlanta with the greatest spirit and feeling. *The future is bright and brightening.* There is no other news here—all pretty well.

Henry L. Benning To Howell Cobb. E.

Columbus ga., *2 Sept., 1852.*

Dear Howell,... I thoroughly reciprocate your sentiment of happiness at seeing that we are likely soon to be together again.3 You are not much mistaken when you say there seems to be an unusual feeling in favor of conciliation so far as we in this region are concerned. The feeling is not precisely 'universal' but it is very general. Union Democrats and Southern Rights Democrats are I believe acting together now as if nothing had ever happened to make them cut apart, with the exception of some ten or a dozen, mostly S. R. men. These men will not support Pierce but will support nobody else.

Johnson,4 our Member of Cfongress, is an exception from the Union Democrats. He I hear avows himself to be a *Whig,* a Webster Whig if the Webster movement can go on— if not, a Scott Whig. I believe what I hear. There are many reasons for this, outside of principle.

The Whig S. R. men here will pretty generally support Pierce and King. I regret that it will not be in my power to be in Atlanta on the 18th inst., for I want much to have a full and free talk with you 1 Herschel V. Johnson.
2 A conference scheduled with a view to the fusion of the two Pierce tickets in Georgia. 'Benning and Cobb were members of opposing wings in the Democratic party. James Johnson, of Columbus, Member of Congress, 1851-1853; provisional governor of Georgia, 1865. and such of your friends as I should probably meet there, in respect less to the present than the future.

You know well that it has been my conviction for the last two or three years that nothing we could do, short of general emancipation, would satisfy the North. Your idea was that the measures of the Compromise would substantially effect that object, and you went for them for that reason chiefly, I think. Should it turn out that I am right and you are wrong it will not be long before it must be known. And it is therefore now time for you to be making up your mind for the new "crisis". Suppose the Whig party shall be beaten, and especially at the North, will not that disband it and send the elements of which it has been composed into union with this late Pittsburg free-soil anti-slavery concern? Manifestly. What then? That concern takes the North. The Democratic party there, in conjunction with pretty much the whole South, may be able to make one fight, say in 1856—a grand Union Rally—but then the thing will be out. Is it not so? You must have thought of all this. Have you made up your mind as to what is to be done?

George D. Phillips To Howell Cobb.
E.
Marietta ga., *Sept. 15th, 1852.* My Dear Sir: It was my intention when I left home to meet you and other friends at Atlanta on the 18th and cordially to cooperate with any and all Pierce and King men in bringing about if possible reunion and harmony in the Democratic party. But domestic matters render it necessary for me to return home as soon as possible. I sincerely hope there will be a numerous turnout from both wings of the democracy and that all will agree to let bye gones be bye gones, and meet at the polls in Novr. as in days of yore, to achieve as we can (if united) a glorious victory for Georgia, our principles, and the South. And why should we not reunite? Is there anything morally or politically wrong in our reunion; and may not our continued division lead to an irreparable estrangement of the party and the immediate loss of the nominees of our choice? It is true that twelve months since we were in excited, not to say angry debate on the course of action it became the South to pursue touching the so-called compromise measures. We honestly differed and respectively pressed upon each other our opposing views, until unkind feelings were in many instances produced, nor can we now venture to rediscuss those questions without reviving angry feelings. As a States Rights democrat I can concede no principle involved in my opposition to the Compromise measures. I believed them grossly oppressive and unjust, if not unconstitutional, and still thinking so, can never give them my approval; but I am willing to abide by them because an overwhelming majority of the people of Georgia have pronounced in their favour; and such I think are the feelings and sentiments of a great majority of the Southern Rights men. Right or wrong, the whole people have agreed to abide by the Compromise Measures as the best we could get, and the democratic nominees for President and Vice-President have avowed their *early* and cordial approval of those measures. What grounds then exist for the continued division of the party? Our object and wishes being the same, let us forget the past and act in unison with reference to the future. But the great difficulty seems to be in wiping out and beginning anew; how the Democratic electoral ticket shall be remodeled, and shall it be touched at all.

Now it seems to me that a spirit of liberality, justice and fair play should settle those matters in a moment. The executive committee of the Constitutional Union wing (with a view to harmony) has withdrawn their ticket. Let the gentlemen composing the other ticket withdraw themselves and a new ticket be formed composed of four from each wing; the two electors for the state remaining untouched. I am fully aware that many sagacious and able men are opposed to touching the ticket as it now stands and think any change in it would bring weakness rather than strength; but such I am satisfied will not be the case unless it be true that division gives strength. In Habersham and the adjoining counties I know it will strengthen us greatly, not that any democrat personally or politically dislikes or objects to anyone of our electors, but because they think it unfair and unjust to have no elector on the ticket from that wing of the party to which seven tenths of them belong.

But time presses, and amidst the noise and confusion around me I find it impossible to write as I desire and will conclude by expressing my sincere hope that the cause, the great cause of Democracy triumphant will guide the deliberations of the whole party on the 18th and result in securing beyond all contingencies the vote of Georgia for Pierce and King.

Howell Cobb To John B. Lamar. E.
Atlanta ga., *18th Sept., 1852.* Dear John, Our convention met today. It was small in numbers and much divided in sentiment. A correspondence was had with the Executive Committee of the Southern Rights' party, which resulted in nothing though it was couched in kind and conciliatory language. The policy finally adopted was simply to run no ticket. You will observe that it is just what your committee originally determined. I desired to run a ticket, but I found such dissensions about it in our own ranks as to render it impracticable and unwise, though *my feelings* to the last urged me to that policy.

We have now to contend with our

enemies *in* the organization of the democratic party instead of *out* of it. Time alone can tell what is to be the result. At present we are certainly under a cloud; but with proper energy and spirit we shall have a brighter day to dawn upon us, and *we must hide our time.* There will be an exhibition of much bad feeling in our own small column, though I think it will die away. Col. Holsey is not here; but from his known feelings on the subject I look for an awful outbreak from him. I fear that he will not wait for the operation of his better judgment but will be carried away by the first impulses of his indignation and passion. Such seems to be the feeling of every Union democratic editor (Burke and Goodman are here), so you see that things look badly. The electoral ticket *unchanged* will fail to carry the State, but we will not be responsible for it.1

Francis J. Grund2 To Howell Cobb. E.

Phila. pa., *29th October, 1852.*

My Dear Sir: There is no doubt about Pennsylvania. I have stumped it among the Germans, and the state will go by a majority of from 12 to 15,000 for Pierce and King. The victory is easy; but it will require great wisdom and consideration not to turn the battle of Cannae in spite of the trophies into a defeat. The coalition has been victorious; but will the coalition remain united after the inauguration of Genl. Pierce? If Pierce attempts to satisfy the politicians instead of responding to the sense of the people, we shall have troublesome times and I for one look to you as called upon to perform an important part. As far as half a million of readers is concerned I answer for myself as ready to do my duty.

While addressing a Democratic meeting at Pottsville I heard the news of the demise of Daniel Webster, and wrote the enclosed letter as a self-imposed act of piety to his memory. I send it to you as a specimen of my views on material subjects, expecting to be enlightened where I am in the dark.

There is some talk here of reviving the Polk Cabinet, with James Buchanan at the head.... I trust he Pierce will take better counsel from his friends and the friends of the Union generally. Should he touch either extreme he would be involved in difficulties and logical contradictions from the beginning of his administration, and finish by dividing the party. I have not time to say more.

1 At the polls In November the result in Georgia was: For the " regular" or Southernrights Pierce ticket, 33,843; for the Tugalo Pierce ticket, 5,733; for the Scott electors, 15,779; for the Webster and Jenkins ticket, 5,289; and for a ticket of Southern-rights Irreconcilables pledged for Troup and Quitman, 119. 2 Newspaper correspondent; author of "The Americans in their Moral, Religious, and Social Relations "; United States consul at Antwerp, etc. 73566—13 21

Robert Toombs To John J. Crittenden. L. C.

Roanoke Plantation, Stewart Co., Georgia, *Dec. 15th, 1852.*

Dear Sir:... Mrs. T. and myself and both of the girls have been spending the last six weeks in this wild and out of the way country on plantation and have found it very pleasant and regret that the time has come for us to take up the line of march for the North. We leave in a few days, and shall be with you all by the 20th inst.

The Presidential election went very much as I hoped and expected, except in Ten. and Kentucky. I suppose it must have satisfied the Northern Whigs that free-soil don't pay any better at the North than at the South. They have no excuse now for not seeing the truth. They swore if their candidate had no other merit, he was certainly *available.* What would they have done with an unpopular candidate? The nation, with singular unanimity, has determined to take a man without claims or qualifications, surrounded by as dishonest and dirty a lot of political gamesters as ever Cataline assembled, rather than the canting hypocrites who brought out Genl. Scott. The decision was a wise one. We can never have peace and security with Seward, Greeley and Co. in the ascendant in our national counsels, and we had better purchase them by the destruction of the Whig party than of the Union. If the Whig party is incapable of rising to the same standard of nationality as the motley crew which opposes it under the name of the Democracy, it is entitled to no resurrection. It will have none.

Lewis Cass To Howell Cobb. E.

Washington, D. C., *Dec. 18, 1852.*

My Dear Sir: I wish I could give you any satisfactory information respecting the subjects to which you refer, for I am well aware of their importance to our friends, to all true friends of the Union in the South. But I can tell you nothing with any certainty more than all the world knows, and that I believe is just nothing at all. I have no communication, none at all, with Gen. Pierce direct or indirect, verbal or written, except one short note I wrote him the day after the nomination to put him on his guard against answering letters, to which I received a very satisfactory reply, and then our intercourse terminated. There are a thousand speculations as to the composition of the Cabinet but they are entitled to no attention. Gen. Pierce desires to keep his counsels well and perhaps he has yet formed no decision, merely turning the subject over in his mind. I have not the least idea whether he will consult with any one or whether he will depend upon his own knowledge of the public men of the country.

I see the rest? of your views?, but it would be wholly useless for me to speculate upon that subject. I had hoped to see you here; and I say it to you because I have made no secret of it. But you will perceive that I have no other reason to expect it than your own claims and the public good. I wish I could have given you more satisfactory information; but it is out of my power. Gen Shields and Dr. Gwin saw Gen. Pierce this day week at Boston and had a good deal of conversation with him. But I do not understand from them that they learned? anything of his

John B. Lamar To Howell Cobb. E. Macon ga., *Jan. 12/53.*

Dear Howell, I have reed. and return the letters. There is nothing encouraging, as you say; but it looks like things have got to the bottom and must now take a turn. The darkest hour is just before daybreak and I think we shall begin to see light before long.

The spies who are in Washington to feel the public pulse I think will convey a bad account home of the state of feeling toward the "black spirits and white, blue spirits and grey "—and a reaction will take place.

George W. Jones To Howell Cobb. E.

Washington D. C., *February 11, 1853.*

My Dear Sir: I should have written before this and perhaps more than once; but really such is the uncertainty here as to what is in the future that I have not ventured even a prediction as to what Genl. Pierce will do in the organization of his Cabinet.

Judging from present rumors, and what seems to be settled public opinion here, the prospects before us are much more promising than they were a short time since. It is, or rather seems to be, understood on all sides, that *Dix* will not be in the Cabinet. So fax so good. But it is not so well understood who will be in as that he will be out. One of the most current rumors for the last few days is that Howell Cobb and Jeff Davis are both certainly to be in the Cabinet—for the correctness of the rumor of course I cannot vouch—there must be some concessions and compromises in order to get together and reunite the Democratic party, and though Davis is an ultra I suppose if the worst comes we must take the bane with the antidote, as we feel every confidence that the latter will prove efficacious in the present case.

I was told on yesterday in the most confident and confidential manner by a man who professes to be in correspondence with General Pierce on the subjects of his Cabinet, he, the President-elect, having asked the opinions of this gentleman, that William L. Marcy will certainly be the Secretary of State, though he did not profess to have received this information from Genl. Pierce but from a New York Democrat, a friend of Marcy. I was assured that about this there was no sort of doubt—that it was a fixed fact. I hope it may be so. I do not think Genl. Pierce can better that, if it is true, and my informant who was A. W. T. expressed cordial and entire approbation in the propriety of such an appointment. What say youl

On this day three weeks the Inauguration will take place, when all suspense will end as to the subject of the Cabinet, as then all guesses, predictions, and speculations will have to yield to facts; the time is short and will be here in almost no time. There is to be an unprecedented number of applicants for office—Beverly L. Clark of Kentucky—James S. Greene of Missouri, Alexander W. Buel of Michigan are here, each desiring a full Mission.

Our friend Loren P. Waldo of Connecticut is here desiring the appointment of Commissioner of Pensions—this strikes me favorably—he is honest, has the reputation of being a good lawyer, and is a working man. I am decidedly for him. James B. Bowlin desires to be Commissioner of the Genl. Land Office, and David K. Carter of the Patent Office. Orlando B. Ficklin I understand aspires to the Solicitor-ship of the Treasury. But it is unnecessary to attempt to enumerate. I believe almost every Democrat in the present Congress who has not been elected to the next Congress, and does not expect to be, is an applicant for office. Great will be the disappointment in the coming twelve months. But then we are doing something in the way of making places; the House has passed two bills, one to divide Oregon and organize the new Territory of Washington there—the other to organize the Territory of Nebraska west of Missouri and Iowa. Should the Senate pass them there will be several fat offices of Governors, Secretaries, Marshalls, Attorneys, Judges, etc., etc., to bestow. I believe all who are going out of Congress voted for these bills. I said *Nay* to both.

John B. Lamar To Howell Cobb. E. Macon, Ga., *Feb. U, 1853.*

Dear Howell, Herewith I send you enclosure of Washington correspondence. I received it on Saturday as I was leaving for Swift Creek, and all day yesterday I was keeled up with head ache and cold, or I would have returned the letters before.

Stephens seems to be anxious. When he could have served you last year he held aloof. Now that he finds himself in "Coventry" among his Whig friends at Washington, and needs a friend to help him break up old parties and organize a new one to get him out of his troubles, he looks to you. He mocked at our calamities last year, and I can't say I feel like crying when his fear cometh this year.

I believe as he says however a new state of things is coming about. If the California rail road bill is passed, away goes all barriers to internal improvements; and a splendid government (based on prodigality and corruption) will be the order of the day. I think a statesman quite as safe out of Pierce's Cabinet as in it so far as future prospects are concerned.

Thomas D. Harris To Howell Cobb. E.

Washington D. G, *Febry. 15, 1853.*
Dear Governor, General Pierce, as Speaker Boyd has just informed me, will reach Washington on Thursday or Friday next. He thinks with me that Jef. Davis is certainly in the cabinet, and *fears* greatly that Cushing is also. The circumstance of his (Genl. P's) coming to this city at so early a day is evidence we think that his cabinet is not yet definitely formed, As soon as he gets here an avalanche will be let loose upon Cushing which will, if such a thing be possible, crush him—so Boyd says. He thinks further that Dobbins will be appointed. I write you this because I know your anxiety to hear anything and everything in connexion with the Cabinet.... Any new rumors will be communicated to you as they arise. Look for letters, value-

less though they be, every 48 hours.

Alexander H. Stephens To James Thomas. L. C.

Washington, D. C., *Feb. 22, 1853.*

Dear Shi: Your letter of the 14th inst. was received a few days ago. I have made inquiry at the Pension Office after the claim of Mr. Strother for bounty land, etc., but it may be some time before I can get an answer. There is such a press of business in that office that sometimes weeks pass before one's turn comes to be served; and now as they are all preparing to go out I expect they will not be unusually diligent or laborious in keeping their business. When I get an answer I will write to you on that matter.

In reference to the judgeship in our circuit I need not say that I should be highly gratified myself to see you on the bench, and I think it would be generally agreeable to the bar in the circuit. However on that point I can not speak authoritatively, for I have never heard a single one of our brethren there mention the subject except Mr. Toombs. I took the liberty to read that part of your letter that referred to this subject to him (for which I know you will excuse me) and he concurred with me in expressing the opinion that such arrangement would be agreeable to the members of the bar. The subject however seemed to be one that he had not thought much about, or at least he was wholly uninformed, as I am myself, as to who will likely aspire to the place. I had not supposed that Col. Thomas of Elbert would desire the place, ndr do I *now think* he will be a candidate; but how is it with Judge Baxter, and how is it with Judge Andrews? When I get home I will talk over this subject with you. I feel confident from my conversation with Mr. Toombs that he would like to see you on the bench. Still I do not know what he might advise in case Andrews or Baxter or both should be candidates. At present I would simply suggest that you allow the matter to rest until our spring courts open. I have no doubt you would beat any man in the circuit in those counties where you are personally known to the people.

Mr. Pierce is here. He keeps secluded. I am much pleased with his conduct so far. How I shall like his cabinet I do not know until I know who it is. But I *fear* he has not the *nerve* to stand up against the great *Democratic party* clamour of those who force themselves upon him. If he were a man of stern nature and principle he might do a great service to his country. I hope for the best but fear the worst. I shall give him a fair trial. I shall not factiously oppose him.

Georoe W. Jones To Howell Cobb. E.

Washington D. C., *March 10th, 1853.* Dear Cobb, The administration is just getting fairly under way. I hope and expect its success. The Inaugural is excellent. It could not be better. An administration based upon that and conducted upon the principles therein declared cannot be otherwise than successfull. But the best of all is the understanding here that each member of the Cabinet before his appointment was furnished with a copy of that Inaugural, and his adoption of, and concurrence therewith, made a *sina qua non* to his appointment. And the further understanding here is that no man can remain in that Cabinet five minutes after it is understood that he cannot cordially cooperate in administering the Government accordingly. What a triumph for you and me! We contended for principles: we have seen theii triumph. Others have offices; very well....

L. B. Mercer To Howell Cobb. E.

Palmyra, Lee Co., Geo., *April 10th, 1853.* Dear Sir: The question as to who shall be the next nominee of the party for the office which you now hold is I observe beginning to be agitated, but I have seen no intimation of what are your own wishes in the premises. My object is to inquire as far as you may feel inclined to disclose them; for I have not the honour of such an intimate personal acquaintance with your Excellency as would authorize me to ask for a confidential communication.

Although no *secessionist,* I am identified with the so-called wing of the party, as I suppose you know, and am very solicitous for the *thorough* pacification of the party. It was with extreme regret that my illness last summer prevented me from taking any part as one of the Executive Committee in promoting that object.

In addition to my high personal esteem, I appreciate the course which you have pursued to secure this most desirable end; and I therefore tender to your Excellency my feeble aid with great cordiality in forwarding any political aim which you may have, whether it be gubernatorial or otherwise.

I entertain great hopes of Gen. Pierce; he starts well; his inaugural admirable. Let him stick to strict construction like Mr. Polk, the best President we have ever had, and all will be well; no danger from expansion then. Centralization will be our ruin, if we are ever ruined, which may God forbid. I have the honour to coincide with your Excellency in your views about secession. *Abstract* right of secession would turn out *practical* nonsense, for the *abstract* right might be demonstrated a thousand times, and then when it is put in *practice* it would turn out revolutionary. War would be inevitable, and it would be better far to fight for our rights in the Union than out of it. But enough of this. I hope such a question will never be started again.

George W. Jones To Howell Cobb. E.

Fayetteville, Tenn., *May 19, 1853.*

Dear Cobb, Yours of the 14th inst. was received last night. I agree with you that "things have been going on after a strange fashion at Washington of late." Or at least appearances justify such conclusions. The President seems to have determined to avow and act upon the principles of the Compromise Union men, and distribute the patronage among the fire-eaters and free-soilers. Various causes may press upon the President the course which has given things the appearance they seem to wear. These same fire-eaters and freesoilers are I doubt not much more importunate for office than the others, for one of the best of all reasons—they have less popularity and consequently find less favor at the hands of the people. The appointments will doubtless be felt disadvantageously by the democracy throughout the country, and particularly in the South where all of our elections to the 33rd Congress are now pending. I think Genl. Pierce has been imposed upon in this matter.

But then as to the appointments of Sovle1 and Borland,2 I am not certain but it was the very best possible policy. They were both in 1 Pierre Soul6, Senator from Louisiana, 1847-1853, United States Minister to Spain, 1853-1855.
a Solon Borland, Senator from Arkansas, 1848-1853, United States Minister to Nicaragua, etc., 1853-1854. the Senate where no instructions could reach, nor wise counsels influence their action. And where they could propagate their heresies and revolutionary dogmas....

They are now in positions wherein they are under the instructions of the President through the State Department. I have confidence that their instructions will be right and if not fully observed and obeyed their missions will be vacated. Slidell for Soule in the Senate is certainly not a bad exchange.
...

I am not certain but it is better to have these ultra men North and South in under Executive appointments than in legislative positions— particularly if the President be right. I have learned that Pierce's intention was to have taken two Compromise Union men and one opponent, from the South, into his Cabinet, and he believed at the time that Dobbin belonged to the former wing.

I saw in the " XX " letter of the Baltimore Sun of the 12th inst. that H. R. Jackson is to receive the mission to some one of the South American States. I hope it is so.

Our friend Andrew Johnson is the Democratic candidate for Governor. I have not heard from him since his nomination. I doubt not he will make a bold, vigorous and energetic canvass. I hope he will succeed; I know he ought. But then he and his competitors have not met yet. The canvass has hardly opened in any part of the State. And like yourselves we are threatened with distraction and ruinous divisions in some localities growing out of the " *Maine liquor law* ", and then the weight of the Executive appointments seemingly against that wing of the party to which Johnson belongs, all taken together makes the result rather doubtful, too much so for me at this time to give an opinion with which I would feel satisfied. The last Legislature made a most villainous apportionment of our legislative districts and representation which almost precludes the hope and possibility of our carrying the Legislature this summer. They gave us two out of ten Congressional districts. I think we shall carry three certainly—possibly four. I am a candidate without opposition so far. I am pretty confident that I shall have none. I was at Columbia last week, the residence of W. H. Polk, J. H. Thomas, Barclay Martin and others. All is smooth and easy with me in that county and throughout the district. My health is tolerable good, and if I live I expect to be in Washington next December as usual, where I shall be more than gratified to meet and to greet you as a member of one or the other house. It is all important that we have good men and reliable in Congress. And unless it is certain that you can be elected to the Senate you had better secure an election to the House. It is of the highest importance that you be there. Your presence is indispensable for the success of our principles. *Your successor* is a very good man....1 Will he be a candidate for reelection? I know he desires to return.

Will Chastain be a candidate? What is Stephens doing—and what is his position at present? also Toombs? Write me fully on the receipt.

John H. Lumpkin To Howell Cobb.
E.
(Private.)

Rome ga., £ *July, 1853.*

Dear Cobb, I reed your letter immediately after the adjournment of the gubernatorial convention giving me the result of its deliberation.2 I am perfectly satisfied that my friends pursued the proper course with my name and my only regret is that I permitted my name to be used before the county meetings in this section of the State. I would like very much to close my political career with this position, and my anxiety on this subject induced me to believe that this was a favorable time to accomplish my desires. It was a mistaken calculation and I feel that I have manifested the disposition without receiving any corresponding support. And I regret that any movement was made at all. I am satisfied with the nomination and will give it a cordial support. The nomination of the candidates for Congress and for the Judgeship has been made: Chastain, Unionj Democrat, for Congress and L. W. Crook, Southern Rights, for Judge. I am not only satisfied but pleased with the nomination of both of these men. Indeed, it was understood at the convention that both of these men were my first choice. I did not think that Wright, Underwood or Milner ought to aspire to the honor of a *democratic* nomination for the judgeship, and inasmuch as I had declined the nomination, Col. Crook was the only man the democrats could nominate, and he was and had been my friend. All the others had either secretly or openly opposed my nomination, and if Crook was nominated Chastain was the man to be nominated under existing circumstances. Tumlin I learn will be a candidate, and if Dr. Lewis continues to run the chances will be in Tumlin's favor. If Dr. Lewis declines, as it is hoped and believed that he will, then Chastain will be elected without much difficulty. And Col. Tumlin and all those who act with him will go by the board. There is a great deal of confusion here and much unwillingness to support the nominees. But I hope that all will be well in the end. I shall give to all the nominees a cordial support.

Have you seen any allusion to my strength in the Southern Banner that was of a disparaging character? My father wrote me that 1 Junius Hlllyer, Congressman from the sixth district of Georgia, 1851-1855. 1 Herschel V. Johnson, governor of Georgia, 1853-1857, had just received the DemocraUc nomination for the governorship.

he had, and was much afflicted on account of it. I take the Banner, but that number did not reach me. I have written to him and hope I shall succeed in relieving his mind of some of his impressions....

Alexander C. Morton To Howell Cobb. E.

Columbus, Geo., *July 2, 1853.*

Dear Sir: Our Albany convention have, as I announced to you they would do, nominated A. H. Colquitt1 for Congress.

The result will be that Johnson will walk over the course. If Clark had been nominated a respectable race might have been had; but Colquitt has not a political antecedent and will fail to rally the party. I may not be here to chronicle the result, but I tell you *now* we will lose the district so far as Member of Congress is concerned by 500 votes. The nomination of H. V. Johnson has fallen still-born. Not a shout or an approving word has followed it; even his old friends (the Southern Rights Wing) take it coldly....

Toombs has been here and rallied the whigs. They are enthusiastic for Jenkins and are preparing for an early and active canvass.

I fear, my good sir, from all the signs of the times that we are doomed to utter defeat.

John W. Forney 2 To Howell Cobb. E.

Washington, D. C, *July 29, 1853.* My Dear Cobb, I got yours this morning and at once called on the President. Daniel is appointed, but the President was amazed when I told him how you had been assailed by him, and was evidently deeply mortified and chagrined. He said if he had known it things would have been very different. Campbell avowed his ignorance of it in positive terms. It is not true that Gov. McDonald protests against *Frierson*—at any rate he will not be removed. The President and Campbell both authorize me to say so. Gen. Pierce also said that as soon as you got here that the case of Davis should be looked after. He is greatly pleased at Gardner's course. G. is here but I have not yet seen him,—and said that G. was greatly your friend and said you had served them (the Southern Rights men) nobly and told P. they were resolved you should go to the U. S. Senate. Pierce hopes you will see G. in New York. If you don't get here by Wednesday next I will have to meet you in New York where I go to see Buck off. I think Sickles is safe. Corcoran is very anxious to meet you.

1 Alfred H. Colquitt, who was a brilliant speaker, defeated James Johnson for Congress In the third district of Georgia In the election of 1853. Editor of prominent newspapers In Philadelphia and Washington; Clerk of United States House of Representatives, 1851-1855, as Democrat; 1859-1861, as Republican, Secretary of United States Senate, 1861-1867.

F
John L. Ketcham To Howell Cobb. E.

Indianapolis ind., *August 9, 1853.* Dear Sir: One Pleasant Ellington, formerly of Kentucky, but now of Missouri, on the 21 June made his affidavit before the U. S. Comr., under the Fugitive Slave law, claiming a colored man of this place by the name of John Freeman, alledging that he escaped from him in March 1836. Freeman has lived in this place since August 1844, has always demeaned himself with propriety, was sexton to one of the Presbyterian Churches for some three or four years, very industrious and economical, known by all our older citizens, and has acquired a handsome property worth say $4,000. In the meantime he married a very smart yellow girl and they now have three or four children.

Freeman upon his arrest told his counsel that he knew nothing of Mr. Ellington and that he was a free man; that he was born and raised in Virginia and in 1831 went into Walton County, Georgia, and resided at Monroe, Georgia from that time until he left in 1844. He also placed in our hands a mass of papers principally showing business transactions: but amongst them was an old letter dated 15 March 1831 from L. B. Jennings directed to Creed M. Jennings stating that Freeman was sent by L. B. J. to C. M. J. with a horse called the Bald Hornet and that Creed M. was to see to getting Freeman back. There was a copy from the records of the Walton Court showing that on the 22 Febry. 1832 Creed M. Jennings was appointed Freeman's guardian, and another in 1837 showing that Creed M. Jennings having left the State, Warren I. Hill was appointed his guardian. He had also two papers from Hill, the one in 1837 the other in 1844, stating that Freeman was a free man and requesting all persons to allow him to pass unmolested, etc. We applied for, and got a continuance of the case for sixty days. I went to Georgia and found everything just as Freeman told me. Showed the papers to Judge Hill, who recognized the Court papers and his own certificates and said he was personally acquainted with almost all the transactions shown by his business papers. He also knew the handwriting of L. B. Jennings and stated that the letter was a genuine one. I took the depositions of Judge Hill, Judge Briscoe, I. I. Selman, Col. Johnson and Dr. Galoway, all of whom testified that Freeman came to Monroe in 1831 and continued to reside there until 1844 without being absent at any time during that period longer than perhaps a few days at a time, except in 1836 he went with a volunteer company raised in Walton County down to Florida to join in Indian war and that he returned with the Company in about two months.

Leroy Pattillo came home with me to see if the John Freeman in jail were the identical John Freeman that had resided in Monroe.

We went in company with a dozen to the jail, Freeman not knowing that I had returned, and not a soul in Indiana knowing Mr. Pattillo's name, it not having been mentioned by either of us after we got into Indiana. We were placed in a large room and Freeman was brought in. After shaking hands with me I told him to look about him and see if there were any person present from a distance whom he could recognize. He deliberately looked around upon those present, one after another, when at last his eye rested on Mr. Pattillo. For an instance it was rivetted! Then with one bound he seized the old man with great energy, at the same time shouting his name. Mr. Pattillo also recognized him at the same moment and for a moment they were both overcome and wept together! Indeed sir it was the most thrilling meeting I have witnessed. None present could refrain his tears. Mr. P. and Freeman then entered into a familiar conversation about persons and things about Monroe, etc. etc. Mr. P., unable to remain till the 29th inst., the day of trial, we took his deposition in which he states that Freeman came to Monroe in 1831 remained till 1844 and that he is as certain of his being the same Freeman as he is of his own personal identity.

Ellington brought three men from Kentucky to see Freeman, who after as full examination of him as could be made without stripping him, said they were not satisfied but would like to see his body— that Ellington's boy had certain scars, etc. We insisted that they should *first* describe the scars and then he might be strip'd. But the Marshal, J. L. Robinson, who voted *against* the Fugitive Slave law but who now wants to atone for his mistep by endeavoring to enforce it against a free man, took the claimant and his three witnesses to the jail in the absence of Freeman's counsel and made F. strip himself and the witnesses took accurate note of his scars, and it was immediately given out that Freeman is Ellington's slave. These three men have returned to Kentucky and since then we have received notice to take depositions in their neighborhood! Although Ellington had heretofore while I was in Georgia taken the deposition of several at the same place to prove his loss of a slave, where he never asked the first witness as to any scars. And upon our cross-examination the witnesses all stated that they knew of no marks or scars. Now you at once see how this matter will be managed. These three men have a description of Freeman's scars; they will swear to them, and doubtless others will be found who *now* can recollect that " Sam" had just such scars.

Accidentally while at the taking of Ellington's depositions my associate counsel got track of " Sam ", E's negro, and after several days search through Ohio found where Sam had lived until the last three years and that he now resides in Canada—he talked with a man on whose land "Sam " now resides! We were sure of his identity from the account he gave of himself. He had once before run off and was after an absence of three years captured in a canal. He showed a scar on his leg which he says he got at the furnace—gave his master's name, etc. etc. All of which is precisely the account which Ellington had given of his slave.

My associate counsel started Monday of last week to Canada to see Sam, and on Saturday night last I received a letter from him at Sandusky stating that he had seen "Sam " and that there is no mistake about it. When Coburn told Sam that Pleasant Ellington had arrested a negro in Indianapolis claiming him to be his "Sam ", the darky started up with great energy and exclaimed "that's a lie, I am his man, here is his body," striking his own breast with violence. We had proposed to Ellington's counsel upon our first information about Sam, that if Ellington would get a respectable man from his former residence in Ky. to go with one of us to Canada, if we did not show him the veritable Sam to his full satisfaction we would pay all expenses of the trip and the man for his time, which was declined.

Since receiving the above information from Mr. Coburn, I have proposed that if Mr. Ellington will manumit the Canada "Sam" that we will have him on the spot, and if he is not the identical boy that Ellington lost from Ky. in 1836, he may take Freeman. You will be surprised to hear that both propositions have been rejected, with the declaration that Record proof of the escape of Sam will be produced and the affidavits of persons to identify John Freeman as "Sam" will be produced, upon which they say they will be entitled to the Court's Certificate to remove him.

Allow me to ask whether in such a case such a course is not calculated to scandalize the law and to work immense injury? I trust it may be avoided. I have no doubt but the Comr. will hear all our evidence on the subject of personal identity. It behooves us then to have all the evidence in our reach. Coburn when he wrote from Sandusky was on his way to Kentucky to get some one there if possible who knew Sam, to go with him back to Canada to see Sam. If we succeed in this we shall probably have little trouble. If we do not we shall have a hard fight. You will say what of all this? Just this, Freeman says he knows you well and thinks you would know him. Says you have often eat oysters in his shop—especially mentions that you with Dr. Delemater and others had some oysters, etc., at his shop one night, and upon his answering to the inquiry "What is the bill?", "Fifty cents," that *you* replied that such a supper could not be afforded for "fifty-cents" and threw down a dollar. The poor darkey thinks that you will remember this!

I hope you may have some recollection of him *prior* to *1836*. If so *then* will it not be in your power to visit us? The case is set for the 29th inst. I use no flattery when I say that your statement made to the Commissioner that you knew Freeman prior to and at the time that Ellington's boy escaped would set the matter at rest.

If your business is such as to allow you to visit us at this time we will make your stay as pleasant as possible. I trust such a visit to our part of the country would be gratifying to you. Indiana has always been foward to furnish every facility to the South in reclaiming her fugitive slaves. And now when one is seized as a slave whom we know to be free we feel an interest that justice should be done. Pardon me for saying the expense of your trip will be paid.

If you cannot come then please write me a line stating what you know of John Freeman prior to 1836. Will you also state in it what is the character of Leroy Pattillo generally and especially for truth and veracity.

P. S.—I need not say to you that I am no abolitionist; I am a Kentuckian by birth and a democrat from the cradle.

William Hope Hull To Howell Cobb. E.

Decatur ga., *Aug. 16, 1853.*

Dear Howell, I am here reporting for Tom1—have been here a week. There has been a very considerable collection of lawyers and a good deal of political chat. Both sides are very confident and in good spirits. I think myself that Johnson's prospects are getting better. A month ago I thought Jenkins2 would sweep the State; I now doubt seriously if he can be elected. I heard Jenkins speak the other night in Atlanta. He took the Union line very distinctly repudiating for himself and party all alliances with national parties as at present organized, but striking out for a national Union.organization—a false move in my humble judgment. He would have run better under the name of Whig. He will not get a Democrat now that would not have voted for him as a Whig, and he will lose many an old fogey Whig.

In this district the contest is very doubtful. Bailey will carry his and Chastain his. So I learn by talking round. Johnson is speaking all about but I have not got a chance to hear him. I was informed that in Atlanta he repudiated the heretical doctrine of the right of secession. The legislature I consider very doubtful. The fire-eaters have acted everywhere with their usual good feeling and policy. They have proscribed the Union Democrats wherever they have the power to do so, as for instance in Gwinnett where with a bare majority of the party they have nominated a full ticket of fireeaters, while in Walton the Union men have given them two. As to 1 Thomas R. R. Cobb, supreme-court reporter, 1849-1857.
3 Charles J. Jenkins, Whig or Union nominee for the governorship in 1853; governor of Georgia, 1885-1868. the election in our district, I have no opinion about it. Holsey could have carried it if he had come out a month ago or before Morton and Stanford did; but they will get too many votes for him to be elected.

My father has accepted the nomination for the Senate in Clarke. In case of a contest between Democrats you will have whatever help he can afford you. You have heard of course that Chappell has announced himself for the U. S. Senate.

The fire-eaters are expecting you to take the stump for Johnson. My advice would be to do no such thing; there is no good reason why you should. It is against the proprieties of your position anyhow, and that is a good reason for declining; but a better one is that you will do yourself more harm than you will do Johnson good. It will be so late when you can get into the field that men will have taken their positions on the Governor's election, and the chance of changing a man after he is once committed is very small; so that I think you could do little for him. On the other hand there is a very kind feeling towards you on the part of all Union men, whether Whigs or Democrats, and in case of a fight with any fire-eater you would receive their support; but whenever you begin a battle in person against them you will alienate them from you while if you are quiet there are some like Nash, Dunnagan, Irwin and others, that would hate to vote against you for anybody. As to gaining any votes from the fire-eaters, I do not take that into the account. Their hatred of you will only end with life. I do believe that many of them will secretly drop Johnson only because he is understood to be your friend.

The nomination in Chatham is a great lick. I have felt more encouraged ever since I saw it.

Lucius Q. C. Lamar To Howell Cobb. E.

Covington ga., *Septr. 21st, 1853.*

Dear Sir: I presume that during our last interview I told you that in the reunion of the two divisions of our party I had again become your political friend and should advocate your election to the U. S. Senate. Whether I did so or not, such was certainly my feeling and my intention. Accordingly I have been for some time zealously urging your claims to that office in every quarter where I thought I could do so with any effect. But I learned recently from unquestionable authority that Col. Chappell has come out as a candidate for the same office. When I was with you it did not occur to me that there was the remotest possibility of my having to support *you* at *his* expense. I cannot express the pain and embarrassment which the present state of things causes me; but I must make known to you the course which I shall deem it my duty to take in this matter. I love and honor Col. Chappell above any other man; and my personal obligations to him are such as you would be the last man to have me disregard if you knew them. As long therefore as Col. Chappell remains in the field I shall give him my support. After him I would prefer you to any other public man in our state and shall act accordingly. The course of my conduct appears inconsistent, but it arises entirely from circumstances that I did not anticipate. I hope that I may yet be enabled to attest my appreciation of your character as a statesman and my attachment to you personally.

Thomas D. Harris To Howell Cobb. E.

Washington D. C., *Oct. 13, 1853.*

Dear Governor, I rejoice at the complete victory just achieved by the Democracy of Ga.,1 but should rejoice less if I did not feel and believe that your election to the Senate would follow. This is the goal now of my heart's livliest wishes, and I feel that all things else must be laid aside till the great work is accomplished. Standing a thousand miles from the seat of Government in Ga., with no special information as to the views of individual members of the Legislature touching this interesting matter, I yet feel and almost know to a certainty that you are to be elected.

I saw Sturgis yesterday and sought with all the keenness I could command to penetrate his real heart as to yourself. As a matter of course he is for Iverson and will support him in caucus. and will vote only for the nominee of the caucus; but I verily believe that you have his first and best wishes. This is enough, and indeed all I can say. Thad. Sturgis is for you and wishes he had twenty votes to give you. This fact may be taken too as a fair clue to the feelings of the old man.

I never was so anxious to see the figures of the various counties before. I hope to God that your old district gave a generous vote to Johnson and returned a goodly number of Democrats to the Legislature.

Dug. Wollack who, you know says a great many things, some true and some perhaps not so—tells me that Jef. Davis is anxious for your election and that Pierce is doubly so. The latter I doubt not is so, and I am not prepared to dispute the former. If this be so and the legislature is an Administration legislature it seems to me there can be no such thing as fail with you.

In a week from to-day I expect to be in W. Point, and if you have not lost all regard for the only true friend you have on earth I shall hear from you in two days after I get there.

1 Johnson was elected governor by 47,638 votes against 41,128 for Jenkins.

John T. Grant To Howell Cobb. E.
Monroe ga., *Oct. 18th, 1853.*

Dear Howell, Feeling a very warm interest in your election as senator, I have been trying to get all the information I could in relation to your prospects. The Whigs I find are generally exceedingly hostile to you in consequence of the active part you took in Johnson's election. I met with Reynolds (member from Newton) a few days ago, and he told me he should write to every Whig elect and do all in his power to defeat you. Although a union whig he prefers McDonald or *anybody* else to you. He desires that the Whigs should unite upon Chappell. By doing so he thinks they can elect him by the assistance of the votes he can get from the Democratic party.

I slept with Toombs a week before the election and I was both surprised and gratified to hear him say that he preferred your election to that of any other man of *either* party who had been spoken of.

I have been urging upon Warren to go to Milledgeville. He says he does not yet know whether he can go, but I think there is no doubt of it. He is warmly for you and I think can do you much good.... Our members are a little cautious about expressing an opinion farther than that they will vote for the nominee, but I think there is no doubt about their being right by the time the election takes place. Major Hill has always been your friend.

Bleckley1 of Atlanta, Southern Rights Democrat, I learn is for you. He is a candidate for Solicitor and if you can give him a little lift without injury to *yourself* I hope you will do it, but I would rather all others should fail than that you should injure yourself....

Thomas C. Howard And H. K. Green To Howell Cobb. E.
Milledgeville ga., *Deer. 3rd, 1853.*

Dear Sir: We have after much thought and great solicitude for the future interests of the Democratic party in Georgia come to the conclusion to address you this note. We are convinced, and are also assured that you are, that the sort of internecine warfare now waging between members of our party can only result in disaster to all of us. So far as concerns the particular fact that has raised the unfortunate issue between our party adherents it is now useless to speak. That matter we believe you regard as foreclosed and that nothing is left for it but to carry out the expressed will of the party. We propose to speak of yourself and we ask your forgiveness for speaking plainly. Upon you and you alone of all the men in Georgia must rest the 1 Logan E. Bleckley, solicitor-general of the Coweta circuit, 1853-1857; associateJustice of the Georgia supreme court, 1875-1887; chief-justice, 1887-1894, 73566—13 22 great labor of composing the unhappy dissensions between the wings of the party. *We are well aware that you have made the effort to bring about this consummation.* Our Union Democratic friends are well assured of this and so are many of the Southern Rights Democrats. But what we greatly desire as a thing that will most materially affect us in Georgia in the future *is to have your conduct* in reference to the Senatorial nomination *fairly and justly appreciated.* With you at the head of our forces, the whole party at peace and marshalled as you *could* marshall it, we could sweep Whiggery from the face of the land. Permit us to ask if you were *properly* invited here will you not come and address us upon the state of party affairs. Personally, it would be a high gratification, and we are morally certain that it would make you the *strongest* man in Georgia. We declare it to be a fact in our belief that the sight of you here with such a purpose would melt the hearts of all. Pardon the freedom we use. We are anxious to see the unhappy state of things that now distract us changed, and changed they will be through your agency if changed at all. Permit us then to hope that we shall have the great satisfaction of greeting you here soon with such a cordial and affectionate reception and shall convince you we are in very truth your friends.

P. S.—Will it be necessary for us to say that what we have written has no connection with Govr. McDonald's interests, *at least directly?* Upon our honors we assert this as the fact.

John H. Lumpkin To Howell Cobb. E.

(Private and confidential.)

Rome ga., *28th Deer., 1853.* Dear

Cobb, I see from the papers that you have been to Milledgeville and that you there made the great speech of your life. It was a great occasion, and made by you under very trying circumstances. In fact there are but few men that could have made a speech under such circumstances. I frankly confess that I could not, and I am therefore astounded from the report that this was the greatest effort of your life, and that no such speech was ever made in Milledgeville before. I congratulate you upon the success of the effort. It has at one stroke put you where you ought to have been by common consent of the political party to which, you have always been attached. You have placed yourself now at the head of the Democratic party of the State of Georgia. I rejoice at the evidences that surround me that such is now a conceded fact.. I hope that the feeling that now prevails may be sufficient to elect you yet United States Senator at this session of the legislature. I understand, that Govr. McDonald will after the legislature convenes resign into the hands of the Democratic party the nomination that has been given to him and will urge them to make an election at the present session of some democrat while they have the power. This will be acting magnanimously and very correctly in my opinion. And if he had failed to have done so it would under all the circumstances impaired his standing with the democrats throughout the State and country. I am not advised as to what are his partialities in regard to the man who may be elected. He ought to go in for your election, and in this way secure for himself a position in the Cabinet of Genl. Pierce and strength to the party in this state and throughout the country....

Colin M. Ingersoll1 To Howell Cobb. E.

"washington D. C., *Jan. 20, 1854.* Dear Sir: I thank you for your highly esteemed favor of the 13th inst., and at the same time I reciprocate the friendly confidence in which it was written. From what I have already told you on paper it is hardly necessary for me here to renew to you assurances of high regard personal and political or to tell you what I have been free to say to everyone, that among the living Democratic statesmen of the Union there is no one in my opinion to whom the Northern Democracy owe more than to you—or in whom they have greater confidence. With these feelings I write to you at the present time, and as you ask for a frank and full letter you shall have it in the spirit of that confidence which marks your own. To give "a full view of the bearings in the democratic party" here is a somewhat difficult task just at this time. Over everything there seems to hang a cloud which, whether it portends coming storm or whether it is soon to give way to " bright skies" I am not the seer to foretell, and if I hope for the best I almost fear the worst. You have seen by the votes in Congress that the Democratic party has thus far kept together in refusing to join in an attempt to break up the Administration. The general feeling among the members seems to me to be this: They have come on here determined to give the Adm. an honest support so long as it is true to democratic measures—but in so doing they do not consider themselves obligated to endorse the blunders of the Administration or the ethics of the Washington Union. They have no more love for John Van Buren, his adherents, and their heresies than they had when these gentlemen were plotting treason openly against the party and the interests of the Union. Nor do they think the Guthrie letter and the Bronson removal right in principle or wise in policy: and finally they think that "Union" men generally have been neglected to some extent in the policy of the Administration. There is not that healthy state of feeling here that I wish there was—there is not that eagerness to defend the 1 Congressman from Connecticut, 1851-1855.

Administration policy which is so necessary to Administration success. Matters may right themselves after a while—I hope they will. But let us look at the question broadly and see where we stand now. Who among your Southern Representatives will make bold to meet his constituents with a speech delivered in Congress full of commendation for the "softs" and denunciation of the course of Dickinson Bronson and the "hards"? And what will you say when Whig orators charge upon you the "democratic policy" which brought all this about? Who of your States Rights men will endorse before the people the principle of the Guthrie letter and Cushing's which followed? You perceive that I look at the question as it may present itself one, two or three years hence—and here let me say that the policy of the " hard " members of Congress is first to strengthen their cause at home and then to so place their cause before the Nation that Southern men will be forced by the popular feeling to take sides with them by and by. I choose to present it thus to you whose present position is enviable and for whose future I have great confidence and the highest hopes. As a Southern man you can best judge how these questions will be met, if ever presented, by your people. I throw them out as suggestions which may after all have nothing in them worthy of reflection. But the Administration must be sustained—it has thus far been true to principle, and so long as it continues so I intend to support it. Whoever leaves it for a new organization will as you will observe be " utterly ruined and wrecked politically." Hence I have seen with deep regret the course of our "hard" friends in Congress. They have acted with little prudence or sagacity it seems to me. From the start they evinced a determined spirit of opposition to the Administration, and this has caused many an honest democrat to pause while he at heart sympathized with them in what they considered the hard usage they had received at the hands of the Administration. The "hards" say they do not mean to leave the party. If they do not—if they stand by Gen. Pierce and his measures, the sympathy of the popular heart the Union through will be with them as it was in times gone by when the seal of condemnation was put upon Van Buren, Seward and the pernicious doctrines of abolitionism at the North and the men who advocated secession at the South. In the New York quarrel I have no disposition to participate, and the mistake of the Adm. has been in meddling with it; but I cannot if put on my confession say that I sympathize with the "softs" or deny that remaining true to the party and its organization I wish the " hards " success.

You ask what I think of the sincerity of the free-soil democrats in New York generally? Some of them are honest in their repentance doubtless; but the majority of them are jockey politicians at best. Dean, M. C. from New York, stated yesterday in the H. R., I understand, that he and a majority of his " soft " colleagues would vote the Nebraska Bill, etc. Perhaps they will. I shall believe it when I see it and be glad to see it although it may prove how recklessly these same gentlemen were sporting with the interests of the Union hardly three years ago. *Query,* if they do so vote, is not the *morale* of their party at home gone, and will not all this go to strengthen still more the "hards" at their next election? Passing from one point to another, R. K. Meade of Va., who is here on a visit, assured me the other day that in spite of what they wrote for the Enquirer their sympathies were with the " hards " in New York! What times have we fallen upon? as Mrs. Partington would say, judging from circumstances like these, "things is in an awful perdition."

I have thus, my dear Sir, attempted in a poor way and with the familiarity and confidence of one writing to an elder brother, to answer the queries propounded in your letter. It has at least the merit of frankness, and as such I send it to you "Greeting". A word in conclusion. I like General Pierce very much—he has treated all my applications to him with consideration and favor. I believe that he is honest and that he means to do right and I am a friend to him ready to raise a voice in his defence. I have upon more than one occasion spoken of the high opinion I had of you to him and he has invariably reciprocated the feeling. I saw him only a day or so ago—I told him that I had received a very gratifying letter from you—he replied "how like a prince Cobb has acted— he's a glorious fellow "—and before I left him he said, "make my best regards to Cobb when you write to him. I have the highest opinion of him, and I mean to show my appreciation of him on the first occasion which presents itself"— this was very nearly the remark, and although he did not seem to speak to me in confidence yet I trust you will consider it as confidential between us.

If the President is to be relied upon, he means to straighten things in New York. His antecedents are all with the professions of the "hards" and he leans that way now I think; but the " hard" leaders have managed badly. They have abused the President, and now attempt to drive him; and I don't believe he'll be "*driven* from the temple" though the pillars of the edifice are carried off and he and his chosen companions left to lie buried in the ruins. I shall be very glad to hear from you soon again....

Robert Toombs To W. W. Burwell. 1 L. C.

U. S. Senate Chamber, *Feb. 3, 1854.*

My Dear Sir: I thank you for your reply to my dispatch and letter of this morning. I have some servants and horses in Charleston waiting for the Bal. Steamer and I am anxious to know when she will resume her trips, in order to give instructions to my agents touching their movements.

I feel great solicitude about your course on the Nebraska bill. We had a caucus this morning of the friends of the bill. Every Southern Whig Senator for the bill and every Southern Democrat whose opinions are known also for it. The meeting was composed of a large majority of the Senate—who unanimously determined to carry the bill as it stands on the slavery issue. There cannot be a doubt as to the propriety and policy of repealing the Missouri compromise. The North never did agree to it and never would sanction it since its adoption. They have adhered to its prohibitory provisions, but uniformly and nearly unanimously trampled its principles under foot so far as the South was to be benefited by it. The measure was originally passed by Southern votes with a few Northern men, every one of whom were defeated for voting for it but three. When the territory of Oregon was organized with the prohibition in it, the North nearly unanimously refused to accept the prohibition with the recognition of the Missouri compromise. In the long struggle for govmts for California and N. Mexico, the whole North (with I think but four exceptions) repudiated and refused to recognize the Missouri Compromise; and even today the free-soil scoundrels who talk of the breach of compact repudiate it in principle (which was division on a line of latitude) and insist only on the prohibition. In sustaining it they only sustain the Wilmot Proviso. Therefore the North having both refused to adopt or recognize it, there is no pretence that it is or was a compact between the sections; but the compromise of 1850 was a compact—a compact recognized by a majority of the North and adopted by both parties North and South in their party platforms. It has therefore the almost universal sanction of the nation, and the Nebraska bill but applies its principles to the present and all other cases for the future. This will settle the question—settle it in conformity with the declared will of the whole people, and offer the only possible mode of final disposition of this dangerous question. It is a measure of peace, equality and fraternity; and if we let this opportunity of finally settling it escape I see no hope in the future. Dissolution will surely come, and that speedily. I write hastily under the speech 1 Editor of the Baltimore Patriot, and for a time editor of the Southern Quarterly Review. of Mr. Chase. When you next come to the city call on me and we will talk over the matter more fully than I have time to write.

Stephen A. Douglas To Howell

Cobb. E.

Washington D. C., *April 2d, 1854.*

My Dear Sir: I am greatly indebted to you for your kind letter, and regret that the pressure of business and multiplicity of engagements have rendered it impossible for me to answer letters, even from distinguished and esteemed friends, among whom I am happy to rank you. I could not doubt that the Nebraska Bill and the principle asserted therein would meet your hearty approval. It is the principle with which your public life is especially identified. It will triumph and impart peace to the country and stability to the Union. I am not deterred or affected by the violence and insults of the Northern Whigs and Abolitionists. The storm will soon spend its fury and the people of the North will sustain the measure when they come to understand it. In the meantime our Southern friends have only to stand firm and leave us of the North to fight the great battle. We will fight it boldly and will surely triumph in the end. The great principle of self government is at stake, and surely the people of this country are never going to decide that the principle upon which our whole republican system rests is vicious and wrong.

I shall be glad to hear from you at all times and to receive suggestions from your pen as to the best mode of conducting the great movement in which we are all engaged.

Thomas H. Bayley 1 To Howell Cobb. E.

Washington, D. C., *May 6,1854...* . The Nebraska bill is in great danger. The Softs almost to a man will oppose it—and the Hards give it a cold support. They say they are not disposed to go out of their way to support a leading measure of an administration, upon the success of which its salvation depends, that has put its iron heel upon them. I do not approve of course of this reasoning, but human nature is human nature, and I for one am not disposed to judge them too harshly...

Alexander H. Stephens To W. W. Burwell. L C

Washington, D. C., *May 7, 1854.*

Dear Sir: Your letter was duly received and I feel obliged to you for it. Your lick on Benton was appropriate and was well calculated to lessen the effect of his speech with his old party. His speech by the by is very valuable in many points. Tomorrow I think we 1 Congressman from Virginia, 1844-1856.

shall get the Nebraska bill up in committee. The contest will be hard and the vote close, but we have the count. How the result will be I cannot positively state. Any thing that you may feel disposed to say favourable to the measure will be very timely this week. Perhaps *Franklin* might be induced not to vote against the bill if he should be assured that the sentiments of the people of Maryland were for it. I feel a deep interest in the success of the measure as a Southern man. The issue presented by the bill is one which in the main has arrayed the *free-soilers* in solid ranks against the South. The moral effect of the victory on our side will have a permanent effect upon the public mind, whether any positive advantages accrue by way of the actual extension of slavery or not. The effect of such a victory at this time is important. We are on the eve of much *greater issues* in my opinion. The Cuba question will soon be upon us. Politicians may attempt to stave it off; but come it will and that soon. We cannot permit the injurious policy of England and France to be carried out on that island! The Black Warrior affair it seems is not settled, etc. But I can say no more now. One word more about the Nebraska bill. The Clayton amendment will be dropt. This will be the ground upon which Southern *defectionists* will attempt to justify their *alliance* with the free-soilers. It will however only be a pretext, and as such they should not be permitted to escape on it. The great question for the South is whether she can be in a *worse* condition than she now is with the "naming sword" of a public act denying her entrance into the territory on any condition or the votes of any body. But enough.

P. S.—Please tell your business man to have the Patriot sent to me here—the daily. I will send the subscription when I see the terms.

N. B.—One other word about Nebraska and the Clayton amendment. I think it of great importance for the South to have the kind feelings of the foreign population. Come that population will, and why should we make them our enemies upon the small question of whether they should vote in a *Territory only* within one year or five? If you concur, a *leader* on that point would help much.

Alexander H. Stephens To W. W. Burwell. L. C

Washington, *D. C, May 8, 185b.*

Dear Sir: Allow me to express my gratification at the views given in an article in this Evening's Patriot in reply to the Chamber of Commerce of New York favouring an abandonment of privateering in war. The position of the Patriot is right on this great question. *We* ought not to think of abandoning privateering in case of war.

Mr. Buchanan was wrong, altogether wrong, in the policy indicated by him in his late speech. And the Intelligencer was wrong in commending that speech. Our merchant marine is our *naval militia.* If we were to adopt the policy of the Chamber of Commerce in New York we should have to keep as large a navy as England in order to cope successfully with her on the ocean. We could not please her better than to follow Mr. Buchanan's lead which the New York men have so readily fallen into. I am truly glad to see that the Patriot has taken hold of the subject.

Alexander H. Stephens To J. W. Duncan. Pa.

Washington, *D. C, May 86, 1854.*

Dear Duncan, Long before you get this, you will have heard the glorious news of the result of the Nebraska bill and the triumph of the compromise of 1850. The contest in the House was close and hot but we whipped the opposition out and carried the measure by 13 majority. The excitement has nearly all passed away. Nobody says anything now against it but the abolitionists. Let them howl on—" 'Tis their vocation."

We shall soon have another question which will absorb all others. That is our relations with Spain growing out of the state of affairs in Cuba. What is to become of this no one now can tell. The *position* of the Administration is not known upon it. You need put no reliance on rumours from this city on that point. They are as yet *mum*. But of one thing I am pretty well persuaded at this time and that is there will be a *revolt* in Cuba before the late *registration edict* of the Gov. of Cuba goes into effect in August. By that edict about half of the slaves of the island will be declared free. The planters there will not submit. Will not aid in that struggle go from the United States? I think it will, in spite of proclamations and indictments. My sympathies will be with the revolutionists and so will the sympathies of a majority of our people. But I can say no more now.

I expect to start home Monday. I am to be at LaGrange at court on the first Monday in June. I wish to get you to do me a favour and that is to look over the files of the Federal Union and copy an editorial of that paper, printed I think on the 7th July, 1844, reviewing a speech I made in Milledgeville on the night of the 4th July 1844. It was the first paper printed after the 4th and I think its date was the 7th. A copy of that editorial I wish you to send me at Crawfordville. I will get it there when I return from LaGrange. Your attention to this will greatly oblige me.

Alexander H. Stephens To W. W. Berwell. L. C.

Washington, D. C., *June 26, 1854.*

Dear Sir: Mr. Toombs a few days ago showed me a letter from you enclosing some editorials from the Patriot. It so happened that only one of my papers in which these editorials appeared ever came to hand. That was the one containing the last. How this occurred I do not know. There has been no failure to receive the paper (save in these instances) since I ordered it. I mention the fact that you may if you choose make inquiry to ascertain if a suppression of the issues was general towards the South or Southern subscribers.

I was highly pleased with the position assumed and the views presented in the articles alluded to—and I will also add that I showed them to a number of Southern Whigs of the House, including Preston of Ky., Zollicoffer of Tenn. and Caruthers of Mo., who were quite as well pleased with them as I was myself. The truth is the Southern Whigs must strike out a lead for themselves. They can not afford either for their own sake or that of the country to fall into the ranks of either of the great nominal parties as they are now organized and constituted. I see the Columbus Enquirer of Georgia is advocating the policy of our starting a ticket of *Southern* men for Pres. and Vice President. This I am decidedly opposed to and have so written to the author of the articles in that paper of this character. What we want is a sound national organization upon broad—national—republican principles. We want no sectional men or sectional issues—at least so long as national men enough can be found to make a party on national issues and principles. If the Southern Whigs will but maintain their position of 1850 and the principles of the Kansas and Nebraska bill just passed, and hold no affiliation with any party North or South which does not make these principles the test of their organization, all will be well and a most glorious triumph in a short time will be the result. Decision, firmness and boldness in the maintenance of this position is all that is wanted. Hundreds and thousands of Northern Whigs when they see that this is our fixed determination will abandon the Seward ranks of Antislavery agitators. There is nothing that will tend so much to a speedy purification of both parties North as a resolute purpose on our part to adhere to this course. I have no time to say more now but to bid you good cheer and to invoke you to keep the flag flying. The National Intelligencer has already calmed on the question of repeal, and many more papers worse than that will follow suit when they see that we are in earnest.

P. S.—Mr. Toombs went home Saturday.

Alexander H. Stephens To W. W. Burwell. L. C.

Washington, D. C, *June 27, 1854.*

My Dear Sir: Your letter of the 22d Inst. by some strange and unaccountable delay was not received until this moment. The *papers* have not yet come to hand. I wrote to you yesterday and hope my letter met better luck on the way than yours did. If you got my letter of yesterday you are fully apprized of my views and opinions upon the subject of yours. I fully agree with you in the views given in the editorials which Mr. Toombs got from you some days ago. There will doubtless be a very general expression of Southern Whig sentiment in the Senate and House before long on the present condition of parties. Mr. Jones led off in the Senate yesterday—Jones of Ten. I did not hear his speech, but hear it spoken of very highly. He took strong Southern ground—or rather I should say National ground. (It is the Northern Whig Abolition party now which occupies sectional ground exclusively and wish to bring Southern Whigs to their sectional organization.) But if they are but true to themselves and true to the country they will continue to stand where they now stand and hold affiliations with no organization North or South which does not stand upon their own broad National Platform. I have heard of no meeting of the Southern Whigs in Congress. What we have done thus far is to confer freely with each other upon the present as well as the future. I wish you would send to Senator Badger[1] your papers of last week with the editorials marked so as to attract his attention. He will speak soon in the Senate on the Boston Memorial and it is all important that he should be fully apprized of the outside state of public feelings amongst the Southern Whigs. I do not know that he is thoroughly with us. Kerr[2] of the House is, but still your paper might strengthen him. "Verbum sap."

Howell Cobb To His Wife. E.

Clarksville *ga., 1st Oct., 1854*My Dear Wife,... I have met with leading Democrats from all these upper counties of my district and with one voice they call upon me to return to Congress. I believe that if the election was tomorrow I would get *every* vote in Kabun county and a larger vote in all the other counties than I ever got before. The Southern Rights men seem to be the warmest friends I have, whilst the Union men are as true as ever. This is gratifying I assure you; whether I will avail myself of it remains to be determined....

1 George E. Badger, Senator from North Carolina, 1846-1855.

3 John Kerr, Congressman from North Carolina, 1853-1855.

Howell Cobb To James Buchanan. Pa. (Private.)

Athens, Ga., *5th Dee., 1854,.*

My Dear Sir: When we parted in Philadelphia I promised to write you if anything should occur which might render a letter from me of any interest. I don't know that I can now redeem the condition of that promise but I have determined to submit to you some thoughts suggested by the recent elections.

As you have seen, the Democratic party has been literally slaughtered in the Northern, Middle and Western States, whilst of the Whig party there is not left even a monumental remembrance. It is with the Democracy however that we have to deal, leaving "the *whigs* to bury *the whigs"*. After looking at the defeats and disasters which have come upon us until the heart is sickened at the sight it is natural that we should look to the future to see what, if anything, can be done to retrieve our lost ground. I am not disposed to look too gloomily upon the future. I cannot but feel that 1856 will see an overwhelming reaction in the public mind. Whether it should be so or not depends in a great measure upon the course of policy of the Democratic party. At present it would seem that the presidential contest of 1856 will be between the National Democratic party on the one hand, and on the other two Sectional parties, a northern one headed probably by Seward and a Southern one possibly by Toombs. This will certainly be the fight unless the whigs should become partly nationalized through the instrumentality of the " Know Nothings ", of which there is some chance. At all events we may regard it as settled that the democracy will have to fight the one or the other of the issues above suggested. In view of these things the question is beginning to be discussed pretty freely, who shall be our candidate? In deciding this matter the public mind naturally turns first to the present executive as being in office and thereby having a claim upon the party. In this communication you will allow me to speak freely and candidly. The renomination of Genl. Pierce is certain and inevitable defeat. I care not to discuss the reason for this state of things but of *the fact* there cannot be a reasonable doubt. The same remark may with equal truth be applied to every member of his cabinet. The *present* is not the proper time for any of them. Without disposing seriatim of all the candidates spoken of, allow me to say to you frankly that it is in this section of the country very generally agreed that you are not only the strongest but perhaps the only man that can succeed in 1856. I could give you the reasons upon which this opinion is founded but a reference to two considerations will show you that there are good reasons for the opinon. First, you have been absent from the country during this bitter Nebraska contest and are not therefore complicated with it personally. Whilst we hold that the democratic party is fully committed to the principles of that measure and must stand or fall by it yet it is important that in the next presidential race we should be relieved from the bitter personal feeling which exists towards those who were most prominent in that matter. The other consideration to which I refer is this—there is a very general averseness to a speculative candidacy. There is a desire everywhere that our next President shall be a man whose position and character as a statesman shall be known and appreciated. I might become fulsome if I went farther on this point. You understand my meaning and that is sufficient.

I have reason to believe that a similar feeling exists in other portions of the Union, making the prospect for your nomination and election *fax brighter* than it ever has been at any past period. I have not written this letter to seek your confidence but to communicate to you what I believe to be a very general feeling on this important question of a democratic candidate for the presidency.

Alexander H. Stephens To W. W. Burwell. L. C.

Washington, D. C, *Bee. SO, 1854.*

Dear Sir: Yours of yesterday's date was received last night and by the same mail I got the advance sheets of your leader for the next Southern Quarterly Review. I am very much pleased indeed with the article. Your plan of treating this sectional question meets my hearty approbation. And I have for a long time desired to see an able Southern periodical established upon just such a basis. I was only a subscriber to the Southern Quarterly and quit it because I could not sanction or even patronize such heresies as I thought it circulated. You take an enlarged view of the subject, a national view, a patriotic view which looks no less to the maintenance of our just rights than to the preservation of the Union to which all sections, ours as well as others, are so much indebted for our common growth, prosperity, happiness and renown.

I have never met with the pamphlet The North and the South which you review. Indeed I never heard of it before. Will you send me a copy if you have one to spare. With this I send you a copy of Stringfellow's which you may not have seen.

I shall keep your sheets a few days longer to show them to some Southern gentlemen, then I will return them. I will also confer with Messrs. Hunter and Mason as you request. It is too cold for me to get out today but I hope to be able to face the wind in a day or two. I have improved some in health since November. I was quite ill then but have not much in that way to brag of yet.

I trust you will not permit your connection with the Review to hang upon the contingency of the opinion of the South Carolina delegation and that of the Southern men of the same school. The truth is this class of men never did give utterance to the real sentiments of the South; and hence the Review under their lead and management has always been a sickly and languishing plant. My opinion is that if the Review was put upon the basis you propose it would take on new life, draw new sustenance and soon be one of the most vigorous and widely circulated and generally read quarterlies of the kind published in this country.

Thomas W. Thomas To Alexander H. Stephens. R.

Elberton, Geo., *5 May, 1855*. Dear Sir: A rumor is becoming spread abroad among your late constituents that you will decline to serve them in the next Congress. The reason assigned is that you are opposed to the secret political associations called Know Nothings into which it is supposed a large number of your political friends have gone. It is at the request of numerous personal and political friends that I ask you to state your views and intentions in reference to this matter. I believe I express the unanimous wish of the people of Elbert County, whigs and democrats outside of the Know Nothing organization (and doubtless of many in the order) when I say we desire you to serve us again in the next Congress, and that no other man can do it so well at this particular juncture of our political affairs. Your past life is a pledge to us better than a thousand secret oaths that our constitutional rights will be safe in your hands and we ask you to put on your armor and do battle once more for Georgia and the South. Mysterious whispers float about of the almost countless number of those who think that republicanism can be protected only in the dark, but some yet remain who have American spirit enough to believe that the rights and liberties which our fathers wrested from foreigners, sword in hand, can be preserved to their posterity by open and manly action without secret oaths and midnight consultations.1

Robert Toombs To T. Lomax.2

Boston, Mass., *June 6th, 1855*. Dear Sir: More than three weeks ago, in compliance with my promise, I wrote to you giving my opinions of the new political organization commonly known as " Know Nothings" or the American party. I did not learn until I reached Augusta on my way here, that you had not received it. If it should yet come to hand I wish 1 Stephens replied to this in a public letter, dated May 9, 1855, elaborately denouncing the Know-Nothing party. This was published in the Federal Union, MlledgeYllle, Ga., May 22, 1855. and in other contemporary newspapers. It is reprinted in Henry Cleveland, "Alexander H. Stephens", Philadelphia. 1806, pp. 459-471.
3 From the Federal Union, Milledgeville, Ga., June 19, 1855. Mr. Lomax was the editor of the Times and Sentinel, Columbus, Ga. you to publish it, as it was a much fuller and more carefully prepared exposition of my opinions than this letter can be. I shall embark today for Liverpool, and for want of time must confine myself to a very brief statement rather than an argument on the subject.

My first objection to the new party is one independent of its principles. I am opposed to it because it is a *secret* political society. Society has a right to know the men and the principles and the policy of the men who seek to direct its affairs and control its destiny. Publicity is the lifeblood of a representative Republic. Without it public liberty must soon perish, and no necessity short of that which would justify revolution can justify the surrender of this great security of popular government. All party associations are constantly liable to be used by the cunning, the unprincipled and enterprising members for the promotion of personal objects rather than the public interests, and it needs no argument to prove that secrecy greatly increases this tendency and facilitates the accomplishment of such unworthy ends. Secrecy is the natural covering of fraud, the natural ally of eror and the enemy of truth. The patriots who framed our constitution gave it a fatal blow, by provisions which secure the freedom of speech and the liberty of the press.

This objection to the *new party* derives additional force from the obligation which is said to be imposed upon the applicant for admission, that he will carry out its decrees whether his judgment approves them or not. If this be true it is a surrender of the dearest rights of freedom and is a crime against society.

My next objection to the American party is that it proposes in some way to invade the rights of conscience or to call men in question for the free exercise thereof. I am opposed to all religious tests of every sort and for every purpose. Our constitution protects us against the putting of such tests upon the statute book, but the principle is founded on truth and justice and ought to be the rule of the individual action as well as of the public conduct of every citizen. Centuries of unavailing persecution taught our fathers the folly as well as the wickedness of attempting to control men's conscience by penal statutes or civil disabilities; they therefore put the sting of disability into the temptation to disgrace our statute book with this sort of legislation. We will defeat their noble objects, in part at least, by enacting a different rule in the exercise of our political rights.

It is charged that the Roman Catholic policy is cruel, intolerant and despotic. The charge is not wholly unfounded. If it be true it is greatly to be condemned and deplored, and above all things we should avoid imitating their vices and thereby justly subjecting ourselves to this great condemnation. We can neither conquer or eradicate the vices of Romanism, whatever they may be, by imitating them, or by persecution. The world has tried these remedies for centuries past, and tried them in vain. Let us rather oppose her cruelty with kindness, her intolerance with free toleration (in substance as well as form), her despotism with freedom, and then we may reasonably look for different and better results. The moment that the simple yet sublime truth got itself acknowledged by our government that the citizen is responsible to the State for his civil conduct but to God only for his religious faith, the unholy bonds which unite the church to the State were broken, persecution for conscience sake became impossible here, and religious toleration entered upon its career of universal dominion. Its first great triumph was to strike the fetters from the consciences of Irish Roman Catholics. It has begun a similar good work for the Protestants in Spain and Sardinia, and for the Greek in Turkey, and it will go on " conquering and to conquer "; until the demon of persecution—blind, deaf and stupid—shall have no more abiding place upon the face of the earth.

The naturalization laws are greatly complained of by the American party. I think them founded on just principles, and are in the main wise and good laws. To naturalize an intelligent foreigner of good moral character and attached to free government and the principles of our constitution and who has resided among us long enough to test these qualifications is a great benefit to the State as well as to the individual who receives the high privilege. These are the conditions and safeguards which our laws seek to throw around the right of citizenship. These laws are no doubt frequently violated; they are doubtless imperfect and do not fully effect the objects intended by them. Let all proper additions and amendments necessary to carry out these objects be made and then let the law be faithfully administered, and these things can be done without the aid of secret societies.

There is another objection to this party, which should be put under the ban of Southern opinion. We have had a great struggle for the last six years upon an intensely exciting sectional issue. This issue has been settled by the wisdom of the representatives of the people. This issue found its solution in the legislation of 1850 and 1854. The peace and safety of the Republic demand that this legislation should not only be undisturbed, but vigorously upheld by the nation. The American Party in the north whenever it has had power has shown the most vigorous hostility to this legislation. The Know Nothings of Massachusetts have attempted to nullify it, and have shown a total disregard of their *public* oaths, and therefore are wholly incapable of giving any pledge, open or secret, that a man of honesty ought to accept. Political association with these men is moral complicity with their crimes,

The true policy of the South is to unite; to lay aside all party divisions. Whigs, Democrats and Know Nothings should come together and combine for the common safety. If we are wise enough to do this, to present one unbroken column of fifteen states united for the preservation of their own rights, the Constitution and the Union, and to uphold and support that noble band of patriots at the North who have stood for the Constitution and the right against the tempest of fanaticism, folly and treason which has assailed them, we shall succeed. We shall then have conquered a peace which will be enduring, and by means which will not invite further aggression.

Alexander H. Stephens To Thomas W. Thomas.1 crawfordsville, Ga., 7 *June, 1855.* Dear Thomas, I got back from Lexington last night, and this morning got your letter. I have not time to say but a word. I am glad to hear so good a report from Elbert. All is right in Oglethorpe for the present at least. I had a large audience and all appeared satisfied with my position and course? except Shackelford. He was the only *murmurer* I heard. I want to go over to Washington tomorrow if I can. Monday I shall be in Augusta, Tuesday in Warrenton—so you see I am busy. I will not make the draft upon you to go to the Chron. and Sentinel office. I deeply regret that you cannot buy? the press; but you do right in not thwarting or opposing your mother's wishes. Your first obligations are due to her. Parental duties above all others ought to be discharged next to those of a higher order which belong not to this earth.

I don't know what is to become of the Chron. and Sentinel in the fight. I hear that *battery* will be taken by the enemy. If so, it will be a great loss to us. But how to prevent it now I do not see. Perhaps *events* or the turn that things may take will secure it on our side, but I hope in this matter almost against hope. Enough however of this. I have not heard what the Democracy have done at Milledgeville or the K. N.'s at Phila. The latter I expect has blown up and the first ought to have done the same thing.

Robert Toombs To Alexander H. Stephens. R.

London, *June 21st, 1855.* Dear Stephens. We have had no mishaps since we left you in Augusta and scarcely an incident worth jotting down. We left Boston on the 6th Inst. and had a pleasant run for eight days (barring our detention off Halifax for fourteen hours) when a N. Wester 1 MS. in the possession of Mr. J. K. Smith, 1145 West Bridge Street, Grand Rapids, Mich.

73566—13 23 struck and continued until the day we reached Liverpool, Sunday the 17th. Our ship took the Northern passage away up towards the North pole (we were in 57 11") and dropped down between Scotland and Ireland and it was as cold as any weather we had last winter in Georgia. The weather since we came here has been cool but very pleasant. London having had three sun-shiny days together (including this one) is overjoyed, and if it were a Catholic country I dare say they would celebrate a "Te deum." I have not time today to give you a minute account of my peregrinations thus far altho' there is in the main nothing of interest until we got here.

Liverpool is precisely such a place as I expected to find. In the country between here and there I was disappointed. The two hundred and five miles is mostly in grass—not as striking as Culpeper county, Virginia, and gives you no idea of its great value. The whole country seemed covered with sheep, a few cattle (all good) and a little (not much) wheat. But after being here three days today I begin to realize the grandeur and magnificence of this capitol of the world. It is much greater than I had ever pictured to my imagination, and one is bewildered with the wealth, the magnificence, the beauty, and the thousand objects of grandeur and interest which arrest him at every turn. Night before last I went to parliament and had the good luck to hear quite a number of their speakers—Palmerston, name illegible, Fred Peel, and a score of others of lesser note. The speaking was poor, very poor, the matter commonplace, and the style perfectly genteel but perfectly insipid. You could not have stood it half an hour. I braced myself up to listen to them three mortal hours. I shall go again this evening. Yesterday I spent the day in Westminster Abbey and regretted being compelled to leave when the evening service began. I much enjoyed the thousands of historic memories which cluster within its old walls. Today we spent almost entirely in the Tower which has objects enough for a week's examination. I shall leave here for France (Paris) on Monday and now fear I shall lose the prime object of my visit this year, that is a trip to Italy. The cholera is in Venice and Naples, and Home is said to be dreadfully scourged with something like yellow fever. But I think I must go to Rome anyhow. Julia and Sallie and Felix all keep well, except Sallie's cold which troubles her a good deal. They and Geo. H. Shorter compose all of my party. Van Buren, Fillmore, and Abbot Lawrence are all here and lionizing themselves. As well from our recent great calamity as from preference otherwise, I avoid all social intercourse and decline all invitations and am trying to turn my trip to advantage. Write me all the news at home by every steamer, care of George Peabody & Co., London, who will forward to me. All send their best regards.

Thomas D. Harris To Howell Cobb. E.

Washington D. C, *Oct. 15, 1855.*

Dear Governor, Here I am again amid the scenes which have known me for twelve long and eventful years but which are soon to know me no more forever. I could desire to remain attache of the House of Representatives for another Congress at least, on your's and Lumpkin's account; but that cannot be according to any sensible reading of the future which I am able to give....

The presence of so few knowing ones about the capital at this early day or of those who pretend to speculate as to the chances and character of the organization of the next House prevents the giving an idea beyond my own crude and clumsy head.

The late sickly movement of those few whigs in a few states of the North who call themselves " National Men " constituting less than a corporal's guard at home and without a solitary representative or sympathizer on the floor of the House from all the opposition of the North, cannot of course aid in the remotest degree, as some have supposed, to a democratic organization.

That movement amounts to nothing at all now and will in the end prove worse than nothing because, failing in their purpose of reorganizing the old Whig party, just nine in ten of them, rather than affiliate with the Democracy, will go to Seward or Republicanism. In this view of the case I cannot but fear that the good old Commonwealth of Pennsylvania who today rejoices in her Democratic strength will next year by the treachery of this same sort of cattle who refused to go to the polls at the last election cast her vote against us. But we shall be able to judge more satisfactorily when the aggregate vote of the state shall be known.

. The New House stands thus—Norton. Representatives 144

Northn. Democrats 22

Abolition, K. N., Anti-Nebraska, total 122

Total Soutlm. Reps 90

Northn. Nebraska democrats 22 112 which deduct 112

Northn. Abfolltion, K. N., Anti-Nebraska majority— 10

These figures make in my judgment the nearest approach to a democratic organization which any contingency can possibly bring about, and the chances are as now advised that Ky., and perhaps Tennessee. will go against the South in any plan or programme that shall be proposed by the North.

Now, sir, if you can pick a flaw in the above your vision is keener than mine. I would I could see a chance to replace you in a position the duties of which you discharged with such acknowledged honor and ability during the 31st Congress.

In all that I have said in connexion with the Speakership I have taken care to declare it as *my opinion* that you had no aspirations either for the office itself or for the nomination of the party and that you would not in *my opinion* permit your name to be used unless it shall be considered and believed that some important party end is to be accomplished; that nothing of selfishness entered into your feelings or wishes in connexion with it, etc. etc....

Richardson is here today and says the party must rally upon you for Speaker and Sproule says that the two Democrats from Indiana are also for you.

What is your majority? I have said in all my talk here and letters abroad to absent clerks that it was about 4,000— I suppose it is all of 3,000.

Howell Cobb To His Wife. E.

Washington City, *Dec. 23rd, 1855.*

My Dear Wife, The third week of the session is gone and no Speaker yet. As usual the town is full of rumors that we will elect to morrow but I do not see that there is any better prospect for it now than there has been all the time.

It is with a sad heart that I thus see the last hope of spending Christmas with you gone. You ask if I will go to New Haven to see my friend Ingersoll. Certainly not, as it would take half the time it would to go home and if I leave here at all I shall certainly travel southward. As you will see from the papers I have made a speech. You will see a very correct report of it in the Union. I may say to you what I could not say to any body else and that is that I never made a speech here before that produced such an effect. I give you a very high evidence of it in the fact that over thirty thousand copies have been subscribed for by the members for circulation. I cannot even to you repeat all the handsome things that have been said to me by my Democratic friends. The truth is that I now feel that the great object I had in returning to Congress has been effected. This speech has fully reinstated me with the national democracy. "Richard is himself again. " Don't chide my vanity— but do justice to one who has for some years failed to get it at the hands of his friends. All is right now so far as the political world is concerned, and I am now ready to quit and go home and would today give a year's salary to resign my seat in the morning, return to the only place of true happiness in this world, the bosom of my own family. This cannot be, but I will try to avoid creating the necessity for returning here again....

1 Cobb had just been elected to Congress from the sixth district of Georgia with a vote of 9,203 against 0,227 for Franklin, his Know-Nothing opponent.

Robert C. Winthrop1 To Howell Cobb. E.
(Private.)
Boston, *5 J arty, 1856.*

My Dear Sir: The long agony in the organization of the House carried me back to the day when you and I were *pitted* against each other for the Speaker's Chair. There seems to have been less bitterness and violence in the present contest than in that to which we were parties. Perhaps this is the reason why our strife was ended soonest. The present struggle burns along like a *slow match* smoking and smouldering but with little flame. Ours was soon kindled into a conflagration and went off in a blaze.

I cannot help feeling now as I did then that the great thing to be accomplished is an *organization* of some sort. The present spectacle is likely to involve our Government in contempt both at home and abroad. Great Britain will laugh at the idea of our asserting the Monroe doctrine while we cannot choose a presiding officer. I do not doubt that you feel all this even more strongly than any mere outsider. Looking on however from "this loop-hole of retreat" I cannot help thinking that something might be done to bring this interminable game of political chess to an end. I think I can see how the Republicans (as they are called) could do something creditable to themselves and to the country towards ending the controversy. But I have no correspondence with any of them and am one of the last whose counsel they would be likely to heed. But I think I can see also how *you* and the Democratic members could adopt a course which would redound to your honor. You have thus far held out with signal firmness making no compromises and entering into no arrangements. You may still avoid. everything inconsistent with this policy and yet accomplish the result which is so desirable. If the Democratic members were to come to a resolve that the honor of the country and the existence of the Government required an *organization* of the Representative branch without further delay and that the Democratic party having the Administration in its own hands is especially responsible for securing to that Administration the means of *carrying on the Government;* if they would resolve next, that to this end they were ready to sacrifice any personal or party preferences or advantages and to give evidence of this readiness by voting for a candidate not of their own number—provided only that he were not identified with any mere Sectional Organization and provided further that this step was to be taken as the result of no bargain or compromise of principles;—and if then you could select out of the Fuller men or out of any other men, a candidate to whom your 90 votes would secure a majority, I think it would be a 1Con pressman from Massachusetts, 1840-1842, and 1843-1850; Speaker of the House, 1847-1849.

stroke of policy and patriotism which your opponents might well envy you. If the old Whig party of which I am one of the survivors had such cards-in their hands and I was in a position to lead off I should jump at the chance of taking this precise course. At any rate it has impressed itself so strongly on my mind within a few days that I have ventured to write you this confidential and friendly letter on the subject.

I have not forgotten Shakespeare's rebuke upon those " who sit by the fire and presume to know what's done in the Capitol" but I know you will receive my suggestions kindly and attribute them to the right spirit. I cannot suppress the " Union—however bounded" spirit on these occasions of National exigency and it really seems to me that the scene of disorganization at Washington has gone on as long as any true patriot could be willing to see it.

I rely on our old friendship surviving all personal and political competitions to secure my letter a *confidential,* as well as kind reception and I shall be very glad to hear from you at any time. I see our old friend Berrien is gone at last. There were few abler and better men, tho' like all of us he had his angular points.

Strange as it may seem to you, there is not one Massachusetts member of either Senate or House in the present Congress with whom I correspond or from whom I have any reason to expect even a *public document* this winter. If therefore you are distributing anything interesting from time to time and are troubled with surplus copies (particularly of your own speeches) I shall be glad to be remembered.

Howell Cobb To His Wife. E.
. Washington City, *2 Feby., 1856.* My

Deab Wife, I am writing this letter whilst the intensest excitement exists in the house. We have adopted the plurality rule and we are now voting under its operation. The candidates. are Banks and Aiken of S. C. and the result extremely doubtful. Each side afraid and each side hopeful. About the same state of things exists as when I was elected in 1849. It will be perhaps two hours before we get to the end and I will not keep this letter open but will write you again by this mail if an election is had. Gov. Aiken little dreamed that he would be the man for Speaker when he came here, and now regrets exceedingly the necessity of his position. You have doubtless some curiosity to know how he came to be the favorite. He is personally the most popular man in the house, universally liked by everybody. He *is a democrat* and as national as a South Carolinian ever gets to be. He was not in our caucus, though approving our platform, and for that reason the National Know Nothings have agreed to vote for him. This result in some respects will do good *if Aiken is elected.* We shall have beaten Banks which will be a great point but at the same time I would have preferred no complication with the Know Nothings. I have consented to this arrangement as an expedient not as a choice. If Banks is elected the responsibility will be on the Southern K. N's. and their allies. The excitement grows more and more intense. In my next letter I will give you my ideas about the effect of the election no matter how it ends...

P. S.—I forgot that you would get the news by telegraph before my letter reaches, still I will enclose a memorandum after the election is over to secure your hearing the result.

Enclosed memorandum.

My Dear Wife, I regret to say that Banks is elected as I have feared all the time.

Robert Toombs To Thomas W. Thomas.1

Washington, D. C., *Feby 9th, 1856.*

Dear Thomas, Your letter of the 4th inst.2 was blocked up eight or ten days by the snows and reached me just before I left for Boston to lecture the Yankees,3 and found me much engaged in preparation for that work, and after ten days' absence I have been much bothered in getting it out of the press. It has attracted a good deal of attention, and therefore it is necessary at least to have it printed decently and correctly.

I agree with you as to the very small amount of wisdom with which our friends are managing public affairs in Georgia; but it is fully equal to the quantity manifested here. I have less hopes of being able finally to cooperate with them than I ever had. Every consideration of duty and public interest requires that we should sustain them in the present conflict, whatever may be our future course towards them. There is no safety for our constitutional rights at this time in any other organization, and we must therefore do the best we can with them. One of their great mistakes is that from the great support we have given them they think themselves perfectly secure in power and are forgetfull of the instrumentalities which saved them from ruin and which alone can maintain them. Your strong sense of justice and hatred of selfishness makes your judgment severe on Cobb. You looked for a lofty self-sacrificing patriotism and devotion to public principle, and were disappointed. And yet with the 1 MS. in the possession of Mr. W..1. DeRenne, Wormsloe, Savannah, Gn. Error in original, should be 4th ult.

» Refers to the lecture on slavery which Toombs delivered in the Tremont Temple, Boston, Mass., Jan. 24. 1856. The lecture is printed in A. H. Stephens, "War between the States", I, 625-647.

want of these he is not wholly without good points. That you are right in thinking he will turn me out1 if he has a chance I think very likely, but I still think he would only do it for *himself* and not for another. The great defect of Cobb's character is that as a public man (outside of his own family and particular friends) he is without attachments or resentments and careless of means by which he accomplishes his ends. He has always worked with very bad materials, and therefore has a low morality in politics, and therefore he has no recuperative power. When once the tide sets against him he is powerless forever. This is the appointed punishment, and you will see that he cannot escape it. I do not know a more powerless public man here and in Georgia at this time than Mr. Cobb. He is valuable in action; not worth a sixpence in council. This is of course confidential. He is now playing between Pierce and Buchanan, and I know one of them knows it and think it very probable that the other does too.

I was invited to a Democratic caucus of Senators the other day to adopt a platform. Considering that a work that it was my duty to participate in, as my own and my friends' cooperation with that party depended upon their adoption of a sound one, I went. The subject had been referred (upon Iverson's motion) before I came on, to a committee with Genl. Cass at the head of it. They reported a sound one; but as soon as we assembled I found Dodge, James Allen and others who had voted against the Kansas act in the meeting, and all against adopting any platform whatever. A motion was made, discussed and *adopted* that it was inexpedient to adopt any until the Cincinnati convention! Of course I considered myself out of the ring and retired without saying a word. What fools! They have already all the odium of their pro-slavery action on their heads, and now would throw away all the strength it gives them. They have already commenced running from a defeated foe. Their anxiety to begin plundering the enemy's camp disables them from following up their victory and it may happen as it has happened frequently before, that the enemy may rally and destroy them.

I am strongly inclined to the opinion that you are right in your estimate of Johnson.2 I firmly believe he is sincere and reliable upon the Georgia platform and would risk himself in defence of

great public principles—and that is a rare virtue. I never could understand Jim Gardner's8 toadyism of McMillen. It has always been the strangest thing to me in all of our local politics. What can be the seat of his power over him? He certainly knows him to be an unmitigated scoundrel, and yet he is constantly puffing him.
11. e., defeat Toombs for reelection to the Senate.
= Herschel V. Johnson.
James R. Gardner, editor of the Augusta Constitutionalist.

After your retirement the Democratic party could have done nothing which would have so much benefited themselves and the country as the election of Jenkins to the Supreme Court, and they stupidly "threw away a pearl richer far than all their tribe " at the instance of that dirty demagogue McMillen. Unless they adopt wiser counsels they cannot hold Georgia either with or without their Whig allies. However great they may esteem our power, at this rate their weight will soon get be3rond our strength.

I expect there is some mistake about Dr. Landmen's account of the Buchanan letter. I saw Buck in London last summer and he talked to me very satisfactorily on the slavery question. But if he has been misled to take the position you have heard, it will be fatal to him. I will not support any man who is not clear, distinct and unequivocal on this subject. I have fought long enough, and will be content with nothing but a plain straightforward fight on principle. The question is in a critical condition, more so than it has been for twenty years, and nothing but iron firmness can save either our rights or the country.

The election of Banks has given great hopes to our enemies, and their policy is dangerous in the extreme to us. They will affect great moderation and seduce some Southern men into their ranks, very much with the same policy as that adopted in 1852. Yet they will have all substantial power in the event of success. This will finally result in division at the South, which will be the most fatal result that could happen to us. Pierce is anxious for the nomination, is fighting Buck hard. As things now stand I rather incline to think we cannot do much better than to run him. I am glad you are in the delegation. Hold on, "watch and wait," as Calhoun said, until the time comes, and then we can see clearer into the future and be able better to decide what is best for the country. Mrs. T. and I both have been very unwell for a week past with colds. Weather desperate. I shall be at home to Elbert court and remain till after Warren. Have our Warren (Battle) cases all right for a trial. My best regards to Mrs. Thomas.

Thomas W. Thomas To Aijcxander H. Stephens. R.

Elberton, Geo., *25th Feb., 1856.*

Dear Sir: Your request in behalf of Mr. Thornton concerning the corn shall be attended to. Last Friday I got a letter from you dated 30th January. It was written in reply to mine reminding you to send documents to Dr. Hearn. How it was detained so long on the road I cannot imagine.

I see by the papers Shannon's appointment has been confirmed by the Senate and that he has gone back to Kansas. I read this announcement with none of the pain of disappointment, but on the contrary with a sense of relief. The position was full of responsibility, and while I did not intend to shun it, mature reflection since you first mentioned the matter had taught me not to covet it. If Kansas comes in as a free state the Kansas party at the South— the true Southern Rights party, of which I consider you and Toombs the head and front—will go down. The masses on this as on all other subjects will take no test of reliability, soundness and good policy, except success. Integrity, courage and sense defeated become trickery, cowardice and folly. This has been the case in all ages and will be to the end of the chapter. Expectation has been excited, our enemies at home have charged that the measure was a free-soil measure, that foreigners would rush in and defeat the South. It will be in vain that we say and prove the status was anti-slavery that the repeal gave us at least a chance,—they will bring up their prophecies and the result and all the reasoning and truth in the world cannot withstand the effect that will be made on the popular mind. I verily believe the effect will be the utter prostration of every man at the south who has stood up for us and the complete triumph of a set of traitors and fools. If the question could be decided this summer and the anti-slavery party prevails in the Territory, I believe Kenneth Rayner would beat Pierce for President. It was with my mind fully impressed with these views that I had resolved to accept the appointment, fully conscious that while success would have elevated me immensely, defeat would crush me and the cause of slavery with ine. You can easily imagine therefore that it is not unpleasant to think I shall not be called on to hazard so much. These are my opinions and I am fixed and settled in the belief that the next twelve months will show I am right. To one who has observed the signs of the times for the last six months it seems to me it ought to be plain that this struggle in Kansas is the very turning point of the battle between the North and South which has raged for 35 years. Of all men in the country the President is most interested to have the cause of slavery prevail in that new State. He has cast in his lot with the South and he must sink or swim with us.

So far as I am personally concerned I am perfectly satisfied with the turn events have taken and am under lasting obligations to you for the confidence and high opinion you have manifested for me. Do you intend to come home to any of the spring courts, and when is it likely I shall see you?

Thomas R. R. Cobb To Howell Cobb. E.

Washington, Wilkes Co. ga., *Mar. 4,1856.* Dear Brother... Thomas W. Thomas speaks kindly of and about you and you need have no fear about his action in Cincinnati unless *Toombs and Stephens* are adverse to you—if they are Thomas will act on their line of policy. He has determined to go to Cincinnati. T. & S. are very warm for Pierce. This is the universal feeling in Georgia. Next to him they (T. & S) want Douglas. I can't get either of them to come to the contingency of a Southern candidate. My own opinion is from their studied silence that they are *averse* to anything that we contemplate. I intend before leaving this court to have a still plainer talk with Thomas and will write you the result. I intend to open certain contingencies to him and get him committed. Ward1 is here. He is your devoted friend. I don't think Jim Jackson will go under any circumstances. I have not seen him. Ward tells me he has written to him. Old Thos. Stewart of our County has a claim before Congress—started thirty years ago. He is bothering me about it and it seems to me he has a good claim. He says you are managing it. Can you find time to look to it and let me know its situation. I suppose it has to run through the new mill.

I saw sister Mary Ann before I left Athens. She and the children look *very well.* My wife's health is very bad. I am determined to take her to N. Y. this summer. There is no other news.

Howell Cobb To. Pa. (Private and confldentlal.)

Washington City, *21 April, 1856.* My Dear Sir: Since I conversed with you I have met and talked with several of those who are disinclined to the support of Mr. Buchanan, who put their opposition on the ground of his want of complicity with the Kansas bill. I desire to state to you the manner in which I met the objection, that Mr. B. may be informed of the position of his friends in the matter. I state my argument briefly thus.

Mr. B. was in favor of the Missouri compromise as the best mode of settling the slavery question on the basis of a fair and equitable division of the common territory. He was in favor not merely of the letter but the spirit of the Missouri compromise and therefore advocated its extension to the Pacific Ocean. In this position he was cooperating with the *entire* South and a few of the soundest and most rational men of the North. In that movement he was opposed by the present pretended friends of the Missouri compromise. He advocated it *then* as a *national* measure, they advocate it *now* as a *sectional* measure. They commenced their advocacy at the point where his ceased. Had his counsels prevailed, the South would have been satisfied and the North would have had no just cause for complaint. The united effort of himself and the 1 John E. Ward, of Savannah, Ga., president of the Democratic convention at Cincinnati, 1850. south failed and in 1850 a new principle was inaugurated by the adoption of the compromise measures of 1850. The country by that act repudiated the principle of division (which was the principle of the Missouri Compromise) and substituted for it the principles of the Compromise of 1850. The incorporation of this latter principle into the Kansas act was the necessary result of the legislation of 1850; and the repeal of the Missouri restriction finds its justification, not only in any inconsistency in the former friends of that compromise, but in the refusal of its *former* enemies and present false advocates to adopt it and extend its provisions to the Pacific Ocean in 1850. In this view of the matter the friends of the Missouri compromise prior to 1850 find no difficulty in sustaining the legislation of 1854 in the Nebraska Kansas bill.

You will see that the point which they are trying to make upon Mr. B. is not that he is now opposed to the principles of the Kansas bill but that he would have opposed it at the time it passed. The view I have presented above meets that issue, and I think triumphantly. I thought it would be well enough for Mr. B. to be informed of the manner in which his friends were meeting this question and for that reason I have addressed you this letter. I need not say to you that for myself I regard the idea of Mr. B's unsoundness on this question as monstrous and not to be entertained by a southern man for a moment. The prospect for his nomination and election is now so promising that I desire every point of danger guarded against.

BOBEET TOOMBS TO GEORGE W. CRAWFORD. L. C.

Washington, D. C, *May 17, 1856.* Dear Crawford, I saw Mr. Baynes, the brother-in-law of Mrs. Catlett a few days ago. She has had nothing from Texas, and being without the means of supporting herself and children is somewhat in debt. She is anxious for aid to the extent of one thousand dollars, which she says will relieve her and enable her to go on. What shall I do? If you approve it I will let her have it on the security you suggested, and as you advanced in Texas during my absence and I am indebted to you for my part of your Texas trip, there will be but a small portion (about $125 I think) coming from you. Write me on the subject. I have not heard from my New York man who is now due here (about correcting the certificates). I think Beverly, to whom I have written, has the authority to make all right without him. I will give it thorough attention and endeavor to straiten? that point. All are busy about Kansas affairs, Navy Board, and squandering money generally. The Pres. nomination is now exciting great interest. Buck and Douglas are the most prominent, and are likely to beat each other and give place to some incompetent outsider. Give my best respects to Mrs. Crawford and your family.

Junius Hillyer To Howell Cobb. E. Monroe ga., *May 28th, "56.*

Dear Howell,... Brooks and Sumner have had some sport in the Senate. I don't see what your house has to do with it. When you see Mr. Brooks give my respects to him and offer him my sympathy and most sincere regard.

Of course the action of your committee and of your house will fizzle out.

Nothing new here in politics; we are getting up our July convention and preparing to make a rally for somebody, we don't know nor care who.

Are you seeking the Vice Presidency? You might make capital in the Senate; but you will do better in the cabinet.

Robert Toombs To George W. Crawford. L. C.

Washington, D. C. *May 30, 1856.*

Dear Crawford, Your letter of the 22nd inst. is recd. and I have seen Mr. Baynes and sent by him the proper papers to be executed in order to the payment of the $1,000. Mrs. Catlett and her brother are very willing and seem very grateful for the favour. Wilcox has not yet called to see me according to his promise, and as we have a recess now in order that the faithful may go to Cincinnati, I will go over to N. York and try to see him and arrange those certificates with him. I will leave tomorrow.

The politicians have generally left for Cincinnati. Douglas and Buchanan are still the favourites, very probably awaiting the fate you predict for both; but it is my opinion that one of them will get it, as there is much grumbling about the interference and intrigues of "outsiders." But I have too little interest to speculate upon so uncertain an event.

The Yankees seem greatly excited about Sumner's flogging. They are afraid the practice may become general and many of their heads already feel sore. Sumner takes a beating badly. He is said to be ill, tho' I don't believe it. Kansas seems to surrender at discretion, and no more can now be made out of the "border ruffians." They have taken away all of the Sharp's rifles from the friends of liberty, who are whining like whipped curs.

Gaza Way B. Lamar1 To Howell Cobb. E.

New York, *May 31, 1856.* My Dear Sir, You are in the midst of exciting scenes and words provoking and sometimes insulting perhaps to Southern blood and so prone to them as perhaps to mislead your usual good judgment.

1 A prosperous banker who had removed from Savannah to New York. Upon the organization of the Southern Confederacy he served for a time as its fiscal agent at New York. He then returned to Savannah and became a promoter of blockade-running.

I arrived here this morning from Savh. and saw you are on the committee of the House to investigate the matter of the assault of Mr. Brooks upon Senator Sumner, and I presumed to suggest to you my views as to the course you ought to pursue, independently and honestly, let the consequences, temporarily or permanently be as they may.

Viewed dispassionately in every light, the assault was unjustifiable, unmanly, illtimed, illadvised, injudicious to the cause of the South, and totally indefensible as to time, place and manner; and it is my deliberate opinion that to attempt to sustain it by the South or any portion of it will prove disastrous in the extreme,—for the public opinion can never be brought to approve of it. Senators had accused him of *fanaticism* and had in various ways insulted him as much or more than he did Senator Butler in his speech as I have seen it reported. He was therefore (give the Devil his due) justifiable under the *lex talionis* for his language and his sarcasm and ridicule.

Then, for a gentleman and a man of honor to assault another with a stick, giving him no opportunity of defence was cowardly and unmanly and cannot be justified. Then, doing it in the Senate Chamber and for words spoken in debate in which he has the Egis of the Constitution to shield him. Then, unfortunately and worst of all, for the South or the Democracy to sustain it is abominable and will draw down tenfold force upon them with all right minded men. *Now Sir* is the *crisis* for *you*. "Fiat justitia ruat coelum." Take the Bull by the horns and shake him lifeless. If Mr. Brooks cannot justify himself, *expel him;* and at any rate even with the best case he can make, if any be possible, he has so outraged decency, propriety and manliness, let him not escape severe punishment, that the constitutional right of speech be properly vindicated, that at least one Southern man in high place can be honest and independent and do right even to an Abolitionist. Be fearless and *lead* the public mind the right way, the best for the South, the best for the East the West and the North and the best for you. If fanaticism strike at you, and there is plenty of it at the South to do it, meet it and crush it by manly honest upright argument and you'll soon ride upon the storm.

You can do it without truckling to the North and without offence to any but the most infatuated prejudices of the South. If Mr. Brooks dare assail you as opposing him and threaten, let him be defied. Shield yourself under your official position on the Committee and let the world know that you dare to act honestly and independently even with Southern prejudices against you. They will soon evaporate and you will stand as a pillar unshaken by the storm and admired by them as well as the whole country.

John E. Ward To Howell Cobb. E.

Cincinnati, *June 3, 1856.* My Dear Gov., You will have heard by telegraph that the convention is organized and that I have most unexpectedly been elected the President of the Convention. The labors are very arduous and I will struggle hard to maintain the honor and dignity of our old State. I am grieved and mortified about our own delegation; the Buchanan delegates are few and very far between in our delegation. Dr. Lewis and your friend Buchanan are among the strongest Douglas men. Buchanan is rabid. According to my opinion, there is only one chance. That is, to keep them on Pierce as long as possible. The Buchanan strength may then be so fully developed as to induce them to go to him. Buchanan has only Murphy, Hull, Irwin and myself, but we will divide if necessary. The indications are so strong in favor of Buchanan that it is difficult to see how men can resist. Yet they do resist, and the intrigues to defeat him are disgusting, and I fear will succeed, and their success will be the defeat of our party, and this you may regard as a fixed fact. We will probably commence voting on Thursday, and will not adjourn before Saturday night, if then. Buchanan in my opinion will *not* be nominated, but I doubt if either of the others will be. Douglas in my opinion has the best chance of the three, though his vote at first will be small. I am however singular in this opinion, and certainly the wish is not father to the thought. But you know with what ardor I will support him if nominated.

Alexander H. Stephens To Thomas W. Thomas.1

Washington, D. C., *16 June, 1856.* My Dear Sir: Your letter of the 11th inst has just reached me. I by no means concur with you in the opinion that Buchanan as a matter of course could be elected. I look upon the approaching contest as one of great heat and fierceness, nor is the result free from doubt. On the most probable result however I cannot yet venture even a speculation satisfactory to myself until I see what the present fusion movement at Philadelphia will accomplish. Nor do I concur with you at all as to the reason Mr. Pierce was not nominated. It was not because he "shot down" the abolition traitors in Kansas but rather because he " shot down " all the true friends of the Kansas Bill in the Northern States two years ago— not with gunpowder it is true but with executive patronage by putting their enemies in power over their necks and heads. Many of our best friends at the North were *hostile* to Pierce, and to my knowledge they had reason to be. It is only within the last six months that the position of Mr.

1 MS. In the possession of Mr. W. J. DeRenne, Wormsloe, Savannah, Ga.

Pierce has been such as to receive my commendation. I know the position of his administration. That there has been a change in his policy I have no doubt. When he sent Reeder to Kansas his design or that of his Cabinet I am clearly of opinion was to make Kansas a free State. The reason the change in that policy took place I will not now stop to enquire into. Perhaps it sprang? from the same motive which caused weak and vacillating councils to change their tactics on the original proposition when it was first introduced into the Senate. It may have been discovered that the question was strong enough to override "puny opposition." But his conduct towards those men who stood in the front of the fight could not be forgotten by them barely because at the last hour he seemed disposed to mount the tide that he could no longer stay back and be borne upon its bosom again into power. I am now speaking of the reasons and motives on the part of those Northern men in the Convention who were opposed to his renomination. And while I would have voted for him if he had been the choice of the Convention, upon the ground that he is *now* right or has been lately, I am free to confess to you, as you already know, he was no *favorite* of mine— and he is one of the last men in the country I would head a rebellion for. I believe most of the difficulties we now have in Kansas have arisen from the fickleness, weakness, folly and vacillations of his policy in regard to that territory. Mr. Buchanan is not indebted for his nomination to any *abolition* or *free soil* or *anti-Kansas* feeling on the part of any of the members of the Cincinnati convention. The truth is there were no such members there. But I could give instances of men in that convention, true as steel to Kansas, who were against Pierce because of his course toward the true Kansas men "at the period that tried men's souls" on that question. But I need not open those points. The fact is as I state it, and you will find that there will be but few men at the North of previous free-soil proclivities who vote for Buchanan. *Som-e may* but it will be those only who have or will make up their minds to abandon their heresies and for the future stand with the party upon the *status* of existing legislation. My word for it you need have no apprehensions for the Wilmot Proviso hereafter if Buchanan should be elected. All men who look to any such result or who have a desire to produce it will fall into the fusion ranks of Black Republicanism which now seriously threatens to sweep the entire North. If I could today be assured of carrying the whole South, 120 votes, and Penn. , and New Jersey I would be willing to illegible. I am however not without hopes of carrying several other Northern States, to wit Illinois, Iowa, California, Connecticut and perhaps New Hampshire and Maine— and it may be Indiana also. But the contest in all these states will be the hottest ever waged in pollitticks, and just as directly on the line as if Pierce had been the nominee. Apart from Buchanan's declarations which I have heard of, that he would have voted for the Bill if he had been in Congress, apart from his public speech in response to the resolutions of the Penn. Democratic convention affirming that the Kansas bill was not an " act of unnecessary legislation" but an act of justice and equality, which resolutions he approved; apart I say from these considerations he has fully and cordially endorsed the Cincinnati Platform which fully identifies him with it; and upon it with all of us must stand or fall as the people in the contest may decide. Nor is his case at all analogous to that of General Scott in 1852. The Whig Platform of that year it is true was sound enough upon the slavery question. It was satisfactory to me for I *drew it* or helped to draw it. But General Scott would not *express his approval of it.* He took the nomination *with the resolutions annexed.* And it is well known that I never took any position against Scott until he refused *to endorse or approve the Platform.* Indeed after the nomination I stated to friends of his that I would vote for him if he would in his letter of acceptance give his approval to it. This he declined to do, and so far from it, distinctly stated in his letter that he would not make those principles the policy of his administration so far as the conferring of patronage was concerned. It was when this letter of acceptance made its appearance that I for the first time announced my determination not to support him. Up to that time I had not committed myself against his support. I expressly refused so to commit myself in conversation with Mr. Dawson and others just before they went to the convention, though Dawson and other Fillmore men were open and positive in their declarations that they would not vote for Scott if nominated. Dawson said if Scott should be nominated there could not be an electoral ticket got up in Georgia for him. I told Dawson if *Seward* were nominated an electoral ticket would be run in Georgia for him. That if the convention would put forth a sound and national platform, such as that which was adopted and which I alluded to, and should nominate Scott on it and if he would plant himself upon it, though I was very much opposed to his being the candidate on it, but nevertheless I would vote for him. These are facts. The Platform was adopted. Scott was nominated. He refused to give the Platform his approval and I opposed his election while Mr. Dawson voted for him. Now in the present case I have seen nothing from Mr. Buchanan tending to show that he was not in sentiment with us in the original Kansas movement. I know many of the warmest friends of his nomination were also the staunchest friends we had in that fight. I know he has publickly endorsed the declaration that the measure was not an unnecessary act, and above all I 73566—13 24 know that he is now openly and fully committed to the policy of the measure not only in the past but in the future, and I also know that the great body of the enemies of that measure both North and South will make the greatest possible efforts in their power to defeat him, and mainly because of his *present* open and avowed position. But in the case of Scott the *great mass* of those at the North who ran him and whom his election would have tended more or less to bring into power openly repudiated the platform upon which he was nominated. So much for this digression, which I hope you will excuse, especially as you think I had not " half so strong a case for going against Scott" as I have for heading a rebellion against Buchanan in favour of Pierce or Douglas. Now I assure you again I look solely in all these questions to *principles* and not to men—at least I look more to principles than I do to men. Douglas was my choice, and if for either of these men I would have been induced to head a rebellion it would have been for him. But in this case *duty* does not point that way, as I feel the pressure of its sense. On the contrary I feel in this matter very much as Douglas expresses his own feelings on the subject. And here I will remark that I feel fully assured and satisfied that you are mistaken in supposing that Douglas was not nominated because he backed Pierce. I know the most influential men from the North in that convention who favoured Buchanan's nomination were just as true and sound as Douglas himself. I have been with them in council in the darkest hours which ever enshrouded our cause. Their preference for Buchanan grew out of no opposition to Douglas's position or principles, from no disposition to yield an iota to the anti-Kansas feeling, but from a personal preference, and from the fact that Douglas's putting in for the nomination defeated Buchanan and caused Pierce an outsider to be taken up and whose whole policy until lately has been to strike down national men North and South. This is the reason for their preference; and it is not only a natural one and a legitimate one but an *excusable* one in my opinion. These are my views given to you as you gave yours to me. I am on the ground and speak of things I know. And as I understand the dictates of duty in the almost death struggle before us on the part of the friends of the Union under the constitution— as it is and ought to be maintained on our side, and the open and avowed enemies of both on the other side, they prompt me strongly not only not to opose Buchanan and thus cripple the efforts of the patriots throughout the land but to give them my cordial and warm cooperation. Whether this course will be the beginning of the end of my political ruin is a question of but little weight with me. If the country can be saved by a union of its friends who make common cause to preserve it on the only basis on which it ought to be preserved, I shall be content whatever future may betide myself. You express a sympathy for those true, national, constitution abiding men at the North who have been cut down for their maintenance of the right in days past. I feel the same. But you must allow me to say to you that more of them *fell under the hands* of Pierce and his administration than by any other means. These are the men who were most anxious for Buchanan's nomination. Some of them I know, and the cause of their grievance I also know. And it was "natural" as you say to look to some other quarter for a leader than to the hand that smote them. I know it has been said that Buchanan's friends were looking to free-soil support. This, I tell you candidly from an observation on the ground, in my opinion is a misrepresentation. Those who were desirous of the nomination of Pierce favoured such rumors. I could never find any real friend of Buchanan's that ever put forth such an argument. I was very anxious that the contest between the several candidates for the nomination should not descend to such a system of warfare. I am well satisfied that it was not founded in truth and justice. Buchanan's antecedents were also brought up— his expressions on Slavery expressed in his Texas speech, etc. Now upon all these points I have acted upon the principle of letting men's antecedents before 1850 be forgotten. On this principle only could I have supported Webster or Fillmore in 1852. And ever since the passage of the Kansas bill in 1854 I have not been disposed to make opposition to that measure a test for perpetual exclusion. I am willing to affiliate now with all who from this time henceforth will make the principle of that bill in our territorial policy the basis of legislation—those who will not only agree to let that bill remain untouched upon the statute book but who will in future apply the same principles to all analogous cases. The great result of getting this policy sustained and established in our Government is the object to which I am looking. If in Georgia there should be a union of parties as you anticipate in support of Buchanan I should be rejoiced. But you or I certainly do not understand the position of the leaders of the Georgia K. N's if you suppose their position is the same as Buchanan's. In their platform in Phila. in Feb. last, which Mr. Fillmore has endorsed, the taking off of the Missouri restriction is one of the grave offenses charged against the Administration. That act Buchanan approves. Neither Fillmore or any of his Georgia leaders have ever signified any disposition to make the principle of the Kansas bill as to slavery the basis of future-legislation in the creation or formation of territorial governments. To this policy Mr. Buchanan and the whole party, every man that nominated him. is fully committed. To get the whole country—all parties in Georgia and everywhere else brought to the same committal and acknowledgement—is the height of my ambition. This is what I wish above all things to see accomplished. If John Van Buren for instance shall take down what he has said and give in his adhesion to sound and right doctrines even at the eleventh hour I would not close the door against him. The triumph of the truth is what I wish to see and on this point I can say with earnestness and zeal to all who have heretofore fought us

While the lamp holds out to burn,
The vilest sinner may return.

I am not looking to the success of mere men or parties. I am looking solely to the success of principles. And I do verily believe if in the approaching contest we shall succeed, there will never be another sectional or slavery struggle in the United States, at least in our day. For the first time in the history of the country has the issue been presented. A right Platform presented by a unanimous party with a candidate running squarely upon the principles announced was never before submitted to the American people. Upon the result of the issue the fate of the country may depend. I shall not now anticipate contingencies or what may happen in case of defeat. I have a strong attachment for the Union as it was made and so long as it may be maintained under the Constitution. I have strong faith in its being thus preserved. But now is the time when it is to be put to the trying test. My utmost efforts will be made on the side of those who look with the same objects and hopes that I do to the future. But I must stop. I can say no more now. I have written already more than I had any idea of writing when I took up my pen. My fingers are tired out. I fear you can not decipher what is already written or rather scribbled. I have given you however my views with that freedom and frankness which I thought was due no less to you than myself.

John E. Ward To Howell Cobb. E. (Strictly private and confidential.) savannah, Ga. *July 5, 1856.* My Dear Gov.,... The Georgia delegation to the last convention were *not* your friends and would not have been if the opportunity had occurred. The feeling for you at the North, at the East, and at the West was overwhelming, but the South will strike you unless their fangs are drawn, and this can only be done by a distinct recognition by the next Administration. If this is not done I shall be content forever to abandon politics and pursue my profession in which I have no doubt I shall have more happiness. I think all of your friends will tell you that if the South is not *opposed* to you at the next convention you will most assuredly receive the nomination. There is but one man in your path and the reasons are many in your favor. If the selection is made from the South I regard it as certain, if Southern opposition can be overcome. You must solve for yourself the question how to do this and yet maintain your power at the North. If the parties were all united in the different States I would say go into the Cabinet yourself. I do not think this is now your policy. In the present condition of the country no President or any member of his Cabinet can be nominated, and the experience of both parties clearly demonstrates this fact in the last two conventions. I may be governed by selfish considerations, but I must let the record of the past answer if I could for personal promotion thwart the wishes of friends who have higher claims whilst I am professing to serve them. I write freely because I see the dangers which surround us, the necessity of united action and promptness. I must also say that since my return I find the very position occupied by me in the convention has excited jealousy of little men and family cliques. Such is human nature; and my power of serving my friends is diminished unless I am placed in a position where I can make it felt by friends and foes. There is only one in the whole range of offices which my circumstances will permit me to take, or for which I think I can qualify myself. If you shall think it advisable for me to have that I should for the reasons before stated be glad to get it. If you think your views will be better promoted by going into the Cabinet yourself, and write me that you are satisfied with the condition of things, you will witness the cheerfulness with which I will labor to promote those views in a private station. I have opened my whole heart to you. It would not be a human heart if much that was selfish was not seen therein; but if I understand myself my first wish is to witness your complete triumph. I have therefore made these suggestions; but you ought to determine on your course and then *quietly* but by every *means* pursue it.

James Buchanan To Howell Cobb. E. Wheatland pa., *10 July, 1856.* My Dear Sir: I have received your kind favor and am sorry to learn that the article in the Lancaster Intelligencer about Col. Benton has produced such an unhappy effect in Washington. It only illustrates the truth of the remark that grave consequences often flow from the most trifling causes. I am as little responsible for this article as I am for " Squatter Sovereignty ", although my friends in the South charge me with both, and this with equally good reason. I never saw the article and knew nothing of it until some days after it had appeared in the Intelligencer. The Editor has a correspondent in St. Louis who has written him letters gratis for publication for a number of years and they have been quite interesting and increased the circulation of his paper. It appears this correspondent, who went from Lancaster and whose relatives, all excellent Democrats, reside in the neighborhood, is a strong Benton man. The Editor told me he thought it was bad policy in the Washington Union to be assailing Col. Benton or any other man who was supporting me and therefore he wrote and inserted the article. There shall be no more of this thing, though it would give the affair too much importance formally to recall the article. Whether Benton be sincere or not (I believe he is) I cannot perceive the necessity for assailing him and thus affording him a reason or a pretext for keeping his electoral ticket in the field. Governor Price voluntarily assured me and pledged his honor for the event that if they would not compromise with their opponents they would withdraw their ticket. In a short time Col. Benton's sincerity must be tested. I presume it is not intended to drive from my support all who do not agree with the platform with which I am identified, heart and soul, and who prefer me rather than support a Know Nothing or a disunionist. There are very many such among the old Whig party in this State.

Maryland is a prodigy. The Black Republicans here calculate upon her vote for Fillmore with perfect confidence. Their hope is that I will have sufficient strength in the South to carry the election into the House and then they would consider Fremont's election as certain. Fillmore has not the most remote chance of any Northern State. He will not get an electoral vote in the Union unless it be in the South. Under these circumstances is it not amazing that the old line Whigs of Maryland should play into the hands of the abolitionists and disunionists. I speak of Maryland particularly because the Black Republicans speak of it in such a manner as to induce a belief that they have some real foundation for their hopes. In case of a dissolution of the Union, which Heaven forbid, Maryland and Pennsylvania would most probably be frontier States; and whilst we and generations yet to come would have bitter cause to deplore the dreadful catastrophe these two States would suffer more than any other members of the Confederacy....

Howell Cobb To James Buchanan. Pa.

Washington City, *14 July, 1856.*

My Dear Sir: I hope you may be right about Col. Benton; but I can't think so. As a matter of course we should be glad to get all the support we can, and no fair man will object to it though I can't answer for everybody on that.

My object in writing today is to give you the benefit of a conversation I have had with Mr. George of N. H. , the confidential friend of the President. I learned from him that the President is far from being pleased with the present state of things. He thinks that the support of himself and friends is not sought in the election. He refers to the fact that while Breckinridge wrote him a handsome letter on receiving his speech made here, that he has never received either from yourself or any friend of yours the slightest evidence of any appreciation of that act. In a word I fear that the President and his cabinet are *sore* and unless something is done to conciliate their feelings we shall receive less aid from that quarter than we ought to have. Col. George suggested to me that the President desired to make a visit to N. H. before the election for the purpose of making some arrangements preparatory to his final return, and that he thought that such a visit could be made the means of enlisting the enthusiasm of the President's friends in the election; but he felt at present that as your friends did not seem to desire any such support from him, he could not do it. The plain English of all this is that the President and his friends feel slighted and want some little attention. Perhaps another idea has entered their heads and that is that Burke and other enemies of the President being now very active for you are to be put ahead of them in the counsels and favors of your administration. I do not write to make any suggestion on the subject; but I deem it important that you should be in possession of all the facts that you may best know how to meet any contingency that may arise. The feeling of Mr. Pierce and the most of his cabinet towards me is such that I cannot approach them, or I would inform myself more particularly about them and their feelings towards you and your election.

We are poorly organized here as yet, but I hope it will now be improved as Glancy Jones 1 has taken hold of the matter and I have no doubt will throw new life and energy into the committee.

The accounts we have from the South are all that we could ask them to be,—not so from the east and west, though we hope for a reaction. I will not permit myself to doubt the result of the election; but at present things are not as favorable as I thought they were when I last wrote to you. Now that the House has acted upon the Brooks case I have no doubt in a few weeks the excitement will die away.

William Hope Hull To Howell Cobb. E.

Athens ga., *July U, 1856.* Dear Howell, Things are here about as I supposed they would be. The Calhounites are very sore-headed and would gladly defeat Buchanan if they dared, but I believe they will not venture to attack him except in an underhanded way. They have commenced the war 1 Congressman from Pennsylvania, 1S51-1858; United States minister to Austria, 18581861.

on "squatter-sovereignty," as you have seen in the papers, and will injure you and Buchanan somewhat in that way. I write this to get your views on that point.

Is it worth while for your friends to

defend that doctrine through the Banner? For we have no other paper in the State. I do not know whether it is best or not. On the one hand if you stand by and let the whole press denounce squatter sovereignty as being abolitionism and get the mass of the people to thinking that way, may they not use it against you hereafter with fatal effect? And also may it not injure Buchanan's prospects for his professed supporters to be making an issue so manifestly untenable, as that his letter does not avow that doctrine? On the other hand they have the whole press against us, and the Banner alone could do but little out of our own district, and a division and strife among ourselves may do us more harm than the other course. My own judgment is that we have the vantage ground, and that if we are ever to make a stroke at Calhounism now is the time. We have the national party and its platform, we have every national man at the North, we have the candidate of the party. So I should meet the issue if I were you, at all hazards. This is however a matter for yourself. I am ready to go into the fight, or keep still, just as you think best. Judge Jackson thinks we had better be quiet.

Write me immediately. I stirred them up *some* in a little speech I made on Saturday night. I couldn't help giving sound views a showing.... I want you to tell me in your letter whether any action on the slavery question has ever been had in the Legislatures of Nebraska, New Mexico and Utah, and if any, what? Find this out for me and don't forget it.

James Buchanan To Howell Cobb. E.

Wheatland pa., *22 July, 1856.*

My Dear Sir: As in duty bound I should have acknowledged yours of the 14th instant sooner but for incessant company.

I am at a loss to know what the real object of Mr. George is. I have too good an opinion of the President to suppose for a moment that he would require a request from me to induce him to employ all proper exertions to render the Democratic cause triumphant. This I feel confident he will do. Should I be elected his friends shall be treated by me according to their deserts, nothing more and nothing less. It would have been " comme il faut" if I had written a letter of thanks to the President, Gen. Cass and Mr. Douglas for their noble speeches, immediately after the result of the Cincinnati Convention was known. I wish I had done so; but the truth is that my house was filled with company to such a degree that I had no time to put pen to paper at the moment, and I did not suppose that either of these gentlemen would doubt my gratitude for their truly generous conduct. To write now for the purpose of putting the President and his friends in motion to support the ticket would be altogether a different affair; I feel much disinclined to do it. Perhaps some occasion may offer for me to write to the President on another subject; and if so I may adopt your suggestion.

I am glad to learn that your accounts from the South are all you "could ask them to be". The Black Republicans, in these parts either entertain, or affect to entertain, strong hopes of Kentucky, Tennessee, Missouri and Maryland. I say the Black Republicans because they expect to carry the election into the House by the strength of Fillmore and the Know-Nothings in these states. In the North F. is nowhere because the Northern Know-Nothings are always transferable. He cannot by any possibility obtain a single electoral vote in any free State. The news from Maryland is not favorable and if our friends in that state are making exertions they are unknown to me.

In this State, although not naturally very sanguine, I do not think there is room for doubt. My information is all which could be desired from every part of the State except Wilmot's district and three counties in the extreme west on the Ohio line. In all these counties my friends are up and doing. In this, the strongest Whig county in the United States, I think I am quite safe in saying that the majority will be reduced at least 3,000, which is equal to the majority which will be given against us in Wilmot's district. Our friends here are willing to wager that I will carry the county, but I have discouraged this because it could do no good and might injure the cause. I think we have more to apprehend from Fillmore in the South than any other cause.

My information from Illinois, Indiana and Wisconsin, especially the latter, is satisfactory.

I have always had a pretty firm conviction that the danger to the Union would eventually make us stronger in the North than our friends have imagined.

Howell Cobb To James Buchanan. Pa.

Washington City, *27 July, 1856.* My Dear Sir: I have just returned from Georgia. My trip to the South confirms my information from there. I do not fear the result in any southern state. In Georgia the majority will be the largest ever given in any presidential election, and I judge of other Southern States from the feelings of the people there. I feel confident about the South. If Mr. Fillmore had any prospect of an election, it would be somewhat different. He would then contest the states you mention, and perhaps others; but every day makes it more and more manifest that he has no showing and that a vote given to him only strengthens Fremont, and this conviction will ensure for you every Southern State. I calculate more upon the influence of general causes than upon mere detail information.

In my judgment the election turns upon your October elections. If we can carry Pa. for our state ticket every thing is safe—if we lose that election I fear that all is lost. Too much importance cannot be attached to the result of your state elections.

In writing to you about the interview I had with Mr. George, I did not intend to suggest any line of policy. I only desired to let you know the state of feeling in that quarter.

Don't bother yourself about answering my letters; I know that you have much of mere formal letter writing. I beg that you will not permit my letters to add to the burthen.

Howell Cobb To James Buchanan. Pa. (Strictly private.)

Washington City, *3 Aug., 1856.* My Dear Sir: I confess to you that I fear the administration is not as active in your support as they might be and I attribute it to the cause mentioned in a former letter. I speak *advisedly.* I have no idea that any thing will be done to injure your election that you will ever see or know; but you have been in an administration and therefore know how much can be done in a quiet way to affect the election, of which the world sees and knows nothing. An impolitic or injudicious appointment will tell upon a town, county or state, and in a thousand other ways can an administration do much good or harm, without attracting public attention. It is then important to have their *cordial* support if it can be done without any sacrifice of feeling or principle. The President as well as Mr. Marcy would be flattered with a kind word from you; and a kind message to the P. M. Genl. through some mutual friend would effect what I regard as important. I have had no intercourse with either of them, for my relationship towards them would not perhaps authorize it; but I *know* what I say to you deserves consideration. I need not say that it is on *your* account not *theirs* that I feel a solicitude on this subject. I have no suggestion to make further than what I have said, and you must attribute the repetition to the motive I have avowed for again mentioning it to you. I cannot write *all* that I would say if I could see you, and if practicable I would go to Wheatland but it is impossible.

Our accounts here from Illinois and Indiana are highly favorable; not so from Iowa though the indications of a reaction throughout the North and West are very strong. I repeat that you have nothing to fear from the South.

Howell Cobb To James Buchanan. Pa. (Trivate.)

Washington City, *4 Aug., 1856.*

My Dear Sir: If an arrangement can be made in reference to the electoral ticket of Maryland we can make that State *certain.* At present the ticket is composed entirely of old time Democrats. The last elections there show that we made very heavy gains in the Whig districts—indeed the only districts we carried were the old Whig districts of the State. Under these circumstances it is of great importance that there should be on our electoral ticket some old time whigs. So important is it that I think you ought to write some of your leading friends there, urging upon them the importance of this change in the ticket—some of the present ticket could be induced to resign and their places filled as suggested. This, as I am well informed, will save Maryland—otherwise it may be lost. You have seen the letters of Pratt and Pearce. Reverdy Johnson will be out in a similar letter, and I am informed from a reliable source that as soon as Congress adjourns the National Intelligencer will take similar grounds. This change in the electoral ticket will greatly strengthen all these influences.

My acquaintance with the leading men of Md. is too limited to admit of my having any influence with them. I do not think that I overestimate the importance of this matter. You have the facts and can judge for yourself. I think it would justify a special messenger from you to Md., if you feel disinclined to write on so delicate a subject.

I fear that I trouble you with my frequent suggestions; but you must appreciate the motives and pardon the intrusion.

P. S. My allusion to the Intelligencer is founded upon a confidential communication, and must not therefore be spoken of for the present.

Howell Cobb To James Buchanan. Pa. (Private.)

Washington City, *H Aug., 1856.* Dear Sir: I am so impressed with the necessity and importance of a change in the electoral ticket of Maryland that I make another suggestion to you. I understand that there is a gentleman on the ticket by the name of Bowen (Levi K.) who will do anything you want him to do. Could you not write to him to come and see you and get him to arrange for his own place to be supplied with an old time whig? I have written to other friends in Md. on the same subject. I have just returned from Maine. The prospect there is better than I expected to find it. Our friends there talk confidently of carrying the State. My own opinion is from all I could gather, that it will be a close contest but that we shall carry the State. If Hamlin is beaten for you by the combined votes of the Dem. and straight Whig candidates for Gov., we shall pretty certainly carry the State.

You see that the South is all right, as I wrote you it would be. Everything looks brighter and improves daily. I go home directly, filling some appointments on the route, and *if possible* shall then go to the West—Indiana and Illinois, and give what help I can to our friends there.

Kobert Toombs To Alexander H. Stephens. R.

Washington, Geo., *Sept. 3rd, 1856.*

Dear Stephens, I recd. your letter of the 29th this evening on my arrival at home from Columbia. Columbia court adjourned until the 5 Monday in Sept. on account of a very great freshet which washed away bridges, fences, etc., and prevented juries, etc., from attending. I would have written you before but I have been expecting you home every two or three days. I have been very active since I got home. Have spoken in Hancock, Taliaferro. Columbia and at Bulah, and tomorrow I speak at Lexington. The K. Ns are active and violent and were making some impression on the 8th Dist. The canvass was not well managed by Gardner and not very well by our local friends. I found them on issues that would have hurt them badly, but the tide is turning very preceptibly and many are coming back, and they are wavering all along the line. The order is vigilant and untiring and fighting for their necks,— in truth many of them deserve to lose them. All of us are in good health, the county generally healthy, but crops are miserable and what little was made "was in the bottoms and that was swept away by the freshet of Sunday last. It was worse in Columbia than anywhere I have heard of. I cannot possibly leave here before week after next. My business in Greene and Elbert is imperative. but after then I will come on if necessary. Write me to Greene next week. I shall speak there on Tuesday and at Elberton on Thursday next. Nothing else new.

P. S.—We hear today thro' Nashville (our telegraph being down) that you adjourned on the 30th. I do not credit it but hope it may be so.

Thomas W. Thomas To Alexander H. Stephens. R.

Elberton Tga., *5 Sept., 1856.* Dear Sir: The last letter I received from you was a hasty note requesting me to attend the meeting at Appling. I went, and was also at Bulah in Wilkes Co. This week I have spoken at Danielsville and Lexington and shall continue actively in the harness to the end of the chapter. But you must not think we can do without you in Elbert. You must come up here and canvass the whole county like you did before, and I want you to write to some one (Wm. B. Nelms, I suggest, lest I be out of the way) and say when we can look for you. I want you to make three speeches in'the county if possible, and the people of Madison and Franklin counties are exceedingly desirous that you should make an appointment to Madison Springs. But the great fight is in the 8th. They have boasted they intended to make this district the battle ground. It will never do for us to fall back here. All that I have hoped to do was to keep matters right until you appeared. Don't listen to what some may tell you. *This district is not safe unless you put in strong.*

You have perhaps noticed in the papers that I denied the correctness of the item purporting to be an extract from a speech of yours at Griffin in 1848 about the soundness of Mr. Fillmore. The newspapers don't represent the matter correctly—one says I *unequivocally* denied it—another says I *absolutely* denied it. Neither of these are true—I denied it absolutely and unequivocally so far as my belief went, and I stated the reasons—to wit, I understood at the time (1848) your opinion of Mr. Fillmore to be quite different and I did not believe you expressed an opinion you did not entertain. Linton denied it just as I did, at Lexington on the 12th, in a discussion with Hill1 and upon comparing notes with him we came to the conclusion the extract was false. He so said at Lexington and I so said at Augusta. One Murray, calling himself the editor of the Griffin Union in 1848, has come out and says the extract was submitted to and approved by you before it was published.

I suggest that in case Linton and I represented you correctly, if it is not advisable for you so to state in the papers. So far as I am concerned I care nothing about it. My denial was true as made, but it is due to justice that the truth be stated whichever way it is.

J. Branham To Howell Cobb. E.

Gainesville ga., *15 Sept., 56.* Dr. Sir: The news from Maine is alarming, showing the abolition tendency every where North. If Pensylvania fails to sustain Buckhannan at her October election, all will be lost, the South distracted. confidence shaken, and every thing uncertain. I would consentrate the *entire* canvassing strength from *all quarters,* North, 1 Benjamin H. Hill, of La Grange. Ga., then a leader of the Georgia Know-nothings. He was defeated as a candidate for Congress in 1855 and for the governorship of Georgia in 1857. He was afterward a Confederate Senator from Georgia; United States Congressman from Georgia, 1875-1877; Senator from Georgia, 1877-1882.

East, and South in that State untill the October election. Will it not be best to carry Toombs and Stevens at once to that theater? There will be time then to canvass the other states, Illinois, Indianna and Misshigan. The South is now safe. Should Florida and California go against Buckhannan, success in Pensylvania will restore them. Georgia is all safe; Jenkins's and Judge Nesbit's letters will settle it. I write in great haste. If you can spare a moment, say is *Pensylvania safe?*

Jeremiah S. Black 1 To Howell Cobb. E.

Somerset, Pa., *Sept. 22, 1856.*

My Dear Sir: I have been seeing a good many friends lately and have made some calculations. I do not see the least reason to doubt that our election in October will be a triumph for the truth. Thus far I have bated no jot of heart or hope. It is probable however that you understand the subject better than I do and that you have watched the current of the fight with an eye more skilful than mine.

When I speak thus confidently I say what I believe sincerely; but I will not deny that there is a possibility of Fremont's election, though it is but a bare possibility. What is to be done in that event? I do not ask you for a reply to this question, for I dare say you have not made up your mind. But the mere thought that such a thing *might* occur is enough to startle one.... His election would place the country in a condition so totally new that we could be guided in our course by no precedents which have been set since the days of the revolution. If he means to be faithful as other successful candidates have been to the party electing him he must remove every sound constitutional democrat from office and fill their places with men who have distinguished themselves by ferocious and senseless abuse of the South. Such men of course he cannot find in the South, and better men I suppose would hardly accept office under him. There is but one policy left for him to adopt (and that I suppose he will adopt), which is to repudiate the Black Republican platform altogether, declare himself the champion of Southern Rights, offer to pacify Kansas on the basis of Toombs's bill, and cover himself with infamy as with a garment by acknowledging that he has obtained the highest office in the world under false pretences. This would suit the moral and political calibre of the Know Nothings exactly, and I do believe that three fourths of the Black Republicans would be hugely tickled with the smartness of such a manoeuvre. Not more than one fourth of them believe what they profess; with the balance this campaign is a wild, heartless and unprincipled hunt after office. But suppose 1 Judge of tbe Pennsylvania supreme court, 1851-1857; United States Attorney-General. lt,57-1860; United States Secretary of State, 1860-186L

Fremont to be elected on the principle of avowed hostility to a large part of the Union, and that principle to be carried out in his administration: what would be the upshot of that? As to you yourself, your blood and judgment are too well commingled to allow of a doubt that you would behave calmly; but some of your people might need holding back. Do nothing rashly, and take no decisive step without first having a full and free consultation with your Northern friends. Remember that if the worst comes to the worst we will be sharers in a common calamity and something more than sharers in the disgrace. I am very sure that our united efforts can accomplish more for the cause of justice and right than anything which you of the South can achieve alone and unaided. At the worst we can aid in giving to you and ourselves the moral position in the face of the world to which we are fairly entitled. What I ask is this and this only: that if you should be of opinion (from anything which may hereafter occur) that the South is bound to right herself by taking a measure which the Constitution does not provide for, you will hear us, your true friends of the North, before you give it a shape which cannot be changed. If you will do this, even the election of Fremont may result in nothing worse than turning New England with her ignorance, bigotry and superstition out of the Union; and that is a consummation most devoutly to be wished. But this is the gloomy view of the subject. We are safe yet, and Buchanan's election will enable us to crush the rascals. Be of good cheer. Let hope elevate and joy brighten your crest.

Robert Toombs To Alexander H. Stephens. R.

Washington, Geo., *Deer. 1st, 1856.*
Dear Stephens, I got home Saturday night from Athens and found myself a good deal incommoded in the throat from arguing my cases in the Supreme Court, and besides took an additional cold which does not mend the matter. I think I shall stay at home this week and next to recruit. I need rest, even much conversation is hurtfull to me, and I think I shall keep quiet until the 15th Deer. and leave as soon thereafter as the weather will permit. We have had warm and wet weather for ten days past and it is now raining a northeaster at this present writing (7 o'clock p. m.). If it clears off in a day or two I shall go down to my plantation again for a few days. Nothing at all new here; Julia and Sallie and Clara all well and anxious to get to Washington before cold weather sets in. Some of our friends ire much dissatisfied with Buck's California letter, I among the number. Apart from every other consideration it was not done at the right time nor in the right way, and therefore it does more harm than simply being wrong. What will he do about his Cabinett? Cobb, Johnson and Ward are in the field thro' their friends—none of them offensively but in good taste—as far as I have heard. If he will observe two rules he will get along smoothly, and if he departs from either he will never touch bottom till he gets back to Wheatland: 1st. His cabinett must be composed of men thoroughly with us on the Kansas Nebraska issue—no dodging, no compromising it. 2ndly. They must be men who have the confidence of the section from which they are taken, especially of the party in it, and fit to lead. With these requisites I don't care who the men are; without them I should only care that no friend of mine should be buried under the ruin.

Write me the signs to this place until the 15th inst. My best wishes and congratulations to Douglas on his success personal and political.

Alexander H. Stephens To Thomas W. Thomas.1

Washington, *D. C, 12 Dec., 1856.*
Dear Thomas, Your letter from Atlanta enclosing Hill's refusal of my demand 2 did not reach me until late last night. His reply is truly an enigma to me. I have prepared and sent to the Constitutionalist a short card which seems to me proper. I know no other course to pursue. What I say is short and to the point. You were perfectly right about the pistols. I should not have hesitated to fight with any weapon I could have used. I meant only to exclude the right of choosing any kind of weapon, such as rifles, broad swords, &c., on the part of the challenged party. My letter was written in great haste for the mail, and I only intended to put you on your guard on that point, as it might not have occurred to you that a rifle was too heavy for me. I had a particular reason also for what I said about the pistols. You will see how I bring the subject before the public. I have been waiting the result of this correspondence to make a reply to his letter to the Savannah Republican. But for this I should have replied to that the day I was in Augusta. I never saw in the same space more lies, palpable lies of the meanest sort—just enough truth to give semblance to the whole—than that letter contains. In several particulars he states just the reverse of the truth. The fact was directly contrary to what he states it to have been. Write to me fully what you think of the course I have taken with him. It seemed to me that what I said ought to be short,—pointed but short. That was my judgment. I did not wish to be coarser in my language than the necessity required. Was I enough so or not? Was I too short or not?

1 MS. in possession of Mr. J. K. Smith, Grand Rapids. Mich. 1 As a sequel to a joint debate between Ihem In the presidential campaign. Stephens bad sent to Benjamin U. Hill a challenge to a duel, which Hill declined.

Lucius Q. C. Lamar To Howell Cobb. E.

Abbeville, Mississippi. *Dec. 17th 1856.*

My Dear Sir: I have been wanting

to drop you a line or two, but never felt certain as to the point at which a letter would reach you. My non-attendance at the Cincinnati Convention was owing, I assure you, to no abatement in my devotion to your interests, but to the firm conviction that I could do you no good there in any way. I presume you saw what a mob of a delegation went from this state. I was almost wholly unknown to them; and the only men who could have obtained admission for me as a regular delegate were most anxious to get themselves in, for their own purposes. My feelings towards you are, dear sir, just what they were when I stood by you, to the last, in Georgia. And if you should ever be engaged in any enterprise which may require the cooperation of true friends *outside of your own State,* I hope you will *think of me as one ardent, devoted and ready at a minute's warning.* Do continue to treat me as you did in Georgia as a friend on whom you may rely and in whom you may confide with security.

Dr. Branham, who has just returned from Georgia, says that your vote on the increase pay to members etc., will hurt you in your next race, that it will defeat Foster,etc! Anything in it? If there is anything interesting in Washington—anything about Mr. Buchanan— his future policy, who are to be his Cabinet, who his *peculiar* friends, what are to be *your* relations to the incoming administration, what Toombs's and Stephens's—and what your relations (personal and political) with the two latter gentlemen; and if it be not asking too much of you, I would be most happy to have the benefit of such views and suggestions as you might feel at liberty to send me. Your letters will be kept sacred, or if you wished it, consigned to an element more oblivious than the waters of Lethe. I have done but little for myself out here. I have attracted no attention worth mentioning. I may go to the Legislature next year, but outside of my own county there seems to be no movement towards me for Congress. I made four or five speeches during the campaign and they took well. I think I shall be able to get pretty much what I please from the people out here. I shall never want anything from anybody else, not from the Federal Executive at least. Is it true that the President elect offers you your choice in his Cabinet? Don't you think I ask very plain questions? I do hope you and Stephens are friendly. I have become a great admirer of him. If you and he *are friends* give him my very highest respects.

73566—13 26

Alexander H. Stephens To Thomas W. Thomas.1

Washington, D. C., *29th December, 1856.*

Dear Thomas, Your letters of the 22d, 23d, and 24th insts. are all before me.... I was glad that my *card* met your approbation, as well as that of McIntosh and other friends in Elberton.... If I had had the correspondence here at the time I should have sent that along with it, accompanied with a few words of comment thereon, specifying for instance the points wherein Hill in his letters to me had most grossly lied— such as the epithets against the "Know Nothings," which he put into my mouth most gratuitously and villainously, in order, seemingly, to justify him in using the retort, as he calls it, by way of reply, and for bringing it in in the manner stated by him, etc. , and especially his reply to the first question in my second letter. His answer to this question put to him by me is one of the most unscrupulous lies that was ever uttered by the most abandoned and profligate scoundrel on earth.

In his speech when he gave the Judas illustration he *did expressly* and *instantly* state: "Fellow citizens, I don't apply that to Mr. Stephens." The words and the whole fact is indelibly fixed upon my brain, for as he was proceeding with the sentence my ire was kindling at the offensive character of the remark. But no sooner had the words fallen from his mouth than he instantly said what I have stated, and this was followed up immediately with a most fulsome eulogy upon my character and ability, etc., and his high admiration for me, etc., which totally disarmed his remarks or the illustration of everything like intended personal offense in its application. It was in *reply* to nothing that I had said. It seemed to me at the time altogether out of place. I recognized it however instantly as the property of another. I knew it was borrowed or stolen from Underwood, who was the author of it. But I cared nothing more for it or about it, introduced, qualified and restricted as it was, than I did when it was told to me long before by you—with the exception that Hill lessened himself somewhat in my estimation by not crediting it where he ought. This was in his first three-quarter hour reply. I made no allusion to it in my fifteen minutes' reply because there was no occasion.... He made no allusion to it again whatever in his second reply. And it was only after the *boasting* reference he made to this remark elsewhere, and without the qualification, that it became offensive. His answer, therefore, to the first question in my second letter is simply an insulting response and an unscrupulous lie to cover his own mendacious gasconade afterwards. Besides these I might have noticed 1 MS. In the possession ot Mr. J. K. Smith, Grand Rapids, Midl.

some other points where he undertakes to set forth what I said, which are false, etc. But, upon the whole, I do not know if it is not best as it is. The correspondence was between ourselves upon matters known to each of us, and when he proved himself to me to be an unscrupulous liar and refused to give that satisfaction which was due to a gentleman, it was my right to post him or publish him. That act or fact of my so doing was on my own responsibility. That concerned him and me. The public had nothing to do with my reasons for doing it, or rather the reasons for the language used.... My challenge was based upon *his version* of what he had said to me in my presence, as well as upon the report of what he said at Thomson and Augusta, taking his entire explanation together. And the denunciation was based upon the same. It was not done with a view of justifying myself before the public for what I had done, but mainly to give him that *insult* which he deserved and which might change his feelings so far as to induce him, perchance, to call "in a friend." This I thought, too, he might be more likely to do with the correspondence unpublished. The whole tenor of his letters to me showed an insulting tone and bullying temper, and was intended to hold out the idea to the last that he would fight if a case should be made. Indeed, I was myself in great doubt whether he would or not. Hence I carefully, according to your suggestion, avoided everything that might seem, even, to close the door against him on that line. But whatever doubt I had on that point is now removed. I see he has gone to the papers with a publication which answers my card as "its merits demand" in his estimation. In other words, the spiritless cur tucks his tail, runs, barks and howls. Well, let him bark and howl on—and I may add, lie on, too. For his communication to the Chronicle and Sentinel is nothing but a tissue of falsehoods from beginning to end.... I am glad the correspondence is out. The people can see it and from that can judge whether I was too severe on him, or not severe enough, or form any other judgment they please. I have done just what I conceived to be my duty to myself. Every man can act as he pleases, but no man of recognized position shall insult me with impunity unless he *shirks* responsibility. This is equivalent to outrunning in a fight. A man who might call me a "damn liar" and then take to his heels might escape punishment from me, for I could not catch him. But the damn lie from such a craven would not greatly excite my ire. And that is the present position of Mr. Hill—he calls hard names, but keeps out of the way. It is true I cannot horsewhip him, even if I could catch him, which I would be justified in doing. But really I have no disposition to do this if I could. That some may presume upon my inability to use the cudgel or the whip I have no doubt; and that Mr. Hill is one of this class I have no doubt. But if I had the strength of Samson I should have done just what I have and no more. The man that cannot maintain his words by fighting if called on to do it is like one who says something and runs. But what depth of infamy can be found low enough for one who after *boasting* that he had insulted another *to his face* and that other had *cowered under it* (when in truth he had at the time disclaimed all intention to insult) upon being called on to stand up to the *language of his boast* actually backs out and runs!..

The most striking feature of Hill's communication, as well as his letters to me, is the villainous attempt to assume that my grievance against him was a *retort* in reply to what I had said in argument, which he holds to have been legitimate. This was not the grievance at all, as he knows veiy well. For nothing occurred in the discussion of which I complained or had any disposition to complain at the time. It was his *boastful* and *lying* account elsewhere of what had occurred and his *lying* and *insulting version* of it in his letter to me that I complained of. This was my grievance, and it was for this I called upon him to meet me face to face and maintain as a gentleman if he could. This he could not do. He had not the nerve. He *skulked*—and let him skulk.

I beg pardon of you for imposing so much of my private matters upon your attention. I should like however to have your opinion and judgment upon the propriety of writing out and publishing the speech I made in Lexington on this occasion. I have the notes I took at the time of his speech and can give the substance of what I said on every point in the speech of two hours, as well as the fifteen minutes' speech. From this it would appear how completely he was exposed if not disgraced in the argument on the points he made. And it would furnish the true key perhaps to his Judas illustration. The one he assigns is false. In his letters to me and in his communication he has given a *version* to my speech which, if not put right, may hereafter do me injury. Would it not be well for me to give that speech a durable form, according to my own account and report of it? Let me have your suggestions on this point and give me your suggestions fully and freely upon all others connected with the affair.

And now, having said so much about myself, allow me to say that I should be exceedingly gratified at your appointment on the Supreme Bench in case McDonald resigns. Johnson could not do anything that would give me more pleasure. And I tell you now, if events take that course you must not decline for any consideration whatever. I am not surprised at your disgust with politics, as well as the administration of the law. I have felt the same for both for some time, and for the former, that is, politics, a little more lately than ever. Perhaps you may think I have good reasons for it, as this letter abundantly shows. However, we live in a very bad world and must do the best we can in it, both for our own and its good. too....

Howell, Cobb To His Wife. E. Washington City, *6 J any., 1857*.

My Dear Wife, This morning's mail brought both your's and your brother John's letter in reply to mine. I have read them with care and interest, and shall reflect well upon the subject before I determine the matter finally.

The southern men who had been urging so strongly the name of my venerable old friend Genl. Cass begin to withdraw from him their support. Finding, as some of them have done, that a contest could not be got up between the old Genl. and myself, they now say that it is all a mistake about the south wanting his appointment, and not a few of them declare that they prefer that I should take the State Department. If I had made a fight upon Cass it would have played into their hands; but to their surprise I cordially endorsed the suggestion, and that knocked all their calculations into "Pi." How it is to work out in the end I cannot say. Mr. Buchanan I know is much embarrassed. I had a visit last night from Appleton of Maine who has been staying with Mr. Buchanan and who is to edit the Union. I learn from him nothing new but he confirms what I have heard from others. Appleton has been my friend and has urged all the time my name for the State Dept. in preference to Genl. Cass, and I have no doubt that in this particular he reflects the views and feelings of Mr. Buchanan....

Thomas W. Thomas To Alexander H. Stephens. R.

Elberton ga., *12 January, 1857.* Dear Sir: I wrote you by the last mail in reply to yours of the 29th December and closed with a promise to write again in a few days. My suggestions in relation to the course proposed by you of publishing your Lexington Speech were hastily penned and I have carefully considered the matter since. This more mature consideration has strengthened the conviction that you ought not for any reason to open or give a pretext for opening the controversy in the newspapers. If a false impression has been made by Hill in regard to that meeting, it must remain—there is no help for it. But I have not the remotest idea that anything he has said can hurt you or that anything he may say or do can help him. His plea of conscience and religion is ridiculous, and there is not a man in the world so much a fool as not to see it. The whole matter has convinced me not only that he is without courage but also that he is destitute of good judgment and sense. If he had any judgment he would have foreseen from your first letter that you intended to make a point on him, I mean a fighting point, and knowing he would not fight (for certainly he knew it at the start) he ought either to have given the necessary denial unaccompanied with a fresh provocation or else begun then his character of Christian and played it consistently from the beginning. As it is, there is no consistency in-his professions, and every body can and do understand that he is merely a gasconading coward who puts on the livery of heaven to save his bacon. In this land of Bibles all know it is as much against God's law to revile even when you have been reviled or to call one a liar as it is to kill. This is obliged to be the judgment of every man of sense, and yet I have no idea it has ever occurred to him that such will be the opinion even of his friends who have the faculty of reasoning. I am well satisfied there is a screw loose somewhere in his intellectual machinery. In your next race for Congress there will be some talk about voting for a duelist and all that but the result will not vary fnre votes against you on account of recent transactions, and upon the whole I think you will gain. for out of the two or three thousand Know Nothings in the 8th dist. there must be some two or three hundred who are men of courage and in their hearts despise a coward.

I fully subscribe to all you say about having done what you felt to be your duty in the matter and not caring what outsiders may say or think. No gentleman will fail to do anything for his own vindication because popular clamor may arise. So to fail would be the meanest cowardice. But I would regard public opinion this much—it is frequently a weapon to annoy or destroy your enemy, it is the very breath of a coward's nostrils and I would hurl it upon him with all the force I could give it. I was about to say I regarded it just as a soldier does his gun but this would be too respectable a figure—I would rather compare it to a Yankee wire trap, it is a capital thing to catch and choke vermin to death. One loses nothing by having public opinion on his side and it may greatly annoy one's enemy—if he is a weak man and a coward it will destroy. A coward alone it cannot destroy. witness Cone's case: he is not weak in the upper story and has no screw loose. Upon the whole I don't think it a very valuable weapon. but worth taking along. These were the considerations which induced me to urge the publication of the correspondence; that your card might have that justification in the opinion of the public which the whole truth entitled it to. The card had my full approbation, and in view of the insulting and bullying tone of his second letter it would have been weakness in you to have spared him. I can say to you now that if he had met you on the field I saw no way of stopping the combat short of bloodshed or an unconditional apology from him for writing it. If he had been game, that letter could only have been written to make the meeting bloody; and knowing that no man in senses would do that on the case between you prior to that, I was able to come to the conclusion that he would not fight and so told Linton when he brought me your challenge. Linton thought he was going to fight but I never did, either before or after your card. To tell you the truth I rather expected he would have me arrested for carrying him the challenge and I got Linton to go along to Atlanta for the purpose of giving him for security if he did. Indeed I shall not consider myself safe until after the next term of Troup court—he may yet procure an indictment from the grand jury. If he does I shall plead guilty and not trust an infernal Know Nothing jury in that county on the point of a recommendation to put me in the penitentiary, for the scamps might do it. But enough of him—one good has resulted at least: he is killed off I think so far as the next race for Governor is concerned, which he probably would have made on his side but for this quarrel and its consequences.

Our county elections went here to our entire satisfaction, so I understand they did in Oglethorpe. The Know Nothings were turned out there I heard. We agreed upon a ticket in this county for judges, taking three and giving them two. For Receiver two antis ran, so also for Collector, and no Know Nothing. For Ordinary our friend Buck Edwards beat his opponet 130 votes out of six hundred polled—no election held at two decided Democratic precincts. Buck was beat one year ago for Clerk of the Superior Court. They are entirely dispirited in this county and we shall gain on them rapidly and surely. I think we may count on 250 in this county, perhaps three hundred. Heretofore they have always controlled the two groceries in this county and through that means caught *every* floater. I am laying plans to break into that arrangement hereafter and if I fail I shall see to it that a new Buchanan grocery out and out is established and well stocked before the next election.

I am strongly solicited to run for the Senate next summer, and believe I would have no opposition; but I have no idea of doing it. My future connexion with politics (if any) *must pay* or I am ruined, and I don't intend that shall take place. In truth I am tired and sick of the whole matter, too much so ever to get into harness for the love of the thing. We are making a great to do about the rights of our section, when the fact is there are results in our state government which would induce me a thousand times quicker to resistance by arms than anything Fremont's party ever did or threatened. I say this, and I will stand by it and maintain it against all controvertors. If my state were to call on me tomorrow to take arms in her defence I would do it and adjourn my grievances; but so help me God, I for one would be for never laying them down until some matters were settled at home. The blood and humours of the body politic have become so vitiated and corrupted that it needs a thorough shaking and purging to be purified, and I am getting to be willing to give it this shaking and purging even at the risk of the death of the patient.

I see many rumors and letters in the papers about Buchanan's intended course in relation to Kansas. I have some fear that all will not be well. *Kansas must come in as a slave state or the cause of southern rights is dead.* And I don't refer here to any balance of the federal system or any fool idea of that sort. I care nothing how her Senators and Representatives may vote. It has been predicted by the enemies of Southern rights at home that the plan of her organization would lead to free soil. We have led the people to believe otherwise; if their prediction is fulfilled and history should write the verdict against us, we go down, and such knaves as Ben Hill & Co. will rule during the present generation. Mark this prediction. I am here away from the steam and smoke of the boiling cauldron and in many respects better able to judge than those who surround it. We can't afford to lose the point. We must have it our way or we are ruined. To stop to cavil and dispute about this or that course being in accordance with the act of organization or not is as great folly as to open moot courts to argue constitutional questions when the citadel of our liberties and existence is surrounded and assaulted. If Buchanan should secretly favor the free-state men of Kansas, as I see it charged he will, and succeed in bringing it in as a free State, he will richly deserve death, and I hope some patriotic hand will inflict it. In such an event there will be no hope for the South but a bloody revolution, and the stake will be worth the contest. Pierce, notwithstanding his fine writing, has been paltering with us all the time, keeping the promise to the ear and breaking it to the hope. He has all along done everything in his power to bring it in as a free state and but for his natural deficiency of intelectual calibre on this and all other matters he would have succeeded. Hence he never would appoint any but a Northern man Governor there. If he had been with us he would after Seeder's treachery have appointed Atchison or Whitfield. In the late case when the Judge bailed one of our friends and Geary re-arrested him and held him in custody after the order discharging him, Pierce showed his real hand. The order of Judge Lecompte until reversed by a higher tribunal was the law of the land, and Geary committed perjury, a breach of his official oath, when he violated and disregarded it, and Pierce did the same thing when he made the act his own by approving it and discharging Lecompte. This thing has been done and avowed, and no one opens his mouth, yet we are the sons of the sires of '76. We be dammed—we are a disgrace to our lineage. Such executive interference with the independence of the judiciary would have set England in a blaze and discharged any ministry in ten days, and yet we Constitution-governed and Constitution-loving Americans submit without a murmur. An impeachment neither of the President nor Geary has been hinted at. As gross an infraction of the Constitution occurred in Polk's time and nothing was said about it. It was the Mexican insurection near Santa Fe after General Kearny had conquered the country and left Col. Sterling Price of Missouri in command. He hung one of the parties for treason. Polk said the Del Norte was our boundary and on this alone he placed his justification for beginning the war. He could place it on no other; if the Del Norte was not our boundary he, Polk, had grossly violated the Constitution and ought to have been impeached. If the Del Norte was our boundary the Mexican whom Col. Price hung was guilty of murder if he killed and treason if he levied war. In the account of the transaction we read of a clerk of the court, a sheriff, district attorney and all the usual machinery for executive civil justice, and yet the offender was hung by sentence of a drum-head court martial. Polk instead of having him, Price, tried and hung for this act of usurpation and murder, promoted him to a Brigadier. Benton pretends to write a history for the purpose, he says, of " showing the workings of our system." This transaction he dispatches with these words: "many were killed in action and others hung for high treason—being tried by some sort of a court which had no jurisdiction of treason." He occupies forty pages with the mutiny on board the brig Somers, commanded by Slidell McKenzie. He is a humbug—he does not understand our system nor constitutional principles and does not know the truth by sight—McKenzie committed a murder prompted by his cowardly fears but he violated no principle of the constitution. The great principle of civil government which lies at the foundation of all liberty, that the military shall be subordinate to the civil power and which limits the power of a military commander to his muster roll, was here disregarded and trampled under foot and Polk rewarded the usurper and criminal—the Senate who ought to have judged and condemned him confirmed his deed and gave their sanction to the reward. Benton does not see and does not tell it. I called public attention to it in a communication at the time in the Constitutionalist signed Taos but those sleepless guardians of the public weal, as they style themselves, called editors, took no notice and could not understand what was as plain as the nose on one's face.

But I must close—it is late and I am tired and have written this by snatches as I had leisure.

Robert Toombs To Thomas W. Thomas.1

Washington, D. C., *Feby 5th, 1857?*

Dear Thomas, I received your letter of the 26th ult. a few days ago and called on a friend of mine well skilled in the laws of Alabama to ascertain what the law of that State was upon the case submitted by you. He was kind enough to look fully into the matter and give me a full and satisfactory opinion. The result is that Mrs. Ashworth has no right of action against either owners or officers of the steamboat. The steamboat law of that state gives a right of action to the personal representatives of any person killed by *bursting* a *boiler,* but is confined exclusively to that class of injuries; in all other respects the common law applies, which gives no remedy for personal injuries to survivors of the person injured. I am very sorry to find the poor woman remediless, for the case calls loudly for redress.

Why did you not come to Washington to attend to my bill as you promised? I could not account for your absence.

I concur with your strictures upon the administration in relation to Kansas affairs, but you are wholly mistaken as to Mr. Stephens's speech which you have doubtless seen before this time. I am certain Pierce for the last six months has done all he could to make Kansas a free State. Our friends there are now satisfied that that is his and Geary's policy, and he removed Judge Lecompte because he could neither be intimidated or seduced. I have arrested him in the Senate and if our friends will stand up to me I will give him great trouble in consummating his policy. At all events I will do my own duty and leave the rest to God and the people. I am afraid that Mr. Buchanan will fall into the same policy, tho' it is due to him to say he utterly repudiates the policy, and I do not think that he is at all solicitous that it should come in as a free state. I do not know what will be the prime? cast of Buck's cabinett. I think it probable that Cobb and Floyd of Va. will go in from the South, but I cannot tell who else will go in from our country. And at the North all is uncertainty. The scramble is not only not interesting to me but is positively loathsome, and I hardly feel the least interest in how it will terminate. Buchanan has been here for a week, until yesterday; he talked a great deal to every body *but said nothing.* I supposed he had his program in his pockett and therefore he got as little out of me as I did out of him. Outrages are so common in our territories that they cease to attract attention. The House of Reps. ought to have impeached Geary, but we being Judges could not move. We shall be badly complicated with England as the Dallis treaty will certainly be rejected, as it ought to be by a large majority.

1 MS. in the possession of W. J. DeRenne, Wormsloe, Savannah, Oa.
3 Dated erroneously 1856 In the original.

Stephens left yesterday in great distress about Linton and his domestic misfortunes. He left it doubtful whether he would return again this session. I shall leave here as soon as possible after the 4th March and will certainly reach home by our court unless providentially prevented. We are all in excellent health and now are having fine weather after a terrible cold spell. Write to me.

Robert M. Mclane1 To Howell Cobb. E.
(Private.)

Baltimore md., *Saturday Night—H Feby., 1857.* My Dear Cobb, I did not get to see you last night, as I waited after my dinner to see Bright2 who got back to Washington last night— and after seeing him it was the hour of an engagement. I had formed with some ladies of this city who were dependent upon me for the evening. I wrote you however a few lines which I sent to the boat this morning; but the messenger returned without finding you there. Bright told me that though he expected his visit to Wheatland would be no secret yet he was unwilling to refer to it or to the matters there discussed in any general way. Nevertheless he was sorry to miss you, as he had intended to communicate with you. Of course I will make no reference to that part of his intercourse with Mr. B. which had reference to himself except to say that he put himself entirely at ease in regard to all issues made between Douglas and himself in the conversation had between the former and Mr. B., and in regard to his own connection with Mr. B's cabinet, explaining fully to Mr. B. his desire to be left in the Senate. Bright has not changed his own original view that Gen'l Cass should be in the State and yourself in the Treasury; but I do not think he was encouraged to think that Mr. B. would concur with him in this view, and although he said it was clear that the *solicitation* of certain parties had induced Mr. B. to entertain the consideration of the suggestions made in support of Mr. *Walker,* yet he had no reason to suppose that the result of such *consideration* would induce him to select Mr. Walker for the State Department. In fine, though it is still *possible* that Mr. B. may be induced to invite Gen'l Cass to the State Department, supposing no other solution can be found for the North Western difficulties, yet it is not *possible* that he will in the absence of such a necessity prefer Mr. Walker to yourself for that post. Such at least is the conclusion to which I have

come from a full and unreserved conversation with Bright, and such I believe is his own conclusion and the one he would have communicated to you had he met you prior to your leaving 1 Congressman from Maryland, 1847-1851; United States minister to China and to Mexico, etc.
Jesse D. Bright, Senator from Indiana, 1845-1862.
Washington this morning. I urged Gen'l Cass to abandon absolutely all idea of a personal connection with the Govt. and to express directly his real feeling and judgement of your personal and political fitness to the Prest., but he was unwilling *for many reasons* to adopt my counsel, though I am sure he respected me for offering it. In truth however he could not divest himself of the feeling, which some have encouraged, that *he* ought and might get invited to the Helm himself.

I went over fully with Slidell last night the views I presented to you in the morning and urged him to write to Mr. B. explaining in detail all the motives and impulses that prompted certain Southern States Rights senators in their counsels, challenging Mr. B's attention to the fact that the senators from Delaware, Maryland, Virginia, North Carolina, South Carolina, Georgia, Louisiana and Texas had not and would not assume the responsibility of recommending Mr. Walker for the State Department and that the senators from Florida, Alabama, Mississippi and Arkansas had not and would not be *united* in such a recommendation, there being in truth but *one* from each of these states that *had* or *would* take the responsibility. *Slidell said he would write and write fully....*

I will myself write to some friends in New York who have access to Mr. B. and for whose opinion he has considerable regard and who were conspicuous and influential in the canvass *and who have intimated to him how such a preference would be received by the enlightened and conservative men of the country and I am sure they will embrace the occasion to renew and strengthen the expression of their feelings.*

I shall return to Washington this day week and if you have any occasion to communicate with me address me there at Willard's Hotel.

John W. Forney To Howell Cobb. E.
Phila. pa., *Feb. 18,1857.* My Dear Cobb, Just from Lancaster where I have heard *my doom;* and I find on my table your letter. It wounds me like a blow. Let me say you are wholly and utterly mistaken. It was only when I was informed by Col. Johnson of New York that you were willing that Walker should go into the State Dept. and only when I was informed that it was reduced to a clear choice between *Hunter* and Walker that I moved and that my friends moved. For Hunter we never will go or can go. Against him we shall wage war to the knife and the knife to the hilt. He and his friends in Va. and in the South, including Toombs, have ruthlessly, cruelly, and ungratefully attacked me and my friends, and by the Great God they shall find that if we are Democrats we are not negro slaves and dogs. But you are our first choice for State and several words illegible. You are in our hearts, and I said it today at Wheatland to Mr. B. and so did Magraw, that you were our choice before Walker, before Cass, before Hunter, before the whole world—*but anybody before Hunter.* It was given out oracularly that you were not to go into the State; that Hunter was; and we ran to Walker as our only harbor, but this only when we are assured that you would not object— indeed that you were with him (W.) and his friends at the National and gave Walker public credit for ability, statesmanship and versatility of talent. Now all is changed and Hunter out of the way and you or Cass is certain. Had Mr. Buchanan behaved like a bold Jackson and put you in at once into State no trouble would have ensued; but when Hunter our foe, *your foe,* and Mr. Buchanan's foe, is to be forced upon us, we say "take any shape but that." Give me some credit for fidelity, my dear Cobb, and let me know if your friends do not *stand justified by the facts.* Sickles, Magraw, Reynolds, Geo. Martin, Westcott illegible, Judge Black, Sam Black, all agree in this. They are for you *first,* for Hunter *never, never, never!* We shall go for Marcy first.

I go to Washington at the Inauguration to sell my furniture and to retire to a country newspaper. Vive Jones!

James Buchanan To Howell Cobb. E.
Wheatland pa., *sl February, 1857.* My Dear Sir: It affords me great pleasure to tender to you the appointment of Secretary of the Treasury. This you have doubtless anticipated. It was both my desire and intention from the beginning, as well for personal as political reasons to avail myself of your able and valuable services, either in the State or Treasury Department according to circumstances. I shall by this mail offer the State Department to our venerable and patriotic friend General Cass, who cannot fail to be agreeable to you. I shall be happy to learn your willingness to accept this appointment and in that event have no doubt we shall get on together for the public good in peace, harmony and friendship.

Robert Toombs To Alexander H. Stephens. R.
Washington D. C, *Feby. Uth, 1857.* Dear Stephens, Since I wrote you last some important events have transpired which you may take some interest in. Glancy Jones is out of cabinett. Buchanan wrote him he was embarrassed and asked him if a foreign mission would not do, he promptly wrote him that he disembarrassed him. Cass and Cobb have been definitely appointed, none others have been, but Floyd and Jake Thompson and A. V. Brown are pretty sure, but Toucey is in danger and Jones at sea. The tariff bill as it passed the house merely increases the free lists and reduces duty on wool. The Senate will amend it by reducing duties generally; its passage in the house is doubtfull.

I had a communication today from what I thought was very good authority that Pierce1 is preparing to run away to the free states. I believed in the truth of the statement but under your instructions have taken no steps about it.

Robert Toombs To Alexander H. Stephens. E.

Washington, D. C., *10th Mar., 1857.*

Dear Stephens, I have been so busy that I really have not had time to answer your letter of the 4th reed. a few days ago. Cobb says he does not want Pierce, he is becoming lazy and worthless. He and Felix had made arrangements for running away last Saturday night and Clark the owner of Felix had a police on the watch for Felix and took him and put him in jail and sent him to Richmond for sale next day. Pierce being in with him, they arrested him as a runaway and were carrying him to jail; but he got the constable to bring him by my house and I ordered him to release him and sent him to the kitchen. That night he was taken quite sick, and is yet with me. I hope to leave at the furtherest next Monday and shall bring him home with me if he wants to come; if not shall let him run at large as you requested me.

Things go off here calmly but without enthusiasm, indeed rather with indifference. Buck will vacate all the offices, or rather when the commissions expire consider them open. We have lots of office seekers here who are a great pest to those of us who are compelled to stay here.

I am glad to hear Linton is improving. Give him my best respects. Howell Cobb To.2 *March 30, 1857.*

Dear Sir: I reply to your letter at once, that you may not misinterpret my silence into an approval of your suggestions. I do not think that a citizen loses his political identity or independence by accepting office under the government. He does, however, commit himself to the service of the country, to the utmost extent required for a faithful discharge of the duties of his position. His political associates ought not to expect of him any service to his party at the expense of his duty to the government. Holding, as you 1 Pierce and Felix, mentioned below, were negro slaves.

M. W. Cluskey, "The Political Textbook," 12th edition, Phlla., 1860, p. 117.

do, an office of great pecuniary responsibility, and one requiring your constant personal attention, I cannot sanction the propriety of your absence from your post for the purpose of an active engagement in the approaching election of your state.

No one regards with more interest than I do the success of the national Democratic party at this important period in our history. But that success must not be purchased at the expense of the public interest, which might be the case if those holding high and important offices should absent themselves from their posts to conduct the canvass. Regarding your letter in the light of an application for leave of absence, I have withheld my approval for the foregoing reasons.

Robert Toombs To W. W. Bur Well. L. C.

(Private.)

Washington, Ga., *Mch. 30, 1857.*

My Dear Sir, Your letter of the 22nd inst. is reed. and I am obliged to you for the kind interest you take in my personal affair with Davis. I am very glad it is settled, and the mode is one to which from the attitude I have held in the matter I could at no time have objected.

You are right about the Mexican mission. I had a very long and satisfactory interview with Buchanan about our Mexican policy, in which I was happy to find he generally concurred. I advised him to send Benjamin to Mexico, of which he seemed to think well. He spoke some of Cuba also—I told him England, Spain and Mexico were his three important missions, the others were mere feathers for peacocks and genteel illegible friends. My proposition to him to acquire Cuba was to get American citizens to buy up the Spanish debt to British subjects, which now amounts to about 200 millions of dollars and can be bought at 17 per cent, or thirty-four millions for the two hundred, and then negotiate for payment to our citizens, and if not done to force it by running " negro law" on Spain. If we can do this and get a charter from the Rio Grande to Tiberon from Mexico *before* we buy Sonora and secure the Tehauntepec route, we shall do pretty well for four years. The charter, etc., must be gotten before we buy, to get ridd of grants for the Northern and Central Pacific routes which the North will insist on before they would give us such a charter and proper grant. The Tehauntepec route can be secured by Benjamin in Mexico in a week. I sent for Hargess? and had a long talk with him on Mexican affairs and very readily agreed to cooperate in both objects. I am a good deal urged to undertake this Cuban business in England, but I do not like to leave the Senate. Do not mention this to a single soul but tell me what you think of it. It is my decided strong conviction that I ought to be on this side the water and it is my present purpose to act on it. If I should go away I should by all means wish you at Washington. Indeed I hope this summer to make that arrangement any how. I am obliged to go to Texas in about a fortnight but return again about the 1st of June. All quiet in Georgia, some anxiety about our nomination for govr., but it will pass away after the convention. My election comes off this fall, but it does not seem as tho' there will be any serious opposition to me.

Howell Cobb To Alexander H. Stephens. R.

(Private.)

Washington City, *10 June, 1857.*

Dear Stephens, I have received your letters and would interpose in the case of your friend Sturdevant but for the rule I mentioned to you and which I am more and more convinced every day I must adhere to.

I sincerely hope you have no serious idea of declining to run for Congress. It would be bad policy for yourself, but of that I have no right to speak. It would be a hard blow upon your friends in Ga. and the principles which I know you are anxious to see triumphant. Your withdrawal would endanger your own district and almost render certain the loss of the 7th and 3rd. It would weaken our ticket throughout the State. These are considerations enough, but there is another of more importance. Your place cannot be filled in the House. You know that as well as I do. Would it be right then for you at this juncture to withdraw? The question admits of but one answer, and I can assure you that I speak the earnest voice of all our friends here in urging upon you not to think of leaving Congress at this time.

I am still hard pressed with my business, but I felt that I must write you these hasty lines.

Thomas W. Thomas To Alexander H. Stephens. R.

Elberton ga., *15 June, 1857.* Dear Sir: The spirit moves me to write you a letter. I am in trouble and would give ten dollars for the opportunity of talking to you one hour. My trouble is this—I have just read Walker's inaugural in Kansas and if the document I have seen is genuine it is clear Buchanan has turned traitor. I have read and reread, I have thought over and turned the thing in my mind every way, and there is no way to escape the damned spectre. It stands there and glares upon us. *We are betrayed.* He, Walker, is reported as travelling to that country through the North, gathering up a freesoil suite and speaking with them (Wilson and Robinson) to the same crowd, taking introductions to the people from Robinson, and attempting to mask his vile hypocrisy with the flimsy twaddle of a slave state in the Indian country south of Kansas. He says Buchanan and his cabinet knew his opinions before he left Washington. If this be true or if Buchanan retains him thirty days we are ruined, and ought to be if we sustain Buchanan. I want you to give me your views in a letter directed to Milledgeville as I shall not have time to hear from you here before I leave for the convention to be held the 24th. I see no escape from the conclusion I have come to about this inaugural. He puts himself in thought, feeling and hope with our enemies, and that's the truth. Our victory is turned to ashes on our lips, and before God I will never say well done to the traitor or to his master who lives in the White House. In all your public career you have never been placed in a situation of as much difficulty or in one which called for so much firmness. If I had seen Walker's inaugural prior to the 1st Tuesday in May I would have cut off my right hand before it should have written the resolutions passed here approving Buchanan's administration. I believe all the counties have nominated you, and I believe it is a high public duty that you should serve in Congress again; but it strikes me you never can approve the administration in this Kansas business. I take this for granted, and I know I cannot be mistaken unless the papers lie about what Walker said. Now if you run, differing with the administration on this, which is all we elected it for, what policy will you run on? Can the party in the 8th, flushed with success and just beginning to suck the spoils pap, be induced to peril their present happy condition by striking for Southern rights? I have always said, and I think so now, that if Kansas is admitted as a free state we are ruined. It will be useless to attempt explanations and excuses, we are condemned, and I think justly. We have made the people believe it will be a slave state and we ought to make it good or not assume to hold the reins of power. With my present views I can never vote in the democratic convention for a resolution approving this vile treachery of Buchanan. I speak freely to you as I have always done—you will give it only such weight as it deserves.

Howell Cobb To Alexander H. Stephens. R.
(Private.)

Washington City, *17 June, 1857.* Dear Stephens, I have this moment placed your letter in the hands of Joseph Baker, Collector at Philadelphia, who promises me to obtain and have forwarded to you at an early day the information you want about the vote last fall in Pa. If he fails let me know; but *he will not fail* as I have impressed upon him the importance of attending to it promptly.
73566—13 26

From what you write and what I see in the papers I fear that Walker's inaugural address is to do us harm in the South. That part that you object to I never saw or heard of until I read it in the papers. It could have been omitted without injuring the object which I think he had in mind. I confess that I did not like the argument or presentation of the question by him. My opinion is that he thought at the time he wrote it that Kansas would come in as a slave state and his object was to satisfy the other side that they would have a fair chance to be heard. This is my reading of it though I never heard any thing from him on that point before he left.

The point made by the Constitutionalist against submitting the constitution to the people I do not think is well taken. The true policy is to say nothing about slavery in the constitution, and let the state be admitted as it is, and the question of slavery can be decided by them afterwards. That is my idea, and I believe the correct one, and will in the end be adopted by the convention if our friends there act wisely. Now that the principle of the Kansas bill is fully and thoroughly recognized by the administration, just *as our own people* demanded it, it would be a hard blow to lose the whole benefit of it by having a false issue made before the country. I write this hasty note with constant interruptions and no time to look over what I have written.

Howell Cobb To Alexander H. Stephens. R.
(Private.)

Washington City, *18 June, 1857.*

Dear Stephens, I have this moment received yours of 15th and though I wrote you a hasty note last night, I reply at once.

It is proper that you should know the view of the administration in sending out Gov. Walker to Kansas. This I attempted to give you at the time and I now repeat what I then said. The President desired in good faith to carry out the principle of the Kansas bill as laid down by himself and in conformity to the doctrines of the Supreme Court in the Dred Scott case. This was entirely acceptable to our people. He did not wish Gov. Walker or any other official of the Government to use his position to affect the decision of the slavery question, one way or the other. He was indifferent to that decision, so it was fairly and honestly made by the people of Kansas, and this was the position of every member of the cabinet. Since the reception of Gov. Walker's inaugural there has been no mention of the subject in cabinet, and I now write this hasty note as the reflection of my own mind. I think it unfortunate that Gov. Walker made any argument in his inaugural on the subject, but I feel satisfied that I gave you in my note of last night the true solution of his motives. The propriety of submitting the constitution to the people for ratification was discussed and approved but with no view to affecting the result. It was believed that without such submission we could not justify and carry through the admission. I feel fully justified in repeating that the President and his cabinet were not only willing but anxious that this question should be settled without any outside influence from Government.

AVhen I read Walker's address I feared that the construction you indicate would be placed upon it. *My* reading of it was cursory and I have not since read it, but it did not impress me as unfavorably as you seem to be. I should like exceedingly to see and talk with you fully and freely about this matter as I find it impossible to say on paper just what I wish to say. Since I commenced this letter I have been interrupted more than a dozen times—and will be again before I get through. It is all important that we should make no issue that cannot be fully maintained on the line of our past policy on this subject. That you understand fully, and must see that our people do not get off the line.

Robert Toombs To W. W. Bur Well. L. C.

Washington, Ga., *July 11, 1857.*

My Dear Sir: I returned about two weeks since, after a very long and except an accident a very pleasant trip in Texas, and I took? the woods and prairies, camped out, and gave the country a pretty thorough general exploration. Just as I left Northern Texas, a horse ran away with a friend's buggy with whom I was travelling, threw us out and badly sprained one of my ankles, which has kept me on crutches until within the last two or three days. I am now improving and doing pretty well with a walking cane for short distances.

I very fully concur with you on the propriety of my remaining in the country and have recently again authorized the use of my name for the Senate. As yet there seems to be no opposition from within, but I can not tell what may turn up.

Was there ever such folly as this Walker has been playing in Kansas? Everything was quiet, going on smoothly, to some decision and determination, and the country was quite indifferent what that should be, when he puts in, and merely to give himself consequence and to seem to settle what was rapidly settling itself, raises the devil all over the South. And this is not the worst of it. Buchanan intends to sustain him, and thereby rain himself and his administration. I marked with great pain the article in the Union of the 7th inst. It is disingenuous and does not state the case. He argues that the convention ought to submit the new constitution to the people. Admit it and it does not justify Walker. In the first place it is none of his business whether they do or not. It is their business and not his, and he was in no way called upon even for his advice, much less his arrogant and insolent threats that unless they carried out his will in the premises Congress *ought not, would not* admit the state, and he would join the free-soilers. Now the convention ought never under any circumstances to comply with his demand that it be submitted to all the people who may happen to be in Kansas when the ratification takes place, and I trust they will give him a chance to carry out his threat and join the free-soil traitors. His "isothermal" and "thermometrical" arguments and follies I suppose simply means that Kansas is too cold for " niggers," and that is the very question which the people in convention are called on to decide, and his argument (in his position) is a direct government interference, unless he is recalled, and it is this which so much aroused the South. The condemnation of him is universal as just. I did not see the list of your Senators elect, but hope you have succeeded. I would be glad to sell your friend if he likes my part of Texas a good tract of land cheaply and on any terms he wants and could doubtless make his residence there useful and advantageous to both of us. Let me hear from you.

Thomas R. R. Cobb To Howell. Cobb. E.

Madison Springs ga., *July 15th, 1857.* Dear Brother, We are here spending a few days. Your letter was forwarded to this place. Judge Tom Thomas has been here for the last 24 hours, and has talked about nothing except Walker and Kansas. He professes the greatest friendship for you, and says that Toombs and Stephens have the same; but he says that they will undoubtedly denounce the Administration on this Walker business. In fact he tells me that Toombs has already denounced it publicly in a speech in Washington. I have endeavored to allay him and to present to him the inevitable result—a division of the Democratic Party—and the fusion of the seceders with the Americans. This he denies, but professes great concern that the Administration should do something to manifest its disapprobation of the objectionable features in Walker's inaugural. The complaint is now narrowed down to the Isothermal line and the dictation of *the persons* to whom the constitution should be submitted for ratification. He insists that there is very great difference between Walker and the position taken by the Union (Judge Black). The latter refers properly the question of the qualification of voters to the convention. We have disputed as to Walker's position, he insisting that Walker *dictates* that. hey *shall* submit it to a vote of *all* the persons in the Territory at th?ate of the voting. and that he says that Mr. Buchanan stands on the sSft016 Position. We have not the Inaugural or Topeka speech here and caylnot aSree as to their contents. I give you these items / " that you may understand the points made. They clamor for *removal* and Toombs swears his appointment shall never be ratified in the Senate. I asked Thomas how it was possible for the Administration *now* to remove him. He says he *lies* on Mr. Buchanan, alleging instructions which he never had, and that Mr. B. ought to yield to his friends. I suggested that if Mr. Walker was sent on a foreign mission, would that satisfy them. He replied,—send him anywhere so he is gotten out of Kansas.

A split in Georgia is inevitable. I believe the people if properly enlightened will sustain the Administration although I sincerely believe *Walker* to be *its foe.* He is playing for the succession. Simmons in this district will try to make a point on him here and put himself among the ultras. There is trouble ahead. Nothing new. I cannot go North before Fall.

P. S. The article in the Constitutionalist signed "Southern Rights" was by Genl. Gerdine.

Lucius Q. C. Lamar To Howell Cobb. E.

Oxford, Miss., *July 17th, 1857.*

Dear Sir: For the first time in my life I write to you with a feeling of embarrassment. But I am acting from the same impulse which linked me to your name and fortunes in Georgia, admiration of the statesman and love of the man. The cloud which obscures *your* prospects will ever cast its shadow over mine.

You doubtless have learned ere this that I have been nominated for Congress. I was anxious to go under your Administration in order to give you a more efficient support than I had been able to give. If I cannot do this it will give me no pleasure to go to Congress. I presume you have seen my resolutions on Walker and the report of my remark about yourself. I felt confident from what I knew of you that you could not sanction such detestable conduct. But the givings out of the Union and of the Examiner give me some uneasiness. Those papers have taken up the defence of Walker in a real *ex-cathedra* style. If they express the views of the Administration I regret that they so palpably misconceive the grounds of our opposition to Walker's conduct. We are represented as being opposed to the Kansas convention submitting their constitution for adoption or rejection to the people of Kansas. This is not true. So far as this point is concerned our objection goes no farther than to Walker's threat to make such a course a *sine qua non* of admission as a state into the Union. He says in his Topeka speech and intimates in his inaugural that the constitution to be formed, unless so submitted, will be destitute of any binding authority. He certainly cannot speak the sentiments of the Administration in that. I cannot entertain the thought that *you* would oppose the admission of a slave state merely because her constitution was not submitted back to the people. I think the argument of the Union that the people of Kansas are not acting under the authority of Congress in preparing to form a state constitution is utterly empty and ridiculous. Why Robert J. Walker himself admits that act convoking the convention is fully authorized by the organic law of the territory. But suppose there was not? Was there any law authorizing the people of California to form their constitution? Are we of the South to be made to see California hurried into the Union against all law and all precedent *because she fa a free state* and Kansas subjected to the rigors of the inquisition because she *has a chance* of being a slave state? I do not wish to argue the point because I fear it is too late. Great injustice is done to those of us who denounced Walker. They are not enemies of the Administration. As God is my witness my main object was to give you and the Southern members of the Cabinet moral support in your effort to have Walker repudiated and condemned by the administration; for I felt sure you would make such an effort. It is a great error to think that this feeling is confined to a few. It pervades the whole mass of the Democracy here. You can't find one man who avows his approval. If the administration adopts Walker's policy it may cause, the Missi. Democracy to cease their *expressions* of indignation. For we feel that there is no other party which will do us any justice at all. But the enthusiasm of the party will vanish, the energy and momentum of an approving public sentiment will be irretrievably lost to the Administration....

Howell Cobb To Alexander H. Stephens. R.

(Private.)

Washington City, *21 July, 1857.*

Dear Stephens, The letter of Mr. Gordon to which you referred was not enclosed in your letter, and as you made no reference to its contents I am at a loss what to say or do about it. I shall have to await something further from you on the subject....

There seems to be but one point on which there is much difference of opinion between us about the Walker embroglio, and that is who shall be qualified voters on the question of ratification. I think you are wrong on that point and that the rule I lay down would be the correct one. It would be applying to Kansas the same principle which is enforced in every state in the Union as far as I know—certainly the rule in Ga. when our people rejected a constitution which had been formed by them by a convention. But I will not argue the question further as it is one for the decision of the convention and I have no doubt will be satisfactorily disposed of by them.

I think you do injustice to our northern friends in your suspicion that they are willing to stand by a principle *only* when it works in favor of their section. I have seen nothing in my intercourse with them on this Kansas question to justify such a suspicion. The truth is they seem more willing to abide the principle than some of our extreme Southern friends. I have never heard the President or a member of his cabinet express a wish that the question in Kansas should be decided one way or the other except the southern men who desired Kansas to be a slave state and one of them from the North who expressed the same opinion and wish. Since I wrote to you I have seen Orr and other southern men directly from Kansas. From all of them I hear the same statement as to the condition of things there. Orr says that Walker *has made* no public opinion in Kansas but only conformed to what was public opinion among our friends when he got there. This I have no doubt is the fact. If he had avoided the blunder to which I have heretofore referred the same results would have followed and he would have escaped the heavy reproaches which his course has brought both upon himself and the Administration. You see by the papers that he is now engaged in a fierce contest with the Topeka men. There is not and never can be the slightest sympathy between them. Walker I am satisfied has acted in concert and cooperation with our friends throughout. Such is our information from *everyone* who either comes or writes from the territory. I have no doubt that the action of the convention will be sustained by all our friends and be such as to unite the entire democratic party in its support. I hope that the storm has blown over in Ga., and that we may regain all lost ground.

Howell Cobb To Alexander H. Stephens. R.
(Private.)

Washington City, *July 23,1857.*
Dear Stephens, I have this moment received yours of the 18th inst. By this mail I forward you a pamphlet copy of the decision of the Supreme Court in the Dred Scott case and hope it may reach you safely and in time for your purposes. I am glad to hear that things look better in Ga. Such are my advices from various quarters. I see that Goulden has been nominated in the 1st district. This I fear is a bad move and if Seward runs as I expect he will we shall lose that district.1 I was delighted to hear of Crawford's2 renomi 1 In the congressional election of 1857, in the first district of Georgia, James L. Seward, Democrat, received 5,870 votes; Francis S. Bartow, American, 5,093; and W. B. Goulden, Independent Democrat, 508.

2 Martin J. Crawford, judge of the superior court of Georgia (Chattahoochee circuit), 1863-1855 and 1875-18S0; congressman from Georgia, 1855-1861; associate-justice of the supreme court of Georgia, 1880-1883. nation. Unless Linton1 can be elected in the 7th I fear we shall not carry more than five districts. Will you have opposition, and who will it be? I am glad to hear that Toombs is in good spirits, for the late issues may endanger his election. I hear that McDonald is after him. Toombs must not fall into the error of thinking that his success will be promoted by competing with McDonald for the extremists. His reliance is and should be upon the main body of the party, composed of the most conservative and national men. His speech at Washington was rather fiery, though pretty well guarded on the main points. I had hoped to have been in Athens at Commencement, but it is now doubtful. The President wants to go to Bedford Springs about that time and seems unwilling that any of us should be away during his own absence. It would be well if our friends could get together at Athens and relieve the embarrassments which the unfortunate resolution of our convention has thrown around the canvass. I know Judge Brown2 very well and he will conform to the judgment of his friends, but if left to his own may blunder. This canvass is deep water and it requires prudence, sagacity and reason? to conduct it successfully. I should be happy to hear from you as your convenience may admit of your writing.

P. S.—In regard to Forney's paper, I have no fear of its going into opposition now, as I believe that it will be identified with the Walker movement for the succession. There is no doubt of the fact that Walker is playing a bold game for the succession and is strongly backed up in N. Y. How far the Herald is committed to it I don't know. My opinion is that any man who puts in *now* for the succession will have his hand ruled out before the game begins. We shall carry Pa. this fall by an overwhelming majority. You may bet on that.

Robert Toombs To Alexander H. Stephens. R.

Washington, Geo., *Aug. 3rd, 1857.*
Dr. Stephens, Have you a copy of the names of the members of the last Legislature and their addresses. If so, please send it to me. I am getting off all my congressional documents, seeds, etc. I think that I shall clear them out this week if I keep well and meet with no unexpected interruption. I think it about as well to set my house (political) in order as I hear from different quarters some "better Democrats" than I am are after me. Bah! what fools! If they succeed and shall labour half as hard as I have and succeed no better I pitty them from the bottom of my soul.

Julia and I are alone except Gabriel's children. He expects to be at home this week, his little son has been operated upon and it seems 1 Linton Stephens was defeated for Congress In 1857, receiving 4,525 votos as against 4,800 for Joshua Hill.

a Joseph E. Brown then the Democratic nominee for the governorship. He was elected by 57,631 votes against 46,880 for Bejamin H. Hill, the American candidate. thus far with entire success. If I was not so busy I would go at once to the Virginia Springs for the summer as I am getting very feeble under this desperate weather, altho' well except my bowels. Come over when you have liesure.

Robert Toombs To Alexander H. Stephens. R.

Washington, Geo., *Aug. 4,, 1857.*
Dear Stephens,... I got a letter Monday last from Lexington asking me to go

to Lexington Friday to meet Ben Hill. I wrote by the messenger that if our friends would see Ben's committee and they would agree to accept debate (on the terms proposed by me and accepted by Hill last fall) that I would come, but not otherwise, and I did not choose to go so far on a fool's errand. I did not like the employment of fighting skunks nohow, but supposed there was a necessity in this district at least. Yesterday the Democracy nominated Hunter C. Pope for the State Senate in lieu of A. Pope, Jr., declined. The K.Ns put up Anderson, Wingfield and Tal Jones, a strong ticket for the county, which will make a good run, especially as there is a good deal of bad feeling with some of the Democrats towards our ticket. The Democracy seem to lie by when out of joint, and if they do not improve soon we shall be fighting to carry the State in one month. I hear a good deal of Johnson's movements; his friends are active and I think have had success in county movements. The leading men in Lumpkin's, Warren's, Bailey's and Cobb's districts are against me. We look for my brother tonight.

Alexander H. Stephens To The Voters Of The Eighth CongresSional District Of Georgia.1 crawfordville, Ga., *Aug. 14, 1857.1* To The Voters Of The Eighth Congressional District:

It may be unnecessary perhaps for me to say much by way of apology or explanation of my reasons for addressing you at this time and in this way. The numerous calls that have been made upon me by personal and political friends in primary meetings of the people and otherwise to allow my name to go before the District again for re-election to Congress without the formality of a regular nomination require a response. This should have been made earlier, and would have been but for matters of a personal nature that prevented and which in no way concern the public.

To reply however to each separately would take considerable time and devolve upon me a great deal of useless labor; while to select one in preference to others might be deemed invidious. I therefore take 1 From the Constitutionalist, Augusta, Ga., Aug. 18, 1857. this method of answering all together and at the same time saying briefly not only to those who have thus manifested their wishes in this particular but to the other voters of the District generally that if it is the will and pleasure of the people that I shall serve them again in the national councils, I have no sufficient reason consistent with my sense of duty to the country and my obligations to them to justify me in refusing, particularly at this juncture. I feel profoundly sensible of the signal marks of confidence repeatedly shown towards me by the people of this District. The present may not be an improper occasion to make some allusion to them and the past relations between us of Representative and constituents.

During the whole time I have represented the district, the honor has been conferred without any party nomination—this is unusual in our day—and the honor on that account has been more highly appreciated by me. It has caused me if possible to feel more sensibly the weight of the responsibility resting upon me to watch over, look after, guard and protect equally, the rights and interests of all. How far I succeeded in meeting their expectations in the discharge of the great trusts thus confidingly placed in my hands they must judge for themselves. But it is quite a gratification to me to know that since I have been so chosen not a single vote or act of mine as their representative was ever subject of complaint at the time, as far as I am aware of, by a single man of any party in the district. All approved at the time it was done of every thing I did as their representative. At least nothing was heard to the contrary, no censure was made, no disapprobation ever was expressed. Party and national questions of the greatest magnitude and most exciting character were acted on during the time. At the first session of that term of service the Kansas bill which is still the topic of so much discussion was brought forward. I gave it, as you all know, my warm and zealous support. Its success was hailed, not only in this district but by all parties throughout Georgia, as a great triumph, a triumph not of one section of the country over another, not of the South over the North farther than her restoration to equality was concerned, but of the friends of the Constitution everywhere over those who for thirty years had been endeavoring to wrest that instrument from its true spirit, to accomplish selfish and sectional purposes against Southern institutions. And though I have seen up to this day no direct attack upon me individually for my position in connection with that measure, yet I regret to say it is but too apparent, and has been for some time past, that a party in Georgia, and particularly in the 8th District, is rising up, whose object is, if not openly, covertly at least, to get a popular condemnation of it. They now clearly insinuate that it was the work of *tricksters* and *demagogues* for the purpose of *agitation* and excitement. To this it might be a sufficient reply to say that those who bring this charge are estopped from making any such accusation, for they gave it *professedly* as hearty an approval at the time it passed as anybody else. If *tricksters* were the authors of it, they were the *tricksters' backers*.

The *pretext* now that they then gave their approval with a reservation or exception as to the "alien suffrage" and "squatter sovereignty" features as they are called, will not do. This is but an afterthought, and wholly untenable at that. All the "alien suffrage" the bill ever had in it was in it when it met the approval of the Georgia Legislature in February, 1854, and when they declared that hostility to the principles of the bill should be regarded as hostility to the South. And as for the "squatter sovereignty" feature, that was nothing but a fancy of the brain from the beginning, which was conjured up some time afterwards, about the time it was discovered that the only defenders of the bill at the North, with few exceptions, were Democrats. No such principle however ever was in the bill.

This was conclusively shown during the canvass last year, and is now generally admitted. In fact the main argument last year was not so much to show that any such principle was really in the bill as to prove that such was the Northern construction of it. It was strenuously contended that Mr. Buchanan had put that construction upon it in his letter of acceptance. But by his inaugural even that ground of complaint (altogether imaginary and unsubstantial as it was) was removed. This is now also openly acknowledged, and a very important acknowledgment it is, for with the last vestige of that *pretext* for opposition or objection vanishes. It is a matter to be noted and remembered that the Warrenton convention of the 6th inst. that nominated my honorable competitor1 expressly state and proclaim:

We confess, then, our surprise, when his (Mr. Buchanan's) inaugural address *renounced squatter sovereignty,* and the edge of our opposition to his administration was blunted by the apparent boldness and honesty of his sentiments.

This is an honest and timely confession. It is a complete answer to most of the arguments of their orators and newspapers last year. Buchanan's "squatter sovereignty" principles was then the staple of their speeches and editorials, it was the burthen of their song, "the Iliad of their woes." It was this phantom that caused some in their maddened rage to say that the bill with this construction was worse for the South than the Wilmot Proviso itself. Most blinding indeed must have been that rage which could have caused anybody to see that *anything* could have been worse for the South than that 1 T. W. Miller, Know-nothing nominee for Congress In the eighth district of Georgia was defeated by Stephens in the election of 1857 by 5,151 votes, against 4.090.
positive, absolute and *perpetual prohibition* against slavery in the Territory, put on in 1820, and which the Kansas bill removed!

But such things we have witnessed, and perhaps stranger ones are in store for us yet. It is not so much however with the past as with the present and the future we have to deal. The past it is true frequently throws light upon the future, and for this reason it is not to be neglected or forgotten. I need not assure you that I was for the bill in the beginning and am for it yet and shall stand by it to the last, notwithstanding the new "fire in the rear" as well as the one " in the front."

From late indications the next Congress will have before it deeply interesting, if not unusually exciting questions—not less so than those before the last. In the elections for the last Congress the repeal of the Kansas bill was a prominent issue at the North. Upon the assembling of that body a large majority of the House were claimed to be in favor of its repeal. But they did not succeed in their object. If however it was an unwise measure, got up by agitators and *tricksters* to serve selfish and party ends, ought it not to have been repealed? On this point the Warrenton convention, if such be the drift and tendency of their policy, are again estopped—at least their party is— for as late as the 28th of January of last year the following resolution was offered in the House of Representatives by Mr. Meacham of Vermont:
Resolved, That in the opinion of this House the repeal of the Missouri Compromise of 1820, prohibiting slavery north of latitude 36 30', was an example of useless and factious agitation of the slavery question both in and out of Congress, which was unwise and unjust to a portion of the American people.

This resolution is but a short statement of the substance of the commentary of the Warrenton convention, and if they are right their representative ought to have voted for it. But he did not, nor did a single member of the American party, or any party from the South, vote for it except Mr. Etheridge from Tennessee. Messrs. Foster and Tripp from this State voted against it, so did the two Marshalls from Kentucky, Mr. Zollicoffer from Tennessee—all the leaders of the party, and every member of it from the South, with the exception stated. Were these all *tricksters, agitators* and *demagogues,* or the *backers* of such paltry characters? This resolution passed the House, but the majority did not succeed in their attempts to carry a repeal of the measure by law. Their whole efforts then were directed to another election. In this they were signally defeated again, as well in their attempts to get control of the Executive as of the next House. Thus opened and thus ended the last Congress so far as the Kansas bill was concerned. It passed the ordeal of three stormy sessions intact and untouched, and came out of the Presidential contest sustained and endorsed by the people of the United. States and by every Southern State save one.

It was after this memorable popular verdict in its favor last fall—. after its principles seemed to be settled so far as the action of Congress was concerned—after everything pertaining even to a doubtful construction was put to rest by the inaugural of Mr. Buchanan, and after the main principles of the bill were fully affirmed by the Supreme Court of the United States in the Dred Scott case, that I did indulge a strong desire and wish to retire. It was with this measure above all others I had become identified in my public career. With the prospect of its being firmly established in every department of government, the time seemed suitable as well as propitious for me to take that course which was so agreeable to my feelings.

But since the indications to which I have alluded have furnished grounds to apprehend that these and kindred questions will come up before the next Congress, I deem it due to you to say that I feel no disposition to shrink from the responsibility of meeting them. Whatever may have been my wishes for repose, however congenial to my feelings and health quiet and rest might be, I have no inclination *voluntarily* to quit the field of action so long as the fight lasts on this measure. I shall, if the people so will it, stand by it to the end, let that be what it may. As to my course, if elected, I have no new pledge or promise to make. The form in which this question will present itself most probably in the next Congress will not be on a repeal of the measure; that idea is abandoned. It will be upon the point whether its principles shall be truly and faithfully carried into effect. It will be my object to the utmost extent of my power to see to it that this is done; not only in Kansas but in every other Territory of the United States. The principles were set forth in the Cincinnati platform of last year, in the following words: *Resolved,* That we recognize the right of the people of all the Territories including Kansas and Nebraska, acting through the legally and fairly expressed will of a majority of actual residents, and whenever the number of their inhabitants justifies it, to form a Constitution with or without domestic slavery and be admitted into the Union upon terms of perfect equality with other States.

This resolution not only embodied the principles upon which the Kansas bill was founded (thereby fully endorsing them), but it proclaims them as the permanent and settled future policy of the general government towards all the Territories, so far as the action of that party uttering them can make it. It rests upon the basis of removing the question of slavery in the Territories from the control of the General Government and leaving it to be settled in the proper way and at the proper time by the people most deeply interested in it. It secures the right of perfect equality between the citizens of all the States in the Union in the enjoyment of the public domain as long as the Territorial *status* continues. Since 1820 an effort has been made by the anti-slavery men at the North to use the powers of the General Government against southern institutions. The first point of attack was the Territories. Their policy was to hedge in, hem up, bind round, and by restrictions to prevent the South from any further growth and expansion. That this might ultimately weaken, cripple and perhaps destroy the institution in the States was the main object. On the part of the South it was justly insisted that her right of expansion was equal to that of the North. This right, after a struggle for years, was first secured in 1850 after the defeat of the Wilmot Proviso, or Congressional restrictive policy. The Kansas bill did but follow up and carry out the policy of 1850—while the resolution just quoted adopts and looks to the establishment of this as the future policy of the Government. In my judgment the principles upon which this policy rests are worth the Union itself. Its objects were and are, not to make Kansas or any other Territory either a slave or a free State by the action of Federal authority, but to let the people in each, when they come to form their State Constitution, make it for themselves "in their own way," subject to no limitation or restriction except the Constitution of the United States. It was to *prevent* the General Government from having anything to do with or exercising any influence over the formation of the Constitution of the new States either for or against slavery. If carried out in good faith it secures to the South unlimited right of expansion to the utmost extent of her capacity. More than this she has no reason to ask. And with this she has no reason to fear now or hereafter, either from "British philanthropists" or "American abolitionists," or the "moral sentiment of Christendom." Secure in her own State institutions, without the power of molestation on the part of Federal authorities, with the full enjoyment of the right to grow as the country grows, to enlarge as that enlarges, and to carry her slave population wherever climate, soil and productions invite them in our immense public domain, she has nothing to fear from any quarter. I am not one of those who indulge in forebodings of evils to the South in any contingency, either in the Union or out of it. She holds in her hands not only her destiny and the destiny of the Union but the destiny of much greater interests than all these combined. One of her great staples alone now forms the basis of the commerce, enterprise and wealth of the world. Not only the Northern States but most of the nations of Europe are fast becoming dependent upon her. The idea that the question of African slavery is one of vital interest only to those who own the slaves, and to the extent of the money invested in them, is one of those chimeras which might be expected to emanate from the brains of those who think it a divine mission to war against divine decrees.

The amount of capital invested in slaves is but a drop in the bucket compared with the much vaster amount put in motion and sustained by the products of their labor. There is not a flourishing village or hamlet in the North, to say nothing of their towns and cities, that does not owe its prosperity to Southern cotton. England, with her millions of people and billions upon billions of pounds sterling, could not survive six months without it. This they begin to feel and lament. We emphatically hold the lever that wields the destiny of modern civilization in its widest scope and comprehension; and all' we have to do is to realize the consciousness of our power and be resolved to maintain it.

In this connection it may not be amiss or out of place to notice an article in one of our own journals of a recent date. The Columbus *Enquirer* in its issue of the 12th May last says:,

From the commencement of the government until the present period the South comparatively has been growing "small by degrees and beautifully less" in wealth, population, in literature, and in all the elements which add power and greatness to a State. If any one should be incredulous of the fact, let him examine the different census reports which have been made, and the truth will reveal itself in all its fearful proportions.

This ought to be a most mortifying reflection to every southern man if upon reference to the authorities cited the facts were found to sustain the statement. But the censuses furnish no material for such a depreciation of our section. It is true the North has a larger population than the South, and this she had at the beginning. At the first census in 1790 the population of the present non-slave holding States was (1,900,976) nearly two millions, while the white population of the South was only 1.271,488, not much over one. It is also true, when we look not only to this great disproportion between the numbers of the white population of the North and the South but also to the still more comparatively small number of slaves at the South, the prospect for future settlement of new States to be admitted to the Union out of the public territory would seem to be greatly in favor of the North. These very census reports, however, render this prospect much less discouraging to us, for with a white population of only a little over twelve hundred thousand in the South against a like population of near two millions in the North, and with a slave population of only about eight hundred thousand when the government was formed, the South has certainly lost nothing in comparison with the North in her spirit, energy and enterprise in rolling the tide of civilization onwards by the settlement and colonization of new States. Since then under her auspices, and under her institutions, there have been settled, colonized and admitted into the Union the following States: Kentucky, Tennessee, Alabama, Florida, Louisiana, Arkansas, Missouri, Mississippi and Texas—nine in all—and all slave States, while the free States which have been admitted and which properly speaking have been settled and colonized in the same time are only seven in number. They are Ohio, Michigan, Wisconsin, Indiana, Illinois, Iowa and California. Vermont and Maine can hardly properly be taken into this account, for the former was part of the New Hampshire plantations and was settled as early as that State—indeed at the Revolution she claimed a separate existence— while Maine was cut off from Massachusetts. But if these two also be put in the count, it will make but nine—the same number of *free States* admitted as of *slave States* since the government was formed.

In point of wealth, the South has nothing to fear by a comparison with the North. Upon all fair principles of estimation and comparison, the advantages are on her side. And as far as our own State is concerned the census shows that no portion of the United States excels her in all the elements of power, greatness and progress.

If then, with such great disproportion in population against them in the beginning and with such a small number of blacks, the South has held her own so well and lost nothing even under a partial restriction against her from 1820 to 1854, what need she to fear now with the unlimited right of expansion and diffusion according to the means, inclination, and character of her population? The maintenance of this principle is of vast and vital importance to her. And the great Object with her men and statesmen should be to see that it is faithfully carried out in Kansas, let the result under its operation be what it may. I have said that this will be an important question probably before the next Congress. This arises from the doctrines and position of Governor Walker in his inaugural and late speeches in that Territory. There can be no question, it sems to me, that he has violated the plain letter and meaning of the Kansas bill, as well as the resolution quoted from the Cincinnati platform upon which the present Administration was elevated to power. The one declared it to be the true meaning and intent of the act to leave it to the people to settle their own institutions in their own way for themselves. His argument against the possibility of slavery ever going there was intended to influence the public mind against its introduction. He threw all the weight of his high official position against it. If what he says be true it was no less unjust than unnecessary to say it. But a grosser violation of principle he committed in urging that the constitution of the new State should be made in a particular way to suit him and in declaring that if it was not she would not and ought not to be admitted into the Union. Under the Kansas bill the people there have the right to make their Constitution "*in their own way*" "*acting*" (in the language of the resolution before quoted) "*through the legally and fairly expressed will of a majority of the actual residents*"

Now the convention which has been elected to form a constitution there, has been chosen under " the legally and fairly expressed will of a majority of the actual residents" as far as it could be ascertained by law. This no one can gainsay. If anyone refused to vote it was their own choice not to do it. The convention thus elected have plenary powers in conformity to law, to form a constitution. It is their right to submit it for ratification or not as they may choose. The question of the propriety of submitting it or not is one for themselves to determine. This it is their peculiar province to decide. If Gov. Walker had barely suggested, recommended or advised its submission, I should not complain of that part of his address. But he goes on to say that if they do not do it the new State will not be and ought not to be admitted. This is virtually saying that the people "acting under the legally and fairly expressed will of the majority" shall not form their Constitution " in their own way " but in his way or that in which Congress shall see fit to dictate. This is opening up the whole question in a new shape. It goes further. It brings up the old Missouri question—that is, the right or power of Congress to impose conditions or restrictions upon the new States in the formation of their Constitutions, when by the plain letter of the Constitution of the United States Congress can only look into the Constitution of the new State applying and see that it is republican in form. If it come from the legally constituted authorities, Congress has no right or power to inquire into or take jurisdiction over the question as to how it was made—no more in the case of Kansas than in the case of Georgia or Rhode Island. And if Kansas should be rejected on that ground then an enquiry might be instituted as to how all the other State constitutions have been made. The question is one which involves our whole federative system. The main point, it seems to me, is always overlooked by those who see no error in Gov. Walker's address. Their minds are directed simply to the *propriety* of submitting the constitution for ratification. On that point I have nothing to say, because it properly and directly concerns nobody but the people of Kansas. It is the right of the convention, their chosen organ, to do it or not to do it, as they please. But suppose they chose not to do it? Who clothed Gov. Walker or anybody else with authority to say, either that she would not or ought not to be admitted into the Union? Certainly his written instructions which we have seen warrants him in holding no such language. This may or may not become an important question in the next Congress, according as the convention then may or may not determine to conform to Gov.

73566—13-27

Walker's views. If they do thus conform, the question will most probably be ended. But if they do not—if they adopt a pro-slavery constitution without submitting it and present themselves for admission under it just as several other States have done—then the question will come up with all its interest and magnitude. It will be one of much wider, broader and deeper range than any one heretofore connected with Kansas matters. It strikes at the foundation of our government. It involves everything recognized as State Rights and State Sovereignty. It is of higher import than anything connected with the position of any man, party or Administration.

If the present Administration takes sides with Gov. Walker on it, he and they will share the same fate. I cannot however permit myself to believe for a moment that they will in that contingency take such grounds. The doctrine is too outrageous and monstrous to allow any such inference. So far as Mr. Buchanan is concerned—to say nothing of the individual members of his cabinet—there is nothing in his past history to warrant any such conclusion; nothing in his administration thus far affords any grounds even to *suspect it,* except the fact that he has not removed him. Apart from this Walker business no administration has ever in my day so fully mef my cordial approval. I am not however in the habit of condemning without a hearing. Mr. Buchanan may have reasons for his course we know nothing of. In the meantime he must and will be held responsible for the consequences attending his retention, whatever they may be. These he cannot escape from.

But as matters now stand what ought to be done? I mean what ought to be done by those who really and in gooth faith intend to stand by the principles that brought the present Administration into power? The clamor by our opponents is loud for the rebuke and condemnation of the President on account of the Walker policy in Kansas. And who are those whose indignation at these outrages against Southern rights has been so suddenly awakened? Men who consider the passage of the bill that secured these rights which have thus been outraged as nothing but the work of *tricksters,* got up for excitement and agitation— men who twelve months ago could see nothing in it but " squatter sovereignty," more odious and hurtful to the South than the Wilmot Proviso itself, but who now say that but for Walker, Kansas would certainly have come in as a slave State— men who now find it convenient to express much *feigned* wrath at the wrongs that have been done us, who could not suppress their delight when they first heard of these wrongs! One of the leading organs of this party in Georgia, the Macon *Journal and Messenger,* headed an article announcing Gov. Walker's address with "Something to rejoice at." Verily out of the abundance of the heart the mouth sometimes speaketh. Sumner or Seward could not have been more exultant when that address first met their eyes. But to you, voters of the 8th district, I put the question, are these the men you should join to place their nominees in power for the purpose of rebuking the Administration, or even Walker? Surely this would be a rebuking him with a vengeance!

It may be true, as stated, that but for his course in Kansas she would certainly have come into the Union as a slave State. But to whom are we indebted for that policy which was leading so certainly to that result? Not to those who are now so indignant. though lately so full of "something to rejoice at," but to those true and gallant constitution-abiding men at the north, whom it was the pleasure, not twelve months ago, of these latter day "indignationists" to assail and denounce with a rancour not surpassed by anything uttered by Hale or Giddings. This is no time to follow any such leaders. If Walker or others we trusted have or shall prove untrue to us upon this great question, we should at least be true to ourselves. If a rebuke is to be given it ought to be given by those who feel the wrongs committed and who have the fit and proper spirit to give it. This above all other times is the one when every dictate of patriotism requires all the real and true friends of the Kansas bill, North and South, to stand together and see that it is faithfully executed—and deal with all who oppose it as they deserve to be dealt by. The whole South in the next Congress will approach nearer to unanimity, in its party character, than ever before—she will present almost a united front—so nearly so as to warrant the division of the House for all practical purposes into but two parties, the Democratic and the Black Republican. The American party North is utterly defunct—they have not a member elected to the next Congress that I am aware of. At the South thus far they have elected but five, I believe; two in Kentucky, two in Tennessee, and one in Missouri—five in all. Should Georgia send her entire delegation of that party they could do nothing. however willing they might be, without the cooperation of the National Democracy. From the North fifty-one Democrats have been elected, pledged to the principles of the Kansas bill as set forth in the resolution of the Cincinnati Convention I have quoted. The paramount object therefore in securing the rebuke of Walker as well as the maintenance of our principles in any and every contingency should be to select for Congress men true to the principles themselves and who will cordially unite with and cooperate with those North and South who have the same great end in view. This is no time for those devoted to those principles to abandon their organization, either State or national. It is a time when they should stand in firmer and in more solid column. It is the time when all true men who look to principles as an object higher than party should strike for the country, and strike in that way in which their power can be most efficiently felt.

These views, my fellow-citizens of the Eighth District, I submit to you. They are given with that frankness with which I have always spoken to you. If there is anything in them which falls harshly upon the ear of anyone, he will please pardon it. It is not my intention to be offensive to anyone. They are my own sentiments upon some of the public topics of the day which you are entitled to know upon the announcement of my name as a candidate for your suffrages. Consider them and weigh them as the importance of the subjects demand. If you see fit to elect me, the utmost of my ability as in times past shall be devoted to your service. I shall assume the trust without any personal objects or aims to accomplish. I have no ambition but to serve my country and to see it advancing throughout its whole length and breadth in all that will add to its peace, development, happiness, prosperity and greatness. So far as I am personally concerned, I can say with truth, I would not give a day of rest at my cherished home for a whole life spent in Washington. If you think that my competitor, the nominee of the Warrenton convention, will serve you better, abler, more efficiently or more faithfully, you have but to say so. And if he shall succeed in doing it, I assure you no one will be more gratified at it than myself.

Robert Toombs To Alexander H. Stephens. R.

Washington, Geo., *Aug. 15th, 1857.* Dear Stephens,... I am compelled to go to Atlanta on Monday to argue the case of the Colonization Society vs. Gartrell, Admr. of Gideon, which will prevent my being at Hancock Court the first of the week if at all. I hoped that case would come on this week; if I find it will not come till the end of the next I will come down to Hancock Tuesday night. I wrote tonight to Willis that you would be at Bulah on Friday the 28th inst., which I think will be better than Saturday as we shall have a better time to get home and get off the next week if you have other appointments then. The next two weeks after that I think I shall be in So. Western Georgia. I have nothing new. The K. Ns. here open vigorously with a very reputable ticket and are quite fierce against both you and me. But if we can get their candidates on that issue we shall beat their firm in this county and I think in some of the adjoining ones. You-must let nothing but Providential cause prevent your being at Bulah. You and Linton ran a terrible narrow risk in the stage. Julia says she is certain you were not born to be killed by a casualty. I hope it will not keep Linton long out of the canvass. Tell him if he has any engagements on hand or if I can serve him in any other way that I will do it with pleasure. Tell him to write me *at Atlanta* when he wants the *Washington Comity* meeting, and I will make my arrangements accordingly.

Jack Howard has written me a long letter asking my opinions of Walker's policy. I am writing a reply and will send it day after tomorrow. There is nothing new in it. I condemn Walker, disapprove the retaining of him by the administration, but advise a strong and active adherence to the Democratic organization, and show the utter untrustworthiness of the American party on any question. I should like to have a chance to show you the letter. Can't you come over tomorrow night, you could get back Saturday evening. Julia has been very unwell for two days past but is now again improving and out again—the rest all well. Gabe got home last Friday night, his health is much improved and he has strong hopes of his final recovery. Nothing else new.

Howell Cobb To Alexander H. Stephens. R.
(Private.)

Washington, D. C. *3 Sept., 1857.* Dear Stephens, I have just received your letter and am much gratified to learn from it the brightening prospects in our election. I do hope and trust that Linton will carry his district, and from what I hear of Josh Hill's position he will be able to do it. I understand that Hill openly *denounces* the Kansas bill and *advocates* the Missouri Compromise. If so and Linton could canvass he would certainly whip the fight. I read your letter with much pleasure; it is able, clear and convincing. You put the Walker point in as good a light as the position of things and your own opinions would admit of. You saw no doubt the editorial comment of the Union, which expressed the feeling here on the subject—as much as I now recollect the article. I am glad to know that things are settling down in Ga., for I had feared that it might result disastrously in some of the districts. My accounts from the 6th are satisfactory. Jackson will be elected easily.

Today's Union contains Mr. Buchanan's letter to the Silliman crowd. I think it a great document and will tell powerfully in our state. I am extremely anxious to know your opinion of it and the effect it is likely to produce. If our editors will take hold of it in the right spirit they can make it do immense good. I am not overrating its importance. Like yourself I judge the effect upon others by my own feelings. Be sure to write me at once your opinion of it. I write this very hastily for the mail. The messenger is waiting.

P. S.—I have just heard that Judge Curtis has resigned. I have not seen the President or talked with anyone about his successor; but what do you think of Toucey or Choate? It is a mere suggestion in my own brain. Give me your ideas.

Howell Cobb To Alexander H. Stephens. R.
(Private.)

Washington City, *12 Sept., 1857.*
Dear Stephens, Your letter has just reached me. I have sent to the War Department for the paper you wanted for Mr. Nisbet, and if such a document is to be had I will send it to him by to-morrow's mail.

Nothing has been done about the vacant judgeship. I think the President is inclined to Toucey. The *only objection* to Choate is the doubt of his soundness on the constitutional questions of so much interest and importance at this time. In his late speeches I can find nothing to justify the opinion that he is with us on these questions. Otherwise that would clearly be the appointment to be made. The President will appoint no man who is not known to be perfectly sound on those questions. In this he is clearly right and you will approve the determination.

I saw Whitfield[1] and conversed fully and freely with him; and I will give you in a very few words the substance of his information. He says that Gov. Walker is fully sustained by our friends in Kansas and that the constitution will be submitted to the people for ratification but that the convention will prescribe the qualification of voters. He says that a large majority are against slavery and that our friends regard the fate of Kansas as a free state pretty well fixed. He gives this account of what had transpired in the territory before Walker got there: That the pro-slavery men finding that Kansas was likely to become a Black Republican state determined to unite with the free-state Democrats, the pro-slavery men being determined if Kansas was to be a free state it should be a national state, and the free-state Democrats preferring that it should be a slave state to its being an abolition state. Upon this understanding they were cooperating together. The probability is that the convention will be silent in the constitution on the subject of slavery, which would result in the admission of Kansas as a slave state; but how long it would remain so is doubtful. Doniphan was also here. and from my conversation with him, he agrees with Whitfield.

I say that I talked fully with Whitfield. Perhaps I ought to qualify that expression, as my interviews were not very long but very pointed on the question. Speculation however will soon be at 1 John W. Whitfield, Delegate in Congress from the Territory of Kansas, 1855-1856.
an end, as the convention is now in session and we shall know at an early day what they will do.

I sent you yesterday a Union with your letter and comments to which I referred. I read your speech in reply to Miller as reported in the Constitutionalist to the President and his cabinet. All were pleased with it and the President was much gratified with your defence of the Administration in reply to Miller's interrogations. What has he done?

I don't think you all are making as much capital out of the President's letter as you ought. It will secure Linton's election if it could be put in the hands of every voter in his district with appropriate comments. Let me hear from you as the canvass progresses.

Howell Cobb To Alexander H. Stephens. R.
(Private.)

Washington City, *19 Sept., 1857.*
Dear Stephens, I suppose that you have received my letter in answer to your last in which I gave you what Whitfield had to say about Kansas. I reply at once to yours of 16th. I can add nothing to my last about the condition of things in Kansas for we have heard nothing more. The adjournment of their convention until next month is not understood here and we are at a loss to account for it. We shall probably hear in a few days on that point and I will write to you if it is of any importance.

In reference to the pamphlet about Kansas, I have seen and hastily read portions of it. It contains palpable misstatements as well as false arguments. The statement that Walker's Inaugural was submitted to and approved by the President and his cabinet is untrue. We never saw it until it was published in the papers after Walker got to Kansas. I think I have said as much to you before. The argument of the pamphlet on the Badger amendment is wholly at war with our construction of the Kansas bill; and I might refer to other points but it is unnecessary. The author attempted to get up the idea that it was semi-official, which was repudiated by the Union, the States and other papers.

Upon the other point of your letter, which looks to the contingency of the convention refusing to submit the constitution to the people for ratification, I frankly confess that it is full of difficulty. I have thought *much* about it and said but little. With all my heart I trust that such an issue will not come upon us. I am not authorized to say what course the Administration will pursue. We have not anticipated it and have made no programme. My own individual opinion is that it will produce the most dangerous crisis we have yet had on the Kansas question. I know your argument. I have read and thoroughly studied it, but the reply can be made with overwhelming power that the refusal to submit was the result *alone* of a fear that a majority would condemn it. I tell you that an effort to get a free state into the Union over *the will* of a majority of its citizens would never be submitted to *at the South.* But I don't invite a discussion of a question) which I trust in God will not arise. In the frankness and confidence of our correspondence I throw out the above suggestions which I have before made in some of my letters to you.

I have written this hasty reply that it may go by return mail. Let me hear from you how the canvass goes. Jones of the C. and S.1 professes to look for

Howell Cobb To Alexander H. Stephens. R.
'(Private.)

Washington City, *9 Oct., 1857.*

Dear Stephens, I have time to write only a line—being more pressed than ever with business. The financial crisis keeps me busy with *facts* and *figures*. Things look no better in New York, and I am preparing for the storm if it comes and lasts.

The news from the Ga. elections is not as good as I expected. I hoped to the last for Linton's election. I did not expect Bailey's.2 The rest will do very well under the circumstances. I shall die under the conviction that Linton would have been elected if our convention had not passed that third resolution—but it is too late now to discuss that.

Nothing yet from Kansas. I hope our friends have succeeded; but have my fears. I agree fully with your last suggestion that the best policy for their convention is to say nothing in the constitution about slavery and submit it to the qualified voters under the constitution, and to require a new registration of voters so as to require all who vote for it to recognize the existing government. It seems to me that all our friends could unite upon that basis and it presents the only fair mode that I see of making Kansas a slave state, a result most desirable, if it can be brought about upon the recognized principle of carrying out the will of the majority, which is the great doctrine of the Kansas bill. I expect to write today to one of the members of the convention, Batt Jones, to that effect. Pardon the haste of this letter, but I am run to the eyebrows, and I confess that my mind is much and anxiously exercised about the business of my department which is involved in every thing that effects the money market. I wish I could write more but I cannot now.

Gov. Brown iThe Chronicle and Sentinel, Augusta, Ga.

2 David J. Bailey, Congressman from Georgia, 1851-1855; defeated for reSlection in 1857 by Robert P. Trippe. and our friends in the legislature ought to be warned not to make *hasty and unnecessary issues.* They should remember the fate of Gov. Towns and the democratic party in 1850.

Howell Cobb To Alexander H. Stephens. R.
(Private.)

Washington City, *19 Oct., 1857.*

Dear Stephens, Yours of 17th just received. I concur fully with you about the importance of Toombs's election and as I said in my former letter I have said so to my friends and shall continue to press it upon them. You say that McDonald expects to beat him on the extreme Southern rights line with the aid of the Americans who have become quite extreme in their feelings. This is just as I would have it. That game can't win. I felt sure that Toombs would be right upon the issue when it came. Such I now know to be the fact and McDonald will utterly fail to get up a new Southern Rights party. "Burnt children dread the fire," and he can't get up as strong an organization as he did in 1850. Still it is necessary to guard every point, as McDonald is a hard hand to deal with.

I enclose you a letter to read and return to me. It may be necessary to look to the suggestions it contains. You see it is private and confidential. You will so regard it but you can act upon the information it contains. I shall reply to it and avail myself of the opportunity to press Tombs's election, independent of his suggestion. You can analyze this letter, the motives which prompt it and all that kind of thing as well a's I can. Still it is important that you should see and know exactly the points that will be made and then can judge best how to meet them.

I have written to Lumpkin on the subject of Toombs's election but have not received an answer to my last letter.

I will postpone further discussion of the Third resolution and its effects until we meet and then I will satisfy you that I am right about it.

P. S.—About the Custom House in Augusta I have not time to write.

Robert Toombs To W. W. Burwell. L. C.

Roanoke Plantation, Stewart County, Ga., *Nov. 20,1857.* My Dear Sir: Your letter of the 6th inst. was forwarded me at this place and received only yesterday. I have been spending the last month (except a few days in Milledgeville two weeks ago) on plantation enjoying myself keenly with farming operations, hunting, etc., etc., and regret that my vacation is running rapidly to a close. I found no difficulty whatever in my election. Govr. McDonald came down to the capital and urged his own claims vigorously up to the nomination but was not able to command half a dozen democrats against me and the Americans thought it quite unnecessary to throw away their votes on a "dead rabbit," altho' some of them were excessively hostile. I very fully agree with you upon the necessity of defeating the Kansas policy of Walker and those who *palliate, justify or support it.* Before my election at Milledgeville I made a *"clean breast"* of it upon this subject and was warmly and cordially supported by the great mass of the party, the few "King's men" who dissented were not strong enough to raise the standard of rebellion and therefore quite gracefully acquiesced; I determined that my future should be untrammelled, and I was much gratified to find the great majority of the Democrats of Geo. fully up to the same mark.

I have been trying for several years past to bring around to Mr. Hunter, who is really an able and honest and *faith full* Southern man, all those persons at the South who were struggling for sound principles and just government rather than for the promotion of themselves thro some particular aspirant to the Presidency; but his own timidity and especially his dread of the great power of old Tom Ritchie in Virginia has frequently embarrassed me a good deal. I deem his cooperation of primary importance to defeat those Southern men with Northern principles to whom you refer. They can be easily defeated with his cooperation. They must be at all hazards, with him or without him. I will seek an early opportunity to have a full understanding with him when I get to Washington and I do not doubt but that we shall agree thoroughly for the future. Our policy is the same and there shall be nothing on my part to prevent a cordial co-operation. Mr. Wise? can do nothing except thro' the folly of his opponents. Besides he is crazy for the Presidency and that disease unsettles the best of intellects.

I shall be very glad to have you at Washington next winter, and have already been endeavoring to make satisfactory arrangements. At the last session Judge? Butler offered to decline the chairmanship of the judiciary committee in my favour, the committee were also desirous of the arrangement. I privately urged him not to do so because I preferred waiting until the result of my re-election was known. If the same counsels prevail and it is tendered me I shall accept it this winter, in which event if that place (Clerk of that Com.) suits you it shall be at your disposal; and besides I should esteem it a great personal favour for you to accept it. We are all in good health. It is a little uncertain when I will be in Washington.

P. S.—There is a strong disposition in the South to make Stephens Speaker, especially to defeat Orr who is in full sympathy with the Walker people. Stephens does not want it, would prefer Letcher of Va. One or the other might be elected, and I wish you would press that view before the public in some suitable form.

Thomas W. Thomas To Alexander H. Stephens. It.

Elberton, Geo., *12th January, 1858.*

Dear Sir: T received your last enclosing the package from Martin a few days ago. You say " write to me ", and you evince also some repugnance to "sentimental speculations". What am I to do? I have no news to send. All the incidents which happen here in a twelvemonth could be told on one page, and would not be worth the telling at that. I *must* send you sentimental speculations as you call them, or nothing. But for being restrained by the intimations contained in your last already alluded to, I should like to *speculate sentimentally* a little more on the Kansas question and show as I think I could how utterly disastrous must be eventually the course of the Southern Democracy in relation to the Administration. In the judgment of every democrat, in Georgia at least, the President has violated or permitted to be violated the principles of his party, his own personal pledges, and the law of the land. And yet the Democrats in the Georgia Senate when these facts were stated in a resolution in moderate and respectful language, voted all except six to lay it on the table. I have not examined the vote myself with a view to see its party character and I speak from the information of a member of the Senate a few minutes after the vote was taken. In view of these facts I have no reproaches for Douglas. I grieve that he has pursued the course he is now in, but he had no inducement to do otherwise. When Southern men persisted in shouting hozannas and praises after the man whom we had trusted and who had betrayed us what motive had Douglas for remaining true? We betrayed our own rights by the long silence we maintained (unbroken to this day) in relation to the villainy of Buchanan. We proved ourselves unworthy of the co-operation of true men, and Douglas did well for himself and no wrong to us by looking to his own interest at home. Douglas has as much right to be President as Cobb. Cobb has been openly playing for the free-soil support of the North in the next nomination, and we notoriously refused to utter one word of condemnation. I say Cobb has been doing this, because he is the President as much as if he were sworn in. Douglas has heretofore been bravely standing by us. He sees we have not the courage to denounce our enemies and he has come to the conclusion that our alliance is not worth looking after. I agree with him in the judgment he has formed. Until we become better ourselves we have no right to censure him.

In the reply of the President through the secretary of State to Walker's letter of resignation it is gravely stated that he learns with pleasure from Walker's dispatch of the 18th July last that in all his speeches he had refrained from expressing any opinion whether Kansas should be a slave or a free state. When he got the dispatch in July and when he sent the reply to Walker he had Walker's inaugural signed with his name and he had the Topeka speech and he knew as well as he knew his own name that the statement in the July dispatch was a wicked and willful lie. Yet he publishes it to 25 millions of people as the truth and says he is glad to learn it. Such infamy is revolting. And old Cass, a soldier who followed his country's flag with a sword by his side, makes himself the conduit to convey this monstrous lie to the public. You say you can't afford to quarrel with Buchanan now—that the admission of Kansas as a slave state is at stake. You know my opinion of the importance of that measure, but before God when to accomplish it I am required to tolerate such treachery and falsehood as has characterized the Administration from the beginning until now, my answer is it is not worth the price. This is my judgment. I have all my life spoken to you with candour. Never did I deceive you in the smallest particular, and I can't begin it now. Therefore if my views are not acceptable I can't help it. I know if you have any interest in hearing from me you desire to hear my real opinions and not something varnished up.

I am under obligations to you for numerous valuable favors in the way of books and seeds.

Thomas W. Thomas To Alexander H. Stephens. R.

Elberton, Geo., *21st January, 1858.*

Dear Sir: Yours of the 12th inst. was received yesterday. I trust the event may show there was not so much cause for apprehension as you were impressed with when you wrote. It seems to me we have gotten to that place where nothing can save the Democratic party of the South, or anything else worth saving, from utter annihilation, except the admission of Kansas as a slave state. If we *could* get it in as a slave state we would tumble into a pit of their own digging the shabbiest set of knaves and tricksters north and south that ever disgraced a commonwealth. For these reasons I pray thrice daily that you may succeed.

You say Wise's letter1 will do us great injury. I have read the letter and I cannot understand how it can injure any one save the writer. It has nothing in it but egotism and the most absurd and pitiful self-contradictions....

1 Henry A. Wise, governor of Virginia, had issued a public letter, Dec. 30, 1857, indorsing the policy of Douglas and Walker in relation to Kansas.

He has descended at last avowedly to his true place, that of a parasite and hero-worshipper. And so determined is he to have a hero to worship that he bows down and licks the foot of that detected old villain who dispenses the patronage of this government and lives in the White house. Even such an idol he will set up rather than refrain from his filthy devotions.... If such a letter from such a man can influence the Congress of the United States I think it time we had exchanged our social system for that of the Yahoos of whom we read in Gulliver's travels.

I am compelled to differ with you as to the sources of the danger to Kansas. It lies not in the defection of Douglas or of this or that man even in the South. It lies in that profound and placid homage with which our public men deport themselves towards the occupant of the throne, no matter what may be his crimes and malpractises....

I have spoken plainly as becomes a freeman speaking to his representative. I do not doubt *your* patriotism or your moral courage and if I *can* see where a different course on your part would have produced different results in my judgment yet I am not disposed to thwart you or annoy you with complaints. I know no man as able to put in your place; therefore I am duly grateful for valuable services in the past and hope still more glorious success may crown your efforts in the future.

Thomas W. Thomas To Alexander H. Stephens. R.

Elberton Geo., *7th Feb., 1858*. Dear Sir: I have received your letter dated 26th of last month, also your printed speech on Walker's case.1 I was more curious than usual to see this speech because I had read in so many of the Georgia Know Nothing papers little brief paragraphs that it was a failure, and they seemed to take great pleasure in so characterizing it. I think I understand thoroughly all your points, and I must say you sustained them fully in my judgment. I would like much to see a reply to it, and if any was attempted (I mean on the points made) please send me one or two of the best if they are in print. Some of the points are nice but they are exceedingly clear. I don't care to trouble you to send or myself to read any reply if it did not attempt to answer the argument. There is however a certain air of carelessness about the style, which is not usual with you. It reminds me somewhat of the manner I have seen you exhibit on the stump when weary and jaded. This defect (if I am not mistaken in so calling it) does not however impair the force of the argument 1 William Walker while on a second filibustering expedition to Nicaragua had been arrested by Commander Hiram Paulding of the United States Navy. Stephens denounced the arrest as illegal.

to a discriminating mind. I see it stated in the papers that the grand jury at New Orleans refused to find a true bill against Walker. What will the government say now? It's own tribunal (for the grand jury is a tribunal) not only acquits Walker but says there is not even suspicion enough against him to put him on trial, and this after hearing all the government could allege and hearing nothing from Walker. If after this they do not send him back and make complete restitution they ought to be ashamed to look one another in the face. As for my own part I would as soon be caught stealing. Their worst enemy could not wish them in a more humiliating condition. The situation of the rogue who thrust his hand through the crack of a corn crib and got it caught in a steel-trap and had to stand there till morning is respectable compared to them.

I have just read in the National Intelligencer the documents in relation to Kansas, among others Gov. Walker's dispatch of the 15th July last. If evidence was lacking before that the rights of the South had been deliberately betrayed to build up the Democratic Party at the North, it seems to me this dispatch abundantly supplies it. I declare in all candor and coolness that it exhibits such a picture of infamous unmitigated villainy as makes a freeman think of bloodshed. If the President had had the least regard for his pledges or his oath he would not have allowed him to remain a single moment governor of the Territory after receiving this dispatch. Nothing short of seeing the Holy Ghost descending upon old Buck in the shape of a dove patent to my eyesight could ever make me trust him again.

The same mail which brought me your letter and printed speech brought me also another document marked on the back "*Free. L. J. Gartrell, M. C*," which upon opening I found to contain a speech of that honourable gentleman " in defence of slavery and the South. " I have given this speech a very attentive consideration, and I must say (judging from the effect you say Wise's letter had on Congress) it certainly had a powerful effect on that body. It is just the sort of effort to affect powerfully such intellects as could be controlled by Wise's letter. What a magnificent reply he made to Lovejoy about the passage of Scripture quoted on. him against returning fugitive slaves—" Will the gentleman answer me categorically—Does he believe the negro to be equal to the white man?" Now what this had to do with the free-soiler's question and Scripture does not clearly appear; but wasn't it a thunder clap? and though the Yankee answered it rather pointedly and with much sharpness, yet where was the *categorical* answer? There's where the Georgian had him. One thing at least is very clear from the speech—Gartrell was in Congress on that day—for he says so three times on one page. He tells us also some news, for instance he informs us once or twice he (Gartrell) is a " Christian man ". This is strange if true, and in my judgment stranger than true.

P. S.—Send me more seeds. It is all I shall be able to get from the government during this administration. The latest news I have from the administration party in Geo. is to the effect that you and Toombs being determined to make Douglas president have raised this fuss about Gen. Walker to cover up Douglas's sins on the Kansas question. I have this direct from Athens. If it's true it is a pretty smart trick of yours.

Joseph E. Brown1 To Alexander H. Stephens. R.

Executive Department, Milledgeville, ga., *Feby. 9th, 1858.*

Dear Sir: Your kind letter reached my office while I was absent in the up-country on a visit to my father who has had a severe attack of pneumonia.

I have ordered the Secretary of State to make out and send you a commission for Mr. Nettleton as Comr. of Deeds for New York, as requested by Mr. Whitin in his letter to you.

I am very happy to have your approval of my course in vetoing the bank suspension bill. I think its passage most unfortunate for the state. It is a very bad example in legislation. The people in all parts of the state sustain me with very great unanimity, with the exception of the cities. And I am informed that a large party in Augusta and Savannah sustain me. I feel sure I am right and I bid defiance to the bank warfare which is being made up on me.

I am looking with great interest to the action of Congress on the Kansas question. If Kansas is rejected, one of the contingencies of the Georgia platform has clearly happened, and the statute makes it my imperative duty to call the convention which must determine the *status* of Georgia with reference to the Union. We must and will maintain our platform, come what may. While I have any voice in the counsels of Georgia I shall never consent to the disgrace which must follow an acknowledgment of her inferiority and inequality in the Union. If Kansas is rejected I think self respect will compel the Southern members of Congress and especially the members from Georgia to vacate their seats and return to their constituents to assist them in drawing around themselves new safeguards for the protection of their rights in future. When the Union ceases to protect our equal rights, it ceases to have any charms for me.

I shall be glad to hear from you when you have leisure to write, should you have a moment. I am aware of the labor you now have 1 Judge of the superior court of Georgia (Blue Ridge Circuit), 1S55-1857; governor of Georgia, 1859-1865; chief-justice of Georgia, 1868-1870; United States Senator, 18801891.
to perform. I have great confidence in your wisdom and prudence. May the Ruler of the Universe direct your steps through this important crisis.

Robert Toombs To James Buchanan. Pa.

Washington, D. C., *Mch. 2, 1858. Provided,* That nothing in this act shall be construed to abridge or infringe the right (as asserted in the constitutions of Kansas and Nebraska) of the people at all times to alter, reform or abolish their form of government in such manner as they may think proper.

Senate Chamber, *2nd March 1858.* My Dear Sir: I send you the proviso as adopted by the Dem. caucus. I think the opposition is gradually giving away on both sides of the line and that we have a good prospect of union and harmony among the friends of the immediate admission of Kansas.

Joseph E. Brown To Alexander H. Stephens. (Private.)

Executive Department, Milledgeville, Ga., *March 26th, 1858.*

Dear Sir: I have the pleasure to acknowledge the receipt of your letter of 19th inst.

I very much regret to learn that there is now great doubt of the admission of Kansas with the Lecompton Constitution. I thank you for your kindness in giving me the true state of things there in reference to this question.

If Kansas is rejected by a direct vote I can see no other course for Georgia to take but to stand by her rights, upon her platform, and act, or confess to the world that she has backed down from her solemn pledges. I should feel that our humiliation was deep and painful should we adopt the latter course. If Kansas is rejected by the indirect mode which you mention, of smothering the bill in its long agonies in the Select Committee room, our position will be still more embarrassing. Would not this amount to a rejection, and could we doubt that the existence of slavery in the Constitution was the cause of the rejection? There might however be difficulty in uniting our people or in obtaining a majority for action, in this latter event. I confess I do not see how I could consistently with my official duty neglect to call the convention in case Kansas is rejected in the one as the other way. The statute is imperative unless she is rejected on other grounds than the existence of slavery in her constitution. If Minnesota and Oregon are admitted with free constitutions, and Kansas is rejected, what will the people say was the reason? I know that this is a grave question, and requires the most serious and cautious consideration. I hope to do nothing rashly. I am sure you do not wish me to shrink from the discharge of any duty. I would with great pleasure hear the advice of our distinguished Senators and Reps. in Congress as you suggest. I cannot doubt their determination to preserve the honor of Georgia unstained. What assurance have I that some of them would not refuse their advice and leave me to act without it? Would the united delegation respond to the call? The call of the convention might create great confusion in Georgia. Its meeting would not necessarily involve separate state action. It might be proper to adopt ordinances to take effect so soon as a majority of the Southern states concurred. I know you will do all in your power to guide us safely through the difficulty. I shall thank you for information of the state of things as often as you have time to give it.

Robert Toombs To Alexander H. Stephens. R.

Washington ga., *28 Mar., 1858.* Dr. Stephens, I had a fine pleasant run home and got to your town Saturday night, took Monk's hand car and started home and reached safely 11 o'clock. All well in Geo. The weather is delightfull, trees and flowers in full bloom and nature looks charming, and but for the sad recollection of public events at Washington I should almost feel as tho' I were transferred to a new and fairer land. I have seen but little of the people since I reached the State, but everybody I have seen of every party look with shame and indignation upon the course of Crittenden and the Americans1 and I must do the K.Ns. the justice to say that none seem more earnest or decided in their condemnation of them than they do. The people generally seem better informed of the real state of the case and the treachery of these men than I had any idea of and condemn them I think with real earnestness. My court adjourned until Thursday and will sit until Saturday night. I shall stay two or three days at Warren Court if possible. Telegraff me the events of Thursday and let me know if my presence is necessary. If so I will come immediately. Nothing new here.

Robert Toombs To James Buchanan. Pa. 248 F. Street washington, D. C, *18th April, 1858.*

My Dear Sir: I send you by the bearer of this the Tribune of yesterday containing the Leavenworth constitution.

The prospect for a settlement of the Kansas question is good today. The suggestion of Mr. English, to which you referred last night, meets with a good deal of favour among our friends, and if it meets your approbation I think it will pass....

1 Crittenden and Bell in the Senate and about half of the "Americans" in the House had voted against the admission of Kansas under the Lecompton constitution without the submission of that constitution to a vote of the people. 73566—13 28

Joseph E. Brown To Alexander H. Stephens. R.

Executive Department, Miludgeville ga., *May 7th, 1858.*

Dear Sir: I have written you since I have received a letter from you but I trust you will excuse me for again troubling you. I cannot forbear to express to you my great gratification at the success of the Kansas bill. I am truly glad we are rid of this vexed question. I feel that the South has lost nothing of principle by the passage of the bill reported by the conference committee, and I regret to see some of our democratic presses condemning the act. It will however receive the hearty approval of the great mass of our people. Had the bill not passed, there would have been great confusion in Georgia. The storm was suspended in a breathless calm awaiting the result at Washington. My position enabled me to learn a great deal of the feelings and anxieties of the people upon the subject. The democratic party of the state would have been divided and distracted. No action which you or I or any one else could have taken would have prevented it. We all here rejoice at the result and feel that your services have been invaluable to the country in bringing about the result. Had you not been a member of the House, I have no hesitation in saying that the result would have been different. It was a very delicate question and required great firmness, ability and experience. I rejoice at the result.

I trust we may not soon be called upon to meet another question of so much embarrassment. I am at present getting along very well with the W. & A. R. Road.1 We are making regular monthly payments into the Treasury of the State, and I apprehend no difficulty about a continuance of this state of things to the end of my administration. We are putting the road in fine condition and keeping it out of debt. The payment for April into the treasury was $22,000. The Supt. has had all the old scrap iron and castings gathered up and has sold it on three months time with note and two good securities. The amount realized by the collection and sale of this old iron, etc., which was of no use to the road, is about $20,000. The road is being managed on as good a system of economy as any road in the State. I know how laborious your duties are, but I must request that you write me when you can spare a little time.

Howell Cobb To William F. Colcock.2

Treasury Department washington, D. C,

May 22, 1858.

Sir: It appears from your letter of 20th April, 1858, that application has been made to you by Messrs. E. Lafitte and Co., merchants of 1 The Western & Atlantic Railroad, running from Atlanta to Chattanooga, owned and operated by the state of Georgia.
2 M. W. Cluskey, "The Political Textbook ", 12th edition, Phila., 1860, pp. 593-595. William F. Colcock was then U. S. collector of the customs at Charleston, S. C.

Charleston, S. C, "to clear the American ship Kichard Cobden, W. F. Black, master, burthen 750 31-95 tons, for the coast of Africa, for the purpose of taking on board African emigrants, in accordance with the United States passenger laws, and returning with the same to a port in the United States ".

You ask the opinion of the Department upon the propriety of your granting or refusing the application.

The question is an important one, and I have delayed an answer to your letter until I could give the subject a proper examination.

The form in which this application is presented involves the question in some embarrassment. The objects of the applicants must be either to import Africans, to be disposed of as slaves, or to be bound to labor or service—or else to bring them into the country like other emigrants, to be entitled, on their arrival, to all the rights and privileges of freedom. In either of the two first-named contingencies, the object would be so clearly and manifestly against the laws of the United States, as to leave no room for doubt or hesitation. I deem it proper, however, to call your attention to the provisions of those laws, as they indicate very clearly the general policy of the government on the subject of African importation.

Prior to the 1st January, 1808, the time fixed by the Constitution when Congress would be authorized to prohibit such importation— the Acts of 2d March, 1794, (1347) and 10th May, 1800, (270) were passed. These laws indicate the strong opposition felt at that time to the African slave trade. The subsequent Act of March 2d, 1807. (2426) and 20th April, 1818, (3450) as well as the acts of 3d March, 1819, (3532) and 15th May, 1820, (3600) show not only the promptness with which the power was exercised by Congress of prohibiting this trade to the United States, but they also bear evidence of the stem purpose of enforcing their provisions by severe penalties and large expenditures. The legislation of the slaveholding states prior to 1808, exhibits the fact that the first steps taken for its suppression were inaugurated by them.

There is no subject upon which the statute books of our country afford more conclusive evidence than the general opposition everywhere felt to the continuance of the African slave trade.

By reference to the acts of 1794 and 1800, against the slave trade generally, it will be seen that their operation was confined to slaves *eo nomine*.... Both contemplate in general terms the prevention of the trade in slaves. When, however, in 1807, and subsequent thereto, Congress undertook to prevent the importation of slaves into the United States, the language of the law was made more stringent and comprehensive. The first section of the act of 1807 provides: " That from and after the first day of January, one thousand eight hundred and eight, it shall not be lawful to import or bring into the United States, or the territories thereof, from any foreign kingdom, place or country, any negro, mulatto or person of color, with intent to hold, sell or dispose of such negro, mulatto or person of color, as a slave, or to be held to service or labor."

This law seeks not only to prevent the introduction into the United States of slaves from Africa, but any negro, mulatto, or person of color, whether introduced as slaves, or to be held to service or labor. Whether or not the wisdom of our fathers foresaw at that early day that efforts would be made under a pretended apprentice system, to renew the slave trade under another name, I cannot undertake to say, but the language of the law which they have left to us in the statute-book, leaves no doubt of the fact that they intended to provide in the most unequivocal manner against the increase of that class of population by immigration from Africa. No one could then have contemplated an object for which African emigrants would be brought to this country, which is not clearly guarded against and forbidden by the law to which I am now referring. It is only necessary to add, that subsequent acts on the subject contain the same language. This view of the subject is strengthened by reference to the provisions of the act of 28th February, 1803 (2205). The first section of that act is as follows: "That from and after the first day of April next, no master or captain of any ship or vessel, or any other person, shall import, bring, or cause to be imported or brought, any negro, mulatto, or other person of color, not being a native, a citizen, or registered seaman of the United States, or seamen natives of countries beyond the Cape of Good Hope, into any port or place in the United States, which port or place shall be situated in any state which by law has prohibited, or shall prohibit, the admission or importation of such negro, mulatto or other person of color; and if any captain or master aforesaid, or any other person, shall import, or cause to be imported or brought into any of the ports or places aforesaid, any of the persons whose admission or importation is prohibited as aforesaid, he shall forfeit and pay the sum of one thousand dollars for each and every negro, mulatto, or other person of color, aforesaid, brought or imported as aforesaid, to be sued for and recovered by action of debt, in any court of the United States, one-half thereof to the use of the United States, the other half to any person or persons prosecuting for the penalty; and in any action instituted for the recovery of the penalty aforesaid, the person or persons sued may be held to special bail: Provided always, that nothing in this act shall be construed to prohibit the admission of Indians."

It will be seen that Congress, by this act, undertook to co-operate with those states which, by state legislation, had interposed to prevent the importation of negroes into this country. At that time the constitutional prohibition to which I have before referred, restrained Congress from the exercise of the absolute power of prohibiting such importation. The states, however, being under no such restraint, had, in several instances, adopted measures of their own; and the act of 1803 shows the promptness of the general government in exercising whatever power it possessed in furtherance of the object.

The language of this act is important in another view. It will be observed that its object is to prevent the importation into the United States of " any negro, mulatto, or other person of color, not being a native, a citizen, or registered seaman of the United States, or seamen natives of countries beyond the Cape of Good Hope ". It is not confined to slaves or negroes bound *to* labor, but contemplates the exclusion, in the broadest terms, of all such persons, without regard to the character in which they may be brought. It excludes free persons as well as slaves and persons bound to labor or service. The only limitation in the act is, that it is confined to such persons as are prevented by the laws of any of the states from being imported into such states.

At that time there existed laws of some of the states not only prohibiting the introduction of negro slaves, but also free negroes. Indeed the policy of the slaveholding states has always been opposed to the increase of its free negro population; and it is proper here to remark that at the present time that policy is more earnestly sustained in those states than at any previous period of their history. After this reference to the laws on the subject, it is hardly necessary to repeat, that if the application of Messrs. Lafitte and Co. contemplates the introduction of negroes into the United States from Africa, either in the character of slaves or as apprentices bound to service or labor, it is clearly in violation of both the letter and spirit of the law, and cannot be granted.

The form of application made by Messrs. Lafitte and Co. would seem to contemplate the introduction into the United States of negroes from Africa, entitled on their arrival to all the rights and privileges of freemen. The proposition upon its face is so absurd, that it is hardly worthy of serious refutation. Messrs Lafitte and Co. ask us to believe that their vessel, fitted out in the port of Charleston, S. C., is going upon a voyage to Africa to bring to some port in the United States a cargo of free negroes. The port to which the vessel expects to return is not indicated. It cannot be the one from which it sails—nor any other port in the state of South Carolina—as the introduction of free negroes into that state is wisely prohibited by stringent laws and heavy penalties. It cannot be the port of any other slaveholding state, as similar laws in each of those states alike forbid it. The reason for such laws is so manifest, that I do not feel called upon either to produce the evidence of their existence, or to justify the policy which led to their adoption. It is sufficient to know that the public mind of that section of the Union is not more cordially agreed upon any one subject than upon the propriety and necessity of prohibiting, as far as possible, an increase of the free negro population, and hence the laws to which I refer, prohibiting their importation from any place.

Can it be that Messrs. Lafitte and Co. propose to return with their cargo of free negroes to a port in some of the non-slaveholding states? I am not aware of a single state where these new comers would receive a tolerant. much less a cordial welcome; whilst, by stringent laws and constitutional provisions, some of them have provided for their unconditional exclusion.

Looking beyond the legislation which has been had on the subject by the general government and both the slaveholding and the non-slaveholding states, I may be permitted to refer, in this connection, to the various repeated and earnest efforts which have been made in every section of the Union, to provide for the removal from our midst of this most unfortunate class. However variant the motives which have induced these efforts with different persons in different sections of the country, they all exhibit an earnest desire to diminish rather than increase the free negro population. This public opinion, thus manifested in every form, is familiar to every one. and it would be doing great injustice to the intelligence of Messrs. Lafitte and Co. to suppose that they alone were ignorant of it. Where then, do they propose to land their cargo of free negroes? What is the motive which induces the enterprise? It cannot be the profits of the voyage. There are no African emigrants seeking a passage to this country; and if there were, they have no means of remunerating Messrs. Lafitte and Co. for bringing them. The motive cannot be mere philanthropy, for it would confer no benefit upon these negroes to bring them to our shores, where, if permitted to land at all. it would only be to occupy our pest houses, hospitals and prisons.

To believe, under the circumstances, that there is a *bona fide* purpose on the part of Messrs. Lafitte and Co. to bring Africans emigrants to this country to enjoy the rights and privileges of freemen, would require an amount of credulity that would justly subject the person so believing to the charge of mental imbecility. The conviction is irresistible, that the object of the proposed enterprise is to bring these "African emigrants" into the country with a view either of making slaves of them, or of holding them to service or labor. If so, it is an attempt to evade the laws of the country on the subject of African importation to which I have called your attention.

Ordinarily, it would be an unsafe rule for a public officer to act upon the suspicion of a purpose on the part of another to violate the laws of the country, but in this case it is put so clearly beyond the reach of doubt that I think you not only can, but that you are in duty bound to act upon the presumption that it is the intention of Messrs. Lafitte and Co. to evade the laws of the United States, and you should accordingly refuse their vessel the clearance asked for.

Stephen D. Dili-aye To Howell Cobb.1

New York, *June 8, 1858...* . Afraid of the shadows of Daniel S. Dickenson and John B. Floyd, which Mr. Sickles has studiously taught you to believe covered your presidential prospects for 1860, you have, from the hour of your inauguration as Secretary, treated their friends with a concentration of treachery and meanness without a parallel in the annals of corrupt and selfish ambition, under the guise of a faithful servant on guard over the interests of the Treasury; in fact you have systematized corruption, given reward to traitorous spies, and treated Collector Schell of this city with a false-hearted baseness which no language can fitly characterize or no degree of despotism excuse. Not only this, sir, but you are a traitor in camp to the very administration upon which you were foisted by the zealous colporteurs of your political importance. For madly impelled onward by the beatific visions of a false ambition, you have employed such bastard Democrats as Samuel

Butterworth, Superintendent of the Mint, of this city, Daniel E. Sickles, your Congressional adviser, and John B. Haskins, the Man-Friday of Sickles, to strike down one of your associates in the counsels of the nation—one of the purest of Virginia's sons, the present Secretary of War, John B. Floyd.. ..

Howell Cobb To John Robbins, Jr., And Others.2 Pa.

Washington City, *3d. July, 1858.*

Gentlemen: My official engagements prevent the acceptance of your invitation to be present at your celebration of our approaching national anniversary.

The occasion is one always of deep interest, and should never be permitted to pass without awakening our grateful recollections of the past, and renewing our vows of fidelity to the future.

1 This attack upon Cobb was printed by its author as a pamphlet: "Letter to the Hon. Howell Cobb, Secretary of the Treasury ", by Stephen D. Dlllaye, of New York, N. Y., 185S. 10 pp. A copy is in the New York Public Library. The theme of the pamphlet is the disruption among Now York Democrats caused by Cobb's use of the patronage. The contents are summarized as follows: " Howell Cobb's reasons for his removal of Stephen B. Dlltayc from the office of United States General Appraiser. Howell Cobb's complicity with the notorious Daniel E. Sickles. The authors of the assault upon the character of the Hon. John B. Floyd, Secretary of War. Howell Cobb's treason to the administration and to the Democratic Party." The extract from the letter here printed, typical of the whole tirade, is taken from page 14 of the pamphlet.

'Robbins was chairman of a committee of arrangements for a Fourth-of-July celebration at Philadelphia.

The presnt conditon of our country renders the celebration of this anniversary peculiarly interesting. We are just emerging from a disastrous revulsion which had paralyzed the arm of industry and cast a gloom over the business and commercial prosperity of the whole land. and with confidence our countrymen begin to look for a revival of trade and a return of prosperity at an early day.

An angry controversy for years has distracted the peace and quiet of the country and seriously threatened the integrity of the Union. The wisdom of our statesmen and the patriotism of our people have proven equal to the emergency, and the whole country rejoices in the restoration of that harmony and good feeling so essential to our existence as a nation and our happiness as a people. Every section of our noble Union reposes in confidence upon the recognition of its rights and rejoices in the prospect of a return of the era of good feeling and true brotherhood. Peace within our own borders and peace with the world, preserved and maintained upon the principles of constitutional equality and national honor, present ample causes for the free and cordial interchange of congratulations upon the anniversary day of our national independence. I trust that it will not be regarded as indelicate in me to add that the Democracy of Pennsylvania have an additional cause of congratulation in the fact that these happy results have been effected under the administration of Mr. Buchanan and that to his wisdom and firmness we are indebted for their successful accomplishment.

Howell Cobb To James Buchanan. Pa.

Washington City, *2 Aug., 1858.*

My Dear Sir: I have nothing of importance to communicate. As far as I know, everything has gone on well since you left. Such is the case in the Treasury Department. Our receipts from Customs continue to improve. At New York we averaged $172,000 a clay during the last week. The previous week averaged $140,000. The returns from other ports indicate similar improvement. *Save us from deficiencies* and the Treasury will walk through the fiscal year "like a thing of life."

Gov. Floyd I understand has returned. I have heard nothing from our other absentees but their respective Departments are doing very well in their absence.

Howell Cobb To James Buchanan. Pa. (Private.)

Washington City, *4 Aug. 1858.* My Dear Sir: The receipts in New York on yesterday were $217,000. Encouraging accounts from other ports. Less improvement at Philadelphia than at other important points. Every thing progressing smoothly in all the Departments as far as I have heard. Nothing to the contrary was brought to light at the Cabinet meeting on yesterday. Mr. Schell writes me today that he will visit you at Bedford. I regretted to hear that your quiet there was to be disturbed by any business matters and should not allude to the subject but for notice of this proposed visit. I will only say that letters from Cochrane, Sickles and Rand full of complaints come to me, from Cochrane and Sickles *daily.* Cochrane says in his letter of this morning " that a few more weeks of this miserable suspension, and the Administration will have defeated every friend that shall then dare to be a candidate. The Germans are literally enraged." I allude to these things that in the event the matter should be brought to your attention by Mr. Schell you may be notified of the state of feeling on the other side. From all I can learn I infer that the feeling between the two factions is worse than ever. It is the only thing that now mars the harmony of the party so far as the patronage of this Department is concerned. For your own relief as well as mine, we must prescribe some positive bill which will have the effect at least of terminating the endless scramble. I hope that Schell will consent to yield to the wishes of the members to the extent at least of showing to them and the country that he desires to advance their success as far as he can with propriety do it. It is a subject however which I would advise you to dismiss from your mind until your return to Washington and to which I should not have alluded but for the reason of Mr. Schell's visit to Bedford.

Howell Cobb To James Buchanan.

Pa.

Washington City, *6 Aug., 1858.*

My Dear Sir: I received your letter this morning. Before this time I presume you have seen Mr. Schell and he will explain his side of the question. I feel with you that it is absolutely necessary to take a decided stand about the appointments at New York. The articles in the Herald on the subject of the Custom House, etc., are the emanations of the evil counsellors of Mr. Schell. The pretended attack upon Mr. Schell as well as myself is a flimsy gauze to conceal the author. The articles bear internal evidence of the quarter from which they come. As soon as you return I think we will be able to bring matters to a satisfactory solution. It cannot be temporized with any longer. I regret as much as you do that Mr. Schell yields to the influences around him; but if he persists in that course he cannot be sustained. The simple question is whether your policy or that of Fernando Wood, Mather, Tucker, etc., is to be carried out.

I saw the editors of the Union and communicated to them your suggestion about the Ohio convention. I prepared a short article on the subject and handed it to them for tomorrow's paper. It requires a series of articles so as to keep it all the time before the public.

A gentleman from New York in my office today was at the meeting of the State Central Committee of New York which was recently held at Albany. He says that Fernando Wood (who is a member of the committee) introduced Douglas and Wise resolutions but they were voted down. I mention the fact as one of the signs of the times.

The mail failed from New York, that is, no letter from the Collector, and I cannot therefore give you the receipts for yesterday but all my information confirms the constant improvement in business and revenue.

Howell Cobb To James Buchanan.
Pa.

Washington City, *7 Aug., 1858.*

My Dear Sir: I received this morning yours of the 4th inst., and have addressed Mr. Baker on the subject. Receipts in New York on yesterday $216,000. The day before $279,000. The week will average $220,000 per day.

I learn that Mr. Schell has postponed his visit to you until your return to Washington. I hear that Mather is the author of the editorial in the *Herald* suggesting the removal of Schell and myself. That clique is suffering badly for the want of being dealt with. I don't think it will give much trouble to bring them to their senses.

Everything seems to be going on well in the different Departments. It is gratifying to your friends to know that your visit to Bedford has proven a pleasant one and no doubt beneficial to your health. There is no public reason to hasten your return as far as I am informed of the public business.

Mrs. Cobb, I regret to say, has been quite unwell for several days, but is better today.

Howell Cobb To Alexander H. Stephens. R.
(Private.)

Washington City, *8 Sept., 1858.*

Dear Stephens, By yesterday's mail I received your last letter. I had previously received your letter from Chicago and was waiting for your arrival at home to reply to it. I have been intending for several days to write to you but have been unavoidably prevented and now write you from a sick room.

I cannot agree with you about Douglas; and I trust that his unjust and outrageous conduct towards myself personally has not improperly influenced my judgment in the matter. At all events I have endeavored to look at the question free as far as possible from such influences. If Judge Douglas had done as he promised he would do on his return to Illinois—that is, acquiesce in the action of his party in the passage of the English bill—and ceased his war upon the Administration then you would be right and all of us ought to have sustained him. Such has not been his course. *Publicly* he attacks the administration and the Democratic party as having attempted to perpetrate a fraud. and is doing today more than any other man in the country to arouse and organize opposition to the only feature in the English bill which made it acceptable to the South. I allude to the representative population provision. *Privately* he indulges in the coarsest abuse of the President and on all occasions is peculiarly abusive of myself. Under these circumstances to ask our support is in my opinion asking too much. If the true men of Illinois could receive the support they are entitled to from the Democratic party of the whole country and especially the South, they could defeat both Douglas and Lincoln and form the basis of a reorganization of the Democratic party of Illinois upon its national principles. If Douglas is to be sustained then we should sustain Raskins, Hickman. Montgomery. Davis of Indiana, Clark of New York. and all the balance; and I ask you what becomes of the Democratic party and its principles and what hope is there in the future of keeping the party to its principles? With what propriety can the South ask their friends in the North to stand by them if we show such anxiety to clasp to our confidence the men who have opposed and still continue to oppose our principles? This is a deeper and more important question than the election of Douglas. In my judgment it is a question of maintaining the Democratic party upon its true principles. Have you seen Forney's speech at Tarrytown in New York where the opposition met to renominate and sustain Haskins? Look at that speech and the letters to that meeting from Winter Davis, Horace Greeley and *Thomas L. Harris* of Illinois. You will see in all this the programme of Douglas and his followers. They are determined to break up the Democratic party or else to force us to confess " the fraud " and organize upon their line. Forney announces in plain language his purpose and that of his friends to unite with anybody and everybody to defeat us. You know as well as I do the relationship that both Forney and Harris bear to Douglas, and you may rest assured that' the purpose of *one* is the purpose of *all*. It is only a question of time and policy when and how they shall make the most successful war. Don't allow your kind feelings and past confidence in Douglas to deceive you in this matter. The Democratic party and the South have nothing to hope for from his success. Whilst upon some of the old issues Douglas makes strong professions, you see nothing in his course upon new issues to inspire hope and confidence in him. His confidential friends Forney and Harris indicate very clearly by their course what you may in the end expect from Douglas. I have written hastily but you will see the points. I am too unwell to write more but felt anxious to make these suggestions to you. I shall be happy to hear from you when you can write.

Joseph E. Brown To Alexander H. Stephens. R.

Executive Department, Milledgeville ga., *May 5th, 1859.*

Dear Sir: Your letter inclosing application of Mr. J. E. Growland of Washington City to be appointed Commissioner of Deeds for Georgia has just reached this office and upon your recommendation I will appoint him with great pleasure. I have just directed a secretary to inform him that his application has been received here with your recommendation and that he will receive a commission on forwarding to this office the usual fee in such cases. I am much gratified to learn that in your opinion the people generally sustain my administration. I have seen nothing in the published proceedings of any public meeting except the first one at Atlanta which indicates opposition. I beg you to accept assurances of my highest esteem and kindest personal regard.

Joseph E. Brown To Alexander H. Stephens. R.
(Private.)

Executive Department, Milledgeville ga., *June 4th, 1859.*

Dear Sir: Your very kind and welcome letter reached me today and afforded me much pleasure. I agree with you in every essential particular, and am gratified at the just views you have taken of the duty of the democracy of this state. Indeed I could not believe that any wing or section of the party could desire anything but harmony and was disposed to think that the difficulty arose more in the imaginations of certain influences and gentlemen than from any foundation in fact. Certainly a very general indorsement of the national administration is all that could be expected in Georgia, and that much I think it the duty of the convention to give. I differ from the Administration on several points and warmly sustain it on others. And in my opinion your remark that it is our duty to indorse it as far as we can without a sacrifice of principle and to thus strengthen and not weaken it, is wise and just. While I think the President has committed some errors I have no doubt of his patriotism nor of the purity of his motives, nor have I any doubt that the opposition now so clamourous against him would if in power conduct a much more extravagant and unwise administration. I am led to conclude from the action of the LaGrange meeting of the opposition, and from some things I learned while in Savannah, that an effort will be made to organize a new party in Georgia, to be called the opposition party. The LaGrange meeting as you have doubtless noticed disbands the American party. I do not think the people are prepared again to be humbugged by the cry for a new party. Indeed I very much doubt whether they can organize with as much strength as the American party possessed. If wise counsels prevail in our convention, and the different sections of the party meet in a proper spirit, I think we shall have an easy canvass, at least a safe one. I am always much gratified to hear from you. I think the particular interest which was intended to be advanced by this hasty move may have suffered by it. The indications seem to be that we shall have two delegations at Charleston. If so the influence of the State in that convention will be greatly weakened, and if we do not have another set of delegates, the wishes of probably a very large majority of the democracy will not be consulted. While you take no active part in these matters at present, I know that you observe closely and feel an interest in the questions which most affect the interests of the democracy and the South. I do not wish to be troublesome, as I doubt not your correspondence is burdensome, but I should be much pleased to have a suggestion from you occasionally.

Joseph E. Brown To Alexander H. Stephens. R.
(Unofficial.)

Milledgeville ga., *June 21st, 1859.*

Dear Sir: Your favor was received on the day of the meeting of the convention and I took occasion in compliance with your request, when I heard the subject mentioned, to state to several gentlemen the substance of its contents, which seemed to be a source of regret. They were generally of opinion that you ought not to say positively that you would not accept the nomination of the Charleston Convention if tendered, as circumstances might then be found to exist which would make your determination a matter much to be regretted. While your position as no aspirant is beyond doubt correct I doubt whether your duty to your country would not require you to obey the call of such a body, if made, and whether you could do your duty and decline it. There may be developments within a year which will greatly change the present aspect of affairs. You have before this time no doubt seen the result of the deliberations of our late convention. It went off as harmoniously as could have been expected. and I trust its actions may give general satisfaction. The platform I think a safe one and believe that the resolutions went about far enough. Those who voted against them seemed to acquiesce cheerfully and I saw no exhibition of ill feeling on the part of any.

I feel that I have a right to be proud of the unanimous indorsement of a convention so large and composed of such respectable material. I shall labor hard to continue to deserve this confidence. As you have doubtless learned,

I have declined to canvass the state. The condition of my health and my official duties forbid it. And indeed I greatly doubt the propriety of it in case of an incumbent in the office. I trust my decision may be satisfactory to my friends. If my health were perfect there are so many collateral issues that might be sprung in the canvass, upon which an expression of opinion would be desired and upon which the public mind is divided, that I doubt whether any gains could be expected by the party from such course. I shall attend to my executive duties and tiy to recruit my health.

Howell Cobb To James Buchanan. Pa.

Washington City, *25th July, 1859.*

My Dear Sir: The business of the Department has been carried on without any interruption since you left. The receipts were even larger for the last week at New York than I anticipated, amounting for the week to $1,543,962. At this rate the Treasury will be overflowing, and *in less than two years another remUsion.* The country can hardly stand such importations. The news of peace in Europe has just reached us and I doubt not that the effect will be to make the money market easier and enable us to negotiate all the treasury notes we may desire to re-issue. The business of the Department is all so arranged as to admit of my absence at the time I mentioned to you without the slightest inconvenience or difficulty.

To enable me to reach Athens in time to hear my son speak (the principal object of going at *this particular time),* I must leave here on Sunday the 31st of this month. I will then get to Athens on Tuesday the 2nd of August, and he speaks on the next day. As you may not return by that day, I enclose an appointment for my assistant to act in my absence, commencing on the 2nd of August. If it meets your approval, I would request its return in time for me to leave on Sunday. If, however, you prefer that I should remain until you return I will cheerfully postpone my departure until you get back....

Alexander H. Stephens To J. Henly Smith.1 S.

Crawfordville ga., *July 29th, 1859.* Dear Smith, Your highly esteemed favour of the 26th was duly received....

I have been struck with the various comments that have been made on my speech and the sensation it seems to have produced. On the slave trade question I certainly meant to say nothing except what is 1 A newspaper correspondent at Washington, D. C, a close friend of Stephens.

clearly expressed—that was that unless we get immigration from abroad we shall have but few more slave states. This great truth seems to take the people by surprise. Some shrink from it as they would from death. Still it is as true as death. On the policy of opening the trade I said nothing, and meant to say nothing. The people must consider that for themselves. But a man has called to see me on business and I must stop.

Robert Toombs To Alexander H. Stephens. R.

Washington, Geo., *Aug. 27th, 1859.* Dear Stephens,... I had a good meeting in Oglethorpe yesterday—the day to myself. I intended to keep out of this campaign but I find it necessary to put in. Crawford calls for help " in Macedonia ". I have responded according to his wishes. I shall go to Cuthbert and as the missionaries say wherever else Providence may direct, but I have accepted for Elbert, Warren, Richmd. , Scriven, Jefferson and Randolph already and will fill up with spare time but will have all of our cases in Warren, Hancock and Oglethorpe ready. My Sept. courts must go to the Devil. Write me about the Warren case. All well but the " baby ", and he is quite sick.

Howell Cobb To James Buchanan. Pa.

Washington City, *7 Oct., 1859.*

My Dear Sir: I enclose to you the two last dispatches from New Orleans. You will be gratified to learn that the Walker expedition has in all probability been frustrated by the energy of our officers.

We heard that illegible and two hundred men were to go from New York in the St. Louis when I directed the proper steps to be taken there to prevent it. The St. Louis was accordingly refused a clearance. As such a movement was on hand there I have kept the Harriet Lane at New York for the present but shall send her next week to the Florida coast to look after the slavers. No news. All well.

Alexander H. Stephens To J. Henly Smith. S.

Crawfordville ga., *Nov. 10th, 1859.* Dear Smith, Yours of the 5th inst. came to hand last night. What could have become of your other letters I do not know. They may have been misplaced among my mail matter accumulated in some of my absences. The other day in clearing off my table I found a letter that must have come to hand last July. It was unopened and covered up with papers on my table. Yours may be in some similar predicament. I have now about fifty opened letters unanswered. From this you will see how much overlooking might happen, though my custom is always to reply promptly to anything from you and several others who are on my special list, etc.

I have today sent the $12.25 to B. C. Smith at Webster Place as you directed. I am in very good health now and at work 14 hours out of the 24. I have but little time for general reading. Yet I have taken time to read all the papers in the Douglas controversy except Hon. Reverdy Johnson's. That I got from you last night and have not had time yet to look into it. I have not seen any new light thrown upon this vexed question from any of the papers this controversy has brought out. It was a subject I was familiar with and have been for years. Douglas stands just where he has always stood on the points. He is consistent in my judgment. I have not time to say more now. Several gentlemen are in waiting for me to attend to legal business for them, and I must close with renewed good wishes and gratification at the improvement in your health. I wish you would see Rives and learn what has become of my extra Globes of last session? Give my best wishes to Mac. I will do everything in my power for him. I wrote to him soon after my last to you, recommending him to Kennedy of the Census Bureau. I thought it more likely that he could get a situation under him. If he cannot I will do all in my power for any other place. Let him write to me immediately what his prospect is with Kennedy. Gov. Gilmer is very low.

Howell Cobb To Alexander H. Stephens. R.
(Private.)

Washington City, *H Nov., 1859.*

My Dear Sir: I have received yours in reference to allowing rent to the collector at Augusta. I will look into the matter and see what can be done. You know however that I cannot make an exception to a universal rule *in my own state.* I will do however what I can to gratify your wishes in the case.

I do not know that I can give you a very cheering prospect for the future of the country. On the contrary I feel less hopeful than I ever have done before. The recent election in New York fixes the nomination of Seward as the Black Republican candidate. It would seem that the opposition of the North are prepared to put upon us the fearful issue of submission to Sewardism or disunion. Most of our Northern friends with whom I have talked are decidedly of opinion that we can beat Seward more easily than any other man; I doubt it. I rather incline to the opinion that he is their strongest man. For two years the issue has been distinctly made in New York and at both elections the people have declared in favor of Seward, first in the election of Morgan as governor and next in the election that has just taken place. In both cases the issue was accepted by Seward's friends. This looks to me like Seward was *the* strong man in New York. If so why is he not strong with the Black Republicans everywhere? Our success depends upon the nomination and action of the Charleston convention. If we make a nomination that will secure every Southern state and will at the same time be sufficiently acceptable to the Northern Democracy to secure the soundest of the Northern states we may save the country from the effects of Seward's election. Will that be done? Douglas is now out of the way. His strength is gone even at the North. His strongest adherents admit that policy requires the nomination of a Southern man. No other Northern man professes to look for a nomination. Under these circumstances it seems to me that there should be no serious trouble at Charleston.

There is much speculation about the organization of the House. I fear that there will be a Black Republican organization without much difficulty. They need only six votes to give them a clear majority. There is Hickman and Swartz of Pa., Haskin, Clark and Reynolds of N. Y., Adrian and Riggs of N. Jersey, Jno. G. Davis of Indiana, all elected by the Black Republicans, not to speak of Morris of Illinois and other Douglas Democrats whose Democracy sits very lightly upon them—and Winter Davis and Harris of Md., and Etheridge of Tenn., and Gilmer of N. C., and other Southern oppositionists who are supposed to be quite ready for a bargain. With this material to work upon I don't think the Black Republicans will lose the organization for the want of six votes.

After Congress meets we shall be better able to speculate upon the future as we shall then hear from every section of the country. I shall be glad to hear from you whenever you can write.

Robert Toombs To Thomas W. Thomas.1

Washington, Geo., *Dec. 4th, 1859.*
Dear Thomas, When I went to Sparta to make my great agricultural speech, which the world has already forgotten without being at all conscious of the magnitude of its loss, the tavern keeper there handed me three dollars to give you on sight, alleging that you had overpaid him in some of your money matters. I forgot it when I saw you in Milledgeville and the specter of the three dollars keeps rising before me. I cannot forget it, and therefore to ease my conscience I hereby enclose it to you. I came from Athens Friday last. The Supreme Court gave me my Fraley and Ingram case, also Lindsay Smith and Seals case, but they would not give me my 1 MS. In the possession of Mr. W. J. DeRenne, Wonnsloe, Savannah, Ga.
73566"—13 29

Pulliam will. Dougherty took us up in the Oliver and Persons also, and the court sustained us in that also. I did not care for any of them but the Fraley case where my clients had great interest and I had great confidence in the case and it was brought on my judgement. If I had argued as well before you as I did before the Supreme Court you would have given me the case yourself, and I reproached myself for losing it. I hunted up two strong English decisions right on the point and sustaining my distinctions on Tom Cobb's authorities.

I shall leave day after tomorrow for Washington and must dismiss law and plantations from my mind at least for another winter and perhaps for a much longer time. I do not like the look of things either in Washington or in the North. Old Buck is determined to rule or ruin us. I think he means to continue his own dynasty or destroy the party, and the times are at least favourable to his accomplishing the latter result and the country with it. We must succeed next year with some sound, reliable Southern Democrat or the future is gloomy enough. If we can beat the Black Republicans next year with Hunter or as wise a man as he is, I think the North will put down Republicanism itself. If they beat us I see no safety for us, our property and our firesides, except in breaking up the concern. I do not think it wise for the South to suffer a party to get possession of the government whose principles and whose leaders are so openly hostile not only to her equality but to her safety in the Union, and my present opinion is that if such a calamity should come, we should prefer to defend ourselves at the doorsill rather than await the attack at our hearthstone. I think it madness to wait for what some people call "an overt act." They have already declared war, and if the North elect them it is endorsing the declaration, and we ought to meet it with promptness and decision. What do you think of these matters? Write me fully to Washington, D. C., for I want your opinion and co-operation in whatever policy I may deem it necessary to pursue. My wife has improved slowly but thinks herself able to travel by laying up at night. Nothing new. Give my best regards to Mrs. Thomas.

Alexander H. Stephens To J. Henly Smith. S.

Crawfordville ga., *Dec. 17th, 1859.* Dear Smith, Your letter of the 10th inst. came to hand two days ago. Only one of the packages you were kind enough to forward to me has reached me yet. The other is on the way I suppose. I am obliged to you for your attention in this matter. Please tell them at the office there to forward all matter to me here unless otherwise directed. I have no idea of being in Washington this winter. I regret to hear that things are in as bad condition there as you consider them to be in. I have from the beginning thought that the Southern opposition would unite with the Northern wing either directly or indirectly in the organization of the House. But for the Harper's Ferry movement this would have been done openly and at once in my opinion. That affair has made the Southern men a little more coy. But the ultimate end will be the same. How long it will be before it is reached or by what road I am unable to say. My expectation is that the plurality rule will be one of the ways. But we shall see. On one point I feel quite assured you are in error—that is as to the action of the Charleston convention. In the first place I have no idea that any such feeling as you suppose exists, generally I mean. And in the second place I feel quite confident that it will not be when my views upon the subject are really understood. At present there are those who doubtless look upon me with distrust and suspicion and honestly believe that I have personal aspirations that way. But how I pity and commiserate all such. Their eyes will be opened in due time. Do me the favour as well as them to open them on all occasions when you meet with such cases of lamentable delusion.

I was up in Elberton last Monday on professional business. Saw some of your acquaintances there and subscribed for the Star of the South. By the by, I am well pleased with the articles you have written in that paper upon the subject of our free negro population. I forgot to tell you this before. I take it for granted you wrote the article in the last week's paper in reply to the Constitutionalist on Reid's bill. I found the people in Elbert complaining of the scarcity of corn. But the same complaint is heard here and in all the adjacent counties. It sells no higher there than here—at a dollar a bushel. The weather for the last ten days has been cold. Yesterday we had a Northern cold rain—today the wind is up and we shall by night I think have a hard blow from the North West cold enough. Write to me often during the session. I have rheumatism today in my hand and can say no more. Indeed I fear you cannot read what I have attempted to scribble. Remember me to Mac. I do hope he may get a place somewhere in Washington for another year, as he desires it. But if I were in his place I would not stay there. To all other inquiring friends give my kind regards, particularly to Burch and Spencer if you meet them.

Robert Toombs To Alexander H. Stephens. R.

Washington, D. C, *26th Deer., 1859.* Dear Stephens,... We are all at sea here; no organization of the House and no appreciation of the real state of the times by our friends in either house. It is a mere Gallipago's turtle business with them. You remember old Saml. Houston's story. The Black Republicans are stern, confident and defiant. They manage their side of the house with ten times the skill of ours. Indeed ours is not managed at all but everything on our side is done precisely as they would order it if they had the making of the programme. The old fogies in the Senate are all candidates for the Presidency from highest to lowest, and are as silent, sanctimonious and demure as a wh—e at a christening. Buchanan and his cabinett are as rabid and imbecile as ever and much more profligate; they hesitate at no abuse of patronage to compass their petty party ends. God almighty have mercy on these poor people! I am quite sure no mortal arm can save them. Sherman will be elected with absolute certainty; either the four Anti-Lecomptons will go over to them or the South Americans will lend enough of their traitors from the border to pass the plurality rule. About half the S. Americans are with us. The rest are in full sympathy with the Blk. Republicans, therefore you can readily see how all this will end.

Douglas I think begins to see the great folly of his Harper article and would recall it if he could gladly. But the folly is written and must stand to plague him the balance of his political life. He told me last night week that he would vote for any nominee of the Charleston convention on any platform he might be put! and his friends have so announced in the House. This has cutt him off from Clark, Adrian, Jno. G. Davis and Reynolds and Carter. Briggs was never with him and will vote with us if we need him.

Douglas will be very strong in the Charleston convention. He cannot possibly be elected, but I think will nominate whom he pleases. His friends are very strongly for you and I regret very much if we are to continue the govmt. that you have taken the position not to accept. I think it very unwise in you and hurtfull to the country. I think you could be nominated, especially after the old fogies are done fighting their battle of weakness, for none of them have any strength.

I shall make a speech very early after the holidays reviewing calmly the state of the country, the evils, remedies, effects and consequences. I shall make a clean breast of it, " nothing extenuate nor set down aught in malice"; but I shall not withhold the truth because it may be unpalatable or even dangerous to anybody or any section. Let me hear from you soon. All well.

Robert Toombs To Alexander H. Stephens. R.

Washington, D. C, *88th Deer., 1859.* Dear Stephens,... No news—still no speaker. I still think they will elect Sherman in a few days. The Message is out and is satisfactory to the South on the slavery question. Everything has been dull and stagnant during the Christmas, even negroes cease to excite on either side. The social intercourse between North and South or rather between Denis, and Eeps. seems almost wholly to have ceased, and all sides seem sullen and ill-natured....

Joseph E. Brown To Alexander H. Stephens. R.
(Confidential.)

Executive Department, Milledgeville ga., *Deer. 29th, 1859.*

Dear Sir: You have doubtless noticed with interest the difficulties growing up in the democratic party of our state in reference to the appointment of delegates to the Charleston convention, and I should be gratified to have your opinion as to the proper course to be pursued. I was fully satisfied that the people did not have an opportunity for a fair expression of their will in the convention which was called by the members of the legislature and which met on the 8th inst.1 The notice was so short that they could not act, and the selection of delegates was left mainly to such senators and representatives as were willing to take the responsibility to act for the party. I did not hesitate to say that in my opinion the convention should be adjourned over to the time fixed by the executive committee of the democratic party. Other courses prevailed however and the question now is, what had best be done.

Robert Toombs To James Buchanan. Pa.

Washington, D. C, *Dec. 29th, 1859.* My Dear Sir: I send you Hobbes's Thucydides; on page 69 you will find the message of the Lacedemonians and the beginning of the speech of Pericles. You will perceive that even if the repeal of the decree against the Megarians would prevent war he advised his countrymen rather to accept war than to repeal it, for what I consider solid and statesmanlike reasons, as valid today as then. Indeed the experience of more than twenty centuries has fully established the soundness of his position.

Joseph E. Brown To Alexander H. Stephens. R.
(Private.)

Executive Department, Milledgeville ga., *J any. 5th, 1860.*

Dear Sir: It affords me pleasure to acknowledge the receipt of. your kind letter and to thank you for the frank manner in which you have responded to my request. I desired your opinion only for 1 This convention had adopted a resolution to present the name of Howell Cobb to the Charleston convention as a candidate for the presidency, and appointed a set of delegates from Georgia favorable to Cobb's nomination.
my own satisfaction and not for public use. I shall certainly not complicate you with the matter. I agree with you on almost every suggestion you have made. It would be a great misfortune for the democracy to be divided upon the question of appointing delegates to Charleston. If the influences which brought about the other convention will unite in the convention in March I should feel quite willing that your suggestion be carried out and that the persons appointed in December be considered as nominated in March and the nominations confirmed. If they should fail however to unite in the convention in March, I should doubt the propriety of re-appointing all of them. It would be a greater concession than they could reasonably ask. I am however willing to do any thing that can be honorably done to promote harmony. I am always glad to hear from you.

Alexander H. Stephens To J. Henly Smith. S.

Crawfordville ga., *Jan. 5th, 1860.* Dear Smith:... My being out of sorts in health I think is owing to the weather. We have no news. Times rather hard and some complaint with the people for money. Provisions are high and property of all kinds higher than I ever knew it to be.

The country is waiting patiently to see what the Congress will do. But I verily believe they do not care a button what is done. There is really not the least excitement in the public mind upon public affairs. No man that I have seen for weeks or months seems to take any interest in what is going on in Washington. The message of the President has been here a week and I have not seen the first person who has read it. I have alluded to it several times when in company with our most intelligent and reading people and I have not met with one yet who has read it except myself, not even the lawyers in town—we have two, Bristow and Beaseley. How the honor of being a member of Congress and working and worrying oneself half to death there for the good of the people at home vanishes into thin air and becomes perfectly nothing in the estimation of one mingling with the people and seeing how little they care for such things. I had no idea that what was going on at the seat of government produced so little effect upon the public mind as it does. If I had known the fact, I think I should have quit long time ago. But enough of this....

Robert Toombs To Alexander H. Stephens. R.

Washington, D. C, *J any. 5th, 1860. 1* Dear Stephens,... Gilmer never got a Democratic vote on any ballot. I strongly advised them against it, and so far they have 1 Erroneously dated Jan. 5th, 1859, in the original.
firmly adhered. I think Sherman will certainly be elected. He lacked but three votes yesterday, owing to the absence of Dan Sickles without a pair. I understand he could not pair and was obliged to go home. He is looked for today. Stalworth is still drunk and ab-

sent in Alabama. Our Kentucky young friend Brown can't vote on account of non-age and I suppose as soon as one or two more of them get drunk or sick the Blacks will get in range of Winter Davis, Harris and Reynolds, and they will settle it. One of our great difficulties is that there is no leader in the House. None of our people have any control over the Northern Democrats, and therefore an election outside of the Black Republican party is impossible...

Robert Toombs To Alexander H. Stephens. R.

Washington, D. C, *11 J any., 1860.*

Dear Stephens, I recd. your letters of the 1st, 3d, and 6th and 7th inst. yesterday morning and last night. The freezing up of the Potomac piled up all the mails at Acquia Creek and expect kept mine to you here. Yours of the 7th inst. contained your check, for which I am obliged to you. I must have left my brief in the Swan case at home with the bill of exceptions, as I can find it nowhere; but I do not know that I have anything new in it. The Missouri case I suppose you can find in Savannah.

I should pay no attention to the letter of Judge Warren. You have said your say and ought to let it rest. If you answer all the suggestions of the same nature which will be made before the Charleston convention you will get tired of it. Hunter is hurt in Virginia by Wise tho' he is very confident of carrying a majority of the delegates. Wise's friends are willing to support him if he can get the greater outside of Virginia influence, about which there can be no doubt if he has any chance at all. There are very decided indications of the North in favor of Breckinridge. Pennsylvania is certainly for him and so is N. York *if she can carry him.* His great difficulty is with Douglas. Douglas is very much opposed to him, indeed he told me in private that he *was Ms last choice,*—but keep this to yourself. I am very sorry for it. I do not see how we can elect a President or even nominate one without Douglas men, and he is not cordial in favour of Hunter; in fact he would go to him with reluctance. I fear Hunter's want of vim will defeat his nomination. I am quite sure if we could get him up he would make the best race and the best President of any in the lot. But I much fear that he is too honest for the tricksters and too modest to make his way even with the better materials. Douglas's friends and he himself seem more inclined if he can not get it himself to go for you. This may be because you are not in the ring by your own act of exclusion.

I think Mr. Buchanan would like to prevent the nomination of another in order to make himself necessary. This is impossible. He weakens with the party every day. You can understand how little he knows of the use of patronage when he sends Grund to Havre and Faulkner to Paris. Grund caught a senatorial veto. I suppose they will pass Faulkner.

The weather here has been warm and foggy for the last three days, as disagreeable as possible overhead and underfoot. I intended to speak this week but my throat has been sore and I have had a very bad cold. I think I shall speak early next week. I shall give a very thorough review of the present and urge the union of all sound elements to drive out the Black Republicans next fall as the only mode of giving peace and security to the country.

Julia is well. I saw Ward a few days ago, he has not yet finished your bust, he says it will be ready in a week or two.

Howell Cobb To John B. Lamar. E. (Private)

Washington City, *15 Jany., 1860.*
Dear Col.,... In reference to the two conventions in Ga., I have felt much embarrassed but have concluded to write to my friends my views and feelings about the matter and there leave it. I do not entertain any doubt about the regularity and policies of the December convention. According to the past usage of the party it is the only regular and legitimate convention that can be held. At the same time I am not willing to be placed in the position of having obtained by management the delegation from the State to Charleston and being then unwilling to allow the Democracy of the State to pass upon my claims. I attach more importance to the action of the December convention as affording evidence of the confidence in me by the democratic party of Ga. than I do to the votes of their delegates. If the democracy of my own State are against me, I would neither accept the votes of the delegates, nor a nomination even, at Charleston—if I could obtain it—and I am perfectly willing that my enemies should know that such is my position. Let the fact be manifested in any way, shape or form that the democracy of Georgia are against my nomination at Charleston, and that moment my name shall be peremptorily and unconditionally withdrawn from the public consideration in that convention. Entertaining these views and feelings, I have said to my friends who have written to me on the subject: Go into the March convention and accept the issue which has been made. If the democracy are for me, it will be a plain and simple duty to affirm and approve the action of the December convention; if against me, then let them adopt a new platform, select new delegates and present the name of some other favorite for the Presidency. In this matter I can speak only for myself, but all parties may rest assured that my name shall not be used to distract the democratic party of the State at a time when a united South is so imperatively required for our common protection. These views I have freely expressed in all the letters which I have written on the subject. I have not written anything for publication, but I am not only willing but desirous that my position should be made known in the most public and emphatic manner.

From all that I can learn from different portions of the state I do not entertain a doubt that an overwhelming majority of the democracy are with me, and if proper efforts are made to send the right kind of delegates to the March convention it will be made so to appear in that convention.

To my mind the future of the country looks gloomy and for that reason I may feel less solicitous about this matter than I would under other circumstances. I say to you in all candor and sincerity— I am more desirous of obtaining the full confidence of the people of Ga., that I may serve them in the trying crisis that is before us, than I do to obtain even presidential honors....

Alexander H. Stephens To J. Henly Smith. S.

Crawfordville ga., *Jan. 22d, 1860.* Dear Smith, Your long letter of the 9th inst. was not received by me until my return the other day from Savannah, where I was at the Supreme Court for ten days. Since my return I have been very busy with a case in Hancock county. I have noticed Major Cooper's articles in the Constitutionalist but I have not had time to read a single one of them and therefore cannot give you an opinion upon the subject. In relation to the matter of Union or disunion I have only a word to say and that is, if I thought our own people, our public men and private men, were prepared for it, had the proper elements of character, stability of purpose, loyalty to principle, devotion to country, etc., I should not look upon such an alternative with the apprehension I do. The truth is I fear that if disunion should result, if by necessity it should come, we should be no better off in a new republic than we are in the present one. We should have the same or similar wrangling and confusion. Indeed if we were now to have a Southern convention to determine upon the true policy of the South either in the Union or out of it, I should expect to see just as much profitless discussion, disagreement, crimination and recrimination amongst the members of it from different States and from the same State, as we witness in the present House of Representatives between Democrats, Republicans and Americans. The troubles that now beset and environ us grow not out of the nature of our government or any real "irrespressible conflict" between adverse interests. No such things; they grow out of the state of public opinion and the character of our public men North and South. There is a general degeneracy, confined not to one section or the other. The government in itself is good enough—the danger lies in no inherent defect in it. It is in the men who have charge of it, and the people who put such men in charge. The danger is much more radical, I fear, than the Southern people generally imagine, especially those who think disunion would be a remedy for the evils they feel. One may talk as flippantly or as seriously as one pleases of disunion, but one thing is evident to my mind, it will only render confusion worse confounded unless our people can agree upon some line of policy to be pursued and shall generally at least unite and agree to stand together in its maintenance. And if they would do this there would be no necessity for disunion. If they will not do this beforehand have we any reason to hope that they will do it afterwards? I fear not. When the passions of men are once let loose, without control legal or moral, there is no telling to what-extent of fury they may lead their victims. Republicks can only be maintained by virtue, intelligence and patriotism. We have but little public virtue, heroic virtue or patriotism now amongst our public men. They are generally selfish, looking not to country but to individual aggrandisement. There are but few now in Congress who consider anything so much as how their own votes affect them at home. This is a lamentable truth. And if we should break up, all these fellows would be striving to get the inner track of each other, each to take the lead of all the rest. It would be a race between demagogues to see who could pander most to the passions, prejudices and ignorance of the people, that they might profit thereby—just such a sort of thing as was seen in France, 1792, and in Mexico now. This is my apprehension. If the necessity comes I shall hope for the best; but I am by no means sanguine. I wish I were. I can but look upon the alternative as little better than jumping out of the frying pan into the fire. We would quit one set of demagogues to try another. But enough. These sentiments I give to you. They are hastily penned and not intended in this shape for anybody's use and reflection but your own.

Robert Toombs To Alexander H. Stephens. R.

Washington, D. C, *31st Jany., 1860.* Dear Stephens,... I send you a copy of my speech today. The account in the Union by mistake cutts off a column and a half of it. We have whipped out Sherman and the Helperites. Pennington will be elected today or tomorrow; but he professes to be only a New Jersey opposition man. Seward died hard but he is slain. The common impression here is that my speech did them great harm. It had the tendency to bring us together. Every Southern vote stood together solidly for two days and every Northern Democrat but two stood with them, even on a Southern Whig. Smith declared himself independent of all parties and declared he had never belonged to any party but the old Whig party and bolted that in 1852 on Scott. If we could get a fair man for a candidate we could elect him, but the factions here are terrible and destructive....

Alexander H. Stephens To J. Henly Smith. S.

Crawfordville ga., *Feb. 4th, 1860.*

Dear Smith, I have just got back from Augusta where I have been all the past week attending court, and now have your letter of the 30th ulto. before me. The news of the organization of the House reached Augusta while I was there and I saw no man there or anywhere else since that was not gratified at it. I think our friends made some. good points by the course they have taken and ought to feel that the triumph was theirs. They broke the line of the Republicans. They rebuked the endorsers of Helper (I believe Pennington was not on the list of these). They broke the Seward line—he is I believe not the favorite of Pennington—though I have never looked upon Seward as formidable at all, but others have so considered him. I have never thought that he stood any chance for a nomination, and if he were nominated I think he is the weakest man they could run.

Still the moral effect of breaking the prestige of the *ultra* wing of the party is a great point gained. I look upon Pennington as a sort of moderate anti-slavery man with a good deal of national feeling, who is in his present position more by accident than by choice. This is the idea I have of him. WThat a mistake Sherman committed in giving or allowing the use of his name to the friends of Helper as he did, and what greater mistake he made in not coming out in a manly way and saying that he did not approve the sentiments of his book as he has since seen the work! This was just such weakness as a large class of men have who have not the nerve to meet questions at the right time in the right way. Such men can never be leaders. They are by nature only third or fourth rate, and can never rise except by accident to high position. I take it for granted that Sherman does not in fact approve Helper's doctrines. I always regarded him as more decided in his anti-slavery opinions than Pennington, but as by no means amongst the rabid and ultra men on his side of the House. I think that so fur as the duties of the chair are concerned he would have made a better speaker than Pennington. The latter I fear will make an inefficient officer. Sherman would not have come up to the grade of any of his late predecessors; Pennington I apprehend will fall far below them. Banks made one of the ablest if not the ablest Speakers I ever saw in the chair. He was without doubt the most impartial Speaker I ever saw in the House of Representatives. In some things I think Cobb was his superior. It is a matter of vast importance to have an able, quick and prompt presiding officer over any deliberative body and especially in our Ho use of Representatives where there is so much excitement and animosity. Impartiality too is the crowning gem of a Speaker's character. I fear this will be wanting in Pennington. Still I hope all will go along smoothly. I was much pleased with Mr. Toombs's speech. It is exactly on the right line. It is in better tone, temper, and shows more real statemanship with less impulse of bare? passion than any speech I have ever seen from him. If the South would but see the deep truths it teaches, the profound philosophy it inculcates, the true national patriotism it breathes throughout, and would to a man stand unitedly upon the policy it marks out, we should not only carry the next elections. but the country would be safe? just so long as they would maintain sternly that line. Their destiny is truly in their own hands. But if they can not see these things, these truths, and can not be got to adopt so plain, so safe and so wise a policy, what can be expected of them in any other emergency or alternative that their folly may drive them into? That is a question that oppresses me in looking after a solution of it. How can I be sanguine in hope as to what a people will do on a new line when they make so fatal a blunder on one so plain and clear? But let the worst come that may, we must all meet. act according to the necessities of the occasion. It is immaterial by what blunder, foolishness or wickedness the necessity is brought about. We can only hope for the best, while we should at all times be prepared for the worst.

P. S., written on a separate slip of paper.—You may show this to Mr. Toombs if you think proper.

Robert Toombs To Alexander H. Stephens. R.

Washington, D. C., *Feby. 10th, 1860.* Dear Stephens, I have recd. your letters of the 4th and 5th inst. I merely felt a curiosity to know where they had tripped old Holt. He is so blind in his rage against all persons indicted for crimes that he is incapable of giving any man a fair trial, and therefore does more to obstruct public justice than any man in the state. I am glad poor Jones got his neck out of the halter, especially as I did not want his blood on my hands....

There is a lull in politics here just now. Poor Pennington seems wholly incompetent to discharge the duties of the chair, and has been in sad trouble about his committees. The Blacks are likely to break down on their printer unless they can fix up by Monday night. Pennington is not an endorser of Helper's book but he is a Whig, K. N. Fremonter, anti-Seward. The defeat of Sherman was gall and wormwood to the Seward division of the Blacks. It brought them into national discredit and strengthened the opposition to Seward inside his party. My points on them, especially in the fugitive slave case, have told even stronger than I supposed at the North. The party are dumfounded here. No man among them as yet has dared to come up to their defence, tho' next week I am told Hale, Foot and Fessenden will come back at me. If they are fools enough to keep up that fight we shall whip them even in several of the New England states. The Northern members are circulating it largely and say that it has and is producing a very healthy reaction against the Blacks. You have doubtless seen that Brown, Davis and Pugh have all introduced resolutions concerning slavery in the territories. Davis's are those approved by the President and are in the main good; but I think all of them are wrong. It is the very foolishness of folly to raise and make prominent such *issues now.* By the Kansas act of 1854 we repealed the Missouri restriction, declared our purpose as far as possible to remove the question of slavery from the halls of Congress, and therefore gave the territorial legislatures all the power over it which the Constitution allowed them to exercise, and to test that limit provided that all cases involving liberty might be appealed to the Supreme Court. The court has decided that Congress can not prohibit slavery in the territories, and altho' I think it involves the power of the territorial legislatures also, yet it is true that that precise point has never come directly before the Court and never may. It has not arisen in seventy years; it may not arise in seventy years more. Why then press it now when we have just as much weight as we can possibly carry? Hostility to Douglas is the sole motive of movers of this mischief. I wish Douglas defeated at Charleston, but I do not want him and his friends crippled or driven off. Where are we to get as many or as good men in the North to supply their places? Can we get them from the Blacks? From the Fillmore K. Ns? From the old Whigs? There are none such in either ranks. Then it is naked folly to turn out a quarter of a million at least of such men on such pretenses. If this folly shall succeed, God save these poor people, for I can see no other arm in that case. The Democratic caucus meets tomorrow to try to carry out this business. I shall resist it to the last extremity.

The election of Pennington has brought another large brood of abolitionists into this district, and together with those brought here by Banks will abolitionize it completely. The effects here are plainly visible. In view of such effects and consequences here from the mere possession of one branch of Congress we ought not to shut.our eyes to the effects of the possession of the government in all of its departments by *any Black Republican.* It would abolitionize Maryland in a year, raise a powerful abolition party in Va., Kentucky and Missouri in two years, and foster and rear up a free labour party in the whole South in four years. Thus the strife will be transferred from the North to our own friends. Then security and peace in our borders is gone forever. Therefore I deeply lament that any portion of our people shall hug to their bosoms the delusive idea that we should wait for some "overt act." I shall consider our ruin already accomplished when we submit to a party whose every principle, whose daily declarations and acts are an open proclamation of war against us, and the insidious effects of whose policy I see around me every day. For one I would raise an insurrection, if I could not carry a revolution, to save my countrymen, and endeavor to save them in spite of themselves. I did not press these views in my speech, for obvious reasons which you will readily perceive. I am now endeavoring to avert this calamity by and thro' the aid of good men in the North and would not therefore weaken them by this view of the future. I may find it necessary to press it in some form before Congress adjourns. My next speech will be in defence of the "slave power." The denunciations of us everywhere in the North under this name is doing us much harm. By reviewing the government from the beginning I can not only vindicate our section to the North but show the South how little portion they have in David, what little inheritance in the son of Jesse. I am now gathering up and analyzing facts for this purpose. I have written you a longer letter than I intended. Send it to Linton when you read it. All well.

Alexander H. Stephens To J. Henly Smith. S.

Crawfordville ga., *Feb. 24th, 1860.*

Dear Smith, Some time has past since I heard from you last. I fear you are sick again. Sam McJunkin got home three days ago. He came here but I was at Glascock Court. He doubtless would have been able to give me full information about you but as I did not see him I am the more anxious. In my last I inquired of you after Ward's bust. Has he finished it or not? Some friend sent me a copy of the proceedings of some art association of which Dr. Stone is President in Washington City. At the exhibition I see this bust of Ward's mentioned. Still I do not know whether it is finished or not. I have not heard a word from him on the subject since last November or October. If you are well I wish you would find it and after looking at it tell me what sort of a thing it is—is it good or not— well executed I mean—would you from seeing it know for whom it was taken, that is the question, and is the association quick? Nobody here ever thought of me in looking at Sander's bust! Another thing I would inquire about——that is what has become of Peyton's article or sketch that you told me some time ago would appear in the Constitutionalist? Is it still on hand, will it appear, or is the idea abandoned? I simply wish to know how the matter stands. If you are not sick I wish you to write to me and give me the news generally. I should like to know what Bright and Fitch are after—who are they for in the Charleston convention—they seem to be dead against Douglas. Who is Vallandingham for? What is the present prospect for Hunter? He is the man above all others I should prefer to see nominated. Still if Douglas should be, I should support him most cordially if he does nothing worse than he has yet done. This is of course for yourself; I do not wish to have anything to do with public affairs further than to act my part as a private citizen and do not wish to be figuring in the newspapers in any way. I have been excessively annoyed by the use made of my name in our own newspapers. I do not intend to allow the Milledgeville March convention to connect my name in any way with the Charleston convention. The Presidency is an office I do not want and would not have if I could get it by my own mere volition. Write to me soon. I am now at home but will soon be on the circuit again.

Alexander H. Stephens To Dk. Henry R. Casey.1

Crawfordville ga., *March 9th, 1860.*

Dear Sir: You will, I suppose, be in the convention at Milledgeville on the 14th inst., and I therefore address these lines to you there. The subject relates particularly to myself, but I trust you will under the circumstances excuse the obtrusion.

From the allusions to my name in the newspapers in connection with the probable action of that body I feel warranted and justified in authorising you as a friend to make known generally to your fellow members what you and all others who have conferred with me either directly or indirectly about the matter already know, that so far from wishing to be the cause of any embarrassment in their deliberations, I do not wish my name connected with the Presidency in any way. This is certainly no time for the people of the South 1 From the Constitutionalist, Augusta, Ga., Apr. 10, 1860. Dr. Casey was a delegate from Columbia County to the Georgia Democratic Convention then about to assemble at Milledgeville.

to be weakening their strength by divisions and struggles to promote or advance the aspirations of particular favorites to the office of Chief Magistrate of the Union. It is eminently a time for harmony among the friends of the Constitution every where, South as well as North. So far as I am individually concerned, I wish it distinctly known that I have no aspirations for that high office—none whatever; and whatever comment it may subject me to by those who do not know me, I assure you I would not of my own free choice assume its great trusts, if nothing were necessary to enable me to do so but my bare volition. Its duties, cares, anxieties and heavy responsibilities would, with me, far outweigh all fancied honors that may be supposed to attend it.

It is well perhaps for the country that we have quite a number of able and true men who look upon it differently and who have a taste and inclination for the position. By all means let some such one, who can unite the greatest strength in the coming contest be selected as the standard bearer of our cause. Let there be no useless and mischievous wranglings for individual favorites, either at Milledgeville or at Charleston, and all may be well. The only interest I feel in the question is that which all good citizens should feel who desire from the Government nothing but a wise, safe, sound and vigorous administration upon such principles as will secure the rights of all, and the peace, quiet, happiness and prosperity of our common country. In no event do I desire my name connected with it in any way.

You can do with this letter as you think best to accomplish my wishes. If need be, you may read it to the convention.

Robert Toombs To Alexander H. Stephens. R.

Washington, D. C, *Mar. 16th, 1860.* Dear Stephens,... We are getting on badly. The Black Reps, are now strong enough to do mischief in the Senate and are using their power. The Nicaragua Treaty was beaten yesterday and injunction of secrecy taken off by us to expose them. It is nothing to us and I don't care a fig for it, but they are such fools as not to understand their own interest. They will also defeat the Mexican treaty when action is had on it. You will see Ohio refuse to give up old Brown's son and another of the refugees from Harper's Ferry. So we go. New Hampshire has increased her Republican majority and we shall lose every Northern State in the Union except California and perhaps Oregon. The strife here runs " fast and furious" between the friends of the different candidates. It looks to me very much like the officers of ships being engaged in cheating one another at " three up " in the forecastle while the vessel is labouring among the breakers. Douglas I think cannot weather the storm. Penn. and N. York are against him and he is weak in New England, but the great element of his weakness in the North is the hostility of the South to him. I fear he is not patriot enough to struggle for the country with the banner in any other hand than his own. Hunter's prospects have greatly improved within the last week but he by no means shows strength to command the nomination. Penn. wants a tariff man and of course expects the Dem. party now to swallow its past history to secure her support, doubtful at least. Seward has the ascendant with the Blacks and I think will be nominated but it is not certain. Neither New England nor Penn. politicians want him; but I think their people do, and that may finally settle it in his favour. The Democratic wing of the Blacks are rampant for the candidate but as they are a majority I suppose they will be whipped in. Buchanan is at his old game of breaking down in succession all democratic aspirants in order to get it himself, and is laughed at by his own menials and dependants.

I went to see Holt about N. I did not find him in and wrote him a note. I have not yet heard from him. We hear there was trouble in the Geo. convention.1 Our accounts tho' are only up to 12 o'clock the first day of the session. It will be bad to have a split in Geo. and worse still to send two delegations. God knows one is as much as any people ought to stand in such a crowd. Crawford is well, and the House is getting on badly. Julia has thrown away her stick and improves slowly.

Alexander H. Stephens To J. Henly Smith. S.

Crawfordville ga., *Mch. 18th, 1860.* Dear Smith, Your letter of the 14th inst. was received last night. The catalogue of books came duly to hand. It was from that that I gave Mr. Shockly the information about where he could get Niles's Register, and he authorized me to get some one, I named you, to purchase the set for him. But I did not know who sent the catalogue to me at the time. Your letter however to which you allude giving me the information that you had sent it *did come* after a while. I got it just before going to Greene Court the past week. It was delayed somehow and somewhere, I know not how or where. It is safely at hand now however. This I state that you may not 1 A second Georgia Democratic convention met at Mlledgevllle, Mar. 14, 1860. After much wrangling between the Cobb and anti-Cobb factions the latter withdrew temporarily and nominated a ticket of delegates to the Charleston convention. The convention then reassembled and elected a delegation to Charleston of twice the usual size comprising an equal number of Cobb and anti-Cobb men, but instructed the whole delegation to vote as a unit. This convention rejected the resolutions which the December convention had adopted.

73566—13 30 be uneasy about it, as you express some anxiety on that point. The letter gave me a good deal of information on subjects that I was glad to be informed about, and I am obliged to you for it. I have been a good deal annoyed by the use I have seen made of my name in connection with the Charleston nomination, particularly in our own State. An effort has been made to get up a sort of "a tempest in a tea pot " here between Mr. Cobb and myself. Now this I need not assure you was all against my will and wishes. I have done all that I could to prevent any reference to me whatever. And I have felt truly mortified at hearing as I have that Mr. Cobb's friends thought I was at the head of the opposition to him. This is utterly groundless. How little do men who so talk know of what I have done to harmonize that opposition. Our convention is just over and to my surprise the December recommendation of Mr. Cobb was voted down! This only shows the strong opposition to him in the state that nothing could allay. The truth is Mr. Cobb is not the choice of the Democracy of Georgia, not as between me and him but as between him and any other prominent man of the party. He would be the weakest man that there is any probability of being nominated so far as the State of Georgia is concerned. This is my deliberate judgment; it is needless to say why it is so. I regret that it is so. I give the judgment with no pleasure for I esteem Mr. Cobb highly and would support him warmly. As for anv individual rivalship with him I scorn the imputation. I have none of it. I do not wish the office and have no personal favouritism for any other one over him for it. But what I say is simply what I believe to be the naked, unsophisticated truth. Mr. Cobb's friends ought to be able to account for this fact without attributing it directly or indirectly to me. Did he not tiy his strength with his party for the Senate when he and they thought his election almost certain, and yet instead of getting the nomination by a 2/3 vote he did not get even 1/3 I believe. I was not then acting with the party, and was openly for him with the opposite party then against any other man of his own party. I mean I did with the opposite party with which I acted all I could for him if the election came into the Legislature between him and any other of his own party. I preferred him to all others of his party. I have always esteemed him highly and have been on good terms with him personally. All this I say to you, for it is the truth. But I do not wish you to say anything of the opinion I have given of his standing in the State, for my motives would be questioned by an ignorant uncharitable world and I would not have him injured even to the extent that my opinion, if known, would do it. I wish him to keep hold and maintain all the strength he has got. I would do or say nothing to weaken it. Whether he or his friends would act the same magnanimous part by me I know not and care not, for I have no wishes to be gratified or vanity to be flattered. I feel as independent of the world as any man ever did. Had my name been presented to our late convention I have no doubt it would have been substituted for his by a large majority, much larger than the vote against his recommendation was, for I know several of my warmest friends voted for him, knowing it was my wish, and I had written several letters to particular friends urging them most positively and earnestly not to offer my name or permit it to be offered. These are the facts; but I have not time to say more.

Alexander H. Stephens To J. Henly Smith. S.

Crawixjrdville ga., *April lth, 1860.* Dear Smith, I got home last night from Hancock court and found your letter of the date I forget but the one about your correspondence with the Confederacy. I would advise you to write as requested. I do not know what the prospect for your pay will be; but he is a clever man personally. I would simply give him the news. He is not a disunionist per se as I understand him. He is not in favour of opening the African slave trade either, as I understand him. He does no good however to any cause, in my opinion. He is too violent. This I say to you. His judgment is not good. I would advise you, if you write, neither to advocate disunion or the opening of the slave trade. The people here at present I believe are as much opposed to it as they are at the North; and I believe the Northern people could be induced to open it sooner than the Southern people. It would be useless to write on that subject at this time. I have nothing more to say; no time rather to say more.1

Robert Toombs To Alexander H. Stephens. R.

Washington, D. C., *Wth Apl, 1860.* Dear Stephens,... The city is pretty well vacated. All the scheming active politicians have " hied away " to Charleston to select an almoner for the Great Democratic party. The uncertainty of the result is even greater now than at any former period of the contest. Hunter cannot be nominated; nobody will go for him at the North simply because he is an honest man and they want no such a person to guard the exchequer; they pretend that he cannot run at the North on account of his free-trade opinions, which simply amounts to saying that the northern democrats will not support any man who holds the principles of the party. Breckinridge it is said can get Penn. but N, York will not touch him. his character is too good for them.

1 Endorsed in pencil on a blank pane at the end of this letter is the following by J. Henly Smith:

"James P. Hamilton, Editor of the Southern Confederacy, published at Atlanta, Ga., has requested me to correspond for him. As Mr. Stephens udviscs it, I will comply.— J. H. 8."

Guthrie I think will show more Northern strength than any of our Southern men. Douglas will be beaten, I think, with absolute certainty. He will get as good as no support in the North but of the Northwest, and his enemies are numerous, vindictive and remorseless. His aggressive policy makes all opponents enemies both North and South, and nothing but a large break in the South in his behalf can possibly elect him. This I do not look for, altho' I am quite sure he is stronger in the South than he will be with her representatives at Charleston; but I suppose speculations will be of no use now as the end is near. Julia and Sallie and the

Capt. are all in good health and send their best regards.

Robert Toombs To Alexander H. Stephens. R.

Washington, D. C., *May 5th, 1860.* Dear Stephens, Your letter from Lexington was duly recd. and I had intended an earlier answer but could not lay my hands upon my scattered fragments of briefs in the Persons and Oliver cases until yesterday. We have been all excitement here until yesterday when we heard of the final break up at Charleston, and things are now so complicated that it is difficult to tell what is best to be done. Douglas's men made a great mistake in voting to go to the platform before nominating a Prest. A rupture then became inevitable; but he and his friends expected to profit by the secession of two or three states and therefore urged it in common with the various elements of combustion in the So. West. When they resolved to go to platform making I telegraphed Irwin to get a good one and a Southern man on it or bolt. Subsequently when we heard here that the convention had adopted the Tennessee platform I advised Nelms to go back and stand on it; but it appears now that the convention never did adopt except to the extent of the 2/3 of the whole number of delegates from all the states. The nomination of Douglas is now impossible under this. rule, and if it were possible to nominate him he cannot be elected. The amount of discontent with him in the free states would beat him there even if the South would vote for him as a unit, which I do not think possible under existing circumstances. The truth is the rivalry and rancor between the friends of Douglas and all the rest was so great and is now so great that I do not see how it can possibly be reconciled without the withdrawal of the combatants on both sides, which I think none of them have patriotism enough to do. But everything here is at sea. The only chance I see is to get all of them back upon some arrangement made outside and before the Balto. meeting. If this cannot be done I shall stand by the bolters and let things rock on. The Central states disgraced themselves by making an ultimatum and backing down from it. I think if they had stood by the Tennessee resolution an accommodation could be made. The real difficulty at Charleston was that a large number of Democrats North and South had committed themselves so far against Douglas that they were lost if he was nominated, and they therefore preferred ruining the party with themselves than ruining themselves without the party. This being the difficulty, it is evident that nothing but the defeat of Douglas can remedy it. I think tho' he got within a few of his last vote when he reached 152. My health is good as also Julia's and the rest of the family. I am heartily sick of this turmoil and regret that I had not taken your course last winter.

Robert Toombs To Alexander H. Stephens. R.

Washington, D. C., *May 7th, 1860.* Dear Stephens, The late events in Charleston have created a great sensation here. The result of general consultation among the Southern Senators seems to be this—that admitting the propriety of the secession when it was done, that Virginia, Kentucky and Tennessee having preferred an ultimatum which was sustained by N. York and can be carried by those votes in connection with those of the seceding states, that the seceders shall return to Balto., unite with Virginia and Tenneessee and Kentucky in the ultimatum, upon the agreement beforehand that all will secede together if the ultimatum be rejected. I think this programme will be adopted this morning at a meeting of the Senators and Reps. of the seceding states, and will be offered by the Tennessee platform states, upon which a joint address will be made to the South.

I am sorry to see an effort making in Georgia to call a new convention, doubtless simply to send delegates for Douglas. The present delegation would be sustained unless condemned by the convention which sent them to Charleston, which it would be much better to recall than to get up a new one under the notice I see given in Augusta. A bogus delegation would only complete the demoralization and ruin of the party in Georgia, and would certainly be fatal to Douglas even if he should carry the nomination at Charleston. I see but little hope for a favourable issue of the business. The rancor existing between the Douglas and anti-Douglas factions has swallowed all sense of public danger or public principle. For myself I shall approve the above described programme and let it go. I do not think any considerable portion of those who professed to be for Hunter were really for him but were all the time looking to other results. Douglas has pressed his name upon us until I shall accept it and resist him to the bitter end, tho' I see nothing but disaster and defeat in the future. The true policy would be for him to withdraw. That I am now satisfied he never intended to do in any event whatever. Pennsylvania was really for the platform of the So.? States. So was New Jersey, but Wright violated his instructions. I am sick of the very contemplation of such a lot of rogues as those Northern delegates proved themselves to be, and I now see that the contest is to be transferred to the South, which is the greatest calamity that could befall us. We are all in good health. Nothing else new or talked of but the late events in Charleston.

Alexander H. Stephens To J. Henly Smith. S.

Crawfordville ga.j, *May 8th, 1860.* Dear Smith, I got the book I requested you to buy for me, but no letter came with it. I am obliged to you for your attention to this matter. The book is different from what I expected to find it. I did not get back from Polk Court until last Friday. On the way down the road I met the news of the "blow up" or "break down" of the Charleston convention. At this I was not much surprised, but for it I was truly sorry. I deeply regretted the withdrawal of the Southern delegations, especially that of Georgia, and particularly for the reason assigned—that is, the unsoundness of the platform adopted. It is the same as the campaign was waged on in 1856 with the addition, I understand, of what the Georgia state convention requested. But as for myself I was satisfied with the Cincinnati enumeration of principles and I think it was all that ought to be asked. Since 1850 I have stood upon non-intervention by Congress on the subject of slavery in the territories. I and all parties at the South at least have been pledged as far as honor can pledge any man to abide by the territorial policy established in 1850 "in principle and in substance." These words were put in the Whig Baltimore platform) in 1852 by Mr. Webster at my own instance, and I drew up the Southern manifesto against General Scott because he would not endorse it. That paper is now in my possession; and I shall never change my views or position then taken, so long as ink will not blush at human inconsistency. What is to become of parties in the country I do not know; but of my own honor I know what shall come. That is in my own keeping, and if I and the country go down together that shall remain untarnished to the last. Parties may rise or fall, but principles with me are the pole star of my existence. What is the matter now with the country is that a class of men are in power who have no loyalty to principle, no attachment to truth for truth's sake. They are governed by a desire for office, for place and spoils, and change principles with any change of popular breeze? in their eagerness to get it. They are out for nothing but to undermine the most glorious structure of human Government ever devised by man. It may be that the people too are degenerate. If so we are in a bad fix indeed. But I do not believe they are half so far gone as their leaders. I believe they have virtue enough yet left to see truth when it is presented and act upon it. I cannot believe that this country is so near the brink of ruin and destruction as the times to a casual observer indicate—a greater, a higher and a nobler destiny awaits. Bad men have got control of the country. The temple must and will be ridden of the money changers who have defiled the most sacred places. This at least is my hope. If in it I shall be disappointed then all hope will go out together—all hope with me, for I have none beyond. If we are to go into a Revolution with men and under the lead of men who have changed their whole line of public policy in ten years, who could trust them for three under a new regime? What trust could be put in their counsels? What reliance in their judgments? What confidence in their professed principles? None by me—and Heaven protect those who may be simple minded enough and weak enough to try them!

Howell Cobb To Robert Collins And Others.1

Washington City, *May 9, 1860.*

Gentlemen: Your letter of the 5th inst. has just reached me. The limited time allowed for action induces me to comply with your request for a "prompt" answer, and I shall endeavor to make it equally " candid."

I sympathise fully in your apprehensions for the future of our country. It cannot be disguised that both the safety of the South and the integrity of the Union are seriously threatened. It is my honest conviction that the issue depends upon the action of the southern people at this important juncture. A firm, wise and unfaltering policy on the part of the South will give security to her own rights and peace and quiet to the Union. Any other course will be equally fatal to the preservation of the one and the maintenance of the other. Like yourselves I have looked to the National Democratic party as the only political organization in which the sound Constitutional ele 1 From the Augusta, Ga., Constitutionalist, May 17, 1860. Copy obtained through the kindness of Miss Julia A. Flisch, of Augusta, Ga. Robert Collins and others, constituting a committee of the citizens of Macon, Ga., had addressed the following inquiry to numerous leading public men of the State:

"Macon, Ga., *May 5th, 1860.* "Sih: We are alarmed by the state of things developed in the Democratic convention at Charleston. The discord and disorganising spirit which prevailed there threaten the integrity and overthrow of the Democratic party. We are filled with painful forebodings at the prospect of the Democratic party being slaughtered in the house of its friends— a catastrophe which will put in equal peril the Union of the States and the safety of the South. Clinging to the fate and fortunes of both, we invoke your counsels in this crisis. We believe the Democracy of Georgia should be represented in the adjourned National convention at Baltimore. Will you please give us your views candidly and promptly for publication?"

The letter of Toombs in reply to this inquiry follows herein. That of Stephens is published in Johnston and Browne, "Life of Stephens," pp. 357-364; Cleveland, A. H. Stephens, 661-667; and in Stephens, War between the States, II, 677-684.

ments of the whole country could be brought into united and cordial co-operation. With this conviction I witnessed the proceedings of the late Charleston convention with intense anxiety and deeply regretted the causes which led to its disruption.

In considering the proper course now to be pursued, we should understand distinctly the reason of the failure of that convention to agree upon a platform and candidates for the support of the Democratic party. If the diiferences which led to the result at Charleston are immaterial and unimportant, then there is no cause for trouble or apprehension. The public mind should promptly pronounce them to be so, and they should be dismissed from our thoughts as unworthy of further consideration. Are the people of Georgia prepared to pronounce this judgment? The answer to this inquiry involves in my opinion the future destiny of the South. There were two points of difference at Charleston which produced the disruption of the convention. 1st. The platform of the party on the subject of slavery. 2d. The nomination of a proper candidate for the Presidency.

The fifteen Southern States in common with the two Democratic States of the Pacific agreed upon a platform which recognized the equality of the Southern States—and the right of their citizens to go with their property into the common territories of the Union—claiming for them and their property the same protection which the Constitution and laws of the land extend to their bretheren of the non-slaveholding States and their property—nothing more—nothing less. The seventeen States which with perfect unanimity agreed upon this platform are all of them certain Democratic States. The candidates to be nominated by the Democratic party for President and Vice-President must receive their votes to give them the slightest prospect of success. The remaining sixteen States by virtue of their superior numbers in the convention refused to recognize these principles. They did not assert by the platform they adopted antagonistic principles to those agreed upon by the southern and Democratic States. Their policy was to leave the question an open issue so far as any declaration of principles was concerned, but to give a practical construction to their platform by the nomination of a candidate whose chief claim to the nomination grew out of his known hostility to the doctrine for which the southern and Democratic States contended.

The seventeen Democratic States were prepared to unite upon any true and worthy man for the Presidency. There was on their part no disposition whatever to force upon their brethren of the other States a candidate unacceptable to them. The issue on their pare was for principle and success, involving no consideration of mere personal advancement of a favorite candidate. The sixteen opposition States, on the other hand, not only refused to unite upon the platform offered to them by their brethren of the Democratic States, but struggled to force upon the party the nomination of Judge Douglas, against the stern and united voice of every certain Democratic State in the Union. I venture to assert that such a spectacle was never before presented in the history of party conventions. The States were as nearly equally divided as it was possible for them to be. On one side was every Democratic State, and on the other all the opposition States—and the latter who were not certain of giving a single vote for the candidates that might be nominated insisted on making both a platform and a candidate for the Democratic States to elect. There certainly could not be a more unjust distribution of responsibility and duty.

Such was the condition of things at Charleston. The delegation from Georgia would not consent to the consummation of this threatened policy of the numerical majority of the convention. In common with the delegates from seven other southern States they withdrew from the body. Their action should be sustained by the Democracy of the State. They were true and loyal to the trust reposed inHhem and deserve the cordial approval and renewed confidence of their constituents. If they had returned from Charleston, bearing to the people of Georgia the humiliating terms of surrender which the majority of the convention sought to put upon them in the platform and candidate proposed, the people would have received their report in sorrow and spurned their candidate with indignation.

It is due to the Democracy of the sixteen States, which I have designated as opposition States, to say that I use the term "opposition States " in no spirit of disrespect, but simply intend to designate them as States in which, unfortunately for the country, the Democratic party is in a minority. In many of their delegations at Charleston there were large minorities who condemned the course and policy of their colleagues as wrong in principle and unjust to their brethren of the South. This was particularly the case in Pennsylvania and other States to whose votes, in connection with the certain Democratic States, we look with the greatest confidence for the election of our candidates.

The truth is, that the sound Democracy of the North are determined to stand by the South in this hour of trial, if the South will only be true and faithful to herself. The unwise declaration of a few southern men in favor of the nomination of Mr. Douglas as a matter of policy and expediency has contributed in no small degree to the present unhappy state of things. These exceptional cases have unfortunately been mistaken in some quarters for public opinion, and will account for the otherwise unaccountable persistence with which the friends of Mr. Douglas press his nomination against the earnest protest of a united South.

I have thus briefly alluded to the difficulties in the Charleston convention and the causes which produced them as proper matter for consideration in determining upon the course of action which the Democracy of Georgia ought now to pursue. As the time is short before the re-assembling of the convention at Baltimore, I would suggest the propriety of an immediate call by the State Executive Committee for the March convention to reassemble. It affords the best opportunity at our command for ascertaining the Democratic sentiment of the State as to our future policy. When assembled, I would urge upon that convention to give the action of our delegates at Charleston their cordial approval and authorise them in co-operation with the delegates of those States with whom they acted at Charleston to renew at Baltimore their efforts for a settlement of the difficulties which led to the disruption at Charleston.

The course of the delegation has been so true that they are entitled to the unqualified confidence of their constituents, and can be safely trusted without embarrassing their action with specific instruct tions. The endorsement of their past action will be the best instruction for their future conduct. The same delegation should be authorised to represent the State in the convention to be held in Richmond, and if practicable the time for the meeting of the latter convention should be postponed to a day subsequent to the convention at Baltimore. It would thus afford every opportunity for healing the dissensions in our party and bringing the different portions once more into united and cordial co-operation upon a sound platform and in the support of a sound candidate. I believe it can be accomplished, and it only requires firmness and decision on the part, of the southern Democracy to bring it about. You may rest assured that your true friends at the North—the men who have never deserted you to save themselves—will not force upon you terms of humiliation, and the rest will not venture to press them unless you first indicate by your action that you are prepared to surrender at discretion.

The Democracy of Georgia must now choose between the two wings of the party at the North. The one has been true and faithful in the past and offers you every assurance of their aid and support in the future. The other abandoned you in the hour of danger and trial and invite the renewal of our confidence with notice in advance that you may expect in the future no better faith or greater security than you have received in the past. With the first you will certainly maintain your honor and have a fair prospect of preserving your rights. If an alliance with the latter promises any greater advantage, I confess my inability to discover it.

Robert Toombs To Robert Collins And Others.1

Washington, D. C, *May 10,1860.*

Gentlemen: Your letter of the 5th instant was duly received, and would have been before replied to but for the fact that I have signed an address containing my opinions somewhat at large upon the questions which you have submitted to me, and which address I expected would have been published before this time; that having been delayed, in the meantime I thought it best to give you a brief reply.

I have looked with interest, but without apprehension, upon the proceedings of the late convention at Charleston. I see in those proceedings unmistakable evidence of the steady advance of sound Constitutional principals. Perhaps the time may not have come for the attainment of the full measure of our Constitutional rights; it may not have been prudent on the part of the representatives of the seventeen States to have sanctioned and presented as much truth on the slavery issue as is contained in what is commonly called the majority platform, but when it was thus sanctioned, approved and presented to the convention, it was well to stand by and defend it, especially against the platform of the minority. Seceding delegates did this with manly firmness, and I approve their action. From the best information I have been able to obtain, I believe the majority platform was not only acceptable to a majority of the States, but also to a majority of the delegates, if their votes could have been taken *per capita*. If this be so, it ought not to have been defeated either by accident, want of foresight or contrivance.

It is asserted that the Democratic party hitherto have affirmed the principle of non-intervention by Congress with slavery, both in the States and Territories; but none pretend that it has ever asserted the right of intervention against slavery by the settlers upon a public domain either before or after a Territorial Government has been granted to them by Congress. But this is in truth the real doctrine held by the minority. They desire to interpolate the party creed with it—to make it its rule of action. We cannot hide this great fact by simply shutting our own eyes. The friends of this political opinion have defended it with ability and zeal, have tendered us the issue and demanded its acceptance; it can no longer be avoided either with safety or honor. I accept it, and will give it the same determined opposition with which I have ever met it, whenever and wherever presented.

After the seceding delegates left the convention, it is understood a proposition was made by the delegates from New York to the delegates from some of the southern States, who did not secede, which 1 From the Augusta, Ga., Constitutionalist, May 19, 1860. Copy obtained through the kindness of Miss Julia A. Flisch of Augusta.
might lead to a satisfactory adjustment of these differences. Under this new state of facts occurring after the secession, and perhaps in consequence thereof, in my opinion, the seceding delegates ought to meet with the convention at Baltimore and endeavor to obtain such an adjustment. This is due to the altered state of facts—to the magnitude of the consequences involved in the struggle—due to their confederates who agree with them in principle but who did not secede. If they should then fail they at least may expect to secure the cooperation of the delegates of other Democratic States in such further measures as they may deem necessary for the maintenance of the just and constitutional rights of their constituents.

This course requires no sacrifice of principle. The proposed Richmond convention, if it should be found necessary to hold it, can be held after, as well as before the Baltimore convention, and, I think, with clearer lights for its guidance. If this policy should meet with any considerable opposition in Georgia, I would suggest that a convention of the party be called by the proper authority, that they may take immediate action on the subject. For myself, no party or other necessity can ever induce me to give my assent to any declaration of principles which affirms or admits, directly or by necessary implication, that there is any rightful power anywhere to exclude slave property from any portion of the public dominion (open for settlement of others) except within the limits of a sovereign State, and by her authority. This plain principle of equality and even-handed justice should not be bartered away, or even put in jeopardy, for the sake of party harmony or party success. I will be no party to such a contract. It is always true wisdom and statesmanship to adopt the best attainable measure under all the circumstances of each case, tending to protect, to strengthen or to advance the policy sought to be established.

Truth is often slaughtered in the house and by the hands of its own friends by a struggle for that which is impossible today but which may easily be accomplished to-morrow. It is sometimes wise to accept a part of our just rights, if we can have the residue unimpaired and uncompromitted by the partial instalment; but nothing can justify a voluntary surrender of principles indispensable to the safety and honor of the State. It is true we are surrounded with danger—but I do not concur in the opinion that the danger to the Union is even one of our greatest perils. Our greatest danger today is that the Union will survive the Constitution. The great body of your enemies in the North who hate the Constitution, and daily trample it under their feet, profess an ardent attachment to the Union—and, I doubt not, feel such attachment for the Union unrestrained by the Constitution. Do not mistake your real danger—it is great. Look to the preservation of your rights. The Union has more friends than you have, and will last at least as long as its continuance will be compatible with your safety.

Robert Toombs To Alexander H. Stephens. R.

Washington, D. C., *12th May, 1860.* Dear Stephens, I reed. your letter of the 8th inst. yesterday. It seems from yours that you had not reed. a letter I wrote you some week ago or more inclosing new brief in the Persons and Oliver case and giving you my action and views on the present state of things. When I saw that Douglas's friends voted to make a platform before electing a candidate, thus playing into the hands of Alabama, I knew his friends looked for and desired secession from the convention; and when their platform appeared refusing even an endorsement of the Dred Scott case, I telegraphed Irwin to show to our delegation to keep the South a unit, get a sound platform and a sound Southern man on it and if they found that was impossible, to bolt. A full view of the facts since the adjournment has satisfied me that my advice was good and I approve the action of the majority of delegates. I fought the campaign of 1848 against the doctrine of territorial intervention against slavery. I am not aware that I ever have by act or deed or thought altered my position on that question. I certainly never intended to do so, and recent events do not at all incline me to modify my hostility. I looked upon it with such contempt that I never made it a test, but I certainly would never submit to such a test. Douglas's Harper article has indoctrinated all of his friends with his folly; and his success without a *party* disclaimer of his doctrines would compromit us forever. Therefore I have determined to have that party disclaimer, if I can get it, at all hazards. Mr. Douglas and his friends seem to act on the idea that our fear of Black Republican rule will make us submit to anything. As to me he is mistaken. I do not concur with you as to the extent of our obligation to maintain *non-intervention,* and if I did I certainly do not feel bound to surrender the judicial question when it has been determined in principle in my favour. I did not agree to *intervention* against us by squatters, and to that point it is sought to bring me and party notwithstanding the Dred Scott decision. I wrote yesterday my opinion more at length to the Macon committee for publication, which I suppose you will see in a day or two. Mr. Douglas himself never did agree personally to stand on the legislation of 1850, and certainly we are entitled to require him and all others to stand by interpretations of the power of the people in the territories as expounded by the Supreme Court. But Mr. Douglas's whole position in the Harper article is adverse to the principles laid down by the court on that point. I concur in your views of Yancey's argument at Charleston; but the difficulty is Douglas and his friends do not. As to the Georgia convention, under existing circumstances one ought to be called, but it ought to be called by the State committee. I think also that the delegates should be approved and sent back to Baltimore and to back Tenn. , Va., and Ky. in their ultimatum. If they will do that I have no doubt there will be a satisfactory adjustment of the matter. Without that I can see nothing but turmoil and disaster; but I shall abide the fortunes of those who will struggle for our equal rights in the territories. We are all well—my own health good.

Robert Toombs To Alexander H. Stephens. R.

Washington, D. C, *May 16th, 1860.* Dear Stephens, I recd. your letter this morning and I find myself quite surprised that while we so nearly, I may say exactly, agree in principle that we differ so widely in action. I agree with you that what we ought to demand is to call upon our Northern allies to stand by their bargain; but I complain of them that they will not do it. In the first place we believed? in non-intervention because we held it to be a fundamental principle of law that slavery existed in the territories without local laws, or to put the case wider that it existed everywhere where not *forbidden by law.* The Supreme Court have decided this case in our favour; but Mr. Douglas will not stand to it. The Illinois resolutions passed 4th Jany. by his friends expressly declare that it cannot go into the territories without positive legislation. Mr. Douglas under his own hand in his controversy with Black holds the same principle. He says you are out and can not get in except by positive law and nobody but squatters can pass that law. You very truly say we did not take non-intervention on these terms. 2ndly. We did agree to leave the question of the power of the people of the territories to the courts. You admit in your letter, and I agree with that, it is decided that Congress has not the power to prohibit it itself and could not therefore give it to the people of the territories; but Mr. Douglas denies that and presses upon us, after the decision, for public acceptance the same doctrine.and with tenfold the vigour that he ever did *before the decision.* He tenders the issue, he forces it on you, he will only take non-intervention *with his exposition, and comes f with it in his hands,* and if you leave it without exposition you accept him and his construction of it. You and I are called upon to accept non-intervention as expounded by Mr. Douglas against our own exposition, that of our people and the Supreme Court. Why shall we do this thing? I am willing to accept non-intervention as you expound it. I askfed nothing more at Charleston; but I will not take Mr. Douglas's exposition. Mr. Douglas in a very able speech delivered by him yesterday (he will continue it today) declares that non-intervention and squatter sovereignty mean the same thing, that they are synonymous. He frequently in his speech spoke of the adoption by the party of nonintervention or popular sovereignty. Your own letter is a triumphant reply to him, and I agree with you and not with him. The minority platform did not offer us the Dred Scott opinion. It was artfully worded. It referred to the dogma that old Story boasted that he slipped into Prigg and Pennsylvania, and that is what it intended to endorse. You say Yancey showed conclusively that squatter sovereignty was not in the Cincinnati platform. I agree with you. Douglas does not; says it is there. Now is it not time to *expound* the Cincinnati platform? It was done in 1852 and 1856. Why in 1856? Because thousands of Democrats then held that the repeal of the Missouri restriction was not consistent with the settlement of 1850 nor with the party doctrine of non-intervention. The party declared that it was consistent with both, and many of them bolted and went to the Fremonters. Therefore I think it due to truth and fair dealing in the party and to the rights of the South that we should understand one another. I would not narrow the basis of party action, but I must stand upon the true intent and meaning of our present declaration of principles. I think the New York resolution would do so, or I would take a man with your opinions as the true exponent of the party. I am not willing now to take Mr. Douglas with his exposition, without a party explanation of the platform. These are in brief the reasons upon which my late action has been based, and it does seem to me they are so exactly your own that I am at a loss to discover why our action should not be the same.

I think I shall be compelled to reply to a portion of Douglas's speech, though in the greater portion of it yesterday I concur with him; but the points of divergence will I expect more fully appear in his continuation today. I see the Constitutionalist is prepared to admit the full right of the squatters to prohibit slavery in the territories. Save us from our friends! We are all in good health.

P. S.--I do not think you did Calhoun quite justice. He was for non-intervention but also firmly held the equality of the states in the territories and denied the existence of any power to injure us there. This is a doctrine wholly different from Mr. Douglas's!

Howell Cobb To John B. Lamar. E.

Washington City, *22 May, 1860.* Dear Col.,... I was extremely gratified at the result of your meeting in Macon and was happy to find your name among the delegates. It is the most important party convention that ever assembled in Ga, I intend if possible to be there myself. I shall be appointed a delegate from Clarke county and unless detained here by some insuperable cause I shall be in Milledgeville on the 3d. June. It is extremely inconvenient for me to leave my office whilst Congress is in session but I shall not allow any ordinary consideration to detain me. From all I can learn the Douglas faction will be whipt badly in the state. We shall have some trouble with our own friends to get them to consent to be represented at Baltimore. But when they see that unless *we* send *true men,* there will be a bogus delegation, I think they should give in to our policy. My programme is to send the old delegates, and by endorsing their past action we give the best instructions for their future conduct, as I said in my letter.

My opinion now is that our friends at Baltimore will be able to defeat Douglas and get both a good man and a sound platform. Whilst my individual choice is still for Hunter yet I believe that old Joe Lane is the best man to make the fight on, both in the convention and before the people. He is as true as steel and then he has " fought, bled and died for his country." I believe that the best chance now is to take a northern man—any of them will be acceptable after we get clear of Douglas.

I am glad you are going to have another paper in Macon. It will at least be a check upon the Telegraph. If it is Ben Martin (Benning's brother-in-law), he is a good and true friend of mine and was in 1850, though Benning was against me.....

I will have sent to you speeches of Toombs, Benjamin and others, which will give you all the points on Douglas. In this morning's Constitution you will find an article which fills up the asterisks in Stephens's letter where he quotes from his Augusta speech. Douglas endorsed the letter. He is now asked if he will endorse it with the asterisks filled up.

I sent an editorial to the Federal Union, headed ".The true issue" in which I have discussed the Dred Scott decision and non-intervention. If they publish it *as I sent it,* it will put the gentlemen who have been writing letters against our line in a tight place, though I don't name any of them. It ought to be in next Tuesday's paper. Do write me how matters are progressing in the different counties around you. All send love to John A. and yourself.

P. S.—I call your attention particularly to *Benjamin's* speech. The trooper? articles are admirable and will make a capital document for circulation. *Send them all over the State.*

Robert Toombs To Alexander H. Stephens. R.

Washington, D. C, *26th May, 1860.* Dear Stephens,... I will probably meet you in Milledgeville if I can with any convenience get off from here. You will see from my speech fully where we differ, tho' I am perfectly prepared to accommodate the party difficulty when you think proper: tho' I would never, never did and never will, surrender the constitutional right of protection. Indeed the 5th resolution1 of Davis passed the Senate by a vote of 42 to 2 (Hamlin and Trumbull) after all of Mr. Douglas's clamour against it, Mr. Crittenden and Mr. Kennedy voting with us and the Black Republicans refusing to vote against it except the two mentioned. Under this state of facts I think we are called on to surrender to Mr. Douglas to great disadvantage. All well.

Robert Toombs To Alexander H. Stephens. R.

Washington, D. C, *June 9th, 1860.* Dear Stephens,... I observe the proceedings of the Milledgeville convention. I do not see but that both wings passed substantially the same resolutions, and why they split I can not tell except under it lies mere personal preferences for the Presidency. I am well satisfied that an explanation of the Cincinnati platform is wise and necessary and made so by the conduct of Mr. Douglas *alone.* He is not passive in his opposition to the opinions of a very great majority of the party North and South, but he is active, and his official conduct if we were to elect him on the old Cincinnati platform would subvert the principles of the party. There is much greater reason for an explanatory article than in 1856, for the Kansas-Nebraska act was a party interpretation (in terms) of the legislation of 1850. Douglas's speech in the Senate after the Charleston convention compelled every man to an unconditional submission to his construction or to fight him. I think the latter was the course of duty. I am fully aware that personal hostilities and personal advantages are at the bottom of the strife; but there is a right and a wrong to the controversy for all that. I think the condition of the party is such that nobody can be elected by it, and I do not see that much could be gained by its success. I have ceased to interest myself further than to give my decided opinions to all who ask for them. I think we will adjourn by the 25th Inst. Julia is well tho' still lame, and sends her kindest regards to you.

Alexander H. Stephens To J. Henly Smith. S.

Crawfordville ga., *June 17th, 1860.* Dear Smith,... What will be done at Baltimore tomorrow I can not even conjecture. I fear the rupture begun at Charleston 1 The fifth of the Davis resolutions was: "Resolved, that if experience should at any time prove that the judicial and executive authority do not possess means to Insure adequate protection to constitutional rights in a Territory, and if the territorial government should fall or refuse to provide the necessary remedies for that purpose, it will be the duty of Congress to supply that deficiency." 73566—13 31 will be complete. I cannot believe that the party will abandon the doctrine of *non-intervention.* The seceders seem to demand that as a condition of their future cooperation, so I fear we shall have a Richmond nomination anyhow and that a split in the national Democracy will be permanent. I shall go with the national flag as long as it bears upon its folds the principles it bore when I first acted with them. I am in hopes however that they will in any event give that exposition to the doctrine of *non-intervention* which was set forth in Gov. Johnson's resolutions in our state convention. Not that I look upon it as essential—I am perfectly satisfied with the Cincinnati platform—but it would remove a mountain load of prejudice off the mind of thousands of the South who have been kept most studiously and wickedly ignorant of Douglas's real and true position. He holds that all property, negroes and all, should stand upon the same footing of equality in the territories. How far a territorial legislature can encourage or discourage any species of property is the question really at issue, and that question the Supreme Court never has as yet decided. They have decided only that negro property stands like all other kinds, and this Douglas affirms too. I must however close.

P. S.—Write often, and when the nominations are made write to me fully how they take and what is the prospect at the capital.

John A. Cobb1 To John B. Lamar. E.

Gilmer House, Baltimore md., *June 20th, 1860.*

Dear Uncle, I would have written to you before, but I could have given you no more information than what was contained in the Sun which I have been sending.

The convention met at 5 o'clock this afternoon but as the committee on credentials were not ready to report it adjourned to 10 o'clock tomorrow morning.

I have heard this evening what the committee will report. There will be a minority and majority report. I have not heard what the minority report is, but it amounts to nothing as it will not be adopted. The majority report is to admit Texas, Miss, and Delaware, reject Louisiana, admit half of our delegation and half of the bogus from Georgia, and admit the bogus or anti-Yancey delegates from Alabama. If that report is adopted and the Douglas men feel confident that they can do it, the delegates from the South will never take their seats.

If the majority report is adopted, whoever goes into the convention goes in with the distinct understanding that they will support the nominee, no matter who he is and what is the platform. 1 Son of Howell Cobb.

Our delegates are united in their opinion upon that subject, and I don't think there is a man among us who will go into the convention if that report is adopted.

I think that we will be in Richmond before three days pass. Mr. dishing sent tickets to our delegates to-day to admit them to the dress circle in the theatre where the convention meets. I have not been in yet. I expect to go in the morning. The Southern delegates here are perfectly indifferent in regard to the action of the convention in regard to their seats—most of them are anxious to return to Richmond.

We have speaking here every night. Our speakers speak from the balcony of the Gilmer House, the Douglasites from Reverdy Johnson's house which is just above, where George Saunders is keeping open house and Douglas men can stay *gratis;* the stands are not more than forty (40) ft. apart and speakers are going it from both stands from 8 o'clock at night until 1 and 2 in the morning....

I will write to you in the morning and let you know what action is taken and will send you the papers every day—will enclose the last Sun in this letter. I hope that we will be able to leave here tomorrow for Richmond. You must excuse the writing, as I have a bad pen and mean light and am writing on the top of the bureau as a substitute for a table.

Every place here is crowded. I was lucky and have a room to myself.

Alexander H. Stephens To J. Henly Smith. S.

Crawfordville ga., *July 2d, 1860.*
Dear Smith, Your letter was received two days ago and I delayed answering it until I should get the paper containing the communication referred to in it. This came to hand last night. I read it with interest and was highly pleased with the general tone and style. You present the strong points of the case. In some minor matters you were not quite so effective as you might have been. These I intended to call your attention especially to, but some person took the paper away last night (there were several at the house) and I have not got it to refer to. But one I recollect very distinctly and will name. After stating Mr. Douglas's position very clearly in which he puts slave property in the territories upon the same footing as all other property, etc., you go on to say, "and yet because the party South disagreed with him upon one *vital point* they warred against him." I have not got your words but the idea. Now you should not have styled this a *vital* point. It should have been *immaterial,* for it is an *immaterial* and not a *vital* point of difference— and if it were a *vital,* as his opponents allege it to be, would it not justify their opposition? Can *vital* points ever be waived? Your whole letter *shows* that it is not a vital point; and if you had used the word *immaterial* instead of vital in this connection it would have added great force to your general argument. There were two or three other matters I intended to call your attention to. These related to your historical narrative, but I have forgotten them. But I assure you this letter and your previous one on the whole present Douglas's claims in a stronger light than I have seen them presented in any Southern paper. I have not seen a speech or an article by a Southern man that has been of real benefit to him except yours— not one that met the issue on the right points. No man ever had more cause to exclaim save me from my friends than Douglas has, particularly from his friends at the South. I was surprised at their course at Baltimore. What could they mean by pushing his nomination in the face and teeth of the secession of Tenn., Ky., and Va., to say nothing of the other states, I cannot understand. I may be mistaken. I have heard no explanation of it. I do not know what they rely upon or what their calculations are. I have no lights except what I get from general views and my knowledge of the workings of causes to their effects. But from these lights it does seem to me that this course was neither wise nor patriotic. Madness and folly must have ruled the hour. They put up their man to be beaten. I do sincerely trust it may be otherwise, but I do not see any probable chance for him. Had he been nominated over the votes of the Tenn., Ky., and Va., delegations—had he got two thirds according to the usages which may be regarded as the constitution of the National Democratic organization, had those states adhered to the nomination, then my opinion is that he would have carried them with Ala., La., and Mo., and with enough Northern votes to secure his election. But with the break of the great border States, who that has got sense enough to get out of a shower of rain does not know that even though a ticket may be run for him in those states, yet that it is impossible for him to carry them or either of them? And who does not know that when it is apparent that he will lose the entire south, thousands of men at the North, some for spite and some to get on the winning side, will quit his standard then, and thus leave him perhaps without the vote of a single state? As for his carrying Ala., under existing circumstances, I have no idea. And why the delegation of that State and La. should have persisted in having him nominated with all these considerations before them, I cannot imagine. I can attribute it to nothing short of dementation. I may be mistaken. I hope I am. I would say nor do nothing to weaken their efforts; but as a quiet observer feeling however a deep interest in the general result upon the welfare of the country, I give you freely my candid impressions and convictions at this present writing. I repeat, I maintain these opinions upon general principles only. I have heard no explanations and have no communication with the outside world except through the medium of the public press. I am pained and grieved at the folly which thus demanded the sacrifice of such a noble and gallant spirit as I believe Douglas to be. I can see but one *possible* good that his nomination may effect, and that is he may get enough electoral votes at the North to defeat Lincoln in the colleges and thus throw it in the House where he may be the stepping stone for his party rival (Breckinridge) to rise into office. His back and shoulders may enable his rival to elevate himself to place and honor and in this way attain the object of his ambition, and in this way the country may possibly be benefitted in the ultimate defeat of Lincoln. But what honor this will be to Douglas his friends must determine. They certainly have much less regard for that than I have. If such a position had been necessary for anyone to occupy I would have assigned it to some other one, someone who while rendering public service would have gained instead of

losing reputation. I would not have called upon Douglas to do it. Indeed I think it was very unwise to put him or anybody in nomination without the 2/3 vote. It will be regarded as a violation of the constitution of the party and would of itself be sufficient to justify any man who felt disposed from any cause to consider himself as absolved from all obligation to conform to party action. The whole affair therefore I regard exceedingly unfortunate. I see nothing but disaster attending it. I assure you the wish is far from being the father to the thought in this case. I give but the honest convictions that are forced upon my mind, and shall be rejoiced if when the smoke of the battle field clears away I shall see a more encouraging prospect. I take no Northern paper and do not know how the public sentiment there is running. But I do know that the *doctrine of non-intervention* was never popular there. It was an up hill business to support and sustain it. It broke down the Democratic party. Those who sustained themselves on it did it only in the defensive. It contained no element that addressed itself to the heart of the people. It had no rallying heart for the masses. No converts would ever be made by appealing in its behalf. It was always a question simply of how many would be lost by its advocacy. I have seen nothing to cause me to believe that any change has taken place in the great popular sentiment on this subject in that section. Hence I do not see where Douglas is to gain. The administration will throw all its power against him. This is his only hope for gains in the North. But the old feeling of hate on the part of the Democrats who quit the party on account of this doctrine will seize the opportunity of pouring out all the vials of their wrath against him when they see a prospect of his humiliation. Had the party not split, had he been run at the South with a reasonable show of success there, he would have made great gains from the conservative Union-loving portion of the people North. But there is now nothing to rally that portion unless they see prospects of electing him solely by Northern votes. This I do not think within the range of possibility. What then is to be the result? God only knows. I can say no more. This letter is strictly and exclusively for yourself. I am still confined to the house; do not go out and have no idea that I shall be able to do anything but rest during the heat of summer. I hope I shall not have to take my bed. If I can keep up I shall be content. I wish if you see anything of interest in any Northern paper, the Times, the Herald, or Tribune, or any other, you would buy a copy of the number and send to me. Keep an account and I will pay the amounts. I take none of these papers but would like to see anything of interest in them. What did you mean by referring to certain dispatches in some of the Northern papers about me during the Baltimore Convention in one of your letters to the Confederacy? I did not understand your allusion and do not now. Write often.

Alexander H: Stephens To J. Henly Smith. S.

Crawfordville ga., *July 4th, 1860.*. .. No news politically—two tickets I suppose will be run in Ga. I shall take no active part—can do no good. The Legislature will have to choose electors if the Democratic party is split to any considerable extent, as it probably may be. The Breck. and Lane ticket will carry much the larger portion I think. I could not favour a movement which in my judgment originated not from principle but hostility to a man. And I feel no disposition to engage in an internecine fight when nothing in the end can be hoped for but a profitless victory even at the very best. I shall therefore take my rest quietly, looking on, hoping for the best, though I greatly fear troubles are ahead. If they come I can bear my share. Those only will be responsible whose folly and madness brought them on. The people must bear them as they do all other misfortunes. What I write to you is always strictly and exclusively for yourself.

Alexander H. Stephens To J. Henly Smith. S.

Crawfordville ga., *July 10th, 1860.* Dear Smith, Your letter of the 6th inst. was received last night. The *paper* came by the same mail. The point in your historical narrative I referred to was in part corrected by yourself. The word *have* instead of *protect* covered the idea. Besides this, one other. My opposition to the Clayton Compromise was not *entirely* or solely because it did not protect but because it *perpetuated* the existing status of the country at the time of acquisition, which was antislavery. I wished that *status* changed either by Congress or that authority might be given to the territorial legislatures to change it. That bill tied the hands of both Congress.and the territorial legislatures forever. This however does not amount to much so far as your letter is concerned. I now mention it that you may know the whole facts of the case. You would do well to read that speech, the one I made on the Clayton Compromise, if you write on that subject. What is to become of the country in case of Lincoln's election I do not know. For one I can only give you my own opinion. As at present advised I should not be for disunion on the grounds of his election. It may be that his election will be attended with events that will change my present opinion, but his bare election would not be sufficient cause in my judgment to warrant a disruption— particularly as his election will be the result if it occurs at all of the folly and madness of our own people. If they do these things in the green tree what will they not do in the dry? If without cause they destroy the present Govt., the best in the world, what hopes would I have that they would not bring untold hardships upon the people in their efforts to give us one of their modelling. All I can therefore say in response to your question is that *I would not* advocate disunion on that ground. Let events shape their own course. "Sufficient unto the day is the evil thereof." In point of merit as a man I have no doubt Lincoln is just as good, safe and sound a man as Mr. Buchanan, and would administer the Government so far as he is individually concerned just as safely for the South and as honestly and faithfully *in every particular.* I know the man well. He is not a bad man. He will make as good a President as Fillmore did and better too in my opinion. He has a great deal more practical common sense. Still his party may do mischief. If so it will be a great misfortune, but a misfortune that our own people brought upon us. This is my judgment—this is the way I look upon it at present. I have not lime now to go more into detail, but I will say this, that I consider slavery much more secure in the Union than out of it if our people were but wise. And if they are not this fact adds no additional grounds to hope for more security out of the Union under the head of those who now control our destinies, than in it. We have nothing to fear from anything so much as unnecessary changes and revolutions in government. The institution is *based* on *conservatism.* Everything that weakens this has a tendency to weaken the institution. But I will stop.

P. S.—I see some of our papers are disputing about my position. I shall vote for Douglas; but I do not intend to take any active part in the canvass. I am out of politicks and intend to stay out. This it seems hard to make the people understand.

Alexander H. Stephens To J. Henly Smith. S.

Crawfordville ga., *July loth, 1860.* Dear Smith, I have but a moment to acknowledge receipt of two letters from you—the dates I forget. I am about to start in a few moments for Augusta where I am to be at court tomorrow. I am glad you corrected the lying report that I was going to support the nomination of the seceders.1 Never could I do such a thing until I became as inconsistent and as regardless of my public record and long cherished principles as those who put upon us this nomination. And I trust I may never live to see the day when I shall feel the personal degradation that such a consciousness would inflict upon me. I shall support the nominees of the National Democratic party as long as its flag floats bearing upon its folds the principles upon which I at first entered its ranks. But I can say no more. I shall take no active part in the canvass. In quitting public life my object was to quit all political strifes and keep out of such contests. I am out. and intend to stay out. As a private citizen I shall exercise my franchise and most cordially shall I vote for Douglas and Johnson. I had forgotten what you wrote about the Cyclopoedia. Do as you propose. Send me the 3 vols, when out as you propose or get Shillington to send them. I have got the newspapers you sent me and am obliged to you. Send me more of the same sort. I have been highly entertained with them. I am better than I have been but am still an invalid. The drought here is distressing. We shall make very little corn. The prospect is gloomy beyond conception. On the 11th inst. the thermometer here was at 102—never before above 98.

Alexander H. Stephens To J. Henly Smith. S.

Crawfordville ga., *July Q4th, 1860.* Dear Smith, Your letter of the 20th inst. came to hand last night. It gave me some trouble on your account. When I saw as I did the extensive circulation that was given to your letters and the marked impression that they were making on the public mind everywhere, I thought the writer would be hunted up. I felt the embarrassment of your situation in that event. All these things I thought of some weeks ago. Now I am at a loss on the question of the advice 1 should give you. I do not know what to say to you; and in this state of mind the best thing I can say perhaps is to follow your own sense of duty. Where duty leads there we may never fear to tread. If I wrote, I would be respectful to all persons in my language. I would not confine my letters to the Confederacy; I would write for the Constitutionalist, and I would write for other papers. Perhaps if you 1 The Breckinridge ticket, whose supporters had seceded from the Charleston and Baltimore conventions.

should be turned out you could make as much by correspondence as you now do. Gardner1 ought to pay you well for such letters as you could write. Hampton I suppose can pay nothing. His paper moreover has no influence. If you write you ought to appear in a paper of more character. I have not time to say more today. The drought continues—crops ruined. Let me know the prospect. How will Pa. go? Do the *seceders* stand any chance there? Has Douglas any hopes in X. York, New Jersey, Ohio or Indiana? Let me know your opinion from the best lights you have on the subject. I had heard of Garland's2 running away. I saw Mr. Toombs last week. Did not talk politicks with him except in a very general way. We differ widely and radically on present issues; but as I do not intend to take any active part again in public matters, I have made up my mind never to let such things interfere with my private relations.

Thomas W. Thomas To Alexander H. Stephens. R.

Madison Springs, Geo., *30th July, 1860.*

Dear Sir: In justice to myself I ask leave to occupy your attention with a brief letter. I am informed that in the argument of the state case which went up from Hancock8 to the Supreme Court at Athens you compared me to the late Judge Kenan and related an anecdote the point of which was to show he was a tyrant and I was like him. I could easily show this was unjust by recapitulating my whole conduct in that matter but my object is not to defend myself.

Nor do I intend to assume that I have a right to complain that you thought proper to use any line of argument that in your own judgment would increase the chances of success, and I am well aware that to disparage me would be favourably listened to by a majority of that court.

Nor do I intend to say or intimate that your course was ungrateful for though I have been your faithful and devoted friend for more than ten years,

I never yet had it in my power to place you under obligations, but on the contrary am indebted myself for many and striking proofs of confidence and regard.

But I have this complaint to make which I think just and wellfounded. Entertaining the opinion you do of my conduct in the case alluded to you ought not to have continued to treat me as an intimate and highly esteemed personal friend. Whenever I acquire such an opinion of you, you will never afterwards while I hold it, be my honoured guest.

1 James R. Gardner was editor of the Augusta Constitutionalist; Hampton was editor of the Southern Confederacy, published at Atlanta. 2 Body-servant of Robert Toombs.

Thomas was at this time Judge of the Superior Court of Georgia (northern circuit), from which Stephens had taken a case on appeal to the State Supreme Court.

I will not deny that I have felt most keenly this reproach from you—few men live who could have wounded me so deeply. It is putting out of remembrance many pleasant years to write you this letter but justice to myself demands that I should do it and my feelings dictate that I should do it as I have endeavoured to do without any mixture of bitterness and without any design to give you offence.

I heard of what you said a few days after but it is unnecessary to explain the delay as I am not demanding redress or seeking explanations.

Thomas W. Thomas To Alexander H. Stephens. R.

Elberton Geo., *8th August, 1860.*

Dear Sir: Your letter of the 31st ult. was received last Monday. It was not deemed by me obtrusive. It is true I did not ask for explanations but surely I never said I did not want them. Your conclusion that I did not desire explanations because I did not ask for them seems to me to be illogical. I desire a great many things that I do not ask for. I deemed you an old and valued friend. I learned you had treated me in a manner entirely incompatible with that friendship. I laid the case before you in a manner perfectly friendly, candid and respectful, and I still insist that it was all these. I did not say give me explanations, give me redress. This sort of demand precedes hostility. I felt no hostility and wanted no revenge; and I expressly stated that I was not demanding redress nor explanations, in order that you should not by any possibility mistake the true spirit and intent of my letter by construing it to be one in any event whatever looking to hostility. This is the whole reason and cause why I did not ask for explanations. Now if it be less respectful to you to leave it wholly to your own judgment and sense of justice to say what atonement or explanation shall be made for a supposed injury than to demand these *a la mode,* then have I offended on this point, and not without.

But you are careful to say you do not offer the remarks in your letter as explanations. Therefore I can only say if they had been so offered they would have been entirely acceptable and satisfactory. You further say you make them as vindications of yourself and character. To this I can only reply that your labor has been lost, for neither you nor your character ever needed any vindication *to me.* 1 hope you will excuse me for troubling you. I have been as short as possible and shall close by saying in truth and candor I can still subscribe myself truly your friend.

Alexander H. Stephens To J. Henly Smith. S.

Crawfordville ga., *Aug. 8th, 1860.*
Dear Smith, Yours of the 1st inst. was received some days ago but I have not been in much condition to write with much ease to myself since. About ten or twelve days ago I got a fall as I was going out of the door which gave me some ugly looking bruises on the chin, nose, lips and face generally. Besides this my wrists and both hands suffered. I have not been able to use them well since. The thumb on the pen hand is still out of order. It is with difficulty I write. The accident happened by the heel of my shoe catching or rather heavily touching the carpet strip at the door which gave me a illegible. The balance being lost I fell head and face foremost down the steps to the ground. near eight feet, the face striking the hard gravelled ground. It is a wonder the injuries were not more serious than they were. It was truly a frightful fall. But enough of this. I was very sorry indeed to hear of your interview with Mr. Cobb. Sorry to see the vindictive spirit of persecution which the Administration seems determined to carry out. For your own sake I hope nothing further will be done in the matter. Any thing that I could do for you in bringing you in communication with the Constitutionalist or any other papers as a correspondent will be most cheerfully done. I look upon the election of Douglas as hopeless; yet it is important that the truth should be vindicated before-the people. It is not my intention to take very active part in the canvass or ever in any political canvass again. This I have told you before. When I quit Congress I quit politicks, particularly its strifes on the hustings, forever. My dislike for that sort of business was one of my reasons for going into retirement.

Linton's resignation of his seat upon the Supreme Court bench1 was not with any view of entering into politicks. Far from it. He looks upon such struggles with even greater aversion, I believe, than I do. His object was to go like myself into perfect retirement where he can pursue such objects as are more agreeable to his feelings and tastes than the wranglings of a multitude can afford, either on the "stump" or in the forum. His fondness for books will afford him ample sources for entertainment and amusement. The country at present I think presents nothing attractive to the mind of a patriot. Everything it seems to me is tending, or rather rapidly rushing to national disruption and general anarchy. There is not political virtue enough in the land to save it. This is my present conviction; and while I may still hope, for one may hope as long as life lasts, yet I am fully prepared in mind at least for the greatest and worst calamities that can befal a people. Write often.

Alexander H. Stephens To J. Henly Smith. S.

Crawfordville ga., *Aug. 25th, 1860.* Dear Smith, I have been absent two weeks—went over to Sparta where I could be more completely retired and at rest—got back 1Of Georgia.
day before yesterday a good deal improved in strength and general health—found your letter of the 18th inst., etc. I have promised to make a speech next week in Augusta. This was in response to a call from some 130 or 40 persons of that place. It was very much against my will to do it, but the call was of such a character I could not refuse. I suppose I shall have to permit the use of my name as an elector. This is a great embarrassment to me. I was almost offended at those who put it forward. I had expressly forbidden it. They ought not to have done it. But now the question for me is whether I shall sacrifice my individual feelings or permit myself to be the cause of injury to principles which lie so near my heart. Were I to decline, the reasons would never go with the act. I therefore think it better to suffer individually than for the public to suffer through me. This is the light in which I view it. I cannot write my letter immediately. Our court sits here next week. I must attend to its business. That being on my mind I am not in condition to write on public affairs. Douglas is gaining rapidly in Georgia. The idea that Breckinridge must carry the State by 40,000 majority is all gammon in my judgment. He will however carry the State I think—if not by the popular vote at least before the Legislature. But if he carries the popular vote it will not be by a large majority unless I am greatly mistaken, and if he loses the popularity in the State, and Ky., Tenn., and Va., with N. C. and Mo. vote for Bellj I think there will be a chance for his losing the vote of the Legislature. That body will in that event be much more impressible than at present. How it will turn out however I can not now venture any satisfactory opinion. Public sentiment in the State is now in a tumult.

The caldron is just beginning to boil. It will get worse daily. Fermentation sometimes seems much higher than is expected when it first set in. Contrary to my expectations and what I knew at the time to be his feelings when I wrote you last, my brother Linton has taken the stump. He is to speak tonight in Augusta. He had no idea of this two weeks ago—none in the world—but his feelings have become very warmly enlisted in the national cause. Men who a few weeks ago cared or thought but little of the questions crowding themselves upon public attention are now like him beginning to realize the dangers ahead. To what extent this reaction, if it may be so termed, will go I cannot say. As for myself I look to the future with but little hope. The great evil of the day is the want of that high tone of political integrity and loyalty to principle which constitute the basis and lie at the foundation of all republican or representative government. These are virtues without which our Govnt. cannot stand. I doubt if there is enough pure disinterested patriotism in the land to save it. The signs now point to a speedy national rupture; and the same causes that will bring about that result will inevitably lead very soon to general anarchy. When a people lose or fall from a high tone of political morality they like individual men who have lost character and principles, become ready for anything. The right and the truth of any matter is not what they desire or look for but everything that will provide indulgence to their base propensities. This has been the history of the world and mankind everywhere. We are no better by nature than other people—no better than were the Greeks, the Romans or the French. The only difference thus far between us and the last named nation has been that our public men have been more thoroughly schooled in sound principles of political morality. In our worst crises of corruption there has been a predominance of public virtue and loyalty to the country in the national councils. This I fear is not the case now. Who in the Senate or House of Representatives would risk his reelection upon the advocacy of what his convictions assured him was right in itself, if he apprehended even that his seat should be hazarded thereby? This is our trouble South as well as North. But I must close this homily. Continue to let me know the varying prospect as new features present themselves in the canvass in the different sections and states. These are always better and sooner perceived and understood at the centre than in the more distant parts. Send me the vol. of the Cyclopoedia when the one you mention is ready for delivery.

Alexander H. Stephens To J. Henly Smith. S.

Crawfordville ga., *Aug. 30th, 1860.* Dear Smith,... Douglas is gaining very rapidly just at this time in Ga., from all I can hear. But of course there is no prospect of his getting the vote of the state. If he gets 20,000 votes it will be a wonderful success, with all the leading men of the party and the press, except two or three papers, against him. If his friends should carry Maine next Monday week it will give him a much stronger impetus. But I have no *expectation* of that. I hope but do not look for it. Let me hear from you often.

Alexander H. Stephens To J. Henly Smith. S.

Crawfordville ga., *Sept. 6th, 1860.* Dear Smith, I wrote you from this place last Sunday. I am again at home. Got back from Warren Court yesterday and am to start tomorrow to Hancock. I am improving daily in health and strength. I hope by tomorrow to get a letter from you. I have received but one lately and that was at Kingston. Next Tuesday the election takes place in Pa., and Ohio. I feel great interest in hearing the result but greater still in knowing how the discordant elements in Pa. will cooperate after the State elections. I expect Foster to be. elected Gov. from what I have heard. But will he after his election come out for Breckinridge as Jackson has done in Mo., or will he go for Douglas? Will a united Democratic vote be cast in that state for either Douglas or Breckinridge, and if so for which? This is an important question and one that will affect us here seriously. Foster is claimed here as a Breckinridge man and his election will be hailed from what I hear as a Breckinridge triumph. From an extract of his speech at Philadelphia I saw I should infer that he was a Douglas man. It was on his line of *non-intervention, etc.* Write to me just as soon as you get this. The election will be over in those states. Let me know the *on dits* at Washington. I shall be here tomorrow week—time enough to get your reply to this. The cause is still gaining in this state. If Foster should be elected and he should be shown to be for Douglas and there was good prospect for Douglas to carry Pa., it would give us thousands of votes in Ga.

Alexander H. Stephens To J. Henly Smith. S.

Crawfordville ga., *Sept. 10th, 1860.*

Dear Smith, I am now at home—returned or got here from Appling Court Friday last, but have been too unwell to do any business... or answer letters since.... I went through my business at our court, made a political speech and then went to Augusta where I again spoke Saturday night. I was completely exhausted there—I did not get through with what I intended and wished to say. You have seen a very good report of what I did say in the Constitutionalist. I had not prepared anything further than in thought. I had committed nothing to paper. I however revised the report of it. I do not intend to attempt to speak again unless I recover more strength. I am exceedingly weak and debilitated....

We have no news here. The Douglas cause is gaining daily in Georgia. But then it is fighting without hope. If the indications from the elections in Maine today should be favourable to him it will give a new impetus to his cause in the whole country. But my apprehension is that the Black Republican majority will be increased there. The division in the Democratic ranks will it seems to me tend to that result. I look upon it as the most natural result. Indeed I *look for* nothing but disasters ahead of us. May Heaven avert them. This is all I can say.

Alexander H. Stephens To J. Henly Smith. S.

Crawfordville ga., *Sept. 12th, 1860.* Dear Smith, Your letter of the 8th inst. enclosing editorial of the Constitution was received last night. I wrote to you a few days ago.

In that letter I believe I told you I expected this week to go to the mountain country with a view of recruiting strength, health, etc. But I am still here as you perceive. A very sudden change of temperature caused me to postpone my travel. It is now very cool here. In the up-country I suppose it is quite uncomfortable in the mornings and evenings for an invalid, without fire. Such weather is unsuitable for me to be away from home in. But enough of this. I only meant to let you know why I am still at home. As to the article in the Constitution, I do not think it requires any answer or reply—not even a notice, at least from me. The Va., Ky., Tenn., and N. C. and Ga. delegations bolted at Baltimore because the seceders from Ala. and La. were not permitted to take the seats that they had abandoned and because the convention assigned the seats to those delegates which the Democracy of Ala. and La. had sent up to fill the vacancies etc. according to the call of the convention. This is the whole of it. These very states of Va., Tenn., Ky., etc., had asked the Democracy of the states whose delegates had seceded at Charleston to send up other delegates to fill their places. This they did and then instead of standing by those who had been sent at their call they turned and joined the seceders themselves. The pretence was that the seceders were the true representatives of the Democracy of their states—and that too after they had joined another organization, adopted another name and had even been commissioned to another convention to be held at another place, etc. My judgment was and is that the seceders had unpartyed themselves and should not have been admitted from any state whether there was a representation of the National Democracy from it or not. But when all the States seceded who chose to do so, from whatever cause, there was a quorum of the convention left—and Douglas got a two-thirds vote of that quorum and is the regular nominated candidate of the party. That is my point, and there is no getting round it or under it or over it. Men may bolt when they please, but they cannot escape the proper characterization of their deed. My opinion is that the whole rupture at Charleston and Baltimore is chargeable entirely upon the Southern *bolters.* They ran not from a platform but from a man. The platform was a pretext. The whole rupture originated in personal ambition, spite and hate. This is my deliberate opinion. I cannot however say more. I have not yet seen Mr. Breckinridge's Lexington speech—am anxious to see it—am anxious also to hear from the Maine election. Not a word yet have we heard from that. I am apprehensive that the Republicans have increased their majority. In this State the *tendencies* are favourable to Douglas—becoming more so daily. If there was any prospect of his election a perfect enthusiasm could be got up for him—much more than for any other candidate. But his chances seem to be a hopeless battle before the people and in the House, and hence the indifference of thousands who would otherwise be active, warm and zealous in his cause. It is now thought here that Lincoln will be defeated, that the election will go into the House and if Douglas, Lincoln and Bell should be the three returned to the House *may be* Douglas might be chosen. But we shall see what we shall see. My greatest desire is to defeat Lincoln and thus prevent the evils that such an event might precipitate upon us.

Alexander H. Stephens To J. Henly Smith. S.

Crawfordville ga., *Sept. 15th, 1860.* Dear Smith, The second slip from the Constitution was received last night. I still see in this review not one thing that I desire to answer or see answered. As to the remarks and comments of the writer on my *candour*, etc., of course that is a matter beyond the reach of proof or disproof. Those who know me must judge of it for themselves and those who do not would be influenced very little by any discussion upon the subject. The truth is I have almost despaired of the Republic. Sometimes I take or catch the glimpse of a faint hope, and then the stunning truth seems to flash me full in the face that we are rushing rapidly to the brink of destruction! The times are all sadly out of joint. Men have no regard for past principles or professions. Consistency is wholly disregarded. Passion and prejudice rule the hour; reason has lost its sway. The truth and the right are not sought after. Public virtue is no longer held in its proper estimation, and all our discussions remind me more of the wranglings of the Jacobins in France than anything else. I mean the discussions on the stump and in the newspapers. Perhaps I should not say all. Mr. Douglas's speeches are an exception. In all of them that I have seen he holds a high and statesmanlike position and in them breathes a lofty, national and patriotic tone. But I see no response to this tone either North or South. Most of the Douglas papers and speakers with us seem to me not to rise to the real gravity and dignity of the questions before the country. I do not believe they realize the magnitude of the issues involved. Douglas's speech at Baltimore I think is decidedly the best he has made. Had the whole South planted themselves upon the doctrines and principles of that speech as they ought, all would have been well with us. But they will not, and as I look out upon the country and contemplate the probable future I feel as Jesus did when he came near the city of Jerusalem and wept over it, " saying if thou hadst known even thou at least in this thy day the things that belong unto thy peace, but now they are hid from thine eyes!" Such are my feelings. I may be in error, and those who are driving events as they go may come out right at last. If they do no one will be more rejoiced than I; but I can see no probability of such a fortunate result. To me at present all is gloom and darkness. I have seen partial returns from the election in Maine. This I fear is but a sample of the public sentiment at the North generally. With a divided Democracy what better could have been expected? This is but the realization of my first conviction when the rupture was consummated at Baltimore. What will now come of the attempts of fusion in N. Y. and Pa.? There lie our only hopes for the defeat of Lincoln. Will these attempts succeed, or will not the prevailing sentiment of the North, encouraged by our divisions sweep everything before it? This I now seriously fear. And if so what then? Yes, as I said in Augusta, what then? The question oppresses me. I feel well assured that the bare election of any man under the constitution is not sufficient cause for the withdrawal of any State. But are there not several States that will do it? And if the attempt even is made, who can tell the ultimate consequences? Oh my country, what is to become of it?

I am as you see still at home. I have improved a good deal in strength within the last week since the cool weather set in, but am yet unable to undertake any physical exertion. I have given up all idea of taking any active part in the present canvass. I see no good that anything I can say will accomplish, even if I had the strength to say anything without serious injury to myself. I may be too desponding, but I really look upon all as lost, not only the party and its principles, but the country. These sentiments you may keep to yourself, for I do not wish my depression of spirits to affect in the least those who are more sanguine. Let those who have hopes remit no effort to attain their object. Write to me forthwith to Kingston what you think from a survey of the whole field. I shall go to the upcountry next week and remain there the week after. At Kingston I can get your letter.

Alexander H. Stephens To J. Henly Smith. S.

Crawfordville, ga., *Sept. 16th, 1860.* Dear Smith, This is Sunday as you see from the date. Yesterday I wrote you a long letter. Last night I got the third and last slip from the Constitution in review of my Augusta speech. I notice nothing in any of these pieces that I feel any desire to answer or to have answered. The last piece is very disingenuous in one particular—that is in its attempt to make me inconsistent with myself on the matter of *abstract principles*. But this is quite apparent to all who are familiar with the facts. In my speech of July 1859 on the importance of maintaining abstract principles at any cost and hazard 73566—13 32

I spoke definitely and particularly of those *abstract principles* effecting any *essential* interest, right or *honor;* and in the speech of 1st Sept. 1860 I stated distinctly that the principle of allowing the territorial legislatures to settle the question of slavery did not involve any *essential* right, our present security, future safety, or *honor.* So the effort to show off my inconsistency was a vain and futile one. Indeed in that speech of July 1859 I stated that it was useless to war against those who refused to give us congressional protection in the Territories—that there was nothing practical or essential to our rights, interest or honor in it. I have not the speech before me, but I know this was the substance of it; and I doubt not the reviewer knew it too very well. But let it all pass—as I said yesterday the right and the truth is not what these secessionists and revolutionists are after. Their object is to hide the truth. Personal spite is their aim, and not the public good. They rely upon misleading the people by appeals to their passions and prejudices. This is the policy of all bad men bent upon mischief. Their game is that of the demagogue always a low, mean and, base one. The people by nature are prone to error. Their inclinations in politicks are that way as in morals they are to sin. To do right, to counteract these inclinations in the one sphere or the other, requires an effort. The high mission of a patriot and a statesman is by appeals to truth and virtue to raise the good sense of the masses above their natural propensities, to get them to do right against their natural inclinations. Herein lies the difference between a demagogue and a statesman. It was this high and ennobling quality that caused Webster to tell the men of Boston that they must "conquer their prejudices", as the same great quality caused Aristides on one occasion to say " O Athenians, what Themistocles proposes is greatly to your interest, but it is *unjust.*'" Our demagogues look to nothing but success and rely upon nothing but the weakness of human nature in yielding to their selfish propensities. Such practices have always been the forerunners of the overthrow of all republics. Free institutions, representative government, can be maintained only by the intelligence and virtue of the people. These are the sustaining fountains of patriotism, and when these fountains fail or become polluted patriotism ceases, love of country sours into a rabid passion of undefined rage and hate without aim or object, driving the unfortunate subjects to the wildest and most reckless ends. Such has been the history of all popular governments. The first fatal step has been that of those who, entitled to their confidence, misled the masses instead of keeping them ton the right, even against their seeming interests and their strong natural erroneous inclinations and propensities. This in all times past has most generally, as is the case in our country now, originated in the selfishness and ambition, in the personal likes, dislikes and hates, in the rivalships of public aspirants. For it is a sad and melancholy truth, such is the frailty and weakness of human nature, that even the best of patriots generally hate their enemies or rivals more than they love their Country. From this weakness or imperfection of man's constitution come most of the evils and troubles which disturb the peace, unsettle the foundations and destroy the prosperity and happiness of the wisest and best constituted human societies and governments. These are the evils and troubles that now beset and threaten this fair and happy land, this land of hope and promise to the world. There is a war among the leaders and aspirants for public favour and public trust. It is not a contest for the wisest, safest and soundest policy looking to the security of the rights, interest, welfare and prosperity of all parts and sections of the country. So far from it, it is a contest based upon disloyalty to principle, upon abandonment of principle, and waged with an audacious effort to make the public believe a lie, that there is no abandonment of principle but that the object is to subserve their interests.

This is the state of things here at this time. Its parallel or prototype is to be found in all incipient revolutions. I can look upon it in no other light; and as like produces like in the moral and political as well as the physical world, I look to the same almost inevitable result. The contemplation is a sad one. It presents but little ground of hope. Had revolution been forced upon us as it was upon the colonies by a violation of principle, by the assertion of unjust power incompatible with our security and safety, my hopes and views of the future would be altogether different from what they are. Men who set out in a revolution by an abandonment of the principles and professions of their lives offer no guaranty to me that they will conduct it to any good result. Their conduct shows that other objects than the public welfare are at the bottom of their movement. These objects are personal, and all things in the end as in the beginning will be made to tend to these same purposes, which purposes are utterly inconsistent with any wellgrounded hope for good government. The future to me therefore is gloomy enough! Whether there is virtue and patriotism sufficient in the country to realize its situation and arrest the evil tendency before it is too late I do not know. I cannot answer that question satisfactorily to myself. But perhaps I have tired you with this long Jeremiad, as you may consider it, and therefore I will say no more. Why do you not continue to send me the New York papers? I have got none lately. Have they ceased to be interesting? Have they become as dark and as incapable of throwing light upon the future as my own incoherent speculations? I feel anxious to know how the fusion movements succeeded in N. Y. and Pa. In them lay my only hope for the defeat of Lincoln. I have seen nothing about that matter in Pa. In New York I saw that the Americans and National Democrats had united and that it was expected that the Secession Democrats would also join in the union. But whether they have or not I have not seen. And I am intensely ignorant or uninformed as to how matters stand in Pa. Write to me to Kingston on these points and send your newspapers to that place. I am feeling better today in health than I have felt for several weeks. The weather is still pleasantly cool.

Alexander H. Stephens To J. Henly Smith. S.

Crawfordville ga., *Sept. 30th, 1860.*
Dear Smith. I have just got back from my up-country trip—am to go to Warren court tomorrow—health somewhat improved, would have been more so but for speechmaking that I could not get round. I spoke at Atlanta. Marietta, Floyd Spring and Dalton. There is quite a strong feeling springing up for the national cause in that section of the country. Linton has stirred them up greatly. He has spoken in Gwinnett, Newton, Hall, Cobb, Cass, Whitfield, Catoosa, Walker and Dade—and with great effect. I verily believe that if we had three months to go on we should carry a majority of the Democracy with us. The meeting yesterday at Dalton was large—two thousand perhaps—and enthusiastic. Where four weeks ago there were not ten Douglas men to be found, our friends assure me that Douglas and Johnson will get 3,500 votes in the 5th district. I can hardly think it is so, but such is their belief. The changes are daily and numerous. From all parts of the State I hear that our cause is gaining daily and rapidly. How far this opinion enter-

tained by those who give it is well founded I cannot say. I give it as it is given to me. I saw some gentlemen from Tenn. yesterday who say that Bell will certainly carry that State. I saw one on the cars today from La. who says that Bell will carry that State too. I have all along counted La. for Breckinridge. Send your papers for the future here, and write to me here the present prospect. I shall be back next Saturday. I have no time to say more.

P. S.—I got a great many papers from you at Kingston and *one* letter.

Alexander H. Stephens To J. Henly Smith. S.

Crawfordville ga., *Oct. 13th, 1860.* Dear Smith, I got back from Hancock court this evening and found your letter of the 8th Inst. The news of the elections in Pa., Ohio and Indiana reached me at Sparta. I was not much disappointed though greatly saddened by the result. I have as you know ever since the final rupture at Baltimore been prepared for a general rout of the Democracy everywhere and the triumph of the Republicans in November. This conviction of the mind I have not been able to get rid of all the time. It is true I still hope for New York to prevent the catastrophe, but I see but little grounds upon which to rest a hope. We shall I fear very soon see the "beginning of the end " we have often heard so much of. I foresaw or thought I foresaw these coming events when the Administration began their war on Douglas on the grounds of his Freeport speech. That wickedly foolish policy has brought upon us all these troubles and those. far greater troubles just ahead of us. Present appearances however will not cause me to relax in the least my endeavours to arrest the evils if possible. Should Mr. Breckinridge get the entire South and Lincoln the entire North no earthly power could prevent civil war. I do not know that it can be anyhow should Lincoln be elected. Still if those whose folly and wickedness brought it about should not be sustained at the South by public sentiment in their secession movement they may pause before pushing their projects to extremes. I do trust the popular vote of this State at least will not sustain them. How it will be I cannot venture a conjecture at this time. Had Indiana, Ohio or Pa. gone Democratic it would have aided us greatly. As it is I fear the sectional tendency in the popular mind will be increased by the result in all those States. I have not yet seen or witnessed the effect of these elections upon our people. The time has been too short. I shall fight on to the end. I made a speech on Wednesday in Sparta. It produced I was told a powerful effect. Many said it was the greatest speech I ever made. This I say to you though but to few would I so express myself. My health has greatly improved. I spoke two hours and a half. Next Wednesday I am to speak at Lexington—Saturday at Elberton, then at Savannah, and other places. Douglas is to be in Georgia on the 29th. We will keep the flag afloat even though he does not get a single electoral vote. Should the Government survive, the principles will live, they will form the basis for future action and organization. These are my views. I see the States and Union published the Confederacy's report of my Atlanta speech. I was sorry for that. The report was a miserable one. The speech was one hour and a half long and the best parts were not alluded to, and in some instances I was very inaccurately reported. Indeed it was no report at all, it was simply an account of the speech put in the form of a verbatim report. I send you an account of our Dalton meeting, cut from the Rome Southerner. Judge Wright is the author of this. He was wonderfuly pleased with that demonstration. Mr. Cobb I see has come home and gone to stumping. Mr. Toombs is active. He spoke at Warrenton and Sparta during court. His speeches had no effect at either place. Linton is going up to a mass meeting at Turnpike Gate near Cuhutta Mountain in Murray County next Saturday. It is on the line of Gilmer and Murray counties. The popular mind is fast beginning to be awakened to the importance of the issues. If we had but six months to go upon I do verily believe the state could be carried for Douglas. All I now *hope* for is to defeat the seceders before the people. Continue to write to me. The letter of the 8th is the only one I have got from you since the one at Kingston. I fancy that I see a letter from you occasionally over the signature of Cleaveland in the Cincinnati Enquirer. Am I right or not? And if so, am I not good at guessing? I shall go to Oglethorpe Court Monday, and I shall not be home until Monday week. Then I wish to get a letter from you. Jones, our member of Congress, is out canvassing the district for the seceders' ticket. I understand he spoke in this place Thursday of this week. He had a small crowd. Breckinridge will not get exceeding fifty votes in this county I think. Bell will probably get a plurality. Douglas and Bell together will get a large majority in the district. If Bell could sustain Akin's vote in the State, there would be no difficulty in defeating Breckinridge before the people. But I fear he will not. He will I think lose several thousand of Akin's vote. Some will vote for Douglas but most of them who fall off will illegible vote for Douglas. I have not time to say more—so good night.

Alexanrer H. Stephens To J. Henly Smith. S.

Crawfordville ga., *Nov. 8th, 1860.* Dear Smith, I got home Sunday night last—was here at the election. Taliaferro County did well; but the State I fear has gone for Breckinridge by the popular vote. The old Eighth is all right, I feel confident. I have just heard that Judge Andrews1 has been elected to fill Irwin's place in the House of Rep. in our State Legislature. This shows that Wilkes county does not endorse the course of the seceders at Charleston and Baltimore. I see by the papers received this morning that Lincoln is elected President. It does not surprise me in the least. I have been expecting it ever since the burst up at Baltimore, as you know very well. What is to be the result I cannot tell. We shall I apprehend have trouble.

The people here are taken greatly by surprise at the result. They did not anticipate it and thought I was only indulging in unnecessary apprehensions when I told them months ago how it would most probably be. I have never been disappointed in a Presidential election since 1840. I do not feel so much oppressed in spirits at the result 1 Judge Garnett Andrews, of Washington, Ga., was one of the most thoroughgoing unionists In the State.

now actually upon us as I did months ago in looking forward to it. But enough of this.

I got your letter enclosing the States and Union with extract of my letter to you. I should have preferred that you had only given the first part and omitted that which spoke of my reasons for the course I was taking. The first part would have answered the misrepresentation of my position. But the whole makes no difference. The truth seldom does any harm; and in this case I have been actuated from the beginning by disinterested patriotism looking to the safety, peace, security and best interest of the whole country. I can say no more. Let me hear from you often.

Alexander H. Stephens To J. Henly Smith. S.

Crawfordville ga., *Nov. 21st, 1860.*

Dear Smith, I got home yesterday from Milledgeville after an absence of ten days. I was expecting a letter from you and some papers but found none. I wrote to you soon after our election before I left home. I am anxious to see the tone of Northern leading papers on the present state of public affairs and prospect for the future, and also anxious to know the state of feeling among the public men at Washington, what will be the course of the President and the Administration when South Carolina declares herself out of the Union, as it is generally supposed here that she will certainly do at an early day.

My views of the state of the republic were given to the Legislature last week. You will see a tolerable report of them in the Southern Recorder, republished in other papers. The report was by no means full or clear in some particulars but the outline of the policy I advocated will be seen in it. Let me know how it is received at Washington by all sides. I fear we are past salvation—that there is not patriotism enough in the country North or South to save it.

Alexander H. Stephens To J. Henly Smith.

Crawfordville, Ga., *Nov. 23,1860.*
Dear Smith, I have just received your letter of the 16th Inst. By some strange mishap it has been delayed. I wrote to you day before yesterday stating I had received nothing from you lately. Last night I got the Tribune and N. Y. Herald of the 16th Inst. When I see the Elberton Star I will write to you what I think of your article on retaliatory legislation. You will see from my last speech that I am inclined to favour that policy. I think a course perfectly constitutional might be pursued on that line that would effect the desired result. What our State convention will do is very uncertain. I should not be at all surprised to see secession adopted by them as the proper remedy. The country is in a panic and there is no telling where it will end. I do not know whether I shall be in the convention or not.

I have not made up my mind to go yet. I am inclined to let those who sowed the wind reap the whirlwind, or control it if they can. It does seem to me that we are going to destruction as fast as we can.

Alexander II. Stephens To

Crawfordville ga., *Nov. #5,1860.*

Dear Sir: Your kind and esteemed favor of the 19th instant is before me, for which you will please accept my thanks. I thoroughly agree with you as to the nature and extent of the dangers by which we are surrounded, and the importance of united action on the part of our people in the line of policy to be pursued.

I know also that there breathes not a man in Georgia who is more sensitively alive to her rights, interest, safety, honor and glory than myself; and whatever fate befalls us I earnestly hope that we shall be saved from the worst of all calamities, internal divisions, contentions and strifes. The great and leading object aimed at by me in Milledgeville was to produce harmony on a right line of policy. If the worst comes to the worst, as it may, and our State has to quit the Union, it is of the utmost importance that all our people should be united cordially in this course. This, I feel confident, can only be effected on the line of policy I indicated.

But candor compels me to say that I am not without hopes that our rights may be maintained and our wrongs be redressed in the Union. If this can be done it is my earnest wish. I think also that it is the wish of a majority of our people. If, after making an effort, we shall fail, then all our people will be united in making or adopting the last resort, the "*ultima ratio regurw*". Even in that case I should look with great apprehension as to the ultimate result. When this Union is dissevered, if of necessity it must be, I see at present but little prospect of good government afterwards. At the North I feel confident anarchy will soon ensue. And whether we shall be better off at the South will depend upon many things that I am not now satisfied that we have any assurance of.

Revolutions are much easier started than controlled, and the men who begin them, even for the best purposes and objects, seldom end them. The American Revolution of 1776 was one of the few exceptions to this remark that the history of the world furnishes. Human 1 Prom the National Intelligencer, Washington, D. C, Dec. 6, 1860, reprinting the letter from the New York Journal of Commerce, with a notice that It was addressed by Stephens to a friend in New York. Copy obtained through the courtesy of Mr. J. K. Smith, ot Grand Rapids, Mich.

passions are like the winds; when aroused they sweep everything before them in their fury. The wise and the good who attempt to control them will themselves most likely become the victims. This has been the history of the downfall of all Republics. The selfish, the ambitious, and the bad will generally take the lead. When the moderate men who are patriotic have gone as far as they think right and proper, and propose to reconstruct, then will be found a class below them, governed by no principle but personal objects, who will be for pushing matters further and further, until those who sowed the wind will find that they have reaped the whirlwind.

These are my serious apprehensions. They are founded upon the experience of the world and the philosophy of human nature, and no wise man should condemn them. To tear down and build up again are very different things; and before tearing down even a bad Government we should first see a good prospect for building up a better. These are my views candidly given. If there is one sentiment in my breast stronger than all others, it is an earnest desire for the peace, prosperity, and happiness which a wise and good government alone can secure. I have no object, wish, desire, or ambition beyond this; and if I should in any respect err in endeavoring to attain this object it will be an error of the head and not of the heart.

Howell Cobb To The People Of Georgia.1 washtngton, D. C, *December 6, 1860*1 I have received numerous communications from different portions of the State asking my views on the present condition of the country, accompanied with the request that they might be placed before the public.

It is impossible to answer each of these communications, and I have therefore taken the liberty of addressing my reply to the people of the State, asking for what I have to say that consideration only which is due to convictions deliberately formed and frankly expressed.

The whole subject may properly be considered in the discussion of the following inquiry. Does the election of Lincoln to the Presidency, in the usual and constitutional mode, justify the Southern States in dissolving the Union?

The answer to this enquiry involves a consideration of the principles of the party who elected him, as well as the principles of the man himself.

The Black Republican party had its origin in the anti-slavery feeling of the North. It assumed the form and organization of a party 1 This address was issued as a pamphlet with the following title: "Letter of Hon. Howell Cobb to the People of Georgia, on the Present Condition of the Country." Washington, 1860, 16 pp. The present text is derived from the pamphlet.
for the first time in the Presidential contest of 1856. The fact that it was composed of men of all previous parties, who then and still advocate principles directly antagonistic upon all other questions except slavery, shows beyond doubt or question that hostility to slavery, as it exists in the fifteen Southern States, was the basis of its organization and the bond of its union. Free-trade Democrats and protective-tariff Whigs, internal improvement and anti-internal improvement men, and indeed all shades of partizans, united in cordial fraternity upon the isolated issue of hostility to the South, though for years they had fought each other upon all other issues. The fact is important because it illustrates the deep-rooted feeling which could thus bring together these hostile elements. It must be conceded that there was an object in view of no ordinary interest which could thus fraternize these incongruous elements. Besides, at the time this party organized there was presented no bright promise of success. All the indications of the day pointed to their certain defeat. So deep however was this anti-slavery sentiment planted in their hearts that they forgot and forgave the asperities of the past, the political differences of the present, and regardless of the almost certain defeat which the future had in store for them, cordially embraced each other in the bonds of anti-slavery hatred, preferring defeat under the banner of abolition to success, if it had to be purchased by a recognition of the constitutional rights of the South. The party has succeeded in bringing into its organization all the Abolitionists of the North except that small band of honest fanatics who say, and say truly, that if slavery is the moral curse which the Black Republicans pronounce it to be, they feel bound to dissolve their connection with it, and are therefore for a dissolution of the Union. Such I may denominate the *personnel* of the Black Republican party, which, by the election of Lincoln has demonstrated its numerical majority in every Northern State except New Jersey.1...

There is one dogma of this party which has been so solemnly enunciated, both by their national conventions and Mr. Lincoln that it is worthy of serious consideration. I allude to the doctrine of negro equality. The stereotyped expression of the Declaration of Independence that "All men are born equal," has been perverted from its plain and truthful meaning, and made the basis of a political dogma which strikes at the very foundations of the institution of slavery. Mr. Lincoln and his party assert that this doctrine of equality applies to the negro, and necessarily there can exist no such thing as property in our equals. Upon this point both Mr. Lincoln and his party have spoken with a distinctness that admits of no 1 The material here omitted, filling six pages of the pamphlet, mainly comprises quotations hostile to slavery from the platforms of the Republican party and from Lincoln, Seward, Chase, Sumner, and Wilson.
question or equivocation. If they are right, the institution of slavery as it exists in the Southern States is in direct violation of the fundamental principles of our Government; and to say that they would not use all the power in their hands to eradicate the evil and restore the Government to its *"ancient faith?"* would be to write themselves down self-convicted traitors both to principle and duty. These principles have not only been declared in the impassioned language of its advocates and defenders, but have at length found their way into the statute books

of ten of the Northern States.

Every good citizen, North and South, admits that the Constitution of the United States in express terms requires our fugitive slaves to be delivered up to their owners, when escaping into another State. Congress has discharged its duty in passing laws to carry out this constitutional obligation; and, so far, every Executive has complied with his oath of office, to see this law duly executed. The impediments thrown in the way by lawless mobs, the threats of violence to which the owner has been on different occasions subjected, and the expense to which both the Government and the owner have been put are matters of small consideration compared with the more pregnant fact that ten sovereign States of the Union have interposed their strong arm to protect the thief, punish the owner, and confiscate the property of a citizen of a sister State. Such are the laws passed by these Northern States to defeat the fugitive slave act of Congress and annul a plain provision of the Constitution of the United States.

These laws are the legitimate fruit of the principles and teachings of the Black Republican party, and have therefore very naturally made their appearance upon the statute books of States under the control and in the hands of that party. Their existence cannot and should not be overlooked by those who are desirous of knowing what this party will do on the subject of slavery whenever they have the power to act. I call attention to them not only as an important item in the evidence I am offering of the principles and objects of the Black Republican party, but for the more important purpose of presenting a plain and palpable violation of the constitutional compact by ten of the sovereign parties to it. These very States are among the loudest in their demands for unconditional submission on the part of the South to the election of Lincoln. The inviolability of the Union is the magic word with which they summon the South to submission. The South responds by holding up before them a Constitution basely broken—a compact wantonly violated. That broken Constitution and violated compact formed the only Union we ever recognized; and if you would still have us to love and preserve it. restore to it that vital spirit of which it has been robbed by your sacrilegious hands, and make it again what our fathers made it—a Union of good faith in the maintenance of constitutional obligations. Do this, and the Union will find in all this land no truer or more devoted supporters than the ever-loyal sons of the South. This, however, the Black Republicans will not do, as the facts I am now developing will show beyond all doubt or question.

In the election which has just transpired, the Black Republicans did not hesitate to announce, defend and justify the doctrines and principles which I have attributed to them. During the progress of the canvass I obtained copies of the documents which they were circulating at the North, with a view of ascertaining the grounds upon which they were appealing to the people for their support and confidence. With the exception of a few dull speeches in favor of a protective tariff, intended for circulation in Pennsylvania and New Jersey, and a still fewer number of pitiful appeals for squandering the public lands, the whole canvass was conducted by the most bitter and malignant appeals to the anti-slavery sentiment of the North. Under the sanction of Senators and Representatives in Congress the country was flooded with pamphlets and speeches holding up slave-holders as "barbarians, more criminal than murderers," and declaring unhesitatingly in favor of immediate and unconditional abolition in every State in the Confederacy where it now exists—doctrines which are the necessary and legitimate consequences of the universally recognized dogmas of the Black Republican party. It is worse than idle to deny that such are the doctrines and principles of their party because all of them have not reached that point of boldness and honesty which induce men to follow principles to their legitimate conclusions. One thing at least is certain: The managers of the canvass believed that such doctrines were popular, or they would not have spent both their time and money in giving them such general circulation to the exclusion of all other matter. The election of Lincoln in response to such appeals show that these men properly understood the popular sentiment of their section, to whom alone they appealed for votes to elect their candidate.

From these doctrines, principles and acts of the Black Republican party I propose to extract the aims and objects of the party. It will be borne in mind, that I rely upon the declaration of their principles: 1st. As made by their national convention. 2d. As contained in the deliberate and repeated declarations of their successful candidate for the Presidency. 3d. As announced by their most honored and trusted leaders in the Senate of the United States. I invite attention to the following propositions, as the plain and legitimate objects proposed to be carried out to the extent of their power: *First.* That slavery is a moral, social and political evil: and that it is the duty of the Federal Government to prevent its extension. *Second.* That slavery is not recognized by the Constitution of the United States; and that the Federal Government is in nowise committed to its protection. *Third.* That property in slaves is not entitled to the same protection at the hands of the Federal Government with other property. *Fourth.* That so far from protecting, it is the duty of the Federal Government, wherever its power extends, to prohibit it, and therefore it is the duty of Congress by law to prevent any Southern man from going into the common territories of the Union with his slave property. *Fifth.* That slavery is such an evil and curse, that it is the duty of everyone, to the extent of his power, to contribute to its ultimate extinction in the United States. *Sixth.* That there is such a conflict between slave and free labor that all the States of the Union must become either slave or free; and as all

Black Republicans are opposed to slavery and slave States their policy and doctrines look to all these States becoming free, as not only the natural but desired result of the "irrepressible conflict." *Seventh.* That the Declaration of Independence expressly declares and the Constitution recognizes the equality of the negro to the white man; and that the holding the negro in slavery is violative of his equality as well as of that " *ancient faith* " which Mr. Lincoln says is violated in the present relation of master and slave in the Southern States. *Eighth.* That the Southern States do not stand upon an equality with the non-slaveholding States, because, whilst it is the recognized duty of the General Government to protect the latter in the enjoyment of all their rights of property and would especially be required to protect their citizens from any act of confiscation in the common territories of the Union, it would b the duty of the same General Government not only to withhold Bach protection from the citizen of a Southern State with his slave property in the common domain, but to exercise that power for his exclusion from that common territory. *Ninth.* That the admission of more slave States into the Union is rendered a moral if not a physical impossibility.

To appreciate the full import of these doctrines and principles of the Black Republican party, they should be looked at in connection with the constitutional rights and guarantees claimed by the Southern States. They are briefly: 1. That the Constitution of the United States recognizes the institution of slavery as it exists in the fifteen Southern States.

2. That the citizens of the South have the right to go with their slave property into the common territories of the Union, and are entitled to protection for both their persons and property from the General Government during its territorial condition. 3. That by the plain letter of the Constitution the owner of a slave is entitled to reclaim his property in any State into which the slave may escape, and that both the General and State Governments are bound under the Constitution to the enforcement of this provision; the General Government by positive enactment, as has been done; and the State Governments by interposing no obstacle in the way of the execution of the law and the Constitution.

I decline to enumerate other constitutional rights, equally clear, because I prefer to confine myself in this argument to those which have been fully recognized by the highest judicial tribunal in the country. No law and Constitution-abiding man will deny that the rights here enumerated are within the clear provisions of the Constitution, and that the South is fully justified in demanding their recognition and enforcement. Otherwise we are asked to pay tribute and give allegiance to a government which is wanting either in the will or power to protect us in the enjoyment of undoubted rights. I apprehend it is equally clear that the antagonism between these recognized rights and the doctrines and principles of the Black Republican party is plain, direct and irreconcilable. The one or the other must give way. Surely no right-minded man who admits the existence of the rights claimed by the South will say that she ought to yield. It only remains to enquire whether the Black Republican party will recede from its position and thus end the "irrepressible conflict" which their doctrines have inaugurated. Those who indulge the hope that such will be the case are, in my honest judgment, greatly deluded. The boldness and earnestness with which this party have avowed their principles, the sacrifices they have made to secure their triumph, the deliberation with which their position has been taken, the clear and emphatic committals of their conventions, their candidate and all their leading men; the solemn acts of their State Legislatures—all indicate with unerring certainty that there is no reasonable hope of such a result.

I know that there are those who say and believe that this party is incapable of exercising the power it has obtained without breaking to pieces, and they look confidently to its overthrow at an early period. It may be that a cool philosophy located at a safe distance from the scene of danger may reason plausibly upon the chances of overthrowing a party so utterly unworthy of public confidence; but men looking to the security of property, and fathers and husbands anxious for the safety of their families, require some stronger guarantee than the feeble assurance of partisan speculations to quiet their apprehensions and allay their fears. This may be the case; but unfortunately for the future peace and security of the South, the causes which may lead to its dissolution and defeat arise outside of the slavery question. So far from the question of slavery leading to such a result, it is the only subject upon which the party thoroughly harmonizes. Hostility to slavery is the magic word which holds them together; and when torn to pieces by other dissensions, hatred to the South and her institutions swallows up all other troubles and restores harmony to their distracted ranks. On this point we are not left to mere conjecture; the history of the party in the ten nullifying States affords practical proof of the fact. In which of these States did the Black Republican party lose power in consequence of their acts repudiating the fugitive-slave law and nullifying the Constitution of the United States? So far from their anti-slavery legislation being an element of weakness, it has proven in all these States the shibboleth of their strength. In New York and Pennsylvania the corruptions of this party were so palpable and infamous that their own press cried out against it. Those of the party who made pretension of honesty felt the shame and humiliation brought upon them; and yet, when the Presidential battle was sensions, hatred to the South and her institutions swallows up all and these acts of fraud and corruption were forgotten and forgiven in the greater and more absorbing feeling of hostility and hatred to the South and her institutions. Shall we close our eyes to these historical facts and indulge the vain hope that these men will play a different part, simply because they are transferred to a new theatre of action? I do not doubt that the Black Republican party will be guilty of similar and greater frauds in the Federal Government; nor do I doubt that their wrangling and quarrels over the offices and patronage will plant in their party the seeds of strife and dissension which would lead ordinarily to their speedy downfall and overthrow; but I feel assured by the teachings of the past that the magic word of anti-slavery will again summon them to a cordial and fraternal reunion to renew and continue the war upon slavery, until they shall have accomplished the great object of their organization—" its ultimate extinction."

What are the facts to justify the hope that the Black Republicans will recede from their well defined position of hostility to the South and her institutions? Are they to be found in the two millions of voters who have deliberately declared in favor of these doctrines by their support of Lincoln? Is the hope based upon the fact that an overwhelming majority of the people of every Northern State save one cast their vote for the Black Republican candidate? Is it drawn from the fact that on the fourth of March next the chair of Washington is to be filled by a man who hates the institution of slavery as much as any other abolitionist, and who has not only declared but used all the powers of his intellect to prove that our slaves are our equals and that all laws which hold otherwise are violative of the Declaration of Independence and at war with the law of God— a man who is indebted for his present election to the Presidency alone to his abolition sentiments—and who stands pledged to the doctrine of "the irrepressible conflict," and indeed claims to be its first advocate? Or, shall we look for this hope in the whispered intimation that, when secure of his office, Lincoln will prove faithless to the principles of his party and false to his own pledges, or in his emphatic declaration of May, 1859, that he would " oppose the lowering of the Republican standard by *a hair's breadth,"* or in the public announcement made by Senator Trumbull of Illinois, since the election, *in the presence* of Mr. Lincoln, that he, Lincoln, would "*maintain and carry forward the principles on which he was elected"* at the same time holding up the military power of the United States as the instrumentality to enforce obedience to the incoming abolition administration, should any Southern State secede from the Union; or in the prospect of a more efficient execution of the fugitve slave law, when the marshals' offices in all the Northern States shall have been filled with Lincoln's abolition appointees; or in the refusal of Vermont, since the election of Lincoln, by the decisive vote of more than two to one in her Legislature to repeal the Personal Liberty Bill of that State; or shall we look for it in the doctrine of negro equality which finds among its warmest supporters the brightest lights of the Black Republican party; or in the announcements solemnly made by conventions, speakers, papers, and all other organs of the party that the recognized rights of the South to equality and protection of slave property shall never be tolerated; or in the fact that the party is not only sectional in its principles but sectional in its membership, thereby giving to the South the promise of such boon as she may hope to receive from Black Republicans in their newly assumed character of guardians and masters; or in the warning voice of their ablest statesmen that the decisions of the Supreme Court in favor of our constitutional rights are to be met not with reason and argument for reversal but with the more potent and practical remedy of "reorganization of the Court," by adding a sufficient number of abolitionists to reverse existing decisions; or in the pregnant fact developed by the census returns now coming in, that the numerical majority of the North is steadily and rapidly increasing, with the promise of still further increase by the addition of more free States carved out of that common territory from which the South is to be excluded by unjust and unconstitutional legislation; or in such manifestations of Northern sentiment as led to the nomination by this party of John A. Andrew for Governor of Massachusetts after he had declared his sanction and approval of the John Brown raid; or in the election of that same Andrew to that office by seventy thousand majority after he had declared in his anxiety to abolish slavery that "he could not wait for Providence" to wipe it out, but must himself undertake that duty with the aid of his Black Republican brethren; or shall we be pointed to the defiant tones of triumph which fill the whole Northern air with the wild shouts of joy and thanksgiving that the days of slavery are numbered and the hour draws nigh when the "higher law" and "hatred of slavery and slave holders" shall be substituted for " the Constitution " and the spirit of former brotherhood; or to the cold irony which speaks through their press of the "*inconvenience*" of negro insurrections, arson, and murder which may result in the South from the election of Lincoln. In none of these, nor of the other facts to which I have before referred, can anything be found to justify the hope suggested by those confiding friends who in this hour of gloom and despondency are disposed to hope against hope.

Turning from these indications in the political world to the more quiet and peaceful walks of social and religious life, let us pause for a moment and look to the pulpit, the Sunday schools, and all the sources of Christian influence, for one cheering beam of light. Unfortunately wherever you find the presence of Black Republicanism it is engaged in this work of educating the hearts of the people to hate the institution of slavery. The pulpit forgets every other duty and doctrine to thunder its anathemas against this institution, whilst the Sunday-school room is made the nursery of youthful Abolitionists. This hope we are asked to adopt will find in these sources no encouragement or support. On the contrary nothing has contributed more to the creation of that bitter feeling of hatred which now pervades the two sections of the country than the religious teachings of the North. It has broken social relations, severed churches, and now threatens, in company with its political handmaid, Black Republicanism, to overthrow our once happy and glorious Union.

I refer to one other source upon which the South is asked to rely, and will then close the argument. We are expected, in view of all these facts, to rely for our safety and protection upon an uncertain and at best trembling majority in the two Houses of Congress, and told, with an earnest appeal for further delay, that with a majority in Congress against him Lincoln is powerless to do us harm. I doubt not the sincerity of those who present this appeal against Southern action; but their confidence in its merit only shows how superficial has been their consideration of the subject. It is true that without a majority in Congress Lincoln will not be able to carry out *at present* all the aggressive measures of his party. But let me ask if that feeble and constantly-decreasing majority in Congress against him can 73666—13 33, arrest that tide of popular sentiment at the North against slavery which, sweeping down all the barriers of truth, justice and constitutional duty, has borne Mr. Lincoln into the Presidential chair? Can that Congressional majority, faint and feeble as it is known to be, repeal the unconstitutional legislation of those ten nullifying States of the North? Can it restore the lost equality of the Southern States? Can it give to the South its constitutional rights? Can it exercise its power in one single act of legislation in our favor without the concurrence of Lincoln? Or can it make Christians of Beecher, Garrison, Cheever and Wendell Phillips, or patriots of Seward, Chase and Webb? Can that majority in Congress control the power and patronage of President Lincoln?" Can it stay his arm when he wields the offices and patronage of the Government to cement and strengthen the anti-slavery sentiment which brought his party into existence and which alone can preserve it from early and certain dissolution? Can it prevent the use of that patronage for the purpose of organizing in the South a band of apologists—the material around which Black Republicanism hopes during his four years to gather an organization in Southern States to be the allies of this party in its insidious warfare upon our family firesides and altars? True but over-anxious friends of the Union at the North, faithful but over-confiding men of the South, may catch at this congressional majority straw, but it will only be to grasp and sink with it.

The facts and considerations which I have endeavored to bring to your view present the propriety of resistance on the part of the South to the election of Lincoln in a very different light from the mere question of resisting the election of a President who has been chosen in the usual and constitutional mode. It is not simply that a comparatively obscure abolitionist, who hates the institutions of the South, has been elected President, and that we are asked to live under the administration of a man who commands neither our respect or confidence, that the South contemplates resistance even to disunion. Wounded honor might tolerate the outrage until by another vote of the people the nuisance could be abated; but the election of Mr. Lincoln involves far higher considerations. It brings to the South the solemn judgment of a majority of the people of every Northern State—with a solitary exception—in favor of doctrines and principles violative of her constitutional rights, humiliating to her pride, destructive of her equality in the Union, and fraught with the greatest danger to the peace and safety of her people. It can be regarded in no other light than a declaration of the purpose and intention of the people of the North to continue, with the power of the Federal Government, the war already commenced by the ten nullifying States of the North upon the institution of slavery and the constitutional rights of the South, To these acts of bad faith the South has heretofore submitted, though constituting ample justification for abandoning a compact which had been wantonly violated. The question is now presented whether longer submission to an increasing spirit and power of aggression is compatible either with her honor or her safety. In my mind there is no room for doubt. The issue must now be met, or forever abandoned. Equality and safety in the Union are at an end; and it only remains to be seen whether our manhood is equal to the task of asserting and maintaining independence out of it. The Union formed by our fathers was one of equality, justice and fraternity. On the fourth of March it will be supplanted by a Union of sectionalism and hatred. The one was worthy of the support and devotion of freemen—the other can only continue at the cost of your honor, your safety, and your independence.

Is there no other remedy for this state of things but immediate secession? None worthy of your consideration has been suggested, except the recommendation of Mr. Buchanan, of new constitutional guarantees—or rather. the clear and explicit recognition of those that already exist. This recommendation is the counsel of a patriot and a statesman. It exhibits an appreciation of the evils that are upon us, and at the same time a devotion to the Constitution and its sacred guarantees. It conforms to the record of Mr. Buchanan's life on this distracting question—the record of a pure heart and a wise head. It is the language of a man whose heart is overwhelmed with a sense of the great wrong and injustice that has been done to the minority section, mingled with an ardent hope and desire to preserve that Union to which he has devoted the energies of a long and patriotic life.

The difficulty is, there will be no response to it from those who alone have it in their power to act. Black Republicanism is the ruling sentiment at the North. and by the election of

Lincoln has pronounced in the most formal and solemn manner against the principles which are now commended to the country for its safety and preservation. As a matter of course they will spurn these words of wisdom and patriotism, as they have before turned their back upon all the teachings of the good and true men of the land, or else they will play with it in their insidious warfare to delude the South into a false security, that they may the more effectually rivet their iron chains and thereby put resistance in the future beyond our power. They have trampled upon the Constitution of Washington and Madison, and will prove equally faithless to their own pledges. You ought not—cannot trust them. It is not the Constitution and the laws of the United States which need amendment, but *the hearts* of the northern people. To effect the first would be a hopeless undertaking, whilst the latter is an impossibility. If the appeal of the President was made to *brethren* of the two sections of the country, we might hope for a different response. Unfortunately, however, Black Republicanism has buried brotherhood in the same grave with the Constitution. We are no longer " brethren dwelling together in unity." The ruling spirits of the North are Black Republicans—and between them and the people of the South there is no other feeling than that of bitter and intense hatred. Aliens in heart, no power on earth can keep them united. Nothing now holds us together but the cold formalities of a broken and violated Constitution. Heaven has pronounced the decree of divorce, and it will be accepted by the South as the only solution which gives to her any promise of future peace and safety.

To part with our friends at the North who have been true and faithful to the Constitution will cause a pang in every Southern breast; for with them we could live forever, peaceably, safely, happily. Honor and future security, however, demand the separation, and in their hearts they will approve though they may regret the act.

Fellow-citizens of Georgia, I have endeavored to place before you the facts of the case, in plain and unimpassioned language; and I should feel that I had done injustice to my own convictions, and been unfaithful to you, if I did not in conclusion warn you against the dangers of delay and impress upon you the hopelessness of any remedy for these evils short of secession. You have to deal with a shrewd, heartless and unscrupulous enemy, who in their extremity may promise anything, but in the end will do nothing. On the 4th day of March, 1861, the Federal Government will pass into the hands of the Abolitionists. It will then cease to have the slightest claim either upon your confidence or your loyalty; and, in my honest judgment, each hour that Georgia remains thereafter a member of the Union will be an hour of degredation, to be followed by certain and speedy ruin. I entertain no doubt either of your right or duty to secede from the Union. Arouse, then, all your manhood for the great work before you, and be prepared on that day to announce and maintain your independence out of the Union, for you will never again have equality and justice in it. Identified with you in heart, feeling and interest, I return to share in whatever destiny the future has in store for our State and ourselves.

Howell Cobb To His Wife. E.
Washington City, *7 Dec., 1860.* My Dear Wife,... I put a printed copy of my address to the people of Georgia in Judge Black's1 hand to be handed to the President. Whether I remain here after its publication to the world 1 Jeremiah S. Blafk, Attorney-General. will soon be decided. I suppose I cannot; but I hope to part from the old gentleman pleasantly. Duty to Georgia compels me to speak and self respect compels me to speak in plain language. This I have done, as you know from having heard the address read....

Howell Cobb To James Buchanan.1
Washington City, *Dec. 8, 1860.*
My Dear Sir: A sense of duty to the State of Georgia requires me to take a step which makes it proper that I should no longer continue to be a member of your Cabinet.

In the troubles of the country consequent upon the late Presidential election, the honor and safety of my State are involved. Her people so regard it, and in their opinion I fully concur. They are engaged in a struggle where the issue is life or death. My friends ask for my views and counsel. Not to respond would be degrading to myself and unjust to them. I have accordingly prepared, and must now issue to them, an address which contains the calm and solemn convictions of my heart and judgment.

The views which I sincerely entertain, and which therefore I am bound to express differ in some respects from your own. The existence of this difference would expose me, if I should remain in my present place, to unjust suspicions, and put you in a false position. The first of these consequences I could bear well enough, but I will not subject you to the last.

My withdrawal has not been occasioned by anything you have said or done. Whilst differing from your Message upon some of its theoretical doctrines, as well as from the hope so earnestly expressed that the Union can yet be preserved, there was no practical result likely to follow which required me to retire from your Administration. That necessity is created by what I feel it my duty to do; and the responsibility of the act, therefore, rests alone upon myself.

To say that I regret—deeply regret—this necessity, but feebly expresses the feeling with which I pen this communication. For nearly four years I have been associated with you as one of your Cabinet officers, and during that period nothing has occurred to mar, even for a moment, our personal and official relations. In the policy and measures of your Administration I have cordially concurred, and shall ever feel proud of the humble place which my name may occupy in its history. If your wise counsels and patriotic warnings had been heeded by your countrymen, the fourth of March next would have found our country happy, prosperous, and united. That it will not be so, is no fault of yours.

The evil has now passed beyond control, and must be met by each and all of us under our responsibility to God and our country. If, 1 From the Constitution, Washington, D. C, Dec. 12, 1860.
as I believe, history will have to record yours as the last administration of our present Union, it will also place it side by side with the purest and ablest of those that preceded it.

With the kindest regards for yourself and the members of your Cabinet, with whom I have been so pleasantly associated.

James Buchanan To Howell Cobb. E.

Washington, *10 December, 1860.* My Dear Sir: I have received your communication of Saturday evening resigning the position of Secretary of the Treasury which you have held since the commencement of my administration. Whilst I deeply regret that you have determined to separate yourself from us at the present critical moment, yet I admit that the question was one for your own decision. I could have wished you had arrived at a different conclusion, because our relations both official and personal have ever been of the most friendly and confidential character. I may add that I have been entirely satisfied with the ability and zeal which you have displayed in performing the duties of your important office.

Cordially reciprocating your sentiments of personal regard, I remain, very respectfully, your friend.

Howell Cobb To His Wife. E.

Washington City, *10 Dec, 1860.* My Dear Wife, As you have already learned through the telegraph, I have resigned my office and am again a private citizen. The President and myself part in the most friendly spirit. We both see and feel the necessity and both regret that it should be so. I shall leave here the end of this week, with a view to stopping a day or two in Columbia, S. C. to attend their convention, and shall reach Macon next week, not later than Wednesday. I shall send appointments at once to speak in my old district where I think I can do more good than anywhere else. I shall commence in Lawrenceville on Monday the 24th and shall speak every day until the election, going from Lawrenceville to Gainesville and thence to the mountains. It will be pretty hard work, but I have set out and must do all I can. To carry out this plan I must have a buggy with two horses, to be at Lawrenceville on Sunday night the 23rd and some one to drive, as I must make the travelling as easy as possible. The boys told me they had a good buggy at Athens that would answer the purpose, and if they can do no better they must get horses from the livery stable at Athens. Don't think of sending your horses, as you will not only need them in Macon but they will not be in a condition to stand the rough treatment of the mountains. If they should want me to speak in Macon let it be on Thursday after I get there, so that I may if necessary speak Friday and Saturday up the country or wherever I may be wanted, so that I get to Lawrenceville on Monday 24. Tell your Brother to consult and if deemed necessary he can arrange for Friday and Saturday. If it could be so, my own opinion is I had better go upon the State road somewhere.

I sent your carriage and horses today to Baltimore and Mr. Guthrie will go with them to Savannah. He will be in Macon and you will see him. I sent to day by Adams Express a bundle of my addresses to the Col.1 for circulation. He need not send any to Milledgeville as I have already sent there. I have written you a political business letter and shall be too much engaged for several days to write again. If Tom is in Macon say to him he ought to meet me in Columbia. It would be a good idea if the Legislature would appoint me at once a Commissioner to S. C. That idea might be sent over to Milledgeville.

Robert Toombs To E. B. Pullin And Others.2

Washington, Ga. *Dec. 13, 1860.*

Gentlemen: Your letter of the 10th. inst., inviting me on behalf of the citizens of Danburg and its vicinity to address you at an early day, was received yesterday. I regret very much that my public duties deprive me of the pleasure of accepting your kind invitation. But I shall be compelled to leave for Washington city day after tomorrow, and unless the state of the public business will allow me to return during the Christmas holidays I shall have no day at my command before your election; if I should return, I will take great pleasure in meeting you in council on the state of the country. The legislature of Georgia have unanimously declared that the present crisis demands resistance, and have unanimously voted to call a convention of the people to determine the mode and measures of redress. This is plain language—it is easily understood. It proposes to resist wrongs at the time and in the manner best calculated to obtain redress. The Legislature also unanimously voted a million of dollars to arm the people of Georgia, in order that they may repel by force whatever force may be brought to resist the measures of redress the people may adopt.

Then, upon the question that we have wrongs and that we intend to redress them by and through the sovereignty of Georgia, the state is unanimous. What then is likely to divide us? It cannot be the mode of redress, for it seems all look to secession, separation from the wrong doers, as the ultimate remedy. The time when this 1 Col. John B. Lamar.
3 From the Southern Recorder, Milledgeville, Ga., Dec. 25, 1860. Pullin was the chairman of a committee of citizens of Danburg, a village near Washington, Ga. remedy ought to be applied seems to be the most important, if not the only point of difference between us; we ought not to divide upon this point. Many persons think the remedy ought to be applied immediately, others at a day not to extend beyond the 4th of March next, others again supposing that too short a time for the convenient action of the

abolition states would extend it only to what might be fairly deemed a reasonable and convenient time within which our wrongs might be redressed by the wrong doers. I would strongly advise that there be no division among those who hold either of those opinions. While I personally favor the position of those who are opposed to delaying longer than the 4th of March next, I certainly would yield that point to earnest and honest men who were with me in principle but who are more hopeful of redress from the aggressors than I am, especially if any such active measures should be taken by the wrong doers as promised to give us redress in the Union. But to go beyond the 4th of March we should require such preliminary measures to be taken before as would with reasonable certainty lead to adequate redress, and in the mean time we should take care that the delay gives no advantages to the adversary and takes none from ourselves.

But let us not deceive ourselves as to what is redress and how we can secure it in the Union. The open and avowed object of Mr. Lincoln and the great majority of the active men of his party is ultimately to abolish slavery in the States. This he himself expressly avows, and there is not a single public man of his party in the United States within my knowledge who does not avow his hostility to the relation of master and servant as it exists among us. The means by which they seek to accomplish this result are many, but all consistent and all efficient to produce that result. The first is that we shall be driven out of the Territories by law. Upon this Mr. Lincoln and his party are unanimously agreed; and it is the corner stone of the entire Abolition party in the United States, and is planted in the Chicago platform. This they propose to do in violation of the Constitution of the United States as generally construed from the beginning of the Government and in express violation of that instrument as expounded by the Supreme Court of the United States.

2. They propose to exterminate slavery by abrogating by State laws, that portion of the Constitution which provides for the return of fugitive slaves to their owners. 3. To weaken and destroy it by protecting those who steal slaves and murder the inhabitants of the slaveholding States in pursuit of revolutionary schemes for its abolition, in direct violation of that clause of the Constitution which requires such criminals to be given up. 4. To destroy it by exciting revolt and insurrection among the slaves; this the pulpit, the press, the political orators, and indeed we may say the great body of the abolition party in Congress, in the State Legislatures, and everywhere else, are daily endeavoring to accomplish.

How is it possible to remedy these enormous evils in the Union? There is but one mode, one only; all others are delusions and snares, intended to lull the people into false security, to steal away their rights, and with them the power of redress. This mode is by amendments to the Constitution of the United States. In the Union the States cannot make contracts with each other; all departments of the government would disregard them. To repeal laws hitherto passed by the Abolition States would not redress; they would reenact them next year. The amendment of the Constitution should be such as could neither be evaded or resisted by the Abolition States, and should not rest for their efficiency upon the oaths of Abolitionists—no oaths can bind them.

The Constitution provides two modes for its own amendment. Article 5th is as follows on the point before us: "The Congress, whenever two-thirds of both Houses shall deem it necessary, shall propose amendments to this Constitution, which shall be valid, to all intents and purposes as part of this Constitution when ratified by the legislatures of three-fourths of the States or by conventions in three-fourths thereof, as the one or the other mode of ratification may be proposed by the Congress," etc.

Thus, you perceive, the road is plain, it is easily tested; you can here find a test which ought to satisfy every honest resistance man in Georgia. Do this: offer in Congress such amendments of the Constitution as will give you full and ample security for your rights; then if the Black Republican party will vote for the amendments, or even a majority of them in good faith, they can be easily carried through Congress; then I think it would be reasonable and fair to postpone final action until the legislatures of the northern States could be conveniently called together for definite action on the amendments. If they intend to stop this war on your rights and your property, they will adopt such amendments at once in Congress; if they will not do this, you ought not to delay an hour after the fourth of March to secede from the Union. This is a constitu- tional and effectual ultimatum, means something, can be tested—can be tested at once. This will be putting planks where they are good for something if they are the right kind of planks; but putting planks in your Georgia platform is putting them where our experience teaches us they are powerless for good, and only subject us to the jibes and jeers of our enemies. A cart load of new planks in the Georgia platform, will not redress one wrong, nor protect one right of the people of Georgia. Demand additional constitutional securities from your confederates, and if they are refused. confederate with such of them as are willing to grant them, or defend them yourselves.

William Henry Trescot To Howell Cobb. E.

Washington D. C., Decern. 14, 1860. Dear Sir: I have no time to tell all that has happened here. I write to say that if you hope to do any good in Columbia, recommend the following plan which I cannot argue but which will explain itself. It has the recommendation of Hunter, Davis and Yulee. Let the State pass its ordinance providing:
1. The *immediate,* absolute, irrevocable secession of S. C.
2. That commissioner or commissioners be appointed to notify the fact and

negotiate. 3. That in order to the proper execution of this ordinance and to avoid all unnecessary business disturbance, all collectors, treasurers post masters and other officers holding commissions under the U. S. be allowed days to wind up the affairs, settle the a/c, etc., of their respective offices, after which date the said offices shall expire within the State.

I have no time, as you can well imagine, in the present confusion to say more; but the whole scope and advantage of the plan both to the State and the country will suggest themselves to you at once.

Thomas R. R. Cobb To Howell Cobb. E.

Athens ga., *Dec. 15/60.* Dear Brother, By all means come *directly to Athens* or else send me a list of appointments for you to speak in the following counties— *Franklin, Banks, Habersham, Union, Lumpkin, Forsyth, Hall* and *Gwinnett*. We have trouble above here, and *no one* but *yourself* can quell it. Have you seen my letter on Co-operation? I intended it for the *So. Co.* Convention. I mailed a copy to Col. Gregg at Columbia.

Mrs. Jacob Thompson 1 To Mrs. Howell Cobb.

Washington City, *Dec. 15/60.* My Dear Mrs. Cobb,... I did not see Gov. Cobb after you left. Mr. Thompson went to see him every day and often invited him to take dinner with us but he never could spare the time. His resignation created great excitement here. Mr. Thomas2 has entered upon the discharge of his duties but I have not seen any of the family since their new laurels have fallen upon them. There is great excite 1 Wife of the Secretary of the Interior in Buchanan's Cabinet.

Philip P. Thomas, of Maryland, Secretary of the Treasury *ad interim.* ment now that Genl. Cass has resigned,1 and before I finish this letter I will see Mr. Thompson and write you the truth about it. The same gloom and depression is still over this city—no parties, no dinners, every body looks sad—but I think we Southern people ought to be looking up. for all seems to be going well with us, but I am afraid to hollow until I am entirely out of the woods. I think if you could have heard some of the Black Republican speeches that have been made here even your devotion to *this Union* would have given away. You will read the President's proclamation for *fasting* and prayer on the 4 of Jan., that tells whether he sees the danger or not. Miss Lane and I continue *our silence* on political questions—I go to see her and the President as often as I can because I know they feel their old friends are many of them deserting them. I will do all I can to stand by them until the 4 of March, and hope that day may come quickly. It is also rumored that Mr. Clayton2 has sent in his resignation to Mr. Thomas—if it is accepted Mr. Thompson says he will try to give Clayton the Comr. of Patents which will give him a place until the end of our term. Mr. Thompson has received an appointment from the Gov. of Missi. to go as Commissioner to N. Carolina, and leaves here on Monday the 17 and I am going with him, he will be absent a week or ten days and I can't stay here by myself. The President approves of his going. Mr. Lamar8 has returned home to be a candidate for the State convention. He is very reasonable on the secession question, does not go as far as your husband nor mine, but he amuses me, telling me how delighted he is with his present home and position in the College and yet he can't stay there more than a month at a time. ...

All your friends here enquire a great deal about you. The Gwins are all well and go up to the Capitol every day. I have been up twice, the galleries crowded. I have made no Senatorial calls except upon old friends. I shall not call upon or leave cards upon a single B. Republican or *Douglas.* "Straws tell which way the wind blows," and to be prepared for any emergency, I had doz. packs of cards for Mr. Thompson struck off and left off the *Sec. of the Interior,* as I have no idea of his cards ever being left anywhere as *Mr. Ex. Sec.* as some of the old broken down politicians here do. Gov. and Mrs. Floyd came over to spend the evening with us last evening and I enjoyed it very much. I find I have a great deal of time to stay at home since you left, as I have no place to go to that fills up your house. I felt like some duty was left undone if I did not go to see you every day for several weeks before you left. Some company has just come in, social visitors, this bad day, and I will lay my pen aside until they are gone.

1 From the secretaryship of state. a Philip Clayton, Auditor of the Treasury. L. Q. C. Lamar.

After dinner.—Mr. Thompson returned from his office after 5 o'clock and brought Mr. Ashe of N. Carolina home to dine with us; he gives good accounts of the secession movement in that state, and will go with us to Raleigh on Monday. Maj. McCulloch has just left, and he has the steam high up for secession and war if we can't do better. Dr. Maynard (the gun man) has been here two hours trying to sell Mr. Thompson 3,000 guns, so my head is nearly crazy and my heart goes *pit-a-pat,* at any sound I hear. What are we all coming to? Where is the end of all this trouble? I trust there is a kind Providence whose hand is directing this great revolution and will all go down to his glory and our happiness....

P. S.—Mr. Thompson says it is all true Genl. Cass has resigned and is a miserable man.

Thomas R. R. Cobb To Howell Cobb. E.

Athens, *Dec. 19/60.*

Dear Brother, Your appointments are received and a man sent around with hand bills to post them up in each county.

I have barely time to write this to get it into the mail.

A thousand cheers for So. Ca.! We have a *torchlight* procession tonight.

A. Hood To Howell Cobb. E.

Cuthbert, Ga. *Deer. 19, 1860.* Dear Governor, I see by the papers you are to be in Macon tomorrow. I am glad to find you again upon Georgia soil; there is work to be done and nobody doing it. I am fearful of the consequences of such supineness and neglect. Where are all our speakers? We have done what little we can here but there is great need for missionaries in every part of the State. The cry of cooperation is injuring us. While it means submission, it deceives a great many brave and patriotic people who would scorn it if they only knew the result of it.

I think our district is in a very good condition unless there is a great change. 20 out of 24 counties will be true; still to hold our own we want enthusiasm that can only be created by speaking. Can you find time to make two or three speeches in So. West Ga. ? Our people are all anxious to hear you, it will do *you* more good than any speeches you can make. You know our district has always been hostile to you. Can you not find time to remove the hostility? If you can spare a few days let me know so that I can make the appointments. We have had nothing from So. Ca.; if they go out at once we are safe, if not we are in danger. Write me.

P. S.—Benning made us a glorious speech on Monday.

Robert Toombs To The People Of Georgia (telegram).1 washington, D. C, *Dec. 23, 1860.*

Fellow Citizens Of Georgia:

I came here to secure your constitutional rights or to demonstrate to you that you can get no guarantees for these rights from your Northern confederates.

The whole subject was referred to a committee of thirteen in the Senate yesterday. I was appointed on the committee and accepted the trust. I submitted propositions, which so far from receiving decided support from a single member of the Republican party on the committee, were all treated with either derision or contempt. The vote was then taken in committee on the amendments to the Constitution proposed by Hon. J. J. Crittenden, of Kentucky, and each and all of them were voted against, unanimously, by the Black Republican members of the committee.

In addition to these facts, a majority of the Black Republican members of the committee declared distinctly that they had no guarantees to offer, which was silently acquiesced in by the other members.

The Black Republican members of this committee of thirteen are representative men of their party and section, and, to the extent of my information, truly represent the committee of thirty-three in the House, which on Tuesday adjourned for a week without coming to any vote, after solemnly pledging themselves to vote on all the propositions then before them on that date.

The committee is controlled by Black Republicans, your enemies, who only seek to amuse you with delusive hope until your election, in order that you may defeat the friends of secession. If you are deceived by them, it shall not be my fault. I have put the test fairly and frankly. It is decisive against you; and now I tell you upon the faith of a true man that all further looking to the North for security for your constitutional rights in the Union ought to be instantly abandoned. It is fraught with nothing but ruin to yourselves and your posterity.

Secession by the fourth of March next should be thundered from the ballot-box by the unanimous voice of Georgia on the second day of January next. Such a voice will be your best guarantee for liberty, security, tranquillity, and glory.

Charles F. M. Garnett To Howell Cobb. E.

Lynchburg, Va., *Dec. 28th, 1860.* Dear Sir: I have thought much of the subject of defence in view of the present position of the South. Everybody knows the im 1 From the True Democrat, Augusta, Ga., extra edition, Dec. 24, 1860.
portance of artillery in modern warfare. Unfortunately the Southern States are entirely unprovided. Now I think Virginia can supply cannon, shot and shell, perhaps to the full extent of our wants.

F. B. Deane Jr. of this place has, in time past, furnished large numbers of shot and shell to the U. S. Government. He is now prepared to furnish 1,000 per day. These could be conveyed by rail road to any point in Georgia. I think also through him and another establishment, arrangements could be made to furnish a large number of cannon.

My leading idea for coast defence is in cannon of long range, mounted on carriages of broad wheels, which could be easily moved from point to point.

If you write to me on this subject, my P. O. is "Junction, Hanover County Va."

Alexander H. Stephens To J. Henly Smith. S.

Crawfordville ga., *Dec. 31st, 1860.* Dear Smith, Yours of the 26th inst. was received last night. I do not think anything can be made of any of the propositions I have seen submitted for the settlement of our existing national troubles. Mr. Douglas sent me his. I got it a few days ago and wrote to him forthwith by return mail that I did not think his terms would ever be agreed to by the South. His first and second would never be agreed to—the one looking to the colonization of the blacks would never—nothing can be made of any such scheme of adjustment. 'I do not think that we stand in need of any new constitutional guarantees—we may hereafter if the Union should last—but at present we do not. All we now want or ought to want is a faithful administration of the government, under the present constitution with all its present obligations and guarantees. All that the South has at present just cause to complain of, and the chief ground of just complaints, is the personal liberty bill s of some of the non-slaveholding states. These ought to be repealed, and I doubt not if the whole South had united in asking their repeal with firmness and decision and with an honest intent to be satisfied with it when they got it that success would have crowned their efforts. Of this I am satisfied. But the truth is our ultra men do not desire any redress of these grievances. They would really obstruct indirectly any effort to that end. They are for breaking up. They are tired of the government. They have played out, dried up, and want something new. Here was all the danger or the great difficulty in the way of making any settlement or adjustment. It seems to me at present insurmountable! I do not see how it can be removed or gotten over. Our difficulties spring not from the government, its frame work or its administration so much as they do from the people, the leaders mainly. I have for now two years been impressed with the conviction that we are approaching "the beginning of the end" of this great republic. The events at Charleston and Baltimore but increased this conviction. They disclosed that distemper in the times that I had before seen showing its symptoms. All is now dark and gloomy. I see no ray of hope. What is to become of us I know not. I have but one guiding principle, let come what may, and that is to do my duty as I understand it. Our election comes off day after tomorrow. It will be over before you get this. I now feel almost confident that this State will go for secession. I think it unwise and have done what I could to prevent it; but it is beyond my control, and the movement will before it ends I fear be beyond the control of those who started it. I saw and noticed the articles you mentioned in the Star of the South. I thought as you did about the authorship of them both. I cared nothing for either. The historical illustrations brought forward to meet? me were exceedingly unfortunate. Hampden, Pym and Hollis were the leading spirits of the Revolution in England beginning in 1640—Hampden fell in battle, Pym died before the war ended, Hollis alone of the three lived to survive it. He was swept away by the current and was one amongst the first to go for a Restoration of the Monarchy under Charles II without one word of guarantee against the prerogative of the Crown which was the cause of the Revolution. Cromwell had nothing to do with the first movement as an active agent. He was unknown. He was a child of the Revolution, grasped all honour and ruled England with more rigour than any king ever did before or since. This he did in the name of Liberty. Nor did Louis Napoleon have anything to do with the French Revolution in 1848 in which Louis Philippe was dethroned. That was commenced by Lamartine and a few other patriots. Louis Napoleon sprang up afterwards. He overthrew the Republic and put himself at the head of an Empire with more despotic power than Louis Philippe ever undertook to exercise. But I cannot dwell on these things. The times are distempered. The people are misled, and will see their course I fear when it is too late. What I say to you is not for any one else—except this, that I have no idea of going to Washington. My health will not permit me even if I wished to go. But I see no prospect of doing any good there and very little here or anywhere. Mr. Buchanan has ruined the country. It is past praying for I fear. His appeal to Heaven was made too lata

Robert Toombs To The Augusta, Ga., True Democrat.1

Washington, D. C, *Jan. 1,1861*. The cabinet is broken up, Mr. Floyd, Secretary of War, and Mr. Thompson, Secretary of the Interior, having resigned. Mr. Holt of Kentucky, our bitter foe, has been made Secretary of War. Fort Pulaski is in danger. The Abolitionists are defiant.

Mrs. Robert Toombs To Alexander H. Stephens. It.

Washington, D. C, *Jan. 1st, 1861*.2 Dear Sot: I write a few lines to you this morning to ask you what I shall do with your furniture that is in our house. I have despaired of the Union and will begin to pack up my own things today. If you can do anything you must be at it. I have given up the ship notwithstanding your old friends' opinion in a telegram of the morning papers; I mean Messrs. Douglas and Crittenden. 3 I shall go home with Mr. Toombs when he goes to the convention. I will take great pleasure in having your things packed and shipped or will do anything with them that you desire. You have the following articles: a carpet, bedstead, feather bed, mattrass, bolster and pillows, bowl and pitcher, bureau, couch, shovel and tongs, etc. Please let me know as soon as you can what to do with them. We will send the most of our things home, for we can't get one cent for them here. I hope you are well.

William Porcher Miles To Howell Cobb. E.

Charleston S. C., *Jan. Hth/61*. Dear Sir: I received your letter yesterday (Sunday) and this morning directed copies of all the ordinances passed and resolutions and addresses adopted by the convention of our state to be forwarded you at Macon. I will bear in mind your further request to telegraph you anything important which may transpire. I think there is more possibility of a peaceful solution of our difficulties here. It does not seem likely that the Administration, now that so many states have seceded, while Georgia, Louisiana, and Texas are on the eve of following suit, will attempt to reinforce Anderson—especially as we have proved that we can make pretty tolerable resistance to the entrance of vessels with either troops or supplies. Moreover we are 1 From the Savannah Republican, Jan. 2, 1861.

Erroneously dated Jan. 1, 1860, In the original.

8 In reply to a telegraphic Inquiry addressed to them by eight citizens of Atlanta asking whether there was any hope of Southern rights in the Union, Crittenden and Douglas had telegraphed, Dec. 30, 1860: "In reply to your inquiry, we hare hopes that the rights of the South, and of every state and section, may be protected within the Union. Don't give up the ship. Don't despair of the Republic." 4 The Georgia secession convention, to which Toombs had been elected a delegate from Wilkes county.

better prepared now than when the Star of the West attempted to get in, to give Uncle Sam a warm reception.

Nothing but special spite and malice can induce the Government at Washington to confine its attentions to our harbor when the fortifications along the entire Southern coast have been seized by the authorities of the several states within whose limits they lie. I have always thought that the forts and navy yard at Pensacola were of so much consequence (if they purpose to wage war upon the South) that their most vigorous efforts would be to secure or retake them. Mr. Buchanan will in all likelihood seek to temporise—to delay positive action as long as possible....

Your letter was very cheering. First because you hold out the hope that the Georgia convention will secede immediately and unconditionally, and secondly because you speak of " perpetual separation." I must confess that on this latter point I have had some nervous anxiety lest after we are all out there may be a disposition to reform the old Confederacy. While I would be most sincerely desirous of forming an alliance offensive and defensive with the Northern Confederacy and entering into a treaty commercial on the most favorable terms, I feel utterly unwilling ever again to live under a common government with the free-soil states. Our pride is enlisted to prove to them and to the world that the South is not so poor, weak and destitute of resources as to be unable to hold her own in the great community of nations. Let us inaugurate on this side of the Atlantic a great free-trade government and perfect the grand commercial idea of the nineteenth century—untrammelled exchange of the productions and manufactures of the world.

Wishing you God speed in the Empire State in carrying on the work of Southern Independence.

William Henry Trescot 1 To Howell Cobb. E.
(Private and confidential.)

Barnwell Islano, Near Beaufort, So. Ca., *J any. H, 1861.* My Dear Mr. Cobb, I reached home on Friday last with the intention of returning to Charleston today; but having been too late for the railroad I find time enough to do what I have been wanting to do for some weeks—write you a long letter. It would indeed have to be a very long one to give you the history of the events in Washington since you left it. A strange, sad, history it is, and if ever truly written will exhibit a marvellous example of folly in high places....

1 U. S. Assistant Secretary of State, 1860, author of "The Position and Course of the South" (1850), " Diplomatic History of the Administrations of Washington and Adams" (1857), etc. 73566—13 34

The papers will have given you by this time Floyd's[1] letter of resignation, the correspondence with the Carolina Commissioners, Thompson's resignation and the President's special message; and I think they tell their tale. But very few persons will ever know how earnestly and faithfully Mr. Buchanan's best friends strove to save him, and I believe would have saved him but for Holt and Black. But you were gone, Floyd had resigned; Thompson and Thomas sure to go, and Black, Holt, Stanton and Toucey inflexible. That the Union was gone was clear, and their home position had to be secured. As Black said to me the morning I left, " You beat us all the way through, and came very near carrying your last point; but fortunately our last card was a trump "—which I suppose means that they threatened resignation. Mr. Buchanan's position was undoubtedly a difficult one.... If, when Anderson moved to Fort Sumter, he had said to the commissioners—" this is against my orders. I would have corrected it but you have taken the forts and I cannot restore the status. I am willing to act in good faith, meet me half way," he would have had any facility furnished him. On Sunday the I went to him at one o'clock and plead with him for an hour. Unfortunately Toucey[2] was there.-And when I left, I went to Hunter of Virginia and asked him to go to the President and say, " If your only difficulty is the occupation of the forts, say to the commissioners that you will withdraw Anderson from Sumter if they will evacuate the others and restore them to you, to be held as property until this question is settled; say so now, altho four days have passed, and it will be accepted." Hunter did go and when he came back, he said, " It is useless to repeat what passed. The case is hopeless. The President has changed his ground and will maintain it to the last extremity. Telegraph your people to sink vessels in the entrance of the harbour immediately. They have no time to lose."

It was not until after this and a great deal more that the letter of the commissioners was written, and then it was meant to be not a diplomatic note to the President but a protest against bad faith and a vindication before the country.

The events which have transpired since, you know—the attempt to send reinforcements; the fire upon them; and civil war depending upon the guns at Fort Sumter. Anderson did not fire but took to writing, and as a matter of course put himself in the wrong, and another chance has thus been afforded Mr. Buchanan: God knows if he is wise enough or strong enough to use it. I hope so. Late on the night before I left, the Governor sent for me to go to Washington, but I declined. I did not see what good was to be done there, 1 John B. Floyd of Virginia, Secretary of War in Buchanan's cabinet.

Isaac Toucey, of Connecticut, Secretary of the Navy In Buchanan's cabinet. and I could not tell what might be done at home while I was away. All things are, I believe, working for good; but neither the government at Washington nor Charleston is helping it forward much. It really does seem that a revolution works its way through the blunders of those who attempt to direct it.

I was not one of the commissioners[1] officially, but the convention upon my return passed a vote of thanks for services, etc., and put me on the footing of a commissioner. I have not seen their resolution, don't understand it exactly, but as it was meant kindly have no criticism to make upon it.

I believe you were right from the beginning, altho circumstances so far have helped us all on wonderfully.

You will be glad to know that you made a very pleasant and wholesome impression upon our people, and the convention paid you a compliment which I think is a very great one from that body. When the election of a commissioner to Georgia came up, a member rose and stated that you had expressed a wish that Orr should be sent, and he was unanimously elected. But whatever policy it may have been wise to urge a month ago, I am sure you will agree with me that now it is all important to take Georgia out at once and organize a Southern government immediately. We must meet Lincoln with a President of our own. We want the military resources of the South concentrated at once; and above all, our foreign relations ought to be assured as quickly as possible. No attempt at foreign negociations ought to be made by single states. I trust that these are your views. I deem them all important. The condition of weakness and confusion which will result from four or five states floating about is indescribable. Weld them together while they are hot.

As to the Presidency, I will say nothing as yet. If you have anything to say, let me know. You will understand me.

I have only one favour to ask—let me have a hand in organising the State Department. There are a great many things I don't understand, but that I do.

I will be very glad to hear from you.

P. S.—I go to Charleston tomorrow—direct to me there care of Messrs. Barnwell & Son, Factors.

Jacob Thompson 2 To Howell Cobb. E.

Washington, D. C, *Jarty 16th, 1861.*
My Dear Cobb, I was glad to receive your letter a few days since. It came the same day that I resigned, and I got Robt. M. McGraw to show it to the President. He folded it up very quietly and returned it to me.

1 From South Carolina.
»Secretary of the Interior in Buchanan's cabinet.

The President and Holt played the meanest trick on me in the world in sending the *Star of the West* to Charleston. When Holt was assigned to the Department of War, I came home, wrote my resignation and went back in the evening to give it to him in person. I told him the assignment of Holt to the War Department1 was considered by me the adoption of his line of policy, which made my withdrawal a necessity. The President replied—not at all, and no order should be issued without being first considered and decided in Cabinet. With this promise I could not resign.

A few days afterwards the question was up, and it was clearly decided to send a messenger to Major Anderson to learn his true condition and wishes. This was all that was decided, and the President's letter to me is an afterthought and deceptive. The movement of the *Star of the West* was a strategetical movement of Gen'l Scott. He convinced Holt he could steal into Fort Sumter without discovery or collision. To do this it was necessary to keep the movement a secret, and as they all knew I would resign for such an order and thus blow the order, it was necessary to keep me in ignorance of it. This is the true theory of the whole matter. Since the expedition failed, I have thought it of no importance to push the facts. But I am determined to fortify myself.

Old Buck, at heart, is right and with us, but after Stanton came in, I have seen him gradually giving way....

Well, Cobb, I withdrew only one day before the secession of Mississippi would have made it my duty to withdraw. I am now very anxious to see a new confederacy formed. The Black Republicans do not intend to give back one inch. It is now naked submission or secession. I consider every Southern State disgraced who will quietly surrender her rights without a struggle, and, by Jove, the work thus far goes bravely on. Va. will be out in time. The feeling is getting up in Tenn. and Ky. , and I think Maryland. I hope Georgia will make quick work of it. You know how much importance I have attached to the action of your State. I have all along felt that as goes Georgia, so goes the whole South.

I have been opposed to the withdrawal of the Senators and Members from the South. But they have decided otherwise, and I am content.

It is impossible to get the President and his cabinet to consider the secession of S. Carolina as a fact. He declared, you know, some time before you left, that he could not and would not know the fact. I think he is gradually realizing the idea that it is a fact, but he will not base any action on it.

1 Joseph Holt, of Kentucky, Postmaster General, 1859-1860, was appointed Secretary of War ad *interim* upon Floyd's resignation, and afterward full Secretary for the remainder of Buchanan's administration.

When he returned the correspondence with the S. C. Commissioners, I sketched out a programme of a message for the President to write, according entirely with your suggestions in your letter. He had not the nerve and backbone to adopt our views.

Since Seward's speech of Saturday, I have no hope of any concession; and further effort to obtain a compromise implies in my mind weakness, if not cowardice.

The President still adheres to his position that he has no power of 'oercion, but he has a most curious idea that enforcing the laws at the point of the bayonet is not coercion....

George I. Durham 1 To Howell Cobb. E.

Austin, Texas, *JarCy 17/61.*

Sir: I am directed by the Executive Committee to apprise you of the true condition of public sentiment in this State respecting our relations with the Federal Government.

Our Executive is hostile to the present movement of the Gulf States and will use every means in his power to prevent like action here, but our legislature meets on the 21st inst. and will sustain the convention which meets on the 28th following; that body will pass a secession ordinance to go into effect so soon as it can be ratified by the people; of our co-operation with the Gulf states there can be no doubt.

Should your State authorities desire to communicate with our convention any documents directed to Clement R. Johns (our State Comptroller), George M. Flournoy (our Attorney General), or myself, all of this city, will be immediately placed before them.

The sanctity of public correspondence trusted to the mail being often violated is the reason for suggesting the above course in preference to a direct communication with that body.

Raphael Semmes2 To Howell Cobb. E.

Washington, D. C.. *Jarty 26th, 1861.* My Dear Sir: Permit me to remind you of the conversation we had just before you left Washington. I think States enough have gone out to determine me as to the course I shall pursue. If invited by the Confederacy of the Cotton States I will accept service in its navy and abandon my present position. The chances are that Maryland (my native State) and all the other border slave states will speedily follow you, but whether they do or not I will cast my destiny with yours if you will permit me. I am in some sort claimed as a 1 Secretary of the Executive Committee of Texas.

"Lieutenant, 1837-1855, commander, 1855-1861, United States Navy; commander and rear-admiral, Confederate States Navy, commanding the cruisers *Sumter* and *Alabama.* citizen of Alabama, having resided in that state several years before I was ordered to Washington upon my present duty, and it is probable that my nomination to the new executive for a post in the navy of the new Confederacy will be made by Gov'r Fitzpatrick and other friends from that State. However this may be, may I ask you also to perform this service for me and to inform me promptly of your action and that of the new President in the premises? Messrs. Toombs, Stephens, Fitzpatrick, Clay, Curry, Sydenham, Moore, Stallworth and other good friends to whom I have written or with whom I have conversed freely on the subject will I have no doubt take pleasure in assisting you to accomplish my purpose. As you are a delegate to the convention to form the new Government I may perhaps not inappropriately say a word or two to you on the subject of the organization of your army and navy. The Southern States being planting and agricultural States and but little engaged in commerce and navigation (though doubtless their separation from the North will make them more commercial and navigating than they have hitherto been), they will require but a small naval force for several years to come; and it strikes me also that it will be bad policy to establish a large army. I would advise therefore that both your navy and army lists be kept within very small compass. I mean the regular forces of each, or such as are to be kept on foot as well in peace as in war. If a war ensue, which I do not anticipate, your regular military establishment can be temporarily increased to meet the emergency by appointments and enlistments to continue during the war and by the commissioning of privateers and other irregular maritime forces to serve during the same period. This will enable you at the end of the war to dismiss, as a matter of course and without complaints, all the personnel of both services excepting only the small army and navy lists before referred to. I have said that I do not think we shall have a war and these are my reasons for the opinion. If the border slave states join you the old confederacy will be split nearly in half, and the idea of coercion would be simply ridiculous; if they do not join you, being retained by compromises that will satisfy them, they will be a barrier and a safeguard to you and will hold the hands of the Vandals who might otherwise be disposed to make war upon you. No slave state could possibly be an ally of the free states in a war upon slave states upon the slave question. Be cool therefore in organizing your military and naval establishments and do not consent to place too great burthens upon the shoulders of the people. It is easier to make armies and navies than to get rid of them when made, and the people will not and ought not to submit to exhorbitant taxation to support large establishments for which they will ordinarily have no use. One word more and I shall have done.

Your naval officers I suppose will be taken from the present navy list of the old government. Preserve their relative rank in their new relations. You know rank is of essence with military and naval men, and the rule I suggest to you is not only just and proper and will work well but it will put an end to all jealousies, rivalries and heartburnings. May I ask the favor of a line in reply?

Junius Hillyeh To Howeul Cobb. E.

Washington D. C., *Jan. 30th, 1861.* Dear Sir: I wish you would take a few moments of your time to drop me a line. Things here are not working right. Since the Southern men have left Washington there seems to be nobody standing up for the Southern movement, and the pressure in favour of the Union is so strong as to silence all opposition. This state of things may be unimportant as to the States that have seceded but it is producing a most melancholy effect in the border States. In fact you may prepare your mind for a defeat in Virginia and all the rest of the border States. But that is not all that I dread. It is proper that occupying the position you do, you should be informed of the worst signs of the times. My fear is that we are in danger of meeting not only the opposition of the border States, but their hostility.

You may give more credence to the strong language of Phil Clayton than you do to what I say. He speaks as he feels; I speak as I see and observe. And I tell you, I warn our friends at Montgomery that unless you proceed with the greatest caution you will have the border slave States strongly bound with our foes against us and making common cause with them to conquer a settlement. That there is danger of this is just as true as we live. The great prolific source of danger is upon three subjects mainly. The idea is extensively abroad that the manufacturing interest of Va. is in danger and that the navigation of the Mississippi will be obstructed and that the slave trade will be reopened. I don't understand the question of the tariff in its details, but if you establish free trade we are certain to lose Va. and Md. The navigation of the Mississippi up and down is important to the States on that river and its tributariea and unless this navigation is properly provided for we will lose Ark. , Tenn., Ken., and Mo. I have no fear about the slave trade. But I tell you, Governor, we must raise revenue from a judicious tariff. This is what our people are accustomed to. And it is desirable that our revolution should be attended with as slight a jar as possible to the habits of our people. You have need of all your wisdom and forecast.

I hope I shall be at home in time to vote for you for President. If the election should come on before the 4th Mar., as it ought, I will come home to vote.... Old Buck and his Cabinet are trying honestly in their bungling way to have a peaceful solution in some way of this matter. I honour him for it and am willing, so long as the country remains at peace, to continue with his administration.1 Write to me and give me your views about this course on my part. I hope you will be elected President and that I may be the Solicitor of the Treas. I could start that bureau on a proper plan and make it efficient.

P. S.—One word more. There is such a likeness between your intellect and mine that I know that you will concur with me—that we ought to keep in view the good old Democratic doctrine of "a tariff for revenue, with incidental protection."

From what I learn the Border Congress that meets here on the 4th will break down. Nothing will be done. And now everything depends upon the wisdom, justice and moderation, at Montgomery. Let such action be had as will inspire confidence in the border slave States and will induce them to cast their destinies with us. Write to me.

Augustus R. Wright2 To Howell Cobb. E.

Augusta, Ga., *Feby. 1st, 1861.* Dear Sir: Suffer me to presume upon a casual acquaintance many years ago and the intimacy that for many years existed between our fathers to ask for letters to such gentlemen of your acquaintance in the State of Maryland and at Washington as may be useful or important to me in the mission upon which our State convention has sent me. I would be highly gratified also to have your views as to the best line of argument or policy to be pursued by me to bring about the cordial cooperation of Maryland in our new Government. Should I go at once and lay before Gov. Hicks our ordinance etc., or do you think it best for me to wait a few days to ascertain whether the legislature will be convened or a convention called?

Howell Cobb To His Wife. E.
Montgomery ala., *3 Feby., 1861.*

My Dear Wife, I have been here for more than a day....

Most of the delegates have arrived, but there has been not much consultation. From all I hear there is a general disposition to make me president of the convention. It is thought that my taking that position will exclude me from the Presidency of the Confederacy and 1 Hillyer continued to hold office as Solicitor of the United States Treasury until Feb. 13, 1861, when he resigned.

2 Commissioner from Georgia to Maryland, 1861; Member of the Confederate Congress from Georgia. some of my friends doubted on that account the policy of my taking it. In this I differed from them and have determined to follow my own judgement. The truth is that the Presidency of the Confederacy is an office I cannot seek and shall feel no disappointment in not getting.

There is at present much diversity of opinion as to the course to be pursued in the formation of a provisional government, but there is a general good feeling and disposition to unite and harmonize on whatever may be found the best policy. I feel confident all will work out well in the end....

Howell Cobb To His Wife. E.
Montgomery ala., *6 Feby., 1861.*

My Dear Wife, Since my election as President of the Congress I have been engaged all the time and had no chance to write.

We have gone into secret session, and on pain of expulsion not permitted to divulge anything that is going on. The details would not however be interesting. I can say to you that whilst there are differences of opinion, there will in the end be great unanimity and our final action will prove satisfactory. I feel the greatest confidence in the entire success of our great movement. The newspaper men are annoyed at their exclusion from our sessions and hence you may expect to see all sorts of rumours in the papers. Our friends may rest satisfied that everything is going on well and will end well.

Little or nothing is said about President of the Confederacy, and yet we shall elect one in a day or two, perhaps before you get this letter. So far from making an effort to obtain that position, I have frankly said to my friends that I greatly prefer not to be put there. All that I have seen and learned since I got here has satisfied me that it is a most undesirable position. I rather think that Jeff. Davis will be the man, though I have not heard any one say that he is for him. The truth is—and it is creditable to our public men here— there is no effort made to put forward any man, but all seem to desire in everything to do what is best to be done to advance and prosper the cause of our independence. I cannot better give you an idea of the sentiment of the Congress than to say that my speech on taking the chair is approved by everybody—Stephens, Hill, Wright and Kenan are as strong against reconstruction1 as any of us. The two first made strong speeches yesterday on that line. The delegation from Georgia are acting with perfect unanimity on all questions.

11, e., delegates who had previously opposed secession now advocated permanent Independence for the South.

Junius Hillyer To Howell Cobb. E.
Washington D. C., *Saturday night,*

Feb. 9th, 1861.

Dear Sir: I recd. your letter tonight. I will resign on Monday and leave for home on Tuesday morning. I did not know of there being any feeling in Geo. on the subject, though my place here was becoming daily more and more unpleasant and I am more than willing to return home. I begin to have strong hope of a settlement of our difficulties that will be satisfactory to the South, particularly to the seceding states.

As to a compromise, it is impossible. Nothing that even Del. would submit to will be granted by the Republicans. But the chances are good that the Republican party will acquiesce in the secession movement. I am sure of it if we can prevent a collision till the 4th of Mar. My kindest regards to Tom and the rest. My life here this winter has been to me an unmitigated misery.

P. S.—If we adopt free trade with direct taxation, we are ruined. I would resign to-night and start home in the morning but there is some unfinished business at the office upon which I must by *promise consult* with Genl. Dix 1 on Monday.

Gazaway B. Lamar To Howell Cobb. E.

Bank Of The Republic,
New York, *Feby. 9, 1861.*

My Dear Sir: Notwithstanding I have no reply to any of my late letters to you, knowing your constant engagements I still write you.

The arms seized here have been put at the command of their owners—the question in dispute being the expenses, some 3 or 400 dollars lawyers' fees, etc., between the owners of the vessel and the shippers and owners of the arms.

Gov. Brown ordered several N. York vessels seized yesterday in Sav'h, and I had a telegram to that effect this morning and immediately telegraphed to have the vessels relieved as the arms had been surrendered.

Col. Hayne has left Washington and from the tone of the correspondence there I fear an attack on Fort Sumter, which would be very disastrous if any blood be shed.

The Democratic Convention in Albany last week (Mr. Lasitter? was in it) has drawn the line? for peace with the South, and the cause of peace is gaining daily in the city and in the Country, and will soon sweep the Republicans into a minority, if there be no collisions or indiscretions at the South to give them aid or comfort.

1 John A. Dlx, of New York, then Secretary of the Treasury.

Rome was not built in a day—a good Government cannot be organized and put into operation in a month. Better meanwhile to submit to evils and even to injustice, to bear and forbear, rather than to give offence to your friends here, and thus aid your enemies.

If the Republicans had shown any conciliatory disposition the past 2 months, they would have had twice the strength they now have. Their obstinacy has made secessionists at the South and sympathisers with them at the North.

The South should be careful not to imitate their example, but be prudent, deliberate and forbearing. All will be settled soon in that way.

But it is all important the Confederacy should take charge of the States so far as foreign relations are concerned, immediately—else diverse counsels will produce disastrous oonsequences in some way or other.

The exchange of the money found in the mint at N. Orleans would command the possession of Fort Sumter, Pickens, and at the Tortugas, and settle also a point favorably to the South as to the propriety of that seizure—which has alienated some opinions here. But that is not all—the Confederacy is to bear the brunt and should have the control of all such actions. It should negotiate anew for the forts in Charleston and elsewhere, and on all other points, and meantime S. Carolina and all other states should commit all action on such points to the Confederacy at once and forever. It is folly to proceed in any other way and will inevitably lead to danger and difficulty.

I do not like the export duty on cotton. Make direct taxation on the Georgia principle, and add to it a tax on income (pretty strong). and with economy the New South will have ample means. Free Trade will command England and France as far as they are desirable, which is only as customers, after you secure a peace with the North. You will soon get all the slave states, and you ought to admit none other unless they will institute slavery. And no State or individual should be allowed to free a slave without the vote of 2/3ds of the Congress of the Confederacy, and then they should be removed beyond the limits.

Again I would call your attention to citizenship. None but those who are citizens now and who were or may be born within the bounds of the Confederacy should be citizens. The emigration from the North and East will overwhelm you within 3 years after peace, and control your government for you.

You don't want treaties, only with the North, France, England and the German States. You need no Navy. But you should have an Army of 15 or 20,000 men to put on the northern line and to put in position within the States to keep the negroes in order.

Again I repeat, be careful to cause no irritation or provocation to the North. Submit to evils for a while and wait till they can be righted by negotiation. Bear and forbear.

T. Allan 1 To Howell Cobb. E.

Washington D. C., *February 11, 1861.* Dear Governor, The glorious news of a Southern Confederacy was received here on yesterday and has created a profound sensation. Whilst the tinkers from the border States are here in secret conclave saving the Union (as if it were not dissolved as far back as 20th December), the Southern Congress is moving on majestically and firmly toward the organization of a powerful independent Govt. which will be in full operation before the inauguration of Lincoln. The news has elevated my feelings wonderfully, for I assure you I have been depressed and felt as if I were (as humble as I am) an incubus to the fag end of what was once a glorious Administration. But alas all its glory has departed with those patriotic counsellors who one by one have left the Cabinet. Secession sentiments have become very offensive to the present powers and particularly with the Census Bureau. No sooner had Mr. Thompson retired than the *creature* of his misplaced confidence, Kennedy, by whose appointment he drew upon himself unmeasured abuse from divers quarters, commenced to exhibit his ingratitude by turning out every man in the Census Bureau who entertains the right of secession and has the boldness to express his sentiments. And so it goes. We all who entertain those sentiments feel like orphans. Yet no one has interfered with me. On the contrary I have been treated with as much respect as ever. I have not hesitated (without being offensive) to express my fealty to Georgia and entire approbation of the step she has taken in seceding from the old Union, as well as my well settled determination to resign my office the moment this Administration comes to an end or that a collision takes place between Georgia and the General Government. Yet our Southern friends keep dropping off until few are left. Many who remain in office are mere truckling time servers and ready to do anything to propitiate the favor of the incoming Abolition dynasty. Others are poor and helpless and succumb from necessity, as the best escape from starvation. The people in the District, influenced by their interests as merchants, butchers and builders, et cet., the flesh pots upon which they have grown fat, are also anxious to curry favor with the party soon to be in power. Hence sociability and good fellowship with me and all such is broken and I feel as if I were *not* in the right place. ... Before the 4th of March I shall be rolling on to my native state to share her dangers as well as glories. My destination is my brother's 1A resident of Banks County. Ga., then holding a government clerkship at Washington.

in Banks. Many noble spirits from the cotton states will soon be set adrift on the wide world without means or employment. Apart from a desire to be provided for my unworthy self I hope these gentlemen will be remembered in the formation and organization of the new Government and provided with suitable places.. I will take occasion now to mention the name of a true and trusty friend,—a man of truth, integrity and talents, with whom I have long been intimately associated officially as well as socially. I mean Win. Hall Esqr., a native of Missi., appointed from Louisiana. He is a $1600 clerk in the Genl. Land Office and belongs to my division. He will go out when I do, determined as I am not to have the smell of abolitionism about his garments. It is to you, my noble friend, we look to represent us before the new authorities.

I shall be gratified to hear from you soon if you can spare a moment from the cares of state in the midst of which you are now engaged. The city is full of insolent soldiers and the Dist. militia in complete organization, ready no doubt to butcher Southern men because they will not submit to be ruled by an abolitionist. But all will be peace I think. My eyes shall not behold the disgrace of this once happy republic by the inauguration of an abolitionist as President.

Juntos Hillyer To Howell Cobb. E.
Washington D. C,
Monday, Feb. 11th 1861.

Dear Sir: Before I close my official term I will use one more frank to you, and that will end a very convenient privilege which I was never fully satisfied ought to have been allowed me.

There is I think a growing tendency here to a peaceble acquiescence in our revolution. My opinion is that the Republicans are as much afraid of us as we are of them, and they are daily becoming more and more impressed with the idea of our resources and strength. And my opinion now is that if you can avoid a collision, assume towards old Lincoln an attitude of respectful determination, that we can so

manage him as to get along till Congress meets, when they will repeal all federal laws so far as they affect the seceding States. This will answer our purpose for the present. And the day is not distant when we may reasonably hope for the establishment of friendly relations with the present Government of the U. S. This will of course depend upon the temper of Lincoln and his cabinet. We must hope for the best.

I had a long talk today with J. B. Guthrie and I am of opinion that he would be glad to take a place in our treasury department. I am sure of it. We will want some experience etc. in organizing our revenue system. You and Tom and Stephens and Toombs and the rest must not fail to provide a place in the law or judicial department of the Government for me. I look forward to the future with a fear of starvation. I tell you that under the present pressure my income is destroyed and is just nothing. Talk to our delegation and get them to unite in providing some employment for me. There must be a solicitor of the treasury or some place corresponding to it. And for that I am better qualified than any other living man.

I am gratified beyond measure to see that you are moving forward with a strength and power that commands the respect of all parties here. The Black Eepublicans are absolutely confounded, and Hunter is in extacies. But there is a dark cloud which gives me trouble. You don't attach the same importance to it that I do. I do greatly fear that this Union sentiment in the Border States means submission. My fear is that they are influenced by an indifference to slavery and that the anti-slavery tide is rolling further South. So that I am more and more earnest every day that they should be conciliated and drawn to us by the most friendly legislation as to their interests. From what I hear about the collector at N. Orleans I am very uneasy that mortal offence will be given to the states north of Louisiana. The conduct of the collector may not be understood.

R. K. Hudgins To Howell Cobb. E.

New Orleans, *February 11th, 1861.*

Sir: The revenue cutter *Washington,* authorised by you while Secretary of the Treasury to be repaired at this place under my superintendence, doubtless you are aware, has been taken possession of by the authorities of Louisiana with the view of ultimately constituting her a part of the Southern navy. Not being a citizen of Louisiana, of course I could not retain the command and the supervision of the repairs on that vessel any longer, which I exceedingly regret.

I yesterday received a dispatch from the Hon. J. A. Dix, Secretary of the Treasury, ordering me to report myself at the Department, which order I feel it incumbent to obey as I still hold a Federal Commission, which commission I purpose throwing up the moment my native state, Virginia, secedes from the Union, which I trust she will speedily do. In any event I am heart and soul with the South, as I ever have been and hereby declare my fixed purpose of sharing her fortunes, be they weal or woe, and will hold myself ready to obey her call, when and wherever the government of the Southern Confederacy may require my services.

You Sir know my reputation as an officer and a gentleman, and if consistent would be much obliged if you would endorse this paper and file it in the proper department of the government of the Southern Union.

Joseph E. Brown To Alexander H. Stephens. R.

Milledgeville ga., *Feby. 12th, 1861.*

Dear Sir: I have appointed Lewis F. Kenan Captain and young Mr. Barrow 2d Lieut. as you and others of the Georgia delegation requested. Col. Kenan's course, while a political opponent, has been towards me high toned and honorable, and it affords me much pleasure to appoint his son who is a worthy and promising young man.

Col. Barrow is here now with his son. The positions are now all filled in the two regiments and we shall go immediately to enlisting men. There will be great difficulty in getting them for 5? years, hence I shall fix the term at 3 years. We hope to transfer them immediately after they are raised to the Govmt. of the Confederate States.

I have just received Gov. Cobb's telegram informing me that the Congress has taken under its charge the question of the forts, etc. I suppose it desires me to hold Pulaski till it has men to garrison it. I am happy to hear of so much harmony in the Congress.

Permit me in conclusion to tender you my sincere congratulations on your election with unanimity to the high position you now occupy.1 I have not the pleasure of a personal/ acquaintance with the President, but regard the selection a good one, as his wisdom and statesmanship are known to all to be of the most profound and highest order. May the God of our fathers, whose aid I try always to invoke, aid and guide the President, yourself and the Congress in this hour of trial.

Richard H. Clark 2 To Howell Cobb. E.

Albany, Ga, *Feb. 16th, 1861.* My Dear Sir: I observe that the Montgomery Congress has taken charge of our difficulties with the administration at Washington and perhaps will pursue the policy of making demands of the Lincoln administration. It has for sometime been my suspicion—it is now my conviction, that Genl. Scott, under a pretence of alarm for the Federal Capital, has concentrated troops and munitions of war, to be ready for Lincoln's use, on the very day of his inauguration. I think Mr. Buchanan has allowed Holt and Scott to exercise the powers they have, from a knowledge that their acts will conform with Lincoln's policy. I think there is now and has been for some time a perfect understanding between Lincoln and the War department. Lincoln is reported as saying on his way to Washington, that he would coerce only to the extent of executing the laws and recover 1 The vice-presidency in the provisional government of the Confederate States.
2 One of the codiflers of the jaws of Georgia, 1861, afterward judge of the city court of Atlanta. ing the public property seized. If I am right the 4th, 5th, or 6th March may find a strong Army and Navy force at Charleston and Pensacola. In apprehension of this, there should be proper and extra preparations to meet the attacks, or rather we should take the initiative and anticipate by an attack of our own in due time, if satisfied coercion will be the policy executed with promptness. The only result of a new commission to Washington will be "to go through the motions," and I think "the motions" should be gone through with, provided we lose no vantage ground thereby. If Mr. Buchanan cannot treat with us; more strongly, Mr. Lincoln will not. The prompt secession of Virginia, together with a peace policy adopted by Congress, are the only things which will prevent Lincoln, Scott and Co. from using force. We should be prepared for the worst. These thoughts have no doubt occurred to yourself and others, but they weigh so heavily on my own mind I have thought you would excuse me for bringing them to your special attention, as one of your constituents.

Howell Cobb To His Wife. E.

Montgomery ala., *20 Feby., 1861.*

My Dear Wife,... President Davis, as you have seen, has arrived and been inaugurated. His inaugural was highly satisfactory and the occasion was one of the most impressive scenes I ever witnessed. The crowd was large and decidedly the finest audience of such numbers I ever saw. It was estimated from five to twenty thousand. I should say there were ten thousand.

The Cabinet is not yet appointed, and no one knows who will be, as Davis consults no one out of his own State, as far as I have heard. I have positively refused to go into the cabinet. I hear that Toombs has been offered either the State or Treasury, but I can't say certainly, as Toombs has been called home by the severe illness of his daughter, and the offer, if made at all, was by telegraph. I give you the names as I hear from the rumors of the street—talked of for the cabinet— viz. Yancey, Capt. Bragg, Benjamin, Judge

Walker of Alabama, Memminger of S. C, Henry Jackson, Benning and Bartow of Ga., also Johnson, but notice has been given that his name will be fought. I really have as little idea as you in Macon who will be the Cabinet.

Mrs. Davis is not here but expects to come on in a short time, as soon as the President gets a house....

C. W. Cottom To Howell Cobb. E.

Democrat Office, Winona, Min., *Feb. ssd, 1861.* Hon. Howell Cobb: The action of the Southern States in seceding from a Union which refused to recognize and protect their constitutional rights, meeting my most cordial approbation, and the absolute proscription of every Journal in the North which defends this action, has induced me to sell my office at this place with a view to a location in the South.

Having always been (permit me to say without intent to natter) an admirer of yourself as a public man, I have taken the liberty to address you as to the eligibility of a location, believing that you would freely communicate such information as I may desire: 1st, as to a good location for a poor man who fully understands his business, and can edit and print a paper which would not discredit any gentlemen who might take an interest in his enterprise. I have had seventeen years experience as an editor and publisher—was in '55 and '56 one of the editors of the State Sentinel at Indianapolis, Ind., and since that time conductor of a paper in this State. Am industrious, sober and energetic, supported Breckinridge and lost a large portion of my patronage for so doing—have since defended the South, and lost the most of what remained. Am soul, body and strength opposed to Abolitionism and all other Black Republican heresies. Can give you such gentlemen as Senators Rice of this State and Bright and Fitch of Indiana as references; and will do my whole duty as an editor and publisher. Would prefer Georgia or Northern Alabama——a healthy location.

If an old (though young in years) political admirer may presume upon your time and patience I will be greatly obliged for an answer to this brief letter.

P. S.—I leave here in a few days for New Albany, Ind., at which place please address me.

Gazaway B. Lamar To Howell Cobb. 'E.

Bank or The Republic, *New York, Feby. Md, 1861.*

My Dear Sir: If the S. Confederacy are going to make a tariff, how will they adjust the navigation of the Mississippi? It is greatly better to put a ten pr. ct. duty on exports; but best of all to go free trade in full. That will settle the Mississippi question at once and without exception from any one. But above all, free trade will commend you to the European powers and cause them to go with you and not with the North.

The police would not surrender the 10 cases muskets, and Gov. Brown has seized more vessels. I regret it because it increases irritation and agitation.

My opinion is that the Republicans will show their teeth after 4 March and blockade and collect the revenues after their fashion to which you will submit of course, after your fashion. 73566—13 35

The interruption of vessels by Gov. Brown causes more damage to Georgia than to N. York. He ought to seize debts or some other property if he retaliate at all—which I think inexpedient at this time.

If you will have a tariff, make everything pay alike, with but few obvious exceptions—don't begin to discriminate for any interest. It is a most unjust and iniquitous system at best, most expensive to collect, and dishonest in every respect. How can you settle with the N. West States with their horde of boatmen? They will overrun Louisiana in 2 weeks when they start. Make them your friends and not your enemies; and in opening the Missi. you will make friends of all Europe too.

Don't be afraid to tax the people; the people will pay taxes to get rid of Abolitionists, and if they will not, let them give up their negroes at once. But they are more intelligent than most people give them credit for. Deal frankly and honestly with them, and they will pay taxes and lend money too.

L. K. Bowen To Howell Cobb. E. Washington D. G, *Feby. 25th, '61.*

My Dear Sir: I enclose you a slip from the Sun of this morning communicating facts you may not otherwise get as to the extraordinary movements of Mountebank Lincoln. Some incidents in Balto. the papers discreetly omit.

At the Calvert station there were not less than 10.000 people, and the moment the train arrived, supposing Lincoln was aboard, the most terriffic cheers ever heard were sent up, three for the Southern Confederacy, three for "gallant Jeff Davis" and three groans for "the Rail Splitter." Had Lincoln been there, contrary to my preconceived opinions, I now believe he would have met with trouble. The cause of the feeling was the impudent appointment the day before of 100 Black Republicans to escort him through the city. It was this fact which induced his friends wisely to anticipate trouble, and it would have occurred. The moment the crowd ascertained his family without him were on board they retired quietly in disgust.

This ruse by Lincoln has produced an active feeling amongst our people and hurried their action, and we thank him for it.

Ere long now we hope to see Va. and Md. move and join your noble confederacy.

Raphael Semmes To Howell Cobb. E.

Richmond, Va., *Feb. 28th, 1861.* Dear Governor, I was dispatched from Montgomery under orders from the President so suddenly that I had not the opportunity of calling on my friends, yourself among the number, as I intended to do; so you must excuse me for my seeming remissness. As I shall not return for some two or three weeks the Departments will probably all be organized in my absence. I had an interview before I left with Mr. Memminger on the subject of the organisation of the Light House Establishment. I proposed to get rid of the cumbrous machinery of a Light House Board, which I found to be useless under the old Government, and to substitute therefor a Light House Bureau to be placed under a naval Captain. Mr. Memminger seemed to be favorably impressed with my idea and I suppose this form of organization will be adopted. If it be agreeable to Mr. Memminger and to the new Secretary of the Navy I should like to have the first charge of this Bureau—although I must confess I am not very fond of the confinement—merely for the purpose of giving form and shape to my bantling before it falls into inexperienced hands. A word from you would probably secure this object.

Remember me very kindly to Mr. Toombs and Mr. Stephens.

Letters addressed to me at Washington to the care of " Richard H. Clarke, Esq.,"1 will be forwarded to me promptly.

John A. Cobb To Howell Cobb. E.
Macon ga., *March 4th, 1861.*

Dear Father,... A package came by express today from Washington containing two presents from Col. Colt (the revolver man) one for Mother and one for you. Yours is a large horseman's pistol (revolver) in a fine case.

Mother's is a book. On the back it has "Colt on the Constitution, Higher Law and Irrepressible Conflict" "Dedicated by the Author to Mrs Howell Cobb." On the inside it is a pistol case containing a fine ivory handle revolver arid in the handle is engraved "To Mrs. Howell Cobb from Col. Colt."

William Babham, Jr., To Howell Cobb. E.
Edenton N. C, *Mar. 6/61.* Dear Sir: Acquainted with no one in the Capital of the S outhern Republic, and my State unfortunately having no representative there, I beg you to furnish me with a little information if the numerous demands upon your time will permit. I am satisfied your ardent nature induces you to contribute in every and the least respect to the advancement of the Government in which you have recently embarked. From present indications Old Rip 2 has *even* pronounced against the propriety and expediency of assembling a convention. If this be so, the necessity of secession must soon be presented again 1 A lawyer in Washington, afterwards prominent in New York City.
North Carolina.
to the people. If however the convention is called and the members, composed as it will be mostly of Unionists, are compelled by the withdrawal of Va. to consign No. Ca, to a similar fate, the people will be called upon to ratify it. In this section they are not even prepared for that, and my object in addressing you is to request that you will furnish me with the name of a proper person in the city through whom I may obtain what documents I desire for the purpose of promoting the Southern feeling and reconciling the majority here to the Southern Republic.

In the recent election we had but one candidate in this section whose ground was immediate secession and opposition to reconstruction. He of course was defeated. I take and have ever taken the So. Ca. and Georgia ground. You will oblige me by also suggesting to me the name of the government organ in Montgomery, and if it has none, the best Southern-rights paper in the city. The provisional Constitution has pronounced against the Afr. slave trade. I hope the permanent one will do likewise.

E. B. Hart To Howell Cobb. E.
(Private.) Custom House, New York, Surveyor's Office, 27 And 29 Pine St., *March 7, 1861.*

My Dear Govr., I have desired greatly to write you for some time, but in the bustle of matters financial and political I have not been able to get a quiet moment until now. To you who I think know I am not of a changeable disposition in everything that relates to yourself as ever and if there be anything I can be of service to you in here you have only to mention it and it will be attended to. For political news and intimations of what we may expect we have to wait and watch our political opponents. The Democratic party is neither dead or sleeping. My judgment, based upon careful study of the elements from the beginning of the present unhappy complications of public affairs, is that in common with all really conservative influences it will in case of hostile action on Lincoln's part take an immediate and decided position as a peace party. The governing sentiment of the Republican party on the contrary is clearly warlike. The ultras of that party are fiercely belligerent. The irrepressible conflict is lively in their ranks everywhere. How it works may be seen from the action of the Republican Club here night before last. Raymond (Daily Times newspaper) C. S. Spencer, ex-member of Assembly, and other Repubn. guns of all calibres fired away for hours. Spencer and others desiring to pass a resolution instructing Mr. Lincoln to let slip the dogs of war at once; and Raymond and the quietists urging a mere vote of confidence in the Administration. Finally the Club passed both. If straws shew which way the wind blows these would seem to shew that whilst the temperate Repubns. may get their milder wishes put into words and used as preambles, the intemperate ones will be too likely to shape the action of their party. All we can do here is to be ready to take advantage of the inevitable revulsion of the popular mind and turn it to peace, reconstruction and justice to the South. We mean to do it.

Gaza Way B. Lamar To Howell Cobb. E.
Bank Of The Republic,
New York, *March 9, 1861.*

My Dear Sir: I have yours 5th inst. I had a letter from Mr. Memminger on the subject of the Loan1 but I could give him no encouragement here at present.

You know that all loans are founded on or have reference to London. At this time money is worth 8 and 10 pet. in London, and Europe has to buy a large amount of bread-stuff as well as to pay for the usual amount of cotton, and to pay in gold; for we are furnishing both the provisions and the cotton and are taking no goods, comparatively. In addition to which they are sending out American stocks of all kinds for sale here, as well to raise money as to secure their investments, which in the disturbed state of the country are in jeopardy. These, with the trouble in the currency at the West, based upon State stocks, which are falling and as they decline are requoted by the Bank Department to be increased in quantity or to be sold to make good the currency. I do not believe Virginia, Missouri or Tennessee will pay their July interest, and perhaps N. Carolina may falter too. These apprehensions no doubt prevent these more cautious men from encountering the expense of Secession.

As you are engaged in revising and making a permanent Constitution I trust that it will be done strictly with the warnings of past experience before you, and that free trade will be prominently set forth. It is your sheet anchor, your best bower, your main stay. It can be made to operate as a two-edged sword in winning Europe to your support and distracting the course of the Northern elements of abolition.

Open your ports by treaty with England or France on the principles of perfect free trade—and what would New York do? She would open free trade too within 6 months, if she had to cut loose at Albany and join the South.

1 The loan of $15,000,000 at 8 per cent, authorized by act of the Provisional Congress of the Confederate States, Feb. 28, 1861.

So too, if England join, France must, as well as Germany; so a treaty with one would necessitate a treaty with all of them. Again, the West in is favor of free trade and they would cut loose from New England and Pennsylvania and join the movement, either in a separate confederation or by joining you; and then where would New England be?

I am glad to know there is to be no reconstruction with the North generally, not even a consideration of such a thing. I tell you the North will sooner or later invade the South to emancipate the slaves, Union or no Union. Did you not see that in the last few days of the recent Congress? They unanimously voted that Congress had no power to interfere with slavery in the States. A few days later, the compromise measures of the Republican party being under consideration, 68 of them refused to vote that the Constitution should not be altered—to give Congress the right. There is the expression of the intention to alter the Constitution as soon as they can do it with that purpose.

I think you will find the expense of impost system very great, with all the cutters, etc., etc., and the guarding all points to prevent smuggling, when a small pr. ct. on taxable property would pay enough and more too. Take Georgia for instance, 6f(on the 100$ pays $450,000 a year, then 60$! would pay $4,500,000, and the collection would not cost exceeding 2£ pet. to receiver and 2£ to collector. The issue of treasury notes by the S. Confederacy in sums of 25$, 50$ and 100$ and 500$ bearing interest at 3 pet. would pay all your debts. These being recd. in payment of all dues would give them currency to amt. 5, 8 or 10 millions to which amount the issue should be limited. And they should be a *legal tender* within the Confederacy *except to and by the banks,* which should be compelled to pay their notes *in coin* to keep a stable currency. Then, when the quantity issued began to exceed the demand they would begin to depreciate and go below par. When parties have taxes or duties to pay they would buy them and pay them in and thus reduce the taxes a little. But they should be fundable also at the beginning of any month for 8 pet. bonds payable on long time and irredeemable till the time expired, which would make them the more valuable; and this would absorb the surplus and keep the notes current and dispose of the bonds at the same time.

The Northern people do not sympathise in the secession movement, and tho' not favorable to war, except the Republican party, yet they would rejoice to hear that Maj. Anderson had repulsed an attack, etc., etc., of that hue.

The Democratic convention did immense good in declaring against war on the South. But the resolutions were hollow and deceptive. In the general that party showed their rottenness and unreliability at the Charleston convention. Their leaders never had any inducements to hold with the South except for the spoils, and as the South can afford no more aid to them in that line within the U. S. Union they must seek bread and butter elsewhere. Their adversaries have the run of the kitchens both in the Federal and state offices; and anything that will enable them to displace them in either will be greedily snatched at. And on the contrary any and every thing to keep them out of doors will be despitefully resisted. So if the South keep the peace, give no occasion to excite the popular feeling against her, the good Democracy will hold with her for popularity's sake. But any error or mistake or outrage, however small, would be so horrible to their prospects they would outrun the Republicans in hostilities against you, the spoils being the motive....

P. S. Get your new constitution out and publish it; have it voted on and then write the other slave states to join, or write them to lay it before their people to be voted on by them....

Thomas R. R. Cobb To Howell Cobb. R.

Savannah ga., *Tuesday Mar. 19,1861.*

Dear Brother, Your letter together with *three* from my wife and some forty others have been lying in the P. O. here for several days while I was in blissful ignorance.

I am perfectly willing to labor for the Confederate States. I will gratuitously give my time and talent to revising the laws; but I cannot abandon my family now to spend two months more in Montgomery. If this is necessary I decline. If I can work *at home* and report to my associates at Montgomery when I return there *in May* then I will accept. Let me know at once, as I will correspond with them and arrange parts.

Understand that I appreciate your willingness to appoint me but I have no anxiety or wish for the place. Nothing but an honest desire to do something for the country induces me to consider the proposition.

A. M. Evans To Howell Cobb. E. gillsvtlle, Hall County, Ga., *March 20, 1861.* Dear Sir: Nothing ever has bin more gratifying to me than the movement of the Southern Confederacy so fare as it has Went. thare seems to be still some among us disposed to act with The Black Republican party. It is uncertain which has the power in our county, the Black Republicans or the true American people thare seems to be some dissatisfaction that thare is no appointments in the North Eastern part of Georgia Neither Cival Nor Military. If they is any office that is to fill By Appointment Should you know of any person in our portion of the State capable of filling the office it would grattify me for you to use your influence in that way and I think would be the means of Reconcilling the people to our great and glorious confederacy. I understand that I. N. Garrison of Gillsville would like to get the appointment of Mail Agt. Now Garrison is one of Our Warmest friends Thorough Going high minded Honorable Man. It would give general sattisfaction in our part of the Stat and in A Good portion of South Carolina as he was Raised thare and has Large connection and acquaintance in that State.

Excuse My Badly Written Letter. I remain your Humble Friend.

Gaza Way B. Lamar To Howell Cobb. E.

New York, *March 85th, 1861.*

My Dear Sir: The differences between the rates of the tariffs North and South are creating great discontent already at the North, and they will in the North have to call an extra Congress to repeal their Morrill tariff. This will be the consequence; and if not, a considerable part of the direct importations usually coming North will go to the South. With free trade at the South all the imports would be diverted to the Southern ports until New York City could redress herself either by dissolving the relations she holds to the Union and adopting free trade or by bringing all the other states to do it. With her thousand millions of real estate, self defence would demand her to do the one or the other.

So, whilst cotton (whilst in the South) is king, free trade is to the rest of the Union explosion. Whilst the South can rule Europe and New England by cotton, she can by free trade explode all the power of the rest of the Union.

The South, with but light taxation now, can increase and pay fifteen times as much as they now do and then not pay as much as New York and many of the other States pay now. But if you destroy Northern revenues by free trade where and how are they to get money to pay expences and stealings, much less to carry on war against the South.

I tell you, there is a latent feeling of opposition generally prevailing against the South, even in this city; and that feeling extends to hostility in the interior towns and country, and if they do not make war it is not for want of inclination but of power. I would bet 100 to 5 that a telegram that an attack had been made on Ft. Sumter and repelled by loss of 5000 men of the South would cause an illumination even in this city, and much more in the West and New England.

Free trade will give direct trade, and direct trade will give prosperity and wealth to the South. There are thousands who would now turn their importations to the South even with the present differences in the two tariffs, but they are restrained because of the uncertainty of the action of the North and the equal uncertainty of what may be the tariff of the South. If you hold to the tariff of 1857 the North may adopt one lower and turn everything from South to North. You may then have to adopt a lower one and so keep everything vacillating. Whereas if you go to free trade they cannot go lower; you paralize the New England States and you draw off New York, and N. Jersey and Pennsylvania must follow her. New York cannot and will not yield up her commercial preeminence for any consideration, but will dissolve with all the rest and kick them to destruction first. You have the power by cotton and free trade to rule all that is worth ruling in Europe and America— only play the powers rightly.

Submit your Constitution to the vote of the people at once whilst they are in the temper to adopt it. Clinch them at once and bind them, and stop the mouths of all croakers. The people must be with you, they cannot but prefer your Constitution to the old one. Make them commit themselves at once and forever. Then all the North will see its solidity and permanency, and rely and act upon it. Nothing else but permanence is wanting, to carry 20,000 people from this city to the South before 1 Oct. next.

Only see what an increased value that will give to property, and by raising its value increase the taxes—or lower the rate—and make them more tolerable to the people. Suppose a man with 10,000$ property pays the first year 100$ to the Confederacy; the same property will be worth 15,000$ the 2d year, and a tax of 700 per 100 will produce more than one pct. did the year before. Just set the tide towards prosperity and it will flow on stimulating itself and increasing wealth as it goes. Instead of tribute every year to the North it will not only retain the tribute but bring tribute from the North.

Moreover all Europe will hail your free trade, not from any real love (though they will profess much of it), but because it suits their interests; but they will laud you as much as if they really loved you and promote your true interests as well as their own. I would vastly prefer to levy an export duty of 10 pct. or more and have none upon imports. It would be so much cheaper and easier to collect, and without the ramifications, simple in all its details, and affording basis for statistics.

I hear of many merchants going South; some to establish branches' and some altogether. You will find a great change, and if you don't confine the privilege of voting, the newcomers will vote you down and reestablish the Union in spite of you.

I want an act to give me the right to establish an India-rubber factory, with a capital of $100,000, to make car springs, hose and belting. If I send you the bill can you attend to it for me? When does Congress meet again?

The war feeling so far as talk is concerned is subsiding, but more because they cannot accomplish anything to suit them than for any more regard to the wants and rights of the South.

It is my opinion that the Administration will attempt to reinforce Ft. Pickens and occupy all the forts and strong places in the other slave states, especially Virginia, N. Carolina, Arkansas, etc.

I rather incline to the idea that Virginia and Maryland had better remain with the North. They will cost too much to get them free from Northern chains and there are too many who sympathise more with the free than the slave states; and moreover they would constitute a very good barrier to stand between the South and the North.

I think the Southern loan will all go at or about par—from N. Orleans to S. Carolina—and with one million of treasury notes fundable in sums of 1000$ at the 1st every month, any balance not subscribed for would soon be absorbed, and thus keep the treasury notes at par.

Please let me hear from you.

Howell Cobb To James Buchanan. Pa.

Macon, Ga., *26 March, 1861.*

My Dear Mr. Buchanan, I intended to address you this letter on the 5th of March, but at that time I was so much engaged at Montgomery that I could not carry out my purpose. In fact I have been constantly employed since my return to Georgia and have not even yet reached my home at Athens.

My heart often prompted me to write to you; but whilst you remained in Washington I declined to do so because I knew that my opinions differed so widely from yours that any suggestions from me would be obtrusive and unacceptable. Though silent I sympathised with you in every embarrassment which you encountered and rejoiced with all my heart when the fourth of March came and relieved you from troubles and difficulties which your counsels would have avoided but which were forced upon you by the folly and madness of your enemies and the enemies of your country. However much we may have differed and widely apart the roads we have travelled for the last few months, I assure you that the strong feeling of personal regard and attachment which your uniform kindness and confidence had created remains unchanged. I know not what the future has in store for any of us but I pray God you may long live to enjoy the peace and quiet of the home to which your old neighbors and friends have welcomed you with so much kindness and cordiality.

As you know, I never doubted the result of Lincoln's election. My opinion was and is that it would and ought to dissolve the Union. Upon this subject no shadow of a doubt has ever passed across my mind. Whilst with the good and true men of the north we could have happily and prosperously lived as brethren, there is between us and the northern abolitionists an intense mutual hatred which was irreconcileable. Separation was a necessity which could not be avoided and reunion an impossibility which will never be realized. The Union is not only dissolved but will *never* be reformed. Of this you may rest assured. Whatever differences existed among our people before the dissolution there is now but one sentiment on the subject of reconstruction; and that is, unalterable opposition to it. Good neighbourhood between the two sections is the universal desire of all our people, beyond that no one seeks to go. Our future relations depend much, if not entirely, upon the policy of Lincoln's administration. If war is their policy we are prepared to meet it, however much we may regret the folly and madness which forces it upon us. But war with all its calamities will be welcomed with shouts of rejoicing in preference to submission to abolition rule or renewed brotherhood with our worst enemies, for such we hold the black republicans of the north to be. So far our movements in establishing the Confederate States upon a firm and lasting basis have been eminently successful. I think you will agree with me in pronouncing our constitution a great improvement upon the constitution of the U. S. in all the amendments we have made. Our people are not only content but joyous and happy, and blessed beyond all calculation with prosperity in every department of business. Providence has smiled upon us, and with grateful hearts we go on our way rejoicing. This is not the picture which you had looked for as the result of disunion, and I confess, with all my sanguine feeling, it promises to surpass even my hopes and expectations.

Gazaway B. Lamar To Howell Cobb. E.

Bank Of The Republic,

New York, *March 28th, 1861.*

Dr. Sir: If Cotton is King, the King must command peace; for peace is essential to your prosperity. And Cotton is King—he commands not only all, all the mills and manufactures of Old and New England, France and Europe, but the allegiance of your own citizens, the interest and sinking fund for your Loan, and all the shipping, large and small, of the states.

If the North make war on the Confederacy their ships could not go South for freights—and that important arm, paying this year 20 and 30 pct. profit. not less than 60 million dollars this year, will be *hors du profit,* for excluded from cotton, rice, sugar and tobacco freights, their competition for the breadstuffs and provisions would so reduce their freights that they could not pay seamen's wages. But though cotton is so very great it must not forget that its power is confined to Southern soil and under Southern control. Once exported to any other location, it is as Samson's locks shorn of its power. Therefore wise legislation will look forward and provide all the means to give force and effect to its action.

Would you command peace with N. England and New York? Make a law that no ship belonging to any citizen of those regions shall be allowed to enter a Southern port on pain of forfeiture if the States in which they are owned contribute in any way directly or indirectly to sustain hostilities in any way against the Southern Confederacy; and to prevent changing the ownership, as they would gladly do, make the law have reference to the ownership of 1st Nov. 1860, enrolment and register, no matter by whom owned. Let it apply to the votes of their Representatives in Congress, and not one of them will vote for war. They are as sensitive as to money as Great Britain is, and would cut the throats of all the negroes rather than leave a ship in jeopardy.

But free trade is your trump card as well as the just and equal mode of taxation, and not only so but the cheapest. Take your own bill of taxation in Georgia. It produces at 60 on the 100$— 450,000$. Put it 10 times as much, and it will produce $4,500,000. But suppose she had to pay $9,000,000, or two pr. ct. That is but little more than is paid in New York, and if Georgia pay 9 millions and the other states in proportion there would be abundant income and the collection would be less than 5 pct. on the amt. Under the impost system it would be 25 and 30 p. ct. on the amt. And Free Trade will be like Cotton, it will command the " good will" of all America and all Europe and cause them to cultivate your amity. If N. England attempt any injurious action, put a tax on the intercourse with them and they will succumb as readily as Gt. Britain will on the cotton question.

The two confederacies, established and moving on, will be constantly competing for the commerce of the world, and at home too. They will lower their duties to rival each other till they come to free trade as the finale; and therefore it is only a question of time, and now is the time for the Confederate States to reap the full harvest of the measure.

The Constitution ought to be submitted to the votes of the people— not that there is any doubt as to ratification but to clinch the people br their support hereafter, when things change and the burdens aliome onerous. And it will convince friends and foes at the North that it is the will of the people and not the action of politicians. It would effectually silence the radical section of the Republicans who advocate entire submission in everything to the people, and who advocate the freedom of Italy, Hungary, etc., and it would convince the world that the people made the new government, and they would then regard it as permanent and well founded.

You have never said any thing relative to the right of suffrage being restricted. That is a most important consideration, for the tide of emigration will be such from the North to South that within two years the new comers South will hold the balance of power and control your government and perhaps vote you back into the Union. I think judges should not be elective, nor negroes allowed suffrage, nor tenures of office be too short. And there should be qualifications for Senators, to distinguish their office from Representatives. And Electors should be appointed by the Legislature.

If the few manufacturers in the South cannot stand free trade let them go at something else, and pay them for their investments, rather than lose free trade. Free trade and cotton will carry the Confederacy beyond all precedent in the world if properly managed.

I think the emigration from this city alone will be 20,000 before 1 Nov. to the South. That will cause an advance in property, and that enhancement of property will reduce the rate of taxation—or increase the amount.

There should be a tax on property, on polls and on income, and thus compounded it would be moderate and tolerable, and the unbounded prosperity it would insure to all classes would redound to the credit of secession, and free trade after three years will take care of itself with the people and the world. But free trade will compel New York to leave New England and join the South or make another confederacy. It will give power to the South at the expense of the North. Every man and every dollar that leaves New York for the South reduces N. Y. and strengthens the South. New York when she loses more than her natural increase will decline, rents will be lower, livings reduced, and adversity succeed to her great prosperity—and the latter will have gone South.

Howell Cobb To His Wife. E.

Mobile ala., *31 March, 1861.* My Dear Wife, We failed to make connection at this point, so I am detained here for a day. I shall leave this evening however for New Orleans and expect to be there early tomorrow morning. I have met many friends and acquaintances and passed the time quite pleasantly....

I attended last night, before going to the theatre, a lecture from Mr. Smith, a Member of our Congress from this place. It was on the same subject with my speech in Macon and was a most able and successful effort. It will be published and I advise everyone to read it. It was really a finished and eloquent defence of our new Constitution.

Mobile looks more like a military barracks than a commercial city. There are some fifteen hundred troops here on their way to Pensacola—most of them from Mississippi and composed of the best young men of the State.

I met here one of my old officers in the Treasury Dept.—Mr. *Ela.* A brother of his died here and he came out to settle his estate. He is a New Hampshire man and still holds his place at Washington. I had this morning a long talk with him. He is very much impressed with the condition of things and says the North has no idea of what is going on. He attended Mr. Smith's lecture last night, and told me that the demonstration of the audience when

Smith announced our *eternal* separation from the North left no doubt of the fact that the Union could never be reconstructed. He will be able to give new wrinkles to the Lincolnites on his return to Washington City

Robert Toombs To Alexander H. Stephens. R.

Montgomery ala., *April 6, 1861.*

Dear Stephens,... We have very urgent requests from our friends at Little Rock for you to come to Arkansas and make some speeches for them at such time as will suit you before their election in August. They would prefer it soon. Dr. Blackburn, a very intelligent gentleman, came here for you, and says he will meet you in Memphis with every provision for your comfort in the canvass. I think it would certainly secure Arkansas and is every way very desirable. Write me at once on this subject that I may let him know that he may make the necessary appointments and provision for you.

We have assurances from our officials at Washington that the govt. is pledged to no hostile movement (reinforcement, etc.) without notice; but their activity in naval and army preparations for the last few days indicate a hostile purpose, which a few days will develop. Until I can see the end of it I cannot leave here. The events in Virginia are exciting and promising but I do not think there can be any results until after their May elections. The present movement of the legislature is in antagonism to the convention, and it is possible that the legislature may submit the question of North or South to the people. The prospect of our loan is good, and unless the military indications at Washington injure us in this matter we hope to be in a very good financial condition within a fortnight. The " lame ducks" (suspended banks) in Geo. and South Carolina will injure us there, and more elsewhere. I have made no arrangements about other questions since you left. I have been on the eve of it once or twice and missed. One good lady who had offered me her house for two thousand dollars a year suddenly raised up to five and gave the naive reason that she had a charitable object in view for which to use the money. It reminded me of the Italian robber, "in the name of the Virgin, give me your purse." I am wearing out my cold slowly but it still annoys my head. Things generally here are working smoothly. Give my best regards to Linton and Judge Jas. Thomas. I should like much to be with you all this week.

Howell Cobb To His Wife. E.

New Orleans, *7 April, 1861.*

My Dear Wife, This is Sunday in New Orleans. I have just strolled " solitary and alone " through some of the streets and found here and there a French store open, but most generally the store doors were closed and things bore the appearance of Sunday in a well regulated Christian town.

This morning however my ears were saluted at an early hour with martial music and the volunteer companies soon appeared in full dress parade, and for some time the streets wore the appearance of a gala day. At the Catholic cathedral there was a most imposing and affecting ceremony. The church was filled with the volunteer companies, who had gone there to have their flags-(the flag of the Confederate States) blessed by the Archbishop. The fathers, mothers and daughters of the soldiers were gathered around and there were few dry eyes during the solemn ceremony. Every heart seemed to beat responsive to the patriotism of the occasion, as the solemn ceremony bound the hearts of all in iron bonds to the cause of our new Confederacy. It was a day not soon to be forgotten in this city.

I hear that the races are continued today but I have not become sufficiently acclimated to New Orleans morality to attend.... My Masonic business is closed, and after devoting a day to my female friends here I shall commence my homeward march. My present programme is to go with Slidell and a party of friends to visit a friend on Red River, where I shall remain only a day, and then I propose to go to Oxford, Miss, and thence on the most direct route to Macon....

This morning I met our old friend Maj. McCulloch of Texas who is here busily engaged in forwarding arms to Texas. I think the Major is anxious for a fight and would regret to see our present difficulties settled in a peaceable way.

I have been gratified to find a universal feeling here against reconstruction. Without exception every one I meet responds most cordially to the sentiment that our separation from the North is "perfect, complete and perpetual."

We had our dinner yesterday at the Lake, and it was a most delightful retreat for a day from the dust and turmoil of the city.

I enclose you an envelop with some letter stamps of our Confederate flag. I think they are beautiful....

John W. H. Underwood To Howell Cobb. E.

(Private.)

Rome, Ga., *April 11, 1861.*

Dear Sir: You will have seen no doubt a few favourable notices of myself for next Governor. My inclination is to write a letter declining to have any such use made of my name. I have been restrained by the consideration, first, that it might possibly be of some use to our friends in the final struggle, even if my strength should be small. I am satisfied that Mr. Stephens intends to press Linton Stephens for that office. Failing in that he will press Mr. Crawford... or Benj. H. Hill.... I *was* very favoury inclined to Mr. Crawford but recent events have induced the belief that Mr. S. again has control of him. I do not know how Mr. Colquitt stands nor what are his prospects. I think James Jackson is the man upon whom we should concentrate our strength.

My own inclination is to retire entirely from all contests involving office. I do not want any, and unless something should be voluntarily tendered in the line of my profession I would not take any; therefore the only interest I feel is to see our ancient foe in his true position. Gov. Brown's friends are pressing him for President, Senator, and Governor.... I desire you to understand my opinion of Brown has not changed, and from a conversation he had in Savannah with some gentleman in the presence of Mr. Bartow as I learn he is watching the contests in Geo. with great interest and is delighted at the prospect of a collision between Stephens, Hill and Mr. Toombs on one side and you and your friends on the other, expecting to benefit by it himself. He has a certain strength and I think we had best let him alone, not advance him. I cannot understand the power by which Mr. S. controls and manages Mr. Toombs. It is to me the greatest mystery of the age.

I do not desire particularly to be informed of any line of policy on hand, and will try and fall in right if Judge Benning or Henry R. Jackson or any other friend believes that the use of myself will damage them in any way. I will promptly take it out of the way, for I say to you with entire truth I want nothing. I don't know what we shall do in our district. Wright is anxious to be elected to Congress again.... I shall not interfere with him myself, having positively declined to run. I would be glad to see you and hope to do so at some point soon.

Gaza Way B. Lamar To Howell Cobb. E.
Bank Of The Republic,
New York, *Apl. 13, 1861.*

Dr. Sir: We have just learned by telegram of the bombardment and surrender of Fort Sumter.

Strange as it may seem to you, it is true that the people of this city who have professed to sympathise with the South have recently changed their expressions to hostility, some for one cause and some for another, and more so since the fleet left a week ago for Charleston. Even many influential Democrats have changed and there are very few reliable. The masses may feel differently, but they are led by a few corrupt, spoils-seeking rascals, and will go with them for or against the South as they may be led.

You may calculate that you may have to fight out and fight long too. And Prest. Davis should enlist and accept all the Volunteers he can from Kentucky and the other border States—which will incline all of each State that way....

The Constitution ought on many considerations to be submitted to the vote of the people: 1st. In order to clinch the people to its support through *evil* as well as good report.
2nd. To convince the world how unanimously it would be sustained. 3rd. To stop the mouths of the Republicans, who insist you dare not do it because the people are against you. 4th. It will give your friends ground to act upon to show that the people are with you and that so immense a majority of the people ought to rule, as these very Republicans are contending for in regard to Italy, Hungary, etc. etc. 5th. To convince the people of the North of the magnitude of the difficulty they will have to contend with when they make war upon you.

I am afraid you will find an elephant in Texas. She will cost more than she is worth, unless old Houston is hanged. And the Indians are so troublesome it will bankrupt the Confederacy to keep them off. And I still incline to the opinion that the Fedl. Govt. are sending most of its forces to Texas under an invitation from old Houston and under the pretext of defending her, but mainly to make war on the Confederacy; and in that they show more wisdom than in sending to Charleston, your strongest point of defence and most easily defended.

I hope Fort Pickens is reduced ere this also—there is no use in waiting; after you are once ready go ahead. Forbearance for 3 months is not appreciated here now because you did not allow 10 73566—13 36 men to remain in Fort Sumter, as though there was such a difference in principle between 10 and 70. They even said you ought to have allowed provisions to be thrown into it and have waited!!! Then they would have put 500 men into it unless you resisted; and if you did the answers were ready. The state of Virginia will not vote to go out by the present convention,—it was elected as Union and it will remain so. Maryland will cost more than it will be worth, and Delaware is not worth having. The contest for the Capital would involve the whole North in the contest on a sentiment of honor, falsely so called, and would cause a war of years. Let Maryland, Delaware and Missouri go. Get Virginia if she will bring her forts in her own possession but don't let her expect you to take them for her. With N. Carolina, Tennessee, Arkansas and Kentucky you can spare all the rest. There will be an advantage in many ways in having some slave border States between you and the North. It will keep your negroes safer and the way the North will deal with them will show your people what they have escaped.

The South cannot prepare too largely and efficiently for war. It will be the best means of insuring peace, or if needs must come, in defending your homes. I do not sympathise with any movement, or even a threat, against the capital or the North. Let your policy be exclusively and strictly on the defensive. Let every orator and every newspaper proclaim defence and by no means provoke aggression. When the North see that you will fight on your own soil and are ready to do it. and mean to confine yourselves to it, they will reasonably conclude it is better to let you alone.

The rumors here are that the Harriet Lane has been sunk at Charleston; I am sure it is entitled to credit.

This failure of Lincoln on Charleston, made contrary to Genl. Scott's advice and military science, will damage the Administration, and if Pickens falls too he will forfeit the confidence of all sensible men.

Robert Toombs To Howell Cobb. E.
Montgomery, Ala., *Apr. 23, 1861.*
Dear Cobb, I recd. your letter by today's mail. The troops of Geo. were sent to assist in taking Norfolk's navy yard at the request of the govr. and convention of Va. Since that time the

navy yard has been taken. The Govt. succeeded in sinking 8 or 10 public vessels and doing other great injuries to the fixtures and other property of the establishment; but we secured between 1,000 and 2,000 cannon of the best description, a considerable amount of small arms, three thousand barrels of powder, and a vast supply of shot, shell and other munitions of war. The troops were then ordered to Richmd. to await other troops (13 regiments) yesterday ordered to the aid of Va. These thirteen regiments are to come from Geo., S. C, Ala., Miss., Tenn., Ky., and Arkansas. Col. Robt. Lee who is considered the best officer in the army is at the head (Maj. Genl.) of the Virginia troops, and our troops will be under his immediate orders and will be used according to the exigencies of the occasion, for the defence of Va. and Md. Maryland is thoroughly with us as far as we can learn, and is calling on us for aid. We are today informed by Stephens who is at Richmd. that the New York 7th Reg. were wholly defeated and cut up yesterday morning between Annapolis and Upper Marlboro in Md. by some Maryland troops. We think it is true, getting it from Norfolk as well as Richmd. God grant it may be true. I would rather such a calamity would happen to that regiment than to any in the North. These boasters threatened to march from N. York to N. Orleans. Washington City is in great consternation. Perhaps anon we shall be there? If they could get off I think now they would run.

Alexander H. Stephens To R. Schleiden.1

Richmond, Va., *26th April, '61*.

My Dear Sir: Your very polite and kind note of this day is before me. The feelings and motives by which it was prompted I can readily understand and fully appreciate. For this reason as well as for the deep interest I can but feel in the questions myself, I gave your verbal remarks the considerate hearing mentioned.

In reply to the matter of your note I can but reaffirm to you what I said in conversation upon the same points. No one can more deeply regret the threatening prospect of a general war between the United States and the Confederate States than I do. Such an unfortunate result, if it should occur, cannot be charged to the seeking or desire of the Confederate States government. On the contrary I feel assured in saying that every honourable means has been resorted to by the government to avoid it. Peace not only with the United States, but with all other Powers, is eminently the policy of the Confederate States. But they will have no peace with any which depends on a sacrifice of either their honor or right. Their independence with absolute jurisdiction over their own soil they will maintain at any and every hazzard.

The bombardment of Fort Sumter was not resorted to until every effort at a peaceful adjustment of all matters of controversy with the United States had failed. This the correspondence between their Commissioners and the Secretary of State at Washington as well as the correspondence between General Beauregard and Mr. Secretary Walker—with which you are fully acquainted—will abundantly and clearly show.

1 Text derived from a copy kindly furnished by Dr. Frederic Bancroft, of Washington, D. C. Schleiden was then minister of the Bremen Republic near the Government of the United States.

As to the future or any terms which our Government might grant or accept with a view to arrest further conflict, I can say nothing. I have no authority from the Confederate States government on the subject. But as a citizen desirous at all times to preserve peace, if it can be done on just and correct principles, I have no hesitancy in saying to you that the course of future events in these particulars will depend to a great extent, in my individual judgment, upon the course to be pursued by the government of the United States. From all evidences and manifestations of their design which have reached me, it seems to be their policy to wage a war for the recapture of former possessions, looking to the ultimate coercion and subjugation of the people of the Confed. States to their power and dominion. With such an object on their part persevered in, no power on earth can arrest or prevent a most bloody conflict.

If, however, such a war is not the object of the government of the U. S.—if they have any idea or disposition for an amicable adjustment of the questions in issue, then a great deal depends upon some early indication of such disposition or willingness and its communication either directly or indirectly in some authoritative way to the government of the Confederate States.

This may be the invitation of other steps leading to a peaceful settlement. But without some such expression or indication of their designs and wishes, in the present posture of affairs I see no prospect of arresting the present tendency of events.

Should such communication as I have indicated be made to the government of the Confed. States, I doubt not it would be responded to in a spirit becoming the intelligence and patriotism of their people as well as the magnitude of the momentous issues now pressing to a crisis. This much I will undertake to say in behalf of the Confed. States, though I have no authority to do it.

In relation to the Proclamation of President Davis inviting offers for commissions in Privateer service mentioned by you in conversation, I will barely add that it was intended as a justifiable and legitimate measure in defensive warfare against the war of aggression so clearly inaugurated by the Proclamation of President Lincoln. This at least was and is my individual view of the subject.

Augustus B. Longstreet 1 To Howell Cobb. E.

Columbia, S. C., *1 May, 1861*. Dear Cobb, Wife and I reached here yesterday, her health greatly improved. But to my point. I was greatly surprised and a little

'Judge of the superior court of Georgia (Ocomulgee circuit), 1822-1829; editor of the Augusta Sentinel: president of Emory College, 1839-1848; president of South Carolina College, 1857-1861; president of the University of Mississippi, 1861-1870; author of Georgia Scenes, etc.

provoked to find among the first acts of the provisional government the adoption of the tariff of '57. But for the Morrill tariff this act would have injured our cause seriously with the foreign powers. I enquired what put it into your heads to adopt such an unwise measure, and was told that it was because your body had not time to arrange a scale of duties and therefore took this as already cut out to their hands. I replied, "Why in reason's name did they not adopt it with a reduction of a half a third or a quarter upon every article, arranging the free list as we have arranged it?"

Do this as soon as possible, and let the news of it go to Europe by the next steamer. It will silence clamors at home and do great good abroad. We can hope for little revenue from any tariff for a time, and a high one does not always produce the most....

Joseph E. Brown To Alexander H. Stephens. R.

Executive Department, Milledgeville, Georgia, *May th, 1861.* Dear Sir: I inclose you a copy of a letter addressed to the Secretary of War dated this day on the subject of our coast defence, and beg you to cooperate with me in pressing this matter upon his attention. Our people feel so great a sense of insecurity on the coast that I cannot too strongly urge upon you the importance of this question. If one of the regiments now at Savannah were distributed along the coast it would give them a sense of security to which I feel that they are justly entitled, and I could readily supply the place of the'regiment by ordering out the Savannah regiment of volunteers under the requisition of the Secretary of War to supply the place of the regiment removed from Savannah to other exposed points upon the coast. Your early attention to this matter will be highly appreciated by our exposed fellow citizens upon the coast and will be regarded by me as a great personal favor.

Howell Cobb To His Wife. E.

Montgomery ala., *10 May, 1861.* My Dear Wife. I have just received yours enclosing John A's letter from Norfolk, which I will send to Ma, that she may see how the mighty have fallen. John A. complains that they can hear no news in camp. That is pretty much the case everywhere else. All we know here is that the most active and vigorous preparations are going on to meet the war when it is forced upon us. It seems that similar preparations are being made by our enemies, but of their movements we are not so fully advised. If we knew better what they were doing and what was their immediate policy a better opinion could be formed of the probable course of things. If no conflict takes place in the next forty days, there will be no fight in my opinion. Such is still my notion, though the current of public opinion is different.

The Va. delegates, Brockenborough, Staples and Hunter, are here. Rives and Campbell have not come, though Hunter tells me they are both all right and Virginia is now a unit with us, with the immaterial exception of a small portion of what is called the " panhandle." Hunter tells me that in passing through Tennessee, he found the revolution in public opinion in East Tennessee very great against Andy Johnson, Brownlow, Etheridge & Co. The people will not allow them to speak, and that State being a unit in West and Middle Tennessee, will soon be a unit throughout. The next thirty days will decide our destiny for peace or for a hard war, and every nerve will be strained to be ready for the issue.

I received a letter from Howell1 two days ago. He was in fine spirits and was waiting anxiously for himself and company to be sent to Virginia. I replied to him, that the duty of a soldier was to be content to serve his country where his country needed his services, but that I would see to it that no injustice should be done to his company if I could prevent it....

I hear that the college 2 is broken up, and must soon suspend. In that event Mr. Rutherford will be without employment, and Tom and myself have determined to try and get for him the place of commissary to one of our regiments. He will make an honest and faithful officer and it will in part compensate for the loss of his salary as Professor....

Williams Ruthehford, Jr., To Howell Cobb. E.

Athens ga., *May Hth, 1861.*

My Dear Gov., Your very kind letter reached me by the last mail. stating the fact that you and your noble brother Tom had obtained for me the appointment of commissary to the Ga. army under Gen. Lawton. I am unable to express to you the gratitude and admiration I feel for you and Tom. This I will say, that *never* did a man have truer friends than you both have been to me.

You are however under a wrong impression with regard to the college.2 It has not been broken up. Although the war excitement has materially lessened our numbers yet we have about 40 now in attendance. The Senior final examination will take place tomorrow. The Commencement you know has been changed to 2nd Wed. July, necessarily requiring the examination to come off sooner. But the Faculty have brought it on two weeks sooner even than this in view 1 Howell Cobb, jr.. afterwards professor of law in the University of Georgia.

3 The University of Georgia.

of the present excitement. When the Senior Class leave there will be left about 26 in the three lower classes. The Faculty you know have no power to suspend the college. Mr. Mitchell who represents the Trustees here says the college must not stop. So you see I would be obliged to resign my professorship to accept of the position which you have so kindly provided for me. In a money point of view it would be a losing business. Including the Librarian's salary of $100 I get here $2,100. The position in the army is $1,800.

I had a conversation with Mr. Mitchell yesterday. He said the college could not spare me. Mr. Walsh will leave, and he says if I leave there will be no mathematical teacher in the college. He spoke very kindly about it however, saying that in as much as there would be very few students, some temporary arrangement might be made during my absence and the place would be kept open for me. I consulted Gov. Lumpkin.1 He advises me against resigning my present position for the one offered. If the question came up as a matter of duty, that is, if I could feel that the claims of patriotism were such as to require my service in the army I should go at any sacrifice. But this is a position that so many " honest" men would be willing and anxious to obtain, that I do not feel that duty calls me to resign a present advantage for one not so good.

This is the money view of the matter. The position of commissary I apprehend would subject a man to *endless* complaints. His honesty will be impugned, and altogether it must be an unpleasant position; yet would be gladly accepted if I were out of my present one.

As to the war my mind is fully made up. I never was better satisfied that a cause was just. The issue now is independence or extermination. My mind is fully made up to this issue.

Whenever therefore a call to the field is stronger than the call that my duties here make upon me, I am prepared to respond at once with the energy of soul and body and any cost of pecuniary or personal sacrifice. It seems to me however that I should prefer a more active position in the army than commissary. If I have to fight, I want to fight where I can do execution.

It is possible that after the senior examination, and they retire, that the remaining students may become so dissatisfied as to drop off until the college may wear out before commencement. It is fortunate for us that the long vacation comes in the summer. The fall term commences 1st Sept.

I suppose that the appointment which you got for me could not be kept open upon any such contingency as the disbanding the college. I have now gone over the ground so that I think you understand my 1 Ex-governor Wilson Lumpkin, then a resident of Athens.

position, and there is no doubt but that you will know how to act in the matter. If the war closes in 40 days as you seem to think possible, I would be in a bad fix to resign my professorship. I feel that in this I am becoming better and better qualified both as a teacher and a disciplinarian, and I have a great aversion to change when I feel I am doing well.

Howell Cobb To His Wife. E. Montgomery ala., *18 May. 1861.*

My Dear Wife, I had hoped that Congress would have completed its business today and that I should have reached home when this letter reaches you. It is however now out of the question and I shall be content if we adjourn by Wednesday, the time first appointed.

To day Arkansas will be admitted and her delegates sworn in, making *nine* states in our Confederacy. We have passed bills for the admission of North Carolina and Tennessee as soon as they secede. Old Ky. hangs fire and Missouri is on the eve of civil war, whilst Maryland is overwhelmed with Federal troops and the spirit of her people sinks under the power of numbers. Such is the present status of affairs. In the meantime we are making the most extensive and vigorous preparations to meet the issue of war, if it must be so, and to secure peace if all sense has not left the northern people.

I was gratified to get the letters from the boys. I hear occasionally from them but not so directly as by their own letters. From all quarters however I hear of their good spirits and good conduct.

I can say to you rather confidentially that there is a fair prospect of a quarrel between President Davis and our *worthy* Joe Brown. The latter is trying to ride the high horse about certain acts of Congress which take out of his hands all control of the Ga. troops. I shall sustain Davis and our Congress, and if they show the right spirit we will thoroughly put down the miserable demagogue who now disgraces the executive chair of Ga.

The proposition to adjourn to Richmond has at last failed, and unless some new movement is made on the subject we shall have to return to Montgomery when Congress meets again. In this case we shall try to prevent any other session before October,—or else give Davis power to call us together at whatever place he may think best at the time he makes the call.

...

Robert Toombs To Alexander H. Stephens. R.

Richmond, Va., *June 8,1861.* Dear Stephens, Your letter of the 4th inst. reed. I am glad you are engaged in the produce loan. It is of the last importance to ns, and it is of the last importance to bring the whole country to it at once with a large subscription. We can meet the exigencies of this contest, which is assuming gigantic proportions. The North is acting with wild and reckless vigour; their present credit (not to borrow) but to buy and put men in the field on credit is immense and is used with a lavish hand. They act as tho' they believe they will be impotent after the first effort (which I believe is true) and seem determined to make that overwhelming and effective. Virginia was in a dreadful condition when we got here. I think Scott could have come to Richmond as easily as he could go to Baltimore, if he had have tried. But he did not know it. Things are altering for the better slowly. We have great want of arms; it is getting to be very serious. The States have wasted or put into the hands of their citizens large numbers of the captured arms, which are wholly inaccessible to us; and our foreign arrangements were tardy and insufficient. We have got to rely greatly on private arms or be overrun. Harper's Ferry was very weak when we came here. We have thrown in 6 or 8 thousand more men, and they are bringing a great force against it and seek to cutt off communication at Manassas Gap; but, thank

God, Scott is slow too and may give us time to get more ready than we are. In my opinion we ought to fight as soon as possible. I think we have a great superiority in the personal material of the men; they greatly in numbers and arms and equipments, but I do not see how we can lessen it by time. I do not think the present status can be maintained until Congress meets nor do I believe that Lincoln intends to maintain it until then. He will aim to strike a decisive blow just before Congress meets in order to give himself the control of that body under the very fire of the guns. We shall not attack except to drive them back from Western Va. and Newport News unless strong military reasons invite or compel it.

The Maryland commissioners only came under the pretence of peace; they wanted help for war and urged us to march into Maryland as soon as possible. Not a sound man in Maryland feels himself safe for one hour even in his own house.

Our fortifications are nearly completed at Pensacola, and we do not now need all the troops there—certainly not half as badly as we do here. Our engineers think we can take Pickens as soon as we mount a few more 10 inch guns now en route for that place.

When we came here Letcher had not 20,000 Virginians under arms, and they were scattered about in twenty places and were inefficient for any good. We have now perhaps fifty thousand in all in Va. under arms. Scott has near eighty thousand threatening Virginia and full command of the bay, rivers and inlets. The prospect ahead looks very gloomy. It will take courage and energy to avert great disaster and we have far too little of the latter for the crisis. I fear the trouble is getting too big for the grasp of some of our most reliable people.

Tom Cobb writes me unfavourably of the produce subscription to the loan. It is of vast importance. I fear that he is too sanguine, and especially that he will let go too quick. Nothing is done while anything remains to be done in a financial question. I will keep you advised of anything of interest. Find out if you can in your journeyings how many private arms can be had in the state. Tell Judge Thomas and Linton that the trouble is great in getting arms for their regiment and I doubt the possibility of doing it here. Arms is the cry everywhere.

Missouri is in a terrible condition,— three fourths of her people with us, but without arms and threatened daily with subjugation. She will be in revolution in ten days. Kentucky is divided and distracted and will have a bloody civil war, expected to break out any day. Upon the whole we are in a terrific struggle and need all hands and all heads for the public course. Julia well.

Thomas W. Thomas To Alexander H. Stephens. R.

Elberton, Geo., *17 June, 1861.*

Dear Sir: If I can form my regiment, which I feel almost certain of doing, I can get them called into service and armed by the Gov. the third regiment from this time. The Gov. will do it if he has arms to arm three more, and though he speaks with some doubt he believes he will be able to do it. I understand him if three more are called mine shall be third. Two regiments he says must be sent off before mine and mine shall be the third. I must report to him in two weeks, and wish to do so in one week. We cannot be received he says except for the war. Will you do me the favour to see your company and ascertain if they wish to go with us for the war. If they do tell them to send me the muster roll of men in a week if possible and at all events in two weeks. Please tell them also what the programme is, that Mcintosh, myself, and Linton if he will, are to be the field officers, at least that is the present expectation; and get them if you can to be satisfied with it.1

I see your appointment here is for the 26th. If you are not otherwise pledged and have got rid of your old propensity for " haunting taverns" to see the boys (the boys don't grow cotton) Mrs. Thomas and myself will be much pleased to have you come direct to our house and be entertained by us during your stay. A word in your ear— no one else here can feed your horses, and I have corn, hay and oats in abundance.

1 This regiment was shortly afterward mustered Into the Confederate service as the Fifteenth Regiment of Georgia Infantry, with Thomas W. Thomas as colonel and Linton Stephens as lieutenant-colonel.

Joseph E. Brown To Alexander H. Stephens. R.

Atlanta ga., *June 25th, 1861.* Dear Sir: Your letter has been forwarded to me at this place. I shall make my headquarters here for the present, as the weather is too hot for me in Milledgeville. It is in contemplation to send Col. Semmes's regiment to Virginia as soon as I can get enough of armed companies from the lower counties of the State to form a regiment to take its place and can get equipments and accoutrements for them. As I now have to equip Genl. Phillips's1 brigade and another regiment which is to rendezvous here next Monday, it will be impossible for me to supply the coast regiment till probably some time in August. The regiment to rendezvous on Monday will be the 10th. Besides this we have two battallions in service, equivalent to a regt., and the enlisted regt., making 12. These have all been fully armed accoutred and equipped *by the state.* I send them into the field with full outfit. Gen. Phillips's brigade is organized under the act of our last legislature for home defence and is equivalent to 3 regiments more, making 15 in all. So soon as they have had a month or two of drill, if our coast is not in the meantime attacked, I shall offer them to the President for service in Va., as I think the climate will protect the coast in August, Sept., and Oct. My arms in the Arsenal are exhausted but I have two or three thousand in the hands of companies. I am informed that troops are accepted only for the war, and many more are tendering for the war than I can arm. I shall therefore be obliged to require those having arms to tender for the war or give the arms to those who do so tender. I suppose the quota of Ga. has been about supplied but doubt not the President will accept all I can arm for the war, and as our troops are anxious to go I do not stop to inquire if the quota is exhausted. The regiments above mentioned include none of the independent or Confederate regiments that have gone from the State. I think there are now three—Bartow's, Conner's and McLaw's Regts. I wish I could get in your company as desired for one or two years, but cannot under the rule laid down for others.

Joseph E. Brown To Alexander H. Stephens. R.

Atlanta ga., *July 8th, 1861.* Dear Sir: Your letter on behalf of Mr. Ford addressed to me at Milledgeville is just received here and I have referred Mr. Ford to the Secretary of War who claims the appointing power in the regiment.

1 William Phillips, of Cobb County, a warm friend of Brown's, was now in charge of a camp of instruction—" Camp McDonald "—in Cobb County. The Confederate authorities refused to accept his troops as a brigade, but took them as separate regiments. Phillips then entered the Confederate service with the rank of colonel, commanding Phillips's Legion.

I had this morning before the mail came issued orders to the companies comprising Judge Thomas's regiment to rendezvous at this place on next Monday, the 15th. The regiment called Stiles's regiment will rendezvous at the same time and place. The quartermaster's arrangements, etc., are all being made here. It will not therefore be in my power now to change the place to Augusta. I wish I had known your desire sooner. Let me beg you to come up to Atlanta Monday and see them here, as I am very anxious to see you before you go to Richmond. I shall hope to meet you here. Circumstances compel me to go to Canton tomorrow and remain till Friday when I expect to return here.

I am spending most of my time in the camp of Genl. Phillips's brigade seven miles above Marietta on the State Road. I am trying to recruit my health a little by camp life, and feel some benefit by it.

I now have at the camp two regiments and three battallions fully armed and equipped. The organization is in strict conformity to the statute of the state. Genl. Wayne and Maj. Capers are both at the camp assisting in the training of the troops, and Wayne says he has never seen a body of troops improve so fast. Since the *stampede* I have filled up the brigade with men who will stand the fire for the war, and a better or more orderly body of men can no where be found. I have tendered the brigade to the President fully *armed* and *equipped,* but he has not yet thought proper to accept the tender. He wishes the 2 regiments, but does not seem to wish to take all together. Genl. Phillips is willing that the President appoint his entire staff, except one confidential aid. I appeal to you to assist me in getting the brigade into service as a brigade. If the President does not accept a brigade, he can accept its parts and appoint Phillips its commander and thus receive the whole. Phillips is very popular with his officers and men and is very rigid in his discipline. If they are ordered to the field without him there will be great dissatisfaction, and I think it would be very bad treatment to him. May I appeal to you to give this matter your special attention and get the President to have them as a whole. I am sure you will never have cause to regret it. I arm and equip the two regiments next week and tender them and the brigade, which is equivalent to five armed regiments tendered at once, and I do think the President should take them under state organization. We now have in service from Ga. the ten volunteer regiments numbered from one to ten, and the regular regiment under Col. C. J. Williams, and the two battallions, one at Norfolk, and one at Pensacola, making say 12 regiments. To this add the 4 regiments and 3 battallions now tendered and it makes about 17J regiments Georgia has supplied fully armed and equipped ready for the field, with blankets, accoutrements, &c., &c. The Confederate or independent regiments are not included in the above calculations. There are I believe 3 or 4 of them. I feel that our state is doing her part and trust she will continue to do so.

Gabriel Toombs 1 To Alexander H. Stephens. R.

Washington, Ga., *July 31st, 1861.* My Dear Sir: I write you as a *friend* to aid me in a matter of the *greatest* consequence to me personally, and if I am not mistaken of importance to our Confederate States. It is to ask your cooperation with me in trying to induce my brother to resign the office of General in the army. In this case my brother's zeal blinds his judgment, and is not according to wisdom. He has never been educated in the science of war and has no experience in the business, and besides is physically unfit for camp life. Since his last severe attack of rheumatism he has but little use of one of his arms, and his throat and lungs have been so much affected this winter and spring as to give his friends great solicitude for him. Without naming other private and personal reasons these are sufficient to decide the case against him.

Now my dear friend, if anybody can change his purpose in this matter it is you and I, with the help of our President. If you can bring about this object, you will confer a favor on me that I can never forget. While I am entirely independent of my brother in the sense the world calls independent, no mortal perhaps was ever more dependent upon another for happiness, than I am upon him. So you can imagine what my feelings must be when I tell you I look upon his going in the army as an unnecessary sacrifice of his life. Please let me hear from you as soon as you have any thing encouraging to write.

Howell Cobb To His Wife. E.

Richmond va., *6 Aug., 1861.* My Dear Wife,... I can give you no news outside of what you read in the papers. From the tone of the Northern papers I infer that the people there are getting sick of the war and since their disastrous defeat at Manassas they begin to talk of peace. Besides their people are not volunteering very freely for the war and their treasury is getting low and their credit lower. From all which it would seem a very natural conclusion that they cannot continue the war much longer. I have no idea it can continue till January. Indeed many think that it will close before the Winter sets in....

1 Brother of Robert Toombs, with whose entrance into the Confederate military service this letter Is concerned.

Thomas W. Thomas To Alexander H. Stephens. R.

Camp Walker, Va., *21st Aug., 1861.*

My Dear Sir: I send my orderly, to place my bay horse at your disposal. I would give myself the pleasure of attending this morning in person again but my gray has been ridden off to the battle field by Capt. Poole who called on me this morning to redeem my promise to that effect made several weeks ago, my gray being the only horse in camp able to carry him.

I was *compelled* yesterday to leave while you were here.

Whenever you visit my camp I will be pleased to have you consider my quarters at your service, as well as my horses and servants at all times.

Joseph E. Brown To Alexander H. Stephens. R.

Atlanta ga., *Aug. 22d, 1861.*

Dear Sir: I should have written you frequently since you have been at Richmond but I have had few leisure moments, and I know that your whole time was occupied. I have sent 20£ regiments of Georgia state troops to the field fully armed, accoutred and equipped, which has cost me a great deal of labor. Add to this the six or seven independent regiments of which I have no record, and Georgia now has fully 25,000 troops in active service. On Tuesday next I am to throw two other regiments into camp of instruction at Camp McDonald, and two at Camp Stephens near Griffin, which I had called in honor of yourself. They will add 3,000 to the number now in the field. I feel that Georgia has not been backward in doing her full share and I trust she never will be. You have I presume seen my late letter to Judge Whitaker in which I take position against the proposed convention, and leave the question with the people whether I shall continue in my present position for another term. The press seems to be pretty generally opposed to my re-election, probably most of the politicians are, but if I am not greatly deceived in the signs of the times the masses of the people are still with me and will continue to sustain me.

I think there will be no opposition in Georgia to President Davis and yourself. You will be elected by acclamation, or you should be.

I have only time now to write a short letter. When you can spare the time give me your views as to the future and say what you think my proper course.

Thomas W. Thomas To Alexander H. Stephens. R.

Centreville va., *12th Sept., 1861.*

Dear Sir: I herein enclose a letter that has reached my hands.

Old Mr. Hardy Culver is in Richmond and wants to come here to this camp. Can't you manage to get him a pass? We would be obliged to you if he could come up.

I am sick, have been for a week, am feeble and bilious, indisposed to action or exertion.

We have left our camp at Camp Walker with about or nearly 300 sick and convalescents. We are here at a very desirable place with almost 400.

Thomas W. Thomas To Linton Stephens. R.

Camp Pine Creek va, *20th Sept., 1861.* Dear Linton, I have received yours and Ellick's1 letters since the ones I got McIntosh to acknowledge. I have been quite sick with jaundice. I am sitting up this morning for the first time since Monday evening last. I have suffered a good real with nausea and fever. I have not strength only barely to allude to some matters mentioned in your letter. I have thought for some time that you would never be able to undergo this life and in fact I have not a doubt of the correctness of that opinion, and yet I can't say I am willing for you to resign; for without you in the regiment I would not have been willing to make it, and if you were to go out I should feel embarrassed. I am at great loss therefore what to say to you and hardly fit from weakness to have any opinion at all. I firmly believe if you persist in staying in the army it will cost your life without conferring benefit on the country (for you would do no good if sick all the time). I have been sick 34 days out of 54, but I think I shall do better hereafter. I think I have far more strength of constitution and elasticity than you have, and with all these advantages over you I do not consider it impossible that I may break down. The events so far would indicate badly for me, but I believe I have passed through the worst. My system has been poisoned by the bad air generated from filthy camps around me. But my strength fails and I must lie down. Remember me to Ellick,—say to him how much I am grateful to him for his kindness to the sick.

Robert Toombs To Alexander H. Stephens. R.

Camp Pine Creek va., *Sept. 22nd, 1861.*2 Dear Stephens, Your letter of the 15th inst. is recd., and I am greatly obliged to you for attending to the commissions. I can get no answer to anything thro' the war office or the government. I hope as Walker is out it will now be different. Johnston is a poor devil, small, arbitrary and inefficient. Like Walker, he undertakes

'A. H. Stephens.

2 In July, 1861, Toombs bad resigned the Secretaryship of State to become a brigadier-general In the Confederate Army. Among his aides were his two sons-in-law, Dudley M. Du Bose and W. Felix Alexander. Among the regimental officers in bis brigade were Thomas W. Thomas and Linton Stephens, colonel and lieutenant-colonel of the Fifteenth Georgia Volunteers. to do everything from a mere fondness for power and does nothing well. He harrasses and obstructs but cannot govern the army. I think it will

be wise to put Cooper in the war office. He is. an efficient and good man, and Davis from his confidence in him will let him do its duties. Felix Alexander goes up tomorrow and will bring down for John anything you may want to send. I am very glad to hear that Linton is improving and hope he will soon get able for duty. Col. Thomas is now quite sick. Dr. Steiner fears he is taking the measles tho' it is not yet developed. The regiment like all the rest are much improving in health and are getting along generally well. I have no trouble with any of them and they are all improving fast. The Regulars went down to Munson's Hill for five days last Thursday on picket and will be replaced tomorrow by Semmes. The next detail will be the fifteenth and I think if Thomas is sick I will go down with that regiment myself about Friday next. John Stephens has gone with his command and will be back tomorrow evening with it. Tell Linton to get his strength before he comes to camp. We have no chance of moving shortly and I fear the whole campaign is thrown away, with this mighty army ready and willing to end the war if they had a man of sense and ability to lead them. The movement towards the peninsula is a mere stampede, just what McClellan wants. There is no security for the Southern coasts this winter except in the capture of Washington, and it is time Davis concentrated all of his army on the Potomac instead of frittering his strength on panic expeditions. What has become of our sick? I fear there is no arrangement to send them back when they get well. I have heard nothing of Smith's regiment and nothing of Berry who is at Pensacola and wishes to join me. I hear we shall have. G. W. Smith over this corps of the army instead of Johnston (who is to be Genl. in Chief). We are glad to hear it. Write me by Alexander and give me news. I hear nothing but what T see in the newspapers, and they are such liars I can not rely on them. I notice with indignation the assault of the Examiner on you. It will do you no harm but I would like to know where it came from.

Joseph E. Brown To Alexander H. Stephens. R.

Atlanta ga., *Sept. 28th, 1861.* Dear Sir: On my return to Atlanta from a visit to my sick son I was informed of the dispatch of Mr. Waters to you asking leave to publish your letter to me on the subject of my candidacy, and have since seen your reply. I very much regret that my secretary in his anxiety and without my knowledge sent such a dispatch. It was not only without authority from me but does not meet my approval, nor do I think it right to complicate you with the present canvass should you consent to the publication of the letter. It is true I have on several occasions mentioned to friends your solicitations for me to run again for the office but never with a view to newspaper comment. Our state is happily a unit (or so nearly so that the opposition amounts to nothing) in the support of President Davis and yourself, and I shall be the last man in Georgia to attempt to create any division on that subject. In my published documents and in my speeches to troops I have invariably said that you ought both to be elected by unanimous acclamation. I thought so then; I think so now. It is true I did not think the President did full justice to the Georgia brigade and I was independent enough to say so, but at the same time I have said that his acts generally have met my highest approval and that I should support him warmly and heartily and oppose all opposition to him. All will tell you that I have been your constant advocate and supporter.

The future will soon determine the result of the gubernatorial election. Had I known that the opposition to my re-election would be so bitter as it has been in some quarters I should not have consented to the use of my name, but I had in my own opinion gone too far to retract with honor before these developments were made. The result will be known to you very soon after this letter reaches you. My opinion is that I shall be elected.1 I thought the above explanation of my position about the dispatch of Mr. Waters proper or I might not now have troubled you with a letter.

Robert Toombs To Alexander H. Stephens. R.

Camp Near Fairfax va., *Sept. 30th ?2, 1861.* Dear Stephens, I recd. your letter of the 23rd inst. I am obliged to you for your attention to my commissions. I believe I am now thro' with Richmond. As to the assignment of Smith's regiment, Benjamin3 wrote me the President instructed him to suggest to me to call Genl. Johnston's attention to it; that he was the commander of both corps of the army. I replied to Benjamin that I had good reasons to know that fact, " and in common with the army, not without reasons to lament it". I never knew as incompetent an executive officer. As he has been to West Point, tho', I suppose he necessarily knows everything about it. We are doing nothing here, and will do nothing. The army is dying. I don't mean the poor fellows who go under the soil on the roadside, but the army as an army is dying, and it will not survive the winter. Set this down in your book, and set down opposite to it its epitaph, "*died of West Point*". We have patched a new government with old cloth, we have tied the 1 Brown was reelected governor by 49,404 votes, against 32,459 for E. A. Nisbet. 2 Dated Sept. 30th In the original, but obviously an error.

'Then for a brief time Confederate Secretary of War, later Secretary of State. 73566—13 37 living to the dead. I am glad to see activity in Kentucky and Missouri. They may preserve the spirit of the people.

Thomas1 broke out a week ago with measles, and to my surprise yesterday morning he came riding up to my tent before breakfast to the utter consternation of Dr. Steiner. He seems to improve on his imprudences, and today is appearing quite well and improving. The health of the regiment is improving tho' not as rapidly as I expected. The measles have eaten themselves out of subjects but there is a decided increase of typhoid fever and I think its malignity is also increasing. I have kept perfectly well, except three or four days' confinement to quarters with dysentery. I took no medicine and wore it out.

We have fallen back from Munson and Mason's hills and Falls Church with a great affected panic in order to draw out McClellan. But he would not bite at such small tricks. I begin to think him a general. With not much more than the 35,000 troops Scott said it would take to defend the city, he has conquered and held Maryland, held a victorious army of 100 regiments in check, sent the Northern recruits to Virginia, Kentucky and Missouri, drove us out of the valley of the Kanawha, overawed Kentucky and saved Missouri, and but for the victorious militiaman Price would have reconquered our half of Missouri; and we are lying down here rotting. We have lost more men by inactivity and bad treatment since the battle of Manassas than it could have cost to have gone to Baltimore and ended the war. Your next news from us will be we are building negro cabins and preparing for winter quarters.

Robert Toombs To Alexander H. Stephens. R.

Camp Near Fairfax C. H., Va. *3rd Oct., 1861.*

Dear Stephens, I enclose you a copy of a letter from Bartow to Dawson. He claims to be the oldest Captain, because he *offered* his company on the 12th May and was notified of acceptance on the 15th, and claims acceptance refers back to tender, in all which I think he is right. On the other side, Capt., of a Rome company, tendered and was accepted on the 14th May, and thereby claims seniority. None of the captains have ever been commissioned. I promised him to send you the paper for submission to the war department.

I hear nothing of Linton, now past due. We fear that he is more unwell. Col. Thomas by sheer dint of imprudence seems to have conquered the measles and is rapidly getting well, riding and walking over camp and attending to all of its duties except drill. I saw John Stephens yesterday and he was very well. We have not one particle 1 Thomas W. Thomas was colonel of the Fifteenth Georgia Infantry, which was comprised In Toombs's brigade.

of news. All eyes turn to Richmond and to the West. We appear to be chained to the rock of immobility there to linger and complain and wear ourselves away until spring comes to our relief. Davis is here. His generals are fooling him about the strength of our force in order to shield their inactivity. He *talks* of activity on the Potomac but I fear he does not feel it strong enough to move this inert mass. I have not seen Genl. Smith but I think this corps of the army has been a great gainer by his appointment. Its administration is already very much improved and I have great hopes that he will prove equal to the great trust committed to his hands. Benjamin's administration of the war office also gives great satisfaction here. People can now get things settled one way or the other and a bad way is infinitely better than no way at all. By this I do not mean to say he does not discharge his duties well for I have seen nothing to complain of. Our sick improve very slowly at Richmond. I fear the hospitals in which they have been placed are inefficient some way. I don't mean the Geo. hospital but those into which they put our first detachment of sick. The campaign is about closing on the Atlantic. We lose eighty or ninety thousand volunteers (12 months men) before midsummer of the next year. The enemy will march on us in May or June with two hundred thousand men, and how are we to meet him? The prospect to me looks more gloomy than at any time since the 11th Aug.

Thomas W. Thomas To Alexander H. Stephens. R.

Camp Pine Creek, Fairfax Co., Va. *5th October, 1861.* Dear Sir:... Eight days ago I was broke out all over with the measles—today I feel entirely well with but slight diminution of strength.

I had an easy time with measles. I had had for 5 or 6 weeks kidney affection, bilious derangements and finally jaundice well developed. The measles seemed to make an entire revolution in the system and drove out all the other complaints—the only evil effects it has left me is some diarrhea (not bad) and a habit of bleeding at the nose, and that not bad. I have had rather a tough time— been sick 45 days out of the 67 I have been in Virginia, but it does seem now I am through with it or at least the worst of it. So far I have staid all the time in camp and have not sought other shelter than my tent.

Pres. Davis was up the other day and reviewed about 12,000 troops at Fairfax Court House. There was not a single cheer, even when some one in the crowd among the staff called out for three cheers there was not a single response, everything was as cold as funeral meats. I wasn't there but I get this from such sources I am sure of it, and you may set it down for a lie when the Richmond papers talk about the enthusiastic cheers. I don't know that this amounts to anything but I tell it as a part of the history of the times.

Some for several days past have been busy circulating it among all the camps that the Pres. "*Mowed up*" the generals when he was here. I use the words generally used in telling it, some say " *cursed them out."* Of the truth of this I am not able to say—from what little drippings have reached me from the inner court circles I am inclined to doubt it.

Matters are managed very badly here, without sense, system or policy. Of this now I am certain, and there also exists partiality and corruption in high quarters. The temper of the army is not good. The troops widely feel the unjust oppression and partial hand that is laid upon them, and in my opinion the spirit of the army is dying. I have seen some things that made my blood boil; and that makes one unconsciously begin to debate with himself whether the assassin's knife be justifiable. So far, however, I have kept cool and silent. The end will come after a while, and then the ballot can rectify the mischief.

Thomas W. Thomas To Alexander H. Stephens. R.

Camp Pine Creek, Fairfax Co., Va., *10th Oct. 1861.*

Dear Sir:... The health of this regiment is improving. We can now bring into action over 500 men which is a better showing then we could make for the last 6 weeks.

The election of Gov. Brown is entirely agreeable to me. It is a triumph of the people over the newspapers and I think teaches a dangerous and evil engine a salutary lesson and administers to it a timely rebuke. Judge Nisbet I think highly of, and have great confidence in him; but the animating spirit which nominated him was the old defeated and defunct spirit of Know Nothingism endeavouring in the absence of a large number of the true men of the State to grasp the reins of power. But enough of all this—all governments are humbugs and the Confederate government is not an exception. Its President this day is the prince of humbugs and yet his nomination for the first permanent presidency meets with universal acceptance, and yet I do know that he possesses not a single qualification for the place save integrity. I know nothing to the contrary of his having that. Imbecility, ignorance and awkwardness mark every feature of his management of this army. He torments us, makes us sick and kills us by appointing worthless place-hunters to transact business for us on which depends our health, efficiency and even our lives. I could demonstrate all this to you in an hour's conversation. He would make a good ordinary1 of a county in Georgia and his capacity is not above that; but he is king, and here where we are fighting to maintain the last vestige of republicanism on earth we bow down to him with more than eastern devotion.

You did me the honor once to express the opinion that I was competent to fill a position in his gift, of high dignity and usefulness, and one which I would like to hold; but I cannot consent to take it from him. It would not be honourable in me to do so entertaining the opinion I do of him unless he was informed of that opinion; and if he was so informed he would (at least ought to) refuse it and I do not want to be subjected to a refusal. I wish therefore you will not mention the matter to him and if you have mentioned it and it has been received with favor please say that I have concluded not to enter into the service of the Confederate Government in any other capacity than the one I now hold—and it is probable I will be courtmartialed out of that in less than 60 days. We have to bear things here that no freeman ought to bear, and perhaps outraged nature may speak out in me and bring me into trouble.

P. S.—If I send this letter by mail I shall be compelled to frank it and let you pay the postage. The rule I fear at our post office here is on all paid letters to receive the money and throw the letters in the fire.

Thomas W. Thomas To Alexander H. Stephens. R.

Camp Near Centreville, Fairfax Co. , Va., *17th Oct., 1861.*

Dear Sir: Yours of the 16th inst. was received tonight. I must write if I write at all with a pencil—I have no ink. It is 12 o'clock at night and raining so I can't go out to borrow some.

Night before last we marched back from Camp Pine Creek to this place— started at 2 o'clock and got here about 7, being 5 hours in coming 5 miles. Toombs's whole brigade came together. Our trains bothered us, being in front. We would move frequently not more than 20 feet and stop; it was very fatiguing, almost killing.

Linton joined us here yesterday morning and is now here well. We are expecting a fight every day. The indications now are that we will back over Bull Run and fight there. The enemy are at Fairfax Court House (9 miles from here)—at least their advance posts are there; they are marching upon us, or making out so. Gen. Toombs don't think they are coming; our head generals (Johnston. Smith and Beauregard) think they are coming. What is the truth I don't know—whether we will advance and fight or fall back and fight or run away entirely I don't know, and I doubt if anybody else does know. We are throwing up fortifications here—how extensive I 1 Judge of probate.

don't know; this brigade (3 regiments) furnishes 70 men a day which ought to be about 500 for all the brigades convenient to Centreville.

I have now about 450 men to carry into the fight if it comes, and we are losing about 15 a day by sickness (at least that's the cause assigned)—how many I will have if it's postponed a week I can't say.

This is all I can think of to tell you as to our position, condition and prospects. And now a few hasty words in reply to your letter. Nothing was farther from my purpose than to give you pain. In your last before this one I am answering you requested to hear from me often and in other letters you made the same request. Now you could not reasonably expect to hear from me on any other subject than my thoughts, views and feelings about the army here, our operations, condition and prospects; as for news you could get earlier and more reliable news at the cabinet councils than you could possibly get from me. On this only subject that I thought you wanted to hear from me, I have spoken right out my honest opinions and I think correct opinions. If I have given you pain therefore I can only say I regret it very much. I can't decide very clearly whether you blame me for the pain or whether you intend to attribute it to the nature of the case; if the first, I am sorry it has happened and can only say truly it was not intended; if the second then it was out of my power to prevent it. I have not said one single word in my letter that I do not believe you know to be true.

You tell me to have patience, heroic patience; there is nothing heroic about me—I don't pretend, never did, to that character, but I *have* been patient and still am; I have been prudent and silent also. I see the immense stake we play for. I see the great importance of standing fast now and the difficulty of recasting the game. But I felt a relief in speaking out to you, and thought that honest words to perhaps our wisest councillor would be useful and certainly could not be injurious. These are my opinions and this my defence if I need any. But enough,—exhausted nature demands sleep. I have been four mortal hours hard at work making calculations about how much baggage each company must be allowed, which is the quartermaster's work. If I were not tired and worn out and if the circumstances were not so solemn I could make you laugh by a short sketch of our debates and my figuring and decisions. I have had to decide how much a frying pan weighed, how much a skillet, how much a tin pail, how much a coffee pot,—even if a credit was to be allowed because the handle was off. I have ascertained one fact very satisfactorily, which you can tell Mr. *Judas* Benjamin, the Hon. Sec. of War, so that he will know *one truth,* and he can send it to his generals and they will know *one thing.* We were ordered to put ourselves in "light marching order "—what that was I had to figure out. Now allowing that the officers have theirs, it requires 2 lbs. of cooking utensils to the man, counting non-commissioned officers and privates— this will do—it is light marching order and less will not do, of such articles as soldiers usually have. Cooking utensils was the most vexed question before me—my ten company commanders were all at points about it and my calculations and decision satisfied every one of them. Is not this a triumph? Talk about *my* being rash and impatient—the most politic man in the world—a perfect diplomat. Why Sir a treaty can be made with England and France, yea with the North itself, with less diplomatic skill and talent than it required to settle that question of skillets. Beside this I settled the officers' clothes question, the knapsack question, the blanket question, the tent question, the mess chest question, and the gun box question, the candle box question, the barrel question, and the extra arms question—all in four hours, among ten disputants, when no two had similar ideas at the beginning; and all expressed entire satisfaction with the decisions. Let me tell *you* to be patient and caution you in speaking of your forbearance when you have never been called on to decide how much skillet1 450 men ought to have to be in light marching order.

May God prolong your life for my country's sake, and good bye.

Howell Cobb To His Wife. E.

Camp Bryan, Near Yorktown, Va., *13th Nov., 1861.*

My Dear Wife, In the last thirty-six hours I have rode seventyfive miles, fatiguing two horses and greatly worrying *one* man. No doubt you wish to know why so much riding. Well you shall know. On day before yesterday I received notice that Tom and the Legion2 were to go on a scouting expedition below Bethel. Col. Ward of Florida (whose regiment is encamped near me), and myself determined to join them and for that purpose we left early on Tuesday morning to join the expedition at Bethel. Getting there, or rather a little beyond, we found that the Legion had gone on a foraging expedition but that Col. Levy's La. Regiment had gone on a scout towards Old Point. Ward and myself regarding that as the most interesting route determined to join the latter party.

After reaching Col. Levy's regiment, he proposed that we take a detail of twenty cavalry and go on to New Market bridge, which is about two miles from Hampton and four miles from Old Point, which we did. It was the point at which on the day before the 1 Final s purposely omitted (footnote In the original).

Thomas R. R. Cobb In command of Cobb's Legion.

Yankees had fired upon and wounded one of our men. But we found no vestige of a Yankee and returned after a pleasant ride which amounted to forty miles when I got back to my own camp.

About 11 o'clk I was aroused from my sleep by Tom, whom I did not see during the day, with a message from Genl. Magruder that I must return today for a more extended expedition. Accordingly this morning we took an early start from my camp to join the General at Bethel. In the meantime Genl. Magruder had ordered the Legion and other regiments to go into an ambuscade near New Market bridge expecting that our appearance would draw them out and the ambuscade would play havoc with them. Before we reached Bethel this morning the report met us that a portion of the Legion during the night had been fired upon by our forces and had resulted in the death of a good many—number not known. When we got there we found the report greatly exaggerated, as always is the case. During the night the officers of the Legion were fired upon through a mistake by a portion of their own men and Maj. Bagley was killed, Capt. Morris was wounded in the hand and one private (not from the Athens company) was wounded in the leg. How it occurred was not satisfactorily known when I was unexpectedly and hurriedly called to my own camp. Just as Genl. Magruder, myself and party were about to start on our expedition a man arrived stating that twenty vessels were making for York river, and as my command was charged with the duty of preventing their landing I had to return in double quick to my own camp where I now am writing this letter.

After I got here Dr. Gordon, the steward of the regiment, was fixing my holsters for me and undertook to clean my pistols when one of them went off and shot him in the leg but not badly wounding him. So you see it has been rather a bad day so far. It is now nearly night and there is no sign of any vessels in the river and I hope to have a quiet night's rest which I assure you I very much need.

The accident in Tom's Legion I deeply regret as it is making him feel very badly, the more so as he was absent from them when it occurred—but for this he is not responsible. He wanted to go with his Legion to the ambuscade, but Genl. Magruder insisted on his coming to my camp for me, and as a matter of course he had to obey orders. I ought to say to you that I did not take either of the boys on either expedition. Your injunction not to expose them unnecessarily shall be obeyed. Tom has received official information that the Troup Artillery is ordered to join him so I hope soon to have Howell here. I thank you for the books though we have not yet got the box, though John has arrived. The box is still in Yorktown. All well.

Howell Cobb To His Wife. E.
Yorktown va., *9 Dec., 1861.*

My Dear Wife, Whilst waiting for Gen. Magruder, with whom I am going to select a new camp, I write you a hasty note. There is much excitement here in anticipation of an attack from the enemy, but I still think there will be no fight. However before you get this letter the telegraph will inform you of the result if it should take place, for it must be in a day or two or not at all.

I saw John on yesterday and urged him not to bring his wife on— but he insisted that there was no danger in bringing ladies to Williamsburg. Today Genl. Magruder has issued an order or request that all non-combatants should leave Williamsburg. Now whether there is danger or not it shews that it is no place for women and children. Johnie Rutherford was at my camp this morning in fine health and reported all well at the Legion. Our boys are in excellent health and all in good spirits. The remote chance for a fight has given new life to the camp— and all hands go to work moving with life and spirit.

Our new camp will be a mile nearer to Yorktown on the road toward Williamsburg. The Legion also move their camp and will be much nearer to us than now. The exact distance has not yet been fixed upon.

The weather is beautiful—indeed I never saw a brighter and sweeter day in my life than it is now. I hear the Genl's. voice—ready to mount, and I must close.

Thomas R. R. Cobb To Alexander H. Stephens. R.

Camp Marion, *Dec. 18th, 1861.*

Dear Sir: Your favor was recd. yesterday, and today Mr. Staunton made his appearance in camp. I would have gone to see you in Richmond had I reed. your message in time, but I got it about ten o'clock at night and I left before day next morning. I was in Richmond only sixteen hours and was very busily engaged. I think this explanation due to you as well as to myself.

Mr. S. has behaved badly—very badly. His disposition to avoid his duty as a soldier is bad enough, but his evasion of orders from his Captain and myself makes his conduct much worse. I would have excused his visit to Georgia when I heard the facts had he not subsequently shirked his duty. The good order of my Legion required that he should be brought to this camp. I could consent to nothing until he made his appearance here. He has come; and I can now listen to the appeals of friends.

For the sake of the hospital I consent to the detail of Mr. S. But in passing I must respectfully request that the officers of that Institution will have no more details made from my command without my consent. I have shown my interest in the enterprise too early in its history to require me to make asseverations of it now.

Permit me to add that the surgeons should send the soldiers to their regiments as soon as they are restored. One of my men (Weaver by name) was retained as a nurse for months after his restoration without a word of communication to me. This is all wrong.

Thomas W. Thomas To Alexander H. Stephens. R.

Elberton, Geo., *31st December, 1861.* Dear Sir: I got yours of the 26th inst. this evening. I had heard of your illness though only through the public prints. The good fortune of your recovery I am glad to be told of. I have been well all the time except that cough which I can't get rid of. It does not seem to affect my health and certainly not my strength. I am stronger than I have ever been. I have a power in my grasp and arms that to me is surprising. If I continue to increase in physical power as I have done for the last 6 weeks I might safely challenge Heenan.

I found my family all well and my children much grown and improved. I have not received any letter from Brown. Since I have been here and seen what the state of public feeling is, how dispirited, uneasy and apprehensive the people are I am in much doubt as to whether I ought to retire or even change my theatre for any provocation whatever. Mr. Davis and the peculiar people he trusts have given sufficient cause to every gentleman in the army to mutiny, but if any, even the smallest, further depletion be caused in the public pulse it looks to me that our affairs will be desperate. To my utter astonishment I find everybody apprehensive that the army of the Potomac will be defeated, when we who belong to it (I mean the soldiers—volunteers) have not the least expectation of such a result. Our generals there share the feelings here I think, as every order that has been sent to me for the last 7 or 8 weeks was evidently bottomed on the expectation that we would be whipped whenever we fought.

Large numbers of people here are whining and complaining and probably thinking of a compromise by going back, and nine tenths would vote for peace tomorrow on the basis of giving up Missouri, Kentucky and Maryland. I found another thing which to me was unexpected. All the complaints made of the Administration in the Army by the volunteers are understood and believed in here. I remember once your saying that no matter what its faults (the Administration's) its continuance was necessary to our success for it had public confidence. This might have been true when you said it but it is not true now. There has been a change and a mighty one. I know I have changed. When I left Virginia I felt against it so deep seated an indignation that it verged upon hate; but now I feel a pitiful anxiety to cover and conceal its weaknesses. Then I was like Ham—inclined to mock and laugh over its infirmities, now I am like Shem and Japhet that would take a cloak and walk backward to cover its nakedness. I believe there is serious danger of the whole thing breaking down, and if this is to be so I hope some friendly bullet will find its way to my vitals, as I don't want to live to see it.

You request me in your letter to write you, and I have done so of that which fills my mind to the exclusion per force of every thing else. Of course I don't expect you or any one to believe me, for it is well known that I am a rash man—one whose perceptions to discern and whose judgment to sift and digest are neither to be trusted.

Howsoever this may be I beg leave to thank you for the trouble you have taken for me and to subscribe myself your true friend.

C. G. Memminger 1 To Howell Cobb. E.

Richmond va., *Jany. 1, 1862.*

My Dear Governor, On receipt of your letter of the 27th I took a proper occasion to see the President and read it to him. He very kindly received the suggestions. The first as to the discharge of men in advance of the expiration of their term, he expressed no opinion about. But in the others he concurred in your views. In the matter of kindness with discipline he says he has done everything to promote that feeling. He has urged it upon the Generals but it is either old habit or a hard nature which prevents conformity to so very just and proper a mode of dealing with volunteers.

I hope you will soon be up here to assist the necessary legislation to carry out these plans. You will see ere this reaches you that the Yankees have been backed down by England. I am very sorry for this, as I confidently hoped for a speedy end to the blockade. I still hope almost against hope for some further complication between them and England.

Howell Cobb To His Wife. E.

Richmond, Va., *18th Feby., 186%.*

My Dear Wife, Since I last wrote to you I have been engaged day and night in winding up the old and opening the new Congress.

Today for the first time I saw the President in reference to my future position. I am now ordered to meet Genl. Wool at Old Point to arrange for exchange of prisoners, etc. etc. I shall go there tomorrow. On my return I am ordered to report to Genl. Magruder at Yorktown and shall probably remain there for a short time and 1 Confederate Secretary of the Treasury.
my future movements are dependent upon the developments of the future.

The terrible disaster at Fort Donelson is a terrific shock upon weak nerves—and somewhat trying to strong ones. I cannot despond, and do not. We must have other reverses and perhaps worse ones before the country will be thoroughly aroused, but all will be well in the end....

We look each day for a fight at Savannah, and I do trust that we shall hear nothing to cause shame to a Georgian. If Savannah falls, be it so—but let it be to the enemy a dearly bought victory and one of ashes.

Tom leaves here in the morning for Ga. He goes to increase his legion to a brigade, and will then be appointed a Brigadier to command them. I started to write you merely a hasty note as I knew you would be anxious to know what my movements would be under the new condition of things. I am to meet the Sec'y of War tonight in reference to my mission to Old Point and if I leave as I expect to do in the morning it will be several days before I can write again.

Howell Cobb To His Wife. E.
Norfolk, Va., *22 Feby., 1862.*

My Dear Wite, I am detained here longer than I expected. I have so far only succeeded in fixing a time and place for meeting Genl. Wool. We meet tomorrow on board a steamer between the outposts of the two armies—below our fortification and this side of theirs. The old chap was not willing for me to take a peep at Fortress Monroe. I hope to close the business on tomorrow and to return to Richmond on Monday.

The enemy are evidently surrounding this place—not with a view as I think to an immediate attack but for the purpose of cutting off all communication with other parts of the South. This being done Norfolk must fall. Their plan is to get possession of Suffolk, and this done the two railroads from here—the one to Petersburg and the other to Weldon. We are now putting up fortifications at or near Suffolk and then the fight will probably take place. The same force, being the Burnside expedition, is aiming to get Weldon, and this would effectually stop all communication between Virginia and the Southern States. You will see that the enemy have laid their plans well but whether they can successfully execute them remains to be seen.

I met a lady this morning who came under a flag of truce from the North. She tells me the Yankees regard the rebellion as ended. They expect Vice-President Stephens to resign at once, and raising the banner of reconstruction to carry the country with him by storm. I am happy to find our army in good spirits and more determined than ever to whip the enemy and buoyant with hope and confidence.

I have not received a line from home since I left but I hope to find letters on my return to Richmond. If Johnnie has not left tell him to meet me in Richmond and tell Howell to remain with you until he hears from me again.

I made a visit on day before yesterday to Hardeman's Batallion and found the health and spirits of the batallion good. Like all our troops here they are ready to give the Yankees a warm welcome.

Howell Cobb To His Wife. E.

Norfolk va., *25 Feby., 1862.* My Dear Wife, I am detained here by the slow coach movements of Genl. Wool. We ought to have closed our business in an hour but he must have time to consult his Govt. and that keeps me waiting. We had our first interview on Sunday and agreed upon the basis of a full exchange of all prisoners, including the privateers, and the surplus, to be paroled in their own country until exchanged. I proposed that each Govt.

should transport their prisoners to the frontier of their country free of expense to the prisoners. This he thought right but had no instructions and hence had to confer with Lincoln. We meet tomorrow to close up the matter. Our meeting took place on board my steamboat half way between our fortifications and Fortress Monroe. To my great astonishment and delight I found on board of his boat Miss Lucy Gwin on her way to the South. She was equally delighted and we had quite an interesting talk on our way back to Norfolk where she remained one night and left for Richmond. She abuses the Yankees worse than ever and says that they are confident since the Roanoke and Fort Donelson affairs of our subjugation. She thinks we have but few friends at the north but says that Baltimore is full of true men ready to revolt. Dr. Gwin is now on board of a British merchant vessel attempting to run the blockade. Lucy expects him to arrive every day as he left Baltimore before she did. Mrs. Gwin is still in New York to come on as soon as she can with Cary.

This place is considered in great danger. It is thought that Burnside will attack them in the rear, but so far no demonstration has been made. I have no news here. The twelve months men are reenlisting better than I expected they would....

Robert Toombs To Alexander H. Stephens. R.

Headquarters 1st Brig., 1 Drv., Army Potomac,

Camp Georgia, Near Bull Run va., *March 4th, 1862.*

Dear Stephens, Last fall the Irwin Guards, 9th Georgia Volunteers, were detached from that regiment by order of Genl. Johnson and assigned to artillery duty. The Col. it seems did not consent to it. He has never commanded the regiment sixty days since it has been in service and it was and is in miserable poor condition. In order to meet the views of the commanding genl. this company gave up its captain, who resigned solely to perfect the arrangement, and elected Capt. Lane (son of old Joe) captain, and another skilled artillerist as 1st lieut. (additional). The company had gone down to near the minimum of companies. Immediately it received large accessions from home of our cleverest young men, who have enlisted in it *for the war* as artillerists. We hear Maj. Monger, now in command of the 9th demands its restoration to his regiment. I want you to see Mr. Benjamin personally and give him all the facts and request him to prevent it. His rule does not apply except to exchanges from one regiment to another. Besides, this business cannot be undone. The men say they have enlisted as artillery and will not serve as infantry, especially in that regiment, and the govt. and company will therefore lose thirty or forty of first rate men and that too under the most disagreeable circumstances to the service. Please attend to this matter for the boys before you leave. I feel great interest in the matter because I know all the men. They are from my town mostly and I got many of them to volunteer for the war in that company as artillery which they would not have done otherwise. Indeed the identical men refused to do so until the change was made.

Nothing new in camp, sending back, stripping the men naked under the same old pretences of a fight or an early movement. The troops are in pretty good health considering all the circumstances here and in good spirits, hoping for some stirring events soon somewhere. I suppose that Miles bill meant Lee for commander in chief and Mr. Benjamin for war. It is the old policy under new arrangements. The President, I thought, must have Lee about him, and they together will be Sec. at War, no matter who is in the office nominally. B. will make them as good a head clerk as they can get. The roads are impassable for waggons with burthens.

Howell Cobb To John B. Lamar. E.

Richmond va., *7 March, 1862.* Dear Col., I had intended before leaving here to have written you fully on the present and probable future of the country but an order just received hastens me off to my post. A brigade of five thousand men from the peninsula, including my old regiment and Tom's legion, have been ordered to Suffolk and placed under my command. The brigade will reach Suffolk to day and I shall go there to morrow. As the order has just been handed to me, I have my hands full to get all things ready. As yet none of my staff are with me and I have every thing to do. I expect/ Johnie, Jim Barrow and Mr. Whitner to night.

For a time the late disasters had a most depressing effect upon almost every one but the panic has passed. All are again in good spirits and new life and energy have been infused into the whole military department of the government.... A commanding Genl. will be put at the head of the army, which will have a good effect in restoring confidence and quieting opposition. Genl. Lee will be the man and I think will make a good officer. The enemy are evidently now pushing with all their might to throw an overwhelming army into Ky. and Tennessee. Their object is to separate those States from the South and to hold military possession of them. On this line their evident policy is to get possession of Norfolk and Weldon and thus separate Virginia first and then North Carolina from the cotton states. The whole programme is to isolate the cotton states. They believe that with the border states subjugated, they bring the balance of us to terms in good time. On our side we have confidence in our ability to defeat these plans of the enemy and the energy with which the Government is now mustering up the army, inspiring hope and confidence. I have never desponded myself and do not now. We have hard work ahead and a good deal of it but we are equal to it and the country is now responding with true spirit.

We are getting arms both from abroad and of our own manufacture and in this respect I am happy to find that we are better off than I had feared. There is still much anxiety about powder but the Government say that they are doing better in that respect than they had expected.

I have given you thus hurriedly a sketch of the true state of things as far as I have been able to learn them. As however I have no confidential relationship with either the President or his cabinet, you must take my suggestions as the best judgment I can form from the lights before me.

P. S.—My opportunities for writing will be bad for a time, still direct to me here care of Mr. Browne.

Robert Toombs To Alexander H. Stephens. R.

Camp Near Orange C. H. va., *March U, 1862.*

Dear Stephens, I am scarce of paper this morning and am compelled to write you on an old soiled sheet. Since they recommenced the delivery of the mail all of yours since I left Richmond have come to hand. I recd. four of the back ones yesterday evening for all of which I am greatly obliged to you. Davis came down here with Lee two days ago (that is to Gordonsville), had an interview with Johnston and the result as far as I hare learned it is, G. W. Smith goes to Aquia District in place of Holmes who goes to N. Carolina. Holmes takes one of his brigades and Wilcox's brigade from this division which leaves today from Richmond. I do not know who will be our immediate commander in Smith's place. We are very sorry to lose him. We hear the Pres. has appointed D. R. Jones a Maj. Genl. and will probably put him in Smith's place. Mrs. Jones says it is so as to the appointment. We hear also that Paul J. Semmes has been made a Brig. Genl. Is it so? I wish to know for special reasons. If it be so I can then perhaps do something with the re-enlistment of his regiment.

Col. Thomas1 has again tendered his resignation, which I have accepted. This time he bases it entirely on the state of his health which is very bad. He will probably leave tomorrow or next day. I think it is well for himself and the service. We have no other camp news except the course of the War Department touching the Irwin Guards. It will break up one of the finest companies in the army to gratify a drunken vagabond who can't recruit, for nobody will join him, and must therefore for his *own account,* not the public service, hold on to what he has got. The rule he refers to does not apply to transfers of companies to other duties and to another arm of the service. If you have opportunity please bring it before Randolph.2 What in the devil has Joe Brown to do with it? I cannot imagine. After the troops go into the Confederate service the govr's power over them is at an end.

You wrote me about the record in the Grimes case in Hancock. I do not think I have one of those papers, but if I have send to Mr. Reese and he will find them in my Hancock bundle. I hope you will try that and the Fraly case, as I had my fee in both of these, which has given me great trouble.

I feel great concern about the Govt. Davis seems determined to perpetuate inefficiency in the Navy and P. Office especially, and the Senate is so small, independent of its material, it cannot maintain itself against the patronage of four hundred millions and all the general offices of the army and all the civil offices of the Republic. Davis will immediately reduce it to a mere *lit de justice.* I should not mind that much if he had capacity himself to carry on the govt. but he has not. We shall get our independence but it will be in spite of him.

If he would take every man he could command at Charleston, Savannah and Mobile, leave those cities to local defence or even to the enemy temporarily, with them strengthen Johnston (Sidney) 1 Thomas W. Thomas. G. W. Randolph, then recently appointed Confederate Secretary of War. and Beauregard, let them put in and whip Buell in Tennessee well and we should thereby save Tenn., Ky., Miss. and Ark. Everything depends on quickness and firmness in Tennessee. I do not know what they are doing there but have very little hope that they are doing anything for the public welfare.

Robert Toombs To Alexander H. Stephens. R.

Camp Near Orange C. H. va., *March 28th, 1862.*

Dear Stephens, I recd. your letters thro' Capt. Harris, and your subsequent notes. I expected to have seen you before you left for the South, until a few hours ago; but we have been in the most curious condition for the last twenty-four hours, I suppose, that an army ever found itself in. Yesterday morning I was ordered to be ready at 7 o'clock and march into the Valley to the assistance of Jackson. Just as I was leading my brigade out of camp that order was countermanded. In the evening we were ordered to be ready at 6 o'clock this morning to march ('twas said) to Fredericksburg. We got all ready, struck tents, loaded waggons, etc., etc.—and that order was countermanded. Then within an hour I was ordered to get all hands ready and take the R. Road to Richmond this evening and send the Battery down by the common roads. I put Blodgett in motion and was about moving again to the depot when another order came suspending this one! and here we are waiting for something to turn up! But we have got used to these things and the boys make a joke of it. It is yet probable we may start to Richmond tomorrow. I suppose McClellan must be demonstrating upon the capital. The weather is clear and warm and the roads rapidly improving. My cough is getting the benefit of it as well as the roads. and it is better than at any time since I came to camp.

Thomas has gone home. I think it was well for him. I do not think with his bad health and tempestuous temperament he would have lived a month longer in camp. We hear Genl. Semmes is made a Brigadier. I suppose it is true. I am sorry to lose his regiment. It is well drilled and fine material. None of them will re-enlist before they go home, and don't think a great many of them then for some time to come.

I think we have the greatest possible need for our best troops, and all we can get. for the next six months. We are in the very crisis of our fate and I see nothing at Richmond which seems to appreciate and prepare for it. All of our troops are in pretty good health—some bad cases of diarrhoea and pneumonia but they lessening from the fine weather. The staff and your nephew in good health. 73566—13 38

Howell Cobb To His Wife. E.

Dam No. 2, Near Yorktown va., *15 April, 1862.*

My Dear Wife, Whilst waiting at headquarters for orders I write you this hasty letter. The two armies are drawn up on opposite sides of the Warwick River, within a half mile of each other, and we have a little skirmishing every day. As neither party is disposed to cross over the line it may be days or weeks before any battle takes place and it may be that the enemy finding us stronger than they expected will retire and strike at some other point. Our army is a fine one and now numbers forty thousand, and reinforcements are arriving daily. Though the enemy have larger numbers I think our army will be large enough, as a greater number of men cannot be used. We are all in excellent health and the finest spirits...

.

We are living in the woods without tents or covering. I have a tent as my headquarters because I am obliged to be protected from the rain to do my writing.... Don't feel uneasy or anxious about us, as we never have a gloomy moment except when we think of the anxiety felt by our loved ones at home for our comfort and safety.

General Toombs and his command arrived on the peninsula yesterday. We have Georgians enough here now to whip the Yankees if we had to do the whole work ourselves. But the whole army is a noble one—as I believe, the greatest army for its size ever assembled on this continent.

It will be difficult to write, but be assured I will give you any important news by telegraph. Therefore put no credit in the thousand rumors that will be put afloat. Why, even here we have the most absurd reports in camp from different parts of the line and it is hard to say what they amount to by the time they reach Georgia. Tell Howell he can come on if he wants to do so, but I think he had better remain with you for the present. My orders are ready and I must close.

Robert Toombs To Alexander H. Stephens. R.

Camp Near Richmond, Va., *17th May, 1862.*

Dear Stephens, I recd. your letter of the 1st May and one since, the date of which I forget, as in pursuance of your directions I destroy them when read. I recd. it on the march retreating from the enemy. We had a rough time in the Peninsula, lost about J of my men by exposure mainly, having only lost some 10 or 12 killed and thirty or forty wounded. The most of them I suppose will come back some time or another. We were kept in the trenches, often times a foot deep in water, for eighteen days, without any necessity or ob ject that I could learn. except the stupidity and cowardice of our officers. McClellan was there with his whole army, a good deal less I think than ours, and we could have whipped as easily there as anywhere else. But as usual we burnt up everything and fled, were attacked in the retreat, and left in the hands of the enemy some ten or twelve hundred of our killed, wounded and sick, and that *after a decided victory.* This is called generalship!!

I have no news. My health continues good—better than when I returned to the army. My cough has pretty nearly left me. I found out that smoking was ruining my throat and I quit it.

This army will not fight until McClellan attacks it. Science will do anything but fight. It will burn, retreat, curse, swear, get drunk, strip soldiers—anything but fight.

Davis's incapacity is lamentable, and the very thought of the baseness of Congress in the impressment act makes me sick. I feel but little like fighting for a people base enough to submit to such despotism from such contemptible sources. Let me hear from you when at leisure. I have poor conveniences for writing but little time and no heart for the business.

Robert Toombs To George Hill And Others (telegram).1

Richmond va., *June 11, 1862.* Gentlemen: Your telegram has been received. I refuse a single hand. My property, as long as I live, shall never be subject to the orders of those cowardly miscreants, the Committees of Public Safety of Randolph County, Ga. , and Eufaula. You may rob me in my absence, but you cannot intimidate me.

Thomas W. Thomas To Alexander H. Stephens. R.

Elberton, Geo., *19th June, 1862.* Dear Sir: There is a matter you can do for me better perhaps than I could do it for myself. I can see no impropriety in asking the favour; but if you see any I cheerfully yield to your better judgement.

I wish to become the editor of the Constitutionalist/ and I would undertake that and the control of the Field & Fireside for twenty five hundred dollars. It is not much to say that I can do it as well as Atkinson who now manages both. Now the service you can do me is to communicate with the proprietor, and test him on the sub 1 I. W. Avery, " History of the State of Georgia from 1850 to 1881." N. Y. 1881, p. 231. This was a telegram sent by Toombs to a committee consisting of George Hill, A. F. Newsom, and William Carter. A widespread movement was In progress through local conventions and committees for the diversion of labor from cotton production to that of food supplies. Toombs, however, was a champion of Individualism, and as a protest against this movement had directed the overseer of his plantation, which lay In Randolph County, Ga., near Eufaula, Ala., to plant a full crop of cotton.

'An Influential newspaper published at Augusta, Oa.
ject. I would be willing to resign now and commence at once. I intend to enter the newspaper business, being induced thereto by reasons (chiefly but not altogether) with which you are acquainted. I would be willing to purchase a half interest but prefer to un-

dertake it simply as a salaried editor. I would suggest that in your first approaches you do not mention the sum I have named, but this is merely a suggestion—do the thing as you think fit.

You are perhaps the best judge living of my fitness for either place and of course I can't expect you to give him any but a perfectly candid opinion. If you do not think me qualified to manage the Field & Fireside, then I leave it in your discretion to mention only the other.

My health is precarious—I have strange attacks about once a week, the head is very hot and painful and the body cold, and all the time I suffer from disorders of the stomach and liver. Still at times I feel so well that I cannot doubt an ultimate recovery.

John C. Whitner To Howell Cobb. E.

West Point ga., *June 28th, 1862.* My Dear Sir: It has been nearly a week since I wrote you that the boxes containing the papers relating to proceedings of Provisional Congress had arrived, and yet I am not prepared to begin writing—nor even to make a full report of what the papers are. I write merely to advise you of " progress." The papers were in great disorder, and as I am rather green in such matters, and having no one to give me information, it took me some time to even begin straightening up. The boxes were opened at my house in presence of three gentlemen whom I duly swore, and after hours of work they concluded that I had better sort up and label packages before they attempted an inventory and report. Early next week they will report to you. Without intending to give a full report I would state as being in the boxes, 1 large leather bound blank book 740 pp—59 pp written up with proceedings of open sessions, nearly thro' 1st sessn. Cong.—balance blank. 1 paper bound book 215 pp—155 pp containing Journals secret sessions thro' 1st session of Congress. A large leather bound book 630 pp containing proceedings of executive sessions thro' 3rd sess. Cong. Journals of executive sessions from 18th Nov. to 17 Feb'y I have not yet been able to find, except fragmentary pieces, and many (perhaps all) of Prest's messages, nominations etc. I hope by patience in collecting and arranging these fragments to be able to get the entire records consecutively. There are two other books which appear to be Registers of Acts of Congress, and any quantity of papers which I have not yet even fully examined. As to what Mr. Hooper has done I will leave for the three men to report fully. He has recorded in books Journals of open and secret sessions as just stated, viz: open sessions to 16 March, secret sessions Do. and executive sessions thro' 3rd session, that is I mean to 20 July, 1861. All else of the Journals are on paper like this or foolscap, with corrections, interlineations, printed matter pasted in, etc., tied in tape and labelled for each day. Of course these, being at best rough drafts or full notes, have to be copied in books before the first Journals of Congress can be said to be complete. Shall I do this? In their present form they are not permanent and would not be creditable to the Govt. to have preserved. For instance in some cases the entry is "A message was reed. from the President through his private secretary, Mr. Josselyn and was read as follows "—but no message inserted. and so on. Mr. Hooper has commenced the Journal of Convention, beginning with 28 Febry, and the Permanent Constitution, and has written up as far as 6th March—I presume about half in relation to that Constitution. But the resolution of Congress requires you to have ready " two copies of Journals of the Provisional Congress and the proceedings of the Convention which framed the Provisional and Permanent Constitutions." I was reading the resolution yesterday. Now ought we not to have begun with the Provisional Constitution first? Another question—where are the original records of proceedings of this Convention? I can't find them in Journals of secret, open or executive sessions, nor to themselves, unless mixed in detached pieces with other papers which I have not yet opened and examined minutely. It would seem as Mr. Hooker had commenced the copy that they should be collected together. Perhaps Mr. Dixon or some of the other old Asst. Clerks could tell. But I will write you again on this point in a few days after a fuller examination of all the papers. I would like information or rather your opinion...1

Joseph E. Brown To Alexander H. Stephens. (Private.)

Marietta ga., *July 2d, 1862.* Dear Sir: Your letter of 20th inst. was handed to me yesterday and I regret that I had not received it sooner. I believe however that I have taken in my reply to the President substantially the same views which I am happy to know you hold on the powers of Congress, etc.2 I deeply regret that the President. whom I have regarded as a leading State Rights man. should have given in his adhesion to the doctrines 1 The remainder of this MS. is missing.

2 The Confederate conscription act, approved April 16, 1862, gave occasions for an elaborate controversy between Governor Brown and President Davis. The correspondence, extending from Apr. 22 to Oct. 18, 1862, Is published in Herbert Fielder's " Life of Joseph E. Brown," Springfield, Mass. , 1883, pp. 355-397; also in the "Confederate Records of the State of Georgia," Atlanta, 1910, 111 107-352. of unlimited congressional powers. His position enables him to give to public opinion a very unfortunate bias for his present views. I am satisfied however that my position is the position of the old State Rights leaders from the days of 1798 till the present time, and I am willing to stand or fall by these doctrines. I entered into this revolution to contribute my humble mite to sustain the rights of the states and prevent the consolidation of the Government, and I am still a rebel till this object is accomplished, no matter who may be in power. I am not certain whether I fully agree with you in reference to the "militia." If by the distinction between volunteers and those drafted or compelled to enter the service you intend

to be understood that regiments of volunteers which have been formed and officered by the States under requisitions for troops made by the President are part of the regular army and that only the troops raised by the States by *draft* to fill requisitions are in the sense of the Constitution militia, I must doubt the correctness of the position. It seems to me that the Government of the Confederacy can only raise armies by voluntary enlistment, and as you say, that it has no power to raise them by draft or conscription but must make requisition on the states when it needs more than it can itself raise by voluntary enlistment. When the requisition is made on the state for a certain number of regiments and it responds by tendering the number raised by voluntary enlistment and not by draft, I think these regiments are part of the militia of the State employed in the service of the Confederacy and that the State has the right to appoint the officers. This is the condition of a large proportion of the troops now in the service from this State. I have filled repeated requisitions but in all cases by the tender of volunteers and have raised no regiment by draft. I do not suppose however that you intend by the general language used to say that all who enter the service by voluntary enlistment are part of the regular forces or army without regard to the fact whether they were raised by direct tender to the Confederacy or under requisition on the State.

I presume you have before this time seen my reply. Please give me your opinion of the correctness of the positions I have taken, and as the correspondence may not end there I will thank you for any additional suggestions. I prepared it at Canton while confined by attention to a sick family and made it longer than I should have preferred, though I wished to cover all the ground I have occupied. I was somewhat astonished at the course taken by the President in the publication. It was not fair to publish part of a correspondence in the manner in which this was done. Can it be that the object was to obtain a verdict of the people without permitting the whole case to go to the jury? If so it was more like the trick of the politician than the act of the statesman. I shall make my headquarters here for most of the summer.

I trust your health is improved and that you may be long spared to your country.

Joining you and our fellow citizens in congratulations and thanks to Almighty God for the splendid victory which has attended our arms at Richmond, I am very truly your friend.

John C. Whitner To Howell Cobb. E.

West Point ga., *July 2, 1862.*

My Dear Sir: I wrote you the other day, mentioning I could not find in the boxes sent me the original Journal of the Convention which framed the Permanent Constitution. On fuller examination I can't yet find those records, and deem it proper to report that fact to you forthwith that you may make enquiries about them or instruct me what to do. I can't find original Journals of executive sessions from 18 Nov. to 17 Febry—only *briefs* (and the briefest sort too), and they not probably all here. What shall I do in reference to these? You perceive these memoranda must first be found before I can write full copies. In addition to questions asked the other day I would enquire whether these different sessions—" open," "secret." "executive," and "Proceedings of Convention" must be copied in separate books?

We humbly trust God has spared the lives of all our loved ones in the late terrible fight. To Him we commend each of you.

Robert Toombs To Alexander H. Stephens. R.

Camp Near Richmond, Va., *July Uth, 1862.*

Dear Stephens, I have reed. several letters from you since my last, all of which I need not assure you were very acceptable and gave me a great deal of pleasure. Since about 12th of May I think I have until day before yesterday been in the immediate front of the enemy, doing the hardest kind of the most dangerous and disagreeable service and in the least desirable positions for any purpose whatever and a large portion of the time without the least conveniences of any kind, most of official work having to be done with a pencil as I could get often neither pen or ink and was debarred the use of lights at night for military reasons arising from close proximity to the enemy.

On the day of the great battle of Gaines's Mill I was stationed on this side the Chickahominy in full view of the raging strife all day, and near night was ordered to advance and attack the enemy to prevent his sending reinforcements over to the other side. I had but about two thousand men for duty and was in four hundred yards of the enemy's entrenchments whom I knew to be in heavy force. I objected to the order and required it in writing and peremptory. It was given me, and I made the attack. The battle raged with terrible fury for about two hours, the enemy trying to drive me from a position I was ordered to hold at every hazard by that old ass Magruder. I finally repulsed him with loss on my part of two hundred in killed and wounded and on his, from his official report which we found in his camp two days after, of 253 killed and seven or eight hundred wounded. My loss was chiefly with the 2nd and 15th Geo., the 17th and 20th being placed on my flanks to protect them and the attack being directly in front. In this action our gallant friends McIntosh and Burch and Jno. Tilly fell. My men fought like lions this unnecessary battle, and the thanks we got for it was a lie sent out from Magruder's headquarters before the action was over that I had attacked without orders and was repulsed. The next day he ordered another attack with 7th and 8th Georgia who were roughly handled and driven back. That too I think he sought to put on D. R. Jones. On Sunday we began the pursuit of the enemy and fought him on Sunday, Monday and Tuesday evenings. Tho' we were in Sunday's fight we had nothing but shells and cannonading in our part of the line which did but little damage, and we got into the Monday evening's fight just as it closed and camped on the battlefield amid the dead and dying and wounded and spent the night in trying to do something for them. It was a scene never to be forgotten. On Tuesday, after Lee and Longstreet had declined to attack the enemy who had near fifty pieces of cannon in an almost impregnable position, Magruder, after sending in a few cannon and having-them knocked into strips in ten minutes, attempted to carry the guns with his infantry. We had three quarters of a mile to march after we got into the open field, under a clear, naked, direct fire of grape and canister and spherical case shot, without the least protection. The result was that from time to time every brigade that attacked them on that plateau, and there were at least ten brigades that did so, were broken up, driven off, and swept from the field, my own among them. I lost 194 men in killed and wounded in ten minutes on that crest, and would have lost them all in thirty minutes more if they had been permitted to remain there. The upshot of the whole matter was that we were utterly repulsed in the attack on the battery. But the enemy were so much worsted and not knowing our condition retreated as soon after dark as he could get away, very luckily for us in my judgment.

But the result of the whole matter is that we have utterly defeated and broken up and demoralized McClellan's army, killed, wounded and took prisoners in all the actions not under twenty thousand of his best men and scattered at least half that number who are over land and water from here to Old Point Comfort, hundreds of them preferring our capturing them to returning to service. I have seen many hundreds of them huddle together and send us in word to come and take them.

But our own loss has been terrible and of many of our best men. They were fought without skill or judgment and were victorious by dint of dead hard fighting, thousands and thousands of them never receiving an order except from brigade or regimental commanders for whole hours upon hours in battle. Longstreet has won more reputation, and I think deservedly, than all of our Major Generals put together. Stonewall Jackson and his troops did little or nothing in these battles of the Chickahominy and Lee was far below the occasion. If we had had a general in command we could easily have taken McClellan's whole command and baggage, whereas he saved all his wagons and stores except what he burned, and far the greater part of his valuable outfit. After the fight of Friday the 27th he was not pursued with the least vigour and never was attacked except when he wanted to be, at his rearguard which of course he made as strong as possible. Then while we have gained so much I cannot but feel sad and disheartened at what we lost. It was Manassas and Shiloh over again, barren victories without results when everything was in our power. McClellan will reorganize his yet powerful army, get reinforcements, and we shall have all this blood and toil to shed over again, and worst of all the poor people cannot see it, and all who will not sing peans to such blunderers and imbeciles will probably be crushed and dishonoured. Such is a brief history of the events of the last fortnight. Jackson has returned to the Valley, part of the army has crossed the James River (Huger's and Holmes's commands) and the rest of us, mainly the old army of the Potomac, are here around the works of Richmond.

I recd. a letter from Linton written the same day as your last and am much obliged by his suggestions which I think extremely judicious and correct. I will write him in a day or two. I will send you this by private hand, and therefore have spoken with freedom. Du Bose is very unwell and will perhaps go home tomorrow. Barrett is unwell at home; the rest of us well except myself. I am a good deal worn out with diarrhoea which threatens to become chronic. Being stationary now I will watch it with more care. I shall leave the army the instant I can do so without dishonor. Davis and his Janissaries (the regular army) conspire for the destruction of all who will not bend to them, and avail themselves of the public danger to aid them in their selfish and infamous schemes. Farewell. Let me hear from you when convenient.

John B. Lamar To Mrs. Howell Cobb. E.

Macon ga., *Aug. 9, 1862.* My Dear Sister,... I have my business all arranged so that I can be absent for several weeks, except my negro shoes. And I leave my measures with Mix with directions to get the best shoes he can at any price. I put no limit because if I did the negroes would go barefooted next winter. I will have to pay $4.00 or $5 a pr. for them, but I will have them if they cost any price. The winter cloth I have stored away in my passage, of good nice Georgia plains, and also the osnaburgs for underclothes. Our negroes know less of hard times than any people I have any knowledge of, black or white (except our overseers who live like princes, and I am willing they should as long as they make plenty of everything). Tobacco is the only thing the negroes can possibly complain of wanting. Their cotton is unsold and they don't handle as much money as usual, but have plenty chickens to buy tobacco.

John C. Whitner To Howell Cobb. E.

West Point ga., *Augt. 12th, 1862.* My Dear Sir: Mr. Dixon reached here yesterday and has been busy overhauling books, papers, etc. You will rejoice to hear that he has perfectly preserved the Journals of the Convention which framed the *Permanent* Constitution. Those of the Provisional Constitution are among the proceedings of *secret session.* These journals Mr. Dixon has always carried in his trunk, never allowed Hooper to have them. The copy written out in book Mr. H. had, and Dixon says he thinks he can find it without any difficulty as well as many of the other missing papers. He leaves with me the Journals and says it is useless for me to go on to Richmond. He takes with him all the notes and papers of executive session, and if he cannot find the Journals in Richmond will rewrite them. As.fast as he gathers up any papers will send them to me by express. Under these circumstances I consider it useless for me to go on, and that I had best proceed with writing. Mr. D. agrees with me that the *Journals of Congress* can't be considered complete till copied in book, that Mr. H. did not have finished by his subclerks this work, and that I should proceed with it myself before commencing the copies proper. He thinks from the wording of the instruction to have copies made that it was intended to make an *excerpt* of the journals of secret session all that relating to adoption of Provisional Constitution and to embrace in one book these proceedings and those relating to Permanent Constitution as Journals of the "*Conventions.*"" What do you say? I shall go to Atlanta and make enquiries as to blank books, etc. I have repeated to Mr. D. what you told me to write from Athens, that he may consider himself employed to assist me and that he will be compensated.

There is one thing I wish you would do—write to Secy, of War to give me and those I have to employ to assist me some showing of exemption from conscription. The poppinjays employed as enrolling officers and the defeated army officers appointed to command the camps delight in harrassing and putting to expense everybody. I have offered to show the law of Congress and your appt., but I have no doubt without the showing asked I shall be forced to go to camp or appeal myself to Secy, of War. I am obliged to have assistants in arranging the confused papers and I have chosen those who have been pronounced unable to do military duty. It is not every man that can work at sucli things, and of course I have selected those competent and thus given offence to *incompetent* enrolling officers.

If you still think it is necessary to go on to Richmond I will do so: Dixon seems to regard himself to be *paid* for that, and will therefore give the matter his attention.

We are all well and hope you are still improving and beg to be remembered to each and all. Mr. Dixon sends his kindest regards.

Robert Toombs To Alexander H. Stephens. It.

Gordonsville, Va., *Aug. 22nd, 1862.*

Dear Stephens, Your letter of the 20th by DuBose was received yesterday evening. DuBose arrived here a few moments after I did. The army is strung out from here to the Rappahannock, the front being yesterday between 25 and 30 miles from this place. The enemy are retreating. Whether they made a stand yesterday on the other side of the Rappahannock I have not learned. If they have not they will fall back on Washington City I think.

I am here under arrest. On the 18th we were near Raccoon Ford on the Rapidan, reached the place near eight and one of my regiments was ordered out on pickett to guard the road leading to the Raccoon Ford. The next morning we were ordered to have all our rations cooked and be ready for marching at a moment's warning. The rations and cooking utensils got into camp that morning, the 19th, and I went out to pickett in order to make arrangements for the 15th to get their food and get it cooked. I found out while there that an entire brigade of A. P. Hill's division were between my pickett and the ford just in front, which made my pickett wholly useless. Upon learning these facts I sent word to Longstreet by one of his aids how matters stood and requested him to relieve my picketts that I might execute the order for the regiment to cook their food and prepare for the pursuit of the enemy. Longstreet was absent. Upon learning this fact, and knowing the very short time the regiment had to cook flour and meat and that it was their only chance, as no waggons were to accompany us, I directed the Colonel to come back to camp to cook &c.

When Longstreet returned and heard of it he ordered me arrested for " usurpation of authority," a new crime to me and to the articles of war.1 This was the sole and only cause of my arrest which of course was very unexpected to me. I then asked to be relieved from following the army during my arrest. He granted it and permitted me to come here to remain "for the present." The next morning a cannonading began in the front and expecting an action that day I rode forward, sent Longstreet an explanation of the facts, which he had never heard, asked that the arrest be suspended until I could fight with my brigade in the action. This I was informed both by Genls. Wilcox, Evans and Pryor, was a very usual and proper course. Unfortunately for me as I got up to my brigade it raised a loud cheer, which so incensed the magnates Lee and Longstreet, &c., who were near by, that I got no reply to my request but was ordered peremptorily to this place and two charges put in against me for breaking my arrest and disobeying orders in not immediately coming here. This is the whole case and I send you a copy of the arrest and will send you all the correspondence tomorrow that you may see the truth officially and be able to correct the thousand lies which my enemies avail themselves of every occasion to propagate. Of course the papers will not be published, but you can make such other use of them as will put me right. Today I have sent another demand to be released for the purpose of battle and when I get the reply will send it to you. The whole, thing was as unexpected to me as that this letter should produce a hostile meeting between you and me. My zeal for the public service and desire to prepare my starving regiment for battle is my sole and only fault. I must think it a pretext. You shall have all the papers so soon as I can have them copied.

Before I recd. John's application (about two weeks ago) I recommended Bidford Loftin, ordnance sergeant of the 15th Geo. for brigade ordnance sergeant. I have heard nothing from it as yet. But for that I would have recommended John with the greatest pleasure.

There is nothing new in the camps.

I hope the army now will continue onward and reach Maryland before Lincoln raises his large reinforcements. This army is now strong, stronger than it will ever be again. It will weaken each day, and you will find it difficult to keep it together next winter. All that is in it should be got out of it 1 Toombs was released from arrest in Ume to participate in the second battle of Manassas, Aug. 30, 1862. For Longstreet's account of the episode see his From Manassas to Appomattox, pp. 161, 166.
now, and I think a quick march into Maryland would cause Washington to be evacuated and close the war.

Let me hear from you. I will write tomorrow or send my letter and papers by first safe hands. All well. My health excellent—has not been so good in five years.

P. S.—I have written this very hastily and there may be verbal inaccuracies which you will detect and correct.

Joseph E. Brown To Alexander H. Stephens. R.
(Private.)

Canton, ga., *Sept. 1st, 1862.*

Dear Sir: I have the pleasure to acknowledge the receipt of your letter of the 26th ult. and am gratified that you take the view which you have expressed about the action of Genl. Bragg in his declaration of martial law over Atlanta and his appoint men t, as the newspapers say, of a civil governor with aids, etc.

I have viewed this proceeding as I have others of our military authorities of late with painful apprehensiveness for the future. It seems military men are assuming the whole powers of government to themselves and setting at defiance constitutions, laws, state rights, state sovereignty, and every other principle of civil liberty, and that our people engrossed in the struggle with the enemy are disposed to submit to these bold usurpations tending to military despotism without murmur, much less resistance. I should have called this proceeding into question before this time but I was hopeful from the indications which I had noted that Congress would take such action as would check these dangerous usurpations of power, and for the further reasons that I have already come almost into conflict with the Confederate authorities in vindication of what I have considered the rights of the State and people of Georgia, and I was fearful, as no other governor seems to raise these questions, that I might be considered by good and true men in and out of Congress too refractory for the times. I had therefore concluded to take no notice of this matter till the meeting of the legislature when I expect to ask the representatives of the people to define the bounds to which they desire the Governor to go in the defense of the rights and sovereignty of the state. I confess I have apprehensions that our present General Assembly does not properly reflect the sentiments of our people upon this great question, but if the Executive goes beyond the bounds where he is sustained by the representatives of the people he exposes himself to censure without the moral power to do service to the great principles involved. I fear we have much more to apprehend from military despotism than from subjugation by the enemy. I trust our generals will improve well their time while we have the advantage and the enemy are organizing another army. Hoping that your health is good and begging that you will write me when your important duties are not too pressing to permit it, I am very truly your friend.

Howell Cobb To His Wife. E.
Camp Sarah, Leesburg va., *6 Sept., 1862.*

My Dear Wife, A wagon train leaves in the morning for Rapidan Station and I take the chance to write a line though I can give you no additional news to my letter of yesterday. We are now under orders to march in a few minutes and from all I hear our destination is across the Potomac and into Maryland. The great body of the army has been assembled at this point and there seems to be a general movement in the direction of Maryland. Genl. Lee is evidently pushing forward with great energy and so far with great success. The campaign in this quarter cannot be a long one and our General is therefore making his hay whilst the sun shines. The army of the enemy is represented as greatly demoralized whilst our own is in the finest spirits. It is astonishing to see how the men submit to every trial. Ordinarily a regiment is entitled to ten wagons to carry their baggage—today we have orders that hereafter a regiment can only have *one,* and yet there is no spirit of complaint.

I have heard nothing more from the late battles since I wrote to you. Pearce Moore and Lewis Kenan were both wounded, but not seriously. I know of no other casualties among those you know. All of our crowd continue well having stood the hard march as well as the most veteran troops in the army.

I have just been informed that two divisions of our army have crossed the river and are now in Maryland. We shall follow and cross either tonight or in the morning.

The weather is beautiful and pleasant. All send love to all.

Howell Cobb To His Wife. E.
Charleston, Va., *17 Sept., 1862.* My Dear Wife, This is the first opportunity I have had to write for some time, and I regret that now my letter cannot wear the same cheerful tone that my former ones did. My telegraph from Richmond will have informed you of the death of your brother1 who fell in the hottest of the fight, struggling to rally our broken columns. He lived until the next day and suffered no great pain. The battle in which he fell was the most terrific one of the war. My brigade and about seven hundred other men, making my whole force about twenty-one hundred men, encountered more than fifteen thousand of the enemy. We were flanked and overwhelmed but our troops gen l Colonel John B. Lamar.
erally fought well. The odds were too great and we were driven back. The force we met were reinforcements on their way to Harper's Ferry. Out battle with them delayed their advance until

the enemy surrendered, and this is the only compensation we have for the heavy loss we have met. Jeff Lamar I fear is dead. We cannot get certain information but all the accounts agree that he was twice wounded and the last time severely. The Ga. Legion under him made as pallant a fight as was ever made by men. Though surrounded and overwhelmed, they continued to fight on, and of the two hundred and fifty men that went into the battle only eighty-three have returned to camp. Some we know are prisoners, among that number is Capt. Camak. Of the others we only have rumors and they are too uncertain and unsatisfactory to repeat. I fear that Dr. MelPs son was killed but even that is not certain. I carried into the fight of my brigade about thirteen hundred men, and the next morning only three hundred answered to their names. The number increased to eight hundred and I hope others may yet come in. Some who were reported as certainly killed have come in, which encourages me to a lingering hope for any and all that are still absent.

The enemy on the morning after our fight the 14th surrendered Harper's Ferry with fourteen thousand prisoners and ammunition and stores innumerable. The two armies still face each other and a decisive battle may be looked for at any moment. Our army is in fine spirits and confident of success.

...

The blow which has fallen upon our own family circle in the death of your noble brother is indeed a severe one. Well do I know how it will grieve your heart when the news shall reach you. I need hardly, my dear wife, say how my own heart has bled and how it flows with sympathy for you in this trying hour. You have however your Comforter who never fails you in the hour of your trials, and to that kind Providence must I commend your wounded heart, not doubting He will prove your truest and greatest solace and comfort....

I shall join my command this evening or in the morning, and I hope that a few days will settle the struggle at this point, which may prove the beginning of the end of this most unjust and unholy war of persecution.

It will be difficult to get another chance to telegraph or write shortly but I will avail myself of any opportunity if it is only to write a line.

Robert Toombs To Linton Stephens. R.

Washington, Geo., *Deer. 1st, 1862.*
Dear Linton, On my return home I found both your letters of October and 24th Nov. (having left on the 28th before the first reached here). I received from you three letters this summer all of which but one I answerd (the one with reference to my planting cotton). That I intended to answer more at leisure and laid it by and from the activity of the campaign found no leisure. Your views in reference to my position in the senatorial election1 were in entire harmony with my own; and if I had recd. it before the event I should have fully approved it as I do now. I have not the least concealment or delicacy in reference to my position as connected with that office. I would at any time have accepted it if it had been presented to me in a manner which in my judgment indicated a frank desire upon the part of the representatives of the people that I should do so. I trust my conduct has shown that I would accept it on no other terms. I did not desire the position but I was willing to serve the state wherever in her judgment I could be of the most advantage to her. It was and is now my opinion that I could best serve the public cause in the army and I intend to stay there as long as I can with honor, and life lasts; but I am well aware that that scoundrel Jeff Davis will avail himself of any opportunity to drive me from it, with dishonor if he could—but that part of it is in my own hands, I thank God, not in his. I will not conceal from you that I feel a deep resentment against the present legislature. When this revolution was inaugurated I honestly buried the hatchet and gave whatever influence I had to destroy party feeling and admit the Know Nothings to a sincere amnesty. I combatted prejudice against them, and helped them to places of honor and public confidence. The scoundrels sneaked into the legislature under the cry of no party, and every act of their stupid, false and treacherous career has proven how unworthy they were of my generosity and how just was the public condemnation of them. But in spite of their villainy, I got a public good out of them. I then seemed to approve what they heartily hated, and obtained an apparent unanimity until the country could get itself into line of battle when their cowardice will be a sufficient guarantee for their acquiesence in whatever may be done, good or bad. They are now the backers of Jeff Davis simply because they are afraid of being suspected of disloyalty to the revolution. They are a terribly whipped set of scoundrels and are afraid even to do right lest they may be thought to be what they really are, traitors to public liberty. But we have but one danger from them and that is if the enemy should gain decided advantages over us and *they think* he is likely to succeed they will instantly join Lincoln who always had more of their sympathies than Davis. Their i Toombs had been elected to the Confederate Senate by a narrow majority In the Georgia legislature In December, 1861, but had declined the seat. He was a candidate for similar election in 1863, but was defeated by Herschel V. Johnson.
main support of Davis is based on the idea that he is daily making the revolution odious.

It is time that our political turn had an end. If I live until the next election I shall take a hand in it and endeavour to get a hearing for the people and their rights, and I do not in the least doubt what will become of these treacherous cowardly impostors.

Our friend Brown has done some very foolish things which I greatly regret on his account and our own. His whiskey proclamation was as unconstitutional and as foolish as anything that Davis or Lincoln have ever done. His recommendations about taxing cotton show a want of knowledge of the first principles of political economy which is absolutely humiliating to his friends. He is running a fool's race with Davis and his tools, Bragg and Hindman, robbing the sick and oppressing the poor. Lincoln could afford to pay them five hundred million dollars if they can succeed in burning all the cotton we have on hand and preventing the growing any more. All that I have learned by study and reflection for twenty five years on the science of government can be uttered in two lines, or rather three words: "*order, security* and *justice.*" Give society these and you will make it happy if it will be. You can do no more without injustice and robbery. For ten years I have referred all my votes to these three objects. Extortion is a crime against God and man; punish that and let the production and distribution of wealth alone. Producers have nothing to do with morality. That is a question for consumers, and not then for the legislative power. I have been quite sick for the last two days, my wound slowly improving. I shall leave for Richmond in ten or fifteen days. Write to me.

James M. Smythe To Howell Cobb. E.
, Augusta ga., *Declr. 17th, 1862.*

My Dear Sir: In performing the sad office of having sent to you today a dispatch of Major Lamar Cobb informing you of the death of your noble and gallant brother,1 I cannot refrain from expressing to you my heartfelt sympathy in this terrible bereavement. His death has cast a gloom over this city. His exalted abilities and shining virtues were duly appreciated by our citizens who feel that his loss is a. public calamity.

Knowing him as I did, I felt stricken down by the sad intelligence of his death. How valued should be the liberties purchased with such precious blood. May God console you and protect you.

1 Thomas R. R. Cobb, killed In *the* battle of Fredericksburg. 73566—13 39

Joseph E. Brown To Alexander H. Stephens. R.

(Private.)
Milledgeville ga., *Jan. 30th, 1863.*

Dear Sir: I do not intend to be a candidate for election to another term in the Executive office. But I feel a deep interest in seeing someone elected who, while he does his whole duty to the Confederacy, will contend for and sustain to the extent of his ability the rights and sovereignty of the state. It is also important that we have a man who will look well to the finances of the state. This is a question of vital importance to Georgia. In looking over the field for such a man my mind rests upon your brother as my first choice. I have said not a word to him upon the subject nor have I ever before written to any my intention to retire nor have I intimated it to but few friends in conversation. I have thought it as well that my enemies and opposers who I believe generally entertain the opinion that it is my intention to run again, be left with that impression for a time yet, as they will then make their arrangements with a view to that state of things and at the proper time they can be informed of the true state of the case.

I think it best that a few of us who are friends and agree upon the great issues which are likely to come before the country should confer in advance about this matter. It may be too early yet to have much said. Will you give me your views and say what you think would be Linton's feelings about it, and if he will not consent to run; say who else in your opinion would be the best man? I think we could elect him or that we can elect any good man who is popular in the state. The contest may be a hot one and it will be best to give the proper direction to the public mind through the proper channels at no very distant day. I do not think there should be any newspaper notice of it yet. I will exert myself to the extent of my power for Linton if he will run.

Joseph E. Brown To Alexander H. Stephens. R.

Executive Department, Milledgeville ga., *Feby. 16th, 1863.*
Dear Sir: I have the pleasure to acknowledge the receipt of your two letters, which I have read with much interest.

I have not said publicly that I will not under any circumstances be a candidate for another term in this office, but my convictions on that subject are so well settled that I do not think there is any state of facts likely to arise which can induce me to change my purpose. If Linton does not agree to be a candidate I could not be better suited than to run Genl. Toombs. I have the highest confidence in his patriotism, ability, statemanship, and soundness on the vital question of state sovereignty. I should be glad to know whether he would consent to be a candidate. I have only heard the names of Genl. Wright and Capt. Lester mentioned by the advocates of arbitrary power. In my opinion neither of them would be a formidable candidate. I shall be happy at all times to hear any suggestions you may be pleased to make. It is a matter of the first importance that a friend to constitutional liberty be selected for the position.

I have read your letter relating to conscription with more than ordinary interest. You go to the bottom of the subject, and I shall file your letter for future reference.

It was not my purpose in my reply to Mr. Hill to enter into the discussion, as I had discussed the question at length with the President, but only to repel his unjust assault and to call the attention of the public to the inconsistency of his own course.

Robert Toombs To Alexander H. Stephens. R.

Richmond, Va., *March 2nd, 1863.*
Dear Stephens, I recieved your last letter of about ten days since and would have replied before but I expected to be at home before this time. I have after full and careful deliberation for four months past made a decision to resign. so that if I have made a mistake it has not been for the want of careful examination and consideration of the situation. I am now only waiting the form of acceptance and hope to leave here for home on Wednesday next. I

am fully satisfied that I can not remain in the service with any advantage to the public or with honor to myself. I know the President has much desired my resignation; but I waited my own time and points, and got them as well as was possible from so false and hypocrital a wretch. I simply resigned without assigning any reason, reserving to myself all the points. It is a long story and therefore I will not bore you with it until we meet. You are right in opposing the assumption of Confederate debt by the States. I would not endorse a dime of it. It is puerile and disastrous. The Confederate States have unlimited power of taxation over everything within its limits and also over imports and exports. What more do they want but sense and nerve? As to Geo., I suppose Joe Brown will run again. It is understood here that Gartrell will oppose him. No news except what you see in the papers.

Eobert Toombs To His Brigade In The Army Of Northern Virginia.1

Kichmond, Va., *March 5th, 1863.*
To the Officers and Men of Toombs's Brigade:

Soldiers: To-day I cease to command you. I have resigned my commission as Brigadier General in the Provisional Army of the Confederate States. The separation from you is deeply painful to me. I do not deem it proper on this occasion to enter into a detail of the causes which impose this duty upon me. It is only necessary now for me to say, that, under existing circumstances, in my judgment, I could no longer hold my commission under President Davis with advantage to my country, or to you, or with honor to myself. I cannot separate from you without the expression of my wannest attachment to you, and admiration of your noble and heroic conduct from the beginning of this great struggle to the present time. You left your wives and children, kindred, friends, homes, property and pursuits at the very first call of your country, and entered her military service as soon as she was ready to accept you—and from that day to this, you have stood, with but a few brief intervals, in sight of the public enemy, or within hearing of his guns. Upon your arrival in Virginia, in the summer of 1861, you were incorporated into the army of the Potomac; you have shared with that army in all its toils, its sufferings, its hardships and perils, and contributed at least your full share to its glorious career. You have been in the front, the post of danger and of honor, on all the great battle-fields in Northern Virginia and Maryland, from Yorktown to Sharpsburg; neither disheartened by the death of comrades and friends, or disease, or toil, or privations, or sufferings or neglect; nor intimidated by the greatly superior numbers of the enemy whom you have been often called upon to meet and to vanquish; you have on all occasions displayed that heroic courage which has shed undying lustre upon yourselves, your State, your country and her just and holy cause.

Nearly one thousand of the brave men who originally composed your four regiments have fallen, killed or wounded, in battle; your dead you have buried on the battle-field, shed a manly tear over them, left "glory to keep eternal watch" over their graves, and passed on to new fields of duty and danger.

Though it may seem to be the language of extravagant eulogy, it is the truth, and fit, on this occasion, to be spoken. You have fairly won the right to inscribe upon your tattered warflags, the proud boast of Napoleon's old guard, "This brigade knows how to die, but not to yield to the foe." Courage in the field is not your only claim to proud distinction. Since I took command over you, I have not 1 From the Savannah, Ga., Republican, Mar. 10, 1863.
preferred a single charge against, or arraigned one of you before a court martial. Your conduct never demanded of me such a duty. You can well appreciate the feelings with which I part from such a command. Nothing less potent than the requirements of a soldier's honor could, with my consent, wrench us asunder, while a single banner of the enemy floated over one foot of our country. Soldiers! comrades! friends! Farewell!

Howell Cobb To His Wife. E. Quincy fla., *13 March, 1863.*

My Dear Wife, I have just returned from Tallahassee1 where I went on invitation to attend a meeting of cotton planters. The delusive idea of an early peace had run the people mad on the subject of planting cotton. It was really becoming an alarming state of things, and I fear that even yet the matter is not properly understood. With all that was done last year it is difficult to feed the army and support the country. What then is to become of us if instead of planting corn and raising hogs we raise cotton? Starvation and ruin would be upon us. It was to counteract this state of things that this and other meetings have been called. I am glad to say that a most happy effect was produced and many left the meeting to go home and give new directions about their crop. If the same steps are not taken in other portions of the country we shall see hard times next season. As to peace I see no prospect of it at this time. If it comes I shall greet it with my whole heart, but our true policy is to prepare for the worst and look forward to a continuance of the war.

You will see by the papers that the enemy attempted two days ago to land a force in East Florida on the St. John's river, at Jacksonville. They already occupied Jacksonville, and I suppose the object was to garrison the place with a view to further operations in that part of the State. It is in Genl. Finnegan's district and he promptly met them and drove them back through the town to their gunboats. Our loss was one man killed and three horses. The loss of the enemy is not known. This is all the information we have but shall probably hear more about it in a day or two. The report was that they had landed some negro regiments; of this there is no certainty though it is likely to be the case as they have had a negro regiment for some time at Fernandina. In my district every thing remains quiet and I hope will continue so, though I keep up the same activity as if we were expecting to see the Yankees every day. From every quarter the Yankees profess to be preparing for active operations but so far it amounts to nothing more than talk. The great demonstration against Charleston and Savannah has come to naught and we are 1 Cobb had recently been transferred from the command of a brigade In the Army of Northern Virginia to the command of the military district of Florida.

all anxiety to know the next point of their threatening. I see that Genl. Toombs has resigned and in his address to his brigade says that he cannot with honor hold a commission under President Davis. Browne writes me that Toombs's reason for resigning is not known. I am at a loss to unravel the mystery, though I shrewdly suspect that it was the refusal of Davis to promote him, of which I think Toombs had just cause of complaint.

Joseph E. Brown To Alexander H. Stephens. R.

Milledgeville ga., *March 16th, 1863.*

Dear Sir: I received your letter some days since and regret to hear that Linton will not consent to be a candidate, as I trust we could elect him and he is the proper man. In this state of things Genl. Toombs is I presume the proper man. I wish you would write him to come to Milledgeville to the session. You have no doubt seen that I have called the legislature into session Wednesday week. I think it a vital matter that we look to the production of provisions to the exclusion of everything else. I am satisfied our ultimate success depends on the bread supply. My opinion is that Genl. Toombs's cotton crop1 of last year will be the hardest thing he has to carry. I am sure it will be better for him to excuse the act on account of his absence in the face of the enemy and the impertinence of the committee than to justify the policy. If he does the latter he cannot be elected. I wish he would come to Milledgeville pretty early in the session. Cannot you come over a few days?

P. S.—Kenan is trying to injure Genl. Toombs I am told by saying that Toombs says he is the President's enemy and the President is his enemy and that he is coming down to take the stump against him, etc. This is to work upon the fear of the timid who fear the effect of opposition to the President upon any ground in the present condition of things.

Howell Cobb To His Wife. E.

Qtjinct fla., *1 April, 1863.* My Dear Wife, Since I last wrote to you I have been to Tallahassee on a short tour of inspection. Reports had reached me that the Yankees had several steamers at St. Marks and it was thought they intended to land a force. The telegraph wires were down and I had no means of getting correct information, so I determined to go in person. Happily I found the rumors unfounded and everything as quiet as usual. Indeed the only blockade vessel had steamed up and gone off.

1 Toombs had resisted the movement for reducing the cotton output In 1862. See his telegram of June 11, 1862, *supra.*

You have no doubt seen the accounts of the Yankees burning and evacuating Jacksonville. Their conduct is a mystery that cannot be solved. Their burning of the town would look as though they had abandoned the idea of taking permanent possession; but the rumor now is that the negro soldiers fired the town in violation of the positive orders of their officers. From all accounts there was a terrible feeling between the white and negro soldiers and it is said that the negroes sent word to our people that they wanted to return to their homes and would come to us if we would let them. I cannot vouch for the truth of this rumor. I have not seen Genl. Finegan who ought to know. My opinion is that it would have had a good effect to have allowed the negroes who are dissatisfied to have returned to their owners. Since the abandonment of Jacksonville by the Yankees everything has become quiet again though we are keeping a lookout in every direction for them.

I sent the Georgia regulars down to reinforce Genl. F., and they were very much afraid they would not get back to my command; but they are now on their way back to me and I intend to put them in the Arsenal at Chattahoochee to recruit.

We have had a wretched spell of bad weather. For several days there has been constant rain and to day it is clear and cold—not cold enough for frost, but sufficiently so to make every one feel uneasy about their gardens and fruit. I ought to tell you that we have had several messes of peas from our own garden. All well except Frank Pope who had a hard chill on yesterday. He is up and attending to business but looking badly. I suppose we will all have to have a shaking spell before the season is over.

Robert Toombs To Alexander H. Stephens. R.

Washington, Georgia, *Apl. SI, 1863.* Dear Stephens, Your two notes of yesterday and day before were received and this morning George came over with my horse and I send you Bastiat by him. Be sure to take care of it and bring it back to me, as it is probable I shall have nothing else to do for the next year. I wish to devote my time as far as possible to the pursuit of my neglected political studies. I fear you will not have time to write an additional chapter or even introduction extending the " harmonies" and demonstrating their existence where it is evident Bastiat never suspected them to exist. If you have it would be very desirable if you would do so and let it go out with the work. I do not think the booksellers would publish such a work as Bastiat now. Too few people would read it. The world is now too busy to read at all. I wish you would enquire and if possible get for me "The principles of Political Economy and Taxation" by David Ricardo, 1 vol. 8vo. My copy is missing from my library, and I fear is with the missing boxes of my congressional library. The last edition was published in 1821, and it is therefore rare, but apt to be found in all old bookstores. I am now improving more rapidly than at any time since I was sick, and hope soon to be able to go out to the So. West. Sallie is doing well, the rest all in good health.

Howell, Cobb To James A. Seddon. 1 (Unofficial.)

Headquarters, District Of Middle Florida,

Quincy fla., *H May, '63.*

Dr. Sir: I reply at the earliest moment to your communication of the 5th inst. I have felt assured that both the President and yourself were disposed to do all in your power to aid and sustain me in my duties at this position. I only regret that the law would not permit a more prompt organization of the regiment and battalion that I have raised. I am happy however to say that the public service has not suffered on account of it, and if you could witness the drill of the companies you would scarcely credit the fact that they have so recently been brought into the field. In a short time I will be able to forward the muster rolls and shall be able to turn over to the field officers the best drilled regiment in the service. The credit is due to the members of my staff—particularly to my A. A. Genl., Capt. Barrow, the best military tactician in the Army—all of whom have labored cheerfully and faithfully in the additional duties I have imposed upon them.

With the exception of the Ordnance Bureau, your officers at Richmond have done all I could ask them to do.. .. I am still waiting for guns to put in the hands of my men; and if consistent with your sense of duty I should be greatly pleased if you could adopt some of the suggestions made in my last letter on that subject.

I beg to assure you that the offer you have tendered to me to take the head of the Q. M. General's Department is received in the spirit in which it was offered. So far from regarding it in an unpleasant light, I receive it as an expression of confidence both on yours and the President's part—to which I do not feel entitled. I do not hesitate to say to you that I have but one desire and purpose during this war—and that is to serve the country where I feel that I can be of the most use, without the slightest regard to rank or position. If I know myself I have no ambition to gratify, and in a military point of view I am fully conscious of the fact that I am now higher than my merits entitle me to go. With this frank avowal you will 1 From a MS. copy among the Howell Cobb papers, Erwin collection. Seddon was then Confederate Secretary ol War.

give me credit for candor in the reasons I give for declining the position you have offered me. I cannot accept it because I feel certain that I am not qualified for the place. I have neither the knowledge nor the experience to take charge of so important a bureau in the midst of the war when its business is heaviest and most complicated. I know enough of that place to know that I could not discharge its duties satisfactorily to myself—or the country.

In addition to this public reason there is one of a private character which I am sure you will appreciate. It is this,—My wife is in very bad health. Recent and repeated afflictions in our immediate family have so greatly affected her that I cannot tell at what moment I shall be summoned to her side. Nothing but the most imperative sense of duty keeps me in the service at all. Though I have spent only eight days with her in the last six months, and indeed only six weeks in two years, yet I am now within less than two days journey of her, and the consciousness that I can at a moment's warning be with her is a great relief both to her and me. I sincerely desire that such may continue to be the case; and I should have appealed to you to be permitted to remain where I am before this time but for my unwillingness to embarrass the President and yourself with my personal affairs.

Joseph E. Brown To Alexander H. Stephens. R.

Executive Department, Milledgeville ga., *May 21st, 1863.*

Dear Sir: I have this day received and read your letter. Col. Thweatt delivered your message, which has had much to do in shaping my' course. I am daily receiving letters from different parts of the State upon the same subject. The people seem to have become restless to know my decision at this early day; and I have today replied to a letter from Messrs. Schley, Warner, Gardner and May? of Augusta, and have consented to the use of my name. 1 I suppose they will publish it at an early day.

I do assure you in all candor that I have taken this step reluctantly and only because friends in whose judgment I have great confidence think that no other State Rights man who will consent to run could carry the State. It will never do for Georgia to back down from her position, and I am prepared to submit to any personal sacrifice sooner than she shall do it. It is now said that Col. Gartrell will be the Administration candidate and that he boasts that he has the promise of the active support of the Government at Richmond. As I go into this race I cannot on account of the cause nor on my own account submit to defeat if it is possible to prevent it. I do not 1 As candidate for reelection as governor.

think there will be any difficulty; but the only certain rule is to work all the time. I know you have the confidence of the army and I must beg you to write to your friends there and do all you can for me. I suppose the opposition will calculate much on the ability of the Government to control the army. I think I can get a good vote in the army.

The letter of which you saw extracts in the Intelligencer was written by Col. Abda Johnson of Bartow county who commands the 40th Ga. Regmt. at Vicksburg. He is son of Col. Lindsay Johnson of Cass and son-in-law of Judge Trippe. All the family there has always opposed me. It is said they will support me now as will also the Wofford family. The Genl.2 in Va. has been opposed to me but now supports me.

I have negatived the idea of an anti-Administration party in my 'letter, which will be something in the way of the Administration candidate who expects success on that ground.

Joseph E. Brown To Alexander H. Stephens. R.

Executive Department, Milledgeville ga., *May 29th, 1863.*

Dear Sir: It affords me much pleasure to acknowledge the receipt of your letter and to learn that the matter and style of my letter to Messrs. Schley and others of Augusta met your approval. I have noticed the papers, and even the most bitter of them towards me hold out but little encouragement to an opposing candidate. Sneed discusses it with a little more abuse of me and by entering his protest, but does not desire to enter into a contest. The Telegraph also hopes if there is a contest the canvass will be kept out of the newspapers. I suppose Gartrell's anxiety for the position is so great that he may run, but the accounts which I have from all parts of the state are not favorable to him as a strong candidate. Col. Thweatt now at Columbus writes me that the editor of the Times says Genl. Colquitt will not be a candidate. Kenan I am told says I shall have opposition but that it is not worth while to run any of these spoken of against me—that Ben Hill is the man. My own opinion is, while I do not give Ben credit for very superior judgment, that he will not put himself in the position of a candidate for Governor just now simply to gratify Kenan. He would hardly be willing to resign his seat in the Senate for the chance he would have to be elected Governor. If he ran and did not resign he would not be a very formidable candidate.

I agree with you fully that independence without constitutional liberty is not worth the sacrifices we are making, and to maintain constitutional liberty we must maintain the rights and the sovereignty of the States. Had I been satisfied that we could elect any other States Rights man who would have stood firmly by the principles I have tried to maintain I would under no circumstances have occupied the position I now do as a candidate. As you and others in whose judgment I have great confidence believe it was necessary to success that I run, I am content to make the race and abide the result. While we are now in the midst of the crisis of the war, I feel hopeful of final success.

Robert Toombs To W. W. Burwell. L. C.

Washington, Ga., *June 10, 186S.*

My Dear Bvrwell, Your letter of the 30th ulto. was duly reed. I considered the question of running for Govr. of Georgia, and Govr. Brown very kindly offered to decline and support me, and I suppose there might have been no opposition to me; but under the present circumstances of the country I was well satisfied that the govr's position now in the states is of less importance to the country than any position whatever in the legislative department of the Govt. We can do nothing now in establishing any state policy whatever, we must wait for that until after the war. The necessities of war control the entire industry of the country, and I fear is greatly endangering public liberty. It is in the legislative department that we must hope to preserve rights and check abuses, and I have determined to stand for Congress in this district. Mr. Davis's friends talk of opposing me. I am content and would rather prefer it. He has greatly outraged justice and the constitution, but the public are disinclined to correct abuses when the empire is rocking to its very foundations, and would not look favourably upon a volunteer opposition; but if they make it upon me I shall be justified in any extremity to which the public interest would allow me to go in hostility to his illegal and unconstitutional course.

I am looking with great solicitude to the West, Vicksburg in particular. The enemy are making very great efforts there. My hopes are in Joe Johnston who I think is equal to the occasion. A few days must determine the fate of the Mississippi river and its valley for some time to come. If we fail we shall have a vast amount of suffering and losses in the whole valley and it will take much blood to re-instate ourselves there. It is a hard case on Johnston to have to carry all the blunders of Pemberton on his shoulders at such a time. What do you think of the tax law? I fear this tax in kind will be the winding sheet of poor Hunter. It will wholly fail and leave our currency in such a condition that we shall have again to change the *color* of our treasury notes, which seems to be the only remedy for the evils of our currency which seems to have occurred to the government. The Yankee Congress have certainly beat us badly in finance. Neither could borrow abroad, we had the best elements of domestic credit, yet Chase keeps his credits at one and a half for one of gold, and ours is six and a half for one, and there is no other reason for the difference than their superior management. We are all in good health. My own is daily improving. Except my hand1 (which I consider lost?) I shall soon be as good as ever. I am glad to see you go again into the Va. legislature. Let us have wisdom and virtue in our State counsels if we can not have them in our National. My best respects to Mrs. Burwell and your daughters.

Thomas W. Thomas To Alexander H. Stephens. R.

Elberton, Geo., *2d July, 1863.*

Dear Sir: This will be handed to you by my brother-in-law, Mr. Drury B. Cade, Junr., with whom you are already acquainted. There are some people in Lincoln and Wilkes who have never been to the war and who never intend to go, trying to have him conscripted—for what reason I am unable to say except that he attends strictly to his own business and will fight if he is pushed upon. A short time ago an old man in that neighborhood named Andres died owing his father (my father-in-law) some $20,000, which he had paid down in cash for him 14 years ago. The heirs and some of their friends have tried to defraud him out of it, and in the effort to do it an altercation arose in which one of them gave an insult to his father and offered to strike him. He was twice as big as Dru, but the exhibition of carnal weapons so frightened him that he With others are and will not be easy until he is carried off. I pledge you my word that the scoundrels who are persecuting him have no cause for it except that they tried to cheat and bully his father and are afraid they will be hurt by him. Under these circumstances I feel a profound interest that they be defeated.

Can you do anything for him without subjecting yourself to any thing unpleasant? I will pledge myself unreservedly that he will be active, thorough and honest in anything he undertakes and that he is a shrewd and capable business man. I tell you frankly all the opposition to him because I know you too well and have known you too long to believe in the least you can be deterred from doing as your judgment dictates for the clamors of a damned yelping pack.

Perhaps he might get a place under Capt. W. F. Holden who has been appointed in the 5th District.

He can't be conscripted at all if equal justice is done. Young men in this country under precisely his circumstances are enrolled and then detailed by the Government to attend to their plantations. Please explain this to him and tell him how to obtain his rights in this respect if necessary.

1 Toombs had been wounded In the left hand at the battle of Antletam.

Robert Toombs To Alexander H. Stephens. R.

Washington, Geo., *July 14-th, 1860.* Dear Stephens, I see by the papers you are in Richmond. I hope you will stay there, if your advice will be received. We are gloomy and in great trouble; North, South, East and West the clouds look dark and threatening. I feel but little like going into civil life; we must fight this thing out, and I shall try to be with the militia of Georgia in the prospective defense of our homes. I wish to go back into the army and intend to do so in some capacity. If we can get up a volunteer regiment in this neighborhood I shall take its command if desired; and if not I shall take such other position as will enable me to do the most good with one hand. I am only now remaining at home for a few days on account of Sally's great anxiety about Col. DuBose. Do telegraph me anything you may hear about him. As soon as I hear I shall go to see Brown about the military prospects for the future. Our volunteering has turned out wretchedly. We will have to call out the "melish." They pretend to be afraid if they go in for six months the Govt. will keep them. I defended the Govt. against so vile an imputation, tho' I owe them no favours; but I thought the cowardly exempts were doing them injustice, and I succeeded so far as to raise our quota of volunteers in Wilkes, but pretty generally elsewhere it was a failure. If you have any news from Dudley and his poor brigade send it to me immediately by telegraph. My whole heart is with them.

Joseph E. Brown To Alexander H. Stephens. R.

Marietta, ga., *Aug. 12th, 1863.* Dear Sir: I was in Atlanta yesterday and found some of the prominent citizens of the place getting up a petition to you to address the people there as soon as convenient upon the present condition of the country, our prosperity, etc., and I promised them that I would write you and urge upon you the importance of your compliance with this wish. There seems to have settled upon the minds of our people a sort of feeling of despondency which is stimulated by the constant croaking of a class of speculators who have made money and are preparing to curry favor with Lincoln if he should overrun the country, with the hope of saving their property. These men put the worst face upon every mishap to our arms, and while they are guilty of no act of positive disloyalty they do all in their power to discourage our people. The fear is that they are attempting to form a reconstruction party, by beginning to advocate reconstruction with the North West if they will adopt constitutions tolerating slavery, etc. This is harmless only as it forms the entering wedge to something worse, as there seems to be no more disposition on the part of these states to do this than there is on the part of Massachusetts. The heaviest blows we are having are from the North West. There is no doubt you now have the ears of the people of the Confederacy and their confidence to an extent that no other man in the Confederacy has, and I have no question that such a speech as you would make in Atlanta would do a great deal to revive the hopes of our people and stimulate them to action. I therefore beg you to respond to the call and make the speech. I am anxious to be at Atlanta and hear you and hope you will set a day when I can attend. I expect to go next Tuesday to Athens with my little daughter to school and get back to Atlanta Thursday evening. If you could be there Friday or Saturday of next week or any time after the Monday of the following week I would try to meet you there.

Robert Toombs To The Editor Of The Augusta, Ga., ConstituTionalist.1

Washington, ga., *August 12,1863.* To The Editor Of The Constitutionalist:

The Confederate Government have committed two radical errors in the management of our finances, which produced our present calamitous condition by the operation of laws of currency as fixed, certain, and immutable as the laws which govern the planetary system.

At the beginning of this struggle we had large national resources and unequalled elements of public credit; we borrowed gold at par for our bonds—wealth laid its treasures at our feet, and poverty itself claimed it as a privilege to augment our resources with its mite. Folly has mainly contributed to the drying up of this living fountain of public supply.

The first great error was in attempting to carry on a great and expensive war solely on credit—without taxation. This is the first attempt of the kind ever made by a civilized people. The result of the experiment will hardly invite its repetition. During the first year of its existence the present Congress neither levied nor collected a single cent of taxes, and postponed the collection of those levied for the second year to a period fatally too late to support our currency.

The second error naturally resulted from the first, and consummated the destruction of public credit. This error was the use of the public credit almost exclusively in the form of currency. The natural result of this policy was plain, inevitable, overwhelming. ' is a well settled and sound principle in currency that a nation iFrom the National Intelligencer, Washington, D. C, Aug. 20, 1863.
which has a sufficient quantity of circulating medium properly to answer the wants of its trade and commerce cannot add to the value of that currency by any further addition to its quantity. In the ordinary state of trade any excess of the proper quantity exhibits itself in the form of the exportation of bullion—any deficiency in importation. When, from any cause whatever, the operation of this law is prevented, any redundancy of currency must necessarily depreciate the whole mass, and this depreciation will exhibit itself in the rise in price of all commodities which it circulates. It is also true that if this redundant currency exists in the form of paper money not convertible into coin at the will of the holder, the measure of this depreciation is the difference between the standard or mint price of bullion and the market price when paid in this currency.

Tested by these plain and sound principles, the solution of the causes of our present financial troubles is easy. When this revolution commenced our currency was in excess of the wants of society. The proof is that nearly all of the banks within the Confederate States had suspended cash payments, and their notes were depreciated; therefore the first treasury note which was put into circulation added its nominal value to this excess; each succeeding issue enlarged it, and increased the depreciation of the whole mass. This depreciation soon began to manifest itself in the rise of commodities; yet the Government has unwisely continued daily by a forced circulation to add to this excess, increase the depreciation, and enhance the price of all the commodities which it is compelled to purchase, and is thus exhausting the national resources in the ratio of geometrical progression.

This ruinous policy would have long since run its course but for the fact that law, intimidation, and, above all, the ardent, sincere, honest but mistaken patriotism of the people have been invoked to uphold it. But the principle being radically wrong, no human power could uphold it long, and in spite of all these powerful proofs our national currency is depreciated more than one thousand per cent. below gold and silver, four hundred per cent. below suspended bank notes, and prices and payments are rapidly adjusting themselves to the inexorable facts.

Many unsound reasons are given for this state of things by the supporters or apologists of this pernicious policy. Many able and excellent persons affirm and honestly believe that from the peculiar circumstances which surround us bullion is no longer a standard of value, or a true measure of the depreciation of our currency. This error has produced infinite mischief. It is true that gold and silver do rise and fall in value like but in a much less degree than other commodities, and it is mainly by this reason that they have been adopted by mankind as the standards of value, and however they may rise or fall that in no degree affects their value as a test of the depreciation of inferior currencies; they certainly still remain if not the infallible yet the most accurate measure of such depreciation which the wisdom of the world has yet been able to discover.

This is no pleasant picture for us to behold; yet this is better than the still more gloomy one which a continuance in the paths of error will speedily present to our visions. The consequences are frightful; let us pursue them a little further. Let us suppose that we have five hundred millions of currency now in circulation, worth fifty millions of standard bullion; the issue of an additional five hundred millions of such currency will not add a single dollar to its value. The thousand millions will be worth no more than the five hundred millions were before the last issue, to wit, fifty millions of bullion. The addition has only depreciated the whole currency by one-half, and this depreciation will invariably exhibit itself in the rise of the commodities for which it may be exchanged. The Government, therefore, if it expends the additional issue in commodities, loses first the whole amount of depreciation existing at the beginning of the issue, also all the additional depreciation produced by its daily expenditure; and the noteholders lose one-half of the value of their notes.

It will therefore follow that if the market price of wheat is eight dollars per bushel under the issue of five hundred millions of treasury notes, it will be sixteen dollars per bushel under the issue of a thousand millions, and the sixteen dollars will be worth no more than the eight dollars, and will exchange for no more of other commodities. This being the uniform law of currency, when you fix an arbitrary price on any given commodity and leave all other commodities to the natural operation of this law, you utterly destroy all sound principles of exchange, and must in the end ruin the producers of the regulated commodity unless they abandon that business, at least to the extent of producing any surplus. This must be the effect of this impressment unless the law is throttled by the wisdom and power of the people.

But is this principle true? "That commodities will rise or fall in proportion to the increase or diminution of money, I assume as a fact which is incontrovertible." This is the language of Mr. Ricardo, and he is supported by Adam Smith and all of the great writers and thinkers on currency who have flourished within the last hundred years. The same great truth is daily pressing itself upon our observation and demonstrating itself before our eyes every day. The pay of our officers and soldiers, the pay of the civil employes of the Confederate and State Governments, the compensation of all, either in military or civil life, at wages established on the old basis of a sound currency, has diminished, and is daily diminishing in real exchangeable value, to a sum for which the actual necessaries of life cannot be purchased. They feel the misery and generally know not its law.

The capitalist lends his money to the Government, and finds that at his first half-yearly dividend he receives in payment Treasury notes not worth one-third in money what they were when he made the loan. Yet the Government wonders why people will not buy its bonds. Investments in gold for the last six months have been the safest and among the best in the Confederate States. They have paid one hundred per cent. per month on the original investment in treasury notes. Can I say more to expose the boundless folly of our present financial system?

The history of the currency of our enemies since the beginning of this war is humiliating to us. Neither had foreign credits, both had powerful and established State Governments to back them. We were united in favor of the war, they were divided. They have kept twice the men in the field that we have upon half the money, and paid their soldiers better than we have. Their Treasury notes sell at a discount of less than thirty per cent.; ours at more than one thousand! The reason is solely that their Government has better understood and more firmly adhered to the true principles of currency than ours. In all else we had the advantage.

I have endeavored to point out the main difficulty in our financial policy, and have, to the best of my judgment, traced it to its true source—excess in currency, not national debility.

I have labored to illustrate the disastrous effect on prices of this excess, and here I wish to be clearly understood. I do not say that currency is the sole element in the price of corn, or of any other commodity, but I do affirm that it is *one* of its main elements, always present, ever active, and, other things being equal, "that the price of commodities must every where rise or fall in proportion to the increase or diminution of the money which circulates them." Suppose I am mistaken in the application of this principle to our present circumstances; suppose, as many able and excellent men do firmly hold, that from our peculiar circumstances gold and silver are not now either the true standard of value or the true test of the depreciation of our currency. What then? I will not deny the truth, but I will waive it in deference to honest patriots seeking the same end— the public good; but I will not waive the terrible truth, as plain as the noonday sun, that any and every standard which any intelligent man can apply, and at a velocity rapid and daily increasing, our currency is depreciating, dying, and without our most vigorous efforts must soon pass away. This depreciation of the currency. therefore, whatever may be its regulation, or by whatsoever standard you may test its amount, is our monster evil. 73566—13 40

The mischief is still within our power, and we may still remedy it if we have the wisdom, firmness, and courage which the crisis demands. It involves our independence. We must do it; we have no alternative'which a freeman should consider; any settlement with those miserable miscreants on our northern border, short of eternal separation and independence, would be the consummation of all evils which even the power of God could inflict on us in this world. Therefore, whatever may be the cost in wealth of a return to a sound currency, we must pay the penalty of our past folly—and pay it now. This depreciation of currency having been shown to have resulted chiefly from the excessive issue of treasury notes, we can only correct this evil by stopping instantly any further issue under any pretence whatever, and by reducing as rapidly as possible our present outstanding.issues. It requires large, comprehensive and efficient measures for their continual reduction until they shall rise in value and approximate as nearly as our circumstances will allow to the standard value of gold and silver.

Taxation and loans are the only means of attaining this result— taxation, comprehensive, simple, rigid and equal. The present tax law does not possess these qualities—it is partial, unequal, and complex; fosters vulgar prejudices, and will gather an abundant harvest of frauds and perjuries. The tax-in-kind principle is subject to many grave objections. This mode of taxation should never be resorted to when the currency is redundant, but with all its faults may be a necessary evil whenever there is a great deficiency in the circulating medium. The execution of such a law is necessarily difficult, irritating, wasteful, and productive of much fraud.

But certainly in our present condition the war cannot be carried on and the currency sustained by taxation alone; we must resort to loans. I am not in the least discouraged by the ill success of the Government lately in funding its Treasury notes. Treasury notes are in great excess; the holders are anxiously hunting for a safe and profitable investment for them. The Government is perfectly able to supply that want; heretofore it has not done so. We must issue new bonds with principal and interest payable in gold and silver or their equivalent, and adopt measures to make such payment certain. This can be done by mortgaging a specific portion of the revenue to the new bondholders, adequate to the payment of both principal and interest as each may respectively fall due, coupled with clear provisions that their taxes shall be irrepealable until the mortgages are paid, and that these taxes shall only be paid in gold and silver or the coupons of the bonds for which they are pledged.

By making the provision for our bonds ample at the beginning, so that no future legislation shall be necessary to preserve the public faith, we give the public creditor the best possible security for his money which we are able to offer. The overthrow of Government will be his only danger; that cannot be provided against. We greatly lessen the chances of repudiation, because in this case it would require the direct concurrence of the Executive and both branches of Congress to defeat the security; whereas in the case of bonds charged on the general revenue, it may be defeated by the Executive or either branch of Congress; even the non-action of either would be fatal to it. What are called the cotton-loan bonds, although they have but one of these principles engrafted upon them—to wit, the payment of interest in cash—sell for a largo premium.

The fifteen million loan was based precisely on these principles, and although the Government has violated its pledge to pay these bonds in coin and they suffer under the great disadvantage of being secured by an export duty on cotton, which is made nearly unavailable for the present by the blockade, their market value is nearly double that of all other eight per cent. bonds. These facts demonstrate the soundness of the theory which I advocate. If the cotton bonds had been secured by a land tax, upon the terms I have briefly sketched, adequate to meet them, their coupons would instantly very nearly approximate to gold and silver in value, and the premium upon them, payable in our currency, would be large.

We must act, and that quickly; the public interest and public safety wiU no longer allow delay. Our present system is utterly insupportable; it is upsetting the very foundations of private rights, weakening daily public confidence in our cause at home and abroad— sowing dangerous discontents among the people, which are daily deepening and widening. Patriotism demands that all good men should unite to correct these evils.

Joseph E. Brown To Alexander H. Stephens. It.

Marietta ga., *Aug. 22d, 1863.*

Dear Sir: I found your letter here on my return from Athens, to which point I had gone to carry my little daughter Mary to school. I regret that you cannot make the speech in Atlanta.

I fully agree with you that our matters are being badly managed, and do not know what may be the result if we have not a change of policy. I am advised by the commissary at Atlanta, Maj. Cummings, *privately* that the supply of meat is now very short and that we cannot subsist the army through the fall unless we can get the cattle out of Florida and Lower Ga. faster than we are now doing. I have called the attention of the President to this and asked him to order details from Genl. Cobb's command, who seems to have but little to do now, to drive out the cattle. I also ask that the citizens be liberally compensated for them and that the commissaries be called together and a schedule of prices fixed as high as the market price for all supplies. I do not know that these suggestions will be regarded worth anything but I have felt it my duty to make them. Maj. C. says we have not 1,000,000 of pounds of bacon in Atlanta and that he is supplying Lee's, Bragg's and Johnston's armies.

If I had the money I could send the Q. M. and Com. Genls. of Ga. into lower Ga. and Florida and get out enough beef to supply the deficiency this fall. But enough of this; the powers that be manage it their own way, and we must bide the result and pray that God will deliver us from our own blunders.

You have noticed that I have opposition;1 I suppose Mr. Hill relies upon the failure of our own Government and disaster of our armies for his success. How ardently he desires our success in such case is not for me to know. I am reliably informed that he refused when in Atlanta to say whether he favored reconstruction or not, or to define his position one way or the other, leaving the people to take him upon his past record. As he resigned his position in the Lincoln Congress long after the state seceded, he of course denied that the ordinance of secession took the State out of the Union and held that he was still her representative in Congress after her secession, and held a commission which had not been abrogated by the ordinance and which he might as a loyal citizen of the United States resign. The movement in placing such a man in the field as a candidate is a bold one. Thus far it has excited no enthusiasm so far as I can see, and falls quite stillborn.

Robert Toombs To W. W. Burwell. L. C.

Washington, Ga., *Aug. 29, 1863.*

Dear Burwell, Your letter of the 24th ult. was received here during my absence on a visit to my plantation in so. western Georgia and since that time I have been illegible absent from home. As it did not suit me to own a servant so far from home, I directed Maj. Alexander to tell Robt. to select his master and to sell him to whomsoever he wished to belong to, and he has done so. He sold him to some person in Richmond. I don't know the name of the purchaser.

Our affairs have taken a very unlucky turn since I last saw you. It does not surprise me. The real control of our affairs is narrowing down constantly into the hands of Davis and the old army, and when it gets there entirely the cause will collapse. They have neither the ability nor the honesty to manage the revolution. Many of our ablest and most reliable colonels who brought our troops into the 1 Brown was opposed in the gubernatorial election of 1863 by Joshua Y. Hill and Timothy Purlow. The vote at the polls was for Brown, 36,558; for Hill, 18,222; for Purlow, 10.024.

field have been killed up by the blunders and jealousies of the old army, and the morale of the army is now pretty much gone. We never had a desertion until we had conscription, for the very good reason that there were thousands outside who wanted to take the places of those inside, and besides men who felt an interest in the cause stepped forward full of energy and enthusiasm for its defence. Conscription and conscription alone destroyed all that feeling. When we began to hunt up men with dogs like the Mexicans, they necessarily became as worthless as Mexicans, and every day has seen the deterioration of the troops brought in as conscripts.

As to opposition, I do not see how anything else is left to me or anybody else except the entire surrender of the country. executive, legislative and judicial departments to Mr. Davis. In the 1st place I feel sure that will ruin the cause of independence; 2ndly, it will make the recovery? of public liberty hereafter impossible without another bloody revolution. Therefore I think we should now hold every department of the govt. to the strictest account. I am fully persuaded that the road to liberty for the white man does not lie through slavery. But the only question for a patriot is, will resistance or acquiescence do most harm to the public cause? I think the latter and must act accordingly.

I fear the fall of Vicksburg is much more serious than you seem to think. We are cut in two by it. The vast number of slaves on both sides of it cannot be taken care of either there or any where else. They cannot be left there with safety and cannot be carried away without the ruin of the owners of them, therefore that vast field of production is blasted and other portions of the country will have to support the multitude of refugees in addition to themselves and the army. I fear next year will tell terribly on us. This year and the last we have been blessed with abundant crops and may get thro' very well until next year, but a bad season would bring great suffering if not ruin upon us.

I have written quite a long article upon impressment and the currency, which I enclose you with this. Unless we change our policy the currency will collapse within ninety days. But govt. seems determined to rely upon force and fraud to sustain the army. Those means have always failed and always will. No power but God's can prevent it and therefore if we fold our arms we must be speedily overthrown The country should arouse itself and be heard, but I have but little hope that it will. The heavy hand of power has smitten them and they are paralyzed.

My best regards to the ladies. We are in good health.

P. S.—Are you not a member of the new legislature?

Robert Toombs To Alexander H. Stephens. R.

Washington, Geo., *Nov. 2nd, 1863.*
Dear Stephens, I came down with Linton and staid all night at your house in hopes of seeing you but was disappointed. Linton wrote you the day before but I suppose you did not get it, which was well, as the President arrived in Atlanta just as we left and wanted to see you.

I shall leave here Wednesday morning for Milledgeville with the purpose, if I can be elected, to run for the Senate. Indeed I am rather inclined to run even if I find myself in a minority, with a view to rally and embody those who agree with me in principle, in order to offer whatever resistance I can to the ruin of the revolution and the destruction of public liberty. I am fully aware of the delicacy of your position and do not intend by this letter to commit you in any way, much less to ask for your interference. I deemed it due to our relations that you should be advised of my purposes, which have been formed after long and earnest if not deliberate consideration. Mr. Davis's present policy will overthrow the revolution in six months if the enemy only give him time enough to stand still and do nothing. I shall do what I can to avert so dire a calamity. Of course in adopting the proposed course towards Davis I am fully aware of the nature of the contest. We shall both fight under the same flag. *Yae victis,*—with this difference: I shall avow it and he will quote scripture, say "God bids us do good for evil" and thus "clothe (his) naked villainy in old odd ends stole forth from holy writ and seem a saint when he plays the devil."

Joseph E. Brown To Alexander H. Stephens. R.

Milledgeville ga., *Nov. 27th, 1863.*
Dear Sir: Your letter in reference to the pardon of Martin and Jones was received today. I do not think I have any power to pardon Martin. I am of opinion the President has the pardoning power in such cases. The principal keeper tells me that his conduct has not been good since he has been here and says judging from his behaviour he could not recommend him to executive clemency. I have never examined the evidence in the case of Jones. From all I had heard of the case I had supposed it was not a proper one for pardon till he had served out more of his time. I will try to find time at no distant day to examine the evidence and see what I can do.

You have before this seen the result of the senatorial election. Genl. Toombs did not have as much strength as I supposed with the members. The Hill element almost if not all voted for Gov. Johnson. While I had no reason to wish ill success to Johnson I regretted the defeat of Toombs. I think we need him in Congress.

The disaster at Chattanooga gives much uneasiness here. I fear it will be followed by other Federal victories which will cost us Upper Georgia for a time and expose our people there to extreme suffering.

I wish we had a more able man at the head of our forces in that Department.

Howell, Cobb To Alexander H. Stephens. R.
(Private)
Head-quarters Georgia State Guard,1
Atlanta ga., *8 January, 1864*
Dear Stephens, I got your letter here on my arrival yesterday. The one you wrote to me at Richmond I did not get but presume it will be sent back here, as I left that direction in Richmond. I regret that you could not have gone on with Harris and myself and think it would be well for you to be there now. What is wanting in Richmond is *"brains?* I did not find the temper and disposition of Congress as bad as I expected, but there is a lamentable want of brains and good sound common sense.

I should like very much to communicate to you freely all my impressions from my late visit but cannot write them. If your health will admit of it you ought to go to Richmond. You can do good there.

I have been kept quite busy in my office since I got back and therefore know nothing of what is going on in the army in front. I shall go up in a few days to see Genl. Johnson.

Joseph E. Brown To Alexander H. Stephens. R.

Canton ga., *J any. 4th, 1864* Dear Sir: Your kind letter addressed to me at Milledgeville which has been forwarded to me here was received by mail of this afternoon. Before I left Milledgeville I reappointed Col. Johnson as *aide de camp* under the 20th section of the new militia bill. I have a good opinion of him and regard him a very useful man. I beg to assure you that it afforded me and my family, as it always will, very great pleasure to be able to be of service to Linton. I admire his talents, his honesty and stern integrity, and highly appreciate his friendship.

I expect if no mishap to get home next Saturday night and will be glad to get your letter and views on the question alluded to in your letter. I would be obliged if you would mark all your letters private across the seal of the envelope, as I often have to leave my mails to be opened by secretaries and prefer that your letters should always be handed to me to open.

1 Cobb had been made major-general, Sept. 9, 1863, and assigned to the command of the Confederate reserve forces in Georgia.

Air. Lincoln's rule that the just powers of the government are derived from the consent of *one tenth* of the governed is as much a perversion of the principles of the Declaration of Independence as his abolition proclamation is a violation of the Constitution. I think his message and proclamation affords an excellent text for the message of which we spoke.

But I have not time to write much more. I am here with Mrs. B. trying to make arrangements to get her bedding and other household furniture to middle Ga. before the opening of the spring campaign. I have full confidence in Genl. Johnston if the President will give him enough of men, but I fear this will not be done.

Joseph E. Brown To Alexander H. Stephens. R.

Milledgeville, ga., *J any. 28th. 1864.*

Dear Sir:»On my return from southwestern Ga., where I have been to prepare a place for my negroes, I found your two letters. I am very sorry indeed to hear of your affliction but trust you will soon be well again. I hope Linton's health may be permanently restored. I had a letter from him yesterday.

I thank you for your suggestions and for advising me of the prospect of a war to be waged against me at Richmond. I regret that such may be the intention of those in authority. If it must come I shall try to be prepared to meet it. To this end I will try to do my duty and not be found in the wrong. I agree with you that there has for some time been a disposition at Richmond to control the State Road 1 and I have been advised by a distinguished Georgian there to give up the control of it for a time to the Confederate authorities as the best mode of getting rid of the vast responsibility resting upon me, etc. All this I shall disregard. I know as well as the Confederate authorities do how to manage the road. In response to a call on me by the President to look well to its management to save Genl. Johnston from falling back I have demanded of him the return of *one fourth* of the engines and cars which Confederate officers under his command have carried off the road and got lost or destroyed and never returned. I say if he will return even less than a fourth of what he has taken from the road I will transport all he wishes promptly. I have called his attention to the necessity of prompt action before the army is reinforced in the spring, have stated that the Tennessee *refugee* trains are now in the Carolinas and Va. engaged in the cotton business, have said he has the power to order them back and I have not, and that if he fails to return the rolling stock in time disaster may be the result, etc., etc., and shall continue to urge this upon him. I have just grounds to 1 The Western & Atlantic Railroad. do so. Today I have a letter from Genl. Johnston saying that his supplies go forward promptly now sufficient to meet his demands and accumulate for emergency, etc. I have plenty of wood now on the road and shall not be found at fault.

I have not yet written a line of my intended message but must commence it soon. I had hoped Congress might take some action or the President issue some proclamation that would obviate the necessity. I noticed a committee was to be appointed to address the people. I wish to see the address if it is to appear soon. I hope even then to be able to do some good by proper state action. I thank you for all your suggestions. There is not as much provision as I expected in S. W. Ga. I have noticed closely. The supply question is a very important one and I greatly fear we are not prepared for it. I am always glad to hear from you. Would come and see you but I am pressed with business.

Joseph E. Brown To Alexander H. Stephens. R.

Milledgeville ga., *Feby 13th, 1864.*

Dear Sir: I will be obliged if it will not be too great a task for you, if you will set a day and meet me at Linton's at Sparta where we can compare notes, etc., on the subject of which we have lately corresponded. I am anxious to have the benefit of your suggestions upon the communication in the shape in which I will soon have it. Any day after next week will suit me and the sooner after the better. If you say Monday week it will suit me. I wish to call the legislature together in the early part of March and I wish to act with caution and prudence. I would come to your house but I am too much pressed with business.

My wife has been very sick with rising on her breast for 10 days past and has required so much of my time day and night as to leave me in bad condition to think and prepare anything with care. If you set a day with Linton, when he will be there, I wish the benefit of his suggestions and hence it will. suit to go to his house.

Joseph E. Brown To Alexander H. Stephens. R.

Milledgeville ga., *Feby. 20th, 1864.* Dear Sir: I have just received your letter and will if not Providentially hindered meet you at Linton's Thursday next. As Mrs. B. is again up and needs a little change of place and travel, I will probably take the liberty to bring her with me. The great wrong which you anticipated has been done by Congress and I confess I contemplate with horror the suspension of the *habeas corpus.* Every state in the Confederacy should denounce and condemn the wicked act.

Joseph E. Brown To Alexander H. Stephens. R.

MILlEDGEVILLE ga., *March 4th, 1864.*

Dear Sir: I have to thank you for the copy of the act abolishing the court of Star Chamber. I shall have it printed as an appendix to my message in the same pamphlet, as I think it will produce a good effect. I agree with you that it would be very desirable if possible to secure the cooperation of Senator Hill in the passage of proper resolutions by our legislature. His prejudices are so strong however against some who will from their position be obliged to take a prominent part in the matter that I fear they will control his judgment and his action. Do all you can to secure his aid. I think it might be best for you to come over and stay a few days at the opening of the session and aid in giving proper direction to our action. If you can do so come to my house on your arrival. I will show the copy act to Linton when he gets here. I have rewritten the article on habeas corpus for the message since we parted and have I think made it stronger and a better article. It is the great question of the day and I do hope our legislators will have nerve and patriotism to put Ga. right. Foster writes me that he met *General* Gartrell on his "way home who boasts of his authorship of the bill and puts its necessity on the state of things in N. Carolina. That it has done great good already, etc., etc. He also saw Gerry of the Senate who said he should sustain the President and the suspension. I regret to hear this, though Gerry's rather a negative sort of a man who does not like to take or meet responsibilities. The timidity of members is most to be dreaded.

Benjamin H. Hill1 To Alexander H. Stephens. R.

Lagrange, Ga., *March 14th, 1864* Dear Sir: I did not receive the governor's message until yesterday. I proceed at once to give you my opinion of its merits and positions as I promised to do when I parted with you.

Beginning with that portion of the Message which treats of " the causes of the war, how conducted, and who responsible "—from that point to the end, I must say I have not read anything during the revolution with half so much pleasure and satisfaction. I know I must thank *you* for it. The whole country will owe you an everlasting debt for it. Gov. Brown can never pay you in kind for the great benefit you have bestowed upon him. You have given him a grandeur of conception, an enlargement of views, and a perspicuity

» Member of the Georgia legislature, 1851-1855 and 1859-1861; defeated candidate of the Know-nothing party for the governorship of Georgia, 1857; Senator from Georgia in the Confederate Congress; Member of United States Congress from Georgia, 1875-1877; Senator from Georgia, 1877-1881. During the war he was generally a supporter of Davis's policies.

and power of style to which he never could have reached. His only trouble can be the footprints are *too plain not to* be recognized.

On my arrival at home I found my speech had been set up and the editor was issuing it in an extra. I stopped that and delayed its distribution generally until Friday the 11th, being the regular day of the issue. Under the circumstances however I concluded I could not with propriety alter it, and it was issued as written. The speech as written is not so full or satisfactory as spoken.

1. We agree on the first main idea: That State sovereignty and self-government are the great stakes at issue in this contest and that recognition of this fact is the only basis of settlement. 2. We both agree there must be a change of administration and policy in the U. States before we can have peace. 3. We both agree that it is our duty *now* to make known in every possible way to the people of the North and to the world that we are ready to negotiate on the basis of State sovereignty and free government. 4. You invoke Georgia to move in this matter *now* and I agree with all my heart. In different language we *certainly* concur in the idea that it is proper for the *States* to *move* in the settlement which is to involve their separate existence and sovereignty. 5. We *appear* to differ on the point as to whether proposals should be made to Mr. Lincoln. You think such proposals should be made *after victory.* I think victory is a condition precedent to any negotiation and that as *matters now stand,* we cannot propose to Mr. Lincoln—The difference is not great.

In my judgment none of the states of the late U. States can ever have peace or good government until the whole idea, spirit, policy and body of abolitionism is *crushed out and destroyed.* Now is the time to crush it out. We must throw upon it the whole weight and odium of this war. We *can* do this and it will crush it. This done we can then settle the forms of government and the terms of association. Any thing attained with abolitionism crushed is better than any thing possible with abolitionism not crashed.

Lincoln's defeat in the ensuing election will ensure that crushing. Peace will follow. His accession to power was the declaration of war. His continuance in power has been the continuance of war. His ejection from power will be the end of war. Here is the weight beneath which the idea, the power, and the hopes of abolitionism and the spirit of Puritanic intermeddling must lie buried forever. I think therefore that policy as well as necessity indicates that we should now make a *direct* appeal to the people of the U. States against Lincoln and his policy and his party and make them join issue at the polls in November—*we shaping that issue.* To make this issue or rather appeal the more distinctly I think we ought to hold intercourse with Lincoln only under the rules of war and as an *enemy,* making prominent as the *reason* that he will not permit any other intercourse consistent with our honor; but that we have always been, are now, and ever will be, ready to negotiate with the U. States, through agents with whom we can have peaceful interviews with honor. That agent we will recognize in those who concede that the states are separate, equal and sovereign political communities and who will be willing to negotiate on this basis.

On the leading idea we certainly agree, and details shall not divide.

6. As to a convention of the states, I think that is the certain conclusion from our common premises. *State* action we both urge. You, *separate* action in certain states. I, joint action for *separate* ratification, to accomplish in *part* the very results you propose. Our paths will meet at the same goal and I am willing to walk along with you for *company.*

That portion of the message in the suspension of habeas corpus I can also plainly see is your work. On this subject I have to say: 1. To the legal principles you announce I agree. I intimate as much in my speech. I will never agree that the *military, as such,* from the Commander-in-chief down, can take charge of and control the *citizen.* Civilians must be governed and governed *only* by *civil* tribunals. Persons in no way attached to, or connected with, or within the lines of the *army* cannot, ought not, and must not be governed by military law or military officers. The suspension of the writ of habeas corpus does not and cannot annul, repeal or modify the citizen's constitutional bill of rights. Here lies deep imbedded the corner stone of Freedom's temple and I will never consent to its removal. The act of Congress if carried out does infringe in this respect and therefore I voted against it.

2. But to a certain extent and for proper cases I think the public safety did demand the suspensions of this writ. There are characters, some in and some *interfering* with the army, who ought to be arrested by military order, held without warrant, and tried without a jury. But these are persons who are subject by law or by *their own act* to military power. As to citizens, I freely and cheerfully admit the only suspensions of the writ that can be, is that they may be held *for trial* after legal arrest and upon proper warrant.

But in all this *I think* you will find that Mr. Davis will agree with us. Should this be so we ought not to denounce him in advance.

Here then is our difference: I must admit I have *confidence* in Mr. Davis. I have not agreed with him in many things. But I think his *heart* is right and that nothing could tempt him to be a dictator. He is *tenacious* of his *opinion* but does not seem to use *power* greedily. I admit the danger of *acquiescing* in such a law; but I confess I fear an issue, *especially* if not *necessary,* will weaken us in winning that victory which we both agree is indispensable to the success of the great movement for peace. I shall certainly vote however to repeal the law.

I might agree that the legislature should assert by resolutions the correct doctrine on this subject if it can be done without asserting or implying a want of confidence in the administration. I am fully satisfied the main movement would be weakened by such an issue.

3. The Act limited the suspension to arrests ordered by the President, or Sec. of War—not, as you seem to suppose, to increase the power of the President but to prevent abuses by *subordinates.* You remember how various subordinates declared martial law and cut various "fantastic tricks" on a former occasion when the writ was suspended. The object was to prevent a recurrence of these and similar exhibitions of petty tyranny. For this reason even the General commanding the Trans-Mississippi cannot order an arrest and a suspension except by authority of the President. 4. So also the provision requiring investigation into arrests was *intended* to prevent improper and prolonged detentions. I confess I think your criticism is right. I made the *same criticism* in the Senate and insisted that this investigation belonged to the *courts.* I was overruled but it is due to those who inserted the clause that I should state their intention.

I see Gov. Vance has announced his determination to submit to this law. I see also the papers in Virginia and Georgia and N. C. are opposing an issue upon it. I fear an issue in Georgia unless carefully confined to abstract principles will not meet with support elsewhere.

I have not seen your brother's resolutions.

As to that portion of the Message written by Gov. Brown in relation to the finances, and secret sessions, etc. , etc., I utterly and entirely disagree. I deeply regret that he has made such issues, so unjust to the motives of the Congress and so unsustained by *facts.* It is horrible that such a lame beginning and such a sublime ending should constitute the same message.

I am invited to Milledgeville. Perhaps I will have to go. If so I shall endeavor to be careful. Would like to see you and Gov. Johnson both go. Think I shall go down the last of this week but am not certain.

Robert Toombs To Alexander H. Stephens. R.

Washington, Geo., *Apl. 1, 1864.*
Dear Stephens, This is "all fool's day," a very proper day for the inauguration of what is facetiously called the new financial policy of the govt. Its friends seem very solicitous about its success in "reducing the volume of currency." I don't see any necessity for their fears. It will not only drive out the old currency but the new also before the 1st of

July next so far as it concerns any useful purpose. To tax currency at all is always a very doubtful financial expedient; to tax it to the extent that you do other property is the utmost limit within the line of good faith; to tax it all is not distinguishable in policy or morals from taking it all. You cannot alter the nature of repudiation by changing its name. But the genius of Congress was unequal to the task of buying in their currency at its market value (the only remedy), and being afraid of the word "repudiate," concluded to follow the poet's advice, " If we can not alter the things, by G—d we can change the name, sir." And therefore with an air that no other two men on earth can put on but they, Ben. Hill and Gartrell triumphantly ask. "Has not Congress the right to tax? tax speculators? tax money changers? Ha! I want to see the man that can deny it!" And the thing is settled.

I am greatly delighted at the vote on Linton's resolutions concerning suspension of *habeas corpus.* It was unexpected to me. After witnessing the purchase and transfer of nearly the whole press of the country, including the Whig and Examiner at Richmond, which seemed the most resolute in stemming the tide of despotism daily pouring itself out upon the country, I confess I had but little hope of seeing such a manifestation of public spirit from our legislature at this time. I knew it would come because I have real faith in the power of truth. I was watching and waiting for our day of deliverance but thought it much farther off than I now find it to be. I have neither seen yours nor Linton's speech, but I heard the best accounts of them at Macon and on the road home, both from friends and opponents who heard them. But if I had heard nothing from them I would know their quality by the magnificent results which they produced, for I well know the sort of speaking it would take to arouse the House of Reps., especially, to such noble utterances as are contained in Linton's resolutions. Davis is a hard taskmaster. Old Cooper's order expounding the law has knocked the last plank from under the feet of his defenders and apologists, in and out of the legislature. It is a great pity but what the speeches of his friends in the two houses could have been published before Cooper's order. Cooper's general order was dated the 10th March and was not printed until the 17th in the Richmond papers when it was thought at Richmond that the legislature had endorsed the action of Congress. This authoritative interpretation of the law exceeds in enormity the worst charges of the most extreme opponents of the measure. It authorizes anybody whatever to whom the President may delegate the authority to arrest and imprison at pleasure and openly defies the judicial tribunals of the country, denying to them even the right to inquire whether or no the arrest is for the causes specified in the act. The officer making the arrest only swears that he holds the citizen by virtue of the authority of the secretary of war. Govr. Brown should avail himself of the first opportunity to test the legality of this proceeding. I shall certainly give Mr. Davis an early opportunity to make me a victim by advising resistance, resistance to the death, to his law. There is one view of this act that escaped Linton. I am not surprised at it for in fact it subverts all rights. Altho' it is clear that the Senate intended to restrict the operation of the act it had not sense enough to do it. It in truth enlarged it. It expressly permits men to be seized and imprisoned for innocent acts, for acts that Congress *does not, has not, dares not make criminal.* Where is the law that punishes me for advising or inciting men to abandon the Confederate cause? To do this thing is a perfectly innocent action which Congress has never made criminal. Yet it allows the President to imprison me for it. A Roman emperor has won immortal infamy by a defective publication of his laws, but still he did not enact them. Our Congress punishes what they have never had the courage to make penal. Our constitution says that no *ex post facto* law shall be passed. The late Congress punishes actions which are even innocent when the punishment is inflicted. But my paper is giving out. Will you be at home next week? I want to show you what I have written and talk over these matters. I hate to write. I want to leave home Tuesday or Wednesday and will call and stay all night if you are at home.

Joseph E. Brown To Alexander H. Stephens. R.

Milledgeville ga., *Apr. 5th, 1861)..*

Dear Sir: I have read your speech as published, carefully, and been much gratified at its clear and conclusive exposition of the subject. It settles the question of the unconstitutionality of the suspension to the clear understanding of all men.1 I trust it will be extensively circulated. *Privately,* the Messers. Wartzfielder of this city say they will pay for L000 copies to be circulated in the army, and I have today written to Steele at Atlanta to know if he struck off enough that I can get them. The Messrs. W. do not wish their names known but they are ardently with us and have plenty of money to pay for the copies and not feel it.

I have sent copies of my message2 and of Linton's resolutions to the captain of each company in the Ga. Regts. so far as known where 1 Stephens's speech denouncing the suspension of the writ of *habeas corpus* by the Confederate Government, delivered before the Georgia Legislature at Milledgeville, Mar. 16, 1864, is published in Henry Cleveland's "Alexander H. Stephens," pp. 761-786.

2 Governor Brown's message to the legislature, Mar. 10, 1864, is published in the "Confederate Records of the State of Georgia," III, 587-655; and in major part in Herbert Fielder's "Life of Joseph E. Brown," pp. 281-306. they are and a copy to the clerk of the court of every county in the Confederacy within our present lines. I wish your speech could take the same range. Though I presume the papers of the Confederacy will publish it more generally than they did my message, both because their readers will wish to see

what *you* say and because it is not so long as the message. I see the Atlanta Register says the message is published *in extenso* in the Northern papers. I have no other account of this.

Say to Mr. Hidell that I have ordered two copies of the message to illegible at Richmond and one to him at Craw ford ville.

I learn that Genl. Cobb is getting in the crazy state of fury. A friend from Atlanta writes me that he denounced me on the R. R. car between Macon and that place the other day as a *traitor,* a *Tory;* said I ought to be hung and would be soon; that he had never been to a hanging but would go some distance to see it done, etc. He is no doubt deeply mortified that he had not influence to defeat the measure I prompted by me but he should not be blamed. He did all he could to serve his master and if the President has any gratitude he will not take from him his easy place nor order him to more distant and dangerous fields. I think he is now a little more under the control of his passions than his judgment, and a man in that condition is apt to do foolish things. I learn he stooped in Athens in conversation to charge that I had stolen the public money or in some other way got rich very suddenly, as I had lately purchased two plantations in S. W. Ga. I will send you *privately* a copy of that part of my letter to my informant which relates to this subject, as you may hear the same charges.

You will see in the Confederate Union of this week a reply to the Savannah Republican's charges of *bribery* of the Legislature. I have sent Steele a statement as in the Union with a different line of argument as suggested by Linton, which I suppose he will make an article from.

Joseph E. Brown To Alexander H. Stephens. R.

Milledgeville ga., *April 12th, 186%*
Dear Sir: I have seen no comments on your speech that can be said to be unfavourable, though I have not kept posted on the newspapers comments. I think they are getting a little tired of the fight and do not care to reopen the war by assaults on your speech.

The editors of the Union have agreed to publish 1,500 copies of your speech in pamphlet in type that will go into 16 pages for $200. This the Messrs. Wartzfielder agree to pay, and Jonas Thweatt, 1 The resolutions adopted by the Georgia Legislature In March, 1864, denouncing the suspension of the writ of *habeas corpus* are published In A. EL Stephens's "War between the States," II. pp. 778-780. myself and Philip M. Russell of Savannah, the member who was here yesterday, each agree to pay $50 and take 1,500 more. This will be 3,000. I will have them distributed to the army by sending to a Lieut. of each Co., as I sent my message to the Capt. of each. If the Capt. is against us and does not let the company have the one, the Lieut. may let them have the other. The soldiers write me that both are in great demand. I sent the message to the Clerk of the court in each county in the Confederacy that can now be reached. I wish to send your speech to the Sheriff of each. If one is not read then it is probable the other will be.

I learn that Cobb is managing to get up the army meetings which we noticed condemning me and the legislature. The one in the 24th Regt., McMillan's old regiment, was conducted by the officers who are in the Cobb interest. That regiment went from the mountains— nearly all voted for me and I could carry it tomorrow over Cobb by two to one. You will see in the Conf. Union today a letter from "Fair Play " of the 38th regmt., showing how the meeting in Gardner's Brigade was conducted. I have just received a letter from a Mr. Lee of that Brigade from Twiggs Co. who gives the same account of it and says the Brigade endorses me and would give me a heavier vote if I were before them than I got last October, that the action of the officers in getting through the Resolutions has caused very considerable excitement in the Brigade, that the message is in great demand. I do not know whether the copies sent to the captains reach them or whether they are stolen or taken from the mail bags on the way by P. O. officials. I am fully satisfied from all I learn that the army is all right upon the question and that a decided majority at home is on the same line.

Joseph E. Brown To Alexander H. Stephens. R.
(Private.)

Milledgeville, ga., *April 19th, 186.*
Dear Sir: Your letter to hand last night. Col. Thweatt sent you Cobb's review of your speech. Erskine of Atlanta told me that a staff officer told him the Genl. was the author and Genl. Wayne said the same to me a day or two since, with the remark that women would talk. I am told his bitterness intensifies as he studies of his defeat with the legislature. Foster writes me that Lamar was, he is told, very severe on us both in Atlanta the other night. He seems to have work to do in his own state judging from the resolutions to which you refer in your letter. I am much gratified at their passage. Waters is on a trip to Troup County to his wife's mother's and he writes that the farmers of Troup generally sustain the message and the speech.

7356C—13 41

Mobley tells me that he did not hear them talk, but is told at Harris court that Ben Hill, Pike Hill and Ramsay were very abusive of both you and myself and particularly of you as a *traitor.* Mobley did not wish me to mention his name but said he was told they were talking to a crowd of old farmers.

You have no doubt noticed the attacks of the Richmond Enquirer and other papers upon my message because the position taken looked to the retirement of Georgia from the contest, leaving her sister states to meet the enemy, etc. To meet this view of the case I wrote a letter to Brig. Genl. Colston commanding brigade at Savannah. A good opportunity afforded and I thought it a proper time. You will see my letter in the Union of this date. Also you will see extracts from letters from soldiers in Gardner's Brigade about the Resolutions. From all I hear I am satisfied the meeting in the brigade has injured their side of the question and that a large majority of it is on the right side of the question.

P. S.—Will you go to Richmond at the meeting of Congress? I think it would be best, as you could in that way mingle with the new members.

Joseph E. Brown To Alexander H. Stephens. R.

Milledgeville ga., *May 5, 1864* Dear Sir: Before I received your letter I wrote Linton tendering him the judgeship if he will accept, but saying that I did not see how he could well be spared out of the House of Reps, in the present state of things. The truth is he is greatly needed in both positions and I am at a loss to know what is best for him to do. In this state of the case I leave him to select his own position as he may prefer. I have not heard from him in reply to my letter though I have a letter written before he got mine in which he presents the names of Col. Johnson and Col. Lofton.

Genl. Toombs wrote to say that Linton is the choice of the bar and people, but does not know whether he would be willing to leave the House, and is willing to have him decide whether he ought. In case he does not accept Genl. T. mentions the names of Akerman, Reese and Barnett, and giving Reese the preference as probably the best lawyer, but says either would make a good judge.

I think the report that Senator Johnson is the author of " Troup" is erroneous. At Atlanta Genl. Cobb's friends openly claim for him the authorship.

Genl. Anderson sends me a letter with a copy of the resolutions passed by his brigade condemning me and the legislature and denying that there was any use for the extra session. As I am pretty fully posted from reliable sources as to the action of the meeting I have replied to the Genl. and will publish the correspondence in the Union next week. I intend to send the correspondence to all the companies of his brigade and am of opinion the whole affair will result unfavorably to the originators of the meeting.

P. S. I think your presence at Richmond while the policy of the new Congress is forming would be valuable. I suppose good may result from an interview with the persons you mention.

Joseph E. Brown To Alexander H. Stephens. R.
(Private.)

Milledgeville ga., *May 11th, 1864.* Dear Sir: I received a letter from Linton last night declining the judgeship of the circuit which I had tendered to him. I had doubts what would be best but felt it my duty to leave him to select his own position.

I see from all the indications that the Consolidation party in the state will make a desperate effort next winter to carry measures through the legislature favorable to their purposes. Cobb as Major Genl. of the *reserves* will act as high priest, and I think Linton's services in the House may be indispensably necessary. If he goes out they can control the House. In this view of it I am inclined to think he did right to decline it.

He mentions Genl. Toombs for the place, but I think his great talents in the forum of more value than they could be in the position of a circuit judge whose decisions would be subject to the review of a higher court with a known consolidationist as its most determined member.

Johnson of Hancock, Akerman of Elbert, Reese and Barnett of Wilkes and Lofton of Oglethorpe are all mentioned by their friends. My mind rather inclines to Reese as a sound man and probably the best lawyer of them all. The appointment of Lofton would be an offering to the army which I should be glad to make if all other things were equal. I do not know his position with certainty on the great questions which are likely to come before the country upon which our future liberties so much depend and I am unwilling to put any one on the bench of that circuit whose position is at all doubtful. His regiment passed resolutions denouncing me and the legislature, but I think he was absent. Mr. Barnes of Augusta writes that he told him a few days since that he was opposed to the *habeas corpus* suspension. I have written Genl. Toombs to-day. If you and he and Linton could agree on what is best to be done and advise me soon I would be glad. You are all in the circuit and all have a decided interest in a proper selection and I wish to give the circuit a man satisfactory to the bar. I should be glad to hear from you all soon,

Joseph E. Brown To Alexander H. Stephens. R.

Atlanta ga., *June 6th, 1864.*

Dear Sir: I received your letter with the inclosed and delivered them to Linton, Col. Johnston and Mr. Hidell.

I regret to hear of your sufferings but trust you will soon be relieved and come up.

Genl. Smith is now here and will assume the command in a day or two. He wishes to look round a little before he makes up his staff. I have tendered the troops to Genl. Johnston and asked him to give them an honorable position, have said that he never commanded better material and have assured him that they will do their duty faithfully in the front if ordered there by him. He replies that it is necessary that they guard the ferries on the Chattahoochee river and the approaches to Atlanta for the present. Genl. Smith wishes Genl. Toombs with him all the time and I have written the Genl. to come up immediately. I expect to stay here most of the time and to be here at the battle though I will assume no active command after I turn Smith over with the organization to Genl. Johnston.

Joseph E. Brown To Alexander H. Stephens. R.

Milledgeville ga., *June 17th, 1864* Dear Sir: A letter from Henry Cleveland informs me that the majority of the stock of the Constitutionalist is now owned by Administration men and that he will be obliged to change his course, keep silent, or be ousted.

Could not enough of the stock be purchased to control and keep the paper on the rights lines? I am satisfied the money can be raised on short notice to purchase half of the stock in addition to what is in the right hands, if necessary, by a little effort on the part of our friends. I can raise part of it here. I wish you would see what can be done as it would be a misfortune for the paper to be lost to the cause of liberty. I expect to return to Atlanta Monday or Tuesday. My family are not very well.

John H. Winder 1 To Howell Cobb. E.

Camp Sumter, Andersonville, Ga., *July 9. 1864.*

General: Matters have arrived at that point *where I must* have reinforcements. Twelve men deserted last night with their arms. There is great dissatisfaction among the Reserves; and they, I am assured, have determined to leave, and I have no force to oppose this determination.

1 Confederate brigadier-general commanding the prison stockade at Andersonville.

Now General it is morally certain that if the Government or the people of Georgia don't come to my relief and that instantly, I cannot hold these prisoners, and they must submit to see Georgia devastated by the *prisoners.* There is not a moment to spare. Can you not get a volunteer force for a short time to come down at once—without a moment's delay. You may depend you have not a moment to spare. Twenty-four hours may be too late.

Howell Cobb To His Wife. E.

Headquarters, Georgia Reserves, Macon, Ga., *July 14,186h.* My Dear Wife, Johnnie arrived this morning bringing your most welcome letters. The steps you have taken and propose to take in reference to the apprehended raid on Athens are just right in my opinion. I do not believe that Atlanta will fall and until it does fall there is no serious danger of a raid upon Athens. The troops at Athens... ought to hold the place against any raiding party that will be sent there. Genl. Johnston will not give up Atlanta without a fight though he may be compelled to uncover the town for a time to enable him to meet and fight the flanking movements of the enemy; hence the policy and propriety of moving all stores, etc. , from the city. From all I can learn I am satisfied he intends to make a decided stand at Atlanta, and I believe it will be a successful one. The statement of Maj. Morgan, which I wrote you, that Mrs. Johnston had gone to Milledgeville turns out to be false; she is still in Atlanta and as I am now informed has not sent off any of her things though Col. Ewell went to Milledgeville to see if a house could be got for her in the event she had to move. I fear that Maj. Morgan is as unreliable in his reports from Atlanta as those who report in Athens that shells are falling in the city of Atlanta. Henry Jackson is just from Genl. Hardee's head quarters which are four miles the other side of Atlanta. Mrs. Hardee was in camp with the Genl. and as a matter of course she would not be there if at that point she was in range of the enemy's shells. I don't suppose that a shell has fallen within five miles of the corporate limits of Atlanta. Whilst I am thus confident of the successful defence of Atlanta, I still desire that you should remove your valuables and be prepared to leave yourself if things turn out contrary to my expectations and Athens should become exposed to a raid. What I said to Col. Barrow was what I wanted you to do in the event you should be caught in Athens by a raiding party; but the more I think about it the more unwilling I feel for you to be in the enemy's line, and whilst I fully approve of your idea of sending the children to Mrs. Clayton's I greatly prefer that you should go with them. I would rather see all that we have at Athens and everywhere else in ashes than that you should receive the slightest insult or indignity from the Yankees. Therefore let all go if they come, but let me have you and the children out of their hands....

Howell, Cobb To His Wife. E.

Headquarters, Georgia Reserves, Macon, Ga., *July 18,1864.* My Dear Wife, I write you after a tedious day's labor produced by various rumors and some exciting telegraphic news from the vicinity of Columbus. It appears that the Yankees have cut the railroad between Opelika and Montgomery and are now marching towards Columbus; their force is represented as ten regiments of cavalry and two pieces of artillery. A dispatch just received from Opelika says that they are tearing up the road at Auburn and are expected to arrive at that place. The excitement seems to be considerable at Columbus and Maj. Dawson, commandant of the post, telegraphs that the Yankees are said to be in thirty miles of Columbus and he is calling for reinforcements. I state all the facts that have come to my knowledge, though you may get them in the papers before you get this letter. I am doing all I can to prepare for the defence of Columbus as well as for the safety of the prison at Andersonville, to which point it is thought they may be working their way. It keeps me quite busy, telegraphing, writing, and sending expresses etc., etc., etc. I am not apprehensive of any serious results, but these things show that the enemy is busy, active, energetic, and will spare no pains to inflict all the injury he can upon us. This raid near Columbus is in the immediate neighborhood of John's plantation, and as a matter of course he feels quite anxious and uneasy. Besides, Dr. Johnson's and Maj. Whitner's families have recently moved from West Point to John's plantation for safety, and I suppose all of them are still there except Dr. Johnson who came to Columbus to look for new quarters before this raid commenced, and I don't know whether or not he had returned to the plantation. He sent here Ma's John and twelve other negroes that he had hired to the engineer department. They got here on Saturday evening and since then I have heard nothing from the Dr. or any of the family. I mention the facts to you, as other rumors may reach Athens and it is better you should know the exact facts. I don't think that there is any cause for uneasiness about the two families though they may be subjected to some annoyances. It is a mere raid and not like taking permanent possession of the country.1 In reference to your own movements, I think it is well enough to continue your arrangements for sending to Baldwin such things as you desire and getting ready to leave yourself. My opinion that Atlanta will not fall remains unchanged; still it is best to be prepared for the worst. If you wish to send off any of your furniture do so. Howell can have it boxed for you. The most important thing is to send such as you will need for housekeeping wherever you may be. I got today a letter from Mr. Clayton which I will enclose if I don't forget it in my hurry,—from which I find that he has made you an offer of his house or so much of it as you may need. My advice is not to hesitate to go there if you have to leave Athens before we get the house ready at the plantation. Indeed I still think it is a good place to go to anyhow. After I wrote to you on Saturday the bucket of butter from my friend Maj. Yancey turned up at the house, and all that I could hear was that a negro brought it there. I don't know of anything new beyond what I have written.

Howell Cobb To His Wife. E.

Macon ga., *20 July, 186b*. My Dear Wife, I can now inform you of the exact whereabouts of Genl. and Mrs. Johnston. They reached Macon today about 12 o'clock by a freight train and hearing accidentally that they were expected I sent a pressing invitation to them to come to our house. They are now with me and will stay I hope during their sojourn here. Mrs. Johnston was complaining of a headache and retired at once to her room, so that I have had no conversation with her. With the Genl. I have had but little conversation except in the presence of other members of the household. He evidently feels his present unpleasant situation in being relieved from the command of the army. Still he indulges in no spirit of complaint, speaks kindly of his successor and very hopefully of the prospect of holding Atlanta. In view of the present position of Sherman's army he thinks that Athens is exposed to a raid though he does not look for it immediately. He tells me that he had instructed Genl. Wheeler to keep a lookout for such a movement, and if the enemy attempted it, to strike him in the rear. The crisis for Atlanta is evidently at hand, and it seems to me cannot be postponed beyond this week. At present the Yankees are evidently using every effort to cut off all railroad communication with the place and are succeeding pretty well, as the Macon & Western road is the only one now running and I am just informed that the train that left here this morning has stopped at Griffin in consequence of the telegraphic wires being cut between there and Atlanta. Such is the state of things as far as I can learn them. I can only repeat my advice to you to go with the children to Greensboro, sending such things as I have suggested. There may be and I hope will be no necessity for it; still it is better to be wise and prudent and take time by the forelock.

The latest news from the raiders in Alabama is that they burned Opelika and were four miles this side tearing up the railroad track. A cavalry force has been sent to' intercept them from West Point and we have a force at Columbus able to protect the place. The raiders are represented to be four thousand strong and to have artillery with them. I hear nothing from John's plantation. It may be that the enemy did not go there, as it is not directly on the route which we understand they travelled.

Col. John Hill Lamar was killed in the battle fought by Genl. Early in his march upon Washington City. The news reached here on yesterday. The family as a matter of course are very much distressed. Really the Lamar name is written in blood in the history of this revolution. A proud honor dearly bought.

Howell Cobb To His Wife. E.

Headquarters, Georgia Reserves, Macon, Ga., *July 22,1864.*

My Dear Wife, When I wrote you on yesterday I was engaged in the defense of a poor soldier charged with murder and I was detained in the Court House until after midnight. The State made a strong case against him but I saved his life though he was convicted of manslaughter and condemned to the penitentiary....

The news from Atlanta today is very confused and unsatisfactory. We have nothing reliable but the town is full of rumors and not of the most encouraging kind. The passengers by the train that arrived today differ so widely in their accounts, that no reliance is to be placed upon any of them. It is perhaps enough to say that the most favorable rumors indicate that there is great danger of the fall of Atlanta, and such news may reach you before you get this letter. I greatly fear that we shall have to regret too deeply the removal of Genl. Johnston from the command of that army. Lamar has just returned from the telegraph office. He learned there that these rumors to which I have just referred have no foundation, that everything remains about the same at Atlanta, and there is nothing more than the usual skirmishing going on. Still I must confess that I do not feel the same confidence I did when Genl. Johnston was in command.

Howell Cobb To His Wife. E.

Headquarters, Georgia Reserves, Macon, Ga., *July 23,186Jh* My Dear Wife, Since I wrote to you on yesterday there has been quite a bloody fight at Atlanta resulting favorably to our army. As yet we have very few details and the extent of the victory is wholly unknown. The result as far as we know it, is encouraging but by no means decisive. No battle will amount to anything of importance that does not drive the enemy to the other side of the Chattahoochee. Up to this hour we can hear of no fighting today. This is not a good sign for us for if we had whipt them badly on yesterday the victory ought to have been followed up today. The loss of generals is severe on both sides. Genl. McPherson was the next man to Sherman in the Yankee army and some people regard him as the ablest man of the two. The other Yankee generals killed were small potatoes. On our side we lost the brave and gallant Genl. Walker, truly a heavy blow, and it is now reported that Genl. Wheeler is killed; that lacks confirmation.

As I get no letters from you I take it for granted that you are busily engaged with your packing and getting your things off. Just a line or two to let me know how you are getting on would be very acceptable.

Johnnie came across some fine peaches on yesterday which Bajon and himself bought and sent to you. There were only a few but they took all the man had. I hope you got them. They were sent to the express office today. I felt more depressed on yesterday about Atlanta than I have since our army fell back. Today I feel encouraged and again look with hope and confidence to the result. I do not think that Atlanta will fall; nothing from Alabama.

Joseph E. Brown To Alexander H. Stephens. R.

Executive Department, Mhxedgeville ga., *Aug. 17th, 1864.*

Dear Sir: I have received your letter in behalf of Mr. Stevens of Brooks and regret that it is not in my power to aid him. When I turned over the militia to Genl. Johnston and then to Genl. Hood it was with the express understanding that I would in no way interfere with the organization while under the control of the commanding Genl. The only power I have reserved over them is the power to disband them or resume the command of them as an organization when I choose. During the time I permit them to remain under Genl. Hood, his control over them is as absolute as is Genl. Lee's over the Georgians in Virginia. This I considered necessary to their efficiency and to harmony between me and the Genl. in command. As he is charged with the defence of Atlanta he should have the entire control of all the troops under him. I do not grant a single furlough or detail nor do I annoy him with applications for persons who wish them. If I did this my time would be too much taxed or I must give offence to those whose applications I refused to indorse. I have no position at present which is not filled and do not see how it is in my power to aid or relieve the applicant.

I have armed and placed at the front under my two calls over 10,000 men. The militia have held for some time about three miles of the entrenchments around Atlanta. Genl. Hood acknowledges that they have been of essential service to him in holding the place. No man acquainted with the facts questions that their presence here and at Macon saved both places from capture by Stoneman's raiders. The enemy came within 3 miles of this place in 3 hours after I got the 1000 armed militia to the place.

Josephus Anderson To Howell Cobb. E.

Qtjincy, Fla., *Aug. 29th, 186b.*

My Dear Genu, Your very welcome letter reached me a few days ago and I thank you for it. I am glad that you still speak so encouragingly of our national troubles. It seems to me that light begins to streak the horizon of the future, that the dawn of peace is appearing in the distance. The " situation " is improving decidedly both in Virginia and in Georgia and the campaign is closing far better for us than any previous one. We are stronger than at this period of the year in any former year of the war and our enemies are weaker. The state of things among the people of the North looks well for our cause. At last reaction is taking place and by the blessing of Providence, I trust it will roll on like the waves of ocean sweeping away all opposition. I can hardly think however that the day which brings peace to us will see the Northern people united and prosperous, enjoying peace and quiet. There are too many powerful elements of discord at work there and too much wrath has been kindled in Heaven for this to be the case. There must be a day of reckoning before them and woe unto them when it comes!

Since I wrote to you, our arms have been successful in this State, by the favor of God. That Christian hero, Capt. Dickinson, with a small force has routed the Yankee force and captured about as many more, I believe than his own force. He deserves a brigadiership and I wish it was given him.... All is not quiet here yet however and will not be while our force is so small. The militia have responded nobly and many large companies have been organized in the counties around here. Judge DuPont commands one and makes an excellent officer. He has seen service in other years and knows his duty. I am sorry to say that there is a great deal of sickness now among us. My health continues very poor. I am so very weak and cannot regain my strength it seems. Dr. Hentz says I ought to drink bitters, but that is out of the question now—no brandy to be found to make them with.

Do you know where I can get flour? Corn-bread does not suit me and flour is now a scarce article. Possibly you may put me on the track of some. I want to get a couple of barrels for money or in exchange for salt if I cannot get it for money. Please remember me to those of your staff here who are with you now. My family join in love to you.

Robert Toombs To Alexander H. Stephens. R.

Atlanta, Geo., *30th Aug., 1864.* Dear Stephens, I wrote you some fortnight ago but hearing thro' a letter from Linton to Genl. Smith that he had heard nothing from either of us and my letter to him being of same date I think it probable from not hearing from you that yours also miscarried. I have been very closely engaged here since the enemy began shelling the city. He hauled off a few days ago and the army seemed as much elated as tho' we had gained a great victory, whereas it was simply changing his mode of attack. Our works were formidable; he felt of them half a dozen times; his men could not be got to charge them. He then wisely fell back, massed himself 6 or 7 miles west so. west of the town on the West Point R. Road, entrenched, and is gradually moving, entrenching as he goes, until he straddles the Macon road, cuts off our supplies, and compels us to fight him in his works or evacuate the place as soon as our rations are out. In the mean time he places a corps on the Chattahoochee defending his line from Vining's Station to Sand Town in his rear and thus protecting his line of communications. In fact, allowing for the topography of the country, it is precisely the Vicksburg movement acted over again, except we can get out when we want to and Pemberton could not. But we shall be equally unable to hold the place. The enemy care nothing for Wheeler and his seven thousand cavalry in the rear. They did not obstruct his trains more than four days, if that; and Wheeler avoided all depots where there were as much as armed sutlers. He has been gone for three weeks. I cannot say he has done no good, for he has relieved the poor people of this part of the country temporarily from his plundering marauding bands of cowardly robbers. It is said he is in Tennessee. I hope to God he will never get back into Georgia. We have a question of famine upon us. His band consumes more than the whole army besides and will accelerate the evil day. This army of Tennessee is in a deplorable condition. Hood is getting ridd of Bragg's worthless pets as fast as he can, but Davis supports a great number of them, and many other incompts. are sent from other places to take their commands. Hood I think the very best of the generals of his school; but like all the rest of them he knows no more of business than a ten year old boy, and don't know who does know anything about it. The longer the war lasts the more and more important it becomes to husband the resources of the country; but ours are wasted with a wild recklessness that would disgrace the Choctaw Indians. One third of the white population in Georgia are in the enemy's lines or so close to them as to make them or their industry unavailable to us. About a fourth of the residue is devastated by our armies and the villains around posts. Behold the prospect! This army has less than thirty thousand musketts present for duty, leaving out the militia who have under four thousand. Sherman I do not think has over 45 thousand musketts, and the possession of empire depends on this small force. Kirby Smith and Dick Taylor have over thirty thousand musketts in La. They have not fired a gun or perhaps marched ten miles since Banks left Alexandria last spring. I have a strong opinion that this force was promised to Hood. I saw Gov. Lubbock of Texas last night, who came direct thro' Dick Taylor's camp and therefore spoke on his personal knowledge of these important events. Therefore upon the whole our affairs here are gloomy enough. A good victory would change them much for the better.

I have been interrupted more than a dozen times in writing this letter and have not written you one tenth part that I want to. I will write you again tomorrow or next. Hood has sent me a request to send out people to collect and send him bacon in waggons to Social Circle en route for this place and a whole crowd of them are now in my tent waiting orders.

I hope if-Linton gets well he will come back. Urge him to do so if his health will allow. There are many reasons for it.

Robert Toombs To Aijixander H. Stephens. R.

Washington, Geo., *Sept. 23rd, 1864.*

Dear Stephens, I recd. your letter last evening, and am sorry you and Linton could not come over this week. Our court sits Monday and I shall be at home until it is over. There are quite a number of cases to be tried where all parties are ready and anxious, so I think it will last three or four days. Tell Linton to be sure to come with you. I want to see you both.

Do not by any means go to see Sherman, whatever may be the form of his invitation. It will place you in a wrong, *very wrong* position. What is said to be Brown's answer in the papers of yesterday is the true position. If Sherman means anything he means to detach Georgia from the Confederacy. Better any fate than that. Davis is impregnable upon the peace issue. In every shape and form and at all times he has professed to seek peace, and in truth up to this time his actions have conformed to his professions. The fundamental law commits it to his hands, and nothing could be of more evil tendency than for other officers of the Confederacy, or state governments, to meet any person, and much less a general of an army, to discuss the question. All well.

P. S.—There are strong indications that Davis intends to remove Hood. If done, it will be solely on account of his relation to the Geo. militia.

Joseph E. Brown To Alexander H. Stephens. R.

Milledgeville ga., *Sept. 30th, 1864.*

Dear Sir: I learn that Hon. Joshua Hill agrees fully with us on the line of policy We have acted upon in Confederate politics. There is a vacancy in the Senate from his district by the death of Adams. We need a leader in the Senate. I have confidentially written Hill asking him to run. He is hesitating. I wish you would write him or see him and try to induce him to run. He can be elected and he would render a public service in my opinion. The loss of Atlanta was a great calamity under the circumstances, and I regret to see by the President's speech at Macon that he has no measure of relief to propose.

You have I suppose seen my reply to Genl. Sherman. I have looked for the administration press to attack the closing paragraph as looking to a possible contingency in which Mr. Davis would not be recognized as supreme. Thus far I have seen no comment. They have generally published without remark. I trust your health is good.

P. S. Has Mr. King visited you and what did you say to him?

Joseph E. Brown To Alexander H. Stephens. R.

Milledgeville ga., *Oct. 12th, 1864.*

Dear Sir: I have the pleasure to acknowledge receipt of your letter with inclosures. I am glad you were pleased with my reply to Genl. Sherman. I expected it to be attacked by ultra administration men at the very point you mention. I see Mr. Davis in his speech at Columbia refers to the traitorous conduct of states that would attempt to negotiate, etc.

I have promised to meet Gov. Vance and some or all of the other Southern Governors this side the Mississippi next Monday in Augusta for consultation. Gov. Vance invited the interview. His request is for a consultation as to the best means of filling up the army and sending forward deserters, etc. I intend to sound them a little upon their feelings in reference to a convention of the states. I wish I could see you but will not have time. I now think I will go to Linton's Saturday night on my way, but this letter will not reach you in time for you to meet me there. If it should, I trust you will do so. I only got a telegram last night from Vance settling the time.

In the matter of Henry G. Cole I am not prepared to act. The matter referred to in Genl. Jones's letter was an anonymous letter written from Augusta to Cole at Marietta developing a plan for blowing up the powder works, etc., and for robbing the banks and burning the cotton in Augusta. The letter was intercepted at Marietta after Cole's arrest, and I think there is no doubt he was in the plot. This however was not the cause of his arrest. Genl. Wright learning that he was holding secret correspondence with Genl. Sherman sent a detective to him who represented himself as a spy from Sherman, and Cole communicated freely with him about plans to burn the R. R. bridges in the rear of Johnston's army and referred to his letters written to Sherman, etc., and gave reasons why he had been unable up to that time to carry the plans into execution. He is a Yankee who has always expressed himself hostile to our cause from the beginning and I think he is one of the worst men I know. Under these circumstances I do not feel it my duty to interfere as the state government had nothing to do in making the arrest.

I am glad you make the proposition in your reply to Sherman for an interview on the terms mentioned by you. It keeps the door open and I think this is wise. I also think your letter should be published and reach the Northern press before the election.

Alexander H. Stephens To The Public.1

Crawfordville, Ga., *10th Nov., 1864.*

To The Public: The following old address is now reprinted in this form, not with any special view to its own merits, but for the purpose of self vindication. Insinuations and *flings,* if not direct charges, have repeatedly been made of late against me as a *new light* on States' Rights, in my advocacy of the doctrine of " the ultimate absolute sovereignty of the several States" as the only sure basis of a permanent peace between the States of the old Union.

This address2 was the first written political speech ever made by me. It was made while I was a student of law, and notwithstanding its many very apparent defects (of which however as a first production I am not ashamed), it clearly shows that States' Rights and State Sovereignty are no new or latter day ideas with me. For this purpose only I ask its perusal at this time by all who may be disposed to do me justice in this particular.

It is true I was not a Nullifier. Nullification as I understood its exposition at that day claimed the right of any State, in effect, to 1 This letter was printed as an introduction to a pamphlet: "An Address delivered at Crawfordville on the fourth of July, 1834. " By Alexander H Stephens. Augusta. Ga, 1864. A copy Is In the New York Public Library.

Extracts from the speech are published In Johnston and Browne, "Life of Alexander H. Stephens", p. 88, render null and void, or inoperative within her limits, any law of Congress, and still remain within the Union. Without any desire to revive any of the questions that then divided State Rights men, I may simply add that in my judgment then and now, the reserved Sovereign Powers of the States could be properly resorted to for ultimate protection only by a full resumption of all powers delegated; in other words by secession. In this way only could the sovereign veto of a State against actual or threatened aggression be effectually and properly interposed. When thus interposed there was no constitutional power in the Central Government to command obedience by coercion.

It is also true that I opposed secession in 1850 and 1860, as a question of *policy,* but not as a matter of *right.* The charge that I ever at any time or on any occasion uttered the sentiment that secession would be " a *crime* " is entirely without the shadow of a foundation. The clear right of a State under the compact of 1787 to resume the full exercise of all her delegated powers by a withdrawal from the Union whenever her people in their deliberate and solemnly expressed judgment should determine to do so, was never questioned by me. This was the doctrine of the States' Rights party of Georgia under the lead of the illustrious and renowned Troup—the correct teachings of the Kentucky and Virginia Resolutions of 1798 and '99. In these principles I was reared, by them I have ever been governed in my political acts, and by them I expect to live and die. Hence when Georgia seceded in 1861, even against my own judgment, I stood by her act. To her alone I owed ultimate allegiance. Her cause became my cause. Her destiny became my destiny. From that day to this that cause has engaged every energy of my heart, head and soul, and in it they will continue to be enlisted to the bitter end. Should that end be the establishment of this principle of " the ultimate absolute sovereignty of the several States," it will in my judgment more than compensate for the loss of blood and treasure of this war so unjustly waged against her and her confederates, great as it has been or may be. This doctrine once firmly established will, I doubt not, prove to be the self-adjusting principle—the Continental Regulator— in our present or any future systems of associations or confederations of States that may arise. I make no boast of consistency so far as party relations are concerned—these I have often changed, but *principles never.*

Howell Cobb To His Wife. E.

Camp Near Griffin ga., *16 Nov., 1864.* My Dear Wife, I have time only to write you a hurried note. When I reached the camp at Lovejoy's station on yesterday evening I found everything in motion to fall back. The enemy had burned Atlanta, destroyed the railroad from Atlanta to the Chattahoochee and burnt the railroad bridge over the Chattahoochee. How much has been destroyed the other side of the Chattahooche is not known, but the rumor is they are destroying the road to Marietta—(all very strange and unaccountable to me). The enemy commenced his movement in this direction with an army estimated by Genl. Wheeler to be not less than thirty thousand, including six thousand cavalry under Kilpatrick. Sherman is believed to be with this army. Our cavalry was driven out of Jonesboro and was last night at Lovejoy's station occupying our old camp, whilst the infantry and artillery are here. We were on the march all night. Remaining in the rear, Genl. Smith and myself were the last to get into camp. So far we have heard nothing this morning from Wheeler or the enemy, and it is now 10 o'ck. If I do hear anything before the train leaves I will send you word by Dr. Crawford who carries this letter down. That Sherman intends to move with this large army upon some point in Georgia I have no doubt, but where it will be is not yet so certain though my opinion is that Macon is the point. With our small force we can do but little to impede his progress, but I hope we shall be reinforced in time to defeat this formidable invasion. It would be well as soon as you see that the movement is in direction of Macon—of which I will try to give you notice—to move down with the family to Americus, for though I have no serious fears now that Macon can be taken, still it will not be so comfortable to be there with a Yankee army around it.

I write very hastily as Genl. Smith is waiting for me to ride and attend to some important matters.

An Anonymous Writer To Howell Cobb. E.

January 3d, 1865. Dear Sir, You will excuse me for making the following suggestions upon the state of the country. Things look rather gloomy and unless something is done and that before the spring campaign opens we are undone. We want more men and where are they to come from? Some will say if the skulkers and deserters were brought up we would have men enough; but they cannot be made available. We cannot get from the militia a sufficient number to recruit our army and if we could it will not do to take all the male population out of the country. If they are, there would be nothing made to support the army and what little might be made it would be destroyed by the negroes and deserters, etc. I see but one alternative left us and that to fill up our army with negroes. I have no doubt but they can be made as good soldiers as the population our enemies are importing from Europe. An army is a machine, and you can make anything fight if they are properly drilled. We are told however that they can not be made to fight. They have done some very good fighting for the Yanks, and I cannot see why they will not do as well for us if we will give them their freedom. If you do not put them in the field they will very soon be taken from us and made to take up arms against us. Why not then move in the matter at once and have an army in the spring sufficient to drive the enemy back. If Georgia and South Carolina would give Hardee an army of one hundred thousand men, Sherman would not move out of Savannah, and Charleston and Augusta would be secure, our communications kept open and the state defended, or rather protected against raids. If Alabama and Mississippi would enforce Hood with one hundred thousand, we could march through Tennessee and Kentucky if Gen. Johnson was reinstated in command of that army. Then if North Carolina and Virginia would fill up Gen. Lee's ranks he would be able to drive Grant back. To say the least of this course we could fight them four years longer and by that time I think the North would be willing to make peace, and if she was not, Europe would interpose and settle matters. Some think that our soldiers would not be willing to have negroes placed in the army. If Gen. Lee would say that it is necessary there would be but few objections. Our Congress is afraid to move unless they could be assured that the move would be popular. Six months since it would not have been, but now almost every man I see is in favor of the measure and the day is not far distant when these gentlemen will regret their want of nerve. If our Governor could know the feeling generally of the people he would assemble the Legislature and have a large army of negroes in the field, if he could under the constitution send them out as militia. The Governor will be however satisfied if he can get a chance to abuse President Davis and have out a few more candidates for justice of the Inferior Court and get his cabbages safely to Dooly. The man that leads off in this thing will be the great man of this Confederacy, for it will save us from subjugation. Now General, if you think as I do, and as a large majority of the people of Georgia, you are the very man to lead off in this thing. In the first place you have more influence than any man in Georgia and in the second place you own a great many slaves and if you are willing to give a portion of your slaves, others could not object and would not. As far as I am concerned I am willing to give up everything and commence the world in my old age without one cent if it will save me from Yankee rule. Anything but reconstruction or subjugation. I feel as confident as I can of anything that if we will levy a sufficient force from our black population that it will save us from either. If the country is unwilling 73566—13 42 to fight the negroes I am willing to propose to England and France if they will recognize us with armed intervention that we will agree to the gradual abolition of slavery. I have believed for the last two years that we would be compelled to put negroes in the army or go up the spout. I am old and have no influence. You are a man of genius, ability and influence, and if you can conscientiously lead off in this matter I believe you will make a name that will live till time will be no more.

Howell Cobb To His Wife. E.

Headq'rs Georgia Reserves, And Military Dist. Of Ga., Macon, Ga., *January 16, 1S65.* My Dear Wife, At the depot I met Pope just ready to leave with an extra train for me with a despatch from Richmond ordering me to remove my headquarters at once to Augusta. I leave here in the morning in obedience to the order. I shall take no one with me at present but Pope, but the rest will have to follow in a short time if the order is not countermanded. The order was very unexpected to me and I am at a loss to account for it. There is no sense in it, and is not only a great sacrifice of my personal comfort and interest but is equally unfortunate for the public service. Whilst I obey the order I have written fully to the Dept. on the subject. and if they have not lost all their senses at Richmond or become inconceivably perverse and obstinate the order will be countermanded and I shall return to Macon in a few days. I shall leave the house and lot here in charge of Maj. Cobb until some of the boys get here. I think it would be well enough for Johnnie to come up for a day or two and see that things are put in proper condition for the new state of things. If this is to become the permanent arrangement then the sooner you and the children can get to Athens the better, as we shall be nearer each other. At all events it is advisable that you get back to Macon, as I will not be here to look after your comfort and safety in Americus. All the arrangements for moving our things to Athens and getting our supplies, as well as the corn, meat, etc., etc., brought to Macon or delivered to the Government, should be carried out as soon as it can be done. I have no reason to look for any raids, more than I have had all the time. Still I think it best that every precautionary step should be taken for such a contingency if it should come. My idea is to get as much provisions as we can here and at Athens and all our surplus delivered over to the Govt. that we expect to sell, so that if the worst should come we will be ready to run our stock out of the way of the enemy and have something to live upon. Tell Johnnie that just as fast as the meat is smoked and ready to move he ought to send it up or deliver to the Govt. Mr. Powers has promised me to furnish transportation for these things when I call for it and I have no doubt he will do it promptly.

We have no reliable news here except that the enemy is advancing in South Carolina. They landed in the neighborhood of Beaufort and attacked our forces at Pocataligo where after a stubborn resistance we fell back. If I hear anything additional before the mail closes I will send it to you. Tommy Glenn is just down from Atlanta. He left all well and brings no news of any interest....

Howell Cobb To His Wife. E.
Headq'rs Georgia Reserves
And Military Dist. Of Ga.,
Macon, Ga., *31 J any. 1865.*

My Dear Wife, I have returned from Augusta and once more established at my old headquarters. Genl. Beauregard passed through to day *en route* for Augusta. He did not stop at all, as he was anxious to get to Augusta at the earliest possible moment. I only had a few minutes conversation with him. When I left Augusta the enemy was reported to be advancing in a heavy force on this side of the Savannah river. He was however only as far as Springfield in Effingham county and in my opinion would cross at Sisters' Ferry and join the forces marching upon Branchville. He may threaten Augusta as he did Macon but will hardly take it if the same resistance is made there that was made here.

Whilst in Augusta an open letter came by flag of truce at Richmond from Genl. H. R. Jackson to you. It was open and I read it. He was at Johnson's Island but was to be sent to Fort Warren. He was well and as cheerful as could be expected. The gentleman who brought it was a fellow prisoner who had been paroled, and from him I learned more of the General's feelings than from the letter. The letter is with my baggage, which I had to leave behind with Mrs. Clay and Pope at Milledgeville, or I would forward it.

You ought by all means to write your threatened letters to Genl. Taylor and Capt. Chisolm,—both of whom will be pleased I know to receive them. The box from Capt. Chisolm has not arrived though it has left Augusta. By the carelessness of the illegible line I only got *two* letters from you whilst I was in Augusta. I wrote almost daily but doubt if you ever got them. judging from my luck in getting yours.

If possible I shall make you a hurried visit during this week. I wrote a short letter to Genl. J. to let him know that all were well. Tell Johnnie we are entirely out of provisions and he must send up some at once....

Robert Toombs To Alexander H. Stephens. R.

Washington, Ga., *Mch. 16th, 1865.* Dear Stephens, I rec'd your letter of the 2nd. inst. through Mr. Reed?. I have been recruiting slowly since you left, am now well but weak and gather strength by small degrees. We get nothing from Richmond or N. Carolina but meager, unsatisfactory and conflicting rumors.

Senator Garland and his brother stayed all night with me a few days ago and they represented great despondency in govt. officials and people about Richmond and they seemed to suppose that Richmond would have to be evacuated long before this. Our later accounts do not seem to confirm it. I suppose they will remain there until it will be too late to remain with safety or fight with success. I suppose the armies must be subsisted by universal pillage, as nothing can be sent on from this part of the country. If Sherman has not got into safe quarters before this he would be in great danger if Johnson has any respectable force with which to meet him, but that I much doubt. I see that Davis has forced the negro bill through congress and I suppose has detained the Junto there for some other crowning inquity, the Lord knows what.

I see Brown has got him an impressment law too. How catching is thieving!! His hobby is soldiers' families. He will let it go now since the legislature has put it in the hands of the inferior courts, who, thank God, will make the whole business stink in the nostrils of putridity itself. They are actuated doubtless by the motive of curtailing Joe's power, but unwittingly they will have done a great good to sound principles without ever dreaming of such results.

I am very anxious to go out to Macon and to my plantation, bui Wilkes, Warren and Hancock courts all interfere and I can not go until after that time, when I suppose the militia will be called out to prevent me from going at all. I get no Macon paper and but meager accounts thro' Augusta papers of the action of the legislature, therefore can tell little what they are at. All or nearly all of the members from this section are at home. Elbert, Wilkes and Lincoln have neither senators nor representatives in Macon and I suppose Georgia has few or none in Richmond. You must come over to see me at Wilkes Court. Julia and Sallie and the children are all well. Mr. Clay? and his wife are still with me, Mr. C's health is very poor. I cannot tell what Wigfall's telegram meant except the congress intended to force the reinstatement of Johnston or raise a row. Johnston's appointment may have quieted them down. That was done by Lee. Wigfall cannot see where the mischief lies and therefore can never remedy it.

Robert Toombs To Alexander H. Stephens. R.

Washington, Ga., *Mch. 23rd, 1865.* Dear Stephens, I find upon examination of my old law papers that I have the exemplication of the record from Greene Court of the case of Nicholson and Grimes and will bring it with me to Hancock Court.

My health is again good, having wholly recovered from chills, fever and jaundice and I am again ready to take the field. I see nothing hopeful from Richmond. They will swear all is right until Lee's defeat or evacuation, and then—chaos. I fear the congress has not nerve enough to see and appreciate the evil and the remedy. There is but one remedy—it is begone Davis. I suppose we have the matter of five hundred idlers and ration-eaters in this town, with several? mules, waggons, etc., doing nothing on earth but harassing the people and eating out their substance. Not a waggon load of provisions has been sent to Abbeville since the impressment of five hundred mules and waggons for that purpose in February. There are daily gathering here dozens of hungry adventurers who are consuming the revenues of the country under pretense of administering them. The crowd in the rear far outnumbers those in the front, and I see Davis vetoed a bill to disperse the vagabonds. Come over next week to our Court and bring Linton if you can. I should like to see you both and talk to you about the prospect before us. All well. Mr. & Mrs. Clay? are with us yet.

Jefferson Davis To Mrs. Howell Cobb. E.
(Private.)

Richmond, Va., *30 March, '65.* My Dear Madam, Accept my thanks for your kind consideration in sending me several newspapers with articles of interest in them.

Faction has done much to cloud our prospects and impair my power to serve the country. That such was not their purpose I am well assured, and if we may be permitted to hope that when they see that the indulgence of evil passion against myself injures not the individual only but the cause also of which I am a zealous though feeble representative, the discovery will lead to a change of conduct and an earnest effort to repair the mischief done, it may be in the end be well for us.

Near the close of the session of Congress, after the recommendations of my annual Message had been debated for four months without result, I sent, as was my duty, a message pointing out the necessitous condition of the country and urging legislation before adjournment. My style was not intended to provoke controversy and does not seem to me to have been wanting in decorum and deference. The Senate however took offence and in secret session appointed a committee to reply to the Message; after their adjournment it was published, and if not intended to destroy the confidence of the people in me is certainly calculated to have that effect. No opportunity was afforded to me to reply and correct the many misstatements of the report.

I send you a paper containing an editorial which answers the main points of the report by citations of the official record. Whether truth can overtake falsehood has always been doubtful, and in this case the race is most unequal, as many are interested in spreading statements for which they have hastily made themselves responsible and the demand of the public taste for spicy articles will render it more to the interest of publishers to copy the assault than the defence.

With most affectionate remembrance of you and your's I am very respectfully and truly your friend.

Joseph E. Brown To Alexander H. Stephens. R.

Augusta ga., *April 25th, 1865.* Dear Sir, I am now remaining here to leam the result of the conference going on under the armistice. When that is announced I will try to shape my course as best I can. I have made up my mind to remain in the state and do all I can to aid in the restoration of order and to mitigate suffering as long as I am allowed to do so. If I am arrested and carried off I have prepared my mind to meet my fate with coolness. As matters now stand I am very anxious to see and confer with you as to what is best to be done. Genl. Toombs is here and I am anxious that you come down. Can you not do so?

Howell Cobb To His Wife. E.
Macon ga., *27 April, 1865.*

My Dear Wife,... Laurence and Riley arrived this evening from Columbus, having flanked the enemy—coming down the river to Eufaula and then up here by railroad. All of our negroes have remained with us and behaved very well. Gilbert in particular has behaved remarkably well, more humble and attentive than ever. I regard him the most faithful negro in the world and intend to treat him accordingly....

I started the three boys with our twelve mules to Sumter yesterday and hope they will get there safely. I have got Doctor back but had to give Sumter for him. Pope has the promise of getting his horse back tomorrow. Laurence tells me that Judge Crawford's house was searched all over for him.... The Judge had left here and got back to Columbus and sends me word that they had ruined his plantation but none of his negroes had left him.

I have arranged for the parole of all the officers and men held by Genl. Wilson, and most of them will get off tomorrow. I cannot say how long I shall be detained here, as I have to see to it that all my command are taken care of before I can look to my own interests and comfort. Besides I have to stay that I may protect the people and country as far as I can from the depredations and impressments of the enemy. This I am trying to do by having his army supplied without his resorting to the impressment of private property. Genl. Wilson has been instructed to pay for all he gets and will not impress unless compelled to do so. The conduct of Genl. Wilson since the capture of Macon has been courteous and gentlemanly. Indeed he went so far as to say to me that he would respond to any request made to him through me that was not in violation of his positive orders. So you see that our position is as pleasant as it could be under the circumstances. Still I am anxious to get away from here and shall do so just as soon as I can.

I have given you all the news that I can, for we hear but little of what is going on out of Macon. We know nothing of the state of things between the negotiators, but the opinion prevails very generally that hostilities will not be renewed....

Howell Cobb To William H. Seward.1

Athens ga., *18 July, 1865.* Sir: In a published account of an interview between two Georgians and yourself you are represented to have manifested surprise that no citizen of the South had appealed to the Government in behalf of Mr. Davis.

You had evidently inferred from this silence on the part of the people of the South that there existed among them—to say the least—a feeling of indifference on the subject. That publication is my apology for addressing you this communication, and my object is to disabuse your mind of such erroneous impression.

During the latter portion of the late struggle public opinion in reference to Mr. Davis and his administration was much divided. There were those who fully approved the policy of his administration and as a matter of course gave it their unqualified support. There were others who differed upon many points from his policy who still gave an earnest, support to his administration from a conviction that such a course alone promised success to the cause which they had so deeply at heart. There was another class even more opposed to his policy and who believed that success under his lead was impracticable and therefore urged a change of administration. Whilst there existed these differences of opinion there was one point upon which

1 From an unsigned draft in Howell Cobb'a handwriting among the Howell Cobb papers, Erwin collection.

all were agreed, and that was that Mr. Davis was true and faithful to the trust which had been reposed in him; and in that view he retained the regard and confidence of the great mass of our people. To suppose that the feeling thus universally entertained could by the fortunes of war be suddenly converted into one of heartless indifference would be doing cruel injustice to proud and generous people—a wrong which I am sure you would not be disposed to do them.

The close of the war finds Mr. Davis a prisoner charged with two offences—treason, in being the head and leader of the revolution, and complication with the murder of Mr. Lincoln and the attempted assassination of yourself and others.

In reference to the first charge the people of the South feel that Mr. Davis did all that a high-minded and honorable man could do to ensure the success of the cause to which he had publicly and unqualifiedly committed himself—thousands of others did the same. The fact that he was called to a more important position than the rest does not in their judgment increase his guilt. They were all engaged in a common cause and should meet a common destiny, and hence they feel that the same privileges and opportunities which have been or may be extended to the rest should be extended to him. If, however, it is otherwise ordered and he is destined to suffer for the offence of all by virtue of the involuntary position of leader which he held, I beg that you will do both him and the people of the South the justice to believe that he will have to the end of his sufferings the same universal sympathy of the people of the South which has attended him from the first hour of his imprisonment to thepresent moment. They only require to know in what way they can alleviate his sufferings and save him from the threatened sacrifice to promptly adopt the necessary measures for the accomplishment of the object. They are silent not from a feeling of indifference but from a conviction that they are powerless.

In reference to the charge of his complicity with the murder of Mr. Lincoln I beg to assure you that the conviction of his entire innocence is universal. I have not heard of a single being at the South that entertains on this subject the shadow of a doubt. It is universally. regarded by all who knew Mr. Davis and appreciated the peculiar traits in his character as a moral impossibility. It is for this reason that the imputation of this offence to him has in no wise diminished the sympathy which your own heart will tell you must be felt by all who were in good faith enlisted in the attempted revolution with him.

That my silence in reference to Mr. Clay, imprisoned with Mr. Davis on the same charge, may not be misunderstood, I beg to say that these remarks are equally applicable to him as well as to others to whom I do not refer by name as they are not in the same position of prisoners.

If you had witnessed as I have the anxious interest with which every item of news in connection with Mr. Davis is looked to by the people of the South you would no longer doubt either as to the extent or the intensity of their sympathy with him in this the hour of his severe trial. It is a point upon which there is no ground for doubt, and you may rest assured that every act of kindness extended to him will not only be fully appreciated by the people of the South but they will bear in grateful remembrance those from whom he may receive them. Do not misconstrue the silence to which you have referred. The causes which have led to it are in no wise inconsistent with the existence of the heart-felt sympathy, which I Lave herein represented.

In conclusion I beg that you will attribute this communication alone to the motive which I have avowed—of giving you a true statement of publick feeling in reference to Mr. Davis at the South. It is an act of simple justice due alike to him and the people of the South, and if by writing it I shall do Mr. Davis no good, I trust at least it will do him no harm.

J. D. Collins To John A. Cobb.1 E. Bauldwin County ga., Hurricane Plantation, *July 31,1S65.*

Dear Sir, Acordin to promis I write you to inform you how the negrows or freedmen air getting on. tha dont doo as well as tha did a few weeks back your propersition to hier them has no effect on them at tall tha say and contend that onley three of them agreed to. stay that was the three that spoke Sam. Alleck. and Johnson the rest claim tha made no agreement whatever an you had as well Sing Sams to a ded horse as to tri to instruct a fool negrow Some of them go out to work verry well others stay at thier houseses untell & hour by sun others go to their houseses an stay two & three days Say enny thing to them the reply is I am sick but tha air drying fruit all the time tha take all day evry Satturday without my lief I gave orders last Satturday morning for them to go to work when tha got the order eight went out I ordered torn to go to mill he said he would not doo so. tha air steeling the green corn verry rapped som of them go when tha pleas and wher tha pleas an pay no attention to your orders nor mine; the commandant of post at milledgeville sent walker back under Gen Wilson order I exsplaind the matter to him but he would send him back unless you had paid him for his work up to the time you ordered him off I told Walker ef he came back he would not get a cent for his work not even his clothes nor those he cam back in the face of all the orders had ben given him. I drove him off the Secont time after you left before I recievd a writen 1 Son of Howell Cobb. Collins was the overseer on Cobb's plantation.

order to take him back I then went down an saw the officer in command an exsplaind the hole matter to him but he said he could not allow him driven off without violating Gen. Wilsons order an he was compeld to carry them out as sutch the matter stands as bove stated it would be best for you to visit the plantation soon or write a verry positive letter to be read to them requiering them to work or leave though I think I will get Som of them by not feeding them which proses is now going on though tha is rather two mutch fruit and green corn to have a good effect. I send Alleck up with wagon an mule pleas write back by Alleck I am sick at this time I have had fevor for three days no other matters of importace at presant. P. S.—we will need som barriels to put syrup in in about six weeks.

J. D. Hoover To Howell Cobb. *E. York, Pa., Aug. 31, 1865.*

My Dr. Governor, I am glad to have the opportunity thro' Lawson to write you once again. Four years and more have elapsed since I had that pleasure—and such years! What struggles—what sufferings, what disasters, disappointments and death! If we have not all realised our expectations let us at least be thankful for what remains. We cannot reverse the decrees of Providence.

Lawson tells me that you and Mrs. Cobb and all your family are in the enjoyment of good health and that he was a near neighbor of yours for the four years he remained in Athens. I need not assure you that all my family were pleased to hear it. Wo have been leading a sort of roving life during the War, sometimes in Balto., again in Philada., then N. York, N. York State, and occasionally at Washington. The latter we found neither compatible or agreeable, owing to the changes of society and the condition of things there. Many of your old friends left, tho' some remained. I sold my house early, gave up housekeeping, and have since lived in trunks. I might have made money and got along well could I have sympathised with views of the Administration. But I could not, and soon found enemies where there were once (professed at least) attached friends. Many changes have taken place and if I could see you I could occupy your time for a day in answering inquiries. The limits of a letter do not permit much elaboration. I have seen "Old Buck" several times recently. He looks well and is publishing a "book." It will appear next week. Miss Lane is reported again to be about getting married. She looks well. Forney by his *devotion* to Lincoln has made money, and is the proprietor of the "organ" at Wash'n and the Press in Philada. Gen'l Pierce (the noblest Roman of them all) I have seen frequently. He has lost his wife and is said to be looking for another. I suppose you have heard of our boy, now 3 years and 1 month old. He came after 17 years, and of course is a prodigy.

His name is Franklin Pierce Hoover and I should like you to see him.

I hope that the policy of Mr. Johnson will early restore you all again to your proper position. He will be antagonised by the Radicals and there will be a hard fight. If true to his promises he will be sustained by the Dem. Party, and should a break take place, which I think inevitable, in the Repub'n party, the Democracy will attain power very soon.

I should be glad to hear from you, Governor, at any time. Please address me at Washington. If I can be of any service to you command me at all times. Please present Mrs. Hoover's and my own regards to Mrs. Cobb and all the family that know me. I write this in haste as Lawson leaves in a few moments and at rather sudden notice.

P. S.—Does any opening present itself at the South to make money and live satisfactorily?

Mrs. Jefferson Davis To Mrs. Howell Cobb. E.

Mill View, Near Augusta, Ga., *Sep. 9th, 1865.*

My Very Dear Friend, I have been waiting from day to day to find out when I should obtain leave to quit Georgia, and that point ascertained, to decide and write to you at what time I could be able to go to see you at your home to which you invite me in your own sweet affectionate way; but the authorities so far do not vouchsafe to me an answer and I do not like to leave here until it is received. I am so racked by anxiety, so unhappy between hopes and fears. At present released from imprisonment "within the city limits of Savannah", I am permitted to go at large in the State of Georgia. Think what a roaring lion is going loose in Georgia seeking whom she may devour—one old woman, a small baby, and nurse; the Freedmen's bureau and the military police had better be doubled lest either the baby or I "turn again and rend them." But I will not talk of these things lest I say more than is right. Let me tell you rather of the "leniency," "humanity" or what not which has been evinced towards me.

I am now allowed to correspond with my dear husband under the supervision of the Atty. General strictly upon family matters, and the permission has relieved me of the dreadful sense of loneliness and agonizing doubt and weight of responsibility. I may ask his advice instead of acting upon my own suggestions, and above all I may know from him how he is. I know dear friend you will rejoice with me over this change in my unhappy circumstances and pray with me that God may bless me yet more by softening their hearts to let us meet. He writes in such a spirit of pious resignation and trust in God's faith with those who put their dependence upon him that he has comforted me greatly.

The children who were so large as to remember their father and the Confederacy I was forced to send out of the country. Their sensibilities were so wounded that I felt it could not be well for them to share my durance, and so sent them to Canada with my mother who will put them in school there.

Mr. Schley's family who reside about five miles from Augusta are very kind to me and urge my remaining here a few weeks longer. Then after a short visit to Mrs. Burt (if I can get permission to go to Abbeville) I will return and pay you and Col. Willis of Greensboro each a short visit. I so much desire to see you before I leave the country. I want to see your children and your kind husband once more. Is Mary Anne near you? Mr. Davis says she has changed but little. How queer it seems for your boys to be married,—they seem little to me yet as memory spans the many happy hours of the past. Do give my best love to them.

I would rewrite this miserable scrawl but that I am anxious to save this mail.

My dear old friend, may God add all unto you which now seems denied to our poor people, and if it is not his blessed will be assured you will ever have the most affectionate sympathy of your sincere friend.

P. S.—When you write pray direct to Mr. George Schley,, Augusta, and the letter will be perfectly safe.

Howell Cobb To Andrew Johnson.1

Athens Geo., *17th Oct., 1865.*

Dear Sir: This letter will be handed to you by my near relative and friend, Genl. Henry R. Jackson of this State. I respectfully request that you will grant him a private interview on the subject upon which I now address you. When summoned to Washington as a witness I directed my application under your amnesty proclamation (which was then before Gov. Johnson) to be forwarded to me under cover to Mr. Seward at Washington. My summons was revoked, but the paper with the approval and favorable recommendation of Gov. Johnson was forwarded as directed. I have since addressed Mr. Seward requesting him to present it to you, with an additional word of explanation in my letter to him.

Disappointed in the hope of Seeing you personally I had intended to leave the matter in your hands with the recommendation of Gov. Johnson and Genl. Steedman, until my good friend Genl. Jackson 1 From a MS. copy among the Howell Cobb papers, Erwin collection.

purely from his feelings of affection and friendship, offered me the opportunity of saying to you thro' him what I had been very anxious to say to you with my own lips.

My application now before you contains a frank statement of my case, as strongly presented against myself as it can be truthfully made. Any and every charge beyond what I have frankly stated against myself is untrue, and especially any imputation that I ever treated a prisoner unkindly myself or countenanced it in another. I believe you know me well enough to know that such conduct would be at war with every impulse of my heart.

The request I now make for a private interview with Genl. Jackson is to enable him to place before you the facts in reference to these matters—that my case when truly presented shall receive your calm and deliberate judgment.

I have employed no intermediate to

approach you in my behalf because you know me as well as any one, and I only availed myself of the kind and friendly offer of Genl. Jackson when it became impracticable for me to see you myself. I trust I have not in doing so trespassed too much upon our former kind and friendly relationship.

George Hillyer To Howell Cobb. E. Washington D. C., *Nov. 7th, 1865.*

My Dear General, I have been in repeated consultation with Genl. Jackson during the past week, was present at one of his interviews with the President, and in any circle where business or accident has thrown me whilst here I have neglected no opportunity to make a point or gain information for you. It does my heart good to remember that when you found me lying helpless with fever in a hospital at Richmond you in person looked after and cared for me and carried me to a place of safety and comfort. Now in God's providence a friend, young, active, vigilant and devoted, may here be of service to you. I am such a friend and I rejoice in it. Not in the misfortune which makes you a sufferer, for that is to be lamented and deplored by us all alike, but in the opportunity which enables me to show the grateful remembrance in which I hold you.

You are aware however that my acquaintance and influence with leading men here is extremely limited, and the men with whom I have talked are chiefly strangers heretofore to me and also strangers to you, and their views are only valuable as an index of general popular or prevailing sentiment. And from all I can learn I do not hesitate to say to you that I think there is a very general disposition to hold you responsible as the only accessible man, and in truth the chief man, of the Buchanan administration against whom the accursed venom of the saints can vent itself. Upon surveying the whole field I am of opinion and so told Genl. Jackson that for you to come here and enter into a canvass amongst "so-called" friends would promise but small results; and if you made yourself at all conspicuous would provoke assaults from a thousand hounds and curs of the press, against whom I fear not many ready and influential pens would in" the present excited state of the public mind be found volunteering in your defence.

But I do think, judging too mainly from President Johnson's manner and the impression made on me by his interview with Genl. Jackson, that for you to come here *quietly* and avoid the public and have a personal interview with Mr. Johnson and with him alone (excepting of course such persons as voluntarily come to you) would do good. I do not mean to say that I think he would give you the pardon at once but I do think from the marked thoughtfulness and *considerateness* of his manner when speaking of you that he might and most probably would give you such assurances as would set your mind at rest as to his final action. Should you adopt this course the place where I am stopping here (Greason House corner of Pa. Av. & 13th St.), kept on the European plan, is sufficiently retired, every way comfortable and the *proprietor a friend.*

If you go to Willard's they will have you in the newspapers and your cause prejudiced. These are my views. You will not doubt the friendly spirit in which they are given. Genl. J. will write you more fully or see you.

Joseph E. Brown To Alexander H. Stephens. R.

Milledgeville ga., *Nov. 9th, 1865.* My Dear Sir: In common with the people of Georgia I was much gratified to hear of your safe return to your home after your long imprisonment. If I had known where a letter would reach you after your discharge I should have written you and asked your consent to the use of your name for Governor, that your position in that matter might have been known at the opening of the convention. If I could then have said that you would accept the office all opposition (of which there was some) could have been silenced and your name run without opposition. When I found Mr. Jenkins's name in the special care of Kenan, Cabaniss & Co. , I said if he did not give an express assurance that he would bury all past party division and know no party in his appointments to office I would run against him. I had an interview with him in which he said all I could require, and I then told him I would support him.1 I certainly did not desire the position any longer and was determined in no case to be a candidate unless it became necessary to meet and defeat party organization. I only expressed what I felt when I l Charles J. Jenkins was elected governor of Georgia in November, 186. without opposition. He was removed from office by order of Gen. George G. Meade, Jan. 13, X868. said repeatedly that I preferred you to any man in Georgia for any office you would consent to hold. It is now hoped by many that you will consent to accept the position of Senator in Congress. If so you will receive my support and I trust and believe almost the united support of the legislature. I should be glad to know your wishes on that subject.

When I was released from prison in Washington in June last, I was very desirous of visiting you but was not permitted to do so. When I went to Washington with your brother I intended to go to Fort Warren with him but I was so feeble with a severe cough and weakness after my hard spell of fever that Linton told me at Washington I ought not to attempt it and said he would make the explanation to you. Besides, the condition of my family made it my duty to return. I should have written you but supposed I could only be allowed to send a letter to you on commonplace subjects. What do you think *confidentially* of the President and of the success of his line of policy? Will the test oath be repealed and our delegates to Congress admitted? We have submitted to all it seems that has been understood to be required even to the disgrace of the state by repudiation. This was the pet measure of the provisional governor who with all the help he got from Washington had hard work to carry it.

I am very anxious to see and converse with you but cannot come over. I have to go to my plantation in S. W. Ga. and then make arrangements to move to Atlanta in December as soon as I can get possession of the house I have purchased.

Howell Cobb To His Wife. E.

Macon ga., *18th Nov., 1865.* My Dear Wife, In my short note from Atlanta I informed you that I had determined not to go to Washington. Farther reflection only confirms that opinion. The account that Genl. Jackson gives of things in Washington is anything but encouraging. He has done all that could be done but I differ widely from the opinion he expressed in his letter to me that the result of his visit was very favorable. My case is before the President, and all the facts that I desire to put before him have been presented clearly by Genl. Jackson, and I must now quietly and as patiently as possible bide my time. From what he tells me the feeling is growing worse at the North, and I fear that the results of the late elections at the North have not been without their influence upon President Johnson. Seward informed the Genl. that they had not yet reached the class of cases to which I belonged and that the time had not yet come for me to be pardoned. His idea was that my time would come when Mr. Davis was pardoned, and my opinion is that it will not come sooner. I give you the opinion to which I have come, and we may now dismiss the hope of any early action of a favorable character. I shall now turn my attention to my business, and if permitted shall give it my earnest and undivided attention. I hardly expect to be interfered with, but it is hard to say what these people will or may do....

I regretted to hear in Atlanta of the death of my old friend of other days, Thos. De Kalb Harris. He died about ten days ago and his niece says he sent a message to me on his death bed,—that notwithstanding all that had happened he loved me still. Peace to his ashes.

Howell Cobb To His Wife. E.

Macon ga., *7 Dec., 1865.*

My Dear Wife, Nothing of interest has occurred since I last wrote to you. Every thing moves on in a quiet way. We have some indications of business in our office;1 and if constant attendance and close attention to business will bring in more we shall get it. Two fees, one of five hundred dollars and another of two hundred, with some smaller ones, have been ensured, and I doubt not others will follow in due season. I expect to go to Pulaski to day and shall return in time to go to Sumter on Tuesday next when I hope to arrange matters satisfactorily for our planting interest another year. My calculation is to get back to Athens by the twentieth of this month.

We have just seen the first day's proceedings of Congress and it presents a gloomy future for the South. If the movement of Sumner in the Senate and Thad Stevens in the House foreshadow the future policy of the Govt. then indeed are our darkest days yet to come. The different propositions of these representative men point to continued oppression and humiliation. The only hope of the South is in the willingness and ability of President Johnson to rescue them from the fate that bigotry, hatred and passion would bring upon them. I look with anxious solicitude to his Message which we have not yet received, though we hope to get it to morrow.

Have you seen the resolutions of the Tennessee Legislature? I have not but was told that they proposed to have Mr. Davis, Seddon, Toombs, myself and others severely dealt with for treason; and some one moved to add the names of Buchanan and Breckinridge, which was adopted. What will old Buck say when he finds himself so prominently associated with the leading rebels? I should like to witness the cut of his eye when he first reads these proceedings. May we not naturally inquire, what next?

Johnnie goes up this evening and will give you local news if there should be any.

1 Cobb had recently begun the practice of law at Macon.

I have heard nothing from Milledgeville of any interest, except the passage by both houses of the constitutional amendment for the abolition of slavery. I think they will get the " peculiar institution" thoroughly disposed of after a while. It has now been abolished by Congress, the President, war, state conventions, legislatures, etc. If all that don't kill it I should like to know what would?

This is Thanksgiving day, Mr. Warren and the Methodist preachers *unavoidably* absent, Mr. Reese too sick to officiate, which leaves the whole matter in the hands of Mr. Wills, and as I don't affiliate with him I hope it will not be considered disloyal for me to spend the day until I take the cars for Hawkinsville, quietly in my office and at home.

Robert Toombs To Alexander H. Stephens. R.

Havanna, Cuba, *Dec. 15th, 1865.* Dear Stephens, Your letter of the 17th ult. was duly recd. intact and unopened. I received one of the day before from my wife and two others since dated respectively 20th and 28th ult. Heretofore "we have had no steam communication with N. Orleans from this side for two months. We had the steamers once a fortnight touching here on the way out to England, but now we shall have three steamers to N. Orleans within the next six days and I suppose from this time hereafter the communications will be more regular and frequent. I am fully satisfied that I acted prudently in avoiding an arrest and leaving the country. I should have certainly been imprisoned and treated with indignity by our beloved brethren of the North, and I am ready to accept death or any other fate rather than to submit to it willingly. I see nothing in the conduct of President Johnson to approve, not a single act. And looking at his policy as carefully and as coolly as I am able I see no difference between him and Sumner and Co., except Sumner wants him to order the white slaves of the South to admit the black ones to suffrage and Johnson while he approves the policy desires it to be done by the states. But he is called a conservative, and Sumner a radical. I am bound to confess that I think the radicals have all the advantage of the argument. They say and say truly that Johnson has as much right to order that as a condition precedent to admission into the Union as he has to demand amending the constitutions of the states and United States, dictating the legislation of states as to slaves, and no man with a thimblefull of brains can defend Johnson on the point of difference between him and the so-called radicals. The fact is I have looked upon their pretended quarrel as a mere swell-mob demonstration to make the poor and unfortunate people of the South more readily subject themselves to their degradation. I cannot believe that either of these parties 73566—13 43 see anything in their difference to quarrel about. I am but too happy in being out of the muss in as much as I see such universal submission in all classes to whatever may be imposed upon them. The mass of the people have my depest sympathy. They cannot move of themselves. But for the Orrs and Perrys and Mannings in Carolina and the Johnsons, Browns, etc. in Georgia I have a contempt that no language can measure. They seem to glory in their shame, and revel in the ruin and degradation of those whom they pretend to serve. Orr says the war has settled this constitutional principle and that constitutional principle, etc.. etc. How does war settle anything except which is the strongest party to the pending contest? Poor fool and knave! To what vile uses may we come at last!!

You seem to think I have strong friends at Washington. My accounts are different, and I do not much see any advantage in it. There is no government there or has not been since the 4th of March last but President Johnson and his cabinett. The laws have ceased to be even quoted, much less regarded. "The life of the nation" is the new spear of Ithuriel which unravels all difficulties, and I do not suppose a man of my ideas can ever have usefull friends under despotic system. Nobody is strong enough to keep me out of Fort Warren except Johnson. All the Supreme Court could not do it if they wanted to do so. "The life of the nation " would be adjudged by the commander-in-chief of the army to require incarceration; and if anything more was deemed needful to the " life of the nation ", a military court could hang me much more rightfully than it could the poor woman (Mrs. Surratt I believe) who was hung in Washington; for I did try to take " the life of the nation ", and sorely regret the failure to do it.

As to the state of public affairs I am obliged to say that I deeply regret your purpose to go back to the Federal counsels. I would enlarge upon my reasons but I know it will be too late. Your own action and that of the legislature will have been taken before you get this letter and therefore I can only express the hope that my opinions may be wrong and that you will be able to promote the public interest and advance your reputation as a member of the Senate. President Johnson's position is wholly untenable. He says the states have never been out of the Union, yet that he has the right (God knows where he gets it from) to prescribe the terms of their rehabilitation to the rights of members of the Union. And under this extraordinary assumption he claims to *make them* suit his views and the views of New England. Thus the Constitution of the U. S. reflects not the will of the people but the will of Mr. Johnson and the New England abolitionists.

This I honestly believe to be a fair statement of the case, and it needs no word of comment. Tho' I admit it will be a little funny hereafter to hear patriotic speakers talk of this Gel-lo-rious Constitution as the surpassing wisdom of the fathers and adopted by the "unbought suffrage of a free people. " Won't it be funny for outsiders? I should like to hear Andy on that point before the " unterrified" "iron-ribbed" democracy of East Tennessee. Bah! My friend let us give no countenance to such transparent villainy! We are conquered, conquered by our own folly. Let us stand until we can do better whatever these people put upon us, but do not let us stultify ourselves. It is said God? sees us. Whether he does or not, posterity will see us, at least those who are big enough to be seen. Let us not make ourselves the mockery and derision of the world as long as the world takes the trouble to remember us. It does appear to me that the reasons given by all the public men of the South who give these balefull counsels are wholly untenable and otherwise deserve a reprobation which I do not trust myself to describe. They say let us get ridd of military law. Poor fools! What comes next? In some form freedmen's bureaus with acts of Congress passed by Sumner & Co., to regulate labour! They will find military rule a positive luxury in comparison to the civil regulation of labour by Congress, and that will be the successor of martial law and will be sustained by negro troops. This is the last stage of civil misery and ruin to which our poor people are to be subjected, and President Johnson is himself now demanding the supervision of the labour question of the South. This is the end of the Federal Govt. as it was made. It makes a new one. That it will end in ruin is clear. That such a government may end in blood I earnestly pray for. The true policy of the South is to stand still, do nothing, let the Yankees try their hands on Cuffee. If you try to help them all failures are yours, not theirs; and one thing my friend you may rely upon as long as " grass grows or water flows,"—that is, you can not grow cotton or corn in the South except by small planters independent of paid labor *without a law for the specific performance of contracts*. This principle involves the whole law and prophets of Southern agriculture. Without that we must abandon the application of capital to agriculture except on two hundred acre (or less) holdings. That is, we must come to the tenant system of Europe. How that will succeed were too long a tale for me now.

I am much pleased with this island. It is very fertile and boundless in wealth, with slave labour. Without it, its history is already written in that of Jamaica and Hayti. It is doomed. England and the Yankees will force Spain into the policy of emancipation. That will again give England the monoply of cotton and sugar from her East India system of slavery, which is what she has been playing for ever since she was bitten by West Indian emancipation. As for myself I am unwilling for my posterity to live in a conquered country and I shall emigrate thence as soon as I can make the necessary arrangements. I now think best of Mexico. It has many advantages for people who seek to establish themselves of the better classes. I do not care for its disorders. That perhaps is not unfavorable to "*novi homines* ". I do not think the Spanish element will long control that country. It must be European or Anglo-Saxon. It will be mixed and I shall stand a better chance than in an old established society. So will my family. But when I have more time I will write more fully. The steamer that takes this got in unexpectedly today and I availed myself of it to write you a hurried letter.

If my wife has not left home, tell her to join me. Give my best regards to Linton, two names illegible and all friends about Sparta. I remember their kindness with great gratitude.

J. B. Eusns To Howell Cobb. E.

New Orleans la., *J any. 6th, /66.*

My Dear General, Although I have frequently inquired after you and your family I have never had news of you from one who could inform me how this state of peace suits you, and I continue to see you in uniform surrounded by staff officers, orderlies, etc., although knowing that your military occupation is gone. Of all my acquaintances of *late* prominence I should like to meet you and have the benefit of your views. We do not know what to think or expect. The people here are trying to work under the most discouraging circumstances, trying to turn their back upon Federal politics, etc.

, but there exists a deed-seated apprehension that our state will more slowly than any other recover from her poverty, and in fact in the sugar district there is an utter want of confidence; within twelve months our rich sugar lands have depreciated fifty per cent.

Of your old military friends there is a large number here. Beauregard is doing well, being president of two railroad companies. Hood is in business here but not doing as well, and a host of others are working hard for a living. The behaviour of our people has been remarkably good, and if we can keep our Governor from designing more mischief nothing need be feared in this quarter.

Our legislature meets this month and will consider the proposed constitutional amendments. I have heard that the committee of your legislature presented an able report upon this subject, and being myself a representative, you would confer a great favor upon me by sending me a copy for reading and perhaps for use. Please send it by mail to my address.

Last fall I saw Genl. Johnston in New York; he was somewhat low spirited and not in good health. Present my kind regards to Mrs. Cobb.

P. S.—I am practising law.

Joseph E. Brown To Alexander H. Stephens. R.

Milledgeville ga., *March 2d, 1866.*

Dear Sir: Since I saw you I have conversed with the up-country members about your speech 1 and find they all approve it. Ellington said he liked the speech very much but did not like the man. He has never forgiven you for going against Know Nothingism but he was much pleased at your effort.

The speeches of the President and of Mr. Seward show that the war is to be a bitter one and that Seward is on the president's side. What think you of the prospect of a *peace* Proclamation by the President? Does not Seward's speech foreshadow it as near at hand? Linton is quite unwell today....

The bank bill, as you have I suppose seen, has passed the Senate. Its fate in the House is very doubtful. Indeed it will be very hard to carry it. I do not however despair of its prospects. If we had a skillful leader in the House it could pass. The prejudices are high and hard to combat. The General Assembly are now working quietly and will I suppose adjourn by the 13th as they have resolved to do. The death of Genl. Jackson cast a good deal of gloom over the feelings of a large number of friends. His loss is in our way about the passage of the bill he was reporting. Mr. Barker is still here doing all he can, but does not know how to manage members. I suppose it will be near the heel of the session before the matter is finally disposed of. I shall always be glad to hear from you. Mrs. Brown is with me. She was very sorry you did not stay with her as you passed through. When in Atlanta we hope you will consider our house home.

Joseph E. Brown To Alexander H. Stephens. It.

Milledgeville ga., *March 3d, 1866.*

Dear Sir: I received your letter yesterday after I had mailed one to you. I am very glad indeed to hear that the President has extended your parole with liberty to go to Washington. I trust you may be able to do good there and trust you will go as soon as your affairs will permit. As he has made up the issue with the radicals so boldly he may be ready to admit you freely to his counsels, which might be of great service to the South.

Linton is up this morning and is much better. No action in the House on the bank bill yet.

William M. Browne To Howell Cobb. E.

Athens ga., *March 28, 1866.* My Dear General, The promptness of your reply to my letter and the pleasure it afforded me are only equalled by the keenness of your 1 Stephens's speech before the Georgia legislature on reconstruction, Feb. 22, 1866, Is published in Henry Cleveland, "Alexander H. Stephens ", pp. 804-818.

rebuke of my silence and my contrition. I cannot plead press of business, professional engagements, or any of the many excuses so confidently urged by tardy correspondents. My only excuse is that I had nothing to say and I said it. You know my silence was not from lack of friendship. Of the whole human race of my own age, I believe you are the only man whom I can confidently call a friend and who cares one straw whether I am prosperous or the reverse. With this firm conviction, made firmer by daily experience, it is impossible that I should fail in anything that constitutes friendship— the genuine article—the pure metal, not the greenback.

The fact is I did not write for I did not wish to inflict my pessimism on anybody. I remembered the sage counsel of your excellent wife—" to be still," and even did not avail myself of my weekly means of letting off steam—the Banner—to utter any of the gloomy illconditioned and ill-natured thoughts which have occupied me for some time. Politics to us now are as completely useless for all practical purposes (I mean the discussion of them) as diamond shoebuckles would have been to Robinson Crusoe on the desert island. To talk without any power to act; to assert rights when we have none except what Thad Stevens would allow us; to invoke the Constitution when no one respects that instrument except those of us who have recently sworn to support it and Lincoln's Proclamation,—is degrading to a man who has self respect and is useless to his fellows. I think Stewart's proposition more infamous than Stevens's subjugation or Sumner's compulsory nigger suffrage scheme, because it affects benevolence and invites us to eat dirt to please the radicals. If I have to eat it, I want to be compelled to do it, not to be hospitably invited to it as a desirable meal. My fears that this iniquitous plan is favored by Andy are great and intensified by recent letters from a noted bummer in the Republican ranks who assured me that there would be "no split in the Union ranks."

If the civil rights bill is vetoed I shall have hopes. It will prove that he is resolved not to allow the spirit or the substance of State sovereignty to be invaded if he can help it.

The civil rights bill does not contain a provision in reference to the legal equality of the nigger and the white man in everything relating to life, liberty and property that our legislature has not already passed. But Congress has no right to pass any such law. I may want to have my field ploughed (and I do by the way and cannot get a freedman to do it) but I will not stand your asserting the right to do it (I wish you would in my case, and I would pocket the invasion of personal right).

Graham's letter to Fessenden is a good thing. It is manly, temperate, and true.

I wish I had heard your speech on the stay-law. I have grave doubts as to the constitutionality of the present bill, but had it secured the debts of creditors I should be in favor of it. What ground did you take? I know you made a good speech and would like to know the points altho' I am a stay-law man and drafted a bill for Adams which, if passed, neither Governor could veto or you object to.

We have no excitement over the stay-law or any other law. A fall of 24 a bushel in meal would cause more pleasurable excitement than the news that Christy had taken his seat....

A. C. Niven 1 To Howell, Cobb. E. Monticello, Sullivan Co., N. Y., *April 9,1866.*

My Dear Sir: Your welcome letter was duly recd. A sea of blood has rolled between us since we had met with each other last. Your agency in that sad business was a stern necessity. Had I been a Southern man my heart and hand would have been zealously with you—as a Northern man my co-operation was of the heart alone. This was all I could give to what I ever considered a righteous cause. Nor did I ever succumb to the threats or overt acts of those tyrants and tools of tyrants who trampling under foot the constitutional rights of the people drove many a right minded man to close his lips and remain silent.

It will always be a matter of conscious pride that I never hesitated anywhere or under any circumstances when my opinion was sought to give it freely. Like Voorhees of Indiana, Stockton of New Jersey and Brooks of N. Y., I have felt the power of vindictive abolitionism, when out of 18,000 votes cast for Senator in this district they by a strictly party vote determined after *weeks* of debate following months of investigation that my opponent had from 1 to 10 votes more than were cast for me!! I allude to this merely as showing that in no respect have I quailed before that class of men so well represented by Wade, Sumner, Wilson, Thad Stevens, etc., at Washington, and that I could accept the proffered hospitalities of any Southern man without feeling that my blood was mantling my cheeks. And most assuredly, my doors will be open to any Southern man however prominent and obnoxious he has been or is to the wretches who are now in the ascendant.

I rejoice to hear you speak so encouragingly of the purposes of your people. I trust they will not give way to despondency. Crush'd though they have been by the overwhelming numerical strength gathered from the world and poured out upon the Confederate States, and even now denied their constitutional rights, I trust 1 Democratic Congressman from New York, 1845-1847.
and pray that they will maintain their character for moral heroism as well as they did for physical courage. "'Tis often dark, very dark, just before the break of day."

The passage of the obnoxious bill which by a palpable misnomer is known as the bill of civil rights is calculated I think to widen the breach between the Radicals and the President; and I trust that he will stand firm, and that the friends of Constitutional liberty will surround him with bayonets if need be to protect him against his jacobinical enemies. I have feared that another conflict is at hand— another bloody strife—but the battle fields will not be south of the Potomac.

I have no doubt that Southern people generally have honestly determined to stand by the Union. They were honest in the belief that Secession was an inherent political right; but as an appeal to arms for the vindication and establishment of such right has been decided against them they have yielded the point and are again part and parcel of the United States.

I shall deeply regret any movement on the part of Southern people to leave that region and seek a home elsewhere. Temporarily and from sheer necessity some may emigrate, but I have a better opinion of your people generally. Above and beyond the *Amor Patriae*, your climate, soil, etc., are far more desirable than almost anywhere else; why then should any seek a new home? Northern man as I am, were I not of an age to forbid it I would seek a home among the brave men and brave women of the South.

You will not object to my speaking of the women of the South—I love them for the part they have acted in the recent tragedy—for what they have *performed*-as well as *endured*. It would rejoice me much to have as many as could be sheltered under my roof, sit down with my wife and daughter to discuss subjects on which I well know they would all agree. An enthusiastic lady of Vicksburg, whom we have never seen, in the exuberance of her good feeling has adopted my daughter as a child of the Sunny South. It is a Mrs. Eggleston who is engaged in getting up a fund for Mrs. Jefferson Davis.

Not to weary you, my dear Sir, I close my letter by expressing to you my earnest hope that we may again meet each other to find that there is no estrangement, because no difference of opinion. May the choicest blessings yet be measured out to you and yours: and your life spared to see the people of the sovereign State of Georgia exercising the rights of sovereignty in a constitutional manner.

Alexander H. Stephens To J. Barrett Cohen. L. C.

Crawfordville, Ga., *June 6, 1866.*
My Dear Sir: Allow me to return you many thanks for your very able and interesting argument on the *Habeas Corpus* case in your court. The pamphlet came to the office here during my absence from home, or it would have been acknowledged sooner. Be assured I was very much pleased indeed with the views you presented. I need hardly add that I consider the argument conclusive upon the points raised.

I have thought of you often since the collapse of the Confederate sic and was exceedingly glad to know from this pamphlet that you are still in the land of the living, once more in the old city of Charleston and in the full vigor of your manly intellect. Please remember me kindly to your father. I hope he is with you and well. I should be highly gratified to hear from you by letter and to know what your prospects are—what hopes if any you have for the future of our country.

Alexander H. Stephens To J. Barrett Cohen. L. C.

Crawfordville, Ga., *July 4, J866.*
My Dear Sir: I have but a moment to thank you for your letter of the 9th June. It was a long one, it is true, and I liked it the better for that. I have just got through reading it. It came to the office here while I was absent attending our supreme court at Milledgeville. I was gone over three weeks and only got back a few days ago. I am now going through with my correspondence which heavily accumulated during the time I was away. The labor in this particular is great, hence I can only thank you for yours. I have not the time to give my views fully on the points alluded to by you and indeed presented, several of them, so thoroughly and clearly. In the main I agree with you in what you have said. The call for the Phila. Convention I have noticed with deep interest. What will come of it I cannot now venture to predict. The terms of the call are in some respects not as they should have been. The same objects, as I understand them, might have been set forth in language modified without marring the meaning or sense and which would have been more politic. If the Northern Democracy shall favour this movement, if they will consent to cooperate with it, much good may come of it. How that will be I do not yet know. I am satisfied that they will never abandon their own organization. Our only hope, the only hope for the country, is with the conservatives of the North. But outside the Democratic party at the North we have but few friends, and constitutional liberty has but few friends there outside of that organization. Hence a great deal will depend upon how they act towards the new movement. You are right about the ultimate destiny of the black race amongst us I think. But I can say no more. Kind regards to Mrs. Cohen and your father. Should I go to Charleston I shall certainly avail myself of your kind invitation.

Josephus Anderson To Howell, Cobb. E.

Thomasville, Geo., *Sept. 8th, 1866.*
My Dear Friend:... The Church is in good and growing condition. We have been greatly blessed during the year with reviving grace and the beneficial effects are manifest among the people. In addition to my white charge I have a congregation of about five hundred negroes to whom I preach once every Sabbath, and a Colored Sabbath School numbering about three hundred scholars. My observation convinces me that freedom has had a decidedly injurious influence upon the moral character of the blacks. I have watched them closely and with special reference to this matter. My heart hoped for good fruits, but the wild grapes are marvellously abundant. The juxtaposition of the two races in a state of freedom engenders perpetual evil. It has been so wherever it has occurred. History points to but the one result. The blacks are ever envious of the superiority of the whites and clamorous for equality while using every means to appropriate their property; and the whites are inspired with contempt for the blacks and constantly irritated and provoked by their bad conduct. Nothing but true religion and the humility,

justice and benevolence learned in the school of Christ can enable the two races to exist together in peace while both enjoy freedom. And alas! the poor ignorant negroes are everywhere to a very great extent seduced by the desire of equality from their former pastors and are organizing under superstitious and ignorant pastors of their own color. It is not so here, except among the Baptists; but I hear of its being so in almost every place. What a mixture of superstitious views, what a system of dreams, visions, and trances without morality or real devotion their religion will be under such instructors and guides! Much depends upon the whites. By forbearance and patience, by pure examples and correct teaching, by personal efforts for the poor heathen at our doors, great good can be done.

At what time do you expect to be in Bainbridge? I want to meet you there if possible. I hope to be able to visit you on my way to Americus to attend the Georgia Conference which meets Nov. 28th.

Howell Cobb To Daniel E. Sickles. 1 (Private.)

Athens, Ga., *12 Sept., 1866.* My Dear General, You were kind enough to say to me in your letter that you would be happy to do me a service when in your power. Emboldened by this assurance I approach you, not in my own behalf but for another whose claims upon a kind and generous 1 From a MS. draft among the Howell Cobb papers, Erwln collection.

heart appeal with more earnestness for friendly aid than my own case—unpardoned and exposed to an unknown destiny as I am.

Our war is at an end, the struggle closed disastrously to the friends of Southern separation. With the results we make no issue—we have accepted them and pledged our faith to abide by them. It is the interest of all that the peace that has come should be lastmg, that the bitterness of the past should be forgotten, and that a sincere reconciliation sic. With those who have been seeking to accomplish these results I have been pleased to see your name associated; and whatever may be the motives of some, I have felt satisfied that your own course was dictated by the generous impulses of your nature. I allude to this conviction not merely to give expression to an opinion I entertain but to explain why it is that I have ventured to address you this letter. I write not to open the discussions of the past—I have no wish to revive anything that is past and gone. Let the past bury the past, whilst we deal only with the present and the future. I come to plead the cause of the sufferer and to speak the words which come fresh and full from the hearts of a million sympathising souls—I speak to you the words of truth, if ever words of truth fell from the lips of man when I say to you: turn the captive loose and you will give to reconstruction a meaning, a life and a vitality that it has never yet possessed. I do not ask you to look upon Mr. Davis in his confinement from my standpoint of view—but from your own. Regard him in the light on your own convictions, but at the same time consider the situation of the dying man whose only fault that is greater than his associates, is the prominence he was summoned to occupy. Remember his long confinement—due if you please to his representative character—and then addressing the generous and kindlier feelings of your own heart answer: do the ends of justice and the work of reconstruction demand longer sufferings? Let me say to you in that candor and frankness with which I desire to approach you on this subject, that the people of the South would be unworthy of your regard and confidence if they could be brought by the gratification of their own selfish wants to a feeling of indifference to the fate of their representative man. Grant to them all their desires, restore to them all their rights, giving both to person and property all the protection which is extended to the unoffending North, and if even then they could forget the sufferings and become indifferent to the fate of their representative man, they would deserve to be spurned of man and forgotten of God. I feel assured that you not only recognise but honor the existence of this feeling with the people of the South; and now I ask you to command for yourself the grateful obligation which this universal feeling is ready to acknowledge to the man who shall step forward and unbar the *prison* door. Your voice ought to be heard and will be heard. It is from such a quarter that Mr. Johnson will listen to words of advice and counsel. And confiding as I do in the sincere desire of the President to produce a lasting peace based upon a sincere reconciliation, I would look hopefully to the result.

Howell Cobb To His Wife. E.

Dominion Place, Sumter County, Ga., *December, 1866.*

My Dear Wife, I avail myself of the first opportunity to send a letter to town. I find a worse state of things with the negroes than I expected, and am unable even now to say what we shall be able to do. From Nathan Barwick's place every negro has left. There is not one to feed the stock, and on the other places none have contracted as yet. I shall stay here until I see what can be done. By Tuesday we shall probably know what they will do. At all events I shall then look out for other negroes. I intend to send Nathan Barwick to Baldwin on Wednesday to see what hands can be got there with the assistance of Wilkerson. I am offering them even better terms than I gave them last year, to wit, one third of the cotton and corn crop and they feed and clothe themselves; but nothing satisfies them. Grant them one thing and they demand something more, and there is no telling where they would stop. The truth is I am thoroughly disgusted with free negro labor, and am determined that the next year shall close my planting operations with them. There is no feeling of gratitude in their nature. Let any man offer them some little thing of no real benefit to them, but which looks like a little more freedom, and they catch at it with avidity and would sacrifice their best friend without hesitation and without regret.

That miserable creature Wilkes Flagg1 sent old Ellick down to get the negroes from Nathan Barwick's place. Old Ellick staid out in the woods and sent for the negroes, and they were bargaining with him in the night and telling Barwick in the day that they were going to stay with him. The moment they got their money they started for the railroad. This *is* but one instance but it is the history of all of them. Among the number was Anderson, son of Sye and Sentry, whom I am supporting at the Hurricane.

I hope you are entirely well again and that all with you are well and happy. I cannot now say when I can come up. *f*

Joseph E! Brown To Alexander H. Stephens. R.

Atlanta ga., *Deer. 8th, 1866.* Dear Sir: The churches of the six different denominations of this city have united for the relief of the poor and have determined to 1 Wilkes Flagg was a negro agitator of Mllledgevllle, Ga.
have a course of lectures prepared and delivered during the winter, or of discourses as the Speaker may prefer, upon such subject as each speaker may select for himself as appropriate to the occasion and to procure the most distinguished speakers whose services they can command, each to deliver one discourse. Season and single tickets to be sold and the proceeds after paying the actual expenses of the lecturers or speakers to be applied to the relief of the suffering poor of the city. If we can procure the aid of such speakers as have popular elocution, with the united influence of all the churches we hope to have the lectures largely attended. We can think of no other mode of raising a very considerable sum so pleasantly and profitably to the contributors.

A committee of six, one from each denomination, has been selected of which I have the honor to be chairman, to correspond with the persons selected as speakers. My associates on the Committee are Father O'Rily, Catholic; Col. Grant, Presbyterian: Mr. Eawson, Methodist; Dr. Sells, Episcopalian; and Col. Atkins of the Christian Church. They are unanimous not only in your selection as one of the speakers but in a most earnest request that you will deliver one discourse before the society on such subject as you may select. It will be desirable to have it some time in January. Suit yourself as to time. Now, my dear sir, I do think you can do us much good by a compliance with our request. We will give you a very large audience, and the proceeds would do much good to the suffering poor of the city. I do trust you will consent to come.

By an early reply you will much oblige the committee.

John C. Rutherford To Howell Cobb. E.

Bainbridge ga., *Mch. 20, 1867.*

Dear Genl., We have been quite uneasy ever since we first heard that you were in Washington City; there were many conjectures that suggested themselves to account for your visit, none of which however allayed our anxiety. I have heard from you several times since your return thro' different persons, but would like very much to hear from you directly if you can spare the time, have the inclination, and deem it *prudent.*

The prospect presents humiliation, degradation, without any guaranty for life, liberty, or property, and a still more bitter persecution reserved for yourself and those who occupied similar positions. I was about to advise, but that I will refrain from, as you can see more clearly and understand more perfectly the situation and the prospects.

What effect will the military bill have upon our judicial organization? Gov. Jenkins cannot take the oath provided in the supplementary bill. Who, then, will preside over the baseless fabric of our government? Will the Judges who are excluded from holding office under the constitutional amendment be allowed to continue their courts, even should the military commandants see fit to continue the existing governments until the convention meets and a new constitution is framed? I write more to know how the future and present prospect will affect yourself than for any other purpose.

Alexander H. Stephens To J. Barrett Cohen. L. C.

Crawfordville, Ga., *May 25, 1867.* My Dear Sir: Your letter of the 20th inst. was received yesterday. I wish I were able to answer you at length. This I would cheerfully do to you as a friend to whom my opinions would be freely given, for your own reflection and not for the public; for I do not take any active part in public questions and do not intend to mingle in public affairs ever again. I say I wish I were able to reply to you at length, but I am not. I am extremely weak and feeble, am suffering very much today, am hardly able to be up and scribble these lines. As a general answer, as " *multum, in parvo"* as something short which will really cover the whole I will say that I do not think that the Congress plan when carried out as it will be can be successfully worked—the two races can not coexist in their proportions in this country on this basis. What is to be the end I do not know. But reason and logic lead me to the conclusion that the system cannot be worked. The wish is not father to the thought with me in this instance. Far from it! Nothing could rejoice me more than the grand spectacle that the exhibition of the successful workings of our system of self govt. would thus present to an astonished world. But I do not think any such grand, moral and even sublime result is in store for us. I do not look to any such result. While I shall do nothing to hinder it or obstruct it yet I tell you candidly that I do not think humanity capable of such a demonstration. The system in my judgment will not work. It will break down and with its breaking down all semblance even of self govt. by both races will go with it. We are upon the verge of a consolidated centralized despotic empire. We are fast abandoning the Teutonic systems on which our institutions were based and are lapsing fast into the Asiatic system of empire. T can say no more. What is said is for yourself only. I am ever glad to hear from you. Write to me often.

Alexander H. Stephens To J. Barrett Cohen. L. C.

Crawfordville, Ga., *July 15, 1867.*
My Dear Sir: Your welcome leter of the 10th inst. was received some days ago. I have not been able to reply sooner. I am quite out of health. When able however I am going on with my work. It is not true that I have expressed the opinion that the confiscation policy of Mr. Thad. Stevens would be carried out. On the contrary I have uniformly given it as my opinion that it would not be, unless some new development should render it necessary for party purposes. No such general purpose is now entertained at the North. This is my opinion. But then it is also my opinion that the action of the majority of Congress is governed by no fixed principles or settled policy. They themselves do not know what they may do. The ruling principle with them is power, and they will do anything to secure that. I think they will secure their object without resorting to confiscation. As I wrote to you before, I think constitutional liberty on the continent is in its last death struggles. Did you get that letter?

Howell Cobb To His Wife. E.

Macon ga., *Sept. 1, 1867.*
My Dear Wife, At Atlanta I met my friend Genl. Benning and at his earnest request remained over the night. We made a hurried visit to Col. Glenn's and met all the family there, found and left them well. I also saw Harvy and Sallie on the streets and they were well and happy. Benning and myself sat up all night talking over the present, past and future, that is we went to bed at half past three and were waked up at five in the morning. I found that our minds had been running very much in the same channel about the future prospects of the country, our final conclusion was that the next three months were pregnant with great events that would decide the ultimate destiny of the whole country.

The firmness of the President in adhering to his late policy, and the fall elections at the North, are the events in the early future which would solve the problem of our fate in the South. If these should be favorable we may yet have a happy and prosperous country. If otherwise we cannot see how the South can possibly remain inhabitable by white people. Let us then wait and pray....

Jeremiah S. Black To Howell Cobb. E.

Washington, *Sept. 23, 1867.* My Dear Sir: I did not approve the amnesty proclamation. It was not and is not what the South needs. *Justice* is the supreme necessity. This hollow show of *mercy* postpones the restitution of their rights. I told the President that I disliked it for the reason above stated and because it was useless to my friend Cobb. He answered, " Never mind, it is easier now to relieve Cobb by a special pardon than it was before," and again he intimated that I should not have to wait much longer. He has no intention of allowing you to suffer of that I feel sure; but he pains and sickens me by delaying to do what ought to be done at once.

I think there is a steady flow in the current of public opinion against the abolition party. I would speak with perfect confidence of Penna. if I had not been so bitterly disappointed on other occasions. I hope however there as well as in N. Y. and Ohio. The policy of the President I think will be developed in a few days. He feels that he must husband the power that is left him for self defence. If he does not they will depose him, perhaps hang him. In making this defence he will be obliged to defend the country and strike at its enemies as well as his own. I feel at this moment more hopeful than I have done for a long time. There are many things I would like to tell you, and some questions I would gladly ask you if I was at Macon or you were at York; but it is no use in a letter. ...

Alexander H. Stephens To J. Barrett Cohen. L. C.

Crawfordville, Ga., *Oct. 20, 1867.*
My Dear Sir: I have but a moment to acknowledge the receipt of your kind favour of the 10th inst. and the newspapers referred to, all of which I found here on my return yesterday from a week's absence on a visit to my brother in Sparta. I am so overwhelmed with business that I can do no more than to say that I read with deep interest the articles alluded to. I was *pained* to read Judge Bryan's decision. This is of course for yourself. I know Bryan well and esteem him highly but I think he has fallen into great errors on constitutional law. With the articles you spoke of I was pleased. What is to become of us I do not yet know or yet see. The signs of the times are some better than they have been. Perhaps deliverance is in store for us some way or other. I hope so—earnestly hope so— indulging a hope to that end even against hope. My opinions on the general situation are not changed. The Congress plan if carried out will end in illegible South as well as North. The best way to defeat a convention is to have nothing to do with it. There is not much prospect of defeating it at all, but this is the only course that presents any prospect of doing it. My opinion is that all persons who do not approve of the military bills should have nothing to do with the election.

Robert Toombs To Alexander H. Stephens. R.

Washington, Geo., *Novr. lbth, 1867.*
Dear Stephens, Your letter of yesterday was duly reed. We all regretted that you could not come over to the wedding. It passed off very well and very agreeably to our young "townsfolk" who assembled in large numbers to see and enjoy the show.

I will aid Linton with pleasure in your case in the Supreme Court, and take charge of it if he should be absent. It does seem to me that the case is wholly free from difficulty, from what I remember of the will; and I do not know what Judge Floyd means by the English stat. of mortmain being in force in Georgia. I have a good deal of law to unlearn if the Baptist convention cannot take in this state. Certainly it has " tuck " a confounded sight of good plunder of one sort and another and a considerable under my own auspices. I do not remember the " uses" declared in the will; but it is difficult to make them too indefinite before a court of chancery, which readily supplies by construction, or *cy pros* whatever is wanting in a devise or bequest to charitable uses. If you have the exceptions and will send them over with the clause of the will in dispute, I will examine them, as I am now at leisure, or rather devoting my time to half dozen cases I have to prepare in the Supreme Court. You know when one is engaged in that line of business it is but little trouble to add a few more cases to the dockett.

I cannot find yet my copy of Sidney nor can I find another one in town. I am quite surprised to find one of the old standard works on government so rare. Thirty-five years ago it was in every lawyer's library and the textbook of the old Republican party. I know it is at Athens and in Milledgeville, and if I do not find mine before I go to M., I will get one for you.

Have you seen the address of the Carolina convention? It is a really creditable paper as the first manifestation of vitality yet discoverable in that poor commonwealth. Popular wrongs never Mere and never will be redressed by silence and inaction. Poor Chesnutt! He is badly whipped—what the Indians call a good whipping, whipped until "he lays still and can't hollow." I have been examining and studying for a few days past the burthen on the production of cotton in the rebel states, and without working out anything new I am perfectly astonished at my own results. I will throw them into shape as soon as I have leisure and present them to our people as a warning against any further efforts to produce it under existing laws. To get at accurate details I took two farms of my brother, one in Stewart and the other in Wilkes. and the result is curious. The 2$ cents tax1 on his Stewart place amounts to *10 per cent interest on his whole investment in Stewart county*!! (say $30,000). Or put it another way, it amounts to 5 dollars per acre rent upon all the land cultivated (both corn and cotton) on his plantation, or eight and a half dollars per acre rent upon all the land in cotton, or a tax of twenty-five dollars per head on each hand to be paid by them *and* fifty dollars a head on each hand to be paid by him; in all seventy 1 Ter pound of cotton produced. 73506—13 44 five dollars per head!! He makes in Stewart 6 bales (500 each) to the hand, cultivates 350 acres cotton and 250 in corn—works 42 hands. Whole investment made 1st Jany. at $30,000, so you can work it out and tell me your results. His Wilkes investment shows equally alarming figures, with a very successfull year's work. The result is starvation to the negro, and poverty to the planter if he will plant cotton.

Robert Toombs To Alexander H. Stephens. E.

Washington, Geo., *2nd Deer., 1867*.

Dear Stephens, Yours of the 30th was duly recd. I am sorry I did not go over yesterday, as I was so bothered with disagreeable company that I lost the day instead of spending it with you. I shall leave here on Wednesday for Augusta on some special business and will come up to your house Thursday night. If anything should prevent this arrangement, I will write to you. I am very anxious to see you before you start North.

I would have gone today, but for some important cases in the court of ordinary, and I lost today by old Beasley's getting drunk, and the court " no go." I am trying to get his wife to sober him by tomorrow, and have adjourned the court on my own action today. Pope1 ought to do better by his slaves. If he will appoint drunken officers, he ought to make them get drunk seasonably; but old Beasly makes it a point always to get drunk at the wrong time and keep perfectly sober when nobody cares a "cuss" whether he is drunk or sober.

All well and send their kindest regards to you.

Howell Cobb To J. D. Hoover, Chairman.2

Macon ga., *4 Jany., 1868*.

Dr. Sir: Your invitation to attend the celebration of the 8th January by the democratic resident committee of Washington City has just been received. It revives pleasant memories of the past—and tempts me to break a self-imposed silence on political questions which I have observed since the close of the War. And yet I hesitate to write—for what I write may not harmonize with the festivities of the occasion which assembles you and I would not mar the happy hours of those who meet to celebrate a national festival under the protecting care of the constitution of our fathers.

We of the ill-fated South realize only the mournful present whose lesson teaches us to prepare for a still gloomier future. To participate in a national festival would be a cruel mockery, for which I 1 Brevet major-general, U. S. A., then in command of the third military district which Included Georgia.
1 From an unsigned draft in the handwriting of Howell Cobb, Erwln collection. frankly say to you I have no heart, however much I may honor the occasion and esteem the association with which I would be thrown.

The people of the south, conquered, mined, impoverished, and oppressed, bear up with patient fortitude under the heavy weight of their burthens. Disarmed and reduced to poverty, they are powerless to protect themselves against wrong and injustice; and can only await with unbroken spirits that destiny which the future has in store for them. At the bidding of their more powerful conquerors they laid down their arms, abandoned a hopeless struggle, and returned to their quiet homes under the plighted faith of a soldier's honor that they should be protected so long as they observed the obligations imposed upon them of peaceful law-abiding citizens. Despite the bitter charges and accusations brought against our people, I hesitate not to say that since that hour their bearing and conduct have been marked by a dignified and honorable submission which should command the respect of their bitterest enemy and challenge the admiration of the civilized world. Deprived of our property and ruined in our estates by the results of the war, we have accepted the situation and given the pledge of a faith never yet broken to abide it. Our conquerors seem to think we should accompany our acquiescence with some exhibition of gratitude for the ruin which they have brought upon us. We cannot see it in that light. Since the close of the war they have taken our property of various kinds, sometimes by seizure, and sometimes by purchase,—and when we have asked for remuneration have been informed that the claims of rebels are never recognized by the Government. To this decision necessity compels us to submit; but our conquerors express surprise that we do not see in such ruling the evidence of their kindness and forgiving spirit. They have imposed upon us in our hour of distress and ruin a heavy and burthensome tax, peculiar and limited to our impoverished section. Against such legislation we have ventured to utter an earnest appeal, which to many of their leading spirits indicates a spirit of insubordination which calls for additional burthens. They have deprived us of the protection afforded by our state constitutions and laws, and put life, liberty and property at the disposal of absolute military power. Against this violation of plighted faith and constitutional right we have earnestly and solemnly protested, and our protests have been denounced as insolent;—and our restlessness under the wrong and oppression which have followed these acts has been construed into a rebellious spirit, demanding further and more stringent restrictions of civil and constitutional rights. They have arrested the wheels of State government, paralized the arm of industry, engendered a spirit of bitter antagonism on the part of our negro population towards the white people with whom it is the interest of both races they should maintain kind and friendly relations, and are now struggling by all the means in their power both legal and illegal, constitutional and unconstitutional, to make our former slaves *our masters,* bringing these Southern states under the power of *negro supremacy.* To these efforts we have opposed appeals, protests, and every other means of resistance in our power, and shall continue to do so to the bitter end. If the South is to be made a pandemonium and a howling wilderness the responsibility shall not rest upon our heads. Our conquerors regard these efforts on our part to save ourselves and posterity from the terrible results of their policy and conduct as a new rebellion against the constitution of our country, and profess to be amazed that in all this we have failed to see the evidence of their great magnanimity and exceeding generosity. Standing today in the midst of the gloom and suffering which meets the eye in every direction, we can but feel that we are the victims of cruel legislation and the harsh enforcement of unjust laws. On the other hand our conquerors are amazed that the sufferings of our people create no joy, and the threatened starvation of our wives and children afford no cause for mirth and hilarity, and above all that our hearts do not overflow with gratitude to those who have brought these calamities upon us, and whose policy foreshadows still greater sufferings and gloomier days. We regarded the close of the war as ending the relationship of enemies and the beginning of a new national brotherhood, and in the light of that conviction felt and spoke of constitutional equality. We felt and spoke as freemen and American citizens, and some were bold enough to present their petitions and grievances before the governing power. Such had always been the right and privilege of an American citizen;—but regarding our status in a far different light, such petitions and complaints were denounced in our legislative halls as impertinent and insolent conduct, and even the representative who offered them was rebuked for his temerity. We claimed that the result of the war left us a state in the Union, and therefore under the protection of the constitution, rendering in return cheerful obedience, to its requirements and bearing in common with the other states of the Union the burthens of government, submitting even as we were compelled to do *to taxation without representation;* but they tell us that a successful war to keep us in the Union left us out of the Union and that the pretension we put up for constitutional protection evidences bad temper on our part and a want of appreciation of the generous spirit which declares that the constitution is not over us for the purpose of protection. It reaches our case only when burthens are to be imposed. If on the other hand we venture to whisper that this theory makes secession an accomplished fact and puts these southern states out of the Union, we stand forthwith charged with a renewal of the old issue and a hidden desire to war upon the integrity of the Union. In such reasoning is found a justification of the policy which seeks to put the South under negro supremacy. Better, they say, to hazard the consequences of negro supremacy in the south with its sure and inevitable results upon Northern prosperity than to put faith in the people of the south who though overwhelmed and conquered have ever showed themselves a brave and generous people, true to their plighted faith in peace and in war, in adversity as in prosperity. If we remain silent in the midst of all these conflicting trials and troubles, we are taunted with a cowardly fear that prevents an honest expression of opinion. If on the other hand a brave, and it may be an imprudent spirit, ventures to give expression to his convictions on questions so vitally affecting the very existence of our people, he is threatened with arrest as a disturber of the public peace and the instigator of a new rebellion. Whatever we may do or say is construed into the exhibition of disloyal sentiments and made the pretext for renewed aggressive legislation. It is one of the strange features of human organization to hate those whom we have wronged, and each additional wrong that we put upon others intensifies the hatred which the first wrong created. In this way alone can I account for the bitterness with which our conquerors have pursued our ruined people. That they do hate us none can doubt who will calmly review the history of the governing power since the close of the war. That it will continue through life I doubt not; and in torment they will raise up their eyes, cursing the good and virtuous who are peacefully reposing in Abraham's bosom, beyond the reach of their malignity.

When to present trials, troubles and sufferings, you add the threatening promises of the early future, growing out of the impoverished condition of both the white and negro population, you will readily understand that we have no heart for festive scenes, even though they come to us consecrated by the memories which bring to our contemplation the virtues and greatness of the noble old patriot who in his day and generation " filled the measure of his country's glory."

Through the gloom and darkness which envelops the South, a ray of light is seen. The appeal made in behalf of the constitution as well as of a ruined people has at length reached the northern heart; and in the recent elections in many of the northern states a response has been spoken which has cheered our hearts and caused a smile even upon the furrowed brow of suffering.

I have never doubted the ultimate verdict which the intelligent and virtuous mind of the north would pronounce when relieved from the baneful influence of passion and prejudice. Fortunately for the North as well as the South the Democratic organization presents the opportunity for concentrating all conservative and constitutional elements in the coming struggle for constitutional liberty. At one time some fears were felt that old prejudices engendered in the party, struggles of the past upon issues now past and gone, would interpose obstacles in the way of that united and concentrated effort so essential to success; but those fears are fast passing away as we see the good and intelligent and virtuous of all parties recognizing the fact that the great battle for the preservation of the constitution must be fought under the banner of that old time-honored party whose records bear the honored names of Jefferson and Jackson.

With an Executive who manifests a resolute purpose to defend with all his power the constitution of his country from further aggression, and a Judiciary whose unspotted record has never yet been tarnished with a base subserviency to the unholy demands of passion and hatred, let us indulge the hope that the hour of the country's redemption is at hand, and that even in the wronged and ruined South there is a fair prospect for better days and happier hours when our people can unite again in celebrating national festivals as in the olden time.

Jeremiah S. Black To Howell Cobb. E.

washington, D. C, *April, 1868*. My Dear Sir: Forgive me for every apparent inattention. I never forgot your interests for a moment. My heart yearns to serve you and I thought I could do you and many others some good. But there is nothing here that I can see besides corruption and tyranny. This whole government is so rotten and dishonest that I can only protest. It is drunk with blood and vomits crime incessantly. The convictions of six judges would have compelled them to give judgment against the infamous system of tyranny established over the South; but Congress interposed, and though the Court might have done its duty in McCardle's case, it has not and will not. The act which takes away the jurisdiction is a legislative decree, an exercise of judicial power, and therefore not constitutional. I asked for a judgment as if the act had not passed, but the question is laid over until,—when do you think? Next December. There has been foul play all around. Johnson and Stanberry might have saved the country, but they did not and won't. Seward has manoeuvered and cheated and lied in all possible ways. The court stood still to be ravished and did not even hallo while the thing was getting done. Among them all I think there has been buying and selling enough to save Johnson,—that is to acquit him on the impeachment. But if that should be proven, he will remain in the hands of Seward who will use him only for the basest purposes. It is better for you and for us that Ben Wade (beast though he is) should take his place and put the responsibility on Abolition shoulders, than that we should be burdened with a President who does everything for the enemy which can help them to oppress you. Honor, justice, everything sacred, has been laid on the altar to propitiate the incarnate lie. "My soul comes not into their counsel and unto their assembly mine honor is not joined."

I have talked to Johnson whenever I got an opportunity, about doing the right thing in your case. But he never does anything because it is proper and just in itself. Reasons which seem irresistible to me make no impression on him, and I could not assure him that a correct disposal of that matter would make votes for him; for I did not known certainly whether it would or not. At all events the necessary motive seemed to be wanting, and I could not supply it. I am ashamed of all this. But I cannot help it.

Mrs. Black is not here at present. If she were she would send her warmest love to Mrs. Cobb. Give my most respectful regards to her.

William M. Browne To Howell Cobb. E.

Athens ga., *May 12,1868*. My Dear General, I was very glad to hear from you last night and was especially gratified that your wiser and better experience fully approves what I had already convinced myself is the only course for the South to pursue. Before I heard from you I had already written on this line to the L. Courier and in the Banner of this place (of which by the way in the absence of Mr. Atkinson I have political control). For the South to mix herself up in the questions which divide the democratic party of the North and which threaten again to wreck the party beyond the power of rescue would be madness. We can stand any platform and candidate that may be chosen at New York.

Had I to choose a candidate I might have a preference, or had I to write a platform I could do so containing a great many wholesome truths. But as it is certain my man and my platform would not suit the gentlemen who gave their men and their money, especially their money, to reduce us to our present condition and who still claim to be democrats, I see no use in Southern utterances. It is evident however that the greenbacks and the coin bond-paying parties will be quite as bitter and envenomed as ever the Douglas and the States Rights parties were, and that the result of 1861 will be reproduced in 1868. To save the Government first and then let the democracy of the whole country settle the bond question would seem to be the part of wisdom, for if the radicals get a renewed lease of power the value of the bonds and the greenbacks will not be much greater than our friend Mr. Memminger's elaborately executed promises to pay.

The Belmont party are very active. They have gained Dick Taylor for their side, who is working hard in Louisiana, and are trying to get other Southern men to ally themselves with their faction. I have little faith in the " Great North West " or in Pendleton. He is ultra, and consequently obnoxious to all moderate democrats and detestable to all conservative republicans. He and his party are going to try to play the Douglas Richardson game at Charleston, and if they do, defeat is as certain as death. I intend in my writing to pursue this line. It gratifies and fortifies me to know that you concur.

We had almost a hurricane and drenching rain last night which blew down half of my fine wheat and greatly damaged my fruit. My black mare is dying, and all around I have nothing to cheer or encourage me, absolutely nothing. The Courier takes now but fortnightly letters instead of weekly, and even for that pays very slowly.... In short things are as blue as indigo.

Gaza Way B. Lamar To Howell Cobb. E.

Ebbitt House, Washington D. C., *May 15, 1868.*

Dr. Sir: I take the liberty to give some idea of the recent developments here in politics. You are aware that feelers have been out in favor of Mr. Chase ever since his party put him aside for Gen'l Grant. What progress they made I never could ascertain because (I presume) that I insisted that he should repudiate negro suffrage or at least refer that to the *white* voters of the States. Afterwards I was not consulted.

Now, since the defection in the Senate on the impeachment, amounting to twelve Senators of the Radicals, it is said that a coalition has been formed between Chase and Seward to institute a new party—" the Conservative."

My informant who is a moderate illegible Radical, tells me that they rely on President Johnson and such of the Democrats as he can lead, and *that they either have Belmont,* the chairman of National Democratic Committee, or calculate on his adhesion, because of the financial doctrines—a resumption of specie payments and the payment of the bonds in gold—which are to form a plank in the new platform to catch all business men everywhere and New York City especially. These are the outlines, and they are anxious to ascertain how the South will go. I could not give any opinion— but I told him I thought the name of Mr. Seward would be repulsive to the South in every section.

Unless they can get the Democratic nomination on the 4th of July this new creation will divide the strength of both the old organizations and probably throw the election into the House next February—when the present Congress will elect Grant. The senators who are to leave the Radicals are Anthony, Fessenden, Fowler, Grimes, Henderson, Trumbull, Wiley, Sprague, Ross, Frelinghuysen, Sherman and Van Winkle. Anthony and Sprague consolidate Rhode Island; Fessenden, Grimes, Fowler, Trumbull, Frelinghuysen and Sherman divide their states respectively; and W. Virginia is consolidated. I have no idea of the effect upon the House members, as to who or how many may follow. I think best to adhere to Pendleton and Hancock, though my faith is very weak in Northern Democrats.

L. Q. Washington To Howell Cobb. E.

Washington D. C., *31 May, 1868.* My Dear Sir: I have been waiting for matters to settle down somewhat before answering yours of 25th Mch., in which I was much interested.

Impeachment is beaten and can never be revived. That is certain. The Republicans lose prestige and have offended business men, etc. The experiment is injurious to them apart from their divisions. What these divisions will amount to it is too soon to say. A war is kept up by ultra Radicals and such papers as the Tribune upon the Senators who voted to acquit; but this is not general, and the Chicago convention prudently avoided reading them out or censuring them except by implication. The body of the Repub. party are either openly or secretly hostile to the seven Senators and mean to put the knife to them at the proper time. I don't think Fessenden, Trumbull and Henderson fully appreciate the consequences of the step they have taken and its effect upon their standing with their party. They are all evidently striving to keep their places in the Republican organization, and I think it is more probable they will stick and thus fall between two stools than pursue a policy of sense and decision. But as I said, I think it too soon to estimate what the divisions will be.

As for Chase it is different. I have the best reason to believe he is quietly trying to secure the New York nomination, and hereabouts where principles sit loosely on men I find a good many quite ready to go for him. I don't think outside of Washington the movement amounts to much. For myself unless the platform promises deliverance from negro suffrage I care nothing about the contest. With a good platform any man who is available is good enough for me. Since I wrote you, Hancock has gained strength, and the Pendleton movement so far checked that I regard its strength as confined to certain limits. It is by no means improbable, judging from such affairs in the past, that Pendleton's friends may be strong enough to defeat Hancock in turn. I am clearly of opinion that we *must* nominate a military man so as to divide the Northern army—1st to carry the election, 2d to secure the fruits of victory against fraud. I regret the necessity of nominating any but an experienced statesman. In event of Hancock not being taken up, Frank Blair and McClellan are names that should be carefully considered. The record of the first is good *for this canvass;* they can make no points on him and *he* will not be cheated out of an election. I have no personal commitments and the only points I am positive about are, first a fight on *principle* and second an available man.

I am working very hard as assistant editor to the Intelligencer, correspondent to the London Telegraph and other papers.

I was at our Conservative convention lately in Richmond. We elected an excellent set of delegates to New York. I hope you will reconsider and meet us on there.

The Radis, seem to be at fault about reconstruction and divided, but I think on the whole will bring in the States and take the chances for their votes in Nov. I am told we can carry Georgia at the Presidential election. How is this?

Our vote in Virga. depends altogether on whether we are to be cheated or not. I am trying for a successor to Schofield who will prevent this.

It is always a favor to have your views and counsels on public matters and I hope to hear from you soon.

Jefferson Davis To Howell Cobb. E.

Lenttoxville, C. E., *July 6th, 1868.*

My Dear Sir: The proceedings against me having left a longer interval in which to cast about for some employment by which to support myself and family I have decided to go to Liverpool to see what may be done in establishing a commission house, especially for cotton and tobacco. An Englishman of very high character and social position who has been extensively engaged in the India trade as a commission merchant has proposed to me a partnership under the belief that I could obtain assurance of the shipments of the staple of our own country. With such assurance I would be willing to attempt a new pursuit confident that if the business was strictly that of commissions my friends would incur no risk and I might hope for an increasing income. I write to you to inquire what may be expected in regard to shipments by your friends and neighbors. I expect to leave here on or before the 20th inst. and to take passage the 25th from Quebec, consequently your answer would not reach me at the latter place later than the 24.

Mrs. Davis is my amanuensis, as I had the misfortune to fall and break two of my ribs ten days ago and am quite feeble from the effects of the fall.

With kind regards to Mrs. Cobb and the family, believe me.

Postscript to above, written by Mrs. Jefferson Davis

P. S.—Bear Burrow, I trust at last that we see our way clear, if the guarantees of cotton to be sent reach us before we go to Liverpool or soon after our arrival there, to be raised above the wretched sense of idle dependence which has so galled us. Unless Mr. Davis has a certain amount promised by reliable men, of course he can predicate no arrangements for the future upon the cotton to be sent. Disappointment will be bitter enough if it comes at the first, but much more so when another person is involved in our failure—therefore I beg that you will write us plainly what has been your success in trying to get promise of cotton. I am sorry to say that Mr. Davis's health has not improved, he looks wretchedly, and I think much of his indisposition is induced by his despair of getting some employment which will enable him to educate our children. There were.many things in our visit to the South which convinces me that for a year or more, until at least civil law prevailed, Mr. Davis could not quietly remain there. These if it should please God that we should ever meet I will tell you. Until then I shall as ever remain yours affectionately.

Mrs. Jeffehson Davis To Mrs. Howell Cobb. E.

Lennoxville, C. E., *July 6th, 1868.*

My Dear Sister Maran, I have not been on my dignity though you have been my debtor for two letters for some time, but there are no scores between us save scores of love, and good wishes. I can scarcely tell you how I have languished out my time while my body worked, for I have worked with my hands in this little out of the way village, and prayed and hoped with my soul, without much expectation of release from my troubles. If I could see you I should not mind telling you, but I cannot write all my anxieties. The children are growing apace.... Mr. Davis's soul is wearing out his body—inactivity is killing him, and since his accident his difficulties, cough, and physical exhaustion have increased. I feel sure that he would recuperate if he could once get something to do, but it is fearful to hold your earthly hopes upon an if. We went South last winter upon a tour, and hoped to find our property available there, but returned without being able to get a dollar, but Mr. Davis paid nearly an hundred to support our superannuated old negroes. I could tell you about this if I were with you but refrain from writing—suffice it to say we came back with no hopes for our children's future save those we have in God's promises. As no distance or time seems to sever my heart from yours, I shall scarcely be further off from you in Liverpool than I am here, but I do so long to say good bye face to face with you, and to give you some of my cares to share with me. A selfish wish, is it not? I so often think of you surrounded by children and grandchildren, a home and a future, and bless God that all I love are not like me, floating uprooted. Do, dear old friend, write to me and tell me *every little* thing about yourself, and your family. I am so much afraid of your feeling yourself a stranger to me, and of each cord becoming loosened by disuse, until we drop off altogether into that mechanical intercourse, valueless because labored. How is dear little Sallie Barrow? Has she a child? Mrs. Robb's death affected me deeply. I saw her while in New York, and she looked like death then, but did not in the least know it. Mr. Robb takes it very hard, but tries to hide it. Maggie and Mr. Davis send love to you and your dear children, and dear reliable old tender friend, I am as ever.

Alexander H. Stephens To J. Barbett Cohen. L. C.

Atlanta, Ga., *July 17, 1868.*

My Dear Sir: Your favour of a few days ago was duly received and would have been answered sooner but for indisposition and pressure of business in the? trial now going on.1 I have at this time but a moment to write to you before going to the barracks where the military commission sits. Allow me therefore briefly to thank you for the letter and papers and also especially for the article in the Courier some weeks ago in relation to the Constitutional View. As soon as I saw that I thought I knew to whom I was indebted for such a favourable commendation of the work. For all this you have my very sincere thanks though I fear you place an over estimate upon the value of the Book. What does Mr. Rhett say of it? Has he yet seen it?

I think well of the nomination of Seymour and Blair and trust they may be elected, but have been too busy to see enough of the tone of the Northern Press to form any opinion of my own as to the result. I have not yet had time to read Gen. Scott's and Gen. Orr's queries?. Have laid them away to read when I get this great? trial off my mind. We shall demolish the prosecution, I think.

P. S. My kindest regards to Mrs. Cohen and your father. My brother wrote to me of your very kind attention to him and family while they were in Charleston. For all this accept my sincere? thanks.

1 The trial of E. G. Kirkscey and other " Columbus prisoners" before a military court at Atlanta for the murder of the Radical politician, G. W. Ashburn.

Bird B. Chapman 1 To Alexander H. Stephens. R.

Elyria, Ohio, *July 21st, 1868.*

Sir: That you may not construe my letter of June 20th as personal or party hostility to Pendleton I write you this. Though I think Seymour a much stronger candidate than Pendleton his quasi support of the war will have a tendency to defeat him. Shakespeare says " there is a tide in the affairs of men, which, taken at the flood leads on to fortune." So the Republicans seem to have acted for the last few years in nominating Colonels and Generals for office that the popularity of the war might carry them into office. In nominating the principal General of the war they seem to have put on the climax, for I believe he does not claim ever to have voted with them.

Thus it will show how matters are viewed here. I sent you the Cleveland paper marked to show that to have been favorable to the war and the proclamation was necessary to get a nomination to office. I am not arguing the justice or injustice of the measure, but simply stating the case as it is, as I am almost the only man disconnected with party that can do so. As lawyers well say, an issue must be joined before trial can be had, so the nomination of Chase would have left the country without an issue. I think he would have polled more votes than any other one named in the 4th of July convention, but if elected would have disappointed his supporters.

The real issue is the public debt, and as he was one of its fathers it would have been hard for him to have dis-own'd it. I am glad that you at the South have not made this a special question. Considering how it was incurred one might have supposed you would, and it would have been counted very much against you. I consider the Government really stronger for having the debt, as it makes so many interested in its perpetuity but not so in the payment of the interest.

There are nine men to want cheap tea, tobacco and whiskey, to one who wants his interest on bonds, and will make their wants known before this is over. I own no bonds nor am I a repudiator, but I can see that the first great issue will be upon the taxing of the bonds, and then the payment of the bonds themselves as claimed by their holders.

To meet these questions fairly and justly is my intention. That to save the Government the debt was incurred I have no doubt, but how much of it was necessary is another question and upon this hangs Tariffs, Internal revenues, etc. I have sent you the Elyria and Sandusky papers that you might see that the feeling of hard times has not reached here yet, and until that does I see no chance for a change.

1 Congressional delegate from the Territory of Nebraska, 1855-1857.

An Anonymous Writer To Howell Cobb. E.

New York, *Augt. 3rd, 1868.*

Dear Sir: About the most telling arguments used here by the Radical party are furnished by such men as yourself and Genl. Toombs. Your speech in Atlanta endorsing the candidates1 is extensively circulated and used as a proof of the temper of the South. You are called one of the representative men of the South. I notice in that speech the following language: "And raising the banner of Constitutional liberty and equality, we hurl into their teeth today the same defiance and bid them come on to the struggle. We are ready if they are. Snatch the old banner from the dust and give it again to the breeze, and if needs be to the God of battles, and strike one more blow for Constitutional liberty."

You can well imagine how a wrong construction may be placed on your intentions and motives.

I was riding to day in a street car and asked a common mechanic how the election would go. His reply was:

"If we could only get the Southern politicians to keep silent there would be a chance for our ticket, but they will ruin every thing again by their speeches." I am a Democrat and don't love the Radicals any better than you do and I do assure you that the best policy is for the prominent Rebels at the South to keep quiet.

Do for the sake of the cause as well as for your sake induce your friend Toombs to stay at home or at least to make no inflammatory speeches, no speeches at all. Your speech in Atlanta will loose the ticket 50,000 votes.

Yours etc., A Friend To The Cause.

Robert Toombs To Alexander H. Stephens. R.

Washington, Ga., *Aug. 9th, 1868.* Dear Stephens, Your letters of the 5th and 8th reed. I only reached home from Athens on Friday night and intended to go over to see you Saturday, but Friday night I was engaged to bring some important cases to the Dist. Court U. S. and was disappointed in going over. The speech you sent me very accurately set forth my leading ideas and I am content for them to stand. The speech at the convention I wrote out hurriedly from rough notes (except that part prepared for another purpose last summer) and I omitted (forgot) a good deal of the best of it and was mortified that I omitted the notice I took of Seymour and Blair, by accident. Your views of the 14th Amendment were precisely my own, but I did not care to say so, as I knew it would pass and I feared that the least encouragement would induce our friends to vote for it and therefore seem to give 1 Toombs, Cobb, and B. II. Hill had been the principal speakers at a great Democratic rally at Atlanta, July 23, 18GS. commonly known as the "bush-arbor meeting." it a public sanction. Tho' while I have no doubt but that you are right in thinking that the C. and Sent.1 is unkind to you, I must say you ought not to have given them so fair a chance at you. The Era for three consecutive days before you left Atlanta *after it was adopted*2 declared that you advised the Democrats to accept it, and really as you were there and said nothing about it I did not feel at liberty to deny it in answer to the many inquiries made of me. I simply stated I did not believe it but that I had heard you say nothing specifically on the point. As to Wright, the poor devil will never co-operate with either you or me, until *he ought not,* if that time should ever come. That is when we promote his perjured views. Let him pass. He asked for my corrected speech and heralds it as tho' he were a special organ. He is gaining ground because the real sentiments of the Constitutionalist are hostile to us, not the editors but the proprietors, and people begin to smell it out.

As to the senatorship I preferred that Brown should be beaten by Joshua Hill to almost any other man. It is impossible for you to think worse of the scoundrel than I do, but it could only be done by a Radical, and there was political justice in making the earliest traitor defeat the worst one and break down his party. I differed with you as to the policy of beating Brown. He had been covert? Govr. of Georgia nearly two years, administering the patronage of the military, had the whole patronage of Bullock 4 at his feet, and put all these with the whole patronage, if he had been senator it would have cost us not far short of 10,000 votes. His special knowledge, especially of all the rogues in the State, is prodigious, and I think it was about worth the State to beat him. Hill is a poor devil. His forlorn condition, powerless under the present circumstances, is conclusive evidence of his weakness, his inability to help himself or hurt us. I did my utmost to elect him, and ask of him no other favour than not to join us or speak to me. Your case if necessary shall be continued (Meadow's case). I am very anxious to go to AVhite Sulphur myself and have expected to do so this summer and am now only waiting to see what will be done with the fall courts. I do not see how they can be held now in any event, and I think those villians at Atlanta intend not to have them held if they could be. I will write to you in a few days at the Springs, that is as soon as I get any definite information as to the courts. All well.

1 The Chronicle and Sentinel, a newspaper printed at Augusta, Ga. 21. c., the fourteenth amendment. 3 In February, 1S67, Joseph E. Brown had given up the effort at resisting the congressional reconstruction programme. ne advised the southern whites to acquiesce In negro suffrage; and he himself entered the Republican party. He returned to the Democracy, however, In 1S70. 4 Rufus B. Bullock, Republican governor of Georgia, 1868-1871. He fled from the State before the end of his term, and at Toombs's instance was indicted for embezzlement of public funds. He was extradited from New York in 1876 and tried and acquitted in Georgia.

John M. Johnson To Howell Cobb. E.

Atlanta, Ga., *Sept..22nd, 1868.*

My Dear General,... The belief is gaining ground that Grant will be elected. The negroes since the expulsion of the colored members from the legislature have been much more turbulent than before. The outbreak at Mitchell Court House last Saturday is but the beginning,—others will follow. As soon as I can get $4,000 for my property I will sell and leave the country. Would it not be well for us all to look to contingencies? And prepare for an exodus?

Property is rising and the no. of buildings in process of erection greater than ever before in Atlanta. I am amazed every time I ride out at the evidences of increasing population as indicated by the hundreds of new buildings now going up....

Mrs. Jefferson Davis To Mrs. Howell. Cobb. E.

Waterloo england, *Oct. 22nd, 1868.* My Dear Afflicted Friend, A telegraphic item from the U. S. bears the woful news to us of your deep bereavement,1 and has filled me with a longing akin to heart sickness to be with you in this greatest grief of your checkered life. May God give you strength and patience to wait for your reunion with the love of your life, your greatest earthly stay. Mr. Davis and I feel deeply our loss in him, and know full well that we have no friend left so judicious and wise in council, so brave and strong hearted, so tender and true to his friends. If we cannot become reconciled to his loss, how are we to speak comfort to you, to whose life his-was a constant glow of warmth and sunshine. My memory conjures a thousand tender recollections of him as I write, and I can only pray that you may be able to say. "not my will but thine, oh Lord, be done;" and that "He with his own hand " may wipe the tears off your face and enable you by faith to see that blissful reunion which has been promised to those who patiently watch and pray. If you can only write a few words *do, do* try to write them to me. If it is a great effort remember how dearly I love you and how truly I am a fellow mourner with you and with his children. Tell me of them all and where they are, where you are, how you are. If you cannot write to me then pray ask my dear little Mary Anne to do so. Words do seem so poor when a heart is so full of love and sorrow as mine, that I will not try to express even a part of what you know I feel. Our poor country is not the least one of the sufferers to be pitied when we realize our great loss. Where will she find so staunch and wise a leader in her hour of peril. It is a poor consolation, yet it is one to know that a whole country mourns with you and that your chil 1 Howell Cobb had died suddenly in the city of New York, Oct. 9, 1868.

dren will be ever dear to our people for the sake of their great good father. The good he has done truly "lives after him." Please write to me. I feel as if it would comfort me to see your handwriting only to be sure you are not gone from me too. No one knows except those who have been poor and in a strange land how doubly dear one's friends become. We have just passed very near the valley of death and are now, thank God, better again; but little Billie was at school at this place, and I was with Maggie and Winnie when I was summoned to see him die with typhoid fever of a kind called gastric. I found him quite delirious, with black lips, and fighting everything in deadly fright. The Dr. gave me no hopes at all but I prayed without ceasing and poured brandy down his throat after he ceased to be able to swallow; and after three weeks had elapsed he became convalescent; he is considered a perfect wonder and is getting fat and rosy. You may judge what a miracle his recovery has been, when the Physician sent by the Privy Council from London to inquire what the endemic condition of the town proceeded from was brought to see him as a miraculous recovery. We were going to leave here immediately after Billie's recovery but I was so exhausted by nursing that I have got into a very low nervous condition and for three weeks have not been able to sit up but have lain on the sofa helpless and with my pulse so low that I felt an almost utter inability to be either glad or sorry—a kind of delirious lull of pain and hope of happiness. Of course this has kept Mr. Davis with us. Margaret H. came to us on the last steamer and as soon as I am able to travel we shall go to Leamington until we hear whether Mr. Davis is to go home and be tried next month. If he goes or does not we shall go to some very cheap place on the Continent to educate the children and tide over the state of military anarchy which in my opinion renders it dangerous for Mr. Davis to remain at home. We are too poor to travel, so that I have seen nothing here except Liverpool and this little suburb yclept Waterloo; it is within ten minutes by rail from Liverpool and most of the merchants have residences out here who have small children. I never saw such an expensive country in my life. It costs so much to dress even decently that I have decided not to try and I never accept any invitations or go anywhere to dinner or elsewhere, not even to an exhibition, except such as are free, for I feel hourly the necessity of pinching at every turn. Mr. Davis will I fear never be able to do much again, for he is knocked up by the least exertion more than ordinary—the least cold lays him up with neuralgia and the least exposure brings dreadful headache. I fear his health is permanently broken; the breaking of his ribs gave it the *coup de grace* and he is at times much of an invalid. I watch over him unceasingly and pray to go first if it must be that 73566—13 45 we are to be parted. Twenty years difference asserts itself when the younger of the two is middle aged, and I am in terror whenever he leaves me. Pray for me, for your prayers will avail. Do give my love to the dear good Brownes. Nobody loves them better than I do. Give my tender love to my little Mary Anne, to Lizzie, and Andrew, and to the Boys and their wives—especially to Howell. Will you mind my putting you in mind of your promise even at this hour of having that young Ambrotype copied of you for me. It brings you back to me in your youth when I first began to wonder whether I loved or respected you most, for from the first I understood you and was as now with perfect trust and tenderest love your devoted friend. P. S.—Dear, dear heart, "heaviness endureth for a night, but joy cometh in the morning." May God give you hope and peace equal to your faith; again, dear precious friend, farewell.

Robert Toombs To Alexander H. Stephens. R.

Washington Geo., *Deer. 11th, 1868.*

Dear Stephens, Your letter of the 8th I found on my arrival at home this evening. Linton I hear is at Atlanta, and as it may suit both of our arrangements best to meet as early as possible I will fix next Tuesday as the day (the 15th inst.). Any other day that would not interefere with our circuit dockett in the Supreme Court would suit me as well if that day should not suit him. I will come over on Tuesday unless I hear from you on Monday. We had a pleasant and agreeable meeting of the trustees of the University at Macon. The creation of the chair of history and political science and the invitation to you to accept it was unanimous and extremely cordial. I think it the real, cordial and hearty approbation of every member of the board present to see you upon the subject and to urge you to enter upon its duties as soon as you can possibly arrange your business to do so, tho' they are willing that you should have all the time you require or wish to arrange for the change. I know that the University and the public will be great gainers by your taking upon yourself these new cares and duties; but I do not know whether you will find the change of life agreeable to you. But we will talk over all these matters when we meet.

"The chair of Belle Lettres was filled by Maj. Morris and that of Modern Languages by Dr. Smead of Montgomery, formerly of Wra. and Mary College. Morris I know personally and think very highly of. Smead I do not know, but both came with the highest recomjnendations possible, especially Maj. Morris.

There was a considerable meeting of Planters and others at the Agricultural, etc., etc., convention.

I did not have an opportunity of attending them which I left still in session when I left Macon yesterday morning.

Julia is still complaining of her old disease, but thinks there has been decided amendment of the symptoms within the last three or four days. All the rest well.

Robert Toombs To Alexander H. Stephens. R.

Washington, Geo., *Jany. 24th, 1870.*
Dear Stephens, I received your letter of the 12th inst. The reason I did not come over as I expected was that my wife had a slight relapse which I apprehended would turn out more serious than it did. tho' it threw her back two or three days and I was detained to await the result. She is now a good deal better but still very weak. She sits up the greater part of the day but not strong enough to sit up the entire day and has to retire early. She has not yet been able to get down into the dining room. I was sorry to hear that you are not so well off as when I saw you last, and I fear this very wet unseasonable weather will retard your progress, if not increase your bad symptoms.

I went to Atlanta to see if I could be of any service in the present *coup d'etat* of Bullock and his conspirators. It is a hard job. He is perfectly reckless, fully supported by the military, stakes all upon success, and offers all the offices, places, money and the plunder of the people for help to aid him to obtain the dictatorship of the state. It has not been without its effect upon some so-called democrats. Many outsiders bite at the bait, and some representatives, but our true men have banded together with a good deal of firmness, hold the weak and timid and overawe and intimidate some of the villains on their own side. They have also good prospects of a strong defection among the enemy if they will "stick." Nearly all of the "ins" are against Bullock and his own, and a pretty good lot of those that could not get " in " when they wanted to. Bryant is the candidate of the Democrats for speaker of the House, and I and Joe Brown are trying to elect him! Rather a strange conjunction is it not? But you know my rule is to use the devil if I can do better to save the country. Upon the whole the prospect was pretty good when I left there. I go back Wednesday or Thursday, Wednesday if I can possibly get ready.

There are strange events working in Warren but I can not tell them on paper *now*. I am extremely anxious to see you and will stop at least until the night train passes if my business (a case in the Macon circuit) does not force me on. All the rest well.

Robert Toombs To Alexander H. Stephens. R.

Washington, Geo., *Feby. 8th, 1870.*
... P. S.—I forgot to tell you about my political adventures in Atlanta. I got into consultations with Brown, Bryant, Caldwell *et id omne genus.* Politics does make us acquainted with strange bedfellows. Brown seems really in earnest in his endeavour to defeat Bullock and his schemes. I don't know whether or not he sees where his present course will land him, but I suppose he does. There were many curious developments which I don't care to put on paper but will tell you all about when we meet. We thought we had the crowd pretty dead two or three times, but the spirit of evil at Washington was too strong for us and poor Grant could not "stick."

Alexander H. Stephens To J. Barrett Cohen. L. C.

Liberty Hall, Crawfordville, Ga., *Apr. 16, 1870.*

My Dear Sir: I have wanted to write to you for some time and return you my thanks as well as acknowledgments for the papers you sent me; but the truth is I have been too unwell to do anything. When I was able to be up at all I devoted what strength I had to the completion of the 2d vol. of my work on the war. All the writing on that as well as nearly all my other writing for twelve months and more has been done by the hands of others. It is painful to me to use the pen. But occasionally I do scribble a letter to particular friends as I am now doing and on matters of private business, but all else is done by others. I can sit up and read what is brought to me but I can not stand or walk or help myself in any way in getting about or even in dressing, without assistance of some sort. The book is now off my hands and I hope to recuperate my nervous energies to some extent though I fear I shall never be on foot again. Can you not come up and see me. You may be assured I should be highly gratified to welcome you here, not only once but often. I feel greatly obliged to you for your review of the Harper? controversy. I take it for granted that you were the author of the piece on that subject which I saw in the Charleston Courier.

Alexander H. Stephens To J. Barrett Cohen. L. C.

Liberty Hall, Crawfordville, Ga., *Aug. 8, 1870.*

My Dear Sir: I wrote to you yesterday and today I received a letter from you and also by express a package. A thousand thanks to you for the books. They came in the very nick of time or just at that part of the History under *revision* in which I wished to refer to them. I wrote to you yesterday about the Harper? controversy. I was very sorry indeed that he as Editor of XIX Century mixed himself up at all with the political questions now agitating the state. In truth it would have been better for him and the magazine if he had not. No good can come of it— harm may. Indeed if I had been in South Carolina, while I could not have approved the *platform* adopted by the *Reformers* I could but have sympathized with their objects and bid them good speed for the local ends aimed at, hoping that success should crown their efforts in rescuing their state government from the hands in which it now is, that all would yet be right with them on sober second thought so far as relates to the great fundamental principles involved in their platform. I do trust that all will yet be well. Allowance must be made for indiscretions of those who mean well. A leading object now should be with all the friends of sound principles not to permit any permanent estrangement to take place between them from discussions during the present canvass. No true friend of constitutional liberty can take pleasure in seeing Scott reelected, and while it is true that there are many objectionable features in the platform of the Reformers, yet there is much more ground for hope that a majority of that party will hereafter rectify their errors in these particulars than that any possible good can come from the triumph of their opponents. The world has to be taken as we find it and it is the part? of the patriot and statesman to do the best he can with public affairs as he finds them under circumstances as they arise. This great duty however in no case should lead him to sacrifice principle for policy. While he often is utterly unable to control events as he would have them yet individually he should so act as to secure the greatest attainable good which can be secured without committing himself to error in principle. But enough of this. I am suffering very much to day and am hardly able to be up while I am writing. Please present my kindest regards to Mrs. Cohen and accept my best wishes for both and all yours now and for ever!

P. S.—Just as soon as my nephew returns, which will be in about two weeks, I expect I will get him to hunt up a copy of the speech to which you refer. If another is to be found I will send it to you. I think there are copies of it about the library but I can not make the search myself.

Alexander H. Stephens To J. Barkett Cohen. L. C.

Liberty Hall, Crawtordville, Ga., *Oct. 25, 1870.*

My Dear Sir: I heard from you as you passed through our village on your return from Cincinnati and regretted very much that you could not stop and spend a day or two at least with me.

Your elections are now over and I am anxious to know the result. This I suppose from what I have seen stated in the papers will be made known tomorrow. But as news through the newspapers is so uncertain and unreliable I wish you would write to me and let me know exactly how the matter stands as to governor, Congress and the State legislature. If any negroes are elected to Congress let me know their status— whether Carolina negroes or carpet-baggers— whether full bloods or mixed—whether intelligent for their class or not.

I have felt an intense interest in the efforts at reform in South Carolina, and while I did not think it could be effected in the way our friends took over there, yet I shall be rejoiced to know by results that they understood this question so far as it affected themselves better than I did. Do let me know how its has all turned out. I was exceedingly glad to see the telegram from Charleston the day after the election that the Reform ticket had triumphed in that city. While I could not endorse the principles upon which the victory was achieved yet I infinitely preferred the personnel as well as the objects of the Reformers to the personnel and objects of their opponents. A *half* a loaf is better than no *bread*. In politicks the first great object should be to have the *worst* men displaced from power and better ones brought in if possible, even if both classes avow the same leading principles. As between *honest* men and *knaves* of whatever professions, callings, business or pursuits of life, my warmest sympathies are ever enlisted towards the former in all strifes and contentions between themselves. But enough. Please let me hear from you.

Robert Toombs To Alexander H. Stephens. R.

Madison, Georgia, *19th Nov., 1870.*

Dear Stephens, I enclose you a letter for my wife which please send over by Jim who I expect will be at your house tonight. I had hoped to be there myself but the arbitration in the Whitfield case is protracted by Hill and his villains with the hope of annoying me out, but you know I commonly take a thro' ticket. The thing is unbearable except by a man of my philosophy!!

I will be at your house on my way home possibly Monday night, probably Tuesday night, but if not as soon as I get thro' with this job. I have never seen such cold-blooded villains as the Madison ring, but I have my grip on them and I shall not let go until it thunders. I was glad to hear yesterday that you are doing well. Tell Jim to go home tomorrow and give him the letter I enclose for Madam.

Dudley M. Dubose1 To Alexander H. Stephens. K.

Washington, Ga., *Dec. 21st, 1870.*

Dear Sir: I was very much gratified to receive your letter of today. Wilkes County is all right and safe. We now have the Radicals beaten and expect to increase our majority on tomorrow. 2 We will certainly carry the county by six hundred majority and probably more—it will depend on the number we can get out to vote tomorrow—we have polled in all 1493 votes.

The last news from Lincoln the vote was almost unanimous for the Democrats. We learn from Columbia that the Democrats are at least one thousand ahead. Pope Barrow of Oglethorpe writes me today that his county is safe but was not able to say what our majority would be; he also stated that all of the McWhorters voted openly for me, Judge Hamp McWhorter leading the crowd. I will send you the earliest news of results at this place. I will be very glad to hear from you tomorrow and the next day.

Robert Toombs To Alexander H. Stephens. R.

Washington, Geo., *Deer. 30th, 1870.*
Dear Stephens, I was surprised to see your name in that State lease.3 Is there anything in it? I hope and believe not of course, unless you have been misled in the business. It is a lot of the greatest rogues on the continent, your name alone excepted. I have heard nothing from Reid about, our fee; will write again. For our great victory God be praised. The most gratifying result is the defeat of the Conservative strongholds (see Fifth Dist., Bibb and Monroe, *et id omne).* Thank God for that too. We are all well. A Happy New Year to you.

Robert Too Jibs To Alexander H. Stephens. R.

Washington, Geo., *Deer. 30th, 1870.*
Dear Stephens, Your letter of this evening is recd. I did not think and do not think you did wrong in seeking to become a lessee of the State road under the facts which you state, and I have no doubt but that it will be immensely profitable in honest profits. But I have had the most invincible repugnance to the whole scheme. It was gotten up solely to defraud the people of the State out of the 1 Son-in-law of Robert Toombs.

a In this portion of the Reconstruction period the law required that at each election the polls be kept open for three days. 8 The Western & Atlantic Railroad, owned by the State of Georgia, had just been leased by the State government to a company known as the Western & Atlantic Railroad Co. , in which Stephens had subscribed to a small amount of stock. Joseph E. Brown and Benjamin H. Hill were prominent members of the company, as were also certain carpet-bag politicians, and several railroad presidents and other capitalists. road, and the act was so contrived and drawn as to make it impossible to have fair competition in the lease. The requisition of eight millions security and five millions of that in the State, placed the whole thing in the power of the R. R. companies of the State without the least reason on earth except to shut out competition. As the rent was payable monthly, one hundred thousand dollars, with a constant supervision over the road, was as good as an hundred millions of dollars, especially with a lien on the rolling stock.

Bullock and his friends had the control of the roads in this matter, or might accept a bid from a part of the roads to the ruin of the rest; and the whole scheme has culminated in a grand conspiracy and combination of Bullock, his gang and the roads to drive out competition and take the road at the minimum price fixed. Of course you knew nothing of these things; but except your own name I do not recognize another individual who is not of the ring. When I saw Ben Hill's letter1 going over to the Rads. I stated to more than a dozen gentlemen before I had ever heard one word, that his price was a share in the State road. The idea of the Albany and Gulf road going security for a jug of whiskey I knew to be bosh. The same may be said of the Macon and Brunswick. Besides I do not believe a single one of the roads are legally bound by the action of their presidents, etc., and therefore that there is no security at all. For myself I look upon the whole action of the Terry legislature as null and void, a pure usurpation binding neither on the State or any inhabitant thereof. And as far as I am concerned it has been, since the day they were put upon us to this hour, my fixed purpose to do whatever I could as long as I lived to "expunge" and draw black lines around the whole of that infamous record. With these strong opinions I must candidly say while I look upon your own conduct as perfectly honourable and free from any reproach I did regret seeing your name among the lessees. And I have hesitated long before saying this much because I do not wish any opinion of mine in the least to affect your action in the matter, and especially to deprive you of a very valuable investment honestly and in good faith made by you. I have not the least, doubt but that the lessees will make at least fifty thousand per month clear money.

I am so pressed with business that I cannot come tomorrow. Tuesday I have to leave for Macon to argue the Mercer University case before Cole, and if I go by Augusta, which I expect to do, I will call up on that day to see you. Julia and all the rest of the family are well except Genl. DuBose and myself,—both suffering with cold and he severely attacked.

1 Benjamin H. Hill bad Issued a public letter Dec. 8, 1870, recanting many of the opinions he had previously held and advocating that negroes be protected In their exercise of the suffrage.

Alexander H. Stephens To Francis P. Blair.1

Liberty Hall, Crawfordville, Ga., *8 May, 1871.*

My Dear Sir: Your esteemed letter of the 3d. Inst. written at St Louis Mo. has just reached me—I thank you for it and also thank you for Genl. Schurz's speech. There seems to be very little difference indeed between my views of the present and future and those of Genl. Schurz so far as practical action is concerned. I can well see how a man could have been most conscientiously and earnestly devoted to the emancipation of the negroes in this country. No man I think was more so or could have been more so than Mr. Jefferson was. However much therefore I may have differed with others upon that question while it was a *living* one, yet I can now not only cordially co-operate with all such men, since that question is forever out of the way, upon all the *really practical* and living questions of the present and future which involve the essentials and essence of liberty itself—and the more so when I meet with men of that class, who show by their acts that they were moved by earnest convictions and devotion to what they deemed the just rights of man on the question of emancipation. The only real difference, as I see it, between myself and Genl. Schurz is the question of having an *affirmance* of the 14 and 15 amendments. He is not very distinct on this point; but this is my inference from what he said. He seems to treat these amendments as irregular acts of the Govmt. growing out of or springing from the war—and should therefore be positively affirmed or accepted as valid parts of the constitution as fully as the 13th ament. Now I do not so consider them—the War was over, peace was declared, the 13 amendment was ratified. Slavery was forever abolished. All the states had returned to their obligations under the constitution. This was what the war had been waged for. At first it was waged solely with a view to compel the withdrawing states to return to their obligations under the constitution—when this was accomplished its end was attained—but under this negro slavery which was the prime exciting cause of it had been overthrown by it. It was abandoned in good faith by the returning states—these states were then certainly entitled to their seats in the Congress of States, for withdrawing from which the war had been waged against them, and which they were assured during the while? war was going on were vacant and awaiting their return. The denial of this return, and the *Revolution* forced by arms on their Govt. by which the 14 and 15 Amt were claimed to have been passed, was certainly a most glaring usurpation—after the war was over—after all its ends 1 Text derived from a copy kindly furnished by Dr. Frederic Bancroft, of Washington, D. C. The original is among the Carl Schurz papers in the Library of Congress.

were attained and not as any thing growing out of the war. But in view of all of these things it seems to me that the way of getting out of all these troubles and entanglements is easy if there be as I think there is on the part of Genl. Schurz an earnest and patriotic desire to save free institutions in this country from the grasp of usurpers bent upon their overthrow. The way is pointed out or clearly indicated in the Ky. Resolutions in the late Democratic Convention of that State, which have just reached me and with which as a whole I am greatly pleased. These Resolutions are brief but significant—they are potent not only in what they affirm but in what they do *not* affirm. If Genl. Schurz and men of his class can stand upon such a Platform as that in the coming general civic struggle in all the States on the great present and future question of whether this is to be a govmt. of laws or a govmt. of bayonets, I, for one at least, of the Southern Democracy, say that I can stand upon it. The New York World I see expresses satisfaction with or willingness to stand upon this Ky. Platform—I am gratified at this. The great breaker ahead in the ranks of the Democracy is a *positive affirmance* of the *validity* of any usurpation caused by federal violence and perfidy.

Under existing circumstances it seems to me that the Democracy in their convention might agree to stand upon any platform which does not commit them to any "new departure" from their time honored creed or cardinal principles or of taking " any step backward," but which does or shall positively and affirmatively commit them to the support of the Federal Union with the reservation by the States of the sacred right of local self Govmt. on all subjects which relate exclusively to their own internal interest, safety, and well being, with a denunciation of usurpations of every character without specification of any in detail—leaving the rectification of all existing wrongs to the true friends of liberty through the proper use of the ballot, and all the instrumentalities of the Constitution—including the three Departments of Govmt.—the legislative, executive and judiciary. The ballot and the checks of the Constitution are the only sure safe guards of the people against the schemes of those who are now aiming at the overthrow of liberty and the establishment of a centralized Despotism in this country. On such a program, if power can be wrested from the hands of those who are now so outrageously abusing it for their ambitious and wicked purposes, all the questions growing out of the 14 and 15 amendments touching either their validity or effect can be *practically* easily settled through the instrumentality of the Constitution without wrong to any person or interest in the Country, by those who are really devoted to the great cause of maintaining and preserving free institutions on this continent—and that is now the only real living and absorbing question. The N. Y. World says, the

Ky. Resolutions to which I allude, and which I approve, *ignore* the past. Well if the World thinks so, so be it with the World. It does not *ignore* usurpations. It denounces them. It is true it does not specify; but it is a raking fire which strikes without exception all which come within its range—either past, present or future. What are usurpations and what not can under this platform be inquired into if the constitutional party comes into power, as well as their effects, including the past as well as the present or future. No harm will be done in it. These are matters to be conferred about, however, by and through private correspondence and not by or through the press or on the stump—and in any way, I say to you that it is a matter of the *utmost importance* that the Democracy at the North in their coming conventions County and State shall *not commit* themselves to the N. Y. World's lead by *endorsing usurpations of any* sort. Let them for the present—this year at least—take *no step backwards.* Let them not lower their flag in the face of the enemy—this is the great point. Let them present a bold front against *centralism* and usurpations of all sorts without specifications.

P. S.—I shall be exceedingly glad to welcome you here. Let me know before hand when to expect you.

P. S. (2nd.)—Senator Morton says in effect that the Democracy *dare* not assail the usurpations by which his present Jacobinical dynasty holds power and by which they expect to extend it. In this he exhibits the usual boldness which characterizes the conduct of all usurpers. The worst indication I have seen lately is that some timid Democrats seem to *quail* before the *dare* and intimate that they do not intend any such thing! Now one thing is certain, if the Democratic Party go into the contest under the lead of such captains as these they will be " licked out of their boots ". Usurpers must be met by as bold a front and even bolder than that presented—the righteous are e er bold as a lion—and those who stand upon the *right,* if they mean to maintain it, must be equally bold and unflinching. In this case the Democracy must tell Senator Morton that they do dare to proclaim the truth on all questions and dare assail usurpations of any character and denounce them on all proper occasions—they do dare assail those now in power for the usurpations by which alone they hold it— their usurpations of test oaths and acts of disfranchisements and all these outrages upon the Constitution by which they aim at an overthrow of free institutions in this country, and for *these acts*—for what they have done as well as what they propose to do—the Democracy does dare not only assail them and denounce them but call upon the people to rally at the polls and put them out of their places. If the Democracy has not the *courage* to meet the dare of the Senator and even beard him if need be in his stronghold as he supposes it to be—that of the Reconstruction act so called— then they may as well quit the field and abandon the contest, write a confession that they do not mean to assail or question their most monstrous acts, but only gently to interpose and save from new usurpations, their roaring as I before stated to you will be of the character of that of "Smug the joiner" and will end about as farcical. The organization of the Democracy must be against usurpations of all sorts. Every Democrat should have the nerve to denounce usurpations of any character. He should illegible at none, connive at none, much less sanction or approve any. The effect of usurpations in the past or what is to be done in rectifying their wrongs are questions which may be left for future adjustment in the hands of the friends of the Constitution under and through the peaceful workings of its own instrumentalities for its own maintenance and preservation, under a proper administration of all its provisions.

Robert Toombs To Alexander H. Stephens. R.

Sunday, *21st Jany., 1872.*

Dear Stephens, I recd. your letter of yesterday by Mr. Burnett. I had written to you before its reception and enclose this 2nd edition. You are mistaken as to Smith's[1] not agreeing with your position in the Sun. I. heard him say several times that he did agree with you and requested the judiciary committee to pass a law on the subject or elect under the existing law, which he said he preferred, but if they wished an Executive appointment, to alter the law accordingly. The law was altered and I suppose escaped your attention. I enclose the notice of it from the Constitution taken from the proceedings of Friday *morning* in the House, the Senate having passed it before. Reese and some of the Senators and members were very dogged about it. In fact every day's experience proves to me that nothing makes people so obstinate as ignorance. The appointment of Warner 2 was very much pressed in the State from very respectable quarters, beginning with Jenkins. I do not think it was a favourite appointment with Smith. It seemed to me from what I saw of Smith that he is a sincere, upright man, but yields too much to the mere solicitation of friends. I do not like some of his appointments, indeed I may say none of his appointments of circuit judges, but it must be confessed that his range of selection is very much restricted by the 14th Amendment to the so-called Constitution.

The legislature is feeble, raw, irresolute and easily led away, but I think the majority in the House is patriotic and honest. I think this class has scarcely a majority in the Senate, if at all. We shall do bet 1 James M. Smith, governor of Georgia, 1872-1876.
2 Hiram Warner, chief-justice of Georgia, 1872-1883. ter when we get another lick at them next fall. Julia is improving slowly; still unable to get out of bed. I will be over Tuesday.

Alexander H. Stephens To J. Barrett Cohen. L. C.

Liberty Hall, Crawfordville, Ga., *July 2, 1872.*

My Dear Sir: Your highly esteemed letter came duly to hand several days ago but I have not been able to acknowledge it and return you my thanks for it until now. I have suffered greatly within the last few weeks, and am now hardly able to be up. The country seems to be seized with as evil? a political mania as it was in 1860. Who could have believed that men who could not vote for Douglas then would be huzzahing for Greeley now. Did the world ever witness such a spectacle before? But I can not write more.

P. S.—I send you by mail today a copy of the supplement to the "War between the States" hoping you may find something in it to interest you.

Alexander H. Stephens To J. Barrett Cohen. L. C.

Liberty Hall, Crawfordville, Ga., *Mch. 2, 1873.*

My Dear Sir: Your kind letter of the 24th Jany. last was duly received and duly appreciated. I have forborne to return you my thanks for it up to this time for reasons I need not state, as perhaps you can understand as well without as with an explanation.

The result of the election for Member to Congress from this district is now known: I have been chosen without opposition. This it is true is gratifying to me as an evidence of the continued confidence not only of my old constituents but of the true Democracy of Georgia. My course in relation to the *Senate* was prompted mainly from a sense of duty in the vindication of principles, and to save the State from the fatal effects of going off after the

New Departure? heresy.1 In my efforts for this object I feel that I was utterly? successful. Georgia is all right I think in the future. My great object was achieved, though the office was given to another. For that I had no special desire—and while I shall accept the position now assigned me, *Deo volente,* it will be from no anticipated pleasure to be derived from either its honor or emoluments. It will be from a sense of duty coupled with the hope that possibly I may do some good to the state and country at this particular juncture.

1 The "Greeley movement" to merge the Democratic party with the Liberal Republicans.

Robert Toombs To Alexander H. Stephens. R.

Washington, Ga., *Mar. Hth, 1874.*

Sir: On my return from Elbert court Thursday evening the 12th inst. I found your letters of the 5th, 7th and 8th inst. The letter of the first to which you refer has never been received. My letter of the 4th inst. was not therefore in reply to it. As soon as I saw "Specks" telegram in the Herald (the day of its publication) I telegraphed that paper and at the same time sent you a copy of that telegram, and after receiving your reply the same evening that you had not seen "Specks" telegram I wrote you the letter of the 4th inst. As this telegram indicated that you had been interviewed by "Specks," I deemed it proper to call your attention to my version of what did occur between us last August touching your £ interest in a share of the Western and Atlantic railroad lease, which you had conveyed to the State of Georgia. After that letter was mailed to you I received your second dispatch, relieving "Specks" from my imputation and making a square issue of veracity with me by asserting that "Specks's" dispatch was in your "exact words." My telegram made no issue with you. While it declared "Specks'" dispatch false, it was made on the express ground that you were incapable of falsehood. With these words before you, you promptly and laconically without one word of explanation assumed "Specks's" "exact words" and tendered me an issue of veracity. Your dispatch took me by surprise and gave me great pain. I retained it without reply for consideration about eight hours, and after mature reflection I deemed it due to truth and my own honor to accept the issue thus tendered by you and to repeat what I had written.

Leaving out for the present the main point at issue between us, that I acted without authority, there were two other reasons why I did not believe that "Specks" had your authority for his utterances. 1st. Because our personal relations, and even common civility among gentlemen required that you should have asked an explanation of me before you assailed me in the newspapers, especially thro' interviewers, a class of men of whom you have had so often to complain. 2ndly. "Specks" asserted that you had written to me enquiring of all these matters " and that no reply had been received to this letter ", thus in substance affirming that I was evading the question or refusing you any explanation. This I know was not the truth, and you without doubt endorsed " Specks's " " exact words " without due caution, as you add to this dispatch in your letter of the 5th instant the additional words "but sufficient time had not elapsed for my receiving an answer from you." These words which were omitted by Specks would have removed the false imputation on me contained in that portion of the dispatch. But it would still have left unexplained your earnest anxiety to get before the public without even awaiting the return mail for explanations which it seems you had demanded. I can see nothing in the case even as stated by yourself which called for such urgency.

But the whole tone and temper of your letters of the 7th and 8th inst. make it due to you and myself that I should give you a full and explicit explanation of my course in the whole matter. It is very evident to me that even now you do not understand what action I have taken and what objects I seek to obtain by the bill which I have brought to the next term of Fulton Superior Court in your name against the W. and A. R. R. and Hazelhurst, and to which the State is invited to appear in the usual mode presented immemorially by courts of Chancery,—that is by ordering the Atty. Genl. waited on with a copy of the bill with the request to appear for the state if he so chooses. Upon examination you will find that, so far from injuriously affecting your honor as the venal Bohemian of the press asserts, the proceeding is perfectly consistent with your original action and conduct in surrendering to the State what you very properly term "ill-gotten spoils ", and is the only way left you by the subsequent acts of the spoliators to consummate that object,—and that is therefore the course of consistency, duty and honor. I never supposed you had the least idea of reclaiming for your own use what you granted to the state, which seems to be the gravamen of your complaint. Your narrative of the time, place, circumstances, and substance of Out conversation as far as you go substantially agrees with my recollection of the matter, except as to your directions to me to bring the suit in the event that the Govr. should conclude that the non-acceptance of your deed by Bullock defeated the State's title. I went to Atlanta to attend the session of the Supreme Court in August. While there I had a conversation with Govr. Smith tendering the of a share in the lease held by you and conveyed to the State, and he then showed me the memorial of Jos. E. Brown and his associates (directors of the W. and A. R. R.) asking the Govr. upon various false, fraudulent and illegal pretenses to refuse your deed, declare it forfeited, and to convey that interest to Hazelhurst, one of their confreres, which Bullock, in an executive order duly entered on his minutes, mainly for the reasons assigned by Brown and his directors, graciously granted on the 19th Oct. 1870, nearly ten months after you made the deed and about two days before his flight from the State and public justice. These papers never came to my knowledge until that term, and Govr. Smith told me that he would examine the question and if he came to the conclusion that Bullock's action did not defeat the deed that he would bring the bill for the State to set aside his action and to recover the lease and profits for the State. We both agreed that if the title was not in the State, it was in you, and in the latter event suit would have to be brought in your name,—the correctness of which opinion nobody I presume really doubts.

On my return home I stopped at your house, narrated to you all these facts and others in connection with the case, and obtained your consent to bring the action in your name, if the Govr. determined the title was not in the State. On his point my recollection is clear and decided. I stated to Govr. Smith that I would do so and stated to several of my personal friends after our interview that I had done so, which greatly strengthens my convictions of the correctness of my memory. I did not return from Virginia until September, went on my circuit which continued until late in December, and never heard from Smith on the subject until the Jany. term of the Supreme Court, when he announced to me his opinion that the title was in you and not in the State, and therefore that he should not order the suit on behalf of the State. I then determined to bring the suit in pursuance of my understanding with you to the March term of Fulton Superior Court. You complain that I ought to have written to you before bringing the suit; under the above state of facts I do not think the complaint well founded. I should certainly have mentioned it to you if it had occurred to me when I was writing to you. I do not remember to have written to you above once or twice after I returned from Atlanta before the bill was brought, and those letters, if more than one, were confined mainly if not exclusively to public questions. I intended to have sent you a copy of the bill as soon as I could get one; I had no further occasion to refer to you about the case; the facts were few and plain, and all in the exhibits, which were the original lease and act of incorporation, your deed, and the exemplification from the Executive department of the action of Brown, Bulloch and Co., and under the prayer of the bill this action could be set aside and your deed to the State declared valid if the Court so held; if not then the title remained in you, and you could reconvey the share and profits to the State, which Govr. Smith would promptly receive. I did not see then and cannot see now what possible objection you could have to that course. It is the only way to execute your original purpose and defeat the machinations of the spoliators to appropriate to themselves your share in a lease which then and now according to your letters now before me you hold to be unfair, illegal and wrong. The bill, or a pretty full abstract of it, was in the newspapers, and was open to inspection, and *if I had remembered what never took place,* or you had *forgotten what did,* or for any other reason desired it, a flash of lightning from you would have dismissed the bill in half an hour, without making issues of fact with me in the newspapers. You order me with considerable emphasis to dismiss the bill. I decline to obey your instructions. I will strike my name from the case, and you can give it whatever direction you may think proper. I very deeply regret that any thing should have occurred to break our long and, certainly on my part, sincere friendship; but I do not feel that it is my work. I have suffered numerous and great wrongs and injuries for my disinterested efforts to serve faithfully in office and out of office my day and generation. They have stung me deeply but have failed thus far to relax my efforts in the cause of the right. I would rather receive and suffer the reproaches of every man in the world than deserve them from the meanest of mankind.

With my best wishes for your personal welfare, very respectfully your obdt. servant.

Robert Toombs To Alexander H. Stephens. R.

Washington, Ga., *Nov. 6th, 1874.* Dear Stephens, Yours of yesterday by Billy is recd. We shall look for you and be very glad to see you on Monday. I shall deliver your message to my brother. The result in Ga. would have been better if Felton1 had been elected; but we ought to be content. I am quite surprised at the vote of Iowa, Wisconsin and especially Illinois. I had supposed that these States would have felt the reaction fully as strong if not stronger than the Middle and Eastern States, and still more surprised at what seems to be the result in Missouri?. I suppose we can see better when the fog clears up. Nothing can arrest the onward tide in favor of the democracy but their own folly, and I am afraid they will supply a plenty of that. Will meet you at the depot Monday.

Robert Toombs To Alexander H. Stephens. R.

Washington, Geo., *Mar. 10th, 1875.* Dear Stephens,... As I expected, the Civil Rights bill passed. It will accomplish its intended work, raise rows, and give Grant excuse for calling in troops, especially about election times. Well it is no funeral of mine. I feel but little interest in which of the two factions of the North triumphs, except I wish the success of the one that speediest brings a change in public affairs and the government of the country. I have no interest in men or parties who recognize the 14th and 15th amendments to the Constitution, and I suppose when the country takes one set of them they will soon wish they had taken the other.

1 Dr. W. H. Felton, of Cartersville, was elected to Congress In 1874, though the early returns appear to have indicated his defeat. He served from 1875 to 1881. 73566—13 46

Julia's health is better than for several years past. All the rest well but myself. Our post-office here is wretched. Morgan is imbecile from drunkenness. I see Gordon and Lamar did not carry N. Hampshire. I am glad they failed on their line. They do as much mischief as such light headed people are capable of.

Robert Toombs To Alexander H. Stephens. R.

Washington, Ga., *Oct. 30th, 1876.* Dear Stephens, Your letter of the 26th inst. was handed to me by Mr. T. K. Oglesby. I was much in hopes and so was my wife that you could have come over during the last week. The weather has been so charming and yet continues. I hope this Indian summer will last all November. It is so fine that, as Lady Blessington once wrote of Italy, " it is a pleasure to live " just to enjoy it. We are all in good health and therefore in good condition to enjoy it. I hope Harry will get through his ginning time enough to allow you to come over before this good weather ends and chilly November gets good hold of us. We are very glad to hear of your continued improvement and hope you will get into snug quarters at Washington before the winter sets in. Tilden's letter is infamous, and I am glad I committed myself from the day of his nomination (and as to that before his nomination) not to vote for him. I never hoped for anything good from an old Van Buren free-soiler trained in Tammany Hall and Wall Street, principles and places more fatal to the rearing prophets than Nazareth of old. I see old 4th Estate has suppressed the original letter, omitted or mutilated it. But it can do him no harm at the South. The mongrel crew who call themselves Democrats have the control of the " organized democracy " would as lief have Beelzebub as God, and prefer Mammon to either if thereby they could perchance reach the treasury. They have none of that " infirmity of great minds, ambition." They want Tilden elected for the same reason that Falstaff rejoiced at Prince Hal's reconciliation with the old King—" Hal, rob me the exchecker." They want "rascalliest sweetest young prince to rob them the treasury ", and they would raise the cry of " stand and deliver" as readily as that of reform, if it promised equal success. But enough of this. "Mankind is the same in every age, etc.," you know the rest. I do not think Tilden's letter can hurt Tilden in the South, for the additional public reason that it is too late to fight him, and his friends are better than his own principles, and the Radicals are intolerable. It may hurt him in Indiana, Ohio and Connecticut where there are many true Democrats who have principles, and these are points where he cannot afford to lose a few hundreds and win. I am in doubt about the result. I have but little special information on the subject and can only judge from partial results which have taken place and general principles. The election will show a large majority of the people against the Radicals but this will result from many close States at the North and a united South; but still I think the radicals may carry, yes will carry, the majority in the electoral college and if they do not they will carry the returns or count out enough Southern votes to put them in and the county will accept it as readily as the Romans did the consulship of Caligula's horse,—"All at once (says a great historian) the Romans became another people." This is our fate.

We hope if you do not come over this week you will be certain to come court week; we shall look for you. Mrs. T. is in good health and sends love. Ask Billy and John to come over with you and stay with us. All the rest well. My health is specially good and I have spent half my time for the last ten days in preparing for and sowing oats and wheat and clover, digging potatoes and fall gardening.

Robert Toombs To Alexander H. Stephens. R.

Washington, Ga., *Bee. 17, 1876.* Dear Stephens, Your letter of the 25th ulto. reached here during my absence from home, and I have only been at home two days at one time since I saw you. I have been to Greensboro, Madison, Fontenoy Mills, etc., on my own and professional business most of the time, besides suffering with a bad cough and cold all the time. I had hoped to be in Washington before this but cannot get there until after the 1st Tuesday in Jany., and perhaps not until the last of that month. Your idea of Grant's patriotism and waiting twentyfive years for justice does not seem to be in accord with the general opinion in Georgia as far as I have had the means of judging. I am very glad that you published your letter adopting the article in the Union. That article in the main is very sound and will answer as a general basis of action by the party. But the truth of the business is that we are in the midst of a revolution. The Constitution was overthrown by the North before the war by their frequent violations of that instrument and their constant efforts ever since to govern the country in their own interest in defiance of its provisions. The Northern Democrats have stood by with indifference and saw the overthrow of the Constitution and even the villainous reconstruction acts in Georgia, by Terry and Co., and in Alabama, Louisiana and Arkansas, and only moved when these usurpations were likely to keep them out of power. Yet still their cause is the cause of all, the cause of liberty entrenched and guarded by republican institutions, and I shall stand by them and am willing to do anything I can (but wait) to restore good government. If the Republican party can hold the government now, the republic is at an end forever. It may rise again in some other form, but the present thing is dead. There certainly can not be a doubt but that Grant and the Republican party intend now to prevent the government of the country passing into the hands of the Democratic party whom they, from Grant down, openly denounce as public enemies, rebels and copperheads. This war is and will be to prevent the Confederates from seizing the government. You will find great power in that cry, a power stronger than the ballot box. They will resist it by force of arms; so the Democrats may as well decide and decide at once whether they will submit to the Pretorian guards or prepare to resist them. A man must be as blind as a bat at noonday not to see in the military events in Louis iana, Florida and South Carolina and the concentration of troops in Washington the whole policy and purposes of the Radicals. They can have but one meaning, and that is to hold the government by force if their frauds fail to secure it to them. As to the question of determining who is elected President or Vice-President of the U. S., there is neither doubt nor difficulty, and the pretences set up to throw doubt on the subject show how vain is the attempt by human language to bind villains. The Constitution says each state may appoint in such manner as the legislature thereof may direct a number of electors, etc. Congress may appoint the time of the election, etc. Then comes the mode of electing Pres. and Vice by Art. 12 amendments, providing that the list of votes to be sent to the President of the Senate illegible, etc. The President of the Senate shall in the presence of both houses " open all the certificates, and the vote shall then be counted." By whom? The President of the Senate? The law does not say so. If it did it would make the President of the Senate the sole judge of the election qualification and returns of a Presidential and Vice-Presidential election, and if he happened to be a candidate make him sole judge in his own case. It is a sufficient answer to say that the organic law does not give it to him, and if it had so intended it would have said so. The law gives him the power to break the seals, open the returns, and even that must be done in the presence of the two houses. Why? Simply to make them spectators? Nonsense. It was to see that the returns had not been tampered with. The Constitution says the Prest. of the Senate shall break the seals before the two bodies, but does not say that he shall count them. There might be a half dozen lists sent up from each state, and whoever counts must decide which to count, and that ends the business, and the President of the Senate is the sole judge of who has been elected. This clause clearly means that the two houses must count. That is why their presence is required, and in my opinion they ought to count the votes as one body, per capita. and decide of course which lists to count and which to reject. The decision against the Pres. of the Senate to count, etc., has been uniform, unvarying, *ab urbe condita.* All the Radicals want is a pretext. This I suppose they think the best they can invent, and arms must silence the law.

Julia's health is again poor, suffering with colds and rheumatism. All the rest well.

Robert Toombs To Alexander H. Stephens. R.

Washington, Ga., *Dec. 28th, 1876.* Dear Stephens, Your letter of the 22d inst. was duly received. The " flings" at you from the Georgia press I have no doubt originated in an alleged interview with you a few days after you reached Washington. The alleged interview took place I think with a correspondent of the Times, N. Y., tho' of this I am not certain. I saw it in the Chronicle and Sentinel and Constitution the same day evening. I received your first letter, which was in two or three days after your arrival. It struck me as singular, as in that letter to me you said you would not express opinions upon events that might never happen and should reserve your opinions until the facts were developed, and this alleged interview about the same time did not appear to be in harmony with your letter to me. I suppose some of the vermin were present at some conversation you may have had with a friend and gave his own version of it and called it an "interview." And it was generally accepted as such 'by the Ga. press, who commented on the single expression that you thought Grant a patriot but did not understand the massing of troops at Washington, but that you would look into the matter when you had time to look around and enquire into it. This is about the substance of the expressions to which reference was made. This I take to be their meaning, but I have seen none of them and do not know that I am right. I am sure it had no reference to anything else but that alleged interview which I have frequently heard commented on by your friends as well as opponents, and I suppose the interview escaped' your notice. It seems to me from what I can see from the Northern press that the action of the Florida court and the S. Carolina court and the developments in La., by the committee has already a noticeable effect upon the Radicals of the North and causes the better part of them in and out of office to pause in their mad career and makes the baser sort fear to tread the desperate role which they set out to play. My opinions are not in the least changed since I saw you. I still think if the Democrats in Congress stand firm, show no symptoms of surrendering or compromising, Tilden & Hendricks will be quietly and peaceably inaugurated and accepted as the true elect of the people. And if they do, it will still be a peacefull consummation of an accomplished revolution, a fall to rise no more. Men who will submit for four years to such a bare, mean, fraudulent usurpation will be still more ready to submit to all future usurpations. I think they have already submitted to too much for a manly resistance to the present, and therefore I illegible submit to the situation without accepting it, hoping at least that anarchy and an expanded empire may soon offer opportunity for new combinations which may overthrow the conquerors of my country even if they fail to establish constitutional liberty. I still think my suggestions to you touching the question of counting the vote are sound and unanswerable. There is nothing in the Constitution of the U. S. or in the cotemporaneous and continued action of both houses of Congress which looks to vesting the power of counting the vote in? the President of the Senate. Some few of the States, Va. and Connecticut for example, voted for senators as separate bodies (all had two bodies), but the two houses *in all cases* finally united when they could not agree and voted per capita. In many of the states original ly the electors were chosen by the legislatures (senate and house) and in all cases per capita. Many of the states, Ga. for instance, elected Govr, state-house officers, judges, solicitors, etc., by convention of the two houses without specifying how, yet the two houses uniformly (finally) voted per capita. I have no argument for a man who says that the President of the Senate can count the vote and decide what vote shall be counted, except that such is not the Constitution nor is it in harmony with either principle or precedent. Whatever follies the two houses may have committed on this subject, nobody was ever yet fool or knave enough to assert such a proposition but the gang of criminals and traitors who now seek to hold the Govt. in defiance of the will of the people. The honest decision of this question and the transfer of the government even into the hands of as poor Democrats as Tilden and Hancock is the end of the Republican party. That organization will cease as completely as the Federalist party did after 1801, and this generation of vipers will become extinct. They know it as well as we do. "*Ilinc lachrymae.*"

I intended to be in Washington by the 11th Dec.; but the Supreme Court refused to advance the tax case of Ga. , dead in the teeth of the law. I will come to review and renew that motion just as soon as they will permit. I shall send on the renewed application as soon as their Christmas holidays are over and come on as soon as they will hear me. We have a dull Christmas, very bad weather, snow, sleet, and a strong north easter with rain all the time. Julia suffers with rheumatism but has kept up. All the rest of us with colds and the blues. The state is quiet and sad, money matters bad, generally apprehensive of the future and becoming daily more restless under the present.

Robert Toombs To Alexander H. Stephens. R.

Washington, Ga., *Apr. 24th, 1877.* Dear Stephens, Your letter of the 8th inst. reached here during my absence at Hancock, Fulton and Oglethorpe courts. I have not been at, home except Sunday for three weeks until yesterday. I am very glad to see your autograph again and especially to hear through the papers that you continue to improve. It gave a great deal of pleasure to your friends to hear of your riding out a few days ago. I have been so busy with my personal and professional affairs for the last three months that I have scarcely had time to keep the run of public events. They seem to me to be in a curious condition. It may result in throwing overboard the worst materials of the radical party, and I am quite sure that nothing worse or even so bad can follow. The fraudulent, coalition calling itself the Democratic party of the South and the North as well are horrified at the Southern policy of Hayes. They fear it may " split the party." So much the better if it does. It certainly needs sifting and cleansing. As to the Northern Democrats they seem ardently to desire bad government at the South, that they may make capital for themselves at home. They do not want redress but grievances to complain of. While that may be fun for the children it is death to the frogs. I hope Hayes will put honest men in office at, the South and care not a copper for their politics. Indeed I have a great aversion for many of the applicants who are being pressed by our Senators and members, especially by Gordon, who I suppose is trying to be office broker under Hayes. What illegible baseness for a senator who knows him so well to commend Bob Alston for Marshall. I can see no other reason for the act than that Alston must, have knowledge of Gordon's secret crimes and therefore has him in his power. The convention question begins to excite a good deal of public interest in this and some other portions of the State. The opposition is mostly secret and is composed of those who wish to prevent additional safeguards against legislative burglary in the shape of bonds, state endorsement or other aid to private speculators. I have concluded to go to the convention from this 29th dist. if one is called and I am elected. It appears to be the general wish of the district....

Robert Toombs To L. N. Trammell. 1

Washington, Ga., *April 26, 1877.* Dear Sir: Your letter of the 17th. ult., requesting my " views upon the subject of calling a convention of the people" to review the present recognized Constitution of this State has been duly received.

1 From the Union and Recorder, Milledgevllle, Ga., May 8, 1877. Col. Trammel was a citizen of Dalton, Ga. The letter was written for publication.

Other pressing engagements have delayed this reply. I do not know a single reason against the call, and the public security and safety demand it. The existing constitution is not the act or deed of the people of Georgia. It was forced upon them by force and fraud. Large numbers of her most worthy, intelligent and virtuous citizens were denied the privilege of even voting for members of the convention, who with but few exceptions were hungry, hostile, alien enemies, domestic traitors, and ignorant, vicious, emancipated slaves. The last legislature passed an act to allow the people to meet in convention and review the work of these military appointees and to amend, change and alter it, or accept it if they like it and thus make it their organic law. It is a public shame that this permission was not given by the first free legislature, and its successor which met after the flight of Bullock. Every other one of the sister provinces exercised the right as soon as they were able to do so, and have greatly benefitted themselves by so doing. The present government of Georgia is a usurpation. It has no moral or legal claim to the support or obedience of the people. It is wanting in the consent of the people—the foundation stone of all rightful government. Therefore it is a public shame, supported only by bad and wicked men for selfish purposes. But independent of the workmen, the work is not good. The present constitution denies the right of the states; subordinates them to their agent, the federal government; in effect asserts that this is a consolidated government; that we owe primary allegiance to the United States. TVe deny it. Let us assert the truth and maintain it when we can, or leave the truth to be defended by our children and children's children whenever opportunity offers. The people wish to review the executive department of the Government; its tenure is condemned by many as too long and its patronage too great. Its power over the judiciary department presents formidable objections to it. The judiciary system itself is defective, totally inadequate to a speedy and impartial trial of either criminal or civil causes. The jury system is vicious and subjects the country to constant danger. Our old grand jury system was far preferable to the present. The legislative department demands review by the people. The senate is a mockery and a nuisance. It has generally defended all the abuses of the corrupt rule of Bullock and his gang, the instrument of all corrupt organizations to deplete the public Treasury and use the public credit for the promotion of local and personal objects and not for the general weal. It is true there have been a considerable number of able and honest patriotic men in that body, but too few to defeat the greater portion or establish a sound policy for the state on many great and vital questions. It has defeated the call of a convention for four years, and last winter sought to defeat it by annexing odious conditions to the bill.

The senate insisted upon submitting the call to the people, hoping to rally ignorant freedmen. all the remnant of the Bullock gang, both inside and outside of the Democratic party, all the friends of the spurious bonds, all "developers of resources" generally, to defeat the convention. They remembered that the call for the present constitution was not submitted to the people but was the work of "sabre sway." Besides, the representation in the senate is grossly unequal. It is neither based upon population, taxation, territory, protection of all interests, nor upon any other sound basis of representation. It is purely arbitrary and was intended by its authors to perpetuate as long as possible the power of the usurpers in spite of the people. The tenure of office is too long and ought to be shortened. Let the people meet in convention and try to adopt a better system.

But the great defect in the constitution is that it does not protect the property of the people against invasion of the legislative power. It is true that was the defect of our old constitution, as well as the present one. The same causes have greatly increased the danger from this source in all free representative governments. The failures to limit by organic law the power of the legislative department have brought the federal and State governments and municipal corporations to the verge of bankruptcy, and impoverished and ruined the people. This has been the most frightful source of our calamities. We must remark and plainly define the dividing line between individual rights and public authority.

The age in which we live has developed new dangers to free representative governments. Even the inventions and discoveries of genius in the arts and sciences, with their benefits and blessings to mankind, have also brought new dangers to good government. This is especially true of those inventions and discoveries which contribute so largely to the promotion and distribution of wealth and the spreading of intelligence among men and nations. The improvements in the application of the illimitable power of steam and utilization of electricity are especially noteworthy elements in their effects upon modern society and governments. They have made great associations of capital, innumerable and gigantic corporations, necessary for their development. These corporations, with large capitals are powerful, and therefore dangerous to society. They first absorb individual capital—all right enough—then all they can borrow, still right enough, and next the treasuries of municipal corporations, public lands and all other public property, then the treasuries and credit of the national and state governments—this is all wrong, violates justice, transfers the sweat of the poor to the coffers of the rich, appropriates the public fund to private use and profit, and opens the flood gates of fraud and public demoralization. What is the remedy for these great evils and dangers? We must find it somewhere, or abandon representative government. We have seen Congress corrupted; state legislatures corrupted; city authorities corrupted; all of our guards over public property and public credit corrupted; a new power is discovered, and political burglary is enrolled among the useful arts of government. The remedy is plain and sufficient for all of these things. We can accept no other security but this: We must put it out of the power of our rulers to injure society if they wish to do it. Let us make a new constitution, and by that constitution make the depository of the public treasury and public credit political burglar proof and put the key in the pockets of the people by declaring that no debt shall ever be created by the legislature or binding upon the State, except for the public defense; that the state shall never be bound for the " debt, default or miscarriage of another." This will save the people and the State from ruin. Nothing else will, and it must be done now or we may be too late. Municipal corporations should be confined to their own limits and not permitted to indorse at all or borrow, except for the good government of their respective corporations. The principal purpose and necessity for a call of a convention is to consider these and such others as the people may desire. All acknowledge the evils. What present reason can be found against the proposed search for a remedy by the people? The people have demanded it again and again almost unanimously through their House of Representatives and all other recognized exponents of the popular will. The people have spoken; let the convention meet. What are the objections to it?

Covert enemies of the convention, those who hope to profit by its abuses, including others who have not well considered the matter, have suggested many. Their principal one is that the convention might endanger the homestead law. One of my own great objections to the present constitution is that it does not secure a sound, substantial real homestead to the women and children of the State. I want such a measure. It is far better for society that the women and children of the State should be secured an ample and sufficient homestead, where they can be comfortable and happy and the children can support themselves and be brought up under virtuous influences, than to be thrown on society houseless and.homeless and penniless, outcast and wanderers, subject to all the temptations to crime in its worst forms, and finally to become tenants of jails and poor houses. Let us demand such a homestead of the convention. It will injure nobody. It will only withdraw from trade and traffic, crime or misfortune, a sacred sanctuary dedicated to humanity. The details may be safely trusted to a convention of the people. We have no such homestead. The present homestead may be waived by the head of the family. It is but a life estate in the hands of the family, and an estate for years only in the minors, and terminates at arrival of age. It is a sham, but even such as it is the objectors well know that such rights as have been acquired under it are so secure that no convention could touch them if they wished to do so. The objection is only intended to deceive the ignorant and unwary. But it is also objected that the convention may remove the capital from Atlanta. Well suppose they do, shall the supposed personal interest of a few thousand people weigh a feather against a good constitution which will protect the rights, liberty and property of all? Away with such nonsense. This is not the true reason. The new constitution would certainly dispose of all future bond questions. There would be no further use for the lobby. Make your constitution right and then there will not be but one remaining question as to the capital, and that would be simply the comfort and convenience of our public servants in discharging public trusts. Atlanta would have no competition in such a contest. It is not worth a thought with freemen. Some of the not very ardent friends of the convention have taken a new disease which a distinguished Senator calls the "apprehensions ". They fear that the convention will put themselves and everbody else in jail for debt, will establish Moses' mode of punishment, and do divers other old and wicked things if ever the people let them come together at Atlanta to consider their organic law. I believe it is not the practice of organic laws to adopt penal codes. That has hitherto been considered the peculiar province of the legislature, and we are content that it shall remain there. But perhaps the " wicked flee when no man pursueth."

Robert Toombs To Alexander H. Stephens. R.

Washington, Ga., *Nov. 2nd, 1877.*
Dear Stephens, I have been trying to take time to write to you for ten days past but I got home the Thursday before Oglethorpe court tired and sick, not able even to attend to the most urgent business letters the balance of that week, and went to Oglethorpe court Monday to defend Ebberhart and it took me until 10 o'clock Saturday night to clear him. Last week I came home and have been extra busy and feeble ever since until two or three days ago. I have been much urged to speak in every part of the state on the convention question,1 but seeing everything going on well and the whole contest being about the capital, about which I care but little, I concluded to let the matter alone and let them fight over the location of the capital as long as all sides went for the new constitution. It is a strange state of things. There are a plenty of interests against the new con 1A constitutional convention at Atlanta in July and August, in which Toombs was the dominating figure, had framed a new constitution for the State. It was ratified by the people in November, by a vote of 110,442 to 40,947.
stitution to have made a serious fight; but they all seem to fear opposition to it, and so far I have not heard of a single candidate for the legislature who opposes it, altho' their name is legion. I feel anxious that the 5th dist. shall arouse while things stand as they do now. Both the Chronicle of Augusta and Constitution of Atlanta are really opposed to ratification, but they are afraid to move against it for fear of the people. If the fidelity of Atlanta to ratification becomes even suspected the capital will be moved back to Milledgeville. Indeed I think the tide is now turning that way already, altho' I am sorry to see it. In national politics all is quiet. Public sentiment is unbroken and increasing in strength in favor of President Hayes. He is on a rock which will never fail him as long as he stays there. The opposition of the Republicans is simply stupid. Their support of his principle that the army is no longer to be used to overawe or control State governments, and his civil reform policy, would do more to strengthen them, than any thing they have done since the war. Well this conduct may bring great good to the country,— "whom the gods intend to destroy they first make mad." The President can never save them by abandoning his present position,—he could only die with them. The day of military has passed until another war comes....

Robert Toombs To Alexander H. Stephens. R.

Washington, Ga., *J amy. 25th, 1878.*
Dear Stephens, Your letter of 2nd Novr. was recd. 3rd inst., and one of our friend Johnson of Balto. who happened to write one to my wife for you upon the same day arrived the same time. The reason is it was directed by your clerk to Washington D. C, remained there two months and took a new start. Johnson's shared the same fate. I have not been well since I left you at Washington, recovered enough to half attend to business until 19th Dec. when I took my bed and have since divided my time between the bed, my room and house, unable to attend to anything but to give directions to the most important matters of my private affairs, and turn over my professional business to other hands, except in one case which I argued in Wilkes very much to my injury. I have

had a succession of colds, welded? on a trouble in the liver. My liver has not been right since I left Atlanta after the adjournment of the convention, and as usual it affected the kidneys. So I am threatened with a general breakdown, and yet I have outlived the Constitution of the U. States. I have looked slightly at the silly reasons given by our three Southern Senators, Hill, Lamar and Butler, for their opposition to the bill for remonetizing silver. Ben says the bonds are not due, and *therefore* it has no effect upon them. What a transparent ass! Butler is afraid it will make money plenty and the cross-road grocers will buy it up and make a corner on bacon!! now dog cheap! Lamar says he opposes because the bill of 1873 *demonetized* and *debased* silver in the markets of the world. Bah! What nonsense, if the act of 1873 demonetized it and thereby debased it, it only debased to the extent demonetization had that effect, and re-monetizing it would as far as that affected restore it where it was. I suppose he knows nothing about it. When the public debt was contracted it was payable in greenbacks (which the Govt. received for the bonds) or in gold and silver at the then legal standard, at the pleasure of the debtor. This is the law of all contracts public or private unless otherwise provided in the contract. The act of 1869 was passed solely to get ridd of the greenback feature by the bondholders' men in Congress. The funding act of 1870 expressly provides that the new bonds should be paid " in coin of the present value." Then gold and silver were both standard value, silver at 412.5 grains to the dollar 9/10 fine and the gold dollar at 25 8/10 9/10 fine to the dollar. That was exactly what we owed, nothing more, nothing less, and the contract would be honestly and legally discharged with either coin of that quantity and fineness if there had not been a single silver or gold coin of the United States in the world. We had the right to coin the silver or gold dollar for that purpose alone if it was to our interest to do so. To pay any less would be robbing the creditor and impairing the obligation of such contract. To pay any more would be robbing the people for the benefit of the bondholder, and that too under false pretences,—robbing the poor (and debtors are generally the poor) for the benefit of the rich. It is as dishonest for an agent (Members of Congress) to pay more than the public owe as to pay less. It is as dishonest to rob the poor as the rich and a great deal more infamous because the rich can take care of themselves and it may not touch their meal tub, but the poor are weak and defenceless and they are God's poor and he has appointed them guardians, they are the wards of humanity and woe to him who betrays the divine trust. Bland's bill is wrong in one respect. Govt. should now at the present price of silver, coin for anybody that comes. Unless a large royalty is put on the coinage it should buy as much bullion as it is wise to coin from time to time, and no more. This is not a question of single or double standard of value. I rather prefer gold as a single standard with silver a subsidiary coin, but of that I am not so confident as I have been. It is not a question of the repeal of the resumption act, tho' it would have an important bearing on that question. But it is a question of whether we shall impose upon the govt. in favor of bondholders and all other debtors1 in the 1 Should be " creditors."

United States a premium of 8 or 10 per cent on their debts amounting in all to not less than 700 or 800 millions of dollars. I would advise the public to take up arms to resist the outrage. It would largely benefit me, as I owe nothing, and f that I possess consists of public and private securities. But the burthen would not only be unjust but too great to be borne by the people. No resumption act should apply to past contracts. If it does, cash payments cannot be maintained under present circumstances 90 days, and this will be true even if gold, silver and greenbacks were of equal value the day of resumption.

I am against all government banking or interfering with paper money in any way. When we can get it I want a sound metallic standard or standards of value and bank paper under the control of the several States redeemable in the coin of the United States on demand. Until we get that we shall be floundering in a Siberian bog, and without it we can never have a free government or ever see prosperity and hopefulness again as a nation. But I must halt, my back is aching and I am wearying you; but I begin to feel a deep interest in this question.

Julia's health is variable but upon the whole better this winter than she usually is in the winter. The bad weather affects her knee, but her rheumatism has disappeared since she left Hot Springs. The rest of the family except her and myself are all in usual health. My cataracts progress slowly; it takes an expert to discover their progress, for I cannot.

Simpson's health is poor, frequent colds and coughs, the rest of his family well. The last year was the most disastrous to the people of Georgia of any since that war; crops poor, prices low, and moneA' of any kind dear and almost unattainable except by those who do not want it. The mass of the people are gradually sinking down to hopeless poverty.

P. S.—Cannot read over my letter to correct omissions or mistakes, but you can read enough to catch the drift of it.

Robert Toombs To Alexander H. Stephens. R.

Washington, Ga., *Jany. 30th 1879.* Dear Stephens, I received your telegram of 28th and your letter from Atlanta. I have been greatly pressed since I reached home cleaning up the business of last year as far as possible and preparing pending cases.1 I was greatly annoyed at the continuance of several cases (5 or 6) by local counsel of Atlanta before I arrived there, altho' I had them set down for the 7th Jany. before I left for Washington, D. C. The continuances were not in the interest of the State.

1 The cases here alluded to were suits for the collection of back taxes from

railroad corporations under an act of 1874. Toombs was the attorney for the State.

I shall try to meet them in 3rd week in March, being the first week of the new term. I was very glad to receive the decision of the Supreme Court in favor of the State, for many reasons. 1st. for sake of principle, next the amount of money secured by the State now and *secula seculorum* as far as this corporation is concerned, next to put down the false clamor of persecution by me of the " poor railroads " when their rights as they called them had been settled by the courts, and lastly and mainly, it is the first great step towards bringing these spoliators under the law and compelling them to contribute their just quota of the public burthens and compelling them to take sides for good government and just taxation, which will greatly benefit the collective body of the people and especially the poor. I think also that the decision is a clear indication that the court is inclined to waver in reference to some of their former bad decisions on these R. Road questions, and especially as Strong delivered the opinion. I have no idea that the court will admit it, but it does nevertheless in principle overrule their decision in Central R. Road vs. the State.

I am sorry to see the new pension bill pass. It seems to me that the Democrats can be driven by the radicals anywhere with clamor about Union soldiers. I would prefer that the villains should remain in power forever than to aid them in such infamous measures. When is it to stop? I wish I could have been heard in the House thirty minutes on illegible bill. I should have reviewed the infamous folly and wrong of further robbing the South to pay extra compensation to the alien and domestic hirelings for overturning the government and plundering the pepole. I would far rather buy rope at the public expense to hang them and to bury them alongside of comrades at Arlington, which Congress stole from an old lame woman the lineal descendant of Martha Washington.

The Hill-Colquitt war still continues without abatement, and will probably intensify as the time for the meeting of the legislature approaches. It will have one good effect—personal hostility will bring out many facts, yea crimes of public men, which it is important that the people shall know in order to do justice to venal and corrupt scoundrels who have so long lived on public plunder and the betrayal of sacred trusts.

The weather has greatly moderated in Georgia and we have had beautiful weather for above a fortnight for preparing for planting. We have already commenced gardening. Pecuniary affairs grow no better but rather worse if possible. In this county more people have gone under, dead broke, this winter than in any previous one in its history. We have reached the point when nobody prospers and no business pays. There seems to be no leading article of production in the State or South which does not cost more to produce it than it will sell for in the markett. This great cost of production is mainly the result of bad government, and in my opinion never can be remedied except by revolution—it may be bloodless, tho' I fear it will not be, but come it must and will. We need a year of Jubilee with amendments suited to our special condition. The bondsman has gone free, let the debtor go free too. Nearly all public debts are thefts, and all corporate property is unquestionably theft—let them cease to vex and harrass the world and let the world take a new start. I am only giving the headings of a few chapters in my forthcoming book on the true science of government. It will give you something to think about and " inwardly to digest " and apply in the execution of your public trust. The public debts (so called) of the United States, the States, the corporations, and the people are certainly greater than the entire property of the country would bring; the balance must be paid by the sweat of the poor. Well how much better is that than imprisonment for debt? It is a great deal worse; for imprisonment for debt compels the creditor to support the debtor. Now you turn loose the debtor and make him work to support the creditor and himself too. Thousands of poor fellows are daily committing suicide notwithstanding that "conscience makes cowards of us all", as Shakespeare says.

My wife's health has much improved this winter, which is a wholly unexpected blessing. My own is good except these eyes of mine which will soon pass away unless the surgeon's art can relieve them. Doubtfull, but I have been thinking probably it is best. I may then be compelled to leave behind me a record that may perchance benefit mankind, which I do not expect ever to do as long as I can see to work for the living around me.

Robert Toombs To Alexander H. Stephens. R.

Washington, Ga., *Mar. 10th, 1879.* Dear Stephens, I suppose you will not come home of course during the recess.1 It would not compensate you for the fatigue and risk of health.

I was glad to see the old House stand firm. I hope you will let the appropriations go and let the army be disbanded before you will continue a single day longer than you can help the test oaths and the election bills. This is the time to test it, as the Northern Democrats for the first time since the war have exhibited the least disposition to vindicate any principle whatever. My correspondence with many leading men of the South indicates that there is a strong disposition manifesting itself over the South generally to begin to 1 Stephens was then Congressman from Georgia, serving la this inter period In that capacity from 1875 to 1882.

reassert principles and cut loose from the Northern Democracy. We have been the servile tools of the knaves and fools, mostly the former, long enough. And many thoughtful men would tremble to see the Democratic party as now constituted in power, even to beat Grant or the devil. I think the true policy of the South is to cut loose from them and run candidates of their own.

The true men of the North would fall into line and reassert the fundamental principles of good government. I see Gordon has " done it at last." The true facts of his political course will now come out and he will be ruined. His letter is as weak as water. His main defence is a plea of condonation, but it is defective in this: such a plea is not good unless the party condoning had full knowledge of the crimes alleged.

My health is good, my wife's health is quite improved. The weather is beautiful for the last week. Thermometer has ranged from 60 at 7 o'clock a. m. up to 80 by 4 p. m., and yesterday it was 74 at sundown.

Robert Toombs To Alexander H. Stephens. R.

Washington, Ga., *April 2nd, 1879.* Dear Stephens, I recd. your letter in reply to my telegram about the Speakership and also about the California wines. I have sent to Hall, Ives and Co. for samples of the latter. I also recd. the Post with your interview. Your positions I think without exception, set forth in that interview, have met with the universal approbation of your friends and also of the public generally as far as I have sampled the crowd. I was 8 or 10 days in Atlanta recently and had a good opportunity of seeing leading men from different sections of the state. I still think it was necessary to the public service to beat Randall, tho' I have rather a personal liking to him and do not know Blackburn even by sight; but Randall's policy will certainly beat the Democratic party in 1880. He and his followers have no principles at all, and are bent upon the election of Tilden, and Tilden cannot be elected. He may be nominated by buying up the venal and corrupt press, which I think is pretty much done now. They will control the "regular organization" which is without principles or policy except " to get in the saddle" and plunder the treasury. Randall has been three times elected, with a largely decreasing majority each time, and the House has not succeeded under his rule in removing a single burthen from the people, correcting a single abuse, restoring a right, or carrying a single reform of sufficient importance to be worthy of public attention. They have run the Govt. in the old rut of the Radicals, 73566—13 47 seemingly as helpless as idiots. I agree with you if the Government is to be carried on upon Radical principles that the Radicals are entitled to run their own machine. I will never support any party who adopts the creed that the fourteenth and fifteenth amendments are any part of the organic law. I may vote for individual men simply because of personal preference, but I will never degrade my intellect, manhood and truth by vindicating in any way such a lie. I will acquiesce in it until I can change it or see some prospects of doing so, but will do no more.

Your criticism on our system of taxation is eminently sound and practical, but the House has not yet sent a revenue bill to the Senate since the Democrats had the majority in it, and never will under Pennsylvania rule. The coalition between the great corporations, bondholders, money-changers and protectionists is now omnipotent, solely from the imbecility and corruption of the Democratic party; and you have struck the keynote of the public calamities by assailing those great combinations. It is wholly immaterial to the poor people which party rules a ruined country while all parties tolerate these intolerable abuses in the administration of the Govt. Your suggestions about currency, gold and silver and paper money, are all indispensable to progress and stability and modern civilization. Let the Govt, take charge of the two first and the state governments of the latter. Your proposed system as to all these are all based upon sound principles and I am getting to be strongly inclined to your goloid? coinage. I have been more at leisure for a few weeks and have given the subject a good deal of attention and have greatly profited by your reports from your committee. I see Liverpool is opening her eyes on the silver question and England will soon come right. International compacts on such questions are impossible and of doubtful wisdom if possible. The Govt. must not control our paper money. Local government is vastly important on this point as well as many others. Jefferson was right when he called the Federal Govt. our Foreign Department. Paper money must be regulated and controlled according to the local wants of business of the people, and can be best managed by each locality. Paper money will necessarily be a monopoly when controlled by the Central Government and this is death to the mass of the people.

I shall have to spend the most of this month in Atlanta attending the Superior Court of Fulton. The Jones, the Western and Atlantic and other rail cases pending there are numerous and will be tedious. I have been labouring in that vineyard so long that they now give me much less trouble than when I began the war, and I am ready for them all. My health has greatly improved this winter. My wife's health is also much improved and she will spend a good deal of the time with me in Atlanta; but her health is by no means firmly established. By the way, my blind eye is taking a curious turn. According to all the doctors and all science it ought to have been totally blind; but instead of that, while they tell me the cataract has spread totally over it, yet it gets no worse and is in fact getting better. While it is yet useless for all purposes of reading and writing, I can now see how to get along about the house pretty well without the aid of the left eye. Well after all it may last as long as I do. I am studying the thing out myself as the doctors are confessedly at fault at its erratic course and seem to be at sea. They console themselves with the idea that the improvement will be but temporary. Perhaps so. How long will Congress sit? Keep them until the dog-days. Perhaps it would be best to lock them up as Constantine did his refractory council. Billy and his wife came over to see the old folks last week; they seem very happy.

Robert Toombs To Alexander H. Stephens. R.

Washington, Ga., *March 25th, 1880.* Dear Stephens, It has been a long time since I have heard directly from you. My eyes are fast failing me, the sight in one being entirely extinct and the other progressing with unexpected rapidity, and I have been labouring as much as possible to finish up my private business and to close my professional business which is now almost exclusively confined to the R. Road tax cases which I now feel will outlast me. The courts, while generally deciding principally against the R. Roads, show an unmistakable purpose to delay them as much as possible, especially in view of the facts that their influence is greatly feared in the election of two supreme judges next winter, besides elections of Govr., Members of Congress and legislature this fall. So I have pretty well despaired of ever seeing the end of them, after six years incessant labour both in the state and federal courts. I cannot bring myself to feel enough interest in politics even to comply with two promises which have been outstanding, each for several months, to give my views upon the condition and future policy of the Democratic party, one promise to the Cincinnati Enquirer and the other to the C. and C. of Augusta. I think the policy of conciliation, even to the extent of wholly sacrificing its own principles, has pretty effectually destroyed the Democratic party, for the present at least. I cannot see any sufficient cause for the decline of the Democratic majority in the H. of Reps, from seventy to nothing within four years, and the loss of many Democratic States, but this: the abandonment of free trading, a sound currency, opposition to Nat. Banks, subsidies and subventions to R. Roads, adopting all the really bad principles of the old Federal party and generally making this a parental government to rob the many for the profit of the few, to say nothing of abandoning to threatened force all securities for presidential elections by the electoral commission. Indeed it were useless to enumerate errors which have been adopted by the Democratic party under the false and cowardly pretext " of accepting the situation ", which simply means abusing all constitutional safeguards and turning over the Federal Government to the present Republican party. The great difficulty is that the Democratic organization has no principles whatever and requires no test of principles. Since the open and shameless action of the Balto. Greeley convention it has recognized nothing but the cry of " anybody to beat Grant, anybody to beat the nominee of the Radicals," which simply means to get power in order to " rob the exchecker." I feel deeply humiliated for the State to have two such Senators as Gordon and Hill, both venal and corrupt, without principles, without policy. They are a reproach to the State. The effort here to run " *Uncle Samivel*" seems to drag in Georgia. I expect he has not soaped the press enough and they are fearfull of the result in the state?. But I have given but little attention to the subject and have but little information as to the movements of party workers. I regret Dr. Felton's course very much. His vote in the ways and means committee added to his foolish letter about David Davis I think will ensure his defeat with absolute certainty; and what is worse I think he has deserved his fate. A half dozen broken iron furnaces in his district by his own confession are too strong for his principles if he has any. The tariff ought to have been the leading subject of Democratic agitation for the last four years. The West is as ready for it as the South, from the enormous amount of her exports of her grain and hog-products, and is, always has been, and always will be the most valuable ally of sound principles. But enough of all this. My wife's health is better than usual and we have bought a nice summer residence in that dead town Clarksville and expect to get up there by 1st July and spend the summer, and we would be very glad if you would spend with us as much of your time as you can. Let me hear from you.

Robert Toombs To Alexander H. Stephens. R.
, Augusta, Ga., *25th Apl., 18S0.*

Dear Stephens, Last Friday week I wrote you a hasty note about the Gilmer trust fund in my hands and promised a reply to your letter received a few days before. The next day I was unexpectedly called to Savannah on account of Judge Wood's argument and try some important cases in lieu of Erskine who was quite sick. I went down to Savannah and returned thus far homeward bound last evening having disposed of all of my business there except Mrs. Stephens's case and set that down positively for Thursday next. When I reached here I had an imparlance with Montgomery and upon my answer and exhibits in the case he agreed to dismiss the bill as to Mrs. Stephens, as he considered he had no case left under the answer and exhibits against her. And further if his client declined to agree to the dismissal, he would not argue that part of the case for fear I might dismiss it. I telegraphed you the result that evening. My wife went with me as far as Waynesboro to visit our niece Eva Jones and is now with me here. She is quite well and we will go up tomorrow.

There is of course a good deal of talk about the correspondence between yourself and Gordon wherein those who do not like you or want your place take sides with Gordon. There are three plain undisputed facts in the case. 1st, that there were not to be but two Democratic supervisors from the five districts in the State; 2ndly, that neither one of those two should be appointed from the 2nd district but that district was to be filled with a Republican; 3rdly, that these determinations of Walker were made to Gordon by Walker himself, as proven by his letter to Gordon used as evidence against you, for what purpose I cannot see. From these facts, Gordon's whole conduct towards you and Casey, especially taken in connection with the fact that he had aided in filling the two Democratic districts, is proven to have been insincere and his professions false and hypocritical. I think you ought to have dwelt more on that letter of Walker. Gordon seems to me to be exposing his imbecility, untrustworthiness and dishonesty more and more every time the public hears from him either thro' himself or others, and his silence cannot conceal his follies. As to national politics there seems to be but one question settled in Georgia. This is that Tilden is dead here. Field stock is decidedly improving; Hendricks, Bayard and Hancock each looked upon as falling within the chances of nomination. As to Congress, the probabilities are decidedly in favour of opposition in the 2nd, 3d, 4th, 5th, 6th, 7th, and 9th. I mean opposition to the incumbents by Democrats of some sort. Felton's conduct in the ways and means has injured him a good deal,—more perhaps than he thinks; and I do not think his defence is at all satisfactory. It is only the modified cry of the old home league,—protect everything in my district. I hope the duty on all materials used in printing will be the last taken off. A tax on such knowledge as they furnish the public in many cases is highly beneficial both to public morals and the cause of truth. It seems that there are many, aspirants for govr. and that Colquitt will have strong opposition. I saw him in Savannah. He seems very earnest and anxious on the subject, and perhaps has reason to be so.

It appears to me at this distance from headquarters that Grant is weakening. The fight of Blaine and the administration seems to be earnest, determined and far more open than I supposed it would be after the results in N. York and Penn. I regret to see his chances lessen for several reasons. I think he would be the easiest one of them to be defeated by a real, honest, true Democrat if one should be started, and I would prefer his election to anybody of his party for several reasons. Among them I think if a crisis should come he would be more apt to destroy the Union, which I so earnestly desire. I do not think the opposition to you in the district grows any or will give you any trouble; it is getting a little more rancorous but no stronger. Write me the current at Washington.

Alexander H. Stephens To J. Barrett Cohen. L. C.

Liberty Hall. Crawfordville, Ga., *June 26, 1881.*

My Dear Sir: Your very kind and highly appreciated letter of the 16th inst. would have been answered sooner but for two reasons. The first is the printed argument in the case you refer to did not come by the mail that brought your letter, and I delayed answering until I could get it. The second reason is, while waiting to receive the pamphlet I was called to Harlem, where under previous engagement I was to make an address on the 23rd inst., from which place I did not get back until day before yesterday. Allow me now without waiting for the argument (for it has not yet come to hand) to return you thanks for the letter and to ask you to send me another copy, hoping it may meet with better fortune in its transit than its predecessor.

I have Mr. Davis's work, and have got about two thirds through the first volume. As far as I have gone I am upon the whole very well pleased with it. It will certainly do less harm than I apprehended it might. In your estimate of his character I agree with you very fully. But I think this book has been a good deal *licked* into shape and its present appearance by other calmer heads and more philosophical minds than Mr. Davis. I can't say more on the point now.

In regard to the matter of the personal memoir, I can only say I have long since desired to do that very thing, but I fear I shall never have time. I am contemplating a big work of another kind for this summer—that is an elaborate history of the United States, set forth in a large octavo thousand page volume. But I do not yet know whether I shall undertake this work or not.

Present my kindest regards to Mrs. Cohen. I wish you and she would come up and spend a few days or a week with me this summer. Alexander H. Stephens To J. Barrett Cohen. L. C.

Liberty Hall, Crawfordville, Ga., *Sept. 18, 1881.*

My Dear Sir: Your very highly appreciated letter of the 16th inst. with P. S. of yesterday was received today—Sunday—and as I was at leisure I enjoyed its perusal very much. Do come and see me "immediately if not sooner." I want to talk over divers matters with you, among other things that law argument which you sent me and which I did receive but did not have time to write you about as I wished. I have been exceedingly busy on my work—devoting all my time and strength to it. I want to get through with it before the meeting of Congress. I will say no more now but to repeat my request for you to come as soon as you can. Drop me a postal a day or two before you start so I will know when to look for you.

Robert Toombs To Alexander H. Stephens. R.

Washington, Ga., *Feby. 19th, 1882.*

Dear Stephens, I read with great pleasure your speech at Savannah. It was a decided success. Nothing could have been more appropriate. The early history of the settlement of Georgia was but little known to her people or the public. Our people will no longer have cause to be ashamed of the humility of her early origin, nor of the noble and wise policy as to her landed system which she pursued from the settlement of the colony to the time when she gave away the last acre to widows, orphans, emigrants, and homes to all including her own citizens—restricted in quantity to all, with exceptions in favour of a few men who did the state great service in her struggle for independence. I hope it will be published in pamphlet form for general distribution, especially among our own people. Perhaps it is only subject to one slight criticism and that an amiable one. Perhaps you were too liberal in your list of her worthies.

The day I left Atlanta (it was very warm weather) the passengers put up all the windows, made it impossible to escape strong drafts of air and gave me a severe cold from which I have not wholly recovered yet, made me unfit for a large amount of unfinished business, and forbade any effort to have an operation on my eyes. I found *my* wife's health not improved but no worse, perhaps upon the whole generally more comfortable. I do not know when I will be able to ?ome to Atlanta. She is anxious to go with me when I go to Atlanta to have my eyes operated on. I dread to carry her and this may lead to an indefinite postponement of the operation. Remember me kindly to your household.

Abolition question, 54-55,61,98. *See also* Slavery.

Adrian, Garnett B., elected toCongress, 449; opposition to Douglas, 452.

Africa, slave-trade, 435-439.

Aiken, William, candidate for Speaker, 358-359.

Akerman, Amos T., mentioned for judgeship, 642,643.

Alabama, political conditions in, 87, 126, 128, 132, 159,166,172,173; Union convention of, 275; laws, 394; admission of, 416; delegates from, 482,484,495;
military operations in, 648.

Albany convention, 101,538.

Albany Evening Journal, 125.

Alexander, *Maj.,* 628.

Alexander, Felix, 576.

Alexander, John R.,position of, 175,208,310.

Alford, of Ga.,campaigning by, 60.

Allan, T.,letter from, 540.

Allen, Charles, committee appointment of, 274.

Allen, James, attitude of, 360.

Alston, Robert, 727.

Ames, H. *V.,* State Documents on Federal Relations, cited, 143,185,215.

Anderson, Ga., stage line from, 105; petition from, 106.

Anderson, Know Nothing candidate in Ga., 409.

Anderson, John, influence of, 215.

Anderson, Josephus, letters from, 650, 682.

Anderson, *Gen.* Robert H., military operations of,

528,530,532,550; letter from, 642.

Anderson, Samuel, 156.

Andersonville. prison at, 644, 646.

Andrew, John A., nominated governor of Mass., 512; elected, 513.

Andrews, Garnett, suggested for chairman, 291; position of, 307; candidate for judgeship, 326;
election to State legislature, Ga., 502.

Anthony, Henry B., 697.

Applet on, John, visit from, 389.

Archer, William S., report on Texas question by, 65.

Arkansas, admission of, 416; secession movement in, 535,558,568.

Armstrong, *Gen.,* editor, 294.

Armstrong, James W., candidate for secretary of
Ga. senate, 176; delegate from Ga., 288,298.

Arnold, of Ga., position of, 307.

Ashbum, G. W., trial for murder of, 700.

Ashe, Thomas S., of N. C, 524.

Ashe, William S., committee appointment of, 272.

Ashmun, George, letter from, 261.

Ashworth, *Mrs.,* case of, 394.

Atchison, David R., of committee on behalf of
Southern members, 138.

Atkins, *Col.,* 685.

Atlanta, Ga., conference at, 318, 320; martial law over, 605; military operations about, 645, 647, 648-649, 650, 651, 653, 656; relief of poor in, 684-
685; constitutional convention at, 731.

Attorney-General, dinner given by, 181.

Averett, T. H., attitude of, 302.

Avery, I. W., *History of the State of Georgia,* 595.

Aycock, of Walker Co., Ga., 117.

Babham, William, jr., letter from, 547.

Badger, George E., speech by, 347.

Bagby, Arthur P., opinion of, 87,88.

Bagley, *Maj.,* Mlled, 584.

Bailey, *Dr.,* of Savannah, 113.

Bailey, David J., candidate for Congress, 334; defeated for reelection,
424.

Baker, Joseph, collector at Philadelphia, 401.

Balche, Benjamin, letter from, 220.

Baltimore, conventions, 57, 58, 93, 101, 102, 106, 244, 275, 280, 281, 282, 284, 290, 299, 312-313, 481-482, 482-483, 495; display of feeling against Lincoln at, 546.

Bancroft, *Dr.,* Frederic, acknowledgment to, 563, 713.

Bank of the U. S., 56.

Banks, Nathaniel P., speakership contest, 358, 359, 361,460.

Barker, of Ga., political work of, 677.

Barnburners, 109, 113,114, 116,125, 169, 263.

Barnett, Samuel, mentioned for judgeship, 642,643.

Barnwell and Son, Charleston, 531.

Barrett, of Confederate army, illness of, 601.

Barrow, *Col,* James, 591, 616, 645.

Barrow, Sallie, 700.

Bartlett, Thomas, jr., committee appointment of, 272.

Bartow, Francis S., defeated for Congress, 407; mentioned for Davis's Cabinet, 544; officer in Confederate army, 571, 578.

Barwick, Nathan, negroes of, 684.

Bass, *Col.* Nathan, 156.

Baxter, Eli H., judge of the superior court of Ga., 291,326. «

Bayard, Thomas F., candidacy of, 741.

Bayley, Thomas H., member of Congress from Va., 57; of committee on behalf of Southern members, 138; candidate for Speaker, 263, 264, 274; leaves caucus, 268; committee appointment of, 271; caucus vote of, 271; letter from, 343.

Baynes, 364,365.

Beaseley, lawyer of Crawfordville, Ga., 454.

Beauregard, *Gen.* P. G. T., correspondence, 563;

military operations of, 593, 659, 676.
Bedinger, Henry, speech of, 96.
Bell, John, proposition of, 188; vote on Kansas
question, 433; candidate for presidency, 496, 500,
502.
  Belmont party, 696.
  Benjamin, J. P., urged for Mexican mission, 399;
speeches of, 480; mentioned for Davis's Cabinet,
544; Confederate Secretary of War, letter of, 577;
administration of, 579.
  Benning, Henry L., letters from, 97, 168, 318; position of, 214; speech of, 524; mentioned for Davis's
Cabinet, 544; support of, 560; visit of, 687.
  Benton, Thomas H., plan of, 61; and Texas question, 62, 65; attack upon Cass by, 75; proposal of,
88; reference to, 110; attitude of, 147; speeches of,
159, 160, 343; opposition to, 160, 169; political course of, 172; article concerning, 373,374; history by, 393.
  Berrien, John McPherson, senator from Ga., 62, 69;
and Texas question, 62, 63, 64; letter to, 64; opposition to, 87; presidential preference of, 104;
speech by, 130; attitude of, 147; political work of,
232-233.
  Bethune, James N., of Ga., candidacy of, 175.
Bird, John, 189.
  Birdsall, Ausbum, letter from, 125; political work of, 132.
  Bishop, of Murray Co., Ga., influence of, 249.
Black, James, member of Congress from Pa., 86.
Black, Jeremiah S., 516; letters from, 382, 687, 694;
preference of, 397; opinion of, 404; influence of,
530.
  Black, Samuel, preference of, 397.
  Black, W. F., master of *Richard Cobden,* 435.
  Blackburn, Dr., of Ark., 558.
  Blaine, James G., 742.

Blair, Francis P., opinion of, 87; opposition to, 276;
mentioned for presidential candidate, 698; nominated for Vice-President, 700; letter to, 713.
  Bleckley, Logan E., support of, 337.
  Bocock, Thomas S., attitude of, 302.
  Borland, Solon, movement of, 293; appointment of,
327.
  Botts, John M., 104,117.
  Bowen, Levi K., on electoral ticket, 379; letter from,
546.
  Bowlin, James B., letter from, 159; bill to be presented by, 221; candidate for Commissioner of
General Land Office, 324.
  Boyd, Linn, address issued by, 144, 164; candidate for Speaker, 177, 263, 264, 267, 268; political work of, 219; elected Speaker, 268, 270, 272; work as
Speaker, 271, 274; appointments by, 272; opinion of, 325.
  Bragg, Gen. Braxton, mentioned for Davis's Cabinet, 544; declaration of martial law by, 605.
  Branham, Dr., opinion of, 385.
  Branham, J., letter from, 381.
  Brazil, supplies for England from, 70.
  Breckinridge, John C, letter from, 375; candidacy of, 455, 467, 486, 488, 492, 494, 495, 500, 501, 502.
  Briggs, George, position of, 452.
  Bright, Jesse D., mentioned for presidency, 278; Interview with, 395; position of, 463.
  Briscoe, *Judge,* deposition of, 331.
  Bristow, lawyer of Crawfordville, Ga., 454.
  Brockenborough, John W., Va. delegate, 566.
  Bronson, David, letter to, 61.
  Bronson, Dickinson, 339, 340.
  Brooks, James, position of, 219; caucus debate by,
270; mentioned, 679.
  Brooks, Preston, assault by, 365, 366,375.
  Brown, Aaron V., campaigning of, 117; mentioned for Buchanan's Cabinet, 398.
  Brown, Albert G., plan offered by, 123; letters to,
210.
  Brown, Charles, speech by, 153.
Brown, James L., 243.
Brown, John, raid of, 512.
Brown, John Y., inability to vote, 455; resolution introduced by, 461.
Brown, Joseph E., delegate, 161; political work of,
207, 424-425; nominee for governor of Ga., 408;
letters from, 431, 432, 434, 444, 445, 453, 565, 571,
574, 576, 597, 605, 610, 614, 617, 618, 621, 627, 630
631, 632, 633, 634, 639, 640, 641, 642, 643, 644, 649,
653, 662, 670, 677, 684; vessels ordered seized by,
538,545,546; political ambitions of, 560; reelection of, 577, 580; controversy with Davis, 568, 597-598;
criticism of, 609; message of, 634-637; impressment law of, 660; enters Republican party, 703;
lessee of Western and Atlantic Railroad, 711.
  Brown, William I., letter to, 133.
  Browne, E. R., 307.
  Browne, William M., letters from, 677,695.
  Brownlow, William G., governor of Tenn., opposition to, 566.
  Bryan, *Judge,* decision of, 688.
  Bryant, J. E., candidate for speaker of legislature,
Ga., 707.
  Buchanan, Hugh, a delegate from Ga., 367.
  Buchanan, James, candidacy of, 92, 102, 244, 277,
294, 296, 297, 298, 299, 300, 348-349, 364, 365, 367,
368-371, 375-376; position of, 94, 98, 100, 219, 263,
264, 297, 345, 383, 456; letters to, 159, 163, 348, 374,
377, 378, 379, 432, 433, 440, 441, 442, 446, 447, 453,
517, 554; letters from, 161, 180, 232, 288, 373, 376,
397, 421, 518; political work of, 269, 274; rumor concerning, 321; position on slavery question, 361;
policy concerning Kansas, 363-364,

392, 398, 400-401, 403, 404, 405, 407, 418; Cabinet of, 389, 394; interview with, 399; administration of, 427, 450, 452; Message of, 452,530; recommendation of, 515; proclamation of, 523; action toward the South, 532, 533, 536; mentioned, 666; accused of treason, 672.

Buckner, Aylett, presidential preference of, 104.

Buel, Alexander W., letter from, 215: candidate for diplomatic appointment, 324.

Buffalo Historical Society, MS. in possession of, 212.

Bulletin, Philadelphia, 195.

Bullock, Rufus B., Republican governor of Ga., 703, 707, 708, 712,719.

Bulwer, *Sir* Henry, British minister, 181.

Burch, of Confederate army, death of, 600.

Burke, John W., 148, 375; letter from, 157.

Burney, J. W., letter from, 62.

Burnside, *Oen.* A. E., movements of, 588,589.

Burt, Armistead, political position of, 128; committee appointment of, 272.

Burt, *Mrs.*, of Abbeville, S. C, 668.

Burwell, W. W., letters to, 342, 343, 344, 346, 347, 349, 399,403, 425, 619, 628.

Butler, Andrew P., chairman of judiciary committee, 426.

Butler, Matthew C., position of, 732.

Butler, William O., vice-presidential candidate, 106, 108,113,125,131,132,133, 219, 277, 280.

Butterworth, Samuel, superintendent of the mint, 439.

Cabaniss, E. G., letter from, 246.

Cabell, E. Carrington, of committee on behalf of Southern members, 138.

Cade, Drury B., jr., 620.

Calhoun, J. C, and annexation of Texas, 58; and Oregon question, 74; political position of, 78, 79, 81, 128, 129, 147, 190, 283; influence of, 87, 88; following of, 110, 281; conference with, 138; of committee on behalf of Southern members, 138; movement led by, 139,141-142,145,154,159,172; *Works,* cited, 143; address of, 144, 156, 157, 164, 168, 169, 172, 173; support of, 178.

California, slavery in, 118,120,121,122,124,135; gold seekers in, 140; admission of, 141,187,199,200, 201-203,211,212, 416; railroad bill, 325; political affairs in, 368,464.

Camak, *Capl.*, captured, 607.

Campbell, Va. delegate, 566.

Campbell, D. C, of Ga., political work of, 232.

Campbell, James, Postmaster General, 330.

Campbell, Thomas J., elected Clerk of H. of R., 181.

Capers *Ma).*, 572.

Carolina movement, 139.

Carrollton (O.), political meeting at, 124.

Carter, Luther C, opposition of, 452.

Carter, William, telegram to, 595.

Cartter, David K., motion by, 268, 269; committee appointment of, 272; political work of, 293; candidate for Commissioner of Patent Office, 324.

Cartwright, letter to, 93.

Caruthers, Samuel, 346.

Casey, *Dr.* Henry R., letter to, 463.

Cass, Lewis, speech by, 75; position of, 92, 98, 100, 111, 263; candidacy of, 96, 102, 110, 113, 114, 115, 125, 126, 131, 132, 133, 194, 277, 280, 288, 289, 290, 293, 294, 296, 297, 298, 299, 300; letters of, 97, 164, 190, 291, 322; nomination of, 106, 107, 108, 110; vote on Wilmot Proviso, 107; position on slavery, 108-109; Southern alliance of, 148; opinion of, 220; opposition of, 230; chairman of committee, 360; mentioned for Cabinet position, 389, 395, 396, 397; appointed Secretary of State, 397; resignation from secretaryship of state, 523.

Cassville Pioneer, 142.

Catholics, Roman, charge against, 351.

Catlett, *Mrs.*, 364, 365.

Census Bureau, secession sentiment in, 540.

Chapman, Bird B., letter from, 701.

Chapman, John G., of committee on behalf of Southern members, 138.

Chapman, Reuben, political position of, 166.

Chapman, S. T., letters from, 232, 236.

Chappell, Absalom H., congressman from Ga., 58; defeat of, 60; call for meeting signed by, 191; letter from, 193; letters to, 221, 227; candidate for Congress, 265; appointed delegate, 288; candidate for U. S. Senate, 335, 336,337.

Charleston (S. C), Webster's reception in, 87; letter to committee of citizens of, 133; military movements at, 544.

Charleston convention, 445, 449, 451, 452, 453, 454, 455, 456, 463, 467, 468, 469, 470, 472-474, 475, 476, 478.

Charleston Mercury, 101, 110, 128,302.

Chase, Albon, editor, 63; letter from, 77.

Chase, Salmon P., election of, 169; speech of, 343; attitude toward slavery, 506; political work of, 696, 697; candidacy of, 701.

Chastain, Elijah W., political opinion of, 137; leadership of, 215; campaign of, 248, 249; nominated for Congress, 329,334.

Chattanooga, Confederate disaster at, 631.

Chickahominy, battles of the, 601.

Chisolm, *Capt.*, 659.

Chisolm, Edward D., Union leader of Ga., 249.

Chivalry, the extreme Southern-rights element, 166, 172, 173.

Choate, Rufus, candidate for judgeship, 422.

Chronicle and Sentinel, Augusta, 62, 82, 174, 196, 282, 353, 387, 424, 703, 725, 732.

Cincinnati convention, 360, 362, 365, 367, 368, 385.

Civil Rights bill, 721.

Clark, Horace F., congressman from N. Y., 443 449, 452.

Clark, *Judge* Richard H., of Ga., 330.

Clarke, Beverly L., address issued by, 144, 164; candidate for diplomatic appointment, 324.

Clarke, Richard H., of Washington, D. C, 547.

Clary, *Gov.* Clement C, sr., candidacy of, 172.

Clay, C. C, defense of, 664.

Clay, Henry, candidacy of, 55, 58, 94, 98, 99, 103, 104, 105, 128; tariff position of, 61; speech of, 89, 183-184; position of, 93, 140; report by, 190; chairman of Senate committee of thirteen, 201, 206; compromise resolutions, 208, 209; opinion of, 220.

Clayton, John M., advocates Taylor's nomination, 89; compromise bill, 117, 198-199, 486-487; of committee on behalf of Southern members, 138; attitude toward Taylor, 140; petition left with, 155; complaints against, 165; amendment of, 344.

Clayton, Philip, Auditor of the Treasury, letters from, 303, 317; resignation of, 523; opinion of, 535.

Clayton, William, political work of, 194.

Cleveland, Chauncey F., position of, 268, 302; caucus vote of, 270.

Cleveland, Henry, *A lexander H. Stephens,* 350, 471, 639, 677; letter from, 644.

Clinch, *Gen.,* chairman of political meeting, 130.

Clinch, Duncan L., elected to Congress, 53; vote on Texas question, 62, 64.

Clingman, Thomas L., duel of, 66; speech by, 93, 183; position of, 181.

Clipper, Baltimore, 195.

Cluskey, M.W., *The Political Textbook,* 215, 398, 434.

Cobb, Howell, chronology, 13-16; letters heretofore printed, 17-30; letters to, 54, 55, 56, 59, 60, 62, 63, 65, 66, 68, 69, 75, 76, 77, 78, 80, 82, 84, 85, 86, 87, 88, 89, 91, 94, 95, 96, 97, 105, 106, 107,109,110, 111, 113, 114,115,116,124,125,126,129,130,131 138,142,148,152,156,157,158,159,160 166, 167, 168, 172, 173, 174, 175, 176, 178, 180, 182, 184,186,189,190,191,193,194, 206, 208, 209, 210,212, 213,214,215,217,218,220,227,229,230 232,233,234, 236, 237, 242, 244, 245, 246,247,260, 261, 264, 265,267, 268, 269,275,277, 279, 280,284, 287,289, 290, 291,293, 294, 295,297, 298,299, 300,301, 302,303,307, 308,311, 316,317,318,319,321,322, 323, 324, 325, 326, 327,329, 330,331, 334,335,336,337, 338,339, 343,355,357, 362, 365, 367,372,373, 375,376, 381,382,385,395,396, 397, 404, 405, 439, 518,522, 524,525,528, 529, 531, 533,535, 536, 538, 540, 541,542, 544, 545,546, 547,548,549,551, 552,555, 560, 561, 562,564,566, 587, 596, 599, 602, 609, 644, 650,656,666, 669,676, 677,679, 682, 685, 687, 694, 695,696, 697, 698, 702, 704; letters from, 75, 76, 79, 81,133,138,145,159,163,176,177,179,1 196,210,215,221,238, 249,278,311, 318, 320, 347, 348, 356,358,363, 374,377, 378,379, 389,398,400,401, 402, 406,407, 421, 422, 423,424,425, 434, 439, 440,441,442, 447,448,456,471,479, 516,517, 518,536, 537,544,554, 557,559,565,568,573,583,585,587,588 606,613,614, 616,631,645,646,647,648,655, 658,659, 662, 663, 668, 671, 672, 682,684, 687, 690; addresses issued by, 144, 505; nominated for Speaker, 177; elected Speaker, 179-180; mentioned for Vice President, 220; mentioned for governor of Ga., 227,231, 232, 234; nominated as governor of Ga., 236-237; nomination accepted, 238; candidacy for governor, 243; election as governor, 261; opposition to, 272, 273,359-360,427,465-466,640; position on the tariff and on slavery, 278-279; mentioned for Cabinet position, 323, 384, 389, 394, 395, 397; influence of, 337-338; reelected to Congress, 356; again mentioned for Speaker, 356; appointed Secretary of the Treasury, 397; resolutions in favor of, for presidency, 453; resignation from Cabinet, 517, 518; military service of, 613, 614, 616-617, 655-656, 658; criticism of speech of, 702; death of, 704.

Cobb, Howell, congressman from Ga.(1807-1812), 56.

Cobb, Howell, of Houston Co., Ga., letters heretofore printed, 24.

Cobb, *Mrs.* Howell, letters to, 75, 76, 79, 81, 138, 145, 176, 177, 179, 181, 182, 183, 210, 318, 347, 356, 358, 389, 516, 518, 522, 536, 537, 544, 557, 559, 565 568, 573, 583, 585, 587, 588, 589, 594, 602, 606, 613, 614, 645, 646, 647, 648, 655, 658, 659, 661, 662, 667, 671,672, 684, 687, 704; pistol presented to, 547; illness of, 617.

Cobb, Howell, jr., letter from, 566.

Cobb, John A., letters from, 482, 547; letter to, 665.

Cobb, *Maj.* Lamar, 609.

Cobb, Thomas R. R., letters from, 76, 88, 106, 191, 362, 404, 522, 524, 551, 570, 585; opinion of, 90; court reporter, 334; military command of, 583, 584, 588; death of, 609.

Cobb, W. R. W., congressman from Ala., 166, 168, 173.

Cobb Co., Ga., political meeting in, 207.

Coburn, lawyer, 333.

Cochrane, John, complaints from, 441.

Coffee, duty on, 82, 83, 84.

Colamer, of Cumming, Ga., 163.

Colcock, William F., supports Cobb, 178.

Cole, Henry G., traitorous conduct of, 654.

Cohen, J. Barrett, letters to, 680, 681, 686, 688, 700, 708, 709, 717, 742, 743.

Cohen, Solomon, delegate, 300.

Coleman, *Mrs.* Chapman, *Life of John J. Crittenden,* 140; letter to, 165.

Collamer, Jacob, Postmaster General, 155.

Collier, Henry W., governor of Ala. , 317.

Collins, J. D., letter from, 665.

Collins, Robert, letters to, 471, 475.

Colonization Society *vs.* Gartrell, 420.

Colquitt, Alfred H., candidate for secretary of Georgia senate, 176; nominated for Congress, 330; candidate for governor of Ga., 741.

Colquitt, Walter T., 59, 60, 68, 69; political work of, 117, 130, 261; mentioned for governor of Ga., 167, 618; letter from, 176; position of, 207, 214, 560.

Colston, *Brig.-Gen.* R. E., 642.

Colt, *Col.* Samuel, presents from, 547.

Columbia, S. C, communication with Raleigh, 68.

Columbia River, free navigation of, 80.

Columbus, Ga., military operations at, 646.

Compromise measures, 191, 218, 219, 232, 249, 266, 267,269,270,271,275,276,277,279-290 *passim,* 293, 295, 296, 297, 298, 303, 305, 312, 319.

Cone, F. H., assault upon Stephens by, 126,127,131.

Confederate States, organization of, 534, 536-537, 539,540,546,547,549-550,553,555-557,561; military preparations, 565, 569; military movements of, 576, 581-582, 584, 588, 591, 593; condition of troops of, 577-578, 579, 580, 582-583, 589, 590, 593, 606, 613, 627, 628, 629, 651; conscription act of, 597-598; financial system of, 622-627,637-638; suspension of writ of *habeas corpus* by, 633, 637, 638-640, 643; conditions after the war, 690-694. *See also* Congress, Confederate; names of officials and particular states.

Confederate Union, 640, 641, 643.

Congress, Confederate, business of, 568,633,639; provisional, organization of, 536,537; loan authorized by, 549, 554, 555, 558, 627; books and papers of, 596-597, 599, 602.

Congress, U. S., tariff proceedings in, 82; supporters of Clay in, 105; petition to, 105; and slavery question, 118, 121-122, 124, 134-135, 138, 194, 197-198, 238-239, 283, 461, 513-514; meetings of Southern members of, 142, 143; and Wflmot Proviso, 151; officers suggested, 174-175; election of Speaker, 178, 179-180,356; observations upon, 188; Powers of, 209; publication of laws of, 233; proceedings of, 324; organization of, 355,357-358, 449, 451-452; and Kansas bill, 412, 413; attitude toward the South, 672.

Congressional Globe, 56,57,96, 146, 153, 183,271,448.

Connecticut, congressional delegation from, 159; political affairs in, 169,368, 722.

Conner, *Col.* Z. T., 571.

Constitution, Atlanta, 725, 732.

Constitution, Washington, 494, 495, 496, 497, 517.

Constitutionalist, Augusta, 82, 87, 90, 110, 115, 152, 174, 316, 393, 402, 405, 409, 423, 451, 457, 463, 471, 475, 479, 488, 491, 494, 595, 622, 644, 703.

Constitutional Union party, 220, 221, 226, 227, 229, 230, 232, 236, 237, 260, 273, 307, 311, 316, 317.

Cooper, James F., superintendent of mint at Dahlonega, Ga., 67, 68; letters from, 86, 130, 137, 233; urged for governor of Ga., 167; candidate for secretary of senate, Ga., 176.

Cooper, Mark A., letter from, 137; articles by, 457.

Cooper, *Gen.* Samuel, mentioned for Confederate Secretary of War, 576; orders of, 638.

Corcoran, W. W., 330.

Corwin, Thomas, political activities of, 104; attitude of, 140,141.

Cottom, C. W., letter from, 544.

Coulter, position of, 208.

Courier, Charleston, 700, 708.

Courier, Louisville, 695, 696.

Crawford, *Dr.,* 656.

Crawford, *Gov.* George W., administration of, 53, 60-61, 73; letters to, 71, 72, 138, 155, 364, 365; message of, 90; proposed for Taylor's Cabinet, 147.

Crawford, Martin J., renomination for Congress, 407; mentioned for governor of Ga., 560; search for, 662.

Crawford, William H., senator from Georgia, 56.

Crittenden, John J., 103, 165; letter for, 104; letters to, 127, 135,139, 140,146, 232, 322; vote on Kansas question, 433; vote on Davis resolutions, 481; amendments proposed by, 525; telegram from, 528.

Crittenden, *Col.* Thomas, 140, 142,147.

Crook, L. W., 161, 329.

Cross, killing of, 83.

Crowell, John, nomination of, 124.

Cuba, relations with, 344,345,399; observations upon, 675.
Culver, Hardy, 574.
Cummings, *Maj.*, commissary at Atlanta, 627, 628.
Currency question, 732-734, 738.
Curtis, *Judge* B. R., resignation of, 422.
Gushing, Caleb, letter of, 340.
Customs, receipts, 440, 442, 446.
Cutter, congressman from Ohio. *See* Cartter.
Cuyler, R. R., position of, 208; suggested for chairman, 291.
Cuyler, Tel., candidate for secretary of senate, Ga., 176.
Dallas, George M., 92,94,98,102.
Dallas treaty, 394.
Danelly, Dr., political position of, 114.
Daniel, J. R. J., committee appointment of, 272.
Daniel, John M., appointment of, 330.
Daniell, W. C, letters from, 109,113,182.
Davis, Jefferson, attitude of, 233, 261; mentioned for Cabinet position, 323, 325; attitude toward Cobb, 336; resolutions introduced by, 461, 481; President of the Confederacy, 537; inauguration of, 544; proclamation issued by, 564; controversy with Brown, 568, 597-598; troops reviewed by, 578; criticism of, 580-581,586,595,608,614, 628, 630, 639; orders of, 591; policy of, 636-637; attitude toward peace, 652, 653; letters from, 661, 698; veto of, 061; imprisonment of, 663-665, 667-658, 683; defense of, 663-665; business plans of, 698-699; family of, 705.
Davis, *Mrs.* Jefferson, letters from, 667, 699, 704; fund for, 680; postscript written by, 699.
Davis, John G., 443; elected to Congress, 449; opposition of, 452.
Davis, Winter, letter from, 443; elected to Congress, 449; mentioned, 455.

Dawson, *Maj.,* 578,646.
Dawson, Oscar, 243.
Dawson, *Senator* William C, reputation of, 231; vote of, 234; letter from, 267; position of, 308; leadership of, 311; conversation with, 369.
Dean, Gilbert, position of, 341.
Deane, F. B., jr., 526.
Dearing, William, 137.
Decatur, Ga., political discussion at, 60.
Delaware, political affairs of, 126; delegates from 482; secession sentiment in, 562.
Delemater, *Dr.,* 333.
De Leon, editor of *Federal Union,* letter to, 282.
Democratic Mirror, 291.
Democratic Taylor Party, of Charleston, 133.
Denison, C. W., letter to, 278.
DeRenne, W. J., MSS. in possession of, 359, 367, 394, 449.
Dickinson, *Capt.,* military operations of, 650.
Dickinson, Daniel S., resolutions of, 92, 97, 98,100, 102-103; position of, 93, 266, 294; political work of, 132, 439; candidacy considered, 274.
Dillaye, Stephen D., letter from, 439.
Disney, David T., candidate for Speaker, 263, 264, 267, 268; committee appointment of, 272.
District of Columbia, slavery in, 91, 138, 139, 170, 183,191,206, 247,250,269; militia, 541.
Dix, John A., 102; Secretary of the Treasury, 538, 542.
DUon, clerk of Confederate Congress, 597,602,603.
Dobbin, James C, letter of, 107; mentioned for Pierce's Cabinet, 325.
Dobbs, Jesse, document requested for, 115.
Dodge, Henry, nominated for vice-presidency, 114; attitude of, 360.

Donelson, Andrew J., interviews with, 219, 266; letters from, 244, 262,264, 293, 294; position of, 303, 317.
Doniphan, conversation with, 422.
Dougherty, *Judge* Charles, position of, 215, 242, 243.
Douglas, Stephen A., bill of, 149,150,154, 190; position of, 263, 448, 477-478, 478-479, 481, 482, 483; candidacy of, 277, 290, 294, 296, 297, 298, 299, 300, 364, 365, 367, 370, 449, 452, 461, 463, 468, 469, 473, 480, 484, 485, 488, 489, 491, 492, 494, 495-496, 500, 501, 502; political work of, 288; letter from, 343; support of, 363; course of, 427, 429, 431, 442-443; oppositon of, 455; propositions of, 526; telegram from, 528.
Downs, Solomon W., of committee on behalf of Southern members, 138.
Dred Scott decision, 407, 413, 477, 478, 480.
Dromgoole, George C, congressman from Va., 56,57.
Du Bose, Dudley M., 601, 603, 621; letter from, 711.
Duncan, J. W., letter to, 345.
Dunnagan, position of, 335.
Du Pont, *Judge,* military service of, 650.
Durham, George I., letter from, 533.
Early, Gen. J. A., 648.
East Indies, supplies for England from, 70.
Eatonton, Ga., meeting at, 156.
Echols, *Col.,* removal of remains of, 95.
Edgerton, Alfred P., committee appointment of, 272.
Edmondson, James, letter to, 161.
Edwards, Buck, election of, 391.
Eggleston, *Mrs.,* of Vicksburg, 680.
Egypt supplies for England from, 70.
Ela, officer of Treasury, 558.
Elberton, Ga., stage line via, 105.
Ellington, Pleasant, affidavit by, 331.
England, negotiations with U. S., 70, 72, 73, 76, 80,

88.

English, William H., suggestion concerning Kansas question, 433.

Enquirer, Cincinnati, 502, 739.

Enquirer, Columbus, 245, 346, 415.

Enquirer, Richmond, 642.

Era, 703.

Erskine, of Atlanta, 641.

Etherbridge, Emerson, vote of, 412; elected to Congress, 449; opposition to, 566.

Eustis, J. B., letter from, 676.

Evans, A. M., letter from, 551.

Evans, *Gen.* Nathan G., 604.

EweU, *Col,* 645.

Examiner, 405, 576. See also *Whig and Examiner.*

Fannin, killing of, S3.

Farris, *Col.* Samuel, candidacy of, 2-18.

Faulkner, Charles J., appointment of, 456.

Federal Union, Milledgeville, Ga., 122,123,126, 142, 156, 163, 282, 311, 345, 350; 480; letter to editor of, 117.

Felch, *Gov.* Alpheus, 291.

Felton, *Dr.* W. H., elected to Congress, 721; course of, 740, 741.

Fessenden, William P., 678, 697.

Ficklin, Orlando B., candidate for Solicitor of the Treasury, 324.

Fidelia, ship, 116.

Field and Fireside, 595, 596.

Fielder, Herbert, *Life of Joseph E. Brown,* 597, 639.

Fifteenth Amendment, 713,714.

Fillmore, Millard, nominated for Vice President, 108, 109; observations upon candidacy of, 128, 220, 233, 263, 2%, 297, 302, 371, 374, 377, 381; dinner guest, 181; letter to, 212; denunciation of, 233; defeated for presidential nomination, 312; in London, 354.

Finegan, Gen. Joseph, military operations of, 613, 615.

Fisher, editor of *Federal Union,* letter to, 282; charge of, 293.

Fitch, G. N., position of, 463.

Fitzpatrick, Benjamin, 534.

Flagg, Wilkes, negro agitator, 684.

Fleming, William B., 178.

Flisch, *Miss* Julia A., acknowledgment to, 471,475.

Florida, political affairs of, 128, 131, 143, 155; admission of, 416; military operations in, 613, 614-615,650.

Flournoy, George M., attorney general, Tex., 533.

Floumoy, Samuel W., letter from, 245.

Floyd, *Judge,* of Ga., 689.

Floyd, John B., mentioned for Cabinet position, 394, 397; attack upon, 439; visit of, 523; resignation as Secretary of War, 528,530.

Floyd Springs, Ga., senatorial convention at, 248; barbecue at, 249.

Foote, Henry S., speech of, 96; of committee on behalf of Southern members, 138; attitude toward, 218; letter from, 242; political work of, 267; resolutions of, 280, 287; support of, 303.

Ford, recommendation of, 571.

Ford, Seabury, candidate for governor of Ohio, 125.

Forman, State senator of Ga., 95.

Forney, John W., Clerk of House of Representatives, 264, 255, 267, 268; political work of, 219; letters from, 330,396; speech of, 443; editor, 666.

Forsyth, John, letter from, 136; charge of, 293.

Fort Donelson, 588.

Fort Pickens, 554, 561, 569.

Fort Pulaski, 528.

Fort Sumter, 530,532,538,539,552,561,562.

Foster, political opinion of, 137; letter to, 281.

Foster, Henry D., plan of, 61; candidate for governor of Pa., 494.

Foster, Nathaniel G., vote of, 412.

Fouche, Simpson, editor, 161,163,207,208.

Foundry, project for a national, 137.

Fourteenth Amendment, views on, 702-703,713,714.

Fowler, Joseph S., 697.

Fowler, Orin, 271.

Fraly case, 449, 450, 592.

France, policy of, 71.

Franklin, *Col.,* 95.

Franklin, John R., attitude of, 344.

Freeman, John, negro, case of. 331-334.

Free soil movement, 126, 133, 138, 139, 261, 271, 306, 319.

Frelinghuysen, F. T., 697.

Fremont, J. C, report of exploration of, 109; candidacy of, 378, 382, 383.

French, Benjamin B., suggested for Clerk of House of Representatives, 174.

French, Richard, letter from, 126.

Frierson, opposition to, 330.

Fries, George, letter from, 124.

Fugitive Slave bill, 250.

Fuller, Thomas J. D., committee appointment of, 272.

Fulton, of Dade Co., Ga., influence of, 248.

Fulton, M. C, letter from, 217.

Furlow, Timothy, defeated for governor of Ga., 628.

Gaines's Mill, battle of, 599-600.

Gales, Joseph, dinner guest, 181; political work of, 218.

Galoway, *Dr.,* deposition of, 331.

Galphin claim, 71, 72, 138,155.

Gardner, James R., editor of the *Constitutionalist,* 82,116,489; attitude of, 330,360; political work of, 380.

Garland, body-servant of Toombs, 489.

Garland, A. H., 660.

Garnett, Charles F. M., letters from, 525.

Garrison, I. N., candidate for mail agent, 552.

Gartrell, Admr., Colonization Society vs., 420.

Gartrell, L. J., speech of, 430; candidate for governor of Ga., 611, 617,618; mentioned, 634,638.

Gartrell's Resolutions, 185.

Gayie, John, 145.

Geary, J. W., governor of Kansas, 392,393,394.

Gentry, Meredith P., political work of, 117; of committee on behalf of Southern members, 138.

George,, of N. H., 374,375,376,378.

Georgia, political affairs of, 53-55, 59-60, 69, 88, 89, 90-91,93, 95,104,107,109,115-116,127-132,136,137, 156,164,167,168,175,176,188,193-194, 206-215, 227, 233-237, 247-249, 260, 261, 280-281, 284-288, 291-292, 297,305,308-316,318,321,326,329,334-338,350,353, 365,377,380-382,391, 409, 421,424,444-445, 447,453, 456,469,478,479-480, 486, 492, 493-495,500-504,519, 522,524,560,576-577,609, 610,614,617-619,633,634, 653,671, 677,698,702-703, 707, 708,711, 716, 717, 721, 731-732,735,741; legislative proceedings in, S3, 95-96,184-185; supreme court of, 69,89,95,449-450,401; delegates from, 110-111,482,495; national foundry proposed for, 137; slavery in, 250; letters to voters of 8th congressional district, 409; Cobb's address to the people of, 505; secession movement in, 519-522, 525, 527, 528, 529, 532; Toombs's telegram to the people of, 525; military preparations in, 570, 571, 572, 574, 621; *Confederate Records* of, 597, 639; military operations in, 644-645, 646, 647, 648, 651, 652,656,659; constitution of, 727-732.

Georgia, University of, suspension of, 566, 567.

Georgian, Savannah, 178, 242.

Georgia Platform, 215, 250, 263, 280, 296.

Georgia Railroad, 105.

Gerdlne, *Oen.,* article by, 405.

Gerry, member of Ga. senate, 634.

Giddings, J. R., instructions of, 91; nomination of, 124; committee appointment of, 274.

Gilbert, servant of Cobb, 662.

Gilbert case, 88.

Gilmer, *Oov.* George R., 448.

Gilmer, John A., elected to Congress, 449; defeat of, 454.

Gilmer House, Baltimore, speeches from, 483.

Glenn, *Col.* Jesse A., 687.

Glenn, Luther J., letters from, 89, 95, 213.

Glenn, Thomas, 659.

Glossbronnor, Adam J., nominated sergeant-at-arms, 268.

Gordon, letter from, 406.

Gordon, Dr., steward, 584.

Gordon, John B., letter of, 737; position of, 740, 741.

Gorman, Willis A., leaves caucus, 268; committee appointment of, 272.

Goulden, W. B., candidate for Congress, 407.

Graham, William A., political work of, 218; nominated for Vice President, 302; letter from, 678.

Grant, John T., letter from, 337; on committee for relief of the poor, 685.

Grant, 17. S., candidacy of, 704; policy of, 723, 724.

Greeley, Horace, political activities of, 104, 322; letter from, 443.

Green, H. K., letter from, 337.

Greene, James S., candidate for diplomatic appointment, 324.

Gregg, *Col.* Maxey, letter mailed to, 522.

Gresham, John J., delegate, 288.

Grieve, Miller, position wanted by, 155.

Griffin, candidate for elector, 107.

Grimes, J. W., 697.

Grimes case, 592.

Growland, J. E., appointed commissioner of deeds for Ga., 444.

Grand, Francis J., 278; correspondent, 178; letter from, 321; appointment of, 456.

Guthrie, J. B., conversation with, 541.

Guthrie, James, letter of, 339, 340; candidacy of, 468.

Gwin, Dr., 323, 589.

Gwin, Lucy, 589.

Habeas corpus, suspension of writ of, 633, 637, 638-640, 643.

Hackett, Thomas C, candidate for Congress, 116; convalescence of, 208; appointed delegate, 160,161.

Hale, John P., and the slave question, 91; candidacy of, 113.

Haley, D. M., letter from, 209.

Hall, Nathan K., contract refused by, 233.

Hall, William, 541.

Hamilton, James P., editor, 467.

Hamlin, Hannibal, candidacy of, 380; vote of, 481.

Hampton, editor of *Southern Confederacy,* 489.

Hancock, W. S., candidacy of, 697, 698, 741.

Hancock Co., Ga., malcontent Democrats in, 113.

Haralson, Hugh A., 60, 96.

Hardee, Gen. William J., 645.

Harden, Edward J., letters from, 81,87.

Hargess, interview with, 399.

Harper controversy, 708.

Harpers Ferry, military preparations at, 569; surrender of, 607.

Harriet Lane, ship, 447,562.

Harris, J. Morrison, elected to Congress, 449.

Harris, Thomas D., letters from, 132, 158, 167, 264, 267,277, 289, 298, 325, 336, 355; death of, 672.

Harris, Thomas L., letter from, 443.

Harris, Y. L. G., urged as representative, 234, 235.

Hart, E. B., letter from, 548.

Haskin, John B., 443; attack upon, 439; elected to Congress, 449.

Hayes, *Pres.* R. B., Southern policy of, 727,732.

Hayne, Arthur P., 538.

Hearn Dr. 361.

Hein, editor, 136.

Helper, Hinton R., 489.

Henderson, John B., 697.

Hendricks, Thomas A., candidacy of, 725, 741.

"Henrico" communication, 195.

Herald, New York, 99-101,303, 408, 441, 503.

Herkimer faction, 92, 93.

Herring, James, urged for postmaster at La Grange, Ga., 155.

Hickman, John, mentioned, 443; elected to Congress, 449.

Hicks, *Gov.* Thomas H., 536.

Hill, *Maj.,* support of, 337.

Hill, A. P. division under, 603.

Hill, Benjamin H., of executive committee of
Union party, 316; discussion with, 381; quarrel with Stephens, 384, 386-388, 389-391; candidate for governor of Ga., 408,560,618; debate with, 409; delegate to Confederate Congress, 537; support of,
634; letter from, 634; mentioned, 638; opposition of, 642; lessee of Western and Atlantic Railroad,
711; public letter of, 712; position of, 732,740.

Hill, Edward Y., candidate for governor of Ga.,
156,167; nominated as delegate to Nashville convention, 187.

Hill, George, telegram to, 595.

Hill, Joshua, elected to Congress, 408; nominee for
Congress, 421, 424; candidate for governor of Ga.,
628; policy of, 653; candidate for senatorship, 703.

Hill, Pike, opposition of, 642.

Hill, W. J., candidate for Ga. senate, 234, 235.

Hill, Warren I., guardian, 331.

Hilliard, Henry W., congressman from Ala., 166,
167,168, 173.

Hillyer, George, letter from, 669.

Eillyer, Junius, letters from, 63, 365, 535, 538, 541;
candidate for elector, 107; position of, 267; candidate for Speaker, 274; letter to, 280; resolution of
289, 290, 312; candidate for reelection, 329.

Hines, political support of, 175.

Hinton, Wood, letter from, 60.

Holden, *Copt.* W. F., 620.

Holden, W. W., editor of N. C. *Standard,* letter to,
133.

Hollingsworth, Ga., postmaster for, 69.

Holmes, Isaac E., letter from, 88; candidacy of, 128;
vote of, 178.

Holmes, T. H., military services of, 592.

Holsey, Hopkins, letters from, 89, 91, 142, 148, 152,
279; attitude of, 116,142,173-174,321; editorial by,
307; candidacy of, 335.

Holt, Hines, of Ga., political support of, 175; delegate, 288.

Holt, Joseph, Secretary of War, 528, 530, 532.

Hood, Arthur, delegate, 298.

Hood, A., letter from, 524.

Hood, *Gen.* John B., 649, 651, 676.

Hooper, *Judge,* position of, 208.

Hooper, Johnson J., secretary of Provisional Confederate Congress, 596-597, 602.

Hoover, Franklin Pierce, 667.

Hoover, J. D., letter from, 666; letter to, 690.

Horner, candidacy of, 176.

House of Representatives, proceedings on Texas question, 62; tariff proceedings in, 81; election of officers of, 176,177, 181. *See also* Congress, U. S. ,

Houston, George S., letters from, 126, 131, 157, 158,
168,172,173; attitude toward, 168; committee appointment of, 271, 272; position of, 273.

Houston, Samuel, 244-245, 561.

Howard, Jack, opposition of, 176; letter of, 421.

Howard, Thomas C, political work of, 130; letter from, 337.

Hoyt, Jesse, 101.

Hubhard, David, candidacy of, 166; election of, 173.

Hubhard, Vinson, toast offered by, 114-115; document requested for, 115.

Hudgins, R. K., letter from, 542.

Hull, Henry, jr., letter from, 295.

Hull, William Hop i, letters to, 77,196; letters from,
78,142,280,334,375; speech by, 130; political activities of, 151,287; delegate, 295-296,298,367; of committee of Constitutional Union party, 236, 238.

Hunker party, 169.

Hunter, George R., influence of, 194.

Hunter, Robert M. T., conference with, 349; mentioned for Cabinet position, 396, 397; political work of, 426; candidacy of, 450, 455, 465, 467, 469, 480; interview with Buchanan, 530; delegate to
Confederate Congress, 566.

Buntsville Democrat, 172.

Illinois, political affairs in, 126,229,368,377,378,382,
721; admission of, 416.

Improvement Bill, 234.

Indiana, vote of, 98; political affairs of, 113,126,159,
169, 174, 175, 229, 368, 377, 378, 382, 500, 501, 722;
admission of, 416.

Ingersoll, Colin M., letter from, 339.

Ingram, Porter, candidate for judgeship,175.

Ingram case, 449, 450.

Internal improvements, Cobb's position on, 278.

Iowa, political affairs in, 126, 229, 368, 378, 721; admission of, 416.

Ireland, Catholics from, 71.

lron, railroad, duty on, 61.

Irwin, David, position of, 335; delegate, 367.

Irwin Guards, 589, 592.

Ivcrson, Alfred, 102; letters from, 129, 175; dinner with, 138; support of, 336; motion by, 360.

Jackson, Henry R., letters from, 110, 178, 284, 316,
659; mentioned, 136, 645, 671; conduct of, 258;
political opinions of, 287,376,560; position of, 307;
information through, 310; mentioned for diplomatic appointment, 328; mentioned for Davis's
Cabinet, 544; interview with, 668, 669; death of,
677.

Jackson, James, 90; letters from, 115,300; candidate for judge, Ga., 176; attitudo of, 293; delegate, 298,
363; influence of, 560.

Jackson, Joseph W., position of, 268; caucus vote of, 269; resolution of, 289, 290, 312.

Jackson, Stonewall, military operations of, 601.

Jacksonville, occupation of, 613; burning and evacuation of, 615.

Jameson, J. F., *Correspondence of J. C Calhoun,* citod, 139.

Jefferson, Thomas, opinion of, 61; letter of, 93; quoted, 113.

Jenkins, Charles J., Ga. Whig leader, 59; declension of appointment by, 212; attitude of, 293; candidate for governor of Ga., 334; letter of, 382; elected governor of Ga., 670; inability to take oath, 685.

Jenkins, Timothy, committee appointment of, 274.

Jennings, Creed M., letter to, 331.
Jennings, L. B., letter from, 331.
Johns, Clement R., State comptroller, Tex., 533.
Johnson, vote of Democratic congressional caucus for, 268.

Johnson, Col., of New York, 396.
Johnson, Dr., 646.
Johnson, Col. Abda, letter of, 618; appointed *aide-de-camp,* 631.

Johnson, Andrew, candidate for governor of Term., 328; opposition to, 566; policy of, 667, 673, 674 675, 687, 688, 694; letter to, 688; interview with, 670.

Johnson, Cave, political opinion of, 133.

Johnson, Herschel V., candidate for governor of Ga., 88,156, 329, 330, 334, 335; attitude of, 318; elected governor of Ga., 336; estimate of, 360; mentioned for Buchanan's Cabinet, 384; political movements of, 409; resolutions of, 482; candidate for vice-presidency, 488, 500; mentioned for Davis's Cabinet, 544; elected senator, 630; mentioned for judgeship, 642, 643.

Johnson, James, position of, 318; candidate for Congress, 330; recommends Cobb, 668.

Johnson, John Calvin, letter from, 234.

Johnson, John M., letter from, 704.
Johnson, Col. Lindsay, 287,331,618.

Johnson, Reverdy, letter of, 379; paper of, 448; speeches from house of, 483.

Johnson, Robert W., amendment offered by, 267; caucus vote of, 269; resolution offered by, 269.

Johnson, W., election of, 173.

Johnston, *Gen.* A. S., interview with, 592; military operations of, 577, 592, 632, 633, 645, 649; removal of, 647,648; reinstatement of, 660.

Johnston, *Gen.* Joseph E., criticism of, 575-576; military operations of, 619.

Johnston, William F., nominated governor of Pa., 303.

J ohnston and Browne, *L ife of A lezander H. Stephens,* 471,654.

Jolly, John, of Camming, Ga., 163.
Jones, of Ga., urged for Commissioner of Patents, 155.

Jones, Union delegate from Ga., 298.

Jones, editor of Augusta *Chronicle and Sentinel,* 424.

Jones, pardon of, (130.
Jones, *Col.,* political support of, 175.

Jones, Batt, member of Kansas convention, 424.

Jones, D. R., military service of, 592,600.

Jones, George W., political work of,117; election of, 173; resolution of, 219; candidate for Speaker, 263, 264; interview with, 260; leaves caucus, 208; letters from, 269, 275, 290, 301, 323,326,327.

Jones, Glancy, political work of, 375; omitted from Buchanan's Cabinet, 397.

Jones, Jack, support of, 176.
Jones, James C, speech of, 317.
Jones, John J., political work of, 502.
Jones, Tal, Know Nothing candidate in Ga., 109.

Jones, W. P., letter from, 260.
Journal and Messenger, Macon, Ga., 275,418.

Journal of Commerce, New York, 192,

504.
Josselyn, private secretary to Jefferson Davis, 597.

Judiciary Committee, of Congress, instructions to, 91.

Kansas, political affairs in, 362; Buchanan's policy concerning, 392.

Kansas Bill, 363, 364, 367, 371, 410, 416, 419, 434.
See also Kansas question.

Kansas question, 394, 400-407 *passim,* 412-419 *passim,* 421-433 *passim. See also* Kansas Bill.

Kaufman, David S., 244.
Kearny, *Gen.* Stephen W., 393.
Kenan, *Judge,* 489.
Kenan, A. H., 155; letter from, 241; speech of, 293; delegate to Baltimore convention, 298; delegate to Confederate Congress, 537; opposition to Toombs, 614; position of, 618.

Kenan, Lewis, wounded, 606.
Kennedy, Anthony, vote of, 481.
Kennedy, Joseph C. G., of the Census Bureau 448, 540.

Kentucky, vote of, 98; political affairs of, 101,103, 126, 127, 159, 322, 355, 377, 462; admission of, 416; delegates from, 495; secession movement in, 532, 535, 568, 570.

Kerr, John, position of, 347.
Ketcham, John L., letter from, 331.
Kilpatrick, H. J., military operations of, 656.

King, John P., letter from, 75.
King, Preston, political position of, 265,266,268, 270, 302, 306; caucus vote of, 270; committee appointment of, 274; political work of, 293.

King, Thomas B., candidate for Congress, 114; considered as Secretary of the Navy, 208.

King, William E., mentioned for vice-presidency, 106; of committee on behalf of Southern members, 138; political activities of, 166; posi-

tion of, 266;
nominated as Vice-President, 299; candidacy of,
308, 309, 310, 311, 313-314, 315, 316, 318, 321.

Kingston, Ga., political meeting at, 214.

Kirkscey, E. G., trial, 700.

Knowles, appointed delegate to Baltimore convention, 287.

Know Nothing party, 348, 350, 359, 371, 377, 380, 382,
391, 409, 420, 608; discussion of, 351-353.

Knox, Samuel, opinion of, 218.

Lafltte, E., and Co., application by, 434, 437-439.

La Grange, Ga., meeting at, 444, 445.

Lamar, Gazaway B., letters from, 365, 538, 545, 549,
552, 555, 561, 696.

Lamar, Jeff, death of, 607.

Lamar, John B., letters from, 80, 82, 116, 182, 191,
242, 280, 287, 289, 302, 307, 316, 323, 324, 602; political opinion of, 144; letters to, 215, 320, 456, 479,
482, 590; addresses sent to, 519; death of, 606.

Lamar, *Col.*, John Hill, death of, 648.

Lamar, Lucius Q. C, letters from, 96, 335, 385, 405;
candidate for Miss, convention, 523; opposition of,
641; position of, 732, 733.

Lancaster convention, 303.

Lancaster Intelligencer, 373.

Landrum, Dr. Z. P., account by, 361.

Lane, *Capt.,* of Confederate army, 590.

Lane, Harriet, 523, 666.

Lane, *Gen.* Joseph, mentioned for presidency, 278,
480; candidate for vice-presidency, 486, 488, 494.

La Sere, Emile, political opinion of, 133.

Lawrence, Abbott, suggested for Taylor's Cabinet,
140; in London, 354.

Lawton, *Gen.* A. E., 566. 73566—13 18

Lecompte, *Judge* S. D., 392, 394.

Lecompton constitution, 432, 433.

Lee, Dr., paper attributed to, 155.

Lee, Eobert E., military operations of, 563, 591, 600,
601, 604, 606.

Leib, Owen D., congressman from Pa. , 86.

Lester, *Capt.,* mentioned for governor of Ga., 611.

Lester, G. N., 212.

Letcher, John, mentioned for Speaker, 427; military
activity of, 569.

Levy, *Col.* William M., 583.

Lewis, Dr. James W., candidate for Congress, 329;
delegate to Cincinnati convention from Ga., 367.

Lincoln, Abraham, observations upon candidacy of, 485, 487, 496, 497, 500, 501; election of, 502;
attitude toward slavery, 506, 507, 508, 509, 511-512,
513, 520; display of feeling against in Baltimore,
546; opposition to reelection of, 635; proposals to be made to, 635; assassination of, 664.

Locofocos, 58, 59, 60, 72, 127, 139.

Loftin, Bidford, ordnance sergeant, 604.

Lofton, Co!. W. A., mentioned for judgeship, 642, 643..

Lomax, T., letter to, 350.

London, description of, 354.

Longstreet, Augustus B., letter from, 564.

Longstreet, *Gen.* James, military operations of,
600, 601, 603, 604; *From Manassas to Appomattox,*
cited, 604.

Louisiana, acquisition of, 61; political affairs of, 109,
129, 133, 276, 500, 676; delegates from, 114, 482, 484,
495; secession movement in, 254, 528; admission of, 416; military operations in, 652.

Lubbock, Francis E., governor of Tex., 652.

Lumpkin, John H., discussion with, 60; money collected by, 69; letters to, 81, 307; letters from, 86, 116,
138, 156, 160, 163, 176, 206, 208, 214, 229, 247, 287,
299, 308, 329, 338; address issued by, 144; mentioned for governor of Ga., 156; circular signed by,
164; opposition to candidacy of, 167; position on
Oregon bill, 185; delegate, 298, 307.

Lumpkin, Joseph H., 207; letters from, 94, 227;
delegate, 161.

Lumpkin, Wilson, governor of Ga., 156, 242, 567.

Lumpkin Co., Ga., political conditions in, 85-86.

McAllister, Matthew H., of Ga., political work of,
117; dinner guest, 181.

McCardle case, 694.

McCay, of Americus, Ga., opinion of, 243.

McClellan, *Gen.* George B., military operations of,
578, 593, 595, 600, 601; mentioned for presidential candidate, 698.

McClernand, John A., mentioned for Speaker, 17.r.

McCulloch, *Ma.,* of Texas, 524, 559.

McDonald, *Gov.* Charles J., letters from, 55, 84; political work of, 207; influence of, 213, 215, 242; position of, 242; candidate for reelection as governor of Ga., 243, 247-248; defeated for governor, 261;
opposition to, 303; support of, 317; opposition of, 330, 408, 425; candidate for U. S. Senate, 337,
338-339, 425-426; resignation from supreme court bench of Ga., 388.

McDougall, political support of, 175.

McDowell, *Gov.* James, suggested for Speaker, 174.

McDuffle, George, relation with Galphin claim, 71.

McFarland, Thomas G., opinion of, 310.

McGauchey, Edward W., election of, 175.

McCra-.v, Robert M,, 531.

Aiclutosh, of Confederate army, death of, 600.

Mcintosh, of Elberton, Ga., approhation of, 386.

Mcintosh, *Col.* Lachlan, removal of remains of, 95.
McJunkin, Samuel. 462.
McKay's Bill, 86.
McKenzie, Slidell, commander of the *Somers,* 393.
McLane, Robert M., of Md., speech of, 96; letters from, 126, 395.
McLaws. Lafayette, military command of, 571.
McLean, John, political activities of, 104.
McMillan, Robert, of Ga., candidate for elector, 107.
McMillen, estimate of, 360-361.
McNew, nominated doorkeeper of House of Representatives, 268.
Macon, Ga., Union celebration at, 221, 227.
Macon and Western Railroad, 647.
Mcl'herson, *Gen.* James B., death of, 649.
McWhortcr, *Judge* Hamp, 711.
Madison, James, opinion of, 252-253.
Magraw, preference of, 397.
Magruder, *Gen.* John B., message from, 584; orders of, 585, 600; order to report to, 587.
Maine, political affairs of, 94, 126, 368, 380, 381, 494, 497; vote of, 98; resolutions of legislature of, 169; admission of, 416.
Manassas. hattle of, 573.
Mann, Job, letter from, 133.
Marcy, William L., political activities of, 263, 294, 296,378; mentioned for Secretary of State, 323,324.
Marshall, Alexander K., vote of, 412.
Marshall, Humphrey, vote of, 412.
Martin, pardon of, 630.
Martin, Barclay, residence of, 328.
Martin, Ben, 480.
Martin, Georgc, preference of, 397.
Martin, Robert E., letter from, 242.
Maryland, political affairs of, 101,126,159, 374, 377, 379,462; slavery in, 247,250; secession movement in, 532, 533, 535, 536, 546, 554, 562, 588; military operations in, 606.
Mason, James M-, conference with, 349.
Massachusetts, political affairs of, 109, 229, 261.
Mather, policy of. 441, 442.
Maynard,Pr.,524.
Meacham, James, resolution offered by, 412.
Meade, *Gen.* George G., order of, 670.
Meade, Richard K., caucus dehate by, 270; position of, 341.
Mell, *Dr.,* rumored death of son of, 607.
Memminger, C. G., Confederate Secretary of the Treasury, 544,547, 549,587.
Memphis convention, 84.
Mercer, L. B., letter from, 326.
Mercer University, meeting of trustees of, 706; case, 712.
Meriwether, James A., Ga. Whig leader, 59; letters from, 210, 236; of committee of Constitutional Union Party, 236,, 238; letter to, 238.
Mexico, relations with Toxas, 66; news from, 75; war with, 76, 83, 95,101; boundary, 201, 204, 205; relations with,399, 464; observations upon, 676.
Michigan, political affairs in, 126; admission of, 416.
Miles, William Porcher, letters from, 528.
Milledge, John, of committee of Constitutional Union Party, 236, 238; letter from, 291; delegate, 208.
Milledgeville, Ga., conventions at, 116, 287, 288, 291.292, 293, 311, 463, 465, 481.
Miller, *Dr.* H. V. M., 60, 208, 287.
Miller, T. W., Know Nothing candidate for Congress, 411; speech in reply to, 423.
Milner, *Col.,* political work of, 287, 329.
Millson, John S., committee appointment of, 272.
Mississippi, political affairs in, 159, 242, 293; convention, 275; admission of, 416; delegates from 482; secession of, 532.
Mississippi River, navigation of, 535,545,546.
Missouri,vote of, 98; political affairs in,377,462;admission of, 416; secession movement in, 535, 562, 568,570.
Missouri Compromise, 62,89,92,93,94,119,120,121, 122, 123, 185, 186, 187, 193, 200, 201, 202, 206, 207, 283,342, 363,364.
Mitchell, William L., 63, 194, 207, 208, 567.
Mobile, military preparations in, 558.
Molse, appointment urged for, 155.
Monger, *Ma.,* command of, 590.
Montgomery, Ala., convention at, 168.
Montgomery, William, 443.
Moore, Pearce, wounded, 606.
Morehead, Charles S., of committee on behalf of Southern members, 138.
Morgan, *Ma.,* 643.
Morgan, Edwin D., governor of N. Y., 448.
Morris, *Cap/.,* wounded, 584.
Morris, *Ma.* Charles, professor at the University of Ga., 706.
Morris, Isaac X.. olected to Congress, 449.
Morris, James, letter to, 161; influence of, 214.
Morton, of Ga., candidacy of, 335.
Morton, Alexander C, letter from, 330.
Morton, Oliver P., position of, 715.
Morton, W illiam H., let ter from, 194.
Moss, Fountain G., proposed for postmaster of Hoillngsworth, Ga., 69.
Murphy, *Col.,*delegate, 161,367.
Murphy, *Judge,* letter to, 275.
Murray, editor of *Griffin* Union, 381.
Nash, position of, 335.
Nashville convention, 186, 187, 194, 206, 207, 263.
National Intelligeneer, 91, 96, 97, 227, 345, 346, 379, 430, 504, 618, 622, 698; letter to editors of, 192.
National party, of Taylor and Fillmore, 148,151.
Naturalization laws, 352.

Nebraska, Territory of, organization of, 324.
Nebraska bill, 341, 342, 343, 344, 345.
Negroes, transportation of, 60; suggested for Confedoratearmy, 656-658; after tho war, 682,684,704.
Nettleton, appointed commissioner of deeds for
N. Y.,431.
New Hampshire, political affairs of, 92.94,126,368,
464, 722; vote of, 98.
New Jersey, political affairs in, 126,133,229,368,470.
New Lisbon, O., political meeting at, 124.
New Mexico, slavery question in, 118,120,121,122,
124, 135, 141, 149-150, 199, 283; military occupation of, 192; establishment of territorial government of, 228.
New Orleans, money in mint at, 539; military demonstration in, 559.
Newsom, A. F., telegram to, 595.
New York, tariff in, 86; political affairs of, 92,109,
126, 129, 229, 302, 340, 442, 448, 465, 497, 499-500,
501; vote of, 98.
New York City, war meeting at, 95; Chamber of
Commerce, policy of, 344-346; customs receipts,
440,442,446.
New York 7th regiment, 663.
New York Journal of Commerce, cited, 192.504.
New York Public Library,copy of pamphlet in,664.
Nicaraguan treaty, 464.
Nicholson, Cass's letter to, 96,108.
Nicholson and Grimes, case of, 661.
Nickelson, James B.,243.
Nile?t Register, cited, 143,465.
Nisbet, Eugenius A., Ga. Whig leader, 59; letter of,
382; paper for, 422; defeated for governor of Ga.,
577,580.
Niven, A. C, letter from, 679.
Norfolk, Va., taking of navy yard at, 562.
North Carolina, vote of, 98; political affairs of, 101,

108, 109, 133, 143, 159; Union sentiment in, 218;
delegates from, 495; secession movement in, 524,
547-548,568.
North 1 nrolinaStandard. 133,158.
Ogle, Andrew J., speech of,303.
Oglesby,T.K.,722.
Oglethorpe, Ga., petition from, 106.
Ohio, political affairs of, 109, 124-125,126, 129, 130.
131,133, 229,302, 600, 601, 722; admission of, 416,
Olds, Edson B., committee appointment of, 274.
Oliver case, 450,468,477.
Oregon, division of, 324; political affairs in, 464.
Oregon question, 65,67,70, 71-72, 73, 74, 75, 76, 77;
79,80,81,85,86,185.
O'Rily, *Father,* 685.
Orr, James L., speech by, 302; statement of, 407,
candidate for Speaker, 426; appointed commissioner, 531; attitude of, 674.
Our Country, 278.
Owen, Robert Dale, amendment by, 76.
Owens, John, of executive committee of Union party, 316.
Pakenham, Sfr Richard, instructions to, 80.
Palo Alto,83.
Parliament,British,354.
Patent Office, report for 1848,189.
Patriot, Baltimore, 344,346.
Pattillo, Leroy, deposition of, 331-332.
Paulding, *Commander* Hiram, 429.
Pearce, James A., letter of, 379.
Peel,Fred, 354.
Peoples, C, of Ga., speech by, 130; political opinion of, 287.
Pemberton, John C, blunders of, 619.
Pendleton, George H., 697.
Penn, A. G., caucus vote of, 269.
Pennington, William, elected Speaker, 458,459,460,
461,462.
Pennsylvania, tariff in, 86; vote of, 98: political affairs of, 109, 130, 131,132, 162, 164, 229, 266, 302,
321,355,368,374,377,378,381,408,

465,470, 493-494,
497, 499-500, 501, 688.
Pcnnsylvanian, 286.
Pensacola, military movements at, 544, 558, 569.
Pension bill, 735.
Persons case, 468,477.
Peyton, article by. 463.,
Philadelphia, political meeting at museum in, 93;
convention, 681.
Phillips, George D., letters from, 65,66,69,184,319;
political opinion of, 137.
Phillips, U. B., *Lifeof Robert Toombs,*cited, 139,146.
Phillips, William, military command of, 571,572.
Pickens, S. C, possession of, 539. *See also* Fort
Pickens.
Pierce,, negro slave, 398.
Pierce, Franklin, nomination of, 299; attitude toward Compromise,
301; candidacy of, 30S-3O9,
310, 311, 313-314, 315, 316, 318, 321, 348, 363, 367;
Cabinet of, 322,323-324,325,326,328;
conversation with, 323; administration of, 326, 327, 339, 340;
appointments by, 330; attitude toward Cobb, 336;
support of, 341; policy concerning Kansas, 367-368,
392,394; attitude toward Buchanan, 375,376,378;
mentioned, 666.
Pittsburg, convention at, 162.
Polk, *Pres.,* J. K., Cabinet of, 62,321; and Texas question, 66; and Oregon question, 72,73; appointment sought of, 81; Democratic treatment of, 85;
appointments of, 85; administration of, 87, 393;
conversation with, 87; and Mexican War, 106.
Polk, William H., resolution introduced by, 267,268,
269, 277; leaves caucus, 268: residence of, 328.
Poole, *Capt.,* 574.
Pope, A., jr., nomination for State senate, Ga., declined, 409.
Pope, Frank, iliness of, 615.

Pope, Hunter C, nominated for State senate, Oa., 409.
Pope, *Maj.-Oen.* John, 690.
Potter, *Dr.,* of Cassville, Ga., 157.
Pottsville, Pa., meeting at, 321.
Pratt, Thomas G., letter of, 379.
Press, Philadelphia, 666.
Preston, William, of Ky., 346.
Preston, William B.,of Va., 141; bill introduced by, 147,154.
Price, Sterling, governor of Mo., 374, 393.
Price, William T., nominated for representative of Ga.,248; appointed delegate, 287.
Printup, D. S., appointed delegate, 160,161; position of, 208.
Privateering, 344.
Pryor, *Ocn.* Roger A., 604.
Pugh, James L., candidate for Congress from Ala., 168; resolution introduced by, 461.
Pulliam, Will, 460.
Puffin, E. B., letter to, 519.
Quitman, John A., political activities of, 106, 242, 303,317.
Raleigh, N. C, communication with Columbia, 68.
Ramsay, of Ga., opposition of, 642.
Rand, of N. Y., complaints from, 441.
Randall, Samuel J., 737.
Randolph, G. W., Confederate Secretary of War, 592.
Rantoul, Robert, jr., 265, 268, 270.
Rawson, Methodist, of Atlanta, 685.
Raymond, Henry J., N. Y. editor, 548,549.
Rayner, Kenneth, 362.
Reconstruction, 621, 690-694, 710, 711.
Reeder, Andrew H., governor of Kansas, 368,392.
Reese, of Macon, Ga., 673.
Reese, Augustus,lawyer of Ga.,proposed for judgeship, 642,643.
Register, Atlanta, 640.
Reid, David S., activities of, 109.
Republic, 317.
Republican, Savannah, 145, 316, 528, 612, 640.

Republican Herald, Rhode Island, 279, 280.
Resaca de la Falma, 83.
Reynolds (E. R. *or* J. H.), congressman from N. Y., 397,449,452,455.
Reynolds, Parmedns, legislator of Ga., opposition to Cobb, 337.
Rhett, Robert Barnwell., speech of, 96, 210; opposition to, 233, 276; toast by, 242.
Rhode Island, political affairs of, 94.
Ricardo, David, *Principles of Political Economy and Taxation,* 615.
Rice, Union delegate from Ga., 298.
Richard Cobden, American ship, 435.
Richardson, Richard, urged as representative of Ga., 234, 235.
Richardson, William A., chairman of caucus, 267; caucus debate by, 270; opinion of, 356.
Richmond, Va., military operations about, 660,661; convention at, 698.
Riggs, Jetur R., elected to Congress, 449.
Riley, Harrison, charge by, 67, 68.
Ritchie, Thomas, editor, 136; letters from, 55, 56, 59; debt due, 69; opposition of, 230; influence of, 426.
Ritchie, W. F., delegate from Va., 59.
Rivers and harbors, bill for, 86.
Rives, William C, Va. delegate, 566.
Roane, W. H., delegate from Va., 57, 59.
Robb, *Mrs.,* death of, 700.
Robbins, John, jr., letter to, 439.
Robert, servant of Toombs, 628.
Robertson, *Dr.,* urged for Inspector of drugs at Charleston, 155.
Robinson, John L., letter from, 174; marshal, 332.
Rome, Ga., meeting at, 160.
Root, Joseph M., 124, 182, 302.
Rosignol, superintendent of mint at Dahlonega, Ga., 67.
Ross, Edmund G., 897.
Rush, Thomas, urged for Congress, 71.
Rusk, Thomas J., of committee on behalf of Southern members, 138.
Russell, Philip M., 641.
Rutherford, John, 585; letter to, 249.
Rutherford, John C, letter from, 685.
Rutherford, Williams, jr., letters from, 189, 566; of University of Georgia, 566.
St. Louis, ship, 447.
St. Louis, Mo., fire in, 160.
Samford, of Ga., campaigning by, 60.
Santa Ti, army at, 192,193; insurrection near, 393.
Saunders, George, 482.
Savage, John H., caucus debate by, 270.
Savannah, vessels seized at, 538.
Savannah Georgian, 286.
Schell, Augustus, collector at N. Y., 439, 441, 442.
Schleiden, R., letter to, 563.
Schley, George, 617, 668.
Schun, Carl, position of, 713-714.
Schwartz, John, elected to Congress, 449.
Scott, Gen. Wlnfleld, candidacy of, 104, 106, 232, 263, 289, 293, 294, 295, 296, 297, 300, 302, 313, 314, 322; position of, 208,369; nominated for presidency, 302; movements of, 532, 569.
Seals case, 449.
Sebastian, William K., of committee on behalf of Southern members, 138.
Secession, sentiment for, 235, 236, 285; right of, 238, 245, 249, 251-259; observations upon, 276, 327, 469, 471, 502, 503-504, 505-516, 519-522, 524, 525-526, 531, 538, 544, 545, 550, 555, 655. *See also* names of Southern States.
Seddon, James A., 182; Confederate Secretary of War, letter to, 616.
Sells, *Dr.,* 685.
Selman, 1.1., deposition of, 331.

Semmes, *Gen.* Paul J., military services of, 571, 592, 593.

Semmes, *Adm.* Raphael, letters from, 533, 546.

Senate, U. S., Texas question in, 62, 63, 64; Oregon question in, 76; discussion on Wilmot Proviso in, 89; Military Committee, 147; Compromise, 191, 201, 203, 204; assault in, 365, 366. *See also* Congress, U. S.

Seward, James L., candidate for Congress, 114; elected, 407.

Seward, William H., influence of, 216, 263, 306, 313, 317, 322, 348, 368, 694, 696; opposition to, 340; candidacy of, 448, 449, 465; attitude toward slavery, 506; speeches of, 533,677; letter to, 663.

Seymour, David L., committee appointment of, 274.

Seymour, Horatio, candidate for presidency, 700, 701.

Shackleford, A. D., of Ga., support of, 176; opposition of, 353.

Shannon, Wilson, appointment of, 361.

Sherman, John, candidate for Speaker, 452, 455, 459, 461; U. S. Senator, 697.

Sherman, Gen. W. T., negotiations with, 652, 653, 654; military operations of, 656.

Shields, of Ala., influence for, 317.

Shields, *Gen.* James, 323.

Shockly, 465.

Shorter, George H., 354.

Shunk, 102.

Sickles, Daniel E., 330; preference of, 397; attack upon, 439; complaints from, 441; absence of, 455; letter to, 682.

Simmons, opinion of, 215.

Simmons, *Rev.* J. C, 246.

Simpson, Richard F., 128.

Singleton, *Dr.*, efforts to become superintendent of mint at Dahlonega, Ga. , 67-68.

Slavery, discussion of, 91, 94-95, 99, 111-112, 116, 118-124, 134-135, 141, 149-150, 169, 171, 179, 184, 186-187, 188, 196-206, 266, 279, 283, 284, 414-416, 461, 498, 505-516, 520-521, 526; resolution concerning, 108; scriptural vindication of, 182; speeches on, 190; abolition of, 673. *See also* Abolition question; Compromise measures; District of Columbia; Dred Scott decision; Fugitive Slave bill; Kansas question; Missouri Compromise; Negroes; Slave-trade; Wilmot Proviso; names of particular States.

Slave-trade, 435-439, 446-447, 467.

Slidell, John, letter from, 275; In Senate, 328; interview with, 396.

Smead, *Dr.*, of Mercer University, 706.

Smith, member of Confederate Congress, lecture by, 557,558.

Smith, B.C., 448.

Smith, Gen. E. K., military service of, 579,644,652, 656.

Smith, O. W., command of, 576; order concerning, 592.

Smith, J. Henly, letters to, 446,447,450,454,457,459, 462, 465, 467, 470, 481, 483, 486, 488, 490, 491, 493, 494,496,497,600,502,503,526.

Smith, J. K., MSS. in possession of, 353,384,386,504.

Smith, Got'. James M., position of, 716; conversation with, 719, 720.

Smith, Lindsay, case, 449.

Smith, Lindsey H., candidacy of, 174.

Smith, Thomas, letter from, 111.

Smyth, influence of, 242.

Smy the, political work of, 261.

Smythe, James M., letter from, 609.

Somen, brig, 393.

Soule", Pierre, appointment of, 327.

South Carolina, political affairs of, 93,101,109,143, 159, 518, 710; secession movement in, 217,228,235, 236,238,258,503,522,532; military movements in, 528-529, 532, 659.

Southern Banner, Athens, Ga., 90,161,163, 173, 174, 230, 233, 235, 279, 280, 311,329, 376, 678, 695.

Southern Confederacy, 467,486,488, 501.

Southerner, Rome, Ga., 501.

Southern Quarterly Review, 349,350.

Southern Recorder, 249,503,519.

Southern Rights party, 223-225, 230, 260, 265, 271, 272,281, 285, 286, 308, 310,315.

"Specks," telegram signed, 718.

Speed, political feeling of, 114.

Spencer, C S.,548.

Sprague, William, 697.

Sproule, opinion of, 356.

Spurlock, James M., 161,249.

Squatter Sovereignty, 373,376,411,479.

Stallworth, James A., absence of, 455.

Stanbery, Henry, attitude of, 694.

Stanford, of Ga., candidacy of, 335.

Stanly, Edward, caucus debate by, 270; committee appointment of, 273.

Stanton, E. M., position of, 530; influence of, 632.

Stanton, Frederick P., replies to, 119; committee appointment urged for, 181; resolution by, 267; motion made by, 269; caucus vote of, 269; position of, 273.

Staples, Va. delegate, 566.

Star, Elberton,503.

Star of the South, newspaper, 527.

Star of the West, ship, 629,532.

State Department, publisher selected by, 233.

States and Union, newspaper, 501,503.

State Sentinel, Indianapolis, 545.

Staunton, of Confederate army, 685.

Steedman, Gen. J. P,., 668.

Steiner, *Dr.,* 576,578.

Stephens, Alexander H., chronology, 13-16; letters heretofore printed, 17-30; letters to, 53,60,63,117, 241, 350, 353, 361, 380, 383, 389, 397, 398, 400, 401, 402, 406, 407, 408, 409, 420, 421, 422, 423, 424, 425, 427, 428, 429, 431, 432, 433, 434, 442, 444, 445, 447, 448, 451, 452, 453, 454, 455, 458, 460, 464, 467, 468,

469, 477, 478, 480, 481, 489, 490, 528, 558, 565, 568,
670, 571, 573, 574, 675, 576, 677, 578, 579, 580, 581,
585, 586, 689, 591, 593, 594, 595, 697, 599, 603, 605,
610, 611, 614, 615, 617, 618, 620, 621, 627, 630, 631,
632, 633, 634, 637, 639, 640, 641, 642, 643, 644, 649,
651, 652, 653, 654, 660, 661, 662, 670, 673, 677, 684,
688, 690, 701, 702, 706, 707, 708, 710, 711, 716, 718,
721, 722, 723, 725, 727, 731, 732, 734, 736, 737, 739,
740, 743; letters from, 57, 58,62,68,71,117,127,138, 146,155, 184,192,195,237,260,264,265,268,271

325, 343, 344, 345, 346, 347, 349, 353, 367, 384, 386,
409, 446, 447, 450, 454, 457, 459, 462, 463, 465, 467,
470, 481, 483, 486, 488, 490, 491, 493, 494, 496, 497,
500, 502, 603, 504, 526, 563, 680, 681, 686, 688, 700,
708,709,713,717,742,743; vote on Texas question,
62; and Galphin claim, 73; appreciation of, 109;
political operations of, 126; assault upon, 127;
131; chairman of committee, 138; dinner with,
138; position on various political matters, 154,
213, 262, 281, 295, 297-298, 311, 362-363; support of, 176; *Recollections,* cited, 195; representation of, 233; tariff vote of, 234; caucus vote of, 274;
War between the States, 359, 471, 640, 717; dispute with Hill, 384, 386-388, 389-391; mentioned for
Speaker, 426; delegate to Confederate Congress,
537; offered chair of history and political science at Mercer University, 706; lessee of Western and
Atlantic Railroad, 711, 718-721; elected to Congress, 717.
   Stephens, Henry, statement by, 106.
   Stephens, John, 576, 578.

   Stephens, Linton, letters to, 188,271,575,607; mentioned, 381, 395, 398, 420, 630, 631, 632, 633, 634, G40, 652, 677, 689, 706; challenge sent by, 391;
nominee for Congress, 408, 421, 423, 424; resignation from supreme court bench of Ga., 491;
political work of, 492, 500, 502,643; mentioned for governor of Ga., 560, 610, 611, 614; military commission for, 570; letter from, 601; resolutions of,
638, 639; judgeship offered, 642; declines judgeship, 643.
   Stephenson, of Cincinnati, 140.
   Steuben ville, O., political meeting at, 124.
   Stevens, of Brooks Co., Ga., recommendation of, 649.
   Stevens, Thaddeus, policy of, 672,678,679,687.
   Stewart, Thomas, claim of, 363.
   Stewart, W. M., proposition of, 678.
   Stiles, William H., political work of, 57,207,248.
   Stockton, John P., 679.
   Stone, Dr., 462.
   Stoneman, Oen. George, raid of, 646,650.
   Strange, *Judge,* of N.C,speech by, 108.
   Street, of Va., information from, 264.
   Stringfellow, *Rev. Mr.,* scriptural vindication of
slavery by, 182,349.
   Strother, claim of, 325.
   Stroud, Orion, letter from, 311.
   Stuart, Charles E.,267; committee appointment of,
272.
   Sturdevant, influence sought for, 400.
   Sturgis, candidate for judgeship, Ga. , 175.
   Sturgis, Thad., position of, 336.
   Sullivan's Island, S. C, meeting held at, 242.
   Sumner, Charles, leadership of, 229; assault upon,
365,366; policy of, 506,672,673,678, 679.
   Sun, Baltimore, 328,482,546.
   Supreme court, Ga., 69,89,95,449-450,491.

   Supreme Court, U. S., decisions of, 118, 120, 407,
413,512; slave question referred to, 123; judges of,
as dinner guests, 181. *See also* Dred Scott decision.
   Surratt, *Mrs.* Mary E., 674.
   Swan case, 455.
   Talley, of Lumpkin Co., Ga., support of, 176.
   Tammany, attitude of, 264.
   Tariff question, 61,70,81,82,86,234,278,398.
   Taylor, *Gen.* Richard, 952,659.
   Taylor, Zachary, candidacy of, 87,89,94,98,99,103,
104, 106, 113, 114, 115, 124, 126, 127, 128, 129, 132;
resolutions in favor of, 95-96; military operations of, 96, 106; nomination of, 108, 109, 112; vote for,
136,137; Cabinet of, 139, 146,147; administration of, 140, 165; policy of, 141; and the Wilmot Proviso, 143, 144, 148; opposition to, 195; illness and death of, 195.
   Tea, duty on, 82,83.
   Tehuantepec route, 399.
   Telegraph, London, 698.
   Telegraph, Macon, 110, 480,618.
   Tennessee, political affairs of, 116-117, 126, 129, 133,
159, 322, 328, 355, 377, 600; Union sentiment in,
218; State convention, 275; admission of, 416;
resolution, 468, 469; delegates from, 495; secession movement in, 532, 535, 566, 568; resolution of legislature of, 672.
   Terhune, Barclay, position of, 208.
   Texas, annexation of, 56, 57,58, 61, 62, 63, 64, 65, 66,
67,71,77,78-79,86,122,123; relations with Mexico,
66; boundary, 141, 204, 205, 210; military preparations in, 192; admission of, 416; delegates from, 482;
secession movement in, 528, 533, 561.
   Thomas, Philip F., Secretary of the Treasury, *ad interim,* 522.
   Thomas, James, of Sparta, Ga., letters to, 57,58,62,
88, 103, 104, 184, 325; suggested for

chairman, 291.

Thomas, James H., congressman from Term., election of, 173; residence of, 328.

Thomas, Stephens, letter sent to, 307.

Thomas, Thomas W., letters from, 105,107,114, 152, 173,230,350,361,380,389,400,427,428

570, 574, 575, 579, 580, 681, 586, 595, 620; of committee of Constitutional Union party, 236, 238, 293; application in favor of, 261; candidate for judgeship, 325-326; letters to, 353, 359, 367, 384, 386, 394, 449; attitude toward Cobb, 359, 362-363; mentioned, 404; military command of, 572; illness of, 576, 578, 579; resignation of military commission, 592.

Thompson, *Judge,* letter from, 133.

Thompson, George, British abolitionist, 228.

Thompson, Jacob, mentioned for Cabinet, 397; Secretary of the Interior, 522,523,524; resignation of, 528, 530; letter from, 531.

Thompson, *Mr».* Jacob, letter from, 522.

Thornton, request concerning, 361.

Thurston, Benjamin B., committee appointment of, 272.

Thweatt, *Col.,* Jonas, 617,618,640,641.

Tilden, Samuel J., letter of, 722; contested election of, 725; candidacy of, 741.

Tilly, John, death of, 600.

Times, Columbus, Ga., 53, 64, 246, 265, 618.

Times, New York, 725.

Toombs, Gabriel, letter from, 573.

Toombs, Robert, chronology, 13-16; letters heretofore printed, 17-30; letters from, 53,60,63, 72, 88, 103, 104, 127, 135, 139, 140, 146, 165, 188, 212, 218, 227, 232, 261, 297, 322, 342, 350, 353, 359, 364, 365, 380, 383, 394, 397, 398, 399, 403, 408, 409, 420, 425, 432, 433, 447, 449, 451, 452, 453, 454, 455, 458, 460, 464, 467, 468, 469, 475, 477, 478, 480,

481, 619, 525, 528, 558, 562, 568, 575, 577, 578, 589, 591, 593, 594, 595, 599, 603, 607, 611, 612, 615, 619, 621, 622, 628, 630, 637, 651, 652, 660, 661, 673, 688, 690, 702, 706, 707, 708, 710, 711, 716, 718, 721, 722, 723, 726, 727, 731, 732, 734, 736, 737, 739, 740, 743; political work of, 127,330, 501; position in various political matters, 154, 213, 262, 295, 298, 311, 362-363; and last illness of Pres. Taylor, 195; support of, 178, 337; tariff vote of, 234; candidate for U. S. Senate, 261, 241, 425; committee appointment of, 273; caucus vote of, 274; leadership of, 348; attitude toward Cobb, 359-360; speeches of, 4C0, 480; military service of, 573, 599-601, 621; arrest of, 603; candidate for Confederate Senate, 608, 630; mentioned for governor of Ga., 611, 614; resignation from military command, 611, 612, 614.'

Toombs, Mrs. Robert, letter from, 528.

Tortugas, possession of, 539.

Toucey, Isaac, mentioned for Cabinet, 398; mentioned for judgeship, 422; Secretary of the Navy, position of, 530.

Towns, George W., candidate for governor of Ga., 156,167,168; letter to, 163; position of, 211; convention called by, 212, 213, 214; legislature reassembled by, 227; policy defeated, 425.

Townsend, Norton S., attitude of, 302.

Trammell, L. N., position of, 208; letter to, 727.

Tremont Temple, Boston, Toombs's lecture in, 359.

Trescot, William Henry, letters from, 622, 529.

Tribune, N. Y., 433,503.

Trippe, Robert P., mentioned for governor of Ga., 156; support of, 176; vote of, 412; elected to Congress, 424.

Trousdale, William, governor of Tenn., 303, 317.

True Democrat, Augusta, Ga., 525; letter to, 528.

Trumbull, Lyman, 481, 512, 697.

Tucker, policy of, 441.

Tugalo party, 311.

Tumlin, *Col.* Lewis, Ga. politician, 161,214, 287, 298, 329.

Turner, Thomas J., 125.

Tyler, John, and annexation of Texas, 58,122; candidacy of, 59; Message of, 69, 70.

Underwood, John W. H., 130,176, 208. 329; letters from, 54, 560; position of, 208; political opinion of, 287; expression of, 386.

Union, Griffin, 381.

Union, Washington, 69, 76, 91, 97, 136,183, 236, 238, 262, 266, 268, 287, 288, 291,294, 317,356,389,403,405, 406, 421, 423, 441, 458, 723.

Union. See also *Confederate Union: Federal Union; LnUm and Recorder.*

Union and Recorder. Milledgeville, 727.

Union party. See Constitutional Union party.

United States, relations with England, 70, 72, 73, 76, 80, 88.

Utah, establishment of territorial government of, 228; bill, 283.

Utica, N. Y., convention at, 101,114.

Van Buren, John (" Prince John"), 101,339, 372,

Van Buren, Martin, candidacy of, 57,58,59,113,114, I 124; Southern alliance of 148; opposition to, 276, 340; position of, 306; in London, 354.

Vance, *Gov.* Z. B., policy of, 637; conference with, 653.

Van Winkle, Peter G., 697.

Vattel, *Law of Nations,* cited, 121.

Venable, Abraham W., of committee on behalf of Southern members, 138; political work of, 219; attitude of, 302.

Vermont, political affairs in, 169, 512; admission of, 416.

Vicksburg, fall of, 629.
Virginia, political affairs in, 56, 87, 93, 143, 155, 159,
218, 462, 698; congressional delegation from, 84;
resolutions, 143, 163, 168, 170, 171; slavery in, 171;
delegates from, 495; secession movement in, 532,
535, 544, 546, 548, 554, 558, 562, 566; military operations in, 569, 571, 588, 593, 594-595, 599-601, 603-604, 606-607.
Voorhees, Daniel W., 679.
Wade, Benjamin, 679, 694.
Waldo, loren P., candidate for Commissioner of
Pensions, 324.
Walker, *Jfaj.,* 70.
Walker, Leroy P., mentioned for Davis's Cabinet,
544; correspondence, 563.
Walker, Robert J., Secretary of the Treasury, 139;
mentioned for Secretary of State, 395, 396, 397;
governor of Kansas, 400-401, 402, 403-404, 405, 406,
407, 416, 417, 418, 419, 422, 423, 426, 428, 430.
Walker, *Gen.* W. H. T., death of, 649.
Walker, William, arrest of, 429-430; expedition of,
447.
Walsh, Pro/., of University of Ga., 567.
Walters, *Col.* Joseph, nomination of, 248.
Ward, killing of, 83.
Ward, *Col,* of Fla., 583.
Ward, John E., letters from, 284, 367, 372; political work of, 287, 298, 363; position of, 307; mentioned for Cabinet position, 384.
Warner, *Judge,* Hiram, nominated for supreme court of Georgia, 69; position of, 95; letter from,
186; mentioned for governor of Ga., 227; delegate,
298; letter of, 455; chief justice of Ga., 716.
Warren, legislator of Ga., support of, 337.
Warren, of Macon, Ga., 673.
Warren case, 447.

Warrenton convention, 411, 412.
Wartzfielder, *Messrs,* of Milledgeville, 639, 640.
Washington, D. C, Southern meeting at, 211.
Washington, L. Q., letter from, 697.
Washington, Territory of, organization of, 324.
Washington, revenue cutter, 542.
Waters, State senator of Ga., 96.
Waters, *Col.,* appointed delegate, 287.
Watkins, *Col.* John D., conversation with, 114.
Wayne, *Gen.* Henry C, 572, 641.
Webster, Daniel, political activities of, 87, 194, 279;
on slave question, 95; attitude of, 140, 147; dinner guest, 181; opinion of, 220; candidacy of, 233, 311,
314; editorial on speech of, 286; death of, 321.
Weems, John B., application in favor of, 261.
Wellborn, Marshall J., vote for, 130; speech of, 189.
Weller, *Col.,* candidate for governor of Ohio, 124, 125.
Westcott, preference of, 397.
Western and Atlantic Railroad, 53, 73, 231, 295, 434,
632, 711; lease of, 711-712, 718-721.
Wheeler, *Gen.* Joseph, military operations of, 647,
651; reported death of, 649.
Whig and Examiner, Richmond, 638. See also
Examiner.
Whitaker, *Judge,* letter to, 574.
White, William B., political work of, 174.
Whitfield, John W., 392, 422.
Whitfield case, 710.
. hitin, request of, 431.
Whitner, John C, 646; letters from, 596, 599, 602.
Wigfall, P. T., 660.
Wilcox, of N. Y., 365.
Wilcox, *Gen.* C. M., 604.
Wilkes, mentioned for judgeship, 643.
Willey, Senator W. T., 697.
Williams, *Col.* C. J., military command of, 572.
Wills, of Macon, Ga., 673.
Willis, *Col,* of Greensboro, N. C, 668.

Wilmington, N. C, coach line from, 68.
Wilmot, David, political position of, 132, 265.
Wilmot Proviso, 88, 89, 95, 96, 97, 98, 101, 107, 112,
121, 135, 143, 144, 151, 170, 182, 183, 197

342, 368.
Wiggins, Southern Rights delegate, 298.
Wilson, Henry, attitude toward slavery, 506, 679.
Wilson, *Gen.* James H., 663, 665, 666.
Winder, John H., letter from, 644.
Wingfield, Junius, attitude of, 318; Know Nothing candidate in Wilkes Co., Ga.; 409.
Winthrop, Robert C, vote of, 91; opposition to, 174,
177; candidate for Speaker, 179, 181; leadership of, 229; letter from, 357.
Wisconsin, vote of, 98; political affairs in, 126, 169,
377, 721; admission of, 416.
Wise, Henry A., charge concerning, 82; attitude of,
426; public letter of, 428, 430; support of, 455.
Wofford, *Capt.* William B., 287, 295; letters from,
69, 295; political activities of, 85, 175, 249; candidate for Congress, 234, 235; of committee of Constitutional Union party, 236, 238.
Wofford, *Gen.* William T., political activities of,
107, 185, 187, 618.
Wollack, Dug., attitude of, 336.
Wood, Fernando, policy of, 441, 442.
Woodbury, Levi, candidacy of, 81, 96, 110, 244.
Woods, William, opinion of, 208, 215; letter from,
212.
Woodward, Joseph A., political position of, 128;
vote of, 178.
Wool, *Gen.* John E., 587, 588, 589.
World, New York, 714, 715.
Wright, Augustus R., political activities of, 176, 329,
501; letter from, 536; delegate to Confederate Congress, 537; candidate for

Confederate Congress, 560; mentioned for governor of Ga., 611; military services of, 654.

Wright, Joseph A., elected governor of Ind., 175.

Wright, William, of N. J., instructions to, 470.

Wynn, candidate for postmaster of Hollingsworth, Ga., 69.

Yancey, William L., duel of, 66; political activities of, 108, 110, 111, 210, 276, 286, 478, 479; mentioned for Davis's Cabinet, 544.

Yost, Jacob S., defeat of, 86.

Young, *Judge,* candidate for clerkship of House of Representatives, 264, 265, 267, 268.

Youngstown, O., political meeting at, 124.

Yulee, David L., 233.

Zollicoffer, Felix K., 346, 412.

o

Lightning Source UK Ltd.
Milton Keynes UK
UKOW022133110113

204779UK00008B/370/P

Besides being a qualified teacher of English, History, Xhosa, and Economics, Solomon Gallant-Page is a prolific author in both his vernacular language and English in the light of the fiction and non-fiction literary works which are in the pipeline: *Decoding the Enigma of the Wealthy few, Your Physical and Mental Wellness the Natural Way, Echoes of the Distant Oceans, Disappearing Humps of the Kalahari Camels, Beyond the Misty Horizon, Ukuthetha Akufani Nokwenza, Ayatheth'amanyange,* etc. As a published author at Vivlia Publishers of Pretoria R.S.A, his book entitled *Inxili kaNgconde* has been studied in some high schools of the Eastern Cape and Western Cape Provinces of the R.S.A. He is currently a candidate attorney, pending his admission after serving his articles of clerkship at any law firm.

He holds the following qualifications: LLB (UNISA), BA (UNISA), Cert. of Legal Practice (LSSA), STD (UNITRA).